W9-AGA-711

# A SHAKESPEAREAN GENEALOGY

This chart reflects Shakespeare's history plays and is thus not historically accurate. Many descendants of Henry II and Edward III are omitted. On occasion, Shakespeare combined or simply invented historical figures. These deviations from fact are explained in the notes.

In the chart, the names of Kings and Queens are printed in capitals, and the dates of their reigns are printed in bold. The names of characters appearing in the plays are underlined.

Henry
d. 1183

Edward, Prince of
Wales 1330–1376

RICHARD II
1367–1400
(**1377–99**)

William of
Hatfield

Lionel, Duke of
Clarence 1338–1368

Philippa
m. Edmund
Mortimer, Earl
of March

RICHARD I
1157–1199
(**1189–99**)

Philip Faulconbridge*
(Richard Plantagenet)

John of Gaunt,
Duke of Lancaster
1340–1399
m. Blanche of
Lancaster
m. Constance of
Castile
m. Katherine
Swynford

HENRY IV
1367–1413
(**1399–1413**)

Thomas Beaufort,
Duke of Exeter
1377–1427

Henry Beaufort,
Bishop of Winchester
1375–1447

John Beaufort,
Earl of Somerset
1372–1409

Joan Beaufort
m. Ralph Neville,
Earl of
Westmoreland

HENRY II
1133–1189
(**1154–89**)
m. Eleanor
of Aquitaine
d. 1204

Geoffrey, d. 1186
m. Constance
of Brittany

Arthur
1187–1203

JOHN 1167–1216
(**1199–1216**)

HENRY III
1207–1272
(**1216–72**)

EDWARD I
1239–1307
(**1272–1307**)

EDWARD II
1284–1327
(**1307–27**)

EDWARD III
1312–1377
(**1327–77**)
m. Philippa of
Hainault

Edmund of Langley,
Duke of York
1341–1402

Edward, Duke of
Aumerle d. 1415

Richard, Earl
of Cambridge
d. 1415  m. Anne
Mortimer (above)

Thomas of
Woodstock, Duke of
Gloucester 1355–1397

Anne

Eleanor
m. Alfonso VIII,
King of Castile

Blanche, d. 1252
m. Louis VIII
of France

William of
Windsor

*Philip Faulconbridge, the bastard son of Richard I, had no historical existence. Such a character appears in the play *The Life and Death of King John* and is referred to in passing in Holinshed's *Chronicles*.

† In the character of Edmund Mortimer, Shakespeare combines two historical figures. The Edmund Mortimer who married Catrin, daughter of Owain Glyndŵr, was the grandson of Lionel, Duke of Clarence, and the younger brother of Roger, Earl of March. He died in 1409. Shakespeare combines him with his nephew, the Edmund Mortimer recognized by Richard II as his heir (d. 1424). This second Edmund was the brother of Anne Mortimer and the uncle of Richard Plantagenet.

‡ The character of the Duke of Somerset combines Henry Beaufort with his younger brother Edmund (d. 1471), who succeeded him as Duke.

Elizabeth Mortimer ("Kate") m. Henry Percy ("Hotspur") 1364–1403

—Henry, Earl of Northumberland 1394–1455

EDWARD IV 1442–1483 (1461–83) m. Elizabeth Woodville d. 1492

—EDWARD V 1470–1483 (1483)

—Richard, Duke of York 1472–1483

Elizabeth of York 1465–1503 m. HENRY VII (below)

—Edmund, Earl of Rutland 1443–1460

Edmund Mortimer†

—George, Duke of Clarence 1449–1478 m. Isabel Neville (below)

Anne Mortimer m. Richard, Earl of Cambridge (below)

—Richard Plantagenet, Duke of York 1411–1460 m. Cicely Neville (below)

RICHARD III 1452–1485 (1483–85) m. Anne Neville (below)

—Edward, Prince of Wales

HENRY V 1387–1422 (1413–22) m. Catherine 1401–1437

—HENRY VI 1421–1471 (1422–61) m. Margaret of Anjou d. 1482

—Edward, Prince of Wales 1453–1471 m. Anne Neville (below)

—Arthur m. Catherine of Aragon (below)

Thomas, Duke of Clarence d. 1421

—Margaret m. James IV of Scotland

—James V of Scotland

John of Lancaster, Duke of Bedford 1389–1435

Mary, Queen of Scots

Humphrey, Duke of Gloucester 1391–1447 m. Eleanor Cobham d. 1454

JAMES I 1566–1625 (1603–25)

John Beaufort, Duke of Somerset 1403–1444

—Margaret Beaufort m. Edmund Tudor, Earl of Richmond

—HENRY VII 1457–1509 (1485–1509) m. Elizabeth of York (above)

HENRY VIII 1491–1547 (1509–47) m. Catherine of Aragon

—MARY I 1516–1558 (1553–58) m. Philip of Spain

Edmund Beaufort, Duke of Somerset 1406–1455

—Henry Beaufort, Duke of Somerset 1436–1464‡

m. Anne Boleyn

—ELIZABETH I 1533–1603 (1558–1603)

—Isabel Neville d. 1476 m. George, Duke of Clarence (above)

m. Jane Seymour

—EDWARD VI 1537–1553 (1547–53)

Richard Neville, Earl of Salisbury 1400–1460

—Richard Neville, Earl of Warwick 1428–1471

m. Anne of Cleves

m. Katherine Howard

—John Neville, Marquess of Montague d. 1471

—Anne Neville d. 1485 m. Edward, Prince of Wales (above)

m. Katherine Parr

Cicely Neville m. Richard Plantagenet, Duke of York (above)

m. RICHARD III (above)

—Mary m. Charles Brandon

—Frances

Jane Grey 1537–1554

—Humphrey, Duke of Buckingham 1402–1460

—Humphrey Stafford d. 1455

—Henry, Duke of Buckingham 1454?–1483

—Edward, Duke of Buckingham 1478–1521

**RICHARD II, 1377–99**   RICHARD was the eldest son of EDWARD THE BLACK PRINCE, himself the eldest son of KING EDWARD III, who ruled England from 1327 to 1377. When the BLACK PRINCE died in battle in France in 1376, RICHARD became the legitimate heir to the throne. He ruled from EDWARD's death in 1377 until he was deposed in 1399 by HENRY BOLINGBROKE, the eldest son of JOHN OF GAUNT, DUKE OF LANCASTER. Because he was the fourth son of EDWARD III, GAUNT and his Lancastrian descendants had weaker hereditary claims to the throne than did RICHARD. When deposed, RICHARD had no children to succeed him, but he recognized EDMUND MORTIMER, FIFTH EARL OF MARCH, as his heir presumptive. This MORTIMER was descended from LIONEL, DUKE OF CLARENCE, the third son of EDWARD III, and therefore also had stronger hereditary claims to the throne than did BOLINGBROKE. SHAKESPEARE combined this MORTIMER with his uncle EDMUND MORTIMER, who married OWAIN GLYNDŴR's DAUGHTER.

**HENRY IV, 1399–1413**   HENRY BOLINGBROKE, eldest son of JOHN OF GAUNT, seized the throne from RICHARD II in 1399. When HENRY died in 1413, he was succeeded by his eldest son, PRINCE HAL, who became HENRY V.

**HENRY V, 1413–22**   HENRY V became king in 1413 and reigned until his death in 1422. He was succeeded by his son, HENRY VI.

**HENRY VI, 1422–61**   HENRY VI was less than one year old when he succeeded his father, HENRY V. In the young king's minority, his uncle HUMPHREY, DUKE OF GLOUCESTER, was named Lord Protector, and the kingdom was ruled by an aristocratic council. HENRY VI assumed personal authority in 1437. He was deposed in 1461 by his third cousin, who was crowned EDWARD IV. HENRY was murdered in 1471.

**EDWARD IV, 1461–83**   EDWARD, the eldest son of RICHARD, DUKE OF YORK, seized the throne from HENRY VI in 1461. His Yorkist claim to the throne derived from his grandmother, ANNE MORTIMER, who was descended from LIONEL, third son of EDWARD III, and was sister to that EDMUND MORTIMER recognized by RICHARD II as his heir presumptive; EDWARD IV's grandfather, RICHARD, EARL OF CAMBRIDGE, was the son of EDMUND OF LANGLEY, fifth son of EDWARD III. EDWARD IV reigned until his death in 1483. His heir was his eldest son (EDWARD), but the throne was usurped by his brother RICHARD, DUKE OF GLOUCESTER.

**RICHARD III, 1483–85**   RICHARD III was the youngeer brother of EDWARD IV. After the death of EDWARD IV in 1483, RICHARD prevented the coronation of EDWARD V with a claim of illegitimacy and succeeded to the throne himself. EDWARD and his younger brother, RICHARD, DUKE OF YORK, were murdered in the Tower of London. RICHARD III was killed at the Battle of Bosworth Field in 1485, and the kingdom fell to the victor, HENRY TUDOR, EARL OF RICHMOND.

**HENRY VII, 1485–1509**   HENRY TUDOR seized the throne from RICHARD III in 1485. He was descended from JOHN OF GAUNT by JOHN's third marriage, with CATHERINE SWYNFORD. He married ELIZABETH, daughter of EDWARD IV, uniting the houses of Lancaster and York. He died in 1509 and was succeeded by his son, HENRY VIII.

**HENRY VIII, 1509–47**   HENRY was the second son of HENRY VII. His older brother, ARTHUR, died in 1502. HENRY VIII's first wife was CATHERINE OF ARAGON, who bore his daughter MARY. His second wife, ANNE BOLEYN, was the mother of ELIZABETH. His third wife, JANE SEYMOUR, bore him a son, who succeeded to the throne as EDWARD VI after HENRY VIII died in 1547.

**EDWARD VI, 1547–53**   EDWARD VI was nine years old when he became king. From 1547 to 1549, the realm was governed by a Lord Protector, the DUKE OF SOMERSET; power then passed to JOHN DUDLEY, DUKE OF NORTHUMBERLAND. When EDWARD VI died in 1553, NORTHUMBERLAND attempted unsuccessfully to prevent the succession of MARY TUDOR by installing as queen his daughter-in-law, LADY JANE GREY, a great-granddaughter of HENRY VII.

**MARY I, 1553–58**   MARY, daughter of HENRY VIII and his first wife, CATHERINE OF ARAGON, came to the throne in 1553. She married KING PHILIP OF SPAIN but died childless. She was succeeded by her half sister, ELIZABETH.

**ELIZABETH I, 1558–1603**   ELIZABETH, the daughter of HENRY VIII and his second wife, ANNE BOLEYN, became queen after the death of her half sister, MARY, in 1558. She ruled until her death in 1603. She was succeeded by her cousin JAMES.

**JAMES I, 1603–1625**   JAMES VI OF SCOTLAND became JAMES I OF ENGLAND in 1603. His claim to the throne of England derived from his great-grandmother, MARGARET TUDOR, a daughter of HENRY VII who married JAMES IV OF SCOTLAND. JAMES ruled England and Scotland until his death in 1625; he was succeeded by his son, CHARLES I.

# THE NORTON SHAKESPEARE

BASED ON THE OXFORD EDITION

SECOND EDITION

*Romances and Poems*

*The original Oxford Text on which this
edition is based was prepared by*

Stanley Wells
Gary Taylor
*General Editors*


John Jowett
William Montgomery

*The Norton Shakespeare*, Second Edition, is based on *William Shakespeare: The Complete Works*,
Second Edition, and is published by arrangement with Oxford University Press,
with additional material from W. W. Norton & Company, Inc.

# THE NORTON
# SHAKESPEARE

*Based on the Oxford Edition*

## SECOND EDITION

*Romances and Poems*

Stephen Greenblatt, *General Editor*
HARVARD UNIVERSITY

Walter Cohen
CORNELL UNIVERSITY

Jean E. Howard
COLUMBIA UNIVERSITY

Katharine Eisaman Maus
UNIVERSITY OF VIRGINIA

*With an Essay on the Shakespearean stage*
*by* Andrew Gurr

W · W · NORTON & COMPANY · NEW YORK · LONDON

W. W. Norton & Company has been independent since its founding in 1923, when William Warder Norton and Mary D. Herter Norton first published lectures delivered at the People's Institute, the adult education division of New York City's Cooper Union. The Nortons soon expanded their program beyond the Institute, publishing books by celebrated academics from America and abroad. By mid-century, the two major pillars of Norton's publishing program—trade books and college texts—were firmly established. In the 1950s, the Norton family transferred control of the company to its employees, and today—with a staff of four hundred and a comparable number of trade, college, and professional titles published each year—W. W. Norton & Company stands as the largest and oldest publishing house owned wholly by its employees.

*Editor:* Julia Reidhead
*Manuscript editor:* Carol Flechner
*Electronic media editor:* Eileen Connell
*Editorial assistant:* Rivka Genesen
*Production manager:* Diane O'Connor
*Photo research:* Rivka Genesen
*Interior design:* Antonina Krass
*Managing editor, College:* Marian Johnson

The Library of Congress has cataloged the one-volume edition as follows:

Shakespeare, William, 1564–1616.
The Norton Shakespeare / Stephen Greenblatt, general editor ; Walter Cohen, Jean E. Howard, Katharine Eisaman Maus [editors] ; with an essay on the Shakespearean stage by Andrew Gurr. — 2nd ed.
p. cm.
"Based on the Oxford edition."
Includes bibliographical references and index.
ISBN 978-0-393-92991-1
I. Greenblatt, Stephen, 1943–  II. Cohen, Walter, 1949–  III. Howard, Jean E. (Jean Elizabeth), 1948–  IV. Maus, Katharine Eisaman, 1955–  V. Gurr, Andrew. VI. Title.
PR2754.G74   2008
822.3'3—dc22
2007046599

ISBN 978-0-393-93143-3

W. W. Norton & Company, Inc., 500 Fifth Avenue, New York, NY 10110
www.wwnorton.com

W. W. Norton & Company Ltd., Castle House, 75/76 Wells Street, London W1T 3QT

3 4 5 6 7 8 9 0

# Contents

# Illustrations

# Preface

Shakespeare's principal medium, the drama, was thoroughly collaborative, and it involved as well continual efforts at revision and renewal. It seems appropriate, then, that this edition of his works is itself the result of sustained collaboration and revision. Two lists of editors' names on the title-page spread hint at the collaboration that has brought to fruition the *Norton Shakespeare*. But the title page does not tell the full history of this project. The text on which the *Norton Shakespeare* is based was published in both modern-spelling and original-spelling versions by Oxford University Press, in 1986. Under the general editorship of Stanley Wells and Gary Taylor, the Oxford text was a thorough rethinking of the entire body of Shakespeare's works, the most far-reaching and innovative revision of the traditional canon in centuries. When many classroom instructors who wanted to introduce their students to the works of Shakespeare through a modern text expressed a need for the pedagogical apparatus they have come to expect in an edition oriented toward students, Norton negotiated with Oxford to assemble an editorial team of its own to prepare the necessary teaching materials around the existing Oxford text. Hence ensued a collaboration of two publishers and two editorial teams.

To what extent is this the *Norton Shakespeare* and to what extent the Oxford text? Introductions (both the General Introduction and those to individual plays and poems), footnotes, glosses, bibliographies, genealogies, annals, maps, documents, and illustrations have all been the responsibility of the Norton team. Andrew Gurr's much-admired essay on the London theater in Shakespeare's time, specially commissioned for the *Norton Shakespeare*, has been moved in this second edition to the front matter.

The textual notes and variants derive for the most part from the work of the Oxford team, especially as represented in *William Shakespeare: A Textual Companion* (Oxford University Press, 1987), a remarkably comprehensive explanation of editorial decisions that is herewith strongly recommended to instructors as a valuable companion to this volume. Several of the textual notes—those to *The First Part of Henry the Sixth*, *Various Poems*, *The Two Noble Kinsmen*, *The Merry Wives of Windsor*, *Troilus and Cressida*, *The Sonnets* and "A Lover's Complaint"—have been substantially updated in the current edition, and all Textual Variants are now gathered in an appendix.

The Oxford text is widely available and already well known to scholars. A few words here may help clarify the extent of our fidelity to that text and the nature of the collaboration that has brought about this volume. The Oxford editors have profited from the massive and sustained attention accorded their edition by Shakespeare scholars across the globe, and of course they have continued to participate actively in the ongoing scholarly discussion about the nature of Shakespeare's text. In the reprintings of the Oxford volumes and in various articles over the past years, the Oxford editors have made a number of refinements of the edition they originally published. Such changes have been incorporated silently here. A small number of other changes made by the Norton team, however, were not part of the Oxford editors' design and were only accepted by them after we reached, through lengthy consultation, a mutual understanding about the nature, purpose, and intended audience of this volume. In all such changes, our main concern was for the classroom; we wished to make fully and clearly available the scholarly innovation and freshness of the Oxford text, while at the same time making certain that this was a superbly useful teaching text. It is a pleasure here to record, on behalf of the Norton team, our gratitude for the personal and professional

generosity of the Oxford editors in offering advice and entertaining arguments in our
common goal of providing the best student Shakespeare for our times. The Norton
changes to the Oxford text are various, but in only a few instances are they major. The
following brief notes are sufficient to summarize all of these changes, which are also
indicated in appropriate play introductions, footnotes, or textual notes.

1. The Oxford editors, along with other scholars, have strenuously argued—in both
the Oxford text and elsewhere—that the now-familiar text of *King Lear*, so nearly
omnipresent in our classrooms as to seem unquestionably authoritative but in reality
dating from the work of Alexander Pope (1723) and Lewis Theobald (1733), represents
a wrongheaded conflation of two distinct versions of the play: Shakespeare's original
creation as printed in the 1608 Quarto and his substantial revision as printed in the
First Folio (1623). The Oxford text, therefore, prints both *The History of King Lear* and
*The Tragedy of King Lear*. Norton follows suit, but where Oxford presents these two
texts sequentially, we print them on facing pages. While each version may be read independently, and to ensure this we have provided glosses and footnotes for each, the
substantial points of difference between the two are immediately apparent and available for comparison. But even many who agree with the scholarly argument for the two
texts of *Lear* nevertheless favor making available a conflated text, the text on which
innumerable performances of the play have been based and on which a huge body of
literary criticism has been written. With the reluctant acquiescence, therefore, of the
Oxford editors, we have included a conflated *Lear*, a text that has no part in the Oxford
canon and that has been edited by Barbara K. Lewalski of Harvard University rather
than by Gary Taylor, the editor of the Oxford *Lears*.

*The Norton Shakespeare*, then, includes three separate texts of *King Lear*. The reader
can compare them, understand the role of editors in constructing the texts we now call
Shakespeare's, explore in considerable detail the kinds of decisions that playwrights, editors, and printers make and remake, witness firsthand the historical transformation of
what might at first glance seem fixed and unchanging. The *Norton Shakespeare* offers
extraordinary access to this supremely brilliant, difficult, compelling play.

2. Among several other plays, *Hamlet* offers similar grounds for objections to the traditional conflation, but both the economics of publishing and the realities of
bookbinding—not to mention our recognition of the limited time in the typical undergraduate syllabus—preclude our offering three (or even four) *Hamlets* to match three
*Lears*. What we have provided in this edition is a convenient selection of parallel passages that will enable teachers to convey some of the complex, often enigmatic issues,
at once stylistic and conceptual, raised by the different texts of the play.

The Oxford text of *Hamlet* was based upon the Folio text, with an appended list of
Additional Passages from the Second Quarto (Q2). These additional readings total
more than two hundred lines, a significant number, among which are lines that have
come to seem very much part of the play as widely received, even if we may doubt that
they belong with all the others in any single one of Shakespeare's *Hamlets*. The Norton
team, while following the Oxford text, has moved the Q2 passages from the appendix
to the body of the play. But in doing so, we have not wanted once again to produce a
conflated text. We have therefore indented the Q2 passages, printed them in a different typeface, and numbered them in such a way as to make clear their provenance.
Those who wish to read the Folio version of *Hamlet* can thus simply skip over the
indented Q2 passages, while at the same time it is possible for readers to see clearly the
place that the Q2 passages occupy. We have adopted a similar strategy with several
other plays: passages printed in Oxford in appendices are generally printed here in the
play texts, though clearly demarcated and not conflated. In the case of *The Taming of
the Shrew* and the related quarto text, *The Taming of a Shrew*, however, we have followed Oxford's procedure and left the quarto passages in an appendix, since we believe
the texts reflect two distinct plays rather than a revision of one. We have similarly repro-

duced Oxford's brief appendices to A *Midsummer Night's Dream* and *Henry V,* enabling readers to consider alternative revisions of certain passages.

3. For reasons understood by every Shakespearean (and rehearsed at some length in this volume), the Oxford editors chose to restore the name "Sir John Oldcastle" to the character much better known as Falstaff in *1 Henry IV.* (They made comparable changes in the names of the characters known as Bardolph and Peto.) But for reasons understood by everyone who has presented this play to undergraduates or sampled the centuries of enthusiastic criticism, the Norton editors, with the Oxford editors' gracious agreement, have for this classroom edition opted for the familiar name "Falstaff" (and those of his boon companions), properly noting the change and its significance in the play's introduction.

4. The Oxford editors chose not to differentiate between those stage directions that appeared in the early editions up to and including the Folio and those that have been added by subsequent editors. Instead, in *A Textual Companion* they include separate lists of the original stage directions. These lists are not readily available to readers of the Norton text, whose editors opted instead to bracket all stage directions that derive from editions published after the Folio. Readers can thus easily see which stage directions derive from texts that may bear at least some relation to performances in Shakespeare's time, if not to Shakespeare's own authorship. The Norton policy is more fully explained in the General Introduction.

5. The Oxford editors have newly prepared complete texts of the multiauthored *King Edward III* and *Sir Thomas More,* in which Shakespeare may have had a hand as collaborator. The texts are available online at wwnorton.com/shakespeare. In addition, the *Norton Shakespeare,* Second Edition, continues to print, with a revised introduction, notes, and glosses, passages from *Sir Thomas More* that appear in the surviving manuscript to be in Shakespeare's own handwriting, and we include for the first time an introduction and bibliography to *King Edward III.*

The collaboration with Oxford was obviously essential to the creation of the *Norton Shakespeare.* But in preparing this Second Edition and making it something fresh and engaging, the critically important collaboration has been with the thousands of people who have used the book. Many of these, teachers and students alike, have generously offered helpful suggestions along with praise. Guided by their responses, as well as by recent developments in Shakespeare scholarship, we determined to look afresh at every detail and to make a wide range of changes. The General Introduction and the individual play introductions have been substantially revised, in some cases wholly rewritten, to make them clearer and more accessible. Textual notes throughout have been updated in response to new findings, and there are hundreds of new and fine-tuned notes and glosses, designed to make this edition an even better tool for learning and pleasure. The General Bibliography has been reorganized and extensively updated, with 7 new sections and over 350 new entries. The Selected Bibliographies, too, have been updated as well as newly annotated. A new introduction provides an illuminating guide to the array of maps, three of them archival and three new, showing places important to Shakespeare's plays. The genealogies have been revised, as has been the text/contexts Timeline. New annotated film lists, including over 50 films, now follow the play introductions. Instructors who emphasize films in their courses may wish to assign *Shakespeare and Film: A Norton Guide* by Samuel Crowl, available packaged with the *Norton Shakespeare.* Finally, in response to many requests, we are making the *Norton Shakespeare* available in three different formats: the familiar one-volume clothbound edition, new two-volume chronological splits (*Early Plays and Poems* and *Later Plays*), and four genre paperbacks, each with a new introduction.

With the Second Edition of the *Norton Shakespeare,* the publisher expands its extensive online resource, Norton Literature Online (wwnorton.com/literature). Students who activate the free password in each new copy of the book gain access to an array of general resources, among them a glossary of literary terms, advice on writing about literature and using MLA documentation style, an author portrait gallery, more than 100 maps, and over 90 minutes of recorded readings and musical selections, among them 80 songs by Shakespeare. With their passwords, students also gain access to a site specifically developed to support the *Norton Shakespeare* (wwnorton.com/shakespeare). Based on content prepared by Mark Rose, University of California, Santa Barbara, this Web site invites students to explore six of the most widely taught plays—*The Merchant of Venice, 1 Henry IV, Hamlet, Othello, King Lear,* and *The Tempest*—through different contextual lenses. For each of these plays, the Web site provides materials on the elements of theater, sources, stage history, and critical receptions, as well as the complete Oxford text. Audio clips and stills from classic productions, etchings, photographs, and costume-design illustrations help students appreciate performance aspects of the plays. The student Web site also includes the redesigned "Shakespearean Chronicle, 1558–1616," an illustrated timeline that interweaves three kinds of chronologies illuminating Shakespeare's life and times. As noted above, a password-protected section of the Web site also includes the complete texts of *The Book of Sir Thomas More* and *The Reign of King Edward the Third,* prepared by the editors of the *Oxford Shakespeare.*

The creation of this edition has drawn heavily on the resources, experience, and skill of its remarkable publisher, the independent, employee-owned company W. W. Norton. Our principal guide has been our brilliant editor Julia Reidhead, whose calm intelligence, common sense, and steady focus have been essential in enabling us to reach our goal. With this Second Edition, we were blessed with the characteristically thoughtful oversight of Marian Johnson, managing editor, college department; scrupulous manuscript editing by Carol Flechner; and the assistance of an extraordinary group of Norton staffers: editorial assistant Rivka Genesen, who, among many other things, coordinated the art program; production manager Diane O'Connor; designer Antonina Krass; editor of the *Norton Shakespeare* Web site Eileen Connell; and proofreaders Paula Noonan and Ann Warren.

The *Norton Shakespeare* editors have, in addition, had the valuable—indeed, indispensable—support of a host of undergraduate and graduate research assistants, colleagues, friends, and family. Even a partial listing of those to whom we owe our heartfelt thanks is very long, but we are all fortunate enough to live in congenial and supportive environments, and the edition has been part of our lives for a long time. We owe special thanks for sustained dedication and learning to our principal assistants: Tiffany Alkan, Lianne Habinek, and Emily Peterson. Particular thanks are due to Noah Heringman for his work on the texts assembled in the documents section and for the prefatory notes and comments on those texts; to Philip Schwyzer for preparing the genealogies and the glossary and for conceiving and preparing the (now online) "Shakespearean Chronicle"; and to Holger Schott Syme for reconceiving and extensively updating the General Bibliography. In addition, we are deeply grateful to Ezra Feldman, Francesca Mari, Douglas McQueen-Thomson, Jeffrey Patterson, and Benjamin Woodring. All of these companions, and many more besides, have helped us find in this long collective enterprise what the "Dedicatorie Epistle" to the First Folio promises to its readers: delight. We make the same promise to the readers of our edition and invite them to continue the great Shakespearean collaboration.

STEPHEN GREENBLATT
WALTER COHEN
JEAN E. HOWARD
KATHARINE EISAMAN MAUS

# Acknowledgments

Among our many critics, advisers, and friends, the following were of special help in providing critiques for particular plays or of the project as a whole: Janet Adelman (University of California, Berkeley), Joel Altman (University of California, Berkeley), Rebecca Bach (University of Alabama at Birmingham), John Baxter (Dalhousie University), Edward I. Berry (University of Victoria), Timothy Billings (Middlebury College), Bruce Boehrer (Florida State University), Barbara Bono (University at Buffalo, SUNY), Gordon M. Braden (University of Virginia), Douglas Brooks (Texas A&M University), Stephen Buhler (University of Nebraska—Lincoln), Richard Burt (University of Florida), Joseph F. Ceccio (University of Akron), Julie Crawford (Columbia University), Christy Desmet (University of Georgia), Heather Dubrow (University of Wisconsin—Madison), Laurie Ellinghausen (University of Missouri—Kansas City), Chris Fitter (Rutgers, State University of New Jersey), Susan Fraiman (University of Virginia), Daniel Gil (University of Oregon), Miriam Gilbert (University of Iowa), Suzanne Gossett (Loyola University), Elizabeth Hanson (Queen's University), Jim Harner (Texas A&M University), Jonathan Gil Harris (George Washington University), Don Hedrick (Kansas State University), Roze Hentschell (Colorado State University), Clifford Huffman (Stony Brook University, SUNY), John Huntington (University of Illinois at Chicago), Sujata Iyengar (University of Georgia), Kimberly Johnson (Brigham Young University), Coppélia Kahn (Brown University), Sean Keilen (University of Pennsylvania), Theodore B. Leinwand (University of Maryland), Zachary Lesser (University of Pennsylvania), Naomi Liebler (Montclair State University), Joyce MacDonald (University of Kentucky), Leah Marcus (Vanderbilt University), Mark Matheson (University of Utah), Robert Matz (George Mason University), Kristen McDermott (Central Michigan University), Ted McGee (University of Waterloo), Scott McMillin (late of Cornell University), Gordon McMullan (King's College London), John Moore (Pennsylvania State University), Carol Neely (University of Illinois at Urbana-Champaign), Lori Newcomb (University of Illinois at Urbana-Champaign), Karen Newman (New York University), Hillary Nunn (University of Akron), Thomas G. Olsen (SUNY at New Paltz), Jim O'Rourke (Florida State University), Paul Parrish (Texas A&M University), Michael Payne (Bucknell University), Rebecca J. Perederin (University of Virginia), Curtis Perry (Arizona State University), Susan Phillips (Northwestern University), Tanya Pollard (Brooklyn College, CUNY), Kristen Poole (University of Delaware), Arnold Preussner (Truman State University), Phyllis Rackin (University of Pennsylvania), Peter L. Rudnytsky (University of Florida), Benjamin Saunders (University of Oregon), Barbara Sebek (Colorado State University), Tracey Sedinger (University of Northern Colorado), Jyotsna Singh (Michigan State University), Andrew Stott (University at Buffalo, SUNY), Garrett Sullivan (Pennsylvania State University), Ramie Targoff (Brandeis University), Henry Turner (University of Wisconsin—Madison), Martine van Elk (California State University, Long Beach), William N. West (University of Colorado at Boulder), Linda Woodbridge (Pennsylvania State University), Lingui Yang (Texas A&M University).

# General Introduction
### *by*
### STEPHEN GREENBLATT

"He was not of an age, but for all time!"

The celebration of Shakespeare's genius, eloquently initiated by his friend and rival Ben Jonson, has over the centuries become an institutionalized rite of civility. The person who does not love Shakespeare has made, the rite implies, an incomplete adjustment not simply to a particular culture—English culture of the late sixteenth and early seventeenth centuries—but to "culture" as a whole, the dense network of constraints and entitlements, dreams and practices that links us to nature. Indeed, so absolute is Shakespeare's achievement that he has himself come to seem like great creating nature: the common bond of humankind, the principle of hope, the symbol of the imagination's power to transcend time-bound beliefs and assumptions, peculiar historical circumstances, and specific artistic conventions.

The near-worship that Shakespeare inspires is one of the salient facts about his art. But we must at the same time acknowledge that this art is the product of peculiar historical circumstances and specific conventions, four centuries distant from our own. The acknowledgment is important because Shakespeare the working dramatist did not typically lay claim to the transcendent, visionary truths attributed to him by his most fervent admirers; his characters more modestly say, in the words of the magician Prospero, that their project was "to please" (*The Tempest*, Epilogue, line 13). The starting point, and perhaps the ending point as well, in any encounter with Shakespeare is simply to enjoy him, to savor his imaginative richness, to take pleasure in his infinite delight in language.

"If then you do not like him," Shakespeare's first editors wrote in 1623, "surely you are in some manifest danger not to understand him." Over the years, accommodations have been devised to make liking Shakespeare easier for everyone. When the stage sank to melodrama and light opera, Shakespeare—in suitably revised texts—was there. When the populace had a craving for hippodrama, plays performed entirely on horseback, *Hamlet* was dutifully rewritten and mounted. When audiences went mad for realism, live frogs croaked in productions of *A Midsummer Night's Dream*. When the stage was stripped bare and given over to stark exhibitions of sadistic cruelty, Shakespeare was our contemporary. And when the theater itself had lost some of its cultural centrality, Shakespeare moved effortlessly to Hollywood and the soundstages of the BBC.

This virtually universal appeal is one of the most astonishing features of the Shakespeare phenomenon: plays that were performed before glittering courts thrive in junior-high-school auditoriums; enemies set on destroying one another laugh at the same jokes and weep at the same catastrophes; some of the richest and most complex English verse ever written migrates with spectacular success into German and Italian, Hindi, Swahili, and Japanese. Is there a single, stable, continuous object that underlies all of these migrations and metamorphoses? Certainly not. The global diffusion and long life of Shakespeare's works depend on their extraordinary malleability, their protean capacity to elude definition and escape secure possession. At the same time, they are not without identifiable shared features: across centuries and continents, family resemblances link many of the wildly diverse manifestations of plays such as *Romeo and Juliet, Hamlet,* and *Twelfth Night*. And if there is no clear limit or end point, there is a reasonably clear beginning: the

1

England of the late sixteenth and early seventeenth centuries, when the plays and poems collected in this volume made their first appearance.

An art virtually without end or limit but with an identifiable, localized, historical origin: Shakespeare's achievement defies the facile opposition between transcendent and time-bound. It is not necessary to choose between an account of Shakespeare as the scion of a particular culture and an account of him as a universal genius who created works that continually renew themselves across national and generational boundaries. On the contrary: crucial clues to understanding his art's remarkable power to soar beyond its originary time and place lie in the very soil from which that art sprang.

## Shakespeare's World

### Life and Death

Life expectancy at birth in early modern England was exceedingly low by our standards: under thirty years old, compared with over seventy today. Infant mortality rates were extraordinarily high, and it is estimated that in the poorer parishes of London only about half the children survived to the age of fifteen, while the children of aristocrats fared only a little better. In such circumstances, some parents must have developed a certain detachment—one of Shakespeare's contemporaries writes of losing "some three or four children"—but there are many expressions of intense grief, so that we cannot assume that the frequency of death hardened people to loss or made it routine.

Still, the spectacle of death, along with that other great threshold experience, birth, must have been far more familiar to Shakespeare and his contemporaries than to ourselves. There was no equivalent in early modern England to our hospitals, and most births and deaths occurred at home. Physical means for the alleviation of pain and suffering were extremely limited—alcohol might dull the terror, but it was hardly an effective anesthetic—and medical treatment was generally both expensive and worthless, more likely to intensify suffering than to lead to a cure. This was a world without a concept of antiseptics, with little actual understanding of disease, with few effective ways of treating earaches or venereal disease, let alone the more terrible instances of what Shakespeare calls "the thousand natural shocks that flesh is heir to."

The worst of these shocks was the bubonic plague, which repeatedly ravaged England, and particularly English towns, until the third quarter of the seventeenth century. The plague was terrifyingly sudden in its onset, rapid in its spread, and almost invariably lethal. Physicians were helpless in the face of the epidemic, though they prescribed amulets,

Bill recording plague deaths in London, 1609.

preservatives, and sweet-smelling substances (on the theory that the plague was carried by noxious vapors). In the plague-ridden year of 1564, the year of Shakespeare's birth, some 254 people died in Stratford-upon-Avon, out of a total population of 800. The year before, some 20,000 Londoners are thought to have died; in 1593, almost 15,000; in 1603, 36,000, or over a sixth of the city's inhabitants. The social effects of these horrible visitations were severe: looting, violence, and despair, along with an intensification of the age's perennial poverty, unemployment, and food shortages. The London plague regulations of 1583, reissued with modifications in later epidemics, ordered that the infected and their households be locked in their homes for a month; that the streets be kept clean; that vagrants be expelled; and that funerals and plays be restricted or banned entirely.

The plague, then, had a direct and immediate impact on Shakespeare's own profession. City officials kept records of the weekly number of plague deaths; when these surpassed a certain number, the theaters were peremptorily closed. The basic idea was not only to prevent contagion but also to avoid making an angry God still angrier with the spectacle of idleness. While restricting public assemblies may in fact have slowed the epidemic, other public policies in times of plague, such as killing the cats and dogs, may have made matters worse (since the disease, as we now know, was spread not by these animals but by the fleas that bred on the black rats that infested the poorer neighborhoods). Moreover, the playing companies, driven out of London by the closing of the theaters, may have carried plague to the provincial towns.

Even in good times, when the plague was dormant and the weather favorable for farming, the food supply in England was precarious. A few successive bad harvests, such as occurred in the mid-1590s, could cause serious hardship, even starvation. Not surprisingly, the poor bore the brunt of the burden: inflation, low wages, and rent increases left large numbers of people with very little cushion against disaster. Further, at its best, the diet of most people seems to have been seriously deficient. The lower classes then, as throughout most of history, subsisted on one or two foodstuffs, usually low in protein. The upper classes disdained green vegetables and milk and gorged themselves on meat. Illnesses that we now trace to vitamin deficiencies were rampant. Some, but not much, relief from pain was provided by the beer that Elizabethans, including children, drank almost incessantly. (Home brewing aside, enough beer was sold in England for every man, woman, and child to have consumed 40 gallons a year.)

## Wealth

Despite rampant disease, the population of England in Shakespeare's lifetime was steadily growing, from approximately 3,060,000 in 1564 to 4,060,000 in 1600 and 4,510,000 in 1616. Though the death rate was more than twice what it is in England today, the birthrate was almost three times the current figure. London's population in particular soared, from 60,000 in 1520 to 120,000 in 1550, 200,000 in 1600, and 375,000 half a century later, making it the largest and fastest-growing city not only in England but in all of Europe. Every year in the first half of the seventeenth century, about 10,000 people migrated to London from other parts of England—wages in London tended to be around 50 percent higher than in the rest of the country—and it is estimated that one in eight English people lived in London at some point in their lives. The economic viability of Shakespeare's profession was closely linked to this extraordinary demographic boom: between 1567 and 1642, a theater historian has calculated, the London playhouses were paid close to 50 million visits.

As these visits to the theater indicate, in the capital city and elsewhere a substantial number of English men and women, despite hardships that were never very distant, had money to spend. After the disorder and dynastic wars of the fifteenth century, England in the sixteenth and early seventeenth centuries was for the most part a nation at peace, and with peace came a measure of enterprise and prosperity: the landowning classes busied themselves building great houses, planting orchards and hop gardens, draining marshlands, bringing untilled "wastes" under cultivation. The artisans and laborers who actually accomplished these tasks, although they were generally paid very little, often managed to accumulate something, as did the small freeholding farmers, the yeomen, who are repeatedly celebrated in the period as the backbone of English national independence and wellbeing. William Harrison's *Description of England* (1577) lovingly itemizes the yeoman's precious possessions: "fair garnish of pewter on his cupboard, with so much more odd vessel going about the house, three or four featherbeds, so many coverlets and carpets of tapestry, a silver salt[cellar], a bowl for wine (if not a whole nest) and a dozen of spoons." There are comparable accounts of the hard-earned acquisitions of the city dwellers—masters and apprentices in small workshops, shipbuilders, wool merchants, clothmakers, chandlers, tradesmen, shopkeepers, along with lawyers, apothecaries, schoolteachers, scriveners, and the like—whose pennies from time to time enriched the coffers of the players.

The chief source of England's wealth in the sixteenth century was its textile industry, an industry that depended on a steady supply of wool. In *The Winter's Tale*, Shakespeare provides a warm, richly comic portrayal of a rural sheepshearing festival, but the increasingly intensive production of wool had in reality its grim side. When a character in Thomas More's *Utopia* (1516) complains that "the sheep are eating the people," he is referring to the practice of enclosure: throughout the sixteenth and early seventeenth centuries, many acres of croplands once farmed in common by rural communities were enclosed with fences by wealthy landowners and turned into pasturage. The ensuing misery, displacement, and food shortages led to repeated riots, some of them violent and bloody, along with a series of government proclamations, but the process of enclosure was not reversed.

The economic stakes were high, and not only for the domestic market. In 1565, woolen cloth alone made up more than three-fourths of England's exports. (The remainder consisted mostly of other textiles and raw wool, with some trade in lead, tin, grain, and skins.) The Company of Merchant Adventurers carried cloth to distant ports on the Baltic and Mediterranean, establishing links with Russia and Morocco (each took about 2 percent of London's cloth in 1597–98). English lead and tin, as well as fabrics, were sold in Tuscany and Turkey, and merchants found a market for Newcastle coal on the island of Malta. In the latter half of the century, London, which handled more than 85 percent of all exports, regularly shipped abroad more than 100,000 woolen cloths a year at a value of at least £750,000. This figure does not include the increasingly important and profitable trade in so-called New Draperies, including textiles that went by such exotic names as bombazines, calamancoes, damazellas, damizes, mockadoes, and virgenatoes. When the Earl of Kent in *King Lear* insults Oswald as a "filthy worsted-stocking knave" (2.2.14–15) or when the aristocratic Biron in *Love's Labour's Lost* declares that he will give up "taffeta phrases, silken terms precise, / Three-piled hyperboles" and woo henceforth "in russet yeas, and honest kersey noes" (5.2.406–07, 413), Shakespeare is assuming that a substantial portion of his audience will be alert to the social significance of fabric.

There is amusing confirmation of this alertness from an unexpected source: the report of a visit made to the Fortune playhouse in London in 1614 by a foreigner, Father Orazio Busino, the chaplain of the Venetian embassy. Father Busino neglected to mention the name of the play he saw, but like many foreigners, he was powerfully struck by the presence of gorgeously dressed women in the audience. In Venice, there was a special gallery for courtesans, but socially respectable women would not have been permitted to attend plays, as they could in England. In London, not only could middle- and upper-class women go to the theater, but they could also wear masks and mingle freely with male spectators and women of ill repute. The bemused cleric was uncertain about the ambiguous social situation in which he found himself:

> These theatres are frequented by a number of respectable and handsome ladies, who come freely and seat themselves among the men without the slightest hesitation. On the evening in question his Excellency and the Secretary were pleased to play me a trick by placing me amongst a bevy of young women. Scarcely was I seated ere a very

elegant dame, but in a mask, came and placed herself beside me. . . . She asked me for my address both in French and English; and, on my turning a deaf ear, she determined to honour me by showing me some fine diamonds on her fingers, repeatedly taking off not fewer than three gloves, which were worn one over the other. . . . This lady's bodice was of yellow satin richly embroidered, her petticoat of gold tissue with stripes, her robe of red velvet with a raised pile, lined with yellow muslin with broad stripes of pure gold. She wore an apron of point lace of various patterns: her head-tire was highly perfumed, and the collar of white satin beneath the delicately-wrought ruff struck me as extremely pretty.

Father Busino may have turned a deaf ear on this "elegant dame" but not a blind eye: his description of her dress is worthy of a fashion designer and conveys something of the virtual clothes cult that prevailed in England in the late sixteenth and early seventeenth centuries, a cult whose major shrine, outside the royal court, was the theater.

## Imports, Patents, and Monopolies

England produced some luxury goods, but the clothing on the backs of the most fashionable theatergoers was likely to have come from abroad. By the late sixteenth century, the English were importing substantial quantities of silks, satins, velvets, embroidery, gold and silver lace, and other costly items to satisfy the extravagant tastes of the elite and of those who aspired to dress like the elite. The government tried to put a check on the sartorial ambitions of the upwardly mobile by passing sumptuary laws—that is, laws restricting to the ranks of the aristocracy the right to wear certain of the most precious fabrics. But the very existence of these laws, in practice almost impossible to enforce, only reveals the scope and significance of the perceived problem.

Sumptuary laws were in part a conservative attempt to protect the existing social order from upstarts. Social mobility was not widely viewed as a positive virtue, and moralists repeatedly urged people to stay in their place. Conspicuous consumption that was tolerated, even admired, in the aristocratic elite was denounced as sinful and monstrous in less exalted social circles. English authorities were also deeply concerned throughout the period about the effects of a taste for luxury goods on the balance of trade. One of the principal English imports was wine: the "sherris" whose virtues Falstaff extols in 2 Henry IV came from Xeres in Spain; the malmsey in which poor Clarence is drowned in Richard III was probably made in Greece or in the Canary Islands (from whence came Sir Toby Belch's "cup of canary" in Twelfth Night); and the "flagon of rhenish" that Yorick in Hamlet had once poured on the Gravedigger's head came from the Rhine region of Germany. Other imports included canvas, linen, fish, olive oil, sugar, molasses, dates, oranges and lemons, figs, raisins, almonds, capers, indigo, ostrich feathers, and that increasingly popular drug from the New World, tobacco.

Joint-stock companies were established to import goods for the burgeoning English market. The Merchant Venturers of the city of Bristol (established in 1552) handled great shipments of Spanish sack, the light, dry wine that largely displaced the vintages of Bordeaux and Burgundy when trade with France was disrupted by war. The Muscovy Company (established in 1555) traded English cloth and manufactured goods for Russian furs, oil, and beeswax. The Venice Company and the Turkey Company—uniting in 1593 to form the wealthy Levant Company—brought silk and spices home from Aleppo and carpets from Istanbul. The East India Company (founded in 1600), with its agent at Bantam in Java, brought pepper, cloves, nutmeg, and other spices from east Asia, along with indigo, cotton textiles, sugar, and saltpeter from India. English privateers "imported" American products, especially sugar, fish, and hides, in huge quantities, along with more precious cargoes. In 1592, a privateering expedition principally funded by Sir Walter Ralegh captured a huge Portuguese carrack (sailing ship), the Madre de Dios, in the Azores and brought it back to Dartmouth. The ship, the largest that had ever entered any English port, held 536 tons of pepper, cloves, cinnamon, cochineal, mace, civet, musk, ambergris,

Cannoneer. From *Edward Webbe, . . . His Travailes* (1590).

and nutmeg, as well as jewels, gold, ebony, carpets, and silks. Before order could be established, the English seamen began to pillage this immensely rich prize, and witnesses said they could smell the spices on all the streets around the harbor. Such piratical expeditions were rarely officially sanctioned by the state, but the queen had in fact privately invested £1,800, for which she received about £80,000.

In the years of war with Spain, 1586–1604, the goods captured by the privateers annually amounted to 10 to 15 percent of the total value of England's imports. But organized theft alone could not solve England's balance-of-trade problems. Statesmen were particularly worried that the nation's natural wealth was slipping away in exchange for unnecessary things. In his *Discourse of the Commonweal* (1549), the prominent humanist Sir Thomas Smith exclaims against the importation of such trifles as mirrors, paper, laces, gloves, pins, inkhorns, tennis balls, puppets, and playing cards. And more than a century later, the same fear that England was trading its riches for trifles and wasting away in idleness was expressed by the Bristol merchant John Cary. The solution, Cary argues in "An Essay on the State of England in Relation to Its Trade" (1695), is to expand productive domestic employment. "People are or may be the Wealth of a Nation," he writes, "yet it must be where you find Employment for them, else they are a Burden to it, as the Idle Drone is maintained by the Industry of the laborious Bee, so are all those who live by their Dependence on others, as Players, Ale-House Keepers, Common Fiddlers, and such like, but more particularly Beggars, who never set themselves to work."

Stage players, all too typically associated here with vagabonds and other idle drones, could have replied in their defense that they not only labored in their vocation but also exported their skills abroad: English acting companies routinely traveled overseas and performed as far away as Bohemia. But their labor was not regarded as a productive contribution to the national wealth, and plays were in truth no solution to the trade imbalances that worried authorities.

The government attempted to stem the flow of gold overseas by establishing a patent system initially designed to encourage skilled foreigners to settle in England by granting them exclusive rights to produce particular wares by a patented method. Patents were granted for such things as the making of hard white soap (1561), ovens and furnaces (1563), window glass (1567), sailcloths (1574), drinking glasses (1574), sulphur, brimstone, and oil (1577), armor and horse harness (1587), starch (1588), white writing paper made from rags (1589), aqua vitae and vinegar (1594), playing cards (1598), and mathematical instruments (1598).

Although their ostensible purpose was to increase the wealth of England, encourage technical innovation, and provide employment for the poor, the effect of patents was often the enrichment of a few and the hounding of poor competitors by wealthy monopolists, a group that soon extended well beyond foreign-born entrepreneurs to the favorites of the monarch who vied for the huge profits to be made. "If I had a monopoly out" on folly, the Fool in *King Lear* protests, glancing at the "lords and great men" around him, "they would have part on't." The passage appears only in the quarto version of the play (*History of King Lear* 4.135–36); it may have been cut for political reasons from the Folio. For the issue of monopolies provoked bitter criticism and parliamentary debate for decades. In 1601, Elizabeth was prevailed upon to revoke a number of the most hated monopolies, including aqua vitae and vinegar, bottles, brushes, fish livers, the coarse sailcloth known as poldavis and mildernix, pots, salt, and starch. The whole system was revoked during the reign of James I by an act of Parliament.

## Haves and Have-Nots

When in the 1560s Elizabeth's ambassador to France, the humanist Sir Thomas Smith, wrote a description of England, he saw the commonwealth as divided into four sorts of people: "gentlemen, citizens, yeomen artificers, and laborers." At the forefront of the class of gentlemen was the monarch, followed by a very small group of nobles—dukes, marquesses, earls, viscounts, and barons—who either inherited their exalted titles, as the eldest male heirs of their families, or were granted them by the monarch. Under Elizabeth, this aristocratic peerage numbered between 50 and 60 individuals; James's promotions increased the number to nearer 130. Strictly speaking, Smith notes, the younger sons of the nobility were only entitled to be called "esquires," but in common speech they were also called "lords."

Below this tiny cadre of aristocrats in the social hierarchy of gentry were the knights, a title of honor conferred by the monarch, and below them were the "simple gentlemen." Who was a gentleman? According to Smith, "whoever studieth the laws of the realm, who studieth in the universities, who professeth liberal sciences, and to be short, who can live idly and without manual labor, and will bear the port, charge and countenance of a gentleman, he shall be called master . . . and shall be taken for a gentleman." To "live idly and without manual labor": where in Spain, for example, the crucial mark of a gentleman was "blood," in England it was "idleness," in the sense of sufficient income to afford an education and to maintain a social position without having to work with one's hands.

For Smith, the class of gentlemen was far and away the most important in the kingdom. Below were two groups that had at least some social standing and claim to authority: the citizens, or burgesses, those who held positions of importance and responsibility in their cities, and yeomen, farmers with land and a measure of economic independence. At the bottom of the social order was what Smith calls "the fourth sort of men which do not rule." The great mass of ordinary people have, Smith writes, "no voice nor authority in our commonwealth, and no account is made of them but only to be ruled." Still, even they can bear some responsibility, he notes, since they serve on juries and are named to such positions as churchwarden and constable.

In everyday practice, as modern social historians have observed, the English tended to divide the population not into four distinct classes but into two: a very small empowered group—the "richer" or "wiser" or "better" sort—and all the rest who were without much social standing or power, the "poorer" or "ruder" or "meaner" sort. References to the "middle sort of people" remain relatively rare until after Shakespeare's lifetime; these people are absorbed into the rulers or the ruled, depending on speaker and context.

The source of wealth for most of the ruling class, and the essential measure of social status, was landownership, and changes to the social structure in the sixteenth and seventeenth centuries were largely driven by the land market. The property that passed into private hands as the Tudors and early Stuarts sold off confiscated monastic estates and then their own crown lands for ready cash amounted to nearly a quarter of all the land in England. At the same time, the buying and selling of private estates was on the rise throughout the period. Land was bought up not only by established landowners seeking to enlarge their estates but by successful merchants, manufacturers, and urban professionals; even if the taint of vulgar moneymaking lingered around such figures, their heirs would be taken for true gentlemen. The rate of turnover in landownership was great; in many counties, well over half the gentle families in 1640 had appeared since the end of the fifteenth century. The class that Smith called "simple gentlemen" was expanding rapidly: in the fifteenth century, they had held no more than a quarter of the land in the country; but by the later seventeenth century, they controlled almost half. Over the same period, the land held by the great aristocratic magnates held steady at 15 to 20 percent of the total.

## Riot and Disorder

London was a violent place in the first half of Shakespeare's career. There were thirty-five riots in the city in the years 1581–1602, twelve of them in the volatile month of June 1595. These included protests against the deeply unpopular lord mayor Sir John Spencer, attempts to release prisoners, anti-alien riots, and incidents of "popular market regulation." There is an unforgettable depiction of a popular uprising in *Coriolanus*, along with many other glimpses in Shakespeare's works, including John Cade's grotesque rebellion in *The First Part of the Contention (2 Henry VI)*, the plebeian violence in *Julius Caesar*, and Laertes' "riotous head" in *Hamlet*.

The London rioters were mostly drawn from the large mass of poor and discontented apprentices who typically chose as their scapegoats foreigners, prostitutes, and gentlemen's servingmen. Theaters were very often the site of the social confrontations that sparked disorder. For two days running in June 1584, disputes between apprentices and gentlemen triggered riots outside the Curtain Theatre involving up to a thousand participants. On one occasion, a gentleman was said to have exclaimed that "the apprentice was but a rascal, and some there were little better than rogues that took upon them the name of gentlemen, and said the prentices were but the scum of the world." These occasions culminated in attacks by the apprentices on London's law schools, the Inns of Court.

The most notorious and predictable incidents of disorder came on Shrove Tuesday (the Tuesday before the beginning of Lent), a traditional day of misrule when apprentices ran riot. Shrove Tuesday disturbances involved attacks by mobs of young men on the brothels of the South Bank, in the vicinity of the Globe and other public theaters. The city authorities took precautions to keep these disturbances from getting completely out of control but evidently did not regard them as serious threats to public order.

Of much greater concern throughout the Tudor and early Stuart years were the frequent incidents of rural rioting against the enclosure of commons and wasteland by local landlords (and, in the royal forests, by the crown). This form of popular protest was at its height during Shakespeare's career: in the years 1590–1610, the frequency of anti-enclosure rioting doubled from what it had been earlier in Elizabeth's reign.

Although they often became violent, anti-enclosure riots were usually directed not against individuals but against property. Villagers—sometimes several hundred, often fewer than a dozen—gathered to tear down newly planted hedges. The event often took place in a carnival atmosphere, with songs and drinking, that did not prevent the participants from acting with a good deal of political canniness and forethought. Especially in the Jacobean period, it was common for participants to establish a common fund for legal defense before commencing their assault on the hedges. Women were frequently involved, and on a number of occasions wives alone participated in the destruction of the enclosure, since there was a widespread, though erroneous, belief that married women acting without the knowledge of their husbands were immune from prosecution. In fact, the powerful Court of Star Chamber consistently ruled that both the wives and their husbands should be punished.

Peddler. From Jost Amman, *The Book of Trades* (1568).

Although Stratford was never the scene of serious rioting, enclosure controversies there turned violent more than once in Shakespeare's lifetime. In January 1601, Shakespeare's friend Richard Quiney and others leveled the hedges of Sir Edward Greville, lord of Stratford manor. Quiney was elected bailiff of Stratford in September of that year but did not live to enjoy the office for long. He died from a blow to the head struck by one of Greville's men in a tavern brawl. Greville, responsible for the administration of justice, neglected to punish the murderer.

There was further violence in January 1615, when William Combe's men threw to the ground two local aldermen who were filling in a ditch by which Combe was enclosing common fields near Stratford. The task of filling in the offending ditch was completed the next day by the women and children of Stratford. Combe's enclosure scheme was eventually stopped in the courts. Although he owned land whose value would have been affected by this controversy, Shakespeare took no active role in it, since he had previously come to a private settlement with the enclosers insuring him against personal loss.

Most incidents of rural rioting were small, localized affairs, and with good reason: when confined to the village community, riot was a misdemeanor; when it spread outward to include multiple communities, it became treason, punishable by death. The greatest of the anti-enclosure riots, those in which hundreds of individuals from a large area participated, commonly took place on the eve of full-scale regional rebellions. The largest of these disturbances, Kett's Rebellion, involved some 16,000 peasants, artisans, and townspeople who rose up in 1549 under the leadership of a Norfolk tanner and landowner, Robert Kett, to protest economic exploitation. The agrarian revolts in Shakespeare's lifetime were on a much smaller scale. In the abortive Oxfordshire Rebellion of 1596, a carpenter named Bartholomew Steere attempted to organize a rising against enclosing gentlemen. The optimistic Steere promised his followers that "it was but a month's work to overrun England" and informed them "that the commons long since in Spain did rise and kill all gentlemen . . . and since that time have lived merrily there." Steere expected several hundred men to join him on Enslow Hill on November 21, 1596, for the start of the rising; no more than twenty showed up. They were captured, imprisoned, and tortured. Several were executed, but Steere apparently cheated the hangman by dying in prison.

Rebellions, most often triggered by hunger and oppression, continued into the reign of James I. The Midland Revolt of 1607, which may be reflected in *Coriolanus,* consisted of a string of agrarian risings in the counties of Northamptonshire, Warwickshire, and Leicestershire, involving assemblies of up to 5,000 rebels in various places. The best known of their leaders was John Reynolds, called "Captain Powch" because of the pouch he wore, whose magical contents were supposed to defend the rebels from harm. (According to the chronicler Edmund Howes, when Reynolds was captured and the pouch opened, it contained "only a piece of green cheese.") The rebels, who were called by themselves and others both "Levelers" and "Diggers," insisted that they had no quarrel with the king but only sought an end to injurious enclosures. But Robert Wilkinson, who preached a sermon against the leaders at their trial, credited them with the intention to "level all states as they leveled banks and ditches." Most of the rebels got off relatively lightly but, along with other ringleaders, Captain Powch was executed.

## The Legal Status of Women

Even though England was ruled for over forty years by a powerful woman, the great majority of women in the kingdom had very restricted social, economic, and legal standing. To be sure, a tiny number of influential aristocratic women, such as the formidable Countess of Shrewsbury, Bess of Hardwick, wielded considerable power. But, these rare exceptions aside, women were denied any rightful claim to institutional authority or personal autonomy. When Sir Thomas Smith thinks of how he should describe his country's social order, he declares that "we do reject women, as those whom nature hath made to keep home and to nourish their family and children, and not to meddle with matters abroad, nor to bear office in a city or commonwealth."

Then, with a kind of glance over his shoulder, he makes an exception of those few for whom "the blood is respected, not the age nor the sex": for example, the queen.

English women were not under the full range of crushing constraints that afflicted women in some countries in Europe. Foreign visitors were struck by their relative freedom, as shown, for example, by the fact that respectable women could venture unchaperoned into the streets and attend the theater. Single women, whether widowed or unmarried, could, if they were of full age, inherit and administer land, make a will, sign a contract, possess property, sue and be sued, without a male guardian or proxy. But married women had no such rights under the common law.

Early modern writings about women and the family constantly return to a political model of domination and submission, in which the father justly rules over wife and children as the monarch rules over the state. This conception of a woman's role conveniently ignores the fact that a *majority* of the adult women at any time in Shakespeare's England were not married. They were either widows or spinsters (a term that was not yet pejorative), and thus for the most part managing their own affairs. Even within marriage, women typically had more control over certain spheres than moralizing writers on the family cared to admit. For example, village wives oversaw the production of eggs, cheese, and beer, and sold these goods in the market. As seamstresses, pawnbrokers, secondhand clothing dealers, peddlers, and the like—activities not controlled by the all-male guilds—women managed to acquire some economic power of their own, and, of course, they participated as well in the unregulated, black-market economy of the age and in the underworld of thievery and prostitution.

Women were not in practice as bereft of property as, according to English common law, they should have been. Demographic studies indicate that the inheritance system called primogeniture, the orderly transmission of property from father to eldest male heir, was more often an unfulfilled wish than a reality. Some 40 percent of marriages failed to produce a son, and in such circumstances fathers often left their land to their daughters, rather than to brothers, nephews, or male cousins. In many families, the father died before his male heir was old enough to inherit property, leaving the land, at least temporarily, in the hands of the mother. And while they were less likely than their brothers to inherit land ("real property"), daughters normally inherited a substantial share of their father's personal property (cash and movables).

In fact, the legal restrictions upon women, though severe in Shakespeare's time, actually worsened in subsequent decades. The English common law, the system of law based on court decisions rather than on codified written laws, was significantly less egalitarian in its approach to wives and daughters than were alternative legal codes (manorial, civil, and ecclesiastical) still in place in the late sixteenth century. The eventual triumph of common law stripped women of many traditional rights, slowly driving them out of economically productive trades and businesses.

Limited though it was, the economic freedom of Elizabethan and Jacobean women far exceeded their political and social freedom—the opportunity to receive a grammar-school or university education, to hold office in church or state, to have a voice in public debates, or even simply to speak their mind fully and openly in ordinary conversation. Women who asserted their views too vigorously risked being perceived as shrewish and labeled "scolds." Both urban and rural communities had a horror of scolds. In the Elizabethan period, such women came to be regarded as a threat to public order, to be dealt with by the local authorities. The preferred methods of correction included public humiliation—of the sort Katherine endures in *The Taming of the Shrew*—and such physical abuse as slapping, bridling, and soaking by means of a contraption called the "cucking stool" (or "ducking stool"). This latter punishment originated in the Middle Ages, but its use spread in the sixteenth century, when it became almost exclusively a punishment for women. From 1560 onward, cucking stools were built or renovated in many English provincial towns; between 1560 and 1600, the contraptions were installed by rivers or ponds in Norwich, Bridport, Shrewsbury, Kingston-upon-Thames, Marlborough, Devizes, Clitheroe, Thornbury, and Great Yarmouth.

Such punishment was usually intensified by a procession through the town to the sound of "rough music," the banging together of pots and pans. The same cruel festivity accompanied the "carting" or "riding" of those accused of being whores. In some parts of the country, villagers also took the law into their own hands, publicly shaming women who married men much younger than themselves or who beat or otherwise domineered over their husbands. One characteristic form of these charivaris, or rituals of shaming, was known in the West Country as the Skimmington Ride. Villagers would rouse the offending couple from bed with rough music and stage a raucous pageant in which a man, holding a distaff, would ride backward on a donkey, while his "wife" (another man dressed as a woman) struck him with a ladle. In these cases, the collective ridicule and indignation was evidently directed at least as much at the henpecked husband as at his transgressive wife.

## Women and Print

Books published for a female audience surged in popularity in the late sixteenth century, reflecting an increase in female literacy. (It is striking how many of Shakespeare's women are shown reading.) This increase is probably linked to a Protestant longing for direct access to the Scriptures, and the new books marketed specifically for women included devotional manuals and works of religious instruction. But there were also practical guides to such subjects as female education (for example, Giovanni Bruto's *Necessarie, Fit, and Convenient Education of a Young Gentlewoman,* 1598), midwifery (James Guillemeau's *Child-birth; or, The Happy Delivery of Women,* 1612), needlework (Federico di Vinciolo's *New and Singular Patternes and Workes of Linnen,* 1591), cooking (Thomas Dawson's *The Good Husewifes Jewell,* 1587), gardening (Pierre Erondelle's *The French Garden for English Ladyes and Gentlewomen to Walke In,* 1605), and married life (Patrick Hannay's *A Happy Husband; or, Directions for a Maide to Choose Her Mate,* 1619). As the authors' names suggest, many of these works were translations, and almost all were written by men.

Starting in the 1570s, writers and their publishers increasingly addressed works of recreational literature (romance, fiction, and poetry) partially or even exclusively to women. Some books, such as Robert Greene's *Mamillia, a Mirrour or Looking-Glasse for the Ladies of Englande* (1583), directly specified in the title their desired audience. Others, such as Sir Philip Sidney's influential and popular romance *Arcadia* (1590–93), solicited female readership in their dedicatory epistles. The ranks of Sidney's followers eventually included his own niece, Mary Wroth, whose romance *Urania* was published in 1621.

In the literature of Shakespeare's time, women readers were not only wooed but also frequently railed at, in a continuation of a popular polemical genre that had long inspired heated charges and countercharges. Both sides in the polemic generally agreed that it was the duty of women to be chaste, dutiful, shamefast, and silent; the argument was whether women fulfilled or fell short of this proper role. Ironically, then, a modern reader is more likely to find inspiring accounts of courageous women not in the books written in defense of female virtue but in attacks on those who refused to be silent and obedient.

The most famous English skirmish in this controversy took place in a rash of pamphlets at the end of Shakespeare's life. Joseph Swetnam's crude *Araignment of Lewd, Idle, Froward, and Unconstant Women* (1615) provoked three fierce responses attributed to women: Rachel Speght's *A Mouzell [Muzzle] for Melastomus,* Ester Sowernam's *Ester Hath Hang'd Haman,* and Constantia Munda's *Worming of a Mad Dogge,* all 1617. There was also an anonymous play, *Swetnam, the Woman-hater, Arraigned by Women* (1618), in which Swetnam, depicted as a braggart and a lecher, is put on trial by women and made to recant his misogynistic lies.

Prior to the Swetnam controversy, only one English woman, "Jane Anger," had published a defense of women (*Jane Anger, Her Protection for Women,* 1589). Learned women writers in the sixteenth century tended not to become involved in public debate but rather to undertake a project to which it was difficult for even obdurately chauvinistic

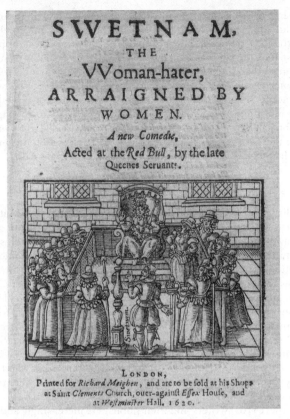

Title page of *Swetnam, the Woman-hater, Arraigned by Women* (1620), a play written in response to Joseph Swetnam's *The Araignment of Lewd, Idle, Froward and Unconstant Women* (1615); the woodcut depicts the trial of Swetnam in Act 4.

males to object: the translation of devotional literature into English. Thomas More's daughter Margaret More Roper translated Erasmus (*A Devout Treatise upon the Pater Noster,* 1524); Francis Bacon's mother, Anne Cooke Bacon, translated Bishop John Jewel (*An Apologie or Answere in Defence of the Churche of Englande,* 1564); Anne Locke Prowse, a friend of John Knox, translated the *Sermons of John Calvin* in 1560; and Mary Sidney, Countess of Pembroke, completed the metrical version of the Psalms that her brother Sir Philip Sidney had begun. Elizabeth Tudor (the future queen) herself translated, at the age of eleven, Marguerite de Navarre's *Miroir de l'âme pécheresse* (*The Glass of the Sinful Soul,* 1544). The translation was dedicated to her stepmother, Catherine Parr, herself the author of a frequently reprinted book of prayers.

There was in the sixteenth and early seventeenth centuries a social stigma attached to print. Far from celebrating publication, authors, and particularly female authors, often apologized for exposing themselves to the public gaze. Nonetheless, a number of women ventured beyond pious translations circulated in manuscript. Some, including Elizabeth Tyrwhitt, Anne Dowriche, Isabella Whitney, Mary Sidney, and Aemilia Lanyer, composed and published their own poems. Aemilia Lanyer's *Salve Deus Rex Judaeorum,* published in 1611, is a poem in praise of virtuous women, from Eve and the Virgin Mary to her noble patron, the Countess of Cumberland. "A Description of Cookeham," appended to the poem, may be the first English-country-house poem.

The first Tudor woman to translate a play was the learned Jane Lumley, who composed an English version of Euripides' *Iphigenia at Aulis* (c. 1550). The first known original play in English by a woman was by Elizabeth Cary, Viscountess Falkland, whose *Tragedie of Mariam, the Faire Queene of Jewry* was published in 1613. This remarkable play, which was not intended to be performed, includes speeches in defense of women's equality, though the most powerful of these is spoken by the villainous Salome, who schemes to divorce her husband and marry her lover. Cary, who bore eleven children, herself had a deeply troubled marriage, which effectively came to an end in 1625, when, defying her husband's staunchly Protestant family, she openly converted to Catholicism. Her biography was written by one of her four daughters, all of whom became nuns.

## Henry VIII and the English Reformation

There had long been serious ideological and institutional tensions in the religious life of England, but officially, at least, England in the early sixteenth century had a single religion, Catholicism, whose acknowledged head was the pope in Rome. In 1517, drawing upon long-standing currents of dissent, Martin Luther, an Augustinian monk and professor of theology at the University of Wittenberg, challenged the authority of the pope and attacked several key doctrines of the Catholic Church. According to Luther, the Church, with its elaborate hierarchical structure centered in Rome, its rich monasteries and convents, and its enormous political influence, had become hopelessly corrupt, a conspiracy of venal priests who manipulated popular superstitions to enrich themselves and amass worldly power. Luther began by vehemently attacking the sale of indulgences—certificates promising the remission of punishments to be suffered in the afterlife by souls sent to purgatory to expiate their sins. These indulgences were a fraud, he argued; purgatory itself had no foundation in the Bible, which in his view was the only legitimate source of religious truth. Christians would be saved not by scrupulously following the ritual practices fostered by the Catholic Church—observing fast days, reciting the ancient Latin prayers, endowing chantries to say prayers for the dead, and so on—but by faith and faith alone.

This challenge, which came to be known as the Reformation, spread and gathered force, especially in northern Europe, where major leaders like the Swiss pastor Huldrych Zwingli and the French theologian John Calvin established institutional structures and elaborated various and sometimes conflicting doctrinal principles. Calvin, whose thought came to be particularly influential in England, emphasized the obligation of governments to implement God's will in the world. He advanced too the doctrine of predestination, by which, as he put it, "God adopts some to hope of life and sentences others to eternal death." God's "secret election" of the saved made Calvin uncomfortable, but his study of the Scriptures had led him to conclude that "only a small number, out of an incalculable multitude, should obtain salvation." It might seem that such a conclusion would lead to passivity or even despair, but for Calvin predestination was a mystery bound up with faith, confidence, and an active engagement in the fashioning of a Christian community.

The Reformation had a direct and powerful impact on those territories, especially in northern Europe, where it gained control. Monasteries were sacked, their possessions seized by princes or sold off to the highest bidder; the monks and nuns, expelled from their cloisters, were encouraged to break their vows of chastity and find spouses, as Luther and his wife, a former nun, had done. In the great cathedrals and in hundreds of smaller churches and chapels, the elaborate altarpieces, bejeweled crucifixes, crystal reliquaries holding the bones of saints, and venerated statues and paintings were attacked as "idols" and often defaced or destroyed. Protestant congregations continued, for the most part, to celebrate the most sacred Christian ritual, the Eucharist, or Lord's Supper, but they did so in a profoundly different spirit from that of the Catholic Church—more as commemoration than as miracle—and they now prayed not in the ancient liturgical Latin but in the vernacular.

"The Pope as Antichrist riding the Beast of the Apocalypse." From *Fierie Tryall of God's Saints* (1611; author unknown).

The Reformation was at first vigorously resisted in England. Indeed, with the support of his ardently Catholic chancellor, Thomas More, Henry VIII personally wrote (or at least lent his name to) a vehement, often scatological attack on Luther's character and views, an attack for which the pope granted him the honorific title "Defender of the Faith." Protestant writings, including translations of the Scriptures into English, were seized by officials of the church and state and burned. Protestants who made their views known were persecuted, driven to flee the country, or arrested, put on trial, and burned at the stake. But the situation changed drastically and decisively when in 1527 Henry decided to seek a divorce from his first wife, Catherine of Aragon, in order to marry Anne Boleyn.

Catherine had given birth to six children, but since only a daughter, Mary, survived infancy, Henry did not have the son he craved. Then as now, the Catholic Church did not ordinarily grant divorce, but Henry's lawyers argued on technical grounds that the marriage was invalid (and, therefore, by extension, that Mary was illegitimate and hence unable to inherit the throne). Matters of this kind were far less doctrinal than diplomatic: Catherine, the daughter of Ferdinand of Aragon and Isabella of Castile, had powerful allies in Rome, and the pope ruled against Henry's petition for a divorce. A series of momentous events followed, as England lurched away from the Church of Rome. In 1531, Henry charged the entire clergy of England with having usurped royal authority in the administration of canon law (the ecclesiastical law that governed faith, discipline, and morals, including such matters as divorce). Under extreme pressure, including the threat of mass confiscations and imprisonment, the Convocation of the English Clergy begged for pardon, made a donation to the royal coffers of over £100,000, and admitted that the king was "supreme head of the English Church and clergy" (modified by the rider "as far as the law of Christ allows"). On May 15 of the next year, the convocation submitted to the demand that the king be the final arbiter of canon law; on the next day, Thomas More resigned his post.

In 1533, Henry's marriage to Catherine was officially declared null and void, and on June 1 Anne Boleyn was crowned queen (a coronation Shakespeare depicts in his late play *All Is True*). The king was promptly excommunicated by the pope, Clement VII. In the following year, the parliamentary Act of Succession confirmed the effects of the divorce and required an oath from all adult male subjects confirming the new dynastic settlement. Thomas More and John Fisher, Bishop of Rochester, were among the small number who refused. The Act of Supremacy, passed later in the year, formally declared the king to be "Supreme Head of the Church in England" and again required an oath to this effect. In 1535 and 1536, further acts made it treasonous to refuse the oath of royal supremacy or, as More had tried to do, to remain silent. The first victims were three Carthusian monks who rejected the oath—"How could the king, a layman," said one of them, "be Head of the Church of England?"—and in May 1535, they were duly hanged, drawn, and quartered. A few weeks later, Fisher and More were convicted and beheaded. Between 1536 and 1539, the monasteries were suppressed and their vast wealth seized by the crown.

Royal defiance of the authority of Rome was a key element in the Reformation but did not by itself constitute the establishment of Protestantism in England. On the contrary, in the same year that Fisher and More were martyred for their adherence to Roman Catholicism, twenty-five Protestants, members of a sect known as Anabaptists, were burned for heresy on a single day. Through most of his reign, Henry remained an equal-opportunity persecutor, ruthless to Catholics loyal to Rome and hostile to some of those who espoused Reformation ideas, though many of these ideas gradually established themselves on English soil.

Even when Henry was eager to do so, it proved impossible to eradicate Protestantism, as it would later prove impossible for his successors to eradicate Catholicism. In large part this tenacity arose from the passionate, often suicidal heroism of men and women who felt that their souls' salvation depended on the precise character of their Christianity. It arose, too, from a mid-fifteenth-century technological innovation that made it almost impossible to suppress unwelcome ideas: the printing press. Early Protestants quickly grasped that with a few clandestine presses they could defy the Catholic authorities and flood the country with their texts. "How many printing presses there be in the world," wrote the Protestant polemicist John Foxe, "so many blockhouses there be against the high castle" of the pope in Rome, "so that either the pope must abolish knowledge and printing or printing at length will root him out." By the century's end, it was the Catholics who were using the clandestine press to propagate their beliefs in the face of Protestant persecution.

The greatest insurrection of the Tudor age was not over food, taxation, or land but over religion. On Sunday, October 1, 1536, stirred up by their vicar, the traditionalist parishioners of Louth in Lincolnshire, in the north of England, rose up in defiance of the ecclesiastical visitation sent to enforce royal supremacy. The rapidly spreading rebellion, which became known as the Pilgrimage of Grace, was led by the lawyer Robert Aske. The city of Lincoln fell to the rebels on October 6, and though it was soon retaken by royal forces, the rebels seized cities and fortifications throughout Yorkshire, Durham, Northumberland, Cumberland, Westmoreland, and northern Lancashire. Carlisle, Newcastle, and a few castles were all that were left to the king in the north. The Pilgrims soon numbered 40,000, led by some of the region's leading noblemen. The Duke of Norfolk, representing the crown, was forced to negotiate a truce, with a promise to support the rebels' demands that the king restore the monasteries, shore up the regional economy, suppress heresy, and dismiss his evil advisers.

The Pilgrims kept the peace for the rest of 1536, on the naive assumption that their demands would be met. But Henry moved suddenly early in 1537 to impose order and capture the ringleaders; 130 people, including lords, knights, heads of religious houses, and, of course, Robert Aske, were executed.

In 1549, two years after the death of Henry VIII, the west and the north of England were the sites of further unsuccessful risings for the restoration of Catholicism. The Western Rising is striking for its blend of Catholic universalism and intense regionalism among people who did not yet regard themselves as English. One of the rebels' articles, protesting against the imposition of the English Bible and religious service, declares, "We the Cornish men (whereof certain of us understand no English) utterly refuse this new English." The rebels besieged but failed to take the city of Exeter. As with almost all Tudor rebellions, the number of those executed in the aftermath of the failed rising was far greater than those killed in actual hostilities.

## Henry VIII's Children: Edward, Mary, and Elizabeth

Upon Henry's death in 1547, his ten-year-old son, Edward VI, came to the throne, with his maternal uncle Edward Seymour named as Lord Protector and Duke of Somerset. Both Edward and his uncle were staunch Protestants, and reformers hastened to transform the English Church accordingly. During Edward's reign, Archbishop Thomas Cranmer formulated the forty-two articles of religion that became the core of Anglican orthodoxy and wrote the first Book of Common Prayer, which was officially adopted in 1549 as the basis of English worship services.

Somerset fell from power in 1549 and was replaced as Lord Protector by John Dudley, later Duke of Northumberland. When Edward fell seriously ill, probably of tuberculosis, Northumberland persuaded him to sign a will depriving his half sisters, Mary (the daughter of Catherine of Aragon) and Elizabeth (the daughter of Anne Boleyn), of their claim to royal succession. The Lord Protector was scheming to have his daughter-in-law, the Protestant Lady Jane Grey, a granddaughter of Henry VII, ascend to the throne. But when Edward died in 1553, Mary marshaled support, quickly secured the crown from Lady Jane (who had been titular queen for nine days), and had Lady Jane executed, along with her husband and Northumberland.

Queen Mary immediately took steps to return her kingdom to Roman Catholicism. Even though she was unable to get Parliament to agree to restore church lands seized under Henry VIII, she restored the Catholic Mass, once again affirmed the authority of the pope, and put down a rebellion that sought to depose her. Seconded by her ardently Catholic husband, Philip II, King of Spain, she initiated a series of religious persecutions that earned her (from her enemies) the name "Bloody Mary." Hundreds of Protestants took refuge abroad in cities such as Calvin's Geneva; almost three hundred less fortunate Protestants were condemned as heretics and burned at the stake.

*The Family of Henry VIII: An Allegory of the Tudor Succession.* By Lucas de Heere (c. 1572). Henry, in the middle, is flanked by Mary to his right, and Edward and Elizabeth to his left.

Mary died childless in 1558, and her younger half sister Elizabeth became queen. Elizabeth's succession had been by no means assured. For if Protestants regarded Henry VIII's marriage to Catherine as invalid and hence deemed Mary illegitimate, so Catholics regarded his marriage to Anne Boleyn as invalid and deemed Elizabeth illegitimate. Henry VIII himself seemed to support both views, since only three years after divorcing Catherine, he beheaded Anne Boleyn on charges of treason and adultery, and urged Parliament to invalidate the marriage. Moreover, though during her sister's reign Elizabeth outwardly complied with the official Catholic religious observance, Mary and her advisers were deeply suspicious, and the young princess's life was in grave danger. Poised and circumspect, Elizabeth warily evaded the traps that were set for her. As she ascended the throne, her actions were scrutinized for some indication of the country's future course. During her coronation procession, when a girl in an allegorical pageant presented her with a Bible in English translation—banned under Mary's reign—Elizabeth kissed the book, held it up reverently, and laid it to her breast; when the abbot and monks of Westminster Abbey came to greet her in broad daylight with candles (a symbol of Catholic devotion) in their hands, she briskly dismissed them with the telling words "Away with those torches! we can see well enough." England had returned to the Reformation.

Many English men and women, of all classes, remained loyal to the old Catholic faith, but English authorities under Elizabeth moved steadily, if cautiously, toward ensuring at least an outward conformity to the official Protestant settlement. Recusants, those who refused to attend regular Sunday services in their parish churches, were fined heavily. Anyone who wished to receive a university degree, to be ordained as a priest in the Church of England, or to be named as an officer of the state had to swear an oath to the royal supremacy. Commissioners were sent throughout the land to confirm that religious services were following the officially approved liturgy and to investigate any reported backsliding into Catholic practice or, alternatively, any attempts to introduce more radical reforms than the queen and her bishops had chosen to embrace. For the Protestant exiles who streamed back were eager not only to undo the damage Mary had done but to carry the Reformation much further. They sought to dismantle the church hierarchy, to purge the calendar of folk customs deemed pagan and the church service of ritual practices deemed superstitious, to dress the clergy in simple garb, and, at the extreme edge, to smash "idolatrous" statues, crucifixes, and altarpieces. Throughout her long reign, however, Elizabeth herself remained cautiously conservative and determined to hold in check what she regarded as the religious zealotry of Catholics, on the one side, and Puritans, on the other.

Shakespeare's plays tap into the ongoing confessional tensions: "Sometimes," Maria in *Twelfth Night* says of the sober, festivity-hating steward Malvolio, "he is a kind of puritan" (2.3.125). But they tend to avoid the risks of direct engagement: "The dev'l a puritan that he is, or anything constantly," Maria adds a moment later, "but a timepleaser, an affectioned ass" (2.3.131–32). *The Winter's Tale* features a statue that comes to life—exactly the kind of magical image that Protestant polemicists excoriated as Catholic superstition and idolatry—but the play is set in pre-Christian world of the Delphic oracle. And as if this careful distancing might not be enough, the play's ruler goes out of his way to pronounce the wonder legitimate: "If this be magic, let it be an art / Lawful as eating" (5.3.110–11).

In the space of a single lifetime, England had gone officially from Roman Catholicism, to Catholicism under the supreme headship of the English king, to a guarded Protestantism, to a more radical Protestantism, to a renewed and aggressive Roman Catholicism, and finally to Protestantism again. Each of these shifts was accompanied by danger, persecution, and death. It was enough to make some people wary. Or skeptical. Or extremely agile.

## The English Bible

Luther had undertaken a fundamental critique of the Catholic Church's sacramental system, a critique founded on the twin principles of salvation by faith alone (*sola fide)* and the absolute primacy of the Bible *(sola scriptura)*. *Sola fide* contrasted faith with "works," by which was meant primarily the whole elaborate system of rituals sanctified, conducted, or directed by the priests. Protestants proposed to modify or reinterpret many of these rituals or, as with the rituals associated with purgatory, to abolish them altogether. *Sola scriptura* required direct lay access to the Bible, which meant in practice the widespread availability of vernacular translations. The Roman Catholic Church had not always and everywhere opposed such translations, but it generally preferred that the populace encounter the Scriptures through the interpretations of the priests, trained to read the Latin translation known as the Vulgate. In times of great conflict, this preference for clerical mediation hardened into outright prohibition of vernacular translation and into persecution and book burning.

Zealous Protestants set out, in the teeth of fierce opposition, to put the Bible into the hands of the laity. A remarkable translation of the New Testament, by an English Lutheran named William Tyndale, was printed on the Continent and smuggled into England in 1525; Tyndale's translation of the Pentateuch, the first five books of the Hebrew Bible, followed in 1530. Many copies of these translations were seized and burned, as was the translator himself, but the printing press made it extremely difficult for authorities to eradicate books for which there was a passionate demand. The English Bible was a force that could not be suppressed, and it became, in its various forms, the single most important book of the sixteenth century.

Tyndale's translation was completed by an associate, Miles Coverdale, whose rendering of the Psalms proved to be particularly influential. Their joint labor was the basis for the Great Bible (1539), the first authorized version of the Bible in English, a copy of which was ordered to be placed in every church in the kingdom. With the accession of Edward VI, many editions of the Bible followed, but the process was sharply reversed when Mary came to the throne in 1553. Along with people condemned as heretics, English Bibles were burned in great bonfires.

Marian persecution was indirectly responsible for what would become the most popular as well as most scholarly English Bible, the translation known as the Geneva Bible, prepared, with extensive, learned, and often fiercely polemical marginal notes, by English exiles in Calvin's Geneva and widely diffused in England after Elizabeth came to the throne. In addition, Elizabethan church authorities ordered a careful revision of the Great Bible, and this version, known as the Bishops' Bible, was the one read in the churches. The success of the Geneva Bible in particular prompted those Elizabethan Catholics who now in turn found themselves in exile to bring out a vernacular translation of their own in order to counter the Protestant readings and glosses. This Catholic translation, known as the Rheims Bible, may have been known to Shakespeare, but he seems to have been far better acquainted with the Geneva Bible, and he would also have repeatedly heard the Bishops' Bible read aloud. Scholars have identified over three hundred references to the Bible in Shakespeare's work; in one version or another, the Scriptures had a powerful impact on his imagination.

## A Female Monarch in a Male World

In the last year of Mary's reign, 1558, the Scottish Calvinist minister John Knox thundered against what he called "the monstrous regiment of women." When the Protestant Elizabeth came to the throne the following year, Knox and his religious brethren were less inclined to denounce female rulers, but in England as elsewhere in Europe there remained a widespread conviction that women were unsuited to wield power over men. Many men seem to have regarded the capacity for rational thought as exclusively male; women, they assumed, were led only by their passions. While gentlemen mastered the arts of rhetoric and warfare, gentlewomen were expected to display the virtues of silence and good housekeeping. Among upper-class males, the will to dominate others was acceptable and, indeed, admired; the same will in women was condemned as a grotesque and dangerous aberration.

One of the Armada portraits (c. 1588). Note Elizabeth's hand on the globe.

Apologists for the queen countered these prejudices by appealing to historical precedent and legal theory. History offered inspiring examples of just female rulers, notably Deborah, the biblical prophetess who judged Israel. In the legal sphere, crown lawyers advanced the theory of "the king's two bodies." As England's crowned head, Elizabeth's person was mystically divided between her mortal "body natural" and the immortal "body politic." While the queen's natural body was inevitably subject to the failings of human flesh, the body politic was timeless and perfect. In political terms, therefore, Elizabeth's sex was a matter of no consequence, a thing indifferent.

Elizabeth, who had received a fine humanist education and an extended, dangerous lesson in the art of survival, made it immediately clear that she intended to rule in more than name only. She assembled a group of trustworthy advisers, foremost among them William Cecil (later named Lord Burghley, also known as Burleigh), but she insisted on making many of the crucial decisions herself. Like many Renaissance monarchs, Elizabeth was drawn to the idea of royal absolutism, the theory that ultimate power was properly concentrated in her person and, indeed, that God had appointed her to be His deputy in the kingdom. Opposition to her rule, in this view, was not only a political act but also a kind of impiety, a blasphemous grudging against the will of God. Apologists for absolutism contended that God commands obedience even to manifestly wicked rulers whom He has sent to punish the sinfulness of humankind. Such arguments were routinely made in speeches and political tracts and from the pulpits of churches, where they were incorporated into the *First* and *Second Book of Homilies,* which clergymen were required to read out to their congregations.

In reality, Elizabeth's power was not absolute. The government had a network of spies, informers, and agents provocateurs, but it lacked a standing army, a national police force, an efficient system of communication, and an extensive bureaucracy. Above all, the queen had limited financial resources and needed to turn periodically to an independent and often recalcitrant Parliament, which by long tradition had the sole right to levy taxes and to grant subsidies. Members of the House of Commons were elected from their boroughs, not appointed by the monarch, and although the queen had considerable influence over their decisions, she could by no means dictate policy. Under these constraints, Elizabeth ruled through a combination of adroit political maneuvering and imperious command, all the while enhancing her authority in the eyes of both court and country by means of an extraordinary cult of love.

"We all loved her," Elizabeth's godson Sir John Harington wrote, with just a touch of irony, a few years after the queen's death, "for she said she loved us." Ambassadors, courtiers, and parliamentarians all submitted to Elizabeth's cult of love, in which the queen's gender was transformed from a potential liability into a significant asset. Those who approached her generally did so on their knees and were expected to address her with extravagant compliments fashioned from the period's most passionate love poetry; she in turn spoke, when it suited her to do so, in the language of love poetry. The court moved in an atmosphere of romance, with music, dancing, plays, and the elaborate, fancy-dress entertainments called masques. The queen adorned herself in gorgeous clothes and rich jewels. When she went on one of her summer "progresses," ceremonial journeys through her land, she looked like an exotic, sacred image in a religious cult of love, and her noble hosts virtually bankrupted themselves to lavish upon her the costliest pleasures. England's leading artists, such as the poet Edmund Spenser and the painter Nicholas Hilliard, enlisted themselves in the celebration of Elizabeth's mystery, likening her to the goddesses and queens of mythology: Diana, Astraea, Gloriana. Her cult drew its power from cultural discourses that ranged from the secular (her courtiers could pine for her as a cruel Petrarchan mistress) to the sacred (the veneration that under Catholicism had been due to the Virgin Mary could now be directed toward England's semidivine queen).

There was a sober, even grim, aspect to these poetical fantasies: Elizabeth was brilliant at playing one dangerous faction off another, now turning her gracious smiles on one favorite, now honoring his hated rival, now suddenly looking elsewhere and raising an obscure upstart to royal favor. And when she was disobeyed or when she felt that her prerogatives had been challenged, she was capable of an anger that, as Harington put it, "left no doubtings whose daughter she was." Thus, when Sir Walter Ralegh, one of the queen's glittering favorites, married without her knowledge or consent, he found himself promptly imprisoned in the Tower of London. And when the Protestant polemicist John Stubbs ventured to publish a pamphlet stridently denouncing the queen's proposed marriage to the French Catholic Duke of Alençon, Stubbs and his publisher were arrested and had their right hands chopped off. (After receiving the blow, the now prudent Stubbs lifted his hat with his remaining hand and cried, "God save the Queen!")

The queen's marriage negotiations were a particularly fraught issue. When she came to the throne at twenty-five years old, speculation about a suitable match, already widespread, intensified and remained for decades at a fever pitch, for the stakes were high. If Elizabeth died childless, the Tudor line would come to an end. The nearest heir was her cousin Mary, Queen of Scots, a Catholic whose claim was supported by France and by the papacy, and whose penchant for sexual and political intrigue confirmed the worst fears of English Protestants. The obvious way to avert the nightmare was for Elizabeth to marry and produce an heir, and the pressure upon her to do so was intense.

More than the royal succession hinged on the question of the queen's marriage; Elizabeth's perceived eligibility was a vital factor in the complex machinations of international diplomacy. A dynastic marriage between the Queen of England and a foreign ruler would forge an alliance powerful enough to alter the balance of power in Europe. The English court hosted a steady stream of ambassadors from kings and princes eager to win the hand of the royal maiden, and Elizabeth, who prided herself on speaking fluent French and Italian (and on reading Latin and Greek), played her romantic part with exemplary skill, sighing and spinning the negotiations out for months and even years.

Most probably, she never meant to marry any of her numerous foreign (and domestic) suitors. Such a decisive act would have meant the end of her independence, as well as the end of the marriage game by which she played one power off against another. One day she would seem to be on the verge of accepting a proposal; the next, she would vow never to forsake her virginity. "She is a Princess," the French ambassador remarked, "who can act any part she pleases."

## The Kingdom in Danger

Beset by Catholic and Protestant extremists, Elizabeth contrived to forge a moderate compromise that enabled her realm to avert the massacres and civil wars that poisoned France and other countries on the Continent. But menace was never far off, and there were constant fears of conspiracy, rebellion, and assassination. Many of the fears swirled around Mary, Queen of Scots, who had been driven from her own kingdom in 1568 by a powerful faction of rebellious nobles and had taken refuge in England. Her presence, under a kind of house arrest, was the source of intense anxiety and helped generate continual rumors of plots. Some of these plots were real enough, others imaginary, still others traps set in motion by the secret agents of the government's intelligence service under the direction of Sir Francis Walsingham. The situation worsened greatly after the St. Bartholomew's Day Massacre of Protestants (Huguenots) in France (August 24, 1572), after Spanish imperial armies invaded the Netherlands in order to stamp out Protestant rebels, and after the assassination there of Europe's other major Protestant leader, William of Orange (1584).

The queen's life seemed to be in even greater danger after Pope Gregory XIII's proclamation in 1580 that the assassination of the great heretic Elizabeth (who had been excommunicated a decade before) would not constitute a mortal sin. The immediate effect of the proclamation was to make existence more difficult for English Catholics, most of whom were loyal to the queen but who fell under grave suspicion. Suspicion was intensified by the clandestine presence of English Jesuits, trained at seminaries abroad and smuggled back into England to serve the Roman Catholic cause. When Elizabeth's spymaster Walsingham unearthed an assassination plot in the correspondence between the Queen of Scots and the Catholic Anthony Babington, the wretched Mary's fate was sealed. After vacillating, a very reluctant Elizabeth signed the death warrant in February 1587, and her cousin was beheaded.

The long-anticipated military confrontation with Catholic Spain was now unavoidable. Elizabeth learned that Philip II, her former brother-in-law and onetime suitor, was preparing to send an enormous fleet against her island realm. It was to sail to the Netherlands, where a Spanish army would be waiting to embark and invade England. Barring its way was England's small fleet of well-armed and highly maneuverable fighting vessels, backed up by ships from the merchant navy. The Invincible Armada reached English waters in July 1588, only to be routed in one of the most famous and decisive naval battles in European history. Then, in what many viewed as an act of God on behalf of Protestant England, the Spanish fleet was dispersed and all but destroyed by violent storms.

As England braced itself to withstand the invasion that never came, Elizabeth appeared in person to review a detachment of soldiers assembled at Tilbury. Dressed in a white gown and a silver breastplate, she declared that though some among her councillors had urged her not to appear before a large crowd of armed men, she would never fail to trust the loyalty of her faithful and loving subjects. Nor did she fear the Spanish armies. "I know I have the body of a weak and feeble woman," Elizabeth declared, "but I have the heart and stomach of a king, and of England too." In this celebrated speech, Elizabeth displayed many of her most memorable qualities: her self-consciously histrionic command of grand public occasion, her subtle blending of magniloquent rhetoric and the language of love, her strategic appropriation of traditionally masculine qualities, and her great personal courage. "We princes," she once remarked, "are set on stages in the sight and view of all the world."

## The English and Otherness

Shakespeare's London had a large population of resident aliens, mainly artisans and merchants and their families, from Portugal, Italy, Spain, Germany, and, above all, France and the Netherlands. Many of these people were Protestant refugees, and they were accorded some legal and economic protection by the government. But they were not always welcome by the local populace. Throughout the sixteenth century, London was the site of repeated demonstrations and, on occasion, bloody riots against the communities of foreign artisans, who were accused of taking jobs away from Englishmen. There was widespread hostility as well toward the Welsh, the Scots, and especially the Irish, whom the English had for centuries been struggling unsuccessfully to subdue. The kings of England claimed to be rulers of Ireland, but in reality they effectively controlled only a small area known as the Pale, extending north from Dublin. The great majority of the Irish people remained stubbornly Catholic and, despite endlessly reiterated English repression, burning of villages, destruction of crops, and massacres, incorrigibly independent.

Shakespeare's *Henry V* (1598–99) seems to invite the audience to celebrate the conjoined heroism of English, Welsh, Scots, and Irish soldiers all fighting together as a "band of brothers" against the French. But such a way of imagining the national community must be set against the tensions and conflicting interests that often set these brothers at each other's throats. As Shakespeare's King Henry realizes, a feared or hated foreign enemy helps at least to mask these tensions, and, indeed, in the face of the Spanish Armada, even the bitter gulf between Catholic and Protestant Englishmen seemed to narrow significantly. But the patriotic alliance was only temporary.

Another way of partially masking the sharp differences in language, belief, and custom among the peoples of the British Isles was to group these people together in contrast to the Jews. Medieval England's Jewish population, the recurrent object of persecution, extortion, and massacre, had been officially expelled by King Edward I in 1290, but Elizabethan England harbored a tiny number of Jews or Jewish converts to Christianity who were treated with suspicion and hostility. One of these was Elizabeth's own physician, Roderigo Lopez, who was tried in 1594 for an alleged plot to poison the queen. Convicted and condemned to the hideous execution reserved for traitors, Lopez went to his death, in the words of the Elizabethan historian William Camden, "affirming that he loved the Queen as well as he loved Jesus Christ; which coming from a man of the Jewish profession moved no small laughter in the standers-by." It is difficult to gauge the meaning here of the phrase "the Jewish profession," used to describe a man who never, as far as we know, professed Judaism, just as it is difficult to gauge the meaning of the crowd's cruel laughter.

Elizabethans appear to have been fascinated by Jews and Judaism but uncertain whether the terms referred to a people, a foreign nation, a set of strange prac-

A Jewish man poisoning a well. From Pierre Boaistuau, *Certaine Secrete Wonders of Nature* (1569).

tices, a living faith, a defunct religion, a villainous conspiracy, or a messianic inheritance. Protestant Reformers brooded deeply on the Hebraic origins of Christianity; government officials ordered the arrest of those "suspected to be Jews"; villagers paid pennies to itinerant fortune-tellers who claimed to be descended from Abraham or masters of cabalistic mysteries; and London playgoers, perhaps including some who laughed at Lopez on the scaffold, enjoyed the spectacle of the downfall of the wicked Barabas in Christopher Marlowe's *Jew of Malta* (c. 1592) and the forced conversion of Shylock in Shakespeare's *Merchant of Venice* (1596–97). Few if any of Shakespeare's contemporaries would have encountered on English soil Jews who openly practiced their religion, though England probably harbored a small number of so-called Marranos, Spanish or Portuguese Jews who had officially converted to Christianity but secretly continued to observe Jewish practices. Jews were not officially permitted to resettle in England until the middle of the seventeenth century, and even then their legal status was ambiguous.

Shakespeare's England also had a small African population whose skin color was the subject of pseudoscientific speculation and theological debate. Some Elizabethans believed that Africans' blackness resulted from the climate of the regions in which they lived, where, as one traveler put it, they were "so scorched and vexed with the heat of the sun, that in many places they curse it when it riseth." Others held that blackness was a curse inherited from their forefather Chus, the son of Ham, who had, according to Genesis, wickedly exposed the nakedness of the drunken Noah. George Best, a proponent of this theory of inherited skin color, reported that "I myself have seen an Ethiopian as black as coal brought into England, who taking a fair English woman to wife, begat a son in all respects as black as the father was, although England were his native country, and an English woman his mother: whereby it seemeth this blackness proceedeth rather of some natural infection of that man."

As the word "infection" suggests, Elizabethans frequently regarded blackness as a physical defect, though the blacks who lived in England and Scotland throughout the sixteenth century were also treated as exotic curiosities. At his marriage to Anne of Denmark, James I entertained his bride and her family by commanding four naked black youths to dance before him in the snow. (The youths died of exposure shortly afterward.) In 1594, in the festivities celebrating the baptism of James's son, a "Black-Moor" entered pulling an elaborately decorated chariot that was, in the original plan, supposed to be drawn in by a lion. There was a black trumpeter in the courts of Henry VII and Henry VIII, while Elizabeth had at least two black servants, one an entertainer and the other a page. Africans became increasingly popular as servants in aristocratic and gentle households in the last decades of the sixteenth century.

pena, El rey deſta tierra es muy podero-
ſo porque es ſeñor de cincuenta y quatro
iſlas muy grādes y en cada vna dſtas ay
vn rey z todos ſon obedientes a el en las
ħles iſlas ay muchas maneras de gētes.

E n la india ay vna iſla en la qual ay
y habitan vna manera de gētes las
quales ſon pequeñas de cuerpo y ſon de
muy maliada natura porque ellas ni

Man with head beneath his shoulders. From a Spanish edition of Sir John Mandeville's *Travels*. See *Othello* 1.3.144–45: "and men whose heads / Do grow beneath their shoulders." Such men were occasionally reported by medieval travelers to the East.

An Indian dance. From Thomas Hariot, *A Briefe and True Report of the New Found Land of Virginia* (1590 ed.).

Some of these Africans were almost certainly slaves, though the legal status of slavery in England was ambiguous. In Cartwright's case (1569), the court ruled "that England was too Pure an Air for Slaves to breathe in," but there is evidence that black slaves were owned in Elizabethan and Jacobean England. Moreover, by the mid-sixteenth century, the English had become involved in the profitable trade that carried African slaves to the New World. In 1562, John Hawkins embarked on his first slaving voyage, transporting some three hundred blacks from the Guinea coast to Hispaniola, where they were sold for £10,000. Elizabeth is reported to have said of this venture that it was "detestable, and would call down the Vengeance of Heaven upon the Undertakers." Nevertheless, she invested in Hawkins's subsequent voyages and loaned him ships.

English men and women of the sixteenth century experienced an unprecedented increase in knowledge of the world beyond their island, for a number of reasons. Religious persecution compelled both Catholics and Protestants to live abroad; wealthy gentlemen (and, in at least a few cases, ladies) traveled in France and Italy to view the famous cultural monuments; merchants published accounts of distant lands such as Turkey, Morocco, and Russia; and military and trading ventures took English ships to still more distant shores. In 1496, a Venetian tradesman living in Bristol, John Cabot, was granted a license by Henry VII to sail on a voyage of exploration; with his son Sebastian, he discovered Newfoundland and Nova Scotia. Remarkable feats of seamanship and reconnaissance soon followed: on his ship the *Golden Hind,* Sir Francis Drake circumnavigated the globe in 1579 and laid claim to California on behalf of the queen; a few years later, a ship commanded by Thomas Cavendish also completed a circumnavigation. Sir Martin Frobisher explored bleak Baffin Island in search of a Northwest Passage to the Orient; Sir John Davis explored the west coast of Greenland and discovered the Falkland Islands off the coast of Argentina; Sir Walter Ralegh ventured up the Orinoco Delta, in what is now Venezuela, in search of the mythical land of El Dorado. Accounts of these and other exploits were collected by a clergyman and promoter of empire, Richard Hakluyt, and published as *The Principal Navigations* (1589; expanded edition 1599).

"To seek new worlds for gold, for praise, for glory," as Ralegh characterized such enterprises, was not for the faint of heart: Drake, Cavendish, Frobisher, and Hawkins all died at sea, as did huge numbers of those who sailed under their command. Elizabethans sensible enough to stay at home could do more than read written accounts of their fellow countrymen's far-reaching voyages. Expeditions brought back native plants (including, most famously, tobacco), animals, cultural artifacts, and, on occasion, samples of the native peoples themselves, most often seized against their will. There were exhibitions in London of a kidnapped Eskimo with his kayak and of Virginians with their canoes. Most of these miserable captives, violently uprooted and vulnerable to European diseases, quickly perished, but even in death they were evidently valuable property: when the English will not give one small coin "to relieve a lame beggar," one of the characters in *The Tempest* wryly remarks, "they will lay out ten to see a dead Indian" (2.2.30–31).

Perhaps most nations learn to define what they are by defining what they are not. This negative self-definition is, in any case, what Elizabethans seemed constantly to be doing, in travel books, sermons, political speeches, civic pageants, public exhibitions, and theatrical spectacles of otherness. The extraordinary variety of these exercises (which include public executions and urban riots, as well as more benign forms of curiosity) suggests that the boundaries of national identity were by no means clear and unequivocal. Even peoples whom English writers routinely, viciously stigmatize as irreducibly alien— Italians, Indians, Turks, and Jews—have a surprising instability in the Elizabethan imagination and may appear for brief, intense moments as powerful models to be admired and emulated before they resume their place as emblems of despised otherness.

## James I and the Union of the Crowns

Though under great pressure to do so, the aging Elizabeth steadfastly refused to name her successor. It became increasingly apparent, however, that it would be James Stuart, the son of Mary, Queen of Scots, and by the time Elizabeth's health began to fail, several of her principal advisers, including her chief minister, Robert Cecil, had been for several years in secret correspondence with him in Edinburgh. Crowned King James VI of Scotland in 1567 when he was but one year old, Mary's son had been raised as a Protestant by his powerful guardians, and in 1589 he married a Protestant princess, Anne of Denmark. When Elizabeth died on March 24, 1603, English officials reported that on her deathbed the queen had named James to succeed her.

Upon his accession, James—now styled James VI of Scotland and James I of England—made plain his intention to unite his two kingdoms. As he told Parliament in 1604, "What God hath conjoined then, let no man separate. I am the husband, and all of the whole isle is my lawful wife; I am the head and it is my body; I am the shepherd and it is my flock." But the flock was less perfectly united than James optimistically envisioned: English and Scottish were sharply distinct identities, as were Welsh and Cornish and other peoples who were incorporated, with varying degrees of willingness, into the realm.

Fearing that to change the name of the kingdom would invalidate all laws and institutions established under the name of England, a fear that was partly real and partly a cover for anti-Scots prejudice, Parliament balked at James's desire to be called "King of

Funeral procession of Queen Elizabeth. From a watercolor sketch by an unknown artist (1603).

Great Britain" and resisted the unionist legislation that would have made Great Britain a legal reality. Although the English initially rejoiced at the peaceful transition from Elizabeth to her successor, there was a rising tide of resentment against James's advancement of Scots friends and his creation of new knighthoods. Lower down the social ladder, English and Scots occasionally clashed violently on the streets: in July 1603, James issued a proclamation against Scottish "insolencies," and in April 1604, he ordered the arrest of "swaggerers" waylaying Scots in London. The ensuing years did not bring the amity and docile obedience for which James hoped, and, though the navy now flew the Union Jack, combining the Scottish cross of St. Andrew and the English cross of St. George, the unification of the kingdoms remained throughout his reign an unfulfilled ambition.

Unfulfilled as well were James's lifelong dreams of ruling as an absolute monarch. Crown lawyers throughout Europe had long argued that a King, by virtue of his power to make law, must necessarily be above law. But in England, sovereignty was identified not with the King alone or with the people alone but with the "King in Parliament." Against his absolutist ambitions, James faced the crucial power to raise taxes that was vested not in the monarch but in the elected members of the Parliament. He faced as well a theory of republicanism that traced it roots back to ancient Rome and that prided itself on its steadfast and, if necessary, violent resistance to tyranny. Shakespeare's fascination with monarchy is apparent throughout his work, but in his Roman plays in particular, as well as in his long poem *The Rape of Lucrece*, he manifests an intense imaginative interest in the idea of a republic.

## The Jacobean Court

With James as with Elizabeth, the royal court was the center of diplomacy, ambition, intrigue, and an intense jockeying for social position. As always in monarchies, proximity to the king's person was a central mark of favor, so that access to the royal bedchamber was one of the highest aims of the powerful, scheming lords who followed James from his sprawling London palace at Whitehall to the hunting lodges and country estates to which he loved to retreat. A coveted office, in the Jacobean as in the Tudor court, was the Groom of the Stool, the person who supervised the disposal of the king's wastes. The officeholder was close to the king at one of his most exposed and vulnerable moments, and enjoyed the further privilege of sleeping on a pallet at the foot of the royal bed and putting on the royal undershirt. Another, slightly less privileged official, the Gentleman of the Robes, dressed the king in his doublet and outer garments.

The royal lifestyle was increasingly expensive. Unlike Elizabeth, James had to maintain separate households for his queen and for the heir apparent, Prince Henry. (Upon Henry's death at the age of eighteen in 1612, his younger brother, Prince Charles, became heir, eventually succeeding his father in 1625.) James was also extremely generous to his friends, amassing his own huge debts in the course of paying off theirs. As early as 1605, he told his principal adviser that "it is a horror to me to think of the height of my place, the greatness of my debts, and the smallness of my means." This smallness notwithstanding, James continued to lavish gifts upon handsome favorites such as the Earl of Somerset, Robert Carr, and the Duke of Buckingham, George Villiers.

The attachment James formed for these favorites was highly romantic. "God so love me," the king wrote to Buckingham, "as I desire only to live in the world for your sake, and that I had rather live banished in any part of the earth with you than live a sorrowful widow's life without you." Such sentiments, not surprisingly, gave rise to widespread rumors of homosexual activities at court. The rumors are certainly plausible, even though the surviving evidence of same-sex relationships, at court or elsewhere, is extremely difficult to interpret. A statute of 1533 made "the detestable and abominable vice of buggery committed with mankind or beast" a felony punishable by death. (English law declined to recognize or criminalize lesbian acts.) The effect of the draconian laws against buggery and sodomy seems to have been to reduce actual prosecutions to the barest minimum: for the next hundred years, there are no known cases of trials resulting in a death sentence for homosexual activity alone. If the legal record is, therefore, unreliable as an index of the extent of homosexual relations, the literary record (including, most famously, the majority of Shakespeare's sonnets) is equally opaque. Any poetic avowal of male-male love may simply be a formal expression of affection based on classical models, or, alternatively, it may be an expression of passionate physical and spiritual love. The interpretive difficulty is compounded by the absence in the period of any clear reference to a homosexual "identity," even though there are many references to same-sex acts and feelings. What is clear is that male friendships at the court of James and elsewhere were suffused with a potential eroticism, at once delightful and threatening, that subsequent periods policed more anxiously.

In addition to the extravagant expenditures on his favorites, James was also the patron of ever more

James I. By John De Critz the Elder (c. 1606).

*Two Young Men.* By Crispin van den Broeck (c. 1590).

elaborate feasts and masques. Shakespeare's work provides a small glimpse of these in *The Tempest,* with its exotic banquet and its "majestic vision" of mythological goddesses and dancing nymphs and reapers. The actual Jacobean court masques, designed by the great architect, painter, and engineer Inigo Jones, were spectacular, fantastic, technically ingenious, and staggeringly costly celebrations of regal magnificence. With their exquisite costumes and their elegant blend of music, dancing, and poetry, the masques, generally performed by the noble lords and ladies of the court, were deliberately ephemeral exercises in conspicuous expenditure and consumption: by tradition, at the end of the performance, the private audience would rush forward and tear to pieces the gorgeous scenery. And although masques were enormously sophisticated entertainments, often on rather esoteric allegorical themes, they could on occasion collapse into grotesque excess. In a letter of 1606, Sir John Harington describes a masque in honor of the visiting Danish king in which the participants, no doubt toasting their royal majesties, had had too much to drink. A lady playing the part of the Queen of Sheba attempted to present precious gifts, "but, forgetting the steps arising to the canopy, overset her caskets into his Danish Majesty's lap. . . . His Majesty then got up and would dance with the Queen of Sheba; but he fell down and humbled himself before her, and was carried to an inner chamber and laid on a bed." Meanwhile, Harington writes, the masque continued with a pageant of Faith, Hope, and Charity, but Charity could barely keep her balance, while Hope and Faith "were both sick and spewing in the lower hall." This was, we can hope, not a typical occasion.

While the English seem initially to have welcomed James's free-spending ways as a change from the relative parsimoniousness of Queen Elizabeth, they were dismayed by its consequences. Elizabeth had died owing £400,000. In 1608, the royal debt had risen to £1,400,000 and was increasing by £140,000 a year. The money to pay off this debt, or at least to keep it under control, was raised by various means. These included customs farming (leasing the right to collect customs duties to private individuals); the highly unpopular impositions (duties on the import of nonnecessities, such as spices, silks, and currants); the sale of crown lands; the sale of baronetcies; and appeals to an increasingly grudging and recalcitrant Parliament. In 1614, Parliament demanded an end to impositions before it would relieve the king and was angrily dissolved without completing its business.

## James's Religious Policy and the Persecution of Witches

Before his accession to the English throne, the king had made known his view of Puritans, the general name for a variety of Protestant sects that were agitating for a radical reform of the Church, the overthrow of its conservative hierarchy of bishops, and the rejection of a large number of traditional rituals and practices. In a book he wrote, *Basilikon Doron* (1599), James denounced "brainsick and heady preachers" who were prepared "to let King, people, law and all be trod underfoot." Yet he was not entirely unwilling to consider religious reforms. In religion, as in foreign policy, he was above all concerned to maintain peace.

On his way south to claim the throne of England in 1603, James was presented with the Millenary Petition (signed by 1,000 ministers), which urged him as "our physician" to heal the disease of lingering "popish" ceremonies. He responded by calling a conference on the ceremonies of the Church of England, which duly took place at Hampton Court Palace in January 1604. The delegates who spoke for reform were moderates, and there was little in the outcome to satisfy Puritans. Nevertheless, while the Church of England continued to cling to such remnants of the Catholic past as wedding rings, square caps, bishops, and Christmas, the conference did produce some reform in the area of ecclesiastical discipline. It also authorized a new English translation of the Bible, known as the King James Bible, which was printed in 1611, too late to have been extensively used by Shakespeare. Along with Shakespeare's works, the King James Bible has probably had the profoundest influence on the subsequent history of English literature.

Having arranged this compromise, James saw his main task as ensuring conformity. He promulgated the 1604 Canons (the first definitive code of canon law since the Reformation), which required all ministers to subscribe to three articles. The first affirmed royal supremacy; the second confirmed that there was nothing in the Book of Common Prayer "contrary to the Word of God" and required ministers to use only the authorized

The "swimming" of a suspected witch (1615).

services; the third asserted that the central tenets of the Church of England were "agreeable to the Word of God." There were strong objections to the second and third articles from those of Puritan leanings inside and outside the House of Commons. In the end, many ministers refused to conform or subscribe to the articles, but only about 90 of them, or 1 percent of the clergy, were deprived of their livings. In its theology and composition, the Church of England was little changed from what it had been under Elizabeth. In hindsight, what is most striking are the ominous signs of growing religious divisions that would by the 1640s burst forth in civil war and the execution of James's son Charles.

James seems to have taken seriously the official claims to the sacredness of kingship, and he certainly took seriously his own theories of religion and politics, which he had printed for the edification of his people. He was convinced that Satan, perpetually warring against God and His representatives on earth, was continually plotting against him. James thought, moreover, that he possessed special insight into Satan's wicked agents, the witches, and in 1597, while King of Scotland, he published his *Daemonology*, a learned exposition of their malign threat to his godly rule. Hundreds of witches, he believed, were involved in a 1590 conspiracy to kill him by raising storms at sea when he was sailing home from Denmark with his new bride.

In the 1590s, Scotland embarked on a virulent witch craze of the kind that had since the fifteenth century repeatedly afflicted France, Switzerland, and Germany, where many thousands of women (and a much smaller number of men) were caught in a nightmarish web of wild accusations. Tortured into lurid confessions of infant cannibalism, night flying, and sexual intercourse with the devil at huge, orgiastic "witches' Sabbaths," the victims had little chance to defend themselves and were routinely burned at the stake.

In England, too, there were witchcraft prosecutions, but on a much smaller scale and with significant differences in the nature of the accusations and the judicial procedures. Witch trials began in England in the 1540s; statutes against witchcraft were enacted in 1542, 1563, and 1604. English law did not allow judicial torture, stipulated lesser punishments in cases of "white magic," and mandated jury trials. Juries acquitted more than half of the defendants in witchcraft trials; in Essex, where the judicial records are particularly extensive, some 24 percent of those accused were executed, while the remainder of those convicted were pilloried and imprisoned or sentenced and reprieved. The accused were generally charged with *maleficium*, an evil deed—usually harming neighbors, causing destructive storms, or killing farm animals—but not with worshiping Satan.

After 1603, when James came to the English throne, he somewhat moderated his enthusiasm for the judicial murder of witches, for the most part defenseless, poor women resented by their neighbors. Although he did nothing to mitigate the ferocity of the ongoing witch hunts in his native Scotland, he did not try to institute Scottish-style persecutions and trials in his new realm. This relative waning of persecutorial eagerness principally reflects the differences between England and Scotland, but it may also bespeak some small, nascent skepticism on James's part about the quality of evidence brought against the accused and about the reliability of the "confessions" extracted from them. It is sobering to reflect that plays like Shakespeare's *Macbeth* (1606), Thomas Middleton's *Witch* (before 1616), and Thomas Dekker, John Ford, and William Rowley's *Witch of Edmonton* (1621) seem to be less the allies of skepticism than the exploiters of fear.

# The Playing Field

## Cosmic Spectacles

The first permanent, freestanding public theaters in England date only from Shakespeare's own lifetime: a London playhouse, the Red Lion, is mentioned in 1567, and James Burbage's playhouse, The Theatre, was built in 1576. (The innovative use of these new stages, crucial to a full understanding of Shakespeare's achievement, is, in this volume, the subject of a separate essay by the theater historian Andrew Gurr, pages 79–99.) But it is misleading to identify English drama exclusively with these spe-cially constructed playhouses, for in fact there was a rich and vital theatrical tradition in England stretching back for centuries. Many towns in late medieval England were the sites of annual festivals that mounted elaborate cycles of plays depicting the great biblical stories, from the creation of the world to Christ's Passion and its miraculous aftermath. Most of these plays have been lost, but the surviving cycles, such as those from York, are magnificent and complex works of art. They are sometimes called "mys-tery plays," either because they were performed by the guilds of various crafts (known as "mysteries") or, more likely, because they represented the mysteries of the faith. The cycles were most often performed on the annual feast day instituted in the early four-teenth century in honor of the Corpus Christi, the sacrament of the Lord's Supper, which is perhaps the greatest of these religious mysteries.

The Feast of Corpus Christi, celebrated on the Thursday following Trinity Sunday, helped give the play cycles their extraordinary cultural resonance, but it also con-tributed to their downfall. For along with the specifically liturgical plays traditionally performed by religious confraternities and the "saints' plays," which depicted miracu-lous events in the lives of individual holy men and women, the mystery cycles were closely identified with the Catholic Church. Protestant authorities in the sixteenth cen-tury, eager to eradicate all remnants of popular Catholic piety, moved to suppress the annual procession of the Host, with its gorgeous banners, pageant carts, and cycle of visionary plays. In 1548, the Feast of Corpus Christi was abolished. Towns that con-tinued to perform the mysteries were under increasing pressure to abandon them. It is sometimes said that the cycles were already dying out from neglect, but recent research has shown that many towns and their guilds were extremely reluctant to give them up. Desperate offers to strip away any traces of Catholic doctrine and to submit the play scripts to the authorities for their approval met with unbending opposition from the government. In 1576, the courts gave York permission to perform its cycle but only if

> in the said play no pageant be used or set forth wherein the Majesty of God the Father, God the Son, or God the Holy Ghost or the administration of either the Sacraments of baptism or of the Lord's Supper be counterfeited or represented, or anything played which tend to the maintenance of superstition and idolatry or which be contrary to the laws of God . . . or of the realm.

Such "permission" was tantamount to an outright ban. The local officials in the city of Norwich, proud of their St. George and the Dragon play, asked if they could at least parade the dragon costume through the streets, but even this modest request was refused. It is likely that as a young man Shakespeare had seen some of these plays: when Hamlet says of a noisy, strutting theatrical performance that it "out-Herods Herod," he is alluding to the famously bombastic role of Herod of Jewry in the mystery plays. But by the century's end, the cycles were no longer performed.

Early English theater was by no means restricted to these civic and religious festi-vals. Payments to professional and amateur performers appear in early records of towns and aristocratic households, although the terms—"ministralli," "histriones," "mimi," "lusores," and so forth—are not used with great consistency and make it difficult to dis-tinguish among minstrels, jugglers, stage players, and other entertainers. Performers acted in town halls and the halls of guilds and aristocratic mansions, on scaffolds erected in town squares and marketplaces, on pageant wagons in the streets, and in inn yards. By the fifteenth century and probably earlier, there were organized companies of players traveling under noble patronage. Such companies earned a living providing amusement, while enhancing the prestige of the patron.

A description of a provincial performance in the late sixteenth century, written by one R. Willis, provides a glimpse of what seems to have been the usual procedure:

> In the City of Gloucester the manner is (as I think it is in other like corporations) that when the Players of Interludes come to town, they first attend the Mayor to

Panorama of London, showing two theaters, both
round and both flying flags: a flying flag indicated that
a performance was in progress. The Globe is in the
foreground, and the Beargarden or Hope is to the left.

inform him what nobleman's servant they are, and so to get licence for their public
playing; and if the Mayor like the Actors, or would show respect to their Lord and
Master, he appoints them to play their first play before himself and the Aldermen
and common Council of the City and that is called the Mayor's play, where everyone that will come in without money, the Mayor giving the players a reward as he
thinks fit to show respect unto them.

In addition to their take from this "first play," the players would almost certainly have
supplemented their income by performing in halls and inn yards, where they could pass
the hat after the performance or even on some occasions charge an admission fee. It
was no doubt a precarious existence.

The "Interludes" mentioned in Willis's description of the Gloucester performances
are likely plays that were, in effect, staged dialogues on religious, moral, and political
themes. Such works could, like the mysteries, be associated with Catholicism, but they
were also used in the sixteenth century to convey polemical Protestant messages, and
they reached outside the religious sphere to address secular concerns as well. Henry
Medwall's *Fulgens and Lucrece* (c. 1490–1501), for example, pits a wealthy but dis-
solute nobleman against a virtuous public servant of humble origins, while John Heywood's *Play of the Weather* (c. 1525–33) stages a debate among social rivals, including
a gentleman, a merchant, a forest ranger, and two millers. The structure of such plays
reflects the training in argumentation that students received in Tudor schools and, in
particular, the sustained practice in examining all sides of a difficult question. Some of
Shakespeare's amazing ability to look at critical issues from multiple perspectives may
be traced back to this practice and the dramatic interludes it helped to inspire.

Another major form of theater that flourished in England in the fifteenth century
and continued on into the sixteenth was the morality play. Like the mysteries, moralities addressed questions of the ultimate fate of the soul. They did so, however, not by
rehearsing scriptural stories but by dramatizing allegories of spiritual struggle. Typically,
a person named Human or Mankind or Youth is faced with a choice between a pious
life in the company of such associates as Mercy, Discretion, and Good Deeds and a dis-
solute life among riotous companions like Lust or Mischief. Plays like *Mankind* (c.
1465–70) and *Everyman* (c. 1495) show how powerful these unpromising-sounding
dramas could be, in part because of the extraordinary comic vitality of the evil character, or Vice, and in part because of the poignancy and terror of an individual's encounter
with death. Shakespeare clearly grasped this power. The hunchbacked Duke of
Gloucester in *Richard III* gleefully likens himself to "the formal Vice, Iniquity." And

when Othello wavers between Desdemona and Iago (himself a Vice figure), his anguished dilemma echoes the fateful choice repeatedly faced by the troubled, vulnerable protagonists of the moralities.

If such plays sound a bit like sermons, it is because they were. Clerics and actors shared some of the same rhetorical skills. It would be misleading to regard churchgoing and playgoing as comparable entertainments, but in attacking the stage, ministers often seemed to regard the professional players as dangerous rivals. The players themselves were generally too discreet to rise to the challenge; it would have been foolhardy to present the theater as the Church's direct competitor. Yet in its moral intensity and its command of impassioned language, the stage frequently emulates and outdoes the pulpit.

### Music and Dance

Playacting took its place alongside other forms of public expression and entertainment as well. Perhaps the most important, from the perspective of the theater, were music and dance, since these were directly and repeatedly incorporated into plays. Many plays, comedies and tragedies alike, include occasions that call upon the characters to dance: hence Beatrice and Benedick join the other masked guests at the dance in *Much Ado About Nothing*; in *Twelfth Night*, the befuddled Sir Andrew, at the instigation of the drunken Sir Toby Belch, displays his skill, such as it is, in capering; Romeo and Juliet first see each other at the Capulet ball; the witches dance in a ring around the hideous caldron and perform an "antic round" to cheer Macbeth's spirits; and, in one of Shakespeare's strangest and most wonderful scenes, the drunken Antony in *Antony and Cleopatra* joins hands with Caesar, Enobarbus, Pompey, and others to dance "the Egyptian Bacchanals."

Moreover, virtually all plays in the period, including Shakespeare's, apparently ended with a dance. Brushing off the theatrical gore and changing their expressions from woe to pleasure, the actors in plays like *Hamlet* and *King Lear* would presumably have received the audience's applause and then bid for a second round of applause by performing a stately pavane or a lively jig. Indeed, jigs, with their comical leaping dance steps often accompanied by scurrilous ballads, became so popular that they drew not only large crowds but also official disapproval. A court order of 1612 complained about the "cutpurses and other lewd and ill-disposed persons" who flocked to the theater at the end of every play to be entertained by "lewd jigs, songs, and dances." The players were warned to suppress these disreputable entertainments on pain of imprisonment.

The displays of dancing onstage clearly reflected a widespread popular interest in dancing outside the walls of the playhouse as well. Renaissance intellectuals conjured up visions of the universe as a great cosmic dance, poets figured relations between men and women in terms of popular dance steps, stern moralists denounced dancing as an incitement to filthy lewdness, and, perhaps as significant, men of all classes evidently spent a great deal of time worrying about how shapely their legs looked in tights and how gracefully they could leap. Shakespeare assumes that his audience will be quite familiar with a variety of dances. "For hear me, Hero," Beatrice tells her friend, "wooing, wedding, and repenting is as a Scotch jig, a measure, and a cinquepace" (2.1.60–61). Her speech dwells on the comparison a bit, teasing out its implications, but it still does not make much sense if you do not already know something about the dances and perhaps occasionally venture to perform them yourself.

Closely linked to dancing and even more central to the stage was music, both instrumental and vocal. In the early sixteenth century, the Reformation had been disastrous for sacred music: many church organs were destroyed, choir schools were closed, the glorious polyphonal liturgies sung in the monasteries were suppressed. But by the latter part of the century, new perspectives were reinvigorating English music. Latin Masses were reset in English, and tunes were written for newly translated, metrical psalms. More important for the theater, styles of secular music were developed that emphasized music's link to humanist eloquence, its ability to heighten and to rival rhetorically powerful texts.

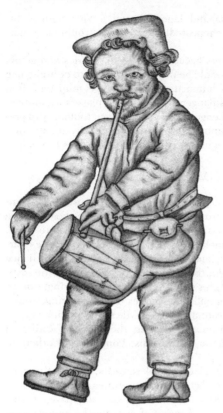

Richard Tarlton. Tarlton was the lead comedian of the Queen's Company from 1583, the year of its founding, until 1588, when he died.

This link is particularly evident in vocal music, at which Elizabethan composers excelled. Renowned composers William Byrd, Thomas Morley, John Dowland, and others wrote a rich profusion of madrigals (part songs for two to eight voices unaccompanied) and ayres (songs for solo voice, generally accompanied by the lute). These works, along with hymns, popular ballads, rounds, catches, and other forms of song, enjoyed immense popularity, not only in the royal court, where musical skill was regarded as an important accomplishment, and in aristocratic households, where professional musicians were employed as entertainers, but also in less exalted social circles. In his *Plaine and Easie Introduction to Practicall Musicke* (1597), Morley tells a story of social humiliation at a failure to perform that suggests that a well-educated Elizabethan was expected to be able to sing at sight. Even if this is an exaggeration in the interest of book sales, there is evidence of impressively widespread musical literacy, reflected in a splendid array of music for the lute, viol, recorder, harp, and virginal, as well as the marvelous vocal music.

Whether it is the aristocratic Orsino luxuriating in the dying fall of an exquisite melody or bully Bottom craving "the tongs and the bones," Shakespeare's characters frequently call for music. They also repeatedly give voice to the age's conviction that there was a deep relation between musical harmony and the harmonies of the well-ordered individual and state. "The man that hath no music in himself," warns Lorenzo in *The Merchant of Venice,* "nor is not moved with concord of sweet sounds, / Is fit for treasons, stratagems, and spoils" (5.1.82–84). This conviction, in turn, reflects a still deeper link between musical harmony and the divinely created harmony of the cosmos. When Ulysses, in *Troilus and Cressida,* wishes to convey the image of universal chaos, he speaks of the untuning of a string (1.3.109).

The playing companies must have regularly employed trained musicians, and many actors (like the actor who in playing Pandarus in *Troilus and Cressida* is supposed to accompany himself on the lute) must have possessed musical skill. Unfortunately, we possess the original settings for very few of Shakespeare's songs, possibly because many of them may have been set to popular tunes of the time that everyone knew and no one bothered to write down.

### Alternative Entertainments

Plays, music, and dancing were by no means the only shows in town. There were jousts, tournaments, royal entries, religious processions, pageants in honor of newly installed civic officials or ambassadors arriving from abroad; wedding masques, court masques, and costumed entertainments known as "disguisings" or "mummings"; juggling acts, fortune-tellers, exhibitions of swordsmanship, mountebanks, folk healers, storytellers, magic shows; bearbaiting, bullbaiting, cockfighting, and other blood sports; folk festivals such as Maying, the Feast of Fools, Carnival, and Whitsun Ales. For several years, Elizabethan Londoners were delighted by a trained animal—Banks's Horse—that could, it was thought, do arithmetic and answer questions. And there was always the grim but compelling spectacle of public shaming, mutilation, and execution.

Most English towns had stocks and whipping posts. Drunks, fraudulent merchants, adulterers, and quarrelers could be placed in carts or mounted backward on asses and paraded through the streets for crowds to jeer and throw refuse at. Women accused of being scolds could be publicly muzzled by an iron device called a "brank" or tied to a cucking stool and dunked in the river. Convicted criminals could have their ears cut off, their noses slit, their foreheads branded. Public beheadings (generally reserved for the elite) and hangings were common. In the worst cases, felons were sentenced to be "hanged by the neck, and being alive cut down, and your privy members to be cut off, and your bowels to be taken out of your belly and there burned, you being alive."

Shakespeare occasionally takes note of these alternative entertainments: at the end of *Macbeth*, for example, with his enemies closing in on him, the doomed tyrant declares, "They have tied me to a stake. I cannot fly, / But bear-like I must fight the course" (5.7.1–2). The audience is reminded then that it is witnessing the human equivalent of a popular spectacle—a bear chained to a stake and attacked by fierce dogs—that they could have paid to watch at an arena near the Globe. And when, a few moments later, Macduff enters carrying Macbeth's head, the audience is seeing the theatrical equivalent of the execution of criminals and traitors that they could have also watched in the flesh, as it were, nearby. In a different key, the audiences who paid to see *A Midsummer Night's Dream* or *The Winter's Tale* got to enjoy the comic spectacle of a Maying and a Whitsun Pastoral, while the spectators of *The Tempest* could gawk at what the Folio list of characters calls a "salvage and deformed slave" and to enjoy an aristocratic magician's wedding masque in honor of his daughter.

An Elizabethan hanging.

## The Enemies of the Stage

In 1624, a touring company of players arrived in Norwich and requested permission to perform. Permission was denied, but the municipal authorities, "in regard of the honorable respect which this City beareth to the right honorable the Lord Chamberlain," gave the players 20 shillings to get out of town. Throughout the sixteenth and early seventeenth centuries, there are many similar records of civic officials prohibiting performances and then, to appease a powerful patron, paying the actors to take their skills elsewhere. As early as the 1570s, there is evidence that the London authorities, while mindful of the players' influential protectors, were energetically trying to drive the theater out of the city.

Why should what we now regard as one of the undisputed glories of the age have aroused so much hostility? One answer, curiously enough, is traffic: plays drew large audiences—the public theaters could accommodate thousands—and residents objected to the crowds, the noise, and the crush of carriages. Other, more serious concerns were public health and crime. It was thought that numerous diseases, including the dreaded bubonic plague, were spread by noxious odors, and the packed playhouses were obvious breeding grounds for infection. (Patrons often tried to protect themselves by sniffing nosegays or stuffing cloves into their nostrils.) The large crowds drew pickpockets and other scoundrels. On one memorable afternoon, a pickpocket was caught in the act and tied for the duration of the play to one of the posts that held up the canopy above the stage.

Syphilis victim in a tub. Frontispiece to the play *Cornelianum Dolium* (1638), possibly authored by Thomas Randolph. The tub inscription translates as "I sit on the throne of love, I suffer in the tub," and the banner as "Farewell O sexual pleasures and lusts."

The theater was, moreover, a well-known haunt of prostitutes and, it was alleged, a place where innocent maids were seduced and respectable matrons corrupted. It was darkly rumored that "chambers and secret places" adjoined the theater galleries, and in any case, taverns, disreputable inns, and whorehouses were close at hand.

There were other charges as well. Plays were performed in the afternoon and, therefore, drew people, especially the young, away from their work. They were schools of idleness, luring apprentices from their trades, law students from their studies, housewives from their kitchens, and potentially pious souls from the sober meditations to which they might otherwise devote themselves. Wasting their time and money on disreputable shows, citizens exposed themselves to sexual provocation and outright political sedition. Even when the content of plays was morally exemplary—and, of course, few plays were so gratifyingly high-minded—the theater itself, in the eyes of most mayors and aldermen, was inherently disorderly.

The attack on the stage by civic officials was echoed and intensified by many of the age's moralists and religious leaders, especially those associated with Puritanism. While English Protestants earlier in the sixteenth century had attempted to counter the Catholic mystery cycles and saints' plays by mounting their own doctrinally correct dramas, by the century's end a fairly widespread consensus, even among those mildly sympathetic toward the theater, held that the stage and the pulpit were in tension with one another. After 1591, a ban on Sunday performances was strictly enforced, and in 1606, Parliament passed an act imposing a fine of £10 on any person who shall "in any stage-play, interlude, show, May-game, or pageant, jestingly or profanely speak or use the holy name of God, or of Christ Jesus, or of the Holy Ghost, or of the Trinity (which are not to be spoken but with fear and reverence)." If changes in the printed texts are a reliable indication, the players seem to have complied at least to some degree with the ruling. The Folio (1623) text of *Richard III,* for example, omits the Quarto's (1597) four uses of "zounds" (for "God's wounds"), along with a mention of "Christ's dear blood shed for our grievous sins"; "God's my judge" in *The Merchant of Venice* becomes "well I know"; "By Jesu" in *Henry V* becomes a very proper "I say"; and in all the plays, "God" from time to time metamorphoses to "Jove."

But for some of the theater's more extreme critics, these modest expurgations were tiny bandages on a gaping wound. In his huge book *Histriomastix* (1633), William Prynne regurgitates half a century of frenzied attacks on the "sinful, heathenish, lewd, ungodly Spectacles." In the eyes of Prynne and his fellow antitheatricalists, stage plays were part of a demonic tangle of obscene practices proliferating like a cancer in the body of society. It is "manifest to all men's judgments," he writes, that

> effeminate mixed dancing, dicing, stage-plays, lascivious pictures, wanton fashions, face-painting, health-drinking, long hair, love-locks, periwigs, women's curling, powdering and cutting of their hair, bonfires, New-year's gifts, May-games, amorous pastorals, lascivious effeminate music, excessive laughter, luxurious disorderly Christmas-keeping, mummeries . . . [are] wicked, unchristian pastimes.

Given the anxious emphasis on effeminacy, it is not surprising that denunciations of this kind obsessively focused on the use of boy actors to play the female parts. The enemies of the stage charged that theatrical transvestism excited illicit sexual desires, both heterosexual and homosexual.

Since cross-dressing violated a biblical prohibition (Deuteronomy 22:5), religious antitheatricalists attacked it as wicked regardless of its erotic charge; indeed, they often seemed to consider any act of impersonation as inherently wicked. In their view, the theater itself was Satan's domain. Thus a Cambridge scholar, John Greene, reports the sad fate of "a Christian woman" who went to the theater to see a play: "She entered in well and sound, but she returned and came forth possessed of the devil. Whereupon certain godly brethren demanded Satan how he durst be so bold, as to enter into her a Christian. Whereto he answered, that *he found her in his own house,* and therefore took possession of her as his own" (italic in original). When the "godly brethren" came to power in the mid-seventeenth century, with the overthrow of Charles I, they saw to it that the playhouses, temporarily shut down in 1642 at the onset of the Civil War, remained closed. The theater did not resume until the restoration of the monarchy in 1660.

Faced with enemies among civic officials and religious leaders, Elizabethan and Jacobean playing companies relied on the protection of their powerful patrons. As the liveried servants of aristocrats or of the monarch, the players could refute the charge that they were mere vagabonds, and they claimed, as a convenient legal fiction, that their public performances were necessary rehearsals in anticipation of those occasions when they would be called upon to entertain their noble masters. But harassment by the mayor and aldermen continued unabated, and the players were forced to build their theaters outside the immediate jurisdiction of the city authorities, either in the suburbs or in the areas known as the "liberties." A liberty was a piece of land within the City of London itself that was not directly subject to the authority of the lord mayor. The most significant of these from the point of view of the theater was the area near St. Paul's Cathedral called "the Blackfriars," where, until the dissolution of the monasteries in 1538, there had been a

Dominican monastery. It was here that in 1608 Shakespeare's company, then called the King's Men, built the indoor playhouse in which they performed during the winter months, reserving the open-air Globe in the suburb of Southwark for their summer performances.

## Censorship and Regulation

In addition to those authorities who campaigned to shut down the theater, there were others whose task was to oversee, regulate, and censor it. Given the outright hostility of the former, the latter may have seemed to the London players equivocal allies rather than enemies. After all, plays that passed the censor were at least licensed to be performed and hence conceded to have some limited legitimacy. In April 1559, at the very start of her reign, Queen Elizabeth drafted a proposal that for the first time envisaged a system for the prior review and regulation of plays throughout her kingdom:

> The Queen's Majesty doth straightly forbid all manner interludes to be played either openly or privately, except the same be notified beforehand, and licensed within any city or town corporate, by the mayor or other chief officers of the same, and within any shire, by such as shall be lieutenants for the Queen's Majesty in the same shire, or by two of the Justices of Peace inhabiting within that part of the shire where any shall be played. . . . And for instruction to every of the said officers, her Majesty doth likewise charge every of them, as they will answer: that they permit none to be played wherein either matters of religion or of the governance of the estate of the commonweal shall be handled or treated upon, but by men of authority, learning and wisdom, nor to be handled before any audience, but of grave and discreet persons.

This proposal, which may not have been formally enacted, makes an important distinction between those who are entitled to address sensitive issues of religion and politics—authors "of authority, learning and wisdom" addressing audiences "of grave and discreet persons"—and those who are forbidden to do so.

The London public theater, with its playwrights who were the sons of glovers, shoemakers, and bricklayers and its audiences in which the privileged classes mingled with rowdy apprentices, masked women, and servants, was clearly not a place to which the government wished to grant freedom of expression. In 1581, the Master of the Revels, an official in the lord chamberlain's department whose role had hitherto been to provide entertainment at court, was given an expanded commission. Sir Edmund Tilney, the functionary who held the office, was authorized

> to warn, command, and appoint in all places within this our Realm of England, as well within franchises and liberties as without, all and every player or players with their playmakers, either belonging to any nobleman or otherwise . . . to appear before him with all such plays, tragedies, comedies, or shows as they shall in readiness or mean to set forth, and them to recite before our said Servant or his sufficient deputy, whom we ordain, appoint, and authorize by these presents of all such shows, plays, players, and playmakers, together with their playing places, to order and reform, authorize and put down, as shall be thought meet or unmeet unto himself or his said deputy in that behalf.

What emerged from this commission was in effect a national system of regulation and censorship. One of its consequences was to restrict virtually all licensed theater to the handful of authorized London-based playing companies. These companies would have to submit their plays for official scrutiny, but in return they received implicit, and on occasion explicit, protection against the continued fierce opposition of the local authorities. Plays reviewed and allowed by the Master of the Revels had been deemed fit to be performed before the monarch; how could mere aldermen legitimately claim that such plays should be banned as seditious?

The key question, of course, is how carefully the Master of the Revels scrutinized the plays brought before him either to hear or, more often from the 1590s onward, to peruse. What was Tilney, who served in the office until his death in 1610, or his successor, Sir George Buc, who served from 1610 to 1621, looking for? What did they insist be cut before they would release what was known as the "allowed copy," the only version licensed for performance? Unfortunately, the office books of the Master of the Revels in Shakespeare's time have been lost; what survives is a handful of scripts on which Tilney, Buc, and their assistants jotted their instructions. These suggest that the readings were rather painstaking, with careful attention paid to possible religious, political, and diplomatic repercussions. References, directly or strongly implied, to any living Christian prince or any important English nobleman, gentleman, or government official were particularly sensitive and likely to be struck. Renaissance political life was highly personalized; people in power were exceptionally alert to insult and zealously patrolled the boundaries of their prestige and reputation.

Moreover, the censors knew that audiences and readers were quite adept at applying theatrical representations distanced in time and space to their own world. At a time of riots against resident foreigners, Tilney read *Sir Thomas More,* a play in which Shakespeare probably had a hand, and instructed the players to cut scenes that, even though they were set in 1517, might have had an uncomfortable contemporary resonance. "Leave out the insurrection wholly," Tilney's note reads, "and the cause thereof and begin with Sir Thomas More at the Mayor's sessions, with a report afterwards of his good service done being sheriff of London upon a mutiny against the Lombards only by a short report and not otherwise at your own perils. E. Tilney." Of course, as Tilney knew perfectly well, most plays succeed precisely by mirroring, if only obliquely, their own times, but this particular reflection evidently seemed to him too dangerous or provocative.

The topical significance of a play depends in large measure on the particular moment in which it is performed and on certain features of the performance—for example, a striking resemblance between one of the characters and a well-known public figure—that the script itself will not necessarily disclose to us at this great distance or even to the censor at the time. Hence the Master of the Revels noted angrily of one play performed in 1632 that "there were diverse personated so naturally, both of lords and others of the court, that I took it ill." Hence, too, a play that was deemed allowable when it was first written and performed could return, like a nightmare, to haunt a different place and time. The most famous instance of such a return involves Shakespeare, for on the day before the Earl of Essex's attempted coup against Queen Elizabeth in 1601, someone paid the Lord Chamberlain's Men (the name of Shakespeare's company at the time) 40 shillings to revive their old play about the deposition and murder of Richard II. "I am Richard II," the queen declared. "Know ye not that?" However distressed she was by this performance, the queen significantly did not take out her wrath on the players: neither the playwright nor his company was punished, nor was the Master of the Revels criticized for allowing the play in the first place. It was Essex and several of his key supporters who lost their heads.

Evidence suggests that the Master of the Revels often regarded himself not as the strict censor of the theater but as its friendly guardian, charged with averting catastrophes. He was a bureaucrat concerned less with subversive ideas per se than with potential trouble. That is, there is no record of a dramatist being called to account for his heterodox beliefs; rather, plays were censored if they risked offending influential people, including important foreign allies, or if they threatened to cause public disorder by exacerbating religious or other controversies. The distinction is not a stable one, but it helps to explain the intellectual boldness, power, and freedom of a censored theater in a society in which the perceived enemies of the state were treated mercilessly. Shakespeare could have Lear articulate a searing indictment of social injustice—

> Robes and furred gowns hide all. Plate sin with gold,
> And the strong lance of justice hurtless breaks;
> Arm it in rags, a pygmy's straw does pierce it.
> (4.5.155–57)

—and evidently neither the Master of the Revels nor the courtiers in their robes and furred gowns protested. But when the Spanish ambassador complained about Thomas Middleton's anti-Spanish allegory *A Game at Chess,* performed at the Globe in 1624, the whole theater was shut down, the players were arrested, and the king professed to be furious at his official for licensing the play in the first place and allowing it to be performed for nine consecutive days.

In addition to the system for the licensing of plays for performance, there was also a system for the licensing of plays for publication. At the start of Shakespeare's career, such press licensing was the responsibility of the Court of High Commission, headed by the Archbishop of Canterbury and the Bishop of London. Their deputies, a panel of junior clerics, were supposed to review the manuscripts, granting licenses to those worthy of publication and rejecting any they deemed "heretical, seditious, or unseemly for Christian ears." Without a license, the Stationers' Company, the guild of the book trade, was not supposed to register a manuscript for publication. In practice, as various complaints and attempts to close loopholes attest, some playbooks were printed without a license. In 1607, the system was significantly revised when Sir George Buc began to license plays for the press. When Buc succeeded to the post of Master of the Revels in 1610, the powers to license plays for the stage and the page were vested in one man.

## Theatrical Innovations

The theater continued to flourish under this system of regulation after Shakespeare's death; by the 1630s, as many as five playhouses were operating daily in London. When the theater reemerged after the eighteen-year hiatus imposed by Puritan rule, it quickly resumed its cultural importance, but not without a number of significant changes. Major innovations in staging resulted principally from Continental influences on the English artists who accompanied the court of Charles II into exile in France, where they supplied it with masques and other theatrical entertainments.

The institutional conditions and business practices of the two companies chartered by Charles after the Restoration in 1660 also differed from those of Shakespeare's theater. In place of the more collective practice of Shakespeare's company, the Restoration theaters were controlled by celebrated actor-managers who not only assigned themselves starring roles, in both comedy and tragedy, but also assumed sole responsibility for many business decisions, including the setting of their colleagues' salaries. At the same time, the power of the actor-manager, great as it was, was limited by the new importance of outside capital. No longer was the theater, with all of its properties from script to costumes, owned by the "sharers"—that is, by those actors who held shares in the joint-stock company. Instead, entrepreneurs would raise capital for increasingly fantastic sets and stage machinery that could cost as much as £3,000, an astronomical sum, for a single production. This investment, in turn, not only influenced the kinds of new plays written for the theater but helped to transform old plays that were revived, including Shakespeare's.

In his diary entry for August 24, 1661, Samuel Pepys notes that he has been "to the Opera, and there saw Hamlet, Prince of Denmark, done with scenes very well, but above all, Betterton did the prince's part beyond imagination." This is Thomas Betterton's first review, as it were, and it is typical of the enthusiasm he would inspire throughout his fifty-year career on the London stage. Pepys's brief and scattered remarks on the plays he voraciously attended in the 1660s are precious because they are among the few records from the period of concrete and immediate responses to theatrical performances. Modern readers might miss the significance of Pepys's phrase "done with scenes": this production of *Hamlet* was only the third play to use the movable sets first introduced to England by its producer, William Davenant. The central historical fact that makes the productions of this period so exciting is that public theater had been banned altogether for eighteen years until the Restoration of Charles II.

A brief discussion of theatrical developments in the Restoration period will enable us at least to glance longingly at a vast subject that lies outside the scope of this introduction: the rich performance history that extends from Shakespeare's time to our own, involving tens of thousands of productions and adaptations for theater, opera, Broadway musicals, and, of course, films. The scale of this history is vast in space as well as time: as early as 1607, there is a record of a *Hamlet* performed on board an English ship, HMS *Dragon,* off the coast of Sierra Leone, and troupes of English actors performed in the late sixteenth and early seventeenth centuries as far afield as Poland and Bohemia.

William Davenant, who claimed to be Shakespeare's bastard son, had become an expert on stage scenery while producing masques at the court of Charles I, and when the theaters reopened, he set to work on converting an indoor tennis court into a new kind of theater. He designed a broad open platform like that of the Elizabethan stage, but he replaced the relatively shallow space for "discoveries" (tableaux set up in an opening at the center of the stage, revealed by drawing back a curtain) and the "tiring-house" (the players' dressing room) behind this space with one expanded interior, framed by a proscenium arch, in which scenes could be displayed. These elaborately painted scenes could be moved on and off, using grooves on the floor. The perspectival effect for a spectator of one central painted panel with two "wings" on either side was that of three sides of a room. This effect anticipated that of the familiar "picture frame" stage, developed fully in the nineteenth century, and began a subtle shift in theater away from the elaborate verbal descriptions that are so central to Shakespeare and toward the evocative visual poetry of the set designer's art.

Another convention of Shakespeare's stage, the use of boy actors for female roles, gave way to the more complete illusion of women playing women's parts. The king issued a decree in 1662 forcefully permitting, if not requiring, the use of actresses. The royal decree is couched in the language of social and moral reform: the introduction of actresses will require the "reformation" of scurrilous and profane passages in plays, and this, in turn, will help forestall some of the objections that shut the theaters down in 1642. In reality, male theater audiences, composed of a narrower range of courtiers and aristocrats than in Shakespeare's time, met this intended reform with the assumption that the new actresses were fair game sexually; most actresses (with the partial exception of those who married male members of their troupes) were regarded as, or actually became, whores. But despite the social stigma and the fact that their salaries were predictably lower than those of their male counterparts, the stage saw some formidable female stars by the 1680s.

The first recorded appearance of an actress was that of a Desdemona in December 1660. Betterton's Ophelia in 1661 was Mary Saunderson (c. 1637–1712), who became Mrs. Betterton a year later. The most famous Ophelia of the period was Susanna Mountfort, who appeared in that role for the first time at the age of fifteen in 1705. The performance by Mountfort that became legendary occurred in 1720, after a disappointment in love, or so it was said, had driven her mad. Hearing that *Hamlet* was being performed, Mountfort escaped from her keepers and reached the theater, where she concealed herself until the scene in which Ophelia enters in her state of insanity. At this point, Mountfort rushed onto the stage and, in the words of a contemporary, "was in truth Ophelia herself, to the amazement of the performers and the astonishment of the audience."

That the character Ophelia became increasingly and decisively identified with the mad scene owes something to this occurrence, but it is also a consequence of the text used for Restoration performances of *Hamlet.* Having received the performance rights to a good number of Shakespeare's plays, Davenant altered them for the stage in the 1660s, and many of these acting versions remained in use for generations. In the case of *Hamlet,* neither Davenant nor his successors did what they so often did with other plays by Shakespeare—that is, alter the plot radically and interpolate other material. But many of the lines were cut or "improved." The cuts included most of Ophelia's sane speeches, such as her spirited retort to Laertes' moralizing; what remained made her part almost entirely an emblem of "female love melancholy."

Thomas Betterton (1635–1710), the prototype of the actor-manager, who would be the dominant figure in Shakespeare interpretation and in the theater generally through

# The Spanish Tragedie:
## OR,
## Hieronimo is mad againe.

Containing the lamentable end of *Don Horatio*, and
*Belimperia*; with the pittifull death of *Hieronimo*.

Newly corrected, amended, and enlarged with new
Additions of the *Painters* part, and others, as
it hath of late been diuers times acted.

## LONDON,
Printed by W. White, for I. White and T. Langley,
and are to be sold at their Shop ouer againft the
Sarazens head without New-gate. 1615.

Title page of Thomas Kyd's *Spanish Tragedie*
(1615). The first known edition dates from 1592.

the nineteenth century, made Hamlet his premier role. A contemporary who saw his last performance in the part (at the age of seventy-four, a rather old Prince of Denmark) wrote that to *read* Shakespeare's play was to encounter "dry, incoherent, & broken sentences," but that to see Betterton was to "prove" that the play was written "correctly." Spectators especially admired his reaction to the Ghost's appearance in the Queen's bedchamber: "his Countenance . . . thro' the violent and sudden Emotions of Amazement and Horror, turn[ed] instantly on the Sight of his fathers Spirit, as pale as his Neckcloath, when every Article of his Body seem's affected with a Tremor inexpressible." A piece of stage business in this scene, Betterton's upsetting his chair on the Ghost's entrance, became so thoroughly identified with the part that later productions were censured if the actor left it out. This business could very well have been handed down from Richard Burbage, the star of Shakespeare's original production, for Davenant, who had coached Betterton in the role, had known the performances of Joseph Taylor, who had succeeded Burbage in it. It is strangely gratifying to notice that Hamlets on stage and screen still occasionally upset their chairs.

## Shakespeare's Life and Art

Playwrights, even hugely successful playwrights, were not ordinarily the objects of popular curiosity in early modern England, and few personal documents survive from Shakespeare's life of the kind that usually give the biographies of artists their appeal: no diary, no letters, private or public, no accounts of his childhood, almost no contemporary gossip, no scandals. Shakespeare's exact contemporary, the great playwright Christopher Marlowe, lived a mere twenty-nine years—he was murdered in 1593—but he left behind tantalizing glimpses of himself in police documents, the memos of high-ranking government officials, and detailed denunciations by sinister double agents. Ben Jonson recorded his opinions and his reading in a remarkable published notebook, *Timber; or, Discoveries Made upon Men and Matter*, and he also shared his views of the world (including some criticisms of his fellow playwright Shakespeare) with a Scottish poet, William Drummond of Hawthornden, who had the wit to jot them down for posterity. From Shakespeare, there is nothing comparable, not even a book with his name scribbled on the cover and a few marginal notes such as we have for Jonson, let alone working notebooks.

Yet Elizabethan England was a record-keeping society, and centuries of archival labor have turned up a substantial number of traces of its greatest playwright and his family. By themselves the traces would have relatively little interest, but in the light of Shakespeare's plays and poems, they have come to seem like precious relics and manage to achieve a considerable resonance.

### Shakespeare's Family

William Shakespeare's grandfather Richard farmed land by the village of Snitterfield, near the small, pleasant market town of Stratford-upon-Avon, about 96 miles northwest of London. The playwright's father, John, moved in the mid-sixteenth century to Stratford, where he became a successful glover, landowner, moneylender, and dealer in wool and other agricultural goods. In or about 1557, he married Mary Arden, the daughter of a prosperous and well-connected farmer from the same area, Robert Arden of Wilmcote.

John Shakespeare was evidently highly esteemed by his fellow townspeople, for he held a series of important posts in local government. In 1556, he was appointed ale taster, an office reserved for "able persons and discreet," in 1558 was sworn in as a constable, and in 1561 was elected as one of the town's fourteen burgesses. As burgess, John served as one of the two chamberlains, responsible for administering borough property and revenues. In 1567, he was elected bailiff, Stratford's highest elective office and the equivalent of mayor. Although John Shakespeare signed all official documents with a cross or other sign, it is likely, but not certain, that he knew how to read and write. Mary, who also signed documents only with her mark, is less likely to have been literate.

According to the parish registers, which recorded baptisms and burials, the Shakespeares had eight children, four daughters and four sons, beginning with a daughter Joan born in 1558. A second daughter, Margaret, was born in December 1562 and died a few months later. William Shakespeare ("Gulielmus, filius Johannes Shakespeare"), their first son, was baptized on April 26, 1564. Since there was usually a few days' lapse between birth and baptism, it is conventional to celebrate Shakespeare's birthday on April 23, which happens to coincide with the feast of St. George, England's patron saint, and with the day of Shakespeare's death fifty-two years later.

William Shakespeare had three younger brothers, Gilbert, Richard, and Edmund, and two younger sisters, Joan and Anne. (It was often the custom to recycle a name, so the firstborn Joan must have died before the birth in 1569 of another daughter

"Southeast Prospect of Stratford-upon-Avon, 1746." From *The Gentleman's Magazine* (December 1792).

christened Joan, the only one of the girls to survive childhood.) Gilbert, who died in his forty-fifth year in 1612, is described in legal records as a Stratford haberdasher; Edmund followed William to London and became a professional actor, but evidently of no particular repute. He was only twenty-eight when he died in 1607 and was given an expensive funeral, perhaps paid for by his successful older brother.

At the high point of his public career, John Shakespeare, the father of this sub-stantial family, applied to the Herald's College for a coat of arms, which would have marked his (and his family's) elevation from the ranks of substantial middle-class citi-zenry to that of the gentry. But the application went nowhere, for soon after he initi-ated what would have been a costly petitioning process, John apparently fell on hard times. The decline must have begun when William was still living at home, a boy of twelve or thirteen. From 1576 onward, John Shakespeare stopped attending council meetings. He became caught up in costly lawsuits, started mortgaging his land, and incurred substantial debts. In 1586, he was finally replaced on the council; in 1592, he was one of nine Stratford men listed as absenting themselves from church out of fear of being arrested for debt.

The reason for the reversal in John Shakespeare's fortunes is unknown. Some have speculated that it may have stemmed from adherence to Catholicism, since those who remained loyal to the old faith were subject to increasingly vigorous and costly dis-crimination. But if John Shakespeare was a Catholic, as seems quite possible, it would not necessarily explain his decline, since other Catholics (and Puritans) in Elizabethan Stratford and elsewhere managed to hold on to their offices. In any case, his fall from prosperity and local power, whatever its cause, was not absolute. In 1601, the last year of his life, his name was included among those qualified to speak on behalf of Strat-ford's rights. And he was by that time entitled to bear a coat of arms, for in 1596, some twenty years after the application to the Herald's office had been initiated, it was suc-cessfully renewed. There is no record of who paid for the bureaucratic procedures that made the grant possible, but it is likely to have been John's oldest son William, by that time a highly successful London playwright.

## Education

Stratford was a small provincial town, but it had long been the site of an excellent free school, originally established by the Church in the thirteenth century. The main purpose of such schools in the Middle Ages had been to train prospective clerics; since many aristocrats could neither read nor write, literacy by itself conferred no special distinction and was not routinely viewed as desirable. But the situation began to change markedly in the sixteenth century. Protestantism placed a far greater emphasis upon lay literacy: for the sake of salvation, it was crucially important to be intimately acquainted with the Holy Book, and printing made that book readily avail-able. Schools became less strictly bound up with training for the Church and more linked to the general acquisition of "literature," in the sense both of literacy and of cultural knowledge. In keeping with this new emphasis on reading and with human-ist educational reform, the school was reorganized during the reign of Edward VI (1547–53). School records from the period have not survived, but it is almost certain that William Shakespeare attended the King's New School, as it was renamed in Edward's honor.

Scholars have painstakingly reconstructed the curriculum of schools of this kind and have even turned up the names and rather impressive credentials of the school-masters who taught there when Shakespeare was a student. (Shakespeare's principal teacher was Thomas Jenkins, an Oxford graduate, who received £20 a year and a rent-free house.) A child's education in Elizabethan England began at age four or five with two years at what was called the "petty school," attached to the main grammar school. The little scholars carried a "hornbook," a sheet of paper or parchment framed in wood and covered, for protection, with a transparent layer of horn. On the paper was written

The Cholmondeley sisters, c. 1600–10. This striking image brings to mind Shakespeare's fascination with twinship, both identical (notably in *The Comedy of Errors*) and fraternal (in *Twelfth Night*).

the alphabet and the Lord's Prayer, which were reproduced as well in the slightly more advanced *ABC with the Catechism,* a combination primer and rudimentary religious guide.

After students demonstrated some ability to read, the boys could go on, at about age seven, to the grammar school. Shakespeare's images of the experience are not particularly cheerful. In his famous account of the Seven Ages of Man, Jaques in *As You Like It* describes

> the whining schoolboy with his satchel
> And shining morning face, creeping like snail
> Unwillingly to school.
>
> (2.7.144–46)

The schoolboy would have crept quite early: the day began at 6:00 A.M. in summer and 7:00 A.M. in winter and continued until 5:00 P.M., with very few breaks or holidays.

At the core of the curriculum was the study of Latin, the mastery of which was in effect a prolonged male puberty rite involving much discipline and pain as well as pleasure. A late sixteenth-century Dutchman (whose name fittingly was Batty) proposed that God had created the human buttocks so that they could be severely beaten without risking permanent injury. Such thoughts dominated the pedagogy of the age, so that even an able young scholar, as we might imagine Shakespeare to have been, could scarcely have escaped recurrent flogging.

Shakespeare evidently reaped some rewards for the miseries he probably endured: his works are laced with echoes of many of the great Latin texts taught in grammar schools. One of his earliest comedies, *The Comedy of Errors,* is a brilliant variation on a theme by the Roman playwright Plautus, whom Elizabethan schoolchildren often performed as well as read; and one of his earliest tragedies, *Titus Andronicus,* is heavily indebted to Seneca. These are among the most visible of the classical influences that are often more subtly and pervasively interfused in Shakespeare's works. He seems to have had a particular fondness for *Aesop's Fables,* Apuleius's *Golden Ass,* and above all Ovid's *Metamorphoses.* His learned contemporary Ben Jonson remarked that Shakespeare had "small Latin and less Greek," but from this distance what is striking is not the limits of Shakespeare's learning but rather the unpretentious ease, intelligence, and gusto with which he draws upon what he must have first encountered as laborious study.

## Traces of a Life

In November 1582, William Shakespeare, at the age of eighteen, married twenty-six-year-old Anne Hathaway, who came from the village of Shottery, near Stratford. Their first daughter, Susanna, was baptized six months later. This circumstance, along with the fact that Anne was eight years Will's senior, has given rise to a mountain of speculation, all the more lurid precisely because there is no further evidence. Shakespeare depicts in several plays situations in which marriage is precipitated by a pregnancy, but he also registers, in *Measure for Measure* (1.2.125ff.), the Elizabethan belief that a "true contract" of marriage could be legitimately made and then consummated simply by the mutual vows of the couple in the presence of witnesses.

On February 2, 1585, the twins Hamnet and Judith Shakespeare were baptized in Stratford. Hamnet died at the age of eleven, when his father was already living for much of the year in London as a successful playwright. These are Shakespeare's only known children, although the playwright and impressario William Davenant in the mid-seventeenth century claimed to be his bastard son. Since people did not ordinarily advertise their illegitimacy, the claim, though impossible to verify, at least suggests the unusual strength of the Shakespeare's posthumous reputation.

William Shakespeare's father, John, died in 1601; his mother died seven years later. They would have had the satisfaction of witnessing their eldest son's prosperity, and not only from a distance, for in 1597 William purchased New Place, the second largest house in Stratford. In 1607, the playwright's daughter Susanna married a successful and well-known physician, John Hall. The next year, the Halls had a daughter, Elizabeth, Shakespeare's first grandchild. In 1616, the year of Shakespeare's death, his daughter Judith married a vintner, Thomas Quiney, with whom she had three children. Shakespeare's widow, Anne, died in 1623, at the age of sixty-seven. His first-born, Susanna, died at the age of sixty-six in 1649, the year that King Charles I was beheaded by the parliamentary army. Judith lived through Cromwell's Protectorate and on to the Restoration of the monarchy; she died in February 1662, at the age of seventy-seven. By the end of the century, the line of Shakespeare's direct heirs was extinct.

Patient digging in the archives has turned up other traces of Shakespeare's life as a family man and a man of means: assessments, small fines, real-estate deeds, minor actions in court to collect debts. In addition to his fine Stratford house and a large garden and cottage facing it, Shakespeare bought substantial parcels of land in the vicinity. When in *The Tempest* the wedding celebration conjures up a vision of "barns and garners never empty," Shakespeare could have been glancing at what the legal documents record as his own "tithes of corn, grain, blade, and hay" in the fields near Stratford. At some point after 1610, Shakespeare seems to have begun to shift his attention from the London stage to his Stratford properties, although the term "retirement" implies a more decisive and definitive break than appears to have been the case. By 1613, when the Globe Theatre burned down during a performance of *All Is True* (*Henry VIII*), Shakespeare was probably residing for the most part in Stratford, but he retained his financial interest in the rebuilt playhouse and probably continued to have some links to his theatrical colleagues. Still, by this point, his career as a playwright was substantially over. Legal documents from his last years show his main concern to be the protection of his real-estate interests in Stratford.

Half a century after Shakespeare's death, a Stratford vicar and physician, John Ward, noted in his diary that Shakespeare and his fellow poets Michael Drayton and Ben Jonson "had a merry meeting, and it seems drank too hard, for Shakespeare died of a fever there contracted." It is not inconceivable that Shakespeare's last illness was somehow linked, if only coincidentally, to the festivities on the occasion of the wedding in February 1616 of his daughter Judith (who was still alive when Ward made his diary entry). In any case, on March 25, 1616, Shakespeare revised his will, and on April 23 he died. Two days later, he was buried in the chancel of Holy Trinity Church beneath a stone bearing an epitaph he is said to have devised:

Good friend for Jesus' sake forbear,
To dig the dust enclosed here:
Blest be the man that spares these stones,
And curst be he that moves my bones.

The verses are hardly among Shakespeare's finest, but they seem to have been effective: though bones were routinely dug up to make room for others—a fate imagined with unforgettable intensity in the graveyard scene in *Hamlet*—his own remains were undisturbed. Like other vestiges of sixteenth- and early seventeenth-century Stratford, Shakespeare's grave has for centuries been the object of a tourist industry that borders on a religious cult.

Shakespeare's will has been examined with an intensity befitting this cult; every provision and formulaic phrase, no matter how minor or conventional, has borne a heavy weight of interpretation, none more so than the bequest to his wife, Anne, of only "my second-best bed." Scholars have pointed out that Anne would in any case have been provided for by custom and that the terms are not necessarily a deliberate slight, but the absence of the customary words "my loving wife" or "my well-beloved wife" is difficult to ignore.

## Portrait of the Playwright as Young Provincial

The great problem with the surviving traces of Shakespeare's life is not that they are few but that they are dull. Christopher Marlowe was a double or triple agent, accused of brawling, sodomy, and atheism. Ben Jonson, who somehow clambered up from bricklayer's apprentice to classical scholar, served in the army in Flanders, killed a fellow actor in a duel, converted to Catholicism in prison in 1598, and returned to the Church of England in 1610. Provincial real-estate investments and the second-best bed cannot compete with such adventurous lives. Indeed, the relative ordinariness of Shakespeare's social background and life has contributed to a persistent current of speculation that the glover's son from Stratford-upon-Avon was not in fact the author of the plays attributed to him.

The anti-Stratfordians, as those who deny Shakespeare's authorship are sometimes called, almost always propose as the real author someone who came from a higher social class and received a more prestigious education. Francis Bacon, the Earl of Oxford, the Earl of Southampton, even Queen Elizabeth, have been advanced, among many others, as glamorous candidates for the role of clandestine playwright. Several famous people, including Mark Twain and Sigmund Freud, have espoused these theories, though very few scholars have joined them. Since Shakespeare was quite well-known in his own time as the author of the plays that bear his name, there would need to have been an extraordinary conspiracy to conceal the identity of the real master who (the theory goes) disdained to appear in the vulgarity of print or on the public stage. Like many conspiracy theories, the extreme implausibility of this one only seems to increase the fervent conviction of its advocates.

To the charge that a middle-class author from a small town could not have imagined the lives of kings and nobles, one can respond by citing the exceptional qualities that Ben Jonson praised in Shakespeare: "excellent *Phantsie*; brave notions, and gentle expressions." Even in ordinary mortals, the human imagination is a strange faculty; in Shakespeare, it seems to have been uncannily powerful, working its mysterious, transforming effects on everything it touched. His imagination was intensely engaged by what he found in books. He seems throughout his life to have been an intense, voracious reader, and it is fascinating to witness his creative encounters with Raphael Holinshed's *Chronicles of England, Scotlande, and Irelande*, Plutarch's *Lives of the Noble Grecians and Romans*, Ovid's *Metamorphoses*, Montaigne's *Essays*, and the Bible, to name only some of his favorite books. But books were clearly not the only objects of Shakespeare's attention; like most artists, he drew upon the whole range of his life experiences.

To integrate some of the probable circumstances of Shakespeare's early years with the particular shape of the theatrical imagination associated with his name, let us indulge briefly in the biographical daydreams that modern scholarship is supposed to have rendered forever obsolete. The vignettes that follow are conjectural, but they may suggest ways in which his life as we know it found its way into his art.

## 1. THE GOWN OF OFFICE

Shakespeare was a very young boy—not quite four years old—when the Stratford council elected his father, John, to a year's term as bailiff (the equivalent of mayor). The office, the town's highest, was attended with considerable ceremony. The bailiff and his deputy were entitled to appear in public in furred gowns, attended by leather-clad sergeants bearing maces before them. On Rogation Days (three days of prayer for the harvest, before Ascension Day), they would solemnly pace out the parish boundaries, and they would similarly walk in processions on market and fair days. On Sundays, the sergeants would accompany the bailiff to church, where he would sit with his wife in a front pew, and he would have a comparable seat of honor at sermons in the Guild Chapel.

Public deference was a matter of law as well as custom: any inhabitant who spoke disrespectfully to the bailiff or other town officer was subject to the penalty of three days and three nights in the stocks. Newcomers who sought employment—notably including traveling players who hoped to stage performances—were obliged to obtain the bailiff's permission. In the year that John Shakespeare held office, two such professional playing companies arrived in Stratford. They must have proceeded to the bailiff's house on Henley Street and presented the letters of recommendation, with wax seals, that showed that they were not vagabonds. They would have spoken with more than ordinary deference, since it was the bailiff who would decide whether they would be sent packing or—as was the case—allowed to post their bills announcing the performances. The first of these performances was usually free to all comers. The bailiff would have been expected to attend, for it was his privilege to determine the level of the reward to be paid out of the city coffers; he would, presumably, have been given one of the best seats in the guildhall, where a special stage had been erected. It is impossible to know whether John Shakespeare took his family to these plays, but his little boy would certainly have been aware of what was happening.

On a precocious child (or even, for that matter, on an ordinary child), the effect of his father's office and the elaborate rituals that attended it would be at least threefold. First, the ceremony would convey irresistibly the power of clothes (the gown of office) and of symbols (the mace) to transform identity as if by magic. Second, it would invest the father with immense power, distinction, and importance, awakening what we may call a lifelong dream of high station. And third, pulling slightly against this dream, it would provoke an odd feeling that the father's clothes do not fit, a perception that the office is not the same as the man, and an intimate, firsthand knowledge that when the robes are put off, their wearer is inevitably glimpsed in a far different, less exalted light.

## 2. PROGRESSES AND ELECTIONS

This second biographical fantasy, slightly less plausible than the first but still quite likely, involves a somewhat older child witnessing two characteristic forms of Elizabethan political ceremony, both of which were well known in the provinces. Queen Elizabeth was fond of going on what were known as "progresses," triumphant ceremonial journeys around her kingdom. Let us imagine that the young Shakespeare—say, in 1574, when he was ten years old—went with his kinsfolk or friends to Warwick, some 8 miles distant, to witness a progress. He would thus have participated as a spectator in an elaborate celebration of charismatic power: the courtiers in their gorgeous clothes, the nervous local officials bedecked in velvets and silks, and at the center, carried in a special litter like a painted idol, the bejeweled queen. Let us imagine further that in addition to being struck by the overwhelming force of this charisma, the boy was struck, too, by the way this force depended paradoxically on a sense that the queen was after all quite human. Elizabeth was in fact fond of calling attention to this peculiar tension between near-divinization and human ordinariness. For example, on this occasion at Warwick (and what follows really happened), after the trembling Recorder, presumably a local civil official of high standing, had made his official welcoming speech, Elizabeth offered her hand to him to be kissed: "Come hither, little Recorder," she said. "It was told me that you would be afraid to look upon me or to speak boldly; but you were not so afraid of me as I was of you; and I now thank you for putting me in mind of my duty." Of course, the charm of this royal "confession" of nervousness depends on its manifest implausibility: it is, in effect, a theatrical performance of humility by someone with immense confidence in her own histrionic power.

A royal progress was not the only form of spectacular political activity that Shakespeare might well have seen in the 1570s; it is still more likely that he would have witnessed parliamentary elections, particularly since his father was qualified to vote. In 1571, 1572, 1575, and 1578, there were shire elections conducted in nearby Warwick, elections that would certainly have attracted well over a thousand voters. These were often memorable events: large crowds came together; there was usually heavy drinking and carnivalesque festivity; and, at the same time, there was enacted, in a very different register from that of the monarchy, a ritual of empowerment. The people, those entitled to vote by virtue of meeting the property and residence requirements, chose their own representatives by giving their votes—their voices—to candidates for office. Here, legislative sovereignty was conferred not by God but by the consent of the community, a consent marked by shouts and applause.

Recent cultural historians have been so fascinated by the evident links between the spectacles of the absolutist monarchy and the theater that they have largely ignored the significance of this alternative public arena, one that generated intense excitement throughout the country. A child who was a spectator at a parliamentary election in the 1570s might well have found the occasion enormously compelling. It is striking, in any case, how often the adult Shakespeare returns to scenes of acclamation and mass consent, and striking, too, how much the theater depends on the soliciting of popular voices.

### 3. EXORCISMS

A third and final fantasy is even more speculative than the second and involves a controversial claim, which has long been hotly debated— that Shakespeare either was a secret Catholic or was at least raised in a Roman Catholic household in a time of official suspicion and persecution of recusancy. A late seventeenth-century Anglican clergyman, Richard Davies, jotted down in some notes on Shakespeare that "he died a papist." In a modern biographical study, E. A. J. Honigmann convincingly linked several of the schoolmasters who taught in Stratford at the time that Shakespeare would have been a pupil to a network of Catholic families in Lancashire with whom one "William Shakeshafte," possibly a young schoolmaster or player, was connected in the late 1570s or early 1580s.

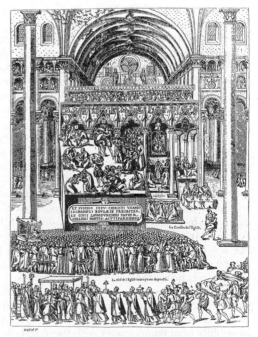

Exorcism: Nicole Aubry in the cathedral at Laon, 1566.

Catholics in Elizabethan England were not free to practice their religion—any more than Protestants, in Catholic countries, were free to practice theirs—and the beleaguered faithful, beset with spies, came together only at great risk to confess and receive Communion from clandestine priests. Under the circumstances, although a substantial portion of the population may have retained a residual inward loyalty to the traditional faith, the vast majority fell away from outward Catholic practice. After all, the churches, great and small, were now the places of Protestant worship; the innumerable local saints' shrines and pilgrimage sites had been systematically destroyed; the monasteries and convents had been abolished, their property bestowed on royal favorites or sold at bargain prices to local magnates. Seeking a spectacular way to demonstrate the enduring spiritual power and authenticity of the Roman Church, the embattled Counter-Reformers turned to an ancient ritual: exorcism. Devils who possessed the souls of troubled men and women had once been exorcised in public, but now the healing rite had to be conducted in secret, in a barn in a remote village, perhaps, or in the attic of the secluded house of a Catholic loyalist. The danger for those who presided was enormous—brutal interrogation, torture, and an unspeakably horrible execution was the usual fate of the missionary priests who were caught—but the vivid demonstration of the Church's triumph over evil was sufficiently compelling to warrant the risk. For despite the lynx-eyed alertness of the Protestant authorities, Catholics staged a surprising number of clandestine exorcisms, many of which drew substantial crowds.

Accepting for the moment that William Shakespeare was raised in the recusant faith of his father and mother, let us imagine that one day in the early 1580s the young man attended an exorcism of which he had learned through the secret network of the faithful. Here, based on an eyewitness account of such an occasion recently transcribed by Gerard Kilroy, is what he is likely to have seen. At the center of a large room, emptied of other furniture in order to accommodate the many observers, stood a bed. A young woman sat on the bed, and a priest, in clerical vestments, stood over her, preaching a sermon. As he spoke, the woman began to writhe and scream. At first the screams, uttered by a deep voice that could not have been the woman's although it came from her mouth, were not intelligible. Gradually, the bystanders began to make out some of the words, blasphemous oaths—"God's wounds! God's nails!"—followed by menaces, spoken as if by a rabid Protestant: "Popish priests, popish priests, to prison with them and hang them, hang them, hang them." The exorcist held up the Eucharist over the writhing woman, and the screams intensified. "Who are you?" he demanded. "I am Modu," the voice replied. "Depart, Modu!" shouted the priest, bringing the consecrated wafer closer to the demoniac. When that did not succeed in driving the devil out, the priest advanced a chafing dish of fire and brimstone, provoking more shouting and cursing, and then displayed a painting of the Blessed Virgin. "I will not behold or see her," screamed the demonic voice.

The longer the scene continued, the more there was confirmation of the contested tenets of the Catholic faith. The devil admitted that the Virgin Mary was a particularly efficacious intercessor, that purgatory existed, that the wafer, consecrated by the priest, actually was the body and blood of Christ. The devil also revealed that all Protestants were his followers. Finally, under the irresistible force of spiritual compulsion, he agreed to depart forever from the body of the possessed. The departure was difficult: again and again the tormented young woman gaped, as if her mouth were being torn open. She screamed in pain, rose up only to be cast down violently by invisible hands, cried out that she was being drowned, and called upon Jesus and his mother to save her. Only when a sacred relic was placed directly on her flesh did the devil finally leave her.

There is no way to know if William Shakespeare actually witnessed such a scene, but if he did, he would have carried away several indelible impressions: an awareness that strange, alien voices may speak from within ordinary, familiar bodies; an intimation of the immense, cosmic forces that may impinge upon human life; a belief in the possibility of making contact with these forces and compelling them to speak. These are, after all, the foundation stones of great tragedy.

Many years later, Shakespeare brooded about demonic possession when he was writing his greatest tragedy about the presence of evil in the world, *King Lear*. "This is the foul fiend Flibbertigibbet," shouts the madman, Poor Tom; "The Prince of Darkness is a gentleman. Modo he's called, and Mahu" (3.4.103, 127–28). But Poor Tom in that play is faking it; he is actually the noble Edgar, who has disguised himself as a madman in order to escape persecution. Did Shakespeare as a teenager already think that the whole compelling event, in all of its metaphysical weirdness, was a powerful theatrical fraud, a piece of pious propaganda? Perhaps. But if so, he also clearly understood that evil exists, that persecution is real, and that illusion has an irresistible force.

These imaginary portraits of the playwright as a young provincial introduce us to several of the root conditions of the Elizabethan theater. Biographical fantasies, though entirely speculative and playful, are useful in part because some people have found it difficult to conceive how Shakespeare, with his provincial roots and his restricted range of experience, could have so rapidly and completely mastered the central imaginative themes of his times. Moreover, it is sometimes difficult to grasp how seeming abstractions such as market society, monarchical state, and theological doctrine were actually experienced directly by peculiar, distinct individuals. Shakespeare's plays were social and collective events, but they also bore the stamp of a particular artist, one endowed with a remarkable capacity to craft lifelike illusions (what Jonson called "excellent *Phantsie*"), a daring willingness to articulate an original vision ("brave notions"), and a loving command, at once precise and generous, of language ("gentle expressions"). These plays are stitched together from shared cultural experiences, inherited dramatic devices, and the pungent vernacular of the day, but we should not lose sight of the extent to which they articulate an intensely personal vision, a bold shaping of the available materials. Four centuries of feverish biographical speculation, much of it foolish, bears witness to a basic intuition: the richness of these plays, their inexhaustible openness, is the consequence not only of the auspicious collective conditions of the culture but also of someone's exceptional skill, inventiveness, and courage at taking those conditions and making of them something rich and strange.

## The Theater of the Nation

What precisely are the collective conditions highlighted by these vignettes? First, the growth of Stratford-upon-Avon, the bustling market town of which John Shakespeare was bailiff, is a small version of a momentous sixteenth-century development that made Shakespeare's career possible: the making of an urban "public." That development obviously depended on adequate numbers; the period experienced a rapid and still unexplained growth in population. With it came an expansion and elaboration of market relations: markets became less periodic, more continuous, and more abstract—centered, that is, not on the familiar materiality of goods but on the liquidity of capital and goods. In practical terms, this meant that it was possible to conceive of the theater not only as festive entertainment for special events—lord mayor's pageants, visiting princes, seasonal festivals, and the like—but as a permanent, year-round business venture. The venture relied on ticket sales—it was an innovation of this period to have money advanced in the expectation of pleasure rather than offered to servants afterward as a reward—and counted on habitual playgoing with a concomitant demand for new plays from competing theater companies: "But that's all one, our play is done," sings Feste at the end of *Twelfth Night* and adds a glance toward the next afternoon's proceeds: "And we'll strive to please you every day" (5.1.394–95).

Second, the royal progress is an instance of what the anthropologist Clifford Geertz has called the Theater State, a state that manifests its power and meaning in exemplary public performances. Professional companies of players, like the one Shakespeare belonged to, understood well that they existed in relation to this Theater State and would, if they were fortunate, be called upon to serve it. Unlike Ben Jonson, Shakespeare did not, as far as we know, write royal entertainments on commission, but his plays were frequently performed before Queen Elizabeth and then before King James and Queen Anne, along with their courtiers and privileged guests. There are many fascinating glimpses of these performances, including a letter from Walter Cope to Robert Cecil, early in James's reign. "Burbage is come," Cope writes, referring to the leading actor of Shakespeare's company, "and says there is no new play that the queen hath not seen, but they have revived an old one, called *Love's Labours Lost*, which for wit and mirth he says will please her exceedingly. And this is appointed to be played tomorrow night at my Lord of Southampton's." Not only would such theatrical performances have given great pleasure—evidently, the queen had already exhausted the company's new offerings—but they conferred prestige upon those who commanded them and those in whose honor they were mounted.

Monarchical power in the period was deeply allied to spectacular manifestations of the ruler's glory and disciplinary authority. The symbology of power depended on regal magnificence, reward, punishment, and pardon, all of which were heavily theatricalized. Indeed, the conspicuous public display does not simply serve the interests of power; on many occasions in the period, power seemed to exist in order to make pageantry possible, as if the nation's identity were only fully realized in theatrical performance. It would be easy to exaggerate this perception: the subjects of Queen Elizabeth and King James were acutely aware of the distinction between shadow and substance. But they were fascinated by the political magic through which shadows could be taken for substantial realities, and the ruling elite was largely complicit in the formation and celebration of a charismatic absolutism. At the same time, the claims of the monarch who professes herself or himself to be not the representative of the nation but its embodiment were set against the counterclaims of the House of Commons. And this institution, too, as we have glimpsed, had its own theatrical rituals, centered on the crowd whose shouts of approval, in heavily stage-managed elections, chose the individuals who would stand for the polity and participate in deliberations held in a hall whose resemblance to a theater did not escape contemporary notice.

Third, illicit exorcism points both to the theatricality of much religious ritual in the late Middle Ages and the Renaissance and to the heightened possibility of secularization. English Protestant authorities banned the medieval mystery plays, along with pilgrimages and other rituals associated with holy shrines and sacred images, but playing companies could satisfy at least some of the popular longings and appropriate aspects of the social energy no longer allowed a theological outlet. That is, official attacks on certain Catholic practices made it more possible for the public theater to appropriate and exploit their allure. Hence, for example, the plays that celebrated the solemn miracle of the Catholic Mass were banned, along with the most elaborate church vestments, but in *The Winter's Tale* Dion can speak in awe of what he witnessed at Apollo's temple:

> I shall report,
> For most it caught me, the celestial habits—
> Methinks I so should term them—and the reverence
> Of the grave wearers. O, the sacrifice—
> How ceremonious, solemn, and unearthly
> It was i'th' off'ring!
>
> (3.1.3–8)

And at the play's end, the statue of the innocent mother breathes, comes to life, and embraces her child.

The theater in Shakespeare's time, then, is intimately bound up with all three crucial cultural formations: the market society, the theater state, and the Church. But it is important to note that the institution is not *identified* with any of them. The theater may be a market phenomenon, but it is repeatedly and bitterly attacked as the enemy of diligent, sober, productive economic activity. Civic authorities generally regarded the theater as a pestilential nuisance, a parasite on the body of the commonwealth, a temptation to students, apprentices, housewives, even respectable merchants to leave their serious business and lapse into idleness and waste. That waste, it might be argued, could be partially recuperated if it went for the glorification of a guild or the entertainment of an important dignitary, but the only group regularly profiting from the theater were the players and their disreputable associates.

For his part, Shakespeare made a handsome profit from the commodification of theatrical entertainment, but he seems never to have written "city comedy"—plays set in London and more or less explicitly concerned with market relations—and his characters express deep reservations about the power of money and commerce: "That smooth-faced gentleman, tickling commodity," Philip the Bastard observes in *King John,* "wins of all, / Of kings, of beggars, old men, young men, maids" (2.1.574, 570–71). We could argue that the smooth-faced gentleman is none other than Shakespeare himself, for his drama famously mingles kings and clowns, princesses and panderers. But the mingling is set against a romantic current of social conservatism: in *Twelfth Night,* the aristocratic heiress Olivia falls in love with someone who appears far beneath her in wealth and social station, but it is revealed that he (and his sister Viola) are of noble blood; in *The Winter's Tale,* Leontes' daughter Perdita is raised as a shepherdess, but her noble nature shines through her humble upbringing, and she marries the Prince of Bohemia; the strange island maiden with whom Ferdinand, son of the King of Naples, falls madly in love in *The Tempest* turns out to be the daughter of the rightful Duke of Milan. Shakespeare pushes against this conservative logic in *All's Well That Ends Well,* but the noble young Bertram violently resists the unequal match thrust upon him by the King, and the play's mood is notoriously uneasy.

Similarly, Shakespeare's theater may have been patronized and protected by the monarchy—after 1603, his company received a royal patent and was known as the King's Men—but it was by no means identical in its interests or its ethos. To be sure, *Richard III* and *Macbeth* incorporate aspects of royal propaganda, but given the realities of censorship, Shakespeare's plays, and the period's drama as a whole, are surprisingly independent and complex in their political vision. There is, in any case, a certain inherent tension between kings and player kings: Elizabeth and James may both have likened themselves to actors onstage, but they were loath to admit their dependence on the applause and money, freely given or freely withheld, of the audience. The charismatic monarch insists that the sacredness of authority resides in the body of the ruler, not in a costume that may be worn and then discarded by an actor. Kings are not *representations* of power—or do not admit that they are—but claim to be the thing itself. The government institution that was actually based on the idea of representation, Parliament, had theatrical elements, as we have seen, but it significantly excluded any audience from its deliberations. And Shakespeare's oblique portraits of parliamentary representatives, the tribunes Sicinius Velutus and Junius Brutus in *Coriolanus,* are anything but flattering.

Finally, the theater drew significant energy from the liturgy and rituals of the late medieval Church, but as Shakespeare's contemporaries widely remarked, the playhouse and the Church were scarcely natural allies. Not only did the theater represent a potential competitor to worship services, and not only did ministers rail against prostitution and other vices associated with playgoing, but theatrical representation itself, even when ostensibly pious, seemed to many to empty out whatever it presented, turning substance into mere show. The theater could and did use the period's deep currents of religious feeling, but it had to do so carefully and with an awareness of conflicting interests.

## Shakespeare Comes to London

How did Shakespeare decide to turn his prodigious talents to the stage? When did he make his way to London? How did he get his start? To these and similar questions we have a mountain of speculation but no secure answers. There is not a single surviving record of Shakespeare's existence from 1585, when his twins were baptized in Stratford church, until 1592, when a rival London playwright made an envious remark about him. In the late seventeenth century, the delightfully eccentric collector of gossip John Aubrey was informed that prior to moving to London the young Shakespeare had been a schoolteacher in the country. Aubrey also recorded a story that Shakespeare had been a rather unusual apprentice butcher: "When he killed a calf, he would do it in a high style, and make a speech."

These and other legends, including one that has Shakespeare whipped for poaching game, fill the void until the unmistakable reference in Robert Greene's *Groats-Worth of Witte, Bought with a Million of Repentance* (1592). An inspired hack writer with a university education, a penchant for self-dramatization, a taste for wild living, and a strong streak of resentment, Greene, in his early thirties, was dying in poverty when he penned his last farewell, piously urging his fellow dramatists Christopher Marlowe, Thomas Nashe, and George Peele to abandon the wicked stage before they were brought low, as he had been, by a new arrival: "For there is an upstart crow, beautified with our feathers, that with his 'Tiger's heart wrapped in player's hide' supposes he is as well able to bombast out a blank verse as the best of you, and, being an absolute *Johannes Factotum*, is in his own conceit the only Shake-scene in a country." If "Shake-scene" is not enough to identify the object of his attack, Greene parodies a line from Shakespeare's early play *Richard Duke of York* (3 *Henry VI*): "O tiger's heart wrapped in a woman's hide!" (1.4.138). Greene is accusing Shakespeare of being an upstart, a plagiarist, an egomaniacal jack-of-all-trades—and, above all perhaps, a popular success.

By 1592, then, Shakespeare had already arrived on the highly competitive London theatrical scene. He was successful enough to be attacked by Greene and, a few months later, defended by Henry Chettle, another hack writer who had seen Greene's manuscript through the press (or, some scholars speculate, had written the attack himself and passed it off as the dying Greene's). Chettle expresses his regret that he did not suppress Greene's diatribe and spare Shakespeare "because myself have seen his demeanor no less civil than he excellent in the quality he professes." Besides, Chettle adds, "divers of worship have reported his uprightness of dealing, which argues his honesty and his facetious [polished] grace in writing that approves his art." "Divers of worship": not only was Shakespeare established as an accomplished writer and actor, but he evidently had aroused the attention and the approbation of several socially prominent people. In Elizabethan England, aristocratic patronage, with the money, protection, and prestige it alone could provide, was probably a professional writer's most important asset.

This patronage, or at least Shakespeare's quest for it, is most visible in the dedications in 1593 and 1594 of his narrative poems *Venus and Adonis* and *The Rape of Lucrece* to the young nobleman Henry Wriothesley, Earl of Southampton. It may be glimpsed as well, perhaps, in the sonnets, with their extraordinary adoration of the fair youth, though the identity of that youth has never been determined. What return Shakespeare got for his exquisite offerings is likewise unknown. We do know that among wits and gallants, the narrative poems won Shakespeare a fine reputation as an immensely stylish and accomplished poet. An amateur play performed at Cambridge University at the end of the sixteenth century, *The Return from Parnassus*, makes fun of this vogue, as a foolish character effusively declares, "I'll worship sweet Mr. Shakespeare, and to honour him will lay his *Venus and Adonis* under my pillow." Many readers at the time may have done so: the poem went through sixteen editions before 1640, more than any other work by Shakespeare.

Patronage was crucially important not only for individual artists but also for the actors, playwrights, and investors who pooled their resources to form professional theater companies. The public playhouses had enemies, especially among civic and religious authorities, who wished greatly to curb performances or to ban them altogether. An act of 1572 included players among those classified as vagabonds, threatening them, therefore, with the horrible punishments meted out to those regarded as economic parasites. The players' escape route was to be nominally enrolled as the servants of high-ranking noblemen. The legal fiction was that their public performances were a kind of rehearsal for the command performances before the patron or the monarch.

When Shakespeare came to London, presumably in the late 1580s, there were more than a dozen of these companies operating under the patronage of various aristocrats.

We do not know for which of these companies, several of which had toured in Stratford, he originally worked, nor whether he began, as legend has it, as a prompter's assistant and then graduated to acting and playwriting. Shakespeare is listed among the actors in Ben Jonson's *Every Man in His Humour* (performed in 1598) and *Sejanus* (performed in 1603), but we do not know for certain what roles he played, nor are there records of any of his other performances. Tradition has it that he played Adam in *As You Like It* and the Ghost in *Hamlet,* but he was clearly not one of the leading actors of the day.

By the 1590s, the number of playing companies in London had been considerably reduced, in part through competition and in part through legislative restriction. (In 1572, knights and gentry lost the privilege of patronizing a troupe of actors; in 1598, justices of the peace lost the power to authorize performances.) By the early years of the seventeenth century, there were usually only three companies competing against one another in any season, along with two children's companies, which were often successful at drawing audiences away from the public playhouses. Shakespeare may initially have been associated with the Earl of Leicester's company or with the company of Ferdinando Stanley, Lord Strange; both groups included actors with whom Shakespeare was later linked. Or he may have belonged to the Earl of Pembroke's Men, since there is evidence that they performed *The Taming of a Shrew* and a version of *Richard Duke of York (3 Henry VI).* At any event, by 1594, Shakespeare was a member of the Lord Chamberlain's Men, for his name, along with those of Will Kemp (or Kempe) and Richard Burbage, appears on a record of those "servants to the Lord Chamberlain" paid for performance at the royal palace at Greenwich on December 26 and 28. Shakespeare stayed with this company, which during the reign of King James received royal patronage and became the King's Men, for the rest of his career.

Many playwrights in Shakespeare's time worked freelance, moving from company to company as opportunities arose, collaborating on projects, adding scenes to old plays, scrambling from one enterprise to another. But certain playwrights, among them the most successful, wrote for a single company, often agreeing contractually to give that company exclusive rights to their theatrical works. Shakespeare seems to have followed such a pattern. For the Lord Chamberlain's Men, he wrote an average of two plays per year. His company initially performed in The Theatre, a playhouse built in 1576 by an entrepreneurial carpenter, James Burbage, the father of the actor Richard, who was to perform many of

Edward Alleyn (1566–1626). Artist unknown. Alleyn was the great tragic actor of the Lord Admiral's Men (the principal rival to Shakespeare's company). He was famous especially for playing the great Marlovian heroes.

Shakespeare's greatest roles. When in 1597 their lease on this playhouse expired, the Lord Chamberlain's Men passed through a difficult and legally perilous time, but they formed a joint-stock company, raising sufficient capital to lease a site and put up a splendid new playhouse in the suburb of Southwark, on the south bank of the Thames. This playhouse, the Globe, opened in 1599. Shakespeare is listed in the legal agreement as one of the principal investors; and when the company began to use Blackfriars as their indoor playhouse around 1609, he was a major shareholder in that theater as well. The Lord Chamberlain's Men, later the King's Men, dominated the theater scene, and the shares were quite valuable. Then as now, the theater was an extremely risky enterprise—most of those who wrote plays and performed in them made pathetically little money—but Shakespeare was a notable exception. The fine house in Stratford and the coat of arms he succeeded in acquiring were among the fruits of his multiple mastery, as actor, playwright, and investor in the London stage.

## The Shakespearean Trajectory

Even though Shakespeare's England was in many ways a record-keeping society, no reliable record survives that details the performances, year by year, in the London theaters. Every play had to be licensed by a government official, the Master of the Revels, but the records kept by the relevant officials from 1579 to 1621, Sir Edmund Tilney and Sir George Buc, have not survived. A major theatrical entrepreneur, Philip Henslowe, kept a careful account of his expenditures, including what he paid for the scripts he commissioned, but unfortunately Henslowe's main business was with the Rose and the Fortune theaters and not with the playhouses at which Shakespeare's company performed. A comparable ledger must have been kept by the shareholders of the Lord Chamberlain's Men, but it has not survived. Shakespeare himself apparently did not undertake to preserve for posterity the sum of his writings, let alone to clarify the chronology of his works or specify which plays he wrote alone and which with collaborators.

The principal source for Shakespeare's works is the 1623 Folio volume of *Mr. William Shakespeares Comedies, Histories, & Tragedies*. Most scholars believe that the editors were careful to include only those plays for which they knew Shakespeare to be ·the main author. Their edition does not, however, include any of Shakespeare's nondramatic poems, and it omits two plays in which Shakespeare is now thought to have had a significant hand, *Pericles, Prince of Tyre* and *The Two Noble Kinsmen*, along with his probable contribution to the multiauthored *Sir Thomas More*. (A number of other plays were attributed to Shakespeare, both before and after his death, but scholars have not generally accepted any of these into the established canon.) Moreover, the Folio edition does not print the plays in chronological order, nor does it attempt to establish a chronology. We do not know how much time would normally have elapsed between the writing of a play and its first performance, nor, with

IF YOV KNOW NOT ME,
You know no body.
OR,
*The troubles of Queene* ELIZABETH.

LONDON.
Printed by *B.A.* and *T.F.* for *Nathanaell Butter.* 1 6 3 2.

Title page of Thomas Heywood's *If You Know Not Me, You Know No Body; or, The Troubles of Queene Elizabeth* (1632 ed.).

a few exceptions, do we know with any certainty the month or even the year of the first performance of any of Shakespeare's plays. The quarto editions of those plays that were published during Shakespeare's lifetime obviously establish a date by which we know a given play had been written, but they give us little more than an end point, because there was likely to be a substantial though indeterminate gap between the first performance of a play and its publication.

With enormous patience and ingenuity, however, scholars have gradually assembled a considerable archive of evidence, both external and internal, for dating the composition of the plays. Besides actual publication, the external evidence includes explicit reference to a play, a record of its performance, or (as in the case of Greene's attack on the "upstart crow") the quoting of a line, though all of these can be maddeningly ambiguous. The most important single piece of external evidence appears in 1598 in *Palladis Tamia*, a long book of jumbled reflections by Francis Meres that includes a survey of the contemporary literary scene. Meres finds that "the sweet, witty soul of Ovid lives in melliflous and honey-tongued Shakespeare, witness his *Venus and Adonis,* his *Lucrece,* his sugered Sonnets among his private friends, etc." Meres goes on to list Shakespeare's accomplishments as a playwright as well:

> As Plautus and Seneca are accounted the best for Comedy and Tragedy among the Latins: so Shakespeare among the English is the most excellent in both kinds for the stage; for Comedy, witness his *Gentlemen of Verona,* his *Errors,* his *Love labors lost,* his *Love labours won,* his *Midsummers night dream,* & his *Merchant of Venice:* for Tragedy his *Richard the 2, Richard the 3, Henry the 4, King John, Titus Andronicus* and his *Romeo and Juliet.*

Meres thus provides a date by which twelve of Shakespeare's plays had definitely appeared (including one, *Love's Labour's Won,* that appears to have been lost or that we know by a different title). Unfortunately, Meres provides no clues about the order of appearance of these plays, and there are no other comparable lists.

Faced with the limitations of the external evidence, scholars have turned to a bewildering array of internal evidence, ranging from datable sources and topical allusions on the one hand to evolving stylistic features (ratio of verse to prose, percentage of rhyme to blank verse, colloquialisms, use of extended similes, and the like) on the other. Thus, for example, a cluster of plays with a high percentage of rhymed verse may follow closely upon Shakespeare's writing of the rhymed poems *Venus and Adonis* and *The Rape of Lucrece* and, therefore, be datable to 1594–95. Similarly, vocabulary overlap probably indicates proximity in composition, so if four or five plays share relatively "rare" vocabulary, it is likely that they were written in roughly the same period. Again, there seems to be a pattern in Shakespeare's use of colloquialisms, with a steady increase from *As You Like It* (1599–1600) to *Coriolanus* (1608), followed in the late romances by a retreat from the colloquial.

More sophisticated computer analysis should provide further guidance in the future, even though the precise order of the plays, still very much in dispute, is never likely to be settled to universal satisfaction. Still, certain broad patterns are now widely accepted. These patterns can be readily grasped in the *Norton Shakespeare,* which presents the plays in the chronological order proposed by the Oxford editors.

Shakespeare began his career, probably in the early 1590s, by writing both comedies and history plays. The attack by Greene suggests that he made his mark with the series of theatrically vital but rather crude plays based on the foreign and domestic broils that erupted during the unhappy reign of the Lancastrian Henry VI. Modern readers and audiences are more likely to find the first sustained evidence of unusual power in *Richard III* (c. 1592), a play that combines a brilliantly conceived central character, a dazzling command of histrionic rhetoric, and an overarching moral vision of English history.

At virtually the same time that he was setting his stamp on the genre of the history play, Shakespeare was writing his first—or first surviving—comedies. Here, there are even fewer signs than in the histories of an apprenticeship: *The Comedy of Errors,* one of his early efforts in this genre, already displays a rare command of the resources of comedy: mistaken identity, madcap confusion, and the threat of disaster, giving way in the end to reconciliation, recovery, and love. Shakespeare's other comedies from the early 1590s, *The Taming of the Shrew, The Two Gentlemen of Verona,* and *Love's Labour's Lost,* are no less remarkable for their sophisticated variations on familiar comic themes, their inexhaustible rhetorical inventiveness, and their poignant intimation, in the midst of festive celebration, of loss.

Successful as are these early histories and comedies, and indicative of an extraordinary theatrical talent, Shakespeare's achievement in the later 1590s would still have been all but impossible to foresee. Starting with *A Midsummer Night's Dream* (c. 1595), Shakespeare wrote an unprecedented series of romantic comedies—*The Merchant of Venice, The Merry Wives of Windsor, Much Ado About Nothing, As You Like It,* and *Twelfth Night* (c. 1602)—whose poetic richness and emotional complexity remain unmatched. In the same period, he wrote a sequence of profoundly searching and ambitious history plays—*Richard II, 1* and *2 Henry IV,* and *Henry V*—which together explore the death throes of feudal England and the birth of the modern nation-state ruled by a charismatic monarch. Both the comedies and histories of this period are marked by their capaciousness, their ability to absorb characters who press up against the outermost boundaries of the genre: the comedy *Merchant of Venice* somehow contains the figure, at once nightmarish and poignant, of Shylock, while the *Henry IV* plays, with their somber vision of crisis in the family and the state, bring to the stage one of England's greatest comic characters, Falstaff.

If in the mid to late 1590s Shakespeare reached the summit of his art in two major genres, he also manifested a lively interest in a third. As early as 1593, he wrote the crudely violent tragedy *Titus Andronicus,* the first of several plays on themes from Roman history, and a year or two later, in *Richard II,* he created in the protagonist a figure who achieves by the play's close the stature of a tragic hero. In the same year that Shakespeare wrote the wonderfully farcical "Pyramus and Thisbe" scene in *A Midsummer Night's Dream,* he probably also wrote the deeply tragic realization of the same story in *Romeo and Juliet.* But once again, the lyric anguish of *Romeo and Juliet* and the tormented self-revelation of *Richard II,* extraordinary as they are, could not have led anyone to predict the next phase of Shakespeare's career, the great tragic dramas that poured forth in the early years of the seventeenth century: *Hamlet, Othello, King Lear, Macbeth, Antony and Cleopatra,* and *Coriolanus.* These plays, written from 1601 to 1607, seem to mark a major shift in sensibility, an existential and metaphysical darkening that many readers think must have originated in a deep personal anguish, perhaps caused by the death of Shakespeare's father, John, in 1601.

Whatever the truth of these speculations—and we have no direct, personal testimony either to support or to undermine them—there appears to have occurred in the same period a shift as well in Shakespeare's comic sensibility. The comedies written between 1601 and 1604, *Troilus and Cressida, All's Well That Ends Well,* and *Measure for Measure,* are sufficiently different from the earlier comedies—more biting in tone, more uneasy with comic conventions, more ruthlessly questioning of the values of the characters and the resolutions of the plots—to have led many twentieth-century scholars to classify them as "problem plays" or "dark comedies." This category has recently begun to fall out of favor, since Shakespeare criticism is perfectly happy to demonstrate that *all* of the plays are "problem plays." But there is another group of plays, among the last Shakespeare wrote, that continue to constitute a distinct category. *Pericles, Cymbeline, The Winter's Tale,* and *The Tempest,* written between 1608 and 1611, when the playwright had developed a remarkably fluid, dreamlike sense of plot and a poetic style that could veer, apparently effortlessly, from the tortured to the ineffably sweet, are known as the "romances." These plays share an interest in the moral and emotional life less of the adolescents who dominate the earlier comedies than of their parents. The romances are deeply concerned with patterns of loss and recovery, suffering and redemption,

despair and renewal. They have seemed to many critics to constitute a deliberate conclusion to a career that began in histories and comedies and passed through the dark
and tormented tragedies.

One effect of the practice of printing Shakespeare's plays in a reconstructed
chronological order, as this edition does, is to produce a kind of authorial plot, a
progress from youthful exuberance and a heroic grappling with history, through psychological anguish and radical doubt, to a mature serenity built upon an understanding of loss. The ordering of Shakespeare's "complete works" in this way reconstitutes
the figure of the author as the beloved hero of his own, lived romance. There are
numerous reasons to treat this romance with considerable skepticism: the precise order
of the plays remains in dispute, the obsessions of the earliest plays crisscross with those
of the last, the drama is a collaborative art form, and the relation between authorial
consciousness and theatrical representation is murky. Yet a longing to identify Shakespeare's personal trajectory, to chart his psychic and spiritual as well as professional
progress, is all but irresistible.

## The Fetishism of Dress

Whatever the personal resonance of Shakespeare's own life, his art is deeply
enmeshed in the collective hopes, fears, and fantasies of his time. For example, throughout his plays, Shakespeare draws heavily upon his culture's investment in costume, symbols of authority, visible signs of status—the fetishism of dress he must have witnessed
from early childhood. Disguise in his drama is often assumed to be incredibly effective:
when Henry V borrows a cloak, when Portia dresses in a jurist's robes, when Viola puts
on a young man's suit, it is as if each has become unrecognizable, as if identity resided
in clothing. At the end of *Twelfth Night*, even though Viola's true identity has been disclosed, Orsino continues to call her Cesario; he will do so, he says, until she resumes
her maid's garments, for only then will she be transformed into a woman:

> Cesario, come—
> For so you shall be while you are a man;
> But when in other habits you are seen,
> Orsino's mistress, and his fancy's queen.
> (5.1.372–75)

The pinnacle of this fetishism of costume is the royal crown, for whose identity-
conferring power men are willing to die, but the principle is everywhere from the filthy
blanket that transforms Edgar into Poor Tom to the coxcomb that is the badge of the
licensed fool. Antonio, wishing to express his utter contempt, spits on Shylocks' "Jewish gaberdine," as if the clothing were the essence of the man; Kent, pouring insults on
the loathsome Oswald, calls him a "filthy worsted-stocking knave"; and innocent Innogen, learning that her husband has ordered her murder, thinks of herself as an expensive cast-off dress, destined to be ripped at the seams:

> Poor I am stale, a garment out of fashion,
> And for I am richer than to hang by th' walls
> I must be ripped. To pieces with me!
> (*Cymbeline* 3.4.50–52)

What can be said, thought, felt, in this culture seems deeply dependent on the
clothes one wears—clothes that one is, in effect, *permitted* or *compelled* to wear, since
there is little freedom in dress. Shakespearean drama occasionally represents something like such freedom: after all, Viola in *Twelfth Night* chooses to put off her "maiden
weeds," as does Rosalind, who declares, "We'll have a swashing and a martial outside"
(*As You Like It* 1.3.114). But these choices are characteristically made under the pressure of desperate circumstances, here shipwreck and exile. Part of the charm of Shakespeare's heroines is their ability to transform distress into an opportunity for

self-fashioning, but the plays often suggest that there is less autonomy than meets the eye. What looks like an escape from cultural determinism may be only a deeper form of constraint. We may take, as an allegorical emblem of this constraint, the transformation of the beggar Christopher Sly into a nobleman in the playful Induction to *The Taming of the Shrew*. The transformation seems to suggest that you are free to make of yourself whatever you choose to be—the play begins with the drunken Sly indignantly claiming the dignity of his pedigree ("Look in the Chronicles" [Induction 1.3–4])—but in fact he is only the subject of the mischievous lord's experiment, designed to demonstrate the interwovenness of clothing and identity. "What think you," the lord asks his huntsman,

> if he were conveyed to bed,
> Wrapped in sweet clothes, rings put upon his fingers,
> A most delicious banquet by his bed,
> And brave attendants near him when he wakes—
> Would not the beggar then forget himself?

To which the huntsman replies, in words that underscore the powerlessness of the drunken beggar, "Believe me, lord, I think he cannot choose" (Induction 1.33–38).

Petruccio's taming of Katherine is similarly constructed around an imposition of identity, an imposition closely bound up with the right to wear certain articles of clothing. When the haberdasher arrives with a fashionable lady's hat, Petruccio refuses it over his wife's vehement objections: "This doth fit the time, / And gentlewomen wear such caps as these." "When you are gentle," Petruccio replies, "you shall have one, too, / And not till then" (4.3.69–72). At the play's close, Petruccio demonstrates his authority by commanding his tamed wife to throw down her cap: "Off with that bauble, throw it underfoot" (5.2.126). Here as elsewhere in Shakespeare, acts of robing and disrobing are intensely charged, a charge that culminates in the trappings of monarchy. When Richard II, in a scene that was probably censored from the stage as well as the printed text during the reign of Elizabeth, is divested of his crown and scepter, he experiences the loss as the eradication of his name, the symbolic melting away of his identity:

> Alack the heavy day,
> That I have worn so many winters out
> And know not now what name to call myself!
> O, that I were a mockery king of snow,
> Standing before the sun of Bolingbroke
> To melt myself away in water-drops!
> (4.1.247–52)

When Lear tears off his regal "lendings" in order to reduce himself to the nakedness of the Bedlam beggar, he is expressing not only his radical loss of social identity but the breakdown of his psychic order as well, expressing, therefore, his reduction to the condition of the "poor bare forked animal" that is the primal condition of undifferentiated existence. And when Cleopatra determines to kill herself in order to escape public humiliation in Rome, she magnificently affirms her essential being by arraying herself as she had once done to encounter Antony:

> Show me, my women, like a queen. Go fetch
> My best attires. I am again for Cydnus
> To meet Mark Antony.
> (5.2.223–25)

Such scenes are a remarkable intensification of the everyday symbolic practice of Renaissance English culture, its characteristically deep and knowing commitment to illusion: "I know perfectly well that the woman in her crown and jewels and gorgeous gown is an aging, irascible, and fallible mortal—she herself virtually admits as much—yet I profess that she is the Virgin Queen, timelessly beautiful, wise, and just." Shakespeare understood how close this willed illusion was to the spirit of the theater, to the actors' ability to work on what the chorus in *Henry V* calls the "imaginary forces" of the audience. But there is throughout Shakespeare's works a counterintuition that, while it does not exactly overturn this illusion, renders it poignant, vulnerable, fraught. The "masculine usurp'd attire" that is donned by Viola, Rosalind, Portia, Jessica, and other Shakespeare heroines alters what they can say and do, reveals important aspects of their character, and changes their destiny, but it is, all the same, not theirs and not all of who they are. They have, the plays insist, natures that are neither transformed nor altogether concealed by their dress: "Pray God defend me," exclaims the frightened Viola. "A little thing would make me tell them how much I lack of a man" (*Twelfth Night* 3.4.268–69).

## The Paradoxes of Identity

The gap between costume and identity is not simply a matter of what women supposedly lack; virtually all of Shakespeare's major characters, men and women, convey the sense of both a *self-division* and an *inward expansion*. The belief in a complex inward realm beyond costumes and status is a striking inversion of the clothes cult: we know perfectly well that the characters have no inner lives apart from what we see on the stage, and yet we believe that they continue to exist when we do not see them, that they exist apart from their represented words and actions, that they have hidden dimensions. How is this conviction aroused and sustained? In part, it is the effect of what the characters themselves say: "My grief lies all within," Richard II tells Bolingbroke,

> And these external manner of laments
> Are merely shadows to the unseen grief
> That swells with silence in the tortured soul.
>                    (4.1.285–88)

Similarly, Hamlet, dismissing the significance of his outward garments, declares, "I have that within which passeth show— / These but the trappings and the suits of woe" (1.2.85 86). And the distinction between inward and outward is reinforced throughout this play and elsewhere by an unprecedented use of the aside and the soliloquy.

The soliloquy is a continual reminder in Shakespeare that the inner life is by no means transparent to one's surrounding world. Prince Hal seems open and easy with his mates in Eastcheap, but he has a hidden reservoir of disgust:

> I know you all, and will a while uphold
> The unyoked humour of your idleness.
> Yet herein will I imitate the sun,
> Who doth permit the base contagious clouds
> To smother up his beauty from the world,
> That when he please again to be himself,
> Being wanted he may be more wondered at
> By breaking through the foul and ugly mists
> Of vapours that did seem to strangle him.
>                    (*1 Henry IV* 1.2.173–81)

"When he please again to be himself": the line implies that identity is a matter of free choice—you decide how much of yourself you wish to disclose—but Shakespeare employs other devices that suggest more elusive and intractable layers of inwardness. There is a peculiar, recurrent lack of fit between costume and character, in fools as in princes, that is not simply a matter of disguise and disclosure. If Hal's true identity is partially "smothered" in the tavern, it is not completely revealed either in his soldier's armor or in his royal robes, nor do his asides reach the bedrock of unimpeachable self-understanding.

Identity in Shakespeare repeatedly slips away from the characters themselves, as it does from Richard II after the deposition scene and from Lear after he has given away his land and from Macbeth after he has gained the crown. The slippage does not mean that they retreat into silence; rather, they embark on an experimental, difficult fashioning of themselves and the world, most often through role-playing. "I cannot do it," says the deposed and imprisoned Richard II. "Yet I'll hammer it out" (5.5.5). This could serve as the motto for many Shakespearean characters: Viola becomes Cesario, Rosalind calls herself Ganymede, Kent becomes Caius, Edgar presents himself as Poor Tom, Hamlet plays the madman that he has partly become, Hal pretends that he is his father and a highwayman and Hotspur and even himself. Even in comedy, these ventures into alternate identities are rarely matters of choice; in tragedy, they are always undertaken under pressure and compulsion. And often enough it is not a matter of role-playing at all, but of a drastic transformation whose extreme emblem is the harrowing madness of Lear and of Leontes.

There is a moment in *Richard II* in which the deposed King asks for a mirror and then, after musing on his reflection, throws it to the ground. The shattering of the glass serves to remind us not only of the fragility of identity in Shakespeare but of its characteristic appearance in fragmentary mirror images. The plays continually generate alternative reflections, identities that intersect with, underscore, echo, or otherwise set off that of the principal character. Hence, Desdemona and Iago are not only important figures in Othello's world, they also seem to embody partially realized aspects of himself; Falstaff and Hotspur play a comparable role in relation to Prince Hal, Fortinbras and Horatio in relation to Hamlet, Gloucester and the Fool in relation to Lear, and so forth. In many of these plays, the complementary and contrasting characters figure in subplots, subtly interwoven with the play's main plot and illuminating its concerns. The note so conspicuously sounded by Fortinbras at the close of *Hamlet*—what the hero might have been, "had he been put on"—is heard repeatedly in Shakespeare and contributes to the overwhelming intensity, poignancy, and complexity of the characters. This is a world in which outward appearance is everything and nothing, in which individuation is at once sharply etched and continually blurred, in which the victims of fate are haunted by the ghosts of the possible, in which everything is simultaneously as it must be and as it need not have been.

Are these antinomies signs of a struggle between contradictory and irreconcilable perspectives in Shakespeare? In certain plays—notably, *Measure for Measure, All's Well That Ends Well, Coriolanus,* and *Troilus and Cressida*—the tension seems both high and entirely unresolved. But Shakespearean contradictions are more often reminiscent of the capacious spirit of Montaigne, who refused any systematic order that would betray his sense of reality. Thus, individual characters are immensely important in Shakespeare—he is justly celebrated for his unmatched skill in the invention of particular dramatic identities, marked with distinct speech patterns, manifested in social status, and confirmed by costume and gesture—but the principle of individuation is not the rock on which his theatrical art is founded. After the masks are stripped away, the pretenses exposed, the claims of the ego shattered, there is a mysterious remainder; as the shamed but irrepressible Paroles declares in *All's Well That Ends Well*, "Simply the thing I am / Shall make me live" (4.3.310–11). Again and again, the audience is made to sense a deeper energy, a source of power that at once discharges itself in individual characters and seems to sweep right through them.

## The Poet of Nature

In *The Birth of Tragedy*, Nietzsche called a comparable source of energy that he found in Greek tragedy "Dionysos." But the god's name, conjuring up Bacchic frenzy, does not seem appropriate to Shakespeare. In the late seventeenth and eighteenth centuries, it was more plausibly called Nature: "The world must be peopled," says the delightful Benedick in *Much Ado About Nothing* (2.3.213–14), and there are frequent invocations elsewhere of the happy, generative power that brings couples together—

> Jack shall have Jill,
> Naught shall go ill,
> the man shall have his mare again, and all shall be well.
> (*A Midsummer Night's Dream* 3.3.45–47)

—and the melancholy, destructive power that brings all living things to the grave: "Golden lads and girls all must, / As chimney-sweepers, come to dust" (*Cymbeline* 4.2.263–64).

But the celebration of Shakespeare as a poet of nature—often coupled with an inane celebration of his supposedly "natural" (that is, untutored) genius—has its distinct limitations. For Shakespearean art brilliantly interrogates the "natural," refusing to take for granted precisely what the celebrants think is most secure. His comedies are endlessly inventive in showing that love is not simply natural: the playful hint of bestiality in the line quoted above, "the man shall have his mare again" (from a play in which the Queen of the Fairies falls in love with an ass-headed laborer), lightly unsettles the boundaries between the natural and the perverse. These boundaries are called into question throughout Shakespeare's work, from the cross-dressing and erotic crosscurrents that deliciously complicate the lives of the characters in *Twelfth Night* and *As You Like It* to the terrifying violence that wells up from the heart of the family in *King Lear* or from the sweet intimacy of sexual desire in *Othello*. Even the boundary between life and death is not secure, as the ghosts in *Julius Caesar, Hamlet,* and *Macbeth* attest, while the principle of natural death (given its most eloquent articulation by old Hamlet's murderer, Claudius!) is repeatedly tainted and disrupted.

Disrupted, too, is the idea of order that constantly makes its claim, most insistently in the history plays. Scholars have observed the presence in Shakespeare's works of the so-called Tudor myth—the ideological justification of the ruling dynasty as a restoration of national order after a cycle of tragic violence. The violence, Tudor apologists claimed, was divine punishment unleashed after the deposition of the anointed king, Richard II, for God will not tolerate violations of the sanctified order. Traces of this propaganda certainly exist in the histories—Shakespeare may, for all we know, have personally subscribed to its premises—but a closer scrutiny of his plays has disclosed so many ironic reservations and qualifications and subversions as to call into question any straightforward adherence to a political line. The plays manifest a profound fascination with the monarchy and with the ambitions of the aristocracy, but the fascination is never simply endorsement. There is always at least the hint of a slippage between the great figures, whether admirable or monstrous, who stand at the pinnacle of authority and the vast, miscellaneous mass of soldiers, scriveners, ostlers, poets, whores, gardeners, thieves, weavers, shepherds, country gentlemen, sturdy beggars, and the like who make up the commonwealth. And the idea of order, though eloquently articulated (most memorably by Ulysses in *Troilus and Cressida*), is always shadowed by a relentless spirit of irony.

## The Play of Language

If neither the individual nor nature nor order will serve, can we find a single comprehensive name for the underlying force in Shakespeare's work? Certainly not. The work is too protean and capacious. But much of the energy that surges through this astonishing body of plays and poems is closely linked to the power of language. Shakespeare was the supreme product of a rhetorical culture, a culture steeped in the arts of persuasion and verbal expressiveness. In 1512, the great Dutch humanist Erasmus published a work called *De copia verborum* that taught its readers how to cultivate "copiousness," verbal richness, in discourse. (Erasmus obligingly provides, as a sample, a list of 144 different ways of saying "Thank you for your letter.") Recommended modes of variation include putting the subject of an argument into fictional form, as well as the use of synonym, substitution, paraphrase, metaphor, metonymy, synecdoche, hyperbole, diminution, and a host of other figures of speech. To change emotional tone, he suggests trying *ironia, interrogatio, admiratio, dubitatio, abominatio*—the possibilities seem infinite.

In Renaissance England, certain syntactic forms or patterns of words known as "figures" (also called "schemes") were shaped and repeated in order to confer beauty or heighten expressive power. Figures were usually known by their Greek and Latin names, though in an Elizabethan rhetorical manual, *The Arte of English Poesie*, George Puttenham made a valiant if short-lived attempt to give them English equivalents, such as "*Hyperbole*, or the Overreacher," "*Ironia*, or the Dry Mock," and "*Ploce*, or the Doubler." Those who received a grammar-school education throughout Europe at almost any point between the Roman Empire and the eighteenth century probably knew by heart the names of up to one hundred such figures, just as they knew by heart their multiplication tables. According to one scholar's count, Shakespeare knew and made use of about two hundred.

As certain grotesquely inflated Renaissance texts attest, lessons from *De copia verborum* and similar rhetorical guides could encourage mere prolixity and verbal self-display. But even though he shared his culture's delight in rhetorical complexity, Shakespeare always understood how to swoop from baroque sophistication to breathtaking simplicity. Moreover, he grasped early in his career how to use figures of speech, tone, and rhythm not only to provide emphasis and elegant variety but also to articulate the inner lives of his characters. Take, for example, these lines from *Othello*, where, as scholars have noted, Shakespeare deftly combines four common rhetorical figures— *anaphora, parison, isocolon,* and *epistrophe*—to depict with painful vividness Othello's psychological torment:

> By the world,
> I think my wife be honest, and think she is not.
> I think that thou art just, and think thou art not.
> I'll have some proof.
>
> (3.3.388–91)

*Anaphora* is simply the repetition of a word at the beginning of a sequence of sentences or clauses ("I/I"). *Parison* is the correspondence of word to word within adjacent sentences or clauses, either by direct repetition ("think/think") or by the matching of noun with noun, verb with verb ("wife/thou"; "be/art"). *Isocolon* gives exactly the same length to corresponding clauses ("and think she is not/and think thou art not"), and *epistrophe* is the mirror image of *anaphora* in that it is the repetition of a word at the end of a sequence of sentences or clauses ("not/not"). Do we need to know the Greek names for these figures in order to grasp the effectiveness of Othello's lines? Of course not. But Shakespeare and his contemporaries, convinced that rhetoric provided the most natural and powerful means by which feelings could be conveyed to readers and listeners, were trained in an analytical language that helped at once to promote and to account for this effectiveness. In his 1593 edition of *The Garden of Eloquence*, Henry Peacham remarks that *epistrophe* "serveth to leave a word of importance in the end of a sentence, that it may the longer hold the sound in the mind of the hearer," and in *Directions for Speech and Style* (c. 1599), John Hoskins notes that *anaphora* "beats upon one thing to cause the quicker feeling in the audience."

Shakespeare also shared with his contemporaries a keen understanding of the ways that rhetorical devices could be used not only to express powerful feelings but to hide them: after all, the artist who created Othello also created Iago, Richard III, and Lady Macbeth. He could deftly skewer the rhetorical affectations of Polonius in *Hamlet* or the pedant Holophernes in *Love's Labour's Lost*. He could deploy stylistic variations to mark the boundaries not of different individuals but of different social realms; in *A Midsummer Night's Dream*, for example, the blank verse of Duke Theseus is played off against the rhymed couplets of the well-born young lovers, and both in turn contrast with the prose spoken by the artisans. At the same time that he thus marks boundaries between both individuals and groups, Shakespeare shows a remarkable ability to establish unifying patterns of imagery that knit together the diverse strands of his plot and suggest subtle links among characters who may be scarcely aware of how much they share with one another.

One of the hidden links in Shakespeare's own works is the frequent use he makes of a somewhat unusual rhetorical figure called *hendiadys*. An example from the Roman poet Virgil is the phrase *pateris libamus et auro,* "we drink from cups and gold" (*Georgics* 2.192). Rather than serving as an adjective or a dependent noun, as in "golden cups" or "cups of gold," the word "gold" serves as a substantive joined to another substantive, "cups," by a conjunction, "and." Shakespeare uses the figure over three hundred times in all, and since it does not appear in ancient or medieval lists of tropes and schemes and is treated only briefly by English rhetoricians, he may have come upon it directly in Virgil. *Hendiadys* literally means "one through two," though Shakespeare's versions often make us quickly, perhaps only subliminally, aware of the complexity of what ordinarily passes for straightforward perceptions. When Othello, in his suicide speech, invokes the memory of "a malignant and a turbaned Turk," the figure of speech at once associates enmity with cultural difference and keeps them slightly apart. And when Macbeth speaks of his "strange and self-abuse," the *hendiadys* seems briefly to hold both "strange" and "self" up for scrutiny. It would be foolish to make too much of any single feature in Shakespeare's varied and diverse creative achievement, and yet this curious rhetorical scheme has something of the quality of a fingerprint.

But all of his immense rhetorical gifts, though rich, beautiful, and supremely useful, do not adequately convey Shakespeare's relation to language, which is less strictly functional than a total immersion in the arts of persuasion may imply. An Erasmian admiration for copiousness cannot fully explain Shakespeare's astonishing vocabulary of some 25,000 words. (His closest rival among the great English poets of the period was John Milton, with about 12,000 words, and most major writers, let alone ordinary people, have much smaller vocabularies.) This immense word hoard, it is worth noting, was not the result of scanning a dictionary; in the late sixteenth century, there were no English dictionaries of the kind to which we are now accustomed. Shakespeare seems to have absorbed new words from virtually every discursive realm he ever encountered, and he experimented boldly and tirelessly with them. These experiments were facilitated by the very fact that dictionaries as we know them did not exist and by a flexibility in grammar, orthography, and diction that the more orderly, regularized English of the later seventeenth and eighteenth centuries suppressed.

Owing in part to the number of dialects in London, pronunciation was variable, and there were many opportunities for phonetic association between words: the words "bear," "barn," "bier," "bourne," "born," and "barne" could all sound like one another. Homonyms were given greater scope by the fact that the same word could be spelled so many different ways—Christopher Marlowe's name appears in the records as Marlowe, Marloc, Marlen, Marlyne, Merlin, Marley, Marlye, Morley, and Morle—and by the fact that a word's grammatical function could easily shift, from noun to verb, verb to adjective, and so forth. Since grammar and punctuation did not insist on relations of coordination and subordination, loose, nonsyntactic sentences were common, and etymologies were used to forge surprising or playful relations between distant words.

It would seem inherently risky for a popular playwright to employ a vocabulary so far in excess of what most mortals could possibly possess, but Shakespeare evidently counted on his audience's linguistic curiosity and adventurousness, just as he counted on its general and broad-based rhetorical competence. He was also usually careful to provide a context that in effect explained or translated his more arcane terms. For example, when Macbeth reflects with horror on his murderous hands, he shudderingly imagines that even the sea could not wash away the blood; on the contrary, his blood-stained hand, he says, "will rather / The multitudinous seas incarnadine." The meaning of the unfamiliar word "incarnadine" is explained by the next line: "Making the green one red" (2.2.59–61).

What is most striking is not the abstruseness or novelty of Shakespeare's language but its extraordinary vitality, a quality that the playwright seemed to pursue with a kind of passionate recklessness. Perhaps Samuel Johnson was looking in the right direction when he complained that the "quibble," or pun, was "the fatal Cleopatra for which

[Shakespeare] lost the world, and was content to lose it." For the power that continually discharges itself throughout the plays, at once constituting and unsettling everything it touches, is the polymorphous power of language, language that seems both costume and that which lies beneath the costume, personal identity and that which challenges the merely personal, nature and that which enables us to name nature and thereby distance ourselves from it.

Shakespeare's language has an overpowering exuberance and generosity that often resembles the experience of love. Consider, for example, Oberon's description in *A Midsummer Night's Dream* of the moment when he saw Cupid shoot his arrow at the fair vestal: "Thou rememb'rest," he asks Puck,

> Since once I sat upon a promontory
> And heard a mermaid on a dolphin's back
> Uttering such dulcet and harmonious breath
> That the rude sea grew civil at her song
> And certain stars shot madly from their spheres
> To hear the sea-maid's music?
>
> (2.1.148–54)

Here, Oberon's composition of place, lightly alluding to a classical emblem, is infused with a fantastically lush verbal brilliance. This brilliance, the result of masterful alliterative and rhythmical technique, seems gratuitous—that is, it does not advance the plot, but rather exhibits a capacity for display and self-delight that extends from the fairies to the playwright who has created them. The rich music of Oberon's words imitates the "dulcet and harmonious breath" he is intent on recalling, breath that has, in his account, an oddly contradictory effect: it is at once a principle of order, so that the rude sea is becalmed like a lower-class mob made civil by a skilled orator, and a principle of disorder, so that celestial bodies in their fixed spheres are thrown into mad confusion. And this contradictory effect, so intimately bound up with an inexplicable, supererogatory, and intensely erotic verbal magic, is a key to *A Midsummer Night's Dream*, with its exquisite blend of confusion and discipline, lunacy and hierarchical ceremony.

The fairies in this comedy seem to embody a pervasive sense found throughout Shakespeare's work that there is something uncanny about language, something that is not quite human, at least in the conventional and circumscribed sense of the human that dominates waking experience. In the comedies, this intuition is alarming but ultimately benign: Oberon and his followers trip through the great house at the play's close, blessing the bridebeds and warding off the nightmares that lurk in marriage and parenthood. But there is in Shakespeare an alternative, darker vision of the uncanniness of language, a vision also embodied in creatures that test the limits of the human—not the fairies of *A Midsummer Night's Dream* but the weird sisters of *Macbeth*. When in the tragedy's opening scene the witches chant "Fair is foul, and foul is fair" (1.1.10), they unsettle through the simplest and most radical act of linguistic equation ($x$ is $y$) the fundamental antinomies through which a moral order is established. And when Macbeth appears onstage a few minutes later, his first words unconsciously echo what we have just heard from the witches' mouths: "So foul and fair a day I have not seen" (1.3.36). What is the meaning of this linguistic "unconscious"? On the face of things, Macbeth presumably means only that the day of fair victory is also a day of foul weather, but the fact that he echoes the witches (something that we hear but that he cannot know) intimates an occult link between them, even before their direct encounter. It is difficult, perhaps impossible, to specify exactly what this link signifies—generations of emboldened critics have tried without notable success—but we can at least affirm that its secret lair is in the play's language, like a half-buried pun whose full articulation will entail the murder of Duncan, the ravaging of his kingdom, and Macbeth's own destruction.

*Macbeth* is haunted by half-buried puns, equivocations, and ambiguous grammatical constructions known as amphibologies. They manifest themselves most obviously in the words of the witches, from the opening exchanges to the fraudulent assurances that deceive Macbeth at the close, but they are also present in his most intimate and private reflections, as in his tortured broodings about his proposed act of treason:

> If it were done when 'tis done, then 'twere well
> It were done quickly. If th'assassination
> Could trammel up the consequence, and catch
> With his surcease success: that but this blow
> Might be the be-all and the end-all, here,
> But here upon this bank and shoal of time,
> We'd jump the life to come.
>
> (1.7.1–7)

The dream is to reach a secure and decisive end, to catch as in a net (hence "trammel up") all of the slippery, unforeseen, and uncontrollable consequences of regicide, to hobble time as one might hobble a horse (another sense of "trammel up"), to stop the flow ("success") of events, to be, as Macbeth later puts it, "settled." But Macbeth's words themselves slip away from the closure he seeks; they slide into one another, trip over themselves, twist and double back and swerve into precisely the sickening uncertainties their speaker most wishes to avoid. And if we sense a barely discernible note of comedy in Macbeth's tortured language, a discordant playing with the senses of the word "done" and the hint of a childish tongue twister in the phrase "catch / With his surcease success," we are in touch with a dark pleasure to which Shakespeare was all his life addicted.

Look again at the couplet from *Cymbeline*: "Golden lads and girls all must, / As chimney-sweepers, come to dust."

The playwright who insinuated a pun into the solemn dirge is the same playwright whose tragic heroine in *Antony and Cleopatra*, pulling the bleeding body of her dying lover into the pyramid, says, "Our strength is all gone into heaviness" (4.16.34). He is the playwright whose Juliet, finding herself alone on the stage, says, "My dismal scene I needs must act alone" (*Romeo and Juliet* 4.3.19), and the playwright who can follow the long, wrenching periodic sentence that Othello speaks, just before he stabs himself, with the remark "O bloody period!" (5.2.366). The point is not merely the presence of puns in the midst of tragedy (as there are stabs of pain in the midst of Shakespearean comedy); it is rather the streak of wildness that they so deliberately disclose, the sublimely indecorous linguistic energy of which Shakespeare was at once the towering master and the most obedient, worshipful servant.

# The Dream of the Master Text

## Shakespeare and the Printed Book

Ben Jonson's famous tribute to Shakespeare—"He was not of an age, but for all time!"—comes in one of the dedicatory poems to the 1623 First Folio of *Mr. William Shakespeares Comedies, Histories, & Tragedies*. This large, handsome volume, the first collection of Shakespeare's plays, was not, as far as we know, the product of the playwright's own design. We do not even know if he would have approved of the Folio's division of each play into five acts or its organization of the plays into three loose generic categories. Several of the plays grouped among the histories—*Richard Duke of York* (3 *Henry VI*), *Richard II*, and *Richard III*—had been printed separately during Shakespeare's lifetime as tragedies; one of the most famous of his tragedies had appeared as *The History of King Lear*. The Folio editors evidently decided to group together as "histories" only those plays which dealt with English history after the Norman Conquest; hence, *King Lear*, set in ancient Britain, appears with the "tragedies," and so, too, despite its happy ending, does *Cymbeline, King of Britain*. One play, *Troilus and Cressida*, was printed first as a "history," then printed in a second version with a preface that describes it as a "comedy," and then printed in the Folio as a "tragedy." As a fitting

Sixteenth-century printing shop. Engraving by Jan van der Straet. From *Nova Reperta* (1580).

emblem of the confusion, *Troilus and Cressida* does not appear in the Folio title page: apparently included only at the last minute, it was placed, unpaginated, after the last of the histories and the first of the tragedies. Modern readers, who remain perplexed by its genre, may take some consolation from the fact that for Shakespeare and his contemporaries generic boundaries were not hard and fast.

Published seven years after the playwright's death, the Folio was printed by the London printers William and Isaac Jaggard, who were joined in this expensive venture by Edward Blount, John Smethwicke, and William Aspley. It was edited by two of Shakespeare's old friends and fellow actors, John Heminges and Henry Condell, who claimed to be using "True Originall Copies" in the author's own hand. (None of these copies has survived, or, more cautiously, none has to date been found.) Eighteen plays included in the First Folio had already appeared individually in print in the small-format and relatively inexpensive texts called "Quartos" (or, in one case, the still smaller format called "Octavo"); to these, Heminges and Condell added eighteen others never before published: *All's Well That Ends Well, Antony and Cleopatra, As You Like It, The Comedy of Errors, Coriolanus, Cymbeline, All Is True (Henry VIII), Julius Caesar, King John, Macbeth, Measure for Measure, The Taming of the Shrew, The Tempest, Timon of Athens, Twelfth Night, The Two Gentlemen of Verona, The Winter's Tale,* and *1 Henry VI.** None of the

*This sketch simplifies several complex questions such as the status of the 1594 Quarto called *The Taming of a Shrew,* sufficiently distinct from the similarly titled Folio text as to constitute for many editors a different play.

plays included in the Folio has dropped out of the generally accepted canon of Shakespeare's works, and only two plays not included in the volume (*Pericles* and *The Two Noble Kinsmen*) have been allowed to join this select company, along with the nondramatic poems. Of the latter, *Venus and Adonis* (1593) and *The Rape of Lucrece* (1594) first appeared during Shakespeare's lifetime in Quartos with dedications from the author to the Earl of Southampton. *Shakespeare's Sonnets* (1609) were apparently printed without his authorization, as were his poems in a collection called *The Passionate Pilgrim* (1599).

Over the centuries, there have been many attempts to discover and authenticate additional works partly or entirely written by Shakespeare. An interesting case has been made for sections of a history play entitled *King Edward the Third* and for some small traces in the eighteenth-century tragicomedy *The Double Falsehood*, allegedly based on a manuscript of the lost Shakespearean play *Cardenio*. The Norton Shakespeare includes a poem, "Shall I die?" whose original inclusion in the 1988 *Oxford Shakespeare* provoked vigorous debate and much skepticism. Still more skepticism greeted the attribution to Shakespeare of a long poem called "A Funeral Elegy," printed in an appendix to *The Norton Shakespeare*'s first edition and now dropped in the wake of widespread consensus that the attribution was false. In the future, other claimants will no doubt come forward, but, with the very few additions already noted, the Folio will always remain the foundation of Shakespeare's dramatic canon.

The plays were the property of the theatrical company in which Shakespeare was a shareholder. It was not normally in the interest of such companies to have their scripts circulating in print, at least while the plays were actively in repertory: players evidently feared competition from rival companies and thought that reading might dampen playgoing. Plays were generally sold only when the theaters were temporarily closed by plague, or when the company was in need of capital (four of Shakespeare's plays were published in 1600, presumably to raise money to pay the debts incurred in building the new Globe), or when a play had grown too old to revive profitably. There is no evidence that Shakespeare himself disagreed with this professional caution, no sign that he wished to see his plays in print. Unlike Ben Jonson, who took the radical step of rewriting his own plays for publication in the 1616 folio of his *Works*, Shakespeare evidently was not interested in constituting his plays as a canon. If in the sonnets he imagines his verse achieving a symbolic immortality, this dream apparently did not extend to his plays, at least through the medium of print.

Moreover, there is no evidence that Shakespeare had an interest in asserting authorial rights over his scripts or that he or any other working English playwright had a public "standing," legal or otherwise, from which to do so. (Jonson was ridiculed for his presumption.) There is no indication whatever that he could, for example, veto changes in his scripts or block interpolated scenes or withdraw a play from production if a particular interpretation, addition, or revision did not please him. To be sure, in his advice to the players, Hamlet urges that those who play the clowns "speak no more than is set down for them," but—apart from the question of whether the Prince speaks for the playwright—the play within the play in *Hamlet* is precisely an instance of a script altered to suit a particular occasion. It seems likely that Shakespeare would have routinely accepted the possibility of such alterations. Moreover, he would of necessity have routinely accepted the possibility, and in certain cases the virtual inevitability, of cuts in order to stage his plays in the two to two and one-half hours that was the normal performing time. There is an imaginative generosity in many of Shakespeare's scripts, as if he were deliberately offering his fellow actors more than they could use on any one occasion and, hence, giving them abundant materials with which to reconceive and revivify each play again and again as they or their audiences liked it. The Elizabethan theater, like most theater in our own time, was a collaborative enterprise, and the collaboration almost certainly extended to decisions about selection, trimming, shifts of emphasis, and minor or major revision.

For many years, it was thought that Shakespeare himself did little or no revising. Some recent editors—above all the editors of the *Oxford Shakespeare*, whose texts the

*Norton* presents—have argued persuasively that there are many signs of authorial revision, even wholesale rewriting. But there is no sign that Shakespeare sought through such revision to bring each of his plays to its "perfect," "final" form. On the contrary, many of the revisions seem to indicate that the scripts remained open texts, that the playwright and his company expected to add, cut, and rewrite as the occasion demanded.

Ralph Waldo Emerson once compared Shakespeare and his contemporary Francis Bacon in terms of the relative "finish" of their work. All of Bacon's work, wrote Emerson, "lies along the ground, a vast unfinished city." Each of Shakespeare's dramas, by contrast, "is perfect, hath an immortal integrity. To make Bacon's work complete, he must live to the end of the world." Recent scholarship suggests that Shakespeare was more like Bacon than Emerson thought. Neither the Folio nor the quarto texts of Shakespeare's plays bear the seal of final authorial intention, the mark of decisive closure that has served, at least ideally, as the guarantee of textual authenticity. We want to believe, as we read the text, "This is the play as Shakespeare himself wanted it read," but there is no license for such a reassuring sentiment. To be "not of an age, but for all time" means in Shakespeare's case not that the plays have achieved a static perfection, but that they are creatively, inexhaustibly unfinished.

That we have been so eager to link certain admired scripts to a single known playwright is closely related to changes in the status of artists in the Renaissance, changes that led to a heightened interest in the hand of the individual creator. Like medieval painting, medieval drama gives us few clues as to the particular individuals who fashioned the objects we admire. We know something about the places in which these objects were made, the circumstances that enabled their creation, the spaces in which they were placed, but relatively little about the particular artists themselves. It is easy to imagine a wealthy patron or a civic authority in the late Middle Ages commissioning a play on a particular subject (appropriate, for example, to a seasonal ritual, a religious observance, or a political festivity) and specifying the date, place, and length of the performance, the number of actors, even the costumes to be used, but it is more difficult to imagine him specifying a particular playwright and still less insisting that the entire play be written by this dramatist alone. Only with the Renaissance do we find a growing insistence on the name of the maker, the signature that heightens the value and even the meaning of the work by implying that it is the emanation of a single, distinct shaping consciousness.

In the case of Renaissance painting, we know that this signature does not necessarily mean that every stroke was made by the master. Some of the work, possibly the greater part of it, may have been done by assistants, with only the faces and a few finishing touches from the hand of the illustrious artist to whom the work is confidently attributed. As the skill of individual masters became more explicitly valued, contracts began to specify how much was to come from the brush of the principal painter. Consider, for example, the Italian painter Luca Signorelli's contract of 1499 for frescoes in Orvieto Cathedral:

> The said master Luca is bound and promises to paint [1] all the figures to be done on the said vault, and [2] especially the faces and all the parts of the figures from the middle of each figure upwards, and [3] that no painting should be done on it without Luca himself being present. . . . And it is agreed [4] that all the mixing of colours should be done by the said master Luca himself.

Such a contract at once reflects a serious cash interest in the characteristic achievement of a particular artist and a conviction that this achievement is compatible with the presence of other hands, provided those hands are subordinate, in the finished work. For paintings on a smaller scale, it was more possible to commission an exclusive performance. Thus, the contract for a small altarpiece by Signorelli's great teacher, Piero della Francesca, specifies that "no painter may put his hand to the brush other than Piero himself."

There is no record of any comparable concern for exclusivity in the English theater. Unfortunately, the contracts that Shakespeare and his fellow dramatists almost certainly signed have not, with one significant exception, survived. But plays written for the professional theater are by their nature an even more explicitly collective art form than paintings; they depend for their full realization on the collaboration of others, and that collaboration may well extend to the fashioning of the script. It seems that some authors may simply have been responsible for providing plots that others then dramatized; still others were hired to "mend" old plays or to supply prologues, epilogues, or songs. A particular playwright's name came to be attached to a certain identifiable style—a characteristic set of plot devices, a marked rhetorical range, a tonality of character—but this name may refer in effect more to a certain product associated with a particular playing company than to the individual artist who may or may not have written most of the script. The one contract whose details do survive, that entered into by Richard Brome and the actors and owners of the Salisbury Court Theatre in 1635, does not stipulate that Brome's plays must be written by him alone or even that he must be responsible for a certain specifiable proportion of each script. Rather, it specifies that the playwright "should not nor would write any play or any part of a play to any other players or playhouse, but apply all his study and endeavors therein for the benefit of the said company of the said playhouse." The Salisbury Court players want rights to everything Brome writes for the stage; the issue is not that the plays associated with his name be exclusively *his* but rather that he be exclusively *theirs*.

Recent textual scholarship, then, has been moving steadily away from a conception of Shakespeare's plays as direct, unmediated emanations from the mind of the author and toward a conception of them as working scripts, composed and continually reshaped as part of a collaborative commercial enterprise in competition with other, similar enterprises. One consequence has been the progressive weakening of the idea of the solitary, inspired genius, in the sense fashioned by Romanticism and figured splendidly in the statue of Shakespeare in the public gardens in Germany's Weimar, the city of Goethe and Schiller: the poet, with his sensitive, expressive face and high domed forehead sitting alone and brooding, a skull at his feet, a long-stemmed rose in his crotch. In place of this projection of German Romanticism, we have now a playwright and sometime actor who is also (to his considerable financial advantage) a major shareholder in the company—the Lord Chamberlain's Men, later the King's Men to which he loyally supplies for most of his career an average of two plays per year.

These developments are salutary insofar as they direct attention to the actual conditions in which the textual traces that the Folio calls Shakespeare's "Comedies, Histories, & Tragedies" came to be produced, reproduced, consumed, revised, and transmitted to future generations. They highlight elements that Shakespeare shared with his contemporaries, and they insistently remind us that we are encountering scripts written primarily for the stage and not for the study. They make us more attentive to such matters as business cycles, plague rolls, the cost of costumes, government censorship, and urban topography and less concerned with the elusive and enigmatic details of the poet's biography—his supposed youthful escapades and erotic yearnings and psychological crises.

All well and good. But the fact remains that in 1623, seven years after the playwright's death, Heminges and Condell thought they could sell copies of their expensive collection of Shakespeare's plays—"What euer you do," they urge their readers, "buy"— by insisting that their texts were "as he conceiued them." This means that potential readers in the early seventeenth century were already interested in Shakespeare's "conceits"—his "wit," his imagination, and his creative power—and were willing to assign a high value to the products of his particular, identifiable skill, one distinguishable from that of his company and of his rival playwrights. After all, Jonson's tribute praises Shakespeare not as the playwright of the incomparable King's Men but as the equal of Aeschylus, Sophocles, and Euripides. And if we now see Shakespeare's dramaturgy in the context of his contemporaries and of a collective artistic practice, readers continue to have little difficulty recognizing that most of the plays attached to his name tower over those of his rivals.

## From Foul to Fair: The Making of the Printed Play

What exactly is a printed play by Shakespeare? Is it like a novel or a poem? Is it like the libretto or the score of an opera? Is it the trace of an absent event? Is it the blueprint of an imaginary structure that will never be completed? Is it a record of what transpired in the mind of a man long dead? We might say cautiously that it is a mechanically reproduced version of what Shakespeare wrote, but unfortunately, with the possible (and disputed) exception of a small fragment from a collaboratively written play called *Sir Thomas More,* virtually nothing Shakespeare actually wrote in his own hand survives. We might propose that it is a printed version of the script that an Elizabethan actor would have held in his hands during rehearsals, but here, too, no such script of a Shakespeare play survives; and besides, Elizabethan actors were evidently not given the whole play to read. To reduce the expense of copying and the risk of unauthorized reproduction, each actor received only his own part, along with the cue lines. (Shakespeare uses this fact to delicious comic effect in *A Midsummer Night's Dream* 3.1.80–88.) Nonetheless, the play certainly existed as a whole, either in the author's original manuscript or in the copy prepared for the government censor or for the company's prompter or stage manager, so we might imagine the text we hold in our hands as a printed copy of one of these manuscripts. But since no contemporary manuscript survives of any of Shakespeare's plays, we cannot verify this hypothesis. And even if we could, we would not have resolved the question of the precise relation of the printed text either to the playwright's imagination or to the theatrical performance by the company to which he belonged.

All of Shakespeare's plays must have begun their textual careers in the form of "foul papers," drafts presumably covered with revisions, crossings-out, and general "blotting." To be sure, Heminges and Condell remark that so great was the playwright's facility that they "have scarce received from him a blot in his papers." This was, however, a routine and conventional compliment in the period. The same claim, made for the playwright John Fletcher in an edition published in 1647, is clearly contradicted by the survival of Fletcher's far-from-unblotted manuscripts. It is safe to assume that, since Shakespeare was human, his manuscripts contained their share of second and third thoughts scribbled in the margins and between the lines. Once complete, this authorial draft would usually have to be written out again, either by the playwright or by a professional scribe employed by the theater company, as "fair copy."

In the hands of the theater company, the fair copy (or sometimes, it seems, the foul papers themselves) would be annotated and transformed into "the book of the play" or the "playbook" (what we would now call a "promptbook"). Shakespeare's authorial draft presumably contained a certain number of stage directions, though these may have been sketchy and inconsistent. The promptbook clarified these and added others, noted theatrical properties and sound effects, and on occasion cut the full text to meet the necessities of performance. The promptbook was presented to the Master of the Revels for licensing, and it incorporated any changes upon which the master insisted. As the editors of the *Oxford Shakespeare* put it, the difference between foul papers and promptbook is the difference between "the text in an as yet individual, private form" and "a socialized text."

But the fact remains that for Shakespeare's plays, we have neither foul papers nor fair copies nor promptbooks. We have only the earliest printed editions of these texts in numerous individual quartos and in the First Folio. (Quartos are so called because each sheet of paper was folded twice, making four leaves or eight pages front and back; folio sheets were folded once, making two leaves or four pages front and back.) From clues embedded in these "substantive" texts—substantive because (with the exception of *The Two Noble Kinsmen*) they date from Shakespeare's own lifetime or from the collected works edited by his associates using, or claiming to use, his own manuscripts—editors attempt to reconstruct each play's journey from manuscript to print. Different plays took very different journeys.

Of the thirty-six plays included in the First Folio, eighteen had previously appeared in quarto editions, some of these in more than one printing. Generations of editors have distinguished between "good Quartos," presumably prepared from the author's own draft or from a scribal transcript of the play (fair copy), and "bad Quartos." The latter category, first formulated as such by A. W. Pollard in 1909, includes, by widespread but not universal agreement, the 1594 version of *The First Part of the Contention (2 Henry VI)*, the 1595 *Richard Duke of York (3 Henry VI)*, the 1597 *Richard the Third*, the 1597 *Romeo and Juliet*, the 1600 *Henry the Fifth*, the 1602 *Merry Wives of Windsor*, the 1603 *Hamlet*, and *Pericles* (1609). Some editors also regard the 1591 *Troublesome Reign of King John*, the 1594 *Taming of a Shrew*, and the 1608 *King Lear* as bad Quartos, but others have strenuously argued that these are distinct rather than faulty texts, and the whole concept of the bad Quarto has come under increasingly critical scrutiny. The criteria for distinguishing between "good" and "bad" texts are imprecise, and the evaluative terms seem to raise as many questions as they answer. Nevertheless, the striking mistakes, omissions, repetitions, and anomalies in a number of the Quartos require some explanation beyond the ordinary fallibility of scribes and printers.

The explanation most often proposed for suspect Quartos is that they are the products of "memorial reconstruction." The hypothesis, first advanced in 1910 by W. W. Greg, is that a series of features found in what seem to be particularly flawed texts may be traced to the derivation of the copy from the memory of one or more of the actors. Elizabethan actors, Greg observed, often found themselves away from the London theaters—for example, on tour in the provinces during plague periods—and may not on those occasions have had access to the promptbooks they would ordinarily have used. In such circumstances, those in the company who remembered a play may have written down or dictated the text, as best they could, perhaps adapting it for provincial performance. Moreover, unscrupulous actors may have sold such texts to enterprising printers eager to turn a quick profit.

Memorially reconstructed texts tend to be much shorter than those prepared from foul papers or fair copy; they frequently paraphrase or garble lines, drop or misplace speeches and whole scenes, and on occasion fill in the gaps with scraps from other plays. In several cases, scholars think they can detect which roles the rogue actors played, since these parts (and the scenes in which they appear) are reproduced with greater accuracy than the rest of the play. Typically, these roles are minor ones, since the leading parts would be played by actors with a greater stake in the overall financial interest of the company and, hence, less inclination to violate its policy. Thus, for example, editors speculate that the bad Quarto of *Hamlet* (Q1) was provided by the actor playing Marcellus (and doubling as Lucianus). What is often impossible to determine is whether particular differences between a bad Quarto and a good Quarto or Folio text result from the actor's faulty memory or from changes introduced in performance, possibly with the playwright's own consent, or from both. Shakespearean bad Quartos ceased to appear after 1609, perhaps as a result of greater scrutiny by the Master of the Revels, who after 1606 was responsible for licensing plays for publication as well as performance.

The syndicate that prepared the Folio had access to the manuscripts of the King's Men. In addition to the previously published editions of eighteen plays, they made use of scribal transcripts (fair copies), promptbooks, and (more rarely) foul papers. The indefatigable labors of generations of bibliographers, antiquaries, and textual scholars have recovered an extraordinary fund of information about the personnel, finances, organizational structure, and material practices of Elizabethan and Jacobean printing houses, including the names and idiosyncrasies of particular compositors who calculated the page length, set the type, and printed the sheets of the Folio. This impressive scholarship has for the most part intensified respect for the seriousness with which the Folio was prepared and printed, and where the Folio is defective, it has provided plausible readings from the Quartos or proposed emendations to approximate what Shakespeare is likely to have written. But it has not succeeded, despite all its heroic efforts, in transforming the Folio, or any other text, into an unobstructed, clear window into Shakespeare's mind.

The dream of the master text is a dream of transparency. The words on the page should ideally give the reader unmediated access to the astonishing forge of imaginative power that was the mind of the dramatist. Those words welled up from the genius of the great artist, and if the world were not an imperfect place, they would have been set down exactly as he conceived them and transmitted to each of us as a precious inheritance. Such is the vision—at its core closely related to the preservation of the holy text in the great scriptural religions—that has driven many of the great editors who have for centuries produced successive editions of Shakespeare's works. The vision was not yet fully formed in the First Folio, for Heminges and Condell still felt obliged to apologize to their noble patrons for dedicating to them a collection of mere "trifles." But by the eighteenth century, there were no longer any ritual apologies for Shakespeare; instead, there was a growing recognition not only of the supreme artistic importance of his works but also of the uncertain, conflicting, and in some cases corrupt state of the surviving texts. Every conceivable step, it was thought, must be undertaken to correct mistakes, strip away corruptions, return the texts to their pure and unsullied form, and make this form perfectly accessible to readers.

Paradoxically, this feverishly renewed, demanding, and passionate editorial project has produced the very opposite of the transparency that was the dream of the master text. The careful weighing of alternative readings, the production of a textual apparatus, the writing of notes and glosses, the modernizing and regularizing of spelling and punctuation, the insertion of scene divisions, the complex calculation of the process of textual transmission from foul papers to print, the equally complex calculation of the effects that censorship, government regulation, and, above all, theatrical performance had on the surviving documents all make inescapably apparent the fact that we do not have and never will have any direct, unmediated access to Shakespeare's imagination. Every Shakespeare text, from the first that was published to the most recent, has been edited: it has come into print by means of a tangled social process and inevitably exists at some remove from the author.

Heminges and Condell, who knew the author and had access to at least some of his manuscripts, lament the fact that Shakespeare did not live "to have set forth and overseen his own writings." And even had he done so—or, alternatively, even if a cache of his manuscripts were discovered in a Warwickshire attic tomorrow—all of the editorial problems would not be solved, nor would all of the levels of mediation be swept away. Certainly, the entire textual landscape would change. But the written word has strange powers: it seems to hold on to something of the very life of the person who has written it, but it also seems to pry that life loose from the writer, exposing it to vagaries of history and chance independent of those to which the writer was personally subject. Moreover, with the passing of centuries, the language itself and the whole frame of reference within which language and symbols are understood have decisively changed. The most learned modern scholar still lives at a huge experiential remove from Shakespeare's world and, even holding a precious copy of the First Folio in hand, cannot escape having to read across a vast chasm of time what is, after all, an edited text. The rest of us cannot so much as indulge in the fantasy of direct access: our eyes inevitably wander to the glosses and the explanatory notes.

## *The* Oxford Shakespeare

The shattering of the dream of the master text is no cause for despair, nor should it lead us to throw our hands up and declare that one text is as good as another. What it does is to encourage the reader to be actively interested in the editorial principles that underlie the particular edition that he or she is using. It is said that the great artist Brueghel once told a nosy connoisseur who had come to his studio, "Keep your nose out of my paintings; the smell of the paint will poison you." In the case of Shakespeare, it is increasingly important to bring one's nose close to the page, as it were, and sniff the ink. More precisely, it is important to understand the rationale for the choices that the editors have made.

The text of the *Norton Shakespeare* is, with very few changes, that published by the Oxford University Press in 1988 and, in a second edition, in 2005. The *Oxford Shakespeare* was the extraordinary achievement of a team of editors, Stanley Wells, Gary Taylor, John Jowett, and William Montgomery, with Wells and Taylor serving as the general editors. The Oxford editors approached their task with a clear understanding that, as we have seen, all previous texts have been mediated by agents other than Shakespeare; however, they regard this mediation not as a melancholy obstacle intervening between the reader and the "true" Shakespearean text but rather as a constitutive element of this text. The art of the playwright is thoroughly dependent on the craft of go-betweens.

Shakespeare's plays were not written to be circulated in manuscript or printed form among readers. They were written to be performed by the players and, as the preface to the Quarto *Troilus and Cressida* indelicately puts it, "clapper-clawed with the palms of the vulgar." The public was, thus, never meant to be in a direct relationship with the author but in a "triangular relationship" in which the players gave voice and gesture to the author's words. As we have seen, Shakespeare was the master of the unfinished, the perpetually open. And even if we narrow our gaze and try to find only what Shakespeare himself might have regarded as a textual resting point, a place to stop and go on to another play, we have, the Oxford editors point out, a complex task. For whatever Shakespeare wrote was meant from the start to be supplemented by an invisible "paratext" consisting of words spoken by Shakespeare to the actors and by the actors to each other concerning emphasis, stage business, tone, pacing, possible cuts, and so forth. To the extent that this paratext was ever written down, it was recorded in the promptbook. Therefore, in contrast to standard editorial practice, the Oxford editors prefer, when there is a choice, copy based on the promptbook to copy based on the author's own draft. They choose the text immersed in history—that is, in the theatrical embodiment for which it was intended by its author—over the text unstained by the messy, collaborative demands of the playhouse. The closest we can get to Shakespeare's "final" version of a play—understanding that for him as for us there is no true "finality" in a theatrical text—is the latest version of that play performed by his company during his professional life—that is, during the time in which he could still oversee and participate in any cuts and revisions.

This choice does not mean that the Oxford editors are turning away from the very idea of Shakespeare as author. On the contrary, Wells and Taylor are deeply committed to establishing a text that comes as close as possible to the plays as Shakespeare wrote them, but they are profoundly attentive to the fact that he wrote them as a member of a company of players, a company in which he was a shareholder and an actor as well as a writer. "Writing" for the theater, at least for Shakespeare, is not simply a matter of setting words to paper and letting the pages drift away; it is a social process as well as an individual act. The Oxford editors acknowledge that some aspects of this social process may have been frustrating to Shakespeare: he may, for example, have been forced on occasion to cut lines and even whole scenes to which he was attached, or his fellow players may have insisted that they could not successfully perform what he had written, compelling him to make changes he did not welcome. But compromise and collaboration are part of what it means to be in the theater, and Wells and Taylor return again and again to the recognition that Shakespeare was, supremely, a man of the theater.

Is there a tension between the Oxford editors' preference for the performed, fully socialized text and their continued commitment to recovering the text as Shakespeare himself intended it? Yes. The tension is most visible in their determination to strip away textual changes arising from circumstances, such as government censorship, over which Shakespeare had no control. ("We have, wherever possible," they write, put "profanities back in Shakespeare's mouth.") It can be glimpsed as well in the editors' belief, almost a leap of faith, that there was little revision of Shakespeare's plays in his company's revivals between the time of his death and the publication of the Folio. But the tension is mainly a creative one, for it forces them (and, therefore, us) to attend to the play-wright's unique imaginative power as well as his social and historical entanglements.

The Oxford editors took a radical stance on a second major issue: the question of authorial revision. Previous editors had generally accepted the fact that Shakespeare practiced revision within individual manuscripts—that is, while he was still in the act of writing a particular play—but they generally rejected the notion that he undertook sub-stantial revisions from one version of a play to another (and, hence, from one manuscript to another). Wells and Taylor point out that six major works (*Hamlet, Othello, 2 Henry IV, King Lear, Richard II,* and *Troilus and Cressida*) survive in two independent substan-tive sources, both apparently authoritative, with hundreds of significant variant readings. Previous editors have generally sought to deny authority to one edition or another ("faced with two sheep," the Oxford editors observe wryly, "it is all too easy to insist that one *must* be a goat") or have conflated the two versions into a single text in an attempt to recon-struct the ideal, definitive, complete, and perfect version that they imagine Shakespeare must have reached for each of his plays. But if one doubts that Shakespeare ever con-ceived of his plays as closed, finished entities, if one recalls that he wrote them for the living repertory of the commercial playing company to which he belonged, then the whole concept of the single, authoritative text of each play loses its force. In a startling depar-ture from the editorial tradition, the *Oxford Shakespeare* printed two distinct versions of *King Lear,* quarto and Folio, and the editors glanced longingly at the impractical but allur-ing possibility of including two texts of *Hamlet, Othello,* and *Troilus.*

The *Oxford Shakespeare* was published in both old-spelling and modern-spelling editions. The former, the first of its kind ever published, raised some reviewers' eye-brows because the project, a critical edition rather than a facsimile, required the mod-ern editors to invent plausible Elizabethan spellings for their emendations and to add stage directions. The modern-spelling edition, which is the basis for Norton's text, is noteworthy for taking the principles of modernization further than they had generally been taken. Gone are such words as "murther," "mushrump," "vild," and "porpentine," which confer on many modern-spelling editions a certain cozy, Olde-English quaint-ness; Oxford replaces them with "murder," "mushroom," "vile," and "porcupine."

The inclusion of two texts of *King Lear* aroused considerable controversy when the *Oxford Shakespeare* first appeared, although by now the arguments for doing so have received widespread, though not unanimous, scholarly support. Other features remain controversial: "Ancients" Pistol and Iago have been modernized to "Ensigns"; *Henry VIII* has reverted to its performance title *All Is True;* demonic spirits in *Macbeth* sing lyrics written by Thomas Middleton. The white-hot intensity of the debates triggered by the *Oxford Shakespeare's* editorial choices casts an interesting light on the place of Shake-speare not only in the culture at large but in the psyches of millions of individuals: any alteration, however minor, in a deeply familiar and beloved text, even an alteration based on thoughtful and highly plausible scholarly principles, arouses genuine anxiety. The anxiety in this case was intensified not only by the boldness of certain crucial emenda-tions but also by the fact that the editors' explanations, arguments, and justifications for all their decisions were printed in a separate, massive volume, *William Shakespeare: A Textual Companion.* This formidable, dense volume is an astonishing monument to the seriousness, scholarly rigor, and immense labor of the Oxford editors. Anyone who is interested in pursuing why Shakespeare's words appear as they do in the current edition, anyone who wishes insight into the editors' detailed reasons for making the thousands of decisions required by a project of this kind, should consult the *Textual Companion.*

## *The* Norton Shakespeare

The primary task that the editors of the *Norton Shakespeare* set themselves was to present the modern-spelling Oxford *Complete Works* in a way that would make the text more accessible to modern readers. The *Oxford Shakespeare* prints little more than the text itself: along with one-page introductions to the individual works, it contains a short general introduction, a list of contemporary allusions to Shakespeare, and a brief glossary. But while it is possible to enjoy a Shakespeare play on stage or screen without any assistance beyond the actors' own art, many readers at least since the eighteenth century have found it far more difficult to understand and to savor the texts without some more substantial commentary.

In addition to writing introductions, textual notes, and brief bibliographies for each of the works, the Norton editors provide glosses and footnotes designed to facilitate comprehension. Such is the staggering richness of Shakespeare's language that it is tempting to gloss everything. But there is a law of diminishing returns: too much explanatory whispering at the margins makes it difficult to enjoy what the reader has come for in the first place. Our general policy is to gloss only those words that cannot be found in an ordinary dictionary or whose meanings have altered out of recognition. The glosses attempt to be simple and straightforward, giving multiple meanings for words only when the meanings are essential for making sense of the passages in which they appear. We try not to gloss the same word over and over—it becomes distracting to be told three times on a single page that "an" means "if"—but we also assume that the reader does not have a perfect memory, so after an interval we will gloss the same word again.

Marginal glosses generally refer to a single word or a short phrase. The footnotes paraphrase longer units or provide other kinds of information, such as complex plays on words, significant allusions, textual cruxes, historical and cultural contexts. Here, too, however, we have tried to check the impulse to annotate so heavily that the reader is distracted from the pleasure of the text, and we have avoided notes that provide interpretation, as distinct from information.

Following the works, the Norton editors have provided lists of textual variants. These are variants from the control text only—that is, they do not record all of the variants in all of the substantive texts, nor do they record all of the myriad shifts of meaning that may arise from modernization of spelling and repunctuation. Readers who wish to pursue these interesting, if complex, topics are encouraged to consult the *Textual Companion,* along with the old-spelling *Oxford Shakespeare,* the Norton facsimile of the First Folio, and the quarto facsimiles published by the University of California Press. The *Norton Shakespeare* does provide a convenient list for each play of the different ways the same characters are designated in the speech prefixes in the substantive texts. These variants (for example, Lady Capulet in *Romeo and Juliet* is called, variously, "Lady, "Mother," "Wife," "Old Woman," etc.) often cast an interesting light on the ways a particular character is conceived. Variants as they appear in this edition, as well as their line numbers, are printed in boldface; each is followed by the corresponding reading in the control text, and sometimes the source from which the variant is taken. Further information on readings in substantive texts is given in brackets.

Stage directions pose a complex set of problems for the editors of a one-volume Shakespeare. The printing conventions for the stage directions in sixteenth- and seventeenth-century plays were different from those of our own time. Often all of the entrances for a particular scene are grouped together at the beginning, even though some of the characters clearly do not enter until later; placement in any case seems at times haphazard or simply incorrect. There are moments when the stage directions seem to provide stunning insight into the staging of the plays in Shakespeare's time, other moments when they are absent or misleading. It is difficult to gauge how much the stage directions in the substantive editions reflect Shakespeare's own words or at least decisions. It would seem that he was often relatively careless about them, understanding perhaps that these decisions in any precise sense would be the first to be made and unmade by different productions.

The Oxford editors, like virtually all modern editors, necessarily altered and supplemented the stage directions in their control texts. They decided to mark certain of the stage directions with a special sign to indicate a dubious action or placement, but they did not distinguish between the stage directions that came from the substantive texts and those added in later texts, from the seventeenth century to the present. They referred readers instead to the *Textual Companion*, which provides lists of the exact wording of the stage directions in the substantive texts.

The editors of the *Norton Shakespeare* share a sense of the limitations of the early stage directions and share as well some skepticism about how many of these should be attributed even indirectly to Shakespeare. Hence, we do not routinely differentiate between quarto and Folio stage directions; we do so only when we think it is a significant point. But there is, it seems to us, a real interest in knowing which stage directions come from those editions of the plays published up to the 1623 Folio (and including *The Two Noble Kinsmen*, published shortly thereafter) and which were added when the editors were no longer in contact with Shakespeare's presence or his manuscripts. Therefore, we have placed brackets around all stage directions that were added after the First Folio. Unbracketed stage directions, then, all derive from editions up through the Folio.

The *Norton Shakespeare* has made several other significant departures from the Oxford text. The Oxford editors note that when *1 Henry IV* was first performed, probably in 1596, the character we know as Sir John Falstaff was called Sir John Oldcastle. But in the wake of protests from Oldcastle's descendants, one of whom, William Brooke, tenth Baron Cobham, was Elizabeth I's lord chamberlain, Shakespeare changed the name to "Falstaff" (and probably for similar reasons changed the names of Falstaff's companions, Russell and Harvey, to "Bardolph" and "Peto"). Consistent with their decision not to honor changes that Shakespeare was *compelled* to make by censorship or other forms of pressure, the Oxford editors changed the names back to their initial form. But this decision is a problem for several reasons. It draws perhaps too sharp a distinction between those things that Shakespeare did under social pressure and those he did of his own accord. More seriously, it pulls against the principle of a text that represents the latest performance version of a play during Shakespeare's lifetime: after all, even the earliest quarto title page advertises "the humorous conceits of Sir John Falstaff." And, of course, it asks the reader to ignore completely and radically centuries of response—elaboration, fascination, and love—all focused passionately on Sir John Falstaff. The response is not a modern phenomenon: it began with Shakespeare, who developed the character as Sir John Falstaff in *2 Henry IV* and *The Merry Wives of Windsor*. Norton thus restores the more familiar names.

Another major departure from the Oxford text is Norton's printing of the so-called Additional Passages, especially in *Hamlet*. Consistent with their decision not to conflate quarto and Folio texts, the Oxford editors adhere to their control text for *Hamlet*, the Folio, and print those passages that appear only in the Second Quarto in an appendix at the end of the play. As explained at length in the Textual Note to the play, the Norton editors decided not to follow this course, but instead chose a different way of demarcating the quarto and Folio texts (inserting the quarto passages, indented, in the body of the text), one that makes it easier to see how the quarto passages functioned in a version of the play that Shakespeare also authored.

The *Norton Shakespeare* follows Oxford in printing separate quarto and Folio texts of *King Lear*, to which we have added a conflated version of the play so that readers will have the opportunity to assess for themselves the effects of the traditional editorial practice. Moreover, we have departed from Oxford in printing the quarto and Folio texts of the plays on facing pages, so that their differences can be readily weighed. In the hundreds of changes, some trivial and other momentous, it is possible to glimpse, across what Prospero calls "the dark backward and abysm of time," a thrilling sight: Shakespeare at work.

# The Shakespearean Stage
*by*
## ANDREW GURR

## Publication by Performance

The curt exchange between the sentries in the first six lines of *Hamlet* tells us that it is very late at night ("'Tis now struck twelve") and that "'tis bitter cold." This opening was staged originally at the Globe in London in broad daylight, at 2 o'clock probably on a hot summer's afternoon. The words required the audience, half of them standing on three sides of the stage platform and all of them as visible to one another as the players were, to imagine themselves watching a scene quite the opposite of what they could see and feel around them. The original mode of staging for a Shakespearean play was utterly different from the cinematic realism we are used to now, where the screen gives us close-ups on a simulacrum of reality, an even more privileged view of the actors' facial twitches than we get in ordinary life. Eloquence then was in words, not facial expressions.

The playgoers of Shakespeare's time knew the plays in forms at which we can only now guess. It is a severe loss. Shakespeare's own primary concept of his plays was as stories "personated" onstage, not as words on a page. He himself never bothered to get his playscripts into print, and more than half of them were not published until seven years after his death, in the First Folio of his plays published as a memorial to him in 1623. His fellow playwright Francis Beaumont called the printing of plays "a second publication"; the first was their showing onstage. Print recorded a set of scripts, written for the original players to teach them what they should speak in the ensemble of the play in production. The only technology then available to record the performances was the written word. If video recordings had existed at that time, our understanding of Shakespeare would be vastly different from what it is today.

Since the texts were composed only to be a record of the words the players were to memorize, we now have to infer how the plays were originally staged largely by guesswork. Shakespeare was himself a player and shareholder in his acting company, and he expected to be present at rehearsals. Consequently, the stage directions in his scripts are distinctly skimpy compared with some of those provided by his fellow playwrights. He was cursory even in noting entrances and exits, let alone how he expected his company to stage the more complex spectacles, such as heaving Antony up to Cleopatra on her monument. There are sometimes hints in the stage directions and more frequently in the words used to describe some of the actions, and knowing what the design of the theater was like is a help as well. Knowing more about how Shakespeare expected his plays to be staged can transform how we think about them. But gaining such knowledge is no easy matter. One of the few certainties is that Shakespeare's plays in modern performance are even more different from the originals than modern printed editions are from the first much-thumbed manuscripts.

## The Shakespearean Mindset

The general mindset of the original playgoers, the patterns of thinking and expectation that Tudor culture imposed on Shakespeare's audiences, is not really difficult to identify.

It is less easy, though, to pin it down in the sort of detail that tells us what the original concept of staging the plays would have been like. We know that all the original playgoers paid for the privilege of attending the plays and committed themselves willingly to suspend their disbelief in what they were to see. They knew as we do that they were paying to be entertained by fictions. Beyond that, we need reminding today that going to open-air performances in daylight in Shakespeare's time meant being constantly aware that one was in a theater, a place designed to offer illusions. On the one hand, this consciousness of oneself and where one was meant that the players had to do more to hold attention than is needed now, when audiences have nothing but the stage to look at and armchairs to sit in. On the other hand, it made everyone more receptive to extratheatrical tricks, such as Hamlet's reference to "this distracted globe," or Polonius's claim in the same play to have taken the part of Julius Caesar at the university and been killed by Brutus. The regular playgoers at the Globe who recognized Polonius as the man who had played Caesar in Shakespeare's play of the year before, and who recognized Hamlet as the man who had played Brutus, would laugh at this theatrical in-joke. But two scenes later, when Hamlet kills Polonius, they would think of it again, in a different light.

Features of the original mindset such as these are readily identifiable. For others, though, we need to look further, into the design of the theaters and into the staging traditions that they housed and that Shakespeare exploited. Invisibility has a part to play in *A Midsummer Night's Dream* that we can easily underrate, for instance. Invisibility onstage is a theatrical in-joke, an obvious privileging of the audience, which is allowed to see what the characters onstage can't. The impresario Philip Henslowe's inventory of costumes used at the Rose theater in 1597, which lists "a robe for to go invisible," indicates a fictional device that openly expects the willing suspension of the audience's disbelief. In *A Midsummer Night's Dream,* the ostensible invisibility of all the visible fairies emphasizes the theatricality of the whole presentation while pandering to the audience's self-indulgent superiority, the feeling that it knows what is going on better than any character, whether he be Bottom or even Duke Theseus. That prepares us for the mockery of stage realism we get later, in the mechanicals' play in Act 5, and even for the doubt we as willing audience might feel over Theseus's own skepticism about the dangers of imagination that he voices in his speech at the beginning of Act 5.

More to the point, though, it throws into question our readiness to be an audience, since we have ourselves been indulging in just the games of suspending disbelief that the play staged by the mechanicals enters into so unsuccessfully. When Theseus disputes with Hippolyta about the credibility of the lovers' story, he voices the very skepticism—about the lover, the lunatic, and the poet—that any sensible realist in the audience would have been feeling for most of the previous three acts in the forest. The play starts and ends at the court in broad daylight, while the scenes of midsummer madness take place at night in a forest. At the early amphitheaters, all the plays were staged in broad daylight, between 2 and 5 o'clock in the afternoon, and without any persuasive scenery: the two stage posts served as trees onstage. So the play, moving as it does from daylight realism to nocturnal fantasy and back again, with a last challenge to credulity in the mechanicals' burlesque of how to stage a play, has already thoroughly challenged the willing suspension of the viewers' disbelief. *A Midsummer Night's Dream* is a play about nocturnal dreams and fictions that are accepted as truths in broad daylight. It was only a small extension of this game to have the women's parts played by boys, as well as plots in which the girls dressed as boys, to the point where in *As You Like It* Rosalind was played by a boy playing a girl pretending to be a boy playing a girl.

The Shakespeare plays were written for a new and unique kind of playhouse, the Elizabethan amphitheater, which had a distinctive design quite different from modern theaters. Elizabethans knew what the standard features in their theaters stood for, and Shakespeare drew on that knowledge for the staging of his plays. The physical features of the playhouses were a potent element in the ways that the plays were designed for the Elizabethan mindset. When Richard III, the archdeceiver and playactor, appears "aloft between two Bishops" to claim the crown in *Richard III* 3.7, his placing on the stage balcony literally above the crowd on the stage would, even without the accompanying priests, have signified his ironic claim to a social and moral superiority that ought to have matched his elevation. When Richard II comes down from the wall of Flint Castle to the "base court" in *Richard II* 3.3, Elizabethans would have seen his descent as a withdrawal from power and status. These theaters were still new when Shakespeare started to write for them, and their novelty meant that the plays were written more tightly to fit their specific design than the plays of later years, when theatergoing had become a more routine social activity and different kinds of theater were available.

## London Playgoing and the Law

This heightened sense of theatricality, or "metatheater," in Shakespearean audiences was far from the only difference in their mindset from that of all modern audiences. Regular playgoing in London only started in the 1570s, and through Shakespeare's earlier years it was always a perilous and precarious activity. The Lord Mayor of London and the mayors of most of England's larger towns hated playgoing and tried to suppress it whenever and wherever it appeared. Playgoing was exciting not only because it was new but because it was dangerous. The hostility of so many authorities to plays meant that they were seen almost automatically as subversive of authority. Paradoxically, the first London companies were only able to establish themselves in London through the active support of Queen Elizabeth and her Privy Council, which tried hard, in the face of constant complaints from the Lord Mayor, to ensure that the best companies would be on hand every Christmas to entertain the Queen's leisure hours. Popular support for playgoing depended on royal protection for the leading companies.

London was by far the largest city in England. Within a few years of Shakespeare's death, it became the largest in Europe. It was generally an orderly place to live, especially in the city itself. Even in the suburbs, where the poorer people had to live, there were not many of the riots and other disorders that preachers always associated with the brothels, animal-baiting arenas, and playhouses clustering there. The reputation that the playhouses gained for promoting riots was not well justified. Any crowd of people was seen by the authorities as a potential riot, and playhouses regularly drew some of the largest crowds that London had yet seen. The city's government was not designed to control large crowds of people. There was no paid police force, and the Lord Mayor was held responsible by the Privy Council, the Queen's governing committee, for any disorders that did occur. So the city authorities found that playgoing challenged their control over their people.

The rapid growth of London did not help the situation. Officially, the city was governed by the Lord Mayor and his council. But he had authority only inside the city, and London now spread through a large suburban area in the adjacent counties of Middlesex to the north and Surrey across the river to the south. Because the court and the national government were housed in London, the Privy Council often intervened in city affairs in its own interests, as well as when orders were needed that covered broader zones than the city itself. The periodic outbreaks of bubonic plague were one clear instance of such a need, because the plague took no notice of parish or city boundaries. The intrusion of the professional companies to play in London provided another. In the early years, they were chronic travelers, and London was simply one of many stopovers. But the Queen enjoyed seeing plays at Christmas, and her council accordingly supported the best companies so that they could perform for her. It protected the playing companies against the hatred of successive Lord Mayors, except when a national emergency such as a plague epidemic erupted. The Privy Council took control then by ordering the 126 parishes in and around London to list all deaths from plague separately from ordinary deaths. Each Thursday, the parish totals were added together. When the total number of deaths from plague in these lists rose above 30 in any one week, the Privy Council closed all places of public assembly. This meant especially the playhouses, which created by far the largest gatherings. When the theaters were closed, the playing companies had to revert to their traditional practice of going on tour to play in the towns through the country, provided that the news of plague did not precede them.

Plague was not the only reason for the government to lay its controlling hand on the companies. From the time the post was inaugurated in 1578, the Master of the Revels controlled all playing. He was executive officer to the Lord Chamberlain, the Privy Council officer responsible for the annual season of royal entertainment and thus, by extension, for the professional playing companies. The Master of the Revels licensed each company and censored its plays. He was expected to cut out any references to religion or affairs of state, and he tried to prevent other offenses by banning the depiction of any living person onstage. After 1594, he issued licenses to the approved London playhouses, too. Later still, the printing of any playbook was allowed only if he gave authority for it. The companies had to accept this tight control because the government was its only protector against the hostile municipal authorities, who included not only the Lord Mayor of London but also the mayors of most of the major towns in the country.

Most mayors had the commercial interest of keeping local employees at work to justify their hostility to playgoing. But across the country, the hostility went much deeper. A large proportion of the population disliked the very idea of playacting. Their reasons, ostensibly religious, were that for actors to pretend to be characters they were unlike in life was a deception and that for boys to dress as women was contrary to what the Bible said. Somewhere beneath this was a more basic fear of pretense and deceit, of people not acting honestly. It put actors into the same category as con men, cheats, and thieves. That was probably one reason why companies of boys acting men's parts were thought rather more tolerable than men pretending to be other kinds of men. The deception involved in boys playing men was more transparent than when men played characters other than themselves. There was also a strong Puritan suspicion about shows of any kind, which looked too much like the Catholic ceremonial that the new Church of England had renounced. Playgoing found much better favor on the Catholic side of English society than on the Puritan side. Different preachers took different positions over the new phenomenon of playgoing. But few would speak in its favor, and most of them openly disapproved of it. Playgoing was an idle pastime, and the devil finds work for idle hands.

In the 1590s, when *Romeo and Juliet* and Shakespeare's histories and early comedies were exciting audiences, only two playhouses and two companies were officially approved by the Queen's Privy Council for the entertainment of London's citizens. The other main forms of paid entertainment were bear- and bullbaiting, which were much harder on the performers than was playing and so could be staged less frequently. The hostility to plays meant that the right to perform was confined to only a few of the most outstanding companies. These few companies were in competition with one another, and this led to a rapid growth in the quality of their offerings. But playacting was always a marginal activity. Paying to enter a specially built theater in order to see professional companies perform plays was still a new phenomenon, and it still met with great opposition from the London authorities. The open-air theaters like the Globe were built out in the suburbs. London as a city had no centrally located playhouses until after the civil war and the restoration of the monarchy, in 1661. And even playing in the city's suburbs, where they were free from the Lord Mayor's control, the companies had to work under the control of the Privy Council. All the great amphitheaters were built either in Middlesex or in Surrey. At the height of their success, in the years after Shakespeare's death, the Privy Council never licensed more than four or five playhouses in London.

Playgoing in London was viewed even by the playgoers as an idle occupation. The largest numbers who went to the Globe were apprentices and artisans taking time off from work, often surreptitiously, and law students from the Inns of Court doing the same. These fugitives were linked with the wealthier kind of idler, "gallants" or rich gentlemen and other men of property, along with soldiers and sailors on leave from the wars, people visiting London from the country on business or pleasure (usually both), and above all the women of London. Women were not expected to be literate, but one did not need to be able to read and write to enjoy hearing and seeing a play. A respectable woman had to make sure she was escorted by a man. He might be a husband or a friend, or her page if she was rich, or her husband's apprentice if she was a middle-class citizen. She might have a mask on, part of standard women's wear outdoors to protect the face against the weather and to assert modesty—and perhaps anonymity. Market women (applewives and fishwives) went to plays in groups. Whores were expected to be there looking for business, especially from the gallants, but they usually had male escorts, too.

The social range of playgoers at the two playhouses approved for use in 1594 was almost complete, stretching from the aristocracy to the poorest workmen and boys. Many people disapproved of plays, but at peak times up to 25,000 a week flocked to see the variety of plays being offered. Prices for playgoing remained much the same throughout the decades up to 1642, when the parliamentary government that was fighting the King closed all the theaters for eighteen years. Until then, one could get standing room at an amphitheater for 1 penny ($\frac{1}{240}$th of a modern pound, roughly 1 cent),

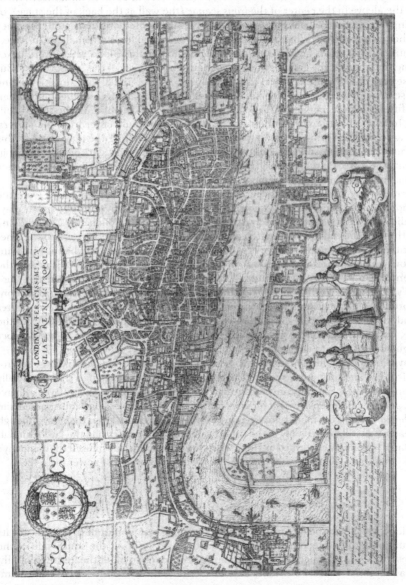

The city of London and its suburbs in 1572.

or a seat on a bench in the roofed galleries for twopence. A seat in a lord's room cost sixpence, which was not much less than a day's wage for a skilled artisan in 1600. The smaller roofed theaters that opened in 1599 were much more expensive. They were called "private" theaters to distinguish them from the "public" open-air amphitheaters, although the claim to privacy was mainly a convenient fiction to escape the controls imposed on the "public" theaters. At the Blackfriars hall theater, sixpence only gained you a seat in the topmost gallery, while a seat in the pit near the stage cost three times that amount and a seat in a box five times, or half a skilled worker's weekly wage.

It was not only the plays and players that were the sights at the playhouses. The richest lords and gallants went to be seen as much as they went to see. At the Globe, the costliest rooms were positioned alongside the balcony "above," over the stage. They were called "lords' rooms," and the playgoers who chose to sit there had a limited view of what went on beneath them. They saw no "discoveries," for instance, such as Portia's three caskets in *The Merchant of Venice,* which were uncovered underneath them inside the alcove in the center of the *frons scenae* (the wall at the back of the stage), or anything other than the backs of the players when they entered. But as audience, they were themselves highly visible, and that was what they paid for. In the hall, or "private," playhouses, with much higher admission prices than at the Globe, there were boxes flanking the stage for the gentry, which gave them a better view of the "discoveries." But at these "select" (because costlier) hall playhouses, where, unlike the Globe, everyone had a seat, some of the most colorful and exhibitionistic gallants could go one better. Up to fifteen gallants could pay for a stool to sit and watch the play on the stage itself, sitting in front of the boxes that flanked the stage. Each would enter from the players' dressing room (the "tiring-house") with his stool in hand before the play started. This gave them the best possible view of the play and easily the most conspicuous place in the audience's eye. Playgoing was a public occasion in which the visibility of audience members allowed them to play almost as large a part as the players.

Through the 1590s, the only permanent and custom-made playhouses were the large open-air theaters. Paying sixpence for a ferry across the river, as the richer playgoers did, or walking across London Bridge to the Rose or the Globe, or else trudging north through the mud of Shoreditch and Finsbury Fields or Clerkenwell to the Theatre or the Fortune in order to see a play, did not have great appeal when it was raining. Consequently, the companies were always trying to secure roofed halls nearer the city center. Up to 1594, they could use city inns, especially in winter, but the Lord Mayor's hostility to playing never made them reliable places for performing. Two constant problems troubled the players throughout these first years of professional theater in London: the city officials' chronic hatred of plays and the periodic visitations of the plague, which always led the government to close the theaters as soon as the number of plague deaths rose to dangerously high levels.

Playgoing was not firmly established in London until the Privy Council chose to protect it in 1594 and to approve specific playhouses for the two companies that it officially sanctioned. By then, Shakespeare had already made his mark. He became a player, a shareholder, and the resident playwright for one of these two companies. That status gained him a privileged place in the rapidly growing new world of playgoing. From then on, although his theater was still located only in the suburbs of the city, his work had the law behind it. That status was amply confirmed in 1603, when the new King made himself the company's patron. The King's Men held their status until the King himself lost power in 1642.

## The Design of the Globe

The Globe was Shakespeare's principal playhouse. He put up part of the money for its construction and designed his best plays for it. It was built on the south side of the Thames in 1599, fashioned out of the framing timbers of an older theater. Essentially, it was a polygonal scaffold of twenty bays or sections, nearly 100 feet in outside diameter, making a circle of three levels of galleries that rose to more than 30 feet high, with wooden bench seating and cushions for those who could afford them. This surrounded an open "yard," into which the stage projected.

The yard was over 70 feet in diameter. Nearly half the audience stood on their feet to watch the play from inside this yard, closest to the stage platform. The stage extended out nearly to the middle of the yard, so the actors could stand in the center of the crowd. The uncertain privilege of having standing room in the open air around the stage platform could be bought with the minimal price for admission, 1 penny (about a cent). It had the advantage of proximity to the stage and the players; its disadvantage was keeping you on your feet for the two or three hours of the play, as well as leaving you subject to the weather. If you wanted a seat, or if it rained and you wanted shelter, you paid twice as much to sit in the three ranks of roofed galleries that circled behind the crowd standing in the yard. With some squeezing, the theater could hold over 3,000 people. It was an open-air theater because that gave it a larger capacity than a roofed hall. The drawback of its being open to the weather was more than outweighed by the gain in daylight that shone on stage and spectators alike.

The stage was a great square platform as much as 40 feet wide. It had over it a canopied roof, or "heavens," to protect the players and their expensive costumes from rain. This canopy was held up by two pillars rising through the stage. The stage platform was about 5 feet high and without any protective rails, so that the eyes of the audience in the yard were at the level of the players' feet. At the back of the stage, a wall—the *frons scenae*—stretched across the front of the players' tiring-house, the attiring or dressing room. It had a door on each flank and a wider curtained space in the center, which was used for major entrances and occasionally for set-piece scenes. Above these entry doors was a gallery or balcony, most of which was partitioned into rooms for the wealthiest spectators. A central room "above" was sometimes used in staging: for example, as Juliet's balcony, as the place for Richard III to stand between the bish-

The second Globe, from Wenceslaus Hollar's engraving of the "Long View" of London (1647). The two captions saying "The Globe" and "Beere bayting h." were accidentally transposed in the original. The Globe is the round structure in the center of the picture.

A photograph of the interior framework of the "new" Globe, on the south bank of the Thames in London, showing the general dimensions of the yard and the surrounding galleries.

ops, as the wall of Flint Castle in *Richard II,* and as the wall over the city gates of Harfleur in *Henry V.* After 1608, when Shakespeare's company acquired the Blackfriars consort of musicians, this central gallery room was turned into a curtained-off music room that could double as an "above" when required. Fewer than half of Shakespeare's plays need an "above."

## The Original Staging Techniques

Shakespearean staging was emblematic. The "heavens" that covered the stage was the colorful feature from which gods descended to the earth of the stage platform. When Jupiter made his appearance in *Cymbeline,* in clouds of "sulphurous breath" provided by fireworks, he was mounted on an eagle being lowered through a trapdoor in the heavens. The other trapdoor, set in the stage platform itself, symbolized the opposite, a gateway to hell. The large stage trap was the place where the Gravedigger came to work at the beginning of Act 5 of *Hamlet.* It was the cell where Malvolio was imprisoned in *Twelfth Night.* The Shakespearean mindset accepted such conventions automatically.

Shakespeare inherited from Marlowe a tradition of using the stage trap as the dreaded hell's mouth. Barabbas plunges into it in *The Jew of Malta,* and the demons drag the screaming Faustus down it at the end of *Dr. Faustus.* Hell was not a fiction taken lightly by Elizabethans. Edward Alleyn, by far the most famous player of Faustus in the 1590s, wore a cross on his breast while he played the part, as insurance—just in case the fiction turned serious. Tracking the Elizabethan mindset about the stage trapdoor can give us a few warnings of what we might overlook when we come fresh to the plays today.

In the original staging of *Hamlet* at the Globe, the stage trap had two functions. Besides serving as Ophelia's grave, it was the distinctive entry point, not used by any other character, for the Ghost in Act 1. When he tells his son that he is "for the day confined to fast in fires," the first audiences would have already taken the point that he

The Globe as reconstructed in Southwark near the original site in London.

had come up from the underworld. His voice comes from under the stage, telling the soldiers to swear the oath of secrecy that Hamlet lays upon them. The connection between that original entry by the Ghost through the trap and the trap's later use for Ophelia is one we might easily miss. At the start of Act 5, the macabre discussion between the Gravediggers about whether she committed suicide and is, therefore, con-

The *frons scenae* of the new Globe.

A gesture using the language of hats, as shown by the man attending the brothers Browne.

signed to hell gets its sharpest edge from the association of the trap, here the grave being dug for her, with the Ghost's purgatorial fires. More to the point, though, Hamlet, as he eavesdrops on the curtailed burial ceremony, makes the same connection when he discovers that it is the body of Ophelia being so neglectfully interred. He remembers the other apparition that came up through the trap and springs forward in a grotesque parody of the Ghost, crying, "This is I, Hamlet the Dane!" It is a melodramatic claim to be acting a new role, that of his father the dead King. The first audiences would have remembered the ghost of dead King Hamlet using the stage trap at this point more readily than we do now. Hamlet's private knowledge of the Ghost and the trapdoor sets him, as so often happens in the play, at odds with his audience. Consequently, centuries of editors, like the characters onstage, have misread this claim as a declaration that young Hamlet ought to be King.

Since his own name is Hamlet, and since he alone could have made the connection between the Ghost and the trapdoor, he was all too likely to be misunderstood. In the next scene, Osric certainly shows that he understands Hamlet's graveside claim that he is his father's ghost to be a claim that he should now be King of Denmark. That explains why Osric insists on keeping his hat in his hand when he comes to invite Hamlet to duel with Laertes. With equals, an Elizabethan gentleman would doff his hat in greeting and then put it back on. Only in the presence of your master, or as a courtier in the presence of the King, did you keep it in your hand. Osric is trying tactfully to acknowledge what he thinks is Hamlet's lunatic claim to be King. He missed the private connection that Hamlet had made with the trapdoor and his father's ghost. Tudor body language, with its wordless gestures and signals that defined human relations, was an aspect of social life so widely understood that it needed no stage direction. The language of hats was a part of the Shakespearean mindset that we now have to register in footnotes.

Other signifiers are necessarily more elusive. We might take heart from the range of the comments made in *Much Ado About Nothing* 4.1 when Hero is accused and is seen to go red. Each of the viewers—Claudio, Leonato, and Friar Francis—gives a different reading (or "noting") of her blush. Different mindsets lead to visual indicators being read in different ways. Each reading tells as much about the observer as about the thing observed. We might add that since the blush is commented on so extensively, Shakespeare must have been concerned to save the boy playing Hero from the necessity of holding his breath long enough to produce the right visual effect.

Costume was a vital element in the plays, a mute and instant signifier of the scene. If a character entered carrying a candle and dressed in a gown with a nightcap on his head, he had evidently just been roused from bed. Characters who entered wearing cloaks and riding boots and possibly holding a whip had just ended a long journey. York,

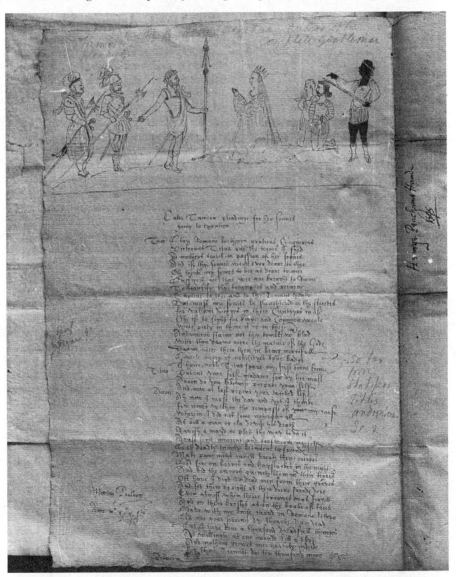

A sketch by Henry Peacham of an early staging of *Titus Andronicus* by Shakespeare's company (1595). Note the attempt at a Roman costume for Titus but not for his soldiers, who carry Tudor halberds, and note Aaron's makeup and wig.

entering in *Richard II* with a gorget (a metal neck plate, the "signs of war about his agèd neck" [2.2.74]), was preparing for battle. Even the women's wigs that the boys wore could be used to indicate the wearer's state of mind. Hair worn loose and unbound meant madness, whether in *Hamlet*'s Ophelia or *Troilus*'s Cassandra.

Comparable audience expectations could be roused by other visual features. Characters with faces blackened and wigs of curly black wool were recognized as Moors,

Johannes de Witt's drawing of the Swan Theatre in 1596, showing two boys playing women greeted by a chamberlain.

alien and dangerous non-Christians. Aaron the Moor in *Titus Andronicus* and the Prince of Morocco in *The Merchant of Venice* acquire that character as soon as they come in view. Othello, by Iago's report and by his own first appearance, takes on the same stereotype. By contrast, Iago is dressed like a simple and honest soldier. Only in the course of Act 1 does it become apparent that it is Othello who is the honest soldier, Iago the un-Christian alien. The play neatly reverses the visual stereotypes of Elizabethan staging. Twentieth-century playgoers miss most of these signals and the ways that the original players used them to show the discrepancy between outward appearance and inner person. As King Lear said, robes and furred gowns hide all.

For *The Merchant of Venice*, Shylock wore his "Jewish gabardine" and may also have put on a false nose, as Alleyn was said to have done for the title role in *The Jew of Malta*. Other national characteristics were noted by features of dress, such as the Irish "strait strossers" (tight trousers) that Macmorris would have worn in *Henry V*. The dress of the women in the plays, who were usually played by boys with unbroken voices, was always a special expense. The records kept by Philip Henslowe, owner of the Rose playhouse and impresario for the rival company to Shakespeare's, show that he paid the author less for the script of *A Woman Killed with Kindness* than he paid the costumer for the heroine's gown.

Women's clothing and the decorums and signals that women's costume contained were very different from those of men and men's clothing. Men frequently used their hats, doffing them to signal friendship and holding them in their hands while speaking to anyone in authority over them. Women's hats were fixed to their heads and were rarely if ever taken off in public. The forms and the language of women's clothes reflected the silent modesty and the quiet voices that men thought proper for women. Women had other devices to signal with, including handkerchiefs, fans, and face masks, and the boys playing the women's parts in the theaters exploited such accessories to the full. A lady out of doors commonly wore a mask to protect her complexion. When Othello is quizzing Emilia in 4.2 about his wife's behavior while she spoke to Cassio, he asks Emilia, who should have been chaperoning her mistress, whether Desdemona had not sent her away "to fetch her fan, her gloves, her mask, nor nothing?" There is little doubt that the boys would have routinely worn masks when they played gentlewomen onstage, and not just at the masked balls in *Romeo and Juliet*, *Love's Labour's Lost*, and *Much Ado About Nothing*.

Other features of the original staging stemmed from the actor–audience relationship, which differs radically in daylight, when both parties can see one another, from what we are used to in modern, darkened, theaters. An eavesdropping scene onstage, for instance, works rather on the same basis as the "invisible" fairies in *A Midsummer Night's Dream*, where the audience agrees to share the pretense. At the Globe, it also entailed adopting the eavesdropper's perspective. In *Much Ado*, the two games of eavesdropping played on Benedick and Beatrice are chiefly done around the two stage posts. In these scenes, the posts that held up the stage cover, or "heavens," near what we now think of as the front of the stage were round, like the whole auditorium, and their function was to allow things to be seen equally by all of the audience, wherever people might be standing or sitting. Members of the audience, sitting in the surrounding galleries or standing around the stage itself at the Globe or its predecessors, had the two tall painted pillars in their sight all the time, wherever they were in the playhouse. And since the audience was in a complete circle all around the stage, if the stage posts were used for concealment there was always a large proportion of the audience who could see the player trying to hide behind a post. It was a three-dimensional game in which the audience might find itself behind any of the game players, victims or eavesdroppers, complicit in either role.

The first of *Much Ado*'s eavesdropping scenes, 2.3, starts as usual in Shakespeare with a verbal indication of the locality. Benedick tells his boy, "Bring it hither to me in the orchard." So we don't need stage trees to tell us where we are supposed to be. He later hides "in the arbour" to listen to what Don Pedro and the others have set for him; this means concealing himself behind a stage post, closer to the audience than the playactors who are talking about him. Don Pedro asks, "See you where Benedick hath hid himself?" a self-contradiction that confirms the game. When it is Beatrice's turn in her arbor scene, 3.1, she slips into a "bower" behind "this alley," which again signals a retreat behind the prominent stage post. These games are played with both of the eavesdroppers hiding behind the post at the stage edge, while the others do their talking at center stage between the two posts.

Such games of eavesdropping, using the same bits of the stage structure, make a strong visual contrast with all that goes on at what we two-dimensional thinkers, used to the pictorial staging of the cinema, call the "back" of the stage, or upstage—where, for instance, the Friar starts the broken-off wedding and where Claudio and Don Pedro later figure at Leonato's monument. These events are more distant from the audience, less obviously comic and intimate. The close proximity of players to audience in such activities as eavesdropping strongly influenced the audience's feeling of kinship with the different groupings of players.

A multitude of other staging differences can be identified. Quite apart from the fact that the language idioms were more familiar to the playgoers at the original Globe than they are now, all playgoers in 1600, many of them illiterate, were practiced listeners. The speed of speech, even in blank verse, was markedly higher then than the recitation of Shakespeare is today. The original performances of *Hamlet*, if the Folio version reflects what was usually acted, would have run for not much more than two and a half hours (the time quoted by Ben Jonson for a play as long as *Hamlet*), compared with the more than four hours that the full Folio or 1605 quarto text with at least one intermission would take today. Quicker speaking, quicker stage action, no intermissions, and the audience's ability to grasp the language more quickly meant that the plays galloped along. The story, not the verse, carried the thrust of the action. Occasional set speeches, like Hamlet's soliloquies or Gaunt's "sceptred isle" speech in *Richard II*, would be heard, familiar as they already were to many in the audience, like a solo aria in a modern opera. In theory if not in practice, the business of hearing, as "audience" (from the Latin *audire*, "to hear"), was more important than the business of seeing, as "spectators" (from the Latin *spectare*, "to see"). The visual aspects of acting, like scenic staging, are inherently two-dimensional and do not work well when the audience completely surrounds the actors. Most of Shakespeare's fellow writers, notably Jonson, understandably set a higher priority on the audience's hearing their verse than on their seeing what the players did with the lines. The poets wanted listeners, although the players did try to cater to the viewers. Yet for all the games with magic tricks and devils spouting fireworks that were part of the Shakespearean staging tradition, spectacle was a limited resource on the scene-free Elizabethan stage. Shakespeare in this was a poet more than a player. Even in his last and most richly staged plays—*Cymbeline, The Winter's Tale,* and *The Tempest*—he made notably less use of such "spectacles" than did his contemporaries.

One piece of internal evidence about the original staging is Hamlet's advice to the visiting players. In 3.2, before they stage the *Mousetrap* play that he has rewritten for them, he lectures them on what a noble student of the theater then considered to be good acting. He objects first to overacting and second to the clown who ad libs with his own jokes and does not keep to the script. How far this may have been Shakespeare's own view it is impossible to say. Hamlet is an amateur lecturing professionals about how they should do their job. His views are what we would expect an amateur playwright with a liking for plays that are "caviar to the general" to hold. His objections to the clown are noteworthy, because once the original performances ended, the clown would conclude the afternoon's entertainment with a comic song-and-dance jig. Thomas Platter, a young German-speaking Swiss student, went to the Globe in 1599 to see *Julius Caesar.* He reported back home that

> on 21 September after lunch I and my party crossed the river, and there in the playhouse with the thatched roof witnessed an excellent performance of the tragedy of the first emperor Julius Caesar with a cast of about fifteen people. When the play

The hall screen in the Middle Temple Hall, built in 1574. Shakespeare's company staged *Twelfth Night* in this hall in February 1602.

was over they danced marvellously and gracefully together as their custom is, two dressed as men and two as women.[1]

The script for one jig survives, probably played by Will Kemp, who was the Shakespeare company clown until he left just before *Hamlet* came to the Globe. Its story is a bawdy knockabout tale of different men trying to seduce a shopkeeper's wife in rhyming couplets, hiding in a chest from her husband, and beating one another up. There is nothing to say what the audience reaction to such a jig might have been after they had seen a performance of *Julius Caesar* or *Hamlet*. It is possible that the Globe players stopped offering that kind of coda when they acquired the clown who played Feste in *Twelfth Night* in 1601. The song with which Feste ends that play might have become an alternative form of closure, replacing the traditional bawdy jig.

Vigorous and rapid staging was inevitable when the half of the audience closest to the stage had to stand throughout the performance. Shakespeare's plays were distinctive among the other plays of the time for their reliance on verbal sparkle over scenes of battle and physical movement, but even the soliloquies raced along. There was little occasion for long pauses and emoting. Dumb shows, like the players' prelude to the *Mousetrap* play in *Hamlet,* were the nearest that the players came to silent acting. There were no intermissions—apples, nuts, and drink were peddled in the auditorium throughout the performance—and the only "comfort stations" were, for the men, the nearest blank wall; for the women, whatever convenient pots or bottles they might be carrying under their long skirts.

Nor were there any pauses to change scenes. There was no static scenery apart from an emblematic candle to signify a night scene, a bed "thrust out" onto the stage, or the canopied chair of state on which the ruler or judge sat for court scenes. Usually any

1. *Thomas Platter's Travels in England* (1599), rendered into English from the German, and with introductory matter by Clare Williams (London: Cape, 1937), p. 166.

special locality would be signaled in the first words of a new scene, but unlocalized scenes were routine. Each scene ended when all the characters left the stage and another set entered. No act breaks appear in the plays before *The Tempest*. *Henry V* marked each act with a Chorus, but even he entered on the heels of the characters from the previous scene. Blue-coated stagehands were a visibly invisible presence onstage. They would draw back the central hangings on the *frons scenae* for a discovery scene, carry on the chair of state on its dais for courtroom scenes, or push out the bed with Desdemona on it for the last act of *Othello*. They served the stage like the house servants with whom the nobility peopled every room in their great houses, silent machines ready to spring into action when needed.

There has been a great deal of speculation about the tiring-house front at the rear of the stage platform: did it look more like an indoor set or an outdoor one, like the hall screen of a great house or palace or like a housefront exterior? In fact, it could easily be either. The upper level of the *frons*, the balconied "above," might equally represent a musicians' gallery, like those in the main hall of a great house, or a city wall under which the central discovery space served as the city gates, as it did for York in *Richard Duke of York* (3 *Henry VI*) 4.8, or *Henry V*'s Harfleur (3.3.78). The "above" could equally be an indoor gallery or an outdoor balcony. The appearance of the stage was everything and nothing, depending on what the play required. Players and playwrights expected the audience members to use their imagination, as they had to with the opening lines of *Hamlet*, or, as the Prologue to *Henry V* put it, to "piece out our imperfections with your thoughts."

## Shakespeare's Companies and Their Playhouses

Shakespeare's plays were written for a variety of staging conditions. Until 1594, when he joined a new company under the patronage of the Lord Chamberlain, the Queen's officer responsible for licensing playing companies, poets had written their plays for any kind of playhouse. The Queen's Men, the largest and best company of the 1580s, is on record as playing at the Bell, the Bel Savage, and the Bull inns inside the city, and at the Theatre and the Curtain playhouses in the suburbs. Early in 1594, it completed this sweep of all the available London venues by playing at the Rose. But in that year, the system of playing changed. The Lord Mayor had always objected to players using the city's inns, and in May 1594 he succeeded in securing the Lord Chamberlain's agreement to a total ban. From then on, only the specially built playhouses in the suburbs were available for plays.

The Queen's Men had been set up in 1583, drawn from all the then-existing major companies with the best players. This larger and favored group at first monopolized playing in London. But it was in decline by the early 1590s, and the shortage of companies to perform for the Queen at Christmas led the Lord Chamberlain and his son-in-law, the Lord Admiral, to set up two new companies in its place as a duopoly in May 1594. Shakespeare became a "sharer," or partner, in one of these companies. As part of the same new establishment, his company, the Lord Chamberlain's Men, was allocated the Theatre to perform in, while its partner company in the duopoly, the Lord Admiral's Men, was assigned to the Rose. This was the first time any playing company secured a playhouse officially authorized for its use alone.

The Theatre, originally built in 1576 by James Burbage, father of the leading player of the Lord Chamberlain's company, was in Shoreditch, a suburb to the north of the city. The Rose, built in 1587 by Philip Henslowe, father-in-law of the Lord Admiral's leading player, Edward Alleyn, was in the suburb of Southwark, on the south bank of the Thames. Henslowe's business papers, his accounts, some lists of costumes and other resources, and his "diary," a day-by-day listing of each day's takings and the plays that brought the money in, have survived for the period from 1592 until well into the next decade. Together they provide an invaluable record of how one of the two major companies of the later 1590s, the only rival to Shakespeare's company, operated through these years.[2] Some of Shakespeare's earlier plays, written before he joined the Lord Chamberlain's Men, including *1 Henry VI* and *Titus Andronicus,* were performed at the Rose. After May 1594, the new company acquired all of his early plays; every Shakespeare play through the next three years was written for the Theatre. Its familiarity supplied one sort of resource to the playwright. But the repertory system laid heavy demands on the company.

Henslowe's papers give a remarkable record of the company repertory for these years. Each afternoon, the same team of fifteen or so players would stage a different play. With only two companies operating in London, the demand was for constant change. No play at the Rose was staged more than four or five times in any month, and it was normal to stage a different play on each of the six afternoons of each week that they performed. A new play would be introduced roughly every three weeks—after three weeks of transcribing and learning the new parts; preparing the promptbook, costumes, and properties; and rehearsing in the mornings—while each afternoon, whichever of the established plays had been advertised around town on the playbills would be put on. The leading players had to memorize on average as many as eight hundred lines for each afternoon. Richard Burbage, who played the first Hamlet in 1601, probably had to play Richard III, Orlando in *As You Like It,* and Hamlet on successive afternoons while at the same time learning the part of Duke Orsino and rehearsing the new *Twelfth Night*—and still holding at least a dozen other parts in his head for the rest of the month's program. In the evenings, he might be called on to take the company to perform a different play at court or at a nobleman's house in the Strand. The best companies made a lot of money, but not without constant effort.

The companies were formed rather like guilds, controlled by their leading "sharers." Each senior player shared the company's profits and losses equally with his fellows. Most of the plays have seven or eight major speaking parts for the men, plus two for the boys playing the women. A normal London company had eight or ten sharers, who collectively chose the repertory of plays to be performed, bought the playbooks from the poets, and put up the money for the main company resource of playbooks and costumes (not to mention the wagon and horses for touring when plague forced the London theaters to close). Shakespeare made most of his fortune from his "share," first in his company and later in its two playhouses.

As a playhouse landlord, Henslowe took half of the takings from the galleries each afternoon for his rent, while the players shared all the yard takings and the other half of the gallery money. From their takings, the sharers paid hired hands to take the walk-on parts and to work as stagehands, musicians, bookkeeper or prompter, and "gatherers" at the different entry gates. The leading players also kept the boys who played the women's parts, housing and feeding them as "apprentices" in an imitation of the London livery companies and trades, which ran apprenticeships to train boys to become skilled artisans, or "journeymen." City apprenticeships ran for seven years from the age of seventeen, but the boy players began much younger, because unbroken voices were needed. They graduated to become adult players at an age when the city apprentices were only beginning their training. Most of the "extras," apart from the playing boys, would be left in London whenever the company had to go on tour.

Because the professional companies of the kind that Shakespeare joined all started as traveling groups rather than as companies settled at a single playhouse in London, the years up to 1594 yielded plays that could be staged anywhere. The company might be summoned to play at court, at private houses, or at the halls of the Inns of Court as readily as at inns or innyards or the custom-built theaters themselves. They traveled the country with their plays, using the great halls of country houses, or town guildhalls and local inns, wherever the town they visited allowed them. Consequently, the plays could not demand elaborate resources for staging. In this highly mobile tradition of traveling

2. See *Henslowe's Diary,* ed. R. A. Foakes (Cambridge, Eng.: Cambridge University Press, 1961).

companies, they were written in the expectation of the same basic but minimal features being available at each venue. Besides the stage platform itself, the basic features appear to have been two entry doors, usually a trap in the stage floor, a pair of stage pillars, sometimes a discovery space, and very occasionally a heavens with descent machinery. Apart from these fixtures, properties such as chairs and a table, a canopied throne on a dais, and sometimes a bed were also in regular use, though in a pinch these could be as mobile as the players themselves. The only essential traveling properties were players, playbooks, and costumes.

Once the two authorized companies settled permanently at the Theatre and the Rose in 1594, they slowly lost some of this mobility. The demands of versatility and readiness to make rapid changes now had to be switched from the venues to the plays themselves. A traveling company needed very few plays, since the locations and audiences were always changing. When the venues became fixed, it was the plays that had to keep changing. The Henslowe papers record that the Lord Admiral's Men staged an amazingly varied repertory of plays at the Rose. Shakespeare's company must have been equally versatile. The practice of giving popular plays long runs did not begin until the 1630s, by which time the number of London playhouses had grown to as many as five, all offering their plays each afternoon. Shakespeare's company in London had only the one peer from 1594 until 1600; and only two from then until 1608, aside from the once-weekly plays by the two boy companies, the "little eyases" mentioned in *Hamlet*, that started with the new century.

From May 1594 to April 1597 at the Theatre, in addition to all his earlier plays that he brought to his new company, Shakespeare gave them possibly *Romeo and Juliet* and *King John*, and certainly *Richard II*, *A Midsummer Night's Dream*, *1 Henry IV*, and *The Merchant of Venice*. But then they ran into deep trouble, because they lost the Theatre. In April 1597, its original twenty-one-year lease expired, and the landlord, who disliked plays, refused to let them renew it. Anticipating this, the company's impresario, James Burbage, had built a new theater for them, a roofed place in the Blackfriars near St. Paul's Cathedral. The Blackfriars precinct was a "liberty," free from the Lord Mayor's jurisdiction. But the plan proved a disaster. The rich residents of Blackfriars objected, and the Privy Council stopped the theater from opening. From April 1597, Shakespeare's company had to rent the Curtain, an old neighbor of their now-silent Theatre, and it was there that the next four of Shakespeare's plays—*2 Henry IV, Much Ado About Nothing, The Merry Wives of Windsor,* and probably *Henry V*—were first staged.

In December 1598, losing hope of a new lease for the old Theatre, the Burbage sons had it pulled down and quietly transported its massive framing timbers across the Thames to make the scaffold for the Globe on the river's south bank, near the Rose. Most of their capital was sunk irretrievably into the Blackfriars theater, and they could afford only half the cost of rebuilding. So they raised money as best they could. Some of the company's more popular playbooks were sold to printers, including *Romeo and Juliet, Richard III, Richard II,* and *1 Henry IV*. More to the point, the Burbage brothers raised capital for the building by cutting in five of the leading players, including Shakespeare, and asking them to put up the other half of its cost. The Globe, its skeleton taken from the old Theatre, thus became the first playhouse to be owned by its players, and, within the limits set by the old frame, the first one built to their own design.

For this theater, one-eighth of which he personally owned, Shakespeare wrote his greatest plays: *Julius Caesar, As You Like It, Hamlet, Twelfth Night, Othello, All's Well That Ends Well, Measure for Measure, King Lear, Macbeth, Pericles, Antony and Cleopatra, Coriolanus, Cymbeline, The Winter's Tale,* and most likely *Troilus and Cressida* and *Timon of Athens*. As the first playhouse to be owned by the players who expected to use it, its fittings must have satisfied all the basic needs of Shakespearean staging. At one time or another, the company staged every one of Shakespeare's plays there.

In 1600, a company consisting entirely of boys started using the Blackfriars playhouse that Richard Burbage's father had tried to open four years before. Companies of boy players had a higher social status than the adult professionals, and, playing only in halls, they commanded a more affluent clientele. The boys performed only once a week, and the relative infrequency of their crowds, plus their skills as trained singers (they were choir-school children turned to making money for their choirmasters), proved less offensive to the local residents than a noisy adult company with its drums and trumpets. Leasing the Blackfriars to the boy company made a minor profit for the Burbages, who took the rent for eight years.

In the longer run, though, this arrangement provided a different means for the Burbage–Shakespeare company to advance its career. The boys' eight years of playing in their rented hall playhouse eventually made it possible for the company of adult players to renew Burbage's old plan of 1596. Shakespeare's company had been made the King's Men when James came to the throne in 1603, and their new patron gave them a status that made it impossible for the residents of Blackfriars to prevent them from implementing the original plan. During a lengthy closure of all the theaters because of a plague epidemic in 1608, the boys' manager surrendered his lease of the hall playhouse to the Burbages. They then took possession for their own company of the playhouse that their father had built for them twelve years before. They divided the new playhouse property among the leading players as they had done in 1599 with the Globe.

A section from Wenceslaus Hollar's "Long View" of London, printed in 1644. Drawn from a standpoint on the tower of the church that is now Southwark Cathedral, Hollar's view shows the roof of the great hall in which the Blackfriars playhouse was built. It can be seen as the long angled roof with two central chimneys, below and to the east of St. Bride's Church.

They were the King's Men, the leading company in the country, and their status after ten years of playing at the Globe was matched by their wealth. By the time theaters reopened late in 1609, the company had established a new system of playing.

The King's Men now had two playhouses, a large open amphitheater and a much smaller roofed hall. Instead of selling or renting one out and using the other for themselves, they decided to use both in turn, for half of each year. It was a reversion to the old system with the city inns, where through the summer they played in the large open yards and in the winter played at inns with big indoor rooms. This time, though, the company owned both playhouses. Their affluence and their high status are signaled by the fact that they chose to keep one of their playhouses idle while they used the other, despite there now being a shortage of playhouses in London. That affluence was needed in 1613, when the Globe burned down at a performance of *All Is True (Henry VIII)* and the company chose the much more expensive option of rebuilding it instead of reverting to the Blackfriars for both winter and summer. That decision, in its way, was the ultimate gesture of affection for their original playhouse. It was a costly gesture, but it meant that the Globe continued in use by the company until all the theaters were closed down by Parliament in 1642.

In 1609, when they reopened after the closure for plague, Shakespeare's company had made several changes in their procedures. The restart was at the Blackfriars, and although they offered the same kind of plays, they began to alter their style of staging. Along with the Blackfriars playhouse, they acquired a famous consort of musicians who played on strings and woodwinds in a music room set over the stage. The new consort was a distinct enhancement of the company's musical resources, which until then had been confined to song, the occasional use of recorders or hautboys, and military drums and trumpets for the scenes with soldiery. In 1608, a central room on the Globe's stage balcony was taken over to serve as a music room like the one at the Blackfriars. From this time on, the King's Men's performances began with a lengthy overture or concert of music before the play.

With that change, the plays themselves now had music to back their singers and provide other sorts of atmospheric effects. Some of the songs and music that appear in the plays not printed until the First Folio of 1623, such as the song that Mariana hears in *Measure for Measure* 4.1, may have been added after Shakespeare's time to make use of this new resource. Shakespeare did use songs, sometimes with string accompaniment, quite regularly in the early plays, but instrumental music hardly ever appears. The last play that he wrote alone, *The Tempest*, was the only one in which he made full use of this new resource.

All the plays containing soldiers and battles used the military drums that in war conveyed signals to infantry formations, as well as the trumpets that were used for signaling to cavalry. These were usually employed for offstage noises, sound effects made from "within" (inside the dressing room or tiring-house behind the stage). Soldiers marching in procession, as in the dead march at the close of *Hamlet*, would have the time marked by an onstage drum. Shakespeare never calls for guns to be fired onstage, even though other writers did, but he did have other noises at his command. A small cannon or "chamber" might be used, fired from the gable-fronted heavens over the stage, as Claudius demands in *Hamlet* and as the Chorus to Act 3 of *Henry V* notes. It was wadding from a ceremonial cannon shot that set the gallery thatch alight at a performance of *All Is True* in July 1613 and burned the Globe to the ground. Stage battles such as Shrewsbury at the end of *1 Henry IV*, written for the Theatre, were accompanied by sword fights that were not the duels of *Hamlet*'s finale but exchanges with broadswords or "foxes" slammed against metal shields or "targets." That action guaranteed emphatic sound effects. The drums and trumpets, with clashes of swords and a great deal of to-ing and fro-ing onto and off the stage, were highlighted in between the shouted dialogue by some hard fighting between the protagonists. The leading players were practiced swordsmen, who knew they were being watched by experts. These were the scenes of "four or five most vile and ragged foils" that the fourth Chorus self-consciously derided in *Henry V* at the Curtain.

The second great reason for noise in the amphitheaters was to mark storm and tempest. Stagehands used the kind of device that Jonson mocked in the Prologue to *Every Man in His Humour*, written for its 1616 publication. His play, wrote Jonson, was free from choruses that wafted you over the seas, "nor rolled bullet heard / To say, it thunders; nor tempestuous drum / Rumbles, to tell you when the storm doth come." For centuries, lead balls rolling down a tin trough were a standard way of making thunder noises in English theaters. The tempest in Act 3 of *King Lear* is heralded several times in the text before a stage direction, "Storm and tempest" (Folio 2.2.450), tells us that it has at last arrived. In 2.2, Cornwall notes its coming twice (Folio 2.2.452, 473). Kent comments on the "Foul weather" in his first line in Act 3, prefaced by the entry stage direction for Act 3, "Storm still," which is repeated for 3.2. Such stage directions appear in both texts (Q has "Storm" for the equivalent Scenes 8, 9, and also at 11, F's 3.4, where F omits any further reference to these noises). These explicit signals indicate that the stagehands provided offstage noises, for all that Lear himself outstorms them with his violent speeches in 3.2.

The main question about the storm scenes in *King Lear* is this: with such consistent emphasis on storm in the language, what was the design behind the stage directions? In the centuries that *Lear* has been restaged, the tempest has been made to roar offstage in a wide variety of ways, often with so much effect that, in the face of complaints that the storm noises made it difficult for the audience to hear the words, some modern productions reduced the storm to solely visual effects, or even left Lear's own raging language to express it unsupported. But the two stage directions indicate that in the original performances the "storm in nature" was not left to Lear himself to convey. The two "Storm still" directions in the Folio suggest a constant rumbling, not the intermittent crashes that might allow Lear to conduct a dialogue with the occasional outbursts of storm noises, as some modern productions have done.

Shakespeare left regrettably few stage directions to indicate the special tricks or properties that he wanted. Curtained beds are called for in *Othello* 5.2 and *Cymbeline* 2.2, and there is the specification "Stocks brought out" in *King Lear* 2.2.132. Small and portable things like papers were a much more common device, from the letters in *The Two Gentlemen of Verona* 1.2.46, 1.3.44, and 2.1.95 to Lear's map at 1.1.35. Across the whole thirty-eight plays, though, there are very few such directions. Shakespeare's economy in preparing his scripts is a major impediment to the modern reader. He hardly ever bothered to note the standard physical gestures, such as kneeling or doffing a hat, and did little more to specify any special effects. Nonetheless, it is important not to imagine elaborate devices or actions where the text does not call for them. On the whole, the demands Shakespeare made of his fellows for staging his plays appear to have been remarkably modest. Since he was a company shareholder, his parsimony may have had a simple commercial motive. Stage properties cost the company money, and one had to be confident of a new play's popularity before investing much in its staging.

There may have been other reasons for avoiding extravagant staging spectacles. Shakespeare made little use of the discovery space until the last plays, for instance, for reasons that we can only guess at. The few definite discoveries in the plays include Portia's caskets in *The Merchant of Venice*, Falstaff sleeping off his sack in *1 Henry IV* 2.5.482, the body of Polonius in *Hamlet*, Hermione's statue in *The Winter's Tale* 5.3.20, and the lovers in *The Tempest* 5.1.173, who are found when discovered to be playing chess. The audience's shock when Hermione moves and comes out of the discovery space onto the main stage is rare in Shakespeare: in every other play, whether comedy or tragedy, the audience knows far more than the characters onstage about what is going on. Shakespeare matched this late innovation in *The Winter's Tale* with his last play, *The Tempest*. After the preliminary and soothing concert by the resident Blackfriars musicians, it opens with a storm at sea so realistic that it includes that peculiarly distinctive stage direction "Enter Mariners, wet" (1.1.46). That startling piece of stage realism turns out straightaway to be not real at all but a piece of stage magic.

# ROMANCES

# Shakespearean Romance

*by*

## WALTER COHEN

What is a romance? Renaissance playwrights inherited two main genres from classical antiquity: comedy and tragedy. Shakespearean drama, however, has never been parceled out into just these two groups. The first relatively complete edition of Shakespeare's plays was published in 1623, seven years after the dramatist's death. John Heminges and Henry Condell, two of Shakespeare's colleagues in the King's Men, the theater company to which he belonged, collected and printed the plays in a single large volume that became known as the First Folio. While the Folio adopted the classical categories of comedy and tragedy, it also added a third division: history. Under "Histories," the editors included Shakespeare's works on English history that take place from the thirteenth to the sixteenth centuries. The Folio's three resulting rubrics—"Comedies," "Tragedies," "Histories"—have considerable value, but they make for a certain conceptual messiness. A Shakespearean history designates a narrowly defined subject matter that may be comic or tragic or neither. Shakespearean comedy and tragedy suggest both a prevailing tone (light or somber) and a likely outcome (happy or sad). None of these designations, however, fits particularly well with the plays included here under the heading of "Romance"—plays that do not concern medieval English history and that often combine a somber feel with a happy ending. The First Folio deals with these plays in three ways. *The Tempest* (1611) opens and *The Winter's Tale* (1609–11) closes the comedies, *Cymbeline* (1609–10) appears last among the tragedies, and *Pericles* (1607–08) and *The Two Noble Kinsmen* (1613–14) are excluded entirely—presumably because they are coauthored works. This essay, however, brings together these five works while also drawing on two other collaborative Shakespearean productions: the lost *Cardenio* (1612–13) and the English history play *All Is True* (*Henry VIII*, 1613). After briefly reviewing their relationship to earlier European literature and theater, it considers them from the three main perspectives that have emerged in modern scholarship. The late plays may accordingly be viewed as the culmination of Shakespearean comedy, as the members of the distinct genre of romance, or as two different versions of tragicomedy.

Although Heminges and Condell did not use the term, the notion of romance was well established by the Renaissance. Based on the word *Rome*, *romance* was used originally as the collective name for the everyday speech derived from Latin and now called the Romance languages. The books written in those languages came to be known as romances. Beginning in the twelfth century *romance* was used to indicate a literary genre, although the genre so indicated differed among the countries—primarily present-day Italy, France, Spain, and Portugal—where Romance languages were spoken. The most influential variation of the romance as a literary form occurred in Old French, where *roman* originally meant "a courtly, or chivalric, narrative." Medieval French romance spread across Europe, inspiring both learned and popular emulation. For their collaborative work *The Two Noble Kinsmen*, Shakespeare and John Fletcher looked to the late fourteenth century and one of Geoffrey Chaucer's *Canterbury Tales*, "The Knight's Tale," itself an adaptation of Giovanni Boccaccio's Italian original from a few decades before.

Such narratives, in prose as well as verse, continued to be composed in the sixteenth century: Ludovico Ariosto's *Orlando Furioso,* Torquato Tasso's *Jerusalem Liberated,* Sir Philip Sidney's *Arcadia,* and Edmund Spenser's *Faerie Queene* are among the most influential contributions to the genre. Like their medieval predecessors, these chivalric romances and many others invited dramatic adaptation.

A second narrative form that had an impact on Shakespearean romance is late classical Greek and, to a lesser extent, Latin prose fiction. A number of these works were translated into English in the late sixteenth century—Heliodorus's *Aethiopica,* the anonymous *Daphnis and Chloe,* and Achilles Tatius's *Clitophon and Leucippe*—and were exploited by Sidney as well as various playwrights. In such tales, faithful lovers are separated and often driven back and forth across the Mediterranean by bad people, bad weather, and bad luck. Ultimately, however, the virtuous couple earns a triumphant reunion that sometimes expands to include the restoration of the relationship between parent and child as well. In *Pericles,* Shakespeare and George Wilkins turned to Chaucer's contemporary John Gower for a story in his *Confessio Amantis* that is taken from an earlier Latin version that, in turn, goes back to a lost fifth-or sixth-century Greek original. In *The Winter's Tale,* Shakespeare borrowed from *Pandosto* (1588), a romance by his contemporary Robert Greene that is generally inspired by Greek fiction.

Along with classical and medieval sources, Shakespeare's final plays were influenced by important predecessors in English drama. Although few texts remain, their titles often survive. The romantic plays of the 1570s and 1580s seem to have combined a certain naïveté with theatrically effective plot twists and concluding scenes of recognition and reconciliation. In the anonymous *Rare Triumphes of Love and Fortune* (1580s), the Olympian gods intervene to set human affairs right. Shakespeare may have drawn on this play in both *Cymbeline* and *The Tempest.* A second legacy from the English theater is the saint's life, a dramatic form that dates from the late medieval period through the 1560s, after which it was suppressed by Protestant authorities. The anonymous work *Mary Magdalene,* preserved in a fifteenth-century manuscript, anticipates *Pericles* in sending a queen to her death at sea, only to be saved, along with her child, by the prayers of the titular character.

Late sixteenth-century Italian pastoral tragicomedy provided yet another dramatic model for Shakespearean romance. Tasso's *Aminta* (1573) is probably the best-known specimen of the genre. Of central importance here is Battista Guarini's *Il pastor fido* (*The Faithful Shepherd,* 1590). Unlike either narrative or dramatic romance, *Il pastor fido* directly engages both Aristotle's *Poetics* (fourth century B.C.E.), the profoundly influential work of theatrical theory, and Sophocles' tragedy *Oedipus Rex* (fifth century B.C.E.). One of Guarini's innovations was to subvert Sophocles' tragic plot at the very last moment, thereby allowing his protagonist to avoid incest and its catastrophic consequences. Shakespeare may have learned of Guarini through Fletcher's unsuccessful adaptation, *The Faithful Shepherdess* (1608–09). Although Shakespeare never borrows as directly as Fletcher did and is more circumspect than his Italian predecessors in finding a providential design in human affairs, most of his romances are indebted either to Guarini or to Italian pastoral tragicomedy in general for their overall shape, settings, and much more.

The most traditional approach to Shakespearean romance approximates the logic of the First Folio's editors in treating the playwright's romantic comedies, problem plays (*Measure for Measure, All's Well That Ends Well*), and romances all as variations on a comic movement from disorder to harmony. Beginning in 1893, when the critic Edward Dowden first applied the term *romance* to *Pericles* and the final three solely authored plays (*Cymbeline, The Winter's Tale,* and *The Tempest*), this first view has gradually been eclipsed by a second, now-dominant paradigm—that the romances differ from the comedies and, indeed, constitute a distinct form within Shakespeare's dramatic oeuvre. That form is marked by its vertical or longitudinal perspective, by a retrospective view that nonetheless leaves room for the future.

Separation and long suffering of families, perilous sea journeys beset by storms that form part of a symbolic geography, near-death experiences followed by spiritual rebirths, the cultivation of patience, the healing power of time, the eventual reunion of royal families whose children (primarily daughters) have been separated from their parents (primarily fathers) at birth, the power of those daughters to redeem their fathers—all these are recurrent motifs. Plot complications are unraveled in ultimate scenes of recognition and reconciliation, where music and visionary spectacle herald the appearance of Greco-Roman gods, who perhaps stand in for a mysterious Christian providence that guides human beings through the labyrinth of life. A third view of the late plays, developed by scholars in recent decades, gives new weight to the three heterogeneous tragicomic works—*Cardenio*, *All Is True*, and *The Two Noble Kinsmen*—on which Shakespeare collaborated with John Fletcher. *The Two Noble Kinsmen* is the only romance extant from this collaboration. *All Is True* is a national history play that treats some of the key events and personalities from the monarchy of King Henry VIII (reigned 1509–47). But it draws on the tone and many of the motifs of romance, with the presumed fictiveness of the standard romance story replaced by a narrative in which all is true. And in the lost *Cardenio*, abandoned lovers are reduced to despair before heaven brings about a romance-style reunion. The two playwrights apparently extracted the plot from an interpolated tale in Miguel de Cervantes's *Don Quixote*, Part 1 (1605, English translation by Thomas Shelton, 1612). In general, the coauthored plays seem to constitute a more pessimistic corrective to the core romances.

Each of these three views of the plays is worth considering in greater detail. Like the romantic comedies, the romances have their roots in seasonal festivity, emblematized in some of the titles: *The Winter's Tale* recalls *A Midsummer Night's Dream* and *Twelfth Night*. In all these plays, the seasonal cycle underlies a movement toward regeneration that is celebrated in the resolution of the plot. Shakespearean romantic comedy is indebted to classical New Comedy, a form invented in ancient Greece whose main surviving examples are the plays of the ancient Roman dramatists Plautus and Terence. With plots confined to the private lives of well-to-do citizens, New Comedy features a series of stock situations (hidden identity) and stock characters (young lovers, restrictive fathers, clever servants, braggart soldiers). The comic action turns on the young man's pursuit of the apparently unsuitable young woman, in the course of which various obstacles must be—and are—overcome. The legacy of Plautus and Terence was revised and elaborated upon in sixteenth-century Italian drama, which introduced to it elements of the Italian novella, or short story, beginning with Boccaccio's *Decameron* in the mid-fourteenth century. Nearly all of Shakespeare's romantic comedies, problem comedies, and romances are indebted to Italian narrative or drama, either directly or via French, Spanish, and English translation. Among the romances, *Cymbeline* borrows from the *Decameron*, *The Winter's Tale* exploits Sicily's association with literary pastoral in its setting, *The Tempest* resembles some of the scenarios from Italian popular theater (the commedia dell'arte), *Cardenio* presumably adapts a Cervantine novella that is itself influenced by Boccaccio and his successors, and, as we've seen, *The Two Noble Kinsmen* also goes back to Boccaccio's narrative poetry.

But Shakespearean comedy and romance depart from classical and Renaissance models in important ways that also sharply distinguish the plays from the classically minded satiric comedy of Shakespeare's contemporary, Ben Jonson. Shakespeare replaces the prosperous private citizens of earlier comedy with aristocrats and rulers, thereby blurring the traditional division between the private concerns of comedy and the public affairs of tragedy. Special attention is accorded to the fate of virtuous young women, whose marriages are crucial to the happy resolution of the plot. That resolution is complicated by a feature common to comedy and romance alike—a paternal or political decree that initially thwarts the romantic aspirations of the young lovers. Such a decree figures in the comedies from *The Two Gentlemen of Verona* through *Love's Labour's Lost* to *Measure for*

*Measure,* and in the late plays from *Pericles* through *The Tempest* to *All Is True.* To avoid its force, the characters flee the society of sanctioned public power for a world of disorder, license, and confused sexual identity. Geographically, this is the pastoral or green world that represents a physical and symbolic alternative to the city or, more often, the court. It is the setting for most of *As You Like It,* for the concluding resolution of both plots of *The Merry Wives of Windsor,* and, indeed, for much else in the romantic comedies. It is also a recurrent locale in the romances, above all in *The Tempest* but to some extent in each of them. The pastoral world is marked by a series of motifs shared by comedy and romance alike. The dreamlike madness of *The Comedy of Errors* and *A Midsummer Night's Dream* is echoed by *The Tempest, Cardenio,* and *The Two Noble Kinsmen.* The male disguise adopted by numerous women in the romantic comedies is also donned by Innogen in *Cymbeline* and, ineffectually, by Dorotea/Violante in *Cardenio* (where the first name, Dorotea, comes from Shelton's translation of Cervantes, while the second, Violante, is from the imitation of *Cardenio* by Lewis Theobald in his tragicomedy *Double Falsehood; or, The Distrest Lovers,* 1728). A lower-class theatrical performance honors the Athenian wedding of Theseus and Hippolyta in both *A Midsummer Night's Dream* and *The Two Noble Kinsmen.*

Both the comedies and the romances also erect barriers to young love very different from the initial prohibition. First, lovers create problems for themselves through their own defects. Katherine's shrewishness in *The Taming of the Shrew* belongs here, but more frequently the difficulty is the failings of men. Proteus comes close to raping Silvia in *The Two Gentlemen of Verona.* Similarly, in *Cardenio,* Ferdinando/Theobald promises his love to Dorotea/Violante, rapes her, abandons her for Luscinda/Leonora, and later abducts Luscinda/Leonora from a nunnery. Just as Claudio doesn't question the slanderous attack on Hero's sexual virtue in *Much Ado About Nothing,* so Posthumus believes the worst of Innogen in *Cymbeline*—outdoing Claudio, however, by ordering his wife's death. In *The Winter's Tale,* King Leontes does not need to be deceived: for no reason he becomes convinced that his wife, Hermione, has been unfaithful. A second barrier is very different, however. The triumph of heterosexual love entails the loss of something valuable, intimacy with another member of one's own sex. In *The Merchant of Venice,* Bassanio must learn to choose Portia over Antonio. In *The Winter's Tale,* Polixenes nostalgically recalls the innocence of his youthful friendship with Leontes. And in *The Two Noble Kinsmen,* the mere sight of Emilia tears apart the kinsmen, Palamon and Arcite, while Emilia herself sadly recalls her childhood love for Flavina, who died when the two girls were eleven.

Nonetheless, the pastoral experience as a whole usually leads to festivity and reconciliation at a deeper level that, through forgiveness, transforms character and restores community. The concluding reconciliation enables some of the characters to get more than they deserve. Just as Proteus is allowed to marry Julia in *The Two Gentlemen of Verona,* Fernando/Henriquez is paired off with Dorotea/Violante in *Cardenio.* Claudio wins Hero in *Much Ado About Nothing,* Posthumus regains Innogen in *Cymbeline,* and Leontes recovers Hermione in *The Winter's Tale.* While the plot mechanisms of the concluding resolutions tend to strain credulity, the happy outcome reveals the power of timely human intervention—whether of Portia in *The Merchant of Venice,* Duke Vincentio in *Measure for Measure,* Prospero in *The Tempest,* or Henry VIII in *All Is True.*

If comedy and romance share so many characteristics, where are the distinctive qualities of romance to be found? One answer lies in the intervening experience of tragedy. During the 1590s, Shakespeare wrote the majority of his romantic comedies. For most of the next decade, he focused on tragedy. The romances depart from the romantic comedies in their incorporation of a tragic perspective, which in most instances is ultimately transcended. Both the storms and the redemptive reconciliation of father and daughter in *Pericles* hark back to *King Lear,* a work that is itself based on a dramatic romance and that seems headed in the

*Le Naufrage (The Shipwreck)* Etching by Claude Lorrain (1600–82).

same direction until catastrophe intervenes. The jealousy of Posthumus in *Cymbeline* and of Leontes in *The Winter's Tale* reprises the fatal behavior of Othello. *All Is True* seems to have raided *Macbeth* for its Porter at the christening of the baby Elizabeth in Act 5. *The Tempest* echoes *Richard II, Julius Caesar, Hamlet,* and *Macbeth* in its concern with usurpation, *Hamlet* in its recourse to a play within a play, and *Othello* and *King Lear* in its dramatization of a father's difficulty in letting go of his daughter. In *The Two Noble Kinsmen,* both Emilia's comparison of pictures and the Jailer's Daughter's madness go back to *Hamlet,* the Daughter's willow song is borrowed from Desdemona in *Othello,* and the Doctor's effort to cure her and the enigmatic prophecies that provide false comfort to the protagonists come from *Macbeth.*

Shakespeare's incorporation of tragic elements in the romances often represents less a break with comedy than a shift in relative weight. Thus, the storm and shipwreck that wash Viola up on the coast of Illyria in *Twelfth Night* anticipate similar scenes not just in *Pericles* but also in *The Winter's Tale* and *The Tempest.* Similarly, the threat of rape that Silvia faces in *The Two Gentlemen of Verona* returns not only for Dorotea/Violante in *Cardenio* but also for Marina in *Pericles,* Innogen in *Cymbeline,* and Miranda in *The Tempest.*

But sometimes in the romances, tragedy is felt more strongly—as a rupture rather than a shift. This is true in the case of mortality—rare in the comedies, routine in the romances. The incestuous Antiochus and his Daughter, like Cleon and his murderous wife, Dionyza, are spectacularly dispatched in *Pericles.* In *Cymbeline,* death comes to both the murderous Queen and her sexually predatory son, Cloten. In *The Winter's Tale,* Leontes' jealousy costs him both his son and Antigonus, the courtier who saves Leontes' daughter, Perdita, from death only at the expense of his own life. In *Cardenio,* a hearse comes by at a crucial moment. *All Is True* chronicles the decline and death of the possibly treasonous Duke of Buckingham, the virtuous Katherine of Aragon, and the corrupt Cardinal Wolsey. It celebrates the corresponding rise of Cromwell, More, Cranmer, and Anne Boleyn, all of whom, however—as at least some of the audience would have known—went on to meet violent deaths as a result of the bloody controversy between Protestants and Catholics in sixteenth-century England. And in *The Two Noble Kinsmen,* only one of the kinsmen can survive: Arcite, the apparent victor over Palamon in a struggle to the death, is fatally injured when thrown from his horse.

While some romance characters die, others experience a quasi-ritualistic symbolic or metaphorical death. This is the fate of Thaisa and Marina in *Pericles;* Innogen in *Cymbeline;* Perdita and Hermione in *The Winter's Tale;* Prospero, Miranda, and Ferdinand in *The Tempest;* Cardenio/Julio in *Cardenio;* and Palamon in *The Two Noble Kinsmen.* The characteristic romance movement from symbolic death to spiritual rebirth is hardly automatic, however. First, it requires time. The passage of the years is necessary if the tragic dimension of life is to be overcome. In general, the romances possess far greater temporal spans than the romantic comedies. In *Pericles* and *The Winter's Tale,* events stretch out over the better part of a generation. *Cymbeline* and *The Tempest* conjure up crucial experiences in the past from the perspective of the present. Reversing the strategy of these two plays, *All Is True* anticipates the supposed triumphs of the audience's present but the play's future from the perspective of the audience's past but the play's present.

Emphasis on the workings of time is tied to a shift in the portrayal of virtuous young women. Shakespeare's romance heroines are less involved in getting their men than are their predecessors in the comedies, and their prospective or reconstituted marriages are less crucial to the restoration of the community. More generally, compared to the comedies the romances arguably feature fewer multiple-plot narratives and certainly stage fewer multiple-marriage conclusions. Both the reduced activity of these women and the reduced significance of their marriages may seem paradoxical, since the redemptive role of the romance heroines tends to exceed that of their predecessors in romantic comedy. But whatever their intentions, that role is directed less toward marriage than toward intergenerational restoration, and usually in particular toward the repair of their parents' suffering or misdeeds. An older man may recover both wife and daughter (Pericles, Leontes in *The Winter's Tale*), a daughter and two sons (Cymbeline), or a son (Alonso in *The Tempest*). Although Marina delivers her father, Pericles, from his misery, that moment of deliverance is just a prelude to the actual climax, in which Pericles is reunited with his wife, Thaisa, while Marina stands mutely by. Similarly, *The Winter's Tale* seems headed toward Perdita's return to the court of her father, Leontes, but the anticipated occasion is narrated rather than dramatized so that the stage can be reserved for the miraculous revival of the statue of her mother, Hermione, and hence for the reconciliation of father and mother, of husband and wife, while Perdita characteristically stands silently by. In *Cymbeline,* Innogen's reconciliation with husband and father alike after comparatively brief separations is followed by Cymbeline's recovery of his long-lost sons, Guiderius and Arviragus. In *The Tempest,* however important the dynastic implications of Miranda's upcoming marriage to Ferdinand may be, the work's conclusion is devoted primarily to her father Prospero's settling of accounts with men of his own age. Finally, rather than displacing the young woman's impact back to the previous generation, *All Is True* projects it forward to the next one. Anne Boleyn matters only as the mother of the future Queen Elizabeth, whose reign unfolds long after the end of the play.

This temporal, intergenerational logic may be understood structurally. *The Winter's Tale* perhaps represents the paradigmatic case. Although in Shakespeare's career comedy precedes tragedy, in this play it is the other way around. The first three acts revive *Othello,* the fourth *As You Like It.* A generation passes between these two movements of the plot. In other words, courtly tragedy is ultimately set in the past, so that its crimes and errors can be redeemed by pastoral comedy, peopled with the rural lower classes, located in the present. The rebirth, recognition, and reconciliation of Act 5 are made possible by the preceding sequence. One kind of variation on this pattern appears in both *Cymbeline* and *The Tempest.* The represented action is confined to the present, but part of what happens in *Cymbeline* and all of what happens in *The Tempest* depend on events as remote as those of the opening acts of *The Winter's Tale.* In all three instances, the potentially tragic moment is located at the birth or during the very early childhood of the youths who, now on the verge of adulthood, will prove crucial to the transcendence of tragedy. In still another variation on the paradigm of *The Winter's*

*Tale, Pericles* and *All Is True* present a sequence of minitragedies. In *Pericles,* these concern both the protagonist and his victimizers, the crucial difference being that Pericles' suffering can be overcome after a generation, whereas the others simply meet their deserved fate. The multiple tragedies of *All Is True* dramatize the fall of one illustrious personage after another from a position of eminence, with the jump forward in time relegated to a concluding prophecy inspired by the birth of the future Queen Elizabeth. Finally, *The Two Noble Kinsmen,* like *The Winter's Tale,* combines a relatively tragic work with a comic one. Like *Troilus and Cressida,* it draws on Chaucer for an account of violently destructive sexuality. Like *A Midsummer Night's Dream,* as we've seen, it offers a popular theatrical performance in the context of Theseus and Hippolyta's wedding. Here, however, the order seems to replicate, not reverse, that of Shakespeare's career. Rather than *A Midsummer Night's Dream* lightening the experience of *Troilus and Cressida,* the latter play seems to darken the outlook of the former.

As these examples suggest, the recapitulation characteristic of the romances places enormous structural pressure on the dramatic narrative. In the 1580s, Sidney's *Apology for Poetry* criticized tragicomedy for its violation of morally appropriate emotional effects in its indifference to the classical separation of styles—of comedy from tragedy.

> But besides these gross absurdities, how all their plays be neither right tragedies, nor right comedies, mingling kings and clowns, not because the matter so carrieth it, but thrust in clowns by head and shoulders, to play a part in majestical matters, with decency nor discretion, so as neither the admiration and commiseration, nor the right sportfulness, is by their mongrel tragicomedy obtained.

This criticism sounds as if it were directed toward Shakespearean drama in general. Sidney also disparages romantic drama for its violation of probability in its indifference to the classical unities of time (a play should last no more than a day) and place (it should take place in a single location).

> You shall have Asia of the one side, and Afric of the other . . . the player, when he cometh in, must ever begin with telling where he is, or else the tale will not be conceived. . . . By and by we hear news of shipwreck. . . . Upon the back of that comes out a hideous monster, . . . and then the miserable beholders are bound to take it for a cave. While in the meantime two armies fly in, represented with four swords and bucklers, and then what hard heart will not receive it for a pitched field? . . . two young princes fall in love. After many traverses, she is got with child, delivered of a fair boy; he is lost, groweth a man, falls in love, and is ready to get another child; and all this in two hours' space.

Here, it is as if Sidney were attacking the late plays in particular—Asia and Africa in *Antony and Cleopatra* (1606–07) and *Pericles;* shipwreck in *Pericles* and *The Tempest;* the hideous monster also in *The Tempest;* the cave in *Cymbeline* and *The Tempest;* the armies in *Antony and Cleopatra, Coriolanus* (1608), and *Cymbeline;* the love affairs followed by children lost for a generation in *Pericles, Cymbeline,* and *The Winter's Tale.*

A generation later Ben Jonson actually did attack Shakespeare's own romances on similar grounds. (See the introductions to *Pericles* and *The Winter's Tale.*) It is easy to see why. Shakespeare goes out of his way to flaunt the primitivism of his materials and methods. Beyond employing Gower as narrator, *Pericles* repeatedly resorts to the outmoded dramatic device of the dumb show. *The Winter's Tale* ostentatiously rings out the old by having Antigonus, savior of Perdita, "*Exit, pursued by a bear*" (3.3.57, stage direction). It brings in the new by sending Time on stage as a Chorus to apologize for the sixteen-year gap in the action. *Cymbeline* goes well beyond the normal range of Shakespearean anachronism by combining ancient Britain, classical Rome, and Renaissance Italy. In the long final-recognition scene, Shakespeare delays the improbable revelations to such an extent that the audience, although more in the know than the characters, sympathizes with Cymbeline's impatience:

I had rather thou shouldst live while nature will
Than die ere I hear more. Strive, man, and speak.
(5.6.151–52)

I stand on fire.
Come to the matter.
(5.6.168–69)

Nay, nay, to th' purpose.
(5.6.178)

In *The Tempest,* where adherence to the unities of time and place requires Prospero to narrate the back story to his daughter Miranda, the conventionality of the device is again laid bare, as Prospero repeatedly accuses Miranda of not listening: "Dost thou attend me?" "Thou attend'st not!" "Dost thou hear?" (1.2.78, 87, 106). And earlier in the same scene, the audience learns that the play's opening storm is nothing more than a trick of the magician's art—nothing more, that is, than a trick of the dramatist's art.

In other words, much of the sophistication of the romances consists in Shakespeare's deliberate recourse to a threadbare stagecraft, in his undermining of the illusion of reality. He wants the audience to see and hear the creaking machinery, to recognize the labor of incorporating incompatible experiences, and nonetheless to find something moving and new. This is an art, however, that for all its artificiality also cooperates with the natural world. But the character of the cooperation between art and nature remains unclear. In Act 4 of *The Winter's Tale,* Perdita speaks against the improvement of nature by art in the cultivation of flowers. King Polixenes disagrees, arguing that

we marry
A gentler scion to the wildest stock,
And make conceive a bark of baser kind
By bud of nobler race.
(4.4.92–95)

But when he discovers that his son is in love with Perdita, whom he believes to be a shepherdess, he violently opposes the marriage of a "gentler scion to the wildest stock" that he has just advocated.

The conflict between Polixenes and Perdita points away from impersonal structures. In the romances, regeneration depends on more than time and artful dramaturgy. It requires a patience often accompanied by suffering and sometimes by repentance. Wronged aristocrats—Belarius in *Cymbeline,* Prospero in *The Tempest*—must spend the better part of a generation in distant rural exile from the court. Pericles is separated from his daughter for a similar period of time, during the last part of which he also grieves over her, believing her dead. The time of mourning lasts an entire generation for Leontes, who justly holds himself responsible for the real death of his son, the supposed death of his daughter, and the apparent death of his wife in *The Winter's Tale.* In *Cymbeline,* Posthumus has to confront his guilt for what he believes is the murder of his wife. And much the same goes for Fernando/Henriquez in *Cardenio.*

The complement of remorse is a self-mastery on the part of the wronged characters that issues in forgiveness far more difficult to offer than in the romantic comedies because there is so much more to forgive. This is the forgiveness Wolsey receives from his enemies at the moment of his fall in *All Is True.* Such forgiveness is linked to the acceptance of social responsibility near the end of *The Tempest,* when in a gesture at once appalling, enigmatic, and moving, Prospero says of the semihuman Caliban, native of the island and would-be rapist of Prospero's daughter and murderer of Prospero himself, "This thing of darkness I / Acknowledge mine" (5.1.278–79). The acknowledgment here seems connected to Prospero's concluding renunciation of magic, emphasis on his own weakness, and consequent humility in the Epilogue he delivers, where the standard appeal for the audience's benevolence takes a sudden religious turn:

> And my ending is despair
> Unless I be relieved by prayer,
> Which pierces so, that it assaults
> Mercy itself, and frees all faults.
> As you from crimes would pardoned be,
> Let your indulgence set me free.
>
> (lines 15–20)

The moment is significant because Prospero is more in control of his own destiny than is any other character in Shakespeare. But in the end, even he must depend on others. The terms of that dependence, moreover, only underscore the infirmity of mortal creatures. Far more than the romantic comedies, the romances reduce the efficacy of human agency. Their virtuous, redemptive young women are less activist than emblematic. They are part of the pattern rather than its creator. Their symbolic names tell the story: in *Pericles*, Marina is of the sea; in *The Winter's Tale*, Perdita is lost; and in *The Tempest*, Miranda is to be wondered at.

All of these features of the romances—violence and literal or metaphorical death, the passage of time, an intergenerational orientation, suffering and repentance, forgiveness and the acknowledgment of human frailty—result in a more encompassing final reconciliation than in the romantic comedies. In those earlier plays, one or two characters often remain unincorporated at the end, less because they are cast out than because they find the terms of inclusion unpalatable. Shakespeare thereby signals the incomplete character of his festive endings, the continuing presence of melancholy, critique, skepticism, or isolation. In the romances, insistence on the partial, provisional nature of the resolution is carried by the previous losses, including, of course, death itself. Hence, all survivors are included regardless of their prior behavior and regardless of whether they have undergone a long period of repentance (Leontes in *The Winter's Tale*), only belatedly confessed their sins (Giacomo, slanderer of Innogen in *Cymbeline*), or not reformed at all (Antonio and Sebastian, murderous usurpers in *The Tempest*; arguably Gardiner, the overly zealous Catholic bishop of *All Is True*).

This inclusive spirit is possible because in the romances' conclusions the natural world with which art cooperates seems connected with an invisible supernatural reality. Like the incorporation of tragedy and the long temporal perspective, the providential guidance of mortal affairs is a signature of Shakespearean romance. The plays opt for resolutions that are rationally inexplicable (*The Winter's Tale, The Tempest*), accessible only through inspired Christian prophecy (*All Is True*), produced by luck but retrospectively coded as Christian providence (*Cardenio*), or manifestly generated by divine intervention that is classical in nomenclature (Diana in *Pericles*; Jupiter in *Cymbeline*; Mars, Venus, and Diana in *The Two Noble Kinsmen*) but Christian in nature (except, perhaps, in *The Two Noble Kinsmen*). The characters wander in a spiritual labyrinth, often stumbling as they go. But the fall is usually a fortunate one, a *felix culpa* that replicates the foundational failure of Adam and Eve, opening the way to earthly redemption and a fleeting glimpse of eternal reality. This vision, often in the form of a dream, is granted only to a character who strives to be worthy of it. Yet the plays suggest that these efforts alone may not be enough. It is the intertwining of divine and human agency that leads to the comic resolution.

Behind this outlook lies the dramaturgy of late-sixteenth-century Italy, based in the religious movement known as the Catholic Counter-Reformation. That dramaturgy also drew on a philosophical tradition known today as Renaissance Neoplatonism for a mystical belief in the unity of opposites, the cosmic harmony that gives meaning to the apparently random vicissitudes of earthly existence. This does not necessarily imply that the romances are Catholic in outlook. It does mean that "the music of the spheres"

Venus and Jupiter (astride an eagle). Engraving by Philips Galle (1585). The classical deities play crucial roles in the resolutions of *Pericles, Cymbeline,* and *The Two Noble Kinsmen.*

(*Pericles,* Scene 21, line 214), indication of divine harmony, is audible to the privileged. It is heard by Pericles ("I hear most heav'nly music," Scene 21, line 218). Cardenio/Julio believes he detects it in the singing of Dorotea/Violante. The revival of Hermione at the end of *The Winter's Tale* is accompanied by music. So, too, is Posthumus's vision of his family in *Cymbeline* and the appearance of the classical deities in *The Tempest.* "Some heavenly music" brings the shipwrecked nobility to their senses in Prospero's charmed circle toward the end of the same play (5.1.52). And music is also heard at the altars of Venus and Diana in Act 5 of *The Two Noble Kinsmen.*

In all these respects, the romances represent a logical development of Shakespeare's earlier dramatic practice and arguably the culmination of his career in the theater. They are also part of a more general movement on the English stage, although it is possible that Shakespeare himself initiated that movement. The romances seem to respond to a series of additional developments, however. One is institutional. In 1608, Shakespeare's company began performing during the winter at the Blackfriars, an indoor, "private" theater that catered to a more uniformly upscale audience than the patrons of the outdoor, "public" Globe, where the King's Men had been playing since 1599. The Blackfriars provided more elaborate theatrical machinery than was available in an open-air theater, and some of the romances take advantage of these resources. For instance, *The Tempest* and *All Is True* adapt the masque, a newly fashionable court theatrical that demanded complex special effects. The shift toward the Blackfriars may be seen as part of an elitist turn in Shakespeare's late plays, also noticeable in the declining role of the clown, a characteristic figure in the romantic comedies often integral to a subplot that comments on the central action. Yet members of the lower classes continue to be prominent in the romances. Such figures include the fishermen and the managers of the house of prostitution in *Pericles;* the Old Shepherd, the Clown, and Autolycus in *The Winter's Tale;* the Boatswain, Caliban, Stefano, and Trinculo in *The Tempest;* the Citizens, the shepherds, and their vicious but witty Master in *Cardenio;* the Porter and unruly citizens in *All Is True;* and the Jailer's Daughter, in addition to the country actors in *The Two Noble Kinsmen.* Equally important, *Pericles,* the earliest of the romances, predates the King's

Men's lease of the Blackfriars. The company continued to use the Globe in the warmer months, and it is certain that *The Winter's Tale* was performed there in 1611 and *All Is True* in 1613. In short, it is easy to make too much of the distinction between playhouses and probably best to view romance as an institutionally transitional form, with one foot in the "public" theater and the other in the "private."

A second motive behind the romances may be biographical. In 1607, Shakespeare's daughter Susanna got married. The next year she had a daughter, Elizabeth, and Shakespeare's own mother died. Thus, the romances coincide with a generational shift in the dramatist's family. The emphasis in the plays on daughters who both marry and help redeem their aging fathers seems compatible with this moment. So, too, does the celebration of the birth of a baby Elizabeth at the end of *All Is True*.

Political changes may also have influenced the romances. Upon assuming the throne in 1603, King James placed each of London's professional acting troupes under the patronage of a member of his immediate family. As the most successful of these troupes, Shakespeare's company, the Lord Chamberlain's Men, became the King's Men. The late plays seem to register this increased proximity to the crown. Just as the romantic comedies shift the focus from the middle class of New Comedy to the aristocracy, so the romances further elevate the social status of the protagonists by concerning themselves with royalty—Pericles, Prince of Tyre; Cymbeline, King of Britain; Leontes, King of Sicilia, in *The Winter's Tale*; Prospero, Duke of Milan, in *The Tempest*; Henry VIII, King of England, in *All Is True*; Theseus, Duke of Athens, in *The Two Noble Kinsmen*; and, more ambiguously, Duke Angelo and his elder son, Roderick, in *Cardenio*. The attention to the younger generation in relation to the older may also respond to the cult that grew up around James's children. The Welsh setting of the cave of Guiderius and Arviragus, Cym-

beline's lost sons, may glance at the 1610 investiture of James's first son, Henry, as Prince of Wales. *All Is True* enthusiastically alludes to the marriage of James's daughter Elizabeth in 1613. Perhaps the same event lies behind the far more somber concluding union of Emilia and Palamon in *The Two Noble Kinsmen*, in this case, however, with Arcite's apparently meaningless fatal fall paralleling the death the previous year of her brother Henry, symbol of the revival of chivalry and martial valor that the play nostalgically evokes. It is unclear if these allusions are flattering to the royal family. And, of course, the point is not to ascertain whether the romances are secretly allegories of that family—they are not—but to understand that the family's prominence, following the long rule of the unmarried and childless Queen Elizabeth, could have helped turn Shakespeare's imagination in a new direction.

The Mediterranean, western Europe, and the northwest coast of Africa. By Joan Oliva (fl. 1580–1615).

Mapping the New World. From Americae sive quartae orbis partis nova et exactissima descriptio, engraved by Hieronymous Cock (1562).

Finally, the romances seem to meditate upon imperial expansion. English merchant ships had aggressively entered the Mediterranean in the 1570s, trading directly with the Ottoman Empire and thereby cutting into Venice's traditional economic dominance in the region. Although many of Shakespeare's plays throughout his career are set in and around the Mediterranean, beginning with *Antony and Cleopatra* (1606) all of them with the exception of *All Is True* are partly or wholly located there. Western European extracontinental voyages—around Africa to India, across the Atlantic to America, and, soon, around the world—had begun in the late fifteenth century, and references to distant lands, peoples, and products are dotted throughout Shakespeare's oeuvre. Yet the foundation of England's first permanent colony in the New World at Jamestown in 1607 apparently sharpened the playwright's interest in the topic. Accordingly, the romances' Mediterranean voyages sometimes feel as if they were also American ones. Unmistakable allusions are rare, however. *All Is True* overtly refers to the New World. The island of *The Tempest,* although clearly located in the Mediterranean, is also connected with Bermuda, and in Caliban it possesses a character whose name is a near anagram of cannibal. Shakespeare would have made the link to America from reading Michel de Montaigne's essay "Of Cannibals" (1580). Prospero colonizes the island and effectively enslaves Caliban, its native, but leaves it behind at the end of the play. Critics have accordingly debated the work's relationship to colonialism. One perspective on this issue is suggested by Thomas More's *Utopia* (1516), which was itself inspired by the European encounter with America and its peoples. In *The Tempest,* the good-hearted, loyal Gonzalo, cast upon the island, presents a utopian vision that is effectively ridiculed by the most treacherous characters in the play. But the redemptive structure of *The Tempest* and the other romances, the providential triumph over adversity following a long period of suffering, is itself a utopian scenario. This scenario distinguishes the late plays from their comic predecessors. If America significantly influences the romances, it does so not through incidental references but at the level of conceptual and dramatic structure.

Most discussions of the romances concentrate on *Pericles, Cymbeline, The Winter's Tale,* and *The Tempest*—and with good reason. Of Shakespeare's three subsequent plays, one is lost (*Cardenio*), another is a history play (*All Is True*), and the third seems very different from the four standard romances (*The Two Noble Kinsmen*). Yet in one obvious respect, the three plays belong together. As already noted, *Cardenio, All Is True,* and *The Two Noble Kinsmen* all are collaborations with Fletcher. English Renaissance playwrights routinely coauthored plays, and early and late in his career Shakespeare was no exception. By 1595, he had probably collaborated on at least *Titus Andronicus, Sir Thomas More,* and *Edward III;* after 1605, he jointly wrote *Timon of Athens* and, as we have seen, *Pericles, Cardenio, All Is True,* and *The Two Noble Kinsmen.* Coauthored works arguably have a less uniformly "Shakespearean" quality than the plays that Shakespeare composed by himself. One effect of attending to the final three plays, then, is to loosen the definition of the romances, to align them with the more general interest in romantic tragicomedy on the English stage at the time, and to underscore the uniquenesss of each of the late plays, the extent to which each deviates from the norms of even such capacious generic categories as romance or tragicomedy.

The Fletcherian collaborations might also be seen as a second stage of Shakespearean romance. Although these last plays share with the earlier romances the assertion of a providential plan, they transmute or eliminate the long temporal vistas previously necessary to the transcendence of tragedy. The final three works thus reduce the thematic depth of divine guidance, the sense that redemption is granted for effort, patience, and suffering, that though the bad may not always be punished, the good are always rewarded. The *Cardenio* story urges patience and the need to trust in time, but the assertions are metaphorical: things are quickly tidied up. *The Two Noble Kinsmen* offers a world of timeless serenity when Palamon and Arcite are first imprisoned, but the ordinary world of time means suffering without redemption. The two works lack the vertical perspective of the preceding romances, instead reverting to the horizontal structure of the still earlier problem plays. *All Is True* seems different. The passage of the years is instrumental in delivering the happy ending, as in the first four romances. But for whom is the ending happy? Not for anyone who has suffered along the way, with the limited and temporary exception of Archbishop Cranmer. Certainly not for Henry VIII, who always gets what he wants, who both does and does not seem responsible for what goes wrong, and whose tortured conscience over his marriage to Katherine is treated with amused skepticism. In other words, *All Is True* is a romance on the model of the earlier plays only if its protagonist is England itself. This plausible conclusion implies, however, the workings of a more austerely impersonal providence than is found in *Pericles, Cymbeline, The Winter's Tale,* and *The Tempest.*

What is true of time also holds for space. The problematic providentialism and foreshortened temporality of the final three plays may be connected to a geographical narrowing of the plot. Each of these works is confined to a single country. Gone, except metaphorically, are the perilous sea journeys of the immediately preceding years. Spatial breadth thus goes the way of temporal depth. The characters' problems are as grave as those in the previous romances, but both human and providential action seems constricted. These landlocked plays may suggest that the initial enthusiasm over the Virginia colony proved difficult to sustain. In retrospect, *The Tempest* appears both to justify and repudiate colonialism. Prospero's decision to leave the island parallels his rejection of magic: both acknowledge limits. Thereafter, although the colonial enterprise may be celebrated, as it is in *All Is True*, it is no longer represented. *Cardenio, All Is True,* and *The Two Noble Kinsmen* accordingly constitute a second movement within Shakespearean romance that reconfigures the entire sequence of plays that begins with *Pericles*.

The same point can be made of the characterization. In *The Tempest*, Prospero, despite his failings, is clearly associated with providence. In the succeeding plays, he is replaced by far weaker providential figures—Duke Angelo in *Cardenio*; Henry VIII in *All Is True*; Duke Theseus in *The Two Noble Kinsmen*. Similarly, daughters lose their redemptive role. Their marriages fail to connote the projection forward, much less the dynastic projection forward, of the family in time. In *Cardenio*, although the fathers are gladdened by the return of their children, the emotional force of the resolution arises overwhelmingly from the pairing off of the young lovers. In *The Two Noble Kinsmen*, Emilia becomes an object of contention and hence a source of destruction rather than reconciliation. Even Elizabeth doesn't save Henry in *All Is True*. He doesn't need saving, and in any case she's a mere babe at the end of the play and never marries. *All Is True* instead proceeds by homonyms, celebrating the marriage of King James's daughter Elizabeth as a substitute for actual familial continuity.

Symptomatically, the actual weddings are transformed from festive into tearful affairs. The hearse in *Cardenio* arrives just before the lovers' reunion. Henry's marriage to Anne in *All Is True* entails the rejection of Katherine and in the event her death. *The Two Noble Kinsmen* opens with the interruption of Theseus and Hippolyta's nuptials by the lamentations of the three widowed queens, is followed by the appearance of Palamon and Arcite on "two hearses" (biers, 1.4.0 s.d.), and ends by echoing its beginning, as the marriage of Palamon and Emilia competes with the mourning for Arcite. The scaling back of the young women's symbolic significance also accords with a casual attitude toward premarital sex. If *Cardenio* follows Cervantes, Dorotea consents to intercourse because she believes the false promises of a cad; if it corresponds to Theobald, she is raped. Either way, she loses her virginity. In the subplot of *The Two Noble Kinsmen*, the Doctor cures the Jailer's Daughter of madness by sending her to bed with someone she mistakenly believes to be Palamon. And in *All Is True*, Anne Boleyn's sexual modesty is treated with irreverence by the Old Lady who waits on her— an irreverence the audience is invited to share.

The last three plays also offer a darker view of violence and death than the previous romances. In *The Tempest*, no one dies. The same is true of *Cardenio*. But the near rape of Miranda by Caliban is replaced by the real rape of Dorotea/Violante by Fernando/Henriquez—a rape for which the perpetrator suffers mild pangs of conscience, fleeting public embarrassment, and the felicity of familial approval and wedded bliss. In *Pericles* and *Cymbeline*, although all who are vicious do not necessarily die, all who die are necessarily vicious. In *The Winter's Tale*, Leontes' son perishes because Leontes must be punished, and Antigonus dies because he has nobly risked everything to save Leontes' daughter, Perdita. Here, too, then, death is part of an ethical calculus. In *All Is True*, however, morality and mortality are randomly related. Buckingham, Wolsey, and Katherine must be removed so that Elizabeth can come to power. Katherine is the finest person in the play, but her death represents neither a voluntary sacrifice for the benefit of England nor a punishment of Henry for his misdeeds. And in *The Two Noble Kinsmen*, Palamon and Arcite seem morally equivalent. Hence, Arcite's death feels at best random, at worst a cruel trick played by providence on shell-shocked mortals. Theseus's assertion of divine wisdom accordingly seems desperate and unconvincing.

In short, the final three plays reveal a growing pessimism, a bleaker outlook, a grimmer universe, a declining belief in the possibility of transcending tragedy. It is unclear how this development relates to the apparently greater tolerance for Catholicism suggested by the Spanish setting of *Cardenio*, unique in Shakespeare's oeuvre, and the admiring treatment of Katherine of Aragon in *All Is True*. Perhaps the point is that all is true, that everyone is right. Both Katherine and Anne are celebrated. But Anne's victory comes in this world, Katherine's only in the next. In other words, this is merely a disguised form of the either-or logic characteristic of all three of the final plays: either Anne or Katherine, either Palamon or Arcite, either Protestants or Catholics. And in an additional sign of the reduced capaciousness of these works, their inability to integrate all the virtuous characters and more, the losers must die.

Finally, the successive views presented here of Shakespearean romance—as a continuation of the comedies, as a distinct and coherent category, and as an internally divided one—are by no means incompatible. They merely provide different ways into the subject. A broad approach to the romances should be open to all of these perspectives—and more.

## SELECTED BIBLIOGRAPHY

Adelman, Janet. *Suffocating Mothers: Fantasies of Maternal Origin in Shakespeare's Plays, "Hamlet" to "The Tempest."* New York: Routledge, 1992. 193–238. The four main romances as efforts to recover the ideal parental couple lost in the tragedies that must nonetheless choose, alternately, either the mother or the father.

Bloom, Harold. *Shakespeare: The Invention of the Human.* New York: Riverhead, 1998. A major critic's personal, sometimes deliberately idiosyncratic, play-by-play analysis that rejects generic categorization of the four main romances, *All Is True* (*Henry VIII*), and *The Two Noble Kinsmen.*

Brown, John Russell, ed. *Later Shakespeare.* New York: St. Martin's, 1967. Ten essays, partly on the late tragedies but mainly on the four main romances and *All Is True* (*Henry VIII*), including both general approaches to the plays from diverse perspectives and readings of individual works.

Frye, Northrop. *A Natural Perspective: The Development of Shakespearean Comedy and Romance.* New York: Harcourt, Brace and World, 1965. Important argument for continuity between the romantic comedies and the romances.

Henke, Robert. *Pastoral Transformations: Italian Tragicomedy and Shakespeare's Late Plays.* Newark: University of Delaware Press, 1997. Compares Italian pastoral tragicomedy to *Cymbeline, The Winter's Tale,* and *The Tempest,* focusing primarily on parallels, while also attending to certain influences.

Jordan, Constance. *Shakespeare's Monarchies: Ruler and Subject in the Romances.* Ithaca, N.Y.: Cornell University Press, 1997. The four main romances as meditations on contemporary debates over the power of the crown, depicting misrule by the monarch and the political and psychological corrections necessary to restore proper government.

Kay, Carol McGinnis, and Henry E. Jacobs, eds. *Shakespeare's Romances Reconsidered.* Lincoln: University of Nebraska Press, 1978. Eleven essays from the 1970s, including readings of individual plays, comparisons to the work of other dramatists, and general studies of Shakespearean romance, with consideration of fathers and daughters and the relation of romance to masque (Frye, Leech), among other topics.

Leggatt, Alexander, ed. *The Cambridge Companion to Shakespearean Comedy.* Cambridge, Eng.: Cambridge University Press, 2002. Essays by Clubb on Italian backgrounds of romantic comedy and romance, and by O'Connell on the innovations of romance.

Palfrey, Simon. *Late Shakespeare: A New World of Words.* Oxford: Clarendon Press, 1997. Argues against conventional readings that stress the providentialism, elitism, and royalism of the four main romances in favor of emphasis on verbal, generic, and political complexity and dissonance.

Richards, Jennifer, and James Knowles, ed. *Shakespeare's Late Plays: New Readings.* Edinburgh: Edinburgh University Press, 1999. A collection distinctive for its insistence on taking into account not only the four standard romances but also the three collaborations with Fletcher—*The Two Noble Kinsmen, All Is True,* and *Cardenio.*

# ROMANCES

ROMANCES

# Pericles, Prince of Tyre:
## *A Reconstructed Text*

*Pericles, Prince of Tyre* (1607–08) was one of the most popular plays of its time and has proven effective in modern productions as well. Coherent and innovative, it brought a new dramatic genre—romance—into Shakespeare's work and, arguably, onto the English stage in general. As a text to be read, however, *Pericles* has sometimes proven more problematic. It is not clear whether the difficulty is intrinsic to the play or results from an almost irresistible but partly mistaken tendency to interpret it in light of Shakespeare's earlier works and thus to make unwarranted assumptions about plot, characterization, morality, dramaturgy, and style. Does the romance pattern fully succeed in mastering the messiness of the play's materials? Does the play raise but not resolve a series of social, political, and sexual anxieties, despite its considerable structural and thematic unity? Are these even the right questions to ask?

Shakespeare's younger contemporary Ben Jonson spoke for many subsequent critics in disparaging *Pericles* as "a mouldy tale . . . and stale," and in attributing its success on the stage to its use of "scraps out of every dish." It is easy to see what Jonson is talking about. In *Pericles,* a King adorns his palace walls with the skulls of his victims. A princess commits incest with her father. Another princess is kidnapped by pirates and sold to a brothel. Famine brings a city to its knees. An entire crew is lost in a tumultuous storm. Two royal families are sent to fiery destruction. And Pericles is almost deposed by his restless nobility.

From the perspective of genre, *Pericles* seems to enact a transition from one kind of romance to another. Pericles first looks like a knight-errant willing to risk death in his quest to win the beautiful maiden. But this standard mode of medieval romance quickly gives way to the manner of late antique Greek romance, in which the faithful and virtuous lovers must suffer separation and all manner of misfortune before their ultimate, triumphant reunion. Characteristically, then, Pericles does not act; he is acted upon. Bad things (as well as good) just keep happening to him. Every member of his family narrowly escapes death: two evade assassins sent by murderous monarchs, and the third survives burial at sea. Each is reported dead, only to experience apparently miraculous rebirth. The play seems consciously to eschew the complex probing of the protagonist's psyche that marks Shakespeare's immediately preceding tragic period in favor of clear-cut moral oppositions and an emphatic poetic justice. By the end of *Pericles,* the good have been rewarded and the bad annihilated, but, for the most part, not as a result of the protagonist's own efforts.

Indeed, Pericles does not even get to act out significant portions of his own destiny before the audience. Much of the story is told by Gower, the onstage presence of the fourteenth-century writer John Gower, whose major work, *Confessio Amantis,* is the most important direct source of *Pericles.* The eighth book of this verse narrative is devoted primarily to the tale of Apollonius of Tyre, which, via medieval intermediaries dating back to a fifth- or sixth-century Latin text, derives from a now-lost late classical Latin or, more probably, Greek romance influenced by *The Odyssey.* A different route through the medieval sources, this time incorporating the lives of early Christian saints who suffered persecution in brothels, leads to the other proximate source of the play, Laurence Twine's *Patterne of Painefull Adventures* (written by 1576; published 1594?). *Pericles* is the first dramatization of these lengthy traditions. The shift in the protagonist's name from "Apollonius" to "Pericles" may derive from still other strains in the Apollonius tradition; from

Woodcut of John Gower, from the title page of *The Painfull Adventures of Pericles Prince of Tyre*, by George Wilkins (1608).

Sir Philip Sidney's *Arcadia* (1590), one of whose protagonists is named Pyrocles; or from one of Shakespeare's favorite sources, Plutarch's *Lives*, which perhaps provides still other characters' names. In addition to praising the renowned fifth-century-B.C.E. Athenian statesman Pericles, it harshly judges his rival and successor Cleon as well as the fourth-century general Lysimachus—all names of characters in the play.

*Pericles* follows its sources more faithfully than do many of Shakespeare's works. One sign of this fidelity is the retention of an episodic plot. More striking still is the appearance of Gower himself as a character. His role as chorus finds its predecessor in *Henry V* (1599), but Gower has the more specific function of giving a (pseudo-) medieval feel to the action. Although he eventually reverts to standard pentameter lines, he starts out primarily in the rhymed tetrameter couplets in which *Confessio Amantis* is written: "To sing a song that old was sung / From ashes ancient Gower is come" (1.1–2). In addition, the theatrical Gower's diction often echoes the medieval poet's, extending even to the use of deliberately antiquated language ("iwis" for "certainly," for example, at 5.2). His moralizing speeches are frequently graced by an unrealistic theatrical device— the dumb show. Further, Gower recounts much of the action in his eight monologues, as if to emphasize that poet's authorship of what sometimes feels like narrative, as opposed to dramatic, material. These strategies are all metatheatrical: they undermine the naturalistic illusion of the play, encouraging the audience to view events from a certain distance, to attend to the larger pattern that unfolds rather than becoming emotionally engaged. Part of the genius of *Pericles*, however, is ultimately to elicit that emotional engagement as well.

Gower's monologues also structure the play more effectively than does the division into five acts introduced by later editors (but not followed here). The scene often shifts within each of the seven main groupings, but there is always a central focus. Gower introduces Antioch and incest (Scene 1), Pentapolis and Pericles' wooing of Thaisa (5), Ephesus and the saving of Thaisa (10), Tarsus and the attempted murder of Marina (15), Mytilene and Marina's virtuous life in the brothel (18), Mytilene again and Marina's reunion with Pericles (20), and Ephesus and the reunion with Thaisa (22), before providing the brief epilogue with which the play concludes.

The actual authorship of *Pericles* is beset by unresolved questions, which are treated at length in the Textual Note. Here it is worth mentioning only that George Wilkins probably wrote most of the first nine scenes and Shakespeare most of the remaining thirteen. Acknowledgment of dual authorship is tied to the long-standing recognition of stylistic differences between the two parts of the play. Wilkins's section of the dialogue is closer to Gower's language than is Shakespeare's. Although both playwrights regularly compose verse in iambic pentameter, Wilkins uses far more end-stopped rhyming couplets than does Shakespeare. By contrast, Shakespeare's predilection for blank-verse enjambment, in which the phrase or idea does not conclude at the end of the line, produces a tension between syntax and verse form.

Thus Wilkins's Pericles decorously repudiates the incestuous Daughter of Antiochus:

> Fair glass of light, I loved you, and could still,
> Were not this glorious casket stored with ill.
> . . . . . . . . . . . . . . . . . . . . . . . . . . . . . . . . . . . . .
> For he's no man on whom perfections wait
> That, knowing sin within, will touch the gate.
> . . . . . . . . . . . . . . . . . . . . . . . . . . . . . . . . . . . . .
> But, being played upon before your time,
> Hell only danceth at so harsh a chime.
>                              (1.119–28)

Shakespeare's Pericles reacts to a storm in imagistically more complex but also more colloquial verse:

>                              . . . O still
> Thy deaf'ning dreadful thunders, gently quench
> Thy nimble sulph'rous flashes. . . .
> . . . . . . . . . . . . . . . . . . . . . . . . . . . . . . . . . .
>                              . . . The seaman's whistle
> Is as a whisper in the ears of death,
> Unheard.—Lychorida!—Lucina, O!
> Divinest patroness, and midwife gentle
> To those that cry by night, convey thy deity
> Aboard our dancing boat, make swift the pangs
> Of my queen's travails!—Now, Lychorida.
>                              (11.4–14)

As a result, Shakespeare's section of the play is theatrically livelier, the contrast with the increasingly frequent monologues by Gower correspondingly sharper. Pericles' meeting with the fishermen is the only episode by Wilkins that seems of a piece with such later parts of the play as the second tempest (quoted from above); the revival of Pericles' wife, Thaisa; the two brothel scenes; and the first recognition scene. And structurally, Pericles breaks neatly in two: in the first nine scenes, Pericles moves from felicity to misfortune and back to felicity; in the remaining thirteen, he simply repeats this pattern but with greater intensity.

Yet such distinctions are misleading. Many Renaissance plays were written by more than one dramatist; Shakespeare collaborated on about a quarter of his plays, mostly near the beginning and end of his career. Especially in performance, such works do not necessarily seem any less unified than single-author pieces. Even though its "feel" shifts, Pericles remains consistent throughout in motif—Pericles as a noble tree, his jewel-like family, destructive eating, providential storms, divine music.

Its episodes also echo one another, within and across the two parts of the play. The deadly skulls at Antiochus's palace are answered by the harmless jousting at Simonides' court, and the bad potential marriage to Antiochus's Daughter is echoed by the good real one to Simonides'. The incestuous relationship between Antiochus and his Daughter is contrasted with the lovingly innocent one between Pericles and Marina. Thaliart's foiled attempt to assassinate Pericles at Antiochus's behest anticipates Leonine's failed effort to murder Marina at Dionyza's. Cleon calls down the "curse of heav'n and men" (4.103) should his family ever prove ungrateful to Pericles, and when his family does so prove, "him and his they [his subjects] in his palace burn" (22.121). The storm that costs Pericles his men but leads him to Thaisa is paralleled by the later tempest that apparently disposes of Thaisa. The vigorous popular culture of the fishermen is set against the degraded popular culture of the brothel. The vow of chastity Simonides attributes to Thaisa to get rid of all her suitors except Pericles is fulfilled both in her genuine vow of chastity when she thinks Pericles gone forever and in Marina's successful defense of her chastity in the brothel. The apparent burial of Thaisa is duplicated in the apparent interment of her daughter. And, more broadly, the excessive love of Antiochus for his daughter and, in a different way, of Dionyza for hers are contrasted with the defective love of Cleon for his daughter and, arguably, of Pericles for Marina—until the end of the play, when Pericles demonstrates the appropriate love of father for daughter: neither too much nor too little.

Throughout, the play insists that the concatenation of miseries inflicted on Pericles and his family ultimately leads to a higher felicity. As noted earlier, this is the structure of tragicomic romance, the genre of nearly all of Shakespeare's final plays. Typically, *Pericles* recapitulates Shakespeare's previous work while reversing its chronology: the tragic mood of the early seventeenth century precedes the comic tone of the 1590s. The play echoes *King Lear* both in its storm scenes and in its reunion of ravaged father and redemptive daughter, who gives "another life / To Pericles thy father" (21.194–95); it then duplicates *The Comedy of Errors,* which draws on the same sources as *Pericles* in its concluding retrieval of the missing wife-turned-priestess from the temple of Diana at Ephesus.

Gower reassuringly emphasizes this larger pattern—"I'll show you those in trouble's reign, / Losing a mite, a mountain gain" (5.7–8)—which becomes especially prominent in Shakespeare's scenes due to the presiding benevolence of Diana. She is first mentioned when, according to Simonides, Thaisa opts for continued virginity (9.9). Then Thaisa invokes her upon awakening in an opened coffin, as does Pericles when he vows not to cut his hair until his baby, Marina, is married (12.102, 13.28). Thaisa becomes her priestess, and Marina places her virginity in the goddess's protection (14.12, 15.4, 16.131). Finally, after Pericles is reunited with Marina, Diana appears to him in a dream, promising him happiness only if he goes to her temple in Ephesus and publicly recounts his loss of Thaisa (21.224–34). This supernatural moment recalls Thaisa's quasi-magical preservation by Cerimon (of whom Pericles says, "The gods can have no mortal officer / More like a god than you," 22.85–86), anticipates Pericles' actual meeting with Thaisa in the final scene (where Diana is repeatedly mentioned), and follows hard upon Pericles' perhaps unique ability to hear "the music of the spheres" (21.214)—the sound of a heavenly harmony that extends to human affairs below. A

Scenic view of the temple of Diana, designed by Inigo Jones for the pastoral *Florentine* (1635).

special sensitivity to music has marked Pericles' family throughout. Pericles is "music's master," Thaisa awakens to "still and woeful music," and, most tellingly, Marina "sings like one immortal" (9.28, 12.86, 20.3).

Although these visual and auditory signs of a divine providence guiding the destiny of Pericles' family are pagan in form, they are Christian in content. Tragicomedy's movement from tribulation to triumph is modeled on the *felix culpa*, the fortunate fall of Adam and Eve that led to the redemptive coming of Christ. Antioch recalls the sinister side of Eden: Pericles will "taste the fruit of yon celestial tree / Or die in the adventure"; Antiochus praises the "golden fruit, but dang'rous to be touched" and later warns, "Touch not, upon thy life" (1.64–65, 71, 130). The eastern Mediterranean of late Greek antiquity in which *Pericles* is set also carries connotations of Judaism and early Christianity. Tyre is connected with the reigns of David and Solomon, and was captured by the Christian forces in the First Crusade. Antioch recalls the rebellion of the Maccabees; in addition, Peter and Paul preached there. Paul was born in Tarsus and had a lengthy ministry in Ephesus. The fishermen on the shore of Pentapolis are literally, like St. Peter, fishers of men. Amid talk of devouring whales (5.63–80), they fish out Pericles, whom "the sea hath cast upon [their] coast" (5.92) in a manner that recalls the biblical Jonah, understood in Christian allegory to prefigure Christ's resurrection. Thaisa later undergoes a similar resurrection; and at Mytilene, the Pander laments, "Neither is our profession any mystery, it's no calling" (16.32–33)—where both "mystery" and "calling" have religious reverberations.

In a final, typically moralistic speech, Gower tells the audience,

> In Pericles, his queen, and daughter seen,
> Although assailed with fortune fierce and keen,
> Virtue preserved from fell destruction's blast,
> Led on by heav'n, and crowned with joy at last.
> (22.110–13)

Although there is no ambiguity here, the play as a whole leaves room for doubts on structural, social and political, and sexual grounds. First, despite the overarching pattern of the triumph over a pagan "fortune" by an implicitly Christian "heav'n," Pericles' sufferings feel arbitrary. It is hard to understand, except according to fairy-tale logic, why his predecessors cannot solve Antiochus's obvious riddle or why the King advertises the very secret he wants to preserve. Similarly, the play does not explain why Pericles leaves his daughter at Tarsus or why Dionyza, eager to be rid of Marina, does not consider sending her home instead of murdering her. More important, the misfortunes in *Pericles* seem unrelenting, unconnected, and unrelated to the character or behavior of their victims. Yet this disjunction fails to inspire any Job-like reflections on injustice. In short, the triumph of divine providence is not fully integrated with the secular saga of misfortune. Perhaps, then, the play reveals a contingent relationship between human vicissitude and redemptive transcendence, thereby raising questions about its own ostensible program.

Second, *Pericles* bears a complicated relationship to its own social and political material. The representation of popular culture provides some of the play's most engaging scenes without, however, always linking up to the larger movement of the plot. The initial storm leaves Pericles "bereft / Unfortunately both of ships and men" (7.79–80). The fishermen who then help him repeatedly receive his praise:

> MASTER ... I can compare our rich misers to nothing so fitly as to a whale: a plays and tumbles, driving the poor fry before him, and at last devours them all at a mouthful. ...
> PERICLES [*aside*] A pretty moral.
> (5.68–73)

This disabused account, which may echo the language of the 1607 Midlands Uprising against landlord enclosures of the common lands, leads to a rebuke of the monarch: "If the good King Simonides were of my mind . . . we would purge the land of these drones that rob the bee of her honey" (5.80–84). But the complaint quickly disappears, leaving only the positive image of Pericles' future father-in-law. Similarly, although Pericles promises the fishermen "if that ever my low fortune's better, / I'll pay your bounties, till then rest your debtor" (5.177–78), the debt, which is usually honored in previous tales of Apollonius (including Twine's), is not recalled when Pericles' fortunes quickly improve.

The anticommercial outlook implicit in the Master's denunciation of "rich misers" also informs the brothel scenes, which, like Pericles' encounter with the fishermen, replaces the predominantly Greek Mediterranean setting of the plot with recognizably English characters. Prostitution is the only market-driven activity depicted in the play, although Gower later reports that Marina graduates to an honest livelihood. Earlier, the Bawd advises her in economic terms: "You have fortunes coming upon you. Mark me, you must seem to do that fearfully which you commit willingly, to despise profit where you have most gain. To weep that you live as ye do makes pity in your lovers. Seldom but that pity begets you a good opinion, and that opinion a mere profit" (16.101–06). Marina is thus urged to perform like an actor at one of London's professional theaters. With commerce almost reduced to the oldest profession, a profession widely practiced in the neighborhoods around the theaters, the play implicitly links itself to the very activity that it simultaneously depicts Marina nobly resisting.

Thus, despite successfully exploiting popular culture for theatrical effect, *Pericles* fails to incorporate that culture into the final reconciliation: the play concludes with a purely aristocratic and royal circle. This ending is tacitly anticipated by the linguistic class divisions of the popular scenes: the fishermen and the brothelkeepers speak prose, whereas Pericles and Marina favor blank verse. Nevertheless, *Pericles* is the only one of Shakespeare's romances written before the King's Men began performing during the winter at Blackfriars, a "private," elite, commercial theater. It was acted at the Globe, the preeminent "public" theater, and its success in the early seventeenth century attests to the enduring, at least partly popular appeal of its traditional romance plot.

Furthermore, *Pericles* seems to take its distance from absolute monarchy—in the fishermen's insistence on their rights and in popular political assertiveness at Tarsus. This is important because the political value of aristocratic leadership is questionable. Antioch has been ruled by an incestuous murderer, and there is no indication of his successor. The Governor of Tarsus lets his city slip into famine; his wife is an attempted murderer. Although the inhabitants eventually kill the couple, their own earlier behavior does not inspire confidence: "All poverty was scorned, and pride so great / The name of help grew odious to repeat" (4.30–31). Under duress they are even worse:

> Those mothers who to nuzzle up their babes
> Thought naught too curious are ready now
> To eat those little darlings whom they loved.
> (4.42–44)

The passage echoes in reverse the riddle's equation of cannibalism with incest—"I feed / On mother's flesh" (1.107–08)—while also recalling numerous other moments where "to eat" is to devour. Ephesus's future remains unspecified: Lord Cerimon acts as a private figure. The Governor of Mytilene frequents a brothel until Marina converts him; at the end of the play, the brothel remains, while the Governor, betrothed to Marina, leaves Mytilene in uncertain hands and goes off to rule Tyre.

Earlier, Pericles' departure from Tyre inspires aristocratic "mutiny" (10.29) and begins the practice of absentee landlordism that reaches its climax near the end of the play when his deputy, Helicanus, appoints Aeschines as *his* deputy and sets out with Pericles. Shortly thereafter, Pericles and Thaisa accede to the throne of Pentapolis, a society whose virtues and defects the fishermen have earlier dissected. The death of Thaisa's father, "the good Simonides," is treated not as an occasion for grief but as an opportunity to dole out kingdoms and break up a family that has only just been reunited.

This outcome may parallel the isolation of the various members of James I's family, an isolation emblematized by James's failure to come to the deathbeds of two of his children. Pericles' absenteeism may also reflect on James's style of governing. Alternatively, it may simply recognize the necessity of intergenerational separation for dynastic continuity, just as the redemptive role of Marina may reflect upon Shakespeare's relationship to his own daughter.

Yet *Pericles* also raises sexual doubts. Although the play subjects its protagonists to debased sexuality only to demonstrate their Diana-like purity, they perhaps do not escape unpolluted. In Gower's *Confessio Amantis*, Pericles' daughter is not Marina but Thaisa. From an extradramatic and extratextual perspective, then, sexual relations with Thaisa, which in Gower would have been incest, are here converted into perfectly appropriate marital intimacy. It is almost as if the name change allows Pericles to have the very experience castigated in Antioch under the protection of the marriage bond. When the nearly catatonic Pericles arrives in Mytilene, Lysimachus agrees that Marina might be the cure:

> She questionless, with her sweet harmony
> And other choice attractions, would alarum [Quarto has "allure"]
> And make a batt'ry through his deafened ports.
>
> (21.34–36)

"Alarum" in the second line works better with the last line, but the Quarto's reading goes well with "choice attractions"; thus, "allure" may be correct. If so, Lysimachus, ignorant of Marina's parentage, is suggesting a potentially unfamilial relationship between father and daughter. So, too, does Pericles. He addresses Marina as "thou that begett'st him that did thee beget" (21.182), a line that may simply express gratitude for bringing him back to life. These words recall the generational reversals of Antiochus's incestuous riddle: "He's father, son, and husband mild; / I mother, wife, and yet his child" (1.111–12).

Tragicomic romance often provides a nontragic resolution to the tale of Oedipus, Pericles' predecessor in solving murderous riddles. Do Pericles' words to Marina reverse or repeat Antiochus's riddle? Ambiguities such as this one trouble the providential pattern. By name Pericles recalls an Athenian virtue at odds with the quasi-allegorical landscape through which he travels, a landscape of Asiatic luxury and decadence, of an incest associated with tyranny whose primary alternative seems to be anarchy. In other words, the various social, political, and sexual ambiguities of *Pericles* bear less on the psychology or morality of the protagonist than on the overall import of the play.

Modern performances of *Pericles* have increasingly embraced the challenge posed by this pattern. Although some productions attempt to create naturalistic settings and complex characters, most respect *Pericles*'s relative indifference to such matters by exploiting what's unrealistic about the play and about Renaissance theater generally. First, the doubling of parts has led to the same actress playing Antiochus's Daughter and Marina, Marina and Thaisa, or Thaisa and Dionyza. This procedure can accentuate the differences between the paired characters; more often, however, it has generated an overtone of incest. Relatedly, when one actor plays all the Mediterranean kings, the stage is able to capture the underlying similarity, the repetitiousness, of Pericles' adventures and, hence, the formal, ritualistic quality of the work. Second, although the figure of Gower can establish intimacy between audience and action, the tendency has been to follow the German dramatist Bertolt Brecht in resisting empathy and identification. Gower's role is thus made to underscore the play's theatricality: it has at various times been sung, treated as a voice-over, and played by a street performer. The dramatized action itself has been represented as street theater, as the work of a traveling troupe, as Chinese opera, as an African-American boatswain's sea chantey to his fellow sailors aboard ship, as a child's picture book, as events in an asylum, as the floor show in a gay brothel. One consequence of these techniques has sometimes been an ironic, farcical approach to the absurdities of the plot. The price, however, is the failure of the climactic recognition scenes, which thrive on psychological nuance. Similar problems may arise with overtly political interpretations, though a feminist or multi-ethnic perspective can be a highly suggestive response to the text. Perhaps the solution, in reading as well as performance, is to refuse to level the unevenness of the play, remaining faithful to its various and complex registers.

Walter Cohen

## TEXTUAL NOTE

*Pericles, Prince of Tyre* poses insuperable textual problems. At some point between 1606 and 1608, most likely in late 1607 or early 1608, Shakespeare probably collaborated on a draft of *Pericles* with George Wilkins, a freelance playwright whose *Miseries of Inforst Mariage* had been successfully staged around 1606 by Shakespeare's company, the King's Men. The exact mechanism of the collaboration is unknown, but Wilkins seems to have composed most of Scenes 1–9 (Acts 1–2 in other modern editions) and Shakespeare most of Scenes 10–22 (Acts 3–5). Each dramatist may also have had a small share in the other's part: for instance, Wilkins seems to have been involved with Gower throughout, writing all of his fifth monologue (Scene 18) and his epilogue (end of Scene 22).

The central evidence for dual authorship and for the attribution to Wilkins is the stylistic disparity between the two sections of the play. The style of the first nine scenes shares a prosaic manner, end-stopped versification, and rhyming couplets with Wilkins's other works during these years. It does not resemble Shakespeare's style at any time (or that of anyone else besides Wilkins proposed so far). By contrast, the final thirteen scenes are in Shakespeare's characteristically idiosyncratic late style, marked by complex imagery and, even more notably, by a radical use of enjambment. At various times, scholars have offered alternative explanations—that Shakespeare wrote the first part of *Pericles* early in his career and came back to it years later; that he wrote it all at once but that the two parts were differently mangled on the path from his manuscript to the printed page; that he deliberately shifted styles midway through the play for aesthetic effect; or that he did collaborate, but with someone other than Wilkins. None of these claims is nearly as plausible as the assumption of joint authorship by Wilkins and Shakespeare.

The play was probably first performed between December 1607 and May 1608, and was apparently a commercial success at the Globe. The King's Men seem to have submitted the company's official promptbook of *Pericles* to the Stationers' Register May 20, 1608, ostensibly with intent to print. Since ownership of the play rested not with the playwright but with the company, however, their real purpose may have been to block Wilkins from illegally exploiting *Pericles*'s popularity by selling it to a publisher himself—something he seems to have done the previous year with *The Miseries of Inforst Mariage*. In the event, the play was not printed in 1608; nonetheless, if the King's Men were trying to stop publication, their strategy failed in at least two respects.

First, Wilkins published a prose rendering of the story entitled *The Painfull Adventures of Pericles Prince of Tyre* sometime in 1608. Its title page advertises its indebtedness to the theatrical version, which for the most part, primarily in Scenes 1–9, it resembles. Yet even in these early scenes, Wilkins's narrative is not as close to the play as might be expected. One purely speculative theory is that he was following not Shakespeare's *Pericles* but an earlier play. It is far more likely, however, that as a collaborating dramatist unattached to an acting company, he would not necessarily have retained a manuscript of the part he wrote and might never have had a personal copy of the entire, jointly authored piece. Indeed, given Wilkins's previous behavior, the King's Men may have made a point of keeping the text out of his hands. *The Painfull Adventures* thus seems to record Wilkins's memory of the play that he recently had helped to write. That memory is less accurate, of course, in the parts he did not compose.

Perhaps the King's Men were unable to prevent publication in another way as well. In 1609, one or more actors who had performed in *Pericles* may have sold it for publication. If so, he or they had to reassemble the text from memory, since an actor routinely possessed a written version of little more than his own part. Since the unauthorized publication of the manuscript would have hurt the interests of the company's actor-shareholders such as Shakespeare, the actors most likely to have gone to press are thus to be found elsewhere. Arguably (although this is disputed), the text was the work of the boy actor who played Lychorida and Marina, as well as some minor other parts, and of a hired man who may have been one of the fishermen and the Pander, again among other small roles. For this claim to hold, these two actors would also had to have acquired a copy of Gower's speeches: perhaps the boy was apprenticed to the actor-shareholder who played Gower.

Almost inevitably, an actor's report significantly differs not only from what Shakespeare wrote but also from what was actually performed. Evidence for this divergence in *Pericles* is to be found especially in the large number of errors in meter, but perhaps also in the repeated confusion of verse and prose (although this may be a product of printing) and in the high degree of verbal repetition. The conjectural identification of the actors who reconstructed the text is based on the relative absence of these defects from the speeches of the characters they presumably played and from the scenes in which they appear. Certainly, the process of reporting cannot account for the stylistic differences between the two parts of the play. The First Quarto (Q1) of *Pericles* was typeset in two printing houses; probably one compositor worked in the first shop, two in the second. But here, again, the division between shops and among compositors does not correspond to the stylistic shift beginning in Scene 10. Neither can compositorial error explain most of the defects in the text. And although the title page names Shakespeare as the author, four other plays published in Quarto before 1623 and attributed to William Shakespeare as well as three more assigned to "W.S." were clearly written by others.

As noted in the Introduction, *Pericles* remained extremely popular in the early seventeenth century. It was revived several times through 1631—at the Globe, on tour in the countryside, and before a more elite audience. The print record is similarly extensive: the Second Quarto (Q2) appeared in the same year as the first, 1609, with subsequent quartos in 1611, 1619, 1630, and 1635. Each was based on the previous Quarto, although Q6 also drew on Q4. But *Pericles* was excluded from the First Folio (F) in 1623, perhaps because the editors thought of it as a collaborative piece. It was published in the second issue of the Third Folio (1664), which relied on Q6; again in the Fourth Folio (1685), which used the Third Folio; and in some major early eighteenth-century editions. But the play then largely dropped out of Shakespeare's works until 1780, when Edmund Malone successfully reintroduced it and provided it with the act and scene divisions—both lacking in Q1—subsequent editors have usually accepted. The play has been routinely included in Shakespeare's canon since then.

Because all editions ultimately derive from Q1, *Pericles* occupies a unique status. For every other Shakespearean play with the ambiguous exception of *Richard III*, at least one early printed version apparently draws directly on either an authorial manuscript or a scribal transcript of it, such as a promptbook. (*Sir Thomas More* remained unpublished during the Renaissance and survives in an authorial manuscript.) Since no reasonably authoritative text of *Pericles* exists, even the claim that Q1 is a report of a performance cannot depend on comparison with a presumably more accurate version but must rely on internal evidence alone. Various unsatisfactory alternatives thus confront an editor. The most commonly adopted strategy in the last fifty years has been to emend the text only conservatively to increase its intelligibility. This approach has the obvious advantage of avoiding the introduction of many new deviations from the original play. On the other hand, it is unlikely to preserve the early printed version, the early performed version, or the authors' original version.

The Oxford editors have taken a different tack. In their original-spelling edition, they reprint Q1. In their modern-spelling edition, followed here, they take advantage of the probable dual authorship of the play and the survival of Wilkins's *Painfull Adventures*, which they treat as a reported text, like Q1. Primarily in Wilkins's share of the play (Scenes 1–9) and in the brothel scenes, this edition draws on *The Painfull Adventures (PA)* when the reporting in Q1 seems to be poor and when Wilkins's prose version seems superior in logic, language, or meter and is not invalidated as a report of the play by dependence on another printed source (Laurence Twine's *The Patterne of Painefull Adventures*, 1594?). Although the rationale for this procedure is clearly strengthened by the assumption that Wilkins wrote the first nine scenes, it is not completely dependent on it.

Wilkins's prose is often metrical, as if he were remembering verse drama. Emendation based on *PA* regularly involves the conversion of prose into verse, as well as a wide variety of discretionary decisions. This policy improves the sense in many places (especially Scene 2). Further, Q1 lacks but apparently refers to a short passage displaying Pericles' musical talent that is reconstructed here (Scene 8a). In addition, by following Wilkins's prose, the rationale for Pericles' marriage to Thaisa is shifted from the nobility of his birth to the nobility of his soul (Scene 9). The same strategy of borrowing, in this instance inspired by the suspicion—disputed by other editors—that Q1 reports a politically censored version of the dialogue between Marina and Lysimachus, initially places Lysimachus in a harsher light (Scene 19). Finally, because this edition's scene divisions often differ from those in other modern editions, the play is divided into scenes but not acts.

Although previous scholars and editors have drawn on *PA* and even engaged in conjectural reconstruction of long passages, this version of *Pericles* pursues such an approach more radically and is bound to remain controversial. It can be criticized not only if some of its underlying assumptions are faulty but even if all of them prove correct. The chance is nil that so many emendations, many of them major, will accurately reproduce what was originally written or performed. Yet this is to say no more than that the Oxford edition takes bigger risks than do its predecessors, but on a play where risk taking makes sense. As already noted, if Q1 is a reported text, other modern editions cannot possibly reproduce the original play at all accurately. This edition may deviate more widely than they do from the original version of *Pericles;* then, again, it may well approximate that version more closely.

So that readers can form their own judgments on this question, for each scene the notes provide the act and scene equivalents in most modern texts of *Pericles.* Where scene division departs from the editorial norm, the deviation is explained. More important, the notes also record every emendation drawn from *PA* that significantly alters the meaning, and every emendation that is one line or longer. Rationales for most of these changes are supplied as well. To avoid overloading the notes to the point of unreadability, less substantial changes appear only in the Textual Variants, which provide selected examples of the conversion in this edition of Q1's prose into verse and a complete record of the verbal borrowings from *PA*, with full quotation except where Wilkins's prose is exactly followed.

## SELECTED BIBLIOGRAPHY

Archibald, Elizabeth. *Apollonius of Tyre: Medieval and Renaissance Themes and Variations, Including the Text of the "Historia Apollonii Regis Tyri" with an English Translation*. Cambridge, Eng.: Brewer, 1991. A study of the literary tradition that provided the source material for *Pericles.*

Frye, Susan. "Incest and Authority in *Pericles, Prince of Tyre.*" *Incest and the Literary Imagination*. Ed. Elizabeth Barnes. Gainesville: University Press of Florida, 2002. 39–58. Focuses on three key scenes (incest, tournament, reunion) to argue that incest—understood physically, politically, and psychologically—is tied to questions of the royal family's legitimacy.

Gossett, Suzanne. " 'You not your child well loving': Text and Family Structure in *Pericles.*" *A Companion to Shakespeare's Works.* IV: *Poems, Problem Comedies, Late*

*Plays.* Ed. Richard Dutton and Jean E. Howard. Malden, Mass.: Blackwell, 2003. 348–64. The play as exploration of the proper love between parent and daughter (neither excessive nor deficient), perhaps rooted in Shakespeare's own family experience.

Halpern, Richard. *Shakespeare Among the Moderns.* Ithaca, N.Y.: Cornell University Press, 1997. 140–58. Weak internal causal logic of the plot combined with transcendent romance plan as symptomatic response to decaying older social order.

Jordan, Constance. *Shakespeare's Monarchies: Ruler and Subject in the Romances.* Ithaca, N.Y.: Cornell University Press, 1997. 35–67. A political reading of the play in light of humanist theory; the work espouses mixed or limited monarchy against divine right of kings.

Nevo, Ruth. *Shakespeare's Other Language.* New York: Methuen, 1987. 33–61. Antiochus as Pericles' double, revealing the incest fear the protagonist must flee in a journey through other doubles to an ambiguous resolution.

Orkin, Martin. *Local Shakespeares: Proximations and Power.* London: Routledge, 2005. 63–81. *Pericles* as meditation on male unruliness, in this way providing a partial critique of its own patriarchal romance resolution.

Palfrey, Simon. *Late Shakespeare: A New World of Words.* Oxford: Clarendon, 1997. 57–78. *Pericles* as a skeptical reworking of romance; Pericles as post-heroic protagonist, dependent on popular support.

Skeele, David. *Thwarting the Wayward Seas: A Critical and Theatrical History of Shakespeare's "Pericles" in the Nineteenth and Twentieth Centuries.* Newark: University of Delaware Press, 1998. Charts the shifts from nineteenth-century negative critical views combined with occasional spectacle-based productions, through modernist emphasis on the play's unity, to contemporary celebrations of its disunity.

———, ed. *"Pericles": Critical Essays.* New York: Garland, 2000. A collection of criticism beginning with Ben Jonson in the early seventeenth century and of theatrical reviews beginning in the mid-nineteenth. Modern critics include Knight, Felperin, Barber and Wheeler, Kahn, Mullaney, Adelman, and Novy, among others.

## FILM

*Pericles, Prince of Tyre.* 1984. Dir. David Hugh Jones. UK. 177 min. Generally praised BBC production, naturalistic by TV-studio standards but not by those of big-budget movies.

# Pericles, Prince of Tyre:
## *A Reconstructed Text*

### THE PERSONS OF THE PLAY

John GOWER, the Presenter
ANTIOCHUS, King of Antioch
His DAUGHTER
THALIART, a villain
PERICLES, Prince of Tyre
HELICANUS
AESCHINES } two grave counsellors of Tyre
MARINA, Pericles' daughter
CLEON, Governor of Tarsus
DIONYZA, his wife
LEONINE, a murderer
KING SIMONIDES, of Pentapolis
THAISA, his daughter
Three FISHERMEN, his subjects
Five PRINCES, suitors of Thaisa
A MARSHAL
LYCHORIDA, Thaisa's nurse
A ship MASTER
CERIMON, a physician of Ephesus
PHILEMON, his servant
LYSIMACHUS, Governor of Mytilene
A BAWD
A PANDER
BOULT, servant to Bawd and Pander
DIANA, goddess of chastity
Lords, ladies, pages, messengers, sailors, pirates, knights,
  gentlemen

### Scene 1

*Enter GOWER[1] [as Prologue]*

|  |  |
|---|---|
| GOWER    To sing a song that old° was sung[2] | *of old* |
| From ashes ancient Gower is come, | |
| Assuming man's infirmities° | *Donning mortal flesh* |
| To glad your ear and please your eyes. | |
| 5    It hath been sung at festivals, | |
| On ember-eves and holy-ales,[3] | |
| And lords and ladies in their lives | |
| Have read it for restoratives.° | *as a medicine* |

**Scene 1** (Q1 lacks act and scene divisions; the present edition numbers scenes consecutively throughout, omitting act divisions [see the Textual Note]. Other modern versions treat Gower's monologue as a prologue and start Act 1, Scene 1, at line 43. This edition, however, assumes that the row of heads referred to by Gower and Antiochus ["yon," lines 40, 77] is seen from roughly the same position both times and is first revealed after line 39. But the heads could be visible from the start.)

Location: The palace at Antioch.
1. Fourteenth-century English poet, whose story of Apollonius of Tyre in the eighth book of his *Confessio Amantis* is an important source of the play. See the Introduction.
2. Like most of Gower's choruses in the play, this one is mainly in rhyming tetrameter couplets.
3. *ember-eves:* evenings before periods of religious fasting. *holy-ales:* country festivals.

|    | The purchase° is to make men glorious, | *benefit* |
| 10 | *Et bonum quo antiquius eo melius.*[4] | |
|    | If you, born in these latter times | |
|    | When wit's more ripe,° accept my rhymes, | *poetry's more advanced* |
|    | And that° to hear an old man sing | *And if* |
|    | May to your wishes pleasure bring, | |
| 15 | I life would wish, and that I might | |
|    | Waste° it for you like taper°-light. | *Use it up / candle* |
|    | This'° Antioch, then; Antiochus the Great[5] | *This is* |
|    | Built up this city for his chiefest seat,° | *capital* |
|    | The fairest in all Syria. | |
| 20 | I tell you what mine authors° say. | *sources* |
|    | This king unto him took a fere° | *mate* |
|    | Who died, and left a female heir | |
|    | So buxom,° blithe, and full of face° | *lively / attractive?* |
|    | As° heav'n had lent her all his° grace, | *As if / its* |
| 25 | With whom the father liking took, | |
|    | And her to incest did provoke. | |
|    | Bad child, worse father, to entice his own | |
|    | To evil should° be done by none. | *that should* |
|    | By custom what they did begin | |
| 30 | Was with long use account' no sin.[6] | |
|    | The beauty of this sinful dame | |
|    | Made many princes thither frame° | *go* |
|    | To seek her as a bedfellow, | |
|    | In marriage pleasures playfellow, | |
| 35 | Which to prevent he made a law | |
|    | To keep her still,° and men in awe, | *always* |
|    | That whoso asked her for his wife, | |
|    | His riddle told not,[7] lost his life. | |
|    | So for her many a wight° did die, | *fellow* |
|    | [*A row of heads is revealed*] | |
| 40 | As yon grim looks do testify. | |
|    | What now ensues, to th' judgement of your eye | |
|    | I give, my cause who best can justify.[8] *Exit* | |
|    | [*Sennet.*]° Enter [*King*] ANTIOCHUS, *Prince* PERICLES,[9] | *Trumpet* |
|    | *and* [*lords and peers in their richest ornaments*] | |
|    | ANTIOCHUS  Young Prince of Tyre,[1] you have at large received° | *fully understood* |
|    | The danger of the task you undertake. | |
| 45 | PERICLES  I have, Antiochus, and with a soul | |
|    | Emboldened with the glory of her praise | |
|    | Think death no hazard in this enterprise. | |
|    | ANTIOCHUS  Music! | |
|    | [*Music sounds*] | |
|    | Bring in our daughter, clothèd like a bride | |
| 50 | Fit for th'embracements ev'n of Jove himself, | |
|    | At whose conception, till Lucina reigned, | |
|    | Nature this dowry gave to glad her presence:[2] | |

4. And the older something good is, the better (Latin).
5. *Antioch . . . Antiochus:* Recalling the Maccabee rebellion and the missions of Peter and Paul.
6. *By . . . sin:* When what they started (incest) became a habit, they no longer experienced it as a sin.
7. If he failed to explain Antiochus's riddle.
8. *my . . . justify:* which (your eye's "judgement") will best perceive the truth of my story.
9. *Pericles:* Named after Pericles, the fifth-century

B.C.E. Athenian leader, from Plutarch's *Lives,* or Pyrocles, a protagonist in Sidney's *Arcadia* (1590).
1. *Tyre:* Associated with David and Solomon; captured by a Christian army in the First Crusade.
2. *At . . . presence:* During pregnancy, until my daughter was born (Lucina was the Roman goddess of childbirth, often equated with Diana), nature gave her this dowry to make her presence welcome (or to make her happy).

The senate-house of planets all did sit,
In her their best perfections to knit.³
       *Enter Antiochus'* DAUGHTER

55 PERICLES   See where she comes, apparelled like the spring,
Graces her subjects,⁴ and her thoughts the king
Of ev'ry virtue gives° renown to men;            *that gives*
Her face the book of praises,⁵ where is read
Nothing but curious° pleasures, as° from thence    *delicate / as if*
60 Sorrow were ever razed and testy wrath
Could never be her mild° companion.         *(modifies "her")*
You gods that made me man, and sway° in love,    *hold sway*
That have inflamed desire in my breast
To taste the fruit of yon celestial tree
65 Or die in the adventure, be my helps,
As I am son and servant to your will,
To compass° such a boundless happiness.         *attain*
ANTIOCHUS   Prince Pericles—
PERICLES   That would be son to great Antiochus.
70 ANTIOCHUS   Before thee stands this fair Hesperides,
With golden fruit, but dang'rous to be touched,
      [*He gestures towards the heads*]
For death-like dragons here affright thee hard.⁶
      [*He gestures towards his* DAUGHTER]
Her heav'n-like face enticeth thee to view
Her countless° glory, which desert must gain;    *(like the stars)*
75 And which without desert, because thine eye
Presumes to reach, all the whole heap° must die.   *your whole body*
Yon sometimes° famous princes, like thyself     *at one time*
Drawn by report, advent'rous by° desire,   *taking a risk out of*
Tell thee with speechless tongues and semblants° bloodless  *appearances*
80 That without covering save yon field of stars
Here they stand, martyrs slain in Cupid's wars,
And with dead cheeks advise thee to desist
From going on° death's net, whom none resist.      *into*
PERICLES   Antiochus, I thank thee, who hath taught
85 My frail mortality to know itself,
And by those fearful objects to prepare
This body, like to them, to what I must;⁷
For death remembered should be like a mirror
Who tells us life's but breath, to trust it error.
90 I'll make my will then, and, as sick men do,
Who know the world, see heav'n, but feeling woe
Grip not at earthly joys as erst° they did,     *previously*
So I bequeath a happy peace to you
And all good men, as ev'ry prince should do;
95 My riches to the earth from whence they came,
[*To the* DAUGHTER] But my unspotted fire of love to you.
[*To* ANTIOCHUS] Thus ready for the way of life or death,
I wait the sharpest blow, Antiochus.

---

3. *The . . . knit:* Astrological forces arranged to give her every perfection.
4. With mastery of all human graces.
5. The anthology of all that is commendable.
6. *Before . . . hard:* The Hesperides (here representing Antiochus's Daughter) were daughters of Hesperus inhab-

iting a garden where golden apples grew, whose entrance was patrolled by a dragon. The "golden fruit, but dang'rous to be touched," like "the fruit of yon celestial tree" (line 64), also evokes Eden.
7. *to what I must:* for death.

ANTIOCHUS  Scorning advice, read the conclusion° then,  *riddle*
    [*He angrily throws down the riddle*]
100 Which read and not expounded, 'tis decreed,
    As these before thee, thou thyself shalt bleed.
    DAUGHTER [*to* PERICLES]  Of all 'sayed° yet, mayst thou prove  *who have tried (assayed)*
        prosperous;
    Of all 'sayed yet, I wish thee happiness.
    PERICLES  Like a bold champion I assume the lists,°  *enter combat*
105 Nor ask advice of any other thought
    But faithfulness and courage.
        [*He takes up and reads aloud*] the riddle
      I am no viper, yet I feed
      On mother's flesh which did me breed.[8]
      I sought a husband, in which labour
110     I found that kindness° in a father.  *kinship; affection*
      He's father, son, and husband mild;
      I mother, wife, and yet his child.
      How this may be and yet in two,°  *only two people*
      As you will live resolve it you.
115 Sharp physic is the last.[9] [*Aside*] But O, you powers
    That gives heav'n countless eyes° to view men's acts,  *(the stars)*
    Why cloud they not their sights perpetually
    If this be true which makes me pale to read it?
        [*He gazes on the* DAUGHTER]
    Fair glass° of light, I loved you, and could still,  *image*
120 Were not this glorious casket stored with ill.[1]
    But I must tell you now my thoughts revolt,
    For he's no man on whom perfections wait°  *(as servants)*
    That, knowing sin within, will touch the gate.
    You're a fair viol,[2] and your sense° the strings  *senses*
125 Who, fingered to make man his lawful music,
    Would draw heav'n down and all the gods to hearken,
    But, being played upon before your time,
    Hell only danceth at so harsh a chime.
    Good sooth,° I care not for you.  *Truly*
130 ANTIOCHUS  Prince Pericles, touch not,[3] upon thy life,
    For that's an article within our law
    As dang'rous as the rest. Your time's expired.
    Either expound now, or receive your sentence.
    PERICLES  Great King,
135 Few love to hear the sins they love to act.
    'Twould braid° yourself too near° for me to tell it.  *upbraid / plainly*
    Who° has a book of all that monarchs do,  *Whoever*
    He's more secure to keep it shut than shown,
    For vice repeated, like the wand'ring wind,
140 Blows dust in others' eyes to spread itself;
    And yet the end of all is bought thus dear,
    The breath is gone, and the sore eyes see clear
    To stop the air would hurt them.[4] The blind mole casts

---

8. Vipers were thought to eat their way out of their mother's body at birth.
9. This final threat is harsh medicine.
1. If your body weren't so sinful.
2. Stringed instrument; vial.
3. Perhaps Pericles makes some movement that Antiochus misinterprets (further Edenic overtones).
4. *For vice . . . them:* For with the breath used to speak word of others' sins, one blows irritating dust in the eyes of the offenders. But the consequence is merely the speaker's death, since the offenders nevertheless see well enough to stop the news-spreading breath.

Copped° hills towards heav'n to tell° the earth is thronged     *Peaked / tell that*
145 By man's oppression, and the poor worm doth die for't.⁵
Kings are earth's gods; in vice their law's their will,
And if Jove stray, who dares say Jove doth ill?
It is enough you know,° and it is fit,     *(that I know)*
What being more known grows worse,⁶ to smother° it.     *conceal*
150 All love the womb that their first being bred;⁷
Then give my tongue like leave to love my head.
ANTIOCHUS [*aside*]   Heav'n, that I had thy head! He's found the
    meaning.
But I will gloze° with him. —Young Prince of Tyre,     *dissemble*
Though by the tenor of our strict edict,
155 Your exposition misinterpreting,
We might proceed to cancel° of your days,     *to the termination*
Yet hope, succeeding from so fair a tree⁸
As your fair self, doth tune° us otherwise.     *move*
Forty days longer we do respite you,
160 If by which time our secret be undone,
This mercy shows we'll joy in such a son.
And until then your entertain° shall be     *entertainment*
As doth befit your worth and our degree.
        [*Flourish. Exeunt.*] *Manet* PERICLES *solus*°     *Pericles remains alone*
PERICLES   How courtesy would seem° to cover sin     *lie*
165 When what is done is like an hypocrite,
The which is good in nothing but in sight.°     *appearance*
If it be true that I interpret false,
Then were it certain you were not so bad
As with foul incest to abuse your soul,
170 Where now you're both a father and a son
By your uncomely claspings with your child—
Which pleasures fits a husband, not a father—
And she, an eater of her mother's flesh,
By the defiling of her parents' bed,
175 And both like serpents are, who though they feed
On sweetest flowers, yet they poison breed.
Antioch, farewell, for wisdom sees those men°     *men who*
Blush not in actions blacker than the night
Will 'schew no course° to keep them from the light.     *eschew no means*
180 One sin, I know, another doth provoke.
Murder's as near to lust as flame to smoke.
Poison and treason are the hands of sin,
Ay, and the targets° to put off the shame.     *shields*
Then, lest my life be cropped to keep you clear,°     *(of blame)*
185 By flight I'll shun the danger which I fear.     *Exit*
    *Enter* ANTIOCHUS
ANTIOCHUS   He hath found the meaning, for the which we mean
To have his head. He must not live
To trumpet forth my infamy, nor tell the world
Antiochus doth sin in such a loathèd manner,

---

5. *The blind . . . for't:* When we blindly protest against the injustice of our superiors, we die (with "mole" meaning "worm"), or, less likely, innocent creatures suffer (here, the "mole" is different from the "worm" and may even destroy it).
6. Since bad deeds become worse for being known.
7. All love the daughter they raised when young (hence,

hinting at incest). The obvious meaning—all love their mother's womb—either is nonincestuous or gets the incest backward.
8. Hope of a correct answer (an heir), with the successful answer (succession) coming from such a fine specimen (Pericles' regal lineage).

190 And therefore instantly this prince must die,
For by his fall my honour must keep high.
Who attends us there?
      *Enter* THALIART
THALIART          Doth your highness call?
ANTIOCHUS   Thaliart, you are of our chamber,° Thaliart,      *my chamberlain*
And to your secrecy our mind partakes°              *imparts*
195 Her° private actions. For your faithfulness           *Its*
We will advance you, Thaliart. Behold,
Here's poison, and here's gold.
We hate the Prince of Tyre, and thou must kill him.
It fits° thee not to ask the reason. Why?            *befits*
200 Because we bid it. Say, is it done?
THALIART   My lord, 'tis done.
ANTIOCHUS   Enough.
      *Enter a* MESSENGER [*hastily*]
Let your breath cool yourself, telling your haste.[9]
MESSENGER   Your majesty, Prince Pericles is fled.     [*Exit*]
ANTIOCHUS [*to* THALIART]   As thou wilt live, fly after; like an
205     arrow
Shot from a well-experienced archer hits
The mark his eye doth level° at, so thou            *aim*
Never return unless it be to say
'Your majesty, Prince Pericles is dead.'
210 THALIART   If I can get him in my pistol's° length°   *(anachronism) / range*
I'll make him sure° enough. Farewell, your highness.   *unthreatening (dead)*
ANTIOCHUS   Thaliart, adieu.         [*Exit* THALIART]
                  Till Pericles be dead
My heart can lend no succour to my head.
      [*Exit. The heads are concealed*]

## Scene 2
    *Enter* PERICLES [*distempered*] *with his lords*
PERICLES   Let none disturb us.         [*Exeunt lords*]
           Why should this change of thoughts,°   *changed state of mind*
The sad companion, dull-eyed melancholy,
Be my so used° a guest as not an hour         *accustomed*
In the day's glorious walk or peaceful night,
5 The tomb where grief should sleep, can breed me quiet?
Here pleasures court mine eyes, and mine eyes shun them,
And danger, which I feared, 's° at Antioch,         *is*
Whose arm seems far too short to hit me here.
Yet neither pleasure's art can joy my spirits,
10 Nor yet care's author's distance comfort me.
Then it is thus: the passions of the mind,°       *obsessions*
That have their first conception by misdread,°     *fear*
Have after-nourishment and life by care,°        *worry*
And what was first but fear what might be done
15 Grows elder now, and cares it be not done.[1]
And so with me. The great Antiochus,

---

9. Use your rapid breathing to cool yourself by explaining the reason for your haste.
**Scene 2** (Act 1, Scene 2, in other modern editions)
Location: The palace at Tyre.

1. *And what . . . done:* And what starts out as simple fear matures into a more rational concern for safety.

'Gainst whom I am too little to contend,
Since he's so great can° make his will his act,      *that he can*
Will think me speaking though I swear to silence,
20     Nor boots it° me to say I honour him      *does it help*
If he suspect I may dishonour him.
And what may make him blush in being known,
He'll stop the course by which it might be known.
With hostile forces he'll o'erspread the land,
25     And with th'ostent° of war will look so huge      *display*
Amazement° shall drive courage from the state,      *Terror*
Our men be vanquished ere they do resist,
And subjects punished that ne'er thought offence,
Which care of them, not pity of myself,
30     Who am no more but as the tops of trees
Which fence° the roots they grow by and defend them,      *shield*
Makes both my body pine and soul to languish,
And punish that° before that he would punish.[2]      *(myself)*

*Enter all the* LORDS, [*among them old* HELICANUS,] *to*
PERICLES

FIRST LORD     Joy and all comfort in your sacred breast!
35     SECOND LORD     And keep your mind peaceful[3] and comfortable.
HELICANUS     Peace, peace, and give experience tongue.
[*To* PERICLES] You[4] do not well so to abuse yourself,
To waste your body here with pining sorrow,
Upon whose safety doth depend the lives
40     And the prosperity of a whole kingdom.
'Tis ill in you to do it, and no less
Ill in your council not to contradict it.
They do abuse the King that flatter him,
For flatt'ry is the bellows blows° up sin;      *that blows*
45     The thing the which is flattered, but a spark,
To which that wind gives heat and stronger glowing;
Whereas reproof, obedient and in order,
Fits kings as they are men, for they may err.
When Signor Sooth[5] here does proclaim a peace
50     He flatters you, makes war upon your life.
[*He kneels*]
Prince, pardon me, or strike me if you please.
I cannot be much lower than my knees.
PERICLES     All leave us else;° but let your cares o'erlook      *except Helicanus*
What shipping and what lading's[6] in our haven,
And then return to us.      [*Exeunt* LORDS]
55          Helicane, thou
Hast movèd us. What seest thou in our looks?
HELICANUS     An angry brow, dread lord.
PERICLES     If there be such a dart° in princes' frowns,      *danger*
How durst thy tongue move anger to our brows?
HELICANUS     How dares the plants look up to heav'n from
60     whence

---

2. *before . . . punish*: before he punishes me ("that").
3. Q1 has "And keep your mind till you return to us peaceful," a phrase that anticipates Pericles' "return to us" (line 55). The omission here eliminates the speaker's clairvoyance about a trip that no one else contemplates until line 111.

4. Lines 37–42 are not in Q1 but are adapted from Wilkins's *Painfull Adventures* (*PA*). They explain why Helicanus thinks Pericles has been, but should not be, flattered.
5. Mock name for a flatterer, a soother of egos.
6. *let . . . lading's*: look carefully to find out what vessels are coming and going and what cargo is.

They have their nourishment?
PERICLES    Thou knowest I have pow'r to take thy life from thee.
HELICANUS    I have ground the axe myself; do you but strike the
    blow.
PERICLES [*lifting him up*]    Rise, prithee, rise. Sit down. Thou art
    no flatterer,
65    I thank thee for it, and the heav'ns forbid
    That kings should let their ears hear their faults hid.
    Fit counsellor and servant for a prince,
    Who by thy wisdom mak'st a prince thy servant,
    What wouldst thou have me do?
HELICANUS                  To bear with patience
70    Such griefs as you do lay upon yourself.
PERICLES    Thou speak'st like a physician, Helicanus,
    That ministers a potion unto me
    That thou wouldst tremble to receive thyself.
    Attend me,° then. I went to Antioch,               *Listen to me*
75    Where, as thou know'st, against the face of death
    I sought the purchase° of a glorious beauty         *acquisition*
    From whence an issue I might propagate,
    As children are heav'n's blessings: to parents, objects;[7]
    Are arms° to princes, and bring joys to subjects.       *weapons*
80    Her face was to mine eye beyond all wonder,
    The rest —hark in thine ear—as black as incest,
    Which by my knowledge found, the sinful father
    Seemed not to strike, but smooth.° But thou know'st this,    *smooth over*
    'Tis time to fear when tyrants seems to kiss;
85    Which fear so grew in me I hither fled
    Under the covering of careful night,
    Who seemed my good protector, and being here
    Bethought me what was past, what might succeed.°    *happen next*
    I knew him tyrannous, and tyrants' fears
90    Decrease not, but grow faster than the years.
    And should he doubt°—as doubt no° doubt he doth—    *suspect / as no*
    That I should open° to the list'ning air             *declare*
    How many worthy princes' bloods were shed
    To keep his bed of blackness unlaid ope,
95    To lop that doubt he'll fill this land with arms,
    And make pretence of wrong that I have done him,
    When all for mine—if I may call—offence
    Must feel war's blow, who° spares not innocence;        *which*
    Which love to all, of which thyself art one,
    Who now reproved'st me for't—
100 HELICANUS                Alas, sir.
PERICLES    Drew sleep out of mine eyes, blood from my cheeks,
    Musings into my mind, with thousand doubts,
    How I might stop this tempest ere it came,
    And, finding little comfort to relieve them,°       *(his subjects)*
105    I thought it princely charity to grieve them.°      *(by my sorrow)*
HELICANUS    Well, my lord, since you have giv'n me leave to
    speak,
    Freely will I speak. Antiochus you fear,

---

7. Objects of affection. This line, composed by the Oxford editors, fills a long-recognized gap in Q1 between lines
77 and 79.

And justly too, I think, you fear the tyrant,
Who either by public war or private treason
110 Will take away your life.
Therefore, my lord, go travel for a while,
Till that his rage and anger be forgot,
Or destinies do cut his thread of life.[8]
Your rule direct° to any; if to me,                                    assign
115 Day serves not light more faithful than I'll be.
PERICLES   I do not doubt thy faith,
But should he in my absence wrong thy liberties?°        jurisdictions
HELICANUS   We'll mingle our bloods together in the earth
From whence we had our being and our birth.
120 PERICLES   Tyre, I now look from thee then, and to Tarsus°   (St. Paul's birthplace)
Intend° my travel, where I'll hear from thee,                     Direct
And by whose letters I'll dispose myself.
The care I had and have of subjects' good
On thee I lay, whose wisdom's strength can bear it.
125 I'll take thy word for faith, not ask thine oath;
Who° shuns not to break one will sure crack both.              He who
But in our orbs° we'll live so round° and safe          places / prudently
That time of both this truth shall ne'er convince:°              refute
Thou showed'st a subject's shine, I a true prince.°   *Exeunt*   prince's

## Scene 3

*Enter* THALIART

THALIART   So this is Tyre, and this the court. Here must I kill
King Pericles, and if I do it and am caught I am like to be
hanged abroad, but[1] if I do it not, I am sure to be hanged at
home. 'Tis dangerous. Well, I perceive he was a wise fellow
5 and had good discretion that, being bid to ask what he would
of the King, desired he might know none of his secrets.[2] Now
do I see he had some reason for't, for if a king bid a man be a
villain, he's bound by the indenture° of his oath to be one.     servant's contract
Hush, here comes the lords of Tyre.

*Enter* HELICANUS [*and*] AESCHINES, *with
other lords*

10 HELICANUS   You shall not need, my fellow peers of Tyre,
Further to question of your King's departure.
His sealed° commission left in trust with me               (with royal wax)
Does speak sufficiently he's gone to travel.
THALIART [*aside*]   How? The King gone?
15 HELICANUS   If further yet you will be satisfied
Why, as it were unlicensed of your loves,°          without your approval
He would depart, I'll give some light unto you.
Being at Antioch—
THALIART [*aside*]       What from Antioch?
HELICANUS   Royal Antiochus, on what cause I know not,
20 Took some displeasure at him—at least he judged so—
And doubting lest° that he had erred or sinned,            And fearing
To show his sorrow he'd correct° himself;               he wished to punish

---

8. In Greek mythology, a person died when the three
Fates "cut his thread of life."
**Scene 3** (Act 1, Scene 3)
Location: The palace at Tyre.
1. *if . . . but:* this is a conjectural editorial addition that

semantically balances Thaliart's reflection on the consequences of failure. *like:* likely. *abroad:* in Tyre.
2. According to Plutarch's *Lives* and Barnabe Riche in
*Souldiers Wishe to Britons Welfare* (1604), the poet Philip-
pides made this request of King Lysimachus of Thrace.

So puts himself unto the ship-man's toil,
With whom each minute threatens life or death.
25 THALIART [*aside*]   Well, I perceive I shall not be hanged now,
Although I would.[3]
But since he's gone, the King's ears it must please
He scaped° the land to perish on the seas.                                      *escaped*
I'll present myself.—Peace to the lords of Tyre.
30 Lord Thaliart am I, of Antioch.[4]
HELICANUS   Lord Thaliart of Antioch is welcome.
THALIART   From King Antiochus I come
With message unto princely Pericles,
But since my landing I have understood
35 Your lord's betook himself to unknown travels.
Now my message must return from whence it came.
HELICANUS   We have no reason to enquire it,
Commended° to our master, not to us.                                           *Directed*
Yet ere you shall depart, this we desire:
40 As friends to Antioch, we may feast° in Tyre.           *Exeunt*   *prepare a feast for you*

## Scene 4

*Enter* CLEON, *the Governor of Tarsus, with* [DIONYZA]
*his wife, and others*
CLEON   My Dionyza, shall we rest us here
And, by relating tales of others' griefs,
See if 'twill teach us to forget our own?
DIONYZA   That were to blow at fire in hope to quench it,
5 For who digs° hills because they do aspire                            *whoever digs up*
Throws down one mountain to cast up a higher.
O my distressèd lord, e'en such our griefs are;
Here they're but felt and seen with midges' eyes,°                     *as small matters*
But like to groves, being topped° they higher rise.                          *pruned*
10 CLEON   O Dionyza,
Who wanteth food and will not say he wants it,
Or can conceal his hunger till he famish?
Our tongues our sorrows dictate to sound° deep                      *proclaim; plumb*
Our woes into the air, our eyes to weep
15 Till lungs fetch breath that may proclaim them louder,
That, if heav'n slumber while their° creatures want,                       *(heaven's)*
They° may awake their° helps to comfort them.          *(creatures) / (heaven's)*
I'll then discourse our woes, felt sev'ral years,
And, wanting° breath to speak, help me with tears.             *when I'm out of*
20 DIONYZA   As you think best, sir.
CLEON   This Tarsus o'er which I have the government,
A city o'er whom plenty held full hand,°                          *generously presided*
For riches strewed herself ev'n in the streets,
Whose tow'rs bore heads so high they kissed the clouds,
25 And strangers ne'er beheld but wondered at,°                     *without admiring*
Whose men and dames so jetted° and adorned°           *strutted / (themselves)*
Like one another's glass to trim them[1] by;
Their tables were stored full to glad the sight,
And not so much to feed on as delight.

---

3. Even if I return home (?); even if that's what I wanted.
4. This line is added by the Oxford editors to explain how Helicanus knows who Thaliart is. Alternatively, Helicanus might simply recognize a leading lord of the dominant regional power.

Scene 4 (Act 1, Scene 4)
Location: Tarsus.
1. Mirror to dress themselves. (Everyone was a model of fashion.)

30     All poverty was scorned, and pride so great
        The name of help grew odious to repeat.
     DIONYZA  O, 'tis too true.
     CLEON  But see what heav'n can do by this our change.
        Those mouths who but of late° earth, sea, and air        *just recently*
35    Were all too little to content and please,
        Although they gave their creatures in abundance,
        As houses are defiled for want° of use,        *by lack*
        They are now starved for want of exercise.
        Those palates who, not yet two summers younger,
40    Must have inventions° to delight the taste        *Demanded novel foods*
        Would now be glad of bread and beg for it.
        Those mothers who to nuzzle up° their babes        *raise*
        Thought naught too curious° are ready now        *exquisite*
        To eat those little darlings whom they loved.
45    So sharp are hunger's teeth that man and wife
        Draw lots who first shall die to lengthen life.°        *(of the other)*
        Here weeping stands a lord, there lies a lady dying,
        Here many sink, yet those which see them fall
        Have scarce strength left to give them burial.
50    Is not this true?
     DIONYZA  Our cheeks and hollow eyes do witness it.
     CLEON  O, let those cities that of plenty's cup
        And her prosperities so largely taste
        With their superfluous riots,° heed these tears!        *excessive indulgence*
55    The misery of Tarsus may be theirs.
        *Enter a [fainting]* LORD *[of Tarsus slowly]*
     LORD  Where's the Lord Governor?
     CLEON  Here. Speak out thy sorrows which thou bring'st in
        haste,
        For comfort is too far for us t'expect.
     LORD  We have descried upon our neighbouring shore
60    A portly sail° of ships make hitherward.        *stately fleet*
     CLEON  I thought as much.
        One sorrow never comes but brings an heir
        That may succeed as his inheritor,
        And so in ours. Some neighbour nation,
65    Taking advantage of our misery,
        Hath stuffed these hollow vessels with their power°        *soldiers*
        To beat us down, the which are down already,
        And make a conquest of unhappy men,°        *(me: Q1)*
        Whereas no glory's got to overcome.[2]
70    LORD  That's the least fear,° for by the semblance        *not to be feared*
        Of their white flags displayed they bring us peace,
        And come to us as favourers, not foes.
     CLEON  Thou speak'st like him's untutored to repeat;[3]
        Who makes the fairest show means most deceit.
75    But bring they° what they will and what they can,        *let them bring*
        What need we fear?
        Our grave's the low'st,° and we are half-way there.        *lowest we can go*
        Go tell their gen'ral we attend° him here        *await*
        To know for what he comes, and whence he comes.

2. Where there's no glory in winning.
3. Like him who hasn't learned (the following lesson) by heart.

80   LORD   I go, my lord.                   *[Exit]*

      CLEON   Welcome is peace, if he on peace consist;°       *resolve*

      If wars, we are unable to resist.

          *Enter [the* LORD *again conducting]* PERICLES *with atten-*

          *dants*

      PERICLES *[to* CLEON*]*   Lord Governor, for so we hear you are,

      Let not our ships and number of our men

85      Be like a beacon fixed t'amaze° your eyes.       *to terrify*

      We have heard your miseries as far as Tyre,

      Since entering your unshut gates have witnessed

      The widowed[4] desolation of your streets;

      Nor come we to add sorrow to your hearts,

90      But to relieve them of their heavy load;

      And these our ships, you happily° may think       *perhaps*

      Are like the Trojan horse was fraught within

      With bloody veins importing overthrow,[5]

      Are stored with corn to make your needy bread,

95      And give them life whom hunger starved half dead.

      ALL OF TARSUS *[falling on their knees and weeping]*   The gods of

          Greece protect you, and we'll pray for you!

      PERICLES   Arise, I pray you, rise.

      We do not look for reverence but for love,

      And harbourage for me, my ships and men.

100    CLEON   The which when any shall not gratify,

      Or pay you with unthankfulness in thought,

      Be it our wives, our children, or ourselves,

      The curse of heav'n and men succeed° their evils!     *follow from*

      Till when—the which I hope shall ne'er be seen—

105    Your grace is welcome to our town and us.

      PERICLES   Which welcome we'll accept, feast here a while,

      Until our stars that frown lend us a smile.     *Exeunt*

## Scene 5

     *Enter* GOWER

      GOWER   Here have you seen a mighty king

      His child, iwis,° to incest bring;         *certainly*

      A better prince° and benign lord         *(Pericles)*

      Prove awe-full° both in deed and word.     *worthy of respect*

5      Be quiet then, as men should be,

      Till he hath passed necessity.[1]

      I'll show you those° in trouble's reign,       *those who*

      Losing a mite, a mountain gain.

      The good in conversation,[2]

10    To whom I give my benison,°          *blessing*

      Is still at Tarsus where each man

      Thinks all is writ he speken can,[3]

      And to remember what he does

---

4. *Since . . . widowed:* This line, adapted from *PA,* replaces Q1's "And seene the"; the substitution prevents the inference that Pericles has "seen" Tarsus's "desolation" "as far as Tyre."

5. *was . . . overthrow:* was laden ("fraught") with Greek soldiers ("bloody veins") who sacked the city.

**Scene 5** (Other editions treat Gower's monologue as a prologue to Act 2 and start Act 2, Scene 1, at line 41. The present edition, however, interprets "here he comes" [line

39] as evidence that the scene does not change.)

Location: The seashore at Pentapolis, which was the coastal area of Cyrenaica, in the northeast corner of what is now Libya. This scene locates it in Greece, however (line 100).

1. *necessity:* the suffering that is his lot.

2. The good man (Pericles) in conduct.

3. Archaic (as is often the case in Gower's speeches): Thinks all Pericles says is holy scripture ("writ").

His statue build to make him glorious.
15 But tidings to the contrary
Are brought your eyes. What need speak I?

*Dumb show.*[4]

*Enter at one door* PERICLES *talking with* CLEON, *all the*
*train with them. Enter at another door a gentleman with*
*a letter to* PERICLES. PERICLES *shows the letter to* CLEON.
PERICLES *gives the messenger a reward, and knights him.*
*Exeunt* [*with their trains*] PERICLES *at one door and*
CLEON *at another*

Good Helicane that stayed at home,
Not to eat honey like a drone
From others' labours, for that he strive
20 To killen bad, keep good alive,
And to fulfil his prince' desire
Sent word of all that haps in Tyre;
How Thaliart came full bent with° sin                             intent on
And hid intent to murdren him,
25 And that in Tarsus was not best
Longer for him to make his rest.
He deeming so put forth to seas,
Where when men been° there's seldom ease,                          are
For now the wind begins to blow;
30 Thunder above and deeps below
Makes such unquiet that the ship
Should° house him safe is wrecked and split,               Which should
And he, good prince, having all lost,
By waves from coast to coast is tossed.
35 All perishen of man, of pelf,°                                     goods
Ne aught escapend° but himself,                           Nothing escaping
Till fortune, tired with doing bad,
Threw him ashore to give him glad.°                                   joy

*Enter* PERICLES *wet* [*and half-naked*]

And here he comes. What shall be next
40 Pardon old Gower; this 'longs[5] the text.                    [*Exit*]

[*Thunder and lightning*]

PERICLES   Yet cease your ire, you angry stars of heaven!
Wind, rain, and thunder, remember earthly man
Is but a substance that must yield to you,
And I, as fits my nature, do obey you.
45 Alas, the seas hath cast me on the rocks,
Washed me from shore to shore, and left my breath
Nothing to think on but ensuing death.
Let it suffice the greatness of your powers
To have bereft a prince of all his fortunes,
50 And, having thrown him from your wat'ry grave,
Here to have death in peace is all he'll crave.

[*He sits.*]

*Enter* [*two poor*] FISHERMEN [*one the* MASTER, *the other*
*his man*]

MASTER [*calling*]   What ho, Pilch![6]

---

4. In Renaissance drama, a brief pantomime performance used to advance the plot.
5. Continuing would lengthen Gower's speech too
much; or, 'longs: belongs to.

6. Nickname derived from a rustic leather garment. The
nicknames, homely references, and social critiques in this
scene have a distinctively English feel.

SECOND FISHERMAN [*calling*]   Ha, come and bring away the nets.
MASTER [*calling*]   What, Patchbreech,° I say!                              (*another nickname*)
    [*Enter a* THIRD FISHERMAN *with a hood upon his head
    and a filthy leathern pelt upon his back, unseemly clad,
    and homely to behold. He brings nets to dry and repair*]
55   THIRD FISHERMAN   What say you, master?
MASTER   Look how thou stirrest now. Come away, or I'll fetch
    th' with a wanion.[7]
THIRD FISHERMAN   Faith, master, I am thinking of the poor men
    that were cast away before us° even now.                                *in our sight*
60   MASTER   Alas, poor souls, it grieved my heart to hear what pitiful
    cries they made to us to help them when, well-a-day,° we could        *alas*
    scarce help ourselves.
THIRD FISHERMAN   Nay, master, said not I as much when I saw
    the porpoise how he bounced and tumbled?° They say they're     (*predictive of storms*)
65   half fish, half flesh. A plague on them, they ne'er come but I look
    to be washed.° Master, I marvel how the fishes live in the sea.         (*by a storm*)
MASTER   Why, as men do a-land°—the great ones eat up the              *on land*
    little ones. I can compare our rich misers to nothing so fitly as
    to a whale: a° plays and tumbles, driving the poor fry before           *he*
70   him, and at last devours them all at a mouthful. Such whales
    have I heard on° o'th' land, who never leave gaping° till they    *of / close their mouths*
    swallowed the whole parish: church, steeple, bells, and all.
PERICLES [*aside*]   A pretty moral.
THIRD FISHERMAN   But, master, if I had been the sexton, I would
75   have been that day in the belfry.
SECOND FISHERMAN   Why, man?
THIRD FISHERMAN   Because he should have swallowed me, too,
    and when I had been in his belly I would have kept such a
    jangling of the bells that he should never have left till he cast°        *vomited*
80   bells, steeple, church, and parish up again. But if the good
    King Simonides were of my mind—
PERICLES [*aside*]   Simonides?
THIRD FISHERMAN   We would purge the land of these drones that
    rob the bee of her honey.
85   PERICLES [*aside*]   How from the finny subject° of the sea[8]         *citizens*
    These fishers tell th'infirmities of men,
    And from their wat'ry empire recollect°                                 *gather*
    All that may men approve or men detect!°                                *expose*
    [*Coming forward*] Peace be at your labour, honest fishermen.
90   SECOND FISHERMAN   Honest, good fellow? What's that? If it be a day
    fits you, scratch't out of the calendar, and nobody look after it.[9]
PERICLES   May° see the sea hath cast upon your coast—                   *You may*
SECOND FISHERMAN   What a drunken knave was the sea to cast
    thee in our way![1]
95   PERICLES   A man, whom both the waters and the wind
    In that vast tennis-court hath made the ball
    For them to play upon,° entreats you pity him.                          *with*
    He asks of you that never used to beg.

---

7. *Look . . . wanion:* Look how quick you are (ironic).
Hurry along, or I'll beat you with a vengeance.
8. Although the Fishermen speak in prose, Pericles
uses verse.
9. *Honest . . . after it:* If "honest" were a day in the calendar that suited someone in your sorry state, you could
remove it without anyone noticing; honesty is so rare

already, no one would notice its departure. (Perhaps a
line is missing before line 89, in which Pericles wishes
the Fishermen good day.)
1. Like St. Peter, the Fishermen are literally fishers of
men, who help save Pericles from the sea. Their discussion of whales also evokes the tale of Jonah. The scene is
full of biblical echoes.

MASTER    No, friend, cannot you beg? Here's them° in our coun-          *There are those*
100   try of Greece gets° more with begging than we can do with            *who get*
working.
SECOND FISHERMAN    Canst thou catch any fishes, then?
PERICLES    I never practised it.
SECOND FISHERMAN    Nay, then thou wilt starve, sure; for here's
105   nothing to be got nowadays unless thou canst fish for't.°           *get it by deception*
PERICLES    What I have been, I have forgot to know,
But what I am, want teaches me to think on:
A man thronged up° with cold; my veins are chill,                       *overwhelmed*
And have no more of life than may suffice
110   To give my tongue that heat to crave your help,
Which if you shall refuse, when I am dead,
For that° I am a man, pray see me burièd.                               *Because*
[*He falls down*]
MASTER    Die, quotha?° Now, gods forbid't an° I have a gown            *says he / if*
here! [*To* PERICLES, *lifting him up from the ground*] Come, put
115   it on, keep thee warm. Now, afore me,° a handsome fellow!           *on my word*
Come, thou shalt go home, and we'll have flesh for holidays,
fish for fasting-days, and moreo'er puddings° and flapjacks, and        *sausages*
thou shalt be welcome.
PERICLES    I thank you, sir.
120   SECOND FISHERMAN    Hark you, my friend, you said you could
not beg?
PERICLES    I did but crave.
SECOND FISHERMAN    But crave? Then I'll turn craver too, an so I
shall scape whipping.°                                                  *(for begging)*
125   PERICLES    Why, are all your beggars whipped, then?
SECOND FISHERMAN    O, not all, my friend, not all; for if all your°    *the*
beggars were whipped I would wish no better office than to be
beadle.[2]
MASTER[3]    Thine office, knave—
130   SECOND FISHERMAN    Is to draw up the other nets. I'll go.
[*Exit with* THIRD FISHERMAN]
PERICLES [*aside*]    How well this honest mirth becomes their
labour!
MASTER [*seating himself by* PERICLES]    Hark you, sir, do you
know where ye are?
135   PERICLES    Not well.
MASTER    Why, I'll tell you. This is called Pentapolis, and our
king the good Simonides.
PERICLES    'The good Simonides' do you call him?
MASTER    Ay, sir, and he deserves so to be called for his peaceable
140   reign and good government.
PERICLES    He is a happy king, since from his subjects
He gains the name of good by his government.
How far is his court distant from this shore?
MASTER    Marry,° sir, some half a day's journey. And I'll tell you,    *To be sure*
145   he hath a fair daughter, and tomorrow is her birthday, and
there are princes and knights come from all parts of the world
to joust and tourney for her love.

---

2. Minor parish official who administered corporal punishment.
3. To improve the motivation of the Second Fisherman's

exit, this edition substitutes "MASTER . . . I'll go" for Q1's
continuation of the Second Fisherman's speech: "But
Master, I'll go draw up the net."

PERICLES   Were but my fortunes answerable
　　　To my desires I could wish to make one° there.          *be one of the princes*
150　MASTER   O, sir, things must be as they may, and what a man
　　　cannot get himself, he may lawfully deal for with his wife's soul.[4]
　　　　　*Enter the [other] two* FISHERMEN *drawing up a net*
　　　SECOND FISHERMAN   Help, master, help! Here's a fish hangs in
　　　the net like a poor man's right in the law; 'twill hardly come out.
　　　　　*[Before help comes, up comes their prize]*
　　　Ha, bots on't,° 'tis come at last, and 'tis turned to a rusty armour.          *a pox (plague) on it*
155　PERICLES   An armour, friends? I pray you let me see it.
　　　*[Aside]* Thanks, fortune, yet that after all thy crosses°          *hardships*
　　　Thou giv'st me somewhat to repair my losses,
　　　And though° it was mine own, part of my heritage          *Even though*
　　　Which my dead father did bequeath to me
160　With this strict charge ev'n as he left his life:
　　　'Keep it, my Pericles; it hath been a shield
　　　'Twixt me and death,' and pointed to this brace,°          *arm armor*
　　　'For that° it saved me, keep it. In like necessity,          *Because*
　　　The which the Gods forfend,° the same may defend thee.'          *forbid*
165　It kept° where I kept, I so dearly loved it,          *remained*
　　　Till the rough seas that spares not any man
　　　Took it in rage, though calmed have giv'n't again.
　　　I thank thee for't. My shipwreck now's no ill,
　　　Since I have here my° father gave in 's° will.          *what my / his*
170　MASTER   What mean you, sir?
　　　PERICLES   To beg of you, kind friends, this coat of worth,
　　　For it was sometime target° to a king.          *once a shield*
　　　I know it by this mark. He loved me dearly,
　　　And for his sake I wish the having of it,
175　And that you'd guide me to your sov'reign's court,
　　　Where with't I may appear a gentleman.
　　　And if that ever my low fortune's better,
　　　I'll pay your bounties,° till then rest your debtor.          *repay your generosity*
　　　MASTER   Why, wilt thou tourney for the lady?
180　PERICLES   I'll show the virtue I have learned in arms.
　　　MASTER   Why, d'ye take it, and the gods give thee good on't!
　　　SECOND FISHERMAN   Ay, but hark you, my friend, 'twas we that
　　　made° up this garment through the rough seams of the waters.          *raised*
　　　There are certain condolements,[5] certain vails.° I hope, sir, if          *tips*
185　you thrive, you'll remember from whence you had this.
　　　PERICLES   Believe't, I will.
　　　By your furtherance I'm clothed in steel,
　　　And spite of all the rapture° of the sea          *plundering*
　　　This jewel holds his building° on my arm.          *its place*
190　Unto thy° value I will mount myself          *(the jewel's)*
　　　Upon a courser° whose delightsome steps          *a horse*
　　　Shall make the gazer joy to see him tread.
　　　Only, my friends, I yet am unprovided
　　　Of a pair of bases.[6]
195　SECOND FISHERMAN   We'll sure provide. Thou shalt have my

---

4. *what . . . soul:* probably ironic: when a man can no
longer "get" (make a living; have children), he can legitimately do so by persuading his "wife's soul" (her conscience; also, "his wife's hole") to trade (prostitute)
herself (with men who will "get"—beget—children with
her). The additions of "himself" and "with" (line 151) in
this edition make the meaning more accessible.
5. Blunder for "dole."
6. Skirts for armored knights on horseback.

best gown to make thee a pair, and I'll bring thee to the court
  myself.
PERICLES    Then honour be but equal to my will,
  This day I'll rise, or else add ill to ill.

                                    [*Exeunt with nets and armour*]

                           **Scene 6**
          [*Sennet.*] *Enter* KING SIMONIDES *and* THAISA *with*
          [LORDS *in*] *attendance* [*and sit on two thrones*]
KING SIMONIDES    Are the knights ready to begin the triumph?°    *tournament*
FIRST LORD    They are, my liege,
  And stay° your coming to present themselves.                    *await*
KING SIMONIDES    Return° them we are ready; and our daughter,    *Answer*
5  In honour of whose birth these triumphs are,
  Sits here like beauty's child, whom nature gat°                 *conceived*
  For men to see and, seeing, wonder at.
                                             [*Exit one*]
THAISA    It pleaseth you, my father, to express
  My commendations great, whose merit's less.
10 KING SIMONIDES    It's fit it should be so, for princes° are    *rulers*
  A model which heav'n makes like to itself.
  As jewels lose their glory if neglected,
  So princes their renown, if not respected.
  'Tis now your office, daughter, to entertain°                  *review*
15   The labour of each knight in his device.[1]
THAISA    Which, to preserve mine honour, I'll perform.
          [*Flourish.*] *The first knight passes by* [*richly armed, and
          his page before him, bearing his device on his shield,
          delivers it to the Lady* THAISA]
KING SIMONIDES    Who is the first that doth prefer° himself?     *present*
THAISA    A knight of Sparta, my renownèd father,
  And the device he bears upon his shield
20  Is a black Ethiop reaching at the sun.
  The word, *Lux tua vita mihi.*[2]
          [*She presents it to the* KING]
KING SIMONIDES    He loves you well that holds his life of° you.  *receives his life from*
          [*He returns it to the page, who exits with the first
          knight.*]
          [*Flourish.*] *The second knight* [*passes by richly armed,
          and his page before him, bearing his device on his
          shield, delivers it to the Lady* THAISA]
  Who is the second that presents himself?
THAISA    A prince of Macedon, my royal father,
25  And the device he bears upon his shield
  An armèd knight that's conquered by a lady.
  The motto thus: *Piùe per dolcezza che per forza.*[3]
          [*She presents it to the* KING]
KING SIMONIDES    You win him more by lenity than force.[4]

---

Scene 6 (Act 2, Scene 2)
Location: Pentapolis, area near the tournament arena,
including a reviewing stand.
1. The ingenuity of each knight's emblem on his shield.
2. Your light is my life (Latin).

3. More by gentleness than by force (Italian). Q1 precedes this phrase with the words "in Spanish"—probably
an error by the reporter. (See the Textual Note.)
4. Not in Q1; adapted from *PA.* Simonides comments
on three of the other five mottoes.

[*He returns it to the page, who exits with the second
knight.*]
[*Flourish. The*] *third knight* [*passes by richly armed, and
his page before him, bearing his device on his shield,
delivers it to the Lady* THAISA]
And what's the third?

THAISA                              The third of Antioch,
30      And his device a wreath of chivalry.[5]
The word, *Me pompae provexit apex.*[6]
[*She presents it to the* KING]

KING SIMONIDES    Desire of renown he doth devise,
The which hath drawn him to this enterprise.[7]
[*He returns it to the page, who exits with the third
knight.*]
[*Flourish. The*] *fourth knight* [*passes by richly armed,
and his page before him, bearing his device on his
shield, delivers it to the Lady* THAISA]
What is the fourth?

THAISA                              A knight of Athens bearing[8]
35      A burning torch that's turnèd upside down.
The word, *Qui me alit me extinguit.*[9]
[*She presents it to the* KING]

KING SIMONIDES    Which shows that beauty hath this power and will,
Which can as well inflame as it can kill.
[*He returns it to the page, who exits with the fourth
knight.*]
[*Flourish. The*] *fifth knight* [*passes by richly armed, and
his page before him, bearing his device on his shield,
delivers it to the Lady* THAISA]
And who the fifth?

THAISA                              The fifth, a prince of Corinth,
40      Presents[1] an hand environèd with clouds,
Holding out gold that's by the touchstone[2] tried.
The motto thus: *Sic spectanda fides.*[3]
[*She presents it to the* KING]

KING SIMONIDES    So faith is to be looked into.[4]
[*He returns it to the page, who exits with the fifth
knight.*]
[*Flourish. The*] *sixth knight* [PERICLES, *in a rusty armour, who, having neither page to deliver his shield
nor shield to deliver, presents his device unto the Lady*
THAISA]
And what's the sixth and last, the which the knight himself
45      With such a graceful courtesy° delivereth?                    *bow*

THAISA    He seems to be a stranger, but his present° is         *presented object*
A withered branch that's only green at top.
The motto, *In hac spe vivo.*°                              *I live in this hope*

KING SIMONIDES    From the dejected state wherein he is
50      He hopes by you his fortunes yet may flourish.

5. (Heraldic term): twisted band that joins the crest and
the knight's helmet.
6. The summit of glory has led me on (Latin).
7. Lines 32–33 are not in Q1; adapted from *PA*.
8. Not in Q1; adapted from *PA*.
9. Who nourishes me extinguishes me.
1. Lines 39–40, adapted from *PA*, replace Q1's "The fift";

the substitution produces symmetry with the other
knights' introductions.
2. Black stone used to check the purity of gold and silver;
symbol of fidelity.
3. Thus is faith to be examined.
4. Not in Q1; adapted from *PA*.

FIRST LORD  He had need mean° better than his outward show    *must intend something*
  Can any way speak in his just commend,°             *on his behalf*
  For by his rusty outside he appears
  T'have practised more the whipstock than the lance.[5]
55 SECOND LORD  He well may be a stranger,° for he comes        *foreigner*
  Unto an honoured triumph strangely furnished.°     *bizarrely equipped*
THIRD LORD  And on set purpose let his armour rust
  Until this day, to scour it in the dust.[6]
KING SIMONIDES  Opinion's but a fool, that makes us scan
60   The outward habit° for the inward man.               *costume*
      [*Cornetts*]°                        *Ceremonial trumpets*
  But stay, the knights are coming. We will withdraw
  Into the gallery.                        [*Exeunt*]
    [*Cornetts and*] *great shouts* [*within*], *and all cry 'The*
    *mean° knight!'*                        *impoverished*

### Scene 7

[*A stately banquet is brought in.*] *Enter* KING [SIMON-
IDES, THAISA *and their train at one door, and at another*
*door a* MARSHAL *conducting* PERICLES] *and* [*the other*]
KNIGHTS *from tilting*

KING SIMONIDES [*to the* KNIGHTS]  To say you're welcome were
    superfluous.
  To place upon the volume of your deeds
  As in a title page[1] your worth in arms
  Were more than you expect, or more than's fit,
5   Since every worth in show° commends itself.         *in practice*
  Prepare for mirth, for mirth becomes a feast.
  You're princes, and my guests.
THAISA [*to* PERICLES]         But you, my knight and guest;
  To whom this wreath of victory I give,
  And crown you king of this day's happiness.
10 PERICLES  'Tis more by fortune, lady, than my merit.
KING SIMONIDES  Call it by what you will, the day is yours,
  And here I hope is none that envies it.
  In framing° artists art hath thus decreed,           *making*
  To make some good, but others to exceed.
  You are her laboured scholar.[2] [*To* THAISA] Come, queen
15     o'th' feast—
  For, daughter, so you are—here take your place.
  [*To* MARSHAL]  Marshal the rest as they deserve their grace.[3]
KNIGHTS  We are honoured much by good Simonides.
KING SIMONIDES  Your presence glads our days; honour we love,
20   For who hates honour hates the gods above.
MARSHAL [*to* PERICLES]  Sir, yonder is your place.
PERICLES                    Some other is more fit.
FIRST KNIGHT  Contend not, sir, for we are gentlemen
  Have° neither in our hearts nor outward eyes         *Who've*
  Envied the great, nor shall the low despise.

---

5. *he appears . . . lance:* he looks more like a manual laborer (a "whipstock" was the handle of a whip used to drive workhorses) than a knight.
6. To polish it in the dust (when he loses).
**Scene 7** (Act 2, Scene 3)
Location: The palace at Pentapolis.

1. Renaissance publishers often advertised the contents on the title page of a book ("volume").
2. Art (creative power) worked hard to make you.
3. Arrange the others according to the honor they deserve.

PERICLES    You are right courteous knights.

25    KING SIMONIDES                                Sit, sir, sit.

[PERICLES *sits directly over against° the* KING *and*                    across from
THAISA. *The guests feed apace.* PERICLES *sits still and*
*eats nothing*]

[*Aside*] By Jove I wonder, that is king of thoughts,
These cates distaste me, he but thought upon.[4]

THAISA [*aside*]    By Juno, that is queen of marriage,
I am amazed all viands that I eat

30    Do seem unsavoury, wishing him my meat.

[*To the* KING]    Sure he's a gallant gentleman.

KING SIMONIDES    He's but a country gentleman.
He's done no more than other knights have done.
He's broke a staff° or so, so let it pass.                              an opponent's lance

35    THAISA [*aside*]    To me he seems like diamond to glass.

PERICLES [*aside*]    Yon king's to me like to my father's picture,
Which tells me in what glory once he was—
Had princes sit like stars about his throne,
And he the sun for them to reverence.

40    None that beheld him but like lesser lights
Did vail° their crowns to his supremacy;                                 lower
Where now his son's a glow-worm in the night,
The which hath fire in darkness, none in light;
Whereby I see that time's the king of men;

45    He's both their parent and he is their grave,
And gives them what he will, not what they crave.

KING SIMONIDES    What, are you merry, knights?

THE OTHER KNIGHTS    Who can be other in this royal presence?

KING SIMONIDES    Here with a cup that's stored unto the brim,

50    As you do love, full[5] to your mistress' lips,
We drink this health to you.

THE OTHER KNIGHTS                    We thank your grace.

KING SIMONIDES    Yet pause a while. Yon knight doth sit too melancholy,
As if the entertainment in our court
Had not a show might countervail° his worth.                          that might equal
Note it not you, Thaisa?

55    THAISA                                What is't to me, my father?

KING SIMONIDES    O, attend, my daughter. Princes in this
Should live like gods above, who freely give
To everyone that come to honour them.
And princes not so doing are like gnats

60    Which make a sound but, killed, are wondered at.[6]
Therefore to make his entertain° more sweet,                          entertainment
Here bear this standing-bowl° of wine to him.                         bowl on a pedestal

THAISA    Alas, my father, it befits not me
Unto a stranger knight to be so bold.

65    He may my proffer take for an offence,
Since men take women's gifts for impudence.

KING SIMONIDES    How? Do as I bid you, or you'll move° me else.        anger

THAISA [*aside*]    Now, by the gods, he could not please me better.

4. *These . . . upon:* (I'm so taken with him that, merely)       6. Which, when dead, appear surprisingly small for all
thinking of him, I lose my appetite for delicacies.              the noise they made alive.
5. Just as you love, fully (all the way).

KING SIMONIDES   Furthermore, tell him we desire to know
70   Of whence he is, his name and parentage.
          [THAISA *bears the cup to* PERICLES]
THAISA   The King my father, sir, has drunk to you,
    Wishing it so much blood unto your life.
PERICLES   I thank both him and you, and pledge° him freely.          *drink to*
          [*He pledges the* KING]
THAISA   And further he desires to know of you
75   Of whence you are, your name and parentage.
PERICLES   A gentleman of Tyre, my name Pericles,
    My education been in arts° and arms,          *liberal arts*
    Who, looking for adventures in the world,
    Was by the rough unconstant seas bereft
80   Unfortunately both of ships and men,
    And after shipwreck driven upon this shore.
          [THAISA *returns to the* KING]
THAISA   He thanks your grace, names himself Pericles,
    A gentleman of Tyre, who, seeking adventures,
    Was solely by misfortune of the seas
85   Bereft of ships and men, cast on this shore.
KING SIMONIDES   Now by the gods I pity his mishaps,
    And will awake him from his melancholy.
          [SIMONIDES, *rising from his state, goes forthwith and*
              *embraces* PERICLES]
    Be[7] cheered, for what misfortune hath impaired° you of,          *deprived*
    Fortune by my help can repair° to you.          *restore*
90   My self and country both shall be your friends,
    And presently° a goodly milk-white steed          *directly*
    And golden spurs I first bestow upon you,
    The prizes due your merit, and ordained
    For this day's enterprise.
95   PERICLES   Your kingly courtesy I thankfully accept.
KING SIMONIDES   Come, gentlemen, we sit° too long on trifles,          *dwell*
    And waste the time which looks for other revels.
    Ev'n in your armours, as you are addressed,°          *dressed*
    Your limbs will well become a soldier's dance.
100   I will not have excuse with saying this,
    'Loud music° is too harsh for ladies' heads',          *The sound of armor*
    Since they love men in arms as well as beds.
          [*The* KNIGHTS] *dance*
    So° this was well asked, 'twas so well performed.          *Just as*
    Come, here's a lady that wants breathing° too.          *exercise*
105   [*To* PERICLES] And I have heard, sir, that the knights of Tyre
    Are excellent in making ladies trip,°          *dance; go astray*
    And that their measures° are as excellent.          *dances; means*
PERICLES   In those that practise them they are, my lord.
KING SIMONIDES   O, that's as much as you would be denied
110   Of your fair courtesy.[8] Unclasp, unclasp.[9]
          *They dance*
    Thanks, gentlemen, to all. All have done well,
    [*To* PERICLES] But you the best.—Lights, pages, to conduct

7. Lines 88–95 are not in Q1; they are adapted from *PA* to improve the transition between lines 87 and 96.
8. *that's . . . courtesy*: that's just what your modesty dictates you should say.

9. Remove (your armor); if the stage direction "*They dance*" is misplaced in Q and really should follow "unclasp," Simonides is presumably ordering Pericles and Thaisa not to dance so intimately.

These knights unto their sev'ral° lodgings.—Yours, sir,                    *separate*
We have giv'n order should be next our own.
115 PERICLES   I am at your grace's pleasure.
KING SIMONIDES   Princes, it is too late to talk of love,
And that's the mark I know you level° at.                                  *aim*
Therefore each one betake him to his rest;
Tomorrow all for speeding do their best.[1]   [*Exeunt severally*]°         *separately*

## Scene 8
*Enter* HELICANUS *and* AESCHINES

HELICANUS   No, Aeschines, know this of me:
Antiochus from incest lived not free,
For which the most high gods, not minding° longer                          *wishing*
To hold the vengeance that they had in store
5  Due to this heinous capital offence,
Even in the height and pride of all his glory,
When he was seated in a chariot
Of an inestimable value, and
His daughter with him, both apparelled all in jewels,[1]
10  A fire from heaven came and shrivelled up
Their bodies e'en to loathing, for they so stunk
That all those eyes adored° them ere their fall                            *that adored*
Scorn now their° hands should give them burial.                            *that their*
AESCHINES   'Twas very strange.
HELICANUS                              And yet but justice, for though
15  This king were great, his greatness was no guard
To bar heav'n's shaft, but sin had his° reward.                            *its*
AESCHINES   'Tis very true.
*Enter three* LORDS [*and stand aside*]
FIRST LORD   See, not a man in private conference
Or council has respect° with him but he.°                 *influence / (Aeschines)*
20  SECOND LORD   It shall no longer grieve° without reproof.            *cause us grief*
THIRD LORD   And cursed be he that will not second it.
FIRST LORD   Follow me, then.—Lord Helicane, a word.
HELICANUS   With me? And welcome. Happy day, my lords.
FIRST LORD   Know that our griefs° are risen to the top,                  *grievances*
25  And now at length they overflow their banks.
HELICANUS   Your griefs? For what? Wrong not your prince you love.
FIRST LORD   Wrong not yourself, then, noble Helicane,
But if the prince do live, let us salute him
Or know what ground's made happy by his step,
30  And be resolved° he lives to govern us,                                 *reassured*
Or dead, give 's° cause to mourn his funeral                               *us*
And leave us to our free election.
SECOND LORD   Whose death indeed's the strongest° in our              *(likelihood)*
      censure,°                                                            *judgment*
And knowing this—kingdoms without a head,
35  Like goodly buildings left without a roof,
Soon fall to utter ruin—your noble self,
That best know how to rule and how to reign,
We thus submit unto as sovereign.

---

1. Each one do his best to succeed (in wooing the   **Scene 8** (Act 2, Scene 4)
Princess).                                          Location: Tyre, the Governor's house.
                                                    1. *both . . . jewels:* not in Q1; taken from *PA*.

ALL [*kneeling*]  Live, noble Helicane!

40  HELICANUS  By honour's cause, forbear your suffrages.°  *voting (for me)*
    If that you love Prince Pericles, forbear.
    [*The* LORDS *rise*]
    Take I° your wish I leap into the seas  *If I accept*
    Where's° hourly trouble for a minute's ease,  *Where there is*
    But if I cannot win you to this love,[2]
45  A twelvemonth longer then let me entreat you
    Further to bear the absence of your king;
    If in which time expired he not return,
    I shall with agèd patience bear your yoke.
    Go, seek your noble prince like noble subjects,
50  And in your search spend your adventurous worth,
    Whom if you find and win unto° return,  *persuade to*
    You shall like diamonds sit about his crown.

FIRST LORD  To wisdom he's a fool that will not yield,
    And since Lord Helicane enjoineth us,
55  We with our travels will endeavour us.
    If in the world he live we'll seek him out;
    If in his grave he rest, we'll find him there.[3]

HELICANUS  Then you love us, we you, and we'll clasp hands.
    When peers thus knit, a kingdom ever stands.  *Exeunt*

## Scene 8a
[*Enter* PERICLES *with* GENTLEMEN *with lights*]

FIRST GENTLEMAN  Here is your lodging, sir.

PERICLES  Pray leave me private.
    Only for instant solace pleasure me
    With[1] some delightful instrument, with which,
    And with my former practice,° I intend  *(of music)*
5   To pass away the tediousness of night,
    Though slumbers were more fitting.

FIRST GENTLEMAN  Presently.°  *At once*
    [*Exit* FIRST GENTLEMAN]

SECOND GENTLEMAN  Your will's obeyed in all things, for our
        master
    Commanded you be disobeyed in nothing.
    [*Enter* FIRST GENTLEMAN *with a stringed instrument*]

PERICLES  I thank you. Now betake you to your pillows,
10  And to the nourishment of quiet sleep.  [*Exeunt* GENTLEMEN]
    [PERICLES *plays and sings*]
    Day—that hath still that sovereignty to draw back
    The empire of the night, though for a while
    In darkness she usurp—brings morning on.
    I will go give his grace that salutation
15  Morning requires of me.  [*Exit with instrument*]

---

2. Love of Pericles (line 41). This line appears in Q1 after line 48, thereby rendering incomprehensible the First Lord's willingness to "yield" (line 53) to the suggestion of searching for Pericles.
3. Lines 56–57 appear after line 29 in Q1. There, they make lines 30–32 problematic and, as in note 2, undermine the First Lord's agreement to travel.

Scene 8a (This scene is not in Q1 or other modern editions. It was adapted from *PA* and provides a reference point for Simonides' compliments in Scene 9, lines 23–28. See the Textual Note.)
Location: The palace at Pentapolis.
1. *pleasure me / With*: grant me.

## Scene 9

*Enter* KING [SIMONIDES] *at one door reading of a letter,*
*the* KNIGHTS [*enter at another door and*] *meet him*

FIRST KNIGHT   Good morrow to the good Simonides.

KING SIMONIDES   Knights, from my daughter this I let you know:
That for this twelvemonth she'll not undertake
A married life. Her reason to herself
5   Is only known, which from her none can get.

SECOND KNIGHT   May we not have access to her, my lord?

KING SIMONIDES   Faith, by no means. It is impossible,
She hath so strictly tied her to her chamber.
One twelve moons more she'll wear Diana's liv'ry.[1]
10   This by the eye of Cynthia[2] hath she vowed,
And on her virgin honour will not break it.

THIRD KNIGHT   Loath to bid farewell, we take our leaves.

[*Exeunt* KNIGHTS]

KING SIMONIDES   So, they are well dispatched. Now to my
daughter's letter.
She tells me here she'll wed the stranger knight,
15   Or never more to view nor° day nor light.[3]                    *neither*
I like that well. Nay, how absolute she's in't,
Not minding whether I dislike or no!
Mistress, t'is well, I do commend your choice,
And will no longer have it be delayed.

*Enter* PERICLES

20   Soft, here he comes. I must dissemble that
In show, I have determined on in heart.[4]

PERICLES   All fortune to the good Simonides.

KING SIMONIDES   To you as much, sir. I am beholden to you
For your sweet music this last night. My ears,
25   I do protest, were never better fed
With such delightful pleasing harmony.

PERICLES   It is your grace's pleasure to commend,
Not my desert.

KING SIMONIDES   Sir, you are music's master.

PERICLES   The worst of all her scholars, my good lord.

KING SIMONIDES   Let me ask you one thing. What think you of
30   my daughter?

PERICLES   A most virtuous princess.

KING SIMONIDES                                    And fair, too, is she not?

PERICLES   As a fair day in summer; wondrous fair.

KING SIMONIDES   My daughter, sir, thinks very well of you;
So well indeed that you must be her master
35   And she will be your scholar;° therefore look to it.°      *student   be prepared*

PERICLES   I am unworthy for her schoolmaster.

KING SIMONIDES   She thinks not so. Peruse this writing else.°      *if you doubt me*

[*He gives the letter to* PERICLES, *who reads*]

PERICLES [*aside*]   What's here?—a letter that she loves the knight
of Tyre?
'Tis the King's subtlety to have my life.

Scene 9 (Act 2, Scene 5)
Location: The palace at Pentapolis.
1. She'll serve Diana, goddess of chastity.
2. Diana, also goddess of the moon.
3. After this line, Q1 has "'Tis well Mistress, your choice

agrees with mine," which is omitted in this edition
because the same thoughts are expressed in lines 16 and
18.
4. *that . . . heart:* replace Q1's "it" (adapted from *PA*).
*that / In show:* outwardly what.

[*He prostrates himself at the King's feet*]

40 O, seek not to entrap me, gracious lord,
A stranger and distressèd gentleman
That never aimed so high to° love your daughter,     *as to*
But bent all offices to honour her.[5]
Never did thought of mine levy° offence,     *give*
45 Nor never did my actions yet commence
A deed might° gain her love or your displeasure.     *that might*
KING SIMONIDES   Thou liest like a traitor.
PERICLES                         Traitor?
KING SIMONIDES                       Ay, traitor,
That thus disguised art stol'n into my court
With witchcraft of thy actions to bewitch
50 The yielding spirit of my tender child.
PERICLES [*rising*]   Who calls me traitor, unless it be the King,
Ev'n in his bosom I will write the lie.°     *(with my sword)*
KING SIMONIDES [*aside*]   Now, by the gods, I do applaud his
      courage.
PERICLES   My actions are as noble as my blood,
55 That never relished of° a base descent.     *gave a hint of*
I came unto your court in search of honour,
And not to be a rebel to your state;
And he that otherwise accounts of me,
This sword shall prove he's honour's enemy.
60 KING SIMONIDES   I shall prove otherwise, since both your practice°     *actions*
And her consent therein is evident
There, by my daughter's hand, as she can witness.[6]
    *Enter* THAISA
PERICLES [*to* THAISA]   Then as you are as virtuous as fair,
By what you hope of heaven or desire
65 By your best wishes here i'th' world fulfilled,[7]
Resolve° your angry father if my tongue     *Inform*
Did e'er solicit, or my hand subscribe
To any syllable made° love to you.     *that made*
THAISA   Why, sir, say if you had,
70 Who takes offence at that° would make me glad?     *what*
KING SIMONIDES   How, minion, are you so peremptory?°     *determined*
[*Aside*] I am glad on't.—Is[8] this a fit match for you?
A straggling Theseus, born we know not where,[9]
One that hath neither blood nor merit
75 For thee to hope for, or himself to challenge°     *claim for himself*
Of thy perfections e'en the least allowance.°     *share*
THAISA [*kneeling*]   Suppose his birth were base, when that° his life     *even though*
Shows that he is not so, yet he hath virtue,
The very ground of all nobility,
80 Enough to make him noble. I entreat you
To remember that I am in love,

---

5. After this line, Q1 has

    KING Thou hast bewitched my daughter,
      And thou art a villain.
    PERICLES By the Gods I have not.

This passage breaks up what is a single speech in *PA*. It is omitted here and replaced by Simonides' speech at lines 47–50, which is adapted from *PA* and is more powerful. *bent all offices*: performed all services.
6. Except for "she can witness," lines 60–62 are adapted

from *PA*; they replace Q1's "No? here comes my daughter, she can witness it," which echoes *Othello* 1.3.169. The reporter of this passage may have played Desdemona.
7. *By what . . . fulfilled*: not in Q1; adapted from *PA*.
8. Lines 72–96, adapted from *PA*, replace Q1's "with all my heart"; inclusion of this passage shifts the emphasis from nobility of birth to nobility of soul.
9. Theseus was an Athenian hero of ambiguous parentage who sometimes mistreated women.

The power of which love cannot be confined
By th' power of your will. Most royal father,
What with my pen I have in secret written
85    With my tongue now I openly confirm,
Which is I have no life but in his love,
Nor any being but in joying of his worth.

KING SIMONIDES    Equals to equals, good to good is joined.
This not being so, the bavin° of your mind         *firewood*
90    In rashness kindled must again be quenched,
Or purchase° our displeasure.—And for you, sir,    *provoke*
First learn to know I banish you my court,
And yet I scorn our rage should stoop so low.
For your ambition, sir, I'll have your life.

95    THAISA [*to* PERICLES]    For every drop of blood he sheds of yours
He'll draw another from his only child.

KING SIMONIDES    I'll tame you, yea, I'll bring you in subjection.
Will you not having my consent
Bestow your love and your affections
100    Upon a stranger?—[*aside*] who for aught I know
May be, nor can I think the contrary,
As great in blood as I myself.
        [*He catches* THAISA *rashly by the hand*]
Therefore hear you, mistress: either frame° your will to mine—    *mold*
        [*He catches* PERICLES *rashly by the hand*]
And you, sir, hear you: either be ruled by me—
Or I shall make you
        [*He claps their hands together*]
105              man and wife.
Nay, come, your hands and lips must seal it too,
        [PERICLES *and* THAISA *kiss*]
And being joined, I'll thus your hopes destroy,
        [*He parts them*]
And for your further grief, God give you joy.
What, are you pleased?

THAISA               Yes, [*to* PERICLES] if you love me, sir.
110    PERICLES    Ev'n as my life° my blood that fosters it.    *as my life loves*

KING SIMONIDES    What, are you both agreed?

PERICLES *and* THAISA            Yes, if't please your majesty.

KING SIMONIDES    It pleaseth me so well that I will see you wed,
Then with what haste you can, get you to bed.    *Exeunt*

## Scene 10

*Enter* GOWER

GOWER    Now sleep y-slackèd hath the rout,[1]
No din but snores the house about,
Made louder by the o'erfed breast
Of this most pompous° marriage feast.    *lavish*
5    The cat with eyne° of burning coal    *eyes*
Now couches fore the mouse's hole,
And crickets sing at th'oven's mouth
As the blither for their drouth.[2]
Hymen° hath brought the bride to bed,    *god of marriage*

Scene 10 (Act 3, Chorus)           2. As if happier for being dry.
1. Sleep has rendered everyone inactive.

10 Where by the loss of maidenhead
A babe is moulded. Be attent,°                                   *attentive*
And time that is so briefly spent°                         *spent onstage*
With your fine fancies quaintly eche.°          *skillfully fill out*
What's dumb in show, I'll plain° with speech.            *clarify*
                        [*Dumb show.*]
              *Enter* PERICLES *and* SIMONIDES *at one door with atten-*
              *dants. A messenger* [*comes hastily in to*] *them, kneels,*
              *and gives* PERICLES *a letter.* PERICLES *shows it* SIMON-
              IDES; *the lords kneel to him. Then enter* THAISA *with*
              *child, with* LYCHORIDA, *a nurse. The* KING *shows her the*
              *letter. She rejoices. She and* PERICLES *take leave of her*
              *father and depart* [*with* LYCHORIDA *at one door;* SIMON-
              IDES *and attendants depart at another*]
15 By many a dern° and painful perch°           *wild / patch of land*
Of Pericles the care-full search,
By the four opposing coigns°                                *corners*
Which the world together joins,
Is made with all due diligence
20 That horse and sail and high expense
Can stead° the quest. At last from Tyre                  *sustain in*
Fame° answering the most strange enquire,°   *Rumor / distant queries*
To th' court of King Simonides
Are letters brought, the tenor these:
25 Antiochus and his daughter dead,
The men of Tyrus on the head
Of Helicanus would set on
The crown of Tyre, but he will° none.                      *desires*
The mutiny there he hastes t'appease,
30 Says to 'em if King Pericles
Come not home in twice six moons
He, obedient to their dooms,°                             *judgments*
Will take the crown. The sum of this
Brought hither to Pentapolis
35 Y-ravishèd° the regions round,                        *Enraptured*
And everyone with claps can° sound                       *started to*
'Our heir-apparent is a king!
Who dreamt, who thought of such a thing?'
Brief° he must hence depart to Tyre;            *In short; quickly*
40 His queen with child makes her desire—
Which who shall cross?—along to go.
Omit we all their dole and woe.
Lychorida her nurse she takes,
And so to sea. Their vessel shakes
45 On Neptune's billow. Half the flood°                        *sea*
Hath their keel cut, but fortune's mood
Varies again. The grizzled° north                          *grisly*
Disgorges such a tempest forth
That as a duck for life that dives,
50 So up and down the poor ship drives.
The lady shrieks, and well-a-near°                            *alas*
Does fall in travail° with her fear,                 *Goes into labor*
And what ensues in this fell° storm                         *cruel*
Shall for itself itself perform;
55 I nill° relate; action may                             *will not*

Conveniently the rest convey,
Which might not what by me is told.[3]
In your imagination hold°                                     *think*
This stage the ship, upon whose deck
60  The sea-tossed Pericles appears to speke.          [*Exit*]

### Scene 11
[*Thunder and lightning.*] *Enter* PERICLES *a-shipboard*

PERICLES   The god of this great vast° rebuke these surges          *vast sea*
Which wash both heav'n and hell; and thou that hast
Upon the winds command, bind them in brass,
Having called them from the deep. O still°                    *quiet*
5  Thy deaf'ning dreadful thunders, gently quench
Thy nimble sulph'rous flashes.—O, ho, Lychorida!
How does my queen?—Thou stormest venomously.
Wilt thou spit all thyself? The seaman's whistle
Is as a whisper in the ears of death,°          *of a dead person*
10  Unheard.—Lychorida!—Lucina,° O!          *goddess of childbirth*
Divinest patroness, and midwife gentle
To those that cry by night, convey thy deity
Aboard our dancing boat, make swift the pangs
Of my queen's travails!—Now, Lychorida.
*Enter* LYCHORIDA [*with an infant*]
15  LYCHORIDA   Here is a thing too young for such a place,
Who, if it had conceit,° would die, as I          *understanding*
Am like° to do. Take in your arms this piece          *likely*
Of your dead queen.
PERICLES                      How, how, Lychorida?
LYCHORIDA   Patience, good sir, do not assist the storm.°          *(by ranting and tears)*
20  Here's all that is left living of your queen,
A little daughter. For the sake of it
Be manly, and take comfort.
PERICLES                      O you gods!
Why do you make us love your goodly gifts,
And snatch them straight away? We here below
25  Recall° not what we give, and therein may          *Demand back*
Use honour with you.[1]
LYCHORIDA                      Patience, good sir,
E'en for this charge.[2]
[*She gives him the infant.* PERICLES, *looking mournfully
upon it, shakes his head, and weeps*]
PERICLES                      Now mild may be thy life,
For a more blust'rous birth had never babe;
Quiet and gentle thy conditions,° for          *circumstances*
30  Thou art the rudeliest welcome to this world
That e'er was prince's child; happy° what follows.          *let be happy*
Thou hast as chiding° a nativity          *upsetting*
As fire, air, water, earth, and heav'n can make
To herald thee from th' womb. Poor inch of nature,
35  Ev'n at the first thy loss is more than can

---

3. Which could not easily "convey" what I've related so far.
**Scene 11** (Act 3, Scene 1)
Location: At sea.

1. *therein . . . you:* so we can criticize you by this standard of honor.
2. For the sake of this child.

Thy partage quit with all thou canst find here.³
Now the good gods throw their best eyes° upon't.                    *look favorably*
    *Enter [the* MASTER *and a]* SAILOR
MASTER   What, courage, sir! God save you.
PERICLES   Courage enough, I do not fear the flaw;°                    *squall*
40   It hath done to me its worst. Yet for the love
    Of this poor infant, this fresh new seafarer,
    I would it would be quiet.
MASTER *[calling]*   Slack the bow-lines, there.—Thou° wilt not,                    *(the storm)*
    wilt thou? Blow, and split thyself.
45   SAILOR   But searoom,⁴ an° the brine and cloudy billow kiss the                    *if*
    moon, I care not.
MASTER *[to* PERICLES*]*   Sir, your queen must overboard. The sea
    works° high, the wind is loud, and will not lie° till the ship be                    *surges / lie still*
    cleared of the dead.
50   PERICLES   That's but your superstition.
MASTER   Pardon us, sir; with us at sea it hath been still° observed,                    *always*
    and we are strong in custom. Therefore briefly° yield 'er, for                    *quickly*
    she must overboard straight.
PERICLES   As you think meet. Most wretched queen!
LYCHORIDA                          Here she lies, sir.
    *[She draws the curtains and discovers the body of Thaisa*
    *in a bed.* PERICLES *gives* LYCHORIDA *the infant]*
55   PERICLES *[to* THAISA*]*   A terrible childbed hast thou had, my dear,
    No light, no fire. Th'unfriendly elements
    Forgot thee utterly, nor have I time
    To give thee hallowed to thy grave, but straight
    Must cast thee, scarcely coffined, in the ooze,°                    *seabed*
60   Where, for° a monument upon thy bones                    *in place of*
    And aye-remaining° lamps, the belching whale                    *ever-burning*
    And humming water must o'erwhelm thy corpse,
    Lying with simple shells.—O Lychorida,
    Bid Nestor bring me spices, ink, and paper,
65   My casket and my jewels, and bid Nicander
    Bring me the satin coffer. Lay the babe
    Upon the pillow. Hie° thee whiles I say                    *Hurry*
    A priestly farewell to her. Suddenly,° woman.                    *Immediately*
                     *[Exit* LYCHORIDA*]*
SAILOR   Sir, we have a chest beneath the hatches caulked and
70   bitumed⁵ ready.
PERICLES   I thank thee. *[To the* MASTER*]* Mariner, say, what coast is this?
MASTER   We are near Tarsus.
PERICLES               Thither, gentle mariner,
    Alter thy course from Tyre. When canst thou reach it?
MASTER   By break of day, if the wind cease.
PERICLES               Make for Tarsus.
75   There will I visit Cleon, for the babe
    Cannot hold out to Tyrus. There I'll leave it
    At careful nursing. Go thy ways,° good mariner.                    *Get to it*
    I'll bring the body presently.
        *Exit [*MASTER *at one door and* SAILOR *beneath*
          *the hatches. Exit* PERICLES *to* THAISA,
          *closing the curtains]*

---

3. *than . . . here*: than your share of anything you find
in this life can make up for.
4. As long as we're at sea (safe from the rocks).
5. *bitumed*: caulked with pitch.

## Scene 12

*Enter Lord* CERIMON *with a [poor man and a] servant*

CERIMON  Philemon, ho!

*Enter* PHILEMON

PHILEMON                 Doth my lord call?

CERIMON  Get fire and meat for those poor men.[1]

                          [*Exit* PHILEMON]

'T'as been a turbulent and stormy night.

SERVANT  I have seen many, but such a night as this

5    Till now I ne'er endured.

CERIMON  Your master will be dead ere you return.

There's nothing can be ministered in nature

That can recover him. [*To poor man*] Give this to th' pothecary°     *druggist*

And tell me how it works.

               [*Exeunt poor man and servant*]

*Enter two* GENTLEMEN

FIRST GENTLEMAN          Good morrow.

SECOND GENTLEMAN  Good morrow to your lordship.

10  CERIMON                        Gentlemen,

Why do you stir so early?

FIRST GENTLEMAN       Sir,

Our lodgings, standing bleak upon° the sea,     *exposed to*

Shook as° the earth did quake.     *us if*

The very principals° did seem to rend     *principal rafters*

15  And all to topple. Pure surprise and fear

Made me to quit the house.

SECOND GENTLEMAN    That is the cause we trouble you so early;

'Tis not our husbandry.°     *good work habits*

CERIMON           O, you say well.

FIRST GENTLEMAN  But I much marvel that your lordship should,

20  Having rich tire° about you, at this hour     *bed furniture*

Shake off the golden slumber of repose. 'Tis most strange,

Nature to be so conversant with pain,[2]

Being thereto not compelled.

CERIMON           I held it ever;°     *always believed*

Virtue and cunning° were endowments greater     *knowledge*

25  Than nobleness and riches. Careless heirs

May the two latter darken and dispend,°     *expend*

But immortality attends the former,

Making a man a god. 'Tis known I ever°     *always*

Have studied physic,° through which secret art,     *medicine*

30  By turning o'er authorities,° I have,     *reading learned texts*

Together with my practice, made familiar

To me and to my aid° the blest infusions     *assistant*

That dwells in vegetives,[3] in metals, stones,

And so can speak of the disturbances

35  That nature works, and of her cures, which doth give me

A more content° and cause of true delight     *greater happiness*

Than to be thirsty after tott'ring° honour,     *unstable*

Or tie my pleasure up in silken bags°     *(of money)*

To glad the fool and death.[4]

---

**Scene 12** (Act 3, Scene 2)
Location: Cerimon's house in Ephesus.
1. Offstage supplicants. Qls "these poor men" might refer to characters onstage.

2. That your nature should be so accustomed to labor.
3. Beneficial substances in plants.
4. To gladden the fool who trusts in wealth, which death inherits.

SECOND GENTLEMAN          Your honour has
40    Through Ephesus poured forth your charity,
      And hundreds call themselves your creatures[5] who by you
      Have been restored. And not alone your knowledge,
      Your personal pain,° but e'en your purse still° open                    *labor / always*
      Hath built Lord Cerimon such strong renown
45    As time shall never—
                *Enter* [PHILEMON *and one*] *or two[6] with a chest*
      PHILEMON    So, lift there.
      CERIMON    What's that?
      PHILEMON    Sir, even now
      The sea tossed up upon our shore this chest.
      'Tis off some wreck.
50    CERIMON          Set't down. Let's look upon't.
      SECOND GENTLEMAN    'Tis like a coffin, sir.
      CERIMON                    Whate'er it be,
      'Tis wondrous heavy.—Did the sea cast it up?
      PHILEMON    I never saw so huge a billow, sir,
      Or a more eager.[7]
      CERIMON          Wrench it open straight.
                *[The others start to work]*
55    If the sea's stomach be o'ercharged with gold
      'Tis by a good constraint of queasy fortune[8]
      It belches upon us.
      SECOND GENTLEMAN    'Tis so, my lord.
      CERIMON    How close° 'tis caulked and bitumed!                          *tightly*
                *[They force the lid]*
                                  Soft,° it smells                            *But wait*
      Most sweetly in my sense.
      SECOND GENTLEMAN          A delicate odour.
60    CERIMON    As ever hit my nostril. So, up with it.
                *[They take the lid off ]*
      O you most potent gods! What's here—a corpse?
      SECOND GENTLEMAN
      Most strange.
      CERIMON          Shrouded in cloth of state,° and crowned,             *royal fabric*
      Balmed and entreasured with full bags of spices.
      A passport,° too!                                                       *An identification paper*
                *[He takes a paper from the chest]*
65    Apollo perfect me i'th' characters.[9]
      'Here I give to understand,
      If e'er this coffin drives a-land,
      I, King Pericles, have lost
      This queen worth all our mundane cost.°                                 *earthly wealth*
70    Who° finds her, give her burying;                                       *Whoever*
      She was the daughter of a king.
      Besides this treasure for a fee,
      The° gods requite his charity.'                                         *May the*

---

5. *call . . . creatures*: owe their lives to you.
6. "Philemon" replaces QI's "two or three" here, "Servant" in the speech prefixes to lines 46–53, and "one" in the stage direction to line 84, in accord with the emphasis on one of Cerimon's assistants in Twine's *Patterne of Painefull Adventures* and in order to make sense of Philemon's appearance at the beginning of the scene.
7. *Did . . . eager*: In QI, these lines appear after "bitumed" (line 58), where the question seems inappro-

priate. The passage is then followed by "Wrench it open," which repeats line 54. Here, "Or a more eager," adapted from *PA*, replaces QI's "as tossed it upon shore" (which repeats QI's "toss up upon our shore," line 49). These changes seek to remedy the possibly faulty memory of the reporters.
8. By the force of uncertain fortune that.
9. Apollo (patron of both scholars and physicians) help me read the writing correctly.

If thou liv'st, Pericles, thou hast a heart
75　That even cracks for woe. This chanced tonight.°　　　　*occurred last night*
SECOND GENTLEMAN　Most likely, sir.
CERIMON　　　　　　　　　　Nay, certainly tonight,
For look how fresh she looks. They were too rash
That threw her in the sea. Make a fire within.
Fetch hither all my boxes in my closet.　　　[*Exit* PHILEMON]
80　Death may usurp on nature many hours,
And yet the fire of life kindle again
The o'erpressed° spirits. I have heard　　　　　　　　*overcome*
Of an Egyptian nine hours dead
Who was by good appliances° recovered.　　　　*medical treatments*
　　　*Enter* [PHILEMON] *with napkins and fire*
85　Well said, well said, the fire and cloths.
The still° and woeful music that we have,　　　　　　　　*soft*
Cause it to sound, beseech you.
　　　[*Music*]
　　　　　　　　　　The vial° once more.　　　　　*(of medicine)*
How thou stirr'st,[1] thou block! The music there!
I pray you give her air.° Gentlemen,　　　　　*(pun on "heir")*
90　This queen will live. Nature awakes, a warmth
Breathes out of her. She hath not been entranced°　　　*unconscious*
Above five hours. See how she 'gins to blow°　　　　*bloom*
Into life's flow'r again.
FIRST GENTLEMAN　　　　　The heavens
Through you increase our wonder, and set up
Your fame for ever.
95　CERIMON　　　　　　　She is alive. Behold,
Her eyelids, cases to those heav'nly jewels
Which Pericles hath lost,
Begin to part their fringes of bright gold.
The diamonds of a most praisèd water°　　　　　　*luster*
100　Doth appear to make the world twice rich.[2]—Live,
And make us weep to hear your fate, fair creature,
Rare° as you seem to be.　　　　　　　　　　*Exquisite*
　　　*She moves*
THAISA　　　　　　　　O dear Diana,
Where am I? Where's my lord? What world is this?
SECOND GENTLEMAN
Is not this strange?
FIRST GENTLEMAN　Most rare.
CERIMON　　　　　　　　　Hush, gentle neighbours.
105　Lend me your hands. To the next chamber bear her.
Get linen. Now this matter must be looked to,
For her relapse is mortal.° Come, come,　　　　*would be fatal*
And Aesculapius° guide us.　　*They carry her away. Exeunt*　*god of healing*

## Scene 13

*Enter* PERICLES *at Tarsus, with* CLEON *and* DIONYZA
[*and* LYCHORIDA *with a babe*]
PERICLES　Most honoured Cleon, I must needs be gone.
My twelve months are expired, and Tyrus stands

---

1. How lively you are (ironic).
2. Once by the precious gold of her eyelids and again
by the jewels they conceal.

Scene 13 (Act 3, Scene 3)
Location: The Governor's house in Tarsus.

In a litigious° peace. You and your lady                                            *conflict-ridden*
Take from my heart all thankfulness. The gods
Make up the rest upon you!¹

5  CLEON                                          Your strokes of fortune,
Though they hurt you mortally, yet glance
Full woundingly on us.

DIONYZA                                 O your sweet queen!
That the strict fates had pleased you'd brought her hither
T'have blessed mine eyes with her!

PERICLES                                 We cannot but obey

10  The pow'rs above us. Should° I rage and roar                              *Even if*
As doth the sea she lies in, yet the end
Must be as 'tis. My gentle babe Marina,
Whom for° she was born at sea I have named so,                            *because*
Here I charge° your charity withal,° and leave her          *saddle / with*

15  The infant of your care, beseeching you
To give her princely training, that she may be
Mannered° as she is born.                            *Instructed in manners*

CLEON                                 Fear not, my lord, but think
Your grace, that fed my country with your corn—
For which the people's pray'rs still fall upon you—

20  Must in your child be thought on. If neglection
Should therein make me vile, the common body°                          *the people*
By you relieved would force me to my duty.
But if to that° my nature need a spur,                                        *that duty*
The gods revenge it upon me and mine
To th' end of generation.

25  PERICLES                                 I believe you.
Your honour and your goodness teach me to't°                            *to do so*
Without your vows.—Till she be married, madam,
By bright Diana, whom we honour all,
Unscissored shall this hair of mine remain,

30  Though I show ill° in't. So I take my leave.                              *look bad*
Good madam, make me blessèd in your care
In bringing up my child.

DIONYZA                                 I have one myself,
Who shall not be more dear to my respect°                                *attention*
Than yours, my lord.

PERICLES                                 Madam, my thanks and prayers.

35  CLEON   We'll bring your grace e'en to the edge o'th' shore,
Then give you up to th' masted Neptune° and                  *ship-conveying sea*
The gentlest winds of heaven.

PERICLES   I will embrace your offer.—Come, dear'st madam.—
O, no tears, Lychorida, no tears.

40  Look to your little mistress, on whose grace°                            *favor*
You may depend hereafter.—Come, my lord.        [*Exeunt*]


## Scene 14

*Enter* CERIMON *and* THAISA

CERIMON   Madam, this letter and some certain jewels
Lay with you in your coffer, which are all
At your command. Know you the character?°                              *handwriting*

---

1. Give you the rest of what you deserve.                    **Scene 14** (Act 3, Scene 4)
                                                              **Location:** Cerimon's house in Ephesus.

THAISA   It is my lord's. That I was shipped° at sea           *on a ship*
5       I well remember, ev'n on my eaning° time,            *birthing*
      But whether there delivered, by th' holy gods
      I cannot rightly say. But since King Pericles,
      My wedded lord, I ne'er shall see again,
      A vestal liv'ry[1] will I take me to,
10      And never more have joy.
CERIMON   Madam, if this you purpose° as ye speak,        *intend*
      Diana's temple is not distant far,
      Where till your date° expire you may abide.        *time of life*
      Moreover, if you please a niece of mine
15      Shall there attend you.
THAISA   My recompense is thanks, that's all,
      Yet my good will is great, though the gift small.      *Exeunt*

## Scene 15

*Enter* GOWER

GOWER   Imagine Pericles arrived at Tyre,
      Welcomed and settled to his own desire.
      His woeful queen we leave at Ephesus,
      Unto Diana there 's a votaress.°               *as a devotee*
5      Now to Marina bend your mind,
      Whom our fast-growing scene must find
      At Tarsus, and by Cleon trained
      In music, letters; who hath gained
      Of education all the grace,
10     Which makes her both the heart and place°      *focal point*
      Of gen'ral wonder. But, alack,
      That monster envy, oft the wrack°             *ruin*
      Of earnèd praise, Marina's life
      Seeks to take off by treason's knife,
15     And in this kind° our Cleon has            *connection*
      One daughter, and a full-grown lass
      E'en ripe for marriage-rite. This maid
      Hight° Philoten, and it is said             *Is called*
      For certain in our story she
20     Would ever° with Marina be,             *always*
      Be't when they weaved the sleided° silk     *divided into filaments*
      With fingers long, small, white as milk;
      Or when she would with sharp nee'le° wound      *needle*
      The cambric° which she made more sound      *fine linen*
25     By hurting it, or when to th' lute
      She sung, and made the night bird° mute,      *nightingale*
      That still records° with moan; or when      *always sings*
      She would with rich and constant pen
      Vail° to her mistress Dian. Still        *Inscribe praises*
30     This Philoten contends in skill
      With absolute° Marina; so             *perfect*
      With dove of Paphos might the crow

---

1. Vestal virgin's uniform of religious chastity.
**Scene 15** (Other modern editions treat Gower's mono-logue as a prologue to Act 4 and start Act 4, Scene 1, at line 53. This edition assumes that the grave Marina goes "to strew" [line 66] "is revealed" during Gower's speech [stage direction after line 42], that Dionyza and Leonine enter here, rather than [as in Q1] at the end of that speech, and hence that the scene does not change.) Location: Tarsus, near the seashore.

Vie feathers white.[1] Marina gets
All praises which are paid as debts,
35 And not as given.[2] This so darks°                        *(by comparison)*
In Philoten all graceful marks
That Cleon's wife with envy rare°                          *extreme*
A present murder does prepare
For good Marina, that her daughter
40 Might stand peerless by° this slaughter.                   *by means of*
The sooner her vile thoughts to stead°                     *help*
Lychorida, our nurse, is dead,
       [*A tomb is revealed*]
And cursèd Dionyza hath
The pregnant instrument of wrath
45 Pressed for this blow.[3] Th'unborn event°                *outcome*
I do commend to your content,°                             *(viewing) pleasure*
Only I carry wingèd Time
Post° on the lame feet of my rhyme,                        *Quickly*
Which never could I so convey
50 Unless your thoughts went on my way.
          *Enter* DIONYZA *with* LEONINE
Dionyza does appear,
With Leonine, a murderer.                    *Exit*
DIONYZA   Thy oath remember. Thou hast sworn to do't.
'Tis but a blow, which never shall be known.
55 Thou canst not do a thing i'th' world so soon°            *quickly*
To yield thee so much profit. Let not conscience,
Which is but cold, or fanning love thy bosom
Unflame[4] too nicely,° nor let pity, which               *scrupulously*
E'en women have cast off, melt thee; but be
A soldier to thy purpose.
60 LEONINE                     I will do't;
But yet she is a goodly creature.
DIONYZA   The fitter then the gods should have her.
          *Enter* MARINA [*to the tomb*] *with a basket of flowers*
Here she comes, weeping her only nurse's death.
Thou art resolved.
LEONINE              I am resolved.
65 MARINA   No, I will rob Tellus of her weed°              *earth of its garment*
To strew thy grave with flow'rs. The yellows, blues,
The purple violets and marigolds
Shall as a carpet hang upon thy tomb
While summer days doth last. Ay me, poor maid,
70 Born in a tempest when my mother died,
This world to me is but a ceaseless storm
Whirring° me from my friends.                             *Hurrying*
DIONYZA   How now, Marina, why do you keep alone?
How chance° my daughter is not with you?                  *Why is it*
75 Do not consume your blood with sorrowing.[5]
Have you a nurse of me.[6] Lord, how your favour°         *appearance*
Is changed with this unprofitable woe!

1. *so . . . white*: so might the crow try to be whiter than the dove. Paphos was a city sacred to Venus.
2. *Marina . . . given*: Marina's virtues compel praise, whether or not one wants to.
3. Has prepared a ready means for the murder.
4. *or . . . / Unflame*: or cooling love blow out the murderous flame in your bosom. Editors variously emend Q1's "in flaming, thy love bosom, enslave."
5. Sighs were thought to consume one's blood.
6. Let me be your nurse.

Give me your flowers. Come, o'er the sea margin°          *seashore*
Walk with Leonine. The air is piercing there,
80  And quick;° it sharps the stomach.° Come, Leonine,     *refreshing / appetite*
Take her by th' arm. Walk with her.
MARINA                          No, I pray you,
I'll not bereave you of your servant.
DIONYZA                          Come, come,
I love the King your father and yourself
With more than foreign heart.° We ev'ry day           *As if we were kin*
85  Expect him here. When he shall come and find
Our paragon to all reports thus blasted,[7]
He will repent the breadth of his great voyage,
Blame both my lord and me, that we have taken
No care to your best courses.° Go, I pray you,        *courses of action*
90  Walk and be cheerful once again; resume
That excellent complexion which did steal
The eyes of young and old. Care not for me.
I can go home alone.
MARINA                          Well, I will go,
But truly I have no desire to it.
95  DIONYZA   Nay, I know 'tis good for you. Walk half an hour,
Leonine, at the least; remember
What I have said.
LEONINE             I warr'nt° you, madam.                *guarantee*
DIONYZA [*to* MARINA]   I'll leave you, my sweet lady, for a while.
Pray you walk softly, do not heat your blood.
What, I must have care of you!
100  MARINA                          My thanks, sweet madam.
                                  [*Exit* DIONYZA]
Is this wind westerly that blows?
LEONINE                          South-west.
MARINA   When I was born the wind was north.
LEONINE                          Was't so?
MARINA   My father, as nurse says, did never fear,
But cried 'Good seamen' to the mariners,
105  Galling° his kingly hands with haling° ropes,          *Irritating / pulling*
And, clasping to the mast, endured a sea
That almost burst the deck.
LEONINE   When was this?
MARINA   When I was born.
110  Never was waves nor wind more violent.
Once from the ladder tackle washes off
A canvas-climber.° 'Ha!' says one, 'wolt out?'[8]       *sailor in the rigging*
And with a dropping° industry they skip              *dripping-wet*
From stem to stern. The boatswain whistles, and
115  The master calls and trebles their confusion.
LEONINE   Come, say your prayers.
MARINA   What mean you?
LEONINE   If you require a little space for prayer
I grant it. Pray, but be not tedious.°                *drawn out*
120  The gods are quick of ear, and I am sworn
To do my work with haste.

---

7. Our universally admired paragon of beauty so    8. So you want to get off ship? (a cruel joke).
blighted.

| | | |
|---|---|---|
| MARINA | Why would you kill me? | |
| LEONINE | To satisfy my lady. | |
| MARINA | Why would she have me killed? | |

Now, as I can remember, by my troth°                                   faith
I never did her hurt in all my life.
125   I never spake bad word, nor did ill turn
To any living creature. Believe me, la.°                               (exclamation)
I never killed a mouse nor hurt a fly.
I trod once on a worm against my will,
But I wept for it. How have I offended
130   Wherein my death might yield her any profit
Or my life imply her danger?

LEONINE                             My commission
Is not to reason of the deed, but do't.

MARINA   You will not do't for all the world, I hope.
You are well favoured, and your looks foreshow
135   You have a gentle heart. I saw you lately
When you caught° hurt in parting two that fought.                      got
Good sooth,° it showed well in you. Do so now.                         Truly
Your lady seeks my life. Come you between,
And save poor me, the weaker.

LEONINE   [drawing out his sword] I am sworn,
140   And will dispatch.

Enter PIRATES [running]

FIRST PIRATE   Hold, villain.

[LEONINE runs away and hides behind the tomb]

SECOND PIRATE   A prize,° a prize.                                     Booty (Marina)

THIRD PIRATE   Half-part,° mates, half-part. Come, let's have her      To be shared
aboard suddenly.°                                                      quickly

Exeunt [PIRATES carrying MARINA]

LEONINE [steals back]

145   LEONINE   These roguing° thieves serve the great pirate Valdes.[9]   law-breaking
An° they have seized Marina, let her go.                               If
There's no hope she'll return. I'll swear she's dead
And thrown into the sea; but I'll see further.
Perhaps they will but please themselves upon her,°                    will only rape her
150   Not carry her aboard. If she remain,
Whom they have ravished must by me be slain.

Exit. [The tomb is concealed]

## Scene 16

[A brothel sign.] Enter [the PANDER, his wife] the BAWD
[and their man BOULT][1]

PANDER   Boult.

BOULT   Sir.

PANDER   Search the market narrowly.° Mytilene is full of gal-        carefully
lants. We lose too much money this mart° by being wenchless.          market time

5   BAWD   We were never so much out of creatures.° We have but        prostitutes
poor three, and they can do no more than they can do, and
they with continual action are even as good as rotten.°               have venereal disease

PANDER   Therefore let's have fresh ones, whate'er we pay for

---

9. Probably named after an admiral in the Spanish
Armada.
**Scene 16** (Act 4, Scene 2)
Location: Mytilene, on the island of Lesbos; before a

brothel.
1. *Pander:* sexual go-between, after Pandarus in *Troilus
and Cressida. Bawd:* supplier of prostitutes. The name
"Boult" may have phallic connotations.

them. If there be not a conscience to be used[2] in every trade,
10 we shall never prosper.

BAWD  Thou sayst true. 'Tis not our bringing up of poor bas-
tards°—as I think I have brought up some eleven—                    *(that enriches us)*

BOULT  Ay, to eleven, and brought them down again.[3] But shall
I search the market?

15 BAWD  What else, man? The stuff we have, a strong wind will
blow it to pieces, they are so pitifully sodden.[4]

PANDER  Thou sayst true. They're too unwholesome, o' con-
science.° The poor Transylvanian is dead that lay with the little      *on my conscience*
baggage.°                                                               *prostitute*

20 BOULT  Ay, she quickly pooped° him, she made him roast meat      *overcame (by disease)*
for worms. But I'll go search the market.                *Exit*

PANDER  Three or four thousand chequins° were as pretty a pro-      *gold coins*
portion° to live quietly, and so give over.°                        *sum / retire*

BAWD  Why to give over, I pray you? Is it a shame to get° when       *earn*
25 we are old?

PANDER  O, our credit comes not in like the commodity, nor the
commodity wages not with the danger.[5] Therefore if in our
youths we could pick up some pretty estate, 'twere not amiss to
keep our door hatched.° Besides, the sore terms we stand upon       *closed for business*
30 with the gods[6] will be strong° with us for giving o'er.          *a strong argument*

BAWD  Come, other sorts offend as well as we.

PANDER  As well as we? Ay, and better too; we offend worse. Nei-
ther is our profession any mystery,[7] it's no calling.° But here    *(religious) vocation*
comes Boult.

*Enter* BOULT *with the* PIRATES *and* MARINA

35 BOULT [*to the* PIRATES]  Come your ways,° my masters,° you say   *Come along / gentlemen*
she's a virgin?

A PIRATE  O sir, we doubt it not.

BOULT [*to* PANDER]  Master, I have gone through° for this piece°   *bargained / (of flesh)*
you see. If you like her, so;° if not, I have lost my earnest.°      *fine / deposit*

40 BAWD  Boult, has she any qualities?°                               *accomplishments*

BOULT  She has a good face, speaks well, and has excellent good
clothes. There's no farther necessity of qualities can° make her    *whose absence can*
be refused.

BAWD  What's her price, Boult?

45 BOULT  I cannot be bated one doit of[8] a hundred sesterces.

PANDER [*to* PIRATES]  Well, follow me, my masters. You shall
have your money presently.° [*To* BAWD] Wife, take her in,         *immediately*
instruct her what she has to do, that she may not be raw in her
entertainment.[9]                     [*Exeunt* PANDER *and* PIRATES]

50 BAWD  Boult, take you the marks of her, the colour of her hair,
complexion, height, her age, with warrant of her virginity, and
cry 'He that will give most shall have her first.' Such a maidenhead were no cheap thing if men were as they have been. Get
this done as I command you.

---

2. If we don't proceed diligently; if conscience can't be
economically exploited; perhaps a comic blunder for "if
conscience is involved."
3. And brought them to prostitution when they turned
eleven.
4. Overboiled in the sweating tub as treatment for venereal disease.
5. Our reputation doesn't accumulate like our profit, nor

does the profit justify the danger (with extended economic wordplay: "credit," "commodity," "wages").
6. This out-of-character admission is part of the religious
undercurrent of the scene.
7. Any secret; any (holy) trade.
8. I cannot get the price reduced a penny (*doit*: small
coin) from.
9. May not be unprepared to entertain customers.

55  BOULT  Performance shall follow.                                    *Exit*

MARINA  Alack that Leonine was so slack, so slow.

He should have struck, not spoke; or that° these pirates,        *if only*

Not enough barbarous, had but o'erboard thrown me

To seek my mother.

60  BAWD  Why lament you, pretty one?

MARINA  That I am pretty.

BAWD  Come, the gods have done their part in you.

MARINA  I accuse them not.

BAWD  You are light° into my hands, where you are like° to live.   *arrived / likely*

65  MARINA  The more my fault°                                          *misfortune*

To scape his hands where I was like to die.

BAWD  Ay, and you shall live in pleasure.

MARINA  No.

BAWD  Yes, indeed shall you, and taste gentlemen of all fashions.

70  You shall fare well. You shall have the difference of all com-

plexions.¹ What, do you stop your ears?

MARINA  Are you a woman?

BAWD  What would you have me be an I be not a woman?

MARINA  An honest° woman, or not a woman.                            *A chaste*

75  BAWD  Marry, whip the gosling! I think I shall have something to

do° with you. Come, you're a young foolish sapling, and must    *some trouble*

be bowed as I would have you.

MARINA  The gods defend me!

80  BAWD  If it please the gods to defend you by men, then men

must comfort you, men must feed you, men must stir you up.

          *Enter* BOULT

Now, sir, hast thou cried° her through the market?              *advertised*

BOULT  I have cried her almost to° the number of her hairs. I      *down to*

have drawn her picture with my voice.

BAWD  And I prithee tell me, how dost thou find the inclination

85  of the people, especially of the younger sort?

BOULT  Faith, they listened to me as they would have hearkened

to their fathers' testament.° There was a Spaniard's mouth       *will*

watered as he went to bed to her very description.

BAWD  We shall have him here tomorrow with his best ruff° on.      *collar*

90  BOULT  Tonight, tonight. But mistress, do you know the French

knight that cowers i' the hams?²

BAWD  Who, Monsieur Veroles?

BOULT  Ay, he. He offered to cut a caper³ at the proclamation,

but he made a groan at it, and swore he would see her

95  tomorrow.

BAWD  Well, well, as for him, he brought his disease hither.⁴

Here he does but repair° it. I know he will come in our shadow   *renew*

to scatter his crowns of the sun.⁵

BOULT  Well, if we had of every nation a traveller, we should

100  lodge them all with this sign.⁶

BAWD [*to* MARINA]  Pray you, come hither a while. You have for-

tunes coming upon you.⁷ Mark me, you must seem to do that

---

1. The variety of appearances (temperaments; ethnici-
ties).
2. Who crouches (from venereal disease).
3. He prepared to leap up and clap his heels together.
4. Englishmen called syphilis "the French disease." This
allusion is one indication of the distinctively English feel
of the scene; see also Scene 5.
5. He will come inside our house to spend his French

crowns; to lose hair from syphilis; to spend his money on
Marina ("sun," if Q1's "in the sun" is retained). With a
play on "shadow" and "sun."
6. We would draw them all here by my pictorial description of Marina.
7. You have prosperity (wealthy men) about to come to
(have an orgasm on top of) you.

fearfully which you commit willingly, to despise profit where
you have most gain. To weep that you live as ye do° makes pity       *(by prostitution)*
105 in your lovers. Seldom but that pity begets you a good opinion,
and that opinion a mere° profit.       *clear*
MARINA   I understand you not.
BOULT [*to* BAWD]   O, take her home,° mistress, take her home.       *inside; to task*
These blushes of hers must be quenched with some present
110 practice.
BAWD   Thou sayst true, i'faith, so they must, for your bride goes
to that with shame which is her way to go with warrant.°       *legitimately*
BOULT   Faith, some do and some do not. But mistress, if I have
bargained for the joint°—       *cut of meat*
115 BAWD   Thou mayst cut a morsel off the spit.°       *deflower her*
BOULT   I may so.
BAWD   Who should deny it? [*To* MARINA] Come, young one, I
like the manner of your garments well.
BOULT   Ay, by my faith, they shall not be changed yet.[8]
120 BAWD [*giving him money*]   Boult, spend thou that in the town.
Report what a sojourner we have. You'll lose nothing by cus-
tom.[9] When nature framed this piece° she meant thee a good       *(of work); (of flesh)*
turn. Therefore say what a paragon she is, and thou reapest the
harvest out of thine own setting forth.
125 BOULT   I warrant you, mistress, thunder shall not so awake the
beds of eels[1] as my giving out her beauty stirs up the lewdly
inclined. I'll bring home some tonight.       [*Exit*]
BAWD   Come your ways, follow me.
MARINA   If fires be hot, knives sharp, or waters deep,
130 Untied I still my virgin knot will keep.[2]
Diana° aid my purpose.       *goddess of chastity*
BAWD   What have we to do with Diana? Pray you, will you go
with me?       *Exeunt.* [*The sign is removed*]

## Scene 17

*Enter* [*in mourning garments*] CLEON *and* DIONYZA
DIONYZA   Why, are you foolish? Can it be undone?
CLEON   O Dionyza, such a piece of slaughter
The sun and moon ne'er looked upon.
DIONYZA   I think you'll turn a child again.
5 CLEON   Were I chief lord of all this spacious world
I'd give it to undo the deed. A lady°       *(Marina)*
Much less in blood than virtue, yet a princess
To equal any single crown o'th' earth
I'th' justice of compare.° O villain Leonine,       *In a fair comparison*
10 Whom thou hast poisoned too,
If thou hadst drunk to him 't'ad been a kindness
Becoming well thy fact.[1] What canst thou say
When noble Pericles demands his child?
DIONYZA   That she is dead. Nurses are not the fates.

---

8. Exchanged or sold (for a prostitute's wardrobe), since
they proclaim her virginity and social status.
9. You'll profit from the resulting increase in our customers; (perhaps) you'll get your turn with Marina.
1. Eels were supposedly roused by thunder.
2. An "Untied . . . virgin knot" presumably means loss of
virginity—not what Marina wants. Perhaps her intent is

suggested by the pun of "knot" and "not"—hence, not
untied.
**Scene 17** (Act 4, Scene 3)
Location: The Governor's house in Tarsus.
1. *If . . . fact:* If you had drunk his health (from the same
poison), the self-punishment would have fit the crime.

15    To foster is not ever° to preserve.                                    *always*
      She died at night. I'll say so. Who can cross° it,                     *deny*
      Unless you play the pious innocent
      And, for an honest attribute,° cry out                                *reputation*
      'She died by foul play.'
CLEON                           O, go to.° Well, well,                       *(contemptuous)*
20    Of all the faults beneath the heav'ns the gods
      Do like this worst.
DIONYZA                          Be one of those that thinks
      The petty wrens of Tarsus will fly hence
      And open° this to Pericles. I do shame                               *disclose*
      To think of what a noble strain° you are,                            *bloodline*
      And of how cowed a spirit.
25 CLEON                              To such proceeding
      Whoever but his approbation added,
      Though not his prime° consent, he did not flow                       *prior*
      From honourable sources.
DIONYZA                              Be it so, then.
      Yet none does know but you how she came dead,
30    Nor none can know, Leonine being gone.
      She did distain° my child, and stood between                        *stain (by comparison)*
      Her and her fortunes. None would look on her,
      But cast their gazes on Marina's face
      Whilst ours was blurted at,° and held a malkin°                     *scorned / dirty peasant*
35    Not worth the time of day. It pierced me through,
      And though you call my course unnatural,
      You not your child well loving, yet I find
      It greets° me as an enterprise of kindness                          *strikes*
      Performed to your sole daughter.
40 CLEON   Heavens forgive it.
DIONYZA   And as for Pericles,
      What should he say? We wept after her hearse,
      And yet° we mourn. Her monument                                     *still*
      Is almost finished, and her epitaphs
45    In glitt'ring golden characters express
      A gen'ral praise to her and care in us,
      At whose expense 'tis done.
CLEON                              Thou art like the harpy,[2]
      Which, to betray, dost, with thine angel face,
      Seize in thine eagle talons.
50 DIONYZA   Ye're like one that superstitiously
      Do swear to th' gods that winter kills the flies,[3]
      But yet I know you'll do as I advise.                    *Exeunt*

## Scene 18

      *Enter GOWER*
GOWER   Thus time we waste,° and long leagues make we short,[1]   *pass quickly*
      Sail seas in cockles,° have and wish but for't,[2]           *seashells*
      Making to take° imagination                              *Proceeding by*
      From bourn° to bourn, region to region.                      *border*

---

2. Monstrous creature with a woman's face and an eagle's
talons.
3. *Ye're . . . flies:* perhaps, You're so afraid of the gods that
you'd feel it necessary to tell them insignificant and unal-
terable things they already know (that winter killed the

flies).
**Scene 18** Scene 18 (Act, Scene 4)
Location: Before Marina's tomb in Tarsus.
1. Here Gower speaks in pentameter couplets.
2. Get something merely by wishing for it.

| | | |
|---|---|---|
| 5 | By you being pardoned, we commit no crime | |
| | To use one language in each sev'ral clime° | *separate region* |
| | Where our scene seems to live. I do beseech you | |
| | To learn of me, who stand i'th' gaps° to teach you | *(between scenes)* |
| | The stages of our story: Pericles | |
| 10 | Is now again thwarting° the wayward seas, | *crossing* |
| | Attended on by many a lord and knight, | |
| | To see his daughter, all his life's delight. | |
| | Old Helicanus goes along. Behind | |
| | Is left to govern, if you bear in mind, | |
| 15 | Old Aeschines, whom Helicanus late° | *recently* |
| | Advanced in Tyre to great and high estate.° | *rank* |
| | Well sailing ships and bounteous winds have brought | |
| | This king to Tarsus—think his pilot thought;[3] | |
| | So with his steerage shall your thoughts go on— | |
| 20 | To fetch his daughter home, who first° is gone. | *already* |
| | Like motes and shadows[4] see them move a while; | |
| | Your ears unto your eyes I'll reconcile. | |

[*Dumb show.*]

Enter PERICLES *at one door with all his train,* CLEON
*and* DIONYZA [*in mourning garments*] *at the other.*
CLEON [*draws the curtain and*] *shows* PERICLES *the
tomb, whereat* PERICLES *makes lamentation, puts on
sack-cloth, and in a mighty passion° departs* [*followed by          sorrow
his train.* CLEON *and* DIONYZA *depart at the other door*]

| | | |
|---|---|---|
| | See how belief may suffer by foul show.° | *false appearances* |
| | This borrowed passion stands for true-owed woe,[5] | |
| 25 | And Pericles, in sorrow all devoured, | |
| | With sighs shot through, and biggest tears o'ershow'red, | |
| | Leaves Tarsus, and again embarks. He swears | |
| | Never to wash his face nor cut his hairs. | |
| | He puts on sack-cloth, and to sea. He bears | |
| 30 | A tempest which his mortal vessel tears,[6] | |
| | And yet he rides it out. Now please you wit° | *know* |
| | The epitaph is° for Marina writ | *that is* |
| | By wicked Dionyza. | |

[*He reads Marina's epitaph[7] on the tomb*]

| | | |
|---|---|---|
| | 'The fairest, sweetest, best lies here, | |
| 35 | Who withered in her spring of year.° | *early in life* |
| | In nature's garden, though by growth a bud, | |
| | She was the chiefest flower: she was good.' | |
| | No visor does become black villainy | |
| | So well as soft and tender flattery. | |
| 40 | Let Pericles believe his daughter's dead | |
| | And bear his courses to be orderèd[8] | |
| | By Lady Fortune, while our scene must play | |
| | His daughter's woe and heavy well-a-day° | *lamentation* |
| | In her unholy service. Patience then, | |
| 45 | And think you now are all in Mytilene. | |

*Exit*

3. Think that his pilot is swiftly traveling thought.
4. Like specks of dust in a sunbeam and like (theatrical) illusions.
5. Cleon and Dionyza's "woe" is "borrowed," not "true-owed" (owned); perhaps also a self-referential comment on the sorrow simulated by the actor playing Pericles.
6. *He bears . . . tears:* His suffering assaults his body.

(Note the internalization of the earlier storms.)
7. The four-line epitaph is from *PA*, which may preserve the author's revised version of this passage. Q1's ten-line version (see the Additional Passage at the end of the play) includes the first two lines here.
8. And allow his fate to be arranged.

## Scene 19

[*A brothel sign.*] *Enter two* GENTLEMEN

FIRST GENTLEMAN  Did you ever hear the like?

SECOND GENTLEMAN  No, nor never shall do in such a place as this, she being once gone.

FIRST GENTLEMAN  But to have divinity preached there—did you
5  ever dream of such a thing?

SECOND GENTLEMAN  No, no. Come, I am for no more bawdy houses. Shall 's go hear the vestals sing?[1]

FIRST GENTLEMAN  I'll do anything now that is virtuous, but I am out of the road of rutting° for ever.         *Exeunt*         fornication

*Enter* [PANDER,] BAWD [*and* BOULT]

10  PANDER  Well, I had rather than twice the worth of her she had ne'er come here.

BAWD  Fie, fie upon her, she's able to freeze the god Priapus and undo the whole of generation.[2] We must either get her ravished or be rid of her. When she should do for clients her fitment°         duty
15  and do me the kindness of our profession,[3] she has° me her         gives
quirks, her reasons, her master reasons, her prayers, her knees,°         (*kneeling to plead*)
that she would make a puritan of the devil if he should
cheapen° a kiss of her.         bargain for

BOULT  Faith, I must ravish her, or she'll disfurnish us of all our
20  cavalleria° and make our swearers[4] priests.         gentlemen customers

PANDER  Now, the pox upon her green-sickness[5] for me.

BAWD  Faith, there's no way to be rid on't but by the way to the pox.°         venereal disease

*Enter* LYSIMACHUS [*disguised*]

Here comes the Lord Lysimachus, disguised.

BOULT  We should have both lord and loon° if the peevish bag-         lowborn
25  gage° would but give way to custom.[6]         worthless woman

LYSIMACHUS  How now, how° a dozen of virginities?         how much for

BAWD  Now, the gods to-bless your honour!

BOULT  I am glad to see your honour in good health.

LYSIMACHUS  You may so. 'Tis the better for you that your resort-
30  ers stand upon sound legs.[7] How now, wholesome iniquity°         healthy whore
have you, that a man may deal withal° and defy the surgeon?°         with / avoid the doctor

BAWD  We have here one, sir, if she would—but there never came her like in Mytilene.

LYSIMACHUS  If she'd do the deed of darkness, thou wouldst say.

35  BAWD  Your honour knows what 'tis to say° well enough.         what I mean

LYSIMACHUS  Well, call forth, call forth.         [*Exit* PANDER]

BOULT  For flesh and blood, sir, white and red, you shall see a rose. And she were a rose indeed, if she had but—[8]

LYSIMACHUS  What, prithee?

40  BOULT  O sir, I can be modest.

---

Scene 19 (Other modern editions divide this scene in two: Act 4, Scene 5 [lines 1–9] and Scene 6 [lines 10–211]. But the location remains in or around the brothel throughout. This edition assumes both that there is no gap in time between the two parts and that the modest shifts in locale within the scene do not violate the relatively unspecific notion of place on the early seventeenth-century stage.)
Location: The brothel in Mytilene.
1. Shall we go hear the vestal virgins (religious devotees) sing?
2. Able to stop the "whole" (hole) work of breeding.

Priapus was the god of procreation, especially of male virility and lechery. "The whole of" emends Q1's "a whole."
3. Enable me to profit from her profession of prostitution; perhaps also homoerotic: have sex with me.
4. Loyal (blasphemous) customers.
5. Moody stubbornness, supposedly caused by anemia in young women; queasiness from lack of experience.
6. Customers; customary behavior. Q1 has "customers."
7. Rather than upon legs bent from venereal disease.
8. If she had but a thorn; if she were sexually experienced.

LYSIMACHUS   That dignifies the renown of a bawd no less than
it gives a good report to a noble to be chaste.[9]
*Enter* [PANDER *with*] MARINA

BAWD   Here comes that which grows to° the stalk, never plucked                    *affixed to*
yet, I can assure you. Is she not a fair creature?

45 LYSIMACHUS   Faith, she would serve after a long voyage at sea.
Well, there's for you. Leave us.
[*He pays the* BAWD]

BAWD   I beseech your honour give me leave: a word, and I'll
have done presently.°                                                              *be done soon*

LYSIMACHUS   I beseech you, do.

50 BAWD [*aside to* MARINA]   First, I would have you note this is an
honourable man.

MARINA   I desire to find him so, that I may honourably know him.

BAWD   Next, he's the governor of this country, and a man whom
I am bound to.

55 MARINA   If he govern the country you are bound to him indeed,
but how honourable he is in that, I know not.

BAWD   Pray you, without any more virginal fencing, will you use
him kindly? He will line your apron with gold.

MARINA   What he will do graciously I will thankfully receive.

60 LYSIMACHUS [*to* BAWD]   Ha' you done?

BAWD   My lord, she's not paced° yet. You must take some pains        *trained (like a horse)*
to work her to your manège.[1] [*To* BOULT *and* PANDER] Come,
we will leave his honour and hers together. Go thy ways.°                        *Come along*
*Exeunt* [PANDER,] BAWD [*and* BOULT]

LYSIMACHUS   Fair one, how long have you been at this trade?

65 MARINA   What trade, sir?

LYSIMACHUS   I cannot name it but I shall offend.

MARINA   I cannot be offended with my trade.
Please you to name it.

LYSIMACHUS                    How long have you been
Of this profession?

MARINA                    E'er since I can remember.

70 LYSIMACHUS   Did you go to't° so young? Were you a gamester°        *copulate / loose woman*
At five, or seven?

MARINA                    Earlier too, sir,
If now I be one.

LYSIMACHUS                    Why, the house you dwell in
Proclaimeth you a creature of sale.

MARINA   And do you know this house to be a place

75 Of such resort° and will come into it?                                            *purpose*
I hear say you're of honourable blood,
And are the governor of this whole province.

LYSIMACHUS   What, hath your principal° informed you who I am?               *employer*

MARINA   Who is my principal?

LYSIMACHUS                    Why, your herb-woman;

80 She that sets seeds of shame, roots of iniquity.
[MARINA *weeps*]
O, you've heard something of my pow'r, and so
Stand off aloof for a more serious wooing.

---

9. Than it gives a noble(wo)man a (falsely) good reputation for being chaste. Q1 has "number" for "noble."

1. To bring her under your control (from horsemanship).

But I protest to thee,
Pretty one, my authority can wink
85   At blemishes,[2] or can on faults look friendly;
Or my displeasure punish at my pleasure,
From which displeasure, not thy beauty shall
Privilege thee, nor my affection,° which                          *lust*
Hath drawn me here, abate with further ling'ring.
90   Come bring me to some private place. Come, come.
MARINA   Let not authority, which teaches you
To govern others, be the means to make you
Misgovern much yourself.[3]
If you were born to honour,° show it now;          *high status; virtue*
95   If put upon you,[4] make the judgement good
That thought you worthy of it. What[5] reason's in
Your justice, who hath power over all,
To undo any? If you take from me
Mine honour, you're like him that makes a gap
100  Into forbidden ground, whom after
Too many enter, and of all their evils
Yourself are guilty. My life is yet unspotted;°          *still free of sin*
My chastity unstainèd ev'n in thought.
Then if your violence deface this building,°                    *body*
105  The workmanship of heav'n, you do kill your honour,
Abuse your justice, and impoverish me.
My yet good lord, if there be fire before me,
Must I straight fly° and burn myself? Suppose this house—    *go immediately*
Which too too many feel such houses are—
110  Should be the doctor's patrimony, and
The surgeon's feeding;° follows it, that I                    *livelihood*
Must needs infect myself to give them maint'nance?
LYSIMACHUS   How's this, how's this? Some more. Be sage.
MARINA [*kneeling*]                          For me
That am a maid, though most ungentle fortune
115  Have franked° me in this sty, where since I came          *shut*
Diseases have been sold dearer than physic—[6]
That the gods would set me free from this unhallowed place,
Though they did change me to the meanest° bird           *humblest*
That flies i'th' purer air!
LYSIMACHUS [*moved*]          I did not think
120  Thou couldst have spoke so well, ne'er dreamt thou couldst.
[*He lifts her up with his hands*]
Though I brought hither a corrupted mind,
Thy speech hath altered it,
[*He wipes the wet from her eyes*]
                          and my foul thoughts
Thy tears so well hath laved° that they're now white.          *cleansed*
I came here meaning but to pay the price,

2. *can wink / At blemishes*: can refuse to see moral short-
comings. Lines 84–89 are adapted from *PA* and replace
Q1's "my authority shall not see thee, or else look friendly
upon thee," which doesn't reflect as badly on Lysimachus. Here and in subsequent passages in this scene,
*PA* may preserve Shakespeare's original words.
3. *Let . . . yourself*: not in Q1 adapted from *PA*.

4. If you were granted rank not by birth but by merit.
5. Lines 96–112 are not in Q1 but were adapted from
*PA*. Q1's lines 94–96 ("If . . . it") and 113–19 ("For . . .
air") seem inadequate to produce Lysimachus's response
at line 113 and dramatic conversion at lines 119–20.
6. Sold at a higher price than medical treatment.

125     A piece of gold for thy virginity;
    Here's twenty to relieve thine honesty.[7]
    Persever still° in that clear way thou goest,            *always*
    And the gods strengthen thee.
    MARINA                The good gods preserve you!
    LYSIMACHUS   The[8] very doors and windows savour vilely.
130     Fare thee well. Thou art a piece of virtue,
    The best wrought up° that ever nature made,[9]     *created*
    And I doubt not thy training hath been noble.
    A curse upon him, die he° like a thief,            *may he die*
    That robs thee of thy honour. Hold, here's more gold.
135     If thou dost hear from me, it shall be for thy good.
          [*Enter* BOULT *standing ready at the door, making his*
          *obeisance unto him as* LYSIMACHUS *should go out*]
    BOULT    I beseech your honour, one piece for me.
    LYSIMACHUS   Avaunt,° thou damnèd door-keeper!     *Begone*
    Your house, but for this virgin that doth prop it,
    Would sink and overwhelm you. Away.         [*Exit*]
140     BOULT   How's this? We must take another course with you. If
    your peevish chastity, which is not worth a breakfast in the
    cheapest country under the cope,° shall undo a whole house-     *sky*
    hold, let me be gelded like a spaniel. Come your ways.
    MARINA   Whither would you have me?
145     BOULT   I must have your maidenhead taken off, or the common
    executioner shall do it.[1] We'll have no more gentlemen driven
    away. Come your ways, I say.
          *Enter* BAWD [*and* PANDER]
    BAWD   How now, what's the matter?
    BOULT   Worse and worse, mistress, she has here spoken holy
150     words to the Lord Lysimachus.
    BAWD   O, abominable!
    BOULT   She makes our profession as it were to stink afore the
    face of the gods.
    BAWD   Marry° hang her up for ever!         *(expresses irritation)*
155     BOULT   The nobleman would have dealt with her like a noble-
    man,[2] and she sent him away as cold as a snowball, saying his
    prayers, too.
    PANDER   Boult, take her away. Use her at thy pleasure. Crack the
    ice of her virginity, and make the rest malleable.
160     BOULT   An if° she were a thornier piece of ground than she is,     *Even if*
    she shall be ploughed.
    MARINA   Hark, hark, you gods!
    BAWD   She conjures.° Away with her! Would she had never     *calls on the gods*
    come within my doors.—Marry, hang you!—She's born to
165     undo us.—Will you not go the way of womenkind? Marry,
    come up, my dish of chastity with rosemary and bays.[3]
          *Exeunt* [BAWD *and* PANDER]
    BOULT [*catching her rashly by the hand*]   Come, mistress, come
    your way with me.

---

7. To assist your chastity. Lines 124–26, adapted from
*PA*, replace Q1's "Hold here's gold for thee."
8. Q1 precedes these lines with "For me be you
thoughten [understand], that I came with no ill intent,
for to me."
9. Line 131 not in Q1; adapted from *PA*.

1. "Executioner shall do" replaces Q1's "hāg-man shall
execute," producing wordplay on "maidenhead" and
"executioner" (one who chops off heads).
2. Would have used her and rewarded her well.
3. The Bawd chides Marina for thinking herself too exquisite a dish (for making too much of her chastity).

MARINA   Whither wilt thou have me?

170   BOULT   To take from you the jewel you hold so dear.

MARINA   Prithee, tell me one thing first.

BOULT   Come, now, your one thing.

MARINA   What canst thou wish thine enemy to be?[4]

BOULT   Why, I could wish him to be° my master, or rather my       (as bad as)

175   mistress.

MARINA   Neither of these can be so bad as thou art,
    Since they do better thee in their command.[5]
    Thou hold'st a place the painèd'st° fiend of hell       most tortured
    Would not in reputation change with thee,

180   Thou damnèd doorkeeper to ev'ry coistrel°       base fellow
    That comes enquiring for his Tib.°       loose woman
    To th' choleric fisting of ev'ry rogue
    Thy ear is liable.[6] Thy food is such
    As hath been belched on by infected lungs.

185   BOULT   What would you have me do? Go to the wars, would
    you, where a man may serve seven years for the loss of° a leg,       only to lose
    and have not money enough in the end to buy him a wooden one?

MARINA   Do anything but this thou dost. Empty
    Old receptacles or common sew'rs of filth,

190   Serve by indenture° to the public hangman—       as apprentice
    Any of these are yet better than this.
    For what thou professest a baboon, could he speak,
    Would own a name too dear.[7] Here's gold for thee.
    If that thy master would make gain by me,

195   Proclaim that I can sing, weave, sew, and dance,
    With other virtues° which I'll keep from boast,       accomplishments
    And I will undertake all these to teach.
    I doubt not but this populous city will
    Yield many scholars.°       pupils

200   BOULT   But can you teach all this you speak of?

MARINA   Prove° that I cannot, take me home again       If you prove
    And prostitute me to the basest groom°       lowest servant
    That doth frequent your house.

BOULT   Well, I will see what I can do for thee. If I can place

205   thee, I will.

MARINA   But amongst honest women.

BOULT   Faith, my acquaintance lies little amongst them; but
    since my master and mistress hath bought you, there's no going
    but by their consent. Therefore I will make them acquainted

210   with your purpose, and I doubt not but I shall find them tracta-
    ble enough. Come, I'll do for thee what I can. Come your ways.

Exeunt. [The sign is removed]

## Scene 20

Enter GOWER

GOWER   Marina thus the brothel scapes, and chances[1]
    Into an honest house, our story says.

4. What is the worst thing you could wish on your
enemy?
5. Since they can command you to do what even they
wouldn't do themselves.
6. To . . . liable: Even the lowest rogue would box your
ear if angry.
7. Would consider beneath him. Q1 follows this sentence with "That the gods would safely deliver me from
this place: here"—a repetition of line 117 that is out of
place here.
Scene 20 (Act 5, Chorus)
1. Unlike Gower's other prologues, which are in tetrameter or, less often, pentameter rhyming couplets, this one
rhymes alternate pentameter lines.

She sings like one immortal, and she dances

    As goddess-like to her admirèd lays.°               *songs*

5  Deep clerks she dumbs,[2] and with her nee'le° composes     *needle*

    Nature's own shape, of bud, bird, branch, or berry,

That e'en her art sisters° the natural roses.               *equals*

    Her inkle,° silk, twin with the rubied cherry;       *linen thread*

That° pupils lacks she none of noble race,           *So that*

10  Who pour their bounty on her, and her gain

She gives the cursèd Bawd. Here we her place,

    And to her father turn our thoughts again.

We left him on the sea. Waves there him tossed,

    Whence, driven tofore° the winds, he is arrived      *before*

15  Here where his daughter dwells, and on this coast

    Suppose him now at anchor. The city strived°     *surpassed itself*

God Neptune's annual feast to keep, from whence

    Lysimachus our Tyrian ship espies,

His° banners sable,° trimmed with rich expense;      *Its / black*

20  And to him° in his barge with fervour hies.              *it*

In your supposing° once more put your sight;      *imagination*

    Of heavy° Pericles think this the barque,°       *sad / ship*

Where what is done in action, more if might,

    Shall be discovered.[3] Please you sit and hark.     *Exit*

## Scene 21

*Enter* HELICANUS [*above; below, enter*] *to him* [*at the first door*] *two* SAILORS [*one* OF TYRE, *the other* OF MYTILENE*]

SAILOR OF TYRE [*to* SAILOR OF MYTILENE]   Lord Helicanus can resolve[1] you, sir.

[*To* HELICANUS] There is a barge put off from Mytilene.

In it, Lysimachus, the governor,

Who craves to come aboard. What is your will?

HELICANUS   That he have his.

              [*Exit* SAILOR OF MYTILENE *at first door*]

5               Call up some gentlemen.

                  [*Exit* HELICANUS *above*]

SAILOR OF TYRE   Ho, my lord calls!

    *Enter* [*from below the stage*] *two or three* GENTLEMEN[; *to them, enter* HELICANUS]

FIRST GENTLEMAN          What is your lordship's pleasure?

HELICANUS   Gentlemen, some of worth° would come aboard.   *some noble visitor*

I pray you, greet him fairly.

    *Enter* LYSIMACHUS [*at first door, with the* SAILOR *and* LORDS OF MYTILENE]

SAILOR OF MYTILENE [*to* LYSIMACHUS]   This is the man that can

in aught resolve° you.              *answer anything for*

10  LYSIMACHUS [*to* HELICANUS]   Hail, reverend sir; the gods preserve you!

HELICANUS   And you, sir, to outlive the age I am,

And die as I would do.

---

2. Her wisdom reduces learned men to silence.
3. *Where . . . discovered:* Where the stage action, which would show more if it could, will reveal what happens.

**Scene 21** (Act 5, Scene 1)
Location: Pericles' ship, off Mytilene.
1. Answer. This line replaces Q1's "Where is Lord Helicanus? He can resolve you, / O here he is sir."

LYSIMACHUS                You wish me well.
   I am the governor of Mytilene;[2]
   Being on shore, honouring of Neptune's triumphs,[3]
15   Seeing this goodly vessel ride before us,
   I made to it to know of whence you are.
HELICANUS   Our vessel is of Tyre, in it our king,
   A man who for this three months hath not spoken
   To anyone, nor taken sustenance
20   But to prorogue° his grief.                             *extend*
LYSIMACHUS   Upon what ground grew his distemp'rature?°    *emotional disturbance*
HELICANUS   'Twould be too tedious to tell it over,
   But the main grief springs from the precious loss
   Of a belovèd daughter and a wife.
LYSIMACHUS   May we not see him?
25 HELICANUS                   See him, sir, you may,
   But bootless° is your sight. He will not speak             *pointless*
   To any.
LYSIMACHUS   Let me yet obtain my wish.
HELICANUS   Behold him.
            [HELICANUS *draws a curtain, revealing* PERICLES *lying*
            *upon a couch with a long overgrown beard, diffused*°    *disorderly*
            *hair, undecent nails on his fingers, and attired in sack-*
            *cloth*]
                   This was a goodly person
   Till the disaster of one mortal° night                    *fatal*
   Drove him to this.
30 LYSIMACHUS [*to* PERICLES]   Sir, King, all hail. Hail, royal sir.
           [PERICLES *shrinks himself down upon his pillow*]
HELICANUS   It is in vain. He will not speak to you.
LORD OF MYTILENE   Sir, we have a maid in Mytilene I durst wager
   Would win some words of him.
LYSIMACHUS                  'Tis well bethought.
   She questionless, with her sweet harmony
35   And other choice attractions, would alarum[4]
   And make a batt'ry through his deafened ports,
   Which now are midway stopped.° She in all happy,°   *half closed / skillful*
   As the fair'st of all, among her fellow maids
   Dwells now i'th' leafy shelter that abuts
40   Against the island's side. Go fetch her hither.     [*Exit* LORD]
HELICANUS   Sure, all effectless; yet nothing we'll omit
   That bears recov'ry's name.° But since your kindness   *That might cure him*
   We have stretched thus far, let us beseech you
   That for our gold we may provision have,
45   Wherein we are not destitute for want,
   But weary for the staleness.
LYSIMACHUS              O sir, a courtesy
   Which if we should deny, the most just gods
   For every graft° would send a caterpillar,        *cultivated plant*
   And so inflict° our province. Yet once more       *afflict (with famine)*

---

2. This line replaces Q1's
   HELICANUS   First what is your place?
   LYSIMACHUS   I am the Governor of this place you lie
      before,
which appears after line 16, where it interrupts the dialogue and attributes to Helicanus a rudeness that seems

gratuitous, since he already knows who Lysimachus is
(see line 3).
3. Observing Neptune's festival.
4. Awaken (as a trumpet). Q1 has "allure," which
introduces a sexual innuendo (see the Introduction).

50 Let me entreat to know at large° the cause       *in detail*
   Of your king's sorrow.
HELICANUS           Sit, sir. I will recount it.
     [*Enter* LORD *with* MARINA *and another* MAID]
   But see, I am prevented.
LYSIMACHUS   O, here's the lady that I sent for.—
   Welcome, fair one.—Is't not a goodly presence?°     *Isn't she attractive*
55 HELICANUS   She's a gallant° lady.           *fine*
LYSIMACHUS   She's such a one that, were I well assured
   Came of gentle kind° or noble stock, I'd wish     *a gentry family*
   No better choice to think me rarely° wed.—     *superbly*
   Fair one, all goodness that consists in bounty
60 Expect e'en here, where is a kingly patient;
   If that thy prosperous and artificial feat°     *artful skill*
   Can draw him but to answer thee in aught,
   Thy sacred physic° shall receive such pay     *treatment*
   As thy desires can wish.
MARINA           Sir, I will use
65 My utmost skill in his recure,° provided       *cure*
   That none but I and my companion maid
   Be suffered° to come near him.         *permitted*
LYSIMACHUS [*to the others*]     Let us leave her,
   And the gods prosper her.      [*The men stand aside*]
     The Song[5]
LYSIMACHUS [*coming forward*]   Marked° he your music?     *Noticed*
MAID   No, nor looked on us.
LYSIMACHUS [*to the others*]   See, she will speak to him.
70 MARINA [*to* PERICLES]   Hail, sir; my lord, lend ear.
PERICLES   Hmh, ha!
     [*He roughly repulses her*]
MARINA   I am a maid,
   My lord, that ne'er before invited eyes,
   But have been gazed on like a comet.° She speaks,     *in awe*
75 My lord, that maybe hath endured a grief
   Might° equal yours, if both were justly weighed.     *That might*
   Though wayward fortune did malign my state,°     *reduce my status*
   My derivation was from ancestors
   Who stood equivalent with mighty kings,
80 But time hath rooted out[6] my parentage,
   And to the world and awkward casualties°     *adverse events*
   Bound me in servitude. [*Aside*] I will desist.
   But there is something glows upon my cheek,
   And whispers in mine ear 'Stay till he speak.'
85 PERICLES   My fortunes, parentage, good parentage,
   To equal mine? Was it not thus? What say you?
MARINA   I said if you did know my parentage,
   My lord, you would not do me violence.
PERICLES   I do think so. Pray you, turn your eyes upon me.
90 You're like something that—what countrywoman?°     *what nationality*
   Here of these shores?
MARINA           No, nor of any shores,

---

5. The song is given in *PA*, which takes it from Twine's   one in particular.
*Patterne of Painefull Adventures.* The early texts of   6. Uprooted me from; obscured; killed.
Shakespeare often call for a song without specifying any

Yet I was mortally[7] brought forth, and am
No other than I seem.
PERICLES [*aside*]    I am great° with woe, and shall deliver          pregnant
  weeping.
95 My dearest wife was like this maid, and such
My daughter might have been. My queen's square brows,
Her stature to an inch, as wand-like straight,
As silver-voiced, her eyes as jewel-like,
And cased as richly, in pace° another Juno,          stride
100 Who starves the ears she feeds, and makes them hungry
The more she gives them speech.—Where do you live?
MARINA    Where I am but a stranger.° From the deck          foreigner
You may discern the place.
PERICLES     Where were you bred,
And how achieved you these endowments which
You make more rich to owe?°          by your owning them
105 MARINA     If I should tell
My history, it would seem like lies
Disdained in the reporting.°          as soon as told
PERICLES     Prithee speak.
Falseness cannot come from thee, for thou look'st
Modest as justice, and thou seem'st a palace
110 For the crowned truth to dwell in. I will believe thee,
And make my senses credit thy relation°          trust your story
To° points that seem impossible. Thou show'st          Even to
Like one I loved indeed. What were thy friends?°          kin
Didst thou not say, when I did push thee back—
115 Which was when I perceived thee—that thou cam'st
From good descending?
MARINA    So indeed I did.
PERICLES    Report thy parentage. I think thou said'st
Thou hadst been tossed from wrong to injury,
And that thou thought'st thy griefs might equal mine,
If both were opened.°          revealed
120 MARINA    Some such thing I said,
And said no more but what my circumstance
Did warrant° me was likely.          assure
PERICLES    Tell thy story.
If thine considered prove the thousandth part
Of my endurance,° thou art a man, and I          suffering
125 Have suffered like a girl. Yet thou dost look
Like patience gazing on kings' graves, and smiling
Extremity out of act.[8] What were thy friends?
How lost thou them? Thy name, my most kind[9] virgin?
Recount, I do beseech thee. Come, sit by me.
  [*She sits*]
MARINA    My name, sir, is Marina.
130 PERICLES    O, I am mocked,
And thou by some incensèd god sent hither
To make the world to laugh at me.

---

7. "Normally," not supernaturally, despite not being born
on "any shores"; perhaps also "fatally"—to her mother.
8. *Yet . . . act:* Yet you seem able to bear even the deaths
of Kings (like statues of Patience personified, perhaps

on royal tombs) and to face down the worst extremities
(especially suicidal despair) with a smile.
9. Sympathetic; related by blood ("kind" also meant
"kin").

MARINA                     Patience, good sir,
Or here I'll cease.
PERICLES                  Nay, I'll be patient.
Thou little know'st how thou dost startle me
To call thyself Marina.
135    MARINA                    The name
Was given me by one that had some power:
My father, and a king.
PERICLES                   How, a king's daughter,
And called Marina?
MARINA                  You said you would believe me,
But not to be a troubler of your peace
I will end here.
140    PERICLES          But are you flesh and blood?
Have you a working pulse and are no fairy?
Motion° as well? Speak on. Where were you born,                 *(of life)*
And wherefore called Marina?
MARINA                     Called Marina
For I was born at sea.
PERICLES                   At sea? What mother?
145    MARINA    My mother was the daughter of a king,
Who died when I was born, as my good nurse
Lychorida hath oft recounted weeping.
PERICLES    O, stop there a little! [*Aside*] This is the rarest dream
That e'er dulled sleep did mock sad fools withal.°              *with*
150    This cannot be my daughter, buried. Well.
[*To* MARINA] Where were you bred? I'll hear you more to th'
bottom°                                                          *the end*
Of your story, and never interrupt you.
MARINA    You will scarce believe me. 'Twere best I did give o'er.°   *stop*
PERICLES    I will believe you by the syllable
155    Of what you shall deliver. Yet give me leave.°              *(to ask)*
How came you in these parts? Where were you bred?
MARINA    The King my father did in Tarsus leave me,
Till cruel Cleon, with his wicked wife,
Did seek to murder me, and wooed a villain
160    To attempt the deed; who having drawn to do't,
A crew of pirates came and rescued me.
To Mytilene they brought me. But, good sir,
What will you° of me? Why do you weep? It may be         *What do you want*
You think me an impostor. No, good faith,
165    I am the daughter to King Pericles,
If good King Pericles be.°                                      *live*
PERICLES [*rising*]    Ho, Helicanus!
HELICANUS [*coming forward*]    Calls my lord?
PERICLES    Thou art a grave and noble counsellor,
170    Most wise in gen'ral. Tell me if thou canst
What this maid is, or what is like° to be,                      *likely*
That thus hath made me weep.
HELICANUS                 I know not.
But here's the regent, sir, of Mytilene
Speaks° nobly of her.                                          *Who speaks*
LYSIMACHUS             She would never tell
175    Her parentage. Being demanded that,
She would sit still and weep.

PERICLES   O Helicanus, strike me, honoured sir,
Give me a gash, put me to present° pain,                                    *immediate*
Lest this great sea of joys rushing upon me
180   O'erbear° the shores of my mortality                                  *Overflow*
And drown me with their sweetness! [*To* MARINA] O, come hither,
        [MARINA *stands*]
Thou that begett'st him that did thee beget,[1]
Thou that wast born at sea, buried at Tarsus,
And found at sea again!—O Helicanus,
185   Down on thy knees, thank the holy gods as loud
As thunder threatens us, this is Marina!
[*To* MARINA] What was thy mother's name? Tell me but that,
For truth can never be confirmed enough,
Though doubts did ever sleep.[2]
MARINA                          First, sir, I pray,
What is your title?
190   PERICLES          I am Pericles
Of Tyre. But tell me now my drowned queen's name.
As in the rest thou hast been godlike perfect,°                    *have been omniscient*
So prove but true in that, thou art my daughter,[3]
The heir of kingdoms, and another life
To Pericles thy father.
195   MARINA [*kneeling*]          Is it no more
To be your daughter than to say my mother's name?
Thaisa was my mother, who did end
The minute I began.
PERICLES   Now blessing on thee! Rise. Thou art my child.
        [MARINA *stands. He kisses her*]
200   [*To attendants*] Give me fresh garments.—Mine own, Helicanus!
Not dead at Tarsus, as she should have been[4]
By savage Cleon. She shall tell thee all,
When thou shalt kneel and justify in knowledge°              *satisfy yourself that*
She is thy very princess. Who is this?
205   HELICANUS   Sir, 'tis the governor of Mytilene,
Who, hearing of your melancholy state,
Did come to see you.
PERICLES [*to* LYSIMACHUS] I embrace you, sir.—
Give me my robes.
        [*He is attired in fresh robes*]
                          I am wild in my beholding.[5]
O heavens, bless my girl!
        [*Celestial music*]
                          But hark, what music?
210   Tell Helicanus, my Marina, tell him
O'er point by point, for yet he seems to doubt,
How sure you are my daughter. But what music?
HELICANUS   My lord, I hear none.
PERICLES   None? The music of the spheres![6] List,° my Marina.      *Listen*
LYSIMACHUS [*aside to the others*]   It is not good to cross him. Give

---

1. The possible sexual complications here, including incest, can be highlighted in performance by doubling the part of Marina with that of Thaisa or Antiochus's Daughter. (For the possible relevance of doubling the part of Marina to the transmission of the text, see the Textual Note.)
2. Even in the absence of doubts.
3. Line is not in Q1; it was added to fill a suspected gap.
4. As she was believed (intended) to be.
5. Unkempt in my appearance, ecstatic at what I see.
6. A sign of celestial harmony, brought about by the proper movement of the heavenly bodies around earth (hence a sign of divine order).

215          him way.

PERICLES   Rar'st sounds. Do ye not hear?

LYSIMACHUS   Music, my lord?

PERICLES   I hear most heav'nly music.

    It raps° me unto list'ning, and thick slumber         *compels*

220     Hangs upon mine eyelids. Let me rest.

      [*He sleeps*]

LYSIMACHUS   A pillow for his head.

      [*To* MARINA *and others*]          Companion friends,

    If this but answer to my just belief

    I'll well remember° you. So leave him all.         *reward; recall*

                [*Exeunt all but* PERICLES]

     DIANA [*descends from the heavens*]

DIANA   My temple stands in Ephesus. Hie thee thither,

225     And do upon mine altar sacrifice.

    There when my maiden priests are met together,

      At large discourse thy fortunes in this wise:

    With a full voice[7] before the people all,

      Reveal how thou at sea didst lose thy wife.

230     To mourn thy crosses,° with thy daughter's, call         *losses*

      And give them repetition to the life.[8]

    Perform my bidding, or thou liv'st in woe;

    Do't, and rest happy, by my silver bow.[9]

    Awake, and tell thy dream.     [DIANA *ascends into the heavens*]

235 PERICLES   Celestial Dian, goddess argentine,°      *silver (like the moon)*

    I will obey thee. [*Calling*] Helicanus!

      [*Enter* HELICANUS, LYSIMACHUS, *and* MARINA]

HELICANUS                 Sir?

PERICLES   My purpose was for Tarsus, there to strike

    Th'inhospitable Cleon, but I am

    For other service first. Toward Ephesus

240     Turn our blown° sails. Eftsoons° I'll tell thee why.    *inflated / Later*

                [*Exit* HELICANUS]

    Shall we refresh us, sir, upon your shore,

    And give you gold for such provision

    As our intents will need?

LYSIMACHUS           With all my heart, sir,

    And when you come ashore I have a suit.

245 PERICLES   You shall prevail, were it to woo my daughter,

    For it seems you have been noble towards her.

LYSIMACHUS   Sir, lend me your arm.

PERICLES              Come, my Marina.

     *Exit* [PERICLES *with* LYSIMACHUS *at one arm,*

               MARINA *at the other*]

## Scene 22

   *Enter* GOWER

GOWER   Now our sands are almost run;

    More a little, and then dumb.°               *silent*

    This my last boon give me,

---

7. *At . . . voice:* Not in Q1; added to fill a suspected gap. *At large discourse:* Tell in detail (in public). *wise:* way.
8. *call . . . life:* speak loudly and repeat exactly what happened.
9. A crescent moon. Diana was goddess of the moon and a renowned hunter.

Scene 22  Scene 22 (Other modern editions divide this scene in two: Act 5, Scene 2 [Gower's monologue, lines 1–20] and Scene 3 [lines 21–125]. But they anomalously keep Thaisa and the temple of Diana onstage across the scene break. Even Gower may remain.) Location: The temple of Diana in Ephesus.

For such kindness must relieve me,
5   That you aptly will suppose°                                        *readily will* imagine
What pageantry, what feats, what shows,
What minstrelsy and pretty din
The regent° made in Mytilene                                            *Lysimachus*
To greet the King. So well he° thrived                                  *(Lysimachus)*
10  That he is promised to be wived
To fair Marina, but in no wise°                                         *way*
Till he° had done his sacrifice                                         *(Pericles)*
As Dian bade, whereto being bound
The int'rim, pray you, all confound.°                                   *skip*
15  In feathered° briefness sails are filled,                           *winged*
And wishes fall out as they're willed.
At Ephesus the temple see:
    [*An altar,* THAISA *and other vestals are revealed*]
Our king, and all his company.
    *Enter* PERICLES, MARINA, LYSIMACHUS, HELICANUS[, CER-
    IMON, *with attendants*]
That he can hither come so soon
20  Is by your fancies' thankful doom.[1]
    [GOWER *stands aside*]
PERICLES   Hail, Dian. To perform thy just° command                      *precise*
I here confess myself the King of Tyre,
Who, frighted from my country, did espouse
The fair Thaisa
    [THAISA *starts*]
        at Pentapolis.
25  At sea in childbed died she, but brought forth
A maid° child called Marina, who, O goddess,                            *girl*
Wears yet thy silver liv'ry.[2] She at Tarsus
Was nursed with° Cleon, whom at fourteen years                          *by*
He sought to murder, but her better stars
30  Bore her to Mytilene, 'gainst whose shore riding[3]
Her fortunes brought the maid aboard our barque,
Where, by her own most clear remembrance, she
Made known herself my daughter.
THAISA                           Voice and favour°—                      *appearance*
You are, you are—O royal Pericles!
    [*She falls*]
35  PERICLES   What means the nun? She dies. Help, gentlemen!
CERIMON   Noble sir,
If you have told Diana's altar true,
This is your wife.
PERICLES             Reverend appearer,° no.                             *reverend-looking man*
I threw her overboard with these same arms.
CERIMON   Upon this coast, I warr'nt you.
40  PERICLES                              'Tis most certain.
CERIMON   Look to the lady. O, she's but o'erjoyed.
Early one blustering morn this lady
Was thrown upon this shore. I oped the coffin,
Found there rich jewels, recovered° her, and placed her                 *revived*

---

1. Thanks to your imaginations' agreement.
2. Still wears your uniform (remains a virgin).
3. *'gainst . . . riding:* where, as we rode at anchor.

Here in Diana's temple.

45 PERICLES             May we see them?

CERIMON    Great sir, they shall be brought you to° my house,                *at*
     Whither I invite you. Look, Thaisa is
     Recoverèd.

THAISA          O, let me look upon him!
     If he be none of mine, my sanctity
50     Will to my sense bend no licentious ear,
     But curb it, spite of seeing.[4] O, my lord,
     Are you not Pericles? Like him you spake,
     Like him you are. Did you not name a tempest,
     A birth and death?

55 PERICLES    The voice of dead Thaisa!

THAISA    That Thaisa
     Am I, supposèd dead and drowned.

PERICLES *[taking Thaisa's hand]*    Immortal Dian!

THAISA    Now I know you better.
60     When we with tears parted° Pentapolis,                 *departed*
     The King my father gave you such a ring.

PERICLES    This, this! No more, you gods. Your present kindness
     Makes my past miseries sports;° you shall do well         *trifles*
     That° on the touching of her lips I may                *If*
65     Melt, and no more be seen.—O come, be buried
     A second time within these arms.

           *[They embrace and kiss]*

MARINA *[kneeling to* THAISA*]*     My heart
     Leaps to be gone into my mother's bosom.

PERICLES    Look who kneels here: flesh of thy flesh, Thaisa,
     Thy burden at the sea, and called Marina
     For she was yielded° there.               *Because she was born*

70 THAISA *[embracing* MARINA*]*    Blessed, and mine own!

HELICANUS *[kneeling to* THAISA*]*
     Hail, madam, and my queen.

THAISA                 I know you not.

PERICLES    You have heard me say, when I did fly from Tyre,
     I left behind an ancient substitute.
     Can you remember what I called the man?
75     I have named him oft.

THAISA    'Twas Helicanus then.

PERICLES    Still confirmation.
     Embrace him, dear Thaisa; this is he.
     Now do I long to hear how you were found,
80     How possibly preserved, and who to thank—
     Besides the gods—for this great miracle.

THAISA    Lord Cerimon, my lord. This is the man
     Through whom the gods have shown their pow'r, that can
     From first to last resolve° you.             *answer everything for*

PERICLES *[to* CERIMON*]*      Reverend sir,
85     The gods can have no mortal officer
     More like a god than you. Will you deliver°           *explain*
     How this dead queen re-lives?

CERIMON             I will, my lord.
     Beseech you, first go with me to my house,

---

4. *my sanctity . . . seeing:* my religious vows will forbid my sense to feel desire, in spite of what I see.

Where shall be shown you all was° found with her,  *that was*
90  And told how in this temple she came° placed,  *came to be*
No needful thing omitted.
PERICLES  Pure Diana,
I bless thee for thy vision,° and will offer  *(in Scene 21)*
Nightly oblations° to thee.—Beloved Thaisa,  *offerings*
This prince, the fair betrothèd of your daughter,
95  At Pentapolis shall marry her.
[*To* MARINA] And now this ornament°  *this hair that*
Makes me look dismal will I clip to form,
And what this fourteen years no razor touched,
To grace thy marriage day I'll beautify.
100  THAISA  Lord Cerimon hath letters of good credit,°  *trustworthiness*
Sir, from Pentapolis: my father's dead.
PERICLES  Heav'n make a star of him! Yet there, my queen,
We'll celebrate their nuptials, and ourselves
Will in that kingdom spend our following days.
105  Our son and daughter shall in Tyrus reign.—
Lord Cerimon, we do our longing stay°  *delay our desire*
To hear the rest untold. Sir, lead 's the way.
*Exeunt [all but]* GOWER
GOWER  In Antiochus and his daughter you have heard⁵
Of monstrous lust the due and just reward;
110  In Pericles, his queen, and daughter seen,°  *you have seen*
Although assailed with fortune fierce and keen,
Virtue preserved from fell° destruction's blast,  *cruel*
Led on by heav'n, and crowned with joy at last.
In Helicanus may you well descry
115  A figure of truth, of faith, of loyalty.
In reverend Cerimon there well appears
The worth that learnèd charity aye° wears.  *always*
For wicked Cleon and his wife, when fame°  *rumor*
Had spread their cursèd deed to° th' honoured name  *against*
120  Of Pericles, to rage the city turn,°  *turned*
That° him and his they in his palace burn.  *So that*
The gods for murder seemèd so content
To punish that, although not done, but meant.
So on your patience evermore attending,
125  New joy wait on you. Here our play has ending.  [*Exit*]

## Additional Passage

Q gives this more expansive version of Marina's Epitaph (18.34–3.7):

'The fairest, sweetest, best lies here,
Who withered in her spring of year.
She was of Tyrus the King's° daughter,  *the King of Tyre's*
On whom foul death hath made this slaughter.
5  Marina was she called, and at her birth
Thetis,¹ being proud, swallowed° some part o'th' earth;  *flooded*

---

5. The second of Gower's speeches in pentameter couplets.
**Additional Passage**
1. A sea nymph here confused with Tethys, wife of Oceanus (in Greek mythology, the ruler of a river that encircled the earth). The image in this passage is of the ocean (because of Thetis/Tethys) surging happily in response to Marina's birth and angrily in response to her death.

Therefore the earth, fearing to be o'erflowed,
Hath Thetis' birth-child on the heav'ns bestowed,
Wherefore she° does, and swears she'll never stint,                                    *(Thetis)*
10    Make raging batt'ry upon shores of flint.'°                                       *rocky shores*

# The Winter's Tale

In his induction to *Bartholomew Fair* (1614), Ben Jonson complained of plays that "make Nature afraid" and "beget Tales, Tempests, and such like Drolleries." His remarks seem aimed directly at his contemporary William Shakespeare, who, in the last years of his theatrical career, had written a number of plays, including *The Winter's Tale* (1609–11) and *The Tempest* (1611), that by some accounts might be said to "make Nature afraid." Jonson implies that such plays, eschewing realism, present fantastic or impossible events that defy the laws of nature. While Jonson found such concoctions unpalatable, most of Shakespeare's contemporaries did not. In prose romances popular throughout the period, characters regularly undertake impossible quests, encounter marvels, and are unexpectedly reunited with lost children. Shakespeare's late plays participate fully in this taste for the marvelous, reveling in, rather than being embarrassed by, the strange and the improbable. In the case of *The Winter's Tale*, we possess a rather full description of the play by Simon Forman, a London astrologer and doctor, who saw it performed on May 15, 1611, and described its complicated plot with no hint that he found either its events absurd or the play defective. On the contrary, Forman's detailed description suggests him to have been fully absorbed by what he saw. Concluding with an account of the deceptive tricks of the play's rogue, Autolycus, Forman moralized: "Beware trusting feigned beggars or fawning fellows."

Modern editors often group *Pericles, The Winter's Tale, Cymbeline,* and *The Tempest* together under the label "romances," although this is not a category used in the Folio (1623). There Shakespeare's plays are divided into comedies, tragedies, and histories. *Pericles* is not included in the Folio; *Cymbeline* is placed at the end of the tragedies; *The Tempest* appears as the first of the comedies and *The Winter's Tale* as the last. These placements are suggestive of the mixed tragicomic nature of these particular dramas. Like Shakespeare's earlier comedies, they all end happily, with families reunited and marriages in prospect; but the late plays also engage with the tragic dimensions of human life to a degree not customary for the early comedies. Before the characters in these plays reach safe harbor, they encounter tyranny, incest, the loss of wives and children, and the treachery of brothers. The protagonists suffer intensely, both because of fortune's blows and because of their own folly. Only by what is experienced as miracle does tragedy turn to mirth and suffering cease. While the miraculous quality of these reversals binds these plays together as a group, it is also at the heart of Jonson's objections. Improbable occurrences and unexpected transformations of sorrow into joy can affront sober common sense, but they also make romance emotionally and theatrically appealing. In defiance of probability, these plays construct a world in which (at least for some fortunate characters) second chances are possible.

By its very title *The Winter's Tale* signals its affiliations with popular storytelling. Within the play, Mamillius, the King of Sicilia's young son, informs his mother that "a sad tale's best for winter" (2.1.27) and offers to tell her one "of sprites and goblins" (2.1.28). The only sprites and goblins in Shakespeare's play turn out to be the internal demons of jealousy and suspicion that erupt in the mind of its protagonist, King Leontes, but *The Winter's Tale* is permeated by sadness, even during its festive conclusion, and its plot is full of wonders. Its starting point is King Leontes' sudden certainty that his wife, Hermione, is pregnant not with his own child, but with that of his childhood friend, King Polixenes of Bohemia, a visitor at Leontes' Sicilian court. Warned of Leontes' jealousy, Polixenes flees back to Bohemia, leaving the King to vent his wrath on Hermione. Imprisoned, she gives birth to a daughter, Perdita, whom Leontes orders

The Bloudy Mother.
1544
OR

The most inhumane murthers, committed by *Iane Hattersley* vpon diuers Infants, the issue of her owne bodie : & the priuate burying of them in an Orchard with her Araignment and execution.

As also, The most loathsome and lamentable end of *Adam Adamson* her Master, the vnlawfull begetter of those vnfortunate Babes being eaten and consumed aliue with Wormes and Lice.

At East *Grinsted* in *Sussex* neere London, in Iuly last. 1609.

Printed for *Iohn Busbie*, and are to be sould by *Arthur Iohnson* in Paules Churchyard at the signe of the White Horse.

In the early seventeenth century, popular pamphlet literature circulated sensational stories of parents, especially unmarried women, who murdered or abandoned their children. In this title page from *The Bloudy Mother* (1609), a serving woman and her master bury the illegitimate child she has killed. On the right, for his part in begetting and disposing of the child, the master is consumed by lice and worms.

to be abandoned in the countryside far from Sicilia. Even when the oracle of Apollo subsequently declares Hermione innocent, Leontes continues to insist on her guilt. As he does, the death of his only son, Mamillius, is announced, and Hermione appears to die of grief. The first three acts of *The Winter's Tale* thus enact a miniature tragedy (not unlike Shakespeare's tragedy of the jealous Othello) in which Leontes' actions result in the loss of wife, daughter, and son. His personal tragedy also affects his kingdom. The oracle proclaims: "the King shall live without an heir if that which is lost be not found" (3.2.133–34). A kingdom without an heir to the throne is a kingdom in danger.

But then something extraordinary happens. The character Time appears onstage, informing the audience that sixteen years have passed and that Perdita, abandoned on the seacoast of Bohemia, has survived. Suddenly, instead of the wintry world of Leontes' Sicilian court, the play bursts with the energies of a Bohemian summer. The

Old Shepherd who rescued Perdita is about to hold a sheepshearing festival, and Florizel, King Polixenes' son, has fallen in love with Perdita. A series of extraordinary events returns the young couple to Leontes' court, where Perdita's true status as his child and heir is revealed. More wonders follow. Taken to see what they believe to be a statue of the long-dead Hermione, the King and his newly recovered daughter witness the seeming miracle of the statue's transformation into flesh and blood.

Shakespeare's chief source for this tale was Robert Greene's popular prose romance *Pandosto,* first published in 1588. Greene provided Shakespeare with the story of a jealous King who loses Queen and daughter but eventually has his daughter restored to him. But the differences between Shakespeare's play and Greene's prose tale are as striking as the similarities. For example, Shakespeare carefully changed the names of most of the characters he borrowed from Greene. In *Pandosto,* the King's lost daughter is Fawnia, but Shakespeare names her Perdita, a word that in Latin means "that which is lost." In Shakespeare's hands, Perdita's lover ceases to be Dorastus and becomes, instead, Florizel, which suggests the young prince's connection with the flowers of spring. Greene's protagonist, Pandosto, is transformed into Leontes, evoking the leonine or lionlike nature of his wrath. Shakespeare also reversed the kingdoms ruled by Greene's Kings. In *Pandosto,* the protagonist is King of Bohemia and his childhood friend rules Sicilia. In *The Winter's Tale,* the reverse is true, and one reason may be the association of Sicilia with the myth of Proserpina, the beautiful daughter of Ceres abducted by Dis, the god of the underworld, as she was picking flowers. Her mother attempted to free Proserpina, but she was allowed to return to the upper world only six months of each year. During that period, spring and summer came to the earth, but winter reigned when Proserpina returned to Dis's kingdom. The sixteen years of mourning Leontes undergoes in Perdita's absence provide a counterpart to aspects of this myth.

Shakespeare, however, made much larger changes in Greene's romance. For example, he enhanced the role of Leontes' son, who is barely mentioned by Greene; he added the characters of Paulina, Emilia, Antigonus, Autolycus, Clown, Time, and rustics such as Dorcas and Mopsa (in *Pandosto,* Mopsa was the name of the Old Shepherd's wife; in *The Winter's Tale,* that wife is long dead). The magnificent sheepshearing festival is Shakespeare's invention; nothing like it exists in *Pandosto.* Most importantly, Greene's romance ends on a tragic note. Although the King and his daughter are finally reunited, Pandosto's wife is never restored to him, and overcome with desire for his grown daughter, he attempts incest and later takes his own life.

Shakespeare clearly saw in Greene's grim tale the basis for a much more resonant narrative of loss and redemption. The play is a diptych of winter and summer, hinged by the appearance of Time. It is probably a mistake to account for this structure by using only one interpretive framework, for the play's elegant simplicity resonates with many narratives of renewal. Some have read the play in Christian terms, seeing Leontes as a sinner who, after a period of suffering and repentance, receives the gift of God's grace through the return of his daughter and the Christlike resurrection of his wife. The play loosely traces the liturgical calendar, moving from the hospitality associated with Christmas to the Lenten period of deprivation and repentance to the joyous celebration of Easter and the Maying festivals associated with Whitsuntide, which occurs seven weeks after Easter. Other critics have stressed the mythic qualities of the play, its resemblance, for example, to the myth of Proserpina, or to fertility rites in which the coming of spring and sexual fulfillment depend on the sacrifice of a figure, usually an old King, associated with winter. In *The Winter's Tale,* Leontes does not die, but he does mourn for sixteen years; and his servant Antigonus, who takes the babe to Bohemia and there names her Perdita, becomes Leontes' sacrificial substitute. Once he has deposited Perdita, Antigonus is mauled and eaten by a bear. As the Old Shepherd who rescues Perdita says to his son, who has witnessed this death, "Thou metst with things dying, I with things new-born" (3.3.104–05), the latter event seemingly dependent on the former. Other critics stress the pattern of generational renewal informing the play as the sins of the father, Leontes, give way to the innocent goodness of Florizel and Perdita. In some productions, the actress playing Hermione also plays Perdita (although a double for one of them usually has to be employed in the statue scene when they are both on stage together), deepening the sense that it is through their children that parents have a second life. Resonating with all these interpretive paradigms, *The Winter's Tale* draws richly on the many narratives and structures of belief through which Western culture has produced and sustained its desire for transcendence and renewal.

In modern productions, the symbolic power of the play's diptych structure is often highlighted by contrasts in the costumes and sets used to distinguish Sicilia and Bohemia. Sicilia, for example, is often a snow kingdom, dominated by white clothing and metallic props; Bohemia is a summer kingdom, the stage carpeted in green, the characters at the sheepshearing festival a riot of variegated colors. When the Bohemian party comes to Sicilia, the winter landscape is literally overwritten with the colorful clothes associated with Whitsuntide.

The play, however, is not simply about the triumph of the young, the rebirth of a world of possibility. *The Winter's Tale,* as befits a tragicomedy, moves from sorrow to joy, but that joy is bittersweet. However important the younger generation is to this old tale, the focus in this and the other romances stays resolutely on the older generation. It is Leontes who sins and must repent, Leontes whose family is reconstituted. Crucially, that reconstitution is only partial and imperfect. Mamillius, the young son, dies, the ultimate sacrifice to Leontes' tyrannous actions; and in the play's last scene, the playwright is at pains to stress that the "statue" of Hermione has wrinkles, the mark of time on her body. Traduced while a fertile wife and mother, Hermione returns as a woman past childbearing. Time, whose appearance marks the hinge of the play, may heal old sorrows and bring new births to pass, but it also shuts down possibilities and destroys youth and strength. The ending of Shakespeare's old tale induces wonder and joy, but it cannot make an old man young or erase all the consequences of rash deeds. Shakespeare's late plays achieve their rich emotional effects from the deep strains of melancholia that underwrite their measured celebrations of the return of love and hope to a chastened social order.

Nor, despite the archaic quality that permeates these plays, are they simple enactments of timeless patterns and narratives. The precipitating event of the play—the eruption of Leontes' jealousy—is a symptom of the faultlines in a particular patriarchal culture. Often said to be "irrational," this jealousy in actuality has its roots in the cultural practices that in Jacobean England made men the heads of families, lineages, and kingdoms, but at the same time made them crucially dependent on women's reproductive powers to generate legitimate heirs. As *The Winter's Tale* opens, Leontes asks Polixenes to extend his stay in Sicilia. Polixenes refuses, but when Hermione entreats him, he agrees. This event, and the sight of his pregnant wife conversing with his friend and holding him by the hand, triggers in Leontes so deep a suspicion of his wife's fidelity that he plans to have Polixenes killed and doubts the legitimacy of his son as well. In part, what disturbs Leontes is the unknowability of the biological origins of his children. Men theoretically had dominion over their wives, but as Leontes says, "No barricado for a belly" (1.2.205)—that is, no absolute defense of a woman's chastity but her own honor, and that lies in her control, not her husband's.

A deep ambivalence toward women and sexuality, moreover, surfaces earlier in the same scene when, reminiscing about his boyhood friendship with Leontes, Polixenes describes the two of them as twinned lambs who experienced a fall from paradise only when they felt sexual passion and had their first encounters with women. In this conversation, the two men echo a strand of early modern thought that viewed men's friendships with men as of greater worth than what were seen as men's more dangerous and unpredictable relations with women, an idea examined as early in Shakespeare's work as *The Two Gentlemen of Verona.* Construed as physically imperfect and as intellectually inferior to men, women were supposedly ruled by their passions and could in turn evoke dangerous and degrading emotions in men. Yet men were enjoined to marry these irrational creatures to procreate and to continue family lineage. Leontes' rage at Hermione seems to stem in part from his dependence on her to give him legitimate heirs.

Other tensions permeate the opening scenes. If in their younger days Polixenes and Leontes were like twinned lambs, in adulthood their friendship is tinged with competitiveness, with Hermione gradually becoming the focus of their rivalry. Polixenes' attendant Archidamus opens the play expressing uneasiness about repaying the generous hospitality provided by Leontes and suggesting rivalry as well as friendship between the two kingdoms; in 1.2 Leontes asks Polixenes if he loves *his* son as dearly as Leontes loves Mamillius, again suggesting competitiveness between the two Kings at the level of paternal affection for their sons. In this general context of subterranean rivalry, Leontes' command that Hermione entreat Polixenes to stay not only expresses his ostentatious generosity (he will even share his wife's attentions with his friend), but also calls forth his rivalrous jealousy (perhaps his friend has taken advantage of his generosity and assumed Leontes' place in Hermione's bed).

Once his jealousy has been triggered, Leontes gives the rein to a deadly rage that finds its chief object in Hermione's pregnant body. This anger is played out in part through Leontes' increasing identification with his young son, Mamillius. In Mamillius, Leontes sees himself as he once was, a young boy not yet wearing either the breeches or the sharp phallic dagger associated with adult manhood (1.2.157–58). It is an image of innocence but also of vulnerability. The name Mamillius, another of Shakespeare's brilliant inventions, suggests one source of that vulnerability. *Mamilla* is the word for the nipple on a breast or a diminutive form of *mamma*, the Latin word for the breast itself. His name thus connects Mamillius to the lactating breast and to the world of women, who in early modern culture presided over childbirth and the early years of children's lives. In a culture in which baby formula did not exist, infants depended utterly on women, either wet nurses or mothers, to provide the crucial sustenance, breast milk. As was often true of women from the upper class, Hermione does not herself seem to have nursed Mamillius. As Leontes bitterly exclaims: "I am glad you did not nurse him" (2.1.58). Nonetheless, the young boy's name and his appearance in 2.1 with his pregnant mother and her waiting women clearly associate him with the feminine sphere of birth, lactation, and early childhood. In identifying with Mamillius, a boy so young his nurse's milk is scarcely out of him, Leontes seems to feel both the vulnerability of the infant dependent on the lactating body of woman and the vulnerability of the adult husband dependent on the pregnant body and the chastity of his wife for legitimate offspring. As if to deny these dependencies, Leontes banishes Mamillius from his mother's presence, and he banishes Hermione to prison. Mamillius dies; Leontes appears to lose all that would link him to the future: wife, son, daughter.

*The Winter's Tale* makes Leontes a dangerous tyrant in Acts 1 to 3 and portrays his anger and paranoia as forces that torture his speech and profoundly isolate him. In the first three acts, Leontes' most characteristic action is to turn away from those who love or attempt to help him. He sends his wife to prison; casts out his infant daughter; refuses the good counsel of his courtiers; rages in misogynistic fury at Paulina, who brings Perdita to him from prison; and finally defies the oracle of Apollo. Lacking trust in his wife and in all those around him, Leontes condemns himself to deathlike isolation. As in Shakespeare's other late plays, much of the language of *The Winter's Tale* is difficult and dense. Normal word order is inverted; speeches begin and end in the middle of a line; figurative language is given elliptical expression. During his period of intense jealousy, Leontes' language becomes even more dense and compressed than is typical of the rest of the play. Looking at his son, he exclaims:

> Can thy dam—may't be?—
> Affection, thy intention stabs the centre.
> Thou dost make possible things not so held,
> Communicat'st with dreams—how can this be?—

> With what's unreal thou coactive art,
> And fellow'st nothing. Then 'tis very credent
> Thou mayst co-join with something, and thou dost—
> And that beyond commission; and I find it—
> And that to the infection of my brains
> And hard'ning of my brows.

                                        (1.2.139–48)

In this difficult passage, Leontes wrestles with the knowledge that his "affection" (the passions of rage, jealousy, and suspicion released in him) wounds him and perhaps leads him to imagine things to be true that are not. On the other hand, his suspicions *may* be justified; he may already be a cuckold. In this horrible state of uncertainty, Leontes' speech verges on incoherence. He interrupts the flow of his own thoughts with questions and ejaculations; his mind darts from boy to mother to his own pain; he realizes he may be wrong, but returns, obsessively, to the coarse and shameful image of his forehead disfigured with the horns of a cuckold.

The inner disorder suggested by this language finds its outward manifestation in Leontes' increasingly tyrannical actions. In the early modern period, the ruler of a king-

In the early modern period, childbirth was largely the affair of women. In this picture from Jakob Rüff's *De conceptu et generatione hominis* (Concerning the conception and birth of man) (1580), several women attend to a woman in labor while, in the background, two men cast the child's horoscope.

dom was often compared to the head of a family. Good order in the commonwealth had its foundation in a well-ordered domestic realm. In *The Winter's Tale*, Leontes oversteps his just authority in both domains, refusing to take counsel from his courtiers, defying the gods, and condemning his wife for adultery with no evidence but his own suspicions. Nowhere, however, does he more certainly exceed his patriarchal authority than when he orders Hermione to stand trial before the proper period of her lying-in has passed. In the Renaissance, childbirth was recognized as an event both important and dangerous. Women gave birth surrounded by other women, usually a hired midwife, as well as by neighbors and female family members. The laboring female body, opened to let the child pass into the world, was considered to be in a particularly vulnerable state, needing to be protected from the unhealthful air that might enter the open womb. Consequently, birthing took place in a closed chamber, and after birth had occurred, women lay in their chambers for an extended period, recovering strength and purging their bodies of the blood and other fluids associated with pregnancy. At the end of this period, often lasting a month but sometimes longer, the woman came out of her house and returned to her normal routines. This occasion was marked by a "churching" ceremony, a rite of purification and celebration in which thanks were given for the safe delivery of a child and the woman's body declared cleansed of the impurities of pregnancy and birth.

When Hermione is made to stand trial, the pathos of her dignified defense of herself is heightened by her weakened state. In many productions, she appears on stage unattended, almost unable to stand. Among the wrongs done her, she accuses Leontes of having "with immodest hatred / The childbed privilege denied, which 'longs / To women of all fashion; lastly, hurried / Here, to this place, i'th' open air, before / I have got strength of limit" (3.2.100–04). Leontes' fury against the maternal body extends to denying that body the privileges of the lying-in period and exposing it to the dangers of the open air of a public place. This is domestic tyranny of a hideous sort.

After such cruelty, what recovery? Bohemia seems to be the place of hope in the play, and that feeling is conveyed in part by the vast expansion of character and event in that pastoral locale. After the claustrophobic focus on Leontes, the action unfolds to encompass the tricks of a wily rogue, Autolycus (whose name links him to the Autolycus of classical mythology, a crafty thief and grandfather of Ulysses; Autolycus's own father, Mercury, was the god of thieves); the sports of a sheepshearing festival; the courtship of Florizel and Perdita; and the intrigues that take many of these players back to Sicilia. The scene depicting the festival at the Old Shepherd's farm, 4.4, is one of the longest in Shakespeare's canon (810 lines), is entirely his own invention, and is a great feast of languages and events. It includes the singing of ballads, a dance of twelve satyrs, Perdita's lyrical catalog of the flowers appropriate to each stage of life, and the painful moment when Polixenes forbids his son's marriage.

As this last moment shows, although Bohemia is a place of healing, it is not a paradise. In Bohemia, "great creating nature" for a time replaces Apollo as the deity who presides over the action. The fertility of the earth and, by extension, the fertility of woman may here seem to be redeemed from the curse laid upon them by Leontes' suspicion of his wife; and Florizel's staunch commitment to Perdita in the face of mounting obstacles to their love augers well. But Polixenes just as staunchly opposes their union, threatening to use his patriarchal power in a way that, as with Leontes, would separate him from his son and from the possibility of future lineage. Bohemia also contains the rogue Autolycus, picking the pockets of country bumpkins and hiding his identity by a series of disguises. Further, Bohemian life is marked by enormous disparities of wealth. The Old Shepherd is rich, in part because of the money he found with Perdita. For the sheepshearing feast, Perdita can afford ingredients—raisins, rice, and spices, for example—that were exotic luxury goods, foodstuffs in excess of the subsistence diet of bread, beer, and cheese that was still the staple for many. It also possible that some of the Old Shepherd's wealth comes from the new profitability of raising sheep. Throughout the sixteenth and seventeenth centuries, land was increasingly enclosed—that is,

In this late seventeenth-century woodcut from the Pepysian collection of early modern ballads, a peddler carries a huge pack and holds several rabbits, or conies, which suggests that he is also a cony-catcher—that is, a con man (like Autolycus), whose victims were popularly called conies.

fenced off for grazing sheep rather than available for communal use in raising food and feeding cattle. These enclosures were popularly blamed for perceived increases in rural poverty and for the creation of masterless men, poor folk who roamed the countryside without fixed places of residence and who were believed to feign sickness or deformity in order to enforce charity from those they met. Autolycus, pretending to have lost his clothes to a highwayman, is a comic version of such a masterless man, yet his presence in the play, juxtaposed to that of the rich shepherd, is a reminder of the social tensions and economic stratifications that permeate the rural landscape with widespread enclosures and other changes in rural life.

Bohemia is also the locale of one of the great set pieces of the play—the debate between Polixenes and Perdita concerning the relative values of art and nature and the relationship between them. This was an ancient debate and one that could give off a decidedly musty odor, even though it was dusted off by a number of Shakespeare's contemporaries. At the heart of this debate lay the question of artifice. Was it a good thing? Did it distort or enhance nature? Given the imperfections of the fallen world and humankind's weaknesses, could art be instrumental in calling into being a better world, or was it merely a temptation to pride or to competition with the divine creator? The refreshing thing about the handling of these issues in *The Winter's Tale* is that the play comes to no abstract resolution concerning them. Rather, it encases the actual debate between Polixenes and Perdita in multiple ironies, and it complexly connects this debate to the actions of characters who seemingly have no involvement with it. For Perdita, product of the pastoral landscape, art is a bad thing. She wants no grafted or hybrid flowers in her garden. Yet even as she speaks her condemnation of art, Perdita is reluctantly dressed as Queen of the sheepshearing feast, a bit of artifice that reveals a truth she herself cannot know: namely, that she is a Queen's daughter. Polixenes, for his part, champions art, declaring that the practice of mixing wild and cultivated plants produces sturdy hybrids and that the art of grafting is itself a gift of nature. Yet when his son wishes to graft himself to a shepherd's daughter, Polixenes finds such a practice abhorrent.

Besides making the obvious point that people don't always act on their stated beliefs, this exchange shows the extreme pressure the play puts on the art-nature dichotomy. In Perdita's case, her "natural" condition as princess is revealed only by means of two kinds of artifice: her dress as Queen of the feast and the role Camillo creates for her as Florizel's Libyan Princess when he devises a way for the two young lovers to return to Leontes' court. Camillo even goes so far as to provide lines for the two to speak. His goal is ameliorative: to satisfy the desires of the young (as well as his own deep longings to again see his homeland) and to heal the breach between the two dissevered kingdoms. The point seems to be not whether in some abstract sense "art" violates "nature," but how artfulness, defined broadly as the representation of the world through painting, statuary, plays, and song, can open new possibilities for imagining what nature is or could be.

This is not an inconsequential point, for in the badly flawed world depicted in *The Winter's Tale* art gradually emerges as one of the resources people can use, either badly

or well, to affect the world around them: to correct old mistakes and to forge new realities. Its effects are determined and limited, of course, by the skill and intentions of the
artist and by the receptiveness of the audience. Autolycus is a subversive con man who
uses disguises and deceptions to fleece money from gulls. By contrast, in the play's final
movement, Paulina emerges as the chief representative of the ameliorative artist who
uses her skills to make better the world around her. Once reviled by Leontes as a witch,
Paulina becomes the King's spiritual guide in the last half of the play (her name linking
her to the New Testament evangelist, St. Paul). This strikingly outspoken woman spends
sixteen years preparing Leontes to be a fit spectator to the tableau of resurrection and
renewal enacted in the last scene. When she had first brought the infant to Leontes from
prison, Paulina had seemed to believe in the self-evident nature of truth. Laying the babe
at Leontes' feet, she proclaimed that the "good goddess Nature" (2.3.104) had made it
an exact copy of the father. Leontes had only to read what nature had written in the face
of his child. But distorting jealousy and rage at his wife had bleared the King's vision.
He would not or could not see himself in the female child he had fathered. So for sixteen years Paulina worked another way, fueling Leontes' remorse and artfully withhold-
ing both from him and from the theater audience the knowledge that Hermione lived.
When the disguised Princess returns to Sicilia, Leontes gets a second chance. Looking
at Perdita, he is finally able to see—not so much himself as the unslandered image of
his wife in the young girl before him. Having admired Perdita, Leontes says to Paulina,
"I thought of her [Hermione] / Even in these looks I made" (5.1.226–27). When he can
believe in the potential goodness of women, and specifically in the chastity of the young
woman who is the simulacrum of his wife, then Leontes can help to create the reality
in which Perdita is truly a Princess and his wife a living being rather than the corpse into
which his rage and distrust had transformed her.

The statue scene itself is one of the most moving dramatic moments in any of
Shakespeare's plays. Like Leontes, the untutored audience does not know that
Hermione lives. Consequently, under Paulina's careful guidance, the spectators both
onstage and off seem to participate in willing the statue into life. When Hermione
descends from her pedestal, the audience can feel itself present at the miraculous resurrection of the dead. In theological terms, this scene touches on controversial matters. Protestants repudiated what they characterized as Catholic idolatry, which
involved the veneration of images, including statues of the Virgin Mary. Protestants, by
contrast, typically stressed the ear over the eye, words over images, faith over works. In
the wake of the Reformation, more radical Protestants went so far as to smash stained-
glass windows and the statues of saints that had for many centuries adorned Catholic
churches. The final moments of *The Winter's Tale* gesture toward this repudiated world
of images and their veneration. While Paulina insists that the audience awaken its faith,
she does so in a scene that is visually organized to focus all eyes on a statue that in its
chapel setting might well evoke memories of prior Catholic practices. In his characteristic way, Shakespeare seems to have things two ways: drawing on the emotional
power of Catholic rituals centered on the image, he simultaneously suggests that there
is no statue on the stage at all, only a living woman roused to new vigor by the recovery of a long lost daughter.

However ambiguous the theological implications of the final scene, ultimately the
old tale ends happily, or mostly so. At the end of the play, patriarchy has been reformed,
but its potential for abuses has hardly been eradicated. In the final scene, the highly
charged image of the pregnant female body is nowhere to be seen. Perdita is not yet a
wife; both Paulina and Hermione are probably too old for childbearing. For Perdita and
Florizel perhaps the greatest tests of faith and mutuality lie ahead, when Perdita's transformation from maid into wife and mother will present new occasions for jealousy and
distrust. Moreover, in *The Winter's Tale* the remembrance of things that were lost and
can never be regained intrudes even on the celebration of the return of Perdita and of
Hermione. Paulina pointedly recalls her husband, Antigonus, lost in carrying Perdita to
Bohemia; Hermione speaks to Perdita of the sixteen long years of their separation; her

wrinkles attest to other losses; Mamillius is gone forever. The point of *The Winter's Tale* hardly seems to be that folly has no consequences or that earthly paradise is possible. Those claims would indeed make nature afraid. Rather, the play celebrates the true miracle of partial restorations, of moments of exquisite joy wrested by work, art, and good fortune from the pains of the imperfect world that men and women have made.

JEAN E. HOWARD

## TEXTUAL NOTE

*The Winter's Tale* was first printed in the Folio of 1623 at the end of the group of comedies. Simon Forman, a London doctor, saw a performance at the Globe on May 15, 1611, and it was performed at court on November 11 of that year. Its exact date of composition, however, is unknown. Largely on stylistic evidence and because *The Winter's Tale* is at several points indebted to Plutarch, a principal source for Shakespeare's classical tragedies such as *Coriolanus* (1608), the Oxford editors place the date of composition in 1609, before *Cymbeline*. Other editors believe the play was written late in 1610 or early in 1611 before the May performance witnessed by Forman. In Act 4, Scene 4, working men at the sheepshearing festival perform a satyr dance that resembles a dance in Ben Jonson's *Masque of Oberon,* which was performed at court on January 1, 1611. In Shakespeare's play, the Old Shepherd remarks that three of the performers had "danced before the King" (4.4.324). This reference has been used to suggest that Shakespeare either was writing *The Winter's Tale* in January of 1611 and so incorporated a contemporary court event into his play, or that he composed the bulk of the play after that date. It is also possible that Shakespeare—or someone else—added this dance to *The Winter's Tale* after the play had already been written and was in performance in order to capitalize on the glamour attached to court occasions, especially if, as the Old Shepherd indicates, members of Shakespeare's company performed in Jonson's masque. If so, the dance would have been recorded in the promptbook but not necessarily in Shakespeare's original manuscript.

The Folio text of the play was probably set from a transcript prepared by Ralph Crane, a scrivener who transcribed a number of plays associated with the King's Men. In many of the manuscripts prepared by Crane, and this is true for *The Winter's Tale,* all the characters who appear in certain scenes, regardless of when they actually come on stage, are listed in the opening stage direction. Crane sometimes modified stage directions in the interest of clarity and imposed his own punctuation and spelling on the playscripts, showing a decided preference for the heavy use of parentheses, hyphens, and apostrophes. The changes Crane made while copying the plays make it difficult to recognize what kind of manuscript lay behind his transcriptions: promptbook or foul papers. As with other plays set from Crane's transcriptions, the Folio *Winter's Tale* is a relatively clean text. Act and scene divisions are carefully and consistently noted, although stage directions are sparse. There are only forty-three in the Folio, and they are regularly supplemented in modern editions.

## SELECTED BIBLIOGRAPHY

Adelman, Janet. "Masculine Authority and the Maternal Body: The Return to Origins in the Romances." *Suffocating Mothers: Fantasies of Maternal Origin in Shakespeare's Plays, "Hamlet" to "The Tempest."* New York: Routledge, 1992. 193–238. Argues that the romances attempt to redress the loss of the idealized parents enacted in *Hamlet* and that *The Winter's Tale* dramatizes the positive restoration of the sexualized mother in the person of Hermione.

Dolan, Frances. "Finding What Has Been 'Lost': Representations of Infanticide and *The Winter's Tale.*" *Dangerous Familiars: Representations of Domestic Crime in England, 1550–1700.* Ithaca, N.Y.: Cornell University Press, 1994. 121–70. Connects *The Winter's Tale* to early modern stories of child abandonment and murder, arguing that the play ultimately forgives the tyrannous father, Leontes, for the exposure of Perdita.

Egan, Robert. "'The Art Itself Is Nature': *The Winter's Tale.*" *Drama Within Drama: Shakespeare's Sense of His Art in "King Lear," "The Winter's Tale," and "The Tempest."* New York: Columbia University Press, 1975. 56–89. Discusses the role of art in rectifying the disordered world of *The Winter's Tale.*

Frye, Northrop. "The Triumph of Time." *A Natural Perspective: The Development of Shakespearean Comedy and Romance.* New York: Columbia University Press, 1965. 72–117. Discusses structures of action and conventions common across Shakespeare's comedies and romances.

Hunt, Maurice. "'Bearing Hence' Shakespeare's *The Winter's Tale.*" *Studies in English Literature 1500–1900* 44 (2004): 333–46. Explores Shakespeare's creative play with the words "bear" and "bear away" in a play in which a bear appears on stage and is often associated with the tyrannous King Leontes.

Mowat, Barbara A. "Rogues, Shepherds, and the Counterfeit Distressed: Texts and Infracontexts of *The Winter's Tale* 4.3." *Shakespeare Studies* 22 (1994): 58–76. Examines the cultural contexts that help make sense of the figure of Autolycus, rogue and con man, in *The Winter's Tale.*

Newcomb, Lori H. "'If That Which Is Lost Be Not Found': Monumental Bodies, Spectacular Bodies in *The Winter's Tale.*" *Ovid and the Renaissance Body.* Ed. Goran V. Stanivukovic. Toronto: University of Toronto Press, 2001. Analyzes the tension between the monumental (stasis and constraint) and the spectacular (metamorphosis and performative freedom) in both the text of *The Winter's Tale* and in its material history as book and as theater piece.

O'Connor, Marion. "'Imagine Me, Gentle Spectators': Iconomachy and *The Winter's Tale.*" *A Companion to Shakespeare's Works. IV: The Poems, Problem Comedies, Late Plays.* Ed. Richard Dutton and Jean E. Howard. Malden, Mass.: Blackwell, 2003. 365–88. Discusses the Renaissance theological debate about the value and truth of images as it bears on a number of early modern plays, including *The Winter's Tale*, in which statues are staged. Argues that Shakespeare insists on the collaboration of word and image, eschewing a total embrace of Reformation logocentrism or Catholic image-worship.

Paster, Gail Kern. "Quarreling with the Dug, or 'I Am Glad You Did Not Nurse Him'." *The Body Embarrassed: Drama and the Disciplines of Shame in Early Modern England.* Ithaca, N.Y.: Cornell University Press, 1993. 215–80. Sets *The Winter's Tale* in an array of Shakespearean texts that anxiously explore early modern cultural practices surrounding reproduction and infant care, especially the practice of wet-nursing.

Wilson, Richard. "The Statue of Our Queen: Shakespeare's Open Secret." *Secret Shakespeare: Studies in Theatre, Religion and Resistance.* Manchester: Manchester University Press, 2004. 246–70. Argues for *The Winter's Tale*'s connection to recusant culture, especially the play's emphasis on the importance of secret spaces dominated by women.

## FILM

*The Winter's Tale.* 1999. Dir. Robin Lough. UK. 170 min. A dark and moving Royal Shakespeare Company production with Anthony Sher as a Leontes truly made mad by jealousy and an impressively dignified Alexandra Gilbreath as Hermione. Imaginative staging of the bear and riveting statue scene as Hermione very slowly comes to life.

# The Winter's Tale

## THE PERSONS OF THE PLAY

LEONTES, King of Sicilia
HERMIONE, his wife
MAMILLIUS, his son
PERDITA, his daughter
CAMILLO ⎱
ANTIGONUS ⎰ Lords at Leontes' court
CLEOMENES
DION
PAULINA, Antigonus's wife
EMILIA, a lady attending on Hermione
A JAILER
A MARINER
Other Lords and Gentlemen, Ladies, Officers, and Servants at
    Leontes' court
POLIXENES, King of Bohemia
FLORIZEL, his son, in love with Perdita; known as Doricles
ARCHIDAMUS, a Bohemian lord
AUTOLYCUS, a rogue, once in the service of Florizel
OLD SHEPHERD
CLOWN, his son
MOPSA ⎱
DORCAS ⎰ shepherdesses
SERVANT of the Old Shepherd
Other Shepherds and Shepherdesses
Twelve countrymen disguised as satyrs
TIME, as chorus

### 1.1

*Enter* CAMILLO *and* ARCHIDAMUS

ARCHIDAMUS    If you shall chance, Camillo, to visit Bohemia on
the like occasion whereon my services are now on foot,[1] you
shall see, as I have said, great difference betwixt our Bohemia
and your Sicilia.

5    CAMILLO    I think this coming summer the King of Sicilia means
to pay Bohemia the visitation which he justly owes him.

ARCHIDAMUS    Wherein our entertainment shall shame us, we
will be justified in our loves;[2] for indeed—

CAMILLO    Beseech you—

10    ARCHIDAMUS    Verily, I speak it in the freedom of my knowledge.
We cannot with such magnificence—in so rare— I know not
what to say.—We will give you sleepy drinks,° that your senses, *drinks to make you drowsy*
unintelligent of our insufficience,[3] may, though they cannot
praise us, as little accuse us.

15    CAMILLO    You pay a great deal too dear for what's given freely.

---

**1.1** Location: Sicilia. The palace of Leontes.
1. On an occasion similar to the one in which I am now
engaged (that is, as attendant lord to a visiting King).

2. Insofar as our less elaborate hospitality will put us to
shame, we will compensate by (the depth of) our love.
3. Unaware of our inadequacy.

ARCHIDAMUS   Believe me, I speak as my understanding instructs
me, and as mine honesty puts it to utterance.

CAMILLO   Sicilia cannot show himself over-kind to Bohemia.
They were trained together in their childhoods, and there
20 rooted betwixt them then such an affection which cannot
choose but branch[4] now. Since their more mature dignities
and royal necessities made separation of their society,° their       *forced them apart*
encounters—though not personal— hath been royally attor-
neyed[5] with interchange of gifts, letters, loving embassies, that°    *so that*
25 they have seemed to be together, though absent; shook hands
as over a vast;° and embraced as it were from the ends of       *wide expanse*
opposed winds.[6] The heavens continue their loves.

ARCHIDAMUS   I think there is not in the world either malice or
matter to alter it. You have an unspeakable° comfort of° your    *inexpressible / in*
30 young prince, Mamillius. It° is a gentleman of the greatest         *(He)*
promise that ever came into my note.

CAMILLO   I very well agree with you in the hopes of him. It is a
gallant child; one that, indeed, physics the subject,[7] makes old
hearts fresh. They that went on crutches ere he was born desire
35 yet their life° to see him a man.                                *hope to live long enough*

ARCHIDAMUS   Would they else be content to die?

CAMILLO   Yes—if there were no other excuse why they should
desire to live.

ARCHIDAMUS   If the King had no son they would desire to live on
40 crutches till he had one.                                *Exeunt*


## 1.2

*Enter* LEONTES, HERMIONE, MAMILLIUS, POLIXENES, *and*
CAMILLO[1]

POLIXENES   Nine changes of the wat'ry star hath been
The shepherd's note[2] since we[3] have left our throne
Without a burden.° Time as long again                           *an occupant*
Would be filled up, my brother, with our thanks,
5 And yet we should for perpetuity
Go hence in debt.[4] And therefore, like a cipher,
Yet standing in rich place,[5] I multiply
With one 'We thank you' many thousands more
That go before it.

LEONTES                         Stay° your thanks a while,          *Postpone*
And pay them when you part.

10 POLIXENES                              Sir, that's tomorrow.
I am questioned by my fears° of what may chance[6]                *I am afraid*
Or breed upon° our absence, that may blow                        *develop because of*
No sneaping winds at home to make us say

---

4. Flourish and spread (as a tree does when it puts
forth branches); divide.
5. Performed by deputies.
6. From opposite ends of the earth. Early modern
atlases often showed the four "corners" of the earth as
the source of the winds.
7. Restores the health of the King's subjects.
1.2 Location: Sicilia. The palace of Leontes.
1. Though listed in the stage direction in F, Camillo has
no part in this scene until line 210, when Leontes says,
"What, Camillo there!" Camillo may be a silent observer

for the first 210 lines, or, as some editors believe, his first
entrance may be marked by Leontes' exclamation.
2. The shepherd has observed nine changes of the
moon (that is, nine months). The moon is "the wat'ry
star" because it governs the tides.
3. Both Kings employ the royal "we," speaking of themselves in the plural.
4. And even then we would depart forever in your debt.
5. Like a zero ("cipher"), which is worthless in itself,
but valuable when it follows another number.
6. Happen by chance.

'This is put forth too truly.'⁷ Besides, I have stayed
To tire your royalty.
15 LEONTES                    We are tougher, brother,
Than you can put us to't.⁸
POLIXENES                    No longer stay.
LEONTES    One sennight° longer.                                  *week*
POLIXENES                    Very sooth,° tomorrow.          *In truth (a mild oath)*
LEONTES    We'll part the time° between's, then; and in that    *split the diffference*
I'll no gainsaying.°                                              *allow no contradiction*
POLIXENES              Press me not, beseech you, so.
20    There is no tongue that moves, none, none i'th' world
So soon as yours, could win me. So it should now,
Were there necessity in your request, although
'Twere needful I denied it. My affairs
Do even drag me homeward; which to hinder
25    Were, in your love, a whip to me;⁹ my stay
To you a charge and trouble. To save both,
Farewell, our brother.
LEONTES                    Tongue-tied, our queen? Speak you.
HERMIONE    I had thought, sir, to have held my peace until
You had drawn oaths from him not to stay. You, sir,
30    Charge him too coldly. Tell him you are sure
All in Bohemia's well. This satisfaction
The bygone day proclaimed.¹ Say this to him,
He's beat from his best ward.²
LEONTES                    Well said, Hermione!
HERMIONE    To tell° he longs to see his son were strong.          *assert*
35    But let him say so then, and let him go.
But let him swear so and he shall not stay,
We'll thwack him hence with distaffs.³
[*To* POLIXENES] Yet of your royal presence I'll adventure°      *risk*
The borrow° of a week. When at Bohemia                           *loan*
40    You take my lord, I'll give him my commission°              *permission*
To let him there a month behind the gest
Prefixed for's parting.⁴—Yet, good deed,° Leontes,              *indeed*
I love thee not a jar° o'th' clock behind                        *tick*
What lady she her lord.⁵—You'll stay?
POLIXENES                    No, madam.
45 HERMIONE    Nay, but you will?
POLIXENES    I may not, verily.
HERMIONE    Verily?
You put me off with limber° vows. But I,                         *weak*
Though you would seek t'unsphere the stars⁶ with oaths,
50    Should yet say 'Sir, no going.' Verily
You shall not go. A lady's 'verily''s
As potent as a lord's. Will you go yet?

---

7. *"that may . . . too truly,"*: an obscure passage. Fearing
the worst, Polixenes hopes that no biting ("sneaping")
winds may blow (that is, no envious forces be active) at
home to make him conclude that his worries were justified.
8. Than any test you put us to.
9. That is, "To hinder me from going home, though lovingly done, would be a punishment ('whip') to me."
1. This good news was announced yesterday.
2. He's forced to relinquish his strongest position. A
fencing metaphor.
3. Wooden sticks, usually about 3 feet long, which
were used in spinning wool. Proverbially, they were
female tools and symbols of female authority.
4. To remain there a month longer than the time
("gest") appointed in advance for his departure.
5. That is, "I love you no less than any noblewoman
loves her husband."
6. To disorder the cosmos. Alluding to the idea that the
stars move in fixed orbits around the earth.

Force me to keep you as a prisoner,
Not like a guest: so you shall pay your fees
55  When you depart,[7] and save your thanks. How say you?
My prisoner? or my guest? By your dread 'verily',
One of them you shall be.
POLIXENES                    Your guest then, madam.
To be your prisoner should import offending,°                    mean I have offended you
Which is for me less easy to commit
Than you to punish.
60  HERMIONE                    Not your jailer then,
But your kind hostess. Come, I'll question you
Of my lord's tricks and yours when you were boys.
You were pretty lordings° then?                    young lords
POLIXENES                    We were, fair Queen,
Two lads that thought there was no more behind°                    (in the future)
65  But such a day tomorrow as today,
And to be boy eternal.
HERMIONE    Was not my lord
The verier wag° o'th' two?                    greater mischief-maker
POLIXENES    We were as twinned° lambs that did frisk i'th' sun,                    identical
70  And bleat the one at th'other. What we changed°                    exchanged
Was innocence for innocence. We knew not
The doctrine of ill-doing, nor dreamed
That any did. Had we pursued that life,
And our weak spirits ne'er been higher reared
75  With stronger blood,° we should have answered heaven                    With more mature passions
Boldly, 'Not guilty', the imposition cleared
Hereditary ours.[8]
HERMIONE                    By this we gather
You have tripped° since.                    sinned
POLIXENES                    O my most sacred lady,
Temptations have since then been born to's; for
80  In those unfledged[9] days was my wife a girl.
Your precious self had then not crossed the eyes
Of my young playfellow.
HERMIONE                    Grace to boot!°                    Heaven help me!
Of this make no conclusion,[1] lest you say
Your queen and I are devils. Yet go on.
85  Th'offences we have made you do we'll answer,°                    answer for
If you first sinned with us, and that with us
You did continue fault, and that you slipped not
With any but with us.
LEONTES                    Is he won yet?
HERMIONE    He'll stay, my lord.
LEONTES                    At my request he would not.
90  Hermione, my dearest, thou never spok'st
To better purpose.
HERMIONE                    Never?
LEONTES                    Never but once.
HERMIONE    What, have I twice said well? When was't before?

7. In early modern England, prisoners were required to pay fees to jailers both for provisions and upon their release.
8. Freed even of the charge of original sin. The doctrine of original sin held that everyone at birth was tainted by sin because the first humans, Adam and Eve,
disobeyed God in the Garden of Eden. Here original sin is linked to the sexual desires that come with maturity.
9. Youthful. An unfledged, or young, bird is one as yet lacking the feathers necessary for flight.
1. Do not follow out this line of reasoning.

I prithee tell me. Cram's° with praise, and make's      *Stuff us; overfeed us*
As fat as tame things. One good deed dying tongueless
95     Slaughters a thousand waiting upon that.²
Our praises are our wages. You may ride's
With one soft kiss a thousand furlongs ere
With spur we heat° an acre.³ But to th' goal.°      *race over / purpose*
My last good deed was to entreat his stay.
100     What was my first? It has an elder sister,
Or I mistake you. O, would her name were Grace!⁴
But once before I spoke to th' purpose? When?
Nay, let me have't. I long.

**LEONTES**                  Why, that was when
105     Three crabbèd° months had soured themselves to death      *bitter*
Ere I could make thee open thy white hand
And clap° thyself my love. Then didst thou utter,      *pledge*
'I am yours for ever.'

**HERMIONE**               'Tis grace indeed.
Why lo you now; I have spoke to th' purpose twice.
The one for ever earned a royal husband;
Th'other, for some while a friend.⁵

         [*She gives her hand to* POLIXENES.⁶
         *They stand aside*]

110     **LEONTES** [*aside*]            Too hot, too hot:
To mingle friendship farre is mingling bloods.⁷
I have *tremor cordis*⁸ on me. My heart dances,
But not for joy, not joy. This entertainment°      *hospitality*
May a free° face put on, derive a liberty      *innocent*
115     From heartiness, from bounty, fertile bosom,°      *generous affection*
And well become the agent.⁹ 'T may, I grant.
But to be paddling° palms and pinching fingers,¹      *caressing*
As now they are, and making practised smiles
As in a looking-glass; and then to sigh, as 'twere
120     The mort o'th' deer²—O, that is entertainment
My bosom likes not, nor my brows.³—Mamillius,
Art thou my boy?

**MAMILLIUS**          Ay, my good lord.

**LEONTES**                      I'fecks,°      *In faith (a mild oath)*
Why, that's my bawcock.° What? Hast smutched° thy nose?      *fine fellow / dirtied*
They say it is a copy out of mine. Come, captain,
125     We must be neat—not neat,⁴ but cleanly, captain.
And yet the steer, the heifer, and the calf

---

2. If one virtuous act goes unremarked, then the thousand more that might have been inspired by it will not come to be.
3. That is, "You'll go much farther with us if you will treat us kindly," with a pun on "ride" as meaning "enjoy us sexually."
4. Would that my first good act were virtuous (full of God's Grace). Hermione may be countering Polixenes' earlier suggestion that she first caused Leontes to sin. With a possible allusion to the Three Graces (Aglaia, Euphrosyne, and Thalia) of classical mythology. Usually depicted nude and dancing in a circle, the three women represented the epitome of earthly beauty and harmony.
5. "Friend" could also mean "lover," a meaning that Leontes takes up in his next speech.
6. It is not certain when Hermione and Polixenes join hands, but by line 117 Leontes remarks that they are

"paddling palms and pinching fingers." Joined hands—or hands separated from one another—are an important and recurring visual motif in the play, culminating at 5.3.107, when Paulina commands Leontes to "present your hand" to Hermione as she ceases to appear a statue.
7. Uniting in passion; having sexual intercourse.
8. A malady marked by an erratic heart rate.
9. And makes the actor of these deeds (Hermione) appear attractive.
1. Early modern texts often represent hands as erotic body parts. Moist palms were believed to be signs of sexual arousal; finger games may suggest sexual penetration.
2. To sigh as loudly as the horn blast that proclaims the death of a hunted deer.
3. Alluding to the proverbial notion that a cuckold sprouted horns from his brow.
4. Punning on neat as meaning both "clean" and "cattle with horns."

Are all called neat.—Still virginalling
Upon his palm?⁵—How now, you wanton° calf—                    *playful*
Art thou my calf?

MAMILLIUS                    Yes, if you will, my lord.

130    LEONTES    Thou want'st a rough pash° and the shoots° that I have,    *shaggy head / horns*
To be full° like me. Yet they say we are                          *entirely; fully*
Almost as like as eggs. Women say so,
That will say anything. But were they false
As o'er-dyed blacks,⁶ as wind, as waters, false

135    As dice are to be wished by one that fixes
No bourn° 'twixt his and mine, yet were it true              *boundary; limit*
To say this boy were like me. Come, sir page,
Look on me with your welkin° eye. Sweet villain,                 *sky blue*
Most dear'st, my collop!⁷ Can thy dam°—may't be?—               *mother*

140    Affection, thy intention stabs the centre.⁸
Thou dost make possible things not so held,°          *things held as impossible*
Communicat'st with dreams—how can this be?—
With what's unreal thou coactive art,°                   *you collaborate*
And fellow'st° nothing. Then 'tis very credent°        *are companion to / believable*

145    Thou mayst co-join with something, and thou dost—
And that beyond commission;° and I find it—             *what is permitted*
And that to the infection of my brains
And hard'ning of my brows.°                          *(with cuckold's horns)*

POLIXENES                    What means Sicilia?

HERMIONE    He something seems° unsettled.                     *seems somewhat*

POLIXENES                            How, my lord!

LEONTES    What cheer? How is't with you, best brother?

150    HERMIONE                            You look
As if you held a brow of much distraction.
Are you moved,° my lord?                                          *angry*

LEONTES                    No, in good earnest.
How sometimes nature will betray its folly,
Its tenderness, and make itself a pastime°          *source of amusement*

155    To harder bosoms! Looking on the lines
Of my boy's face, methoughts I did recoil°                        *go back*
Twenty-three years, and saw myself unbreeched,⁹
In my green velvet coat; my dagger muzzled,°          *in its sheath; blunted*
Lest it should bite its master, and so prove,

160    As ornament oft does, too dangerous.
How like, methought, I then was to this kernel,
This squash,° this gentleman.—Mine honest friend,            *unripe peapod*
Will you take eggs for money?¹

MAMILLIUS                    No, my lord, I'll fight.

LEONTES    You will? Why, happy man be's dole!²—My brother,

5. Still caressing his hand as if playing the virginal, a legless keyboard instrument played on the lap; still acting chastely (like a virgin).
6. Referring to textiles dyed black. Such black cloth was made "false" or weakened by the harsh chemicals in the dye. With a possible reference to Africans, whose dark skin was said to result from overexposure to the sun. It was a commonplace that Africans were prone to licentiousness and were thus sexually "false."
7. That is, "my own flesh." A "collop" is a portion of meat.
8. Passion (probably the passion of jealousy), your

intensity ("intention") pierces my heart or to the core of my being.
9. Not yet old enough to wear men's clothing ("breeches"). Before about the age of six, both girls and boys in early modern England wore a dresslike garment. Giving a boy breeches was a sign of his passage out of childhood and out of the care of women into the world of men.
1. A proverbial expression meaning "Will you accept a trifle in place of something valuable?"
2. Proverbial for "May you have good luck!"

165 Are you so fond of your young prince as we
Do seem to be of ours?
POLIXENES                    If at home, sir,
He's all my exercise, my mirth, my matter;°                    *concern*
Now my sworn friend, and then mine enemy;
My parasite, my soldier, statesman, all.
170 He makes a July's day short as December,
And with his varying childness° cures in me                    *youthful ways*
Thoughts that would thick my blood.³
LEONTES                                        So stands this squire
Officed with me.⁴ We two will walk, my lord,
And leave you to your graver steps. Hermione,
175 How thou lov'st us show in our brother's welcome.
Let what is dear in Sicily be cheap.
Next to thyself and my young rover, he's
Apparent° to my heart.                                        *Heir apparent*
HERMIONE                    If you would seek us,
We are yours i'th' garden. Shall's attend you there?
180 LEONTES    To your own bents° dispose you. You'll be found,                    *inclinations*
Be you beneath the sky. [*Aside*] I am angling° now,                    *fishing; scheming*
Though you perceive me not how I give line.
Go to, go to!
How she holds up the neb, the bill to him,⁵
185 And arms her° with the boldness of a wife                    *herself*
To her allowing° husband!                                        *approving*
                    [*Exeunt* POLIXENES *and* HERMIONE]
                    Gone already.
Inch-thick, knee-deep, o'er head and ears a forked° one!—                    *horned*
Go play, boy, play. Thy mother plays,° and I                    *dallies sexually*
Play° too; but so disgraced a part, whose issue⁶                    *Play a role*
190 Will hiss me to my grave. Contempt and clamour
Will be my knell. Go play, boy, play. There have been,
Or I am much deceived, cuckolds ere now,
And many a man there is, even at this present,
Now, while I speak this, holds his wife by th'arm,
195 That little thinks she has been sluiced⁷ in's absence,
And his pond⁸ fished by his next neighbour, by
Sir Smile, his neighbour.⁹ Nay, there's comfort in't,
Whiles other men have gates,¹ and those gates opened,
As mine, against their will. Should all despair
200 That have revolted° wives, the tenth of mankind                    *rebellious; unfaithful*
Would hang themselves. Physic° for't there's none.                    *Medicine*
It is a bawdy planet, that will strike
Where 'tis predominant;² and 'tis powerful. Think it:

3. Ideas that would make me melancholy, a physical and emotional malady connected with a supposed excess of "thick blood."
4. So this young man performs the same duty for me.
5. How she holds up her face, her mouth to him (to be kissed).
6. Outcome, with puns on "issue" as also meaning "offspring" and "the exit an actor makes from a stage." Leontes' words imply that in playing the part of a cuckold, the result of his role will be disgrace; the illegitimate offspring produced by his wife will bring him disgrace; and his exit from the stage (at death) will be a disgraceful one.
7. Little thinks she has had sexual relations. A sluice

was a trough or channel through which water could be directed. To be sluiced was to have water poured down one's "channel," here probably referring to the vagina where sperm entered.
8. Slang term for the sexual organs of his wife.
9. It is possible that "Sir Smile" is a reference to Polixenes, who may be laughing or smiling in his conversation with Hermione.
1. Another slang term for female genitalia. Leontes imagines the vulva as a gateway that ought to be entered only by a husband.
2. Alluding to the notion that planets control human actions and may exercise malign influences ("strike") when they are in certain "predominant" positions.

From east, west, north, and south, be it concluded,
205 No barricado for a belly.[3] Know't,
It will let in and out the enemy
With bag and baggage.[4] Many thousand on's°                    *of us*
Have the disease and feel't not.—How now, boy?
MAMILLIUS   I am like you, they say.
LEONTES                              Why, that's some comfort.
What, Camillo there!
210 CAMILLO [*coming forward*]   Ay, my good lord.
LEONTES   Go play, Mamillius, thou'rt an honest man.
                                        [*Exit* MAMILLIUS]
Camillo, this great sir will yet stay longer.
CAMILLO   You had much ado to make his anchor hold.
When you cast out, it still came home.°          *always failed to hold*
LEONTES                              Didst note it?
215 CAMILLO   He would not stay at your petitions, made
His business more material.°                                  *important*
LEONTES                              Didst perceive it?
[*Aside*] They're here with me[5] already, whisp'ring, rounding,°       *murmuring*
'Sicilia is a so-forth'. 'Tis far gone
When I shall gust° it last.—How came't, Camillo,         *perceive; taste*
That he did stay?
220 CAMILLO                  At the good Queen's entreaty.
LEONTES   'At the Queen's' be't. 'Good' should be pertinent,
But so° it is, it is not. Was this taken°                      *as / perceived*
By any understanding pate but thine?
For thy conceit is soaking,° will draw in                  *your wit is quick*
225 More than the common blocks.° Not noted, is't,                *dimwits*
But of° the finer natures? By some severals°            *by / individuals*
Of head-piece° extraordinary? Lower messes[6]                   *intellect*
Perchance are to this business purblind?° Say.                     *blind*
CAMILLO   Business, my lord? I think most understand
230 Bohemia stays here longer.
LEONTES   Ha?
CAMILLO   Stays here longer.
LEONTES   Ay, but why?
CAMILLO   To satisfy your highness, and the entreaties
Of our most gracious mistress.
235 LEONTES                      Satisfy?[7]
Th'entreaties of your mistress? Satisfy?
Let that suffice. I have trusted thee, Camillo,
With all the near'st things to my heart, as well
My chamber-counsels,° wherein, priest-like, thou          *secret matters*
240 Hast cleansed my bosom, I from thee departed
Thy penitent reformed. But we have been
Deceived in thy integrity, deceived
In that which seems so.
CAMILLO                  Be it forbid, my lord.
LEONTES   To bide° upon't: thou art not honest; or                 *dwell*
245 If thou inclin'st that way, thou art a coward,

---

3. No means of defending a womb.
4. With full military (or sexual) equipment.
5. They know my secret.
6. Those of lower social status at the dining table. A

"mess" refers to a group of four people who share meals
together.
7. Punning on "satisfy" as meaning both "appease" and
"give sexual pleasure to."

Which hoxes honesty behind,[8] restraining
From course required.[9] Or else thou must be counted
A servant grafted in my serious trust[1]
And therein negligent, or else a fool
250 That seest a game played home,° the rich stake drawn,°    *in earnest / won*
And tak'st it all for jest.

CAMILLO               My gracious lord,
I may be negligent, foolish, and fearful.
In every one of these no man is free,°    *guiltless*
But that his negligence, his folly, fear,
255 Among the infinite doings of the world
Sometime puts forth.° In your affairs, my lord,    *reveals itself*
If ever I were wilful-negligent,
It was my folly. If industriously°    *deliberately*
I played the fool, it was my negligence,
260 Not weighing well the end. If ever fearful
To do a thing where I the issue° doubted,    *outcome*
Whereof the execution did cry out
Against the non-performance,[2] 'twas a fear
Which oft infects the wisest. These, my lord,
265 Are such allowed infirmities that honesty
Is never free of. But beseech your grace
Be plainer with me, let me know my trespass
By its own visage. If I then deny it,
'Tis none of mine.

LEONTES            Ha' not you seen, Camillo—
270 But that's past doubt; you have, or your eye-glass°    *the lens of your eye*
Is thicker than a cuckold's horn—or heard—
For, to a vision° so apparent, rumour    *sight*
Cannot be mute—or thought—for cogitation
Resides not in that man that does not think—
275 My wife is slippery? If thou wilt confess—
Or else be impudently negative°    *shamelessly deny*
To have nor eyes, nor ears, nor thought—then say
My wife's a hobby-horse,[3] deserves a name
As rank° as any flax-wench[4] that puts to°    *indecent / has sexual relations*
280 Before her troth-plight.° Say't, and justify't.    *betrothal*

CAMILLO    I would not be a stander-by to hear
My sovereign mistress clouded so without
My present° vengeance taken. 'Shrew° my heart,    *immediate / Curse*
You never spoke what did become you less
285 Than this, which to reiterate° were sin    *repeat*
As deep as that, though true.[5]

LEONTES            Is whispering nothing?
Is leaning cheek to cheek? Is meeting noses?
Kissing with inside lip? Stopping the career°    *full gallop*
Of laughter with a sigh?—a note° infallible    *sign*

8. Which ensures that frankness is shackled.
9. Keeping (honesty) from the path it must take (to find out truth).
1. A servant who has grown into my confidence as a cutting is grafted onto a plant.
2. Even when the need to do the deed protested against its nonperformance.
3. Whore. The image is of a woman, who, like a horse,

can be mounted. F has "Holy-Horse," an obscure phrase nearly all modern editors emend to "hobby-horse."
4. A girl or woman, usually of low social status, who worked with flax, a fibrous plant used to make candlewicks, clothing, and linen.
5. That is, "As grave as is the sin that you accuse your wife of, even if it were true (which it is not)."

290    Of breaking honesty.° Horsing foot on foot?[6]                                      *violating chastity*
       Skulking in corners? Wishing clocks more swift,
       Hours minutes, noon midnight? And all eyes
       Blind with the pin and web° but theirs, theirs only,                                *cataract disease*
       That would unseen be wicked? Is this nothing?
295    Why then the world and all that's in't is nothing,
       The covering sky is nothing, Bohemia nothing,
       My wife is nothing, nor nothing have these nothings[7]
       If this be nothing.
       CAMILLO                    Good my lord, be cured
       Of this diseased opinion, and betimes,°                                             *quickly*
       For 'tis most dangerous.
300    LEONTES                        Say it be, 'tis true.
       CAMILLO    No, no, my lord.
       LEONTES                        It is. You lie, you lie.
       I say thou liest, Camillo, and I hate thee,
       Pronounce thee a gross lout, a mindless slave,
       Or else a hovering° temporizer, that                                               *irresolute*
305    Canst with thine eyes at once see good and evil,
       Inclining to them both. Were my wife's liver
       Infected as her life, she would not live
       The running of one glass.°                                                         *hourglass*
       CAMILLO                    Who does infect her?
       LEONTES    Why, he that wears her like her medal,[8] hanging
310    About his neck, Bohemia, who, if I
       Had servants true about me, that bare° eyes                                        *possessed*
       To see alike mine honour as their profits,
       Their own particular thrifts,° they would do that                                  *personal gain*
       Which should undo° more doing.° Ay, and thou                                       *stop / sexual acts*
315    His cupbearer,[9] whom I from meaner form°                                         *lower rank or place*
       Have benched, and reared to worship,[1] who mayst see
       Plainly as heaven sees earth and earth sees heaven,
       How I am galled,° mightst bespice a cup                                            *sorely vexed*
       To give mine enemy a lasting wink,[2]
       Which draught to me were cordial.[3]
320    CAMILLO                           Sir, my lord,
       I could do this, and that with no rash° potion,                                    *quick-acting*
       But with a ling'ring° dram, that should not work                                   *slow-working*
       Maliciously,° like poison. But I cannot                                            *Violently*
       Believe this crack° to be in my dread mistress,                                    *flaw*
325    So sovereignly being honourable.
       I have loved thee—
       LEONTES                    Make that thy question,° and go rot!                     *concern*
       Dost think I am so muddy, so unsettled,
       To appoint° myself in this vexation?                                               *put*
       Sully the purity and whiteness of my sheets—
330    Which to preserve is sleep, which being spotted
       Is goads, thorns, nettles, tails of wasps—

---

6. Mounting or rubbing one foot on another. A sexually titillating pastime.
7. Alluding to the proverbial notion that nothing can come of nothing.
8. As though she were a miniature portrait of herself. Ornate lockets containing miniature portraits were popular love tokens among courtiers.
9. In a noble household a male servant whose respon-

sibilities included serving wine to his master.
1. Given authority and elevated to a dignified position. Referring to his "bench" or place at the dining table as a sign of his high rank.
2. To close my enemy's eyes forever.
3. Which drink would be medicinal to me; which drink would cure my heartsickness (perhaps the *"tremor cordis"* to which Leontes referred at 1.2.112).

Give scandal to the blood o'th' prince, my son—
Who I do think is mine, and love as mine—
Without ripe moving° to't? Would I do this?     *good reason*
Could man so blench?°     *stray (from sense)*
335  CAMILLO           I must believe you, sir.
I do, and will fetch off° Bohemia for't,     *kill; rescue*
Provided that when he's removed your highness
Will take again your queen as yours at first,
Even for your son's sake, and thereby for sealing°     *silencing*
340  The injury of tongues in courts and kingdoms
Known and allied to yours.
  LEONTES          Thou dost advise me
Even so as I mine own course have set down.
I'll give no blemish to her honour, none.
  CAMILLO   My lord, go then, and with a countenance as clear
345  As friendship wears at feasts, keep° with Bohemia     *associate*
And with your queen. I am his cupbearer.
If from me he have wholesome beverage,
Account me not your servant.
  LEONTES           This is all.
Do't, and thou hast the one half of my heart;
Do't not, thou splitt'st thine own.
350  CAMILLO              I'll do't, my lord.
  LEONTES   I will seem friendly, as thou hast advised me.     *Exit*
  CAMILLO   O miserable lady. But for me,
What case stand I in? I must be the poisoner
Of good Polixenes, and my ground to do't
355  Is the obedience to a master—one
Who in rebellion with himself, will have
All that are his so too. To do this deed,
Promotion follows. If I could find example
Of thousands that had struck anointed kings
360  And flourished after, I'd not do't. But since
Nor° brass, nor stone, nor parchment[4] bears not one,     *Neither*
Let villainy itself forswear't.° I must     *swear not to do it*
Forsake the court. To do't, or no, is certain
To me a break-neck.°     *(death)*
      *Enter* POLIXENES
                Happy° star reign now!     *Lucky*
Here comes Bohemia.
365  POLIXENES [*aside*]       This is strange. Methinks
My favour here begins to warp. Not speak?—
Good day, Camillo.
  CAMILLO          Hail, most royal sir.
  POLIXENES   What is the news i'th' court?
  CAMILLO             None rare,° my lord.     *noteworthy*
  POLIXENES   The King hath on him such a countenance
370  As° he had lost some province, and a region     *As if*
Loved as he loves himself. Even now I met him
With customary compliment, when he,
Wafting his eyes to th' contrary,° and falling     *Shifting his gaze away*
A lip of much contempt,° speeds from me, and     *sneering*

---

4. That is, since no form of historical record (brass monuments, stone markers, or paper manuscripts) shows an
example of a man who flourished after killing a King.

375 So leaves me to consider what is breeding
That changes thus his manners.

CAMILLO                           I dare not know, my lord.

POLIXENES How, 'dare not'? Do not? Do you know, and dare not?
Be intelligent° to me. 'Tis thereabouts.[5]                                    *informative*
For to yourself what you do know you must,°                                    *(know)*
380 And cannot say you 'dare not'. Good Camillo,
Your changed complexions are to me a mirror
Which shows me mine changed, too; for I must be
A party in this alteration,° finding                                    *(of Leontes' manner)*
Myself thus altered with't.

CAMILLO                              There is a sickness
385 Which puts some of us in distemper, but
I cannot name th' disease, and it is caught
Of you that yet are well.

POLIXENES                           How caught of me?
Make me not sighted like the basilisk.[6]
I have looked on thousands who have sped° the better                           *fared*
390 By my regard, but killed none so. Camillo,
As you are certainly a gentleman, thereto
Clerk-like experienced,[7] which no less adorns
Our gentry° than our parents' noble names,                           *status as gentlemen*
In whose success we are gentle:[8] I beseech you,
395 If you know aught which does behove my knowledge
Thereof to be informed,[9] imprison't not
In ignorant concealment.[1]

CAMILLO                           I may not answer.

POLIXENES A sickness caught of me, and yet I well?
I must be answered. Dost thou hear, Camillo,
400 I conjure thee, by all the parts° of man                                    *duties*
Which honour does acknowledge, whereof the least
Is not this suit of mine, that thou declare
What incidency° thou dost guess of harm                                    *event*
Is creeping toward me; how far off, how near,
405 Which way to be prevented, if to be;
If not, how best to bear it.

CAMILLO                           Sir, I will tell you,
Since I am charged in honour, and by him
That I think honourable. Therefore mark my counsel,
Which must be e'en as swiftly followed as
410 I mean to utter it; or both yourself and me
Cry lost, and so good night!°                                    *good-bye forever*

POLIXENES                           On, good Camillo.

CAMILLO I am appointed him to murder you.

POLIXENES By whom, Camillo?

CAMILLO                           By the King.

POLIXENES                                            For what?

CAMILLO He thinks, nay, with all confidence he swears
415 As he had seen't, or been an instrument
To vice° you to't, that you have touched his queen                           *force*
Forbiddenly.

5. That is, "I'm more or less right (that you are afraid to tell me)."
6. A mythical serpent whose glance was said to be fatal.
7. Also having the experience of an educated man.
8. By succession from whom we are made noble.
9. Which it is necessary for me to know.
1. In concealment that keeps me ignorant; in concealment on the pretense that you are ignorant.

POLIXENES     O, then my best blood turn
To an infected jelly, and my name
Be yoked with his° that did betray the Best!°      *(Judas's) name / Christ*
420  Turn then my freshest reputation to
A savour° that may strike the dullest nostril      *foul odor*
Where I arrive, and my approach be shunned,
Nay hated, too, worse than the great'st infection
That e'er was heard or read.
CAMILLO     Swear his thought over[2]
425  By each particular star in heaven, and
By all their influences,[3] you may as well
Forbid the sea for to obey the moon
As or° by oath remove or counsel shake      *either*
The fabric of his folly, whose foundation
430  Is piled upon his faith, and will continue
The standing of his body.°      *As long as he lives*
POLIXENES     How should this grow?°      *come to be*
CAMILLO  I know not, but I am sure 'tis safer to
Avoid what's grown than question how 'tis born.
If therefore you dare trust my honesty,
435  That lies enclosèd in this trunk° which you      *body*
Shall bear along impawned,[4] away tonight!
Your followers I will whisper to the business,
And will by twos and threes at several posterns°      *city gates*
Clear them o'th' city. For myself, I'll put
440  My fortunes to your service, which are here
By this discovery° lost. Be not uncertain,      *revelation*
For by the honour of my parents, I
Have uttered truth; which if you seek to prove,
I dare not stand by; nor shall you be safer
445  Than one condemnèd by the King's own mouth,
Thereon his execution sworn.
POLIXENES     I do believe thee,
I saw his heart in's face. Give me thy hand.
Be pilot to me, and thy places° shall      *your position*
Still neighbour° mine. My ships are ready, and      *Always be near*
450  My people did expect my hence departure
Two days ago. This jealousy
Is for a precious creature. As she's rare
Must it be great; and as his person's mighty
Must it be violent; and as he does conceive
455  He is dishonoured by a man which ever
Professed° to him, why, his revenges must°      *Professed love*
In that be made more bitter. Fear o'ershades me.
Good expedition° be my friend and comfort      *Let speed (in leaving)*
The gracious Queen, part of his theme, but nothing
460  Of his ill-ta'en suspicion.[5] Come, Camillo,
I will respect thee as a father if
Thou bear'st my life off hence. Let us avoid.°      *be gone*

---

2. You may swear that his allegations are false.
3. Substances that, according to contemporary astrological theories, were emitted by stars and helped to shape human destiny.

4. Shall carry with you as a pledge (of my faith).
5. And make easier the situation of the virtuous Queen, who is a part of Leontes' accusation, but who is not guilty of his unjustified suspicion.

CAMILLO    It is in mine authority to command
The keys of all the posterns. Please your highness
465    To take the urgent hour.° Come, sir, away.    *Exeunt*        seize the moment

## 2.1

*Enter* HERMIONE, MAMILLIUS, [*and*] LADIES

HERMIONE    Take the boy to you. He so troubles me
'Tis past enduring.
FIRST LADY                Come, my gracious lord,
Shall I be your play-fellow?
MAMILLIUS    No, I'll none of you.
5    FIRST LADY    Why, my sweet lord?
MAMILLIUS    You'll kiss me hard, and speak to me as if
I were a baby still. [*To* SECOND LADY] I love you better.
SECOND LADY    And why so, my lord?
MAMILLIUS                            Not for because
Your brows° are blacker—yet black brows they say          *eyebrows*
10    Become some women best, so that there be not
Too much hair there, but in a semicircle,
Or a half-moon made with a pen.
SECOND LADY                        Who taught° 'this?        *taught you*
MAMILLIUS    I learned it out of women's faces. Pray now,
What colour are your eyebrows?
FIRST LADY                        Blue, my lord.
15    MAMILLIUS    Nay, that's a mock. I have seen a lady's nose
That has been blue,[1] but not her eyebrows.
FIRST LADY                            Hark ye,
The Queen your mother rounds apace.° We shall          *grows round quickly*
Present our services to a fine new prince
One of these days, and then you'd wanton° with us,                    *play*
If we would have you.
20    SECOND LADY            She is spread of late
Into a goodly bulk, good time encounter her.°        *good fortune be with her*
HERMIONE    What wisdom stirs amongst you? Come sir, now
I am for you again. Pray you sit by us,
And tell's a tale.
25    MAMILLIUS    Merry or sad shall't be?
HERMIONE    As merry as you will.
MAMILLIUS    A sad tale's best for winter. I have one
Of sprites and goblins.
HERMIONE                Let's have that, good sir.
Come on, sit down, come on, and do your best
30    To fright me with your sprites. You're powerful at it.
MAMILLIUS    There was a man—
HERMIONE                        Nay, come sit down, then on.
MAMILLIUS [*sitting*]    Dwelt by a churchyard.—I will tell it softly,
Yon crickets° shall not hear it.                        *(the other women)*
HERMIONE    Come on then, and give't me in mine ear.
[*Enter apart* LEONTES, ANTIGONUS, *and* LORDS][2]

---

2.1 Location: Sicilia. The palace of Leontes.
1. It is unclear whether Mamillius is making a joke
here or possibly referring to noses made "blue" by the
cold or disfigured by venereal disease.
2. As with many scenes in this play, Ralph Crane, the
scrivener who probably prepared the manuscript for the

printer, massed all the entrances for 2.1 in the initial
stage direction, regardless of when individual characters
actually appeared on stage. Though it is clear that
Leontes, Antigonus, and the other Lords enter only at
2.1.34, in F no entrance is marked for them here, and
their names are included in the direction preceding 2.1.1.

35   LEONTES   Was he met there? His train?° Camillo with him?       *retinue*
    A LORD   Behind the tuft of pines I met them. Never
      Saw I men scour° so on their way. I eyed them       *hurry*
      Even to their ships.
    LEONTES            How blest am I
      In my just censure,° in my true opinion!       *judgment*
40      Alack, for lesser knowledge°—how accursed       *Would I knew less*
      In being so blest! There may be in the cup
      A spider steeped, and one may drink, depart,
      And yet partake no venom, for his knowledge
      Is not infected;[3] but if one present
45      Th'abhorred ingredient to his eye, make known
      How he hath drunk, he cracks his gorge,° his sides,       *throat*
      With violent hefts.° I have drunk, and seen the spider.       *retching*
      Camillo was his help in this, his pander.
      There is a plot against my life, my crown.
50      All's true that is mistrusted.° That false villain       *suspected*
      Whom I employed was pre-employed by him.
      He has discovered° my design, and I       *revealed*
      Remain a pinched° thing, yea, a very trick       *tormented*
      For them to play at will. How came the posterns
      So easily open?
55     A LORD          By his great authority,
      Which often hath no less prevailed than so
      On your command.
    LEONTES          I know't too well.
      [*To* HERMIONE] Give me the boy. I am glad you did not nurse him.[4]
      Though he does bear some signs of me, yet you
      Have too much blood in him.
60   HERMIONE            What is this? Sport?
    LEONTES [*to a* LORD]   Bear the boy hence. He shall not come about her.
      Away with him, and let her sport herself
      With that she's big with, [*to* HERMIONE] for 'tis Polixenes
      Has made thee swell thus.       [*Exit one with* MAMILLIUS]
    HERMIONE           But I'd say he had not,
65      And I'll be sworn you would believe my saying,
      Howe'er you lean to th' nayward.°       *the contrary*
    LEONTES           You, my lords,
      Look on her, mark her well. Be but about
      To say she is a goodly lady, and
      The justice of your hearts will thereto add
70      ' 'Tis pity she's not honest,° honourable.'       *chaste*
      Praise her but for this her without-door° form—       *external*
      Which on my faith deserves high speech—and straight°       *immediately*
      The shrug, the 'hum' or 'ha', these petty brands°       *expressions; stigmas*
      That calumny° doth use—O, I am out,°       *slander / wrong*
75      That mercy does, for calumny will sear°       *stigmatize*
      Virtue itself[5]—these shrugs, these 'hum's' and 'ha's',
      When you have said she's goodly, come between
      Ere you can say she's honest. But be't known

---

3. Alluding to the belief that a spider consumed with food or drink would be poisonous only if its presence were known to the consumer.
4. Women who breast-fed infants were believed to shape an infant's character by substances transmitted in their milk.
5. Leontes seems to mean that calumny (slander) will openly attack virtue, and since Hermione is not virtuous, it is not calumny to attack her. Rather, it is mercy who speaks in indirect "hum's" and "ha's" about her behavior.

From him that has most cause to grieve it should be,
She's an adultress.

80 HERMIONE              Should a villain say so,
The most replenished° villain in the world,                    *complete*
He were as much more° villain. You, my lord,                   *by so much more a*
Do but mistake.

LEONTES              You have mistook,° my lady—                *erred; improperly taken*
Polixenes for Leontes. O, thou thing,
85 Which I'll not call a creature of thy place[6]
Lest barbarism,° making me the precedent,                     *uncivilized rudeness*
Should a like° language use to all degrees,°                   *the same / all ranks*
And mannerly distinguishment° leave out                       *proper distinction*
Betwixt the prince and beggar. I have said
90 She's an adultress, I have said with whom.
More, she's a traitor, and Camillo is
A federary° with her, and one that knows                       *confederate*
What she should shame to know herself,
But with her most vile principal:° that she's                  *partner*
95 A bed-swerver,° even as bad as those                         *adultress*
That vulgars give bold'st titles;[7] ay, and privy
To this their late° escape.                                    *recent*

HERMIONE                    No, by my life,
Privy to none of this. How will this grieve you
When you shall come to clearer knowledge, that
100 You thus have published° me? Gentle my° lord,               *proclaimed / My noble*
You scarce can right me throughly° then to say               *fully do me justice*
You did mistake.

LEONTES              No. If I mistake
In those foundations which I build upon,
The centre° is not big enough to bear                          *earth*
105 A schoolboy's top.—Away with her to prison!
He who shall speak for her is afar-off° guilty,               *indirectly*
But that he speaks.°                                           *Merely for speaking*

HERMIONE                    There's some ill planet reigns.
I must be patient till the heavens look
With an aspect more favourable.[8] Good my° lords,            *My good*
110 I am not prone to weeping, as our sex
Commonly are; the want of which vain dew
Perchance shall dry your pities. But I have
That honourable grief lodged here which burns
Worse than tears drown. Beseech you all, my lords,
115 With thoughts so qualified° as your charities               *tempered*
Shall best instruct you, measure me; and so
The King's will be performed.

LEONTES                    Shall I be heard?

HERMIONE   Who is't that goes with me? Beseech your highness
My women may be with me, for you see
120 My plight requires it.—Do not weep, good fools,°            *dear ones*
There is no cause. When you shall know your mistress
Has deserved prison, then abound in tears
As I come out. This action I now go on

---

6. To whom I'll not give the title of your (high) social
position.
7. That common people call by the coarsest names.

8. Another allusion to the belief that planets can have
an evil effect or "aspect" when situated in certain positions.

Is for my better grace.[9]—Adieu, my lord.
125 I never wished to see you sorry; now
I trust I shall. My women, come, you have leave.°     *permission*
LEONTES     Go, do our bidding. Hence!

            [*Exit* HERMIONE, *guarded, with* LADIES]

A LORD     Beseech your highness, call the Queen again.
ANTIGONUS [*to Leontes*]     Be certain what you do, sir, lest your justice
130 Prove violence, in the which three great ones suffer—
Yourself, your queen, your son.
A LORD [*to* LEONTES]              For her, my lord,
I dare my life lay down, and will do't, sir,
Please you t'accept it, that the Queen is spotless
I'th' eyes of heaven and to you—I mean
In this which you accuse her.
135 ANTIGONUS [*to* LEONTES]          If it prove
She's otherwise, I'll keep my stables where
I lodge my wife,[1] I'll go in couples with her;[2]
Than when I feel and see her, no farther trust her.
For every inch of woman in the world,
140 Ay, every dram° of woman's flesh is false     *smallest piece*
If she be.
LEONTES     Hold your peaces.
A LORD                Good my lord—
ANTIGONUS [*to* LEONTES]     It is for you we speak, not for ourselves.
You are abused, and by some putter-on°     *instigator*
That will be damned for't. Would I knew the villain—
145 I would land-damn him.[3] Be she honour-flawed—
I have three daughters: the eldest is eleven;
The second and the third nine and some five;
If this prove true, they'll pay for't. By mine honour,
I'll geld 'em all.[4] Fourteen they shall not see,
150 To bring false generations.° They are co-heirs,     *illegitimate children*
And I had rather glib° myself than they     *castrate*
Should not produce fair issue.°     *legitimate offspring*
LEONTES             Cease, no more!
You smell this business with a sense as cold
As is a dead man's nose. But I do see't and feel't
155 As you feel doing thus;[5] and see withal
The instruments that feel.[6]
ANTIGONUS           If it be so,
We need no grave to bury honesty;°     *chastity*
There's not a grain of it the face to sweeten°     *to sweeten the face*
Of the whole dungy° earth.     *foul*
LEONTES          What? Lack I credit?
160 A LORD     I had rather you did lack than I, my lord,
Upon this ground;° and more it would content me     *In this affair*

---

9. This trial I am enduring is for my greater honor (when vindicated); *or* This suffering I am enduring is to refine and purge me, leading to greater virtue.
1. An obscure passage, meaning that he'll guard his wife's lodgings as vigilantly as he guards his horses *or* that he will treat his wife's lodgings as he does his stables, where mares are separated from stallions.
2. Have her tied to me (as hounds were leashed together for the hunt).
3. A term of abuse whose exact meaning is unclear. It

may be a dialect form of "lamback" or "lambaste," which means "thrash."
4. I'll make them all barren. Literally, I'll cut out their organs of generation.
5. Leontes here probably does some action (touching a courtier or rubbing his hands together) that shows the immediacy of his sensory reactions.
6. I see the fingers ("instruments") with which I touch things; I see the sinners, Hermione and Polixenes, who touch one another.

To have her honour true than your suspicion,
Be blamed for't how you might.

LEONTES                  Why, what need we
Commune with you of this, but rather follow
165 Our forceful instigation?° Our prerogative      *Our own powerful impulse*
Calls not your counsels,[7] but our natural goodness
Imparts this;° which, if you—or° stupefied      *this information / either*
Or seeming so in skill°—cannot or will not      *cunningly*
Relish° a truth like us, inform yourselves      *Appreciate*
170 We need no more of your advice. The matter,
The loss, the gain, the ord'ring on't,° is all      *of it*
Properly ours.

ANTIGONUS     And I wish, my liege,
You had only in your silent judgement tried it
Without more overture.°      *public disclosure*

LEONTES          How could that be?
175 Either thou art most ignorant by age
Or thou wert born a fool. Camillo's flight
Added to their familiarity,
Which was as gross as ever touched conjecture
That lacked sight only, naught for approbation
180 But only seeing,[8] all other circumstances
Made up to th' deed°—doth push on this proceeding.[9]      *Pointed to the deed*
Yet for a greater confirmation—
For in an act of this importance 'twere
Most piteous to be wild°—I have dispatched in post°      *rash / haste*
185 To sacred Delphos,[1] to Apollo's temple,
Cleomenes and Dion, whom you know
Of stuffed sufficiency.° Now from the oracle      *ample competence*
They will bring all, whose spiritual counsel had°      *obtained*
Shall stop or spur me. Have I done well?
190 A LORD   Well done, my lord.

LEONTES   Though I am satisfied, and need no more
Than what I know, yet shall the oracle
Give rest to th' minds of others such as he,
Whose ignorant credulity will not
195 Come up to th' truth. So have we thought it good
From our free° person she should be confined,      *openly accessible*
Lest that the treachery of the two fled hence
Be left her to perform. Come, follow us.
We are to speak in public; for this business
Will raise° us all.      *rouse (to action)*
200 ANTIGONUS [*aside*]   To laughter, as I take it,
If the good truth were known.      *Exeunt*

## 2.2

*Enter* PAULINA, *a Gentleman[, and attendants]*
PAULINA   The keeper of the prison, call to him.
Let him have knowledge who I am.      [*Exit Gentleman*]

7. My privileges as King do not require that I seek your advice.
8. As obvious ("gross") as any suspicion ("conjecture") ever was that only lacked eyewitnesses ("sight" and "seeing") to confirm its truth.
9. Does urge on this course of action.

1. Delos, often called Delphos by Renaissance writers, was the island where Apollo, the sun god, was supposedly buried. It is here conflated with Delphi, the Greek mainland town where the oracle of Apollo could be consulted.
2.2 Location: Sicilia. A prison.

Good lady,
No court in Europe is too good for thee.
What dost thou then in prison?
    [*Enter* JAILER *and Gentleman*]
                    Now, good sir,
You know me, do you not?

5  JAILER                For a worthy lady,
And one who much I honour.
PAULINA    Pray you then,
Conduct me to the Queen.
JAILER    I may not, madam. To the contrary
I have express commandment.

10  PAULINA             Here's ado,°            *Here's such a fuss*
To lock up honesty and honour from
Th'access of gentle° visitors. Is't lawful, pray you,    *noble; kind*
To see her women? Any of them? Emilia?
JAILER    So please you, madam,

15  To put apart these your attendants, I
Shall bring Emilia forth.
PAULINA    I pray now call her.—
Withdraw yourselves.    [*Exeunt Gentleman and attendants*]
JAILER    And, madam,

20  I must be present at your conference.
PAULINA    Well, be't so, prithee.        [*Exit* JAILER]
Here's such ado, to make no stain a stain
As passes colouring.[1]
    [*Enter* JAILER *and* EMILIA]
                Dear gentlewoman,
How fares our gracious lady?

25  EMILIA    As well as one so great and so forlorn
May hold together. On° her frights and griefs,    *Because of*
Which never tender lady hath borne greater,
She is, something° before her time, delivered.    *somewhat*
PAULINA    A boy?
EMILIA            A daughter, and a goodly babe,

30  Lusty,° and like° to live. The Queen receives    *Vigorous / likely*
Much comfort in't; says, 'My poor prisoner,
I am innocent as you.'
PAULINA           I dare be sworn.
These dangerous, unsafe lunes° i'th' King, beshrew them!    *fits of lunacy*
He must be told on't, and he shall. The office°    *job*

35  Becomes a woman best. I'll take't upon me.
If I prove honey-mouthed, let my tongue blister,[2]
And never to my red-looked° anger be    *red-faced*
The trumpet[3] any more. Pray you, Emilia,
Commend° my best obedience to the Queen.    *Send*

40  If she dares trust me with her little babe
I'll show't the King, and undertake to be
Her advocate to th' loud'st. We do not know
How he may soften at the sight o'th' child.

---

1. To make from no stain at all a stain that exceeds
what the art of dyeing can do; to make of no sin a sin
that surpasses all attempts to justify it.
2. Alluding to the proverb that deceitfulness causes
blisters on the tongue.

3. In early modern warfare, a "trumpet" was a soldier
who, bearing a trumpet, went before the red-coated
herald who carried messages, often angry ones, to the
enemy camp.

The silence often of pure innocence
Persuades when speaking fails.

45 EMILIA                    Most worthy madam,
Your honour and your goodness is so evident
That your free° undertaking cannot miss                    *generous*
A thriving issue.⁴ There is no lady living
So meet° for this great errand. Please your ladyship                    *suitable*
50 To visit the next room, I'll presently
Acquaint the Queen of your most noble offer,
Who but today hammered of° this design                    *mused upon*
But durst not tempt a minister of honour⁵
Lest she should be denied.
PAULINA                    Tell her, Emilia,
55 I'll use that tongue I have. If wit flow from 't
As boldness from my bosom, let't not be doubted
I shall do good.
EMILIA                    Now be you blest for it!
I'll to the Queen. Please you come something° nearer.                    *somewhat*
JAILER    Madam, if't please the Queen to send the babe
60 I know not what° I shall incur to pass it,⁶                    *what (risk)*
Having no warrant.
PAULINA                    You need not fear it, sir.
This child was prisoner to the womb, and is
By law and process of great nature thence
Freed and enfranchised, not a party to
65 The anger of the King, nor guilty of—
If any be—the trespass of the Queen.
JAILER    I do believe it.
PAULINA    Do not you fear. Upon mine honour,
I will stand twixt you and danger.                    *Exeunt*

## 2.3

*Enter* LEONTES

LEONTES    Nor° night nor day, no rest! It is but weakness                    *Neither*
To bear the matter thus, mere weakness. If
The cause were not in being°—part o'th' cause,                    *alive*
She, th'adultress; for the harlot° King                    *lewd*
5 Is quite beyond mine arm, out of the blank°                    *target*
And level° of my brain, plot-proof; but she                    *aim*
I can hook to me. Say that she were gone,
Given to the fire,¹ a moiety° of my rest                    *portion*
Might come to me again. Who's there?
                    [*Enter a* SERVANT]
SERVANT                    My lord.
LEONTES    How does the boy?
10 SERVANT                    He took good rest tonight.
'Tis hoped his sickness is discharged.
LEONTES    To see his nobleness!
Conceiving° the dishonour of his mother                    *Realizing*
He straight° declined, drooped, took it deeply,                    *immediately*
15 Fastened and fixed the shame on't° in himself;                    *of it*

---

4. A successful outcome, with a pun on "issue" as "off-spring."
5. But dared not risk asking a person of higher rank.

6. To let it pass (out of the prison).
2.3 Location: Sicilia. The palace of Leontes.
1. Burned at the stake (for treason against the King).

Threw off his spirit, his appetite, his sleep,
And downright languished. Leave me solely.° Go,                    *alone*
See how he fares.                        [*Exit* SERVANT]
              Fie, fie, no thought of him.°                        *(Polixenes)*
The very thought of my revenges that way
20  Recoil upon me. In himself too mighty,
And in his parties,° his alliance.° Let him be                    *supporters / allies*
Until a time may serve. For present vengeance,
Take it on her. Camillo and Polixenes
Laugh at me, make their pastime at my sorrow.
25  They should not laugh if I could reach them, nor
Shall she, within my power.
              *Enter* PAULINA [*carrying a babe, with* ANTIGONUS,
              LORDS, *and the* SERVANT, *trying to restrain her*]
A LORD                        You must not enter.
PAULINA    Nay rather, good my lords, be second to me.°              *help me*
Fear you his tyrannous passion more, alas,
Than the Queen's life?—a gracious, innocent soul,
More free° than he is jealous.                                    *innocent*
30  ANTIGONUS                        That's enough.
SERVANT    Madam, he hath not slept tonight, commanded
None should come at him.
PAULINA                        Not so hot, good sir.
I come to bring him sleep. 'Tis such as you,
That creep like shadows by him, and do sigh
35  At each his needless heavings, such as you
Nourish the cause of his awaking.° I                              *wakefulness*
Do come with words as medicinal as true,
Honest as either, to purge him of that humour°                    *mental disorder*
That presses him from sleep.
LEONTES                        What noise there, ho?
40  PAULINA    No noise, my lord, but needful conference
About some gossips² for your highness.
LEONTES                            How?
Away with that audacious lady! Antigonus,
I charged thee that she should not come about me.
I knew she would.
ANTIGONUS            I told her so, my lord,
45  On your displeasure's peril° and on mine,                       *At the risk of your anger*
She should not visit you.
LEONTES                        What, canst not rule her?
PAULINA    From all dishonesty he can. In this,
Unless he take the course that you have done—
Commit° me for committing honour—trust it,                        *Imprison*
He shall not rule me.
50  ANTIGONUS            La you now, you hear.
When she will take the rein I let her run,
But she'll not stumble.
PAULINA [*to* LEONTES]        Good my liege, I come—
And I beseech you hear me, who professes
Myself your loyal servant, your physician,
55  Your most obedient counsellor; yet that dares
Less appear so in comforting° your evils                          *condoning*

2. Godparents or sponsors at a child's baptism.

Than such as most seem yours[3]—I say, I come
From your good queen.
LEONTES   Good queen?

60   PAULINA   Good queen, my lord, good queen, I say good queen,
And would by combat make her good,[4] so were I
A man, the worst about° you.                                                                  *lowest in rank of*
LEONTES [to LORDS]                Force her hence.
PAULINA   Let him that makes but trifles of his eyes
First hand° me. On mine own accord, I'll off.                                           *touch*

65   But first I'll do my errand. The good Queen—
For she is good—hath brought you forth a daughter—
Here 'tis—commends it to your blessing.
     [*She lays down the babe*]
LEONTES                                               Out!
A mankind° witch! Hence with her, out o'door—                                 *manlike*
A most intelligencing bawd.°                                                                   *spying go-between*
PAULINA                          Not so.

70   I am as ignorant in that as you
In so entitling me,° and no less honest                                                  *In calling me that*
Than you are mad, which is enough, I'll warrant,
As this world goes, to pass for honest.
LEONTES [to LORDS]                             Traitors,
Will you not push her out?
[*To* ANTIGONUS]              Give her the bastard.

75   Thou dotard, thou art woman-tired,[5] unroosted
By thy Dame Partlet here.[6] Take up the bastard,
Take't up, I say. Give't to thy crone.°                                                    *old woman*
PAULINA [*to* ANTIGONUS]                       For ever
Unvenerable° be thy hands if thou                                                       *Unworthy of respect*
Tak'st up the princess by that forcèd baseness[7]
Which he has put upon't.

80   LEONTES                      He dreads° his wife.                                       *fears*
PAULINA   So I would you did. Then 'twere past all doubt
You'd call your children yours.
LEONTES                             A nest of traitors.
ANTIGONUS   I am none, by this good light.
PAULINA                                          Nor I, nor any
But one that's here, and that's himself, for he

85   The sacred honour of himself, his queen's,
His hopeful son's, his babe's, betrays to slander,
Whose sting is sharper than the sword's; and will not—
For as the case now stands, it is a curse
He cannot be compelled to't—once remove

90   The root of his opinion, which is rotten
As ever oak or stone was sound.
LEONTES [to LORDS]                    A callat°                                             *scold; harlot*
Of boundless tongue, who late° hath beat her husband,                      *recently*
And now baits° me! This brat is none of mine.                                       *provokes*
It is the issue° of Polixenes.                                                                    *offspring*

---

3. Than those who (wrongly) seem most loyal.
4. Prove her to be innocent. Alluding to the chivalric trials by combat in which knights would establish innocence or guilt by means of duels.
5. You are pecked at by women. A metaphor from fal-

conry referring to tearing of flesh with the beak.
6. Expelled from your "roost" or "perch," the position of domestic authority assigned to men. In medieval tales, "Partlett" is a traditional name for a hen.
7. Under that wrongful name of bastard.

95      Hence with it, and together with the dam
       Commit them to the fire.
      PAULINA                 It is yours,
       And might we lay th'old proverb to your charge,°      *apply the proverb to you*
       So like you 'tis the worse. Behold, my lords,
       Although the print° be little, the whole matter            *copy*
100     And copy of the father: eye, nose, lip,
       The trick° of's frown, his forehead, nay, the valley,[8]    *distinctive character*
       The pretty dimples of his chin and cheek, his smiles,
       The very mould and frame of hand, nail, finger.
       And thou good goddess Nature, which hast made it
105     So like to him that got° it, if thou hast                *begot*
       The ordering of the mind too, 'mongst all colours
       No yellow[9] in't, lest she suspect, as he does,
       Her children not her husband's.
      LEONTES [*to* ANTIGONUS]         A gross hag!—
       And lozel,° thou art worthy to be hanged,            *scoundrel*
       That wilt not stay her tongue.
110    ANTIGONUS              Hang all the husbands
       That cannot do that feat, you'll leave yourself
       Hardly one subject.
      LEONTES          Once more, take her hence.
      PAULINA   A most unworthy and unnatural lord
       Can do no more.
      LEONTES         I'll ha' thee burnt.
      PAULINA             I care not.
115    It is an heretic that makes the fire,
       Not she which burns in't.[1] I'll not call you tyrant;
       But this most cruel usage of your queen—
       Not able to produce more accusation
       Than your own weak-hinged fancy—something savours
120     Of tyranny, and will ignoble make you,
       Yea, scandalous to the world.
      LEONTES [*to* ANTIGONUS]        On your allegiance,
       Out of the chamber with her! Were I a tyrant,
       Where were her life? She durst not call me so
       If she did know me one. Away with her!
125    PAULINA   I pray you do not push me, I'll be gone.
       Look to your babe, my lord; 'tis yours. Jove° send her     *(King of the gods)*
       A better guiding spirit. What needs these hands?[2]
       You that are thus so tender o'er° his follies          *gentle with*
       Will never do him good, not one of you.
130     So, so. Farewell, we are gone.                  *Exit*
      LEONTES [*to* ANTIGONUS]   Thou, traitor, hast set on thy wife to this.
       My child? Away with't! Even thou, that hast
       A heart so tender o'er it, take it hence
       And see it instantly consumed with fire.
135     Even thou, and none but thou. Take it up straight.°         *at once*
       Within this hour bring me word 'tis done,
       And by good testimony,° or I'll seize thy life,       *with good evidence*

---

8. Referring to an indentation in the lip or a cleft in the chin.
9. Proverbially, the color of jealousy.
1. The heretic is the one who unjustly makes the fire (Leontes), not the woman who burns in it (Hermione).
2. Why is it necessary for you to push me out? (spoken to Leontes' attendant lords).

With what thou else call'st thine. If thou refuse
And wilt encounter with my wrath, say so.
140 The bastard brains with these my proper° hands          own
Shall I dash out. Go, take it to the fire;
For thou set'st on thy wife.
ANTIGONUS          I did not, sir.
These lords, my noble fellows, if they please
Can clear me in't.
LORDS          We can. My royal liege,
145 He is not guilty of her coming hither.
LEONTES   You're liars all.
A LORD   Beseech your highness, give us better credit.°     think us more honorable
We have always truly served you, and beseech
So to esteem of us. And on our knees we beg,
150 As recompense of our dear services
Past and to come, that you do change this purpose
Which, being so horrible, so bloody, must
Lead on to some foul issue. We all kneel.
LEONTES   I am a feather for each wind that blows.
155 Shall I live on, to see this bastard kneel
And call me father? Better burn it now
Than curse it then. But be it. Let it live.
It shall not neither.
     [*To* ANTIGONUS]     You, sir, come you hither,
You that have been so tenderly officious
160 With Lady Margery³ your midwife there,
To save this bastard's life—for 'tis a bastard,
So sure as this beard's grey. What will you adventure°     risk
To save this brat's life?
ANTIGONUS               Anything, my lord,
That my ability may undergo,
165 And nobleness impose. At least thus much,
I'll pawn the little blood which I have left⁴
To save the innocent; anything possible.
LEONTES   It shall be possible. Swear by this sword
Thou wilt perform my bidding.
ANTIGONUS               I will, my lord.
170 LEONTES   Mark, and perform it. Seest thou? For the fail°     failure
Of any point in't shall not only be
Death to thyself but to thy lewd-tongued wife,
Whom for this time we pardon. We enjoin thee,
As thou art liegeman° to us, that thou carry          loyal servant
175 This female bastard hence, and that thou bear it
To some remote and desert place, quite out
Of our dominions; and that there thou leave it,
Without more mercy, to it° own protection          its
And favour of the climate. As by strange fortune⁵
180 It came to us, I do in justice charge thee,
On thy soul's peril and thy body's torture,
That thou commend it strangely to some place⁶
Where chance may nurse° or end it. Take it up.          nurture; help

---

3. A contemptuous name (like "Dame Partlett") for a
disorderly woman. "Margery-prater" is a slang term for
"hen."
4. Aging was thought to reduce the amount of blood in
the body.
5. Since by some unusual chance; since by the act of a
foreigner (Polixenes).
6. That you take it to some foreign land.

ANTIGONUS   I swear to do this, though a present death
185  Had been more merciful. Come on, poor babe,
Some powerful spirit instruct the kites° and ravens          *birds of prey*
To be thy nurses. Wolves and bears, they say,
Casting their savageness aside, have done
Like° offices of pity. Sir, be prosperous          *Similar*
190  In more than this deed does require;[7] [*to the babe*] and blessing
Against° this cruelty, fight on thy side,          *To counteract*
Poor thing, condemned to loss.°          *Exit* [*with the babe*]          *ruin*
LEONTES                              No, I'll not rear
Another's issue.
          *Enter a* SERVANT
SERVANT                    Please your highness, posts°          *messengers*
From those you sent to th'oracle are come
195  An hour since. Cleomenes and Dion,
Being well arrived from Delphos, are both landed,
Hasting to th' court.
A LORD [*to* LEONTES]    So please you, sir, their speed
Hath been beyond account.°          *without precedent*
LEONTES                              Twenty-three days
They have been absent. 'Tis good speed, foretells
200  The great Apollo suddenly° will have          *at once*
The truth of this appear. Prepare you, lords.
Summon a session,° that we may arraign          *trial*
Our most disloyal lady; for as she hath
Been publicly accused, so shall she have
205  A just and open trial. While she lives
My heart will be a burden to me. Leave me,
And think upon my bidding.          *Exeunt* [*severally*]°          *separately*

## 3.1

          *Enter* CLEOMENES *and* DION
CLEOMENES   The climate's delicate, the air most sweet;
Fertile the isle,[1] the temple much surpassing
The common praise it bears.
DION                              I shall report,
For most it caught° me, the celestial habits—°          *charmed / garments*
5  Methinks I so should term them—and the reverence
Of the grave wearers. O, the sacrifice—
How ceremonious, solemn, and unearthly
It was i'th' off'ring!
CLEOMENES                    But of all, the burst°          *blast (of thunder)*
And the ear-deaf'ning voice o'th' oracle,
10  Kin to Jove's thunder, so surprised my sense
That I was nothing.
DION                    If th'event° o'th' journey          *outcome*
Prove as successful to the Queen—O, be't so!—
As it hath been to us rare, pleasant, speedy,
The time is worth the use on't.[2]
CLEOMENES                    Great Apollo

---

7. To a greater extent or in more ways than this action deserves.
3.1 Location: A road in Sicilia.
1. The island of Delphos (Delos), Apollo's birthplace,
here conflated with Delphi, where Apollo's oracle was located. See note to 2.1.185.
2. The time will have been well spent.

15  Turn all to th' best! These proclamations,
So forcing faults upon Hermione,
I little like.

DION          The violent carriage° of it          *rash handling*
Will clear or end the business. When the oracle,
Thus by Apollo's great divine° sealed up,          *priest*

20  Shall the contents discover,° something rare          *reveal*
Even then will rush to knowledge. Go. Fresh horses!
And gracious be the issue.°          *Exeunt*          *result; the child*

## 3.2
*Enter* LEONTES, LORDS, [*and*] OFFICERS

LEONTES   This sessions, to our great grief we pronounce,
Even pushes 'gainst our heart: the party tried
The daughter of a king, our wife, and one
Of us° too much beloved. Let us be cleared          *By us*

5  Of being tyrannous since we so openly
Proceed in justice, which shall have due course
Even to the guilt or the purgation.°          *acquittal*
Produce the prisoner.

OFFICER          It is his highness' pleasure
That the Queen appear in person here in court.
[*Enter* HERMIONE *guarded, with* PAULINA *and Ladies*]

10  Silence.[1]

LEONTES   Read the indictment.

OFFICER [*reads*]   Hermione, queen to the worthy Leontes, King
of Sicilia, thou art here accused and arraigned of high treason
in committing adultery with Polixenes, King of Bohemia, and

15  conspiring with Camillo to take away the life of our sovereign
lord the King, thy royal husband; the pretence° whereof being          *purpose*
by circumstances partly laid open, thou, Hermione, contrary to
the faith and allegiance of a true subject, didst counsel and aid
them for their better safety to fly away by night.

20  HERMIONE   Since what I am to say must be but° that          *only*
Which contradicts my accusation, and
The testimony on my part no other
But what comes from myself, it shall scarce boot° me          *profit*
To say 'Not guilty'. Mine integrity

25  Being counted falsehood shall, as I express it,
Be so received. But thus: if powers divine
Behold our human actions—as they do—
I doubt not then but innocence shall make
False accusation blush, and tyranny

30  Tremble at patience. You, my lord, best know—
Who least will seem to do so—my past life
Hath been as continent, as chaste, as true
As I am now unhappy; which° is more          *which unhappiness*
Than history can pattern,[2] though devised

35  And played to take° spectators. For behold me,          *captivate*
A fellow of the royal bed, which owe°          *who owns*
A moiety° of the throne; a great king's daughter,          *A portion*

---

**3.2** Location: Sicilia. A court of justice.
1. In F, the word "Silence" is printed in italics and set
as a stage direction. Here it is treated as an imperative

and assigned to the Officer who announces the Queen's
entrance.
2. Than story or drama can show a precedent for.

The mother to a hopeful prince, here standing
To prate and talk for life and honour, fore°                    *before*
40   Who please to come and hear. For° life, I prize° it          *As for / value*
As I weigh° grief, which I would spare.° For honour,              *value / do without*
'Tis a derivative³ from me to mine,°                              *(my children)*
And only that I stand° for. I appeal                             *fight*
To your own conscience, sir, before Polixenes
45   Came to your court how I was in your grace,
How merited to be so; since he came,
With what encounter so uncurrent° I                              *conduct so unacceptable*
Have strained° t'appear thus.° If one jot beyond                 *transgressed / (on trial)*
The bound of honour, or in act or will
50   That way inclining, hardened be the hearts
Of all that hear me, and my near'st of kin
Cry 'Fie' upon my grave.
LEONTES                         I ne'er heard yet
That any of these bolder vices wanted
Less° impudence to gainsay° what they did                        *Were more lacking in / deny*
Than to perform it first.
55   HERMIONE                      That's true enough,
Though 'tis a saying, sir, not due° to me.                       *relevant*
LEONTES   You will not own it.
HERMIONE                    More than mistress of
Which comes to me in name of fault, I must not
At all acknowledge.⁴ For Polixenes,
60   With whom I am accused, I do confess
I loved him as in honour he required;°                           *was his due*
With such a kind of love as might become
A lady like me; with a love, even such,
So, and no other, as yourself commanded;
65   Which not to have done I think had been in me
Both disobedience and ingratitude
To you and toward your friend, whose love had spoke
Even since it could speak, from an infant, freely
That it was yours. Now for conspiracy,
70   I know not how it tastes, though it be dished°                *served*
For me to try how. All I know of it
Is that Camillo was an honest man;
And why he left your court, the gods themselves,
Wotting° no more than I, are ignorant.                           *If they know*
75   LEONTES      You knew of his departure, as you know
What you have underta'en to do in's absence.
HERMIONE   Sir,
You speak a language that I understand not.
My life stands in the level of your dreams,⁵
Which I'll lay down.
80   LEONTES                  Your actions are my 'dreams'.
You had a bastard by Polixenes,
And I but° dreamed it. As you were past all shame—             *merely*
Those of your fact° are so—so past all truth;                    *(guilty) of your crime*

---

3. Something handed on.
4. I must not answer for ("acknowledge") more than
those faults that I actually possess (am "mistress of").
Hermione is denying she possesses the "bolder vices" of
which Leontes accuses her in line 53.
5. As the target ("level") of your delusions. A metaphor
from archery.

Which to deny concerns more than avails;[6] for as
85   Thy brat hath been cast out, like to itself,°         *as it should be*
No father owning it—which is indeed
More criminal in thee than it—so thou
Shalt feel our justice, in whose easiest passage
Look for no less than death.[7]
HERMIONE                     Sir, spare your threats.
90   The bug° which you would fright me with, I seek.      *horrible object*
To me can life be no commodity.°                *profit; comfort*
The crown and comfort of my life, your favour,
I do give° lost, for I do feel it gone               *reckon*
But know not how it went. My second joy,°      *(Mamillius)*
95   And first fruits of my body, from his presence
I am barred, like one infectious. My third comfort,
Starred most unluckily,[8] is from my breast,
The innocent milk in it° most innocent mouth,          *its*
Haled° out to murder; myself on every post[9]      *Dragged*
100   Proclaimed a strumpet, with immodest° hatred     *excessive*
The childbed privilege[1] denied, which 'longs°       *belongs*
To women of all fashion;° lastly, hurried           *ranks*
Here, to this place, i'th' open air,[2] before
I have got strength of limit.[3] Now, my liege,
105   Tell me what blessings I have here alive,
That I should fear to die. Therefore proceed.
But yet hear this—mistake me not—no life,
I prize it not a straw; but for mine honour,
Which I would free:° if I shall be condemned       *vindicate*
110   Upon surmises, all proofs sleeping else°           *except*
But what your jealousies awake, I tell you
'Tis rigour, and not law.[4] Your honours all,
I do refer me° to the oracle.                   *appeal*
Apollo be my judge.
A LORD               This your request
115   Is altogether just. Therefore bring forth,
And in Apollo's name, his oracle.    [*Exeunt certain Officers*]
HERMIONE    The Emperor of Russia[5] was my father.
O that he were alive, and here beholding
His daughter's trial; that he did but see
120   The flatness° of my misery—yet with eyes      *boundlessness*
Of pity, not revenge.
         [*Enter* OFFICERS *with* CLEOMENES *and* DION]
OFFICER    You here shall swear upon this sword of justice
That you, Cleomenes and Dion, have
Been both at Delphos, and from thence have brought
125   This sealed-up oracle, by the hand delivered

6. Your denial of the truth costs you more effort than it's worth.
7. In the mildest course of justice, you can expect death. The implication is that death may well be preceded by torture.
8. Born under most unlucky stars.
9. Alluding to the early modern practice of nailing proclamations to posts in public places.
1. The right to enjoy a period of bedrest and seclusion after childbirth.
2. Exposure to air outside the domestic space was con-

sidered unsafe for women weakened by childbirth.
3. Before I have the strength that follows the customary period of confinement.
4. Playing on the expression "the rigor of the law," Hermione implies that judgment against her would be mere tyranny ("rigor") and not law.
5. Possibly a reference to the legendary Czar Ivan the Terrible, who died in 1584. Many London merchants were interested in trade with Russia, especially after the formation of the Muscovy Company in 1553.

Of great Apollo's priest; and that since then
You have not dared to break the holy seal,
Nor read the secrets in't.

CLEOMENES *and* DION  All this we swear.

130 LEONTES  Break up the seals, and read.

OFFICER [*reads*]  Hermione is chaste, Polixenes blameless, Camillo a true subject, Leontes a jealous tyrant, his innocent babe
truly begotten, and the King shall live without an heir if that
which is lost be not found.

LORDS  Now blessèd be the great Apollo!

135 HERMIONE                              Praised!

LEONTES  Hast thou read truth?

OFFICER  Ay, my lord, even so as it is here set down.

LEONTES  There is no truth at all i'th' oracle.
The sessions shall proceed. This is mere falsehood.

          [*Enter a* SERVANT]

SERVANT  My lord the King! The King!

140 LEONTES                              What is the business?

SERVANT  O sir, I shall be hated to report it.
The prince your son, with mere conceit° and fear                    *thought*
Of the Queen's speed,° is gone.                                     *fortune*

LEONTES                              How, 'gone'?

SERVANT                              Is dead.

LEONTES  Apollo's angry, and the heavens themselves
Do strike at my injustice.

          [HERMIONE *falls to the ground*]

145                              How now there?

PAULINA  This news is mortal to the Queen. Look down
And see what death is doing.

LEONTES                              Take her hence.
Her heart is but o'ercharged.° She will recover.                    *overburdened (by emotion)*
I have too much believed mine own suspicion.

150 Beseech you, tenderly apply to her
Some remedies for life.

          [*Exeunt* PAULINA *and Ladies, carrying* HERMIONE]
                         Apollo, pardon
My great profaneness 'gainst thine oracle.
I'll reconcile me to Polixenes,
New woo my queen, recall the good Camillo,

155 Whom I proclaim a man of truth, of mercy;
For being transported by my jealousies
To bloody thoughts and to revenge, I chose
Camillo for the minister to poison
My friend Polixenes, which had° been done,                         *would have*

160 But that the good mind of Camillo tardied°                      *delayed*
My swift command. Though I with death and with
Reward did threaten and encourage him,
Not doing it, and being done,[6] he, most humane
And filled with honour, to my kingly guest

165 Unclasped my practice,° quit his fortunes here—                 *Revealed my plot*
Which you knew great—and to the certain hazard
Of all incertainties himself commended,°                           *consigned himself*

---

6. That is, "Though I threatened him with death if he did not do it and encouraged him with the promise of reward
if he did do it."

No richer than his honour.[7] How he glisters
Through my rust![8] And how his piety
Does my deeds make the blacker!
[*Enter* PAULINA]

170  PAULINA                         Woe the while!
O cut my lace,[9] lest my heart, cracking it,
Break too.
A LORD          What fit is this, good lady?
PAULINA [*to* LEONTES]   What studied° torments, tyrant, hast for me?          *expertly devised*
What wheels, racks, fires? What flaying, boiling
175  In leads or oils?[1] What old or newer torture
Must I receive, whose every word deserves
To taste of thy most worst? Thy tyranny,
Together working with thy jealousies—
Fancies too weak for boys, too green and idle°          *immature and foolish*
180  For girls of nine—O think what they have done,
And then run mad indeed, stark mad, for all
Thy bygone fooleries were but spices° of it.          *slight tastes*
That thou betrayed'st Polixenes, 'twas nothing.
That did but show thee, of° a fool, inconstant,          *for*
185  And damnable° ingrateful. Nor was't much          *damnably; cursedly*
Thou wouldst have poisoned good Camillo's honour
To have him kill a king—poor° trespasses,          *minor*
More monstrous standing by,[2] whereof I reckon
The casting forth to crows thy baby daughter
190  To be or° none or little, though a devil          *either*
Would have shed water out of fire ere done't.[3]
Nor is't directly laid to thee the death
Of the young prince, whose honourable thoughts—
Thoughts high for one so tender°—cleft the heart          *young*
195  That could conceive a gross° and foolish sire          *stupid*
Blemished his gracious dam.° This is not, no,          *mother*
Laid to thy answer.[4] But the last—O lords,
When I have said,° cry woe! The Queen, the Queen,          *finished speaking*
The sweet'st, dear'st creature's dead, and vengeance for't
Not dropped down yet.
200  A LORD                         The higher powers forbid!
PAULINA   I say she's dead. I'll swear't. If word nor oath
Prevail not, go and see. If you can bring
Tincture° or lustre in her lip, her eye,          *Color*
Heat outwardly or breath within, I'll serve you
205  As I would do the gods. But O thou tyrant,
Do not repent these things, for they are heavier
Than all thy woes° can stir.° Therefore betake thee          *grief / remove*
To nothing but despair. A thousand knees,
Ten thousand years together, naked, fasting,
210  Upon a barren mountain, and still° winter          *always*

---

7. Possessing no fortune but his honor.
8. How he shines ("glisters") in comparison with my rust. The image alludes to polished and rusty armor.
9. It was believed that fainting might be prevented by cutting the stays on the tight bodices characteristic of female dress in this period.
1. A list of early modern forms of torture. The wheel was a device to which a person was tied and his or her limbs broken, usually by beating. The rack typically consisted of a frame with a roller at each end; a person was attached to this frame and his or her limbs stretched by turning the rollers. To "flay" was to strip off someone's skin while he or she was still alive.
2. In comparison with more monstrous ones near at hand.
3. A devil would have shed tears from his fiery eyes (or from hellfires) before he had done it.
4. Presented as a charge you must answer.

In storm perpetual, could not move the gods
To look that way thou wert.°                                      *in your direction*
LEONTES                         Go on, go on.
Thou canst not speak too much. I have deserved
All tongues to talk their bitt'rest.
A LORD [*to* PAULINA]                         Say no more.
215   Howe'er the business goes, you have made fault
I'th' boldness of your speech.
PAULINA                         I am sorry for't.
All faults I make, when I shall come to know them
I do repent. Alas, I have showed too much
The rashness of a woman. He is touched
220   To th' noble heart. What's gone and what's past help
Should be past grief.
[*To* LEONTES]             Do not receive affliction
At my petition.° I beseech you, rather                            *Because of my injunction*
Let me be punished, that have minded° you                        *reminded*
Of what you should forget. Now, good my liege,
225   Sir, royal sir, forgive a foolish woman.
The love I bore your queen—lo, fool again!
I'll speak of her no more, nor of your children.
I'll not remember you of my own lord,
Who is lost too. Take your patience to you,°                      *Be patient*
And I'll say nothing.
230   LEONTES                    Thou didst speak but well
When most the truth, which I receive much better
Than to be pitied of° thee. Prithee bring me                     *by*
To the dead bodies of my queen and son.
One grave shall be for both. Upon them shall
235   The causes of their death appear, unto
Our shame perpetual. Once a day I'll visit
The chapel where they lie, and tears shed there
Shall be my recreation.⁵ So long as nature°                      *my bodily being*
Will bear up with this exercise, so long
240   I daily vow to use it. Come, and lead me
To these sorrows.                              *Exeunt*

### 3.3

*Enter* ANTIGONUS, [*carrying the*] *babe*, [*with*] *a* MARINER
ANTIGONUS   Thou art perfect° then our ship hath touched upon     *certain*
The deserts of Bohemia?
MARINER                    Ay, my lord, and fear
We have landed in ill time. The skies look grimly
And threaten present blusters.° In my conscience,°               *impending storms / opinion*
5   The heavens with that we have in hand are angry,
And frown upon's.
ANTIGONUS   Their sacred wills be done. Go get aboard.
Look to thy barque.° I'll not be long before                     *ship*
I call upon thee.
MARINER             Make your best haste, and go not
10  Too far i'th' land. 'Tis like to be loud° weather.             *stormy*

5. My only diversion; my spiritual renewal or recreation.
3.3 Location: Bohemia. The seacoast. This play, as
does Greene's *Pandosto*, credits Bohemia with a coast.

Only for two brief periods in the late Middle Ages may
Bohemia have controlled a small piece of territory on
the Adriatic Sea, but it was otherwise landlocked.

Besides, this place is famous for the creatures
Of prey that keep° upon't.                                              *live*
ANTIGONUS                           Go thou away.
    I'll follow instantly.
MARINER                  I am glad at heart
    To be so rid o'th' business.                      *Exit*
ANTIGONUS                              Come, poor babe.
15  I have heard, but not believed, the spirits o'th' dead
    May walk again. If such thing be, thy mother
    Appeared to me last night, for ne'er was dream
    So like a waking. To me comes a creature,
    Sometimes her head on one side, some another.
20  I never saw a vessel° of like sorrow,                    *person; receptacle*
    So filled and so becoming.¹ In pure white robes
    Like very sanctity she did approach
    My cabin where I lay, thrice bowed before me,
    And, gasping to begin some speech, her eyes
25  Became two spouts. The fury spent, anon°                          *soon*
    Did this break from her: 'Good Antigonus,
    Since fate, against thy better disposition,
    Hath made thy person for the thrower-out
    Of my poor babe according to thine oath,
30  Places remote enough are in Bohemia.
    There weep, and leave it crying; and for° the babe              *because*
    Is counted lost for ever, Perdita²
    I prithee call't. For this ungentle° business          *unkind; ignoble*
    Put on thee by my lord, thou ne'er shalt see
35  Thy wife Paulina more.' And so with shrieks
    She melted into air. Affrighted much,
    I did in time collect myself, and thought
    This was so, and no slumber. Dreams are toys,°                 *trifles*
    Yet for this once, yea superstitiously,
40  I will be squared° by this. I do believe                        *ruled*
    Hermione hath suffered death, and that
    Apollo would— this being indeed the issue°                     *child*
    Of King Polixenes—it should here be laid,
    Either for life or death, upon the earth
45  Of its right father. Blossom, speed° thee well!                  *fare*
        [*He lays down the babe and a scroll*]
    There lie, and there thy character.³
        [*He lays down a box*]
                              There these,⁴
    Which may, if fortune please, both breed thee, pretty,
    And still rest thine.⁵
        [*Thunder*]
                    The storm begins. Poor wretch,
    That for thy mother's fault art thus exposed
50  To loss and what may follow! Weep I cannot,
    But my heart bleeds, and most accursed am I
    To be by oath enjoined to this. Farewell.

---

1. So filled with sorrow and so beautiful.
2. Latin for "lost one."
3. The written account of your history and parentage.
4. The gold and jewels with which the Old Shepherd grows rich and which are later used to identify the

Princess. See 5.2.29–36.
5. Which may, if you are lucky, be sufficient to pay for your upbringing, pretty child, and still leave you with something besides.

The day frowns more and more. Thou'rt like to have
A lullaby too rough. I never saw
55   The heavens so dim by day. A savage clamour!
Well may I get aboard. This is the chase.°                    *hunt*
I am gone for ever!                    *Exit, pursued by a bear*[6]
        [*Enter an* OLD SHEPHERD]
OLD SHEPHERD   I would there were no age between ten and
three-and-twenty, or that youth would sleep out the rest; for
60   there is nothing in the between but getting wenches with child,
wronging the ancientry,° stealing, fighting—hark you now,           *elderly people*
would any but these boiled-brains° of nineteen and two-and-           *lunatics*
twenty hunt this weather? They have scared away two of my
best sheep, which I fear the wolf will sooner find than the mas-
65   ter. If anywhere I have them, 'tis by the seaside, browsing of°           *on*
ivy. Good luck, an't° be thy will!                    *if it*
        [*He sees the babe*]
What have we here? Mercy on's, a bairn!° A very pretty bairn.           *child*
A boy or a child,° I wonder? A pretty one, a very pretty one.           *girl*
Sure some scape.[7] Though I am not bookish,° yet I can read     *not familiar with books*
70   'waiting-gentlewoman' in the scape. This has been some stair-
work, some trunk-work, some behind-door-work.[8] They were
warmer that got° this than the poor thing is here. I'll take it up           *begot*
for pity; yet I'll tarry till my son come. He hallooed but even
now. Whoa-ho-hoa!
        *Enter* CLOWN°                    *Bumpkin*
75   CLOWN   Hilloa, loa!
OLD SHEPHERD   What, art so near? If thou'lt see a thing to talk
on° when thou art dead and rotten, come hither. What ail'st           *about*
thou, man?
CLOWN   I have seen two such sights, by sea and by land! But I
80   am not to say it is a sea, for it is now the sky. Betwixt the fir-
mament and it you cannot thrust a bodkin's° point.           *needle's*
OLD SHEPHERD   Why, boy, how is it?
CLOWN   I would you did but see how it chafes, how it rages, how
it takes up the shore. But that's not to the point. O, the most
85   piteous cry of the poor souls! Sometimes to see 'em, and not to
see 'em; now the ship boring° the moon with her mainmast,           *piercing*
and anon swallowed with yeast° and froth, as you'd thrust a cork           *foam*
into a hogshead.° And then for the land-service,[9] to see how the     *cask of liquor*
bear tore out his shoulder-bone, how he cried to me for help,
90   and said his name was Antigonus, a nobleman! But to make an
end of the ship—to see how the sea flap-dragoned it![1] But first,
how the poor souls roared, and the sea mocked them, and how

6. One of the most famous stage directions in English drama. A real bear, rather than a man in a bear suit, might have been used in this scene, perhaps discreetly led on a rope by the fleeing Antigonus. There were reports of tame bears in Shakespeare's London, and bearbaiting (setting dogs on chained bears) was a popular Elizabethan sport, sometimes occurring in the same amphitheaters used at other times for stage plays. It is more likely, however, that the bear was impersonated by an actor in a bear costume. Modern productions vary significantly in their representation of the bear. Some strive for realism, having a bearskin-clad actor or a mechanical likeness of a bear pass across a darkened stage illuminated only by the occasional

lightning bolt. Others productions are more stylized, suggesting a bear by the obvious artifice of a mask or symbol.
7. Sexual transgression. English ballads and other popular literature of the period offer numerous accounts of female servants who abandon or kill children born out of wedlock.
8. Some secret sexual affair conducted on back stairs, in chests, or behind doors.
9. Punning on the military and culinary meanings of "service" to suggest both "combat on land" and "food to be served up on land."
1. Devoured it as if it were a flapdragon, a raisin floating on flaming brandy.

the poor gentleman roared, and the bear mocked him, both
roaring louder than the sea or weather.

95 OLD SHEPHERD  Name of mercy, when was this, boy?

CLOWN  Now, now. I have not winked° since I saw these sights.          *blinked an eye*
The men are not yet cold under water, nor the bear half dined
on the gentleman. He's at it now.

OLD SHEPHERD  Would I had been by to have helped the old
100 man!

CLOWN  I would you had been by the ship side, to have helped
her. There your charity would have lacked footing.[2]

OLD SHEPHERD  Heavy° matters, heavy matters. But look thee          *Sad*
here, boy. Now bless thyself. Thou metst with things dying, I
105 with things new-born. Here's a sight for thee. Look thee, a bearing-cloth[3] for a squire's child.

[*He points to the box*]

Look thee here, take up, take up, boy. Open't. So, let's see. It
was told me I should be rich by the fairies. This is some
changeling.[4] Open't. What's within, boy?

110 CLOWN [*opening the box*]  You're a made° old man. If the sins of          *prosperous*
your youth are forgiven you, you're well to live.° Gold, all gold!          *well off; virtuous*

OLD SHEPHERD  This is fairy gold,[5] boy, and 'twill prove so. Up
with't, keep it close.° Home, home, the next° way. We are          *secret / nearest*
lucky, boy, and to be so still° requires nothing but secrecy. Let          *always*
115 my sheep go. Come, good boy, the next way home.

CLOWN  Go you the next way with your findings. I'll go see if the
bear be gone from the gentleman, and how much he hath
eaten. They are never curst° but when they are hungry. If there          *vicious*
be any of him left, I'll bury it.

120 OLD SHEPHERD  That's a good deed. If thou mayst discern by that
which is left of him what he is,° fetch me to th' sight of him.          *his identity or rank*

CLOWN  Marry[6] will I; and you shall help to put him i'th' ground.

OLD SHEPHERD  'Tis a lucky day, boy, and we'll do good deeds
on't.          *Exeunt*

## 4.1

*Enter* TIME,[1] *the Chorus*

TIME  I that please some, try° all; both joy and terror          *test*
Of good and bad; that makes and unfolds error,
Now take upon me in the name° of Time          *with the authority*
To use my wings. Impute it not a crime
5 To me or my swift passage that I slide
O'er sixteen years and leave the growth untried°          *development unexamined*
Of that wide gap, since it is in my power
To o'erthrow law, and in one self-born° hour          *selfsame*
To plant and o'erwhelm° custom. Let me pass          *establish and overthrow*
10 The same I am ere ancient'st order was

2. There you would not have had a secure place to
stand, with a pun on "footing" as meaning "a foundation" (upon which a charity might be founded).
3. The blanket used to wrap an infant in preparation
for baptism. A squire's child, being of a fairly high
social position, would have a rich bearing-cloth.
4. A child secretly substituted for another by fairies. The
term could apply to the abducted child (usually beautiful)
or to the one (often ugly or deformed) left in its place.
5. Riches left by fairies were unreliable. If not kept
secret, they brought bad luck.

6. A mild oath derived from the name of the Virgin
Mary.
4.1 Location: Scene continues.
1. In early modern texts, Time was conventionally represented as an old bald man with wings, signifying how
swiftly time passes. He often carried an hourglass and
a scythe, symbol of the power of time to destroy life. A
common saying was that Time was the revealer of
Truth, or that Truth was the daughter of Time. Robert
Greene's *Pandosto*, Shakespeare's chief source for *The
Winter's Tale*, was subtitled *The Triumph of Time*.

Or what is now received.² I witness to
The times that brought them in; so shall I do
To th' freshest things now reigning, and make stale
The glistering° of this present as my tale                    *glittering shine*
15  Now seems to it.³ Your patience this allowing,
I turn my glass,° and give my scene such growing            *hourglass*
As° you had slept between. Leontes leaving                   *As if*
Th'effects of his fond° jealousies, so grieving              *foolish*
That he shuts up himself, imagine me,
20  Gentle spectators, that I now may be
In fair Bohemia, and remember well
I mentionèd a son o'th' King's, which Florizel
I now name to you; and with speed so pace°                   *proceed*
To speak of Perdita, now grown in grace
25  Equal with wond'ring.⁴ What of her ensues
I list not° prophesy, but let Time's news                    *do not wish to*
Be known when 'tis brought forth. A shepherd's daughter
And what to her adheres,° which follows after,               *pertains*
Is th'argument° of Time. Of this allow,                      *subject matter*
30  If ever you have spent time worse ere now.
If never, yet that Time himself doth say
He wishes earnestly you never may.               *Exit*

## 4.2

*Enter* POLIXENES *and* CAMILLO

POLIXENES    I pray thee, good Camillo, be no more importunate.
'Tis a sickness denying° thee anything, a death to grant this.   *to deny*
CAMILLO    It is sixteen¹ years since I saw my country. Though I
have for the most part been aired abroad,° I desire to lay my    *breathed foreign air*
5  bones there. Besides, the penitent King, my master, hath sent
for me, to whose feeling° sorrows I might be some allay°—or I    *deeply felt / relief*
o'erween° to think so—which is another spur to my departure.     *am bold enough*
POLIXENES    As thou lov'st me, Camillo, wipe not out the rest of
thy services by leaving me now. The need I have of thee thine
10  own goodness hath made. Better not to have had thee than thus
to want° thee. Thou, having made me businesses² which none       *be without*
without thee can sufficiently manage, must either stay to execute them thyself or take away with thee the very services thou
hast done; which if I have not enough considered°—as too         *rewarded*
15  much I cannot—to be more thankful to thee shall be my study,
and my profit therein, the heaping friendships.³ Of that fatal°  *deadly*
country Sicilia, prithee speak no more, whose very naming
punishes me with the remembrance of that penitent—as thou
callest him—and reconciled King my brother, whose loss of his
20  most precious queen and children are even now to be afresh°     *newly*
lamented. Say to me, when sawest thou the Prince Florizel,
my son? Kings are no less unhappy, their issue° not being gra-   *children*
cious,° than they are in losing them when they have ap-          *not proving virtuous*
proved° their virtues.                                           *demonstrated*

---

2. Let me remain as I have been from before the beginnings of civilization even to the time of present customs.
3. As my tale now seems stale in comparison with the
present.
4. Now grown so gracious as to inspire admiration.
**4.2** Location: Bohemia. The palace of Polixenes.

1. F reads "fifteene." At 4.1.6, Time says that sixteen
years have passed. This apparent error may be due to
carelessness on Shakespeare's part or to a misreading of
a Roman numeral by a compositor or scribe.
2. Performed services for me.
3. The accumulation of your kindnesses.

25 CAMILLO  Sir, it is three days since I saw the Prince. What his
   happier affairs may be are to me unknown; but I have missingly
   noted° he is of late much retired from court, and is less fre-      *noted by his absence*
   quent to° his princely exercises than formerly he hath              *less often engaged in*
   appeared.

30 POLIXENES  I have considered so much, Camillo, and with some
   care, so far that I have eyes under my service° which look upon     *spies in my employ*
   his removedness,° from whom I have this intelligence: that he       *retirement (from court)*
   is seldom from the house of a most homely° shepherd, a man,         *simple*
   they say, that from very nothing, and beyond the imagination
35 of his neighbours, is grown into an unspeakable estate.°            *untold wealth*
   CAMILLO  I have heard, sir, of such a man, who hath a daughter
   of most rare note.° The report of her is extended more than can     *quality*
   be thought to begin° from such a cottage.                           *originate*
   POLIXENES  That's likewise part of my intelligence; but, I fear,
40 the angle° that plucks our son thither. Thou shalt accompany        *fishhook*
   us to the place, where we will, not appearing what we are, have
   some question with the shepherd; from whose simplicity I
   think it not uneasy° to get the cause of my son's resort thither.   *difficult*
   Prithee, be my present partner in this business, and lay aside
45 the thoughts of Sicilia.
   CAMILLO  I willingly obey your command.
   POLIXENES  My best Camillo! We must disguise ourselves.

                                                *Exeunt*

                        **4.3**
           *Enter* AUTOLYCUS *singing*
   AUTOLYCUS
          When daffodils begin to peer,
            With heigh, the doxy° over the dale,                       *beggar's wench*
          Why then comes in the sweet° o'the year,                     *sweetest part*
            For the red blood reigns in the winter's pale.°            *skin made pale by winter*

5         The white sheet bleaching on the hedge,[1]
            With heigh, the sweet birds, O how they sing!
          Doth set my pugging° tooth on edge,                          *thieving*
            For a quart of ale is a dish for a king.

          The lark, that tirra-lirra chants,
10          With heigh, with heigh, the thrush and the jay,
          Are summer songs for me and my aunts[2]
            While we lie tumbling in the hay.

   I have served Prince Florizel, and in my time wore three-pile,[3]
   but now I am out of service.

15            But shall I go mourn for that, my dear?
                The pale moon shines by night,
              And when I wander here and there
                I then do most go right.

              If tinkers[4] may have leave° to live,                   *permission*
20              And bear the sow-skin budget,[5]

---

**4.3** Location: Bohemia. Near the cottage where the
Old Shepherd, the Clown, and Perdita live.
1. It was common practice to set clothes out to dry on
hedges.
2. Another slang term for women who take beggars or
vagabonds for lovers.

3. A rich velvet cloth with a thick nap or "pile."
4. Menders of metal pots and kettles. The term was
also applied to itinerant beggars and thieves.
5. Pigskin bag. Bag in which a tinker carried his tools;
hence, a sign of his trade.

Then my account I well may give,
And in the stocks avouch it.°      *acknowledge (my crime)*
My traffic° is sheets. When the kite builds, look to lesser linen.[6]      *trade*
My father named me Autolycus,[7] who being, as I am, littered
25    under Mercury,[8] was likewise a snapper-up of unconsidered
trifles. With die and drab° I purchased this caparison, and my      *dice and whores*
revenue is the silly cheat.[9] Gallows and knock° are too power-      *beatings*
ful on the highway.[1] Beating and hanging are terrors to me. For°      *As for*
the life to come, I sleep out the thought of it. A prize, a prize!

*Enter* CLOWN

30    CLOWN    Let me see. Every 'leven wether tods,[2] every tod yields
pound and odd° shilling. Fifteen hundred shorn, what comes      *one*
the wool to?
AUTOLYCUS [*aside*]    If the springe° hold, the cock's[3] mine.      *trap*
CLOWN    I cannot do't without counters.[4] Let me see, what am I
35    to buy for our sheep-shearing feast?[5] Three pound of sugar, five
pound of currants, rice—what will this sister of mine do with
rice? But my father hath made her mistress of the feast, and she
lays it on. She hath made me four-and-twenty nosegays for the
shearers—three-man-song-men,[6] all, and very good ones—but
40    they are most of them means° and basses, but one Puritan      *tenors*
amongst them, and he sings psalms to hornpipes.[7] I must have
saffron to colour the warden° pies; mace; dates, none—that's      *winter pear*
out of my note;° nutmegs, seven; a race° or two of ginger—but      *not on my list / root*
that I may beg; four pound of prunes, and as many of raisins
45    o'th' sun.°      *sun-dried*
AUTOLYCUS    [*grovelling on the ground*] O, that ever I was born!
CLOWN    I'th' name of me!
AUTOLYCUS    O help me, help me! Pluck but off these rags, and
then death, death!
50    CLOWN    Alack, poor soul, thou hast need of more rags to lay on
thee rather than have these off.
AUTOLYCUS    O sir, the loathsomeness of them offend me more
than the stripes° I have received, which are mighty ones and      *blows*
millions.
55    CLOWN    Alas, poor man, a million of beating may come to a
great matter.[8]
AUTOLYCUS    I am robbed, sir, and beaten; my money and apparel
ta'en from me, and these detestable things put upon me.
CLOWN    What, by a horseman, or a footman?°      *man on foot*
60    AUTOLYCUS    A footman, sweet sir, a footman.
CLOWN    Indeed, he should be a footman, by the garments he has
left with thee. If this be a horseman's coat it hath seen very hot

---

6. The kite, a small bird of prey, supposedly stole small
pieces of linen to make its nest. Autolycus steals sheets,
larger pieces of linen, probably those left to dry on
hedges.
7. In classical mythology, a crafty thief and grandfather
of Ulysses; Autolycus's own father, Mercury, was the
god of thieves.
8. Fathered by Mercury; born when the planet Mercury was ascendant.
9. I was reduced to wearing this garb, and my income
derives from petty swindles.
1. Autolycus fears the penalties meted out to highway-
men. He would rather be a petty thief.
2. Every eleven rams will yield 28 pounds (a "tod") of
wool. The Clown and his father could expect to earn a
substantial amount of money (almost 150 pounds) for

their wool.
3. Woodcock, a bird easily caught and hence proverbial
for its stupidity.
4. Disks used in calculating sums.
5. In rural England, a traditional summer event in
which people of different ranks took part in feasting and
revelry.
6. Men who sing three-part songs.
7. Shrill-sounding musical instruments often played at
country dances and hardly appropriate to accompany
the singing of psalms. Shakespeare may here be satiriz-
ing Puritans, who were notorious for their opposition to
music and dancing.
8. A million blows can be a serious affair, with a pun on
"matter" as "pus," the sign of an infection caused by open
wounds.

service. Lend me thy hand, I'll help thee. Come, lend me thy
hand.

    [*He helps* AUTOLYCUS *up*]

65 AUTOLYCUS  O, good sir, tenderly. O!

CLOWN  Alas, poor soul!

AUTOLYCUS  O, good sir, softly,° good sir! I fear, sir, my shoulder-       *gently*
blade is out.

CLOWN  How now? Canst stand?

70 AUTOLYCUS  Softly, dear sir. Good sir, softly.

    [*He picks the* CLOWN's *pocket*]⁹

You ha' done me a charitable office.°                 *service*

CLOWN [*reaching for his purse*]  Dost lack any money? I have a
little money for thee.

AUTOLYCUS  No, good sweet sir, no, I beseech you, sir.¹ I have a
75 kinsman not past three-quarters of a mile hence, unto whom I
was going. I shall there have money, or anything I want. Offer
me no money, I pray you. That kills° my heart.      *touches*

CLOWN  What manner of fellow was he that robbed you?

AUTOLYCUS  A fellow, sir, that I have known to go about with
80 troll-madams.° I knew him once a servant of the Prince. I can-   *whores*
not tell, good sir, for which of his virtues it was, but he was
certainly whipped out of the court.

CLOWN  His vices, you would say. There's no virtue whipped out
of the court. They cherish it to make it stay there; and yet it
85 will no more but abide.°                   *stay there only briefly*

AUTOLYCUS  Vices, I would say, sir. I know this man well. He
hath been since an ape-bearer,² then a process-server—a bai-
liff—then he compassed a motion° of the Prodigal Son,³ and  *devised a puppet show*
married a tinker's wife within a mile where my land and living°      *property*
90 lies, and having flown over many knavish professions, he settled
only in rogue. Some call him Autolycus.

CLOWN  Out upon him! Prig,° for my life, prig! He haunts      *Thief*
wakes,° fairs, and bear-baitings.              *festivals*

AUTOLYCUS  Very true, sir. He, sir, he. That's the rogue that put
93 me into this apparel.

CLOWN  Not a more cowardly rogue in all Bohemia. If you had
but looked big and spit at him, he'd have run.

AUTOLYCUS  I must confess to you, sir, I am no fighter. I am false
of heart° that way, and that he knew, I warrant him.    *without courage*

100 CLOWN  How do you now?

AUTOLYCUS  Sweet sir, much better than I was. I can stand, and
walk. I will even take my leave of you, and pace softly towards
my kinsman's.

CLOWN  Shall I bring thee° on the way?          *escort you*

105 AUTOLYCUS  No, good-faced sir, no, sweet sir.

CLOWN  Then fare thee well. I must go buy spices for our sheep-
shearing.

AUTOLYCUS  Prosper you, sweet sir.        *Exit* [*the* CLOWN]

---

9. It is uncertain when Autolycus actually picks the
Clown's pocket, but it adds to the humor if Autolycus's
next line, "You ha' done me a charitable office," can
refer both to the kindness the Clown has knowingly
shown Autolycus *and* to the kindness the Clown has
unwittingly done him in making available a purse for
the wily rogue to steal.
1. Autolycus does not want the Clown to find out he

has picked his pocket and so left him with no money.
He may here restrain the Clown from putting his hand
into his pocket.
2. One who carried about a trained monkey.
3. Alluding to the New Testament story of a spendthrift
son who squandered his money only to be forgiven by
his father.

Your purse is not hot° enough to purchase your spice. I'll be                    *full*
110    with you at your sheep-shearing, too. If I make not this cheat°              *deception*
bring out° another, and the shearers prove sheep, let me be                        *lead to*
unrolled⁴ and my name put in the book of virtue.
[*Sings*]          Jog on, jog on, the footpath way,
And merrily hent° the stile⁵-a.                              *grab (to leap over)*
115            A merry heart goes all the day,
Your sad tires in a mile-a.                                    *Exit*

## 4.4

*Enter* FLORIZEL [*dressed as Doricles a countryman*],
[*and*] PERDITA [*as Queen of the Feast*]¹

FLORIZEL    These your unusual weeds° to each part of you              *garments*
Does give a life; no shepherdess, but Flora°                            *goddess of flowers*
Peering in April's front.² This your sheep-shearing
Is as a meeting of the petty gods,
And you the queen on't.°                                                *of it*
5    PERDITA                    Sir, my gracious lord,
To chide at your extremes° it not becomes me—                          *extravagances*
O, pardon that I name them! Your high self,
The gracious mark o'th' land,³ you have obscured
With a swain's wearing,° and me, poor lowly maid,                      *shepherd's costume*
10    Most goddess-like pranked up.° But that our feasts                *adorned*
In every mess⁴ have folly, and the feeders°                             *those who eat*
Digest it with a custom,⁵ I should blush
To see you so attired; swoon, I think,
To show myself a glass.°                                                *mirror*
15    FLORIZEL                    I bless the time
When my good falcon made her flight across
Thy father's ground.
PERDITA                    Now Jove afford you cause!
To me the difference° forges dread; your greatness                     *(in rank)*
Hath not been used to fear. Even now I tremble
To think your father by some accident
20    Should pass this way, as you did. O, the fates!
How would he look to see his work,° so noble,                          *offspring; writings*
Vilely bound up?⁶ What would he say? Or how
Should I, in these my borrowed flaunts,° behold                        *rich garments*
The sternness of his presence?
FLORIZEL                    Apprehend
25    Nothing but jollity. The gods themselves,
Humbling their deities to love, have taken
The shapes of beasts upon them. Jupiter
Became a bull, and bellowed; the green Neptune
A ram, and bleated; and the fire-robed god,
30    Golden Apollo, a poor humble swain,

---

4. Let my name be taken off the list (of thieves and vagabonds).
5. Steps by which people pass over a fence or hedge.
**4.4** Location: Bohemia. In front of the cottage where the Old Shepherd, the Clown, and Perdita live.
1. Again, F lists in the initial stage direction all the major characters who appear in this very long scene. Florizel and Perdita seem, however, to have a private conversation before the Old Shepherd, Polixenes, and

others enter to them at line 54.
2. Peeping out in early April.
3. The one whose graces make him admired by all.
4. A group of four served at table together. See note to 1.2.227.
5. Tolerate it because they have grown used to it.
6. Outfitted in such an inferior way. A bookbinding metaphor.

As I seem now.[7] Their transformations
Were never for a piece° of beauty rarer,                              *person*
Nor in a way so chaste,[8] since my desires
Run not before mine honour, nor my lusts
Burn hotter than my faith.

35  PERDITA                                        O, but sir,
Your resolution cannot hold when 'tis
Opposed, as it must be, by th' power of the King.
One of these two must be necessities,
Which then will speak that you must change this purpose,
Or I my life.[9]

40  FLORIZEL            Thou dearest Perdita,
With these forced° thoughts I prithee darken not          *unnatural; farfetched*
The mirth o'th' feast. Or° I'll be thine, my fair,                     *Either*
Or not my father's. For I cannot be
Mine own, nor anything to any, if
45  I be not thine. To this I am most constant,
Though destiny say no. Be merry, gentle;
Strangle such thoughts as these with anything
That you behold the while. Your guests are coming.
Lift up your countenance as° it were the day                          *as if*
50  Of celebration of that nuptial which
We two have sworn shall come.

PERDITA                                        O Lady Fortune,[1]
Stand you auspicious!

FLORIZEL                             See, your guests approach.
Address° yourself to entertain them sprightly,                       *Prepare*
And let's be red with mirth.

[*Enter the* OLD SHEPHERD, *with* POLIXENES *and* CA-
MILLO, *disguised, the* CLOWN, MOPSA, DORCAS, *and
others*]

55  OLD SHEPHERD [*to* PERDITA]   Fie, daughter, when my old wife lived, upon
This day she was both pantler,° butler, cook,                    *pantry maid*
Both dame° and servant, welcomed all, served all,        *mistress of the house*
Would sing her song and dance her turn, now here
At upper end o'th' table, now i'th' middle,
60  On his° shoulder, and his,° her face afire             *one person's / another's*
With labour, and the thing she took to quench it
She would to each one sip. You are retired
As if you were a feasted one° and not                               *a guest*
The hostess of the meeting. Pray you bid
65  These unknown friends to's welcome, for it is
A way to make us better friends, more known.
Come, quench your blushes, and present yourself
That which you are, mistress o'th' feast. Come on,
And bid us welcome to your sheep-shearing,
As your good flock shall prosper.

70  PERDITA [*to* POLIXENES]                Sir, welcome.
It is my father's will I should take on me

---

7. In classical mythology, Jupiter transformed himself
into a bull and abducted Europa; Neptune took on the
shape of a ram to carry off Theopane; and the sun god
Apollo disguised himself as a shepherd to court Alcestis.
8. Nor ever conducted with so chaste a purpose.

9. One of two things will become necessary: either you
must change your plans, or I must change my life (that
is, risk death).
1. In classical and Renaissance mythology, a woman of
fickle disposition whose favors cannot be relied upon.

The hostess-ship o'th' day.
[*To* CAMILLO]        You're welcome, sir.
Give me those flowers there, Dorcas. Reverend sirs,
For you there's rosemary and rue. These keep°       *retain*
75  Seeming° and savour° all the winter long.       *Color / scent*
Grace and remembrance[2] be to you both,
And welcome to our shearing.
POLIXENES                Shepherdess,
A fair one are you. Well you fit our ages
With flowers of winter.
PERDITA           Sir, the year growing ancient,
80  Not yet on summer's death, nor on the birth
Of trembling winter, the fairest flowers o'th' season
Are our carnations and streaked gillyvors,[3]
Which some call nature's bastards. Of that kind
Our rustic garden's barren, and I care not
85  To get slips of them.
POLIXENES          Wherefore, gentle maiden,
Do you neglect them?
PERDITA           For I have heard it said
There is an art[4] which in their piedness° shares    *streaked color*
With great creating nature.
POLIXENES           Say there be,
Yet nature is made better by no mean°       *means*
90  But nature makes that mean. So over that art
Which you say adds to nature is an art
That nature makes. You see, sweet maid, we marry
A gentler scion to the wildest stock,
And make conceive a bark of baser kind
95  By bud of nobler race.[5] This is an art
Which does mend nature—change it rather; but
The art itself is nature.
PERDITA          So it is.
POLIXENES   Then make your garden rich in gillyvors,
And do not call them bastards.
PERDITA           I'll not put
100  The dibble° in earth to set° one slip of them,    *trowel / plant*
No more than, were I painted,° I would wish    *wearing cosmetics*
This youth should say 'twere well, and only therefore
Desire to breed by me. Here's flowers for you:
Hot[6] lavender, mints, savory, marjoram,
105  The marigold, that goes to bed wi'th' sun,
And with him rises, weeping.[7] These are flowers
Of middle summer, and I think they are given
To men of middle age. You're very welcome.
[*She gives them flowers*]

---

2. Grace ("repentance") and remembrance are qualities associated with rue and rosemary, respectively.
3. Gillyflowers or multicolored carnations. Their variations in color were thought to result from crossbreeding with other flowers, which may be why Perdita calls them "nature's bastards." They were proverbially associated with sexual license.
4. The art of crossbreeding or grafting.
5. We unite a cutting from a highly cultivated plant to the stem of a lesser one and cause the lesser plant to

bring forth a highly cultivated flower, that puns on "gentler scion," "wildest stock," "baser kind," and "nobler race" to suggest a successful union between a highborn heir and a member of the lower social orders.
6. Herbs were divided into "hot" and "cold" varieties based on their supposed temperatures.
7. The marigold, sometimes called "the spouse of the sun," supposedly closed at sunset and opened, filled with dew, in the morning when the sun came up.

CAMILLO   I should leave grazing were I of your flock,
And only live by gazing.
110 PERDITA                Out, alas,
You'd be so lean that blasts of January
Would blow you through and through.
[*To* FLORIZEL]          Now, my fair'st friend,
I would I had some flowers o'th' spring that might
Become your time of day; [*to* MOPSA *and* DORCAS] and yours, and yours,
115 That wear upon your virgin branches yet
Your maidenheads growing. O Proserpina,[8]
For the flowers now that, frighted, thou letst fall
From Dis's wagon!°—daffodils,               *chariot*
That come before the swallow dares, and take°      *charm*
120 The winds of March with beauty; violets, dim,°   *with hanging head*
But sweeter than the lids of Juno's eyes
Or Cytherea's breath;[9] pale primroses,
That die unmarried ere they can behold
Bright Phoebus° in his strength—a malady       *the sun god*
125 Most incident to maids;[1] bold oxlips, and
The crown imperial;[2] lilies of all kinds,
The flower-de-luce[3] being one. O, these I lack,
To make you garlands of, and my sweet friend,
To strew him o'er and o'er.
FLORIZEL             What, like a corpse?
130 PERDITA   No, like a bank, for love to lie and play on,
Not like a corpse—or if, not to be buried,
But quick° and in mine arms. Come, take your flowers.   *living*
Methinks I play as I have seen them do
In Whitsun pastorals.[4] Sure this robe of mine
Does change my disposition.
135 FLORIZEL           What you do
Still° betters what is done. When you speak, sweet,    *Always*
I'd have you do it ever; when you sing,
I'd have you buy and sell so, so give alms,
Pray so; and for the ord'ring° your affairs,       *arranging for*
140 To sing them too. When you do dance, I wish you
A wave o'th' sea, that you might ever do
Nothing but that, move still, still so,
And own° no other function. Each your doing,°   *have / Each thing you do*
So singular° in each particular,             *distinctive*
145 Crowns what you are doing in the present deeds,
That all your acts are queens.
PERDITA            O Doricles,[5]
Your praises are too large. But that your youth
And the true blood which peeps so fairly through't

---

8. In Ovid's *Metamorphoses*, Proserpina, the daughter of Ceres, is abducted by Dis, or Pluto, as she gathers flowers and is taken in his chariot ("wagon") to his underworld kingdom. Sought out by Ceres, Proserpina is allowed to return to earth for six months each year. Her sojourn on earth coincides with spring and summer, her return to the underworld with fall and winter.
9. Juno was queen of the gods; "Cytherea" was another name for Venus, the goddess of love.
1. Alluding to the superstition that women who died of a kind of anemia known as green sickness would be transformed into primroses. Green sickness was espe-cially associated with young virginal women; vigorous sexual activity was sometimes advocated as a cure.
2. A lily first imported into England from Turkey in the late sixteenth century.
3. Fleur-de-lis, the national flower of France.
4. English rural festivities traditionally held at Whit-suntide, a religious festival occurring in the spring, seven weeks after Easter. The festivities, often orga-nized under a festival King and Queen, included mor-ris dances and Robin Hood plays.
5. The name Florizel has assumed.

Do plainly give you out an unstained shepherd,
150 With wisdom I might fear, my Doricles,
You wooed me the false way.
FLORIZEL           I think you have
As little skill° to fear as I have purpose           *reason*
To put you to't. But come, our dance, I pray;
Your hand, my Perdita. So turtles[6] pair,
That never mean to part.
155 PERDITA           I'll swear for 'em.
POLIXENES [*to* CAMILLO]    This is the prettiest low-born lass that ever
Ran on the greensward.° Nothing she does or seems    *grassy turf*
But smacks of something greater than herself,
Too noble for this place.
CAMILLO           He tells her something
160 That makes her blood look out.° Good sooth, she is    *makes her blush*
The queen of curds and cream.[7]
CLOWN           Come on, strike up!
DORCAS    Mopsa must be your mistress. Marry, garlic to mend
her kissing with![8]
MOPSA    Now, in good time!
165 CLOWN    Not a word, a word, we stand upon our manners. Come,
strike up!
[*Music.*] *Here a dance of shepherds and shepherdesses*
POLIXENES    Pray, good shepherd, what fair swain is this
Which dances with your daughter?
OLD SHEPHERD    They call him Doricles, and boasts himself°    *he boasts*
170 To have a worthy feeding;° but I have it    *good pasture land*
Upon his own report, and I believe it.
He looks like sooth.° He says he loves my daughter.    *appears to be honest*
I think so, too, for never gazed the moon
Upon the water as he'll stand and read,
175 As 'twere, my daughter's eyes; and to be plain,
I think there is not half a kiss to choose
Who loves another° best.    *the other*
POLIXENES           She dances featly.°    *nimbly*
OLD SHEPHERD    So she does anything, though I report it
That° should be silent. If young Doricles    *Who*
180 Do light upon her, she shall bring him that
Which he not dreams of.
*Enter [a]* SERVANT
SERVANT    O, master, if you did but hear the pedlar at the door,
you would never dance again after a tabor and pipe.[9] No, the
bagpipe could not move you. He sings several° tunes faster than    *different*
185 you'll tell° money. He utters them as he had eaten ballads,[1]    *count*
and all men's ears grew° to his tunes.    *listened intently*
CLOWN    He could never come better.° He shall come in. I love    *at a better time*
a ballad but even too well, if it be doleful matter merrily set
down, or a very pleasant thing indeed, and sung lamentably.
190 SERVANT    He hath songs for man or woman, of all sizes. No milli-
ner[2] can so fit his customers with gloves. He has the prettiest

6. Turtledoves, which proverbially mate for life.
7. Referring perhaps to a cream custard known as
"white pot." In some May games, a woman was chosen
as Queen of white-pot cream.
8. To make her breath sweet (said ironically).
9. A small drum and fife used for morris dancing.

1. Alluding to the broadside ballads that were sung
and sold by peddlers who traveled throughout the
country.
2. One who sells fashionable articles of clothing such
as hats and gloves. Originally, the word meant one who
sells items imported from Milan.

love songs for maids, so without bawdry, which is strange, with
such delicate burdens° of dildos and fadings, 'Jump her, and       *refrains*
thump her';[3] and where some stretch-mouthed° rascal would,     *obscene*
195   as it were, mean mischief and break a foul gap into the matter,[4]
he makes the maid to answer, 'Whoop, do me no harm, good
man'; puts him off, slights him, with 'Whoop, do me no harm,
good man!'

POLIXENES   This is a brave° fellow.                                *fine*

200  CLOWN   Believe me, thou talkest of an admirable conceited° fel-   *very witty*
low. Has he any unbraided° wares?               *new; not shopworn*

SERVANT   He hath ribbons of all the colours i'th' rainbow; points[5]
more than all the lawyers in Bohemia can learnedly handle,
though they come to him by th' gross; inkles, caddises, cam-
205   brics, lawns[6]—why, he sings 'em over as they were gods or goddesses. You would think a smock° were a she-angel, he so  *a woman's undergarment*
chants to the sleeve-hand° and the work about the square on't.[7]   · *wristband*

CLOWN   Prithee bring him in, and let him approach singing.

PERDITA   Forewarn him that he use no scurrilous words in's
210   tunes.                                        [*Exit* SERVANT]

CLOWN   You have of these° pedlars that have more in them than   *There are some*
you'd think, sister.

PERDITA   Ay, good brother, or go about° to think.            *intend*

    *Enter* AUTOLYCUS [*wearing a false beard, carrying his*
    *pack, and*] *singing*

AUTOLYCUS   Lawn as white as driven snow,
215         Cypress[8] black as e'er was crow,
        Gloves as sweet° as damask roses,              *perfumed*
        Masks for faces, and for noses;[9]
        Bugle-bracelet,[1] necklace amber,
        Perfume for a lady's chamber;
220         Golden coifs,° and stomachers[2]               *caps*
        For my lads to give their dears;
        Pins and poking-sticks of steel,[3]
        What maids lack from head to heel
        Come buy of me, come, come buy, come buy,
225         Buy, lads, or else your lasses cry. Come buy!

CLOWN   If I were not in love with Mopsa thou shouldst take no
money of me, but being enthralled as I am, it will also be the
bondage of certain ribbons and gloves.[4]

MOPSA   I was promised them against° the feast, but they come   *in time for*
230   not too late now.

DORCAS   He hath promised you more than that,[5] or there be
liars.

---

3. Though the servant claims that the songs are without bawdiness, the refrains are in fact full of sexual
puns that the servant may not understand. "Dildos" are
artificial penises; "fadings" can mean "orgasms"; and
"jump her and thump her" denotes sexual relations with
a woman.
4. Would interrupt the song with an indecent insertion.
5. Laces for fastening garments, with a pun on "points"
as meaning "legal arguments."
6. "Inkles" were linen tapes; "caddises" were worsted
tapes used for garters; "cambrics" and "lawns" were
heavy and sheer linens.
7. The stitching about the yoke of the garment.
8. A crepe material imported from Cyprus and used for

mourning clothes.
9. Many upper-class English women wore masks to
protect their skin from exposure to the sun. Some
women's noses were eaten away by syphilis, and masks
would also cover this deformity.
1. A bracelet of shiny black beads.
2. Embroidered bodices for dresses.
3. Metal rods used to iron the ruffs or stiff collars worn
by both men and women. The term is also slang for
"penis."
4. Because I am the prisoner of love, certain ribbons
and gloves must also be put in bondage (bound up in a
parcel).
5. (Perhaps he has promised marriage.)

MOPSA   He hath paid° you all he promised you. Maybe he has        *given; had sex with*
   paid you more, which will shame you to give him again.[6]
235  CLOWN   Is there no manners left among maids? Will they wear
   their plackets where they should bear their faces?[7] Is there not
   milking-time, when you are going to bed, or kiln-hole,° to whis-        *fireplace*
   tle of these secrets, but you must be tittle-tattling before all our
   guests? 'Tis well they are whispering. Clammer your tongues,[8]
240   and not a word more.
MOPSA   I have done. Come, you promised me a tawdry-lace[9] and
   a pair of sweet gloves.
CLOWN   Have I not told thee how I was cozened by the way,°        *cheated on the road*
   and lost all my money?
245  AUTOLYCUS   And indeed, sir, there are cozeners abroad, therefore
   it behoves men to be wary.
CLOWN   Fear not thou, man, thou shalt lose nothing here.
AUTOLYCUS   I hope so, sir, for I have about me many parcels of
   charge.°        *valuable goods*
250  CLOWN   What hast here? Ballads?
MOPSA   Pray now, buy some. I love a ballad in print, alife,° for        *on my life*
   then we are sure they are true.
AUTOLYCUS   Here's one to a very doleful tune, how a usurer's
   wife was brought to bed of twenty money-bags at a burden,° and        *in one childbirth*
255   how she longed to eat adders' heads and toads carbonadoed.°        *cut and grilled*
MOPSA   Is it true, think you?
AUTOLYCUS   Very true, and but a month old.
DORCAS   Bless me from marrying a usurer!
AUTOLYCUS   Here's the midwife's name to't, one Mistress Tail-
260   Porter,[1] and five or six honest° wives' that were present. Why        *truthful; chaste*
   should I carry lies abroad?
MOPSA [*to* CLOWN]   Pray you now, buy it.
CLOWN   Come on, lay it by, and let's first see more ballads. We'll
   buy the other things anon.
265  AUTOLYCUS   Here's another ballad, of a fish that appeared upon
   the coast on Wednesday the fourscore° of April, forty thousand        *eightieth day*
   fathom° above water, and sung this ballad against the hard        *measurement of six feet*
   hearts of maids. It was thought she was a woman, and was
   turned into a cold fish for she would not exchange flesh° with        *have sex*
270   one that loved her. The ballad is very pitiful, and as true.
DORCAS   Is it true too, think you?
AUTOLYCUS   Five justices' hands at it,° and witnesses more than        *signatures on it*
   my pack will hold.
CLOWN   Lay it by, too. Another.
275  AUTOLYCUS   This is a merry ballad, but a very pretty one.
MOPSA   Let's have some merry ones.
AUTOLYCUS   Why, this is a passing° merry one, and goes to the        *very*
   tune of 'Two Maids Wooing a Man'. There's scarce a maid
   westward° but she sings it. 'Tis in request, I can tell you.        *in the west*

---

6. "More" may allude to a pregnancy that will result in
an illegitimate child that she will give to the Clown.
7. That is, "Will they reveal their most private affairs in
public?" There is a pun on "placket," which refers to
both an opening in a petticoat and female genitals.
8. An obscure phrase. The Clown clearly means they
are to be quiet. "To clammer" is a term from bell ringing that means to make the jangling sound characteristic of bells before they grow silent. In F, the phrase is

printed as "clamor your tongues." Many emendations
have been proposed.
9. A cheap, brightly colored scarf associated with St.
Audrey's Fair. St. Audrey was the founder of Ely Cathedral; she died of a throat tumor that she believed was a
punishment for wearing gay neckerchiefs in her youth.
1. The name punningly suggests one who reports gossip ("tales") as well as one who handles genitalia (slang
meaning of "tail").

| | | |
|---|---|---|
| 280 | MOPSA We can both sing it. If thou'lt bear a part² thou shalt<br>hear; 'tis in three parts. | |
| | DORCAS We had the tune on't° a month ago. | *of it* |
| | AUTOLYCUS I can bear my part, you must know, 'tis my occu-<br>pation.° Have at it with you. | *job; act of copulation* |
| | [*They sing*] | |
| 285 | AUTOLYCUS Get you hence, for I must go³ | |
| | Where it fits not you to know. | |
| | DORCAS Whither? | |
| | MOPSA O whither? | |
| | DORCAS Whither? | |
| | MOPSA It becomes thy oath full well | |
| | Thou to me thy secrets tell. | |
| 290 | DORCAS Me too. Let me go thither. | |
| | MOPSA Or thou go'st to th' grange° or mill, | *farm* |
| | DORCAS If to either, thou dost ill. | |
| | AUTOLYCUS Neither. | |
| | DORCAS What neither. | |
| | AUTOLYCUS Neither. | |
| | DORCAS Thou hast sworn my love to be. | |
| 295 | MOPSA Thou hast sworn it more to me. | |
| | Then whither goest? Say, whither? | |
| | CLOWN We'll have this song out anon by ourselves. My father<br>and the gentlemen are in sad° talk, and we'll not trouble them.<br>Come, bring away thy pack after me. Wenches, I'll buy for you | *serious* |
| 300 | both. Pedlar, let's have the first choice. Follow me, girls. | |
| | [*Exit with* DORCAS *and* MOPSA] | |
| | AUTOLYCUS And you shall pay well for 'em. | |
| | [*Sings*] Will you buy any tape, | |
| | Or lace for your cape, | |
| | My dainty duck, my dear-a? | |
| 305 | Any silk, any thread, | |
| | Any toys° for your head, | *small ornaments* |
| | Of the new'st and fin'st, fin'st wear-a? | |
| | Come to the pedlar, | |
| | Money's a meddler, | |
| 310 | That doth utter° all men's ware-a. *Exit* | *put on sale* |
| | [*Enter* SERVANT] | |
| | SERVANT Master, there is three carters,° three shepherds, three | *drivers of carts* |
| | neatherds,° three swineherds that have made themselves all | *keepers of cows* |
| | men of hair.⁴ They call themselves saultiers,° and they have a | *jumpers* |
| | dance which the wenches say is a gallimaufry of gambols,° | *jumble of jumps* |
| 315 | because they are not in't. But they themselves are o'th' mind, | |
| | if it be not too rough for some that know little but bowling,° it | *(a more sedate sport)* |
| | will please plentifully. | |
| | OLD SHEPHERD Away. We'll none on't. Here has been too much | |
| | homely° foolery already. [*To* POLIXENES] I know, sir, we weary | *rough* |
| 320 | you. | |
| | POLIXENES You weary those that° refresh us. Pray, let's see these | *who* |
| | four threes° of herdsmen. | *trios* |
| | SERVANT One three of them, by their own report, sir, hath | |

---

2. Sing a part in the song; play a role (in a sexual
encounter with the two women).
3. F prints "Song" before this line and "Autolycus"
before the next.

4. Probably they have disguised themselves in animal
skins in order to resemble satyrs—mythical woodland
figures, part man, part beast, having the pointed ears,
legs, and short horns of a goat.

|   | danced before the King,[5] and not the worst of the three but | |
| 325 | jumps twelve foot and a half by th' square.° | *exactly* |

OLD SHEPHERD  Leave your prating. Since these good men are
pleased, let them come in—but quickly, now.

SERVANT  Why, they stay at door, sir.

*Here a dance of twelve satyrs*

POLIXENES [*to the* OLD SHEPHERD]  O, father, you'll know more of that hereafter.

330  [*To* CAMILLO] Is it not too far gone? 'Tis time to part them.
He's simple, and tells much.

|   | [*To* FLORIZEL]                      How now, fair shepherd, | |
|   | Your heart is full of something that does take | |
|   | Your mind from feasting. Sooth, when I was young | |
|   | And handed love° as you do, I was wont | *pledged love* |
| 335 | To load my she with knacks.° I would have ransacked | *small gifts; trifles* |
|   | The pedlar's silken treasury, and have poured it | |
|   | To her acceptance.° You have let him go, | *For her to choose* |
|   | And nothing marted° with him. If your lass | *bought from* |
|   | Interpretation should abuse,° and call this | *Should misinterpret* |
| 340 | Your lack of love or bounty, you were straited° | *hard-pressed* |
|   | For a reply, at least if you make a care | |
|   | Of happy holding her.° | *Of keeping her happy* |

FLORIZEL                      Old sir, I know
She prizes not such trifles as these are.

|   | The gifts she looks° from me are packed and locked | *expects* |
| 345 | Up in my heart, which I have given already, | |
|   | But not delivered. | |

|   | [*To* PERDITA]          O, hear me breathe my life° | *make vows of eternal love* |
|   | Before this ancient sir, who, it should seem, | |
|   | Hath sometime loved. I take thy hand, this hand | |
|   | As soft as dove's down, and as white as it, | |
| 350 | Or Ethiopian's tooth, or the fanned snow that's bolted° | *sifted* |
|   | By th' northern blasts twice o'er. | |

POLIXENES                      What follows this?

|   | How prettily the young swain seems to wash | |
|   | The hand was° fair before! I have put you out.° | *that was / interrupted you* |
|   | But to your protestation. Let me hear | |
|   | What you profess. | |

355  FLORIZEL          Do, and be witness to't.

POLIXENES  And this my neighbour too?

FLORIZEL                      And he, and more
Than he; and men, the earth, the heavens, and all,
That were I crowned the most imperial monarch,
Thereof most worthy, were I the fairest youth

| 360 | That ever made eye swerve,° had force and knowledge | *commanded attention* |
|   | More than was ever man's, I would not prize them | |
|   | Without her love; for her employ them all, | |
|   | Commend them and condemn them to her service | |
|   | Or to their own perdition.[6] | |

POLIXENES                      Fairly offered.

CAMILLO  This shows a sound affection.

---

5. This may be a reference to a court performance of Ben Jonson's *Masque of Oberon*, which included a dance of twelve satyrs. It was first put on in January of 1611.

6. Either dedicate my attributes to her service or sentence them to destruction, with a pun on "perdition" and "Perdita."

365 OLD SHEPHERD                  But, my daughter,
    Say you the like to him?
PERDITA                I cannot speak
    So well, nothing so well, no, nor mean better.
    By th' pattern of mine own thoughts I cut out
    The purity of his.[7]
OLD SHEPHERD        Take hands, a bargain;
370     And, friends unknown, you shall bear witness to't.
    I give my daughter to him, and will make
    Her portion° equal his.                         *dowry*
FLORIZEL             O, that must be
    I'th' virtue of your daughter. One° being dead,       *Someone*
    I shall have more than you can dream of yet,
375     Enough then for your wonder. But come on,
    Contract us fore these witnesses.[8]
OLD SHEPHERD            Come, your hand;
    And, daughter, yours.
POLIXENES         Soft,° swain, a while, beseech you.     *Go slowly*
    Have you a father?
FLORIZEL    I have. But what of him?
380 POLIXENES    Knows he of this?
FLORIZEL    He neither does nor shall.
POLIXENES    Methinks a father
    Is at the nuptial of his son a guest
    That best becomes the table. Pray you once more,
385     Is not your father grown incapable
    Of reasonable affairs?[9] Is he not stupid
    With age and alt'ring rheums?° Can he speak, hear,    *debilitating disease*
    Know man from man? Dispute° his own estate?°    *Discuss / condition*
    Lies he not bed-rid, and again does nothing
    But what he did being childish?
390 FLORIZEL                  No, good sir.
    He has his health, and ampler strength indeed
    Than most have of his age.
POLIXENES          By my white beard,
    You offer him, if this be so, a wrong
    Something unfilial.° Reason my son[1]        *Somewhat unbecoming a son*
395     Should choose himself a wife, but as good reason
    The father, all whose joy is nothing else
    But fair posterity, should hold some counsel
    In such a business.
FLORIZEL           I yield° all this;                *grant*
    But for some other reasons, my grave sir,
400     Which 'tis not fit you know, I not acquaint
    My father of this business.
POLIXENES             Let him know't.
FLORIZEL    He shall not.
POLIXENES                Prithee let him.
FLORIZEL                   No, he must not.
OLD SHEPHERD    Let him, my son. He shall not need to grieve
    At knowing of thy choice.

---

7. By my pure thoughts I recognize the purity of his. A
dressmaking metaphor.
8. A pledge of marriage spoken before two witnesses
was legally binding.

9. Unfit to handle matters requiring reason and good
sense.
1. It is reasonable that my son.

FLORIZEL                              Come, come, he must not.
  Mark our contract.
405  POLIXENES [*removing his disguise*]    Mark your divorce, young sir,
  Whom son I dare not call. Thou art too base
  To be acknowledged. Thou a sceptre's heir,
  That thus affects° a sheep-hook?                                    *desires*
  [*To the* OLD SHEPHERD]            Thou, old traitor,
  I am sorry that by hanging thee I can but
  Shorten thy life one week.
410  [*To* PERDITA]                And thou, fresh piece
  Of excellent witchcraft,[2] who of force° must know        *of necessity*
  The royal fool thou cop'st° with—              *you deal; you have sex*
  OLD SHEPHERD                      O, my heart!
  POLIXENES   I'll have thy beauty scratched with briers and made
  More homely than thy state.
  [*To* FLORIZEL]           For thee, fond° boy,                *foolish*
415  If I may ever know thou dost but sigh
  That thou no more shalt see this knack,° as never        *worthless thing*
  I mean thou shalt, we'll bar thee from succession,
  Not hold thee of our blood, no, not our kin,
  Farre than Deucalion off.[3] Mark thou my words.
  Follow us to the court.
420  [*To the* OLD SHEPHERD]    Thou churl, for this time,
  Though full of our displeasure, yet we free thee
  From the dead° blow of it.                                         *deadly*
  [*To* PERDITA]            And you, enchantment,
  Worthy enough a herdsman—yea, him° too,               *(Florizel)*
  That makes himself, but for our honour therein,
425  Unworthy thee[4]—if ever henceforth thou
  These rural latches to his entrance open,
  Or hoop° his body more with thy embraces,                 *encircle*
  I will devise a death as cruel for thee
  As thou art tender to't.              *Exit*
  PERDITA                   Even here undone.
430  I was not much afeard, for once or twice
  I was about to speak, and tell him plainly
  The selfsame sun that shines upon his court
  Hides not his visage from our cottage, but
  Looks on alike.° Will't please you, sir, be gone?          *both alike*
435  I told you what would come of this. Beseech you,
  Of your own state take care. This dream of mine
  Being now awake, I'll queen it no inch farther,°  *play the queen no further*
  But milk my ewes and weep.
  CAMILLO [*to the* OLD SHEPHERD]   Why, how now, father?
  Speak ere thou diest.
  OLD SHEPHERD           I cannot speak, nor think,
  Nor dare to know that which I know.
440  [*To* FLORIZEL]                    O sir,
  You have undone a man of fourscore-three,°       *eighty-three*

---

2. You beautiful young woman skilled in witchcraft.
Some people believed that witches could induce love by
potions.
3. Less linked in kinship than Deucalion, who according to classical mythology was, along with his wife, the
only person to escape a flood sent by Zeus. He thus was
the ancestor of humankind and the most distant rela-

tion one might have.
4. A difficult passage. Polixenes seems to mean that
Florizel, by his actions, has made himself unworthy of
even a shepherd's daughter were it not for the fact that
he is a King's son and so would harm his father's honor
by such a marriage.

That thought to fill his grave in quiet, yea,
To die upon the bed my father died,
To lie close by his honest bones. But now
445 Some hangman must put on my shroud, and lay me
Where no priest shovels in dust.[5]
[*To* PERDITA]                    O cursed wretch,
That knew'st this was the Prince, and wouldst adventure
To mingle faith° with him. Undone, undone!          *exchange vows*
If I might die within this hour, I have lived
To die when I desire.                              *Exit*
450 FLORIZEL [*to* PERDITA]    Why look you so upon me?
I am but sorry, not afeard; delayed,
But nothing altered. What I was, I am,
More straining on for plucking back,[6] not following
My leash unwillingly.[7]
CAMILLO                    Gracious my lord,
455 You know your father's temper. At this time
He will allow no speech—which I do guess
You do not purpose° to him; and as hardly°    *intend / unwillingly*
Will he endure your sight as yet, I fear.
Then till the fury of his highness settle,
Come not before him.
460 FLORIZEL                    I not purpose it.
I think, Camillo?[8]
CAMILLO                    Even he, my lord.
PERDITA [*to* FLORIZEL]    How often have I told you 'twould be thus?
How often said my dignity would last
But° till 'twere known?                              *Only*
FLORIZEL                    It cannot fail but by
465 The violation of my faith, and then
Let nature crush the sides o'th' earth together
And mar the seeds° within. Lift up thy looks.      *sources of life*
From my succession wipe me, father! I
Am heir to my affection.
CAMILLO                    Be advised.°                  *prudent*
470 FLORIZEL    I am, and by my fancy.° If my reason          *love*
Will thereto be obedient, I have reason.[9]
If not, my senses, better pleased with madness,
Do bid it° welcome.                              *(madness)*
CAMILLO                    This is desperate, sir.
FLORIZEL    So call it. But it does fulfil my vow.
475 I needs must think it honesty. Camillo,
Not for Bohemia, nor the pomp that may
Be thereat gleaned; for all the sun sees, or
The close° earth wombs,° or the profound seas hides    *secret / holds in her womb*
In unknown fathoms, will I break my oath
480 To this my fair beloved. Therefore, I pray you,
As you have ever been my father's honoured friend,
When he shall miss me—as, in faith, I mean not
To see him any more—cast your good counsels

5. As a criminal, he would be buried without ritual
under the gallows. In regular funeral rites, the priest customarily placed the first shovelful of dirt on the grave.
6. More eager to go forward because of being pulled
back.

7. Not following this course of action unwillingly (like
a dog dragged by its leash).
8. Camillo may here have taken off his disguise or been
recognized by Florizel even with it on.
9. If my reason will obey love, I will embrace reason.

Upon his passion.° Let myself and fortune           *anger*
485    Tug° for the time to come. This you may know,     *Contend*
And so deliver:° I am put to sea                *report*
With her who here I cannot hold on shore;
And most opportune to her need, I have
A vessel rides fast by,° but not prepared     *anchored nearby*
490    For this design. What course I mean to hold
Shall nothing benefit your knowledge, nor
Concern me the reporting.[1]

CAMILLO                    O my lord,
I would your spirit were easier for advice,°     *to advise*
Or stronger for your need.

FLORIZEL                 Hark, Perdita—
[*To* CAMILLO] I'll hear you by and by.

495    CAMILLO [*aside*]              He's irremovable,°     *unyielding*
Resolved for flight. Now were I happy if
His going I could frame to serve my turn,
Save him from danger, do him love and honour,
Purchase the sight again of dear Sicilia
500    And that unhappy king, my master, whom
I so much thirst to see.

FLORIZEL              Now, good Camillo,
I am so fraught with curious business° that     *matters requiring care*
I leave out ceremony.

CAMILLO            Sir, I think
You have heard of my poor services i'th' love
That I have borne your father?

505    FLORIZEL               Very nobly
Have you deserved. It is my father's music
To speak your deeds, not little of his care
To have them recompensed as thought on.[2]

CAMILLO                    Well, my lord,
If you may please to think I love the King,
510    And through him what's nearest to him, which is
Your gracious self, embrace but my direction,°     *simply follow my advice*
If your more ponderous° and settled project     *weighty*
May suffer° alteration. On mine honour,     *permit*
I'll point you where you shall have such receiving
515    As shall become your highness, where you may
Enjoy your mistress—from the whom I see
There's no disjunction° to be made but by,     *separation*
As heavens forfend,° your ruin—marry her,     *forbid*
And with my best endeavours in your absence
520    Your discontenting° father strive to qualify°     *discontented / appease*
And bring him up to liking.°                  *to giving approval*

FLORIZEL              How, Camillo,
May this, almost a miracle, be done?—
That I may call thee something more than man,
And after that trust to thee.

CAMILLO              Have you thought on°     *of*
A place whereto you'll go?

525    FLORIZEL              Not any yet.

---

1. Would not benefit you to know nor me to report.
2. And no small matter among his affairs to reward your deeds as fully as he values them.

But as th'unthought-on accident is guilty
To what we wildly do,[3] so we profess
Ourselves to be the slaves of chance, and flies
Of every wind that blows.[4]

CAMILLO                                    Then list to me.
530  This follows, if you will not change your purpose
But undergo this flight: make for Sicilia,
And there present yourself and your fair princess,
For so I see she must be, fore Leontes.
She shall be habited° as it becomes                          *dressed*
535  The partner of your bed. Methinks I see
Leontes opening his free° arms and weeping                   *generous*
His welcomes forth; asks thee there 'Son, forgiveness!'
As 'twere i'th' father's person,[5] kisses the hands
Of your fresh princess; o'er and o'er divides him
540  'Twixt his unkindness and his kindness.[6] Th'one
He chides° to hell, and bids the other grow                  *rebukes*
Faster than thought or time.

FLORIZEL                              Worthy Camillo,
What colour° for my visitation shall I                       *pretext*
Hold up before him?

CAMILLO                        Sent by the King your father
545  To greet him, and to give him comforts. Sir,
The manner of your bearing towards him, with
What you, as from your father, shall deliver—°              *say*
Things known betwixt us three—I'll write you down,
The which shall point you forth° at every sitting           *direct you*
550  What you must say, that he shall not perceive
But that you have your father's bosom° there,               *trust*
And speak his very heart.

FLORIZEL                      I am bound to you.
There is some sap° in this.                                  *life*

CAMILLO                        A course more promising
Than a wild dedication of yourselves
555  To unpathed waters, undreamed shores; most certain,
To miseries enough—no hope to help you,
But as you shake off one, to take another;
Nothing so certain° as your anchors, who        *certain (to detain you)*
Do their best office if they can but stay° you              *keep*
560  Where you'll be loath to be. Besides, you know,
Prosperity's the very bond of love,
Whose fresh complexion and whose heart together
Affliction alters.°                              *changes for the worse*

PERDITA                One of these is true.
I think affliction may subdue the cheek°            *make one pale*
But not take in° the mind.                                   *conquer*
565  CAMILLO                        Yea, say you so?
There shall not at your father's house these seven years[7]
Be born another such.

FLORIZEL            My good Camillo,

---

3. But as the unexpected event (Polixenes' discovery of our love) is responsible for our rash behavior now.
4. And like flies blown about by the winds.
5. As if he were your father; *or* as if you were your father.

6. That is, he divides his speech between his past unkindness to your father and the kindness he is eager to perform now.
7. Proverbial expression meaning "for a long time."

She's as forward of her breeding as
She is i'th' rear our birth.[8]

CAMILLO                    I cannot say 'tis pity
570    She lacks instructions,° for she seems a mistress°          *schooling / teacher*
To most that teach.

PERDITA                    Your pardon, sir. For this
I'll blush you thanks.

FLORIZEL                    My prettiest Perdita!
But O, the thorns we stand upon! Camillo,
Preserver of my father, now of me,
575    The medicine of our house, how shall we do?
We are not furnished° like Bohemia's son,          *dressed; equipped*
Nor shall appear so in Sicilia.

CAMILLO    My lord,
Fear none of this. I think you know my fortunes
580    Do all lie there. It shall be so my care
To have you royally appointed° as if          *outfitted*
The scene you play were mine.° For instance, sir,          *written by me*
That you may know you shall not want—one word.

[*They speak apart.*]
*Enter* AUTOLYCUS

AUTOLYCUS    Ha, ha! What a fool honesty is, and trust—his sworn
585    brother—a very simple gentleman! I have sold all my trumpery;
not a counterfeit stone, not a ribbon, glass, pomander,[9] brooch,
table-book,° ballad, knife, tape, glove, shoe-tie, bracelet, horn-          *notebook*
ring[1] to keep my pack from fasting.° They throng who should          *from going empty*
buy first, as if my trinkets had been hallowed,° and brought a          *blessed; made sacred*
590    benediction to the buyer; by which means I saw whose purse
was best in picture;° and what I saw, to my good use I remem-          *looked best (to steal)*
bered. My clown, who wants but something° to be a reasonable          *lacks only one thing*
man, grew so in love with the wenches' song that he would not
stir his pettitoes° till he had both tune and words, which so          *feet (pigs' toes)*
595    drew the rest of the herd to me that all their other senses stuck
in ears.° You might have pinched a placket, it was sense-          *were devoted to hearing*
less.° 'Twas nothing to geld a codpiece of a purse.[2] I could have          *felt nothing*
filed keys off that hung in chains. No hearing, no feeling but
my sir's song, and admiring the nothing of it.[3] So that in this
600    time of lethargy I picked and cut most of their festival purses,
and had not the old man come in with a hubbub against his
daughter and the King's son, and scared my choughs° from the          *jackdaws (silly birds)*
chaff, I had not left a purse alive in the whole army.

[CAMILLO, FLORIZEL, *and* PERDITA *come forward*]

CAMILLO    Nay, but my letters by this means being there
605    So soon as you arrive shall clear that doubt.

FLORIZEL    And those that you'll procure from King Leontes—

CAMILLO    Shall satisfy your father.

PERDITA                    Happy be you!
All that you speak shows fair.

CAMILLO [*seeing* AUTOLYCUS]    Who have we here?

---

8. That is, "She is as superior to her lowly upbringing
as she is inferior to our noble birth."
9. A mixture of sweet-smelling substances made into a
ball and carried about for ornament or to prevent infection.
1. A ring made from horn, which was said to possess

magical qualities.
2. It was easy to cut a purse loose from a codpiece, the
baglike article of dress attached to the front of a man's
hose and covering his genitals.
3. The silliness of it, with a pun on "nothing" and "noting" (meaning "tune"), which were similarly pronounced.

We'll make an instrument of this, omit

610   Nothing° may give us aid.                                   *Nothing that*

AUTOLYCUS [*aside*]   If they have overheard me now—why,
      hanging!

CAMILLO   How now, good fellow? Why shakest thou so? Fear
      not, man. Here's no harm intended to thee.

615   AUTOLYCUS   I am a poor fellow, sir.

CAMILLO   Why, be so still.° Here's nobody will steal that from        *always*
      thee. Yet for the outside of thy poverty,° we must make an    *your ragged clothes*
      exchange. Therefore discase° thee instantly— thou must think     *undress*
      there's a necessity in't—and change garments with this gentle-

620   man. Though the pennyworth° on his side be the worst, yet        *bargain*
      hold thee, [*giving him money*] there's some boot.°          *something more*

AUTOLYCUS   I am a poor fellow, sir. [*Aside*] I know ye well
      enough.

CAMILLO   Nay prithee, dispatch°—the gentleman is half flayed[4]        *hurry*

625   already.

AUTOLYCUS   Are you in earnest,[5] sir? [*Aside*] I smell the trick on't.

FLORIZEL   Dispatch, I prithee.

AUTOLYCUS   Indeed, I have had earnest, but I cannot with con-
      science take it.

630   CAMILLO   Unbuckle, unbuckle.

      [FLORIZEL *and* AUTOLYCUS *exchange clothes*]

      [*To* PERDITA] Fortunate mistress—let my prophecy
      Come home to ye![6]—you must retire yourself
      Into some covert,° take your sweetheart's hat               *hiding place*
      And pluck it o'er your brows, muffle your face,

635   Dismantle you,° and, as you can, disliken°            *Take off your cloak / disguise*
      The truth of your own seeming,° that you may—                  *appearance*
      For I do fear eyes°—over to shipboard                            *spies*
      Get undescried.

PERDITA                     I see the play so lies
      That I must bear a part.

CAMILLO                           No remedy.

      [*To* FLORIZEL] Have you done there?

640   FLORIZEL                                 Should I now meet my father
      He would not call me son.

CAMILLO                           Nay, you shall have no hat.

      [*He gives the hat to* PERDITA]
      Come, lady, come. Farewell, my friend.

AUTOLYCUS                                 Adieu, sir.

FLORIZEL   O Perdita, what have we twain forgot!
      Pray you, a word.

      [*They speak aside*]

645   CAMILLO [*aside*]   What I do next shall be to tell the King
      Of this escape, and whither they are bound;
      Wherein my hope is I shall so prevail
      To force him after, in whose company
      I shall re-view Sicilia, for whose sight
      I have a woman's longing.[7]

---

4. Half undressed (skinned).

5. "Serious," with a pun on "earnest" as meaning both
"sincere" and "an advance payment." See line 628.

6. Let my prophecy (that she be fortunate) be fulfilled.

7. Women, especially pregnant women, were said to be
vulnerable to irrational and very intense cravings.

650 FLORIZEL                    Fortune speed us!
     Thus we set on, Camillo, to th' seaside.
   CAMILLO   The swifter speed the better.
                    *Exeunt* [FLORIZEL, PERDITA, *and* CAMILLO][8]
   AUTOLYCUS   I understand the business, I hear it. To have an open
     ear, a quick eye, and a nimble hand is necessary for a cutpurse.
655  A good nose is requisite also, to smell out work for th'other
     senses. I see this is the time that the unjust man doth thrive.
     What an exchange had this been without boot!° What a boot[9]            even without payment
     is here with this exchange! Sure the gods do this year connive
     at° us, and we may do anything extempore.° The Prince him-            indulge / spontaneously
660  self is about a piece of iniquity, stealing away from his father
     with his clog° at his heels. If I thought it were a piece of honesty      encumbrance (Perdita)
     to acquaint the King withal,° I would not do't. I hold it the                with it
     more knavery to conceal it, and therein am I constant° to my                faithful
     profession.
                    *Enter* [*the*] CLOWN *and* [*the* OLD] SHEPHERD[, *carrying a*
                    *fardel*° *and a box*]                                         bundle
665  Aside, aside! Here is more matter for a hot brain. Every lane's
     end, every shop, church, session,° hanging, yields a careful            court session
     man work.
   CLOWN   See, see, what a man you are now! There is no other
     way but to tell the King she's a changeling,[1] and none of your
670  flesh and blood.
   OLD SHEPHERD   Nay, but hear me.
   CLOWN   Nay, but hear *me*.
   OLD SHEPHERD   Go to,° then.                                                  Go ahead
   CLOWN   She being none of your flesh and blood, your flesh and
675  blood has not offended the King, and so your flesh and blood
     is not to be punished by him. Show those things you found
     about her, those secret things, all but what she has with her.
     This being done, let the law go whistle, I warrant you.
   OLD SHEPHERD   I will tell the King all, every word, yea, and his
680  son's pranks, too, who, I may say, is no honest man, neither to
     his father nor to me, to go about to make me the King's brother-
     in-law.
   CLOWN   Indeed, brother-in-law was the farthest off° you could         most remote relation
     have been to him, and then your blood had been the dearer by
685  I know not how much an ounce.
   AUTOLYCUS [*aside*]   Very wisely, puppies.
   OLD SHEPHERD   Well, let us to the King. There is that in this
     fardel will make him scratch his beard.
   AUTOLYCUS [*aside*]   I know not what impediment this complaint
690  may be to the flight of my master.°                                         (Florizel)
   CLOWN   Pray heartily he be at'° palace.                                       at the
   AUTOLYCUS [*aside*]   Though I am not naturally honest, I am so
     sometimes by chance. Let me pocket up my pedlar's excre-
     ment.°                                                                        hair
                    [*He removes his false beard*]
695  —How now, rustics, whither are you bound?
   OLD SHEPHERD   To th' palace, an° it like your worship.                         if

---

8. F marks a single *"Exit"* here for Camillo, but Florizel    9. Benefit; shoe.
and Perdita undoubtedly exit also, leaving Autolycus       1. A child left or abducted by fairies. See note to
alone on stage to comment on what he has witnessed.       3.3.109.

AUTOLYCUS   Your affairs there? What? With whom? The condi-
tion of that fardel?° The place of your dwelling? Your names?     *nature of that bundle*
Your ages? Of what having,° breeding,° and anything that is     *property / upbringing*
700    fitting to be known, discover.°     *reveal*
CLOWN   We are but plain° fellows, sir.     *simple; smooth*
AUTOLYCUS   A lie, you are rough and hairy. Let me have no
lying. It becomes none but tradesmen, and they often give us
soldiers the lie,[2] but we pay them for it with stamped coin, not
705    stabbing steel, therefore they do not *give* us the lie.[3]
CLOWN   Your worship had like to have given us one° if you had     *(the lie)*
not taken yourself with the manner.[4]
OLD SHEPHERD   Are you a courtier, an't like you, sir?
AUTOLYCUS   Whether it like me or no, I am a courtier. Seest thou
710    not the air of the court in these enfoldings?° Hath not my gait     *garments*
in it the measure° of the court? Receives not thy nose court     *stately walk*
odour from me? Reflect I not on thy baseness court-contempt?
Thinkest thou, for that I insinuate° to toze° from thee thy busi-     *subtly work / tease out*
ness, I am therefore no courtier? I am courtier cap-à-pie,° and     *from head to foot*
715    one that will either push on or pluck back thy business there.
Whereupon I command thee to open° thy affair.     *reveal*
OLD SHEPHERD   My business, sir, is to the King.
AUTOLYCUS   What advocate hast thou to him?
OLD SHEPHERD   I know not, an't like you.
720    CLOWN [*aside to the* OLD SHEPHERD]   'Advocate' 's the court
word for a pheasant.[5] Say you have none.
OLD SHEPHERD   None, sir. I have no pheasant, cock nor hen.
AUTOLYCUS [*aside*]   How blessed are we that are not simple men!
Yet nature might have made me as these are,
725    Therefore I will not disdain.
CLOWN   This cannot be but° a great courtier.     *anyone but*
OLD SHEPHERD   His garments are rich, but he wears them not
handsomely.
CLOWN   He seems to be the more noble in being fantastical.° A     *eccentric*
730    great man, I'll warrant. I know by the picking on's teeth.[6]
AUTOLYCUS   The fardel there, what's i'th' fardel? Wherefore that
box?
OLD SHEPHERD   Sir, there lies such secrets in this fardel and box
which none must know but the King, and which he shall know
735    within this hour, if I may come to th' speech of him.
AUTOLYCUS   Age,° thou hast lost thy labour.     *Old man*
OLD SHEPHERD   Why, sir?
AUTOLYCUS   The King is not at the palace, he is gone aboard a
new ship to purge° melancholy and air himself; for if thou     *rid himself of*
740    beest capable of° things serious, thou must know the King is     *can understand*
full of grief.
OLD SHEPHERD   So 'tis said, sir; about his son, that should have
married a shepherd's daughter.
AUTOLYCUS   If that shepherd be not in handfast,° let him fly. The     *arrested*

---

2. They call us soldiers liars; they cheat us soldiers.
3. Punning on "give the lie" as meaning both "cheat"
and "insult me in a way that requires a challenge to a
duel." The point seems to be that since soldiers pay
with good currency rather than by stabbing (the appropriate response to an insult), vendors can't claim to
have given anything—including the lie—to anyone, and
a duel can be successfully avoided.

4. If you had not stopped yourself in the middle.
5. The Clown thinks "advocate" means "bribe" or
"gift," of which a pheasant would be an example. He is
confusing the King's court with a law court in which
game birds were supposedly given as bribes to local
magistrates.
6. Ornate toothpicks were considered fashionable
accessories.

745    curses he shall have, the tortures he shall feel, will break the
       back of man, the heart of monster.
       CLOWN   Think you so, sir?
       AUTOLYCUS   Not he alone shall suffer what wit can make heavy
       and vengeance bitter, but those that are germane° to him,                    *related*
750    though removed fifty times, shall all come under the hangman,
       which, though it be great pity, yet it is necessary. An old sheep-
       whistling rogue,[7] a ram-tender, to offer to have his daughter
       come into grace!° Some say he shall be stoned; but that death            *favor (at court)*
       is too soft for him, say I. Draw our throne into a sheepcote?°             *pen for sheep*
755    All deaths are too few, the sharpest too easy.
       CLOWN   Has the old man e'er a son, sir, do you hear, an't like
       you, sir?
       AUTOLYCUS   He has a son, who shall be flayed alive, then
       'nointed over with honey, set on the head of a wasps' nest, then
760    stand till he be three-quarters-and-a-dram° dead, then recov-             *a tiny bit*
       ered again with aqua-vitae,° or some other hot infusion, then,               *brandy*
       raw as he is, and in the hottest day prognostication° proclaims,    *almanac prediction*
       shall he be set against a brick wall, the sun looking with a
       southward eye upon him, where he is to behold him with flies
765    blown° to death. But what talk we of these traitorly rascals,              *swollen*
       whose miseries are to be smiled at, their offences being so
       capital? Tell me, for you seem to be honest plain men, what
       you have° to the King. Being something gently considered,[8] I'll       *have to say*
       bring you where he is aboard, tender° your persons to his pres-            *deliver*
770    ence, whisper him in your behalfs, and if it be in man, besides
       the King, to effect your suits, here is man shall do it.
       CLOWN [to the OLD SHEPHERD]   He seems to be of great author-
       ity. Close° with him, give him gold; and though authority be a           *Make a deal*
       stubborn bear, yet he is oft led by the nose with gold. Show the
775    inside of your purse to the outside of his hand, and no more
       ado. Remember—'stoned', and 'flayed alive'.
       OLD SHEPHERD   An't please you, sir, to undertake the business
       for us, here is that° gold I have. I'll make it as much more, and          *what*
       leave this young man in pawn° till I bring it you.                       *as security*
780    AUTOLYCUS   After I have done what I promised?
       OLD SHEPHERD   Ay, sir.
       AUTOLYCUS   Well, give me the moiety.° [To the CLOWN] Are you              *half*
       a party in this business?
       CLOWN   In some sort, sir. But though my case° be a pitiful one,      *condition; skin*
785    I hope I shall not be flayed out of it.
       AUTOLYCUS   O, that's the case of the shepherd's son. Hang him,
       he'll be made an example.
       CLOWN [to the OLD SHEPHERD]   Comfort, good comfort. We
       must to the King, and show our strange sights. He must
790    know 'tis none of your daughter, nor my sister. We are gone°            *lost (dead)*
       else.° [To AUTOLYCUS] Sir, I will give you as much as this old          *otherwise*
       man does when the business is performed, and remain, as he
       says, your pawn till it be brought you.
       AUTOLYCUS   I will trust you. Walk before° toward the seaside. Go      *ahead of me*
795    on the right hand. I will but look upon the hedge,[9] and follow
       you.

       7. An old rascal who whistles while he tends sheep.     will give me a bribe worthy of my high rank.
       8. As I am a highly regarded gentleman at court; if you   9. Slang for "relieve myself."

CLOWN [*to the* OLD SHEPHERD]   We are blessed in this man, as I
    may say, even blessed.
OLD SHEPHERD   Let's before, as he bids us. He was provided to
800    do us good.                            [*Exit with the* CLOWN]
AUTOLYCUS   If I had a mind to be honest, I see fortune would
    not suffer° me. She drops booties° in my mouth. I am courted      *permit / prizes*
    now with a double occasion:° gold, and a means to do the      *opportunity*
    Prince my master good, which who knows how that may turn
805    back to my advancement? I will bring these two moles, these
    blind ones, aboard him.° If he think it fit to shore them[1] again,      *(his ship)*
    and that the complaint they have to the King concerns him
    nothing, let him call me rogue for being so far officious, for I
    am proof against° that title, and what shame else belongs to't.      *impervious to*
810    To him will I present them. There may be matter in it.    *Exit*

## 5.1

*Enter* LEONTES, CLEOMENES, DION, [*and*] PAULINA
CLEOMENES [*to* LEONTES]   Sir, you have done enough, and have performed
    A saint-like sorrow. No fault could you make
    Which you have not redeemed, indeed, paid down
    More penitence than done trespass.[1] At the last
5    Do as the heavens have done, forget your evil.
    With them, forgive yourself.
LEONTES                 Whilst I remember
    Her and her virtues I cannot forget
    My blemishes in them,° and so still think of      *in relation to them*
    The wrong I did myself, which was so much
10    That heirless it hath made my kingdom, and
    Destroyed the sweet'st companion that e'er man
    Bred his hopes out of. True?
PAULINA                Too true, my lord.
    If one by one you wedded all the world,
    Or from the all that are took something good
15    To make a perfect woman, she you killed
    Would be unparalleled.
LEONTES           I think so. Killed?
    She I killed? I did so. But thou strik'st me
    Sorely to say I did; it is as bitter
    Upon thy tongue as in my thought. Now, good now,°      *if you would*
    Say so but seldom.
20 CLEOMENES        Not at all,° good lady.      *Never (say these things)*
    You might have spoke a thousand things that would
    Have done the time more benefit,[2] and graced°      *showed*
    Your kindness better.
PAULINA          You are one of those
    Would have him wed again.
DION              If you would not so
25    You pity not the state,° nor the remembrance      *kingdom*
    Of his most sovereign name,[3] consider little
    What dangers, by his highness' fail of issue,°      *lack of offspring*
    May drop upon his kingdom and devour

---

1. Put them ashore.                       2. That would have been more useful in these times.
5.1 Location: Sicilia. The palace of Leontes.     3. Nor the perpetuation of his royal lineage (through a
1. Performed more penance than your sin warranted.    new child).

Incertain lookers-on.⁴ What were more holy
30    Than to rejoice the former queen is well?°                    *(in heaven)*
What holier, than for royalty's repair,
For present comfort and for future good,
To bless the bed of majesty again
With a sweet fellow to't?
PAULINA                                    There is none worthy
35    Respecting° her that's gone. Besides, the gods              *In comparison to*
Will have fulfilled their secret purposes.⁵
For has not the divine Apollo said?
Is't not the tenor of his oracle
That King Leontes shall not have an heir
40    Till his lost child be found? Which that it shall
Is all as monstrous° to our human reason                         *incredible*
As my Antigonus to break his grave
And come again to me, who, on my life,
Did perish with the infant. 'Tis your counsel
45    My lord should to the heavens be contrary,
Oppose against their wills.
[*To* LEONTES]                          Care not for issue.
The crown will find an heir. Great Alexander
Left his to th' worthiest,⁶ so his successor
Was like to be the best.
LEONTES                                    Good Paulina,
50    Who hast the memory of Hermione,
I know, in honour—O, that ever I
Had squared me° to thy counsel! Then even now                *conformed my actions*
I might have looked upon my queen's full eyes,
Have taken treasure from her lips.
PAULINA                                    And left them
More rich for what they yielded.
55  LEONTES                                    Thou speak'st truth.
No more such wives, therefore no wife. One worse,
And better used,° would make her sainted spirit               *treated*
Again possess her° corpse, and on this stage,                 *(Hermione's)*
Where we offenders mourn, appear soul-vexed,°                *with troubled soul*
And begin, 'Why° to me?'                                      *Why offer this insult*
60  PAULINA                                    Had she such power
She had just cause.
LEONTES                          She had, and would incense me
To murder her I married.
PAULINA                                    I should so.
Were I the ghost that walked I'd bid you mark
Her eye, and tell me for what dull part in't
65    You chose her. Then I'd shriek that even your ears
Should rift° to hear me, and the words that followed          *split*
Should be, 'Remember mine'.°                                  *(my eyes)*
LEONTES                                    Stars, stars,
And all eyes else,° dead coals! Fear thou no wife.            *all other eyes*
I'll have no wife, Paulina.

---

4. And destroy those subjects who are bewildered (by the matter of his successor).
5. Will ensure that their secret purposes are fulfilled.
6. Alexander the Great (356–323 B.C.E.), conqueror of Greece, Persia, and Egypt, died before his own son was born and reportedly urged his followers simply to choose the worthiest man as his successor.

PAULINA                         Will you swear
70    Never to marry but by my free leave?

LEONTES    Never, Paulina, so be blest my spirit.

PAULINA    Then, good my lords, bear witness to his oath.

CLEOMENES    You tempt him over-much.

PAULINA                     Unless another
   As like Hermione as is her picture
   Affront° his eye—                                        *Confront*
75 CLEOMENES                Good madam, I have done.[7]

PAULINA    Yet if my lord will marry—if you will, sir;
   No remedy but you will—give me the office
   To choose your queen. She shall not be so young
   As was your former, but she shall be such
80    As, walked your first queen's ghost,[8] it should take joy
   To see her in your arms.

LEONTES                   My true Paulina,
   We shall not marry till thou bidd'st us.

PAULINA                       That
   Shall be when your first queen's again in breath.°         *alive*
   Never till then.

      *Enter a* SERVANT

85 SERVANT    One that gives out himself° Prince Florizel,      *claims to be*
   Son of Polixenes, with his princess—she
   The fairest I have yet beheld—desires access
   To your high presence.

LEONTES               What° with him? He comes not    *Who comes*
   Like to° his father's greatness. His approach,           *As befits*
90    So out of circumstance° and sudden, tells us        *informal*
   'Tis not a visitation framed,° but forced             *planned*
   By need and accident. What train?°                *retinue*

SERVANT                   But few,
   And those but mean.°                              *of low rank*

LEONTES              His princess, say you, with him?

SERVANT    Ay, the most peerless piece of earth, I think,
   That e'er the sun shone bright on.

95 PAULINA                O, Hermione,
   As every present time doth boast itself
   Above a better, gone, so must thy grave
   Give way to what's seen now![9]
   [*To the* SERVANT]           Sir, you yourself
   Have said and writ so; but your writing now
100    Is colder than that theme. She had not been
   Nor was not to be equalled—thus your verse
   Flowed with her beauty once. 'Tis shrewdly° ebbed     *grievously*
   To say you have seen a better.

SERVANT               Pardon, madam.
   The one° I have almost forgot—your pardon!        *(Hermione)*
105    The other, when she has obtained your eye,
   Will have your tongue too. This is a creature,

---

7. Many editors emend this line to assign "I have done"
to Paulina, rather than Cleomenes. As it stands, the
line suggests Cleomenes' exasperation that Paulina will not
listen to him. If emended to assign the last three words to
Paulina, the exchange may suggest that Paulina is at least
minimally responsive to the pleas of Leontes' courtiers
that she mitigate her opposition to his remarriage.
8. If Hermione appeared as a ghost.
9. As each present time boasts itself to be superior to a
time better than itself, but gone from view, so you, in
your grave, must be superseded by what is now seen.

Would she begin a sect, might quench the zeal
Of all professors else;[1] make proselytes°                          *converts*
Of who° she but bid follow.                                          *Of those who*

PAULINA                          How? Not women!

110   SERVANT   Women will love her that she is a woman
More worth° than any man; men, that she is                           *worthy*
The rarest of all women.

LEONTES                          Go, Cleomenes.
Yourself, assisted with your honoured friends,
Bring them to our embracement.          *Exit* [CLEOMENES]
                          Still 'tis strange
He thus should steal upon us.

115   PAULINA                          Had our prince,
Jewel of children, seen this hour, he had paired
Well with this lord. There was not full a month°                     *a full month*
Between their births.

LEONTES                          Prithee no more, cease. Thou know'st
He dies to me again when talked of. Sure,

120   When I shall see this gentleman thy speeches
Will bring me to consider that which may
Unfurnish me of reason.° They are come.                              *Make me go mad*

          *Enter* FLORIZEL, PERDITA, CLEOMENES, *and others*
Your mother was most true to wedlock, Prince,
For she did print your royal father off,[2]

125   Conceiving you. Were I but twenty-one,
Your father's image is so hit° in you,                               *exact*
His very air, that I should call you brother,
As I did him, and speak of something wildly
By us performed before. Most dearly welcome,

130   And your fair princess—goddess! O, alas,
I lost a couple that 'twixt heaven and earth
Might thus have stood, begetting wonder, as
You, gracious couple, do; and then I lost—
All mine own folly—the society,

135   Amity too, of your brave° father, whom,                           *stouthearted*
Though bearing misery, I desire my life[3]
Once more to look on him.

FLORIZEL                          By his command
Have I here touched Sicilia, and from him
Give you all greetings that a king at friend°                        *in friendship*

140   Can send his brother; and but° infirmity,                          *were it not that*
Which waits upon worn times,° hath something seized                  *accompanies old age*
His wished ability,[4] he had himself
The lands and waters 'twixt your throne and his
Measured° to look upon you, whom he loves—                           *Journeyed across*

145   He bade me say so—more than all the sceptres,
And those that bear them, living.

LEONTES                          O, my brother!
Good gentleman, the wrongs I have done thee stir
Afresh within me, and these thy offices,°                            *greetings*
So rarely° kind, are as interpreters                                 *extraordinarily*

---

1. Of all those who professed other religions.          3. Whom, though I am suffering, I wish to live long
2. Made an exact copy of Polixenes, as a printer pro-    enough.
duces a book.                                           4. Has somewhat deprived him of his desired strength.

150     Of my behindhand slackness.[5] Welcome hither,
    As is the spring to th'earth! And hath he too
    Exposed this paragon to th' fearful usage—
    At least ungentle—of the dreadful Neptune°             *god of the sea*
    To greet a man not worth her pains, much less
    Th'adventure° of her person?                              *risk*
155  FLORIZEL                     Good my lord,
    She came from Libya.
  LEONTES               Where the warlike Smalus,[6]
    That noble honoured lord, is feared and loved?
  FLORIZEL   Most royal sir, from thence; from him whose daughter
    His tears proclaimed his, parting with her. Thence,
160     A prosperous south wind friendly, we have crossed,
    To execute the charge my father gave me
    For visiting your highness. My best train
    I have from your Sicilian shores dismissed;
    Who for Bohemia bend,° to signify                 *make their way*
165     Not only my success in Libya, sir,
    But my arrival, and my wife's, in safety
    Here where we are.
  LEONTES              The blessèd gods
    Purge all infection from our air whilst you
    Do climate° here! You have a holy father,          *reside*
170     A graceful gentleman, against whose person,
    So sacred as it is, I have done sin,
    For which the heavens, taking angry note,
    Have left me issueless; and your father's blessed,
    As he from heaven merits it, with you,
175     Worthy his goodness. What might I have been,
    Might I a son and daughter now have looked on,
    Such goodly things as you?
          *Enter a* LORD
  LORD                   Most noble sir,
    That which I shall report will bear no credit
    Were not the proof so nigh. Please you, great sir,
180     Bohemia greets you from himself by me;
    Desires you to attach° his son, who has,           *arrest*
    His dignity and duty[7] both cast off,
    Fled from his father, from his hopes, and with
    A shepherd's daughter.
  LEONTES            Where's Bohemia? Speak.
185  LORD   Here in your city. I now came from him.
    I speak amazedly,° and it becomes°       *confusedly / befits*
    My marvel° and my message. To your court     *astonishment*
    Whiles he was hast'ning—in the chase, it seems,
    Of this fair couple—meets he on the way
190     The father of this seeming° lady and      *apparent; false*
    Her brother, having both their country quitted
    With this young prince.
  FLORIZEL          Camillo has betrayed me,

---

5. Are reminders of my slowness (in greeting you).     Plutarch.
6. An obscure allusion. The name may be a misprint    7. His royal status and his duty to his father.
for "Synalus," a soldier from Carthage mentioned by

Whose honour and whose honesty till now
Endured all weathers.
LORD                    Lay't so to his charge.°                    *Accuse him directly*
He's with the King your father.
195 LEONTES                              Who, Camillo?
LORD  Camillo, sir. I spake with him, who now
Has these poor men in question. Never saw I
Wretches so quake. They kneel, they kiss the earth,
Forswear° themselves as often as they speak.                    *Perjure*
200 Bohemia stops his ears, and threatens them
With divers deaths in death.°                    *With diverse tortures*
PERDITA                              O, my poor father!
The heaven sets spies upon us, will not have
Our contract celebrated.
LEONTES                              You are married?
FLORIZEL  We are not, sir, nor are we like to be.
205 The stars, I see, will kiss the valleys first.
The odds for high and low's alike.[8]
LEONTES                              My lord,
Is this the daughter of a king?
FLORIZEL                              She is,
When once she is my wife.
LEONTES  That 'once', I see, by your good father's speed
210 Will come on very slowly. I am sorry,
Most sorry, you have broken from his liking
Where you were tied in duty; and as sorry
Your choice is not so rich in worth° as beauty,                    *rank*
That you might well enjoy her.
FLORIZEL [*to* PERDITA]                    Dear, look up.
215 Though fortune, visible an enemy,
Should chase us with my father, power no jot
Hath she to change our loves.[9]—Beseech you, sir,
Remember since you owed no more to time
Than I do now.°  With thought of such affections,                    *when you were my age*
220 Step forth mine advocate. At your request
My father will grant precious things as trifles.
LEONTES  Would he do so, I'd beg your precious mistress,
Which he counts but a trifle.
PAULINA                              Sir, my liege,
Your eye hath too much youth in't. Not a month
225 Fore your queen died she was more worth such gazes
Than what you look on now.
LEONTES                              I thought of her
Even in these looks I made.
[*To* FLORIZEL]                    But your petition
Is yet unanswered. I will to your father.
Your honour not o'erthrown by your desires,[1]
230 I am friend to them and you. Upon which errand
I now go toward him. Therefore follow me,
And mark what way I make. Come, good my lord.        *Exeunt*

---

8. That is, "Chance treats those of high and low rank
identically."
9. Even if Lady Fortune were to make herself apparent
as our enemy and join my father in pursuit, she would
remain powerless to change our love.
1. So long as you have not allowed passion to destroy
your virtue.

## 5.2

*Enter* AUTOLYCUS *and a* GENTLEMAN

AUTOLYCUS  Beseech you, sir, were you present at this relation?°      *when this was told*

FIRST GENTLEMAN  I was by at the opening of the fardel, heard
the old shepherd deliver the manner how he found it; whereupon, after a little amazedness, we were all commanded out of
5   the chamber. Only this, methought I heard the shepherd say
he found the child.

AUTOLYCUS  I would most gladly know the issue° of it.      *outcome*

FIRST GENTLEMAN  I make a broken delivery° of the business, but      *confused report*
the changes I perceived in the King and Camillo were very
10   notes of admiration.[1] They seemed almost, with staring on one
another, to tear the cases° of their eyes. There was speech in      *burst the sockets*
their dumbness, language in their very gesture. They looked as°      *as if*
they had heard of a world ransomed, or one destroyed. A
notable passion of wonder appeared in them, but the wisest
15   beholder, that knew no more but seeing, could not say if
th'importance were joy or sorrow. But in the extremity of the
one,° it must needs be.      *of the one or the other*

*Enter another* GENTLEMAN

Here comes a gentleman that happily° knows more. The news,      *perhaps*
Ruggiero!

20 SECOND GENTLEMAN  Nothing but bonfires. The oracle is ful-
filled. The King's daughter is found. Such a deal° of wonder is      *a great quantity*
broken out within this hour, that ballad-makers cannot be able
to express it.[2]

*Enter another* GENTLEMAN

Here comes the Lady Paulina's steward. He can deliver you
25   more.—How goes it now, sir? This news which is called true is
so like an old tale that the verity of it is in strong suspicion. Has
the King found his heir?

THIRD GENTLEMAN  Most true, if ever truth were pregnant by circumstance.° That which you hear you'll swear you see, there is      *proven by evidence*
30   such unity in the proofs. The mantle of Queen Hermione's,
her jewel about the neck of it, the letters of Antigonus found
with it, which they know to be his character;° the majesty of      *handwriting*
the creature, in resemblance of the mother; the affection of°      *instinct toward*
nobleness which nature shows above° her breeding,° and many    *in excess of / upbringing*
35   other evidences proclaim her with all certainty to be the King's
daughter. Did you see the meeting of the two kings?

SECOND GENTLEMAN  No.

THIRD GENTLEMAN  Then have you lost a sight which was to be
seen, cannot be spoken of. There might you have beheld one
40   joy crown another, so and in such manner that it seemed sorrow wept to take leave of them, for their joy waded in tears.
There was casting up of eyes, holding up of hands, with counte-
nance° of such distraction[3] that they were to be known by gar-      *face*
ment, not by favour.° Our king being ready to leap out of      *features*
45   himself for joy of his found daughter, as if that joy were now
become a loss cries, 'O, thy mother, thy mother!', then asks
Bohemia forgiveness, then embraces his son-in-law, then again

---

5.2 Location: Sicilia. The palace of Leontes.
1. Were the very marks of wonder.
2. Ballads often provided accounts of contemporary

scandals and sensations.
3. So altered by emotion.

worries he° his daughter with clipping° her. Now he thanks the    *he agitates / embracing*
old shepherd, which stands by like a weather-bitten conduit of
50   many kings' reigns.⁴ I never heard of such another encounter,
which lames report to follow it,⁵ and undoes° description to do°    *defies / express*
it.

SECOND GENTLEMAN   What, pray you, became of Antigonus, that
carried hence the child?

55  THIRD GENTLEMAN   Like an old tale still, which will have matter
to rehearse° though credit° be asleep and not an ear open. He    *relate / belief*
was torn to pieces with a bear. This avouches° the shepherd's    *vows*
son, who has not only his innocence,° which seems much, to    *simplemindedness*
justify him, but a handkerchief and rings of his,° that Paulina    *(of Antigonus)*
60  knows.

FIRST GENTLEMAN   What became of his barque° and his fol-    *ship*
lowers?

THIRD GENTLEMAN   Wrecked the same instant of their master's
death, and in the view of the shepherd; so that all the instru-
65  ments which aided to expose the child were even then lost
when it was found. But O, the noble combat that 'twixt joy and
sorrow was fought in Paulina! She had one eye declined for
the loss of her husband, another elevated⁶ that the oracle was
fulfilled. She lifted the Princess from the earth, and so locks
70  her in embracing as if she would pin her to her heart, that she
might no more be in danger of losing.°    *of being lost*

FIRST GENTLEMAN   The dignity of this act was worth the audience of kings and princes, for by such was it acted.

THIRD GENTLEMAN   One of the prettiest touches of all, and that
75  which angled for mine eyes—caught the water,° though not    *(my tears)*
the fish—was when at the relation of the Queen's death, with
the manner how she came to't bravely confessed and lamented
by the King, how attentiveness° wounded his daughter till from    *intent listening*
one sign of dolour° to another she did, with an 'Alas', I would    *grief*
80  fain say bleed tears; for I am sure my heart wept blood. Who
was most marble° there changed colour. Some swooned, all    *unfeeling*
sorrowed. If all the world could have seen't, the woe had been
universal.

FIRST GENTLEMAN   Are they returned to the court?

85  THIRD GENTLEMAN   No. The Princess, hearing of her mother's
statue, which is in the keeping of Paulina, a piece many years
in doing, and now newly performed° by that rare Italian master    *completed*
Giulio Romano,⁷ who, had he himself eternity and could put
breath into his work, would beguile° nature of her custom,° so    *cheat / business*
90  perfectly he is her ape.° He so near to Hermione hath done    *imitator*
Hermione that they say one would speak to her and stand in
hope of answer. Thither with all greediness of affection are
they gone, and there they intend to sup.

SECOND GENTLEMAN   I thought she had some great matter there
95  in hand, for she hath privately twice or thrice a day, ever since
the death of Hermione, visited that removed° house. Shall we    *distant; hidden*
thither, and with our company piece° the rejoicing?    *join*

---

4. Who stands by weeping like a waterspout that has
been around for the reigns of many Kings. Some large
buildings had "conduits" or waterpipes in the form of
gargoyles or gnarled human faces.
5. Which makes any account of it seem deficient.
6. That is, Paulina simultaneously cried and laughed.

7. An Italian painter, a follower of Raphael, who died in
1546 and was most famous for a series of erotic draw-
ings illustrating sexual positions, or "postures." It is not
clear whether Shakespeare, in fact, had ever seen any of
his work.

FIRST GENTLEMAN  Who would be thence, that has the benefit
of access? Every wink of an eye some new grace will be born.
Our absence makes us unthrifty to our knowledge.[8] Let's
along.                                              *Exeunt* [GENTLEMEN]
AUTOLYCUS  Now, had I not the dash° of my former life in me,                     *stain; touch*
would preferment° drop on my head. I brought the old man                         *royal favor*
and his son aboard the° Prince; told him I heard them talk of a      *aboard the ship of the*
fardel, and I know not what. But he at that time over-fond of
the shepherd's daughter—so he then took her to be—who
began to be much sea-sick, and himself little better, extremity
of weather continuing, this mystery remained undiscovered.
But 'tis all one to me, for had I been the finder-out of this secret
it would not have relished° among my other discredits.                          *appeared well*

*Enter* [*the* OLD] SHEPHERD *and* [*the*] CLOWN [*dressed as*
*gentlemen*]

Here come those I have done good to against my will, and
already appearing in the blossoms of their fortune.
OLD SHEPHERD  Come, boy; I am past more children, but thy
sons and daughters will be all gentlemen born.
CLOWN [*to* AUTOLYCUS]  You are well met, sir. You denied to
fight with me this other° day because I was no gentleman born.                  *the other*
See you these clothes? Say you see them not, and think me
still no gentleman born. You were best say these robes are not
gentlemen born. Give me the lie,[9] do, and try whether I am
not now a gentleman born.
AUTOLYCUS  I know you are now, sir, a gentleman born.
CLOWN  Ay, and have been so any time these four hours.
OLD SHEPHERD  And so have I, boy.
CLOWN  So you have; but I was a gentleman born before my
father, for the King's son took me by the hand and called me
brother; and then the two kings called my father brother; and
then the Prince my brother and the Princess my sister called
my father father; and so we wept; and there was the first gentle-
man-like tears that ever we shed.
OLD SHEPHERD  We may live, son, to shed many more.
CLOWN  Ay, or else 'twere hard luck, being in so preposterous
estate[1] as we are.
AUTOLYCUS  I humbly beseech you, sir, to pardon me all the
faults I have committed to your worship, and to give me your
good report to the Prince my master.
OLD SHEPHERD  Prithee, son, do, for we must be gentle° now we                  *act nobly*
are gentlemen.
CLOWN  Thou wilt amend thy life?
AUTOLYCUS  Ay, an it like your good worship.
CLOWN  Give me thy hand. I will swear to the Prince thou art as
honest a true fellow as any is in Bohemia.
OLD SHEPHERD  You may say it, but not swear it.
CLOWN  Not swear it now I am a gentleman? Let boors° and                       *peasants*
franklins° say it; I'll swear it.                                              *small farmers*
OLD SHEPHERD  How if it be false, son?
CLOWN  If it be ne'er so false,° a true gentleman may swear it in          *Even if it is false*

---

8. Makes us squander an opportunity to add to our
knowledge.
9. Insult me so that I must respond with the challenge
of a duel.
1. The Clown probably means "prosperous," but "pre-

posterous" is a nice blunder for it suggests that their
new status as gentlemen is preposterous in the sense of
(1) contrary to nature or (2) putting last what should be
first—that is, inverting the social order by putting "real"
gentlemen behind "false" gentlemen like themselves.

the behalf of his friend, [*to* AUTOLYCUS] and I'll swear to the
Prince thou art a tall fellow of thy hands° and that thou wilt not            *a brave man of action*
be drunk; but I know thou art no tall fellow of thy hands and
150    that thou wilt be drunk; but I'll swear it, and I would thou
wouldst be a tall fellow of thy hands.

AUTOLYCUS    I will prove so, sir, to my power.°                              *as well as I can*

CLOWN    Ay, by any means prove a tall fellow. If I do not wonder
how thou dar'st venture to be drunk, not being a tall fellow,
155    trust me not.
[*Flourish within*]
Hark, the kings and princes, our kindred, are going to see the
Queen's picture.° Come, follow us. We'll be thy good masters.                *likeness*
*Exeunt*

## 5.3

*Enter* LEONTES, POLIXENES, FLORIZEL, PERDITA, CA-
MILLO, PAULINA, LORDS [*and attendants*]¹

LEONTES    O grave and good Paulina, the great comfort
That I have had of thee!

PAULINA                      What,° sovereign sir,                          *Whatever*
I did not well, I meant well. All my services
You have paid home,° but that you have vouchsafed°                           *fully rewarded / vowed*
5      With your crowned brother and these young contracted
Heirs of your kingdoms my poor house to visit,
It is a surplus° of your grace which never                                  *an additional sign*
My life may last to answer.

LEONTES                              O Paulina,
We honour you with trouble.² But we came
10     To see the statue of our queen. Your gallery
Have we passed through, not without much content
In many singularities;° but we saw not                                      *In seeing many rarities*
That which my daughter came to look upon,
The statue of her mother.

PAULINA                              As she lived peerless,
15     So her dead likeness I do well believe
Excels what ever yet you looked upon,
Or hand of man hath done. Therefore I keep it
Lonely,° apart. But here it is. Prepare                                     *Alone*
To see the life as lively mocked° as ever                                   *realistically imitated*
20     Still° sleep mocked death. Behold, and say 'tis well.                 *Quiet*
[*She draws a curtain and reveals the figure of* HERMI-
ONE, *standing like a statue*]
I like your silence; it the more shows off
Your wonder. But yet speak; first you, my liege.
Comes it not something° near?                                               *somewhat*

LEONTES                              Her natural posture.
Chide me, dear stone, that I may say indeed
25     Thou art Hermione; or rather, thou art she
In thy not chiding, for she was as tender

---

5.3 Location: Sicilia. Paulina's house.
1. In F, the stage direction reads: "*Enter Leontes, Polix-*
*enes, Florizell, Perdita, Camillo, Paulina: Hermione (like*
*a Statue:) Lords, etc.*" For a reader of the play, this direction suggests that Hermione is a living character pretending to be a statue. For a theatergoer unacquainted
with the play, by contrast, the immobile female figure
seen on stage is probably first assumed to be an actual
statue of the dead Queen.
2. The honor we pay to you demands much of you (by
way of hospitality).

As infancy and grace. But yet, Paulina,
Hermione was not so much wrinkled, nothing°                    *not at all*
So agèd as this seems.

POLIXENES                  O, not by much.

30    PAULINA   So much the more our carver's excellence,
Which lets go by some sixteen years, and makes her
As° she lived now.                                            *As if*

LEONTES                  As now she might have done,
So much to my good comfort as it is
Now piercing to my soul. O, thus she stood,
35    Even with such life of majesty—warm life,
As now it coldly stands—when first I wooed her.
I am ashamed. Does not the stone rebuke me
For being more stone° than it? O royal piece!°              *hard-hearted / work of art*
There's magic in thy majesty, which has
40    My evils conjured° to remembrance, and                    *summoned*
From thy admiring° daughter took the spirits,               *wondering*
Standing like stone with thee.

PERDITA                  And give me leave,
And do not say 'tis superstition, that
I kneel and then implore her blessing.³ Lady,
45    Dear Queen, that ended when I but began,
Give me that hand of yours to kiss.

PAULINA                  O, patience!
The statue is but newly fixed;° the colour's               *painted*
Not dry.

CAMILLO [*to* LEONTES]   My lord, your sorrow was too sore° laid on,   *painfully*
50    Which sixteen winters cannot blow away,
So many summers dry.⁴ Scarce any joy
Did ever so long live; no sorrow
But killed itself much sooner.

POLIXENES [*to* LEONTES]                  Dear my brother,
Let him that was the cause of this have power
55    To take off so much grief from you as he
Will piece up in himself.⁵

PAULINA [*to* LEONTES]          Indeed, my lord,
If I had thought the sight of my poor image
Would thus have wrought you°—for the stone is mine—        *made you distraught*
I'd not have showed it.
        [*She makes to draw the curtain*]

LEONTES                  Do not draw the curtain.

60    PAULINA   No longer shall you gaze on't, lest your fancy
May think anon it moves.

LEONTES                  Let be, let be!
Would I were dead but that methinks already.⁶
What was he that did make it? See, my lord,
Would you not deem it breathed, and that those veins
Did verily bear blood?

65    POLIXENES                  Masterly done.
The very life seems warm upon her lip.

LEONTES   The fixture of her eye has motion in't,⁷

3. A possible reference to the Protestant attack on the
Catholic practice of kneeling before images of the Virgin Mary.
4. And an equal number of summers cannot dry up.

5. Will make a part of himself.
6. May I die if I do not think it already moves.
7. The setting ("fixture") of her eye gives the appearance of motion.

As° we are mocked with art.                                              *In such a way that*

PAULINA                          I'll draw the curtain.
My lord's almost so far transported that
He'll think anon it lives.

70 LEONTES                          O sweet Paulina,
Make me to think so twenty years together.
No settled senses° of the world can match              *calm state of mind*
The pleasure of that madness. Let't alone.

PAULINA   I am sorry, sir, I have thus far stirred you; but
I could afflict you farther.

75 LEONTES                          Do, Paulina,
For this affliction has a taste as sweet
As any cordial° comfort. Still methinks              *restorative*
There is an air comes from her.° What fine chisel        *she seems to breathe*
Could ever yet cut breath? Let no man mock me,
For I will kiss her.

80 PAULINA                    Good my lord, forbear.
The ruddiness upon her lip is wet.
You'll mar it if you kiss it, stain your own
With oily painting.° Shall I draw the curtain?              *paint*

LEONTES   No, not these twenty years.

PERDITA                          So long could I
Stand by, a looker-on.

85 PAULINA                    Either forbear,
Quit presently° the chapel, or resolve you              *immediately*
For more amazement. If you can behold it,
I'll make the statue move indeed, descend,
And take you by the hand. But then you'll think—

90 Which I protest against—I am assisted
By wicked powers.

LEONTES                    What you can make her do
I am content to look on; what to speak,
I am content to hear; for 'tis as easy
To make her speak as move.

PAULINA                          It is required

95 You do awake your faith. Then, all stand still.
Or those that think it is unlawful business
I am about, let them depart.

LEONTES                          Proceed.
No foot shall stir.

PAULINA                    Music; awake her; strike!°              *strike up!*
    [*Music*]
    [*To* HERMIONE] 'Tis time. Descend. Be stone no more. Approach.

100 Strike all that look upon with marvel. Come,
I'll fill your grave up. Stir. Nay, come away.
Bequeath to death your numbness, for from him°              *(death)*
Dear life redeems you.
    [*To* LEONTES]                    You perceive she stirs.
        [HERMIONE *slowly descends*]
Start not. Her actions shall be holy as

105 You hear my spell is lawful. Do not shun her
Until you see her die again, for then
You kill her double.[8] Nay, present your hand.
When she was young, you wooed her. Now, in age,

8. That is, "If you were to shun her in this new life, you would kill her again."

Is she become the suitor?

LEONTES                              O, she's warm!
110    If this be magic, let it be an art
       Lawful as eating.

POLIXENES    She embraces him.

CAMILLO    She hangs about his neck.
       If she pertain to life,° let her speak too.                    be truly alive
115    POLIXENES    Ay, and make it manifest where she has lived,
       Or how stol'n from the dead.

PAULINA                          That she is living,
       Were it but told you, should be hooted at
       Like an old tale. But it appears she lives,
       Though yet she speak not. Mark a little while.
120    [To PERDITA] Please you to interpose, fair madam. Kneel,
       And pray your mother's blessing.—Turn, good lady,
       Our Perdita is found.

HERMIONE                      You gods, look down,
       And from your sacred vials pour your graces
       Upon my daughter's head.—Tell me, mine own,
125    Where hast thou been preserved? Where lived? How found
       Thy father's court? For thou shalt hear that I,
       Knowing by Paulina that the oracle
       Gave hope thou wast in being,° have preserved                 alive
       Myself to see the issue.°                     the outcome; the child

PAULINA                          There's time enough for that,
130    Lest they desire upon this push to trouble
       Your joys with like relation.⁹ Go together,
       You precious winners all; your exultation
       Partake° to everyone. I, an old turtle,¹        Spread your happiness
       Will wing me to some withered bough, and there
135    My mate, that's never to be found again,
       Lament till I am lost.°                                       dead

LEONTES                      O peace, Paulina!
       Thou shouldst a husband take by my consent,
       As I by thine a wife. This is a match,
       And made between's by vows. Thou hast found mine,
140    But how is to be questioned, for I saw her,
       As I thought, dead, and have in vain said many
       A prayer upon her grave. I'll not seek far—
       For him, I partly know his mind—to find thee
       An honourable husband. Come, Camillo,
145    And take her by the hand, whose worth and honesty
       Is richly noted, and here justified°                         testified to
       By us, a pair of kings. Let's from this place.
       [To HERMIONE] What, look upon my brother. Both your pardons,
       That e'er I put between your holy looks
150    My ill suspicion. This'° your son-in-law                     This is
       And son unto the King, whom heavens directing
       Is troth-plight° to your daughter. Good Paulina,             betrothed
       Lead us from hence, where we may leisurely
       Each one demand and answer to his part
155    Performed in this wide gap of time since first
       We were dissevered. Hastily lead away.              Exeunt

9. Lest they (bystanders?) desire at this crucial moment to trouble your happiness with similar stories.
1. I.e., turtledove, a symbol of faithful love.

# Cymbeline

Toward the end of *Cymbeline,* one of the chief characters, Posthumus Leonatus, awakens from a dream vision to find a tablet on his chest, left there by Jupiter, king of the gods. In the dream, Jupiter had promised that the tablet would explain Posthumus's future fortunes. But when Posthumus reads the writing on the tablet, it is incomprehensible to him:

> 'Tis still a dream, or else such stuff as madmen
> Tongue, . . .
> Or senseless speaking, or a speaking such
> As sense cannot untie.

Yet he concludes: "Be what it is, / The action of my life is like it" (5.5.238–42). By his own estimation, Posthumus's life is a senseless riddle. His immediate circumstances perhaps warrant such a conclusion. When Jupiter appears to him, Posthumus, a Briton crucial to his country's recent defeat of Rome, has subsequently disguised himself as a Roman and been put in a British prison. Posthumus deliberately sought his own capture and death because of the guilt he felt for having wrongly commanded the death of his virtuous wife, Innogen, the British King's daughter, falsely accused of sexual infidelity. Unbeknownst to him, however, Innogen, not dead but also disguised as a Roman boy named Fidele, is likewise among those held captive by the Britons.

Such plot complexities are typical of *Cymbeline,* leading not only Posthumus, but also theatergoers, to find it a baffling muddle. In this play, an inordinate number of characters assume disguises, have more than one name, don't know who their "real" parents are, or find themselves unable to decipher the complicated events around them. In one of the play's most famous (or infamous) scenes, Innogen, traveling in a page's disguise to find Posthumus, wakes up from a drug-induced sleep to find herself lying beside the body of a headless man dressed in her husband's clothing. The man is really Cloten, Posthumus's rival for Innogen's hand and the wicked son of Innogen's evil stepmother. Seeing the headless body, Innogen breaks into a lament for the man she believes to be her husband. Her grief is genuine and affecting, but it is prompted by a profound misreading of the object before her.

The improbabilities and complexities of *Cymbeline*'s plot have given some critics pause, as has the freedom with which times and places are handled. Ostensibly set in Roman Britain at the time of Christ's birth (which, according to the chronicles, occurred during the reign of Cymbeline), the play also contains scenes that appear to take place in contemporary sixteenth-century Italy. It is in this modern Italy, for example, that Posthumus is tricked into believing that Innogen is sexually unfaithful to him. Reacting to the play's unusual features, the eighteenth-century critic Samuel Johnson complained:

> This play has many just sentiments, some natural dialogues, and some pleasing scenes, but they are obtained at the expense of much incongruity. To remark the folly of the fiction, the absurdity of the conduct, the confusion of the names, and manners of different times, and the impossibility of the events in any system of life, were to waste criticism upon unresisting imbecility, upon faults too evident for detection, and too gross for aggravation.

This response, however, may say more about Johnson's neoclassical tastes than about the ultimate value of Shakespeare's play. In *Cymbeline,* the complexity of the action seems deliberate rather than inadvertent or unskillful. It creates in the audience both a longing for clarity and control and an anxiety that the play may afford neither. The pleasure of the final act, therefore, stems from the relief experienced when—after a dizzying whirl of events, reversals, revelations, and disguises—peace descends, all identities revealed and all riddles expounded. The sense of wonder produced by this miraculous untangling of complicated events is one of the signal effects of Shakespeare's late plays: amazement that after astonishing suffering can come new hope, after labyrinthine confusions the solace of questions answered.

This feature of the play is one of the reasons why in modern criticism *Cymbeline* is usually called a romance or sometimes a tragicomedy, even though in the First Folio of 1623 it was grouped with the tragedies, probably because it dramatizes serious historical matter taken from the reign of an early Briton King. Like other plays written late in Shakespeare's career, however, such as *The Winter's Tale, Pericles,* and *The Tempest, Cymbeline* does not end tragically. Rather, it ultimately emphasizes the transformation of suffering into joy. While verging on tragedy, each of these plays wins through to a bittersweet conclusion in which shattered families are reconstituted and plot complexities untangled—but always at a cost. Mistakes have consequences in these plays. Sons die; years are lost in exile and wandering; women suffer from unjust slander. If, in the end, good fortune returns to the sufferers, it does not cancel their former pain but provides a miraculous contrast to it.

The date of *Cymbeline* is uncertain, although it is usually given as 1609 or 1610. Scholars differ as to whether it preceded or followed *The Winter's Tale.* We know that it was in performance by 1611, because Simon Forman, a London doctor and astrologer, wrote about seeing it, probably between April 20 and April 30 of that year. It is not clear whether he saw the play at the Globe, the outdoor theater that Shakespeare's company used after 1599, or at Blackfriars, the indoor theater that they also began to use in 1608. The spectacular scenic effects possible in staging this play, such as the descent of Jupiter on the back of an eagle in Act 5, may have been designed with the more elaborate technical capacities of the Blackfriars venue in mind. Some critics have tried to date the play by relating it to the investiture of Henry, King James's oldest son, as Prince of Wales in 1610, since a number of the key scenes of the play take place in Wales. We have no record of a court performance of the play until 1634, however, when it was played before King Charles, who liked it. Other critics have tried to determine the play's relationship to Beaumont and Fletcher's popular tragicomedy *Philaster,* usually dated 1609, to which *Cymbeline* bears some resemblance. But even though the two plays are related, it is not clear which influenced the other.

Whatever its exact date, *Cymbeline* belongs to Shakespeare's late period, and because of its setting it allowed Shakespeare simultaneously to address his long-standing interests both in British and in Roman history. The play intertwines three plot lines and draws on a variety of source materials. The main plot involves Innogen, the daughter and apparently the only living heir of Cymbeline, King of Britain, and her thwarted attempts to live with her chosen husband, Posthumus. Angry that Innogen loves a man of lesser social rank than herself and that she has not married Cloten, his second wife's son, Cymbeline banishes Posthumus from Britain. Posthumus goes to Italy, where he wagers on his wife's chastity with the villain Giacomo, who ultimately makes Posthumus believe Innogen unfaithful. Whether the love of Innogen and Posthumus can be restored is one of the key questions of this plot. This wager story draws on two sources: Boccacio's *Decameron,* a series of prose tales first translated into English in 1620 but available in a French translation in the sixteenth century, and *Frederick of Jennen,* an English translation of a German version of the same story.

A second plot strand deals with Britain's relationship with Rome, especially Rome's demand that the Britons pay the tribute pledged to Julius Caesar upon his conquest of the isle. For this part of the story, Shakespeare drew primarily on the brief account of Cymbeline's reign in Raphael Holinshed's *Chronicles of England, Scotland, and Ireland* (second edition, 1587). Cymbeline was King when the Roman Emperor Augustus Caesar ushered in the famous time of peace known as the *Pax Romana.* In most of the sources, it was Cymbeline's son Guiderius who refused to pay Rome tribute. Shakespeare modified the story, however, so that Cymbeline, urged on by his Queen and her son, is the one who withholds the tribute and provokes a Roman invasion.

The third plotline has to do with two sons of Cymbeline, stolen from their nursery by a wrongly defamed courtier, Belarius, who raises them in the mountains of Wales. By chance, their sister Innogen, disguised as a boy, stumbles upon their mountain cave on her flight from her father's court in pursuit of Posthumus. Near this cave, Cloten, wearing Posthumus's clothes, is killed by one of these sons; also near this cave, Innogen awakes from her sleep to find herself beside his headless body. For the play to reach its resolution, Cymbeline's sons must be reunited with their father. This reunion occurs, but only after the sons play a decisive role in the final battle against the Roman invaders. Their heroic actions in this battle are modeled on quite another part of Holinshed, *The History of Scotland,* which recounts the story of a farmer named Hay and his two sons, who routed Danish invaders at the Battle of Luncarty in about 976 C.E.

From these complex and diverse materials, Shakespeare wove a play whose rich allusiveness has invited many kinds of topical interpretations. One line of criticism has focused on *Cymbeline's* relationship to events and ideas connected to the reign of King James I. James was interested in linking imperial Rome and the Roman Emperors to modern Britain and to his own kingship. He had himself painted crowned with laurel leaves, in the Roman manner, and had coins stamped with his laurel-crowned profile. Like Augustus Caesar, James presented himself as the great peacemaker after Elizabeth's

James I liked to present himself as heir to Roman greatness. In this 1613 engraving, Crispin van de Passe portrays him crowned with the laurel wreath worn by Roman emperors.

reluctant involvement in wars in Ireland and in defending the Protestant countries of the Continent against Catholic powers, especially Spain. Moreover, just as Augustus ruled over a vast empire, James aspired to unite Scotland and England (along with the already incorporated Wales) into a single entity with one church and one set of laws. His project failed, but he exerted much effort in promoting this union during the first years of his reign. *Cymbeline* uncannily echoes some of James's preoccupations. Sometimes called Shakespeare's last Roman play, *Cymbeline* dramatizes ancient Britain's attempts to come to terms with imperial Rome. Names of Roman gods—particularly Diana, Apollo, and Jupiter—abound (Jupiter alone is mentioned over thirty times); and figures from Roman mythology and history, such as Tarquin, Philomela, and Aeneas, are often evoked. The play's title character, like James, is a British monarch respectful of Rome, even when asserting his independence in the matter of the tribute. The final word of the play, spoken by the King, is "peace." The analogies between the play and the Stuart court, however, have their limits. Cymbeline is also a King duped by his wicked Queen and her doltish son—hardly a compliment to James and the royal family if events in the play are seen literally to mirror their circumstances.

Other allusions expand the play's possible range of meanings. Much is made, for example, of Milford Haven, the port in southern Wales where the Romans come ashore for their invasion of England. This port was famous to Shakespeare's audience as the place where Henry Richmond landed in 1485 to begin his assault on the forces of Richard III. Having defeated Richard, Richmond was crowned Henry VII, first of the Tudor Kings; Henry's daughter Margaret married James IV of Scotland, grandfather to the James who assumed the English throne in 1603. When the Romans land at Milford Haven, they in effect precipitate a transformation of the kingdom, much as Henry Richmond was to do 1,500 years later. At the time of their arrival, Cymbeline believes his two sons dead, and his daughter and Cloten have both fled the court. Britain is without an heir. But through the battle with the Romans, the lost sons of Cymbeline are discovered and the kingdom renewed. So, too, James fancied himself an agent of renewal, a second Henry VII arriving from Scotland to unite the whole island under his rule.

Wales itself is an important symbolic location in this play. Although officially incorporated into England in the 1530s, Wales remained distinct, often stigmatized as rude and uncivilized. The Welsh language, banned from use in public contexts, was taken to symbolize the barbarity of this borderland region. On the other hand, in some narratives, Wales was also the place from which the legitimate rulers of England sprang. The stories surrounding the mythical King Arthur give him a Welsh origin, and traditionally the eldest son of the British monarch was (and still is) given the title Prince of Wales. In *Cymbeline*, Wales is imagined as a harsh pastoral landscape in which Belarius and the King's sons live in a cave, hunt the food they eat, and have little contact with other human beings. These sons, Guiderius and Arviragus, frequently complain that they know nothing of the world and its customs and manners. But Wales shelters these sons as they grow to manhood and protects them from the vices of court life. In fact, as is traditional in pastoral literature, the Welsh scenes contain a good deal of anticourt satire. In the play's spatial and symbolic economies, Wales is the place where true British manhood is preserved. In part, the Welsh material can be seen as a compliment to Prince Henry, who was a staunch champion of the Protestant cause in Europe and showed every promise of being a more martial figure than his peace-loving father.

There can be little doubt that *Cymbeline* works with material imbued with a new kind of significance under the reign of James. Yet it may be a mistake to tie the play too closely to the royal family or to particular events. The play doesn't just reflect the world around it; it transforms the materials from that world into a powerful imaginative and ideological structure. In the largest sense, *Cymbeline* works to define both Britain and proper British manhood by constructing a complex narrative about national origins. The wager plot, with its story of sexual slander and threatened rape, is central to that narrative, not only because Innogen often seems to stand for Britain itself (she is several times addressed as "Britain," and she bears the name of the wife of Brute, the legendary ancient King of Britain), but also because the realignment of gender relations plays a crucial role in the "renewal" of Britain and in the play's turn from tragedy to comedy.

Strikingly, this play about Britain's past never mentions the word "England." In the history plays written in the 1590s, the reverse tends to be true: "Britain" is seldom employed, "England" is invoked with great frequency. There are several reasons for Shakespeare's choice in this later play. He is, of course, deliberately evoking the world of the ancient Britons, the early inhabitants of the island who provide the starting point for his creation of a fictive national past. At the same time, he is to some extent reflecting, and helping to create, the Stuart monarch's sense of the entity over which he ruled. James, after all, was not an "Englander" in the same way Elizabeth had been. He was a Scotsman who spoke with an accent and aspired to bring the entire island into a new political alignment.

Setting the play in the reign of Cymbeline allowed Shakespeare to imagine a primitive Britain that was also the cosmopolitan heir to the westward movement of empire. The treatment of Rome is particularly interesting in *Cymbeline*. Partly, the Romans are figured as an invading force, threatening the island. Yet the British characters most eager to repel the Romans and to treat them as an enemy are the evil Queen and her evil son. Cymbeline himself, while defending Britain's right to live free and under its own laws, is more disposed to come to terms with his great opponents and invariably treats them with respect. There is, in fact, a pronounced tension in the play between Britain's desires to defeat the Romans and to emulate them. This tension is managed in part through the splitting of the Romans into the noble figure of Lucius and the devilish figure of Giacomo, who in his deceit and misogyny embodies sixteenth-century stereotypes concerning the villainous Italian.

When Giacomo comes to Britain to test Innogen's fidelity, he fails in his initial attempt to portray Posthumus as a philanderer upon whom Innogen should seek sexual revenge. He then proceeds more secretly; he has himself conveyed in a trunk into her bedroom, from which he issues in the dead of night to survey her sleeping body and the contents of her room. His stealthy act is framed by references to infamous acts of rape. As he steps from the trunk, Giacomo compares himself to Tarquin, the Roman tyrant who raped Lucrece (a story told in Shakespeare's lengthy poem *The Rape of Lucrece*, written in the 1590s). Furthermore, the book that Innogen had been reading when she fell asleep is opened to the story of Tereus, who raped Philomela and cut out her tongue. Although

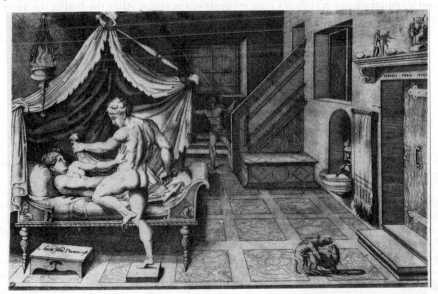

*Tarquin's Rape of Lucrece.* Sixteenth-century copy of an engraving by Agostino Veneziano.

Giacomo does not literally rape Innogen, he violates the privacy of her body with his peering eyes and rapes her honor by lying successfully to Posthumus about her infidelity. At one level, this incident is about the unjust sufferings of a slandered woman. At another level, Innogen is Britain, threatened by a skillful invader. Giacomo penetrates Innogen's bedchamber, and later he penetrates the ear of Posthumus with his poisonous slander.

In the play's denouement, the threat of foreign penetration is graphically repelled when Belarius and the sons of Cymbeline come from the Welsh mountains, joined by Posthumus disguised as a British peasant, and take a stand "in a narrow lane," putting the Romans to flight and instilling courage in the British. The vulnerable narrow lane is thus barricaded against outsiders by the sons of Cymbeline crying, "Stand, stand" (5.5.28). The moment has gendered and sexual overtones. A vulnerable and feminized Britain is protected from invasion by the swords of virile young men whose cry, "Stand," means both to "hold one's ground" and to "have an erection." This event proves pivotal, lending itself equally well to aphorism and to Posthumus's mocking rhyme: "Two boys, an old man twice a boy, a lane, / Preserved the Britons, was the Romans' bane" (5.5.57–58). In the play's symbolic economy, the threat of penetration initiated by Giacomo is thus repulsed by Innogen's long-lost brothers, and in the final scene Giacomo kneels to Posthumus, asking his forgiveness—the Italian subdued by the Briton.

Something quite different occurs with Lucius, the Roman military leader, who embodies the laudable virtues of ancient Rome rather than the hideous vices of sixteenth-century Italy. Even though the Roman army is defeated, Cymbeline decides to resume paying tribute, and in his final speech the King says: "let / A Roman and a British ensign wave / Friendly together" (5.6.479–81). This rapprochement of warring powers is ratified by one of the play's several mysterious visions. Before the battle, a Roman soothsayer told Lucius what the gods had revealed to him:

> I saw Jove's bird, the Roman eagle, winged
> From the spongy south to this part of the west,
> There vanished in the sunbeams; which portends,
> Unless my sins abuse my divination,
> Success to th' Roman host.
>
> (4.2.350–54)

In this play, not even soothsayers have perfect interpretive skills. The outcome of the battle requires some revisions in the exegesis of the vision. After the battle, the soothsayer says:

> For the Roman eagle,
> From south to west on wing soaring aloft,
> Lessened herself, and in the beams o'th' sun
> So vanished; which foreshowed our princely eagle
> Th'imperial Caesar should again unite
> His favour with the radiant Cymbeline,
> Which shines here in the west.
>
> (5.6.470–76)

Conquest has been transformed into concord as the Roman eagle and the British sun merge and as Cymbeline celebrates this peace within the temple of Jupiter.

In stressing the final union of Britain and Rome, the play's conclusion makes Britain the heir of Rome's imperial legacy even as Britain proclaims the integrity of her own land, laws, and customs. In the early modern period, the course of empire was thought to move westward. When Troy fell, the Trojan hero Aeneas bore his father on his back from the fires of the burning city and eventually fulfilled his destiny by establishing a new kingdom in Italy in what was to become the center of the Roman Empire. In the soothsayer's vision, the Roman eagle journeys even farther west, renewing itself, as eagles were believed to do, by enduring the burning fires of Britain's sun to purge away old feathers in preparation for the growth of new.

The eagle, king of birds and emblem of the Roman god Jupiter; according to myth, it could stare at the sun without blinking and fly into the sun in order to burn off its old feathers. From Joachim Camerarius, *Symbolorum et Emblematum* (1605 ed.).

The play's culminating vision of a Britain separate unto itself but also the cosmopolitan heir of an imperial tradition is anticipated in the actions of Innogen and Posthumus. In the final act, both are partly Roman in their dress and sympathies. Posthumus Leonatus comes to Britain in the company of the Italian gentry, but then dresses as a British peasant and fights with Belarius in the narrow lane before reassuming his Italian garb. Innogen is present at the battle as page to Lucius, the Roman general who had found her weeping over the headless corpse of Cloten. In the final moments of reconciliation, Cymbeline's daughter and her husband stand before the British King in foreign clothes. Innogen, moreover, earlier makes a telling speech about Britain's place in the world when discussing with a trusted servant where she would live after Posthumus had come to believe her unchaste. Her father's court, with Cloten present, she finds unthinkable. She then asks:

> Hath Britain all the sun that shines? Day, night,
> Are they not but in Britain? I'th' world's volume
> Our Britain seems as of it but not in't,
> In a great pool a swan's nest.
>
> (3.4.136–39)

Innogen nicely captures the play's most complex view of Britain. Eschewing an insular patriotism associated with Cloten and the Queen, she recognizes a vast world beyond the shores of Britain. Punning on the double meaning of "volume" as "expanse" or "book," Innogen suggests Britain's partial separation from a larger entity. Britain is a little part of a bigger expanse, a page detached from a large book, or a swan's nest in a great pool. As the image of the swan's nest suggests, Britain remains the special seat of grace and beauty. But it is also connected to something larger than itself. There are other pages in the volume to which, even if detached, Britain belongs.

The play, then, seems to be negotiating a new vision of the nation suited for the Stuart moment, a vision resulting from the richly suggestive concatenation of discursive traditions that Shakespeare brought together in this play. Reaching back into the chronicle materials of ancient Britain, he provides a genealogy for modern Britain that (1) insists on the integrity and freedom of the island kingdom but (2) presents it as purged—largely through the efforts of the King's "Welsh" sons—of the corruptions of modern court life as embodied in figures such as Giacomo or Cloten, and (3) aligns Britain with the cosmopolitan values of Rome, positioning the island kingdom as the appropriate heir of Roman greatness: both warlike and peace-loving.

The renewed Britain has a fourth striking characteristic, and that is its decidedly masculine coloration. The wager plot makes plain the role of gender in configuring British national identity. Consider first the changing fortunes of Innogen. At the beginning of the play, she is a beloved and important figure in her father's court. Cymbeline's only living heir, the Princess is also strong-willed and decisive. She chooses Posthumus for her husband even though he has little money and is not of royal birth. By the end of the play, Innogen has been displaced from the succession by her two rediscovered brothers; she has also been ordered killed by her husband, threatened with rape, knocked unconscious by a drug she believes to be medicine, and struck by her husband when, in her page's attire, she steps forward to reveal her identity to him in the last scene. Though cross-dressed for much of the second half of the play, she does not, like Portia in *The Merchant of Venice* and Rosalind in *As You Like It,* use that disguise aggressively to shape her own destiny. Rather, burdened by the knowledge that her husband unjustly and inexplicably desires her death, Innogen grows less powerful and more passive as the play progresses. Her decline can be summarized in the pun on "heir" and "air." Innogen begins as the former and ends as the latter. The mysterious tablet laid on Posthumus's breast contained a riddling prophecy: "Whenas a lion's whelp shall, to himself unknown, without seeking find, and be embraced by a piece of tender air; and when from a stately cedar shall be lopped branches which, being dead many years, shall after revive, be jointed to the old stock, and freshly grow; then shall Posthumus end his miseries, Britain be fortunate and flourish in peace and plenty" (5.5.232–37). When the soothsayer finally untangles this riddle, he declares Posthumus Leonatus to be the lion's offspring; Cymbeline the cedar tree; his lost sons the lopped branches; and Innogen the tender air, because "tender air" in Latin translates as *mollis aer,* which (by a stretch of the imagination) derives from *mulier,* Latin for "wife." When Posthumus is embraced by the "tender air" (no longer an "heir"), his miseries will cease. Apparently because she is now less important to the succession, Innogen is allowed to live with her chosen husband, his masculinity affirmed by his pivotal role in the British victory over the Roman forces.

Victorian critics loved Innogen, idealizing her as a paragon of selfless and long-suffering womanhood. For example, the Princess never protests her demotion from the position of heir apparent; in fact, she says that she considers finding her brothers worth the loss of the kingdom. To many contemporary critics, however, her role in the play's narrative of nation is a troubling one. Britain renews itself as women are disempowered or disappear. Cymbeline's Queen is an embodiment of hypocritical viciousness (Shakespeare does not even bother to give her a name), and her son, a figure whose father is never mentioned or seen, bears her taint. The play's happy resolution occurs only after all traces of this Queen and her offspring have been erased. When finally united with his children, Cymbeline articulates the fantasy of having himself given birth to all three: "O, what am I? / A mother to the birth of three? Ne'er mother / Rejoiced deliverance more" (5.6.369–71). This is the dream of androgenesis, reproduction without union with women.

Much earlier in the play, Posthumus, believing himself cuckolded by Innogen, voices a similar wish: "Is there no way for men to be, but women / Must be half-workers?" (2.5.1–2). In one of the most deeply misogynist speeches in the Shakespeare canon, Posthumus then blames all the vices of the world on "the woman's part" (line 20)—on woman herself and on that part of woman lodged in man, Eve's mark upon the human race. This mistaken projection onto woman of responsibility for evil may partly explain Cymbeline's fantasy of androgenesis and also why, in the last scene, no persons appareled as women are to be seen (Innogen is still dressed as a page). The happy union of Britain and Rome and Wales is overwhelmingly a union of men.

The play's own counterpoint to its exclusion of women from public power is its demonization of the slanderous Giacomo and its depiction of Posthumus's gradual recovery of faith in Innogen. When Posthumus receives a bloody cloth signifying (falsely) that his order to murder Innogen has been fulfilled, he is overcome with remorse and berates husbands like himself for murdering wives "for wrying but a little" (5.1.5). At this point, Posthumus still believes his wife to have been sexually unfaithful to him, yet he castigates himself for having ordered her punished. His words form a remarkable exception to the more usual patriarchal assumption that female chastity is the primary marker of a woman's value and virtue and that loss of chastity is an unforgivable crime. Critics differ as to how much weight to assign this speech. Posthumus makes it when he believes Innogen to be dead; and generally it is easier to forgive the dead than the living. By the time he is finally reconciled to the living, breathing woman, Giacomo's lies have been exposed and Posthumus takes to himself a wife whose chastity is not in question.

The play, however, overtly punishes violence against women when the evil Cloten, who had fantasized raping Innogen, is beheaded, and it punishes misogynous lies when Giacomo must submit to Posthumus in the final scene. Posthumus, who had formerly himself believed slander against Innogen and had attempted to have her killed, repents and becomes the play's image of the proper husband. After Posthumus's performance in battle and when Innogen is no longer heir apparent, Cymbeline withdraws his objections to Posthumus's union with her. Nevertheless, Innogen's formerly dominant position in that marriage now seems to belong to Posthumus, with Jupiter himself providing the warrant for this reversal. In prison, Posthumus has a dream that not only reconnects him to his familial origins but also provides an image of his own future family. As he sleeps, Posthumus's two warlike brothers and his warlike father appear to him. The father is described as "leading in his hand an ancient matron, his wife, and mother to Posthumus" (stage direction following 5.5.123). After this dream, sent by Jupiter, Posthumus recovers his "true" identity as Innogen's husband and Britain's warrior hero. As he assumes his position in the honored line of Leonati men, the place marked for Innogen is that of Roman / British wife, "led in his hand." In its narratives of nation, *Cymbeline* seems able to reprove the most virulent forms of misogyny only when it simultaneously removes women from public power, transforms them into chaste, domesticated wives, and reaffirms the dominance of husbands.

Samuel Johnson was right when he said that *Cymbeline* is a play with many incongruities of time, place, and circumstance. And yet it is not an incoherent play but rather one that richly interweaves the history of the nation with the stories of the figures who take up their positions in that nation. What is eerie about *Cymbeline* is that its characters often understand so little about what is happening to them, and yet each appears to play out the part assigned to him or her by some higher power: Jupiter, destiny, time. In this regard, *Cymbeline* is of a piece with Shakespeare's other romances, plays in which a higher power often seems to steer all boats to shore and reunite long-severed families. But fictions of inevitability can be deceiving. One should remember that the soothsayer had to revise his interpretation of his vision of the eagle and the sun to make his narrative square with events as they actually happened. And to decipher Posthumus's tablet, he could make the prophecy tally with the facts only by means of a tortuous transformation of "tender air" into "wife." This might suggest that in this play, at least, the higher powers determine less than they appear to do; rather, the forms taken by family, nation, and empire are in some measure the result of human efforts, interventions, and narratives. Shakespeare's play is one such narrative. The resolution of its complex plot may invite relieved assent to its culminating vision, but the very artifice of that resolution also reveals its contingency, suggesting that there is nothing either natural or inevitable about the familial and political arrangements that are repeatedly contested and reordered in this tragicomic play.

JEAN E. HOWARD

## TEXTUAL NOTE

*Cymbeline* was first printed in the First Folio (F) of 1623. Its heavy punctuation suggests that it was prepared for printing by a professional scribe—perhaps by Ralph Crane, who is believed to have prepared five of Shakespeare's other plays for the print shop. While not every feature associated with a Crane manuscript is displayed, the use of parentheses, hyphens, and apostrophes in the Folio text of *Cymbeline* is consistent with Crane's practice. Because the scribe regularized the manuscript he copied, it is hard to determine the exact nature of that manuscript. It may or may not have been a promptbook. Although the Folio text contains almost no stage directions relating to sounds, such as trumpet flourishes to mark ceremonial entrances and exits or the noises associated with battle or with hunting parties, this elision of clues to performance practice is characteristic of "literary" transcripts of the sort associated with Crane.

In this edition, several names have been changed from the versions that appear in F. F's "Iachimo" has been modernized to "Giacomo," the Italian name for "James," on the grounds that a modernized text of Shakespeare should also give personal names in modernized forms. Other editors have proposed "Jackimo" as an alternative modernization. F's "Philario" has also been modernized to "Filario." In this instance, F itself uses the form "Filario" at 1.1.98, though elsewhere it employs "Philario." Finally, the heroine's name, given as "Imogen" in F, is here changed to "Innogen." There are several reasons for this alteration. In Holinshed's *Chronicles*, one of Shakespeare's sources for the play, the wife of Brute (an early King of England) was named Innogen. Many scholars assume that this was Shakespeare's source for the name. In addition, Simon Forman, one of Shakespeare's contemporaries, who described a performance of the play in 1611, gave the name of the Princess as Innogen. Forman could have gotten the name wrong, but he might have been accurately recording a fact of performance lost in the printed text. Finally, in *Much Ado About Nothing*, Leonato has a wife called Innogen (who never makes a stage appearance); that couple might thus anticipate the Innogen and Leonatus of *Cymbeline*. The Oxford editors surmise that the compositors who set type for F misread the word "Innogen," mistaking "nn" for "m" and so printing "Imogen." Other scholars disagree, arguing that Shakespeare might well have changed a name he found in his sources and that Forman may have misheard what he observed on the stage or may have remembered the name from his own reading and mistakenly attributed it to the production.

Act and scene divisions in this text follow those employed in most editions since the eighteenth century, with several exceptions, all in Act 5. In most texts, the culminating battle between the Romans and Britons occurs in 5.2. The Oxford editors divide this battle sequence into three scenes—5.2, 5.3, and 5.4—because at two points the stage is momentarily cleared. On the other hand, most editions separate the action that immediately follows the battle into two scenes: Posthumus's arrest by the Britons after this battle, then the actual depiction of his captivity and the appearance of his family to him in a dream. This edition makes these events into one continuous scene, 5.5, since there is no evidence that Posthumus and his jailers ever leave the stage between these two actions.

## SELECTED BIBLIOGRAPHY

Adelman, Janet. "Masculine Authority and the Maternal Body: The Return to Origins in the Romances." *Suffocating Mothers: Fantasies of Maternal Origins in Shakespeare's Plays, "Hamlet" to "The Tempest."* New York: Routledge, 1992. 193–238. Argues that *Cymbeline* recovers the idealized father lost in *Hamlet*, but does so by denigrating maternal authority and the sexualized female body.

Floyd-Wilson, Mary. "'Delving to the root': *Cymbeline*, Scotland, and the English Race," *British Identities and English Renaissance Literature*. Ed. David J. Baker and Willy Maley. Cambridge, Eng.: Cambridge University Press, 2002. 101–15. Partly by associating Cymbeline's evil Queen with Scoto-Britons, Floyd-Wilson argues that *Cymbeline* repudiates the Scottish role in British history, thereby contributing to an Anglocentric historiography.

Hunt, Maurice. "Dismemberment, Corporal Reconstitution, and the Body Politic in *Cymbeline*." *Studies in Philology* 99.4 (Fall 2002): 404–31. Examines the idea of the body politic—its destruction and reconstitution—in *Cymbeline*.

Jones, Emrys. "Stuart *Cymbeline*." *Essays in Criticism* 11 (1961): 84–99. Takes an historical approach to the play emphasizing its links to James I's dedication to peace and the role of Milford Haven in Tudor national mythology.

Kahn, Coppélia. "Postscript: *Cymbeline*: Paying Tribute to Rome." *Roman Shakespeare: Warriors, Wounds, and Women*. London: Routledge, 1997. 160–70. Argues that *Cymbeline* shares much with Shakespeare's other Roman plays, including a preoccupation with Roman *virtu* as the root of masculine identity, but an identity constantly made precarious by the woman's part in its formation.

Knight, G. Wilson. "Cymbeline." *The Crown of Life: Essays in Interpretation of Shakespeare's Final Plays*. London: Oxford University Press, 1947. 129–202. Explores national and religious themes in *Cymbeline*, culminating with a sustained analysis of Posthumus's vision of Jupiter.

Mikalachki, Jodi. "Cymbeline and the Masculine Romance of Roman Britain," *The Legacy of Boadicea: Gender and Nation in Early Modern England*. London: Routledge, 1998. 96–114. From a feminist perspective, explores the respective roles of ancient British savagery and Roman civility in the forging of an all-male national community in *Cymbeline*.

Parker, Patricia. "Romance and Empire: Anachronistic *Cymbeline*." *Unfolded Tales: Essays on Renaissance Romance*. Ed. George M. Logan and Gordon Teskey. Ithaca, N.Y.: Cornell University Press, 1989. 189–207. Examines the pervasive allusions to *The Aeneid* in *Cymbeline*, arguing that the play intimates the passing of Rome's imperial greatness westward to Britain.

Warren, Roger. *Cymbeline*. Shakespeare in Performance series. Manchester: Manchester University Press, 1989. Focuses on performances of the play, especially on striking stage and television versions from the second half of the twentieth century.

Wayne, Valerie. "The Woman's Parts of *Cymbeline*." *Staged Properties in Early Modern English Drama*. Ed. Jonathan Gil Harris and Natasha Korda. Cambridge, Eng.: Cambridge University Press, 2002. 288–315. Traces the history of three stage properties—manacle, ring, and bloody cloth—as they represent Innogen, and woman more generally, in *Cymbeline*.

## FILM

*Cymbeline*. 1982. Dir. Elijah Moshinsky. UK. 175 min. Boasts such cast luminaries as Richard Johnson (the King), Claire Bloom (the Queen), and Helen Mirren (Innogen), among others.

# Cymbeline, King of Britain

## THE PERSONS OF THE PLAY

CYMBELINE, King of Britain
Princess INNOGEN, his daughter, later disguised as a man
   named Fidele
GUIDERIUS, known as Polydore ⎫
ARVIRAGUS, known as Cadwal ⎭ Cymbeline's sons, stolen by Belarius
QUEEN, Cymbeline's wife, Innogen's stepmother
Lord CLOTEN, her son
BELARIUS, a banished lord, calling himself Morgan
CORNELIUS, a physician
HELEN, a lady attending on Innogen
Two LORDS attending on Cloten
Two GENTLEMEN
Two British CAPTAINS
Two JAILERS
POSTHUMUS Leonatus, a poor gentleman, Innogen's husband
PISANIO, his servant
FILARIO, a friend of Posthumus
GIACOMO, an Italian ⎫
A FRENCHMAN     ⎪
A DUTCHMAN    ⎬ Filario's friends
A SPANIARD     ⎭
Caius LUCIUS, ambassador from Rome, later General of the
   Roman forces
Two Roman SENATORS
Roman TRIBUNES
A Roman CAPTAIN
Philharmonus, a SOOTHSAYER
JUPITER
Ghost of SICILIUS Leonatus, father of Posthumus
Ghost of the MOTHER of Posthumus
Ghosts of the BROTHERS of Posthumus
Lords attending on Cymbeline, ladies attending on the Queen,
   musicians attending on Cloten, messengers, soldiers

### 1.1

*Enter two* GENTLEMEN

FIRST GENTLEMAN  You do not meet a man but frowns. Our bloods
  No more obey the heavens than our courtiers
  Still seem as does the King.[1]
SECOND GENTLEMAN        But what's the matter?
FIRST GENTLEMAN  His daughter, and the heir of 's kingdom, whom
5  He purposed to° his wife's sole son—a widow        *intended for*
  That late° he married—hath referred° herself    *recently / given*
  Unto a poor but worthy gentleman. She's wedded,

---

1.1 Location: Cymbeline's court, Britain.
1. *Our . . . King:* Our dispositions ("bloods") are not
more subject to planetary influences than our courtiers'

moods are determined by the King's. (The planets were
believed to affect human actions and emotions.)

Her husband banished, she imprisoned. All
Is outward sorrow, though I think the King
Be touched at very heart.

10 SECOND GENTLEMAN          None but the King?
FIRST GENTLEMAN   He° that hath lost her, too. So is the Queen,          (the Queen's son)
That most desired the match. But not a courtier—
Although they wear their faces to the bent
Of° the King's looks—hath a heart that is not          In accordance with
Glad of the thing they scowl at.

15 SECOND GENTLEMAN              And why so?
FIRST GENTLEMAN   He that hath missed the Princess is a thing
Too bad for bad report, and he that hath her—
I mean that married her—alack, good man,
And therefore banished!—is a creature such
20 As, to seek through the regions of the earth
For one his like, there would be something failing°          lacking
In him that should compare.² I do not think
So fair an outward and such stuff° within          substance; fabric
Endows a man but he.

SECOND GENTLEMAN          You speak him far.°          praise him greatly
25 FIRST GENTLEMAN   I do extend him, sir, within himself;³
Crush him together rather than unfold
His measure duly.⁴

SECOND GENTLEMAN   What's his name and birth?
FIRST GENTLEMAN   I cannot delve him to the root.⁵ His father
Was called Sicilius, who did join his honour°          prowess (as a soldier)
30 Against the Romans with Cassibelan
But had his titles by Tenantius,⁶ whom
He served with glory and admired success,
So gained the sur-addition 'Leonatus';⁷
And had, besides this gentleman in question,
35 Two other sons who in the wars o'th' time
Died with their swords in hand; for which their father,
Then old and fond of issue,° took such sorrow          of his offspring
That he quit being, and his gentle lady,
Big of° this gentleman, our theme, deceased          Pregnant with
40 As he was born. The King, he takes the babe
To his protection, calls him Posthumus⁸ Leonatus,
Breeds him,° and makes him of his bedchamber;⁹          Brings him up
Puts to him° all the learnings that his time          Offers him
Could make him the receiver of, which he took
45 As we do air, fast as 'twas ministered,
And in 's spring became a harvest; lived in court—
Which rare it is to do—most praised, most loved;
A sample° to the youngest, to th' more mature          An example
A glass that feated them,¹ and to the graver
50 A child that guided dotards.° To his mistress,          foolish old men

2. In any man selected for comparison.
3. I set forth his virtues, sir, within the boundaries of
his own merit.
4. *rather . . . duly:* rather than reveal what he is really
worth. The metaphor picks up on the sense of "stuff"
as "fabric" in line 23. Fabric can be crushed together or
unfolded and accurately measured.
5. I cannot completely account for his lineage.
6. Tenantius was Cymbeline's father and the brother of

Cassibelan, who in 3.1.5 is described as Cymbeline's
uncle.
7. The additional name "Leonatus" (born of a lion).
8. In Latin, the word means "after death." As applied to
a child, it means "one born after his or her father's
death."
9. Makes him a personal servant.
1. A mirror that furnished ("feated") them with images
of virtue or elegance.

For whom he now is banished, her own price
Proclaims how she esteemed him and his virtue.[2]
By her election° may be truly read                                   choice (of him)
What kind of man he is.

SECOND GENTLEMAN          I honour him

55   Even out° of your report. But pray you tell me,                  Even beyond the limits
Is she sole child to th' King?

FIRST GENTLEMAN                      His only child.
He had two sons—if this be worth your hearing,
Mark it: the eld'st of them at three years old,
I'th' swathing° clothes the other, from their nursery               swaddling

60   Were stol'n, and to this hour no guess in knowledge°              no informed conjecture
Which way they went.

SECOND GENTLEMAN    How long is this ago?

FIRST GENTLEMAN    Some twenty years.

SECOND GENTLEMAN    That a king's children should be so conveyed,

65   So slackly guarded, and the search so slow
That could not trace them!

FIRST GENTLEMAN                      Howsoe'er 'tis strange,
Or that the negligence may well be laughed at,
Yet is it true, sir.

SECOND GENTLEMAN    I do well believe you.

*Enter the* QUEEN, POSTHUMUS, *and* INNOGEN[3]

FIRST GENTLEMAN    We must forbear.° Here comes the gentleman,       withdraw

70   The Queen and Princess.       *Exeunt [the two* GENTLEMEN]*[4]

QUEEN    No, be assured you shall not find me, daughter,
After the slander of[5] most stepmothers,
Evil-eyed unto you. You're my prisoner, but
Your jailer shall deliver you the keys

75   That lock up your restraint. For you, Posthumus,
So soon as I can win th'offended King
I will be known your advocate. Marry,[6] yet
The fire of rage is in him, and 'twere good
You leaned unto° his sentence with what patience                    You obeyed
Your wisdom may inform° you.                                        instill in

80   POSTHUMUS                      Please your highness,
I will from hence today.

QUEEN                      You know the peril.
I'll fetch a turn about the garden, pitying
The pangs of barred affections, though the King
Hath charged you should not speak together.       *Exit*

85   INNOGEN    O dissembling courtesy! How fine this tyrant
Can tickle° where she wounds! My dearest husband,                   flatter
I something° fear my father's wrath, but nothing—                   somewhat
Always reserved my holy duty—what

---

2. *her . . . virtue:* the price she paid (for loving him) demonstrates how much she valued him and his virtue; her own worth ("price") shows the high esteem in which she held him and his virtues.
3. In F, the name of the Princess is Imogen; but in Holinshed's *Chronicles,* the wife of the ancient English King Brute is called Innogen. A number of scholars have concluded that Shakespeare took the name from Holinshed. For a fuller discussion of the Innogen/Imo-

gen debate, see the Textual Note.
4. F marks *Scena Secunda* (second scene) after the gentlemen exit. Then the Queen, Posthumus, and Innogen enter. There is, however, no change of time or place, and the Queen and the lovers are probably in view at line 69 when the First Gentleman announces their entrance. Most previous editors do not indicate a new scene here.
5. In accordance with the slanderous things said about.
6. A mild oath, from the name of the Virgin Mary.

His rage can do on me.[7] You must be gone,
90 And I shall here abide the hourly shot
Of angry eyes, not comforted to live
But that there is this jewel in the world
That I may see again.
POSTHUMUS                    My queen, my mistress!
O lady, weep no more, lest I give cause
95 To be suspected of more tenderness
Than doth become a man. I will remain
The loyal'st husband that did e'er plight troth;°                    *pledge marriage*
My residence in Rome at one Filario's,
Who to my father was a friend, to me
100 Known but by letter; thither write, my queen,
And with mine eyes I'll drink the words you send
Though ink be made of gall.°                    *bile; bitter liquid*

*Enter* QUEEN

QUEEN                    Be brief, I pray you.
If the King come, I shall incur I know not
How much of his displeasure. [*Aside*] Yet I'll move him
105 To walk this way. I never do him wrong
But he does buy my injuries, to be friends,[8]
Pays dear for my offences.                    [*Exit*]
POSTHUMUS                    Should we be taking leave
As long a term° as yet we have to live,                    *time*
The loathness° to depart would grow. Adieu.                    *unwillingness*
110 INNOGEN    Nay, stay a little.
Were you but riding forth to air yourself
Such parting were too petty. Look here, love:
This diamond was my mother's. Take it, heart;
[*She gives him a ring*]
But keep it till you woo another wife
When Innogen is dead.
115 POSTHUMUS                    How, how? Another?
You gentle gods, give me but this I have,
And cere up[9] my embracements from a next°                    *another wife*
With bonds of death! Remain, remain thou here
[*He puts on the ring*]
While sense° can keep it on; and, sweetest, fairest,                    *the ability to feel*
120 As I my poor self did exchange for you
To your so infinite loss, so in our trifles°                    *love tokens*
I still win of you.[1] For my sake wear this.
[*He gives her a bracelet*]
It is a manacle of love. I'll place it
Upon this fairest prisoner.
INNOGEN                    O the gods!
When shall we see again?

*Enter* CYMBELINE *and lords*

125 POSTHUMUS                    Alack, the King!
CYMBELINE    Thou basest° thing, avoid hence,° from my sight!                    *most lowborn / be off*

7. *but . . . me*: an ambiguous phrase. My holy duty of obedience to my father excepted (a bond put in jeopardy by Cymbeline's act), I do not at all ("nothing") fear what Cymbeline's rage can do to me. Or: My holy duty to my husband excepted (which Cymbeline could disrupt by interfering with the marriage), I do not at all fear what Cymbeline's rage may do to me.

8. But he does endure the consequences of ("buy") my injuries in order to be friends.
9. And wrap up (in the cerecloth, or waxed linen, used in burial shrouds).
1. I still am enriched by you. Posthumus suggests that he is unequal in rank and wealth to Innogen. Correspondingly, his love token is of less value than hers.

If after this command thou fraught° the court                            *burden*
With thy unworthiness, thou diest. Away.
Thou'rt poison to my blood.
POSTHUMUS                            The gods protect you,
130 And bless the good remainders of° the court!                *people remaining at*
I am gone.                                        *Exit*
INNOGEN            There cannot be a pinch° in death                    *pain*
More sharp than this is.
CYMBELINE                            O disloyal thing,
That shouldst repair° my youth, thou heap'st                        *restore*
A year's age on me.
INNOGEN                            I beseech you, sir,
135 Harm not yourself with your vexation.
I am senseless of° your wrath. A touch° more rare       *unable to feel / An emotion*
Subdues all pangs, all fears.
CYMBELINE                            Past grace,° obedience—                *all sense of duty*
INNOGEN    Past hope and in despair: that way past grace.[2]
CYMBELINE    That mightst have had the sole son of my queen!
140 INNOGEN    O blessèd that I might not! I chose an eagle
And did avoid a puttock.[3]
CYMBELINE    Thou took'st a beggar, wouldst have made my throne
A seat for baseness.
INNOGEN                            No, I rather added
A lustre to it.
CYMBELINE        O thou vile one!
INNOGEN                            Sir,
145 It is your fault that I have loved Posthumus.
You bred him as my playfellow, and he is
A man worth any woman, over-buys me
Almost the sum he pays.[4]
CYMBELINE                            What, art thou mad?
INNOGEN    Almost, sir. Heaven restore me! Would I were
150 A neatherd's° daughter, and my Leonatus                        *cowherd's*
Our neighbour shepherd's son.
        *Enter* QUEEN
CYMBELINE                            Thou foolish thing.
[*To* QUEEN] They were again together; you have done
Not after° our command. [*To lords*] Away with her,            *according to*
And pen her up.
QUEEN            Beseech° your patience, peace,                    *I beseech*
155 Dear lady daughter, peace. Sweet sovereign,
Leave us to ourselves, and make yourself some comfort
Out of your best advice.
CYMBELINE                            Nay, let her languish
A drop of blood a day,[5] and, being aged,
Die of this folly.                            *Exit* [*with lords*]
QUEEN            Fie, you must give way.
        *Enter* PISANIO
160 Here is your servant. How now, sir? What news?

2. Redemption. Alluding to the Christian belief that those who despair distrust God and are beyond the reach of grace.
3. A kite, or common predatory bird.
4. *over-buys . . . pays*: pays too much for me by almost the amount he gives for me. (Posthumus both gives himself to Innogen in marriage and also pays the price of banishment.) Innogen insists that Posthumus's worth equals her own and that their marriage consequently does not degrade her.
5. Referring to the popular belief that one lost a drop of blood with each sigh.

PISANIO   My lord your son drew° on my master.                                    *drew a sword*

QUEEN                                                  Ha!
  No harm, I trust, is done?

PISANIO                                There might have been,
  But that my master rather played than fought,
  And had no help of anger. They were parted
  By gentlemen at hand.

165  QUEEN                              I am very glad on't.

INNOGEN   Your son's my father's friend; he takes his part
  To draw upon an exile°—O brave sir!                                             *(Posthumus)*
  I would they were in Afric° both together,                                       *Africa*
  Myself by with a needle, that I might prick°                                     *urge on*
  The goer-back.° [*To* PISANIO] Why came you from your           *swordsman who retreated*
170  master?

PISANIO   On his command. He would not suffer° me                                  *allow*
  To bring him to the haven, left these notes
  Of what commands I should be subject to
  When't pleased you to employ me.

QUEEN                                          This hath been
175  Your faithful servant. I dare lay mine honour
  He will remain so.

PISANIO   I humbly thank your highness.

QUEEN   Pray walk a while.                                      [*Exit*]⁶

INNOGEN   About some half hour hence, pray you speak with me.
180  You shall at least go see my lord aboard.
  For this time leave me.                        *Exeunt* [*severally*]°            *separately*

## 1.2

*Enter* CLOTEN *and two* LORDS

FIRST LORD   Sir, I would advise you to shift° a shirt. The violence            *change*
  of action hath made you reek° as a sacrifice. Where air comes        *emit vapors; stink*
  out, air comes in. There's none abroad so wholesome as that
  you vent.¹

5  CLOTEN   If my shirt were bloody, then to shift it.° Have I hurt      *then I would change it*
  him?

SECOND LORD [*aside*]   No, faith, not so much as his patience.

FIRST LORD   Hurt him? His body's a passable° carcass if he be      *pretty good; penetrable*
  not hurt. It is a thoroughfare for steel if he be not hurt.

10  SECOND LORD [*aside*]   His steel was in debt—it went o'th' back-
  side the town.²

CLOTEN   The villain would not stand° me.                              *confront; stay still for*

SECOND LORD [*aside*]   No, but he fled forward still,° toward your           *always*
  face.

15  FIRST LORD   Stand you? You have land enough of your own, but
  he added to your having, gave you some ground.°                    *fell back before you*

SECOND LORD [*aside*]   As many inches as you have oceans.° Pup-        *(i.e., no inches)*
  pies!

CLOTEN   I would they had not come between us.

---

6. F does not mark a separate exit for the Queen here,
but Innogen appears to be speaking privately to Pisanio,
and only Pisanio, in the following three lines.
1.2 Location: Cymbeline's court.
1. The First Lord flatters Cloten by saying that the
odorous vapors he is giving off are more healthful than

the outside ("abroad") air that is being exchanged for
them.
2. Cloten's sword, like a debtor avoiding creditors, kept
to the backstreets—that is, avoided the thoroughfare or
main street of Posthumus's body (with a possible allusion to anal penetration).

20 SECOND LORD [aside]   So would I, till you had measured how
　　long a fool you were upon the ground.
　　CLOTEN   And that she should love this fellow and refuse me!
　　SECOND LORD [aside]   If it be a sin to make a true election,³ she
　　is damned.
25 FIRST LORD   Sir, as I told you always, her beauty and her brain
　　go not together. She's a good sign,° but I have seen small ⟶ she has a good appearance
　　reflection of her wit.
　　SECOND LORD [aside]   She shines not upon fools lest the reflec-
　　tion should hurt her.
30 CLOTEN   Come, I'll to my chamber. Would there had been some
　　hurt done.
　　SECOND LORD [aside]   I wish not so, unless it had been the fall
　　of an ass, which is no great hurt.
　　CLOTEN [to SECOND LORD]   You'll go with us?
35 FIRST LORD   I'll attend your lordship.
　　CLOTEN   Nay, come, let's go together.
　　SECOND LORD   Well, my lord.　　　　　　　　　　　　*Exeunt*

### 1.3
*Enter* INNOGEN *and* PISANIO

INNOGEN   I would thou grew'st unto the shores o'th' haven
　　And questionedst every sail. If he should write
　　And I not have it, 'twere a paper lost
　　As offered mercy is.¹ What was the last
　　That he spake to thee?
5 PISANIO　　　　　　　　　　It was his queen, his queen.
　　INNOGEN   Then waved his handkerchief?
　　PISANIO　　　　　　　　　　　　And kissed it, madam.
　　INNOGEN   Senseless° linen, happier therein than I!　　　　　*Unfeeling*
　　And that was all?
　　PISANIO　　　　　　　No, madam. For so long
　　As he could make me with this eye or ear
10　　Distinguish him from others he did keep
　　The deck, with glove or hat or handkerchief
　　Still waving, as the fits and stirs of 's mind
　　Could best express how slow his soul sailed on,
　　How swift his ship.
　　INNOGEN　　　　　　　　Thou shouldst have made him
15　　As little as a crow, or less, ere left
　　To after-eye him.²
　　PISANIO　　　　　　　Madam, so I did.
　　INNOGEN   I would have broke mine eye-strings,³ cracked them, but
　　To look upon him till the diminution
　　Of space had pointed him sharp as my needle;⁴
20　　Nay, followed him till he had melted from
　　The smallness of a gnat to air, and then
　　Have turned mine eye and wept. But, good Pisanio,
　　When shall we hear from him?

---

3. A proper choice; with a pun on the Christian doctrine that certain souls are "elected," or predestined for salvation.
1.3 Location: Cymbeline's palace.
1. *'twere . . . is:* the lost letter would be a document written in vain, like an offer of mercy that is not accepted or received (for example, a judge's reprieve that comes too late or God's mercy to an unrepentant sinner).
2. *ere . . . him:* before ceasing to gaze after him.
3. The muscles of the eye, which were supposed to break at death or from overuse.
4. *till . . . needle:* until the distance between us had made him seem as small as the point on my needle.

PISANIO   Be assured, madam,
25   With his next vantage.°                                          *his first opportunity*
INNOGEN   I did not take my leave of him, but had
      Most pretty things to say. Ere I could tell him
      How I would think on him at certain hours,
      Such thoughts and such, or I could make him swear
30   The shes° of Italy should not betray                           *women*
      Mine interest° and his honour, or have charged him     *My entitlement (to him)*
      At the sixth hour of morn, at noon, at midnight
      T'encounter me with orisons⁵—for then
      I am in heaven for him—or ere I could
35   Give him that parting kiss which I had set
      Betwixt two charming words,⁶ comes in my father,
      And, like the tyrannous breathing of the north,°            *north wind*
      Shakes all our buds from growing.
            *Enter a* LADY
LADY                                        The Queen, madam,
      Desires your highness' company.
40   INNOGEN [*to* PISANIO]   Those things I bid you do, get them dispatched.
      I will attend the Queen.
PISANIO                              Madam, I shall.
            *Exeunt* [INNOGEN *and* LADY *at one door,* PISANIO *at another*]

                              1.4

            [*A table brought out, with a banquet upon it.*]¹ *Enter*
            FILARIO, GIACOMO, *a* FRENCHMAN, *a* DUTCHMAN, *and a*
            SPANIARD

GIACOMO   Believe it, sir, I have seen him in Britain. He was then
      of a crescent note,° expected to prove so worthy as since he     *growing reputation*
      hath been allowed the name of. But I could then have looked
      on him without the help of admiration,° though the catalogue    *wonder*
5    of his endowments had been tabled° by his side and I to peruse    *listed*
      him by items.°                                                  *part by part*
FILARIO   You speak of him when he was less furnished than now
      he is with that which makes° him both without and within.       *constitutes*
FRENCHMAN   I have seen him in France. We had very many
10   there could behold the sun with as firm eyes as he.²
GIACOMO   This matter of marrying his king's daughter, wherein
      he must be weighed rather by her value than his own, words
      him, I doubt not, a great deal from the matter.³
FRENCHMAN   And then his banishment.
15   GIACOMO   Ay, and the approbation of those that weep this
      lamentable divorce under her colours⁴ are wonderfully to
      extend him,° be it but to fortify her judgement, which else an    *exaggerate his worth*
      easy battery° might lay flat for taking a beggar without less qual-  *a slight assault*

---

5. To join me in prayers ("orisons"); to assail me (as an
object of devotion) with prayers.
6. Between two words carrying a charm to ward off
danger.
1.4 Location: Filario's house, Rome.
1. No banquet—a light meal of fruit, sweetmeats, and
wine following the main meal—is specified in F, but in
other texts, such as Boccacio's *Decameron,* parallel
wager scenes occur during a meal; and at 5.6.155, Gia-

como, retelling the tale of the wager, says it occurred "at
a feast."
2. Alluding to the popular belief that only eagles could
gaze directly on the sun. At 1.1.140, Innogen described
Posthumus as an eagle.
3. *words . . . matter:* causes his reputation, I am sure,
to be amplified beyond what is true.
4. That is, on Innogen's side (with a pun on "colours"
as meaning both "a military banner" and "pretexts").

|   | ity.° But how comes it he is to sojourn with you? How creeps | *of no rank or merit* |
| 20 | acquaintance?⁵ |   |
|   | FILARIO His father and I were soldiers together, to whom I have been often bound for no less than my life. |   |

*Enter* POSTHUMUS

|   | Here comes the Briton. Let him be so entertained amongst you as suits with gentlemen of your knowing° to a stranger of his | *knowledge* |
| 25 | quality.° I beseech you all, be better known to this gentleman, | *foreigner of his rank* |
|   | whom I commend to you as a noble friend of mine. How worthy he is I will leave to appear hereafter rather than story° him | *give an account of* |
|   | in his own hearing. |   |
|   | FRENCHMAN [*to* POSTHUMUS] Sir, we have known together° in | *been acquainted* |
| 30 | Orléans. |   |
|   | POSTHUMUS Since when I have been debtor to you for courtesies which I will be ever to pay, and yet pay still. |   |
|   | FRENCHMAN Sir, you o'er-rate my poor kindness. I was glad I did | |
|   | atone° my countryman and you. It had been pity you should | *reconcile* |
| 35 | have been put together° with so mortal° a purpose as then each | *(in a duel) / deadly* |
|   | bore, upon importance° of so slight and trivial a nature. | *matters* |
|   | POSTHUMUS By your pardon, sir, I was then a young traveller, | |
|   | rather shunned to go even° with what I heard than⁶ in my every | *refused to agree* |
|   | action to be guided by others' experiences; but upon my | |
| 40 | mended° judgement—if I offend not to say it is mended—my | *improved* |
|   | quarrel was not altogether slight. | |
|   | FRENCHMAN Faith, yes, to be put to the arbitrement of swords,° | *settlement by duel* |
|   | and by such two that would by all likelihood have confounded° | *destroyed* |
|   | one the other, or have fallen both. | |
| 45 | GIACOMO Can we with manners ask what was the difference? | |
|   | FRENCHMAN Safely, I think. 'Twas a contention in public, which | |
|   | may without contradiction suffer° the report. It was much like | *permit* |
|   | an argument that fell out last night, where each of us fell in | |
|   | praise of our country mistresses,⁷ this gentleman at that time | |
| 50 | vouching—and upon warrant of bloody affirmation°—his to be | *affirming it with blood* |
|   | more fair, virtuous, wise, chaste, constant, qualified,° and less | *having notable qualities* |
|   | attemptable° than any the rarest of our ladies in France. | *open to seduction* |
|   | GIACOMO That lady is not now living, or this gentleman's opinion by this° worn out. | *by now* |
| 55 | POSTHUMUS She holds her virtue still, and I my mind. | |
|   | GIACOMO You must not so far prefer her fore ours of Italy. | |
|   | POSTHUMUS Being so far provoked as I was in France I would | |
|   | abate her nothing,⁸ though I profess myself her adorer, not her | |
|   | friend.° | *lover; spouse* |
| 60 | GIACOMO As fair and as good—a kind of hand-in-hand comparison⁹—had been something too fair and too good for any lady | |
|   | in Britain. If she went before° others I have seen—as that diamond of yours outlustres many I have beheld—I could not but | *she surpassed* |
|   | believe she excelled many; but I have not seen the most precious diamond that is, nor you the lady. | |
| 65 | | |
|   | POSTHUMUS I praised her as I rated° her; so do I my stone. | *valued* |
|   | GIACOMO What do you esteem it at? | |

---

5. How does he claim a connection to you? Giacomo implies that Posthumus cunningly insinuated himself into Filario's friendship.
6. Than to appear.
7. The women of our country.

8. I would subtract nothing from my estimation of her.
9. A comparison claiming equality (not superiority); with a possible pun on the "handfast" by which couples pledged their duty to one another at their betrothal.

POSTHUMUS   More than the world enjoys.°                                                           *possesses*

GIACOMO   Either your unparagoned mistress is dead, or she's

70   outprized° by a trifle.                                                                              *exceeded in value*

POSTHUMUS   You are mistaken. The one° may be sold or given,                                       *(the ring)*
or if° there were wealth enough for the purchase or merit for                                       *if either*
the gift. The other° is not a thing for sale, and only the gift of                                   *(his mistress)*
the gods.

75   GIACOMO   Which the gods have given you?

POSTHUMUS   Which, by their graces, I will keep.

GIACOMO   You may wear her in title yours;[1] but, you know,
strange fowl light upon neighbouring ponds.[2] Your ring[3] may
be stolen too; so your brace of unprizable estimations,[4] the one

80   is but frail, and the other casual.[5] A cunning thief or a that-way
accomplished courtier[6] would hazard° the winning both of first                                    *venture*
and last.

POSTHUMUS   Your Italy contains none so accomplished a court-
ier to convince° the honour of my mistress if in the holding or                                      *overcome*

85   loss of that you term her frail. I do nothing doubt you have
store° of thieves; notwithstanding, I fear not[7] my ring.                                           *an abundance*

FILARIO   Let us leave° here, gentlemen.                                                             *stop the conversation*

POSTHUMUS   Sir, with all my heart. This worthy signor, I thank
him, makes no stranger of me. We are familiar at first.

90   GIACOMO   With five times so much conversation I should get
ground of[8] your fair mistress, make her go back° even to the                                       *relent*
yielding, had I admittance and opportunity to friend.°                                               *to assist me*

POSTHUMUS   No, no.

GIACOMO   I dare thereupon pawn the moiety° of my estate to                                          *one half*

95   your ring, which in my opinion o'ervalues it something. But I
make my wager rather against your confidence than her reputation, and, to bar your offence[9] herein too, I durst attempt it
against any lady in the world.

POSTHUMUS   You are a great deal abused in too bold a persua-

100   sion,[1] and I doubt not you sustain° what you're worthy of by                                   *will receive*
your attempt.

GIACOMO   What's that?

POSTHUMUS   A repulse; though your attempt, as you call it,
deserve more—a punishment, too.

105   FILARIO   Gentlemen, enough of this. It came in too suddenly.
Let it die as it was born; and, I pray you, be better acquainted.

GIACOMO   Would I had put my estate and my neighbour's on
th'approbation° of what I have spoke.                                                                 *the proof*

POSTHUMUS   What lady would you choose to assail?

110   GIACOMO   Yours, whom in constancy you think stands so safe. I
will lay° you ten thousand ducats to your ring that, commend                                         *wager*
me to the court where your lady is, with no more advantage
than the opportunity of a second conference, and I will bring
from thence that honour of hers which you imagine so

115   reserved.

1. You may claim her as your legal possession (with a pun on "wear" as meaning "enjoy her sexually").
2. *strange . . . ponds*: strangers may come upon your property (with a pun on "pond" as referring to female genitals).
3. Punning on "ring" as another slang term for "female genitals".
4. So of the two ("brace of") objects you deem invaluable.
5. And the other subject to accident (referring to the ring).
6. A courtier skilled in that way (in the arts of seduction and theft).
7. Am not anxious about.
8. Get the advantage of.
9. To prevent you from feeling personally affronted.
1. A great deal deceived in your too bold belief.

POSTHUMUS    I will wage against your gold, gold to it;° my ring I     *gold equal to it*
hold dear as my finger, 'tis part of it.

GIACOMO    You are a friend, and therein the wiser.[2] If you buy
120    ladies' flesh at a million a dram,[3] you cannot preserve it from
tainting. But I see you have some religion in you, that° you     *since*
fear.

POSTHUMUS    This is but a custom in your tongue.[4] You bear a
graver purpose, I hope.

GIACOMO    I am the master of my speeches, and would undergo°     *undertake*
125    what's spoken, I swear.

POSTHUMUS    Will you? I shall but lend my diamond till your
return. Let there be covenants° drawn between 's. My mistress     *agreements*
exceeds in goodness the hugeness of your unworthy thinking. I
dare you to this match. Here's my ring.

130  FILARIO    I will have it no lay.°     *wager*

GIACOMO    By the gods, it is one. If I bring you no sufficient testimony that I have enjoyed the dearest bodily part of your mistress, my ten thousand ducats are yours; so is your diamond too.
If I come off and leave her in such honour as you have trust in,
135    she your jewel, this your jewel, and my gold are yours, provided
I have your commendation for my more free entertainment.[5]

POSTHUMUS    I embrace these conditions; let us have articles
betwixt us. Only thus far you shall answer: if you make your
voyage upon her and give me directly° to understand you have     *plainly*
140    prevailed, I am no further your enemy; she is not worth our
debate. If she remain unseduced, you not making it appear
otherwise, for your ill opinion and th'assault you have made to
her chastity you shall answer me with your sword.

GIACOMO    Your hand, a covenant. We will have these things set
145    down by lawful counsel, and straight away° for Britain, lest the     *depart at once*
bargain should catch cold and starve.° I will fetch my gold and     *die*
have our two wagers recorded.

POSTHUMUS    Agreed.     [*Exit with* GIACOMO]

FRENCHMAN    Will this hold, think you?

150  FILARIO    Signor Giacomo will not from it. Pray let us follow 'em.
                      *Exeunt.* [*Table is removed*]

### 1.5

*Enter* QUEEN, LADIES, *and* CORNELIUS [*a doctor*]

QUEEN    Whiles yet the dew's on ground, gather those flowers.
Make haste. Who has the note° of them?     *list*

A LADY                             I, madam.

QUEEN    Dispatch.°                  *Exeunt* LADIES     *Make haste*
Now, Master Doctor, have you brought those drugs?

5  CORNELIUS    Pleaseth° your highness, ay. Here they are, madam.     *If it please*
    [*He gives her a box*]
But I beseech your grace, without offence—
My conscience bids me ask—wherefore° you have     *why*
Commanded of me these most poisonous compounds,

---

2. Implying that Posthumus's intimacy with Innogen
("friend" means "lover" or "husband") makes him wise
enough not to risk his ring in a wager on her chastity or
wise enough to know the danger of this wager.
3. Even if you pay a large amount of money for a very
small amount (a "dram") of female flesh.
4. This is merely a conventional way for you to speak.
5. Provided I have your introduction (to Innogen) to
ensure a generous reception.
1.5 Location: Cymbeline's court, Britain.

Which are the movers of a languishing death,
But though slow, deadly.

10 QUEEN                               I wonder, doctor,
Thou ask'st me such a question. Have I not been
Thy pupil long? Hast thou not learned° me how                    taught
To make perfumes, distil, preserve—yea, so
That our great King himself doth woo me oft

15 For my confections?° Having thus far proceeded,        medical compounds
Unless thou think'st me devilish, is't not meet°                    fitting
That I did amplify my judgement in
Other conclusions?° I will try° the forces          experiments / test
Of these thy compounds on such creatures as

20 We count not worth the hanging, but none human,
To try the vigour of them, and apply
Allayments to their act,[1] and by them° gather          (these experiments)
Their several virtues[2] and effects.

CORNELIUS                               Your highness
Shall from this practice but make hard your heart.

25 Besides, the seeing these effects will be
Both noisome° and infectious.                                    offensive

QUEEN                               O, content thee.

*Enter* PISANIO

[*Aside*] Here comes a flattering rascal; upon him
Will I first work. He's factor° for his master,                  an agent
And enemy to my son. [*Aloud*] How now, Pisanio?—

30 Doctor, your service for this time is ended.
Take your own way.

CORNELIUS [*aside*]      I do suspect you, madam.
But you shall do no harm.

QUEEN [*to* PISANIO]            Hark thee, a word.

CORNELIUS [*aside*]    I do not like her. She doth think she has
Strange ling'ring poisons. I do know her spirit,

35 And will not trust one of her malice with
A drug of such damned nature. Those she has
Will stupefy and dull the sense a while,
Which first, perchance, she'll prove° on cats and dogs,          test
Then afterward up higher; but there is

40 No danger in what show of death it makes
More than the locking up the spirits a time,[3]
To be more fresh, reviving. She is fooled
With a most false effect, and I the truer
So to be false with her.

QUEEN                               No further service, doctor,
Until I send for thee.

45 CORNELIUS            I humbly take my leave.            *Exit*

QUEEN [*to* PISANIO]    Weeps she still, sayst thou? Dost thou think in time
She will not quench,° and let instructions° enter    grow cool / good advice
Where folly now possesses? Do thou work.
When thou shalt bring me word she loves my son

50 I'll tell thee on the instant thou art then
As great as is thy master—greater, for
His fortunes all lie speechless, and his name°                  reputation

---

1. *apply . . . act:* apply antidotes to their operation.
2. Their (the compounds') individual powers.

3. Other than the temporary suspension of the vital functions.

Is at last gasp. Return he cannot, nor
Continue where he is. To shift his being°                    *change his abode*
55 Is to exchange one misery with another,
And every day that comes comes to decay°                    *destroy*
A day's work in him. What shalt thou expect
To be depender on a thing that leans,[4]
Who cannot be new built nor has no friends
So much as but to prop him?
    [*She drops her box. He takes it up*]
60                         Thou tak'st up
Thou know'st not what; but take it for thy labour.
It is a thing I made which hath the King
Five times redeemed from death. I do not know
What is more cordial.° Nay, I prithee take it.                *restorative*
65 It is an earnest° of a farther good                          *initial payment*
That I mean to thee. Tell thy mistress how
The case stands with her; do't as from thyself.
Think what a chance thou changest on,[5] but think
Thou hast thy mistress still; to boot,° my son,              *in addition*
70 Who shall take notice of thee.° I'll move the King          *give attention to you*
To any shape of thy preferment,° such                        *any kind of advancement*
As thou'lt desire; and then myself, I chiefly,
That set thee on to this desert,° am bound                   *action deserving reward*
To load thy merit richly. Call my women.
Think on my words.                *Exit* PISANIO
75                  A sly and constant knave,
Not to be shaked; the agent for his master,
And the remembrancer of her° to hold                         *the one who reminds her*
The hand-fast° to her lord. I have given him that[6]         *marriage contract*
Which, if he take, shall quite unpeople her
80 Of liegers for her sweet,[7] and which she after,
Except she bend her humour,[8] shall be assured
To taste of too.
      *Enter* PISANIO *and* LADIES
         So, so; well done, well done.
The violets, cowslips, and the primroses
Bear to my closet.° Fare thee well, Pisanio.                 *private chamber*
Think on my words, Pisanio.
85 PISANIO             And shall do.
           *Exeunt* QUEEN *and* LADIES
But when to my good lord I prove untrue,
I'll choke myself—there's all I'll do for you.    *Exit*

## 1.6

    *Enter* INNOGEN
INNOGEN   A father cruel and a stepdame false,
   A foolish suitor to a wedded lady
That hath her husband banished.[1] O, that husband,
My supreme crown of grief, and those repeated[2]
5 Vexations of it! Had I been thief-stol'n,

---

4. To be dependent on a thing that is about to fall.
5. Consider what opportunity you have to change your service (and become my servant).
6. The box supposedly containing poison.
7. Of ambassadors for her sweetheart.

8. Unless she changes her disposition.
1.6 Location: Cymbeline's court.
1. Who has a banished husband.
2. Those already enumerated. Innogen has already complained of her father, stepmother, and foolish suitor.

As my two brothers, happy;³ but most miserable
Is the desire that's glorious.⁴ Blest be those,
How mean soe'er,⁵ that have their honest wills,°                    *simple desires*
Which seasons comfort.⁶

     *Enter* PISANIO *and* GIACOMO
                          Who may this be? Fie!

10  PISANIO   Madam, a noble gentleman of Rome
Comes from my lord with letters.

  GIACOMO               Change you,° madam?                    *Do you turn pale*
The worthy Leonatus is in safety,
And greets your highness dearly.
    [*He gives her the letters*]

  INNOGEN              Thanks, good sir.
You're kindly welcome.
    [*She reads the letters*]

15  GIACOMO [*aside*]   All of her that is out of door° most rich!        *is visible*
If she be furnished with a mind so rare
She is alone, th'Arabian bird,⁷ and I
Have lost the wager. Boldness be my friend;
Arm me audacity from head to foot,

20  Or, like the Parthian, I shall flying fight;⁸
Rather, directly fly.

  INNOGEN *reads* [*aloud*]   'He is one of the noblest note,° to whose        *reputation*
kindnesses I am most infinitely tied. Reflect° upon him accord-        *Bestow attention*
ingly, as you value

25                       Your truest
                            Leonatus.'
    [*To Giacomo*] So far I read aloud,
But even the very middle of my heart
Is warmed by th'rest, and takes it thankfully.

30  You are as welcome, worthy sir, as I
Have words to bid you, and shall find it so
In all that I can do.

  GIACOMO          Thanks, fairest lady.
What, are men mad? Hath nature given them eyes
To see this vaulted arch° and the rich crop°                    *the sky / harvest*

35  Of sea and land, which can distinguish 'twixt
The fiery orbs above and the twinned° stones                    *identical*
Upon th'unnumbered beach,⁹ and can we not
Partition make with spectacles¹ so precious
'Twixt fair and foul?

  INNOGEN        What makes your admiration?°                    *causes you wonder*

40  GIACOMO   It cannot be i'th' eye—for apes and monkeys,
'Twixt two such shes,° would chatter this way² and                    *women*
Contemn with mows° the other; nor i'th' judgement,                    *Scorn with grimaces*
For idiots in this case of favour° would                    *question of preference*
Be wisely definite; nor i'th' appetite—

45  Sluttery,° to such neat° excellence opposed,                    *Sluttishness / elegant*

---

3. *happy:* I would have been glad or fortunate.
4. But most wretched is the longing for what is exalted (in her case, a longing for Posthumus).
5. However low in status.
6. Which adds spice to their comfort.
7. The phoenix, only one of which existed at any given time. This mythical bird consumed itself in fire every

five hundred years but then rose from its own ashes.
8. The mounted archers of Parthia were famous for their tactics in warfare, which included shooting arrows behind them as they retreated.
9. Upon the beach whose grains of sand are uncounted.
1. Make distinction with organs of sight.
2. Would make their preference (for Innogen) clear.

Should make desire vomit emptiness,
Not so allured to feed.³

INNOGEN   What is the matter, trow?°                                                    *in truth*
GIACOMO   The cloyèd will,°                                                         *sated sexual desire*
50   That satiate° yet unsatisfied desire, that tub                                          *glutted*
Both filled and running,° ravening° first the lamb,                      *emptying itself / devouring*
Longs after for the garbage.
INNOGEN                          What, dear sir,
Thus raps° you? Are you well?                                                        *transports*
GIACOMO   Thanks, madam, well. [*To* PISANIO] Beseech° you, sir,                             *I ask*
55   Desire° my man's abode where I did leave him.                                         *Seek out*
He's strange° and peevish.°                                                  *a foreigner / irritable*
PISANIO                          I was going, sir,
To give him welcome.                                                                    *Exit*
INNOGEN                          Continues well my lord?
His health, beseech you?
GIACOMO                          Well, madam.
INNOGEN   Is he disposed to mirth? I hope he is.
60   GIACOMO   Exceeding pleasant, none a stranger° there                         *none of the foreigners*
So merry and so gamesome.⁴ He is called
The Briton Reveller.
INNOGEN                          When he was here
He did incline to sadness,° and oft-times                                             *seriousness*
Not knowing why.
GIACOMO                          I never saw him sad.
65   There is a Frenchman his companion, one
An eminent monsieur that, it seems, much loves
A Gallian° girl at home. He furnaces⁵                                                   *French*
The thick sighs from him, whiles the jolly° Briton—                                 *lively; lustful*
Your lord, I mean—laughs from 's free° lungs, cries 'O,                             *unconstrained*
70   Can my sides hold, to think that man, who knows
By history, report or his own proof
What woman is, yea, what she cannot choose
But must be, will 's free hours languish°                                              *pine away*
For assurèd bondage?'
INNOGEN                          Will my lord say so?
75   GIACOMO   Ay, madam, with his eyes in flood with laughter.
It is a recreation to be by
And hear him mock the Frenchman. But heavens know
Some men are much to blame.
INNOGEN                          Not he, I hope.
GIACOMO   Not he; but yet heaven's bounty towards him might
80   Be used more thankfully. In himself 'tis much;
In you, which I count his, beyond all talents.⁶
Whilst I am bound to wonder, I am bound
To pity too.
INNOGEN                          What do you pity, sir?
GIACOMO   Two creatures heartily.
INNOGEN                          Am I one, sir?

---

3. *Should . . . feed*: Should destroy sexual desire, not
arouse it (literally, should make desire vomit until it is
empty, not tempt it to eat).
4. Sportive; sexually playful.
5. He exhales like a furnace.

6. *In himself . . . talents*: As regards his own qualities,
heaven's generosity is considerable. In giving him you,
whom I consider his, heaven's generosity surpasses all
abundance.

85      You look on me; what wreck° discern you in me         *downfall*
        Deserves your pity?
     GIACOMO                  Lamentable! What,
        To hide me from the radiant sun, and solace°         *take comfort*
        I'th' dungeon by a snuff?°                          *candle end*
     INNOGEN                I pray you, sir,
        Deliver with more openness your answers
90      To my demands. Why do you pity me?
     GIACOMO    That others do—
        I was about to say enjoy your—but
        It is an office° of the gods to venge° it,        *a duty / revenge*
        Not mine to speak on't.°                       *of it*
     INNOGEN            You do seem to know
95      Something of me, or what concerns me. Pray you,
        Since doubting° things go ill often hurts more      *suspecting*
        Than to be sure they do—for certainties
        Either are past remedies, or, timely knowing,
        The remedy then born[7]—discover° to me         *reveal*
        What both you spur and stop.[8]
100    GIACOMO               Had I this cheek
        To bathe my lips upon; this hand whose touch,
        Whose every touch, would force the feeler's soul
        To th'oath of loyalty; this object which
        Takes prisoner the wild motion of mine eye,
105      Firing° it only here: should I, damned then,         *Enflaming*
        Slaver with lips as common as the stairs
        That mount the Capitol;[9] join grips with hands
        Made hard with hourly falsehood—falsehood as
        With labour;[1] then by-peeping° in an eye        *glancing coyly*
110      Base and illustrous° as the smoky light         *lacking luster*
        That's fed with stinking tallow—it were fit
        That all the plagues of hell should at one time
        Encounter° such revolt.°              *Confront / infidelity*
     INNOGEN            My lord, I fear,
        Has forgot Britain.
     GIACOMO            And himself. Not I
115      Inclined to this intelligence pronounce
        The beggary of his change,[2] but 'tis your graces
        That from my mutest conscience° to my tongue    *most quiet inner being*
        Charms this report out.
     INNOGEN            Let me hear no more.
     GIACOMO    O dearest soul, your cause doth strike my heart
120      With pity that doth make me sick. A lady
        So fair, and fastened to an empery°            *empire*
        Would make the great'st king double,° to be partnered    *twice as great*
        With tomboys hired with that self exhibition[3]
        Which your own coffers yield; with diseased ventures°    *prostitutes; vendors*
125      That play with all infirmities for gold

---

7. *or . . . born:* or, they being known about in time, the remedy is then brought about.
8. *What you both urge on and restrain* (as one commands a horse).
9. *Slaver . . . Capitol:* Offer drooling kisses to whores who, like the stairs to the Roman Capitol building, are available to everyone.
1. *join . . . labour:* clasp hands made as hard with

hourly lies or sexual infidelities as they might have been made hard with work.
2. *Not . . . change:* It is not because I am disposed to give this information that I report the contemptible nature of his change.
3. With whores ("tomboys") hired with that same payment.

Which rottenness can lend to nature; such boiled stuff[4]
As well might poison poison! Be revenged,
Or she that bore you was no queen, and you
Recoil° from your great stock.                                    *Degenerate*

INNOGEN                              Revenged?
130  How should I be revenged? If this be true—
As I have such a heart that both mine ears
Must not in haste abuse[5]—if it be true,
How should I be revenged?

GIACOMO                          Should he make me
Live like Diana's priest[6] betwixt cold sheets
135  Whiles he is vaulting variable ramps,[7]
In your despite, upon your purse[8]—revenge it.
I dedicate myself to your sweet pleasure,
More noble than that runagate° to your bed,              *renegade*
And will continue fast° to your affection,                  *constant*
Still close as sure.[9]

140  INNOGEN                       What ho, Pisanio!

GIACOMO  Let me my service tender on your lips.

INNOGEN  Away, I do condemn mine ears that have
So long attended thee. If thou wert honourable
Thou wouldst have told this tale for virtue, not
145  For such an end thou seek'st, as base as strange.
Thou wrong'st a gentleman who is as far
From thy report as thou from honour, and
Solicit'st here a lady that disdains
Thee and the devil alike. What ho, Pisanio!
150  The King my father shall be made acquainted
Of thy assault. If he shall think it fit
A saucy stranger in his court to mart°                       *do business*
As in a Romish stew,° and to expound                     *Roman brothel*
His beastly mind to us, he hath a court
155  He little cares for, and a daughter who
He not respects at all. What ho, Pisanio!

GIACOMO  O happy Leonatus! I may say
The credit° that thy lady hath of° thee                       *trust / in*
Deserves thy trust, and thy most perfect goodness
160  Her assured credit.[1] Blessèd live you long,
A lady to the worthiest sir that ever
Country called his;° and you his mistress, only            *its own*
For the most worthiest fit. Give me your pardon.
I have spoke this to know if your affiance°                 *faith*
165  Were deeply rooted, and shall make your lord
That which he is new o'er;[2] and he is one
The truest mannered,[3] such a holy witch°             *a charming person*
That he enchants societies into° him;              *crowds of people to*
Half all men's hearts are his.

4. Such diseased prostitutes. Sweating, usually
induced by the steam from boiling water, was a common treatment for syphilis.
5. *a heart . . . abuse:* a heart that my ears must not
abuse by too hastily accepting what they hear.
6. That is, live chastely. Diana was the Roman goddess
of the hunt known for her chastity and her circle of virgin followers.
7. While he is having sexual intercourse with whores
("ramps") of all kinds.

8. In contempt of you, with your money.
9. Always as secret as I am true.
1. *and . . . credit:* and your most perfect goodness
deserves her absolute trust.
2. *and . . . o'er:* and I (by this news of your fidelity) shall
make your lord feel afresh what he already is (that is,
your lord).
3. *he . . . mannered:* he is above all others the most perfect in conduct.

| | INNOGEN | You make amends. | |
|---|---|---|---|
| 170 | GIACOMO | He sits 'mongst men like a descended god. | |

INNOGEN  You make amends.

170 GIACOMO  He sits 'mongst men like a descended god.
 He hath a kind of honour sets him off
 More than a mortal seeming.⁴ Be not angry,
 Most mighty princess, that I have adventured°         *dared*
 To try° your taking of a false report, which hath       *test*
175 Honoured with confirmation your great judgement
 In the election of a sir so rare
 Which° you know cannot err. The love I bear him      *Whom*
 Made me to fan⁵ you thus, but the gods made you,
 Unlike all others, chaffless.° Pray, your pardon.    *without chaff; perfect*
180 INNOGEN  All's well, sir. Take my power i'th' court for yours.
 GIACOMO  My humble thanks. I had almost forgot
 T'entreat your grace but in a small request,
 And yet of moment° too, for it concerns         *importance*
 Your lord; myself and other noble friends
 Are partners in the business.
185 INNOGEN          Pray what is't?
 GIACOMO  Some dozen Romans of us, and your lord—
 Best feather of our wing—have mingled sums
 To buy a present for the Emperor,
 Which I, the factor° for the rest, have done       *agent*
190 In France. 'Tis plate⁶ of rare device, and jewels
 Of rich and exquisite form; their value's great,
 And I am something curious,° being strange,°   *somewhat anxious / foreign*
 To have them in safe stowage. May it please you
 To take them in protection?
 INNOGEN         Willingly,
195 And pawn mine honour for their safety; since
 My lord hath interest° in them, I will keep them     *a stake*
 In my bedchamber.
 GIACOMO        They are in a trunk
 Attended by my men. I will make bold
 To send them to you, only for this night.
 I must aboard tomorrow.
200 INNOGEN         O, no, no!
 GIACOMO  Yes, I beseech, or I shall short° my word     *break*
 By length'ning my return. From Gallia°        *France*
 I crossed the seas on purpose and on promise
 To see your grace.
 INNOGEN       I thank you for your pains;
 But not away tomorrow!
205 GIACOMO        O, I must, madam.
 Therefore I shall beseech you, if you please
 To greet your lord with writing, do't tonight.
 I have outstood° my time, which is material     *overstayed*
 To th' tender° of our present.        *the offering*
 INNOGEN        I will write.
210 Send your trunk to me, it shall safe be kept,
 And truly yielded° you. You're very welcome.   *faithfully returned to*

*Exeunt [severally]*

---

4. So that he appears more than mortal.
5. Winnow. When grain was harvested, wheat was winnowed from the chaff; metaphorically, the good was winnowed from the bad.
6. Objects, often tableware, either made of precious metals or covered ("plated") with them.

## 2.1

*Enter* CLOTEN *and the two* LORDS

CLOTEN   Was there ever man had such luck? When I kissed the
jack[1] upon an upcast,° to be hit away! I had a hundred pound    *on a final throw*
on't, and then a whoreson jackanapes° must take me up[2] for    *an idiotic bastard*
swearing, as if I borrowed mine oaths of him, and might not
5  spend them at my pleasure.

FIRST LORD   What got he by that? You have broke his pate with
your bowl.

SECOND LORD [*aside*]   If his wit had been like him that broke it,
it would have run all out.

10  CLOTEN   When a gentleman is disposed to swear it is not for any
standers-by to curtail[3] his oaths, ha?

SECOND LORD   No, my lord [*aside*]—nor crop the ears of them.

CLOTEN   Whoreson dog! I give him satisfaction? Would he had
been one of my rank.[4]

15  SECOND LORD [*aside*]   To have smelled like a fool.

CLOTEN   I am not vexed more at anything in th'earth. A pox
on't,[5] I had rather not be so noble as I am. They dare not fight
with me because of the Queen, my mother. Every jack-slave°    *lowborn fellow*
hath his bellyful of fighting, and I must go up and down like a
20  cock that nobody can match.°    *equal; fight with*

SECOND LORD [*aside*]   You are cock and capon too an you crow
cock with your comb on.[6]

CLOTEN   Sayst thou?

SECOND LORD   It is not fit your lordship should undertake° every    *take on*
25  companion° that you give offence to.    *fellow*

CLOTEN   No, I know that, but it is fit I should commit offence
to[7] my inferiors.

SECOND LORD   Ay, it is fit for your lordship only.

CLOTEN   Why, so I say.

30  FIRST LORD   Did you hear of a stranger° that's come to court    *foreigner*
tonight?

CLOTEN   A stranger, and I not know on't?°    *of it*

SECOND LORD [*aside*]   He's a strange fellow himself and knows
it not.

35  FIRST LORD   There's an Italian come, and, 'tis thought, one of
Leonatus' friends.

CLOTEN   Leonatus? A banished rascal; and he's another, whatsoever he be. Who told you of this stranger?

FIRST LORD   One of your lordship's pages.

40  CLOTEN   Is it fit I went to look upon him? Is there no derogation°    *loss of dignity*
in't?

SECOND LORD   You cannot derogate,[8] my lord.

CLOTEN   Not easily, I think.

---

2.1 Location: Cymbeline's court, Britain.
1. In the game of bowls, the jack is the target ball. To
"kiss the jack" is to roll one's ball so that it touches the
jack.
2. Challenge me; rebuke me.
3. Shorten, as one bobbed the tails (and sometimes the
ears) of certain dogs. This leads the Second Lord to talk
of cropping the ears of oaths in line 12.
4. Social position. Gentlemen were only supposed to
fight ("give satisfaction" to) men of their own rank. The

Second Lord puns on "rank" as meaning "strong smell."
5. A mild oath meaning "a plague on it."
6. And a castrated cock too if you brag ("crow") that
you are a cock while wearing a fool's cap (coxcomb).
There are puns here on "capon" and "cap on," on
"cock's comb" and "coxcomb."
7. I should assault, with the perhaps unintended secondary meaning of "to defecate upon."
8. You cannot forfeit your dignity; you have no dignity
to lose.

SECOND LORD [*aside*]   You are a fool granted,° therefore your         *an acknowledged fool*
45      issues,° being foolish, do not derogate.                                                        *deeds*
CLOTEN   Come, I'll go see this Italian. What I have lost today at
        bowls I'll win tonight of him. Come, go.
SECOND LORD   I'll attend your lordship.
                                                                              *Exeunt* [CLOTEN *and* FIRST LORD]
        That such a crafty devil as is his mother
50      Should yield the world this ass!—a woman that
        Bears all down° with her brain, and this her son                  *Overcomes everyone*
        Cannot take two from twenty, for his heart,°                       *for the life of him*
        And leave eighteen. Alas, poor princess,
        Thou divine Innogen, what thou endur'st,
55      Betwixt a father by thy stepdame governed,
        A mother hourly coining plots, a wooer
        More hateful than the foul expulsion is
        Of thy dear husband, than that horrid act
        Of the divorce he'd make! The heavens hold firm
60      The walls of thy dear honour, keep unshaked
        That temple, thy fair mind, that thou mayst stand
        T'enjoy thy banished lord and this great land!            *Exit*

## 2.2

[*A trunk and arras.*[1] *A*] *bed* [*is thrust forth with*] INNO-
GEN [*in it, reading a book. Enter to her* HELEN], *a lady*[2]
INNOGEN   Who's there? My woman Helen?
HELEN                                                                   Please you, madam.
INNOGEN   What hour is it?
HELEN                                            Almost midnight, madam.
INNOGEN   I have read three hours then. Mine eyes are weak.
        Fold down the leaf where I have left. To bed.
5       Take not away the taper; leave it burning,
        And if thou canst awake by four o'th' clock,
        I prithee call me. Sleep hath seized me wholly.     [*Exit* HELEN]
        To your protection I commend me, gods.
        From fairies° and the tempters of the night                       *evil beings*
10      Guard me, beseech ye.°                                                *I entreat you*
                [*She*] *sleeps.*
                GIACOMO [*comes*] *from the trunk*
GIACOMO   The crickets sing, and man's o'er-laboured sense
        Repairs itself by rest. Our Tarquin[3] thus
        Did softly press the rushes[4] ere he wakened
        The chastity he wounded. Cytherea,[5]
15      How bravely° thou becom'st thy bed! Fresh lily,                    *splendidly*
        And whiter than the sheets! That I might touch,
        But kiss, one kiss! Rubies unparagoned,
        How dearly they do't![6] 'Tis her breathing that
        Perfumes the chamber thus. The flame o'th' taper

---

**2.2**  Location: Innogen's chambers.
1. Tapestry wall covering.
2. F's stage direction reads "Enter Imogen, in her Bed, and a Lady." The trunk in which Giacomo is concealed is probably brought onstage as the scene opens, either carried on or raised up through the trapdoor in the stage floor. Beds typically were "thrust forth" from a door at the back of the stage. Giacomo mentions an arras in his ensuing description of Innogen's bedroom. One may

have been hung up at the back of the stage for this scene.
3. The ancient Roman Sextus Tarquinius, whose rape of Lucrece (Lucretia) was the subject of a poem by Shakespeare.
4. Reeds commonly used as a floor covering.
5. A name for Aphrodite, or Venus, the goddess of beauty and love, who first set foot on the island of Cytherea after her birth from sea-foam.
6. How dearly do they (her ruby lips) kiss one another.

20    Bows toward her, and would underpeep her lids,
      To see th'enclosèd lights, now canopied
      Under these windows,° white and azure-laced                    *eyelids*
      With blue of heaven's own tinct.° But my design—              *hue*
      To note the chamber. I will write all down.
            [*He writes in his tables*]°                             *writing tablets*
25    Such and such pictures, there the window, such
      Th'adornment of her bed, the arras, figures,
      Why, such and such; and the contents o'th' story.[7]
      Ah, but some natural notes° about her body                    *marks*
      Above ten thousand meaner movables[8]
30    Would testify t'enrich mine inventory.
      O sleep, thou ape° of death, lie dull° upon her,              *mimic / heavy*
      And be her sense but as a monument[9]
      Thus in a chapel lying. Come off, come off;
      As slippery as the Gordian knot was hard.[1]
            [*He takes the bracelet from her arm*]
35    'Tis mine, and this will witness outwardly,
      As strongly as the conscience does within,[2]
      To th' madding° of her lord. On her left breast               *maddening*
      A mole, cinque-spotted,° like the crimson drops               *with five spots*
      I'th' bottom of a cowslip. Here's a voucher°                  *piece of evidence*
40    Stronger than ever law could make. This secret
      Will force him think I have picked the lock and ta'en
      The treasure of her honour.[3] No more. To what end?
      Why should I write this down that's riveted,
      Screwed to my memory? She hath been reading late,
45    The tale of Tereus.[4] Here the leaf's turned down
      Where Philomel gave up. I have enough.
      To th' trunk again, and shut the spring of it.
      Swift, swift, you dragons of the night, that dawning
      May bare the raven's eye![5] I lodge in fear.
50    Though this' a heavenly angel, hell is here.
            *Clock strikes*
      One, two, three. Time, time!
            *Exit* [*into the trunk. The bed and trunk are removed*]

## 2.3

*Enter* CLOTEN *and* [*the two*] LORDS

FIRST LORD    Your lordship is the most patient man in loss, the
      most coldest° that ever turned up ace.[1]                     *least passionate*
CLOTEN    It would make any man cold to lose.

---

7. The design on the tapestry (?). In 2.4.66–91, Giacomo describes in more detail what he saw in Innogen's
bedchamber: a tapestry depicting the story of Antony
and Cleopatra and a chimneypiece carving of Diana
bathing. He could here be referring to the "figures" and
"contents" of either the tapestry or chimneypiece.
8. Less important pieces of property, especially furniture or furnishings.
9. And let her senses be like those of an effigy on a tomb.
1. As easy to open as the Gordian knot was difficult to
untie. Alluding to the myth of Gordius, King of Phrygia,
who tied an impossibly intricate knot and declared that
whoever could untie it would reign over Asia; with a single
thrust of his sword, Alexander the Great cut through it.
Giacomo's unclasping of the bracelet has sexual implications. He is metaphorically violating Innogen's

chastity and, by stealing Posthumus's love token, is
interfering in the marriage bond that links Posthumus
and Innogen.
2. As powerfully as does his inward consciousness.
3. Giacomo means his knowledge of the mole will
make Posthumus believe he has slept with Innogen. To
"pick the lock" is a euphemism for "to have sex."
4. In Greek mythology, Tereus, King of Thrace, raped
his wife's sister Philomela and cut out her tongue so she
could not reveal what had happened. Philomela later
wove the story into a tapestry.
5. May cause the raven to wake. The bird supposedly
slept facing east and awakened at dawn.
2.3 Location: A room near Innogen's chambers.
1. *that . . . ace:* who ever threw the lowest score in a
game of dice, with a pun on "ass."

FIRST LORD    But not every man patient after° the noble temper           *according to*
5      of your lordship. You are most hot and furious when you win.
CLOTEN    Winning will put any man into courage. If I could get
        this foolish Innogen I should have gold enough. It's almost
        morning, is't not?
FIRST LORD    Day, my lord.
10   CLOTEN    I would this music would come. I am advised to give
        her music o' mornings; they say it will penetrate.[2]
            *Enter* MUSICIANS
        Come on, tune. If you can penetrate her with your fingering,
        so; we'll try with tongue too.[3] If none will do,° let her remain;    *suffice*
        but I'll never give o'er. First, a very excellent good-conceited°     *ingenious*
15      thing; after, a wonderful sweet air with admirable rich words
        to it; and then let her consider.
            [*Music*]
MUSICIAN [*sings*][4]    Hark, hark, the lark at heaven gate sings,
        And Phoebus gins° arise,[5]                                          *Apollo (sun god) begins*
        His steeds to water at those springs
20      On chaliced flowers[6] that lies,
        And winking Mary-buds° begin to ope their golden eyes;              *closed marigold buds*
        With everything that pretty is, my lady sweet, arise,
        Arise, arise!
CLOTEN    So, get you gone. If this penetrate I will consider° your         *value*
25      music the better; if it do not, it is a vice° in her ears which       *defect*
        horse hairs and calves' guts[7] nor the voice of unpaved[8] eunuch
        to boot can never amend.                        [*Exeunt* MUSICIANS]
            *Enter* CYMBELINE *and* [*the*] QUEEN
SECOND LORD    Here comes the King.
CLOTEN    I am glad I was up so late, for that's the reason I was up
30      so early. He cannot choose but take this service I have done
        fatherly. Good morrow to your majesty, and to my gracious
        mother.
CYMBELINE    Attend you here the door of our stern daughter?
        Will she not forth?
35   CLOTEN    I have assailed her with musics, but she vouchsafes no
        notice.
CYMBELINE    The exile of her minion° is too new.                           *darling*
        She hath not yet forgot him. Some more time
        Must wear the print° of his remembrance out,                        *imprint*
        And then she's yours.
40   QUEEN [*to* CLOTEN]        You are most bound to th' King,
        Who lets go by no vantages° that may                                *opportunities*
        Prefer° you to his daughter. Frame° yourself                        *Recommend / Prepare*
        To° orderly solicits,° and be friended                              *With / solicitations*
        With aptness of the season.[9] Make denials
45      Increase your services; so seem as if
        You were inspired to do those duties which
        You tender to her; that you in all obey her,

2. Affect her emotions; arouse her sexually.
3. If your instrumental music can move her, that's
good. We'll try to move her with song as well. These
lines also carry an explicitly sexual secondary meaning:
If you can insert your fingers inside her, that's good.
We'll try oral sex as well. It is unclear if Cloten understands the bawdy import of his own words.
4. F does not attribute this song to a particular singer
but simply introduces it as "SONG." It also appears in a

seventeenth-century manuscript located in the
Bodleian Library at Oxford.
5. These lines also echo Shakespeare's sonnet 29, lines
10–12: "my state / Like to the lark at break of day arising / From sullen earth, sings hymns at heaven's gate."
6. Flowers with cuplike blossoms.
7. Both were used as strings for musical instruments.
8. Castrated (lacking stones).
9. And be assisted by appropriate timing.

Save when command to your dismission tends,
And therein you are senseless.[1]

CLOTEN                                    Senseless? Not so.
    [*Enter a* MESSENGER]

50 MESSENGER [*to* CYMBELINE]   So like you,° sir, ambassadors from Rome;   *If you please*
    The one is Caius Lucius.

CYMBELINE                          A worthy fellow,
    Albeit he comes on angry purpose now:
    But that's no fault of his. We must receive him
    According to the honour of his sender,
55 And towards himself, his goodness forespent on us,[2]
    We must extend our notice. Our dear son,
    When you have given good morning to your mistress,
    Attend the Queen and us. We shall have need
    T'employ you towards this Roman. Come, our queen.
                       *Exeunt* [*all but* CLOTEN]

60 CLOTEN   If she be up, I'll speak with her; if not,
    Let her lie still and dream.
        [*He knocks*]
                  By your leave, ho!—
    I know her women are about her; what
    If I do line° one of their hands? 'Tis gold   *fill (with gold)*
    Which buys admittance—oft it doth—yea, and makes
65 Diana's rangers false° themselves, yield up   *gamekeepers turn false*
    Their deer to th' stand o'th' stealer;[3] and 'tis gold
    Which makes the true man killed and saves the thief,
    Nay, sometime hangs both thief and true man. What
    Can it not do and undo? I will make
70 One of her women lawyer to° me, for   *advocate for*
    I yet not understand the case[4] myself.—
    By your leave.
        *Knocks. Enter a* LADY

LADY   Who's there that knocks?
CLOTEN                                    A gentleman.
LADY                                       No more?
CLOTEN   Yes, and a gentlewoman's son.
LADY                                    That's more
75 [*Aside*][5] Than some whose tailors are as dear° as yours   *expensive*
    Can justly boast of. [*To him*] What's your lordship's pleasure?
CLOTEN   Your lady's person. Is she ready?°   *dressed; prepared*
LADY                                                Ay.
    [*Aside*] To keep her chamber.
CLOTEN                                    There is gold for you.
    Sell me your good report.
80 LADY   How, my good name?°—or to report of you   *reputation*
    What I shall think is good?
        *Enter* INNOGEN
             The Princess.   [*Exit*]

---

1. *Save . . . senseless:* Except what pertains to your dismissal ("dismission"), which you are incapable of understanding. Cloten, however, takes "senseless" to mean "stupid."
2. *his . . . us:* in view of the virtue he has shown in previous dealings with us.
3. *yield . . . stealer:* surrender their deer to the place where the thief stands to shoot; surrender what is most dear or valuable (their chastity) to the thief's erect penis ("th' stand").
4. *for . . . case:* for I still do not know how to manage the matter (with wordplay on "stand under" as slang for "sexually penetrate" and on "case" as slang for "vagina").
5. The Lady's speaking all or part of this and her next speech in asides explains the outspokenness of her comments; it also follows the pattern of 2.1 and of later scenes in which Cloten's words are slyly subjected to derogatory commentary by those with whom he converses.

CLOTEN   Good morrow, fairest. Sister, your sweet hand.

INNOGEN   Good morrow, sir. You lay out too much pains
      For purchasing but trouble. The thanks I give
85   Is telling you that I am poor of thanks,
      And scarce can spare them.

CLOTEN                                   Still I swear I love you.

INNOGEN   If you but said so, 'twere as deep° with me.                    solemn; binding
      If you swear still,° your recompense is still                                   always
      That I regard it not.

CLOTEN                         This is no answer.

90   INNOGEN   But° that you shall not say I yield being silent,                Except
      I would not speak. I pray you, spare me. Faith,
      I shall unfold equal discourtesy[6]
      To your best kindness. One of your great knowing°            knowledge
      Should learn, being taught, forbearance.

95   CLOTEN   To leave you in your madness, 'twere my sin.
      I will not.

INNOGEN         Fools cure not mad folks.

CLOTEN   Do you call me fool?

INNOGEN                         As I am mad, I do.
      If you'll be patient, I'll no more be mad;
      That cures us both. I am much sorry, sir,
100   You put me to forget a lady's manners
      By being so verbal;[7] and learn now for all
      That I, which know my heart, do here pronounce
      By th' very truth of it: I care not for you,
      And am so near the lack of charity
105   To accuse myself I hate you,[8] which I had rather
      You felt than make't my boast.°                               than I had to say it

CLOTEN                                   You sin against
      Obedience which you owe your father. For°                            As for
      The contract you pretend° with that base wretch,                       claim
      One bred of alms and fostered with cold dishes,
110   With scraps o'th' court, it is no contract, none.
      And though it be allowed in meaner° parties—             socially inferior
      Yet who than he more mean?—to knit their souls,
      On whom there is no more dependency
      But brats and beggary,[9] in self-figured° knot,                self-contracted
115   Yet you are curbed from that enlargement° by                       freedom
      The consequence o'th' crown,[1] and must not foil°                   defile
      The precious note° of it with a base slave,                      reputation
      A hilding for a livery,[2] a squire's cloth,°                        uniform
      A pantler°—not so eminent.                                  pantry servant

INNOGEN                              Profane fellow,
120   Wert thou the son of Jupiter,° and no more                    king of the gods
      But what thou art besides, thou wert too base
      To be his° groom; thou wert dignified enough,[3]            (Posthumus's)
      Even to the point of envy, if 'twere made
      Comparative for your virtues to be styled

---

6. I shall display discourtesy equal.
7. "Verbal" (talkative; plainspoken) may refer either to Cloten or to Innogen.
8. And . . . you: And I am so near uncharitableness that I can charge myself with hating you.
9. On . . . beggary: Upon whose marriage nothing depends but worthless children and extreme poverty.

1. by . . . crown: by the importance of the crown; by the consequences that flow from your inheritance of the crown.
2. A worthless person fit only to wear the uniform ("livery") of his master's household.
3. You were raised in status sufficiently.

125 The under-hangman⁴ of his kingdom, and hated
For being preferred° so well.                                                    *advanced*

CLOTEN                              The south-fog⁵ rot him!

INNOGEN    He never can meet more mischance than come
To be but named of° thee. His meanest garment                                   *by*
That ever hath but clipped° his body is dearer                                  *encircled*
130 In my respect than all the hairs above thee,°                               *on your head*
Were they all made such men. How now, Pisanio!
                    *Enter* PISANIO

CLOTEN    His garment? Now the devil—

INNOGEN [*to* PISANIO]    To Dorothy, my woman, hie thee presently.°           *at once*

CLOTEN    His garment?

INNOGEN [*to* PISANIO]    I am sprited with° a fool,                           *am haunted by*
135 Frighted, and angered worse. Go bid my woman
Search for a jewel that too casually
Hath left mine arm. It was thy master's. 'Shrew me°          *Beshrew me (plague on me)*
If I would lose it for a revenue
Of any king's in Europe! I do think
140 I saw't this morning; confident I am
Last night 'twas on mine arm; I kissed it.
I hope it be not gone to tell my lord
That I kiss aught but he.

PISANIO                              'Twill not be lost.

INNOGEN    I hope so. Go and search.          [*Exit* PISANIO]

CLOTEN                              You have abused me.
'His meanest garment'?

145 INNOGEN                    Ay, I said so, sir.
If you will make't an action,° call witness to't.                              *a lawsuit*

CLOTEN    I will inform your father.

INNOGEN                    Your mother too.
She's my good lady, and will conceive,° I hope,°                              *think / expect*
But the worst of me. So I leave you, sir,
To th' worst of discontent.                                      *Exit*

150 CLOTEN                    I'll be revenged.
'His meanest garment'? Well!                                    *Exit*


## 2.4

*Enter* POSTHUMUS *and* FILARIO

POSTHUMUS    Fear it not, sir. I would I were so sure
To win the King as I am bold her honour
Will remain hers.

FILARIO                    What means° do you make to him?                     *intercessions*

POSTHUMUS    Not any; but abide the change of time,
5 Quake in the present winter's state, and wish
That warmer days would come. In these seared° hopes                            *withered*
I barely gratify° your love; they failing,                                     *repay*
I must die much your debtor.

FILARIO    Your very goodness and your company
10 O'erpays all I can do. By this,° your king                                 *By now*
Hath heard of great Augustus. Caius Lucius
Will do 's commission throughly.° And I think                                  *thoroughly*

---

4. *if 'twere . . . under-hangman:* if a comparison were
made between your virtues and those of Posthumus and
you were given the job of assistant hangman; if, in
accordance with your virtues, you were given the job of
assistant hangman.
5. A damp fog brought by the south wind and supposed
to breed infections.
2.4 Location: Filario's house, Rome.

He'll grant the tribute, send th'arrearages,°    *overdue payments*
Ere look upon our Romans, whose remembrance°   *the memory of whom*
Is yet fresh in their grief.[1]

15 POSTHUMUS      I do believe,
Statist° though I am none, nor like to be,      *Statesman*
That this will prove a war, and you shall hear
The legions now in Gallia sooner landed
In our not-fearing Britain than have tidings
20 Of any penny tribute paid. Our countrymen
Are men more ordered° than when Julius Caesar   *better disciplined*
Smiled at their lack of skill but found their courage
Worthy his frowning at. Their discipline,
Now wing-led[2] with their courage, will make known
25 To their approvers° they are people such   *those who would test them*
That mend upon the world.[3]

    *Enter* GIACOMO

FILARIO      See, Giacomo.
POSTHUMUS [*to* GIACOMO]  The swiftest harts° have posted° you  *deer / conveyed*
 by land,
And winds of° all the corners° kissed your sails   *from / (of the globe)*
To make your vessel nimble.
FILARIO [*to* GIACOMO]  Welcome, sir.
30 POSTHUMUS [*to* GIACOMO] I hope the briefness of your answer made°  *caused*
The speediness of your return.
GIACOMO      Your lady is
One of the fair'st that I have looked upon—
POSTHUMUS And therewithal the best, or let her beauty
Look through a casement[4] to allure false hearts,
And be false with them.
35 GIACOMO      Here are letters for you.
POSTHUMUS Their tenor good, I trust.
GIACOMO       'Tis very like.

    [POSTHUMUS *reads the letters*]

FILARIO Was Caius Lucius in the Briton court
When you were there?
GIACOMO     He was expected then,
But not° approached.           *had not*
POSTHUMUS    All is well yet.
40 Sparkles this stone as it was wont, or is't not
Too dull for your good wearing?
GIACOMO     If I had lost it
I should have lost the worth of it in gold.
I'll make a journey twice as far t'enjoy
A second night of such sweet shortness which
45 Was mine in Britain; for the ring is won.
POSTHUMUS The stone's too hard to come by.
GIACOMO       Not a whit,
Your lady being so easy.
POSTHUMUS    Make not, sir,
Your loss your sport. I hope you know that we
Must not continue friends.

---

1. The Britons' grief; the grief inflicted by the Romans.
2. Carried aloft (as if on wings); led on each flank (each "wing"). The Second Folio (F2, printed in 1632) has "mingled," an emendation adopted by some editors.
3. *such . . . world:* who improve in the world's estimation.
4. Look out through a window (alluding to the manner in which prostitutes solicited customers).

GIACOMO                          Good sir, we must,
50   If you keep covenant. Had I not brought
     The knowledge° of your mistress home I grant                    *A sexual account*
     We were to question° farther, but I now                         *dispute*
     Profess myself the winner of her honour,
     Together with your ring, and not the wronger
55   Of her or you, having proceeded but
     By both your wills.
POSTHUMUS                 If you can make't apparent
     That you have tasted her in bed, my hand
     And ring is yours. If not, the foul opinion
     You had of her pure honour gains or loses
60   Your sword or mine,[5] or masterless leaves both°                *both swords*
     To who shall find them.
GIACOMO                          Sir, my circumstances,°               *detailed evidence*
     Being so near the truth as I will make them,
     Must first induce you to believe; whose strength
     I will confirm with oath, which I doubt not
65   You'll give me leave to spare° when you shall find               *omit*
     You need it not.
POSTHUMUS         Proceed.
GIACOMO                          First, her bedchamber—
     Where I confess I slept not, but profess
     Had that was well worth watching°—it was hanged                 *staying awake for*
     With tapestry of silk and silver; the story
70   Proud Cleopatra when she met her Roman,[6]
     And Cydnus[7] swelled above the banks, or for°                  *either because of*
     The press of boats or pride: a piece of work
     So bravely° done, so rich, that it did strive                  *splendidly*
     In workmanship and value;[8] which I wondered
75   Could be so rarely and exactly wrought,
     Such the true life on't was.
POSTHUMUS                      This is true,
     And this you might have heard of here, by me
     Or by some other.
GIACOMO                    More particulars
     Must justify° my knowledge.                                     *confirm*
POSTHUMUS                       So they must,
     Or do your honour injury.
80 GIACOMO                        The chimney°                        *fireplace*
     Is south the chamber, and the chimney-piece[9]
     Chaste Dian[1] bathing. Never saw I figures
     So likely to report themselves;[2] the cutter
     Was as another nature; dumb, outwent her,
     Motion and breath left out.[3]
85 POSTHUMUS                      This is a thing
     Which you might from relation° likewise reap,                   *report*

---

5. *gains . . . mine:* makes one of us the winner, the other the loser, of his sword in a duel.
6. Alluding to a meeting, described also in Shakespeare's play *Antony and Cleopatra*, between the Egyptian Queen Cleopatra and Mark Antony, a Roman general who was her lover.
7. A river in Cilicia (now Turkey).
8. *that . . . value:* that craftmanship and monetary worth both competed for preeminence.

9. Ornament above the fireplace.
1. Another reference to the goddess associated in classical mythology with hunting, childbirth, and chastity.
2. So lifelike that they could give an account of themselves.
3. *the cutter . . . out:* the sculptor ("cutter") was like a second nature in creative power. Speechless, the sculpture surpassed nature, apart from its lack of movement and breathing.

Being, as it is, much spoke of.

GIACOMO                          The roof o'th' chamber
With golden cherubins is fretted.° Her andirons—                    *carved*
I had forgot them—were two winking Cupids⁴
90  Of silver, each on one foot standing, nicely°                    *ingeniously*
Depending° on their brands.°                              *Leaning / torches*

POSTHUMUS                    This is her honour!
Let it be granted you have seen all this—and praise
Be given to your remembrance—the description
Of what is in her chamber nothing saves
The wager you have laid.

95  GIACOMO                    Then, if you can
Be pale,° I beg but leave to air this jewel. See!                   *Be unmoved*
        [*He shows the bracelet*]
And now 'tis up° again; it must be married                          *put away*
To that your diamond. I'll keep them.

POSTHUMUS                    Jove!°                       *king of the gods*
Once more let me behold it. Is it that
Which I left with her?

100  GIACOMO                    Sir, I thank her, that.
She stripped it from her arm. I see her yet.
Her pretty action did outsell° her gift,                            *exceed in value*
And yet enriched it too. She gave it me,
And said she prized it once.

POSTHUMUS                    Maybe she plucked it off
To send it me.

105  GIACOMO        She writes so to you, doth she?
POSTHUMUS    O, no, no, no—'tis true! Here, take this too.
        [*He gives* GIACOMO *his ring*]
It is a basilisk⁵ unto mine eye,
Kills me to look on't. Let there be no honour
Where there is beauty, truth where semblance,° love          *the mere appearance of it*
110  Where there's another man. The vows° of women                 *Let the vows*
Of no more bondage be to where they are made
Than they are° to their virtues, which is nothing!          *Than women are bound*
O, above measure false!

FILARIO                    Have patience, sir,
And take your ring again; 'tis not yet won.
115  It may be probable she lost it, or
Who knows if one° her woman, being corrupted,                       *one of*
Hath stol'n it from her?

POSTHUMUS                    Very true,
And so I hope he came by't. Back my ring.
        [*He takes his ring again*]
Render to me some corporal sign about her
120  More evident° than this; for this was stol'n.                  *conclusive*

GIACOMO    By Jupiter,⁶ I had it from her arm.
POSTHUMUS    Hark you, he swears, by Jupiter he swears.
'Tis true, nay, keep the ring, 'tis true. I am sure
She would not lose it. Her attendants are
125  All sworn° and honourable. They induced to steal it?          *bound by oaths*

---

4. Two statues of Cupid, the god of love, with eyes
shut. Cupid was often depicted as a beautiful boy with
wings and a torch and wearing a blindfold to signify the
blindness of love.

5. A mythical reptile able with a glance to kill those it
gazed upon.
6. Another reference to the king of the gods. Only the
most solemn vows would be made in his name.

And by a stranger? No, he hath enjoyed her.
The cognizance° of her incontinency                                    *token*
Is this. She hath bought the name of whore thus dearly.
        [*He gives* GIACOMO *his ring*]
There, take thy hire,° and all the fiends of hell                      *fee*
Divide themselves between you!
130 FILARIO                              Sir, be patient.
This is not strong enough to be believed
Of one persuaded° well of.                                             *thought*
POSTHUMUS                    Never talk on't.
She hath been colted° by him.                                          *sexually enjoyed*
GIACOMO                              If you seek
For further satisfying, under her breast—
135 Worthy the pressing—lies a mole, right proud
Of that most delicate lodging. By my life,
I kissed it, and it gave me present° hunger                            *immediate*
To feed again, though full. You do remember
This stain° upon her?                                                  *mark*
POSTHUMUS                    Ay, and it doth confirm
140 Another stain as big as hell can hold,
Were there no more but it.
GIACOMO                              Will you hear more?
POSTHUMUS   Spare your arithmetic, never count the turns.°            *sexual acts*
Once, and a million![7]
GIACOMO                    I'll be sworn.
POSTHUMUS                              No swearing.
If you will swear you have not done't, you lie,
145 And I will kill thee if thou dost deny
Thou'st made me cuckold.
GIACOMO                    I'll deny nothing.
POSTHUMUS   O that I had her here to tear her limb-meal!°             *limb from limb*
I will go there and do't i'th' court, before
Her father. I'll do something.                              *Exit*
FILARIO                              Quite besides°                    *beyond*
150 The government° of patience! You have won.                         *control*
Let's follow and pervert° the present wrath                            *turn aside*
He hath against himself.
GIACOMO                    With all my heart.             *Exeunt*

### 2.5

        *Enter* POSTHUMUS[1]
POSTHUMUS   Is there no way for men to be,° but women                 *to exist*
Must be half-workers?° We are bastards all,                           *be partners*
And that most venerable man which I
Did call my father was I know not where
5 When I was stamped.[2] Some coiner with his tools[3]
Made me a counterfeit; yet my mother seemed
The Dian of that time: so doth my wife
The nonpareil° of this. O vengeance, vengeance!            *one who has no equal*

---

7. That is, there is no difference between having been unfaithful once and having done it a million times.
**2.5** Location: Scene continues.
1. In F, Posthumus's soliloquy is part of 2.4. He is making a reentry, however, after his departure at line 149, and most modern editions mark the soliloquy as a separate scene.
2. Conceived, as coins are stamped with images when they are made.
3. With pun on "tool" as meaning "penis."

Me of my lawful pleasure⁴ she restrained,
10  And prayed me oft forbearance;⁵ did it with
A pudency° so rosy the sweet view on't°                    *modesty / of it*
Might well have warmed old Saturn;⁶ that I thought her
As chaste as unsunned snow. O all the devils!
This yellow° Giacomo in an hour—was't not?—           *sallow*
15  Or less—at first?° Perchance he spoke not, but        *instantly*
Like a full-acorned boar,⁷ a German one,
Cried 'O!' and mounted; found no opposition
But what he looked for should oppose⁸ and she
Should from encounter guard. Could I find out
20  The woman's part in me—for there's no motion°          *impulse*
That tends to vice in man but I affirm
It is the woman's part; be it lying, note it,
The woman's; flattering, hers; deceiving, hers;
Lust and rank thoughts, hers, hers; revenges, hers;
25  Ambitions, covetings, change of prides,° disdain,   *varying extravagances*
Nice° longing, slanders, mutability,                       *Lustful*
All faults that man can name, nay, that hell knows,
Why, hers in part or all, but rather all—
For even to vice
30  They are not constant, but are changing still
One vice but of a minute old for one
Not half so old as that. I'll write against them,
Detest them, curse them, yet 'tis greater skill°           *cleverness*
In a true hate to pray they have their will.°              *desire*
35  The very devils cannot plague them better.        *Exit*

### 3.1

[*Flourish.*] *Enter in state* CYMBELINE, [*the*] QUEEN,
CLOTEN, *and lords at one door, and at another,* Caius
LUCIUS *and attendants*

CYMBELINE  Now say, what would Augustus Caesar with us?
LUCIUS  When Julius Caesar—whose remembrance yet
Lives in men's eyes, and will to ears and tongues
Be theme and hearing ever—was in this Britain
5  And conquered it, Cassibelan, thine uncle,
Famous in Caesar's praises no whit less
Than in his feats deserving it, for him
And his succession° granted Rome a tribute,              *heirs*
Yearly three thousand pounds, which by thee lately
Is left untendered.
10  QUEEN                    And, to kill the marvel,¹
Shall be so ever.
CLOTEN                  There will be many Caesars
Ere such another Julius. Britain's a world
By itself, and we will nothing pay
For wearing our own noses.²

---

4. The sexual pleasure to which marriage entitled him.
5. And often begged me to defer sexual pleasures.
6. The Roman god of agriculture, usually characterized as cold and melancholy.
7. A boar fed full of acorns (with a pun on "boor" as meaning "a German or Dutch peasant").
8. *found . . . oppose:* found no opposition except the body parts he expected to encounter.

3.1 Location: Cymbeline's court, Britain.
1. And, to put a stop to the amazement (which our nonpayment has caused).
2. Perhaps referring to contemporary theories of phys-' iognomy that identified specific physical features, such as noses, with racial types. Roman noses were notoriously prominent.

QUEEN                                  That opportunity
15   Which then they had to take from 's, to resume°            take back
      We have again. Remember, sir, my liege,°                   sovereign
      The kings your ancestors, together with
      The natural bravery° of your isle, which stands            splendor
      As Neptune's park,[3] ribbed and paled in°                 enclosed and fenced in
20   With banks unscalable and roaring waters,
      With sands that will not bear your enemies' boats,
      But suck them up to th' topmast. A kind of conquest
      Caesar made here, but made not here his brag
      Of 'came and saw and overcame'.[4] With shame—
25   The first that ever touched him—he was carried
      From off our coast, twice beaten; and his shipping,°        ships
      Poor ignorant° baubles, on our terrible seas                silly
      Like eggshells moved upon their surges, cracked
      As easily 'gainst our rocks; for joy whereof
30   The famed Cassibelan, who was once at point°—                ready
      O giglot° fortune!—to master Caesar's sword,                fickle; whorish
      Made Lud's town[5] with rejoicing fires bright,
      And Britons strut with courage.
CLOTEN   Come, there's no more tribute to be paid. Our king-
35   dom is stronger than it was at that time, and, as I said, there is
      no more such Caesars. Other of them may have crooked noses,
      but to owe° such straight° arms, none.                      possess / powerful
CYMBELINE   Son, let your mother end.
CLOTEN   We have yet many among us can grip as hard as Cassi-
40   belan. I do not say I am one, but I have a hand. Why tribute?
      Why should we pay tribute? If Caesar can hide the sun from us
      with a blanket, or put the moon in his pocket, we will pay him
      tribute for light; else, sir, no more tribute, pray you now.
CYMBELINE [to LUCIUS]   You must know,
45   Till the injurious° Romans did extort                         insulting
      This tribute from us we were free. Caesar's ambition,
      Which swelled so much that it did almost stretch
      The sides o'th' world, against all colour[6] here
      Did put the yoke upon 's, which to shake off
50   Becomes a warlike people, whom we reckon
      Ourselves to be. We do say then to Caesar,
      Our ancestor was that Mulmutius[7] which
      Ordained our laws, whose use the sword of Caesar
      Hath too much mangled, whose repair and franchise°          free exercise
55   Shall by the power we hold be our good deed,
      Though Rome be therefore angry. Mulmutius made our laws,
      Who was the first of Britain which did put
      His brows within a golden crown and called
      Himself a king.
LUCIUS                    I am sorry, Cymbeline,
60   That I am to pronounce Augustus Caesar—

3. As grounds owned by Neptune, Roman god of the sea.
4. When Julius Caesar, leading an army into Asia, defeated King Pharnaces and his allies, Plutarch reports that Caesar wrote three words to his friend Anitius in Rome: *veni, vidi, vici* ("I came, I saw, I overcame"). See Plutarch's *Life of Julius Caesar* in his *Lives of the Noble Grecians and Romanes* as translated by Thomas North

(1579).
5. London. Contemporary texts such as Holinshed's *Chronicles* erroneously asserted that "London" was derived from "Lud," the name of the mythological British King who was Cymbeline's grandfather.
6. Without any pretense of justice.
7. According to Holinshed, the first King of Britain.

Caesar, that hath more kings his servants than
Thyself domestic officers—thine enemy.
Receive it from me, then: war and confusion°          *destruction*
In Caesar's name pronounce I 'gainst thee. Look
65    For fury not to be resisted. Thus defied,
I thank thee for myself.
CYMBELINE                    Thou art welcome, Caius.
Thy Caesar knighted me; my youth I spent
Much under him; of him I gathered honour,
Which he to seek of me again perforce
70    Behoves me keep at utterance.[8] I am perfect°          *fully aware*
That the Pannonians and Dalmatians[9] for
Their liberties are now in arms, a precedent
Which not to read would show the Britons cold;°          *lacking in spirit*
So Caesar shall not find them.
LUCIUS                         Let proof° speak.          *the result*
75    CLOTEN   His majesty bids you welcome. Make pastime with us a
day or two or longer. If you seek us afterwards in other terms,
you shall find us in our salt-water girdle.[1] If you beat us out of
it, it is yours; if you fall in the adventure, our crows shall fare
the better for you; and there's an end.
80    LUCIUS   So, sir.
CYMBELINE   I know your master's pleasure, and he mine.
All the remain° is 'Welcome'.          [*Flourish.*] *Exeunt*          *All that is left to say*

## 3.2

*Enter* PISANIO, *reading of a letter*

PISANIO   How? Of adultery? Wherefore write you not
What monster's her accuser? Leonatus,
O master, what a strange infection
Is fall'n into thy ear! What false Italian,
5    As poisonous tongued as handed,[1] hath prevailed
On thy too ready hearing? Disloyal? No.
She's punished for her truth,° and undergoes,          *faithfulness*
More goddess-like than wife-like, such assaults
As would take in° some virtue. O my master,          *overcome*
10    Thy mind to° hers is now as low as were          *compared to*
Thy fortunes. How? That I should murder her,
Upon the love and truth and vows which I
Have made to thy command? I her? Her blood?
If it be so to do good service, never
15    Let me be counted serviceable. How look I,
That I should seem to lack humanity
So much as this fact° comes to? [*Reads*] 'Do't. The letter          *action*
That I have sent her, by her own command
Shall give thee opportunity.' O damned paper,[2]
20    Black as the ink that's on thee! Senseless bauble,°          *toy; worthless object*

---

8. *Which . . . utterance:* His seeking that honor of me
again makes it necessary for me to defend ("keep") it to
the death.
9. Inhabitants of Hungary and Dalmatia, a region on
the Adriatic Sea.
1. In the sea that encircles us (as a girdle does the

body).
3.2 Location: Cymbeline's court.
1. Having as many poisons (lies) in his tongue as in his
hands. Contemporary texts depicted Italians as infinitely skilled in making and administering poisons.
2. O hellish object (referring to the letter).

Art thou a fedary° for this act, and look'st         *an accomplice*
So virgin-like without?°         *on the outside*
    *Enter* INNOGEN
                  Lo, here she comes.
I am ignorant in° what I am commanded.       *will pretend ignorance of*
  INNOGEN   How now, Pisanio?
25   PISANIO   Madam, here is a letter from my lord.
  INNOGEN   Who, thy lord that is my lord, Leonatus?
    O learned indeed were that astronomer°       *astrologer*
    That knew the stars as I his characters°—     *handwriting*
    He'd lay the future open. You good gods,
30     Let what is here contained relish° of love,     *taste*
    Of my lord's health, of his content—yet not
    That we two are asunder; let that grieve him.
    Some griefs are med'cinable;° that is one of them,   *beneficial*
    For it doth physic love³—of his content
35     All but in that. Good wax,° thy leave. Blest be     *sealing wax*
    You bees that make these locks of counsel!° Lovers   *for private matters*
    And men in dangerous bonds⁴ pray not alike;
    Though forfeiters you cast in prison,⁵ yet
    You clasp° young Cupid's tables.° Good news, gods!   *lovingly embrace / tablets*
    [*She opens and reads the letter*]
40     'Justice and your father's wrath, should he take me in his
    dominion, could not be so cruel to me as° you, O the dearest   *but that*
    of creatures, would even renew me° with your eyes. Take   *would revive me*
    notice that I am in Cambria,° at Milford Haven.⁶ What your   *Wales*
    own love will out of this advise you, follow. So he wishes you
45     all happiness, that remains loyal to his vow, and your increasing
    in love,
                         Leonatus Posthumus.'
    O for a horse with wings! Hear'st thou, Pisanio?
    He is at Milford Haven. Read, and tell me
50     How far 'tis thither. If one of mean affairs°     *with unimportant business*
    May plod it in a week, why may not I
    Glide thither in a day? Then, true Pisanio,
    Who long'st like me to see thy lord, who long'st—
    O let me bate°—but not like me—yet long'st     *moderate my speech*
55     But in a fainter kind—O, not like me,
    For mine's beyond beyond; say, and speak thick°—   *speak quickly*
    Love's counsellor should fill the bores of hearing,°   *the ears*
    To th' smothering of the sense⁷—how far it is
    To this same blessèd Milford. And by° th' way     *on*
60     Tell me how Wales was made so happy as
    T'inherit such a haven. But first of all,
    How we may steal from hence; and for the gap
    That we shall make in time from our hence-going
    Till our return, to excuse; but first, how get hence.
65     Why should excuse be born or ere begot?⁸

---

3. For it nurtures love; for it keeps love in good health.
4. Men bound by agreements imposing penalties (which are sealed with wax). Innogen is contrasting the fear with which men in legal trouble greet sealed documents to the joy with which lovers receive a sealed love letter.
5. Although you cast those who default on agreements in prison (because sealed bonds lead to indictments).
6. A port in southern Wales that became important in later British history when Henry Tudor landed there in 1485. Defeating the army of Richard III, he was crowned Henry VII, bringing to an end the civil strife known as the Wars of the Roses.
7. Until the sense of hearing is overwhelmed.
8. Why should an excuse be born even before it is conceived—that is, be manufactured before it is needed?

We'll talk of that hereafter. Prithee speak,
How many score of° miles may we well ride        *set of twenty*
'Twixt hour and hour?°                        *In an hour*

PISANIO              One score 'twixt sun and sun,
Madam, 's enough for you, and too much too.

70 INNOGEN   Why, one that rode to 's execution, man,
Could never go so slow. I have heard of riding wagers
Where horses have been nimbler than the sands
That run i'th' clock's behalf.⁹ But this is fool'ry.
Go bid my woman feign a sickness, say

75 She'll home to her father; and provide me presently°     *at once*
A riding-suit no costlier than would fit°              *suit*
A franklin's housewife.¹

PISANIO            Madam, you're best° consider.     *you'd better*

INNOGEN   I see before° me, man. Nor here, nor here,   *straight ahead of*
Nor what ensues,² but have a fog in them

80 That I cannot look through. Away, I prithee,
Do as I bid thee. There's no more to say:
Accessible is none but Milford way.              *Exeunt*

### 3.3

*Enter* BELARIUS, *[followed by]* GUIDERIUS *and* ARVIRA-
GUS *[from a cave in the woods]*¹

BELARIUS   A goodly day not to keep house° with such     *stay home*
Whose roof 's as low as ours. Stoop, boys; this gate
Instructs you how t'adore the heavens, and bows you°   *makes you bow down*
To a morning's holy office.° The gates of monarchs     *a morning prayer*

5 Are arched so high that giants may jet° through       *swagger*
And keep their impious turbans² on without
Good morrow to the sun. Hail, thou fair heaven!
We house i'th' rock, yet use thee not so hardly°     *badly*
As prouder livers° do.            *those living more grandly*

GUIDERIUS          Hail, heaven!

ARVIRAGUS            Hail, heaven!

10 BELARIUS   Now for our mountain sport. Up to yon hill,
Your legs are young; I'll tread these flats.° Consider,   *this plain*
When you above perceive me like a crow,
That it is place° which lessens and sets off,°     *position / enhances*
And you may then revolve° what tales I have told you   *consider*

15 Of courts, of princes, of the tricks in war;
That service is not service, so being done,
But being so allowed.³ To apprehend thus
Draws us a profit from all things we see,
And often to our comfort shall we find

20 The sharded beetle⁴ in a safer hold°            *refuge*

---

9. *than . . . behalf:* than the sands that run through the
hourglass.
1. The wife of a landowning farmer whose social status
was lower than that of the gentry. Early modern English
sumptuary codes prescribed specific fabrics and styles
of dress for people of different ranks.
2. *Nor here . . . ensues:* Neither (what is) on this side,
nor on that, nor what will happen (after Milford Haven
is reached).
3.3 Location: The cave of Belarius, Wales.
1. In his account of a performance of the play in 1611,
Simon Forman wrote of "the Cave in the woods" and of
the "woods" where Innogen's supposedly dead body
was laid. It is possible that some form of stage foliage

surrounded the entrance to Belarius's cave.
2. The idea of giants wearing turbans may come from
romances in which giants were often equated with
Saracens, or followers of Islam, who wore turbans and
were seen as impious enemies of Christians. See, for
example, the Giant Disdain in Edmund Spenser's *Faerie
Queene*, who "on his head a roll of linnen plight, / Like
to the Mores of Malabar" (6.7.43.5–6).
3. *That service . . . allowed:* That acts of service are not
acts of service simply by being done, but rather by being
acknowledged as such (by superiors).
4. The beetle who lives in dung. "Shard" means "patch
of dung."

Than is the full-winged eagle. O, this life
Is nobler than attending for a check,[5]
Richer than doing nothing for a bauble,
Prouder than rustling in unpaid-for silk;
25 Such gain the cap of him that makes 'em fine,
Yet keeps his book uncrossed.[6] No life to ours.

GUIDERIUS   Out of your proof° you speak. We, poor unfledged,[7]          *experience*
Have never winged from view o'th' nest, nor know not
What air's from° home. Haply° this life is best,          *away from / Perhaps*
30 If quiet life be best; sweeter to you
That have a sharper known; well corresponding
With your stiff age, but unto us it is
A cell of ignorance, travelling abed,°          *only while dreaming*
A prison for a debtor, that not dares
To stride a limit.[8]

35 ARVIRAGUS [*to* BELARIUS]   What should we speak of
When we are old as you? When we shall hear
The rain and wind beat dark December, how,
In this our pinching cave,[9] shall we discourse
The freezing hours away? We have seen nothing.
40 We are beastly:° subtle as the fox for prey,          *like beasts*
Like° warlike as the wolf for what we eat.          *As*
Our valour is to chase what flies; our cage
We make a choir, as doth the prisoned bird,
And sing our bondage freely.

BELARIUS                         How you speak!
45 Did you but know the city's usuries,[1]
And felt them knowingly; the art o'th' court,
As hard to leave as keep,° whose top to climb          *dwell in*
Is certain falling, or so slipp'ry that
The fear's as bad as falling; the toil o'th' war,
50 A pain° that only seems to seek out danger          *labor*
I'th' name of fame and honour, which dies i'th' search
And hath as oft a sland'rous epitaph
As record of fair act; nay, many times
Doth ill deserve° by doing well; what's worse,          *earn ill treatment*
55 Must curtsy at the censure.[2] O boys, this story
The world may read in me. My body's marked
With Roman swords, and my report° was once          *reputation*
First with the best of note.° Cymbeline loved me,          *the most renowned*
And when a soldier was the theme my name
60 Was not far off. Then was I as a tree
Whose boughs did bend with fruit; but in one night
A storm or robbery, call it what you will,
Shook down my mellow hangings,° nay, my leaves,          *ripe fruit*
And left me bare to weather.

GUIDERIUS                         Uncertain favour!
65 BELARIUS   My fault being nothing, as I have told you oft,
But that two villains, whose false oaths prevailed

5. Than acting as a servant only to be rebuked.
6. *Such . . . uncrossed:* Such men win the deference (shown by removing "the cap") of the tailor who is the source of their grandeur, yet continue to have their debts standing ("uncrossed") in the tailor's account book.
7. Lacking the feathers necessary for flight (spoken of a young bird).

8. *that . . . limit:* who does not dare to leave a place of sanctuary (for fear of being arrested).
9. Our confining cave; our cave that pinches us with cold.
1. Financial practices whereby money was lent at excessive or illegal rates of interest.
2. Must defer to the person who finds fault.

Before my perfect honour, swore to Cymbeline
I was confederate with the Romans. So
Followed my banishment, and this twenty years
70 This rock and these demesnes° have been my world,     *regions*
Where I have lived at honest freedom, paid
More pious debts to heaven than in all
The fore-end° of my time. But up to th' mountains!     *early days*
This is not hunter's language. He that strikes
75 The venison first shall be the lord o'th' feast,
To him the other two shall minister,
And we will fear no poison which attends°     *is always present*
In place of greater state. I'll meet you in the valleys.
        *Exeunt* [GUIDERIUS *and* ARVIRAGUS]
How hard it is to hide the sparks of nature!
80 These boys know little they are sons to th' King,
Nor Cymbeline dreams that they are alive.
They think they are mine, and though trained up thus meanly°     *in a humble style*
I'th' cave wherein they bow, their thoughts do hit
The roofs of palaces, and nature prompts them
85 In simple and low things to prince it° much     *to act like princes*
Beyond the trick° of others. This Polydore,     *custom*
The heir of Cymbeline and Britain, who
The King his father called Guiderius—Jove,
When on my three-foot stool I sit and tell
90 The warlike feats I have done, his spirits fly out
Into my story: say 'Thus mine enemy fell,
And thus I set my foot on 's neck', even then
The princely blood flows in his cheek, he sweats,
Strains his young nerves,° and puts himself in posture     *sinews*
95 That acts my words. The younger brother, Cadwal,
Once Arviragus, in as like a figure°     *acting the part as aptly*
Strikes life into my speech, and shows much more
His own conceiving.°     *imagination*
    [*A hunting-horn sounds*]
        Hark, the game is roused!
O Cymbeline, heaven and my conscience knows³
100 Thou didst unjustly banish me, whereon
At three and two years old I stole these babes,
Thinking to bar thee of succession as
Thou reft'st° me of my lands. Euriphile,     *deprived*
Thou wast their nurse; they took thee for their mother,
105 And every day do honour to her grave.
Myself, Belarius, that am Morgan called,
They take for natural father.
    [*A hunting-horn sounds*]
        The game is up.°     *Exit*     *roused*

## 3.4

*Enter* PISANIO, *and* INNOGEN [*in a riding-suit*]
INNOGEN   Thou told'st me when we came from horse° the place     *we dismounted*
Was near at hand. Ne'er longed my mother so

---

3. Editors have conjectured that lines 99–107 are either a non-Shakespearean addition or a section he added in revision. They stand apart from the rest of the speech, providing a hurried summary of information. Moreover, "the game is roused" (line 98) is repeated in "The game is up" (line 107).
3.4 Location: Wales, near Milford Haven.

To see me first as I have° now. Pisanio, man,       *do*
Where is Posthumus? What is in thy mind
5   That makes thee stare thus? Wherefore breaks that sigh
From th'inward of thee? One but painted thus
Would be interpreted a thing perplexed°       *bewildered*
Beyond self-explication. Put thyself
Into a haviour of less fear,¹ ere wildness°       *madness*
10   Vanquish my staider senses. What's the matter?
      [PISANIO *gives her a letter*]
Why tender'st thou that paper to me with
A look untender? If 't be summer news,
Smile to't before; if winterly, thou need'st
But keep that count'nance still. My husband's hand?
15   That drug-damned Italy² hath out-craftied° him,       *outwitted*
And he's at some hard point.° Speak, man. Thy tongue       *in some crisis*
May take off some extremity° which to read       *reduce the horror*
Would be even mortal° to me.       *fatal*
PISANIO           Please you read,
And you shall find me, wretched man, a thing
20   The most disdained of fortune.
INNOGEN *reads*  'Thy mistress, Pisanio, hath played the strumpet
in my bed, the testimonies whereof lies bleeding in me. I speak
not out of weak surmises but from proof as strong as my grief
and as certain as I expect my revenge. That part thou, Pisanio,
25   must act for me, if thy faith be not tainted with the breach of
hers. Let thine own hands take away her life. I shall give thee
opportunity at Milford Haven. She hath my letter for the purpose, where if thou fear to strike and to make me certain it is
done, thou art the pander to her dishonour and equally to me
30   disloyal.'
PISANIO [*aside*]   What shall I need to draw my sword? The paper
Hath cut her throat already. No, 'tis slander,
Whose edge is sharper than the sword, whose tongue
Outvenoms all the worms of Nile,³ whose breath
35   Rides on the posting° winds and doth belie°       *speeding / deceive*
All corners of the world. Kings, queens, and states,
Maids, matrons, nay, the secrets of the grave
This viperous slander enters. [*To* INNOGEN] What cheer, madam?
INNOGEN   False to his bed? What is it to be false?
40   To lie in watch° there and to think on him?       *wakefulness*
To weep 'twixt clock and clock?° If sleep charge° nature,       *continually / overcome*
To break it with a fearful dream of° him       *a dream fearful for*
And cry myself awake? That's false to 's bed, is it?
PISANIO   Alas, good lady.
45   INNOGEN   I false? Thy conscience witness, Giacomo,
Thou didst accuse him of incontinency.
Thou then lookedst like a villain; now, methinks,
Thy favour's° good enough. Some jay° of Italy,       *appearance is / strumpet*
Whose mother was her painting,⁴ hath betrayed him.

---

1. *Put . . . fear:* Adopt a less fearsome manner.
2. That country notorious for its poisons.
3. Alluding to the poisonous serpents associated with Egypt's Nile River. Slander was often personified as a woman with snakes issuing from her mouth. In early modern England, women frequently brought cases in the ecclesiastical courts against those who defamed or slandered them; overwhelmingly, they were defending their reputations against claims that they had committed a sexual offense and were unchaste. Pisanio rightly assumes that Innogen is the victim of just such slanderous accusations.
4. Whose mother was entirely the product of her cosmetics—i.e., who was false.

50 Poor I am stale,° a garment out of fashion,         *out of date; not new*
    And for I am richer than to hang by th' walls
    I must be ripped.⁵ To pieces with me! O,
    Men's vows are women's traitors. All good seeming,°     *appearance*
    By thy revolt, O husband, shall be thought
55 Put on for villainy; not born where't grows,
    But worn a bait for ladies.
PISANIO                 Good madam, hear me.
INNOGEN   True honest men being heard like false Aeneas⁶
    Were in his time thought false, and Sinon's⁷ weeping
    Did scandal° many a holy tear, took pity              *discredit*
60 From most true wretchedness. So thou, Posthumus,
    Wilt lay the leaven on all proper men.⁸
    Goodly° and gallant shall be false and perjured      *Admirable*
    From thy great fail.° [*To* PISANIO] Come, fellow, be thou honest,   *failure*
    Do thou thy master's bidding. When thou seest him,
65 A little witness° my obedience. Look,           *Briefly attest to*
    I draw the sword myself. Take it, and hit
    The innocent mansion of my love, my heart.
    Fear not, 'tis empty of all things but grief.
    Thy master is not there, who was indeed
70 The riches of it. Do his bidding; strike.
    Thou mayst be valiant in a better cause,
    But now thou seem'st a coward.
PISANIO               Hence, vile instrument,
    Thou shalt not damn my hand!
INNOGEN              Why, I must die,
    And if I do not by thy hand thou art
75 No servant of thy master's. Against self-slaughter
    There is a prohibition so divine
    That cravens° my weak hand. Come, here's my heart.    *makes cowardly*
    Something's afore't. Soft,° soft, we'll no defence;       *Gently*
    Obedient as the scabbard. What is here?
    [*She takes letters from her bosom*]
80 The scriptures° of the loyal Leonatus,         *writing; sacred texts*
    All turned to heresy? Away, away,
    Corrupters of my faith, you shall no more
    Be stomachers⁹ to my heart. Thus may poor fools
    Believe false teachers. Though those that are betrayed
85 Do feel the treason sharply, yet the traitor
    Stands in worse case of woe. And thou, Posthumus,
    That didst set up° my disobedience 'gainst the King    *instigate*
    My father, and make me put into contempt the suits
    Of princely fellows,° shalt hereafter find    *those equal to my rank*
90 It is no act of common passage but
    A strain of rareness;¹ and I grieve myself
    To think, when thou shalt be disedged° by her     *surfeited*

---

5. *And . . . ripped:* And because I am too valuable to be discarded (by being hung up and forgotten about), I must be torn apart (so that the material may be reused).
6. Being heard as though they were as false as the hero of Virgil's *Aeneid*, Aeneas, who deserted his love, Dido, the Queen of Carthage.
7. Another deceitful character from the *Aeneid*. Sinon betrayed Troy to the Greeks by inducing the Trojans to let into the city a wooden horse in which Greek warriors were concealed.
8. Will corrupt the reputations of all faithful men (as a portion of inferior dough spoils the rest).
9. Ornamented chest coverings worn by women under their bodices.
1. *It . . . rareness:* My choice was no commonplace action but the sign of exceptional qualities.

That now thou tirest on,[2] how thy memory
Will then be panged by° me. [*To* PISANIO] Prithee, dispatch.    *pierced by thoughts of*
95  The lamb entreats the butcher. Where's thy knife?
Thou art too slow to do thy master's bidding
When I desire it too.

PISANIO                    O gracious lady,
Since I received command to do this business
I have not slept one wink.

INNOGEN                    Do't, and to bed, then.

PISANIO    I'll wake mine eyeballs out first.[3]

100 INNOGEN                              Wherefore then
Didst undertake it? Why hast thou abused
So many miles with a pretence?—this place,
Mine action, and thine own? Our horses' labour,
The time inviting thee? The perturbed court,
105 For my being absent, whereunto I never
Purpose° return? Why hast thou gone so far                 *Intend*
To be unbent[4] when thou hast ta'en thy stand,°      *shooting position*
Th'elected° deer before thee?                              *The chosen*

PISANIO                          But to win time
To lose so bad employment, in the which
110 I have considered of a course. Good lady,
Hear me with patience.

INNOGEN                          Talk thy tongue weary. Speak.
I have heard I am a strumpet, and mine ear,
Therein false struck, can take no greater wound,
Nor tent to bottom that.[5] But speak.

PISANIO                                Then, madam,
I thought you would not back° again.                  *go back (to court)*

115 INNOGEN                                Most like,
Bringing me here to kill me.

PISANIO                            Not so, neither.
But if I were as wise as honest, then
My purpose would prove well. It cannot be
But that my master is abused.° Some villain,              *deceived*
120 Ay, and singular° in his art, hath done you both         *unmatched*
This cursèd injury.

INNOGEN    Some Roman courtesan.

PISANIO    No, on my life.
I'll give but notice you are dead, and send him
125 Some bloody sign of it, for 'tis commanded
I should do so. You shall be missed at court,
And that will well confirm it.

INNOGEN                          Why, good fellow,
What shall I do the while, where bide, how live,
Or in my life what comfort when I am
Dead to my husband?

130 PISANIO                    If you'll back° to th' court—            *return*

INNOGEN    No court, no father, nor no more ado
With that harsh, churlish, noble, simple nothing,

---

2. Whom now you feed on (in the manner of a bird of prey).
3. I'll stay awake until my eyes drop out before I'll do it.
4. To be with bow unready.
5. Nor probe ("tent") the depths of that wound.

That Cloten, whose love suit hath been to me
As fearful as a siege.

PISANIO                   If not at court,
Then not in Britain must you bide.

135   INNOGEN                    Where then?
Hath Britain all the sun that shines? Day, night,
Are they not but° in Britain? I'th' world's volume          *Do they exist only*
Our Britain seems as of it but not in't,[6]
In a great pool a swan's nest. Prithee, think
There's livers out of Britain.[7]

140   PISANIO                I am most glad
You think of other place. Th'ambassador,
Lucius the Roman, comes to Milford Haven
Tomorrow. Now if you could wear a mind
Dark° as your fortune is, and but disguise               *Secret; dismal*
145    That which t'appear itself must not yet be
But by self-danger,[8] you should tread a course
Pretty and full of view;[9] yea, haply° near                *perhaps*
The residence of Posthumus; so nigh, at least,
That though his actions were not visible, yet
150    Report should render° him hourly to your ear            *describe*
As truly as he moves.

INNOGEN           O, for such means,°         *a method of access*
Though peril° to my modesty, not death on't,°      *a danger / of it*
I would adventure.°                       *take the risk*

PISANIO            Well then, here's the point:
You must forget to be a woman; change
155    Command[1] into obedience, fear and niceness°—       *daintiness*
The handmaids of all women, or more truly
Woman it pretty self[2]—into a waggish° courage,      *mischievous*
Ready in gibes, quick-answered, saucy and
As quarrelous° as the weasel. Nay, you must         *quarrelsome*
160    Forget that rarest treasure of your cheek,
Exposing it[3]—but O, the harder heart![4]—
Alack, no remedy—to the greedy touch
Of common-kissing Titan,[5] and forget
Your laboursome and dainty trims° wherein          *apparel*
You made great Juno° angry.            *queen of the gods*

165   INNOGEN                Nay, be brief.
I see into thy end,° and am almost                  *purpose*
A man already.

PISANIO       First, make yourself but like one.
Forethinking° this, I have already fit°—      *Anticipating / at hand*
'Tis in my cloak-bag—doublet, hat, hose, all
170    That answer to° them. Would you in their serving,[6]     *go with*
And with what imitation you can borrow

---

6. Seems part of the world, yet distinct. The metaphor
is of the world as a book in which Britain is a page, but
one not bound into the volume.
7. *Prithee . . . Britain:* I pray you, believe that there are
people living outside Britain.
8. *and but . . . self-danger:* and simply disguise your
appearance, which if it were now to show itself for what
it is would put you in danger.
9. Advantageous and with good prospects.
1. The commanding ways of a princess.
2. *or . . . self:* or, more accurately, womanhood itself.

3. In early modern England, English women of the
upper classes shielded themselves from the sun and
cultivated pale complexions, the "treasure" of their
cheeks.
4. The "harder heart" probably refers to Innogen, who
must harden her heart even as she tans her skin. It may
refer to Posthumus's cruelty to Innogen or to Pisanio's
cruelty in forcing these harsh facts upon Innogen.
5. The sun god who shines on ("kisses") everyone alike.
6. If you would with their help.

From youth of such a season,° fore° noble Lucius     *an age / before*
Present yourself, desire his service,° tell him     *to serve him*
Wherein you're happy[7]—which will make him know°     *convince him*
175   If that his head have ear in music—doubtless
With joy he will embrace you, for he's honourable,
And, doubling that, most holy. Your means° abroad—     *As for means of support*
You have me, rich, and I will never fail
Beginning nor supplyment.[8]

INNOGEN                    Thou art all the comfort
180   The gods will diet° me with. Prithee away.     *feed*
There's more to be considered, but we'll even°     *keep pace with*
All that good time will give us. This attempt
I am soldier to,° and will abide it with     *committed to*
A prince's courage. Away, I prithee.
185 PISANIO   Well, madam, we must take a short farewell
Lest, being missed, I be suspected of
Your carriage° from the court. My noble mistress,     *removal*
Here is a box. I had it from the Queen.
What's in't is precious. If you are sick at sea
190   Or stomach-qualmed° at land, a dram° of this     *nauseous / tiny portion*
Will drive away distemper. To some shade,
And fit you to your manhood.[9] May the gods
Direct you to the best.

INNOGEN           Amen. I thank thee. *Exeunt [severally]*

### 3.5

[*Flourish.*] *Enter* CYMBELINE, [*the*] QUEEN, CLOTEN,
    LUCIUS, *and lords*
CYMBELINE [*to* LUCIUS]   Thus far, and so farewell.
LUCIUS                   Thanks, royal sir.
My emperor hath wrote I must from hence;
And am right sorry that I must report ye
My master's enemy.
CYMBELINE          Our subjects, sir,
5   Will not endure his yoke, and for ourself
To show less sovereignty than they must needs
Appear unkinglike.
LUCIUS          So, sir, I desire of you
A conduct° over land to Milford Haven.     *An escort*
[*To the* QUEEN] Madam, all joy befall your grace, [*to* CLOTEN] and you.
10 CYMBELINE   My lords, you are appointed for that office.°     *duty*
The due of honour in no point omit.
So farewell, noble Lucius.
LUCIUS          Your hand, my lord.
CLOTEN   Receive it friendly, but from this time forth
I wear it as your enemy.
LUCIUS          Sir, the event°     *outcome*
15   Is yet to name the winner. Fare you well.
CYMBELINE   Leave not the worthy Lucius, good my lords,
Till he have crossed the Severn.[1] Happiness.
                    *Exeunt* LUCIUS [*and lords*]

---

7. In which things you are skilled.
8. In providing the initial amount nor in supplement-
ing it.
9. Dress yourself in accordance with your (pretended)
manhood.
3.5 Location: Cymbeline's court, Britain.
1. River flowing between Wales and England.

QUEEN   He goes hence frowning, but it honours us
　　　That we have given him cause.
CLOTEN　　　　　　　　　　　'Tis all the better.
20　　Your valiant Britons have their wishes in it.
CYMBELINE   Lucius hath wrote already to the Emperor
　　　How it goes here. It fits° us therefore ripely°　　　　　　　　　*befits / quickly*
　　　Our chariots and our horsemen be in readiness.
　　　The powers° that he already hath in Gallia　　　　　　　　　*military forces*
25　　Will soon be drawn to head,² from whence he moves
　　　His war for Britain.
QUEEN　　　　　　　　　'Tis not sleepy business,
　　　But must be looked to speedily and strongly.
CYMBELINE   Our expectation that it would be thus
　　　Hath made us forward.° But, my gentle queen,　　　　　　　*well prepared*
30　　Where is our daughter? She hath not appeared
　　　Before the Roman, nor to us hath tendered
　　　The duty of the day. She looks us° like　　　　　　　　　　*seems to us*
　　　A thing more made of malice than of duty.
　　　We have noted it. Call her before us, for
　　　We have been too slight in sufferance.°　　[*Exit one or more*]　　*mild in our tolerance*
35　QUEEN　　　　　　　　　　　Royal sir,
　　　Since the exile of Posthumus most retired
　　　Hath her life been, the cure whereof, my lord,
　　　'Tis time must do. Beseech your majesty
　　　Forbear sharp speeches to her. She's a lady
40　　So tender of° rebukes that words are strokes,　　　　　　　　*sensitive to*
　　　And strokes death to her.
　　　　　　*Enter a* MESSENGER
CYMBELINE　　　　　　　　　Where is she, sir? How
　　　Can her contempt be answered?
MESSENGER　　　　　　　　　　Please you, sir,
　　　Her chambers are all locked, and there's no answer
　　　That will be given to th' loud'st of noise we make.
45　QUEEN   My lord, when last I went to visit her
　　　She prayed me to excuse her keeping close,°　　　　　　　*staying confined*
　　　Whereto constrained by her infirmity,
　　　She should that duty leave unpaid to you
　　　Which daily she was bound to proffer. This
50　　She wished me to make known, but our great court°　　　*court business*
　　　Made me to blame° in memory.　　　　　　　　　　　　　*at fault*
CYMBELINE　　　　　　　　　Her doors locked?
　　　Not seen of late? Grant heavens that which I
　　　Fear prove false.　　　　　　　　　　　　*Exit*
QUEEN　　　　　　Son, I say, follow the King.
CLOTEN   That man of hers, Pisanio, her old servant,
　　　I have not seen these two days.
55　QUEEN　　　　　　　　Go, look after. *Exit* [CLOTEN]
　　　Pisanio, thou that stand'st so for° Posthumus!　　　*so much takes the part of*
　　　He hath a drug of mine. I pray his absence
　　　Proceed by° swallowing that, for he believes　　　　　　　*Results from*
　　　It is a thing most precious. But for her,
60　　Where is she gone? Haply° despair hath seized her,　　　*Perhaps*
　　　Or, winged with fervour of her love, she's flown

2. Be gathered to their full strength.

To her desired Posthumus. Gone she is
To death or to dishonour, and my end
Can make good use of either. She being down,
65 I have the placing of the British crown.
            *Enter* CLOTEN
How now, my son?
CLOTEN                    'Tis certain she is fled.
Go in and cheer the King. He rages, none
Dare come about him.
QUEEN                    All the better. May
This night forestall him of the coming day.³            *Exit*
70 CLOTEN   I love and hate her. For° she's fair and royal,            *Because*
And that she hath all courtly parts° more exquisite            *features*
Than lady, ladies, woman—from every one
The best she hath, and she, of all compounded,
Outsells° them all—I love her therefore; but            *Exceeds in value*
75 Disdaining me, and throwing favours on
The low Posthumus, slanders° so her judgement            *discredits*
That what's else° rare is choked; and in that point            *otherwise*
I will conclude to hate her, nay, indeed,
To be revenged upon her. For when fools
Shall—
            *Enter* PISANIO
80            Who is here? What, are you packing,° sirrah?⁴            *scheming*
Come hither. Ah, you precious pander! Villain,
Where is thy lady? In a word, or else
Thou art straightway with the fiends.
PISANIO                              O good my lord!
CLOTEN   Where is thy lady?—or, by Jupiter,
85 I will not ask again. Close° villain,            *Secretive*
I'll have this secret from thy tongue or rip
Thy heart to find it. Is she with Posthumus,
From whose so many weights° of baseness cannot            *measures*
A dram of worth be drawn?
PISANIO                    Alas, my lord,
90 How can she be with him? When was she missed?
He is in Rome.
CLOTEN            Where is she, sir? Come nearer.°            *Be more precise*
No farther halting. Satisfy me home°            *completely*
What is become of her.
PISANIO   O my all-worthy lord!
95 CLOTEN   All-worthy villain,
Discover° where thy mistress is at once,            *Reveal*
At the next word. No more of 'worthy lord'.
Speak, or thy silence on the instant is
Thy condemnation and thy death.
PISANIO                          Then, sir,
100 This paper is the history of my knowledge
Touching her flight.
            [*He gives* CLOTEN *a letter*]
CLOTEN                    Let's see't. I will pursue her
Even to Augustus' throne.
PISANIO [*aside*]            Or° this or perish.            *Either*

3. That is, kill him. *forestall:* deprive.            4. Fellow (a common form of address to a social inferior).

She's far enough, and what he learns by this
May prove his travel,[5] not her danger.

CLOTEN                   Hum!

105   PISANIO [aside]    I'll write to my lord she's dead. O Innogen,
Safe mayst thou wander, safe return again!

CLOTEN    Sirrah, is this letter true?

PISANIO                  Sir, as I think.

CLOTEN    It is Posthumus' hand; I know't. Sirrah, if thou wouldst
not be a villain but do me true service, undergo° those employ-        *undertake*
110   ments wherein I should have cause to use thee with a serious
industry—that is, what villainy soe'er I bid thee do, to perform
it directly and truly—I would think thee an honest man. Thou
shouldst neither want° my means for thy relief nor my voice for      *find lacking*
thy preferment.°                                           *advancement*

115   PISANIO    Well, my good lord.

CLOTEN    Wilt thou serve me? For since patiently and constantly
thou hast stuck to the bare fortune of that beggar Posthumus,
thou canst not in the course of gratitude but be a diligent follower of mine. Wilt thou serve me?

120   PISANIO    Sir, I will.

CLOTEN    Give me thy hand. Here's my purse. Hast any of thy
late° master's garments in thy possession?                               *former*

PISANIO    I have, my lord, at my lodging the same suit he wore
when he took leave of my lady and mistress.

125   CLOTEN    The first service thou dost me, fetch that suit hither.
Let it be thy first service. Go.

PISANIO    I shall, my lord.                                      *Exit*

CLOTEN    Meet thee at Milford Haven! I forgot to ask him one
thing;[6] I'll remember't anon. Even there, thou villain Posthu-
130   mus, will I kill thee. I would these garments were come. She
said upon a time—the bitterness of it I now belch from my
heart—that she held the very garment of Posthumus in more
respect than my noble and natural person, together with the
adornment of my qualities. With that suit upon my back will I
135   ravish her—first kill him, and in her eyes; there shall she see
my valour, which will then be a torment to her contempt. He
on the ground, my speech of insultment° ended on his dead     *contemptuous triumph*
body, and when my lust hath dined—which, as I say, to vex her
I will execute in the clothes that she so praised—to the court
140   I'll knock° her back, foot° her home again. She hath despised       *beat / kick*
me rejoicingly, and I'll be merry in my revenge.

        *Enter* PISANIO [*with Posthumus' suit*]

Be those the garments?

PISANIO                Ay, my noble lord.

CLOTEN    How long is't since she went to Milford Haven?

PISANIO    She can scarce be there yet.

145   CLOTEN    Bring this apparel to my chamber. That is the second
thing that I have commanded thee. The third is that thou wilt
be a voluntary mute to° my design. Be but duteous, and true         *be quiet about*
preferment shall tender itself to thee. My revenge is now at
Milford. Would I had wings to follow it. Come, and be true.

                                                       *Exit*

---

5. May turn out to be merely a long journey for him.
6. The "one thing" may be how long a time has passed    since Innogen set out for Milford Haven (see Cloten's
question at line 143).

150 PISANIO  Thou bidd'st me to my loss,° for true to thee                    *perdition*
    Were to prove false, which I will never be
    To him that is most true. To Milford go,
    And find not her whom thou pursuest. Flow, flow,
    You heavenly blessings, on her. This fool's speed
155     Be crossed° with slowness; labour be his meed.°     *Exit*    *thwarted / reward*

### 3.6

*Enter INNOGEN [dressed as a man, before the cave]*

INNOGEN  I see a man's life is a tedious one.
    I have tired myself, and for two nights together
    Have made the ground my bed. I should be sick,
    But that my resolution helps me. Milford,
5     When from the mountain-top Pisanio showed thee,
    Thou wast within a ken.° O Jove, I think                    *within sight*
    Foundations[1] fly the wretched—such, I mean,
    Where they should be relieved.[2] Two beggars told me
    I could not miss my way. Will poor folks lie,
10     That have afflictions on them, knowing 'tis
    A punishment or trial?[3] Yes. No wonder,
    When rich ones scarce tell true. To lapse in fullness°    *To do wrong when rich*
    Is sorer° than to lie for need, and falsehood                 *worse*
    Is worse in kings than beggars. My dear lord,
15     Thou art one o'th' false ones. Now I think on thee
    My hunger's gone, but even before° I was                 *just a moment ago*
    At point° to sink for° food. But what is this?         *Ready / for want of*
    Here is a path to't. 'Tis some savage hold.°                  *refuge*
    I were best not call; I dare not call; yet famine,
20     Ere clean° it o'erthrow nature, makes it valiant.          *completely*
    Plenty and peace breeds cowards, hardness° ever            *hardship*
    Of hardiness is mother. Ho! Who's here?
    If anything that's civil, speak; if savage,
    Take or lend.[4] Ho! No answer? Then I'll enter.
25     Best draw my sword, and if mine enemy
    But fear the sword like me he'll scarcely look on't.
    Such a foe, good heavens![5]     *Exit [into the cave]*

*Enter BELARIUS, GUIDERIUS, and ARVIRAGUS[6]*

BELARIUS  You, Polydore, have proved best woodman° and           *hunter*
    Are master of the feast. Cadwal and I
30     Will play the cook and servant; 'tis our match.°            *bargain*
    The sweat of industry would dry and die
    But for the end it works to. Come, our stomachs
    Will make what's homely° savoury. Weariness             *plain*
    Can snore upon the flint when resty° sloth                   *lazy*
35     Finds the down pillow hard. Now peace be here,
    Poor house, that keep'st thyself.°                      *goes untended*
GUIDERIUS             I am throughly weary.
ARVIRAGUS  I am weak with toil yet strong in appetite.

---

3.6 Location: Before the cave of Belarius, Wales.
1. Certainties; charitable institutions.
2. *such . . . relieved:* such certainties, I mean, as
should give mental relief to the wretched; such charitable institutions as should give physical relief (food
and rest) to the wretched.

3. *knowing . . . trial:* knowing that poverty is a punishment or a test of one's virtue.
4. Take everything I have, or help me.
5. May it please heaven I meet such a timid foe.
6. F marks a new scene at this point, but the action is
continuous.

GUIDERIUS   There is cold meat i'th' cave. We'll browse° on that                    *nibble*
    Whilst what we have killed be cooked.
BELARIUS [*looking into the cave*]                Stay, come not in.
40  But° that it eats our victuals I should think                    *But for the fact*
    Here were a fairy.
GUIDERIUS                What's the matter, sir?
BELARIUS   By Jupiter, an angel—or, if not,
    An earthly paragon. Behold divineness
    No elder than a boy.
            *Enter* INNOGEN [*from the cave, dressed as a man*]
INNOGEN                Good masters, harm me not.
45  Before I entered here I called, and thought°                    *intended*
    To have begged or bought what I have took. Good truth,
    I have stol'n naught, nor would not, though I had found
    Gold strewed i'th' floor. Here's money for my meat.
    I would have left it on the board so° soon                    *as*
50  As I had made my meal, and parted
    With prayers for the provider.
GUIDERIUS                Money, youth?
ARVIRAGUS   All gold and silver rather turn to dirt,
    As 'tis no better reckoned but of° those        *better thought of but by*
    Who worship dirty gods.
INNOGEN                I see you're angry.
55  Know, if you kill me for my fault, I should
    Have died had I not made it.
BELARIUS                Whither bound?
INNOGEN   To Milford Haven.
BELARIUS                What's your name?
INNOGEN   Fidele,[7] sir. I have a kinsman who
    Is bound for Italy. He embarked at Milford,
60  To whom being going, almost spent with hunger,
    I am fall'n in° this offence.                    *into*
BELARIUS                Prithee, fair youth,
    Think us no churls,° nor measure our good minds        *base fellows*
    By this rude° place we live in. Well encountered.                    *wild*
    'Tis almost night. You shall have better cheer°                    *provisions*
65  Ere you depart, and thanks to° stay and eat it.        *our gratitude if you*
    Boys, bid him welcome.
GUIDERIUS                Were you a woman, youth,
    I should woo hard but be° your groom in honesty,        *rather than fail to be*
    Ay, bid for you as I'd buy.[8]
ARVIRAGUS                I'll make't my comfort
    He is a man, I'll love him as my brother.
70  [*To* INNOGEN] And such a welcome as I'd give to him
    After long absence, such is yours. Most welcome.
    Be sprightly,° for you fall 'mongst friends.                    *cheerful*
INNOGEN                'Mongst friends
    If brothers.[9] [*Aside*] Would it had been so that they
    Had been my father's sons. Then had my price°                    *worth*

---

7. In French and Italian, the name means "faithful one."        9. *'Mongst . . . brothers*: Yes, certainly I am among
8. Yes, make an offer for you with every intent to buy        friends, if you claim me as a brother.
(that is, to marry you).

75 Been less, and so more equal ballasting°         *equal in weight*
To thee, Posthumus.
        [*The three men speak apart*]
BELARIUS             He wrings° at some distress.         *twists in pain*
GUIDERIUS   Would I could free't.°                  *remove it*
ARVIRAGUS                Or I, whate'er it be,
What° pain it cost, what danger. Gods!        *Whatever*
BELARIUS                    Hark, boys.
        [*They whisper*]
INNOGEN [*aside*]   Great men
80 That had a court no bigger than this cave,
That did attend° themselves and had the virtue      *wait on*
Which their own conscience sealed° them, laying by°   *assured / disregarding*
That nothing-gift of differing multitudes,[1]
Could not outpeer° these twain. Pardon me, gods,      *surpass*
85 I'd change my sex to be companion with them,
Since Leonatus' false.
BELARIUS               It shall be so.
Boys, we'll go dress our hunt.° Fair youth, come in.     *game*
Discourse is heavy, fasting.[2] When we have supped
We'll mannerly demand thee of thy story,
So far as thou wilt speak it.
90 GUIDERIUS             Pray draw near.
ARVIRAGUS   The night to th' owl and morn to th' lark less welcome.
INNOGEN   Thanks, sir.
ARVIRAGUS   I pray draw near.           *Exeunt* [*into the cave*]

### 3.7

*Enter two Roman* SENATORS, *and* TRIBUNES
FIRST SENATOR    This is the tenor of the Emperor's writ:
That since the common men are now in action
'Gainst the Pannonians and Dalmatians,
And that the legions now in Gallia are
5 Full weak° to undertake our wars against         *Too weak*
The fall'n-off° Britons, that we do incite          *rebelling*
The gentry to this business. He creates
Lucius pro-consul,[1] and to you the tribunes,
For this immediate levy, he commends°           *entrusts*
10 His absolute commission.° Long live Caesar!       *authority*
A TRIBUNE   Is Lucius general of the forces?
SECOND SENATOR               Ay.
A TRIBUNE   Remaining now in Gallia?
FIRST SENATOR               With those legions
Which I have spoke of, whereunto your levy
Must be supplyant.° The words of your commission   *auxiliary*
15 Will tie you to° the numbers and the time      *indicate to you*
Of their dispatch.
A TRIBUNE             We will discharge our duty.       *Exeunt*

---

1. That worthless gift offered by a public that cannot agree on anything.
2. Conversation is difficult when one is without food.

3.7 Location: A public place, Rome.
1. One who acted as governor or military commander in a Roman province.

## 4.1

*Enter* CLOTEN [*in Posthumus' suit*]

CLOTEN   I am near to th' place where they should meet, if
Pisanio have mapped it truly. How fit° his garments serve me!    *aptly*
Why should his mistress, who was made by him that made the
tailor, not be fit° too?—the rather—saving reverence of the    *apt; sexually compatible*
5   word[1]—for 'tis said a woman's fitness comes by fits.[2] Therein I
must play the workman. I dare speak it to myself, for it is not
vainglory for a man and his glass° to confer in his own cham-    *mirror*
ber. I mean the lines of my body are as well drawn as his: no
less young, more strong, not beneath him in fortunes, beyond
10   him in the advantage of the time,[3] above him in birth, alike
conversant in general services, and more remarkable in single
oppositions.[4] Yet this imperceiverant° thing loves him in my    *stupid*
despite.° What mortality[5] is! Posthumus, thy head which now    *to spite me*
is growing upon thy shoulders shall within this hour be off, thy
15   mistress enforced,° thy garments cut to pieces before thy face;    *raped*
and all this done, spurn her home to her father, who may haply
be a little angry for my so rough usage; but my mother, having
power of° his testiness, shall turn all into my commendations.    *over*
My horse is tied up safe. Out, sword, and to a sore purpose!
20   Fortune, put them into my hand. This is the very description
of their meeting-place, and the fellow dares not deceive me.
*Exit*

## 4.2

*Enter* BELARIUS, GUIDERIUS, ARVIRAGUS, *and* INNOGEN
[*dressed as a man,*] *from the cave*

BELARIUS [*to* INNOGEN]   You are not well. Remain here in the cave.
We'll come to you from hunting.

ARVIRAGUS [*to* INNOGEN]                    Brother, stay here.
Are we not brothers?

INNOGEN                      So man and man should be,
But clay and clay[1] differs in dignity,°    *social position*
5   Whose dust[2] is both alike. I am very sick.

GUIDERIUS [*to* BELARIUS *and* ARVIRAGUS]   Go you to hunting,
I'll abide with him.

INNOGEN   So sick I am not, yet I am not well;
But not so citizen a wanton as
To seem to die ere sick.[3] So please you, leave me.
10   Stick to your journal course.° The breach of custom    *daily routine*
Is breach of all. I am ill, but your being by me
Cannot amend me. Society is no comfort
To one not sociable. I am not very sick,
Since I can reason of° it. Pray you, trust me here.    *talk about*
15   I'll rob none but myself; and let me die,
Stealing so poorly.[4]

---

4.1 Location: Near the cave of Belarius, Wales.
1. With apologies for my punning.
2. For it is said that a woman's inclination for sexual
intercourse comes intermittently.
3. In the favorable opportunities afforded by the times.
4. *alike . . . oppositions:* similarly acquainted with battle tactics, and superior in single combat or duels (with
puns on "service" and "oppositions" as referring to sexual exploits).

5. Life; humankind.
4.2 Location: Before the cave of Belarius.
1. Yet two humans (alluding to the biblical notion that
humans are formed out of clay).
2. The substance to which all humans return at death.
3. *But . . . sick:* But I am not so city-bred a weakling
("wanton") as to think I am dying even before I am sick.
4. Stealing only from one so poor as myself.

GUIDERIUS          I love thee: I have spoke it;
How much the quantity,° the weight as much,                    *As greatly*
As I do love my father.
BELARIUS                    What, how, how?
ARVIRAGUS    If it be sin to say so, sir, I yoke me°                  *I share*
20    In my good brother's fault. I know not why
I love this youth, and I have heard you say
Love's reason's without reason. The bier⁵ at door
And a demand who is't shall die, I'd say
'My father, not this youth'.
BELARIUS [*aside*]          O noble strain!°               *inherited character*
25    O worthiness of nature, breed of greatness!
Cowards father cowards, and base things sire base.
Nature hath meal and bran,° contempt and grace.           *flour and husks*
I'm not their father, yet who this should be
Doth miracle itself, loved before me.⁶
[*Aloud*] 'Tis the ninth hour o'th' morn.
30    ARVIRAGUS [*to* INNOGEN]          Brother, farewell.
INNOGEN    I wish ye sport.
ARVIRAGUS                    You health.—So please you, sir.
INNOGEN [*aside*]    These are kind creatures. Gods, what lies I have heard!
Our courtiers say all's savage but at court.
Experience, O thou disprov'st report!
35    Th'imperious° seas breeds monsters; for the dish            *imperial*
Poor tributary rivers as sweet fish.⁷
I am sick still, heart-sick. Pisanio,
I'll now taste of thy drug.
          [*She swallows the drug. The men speak apart*]
GUIDERIUS                    I could not stir him.
He said he was gentle° but unfortunate,                 *a gentleman by birth*
40    Dishonestly afflicted but yet honest.
ARVIRAGUS    Thus did he answer me, yet said hereafter
I might know more.
BELARIUS                    To th' field, to th' field!
[*To* INNOGEN] We'll leave you for this time. Go in and rest.
ARVIRAGUS [*to* INNOGEN]    We'll not be long away.
BELARIUS [*to* INNOGEN]                    Pray be not sick,
For you must be our housewife.
45    INNOGEN                    Well or ill,
I am bound° to you.                    *Exit*          *indebted*
BELARIUS                    And shalt be ever.
This youth, howe'er distressed, appears° hath had          *apparently*
Good ancestors.
ARVIRAGUS    How angel-like he sings!
50    GUIDERIUS    But his neat° cookery!                           *dainty*
BELARIUS⁸    He cut our roots in characters,°          *alphabet shapes*
And sauced our broths as° Juno had been sick                    *as if*
And he her dieter.°                                                    *cook*
ARVIRAGUS                    Nobly he yokes

---

5. The litter, or platform, on which a corpse was carried to the grave.
6. yet . . . me: yet who this may be who is loved more
than me is a source of great wonder.
7. for . . . fish: but when it comes to eating, small trib-
utaries breed fish as sweet as does the sea.

8. F assigns this speech to Arviragus, but he has the
next one as well. One editorial solution has been to
assign the lines to Guiderius as an extension of his prior
speech. Another, as here, is to give the lines to Belarius,
who thus joins his adopted sons in praising
Innogen/Fidele.

A smiling with a sigh, as if the sigh
55 Was that° it was for not being such a smile;                        *Was what*
The smile mocking the sigh that° it would fly                         *because*
From so divine a temple to commix°                                   *join*
With winds that sailors rail at.
GUIDERIUS                          I do note
That grief and patience, rooted in him both,
Mingle their spurs° together.                                        *roots*
60 ARVIRAGUS                      Grow patience,
And let the stinking elder,⁹ grief, untwine
His perishing° root with° the increasing vine.                  *deadly / from*
BELARIUS    It is great morning.° Come away. Who's there?      *full daylight*

        *Enter* CLOTEN [*in Posthumus' suit*]

CLOTEN    I cannot find those runagates.° That villain      *runaways; fugitives*
Hath mocked me. I am faint.
65 BELARIUS [*aside to* ARVIRAGUS *and* GUIDERIUS] 'Those runagates'?
Means he not us? I partly know him; 'tis
Cloten, the son o'th' Queen. I fear some ambush.
I saw him not these many years, and yet
I know 'tis he. We are held as outlaws. Hence!
GUIDERIUS [*aside to* ARVIRAGUS *and* BELARIUS]    He is but one.
70     You and my brother search
What companies° are near. Pray you, away.                     *companions*
Let me alone with him.     [*Exeunt* ARVIRAGUS *and* BELARIUS]
CLOTEN                       Soft, what are you
That fly me thus? Some villain mountaineers?°        *lowborn mountain people*
I have heard of such. What slave art thou?
GUIDERIUS                                  A thing
75 More slavish did I ne'er than answering
A slave without a knock.°                             *without striking him*
CLOTEN                     Thou art a robber,
A law-breaker, a villain. Yield thee, thief.
GUIDERIUS    To who? To thee? What art thou? Have not I
An arm as big as thine, a heart as big?
80 Thy words, I grant, are bigger, for I wear not
My dagger in my mouth.¹ Say what thou art,
Why I should yield to thee.
CLOTEN                     Thou villain base,
Know'st me not by my clothes?
GUIDERIUS                     No, nor thy tailor, rascal,
Who is thy grandfather. He made those clothes,
Which, as it seems, make thee.²
85 CLOTEN                         Thou precious varlet,°      *absolute scoundrel*
My tailor made them not.
GUIDERIUS                 Hence, then, and thank
The man that gave them thee. Thou art some fool.
I am loath to beat thee.
CLOTEN                   Thou injurious° thief,                *insulting*
Hear but my name and tremble.
GUIDERIUS                     What's thy name?

---

9. A tree with strong-smelling leaves and flowers on
which Judas, the disciple who betrayed Jesus, is said to
have hanged himself.

1. *for . . . mouth:* for I don't let words substitute for
weapons.
2. Alluding to the proverb "The tailor makes the man."

90   CLOTEN   Cloten, thou villain.

GUIDERIUS   Cloten, thou double villain, be thy name,
I cannot tremble at it. Were it toad or adder, spider,
'Twould move me sooner.

CLOTEN                To thy further fear,
Nay, to thy mere confusion,° thou shalt know        *absolute destruction*
I am son to th' Queen.

95   GUIDERIUS              I am sorry for't, not seeming
So worthy as thy birth.

CLOTEN              Art not afeard?

GUIDERIUS   Those that I reverence, those I fear, the wise.
At fools I laugh, not fear them.

CLOTEN                 Die the death.
When I have slain thee with my proper° hand          *own*
100   I'll follow those that even now fled hence,
And on the gates of Lud's town° set your heads.[3]     *London*
Yield, rustic mountaineer.           *Fight and exeunt*

        *Enter* BELARIUS *and* ARVIRAGUS

BELARIUS           No company's abroad?°         *about*

ARVIRAGUS   None in the world. You did mistake him, sure.

BELARIUS   I cannot tell. Long is it since I saw him,
105   But time hath nothing blurred those lines of favour°   *facial features*
Which then he wore. The snatches° in his voice     *hesitations*
And burst° of speaking were as his. I am absolute°   *sudden rush / sure*
'Twas very Cloten.°                  *Cloten himself*

ARVIRAGUS        In this place we left them.
I wish my brother make good time with him,[4]
You say he is so fell.°                 *fierce*

110   BELARIUS          Being scarce made up,°     *barely full-grown*
I mean to man, he had not apprehension°     *had no consciousness*
Of roaring terrors; for defect of judgement
Is oft the cause of fear.[5]

        *Enter* GUIDERIUS [*with Cloten's head*]
              But see, thy brother.

GUIDERIUS   This Cloten was a fool, an empty purse,
115   There was no money in't. Not Hercules[6]
Could have knocked out his brains, for he had none.
Yet I not doing this,° the fool had borne     *had I not done this*
My head as I do his.

BELARIUS         What hast thou done?

GUIDERIUS   I am perfect° what: cut off one Cloten's head,   *certain*
120   Son to the Queen after his own report,
Who called me traitor, mountaineer, and swore
With his own single hand he'd take us in,°     *capture us*
Displace our heads where—thanks, ye gods—they grow,
And set them on Lud's town.

BELARIUS            We are all undone.

125   GUIDERIUS   Why, worthy father, what have we to lose
But that° he swore to take, our lives? The law     *what*

---

3. The heads of criminals were frequently displayed on poles on London Bridge and other places throughout the city.
4. I hope my brother is successful with him.
5. *for . . . fear:* an obscure passage. It may mean that Cloten's faulty judgment, which led him to know no fear, caused fear in others. A less likely meaning is that while defects in judgment cause fear, Cloten knew no fear because he had absolutely no judgment, being utterly witless.
6. Mythical hero of enormous strength.

Protects not us: then why should we be tender
To let[7] an arrogant piece of flesh threat us,
Play judge and executioner all himself,
130 For° we do fear the law? What company          *Because*
Discover you abroad?[8]
BELARIUS                    No single soul
Can we set eye on, but in all safe reason
He must have some attendants. Though his humour°          *disposition*
Was nothing but mutation,° ay, and that          *changeableness*
135 From one bad thing to worse, not° frenzy,          *neither*
Not° absolute madness, could so far have raved°          *Nor / made him mad enough*
To bring him here alone. Although perhaps
It may be heard at court that such as we
Cave° here, hunt here, are outlaws, and in time          *Live in a cave*
140 May make some stronger head,° the which he hearing—          *raise a stronger force*
As it is like him—might break out, and swear
He'd fetch us in, yet is't not probable
To come° alone, either he so undertaking,          *That he would come*
Or they so suffering.[9] Then on good ground we fear
145 If we do fear this body hath a tail°          *rear end; followers*
More perilous than the head.
ARVIRAGUS                    Let ord'nance°          *destiny*
Come as the gods foresay° it; howsoe'er,          *predict*
My brother hath done well.
BELARIUS                    I had no mind
To hunt this day. The boy Fidele's sickness
Did make my way long forth.°          *my journey tedious*
150 GUIDERIUS                    With his own sword,
Which he did wave against my throat, I have ta'en
His head from him. I'll throw't into the creek
Behind our rock, and let it to the sea
And tell the fishes he's the Queen's son, Cloten.
That's all I reck.°          Exit [with Cloten's head]          *care*
155 BELARIUS          I fear 'twill be revenged.
Would, Polydore, thou hadst not done't, though valour
Becomes thee well enough.
ARVIRAGUS                    Would I had done't,
So the revenge alone pursued me.° Polydore,          *only pursued me*
I love thee brotherly, but envy much
160 Thou hast robbed me of this deed. I would revenges
That possible strength might meet would seek us through
And put us to our answer.[1]
BELARIUS                    Well, 'tis done.
We'll hunt no more today, nor seek for danger
Where there's no profit. I prithee, to our rock.
165 You and Fidele play the cooks. I'll stay
Till hasty Polydore return, and bring him
To dinner presently.
ARVIRAGUS                    Poor sick Fidele!
I'll willingly to him. To gain° his colour          *restore*

---

7. *be tender / To let*: be so meek as to allow.
8. What companions (of Cloten) did you find here-
abouts?
9. *either . . . suffering*: either that he would undertake

it or that they would allow it.
1. *I would . . . answer*: I wish that revenges equal to all
the power that we might muster would find us out and
test our mettle.

I'd let a parish of such Clotens blood,[2]
And praise myself for charity.     *Exit [into the cave]*

170 BELARIUS                            O thou goddess,
Thou divine Nature, how thyself thou blazon'st[3]
In these two princely boys! They are as gentle
As zephyrs° blowing below the violet,                *breezes from the west*
Not wagging his sweet head; and yet as rough,°          *violent*
175 Their royal blood enchafed,° as the rud'st wind       *enflamed*
That by the top doth take the mountain pine
And make him stoop to th' vale. 'Tis wonder
That an invisible instinct should frame° them             *shape*
To royalty unlearned, honour untaught,
180 Civility not seen from other,° valour         *not witnessed in others*
That wildly° grows in them, but yields a crop      *without cultivation*
As if it had been sowed. Yet still it's strange
What Cloten's being here to us portends,
Or what his death will bring us.
        *Enter* GUIDERIUS

GUIDERIUS                    Where's my brother?
185 I have sent Cloten's clotpoll° down the stream        *blockhead*
In embassy to his mother. His body's hostage
For his return.[4]
        *Solemn music*
BELARIUS          My ingenious° instrument!—      *artfully crafted*
Hark, Polydore, it sounds. But what occasion
Hath Cadwal now to give it motion? Hark!
GUIDERIUS    Is he at home?
190 BELARIUS                  He went hence even now.
GUIDERIUS    What does he mean? Since death of my dear'st mother
It did not speak before. All solemn things
Should answer° solemn accidents. The matter?      *correspond to*
Triumphs for nothing and lamenting toys
195 Is jollity for apes and grief for boys.[5]
Is Cadwal mad?
        *Enter [from the cave]* ARVIRAGUS *with* INNOGEN, *dead,*
        *bearing her in his arms*
BELARIUS          Look, here he comes,
And brings the dire occasion in his arms
Of what we blame him for.
ARVIRAGUS                The bird is dead
That we have made so much on.° I had rather         *of*
200 Have skipped from sixteen years of age to sixty,
To have turned my leaping time° into a crutch,°    *youth / (old age)*
Than have seen this.
GUIDERIUS *[to* INNOGEN*]*    O sweetest, fairest lily!
My brother wears thee not one half so well
As when thou grew'st thyself.
BELARIUS                O melancholy,
205 Who ever yet could sound thy bottom,° find      *measure your depths*
The ooze to show what coast thy sluggish crare°      *small ship*
Might easiliest harbour in? Thou blessèd thing,

2. I'd draw blood from a whole parish full of fools like
Cloten.
3. How you proclaim yourself (as in a coat of arms).
4. *His body's . . . return:* I will hold his body hostage

until his head returns (which will be never).
5. *Triumphs . . . boys:* Public celebrations for no reason
and showing great grief for trivial matters are foolish
and unmanly.

Jove knows what man thou mightst have made; but I,°       *I know*
Thou diedst a most rare boy, of melancholy.
[*To* ARVIRAGUS] How found you him?

210 ARVIRAGUS                 Stark,° as you see,       *stiff*
Thus smiling as° some fly had tickled slumber,       *as if*
Not as death's dart being laughed at;[6] his right cheek
Reposing on a cushion.

GUIDERIUS            Where?

ARVIRAGUS                 O'th' floor,
His arms thus leagued.° I thought he slept, and put       *linked together*
215 My clouted brogues° from off my feet, whose rudeness       *hobnailed boots*
Answered° my steps too loud.       *Rendered*

GUIDERIUS                Why, he but sleeps.
If he be gone he'll make his grave a bed.
With female fairies will his tomb be haunted,
[*To* INNOGEN] And worms will not come to thee.

ARVIRAGUS [*to* INNOGEN]            With fairest flowers
220 Whilst summer lasts and I live here, Fidele,
I'll sweeten thy sad grave. Thou shalt not lack
The flower that's like thy face, pale primrose, nor
The azured harebell,° like thy veins; no, nor       *blue hyacinth*
The leaf of eglantine,° whom not to slander       *honeysuckle*
225 Outsweetened not thy breath. The ruddock would
With charitable bill—O bill sore shaming
Those rich-left heirs that let their fathers lie
Without a monument!—bring thee all this,
Yea, and furred moss besides, when flowers are none,
To winter-gown thy corpse.[7]

230 GUIDERIUS            Prithee, have done,
And do not play in wench-like words[8] with that
Which is so serious. Let us bury him,
And not protract with admiration° what       *wonder*
Is now due debt. To th' grave.

ARVIRAGUS            Say, where shall 's° lay him?       *ought we to*

GUIDERIUS    By good Euriphile, our mother.

235 ARVIRAGUS                     Be't so,
And let us, Polydore, though now our voices
Have got the mannish crack, sing him to th' ground
As once our mother; use like° note and words,       *a similar tune*
Save that 'Euriphile' must be 'Fidele'.

240 GUIDERIUS    Cadwal,
I cannot sing. I'll weep, and word° it with thee,       *speak*
For notes of sorrow out of tune are worse
Than priests and fanes° that lie.       *temples*

ARVIRAGUS            We'll speak it then.

BELARIUS    Great griefs, I see, medicine° the less, for Cloten       *cure*
245 Is quite forgot. He was a queen's son, boys,
And though he came our enemy, remember
He was paid° for that. Though mean° and mighty rotting       *punished / lowborn*
Together have one dust, yet reverence,

---

6. Not as if laughing at the approach of death. Death was often depicted carrying a spear ("dart").
7. *The ruddock . . . corpse:* referring to the belief that the robins ("ruddocks") covered dead bodies with flowers and moss. *winter-gown:* clothe for winter.

8. Words appropriate to women. In Shakespeare's plays, speeches about flowers are often delivered by female characters, perhaps most notably in *Hamlet* 4.5.173–82 and *The Winter's Tale* 4.4.73–134.

That angel of the world,⁹ doth make distinction
250 Of place 'tween high and low. Our foe was princely,
And though you took his life as being our foe,
Yet bury him as a prince.

GUIDERIUS                    Pray you, fetch him hither.
Thersites' body is as good as Ajax'¹
When neither are alive.

ARVIRAGUS [to BELARIUS]   If you'll go fetch him,
We'll say our song the whilst.          [Exit BELARIUS]
255                                Brother, begin.

GUIDERIUS   Nay, Cadwal, we must lay his head to th'east.²
My father hath a reason for't.

ARVIRAGUS                              'Tis true.

GUIDERIUS   Come on, then, and remove him.

ARVIRAGUS                                   So, begin.³

GUIDERIUS   Fear no more the heat o'th' sun,
260           Nor the furious winter's rages.
          Thou thy worldly task hast done,
              Home art gone and ta'en thy wages.
          Golden lads and girls all must,
              As° chimney-sweepers, come to dust.                    *Like*

265 ARVIRAGUS   Fear no more the frown o'th' great,
              Thou art past the tyrant's stroke.
          Care no more to clothe and eat,
              To thee the reed is as the oak.⁴
          The sceptre, learning, physic,° must              *medical knowledge*
270       All follow this and come to dust.

GUIDERIUS   Fear no more the lightning flash,

ARVIRAGUS     Nor th'all-dreaded thunder-stone.°                 *thunderbolt*

GUIDERIUS   Fear not slander, censure rash.

ARVIRAGUS     Thou hast finished joy and moan.

275 GUIDERIUS *and* ARVIRAGUS   All lovers young, all lovers must
                    Consign to thee⁵ and come to dust.

GUIDERIUS   No exorcisor° harm thee,                      *conjurer of spirits*

ARVIRAGUS   Nor no witchcraft charm thee.

GUIDERIUS   Ghost unlaid forbear thee.⁶

280 ARVIRAGUS   Nothing ill come near thee.

GUIDERIUS *and* ARVIRAGUS   Quiet consummation° have,             *ending*
                    And renownèd be thy grave.

          *Enter* BELARIUS *with the body of Cloten* [*in Posthumus'*
          *suit*]

GUIDERIUS   We have done our obsequies. Come, lay him down.

BELARIUS   Here's a few flowers, but 'bout midnight more;
285 The herbs that have on them cold dew o'th' night°               *of the night*
Are strewings fitt'st for graves upon th'earth's face.
You were as flowers, now withered; even so

---

9. Reverence (respect for someone because of his or
her social position) may here be called the "angel of the
world" because social hierarchy was thought by some to
imitate heavenly hierarchy.
1. Alluding to two Greeks present at the siege of Troy:
Thersites, a scurrilous coward, and Ajax, a mighty hero.
Both appear in Shakespeare's *Troilus and Cressida*.
2. An allusion to classical or Celtic burial practices. The
English Christian custom was to lay the head to the
west. This detail reinforces the pagan world of the play.

3. In F, the following duet is introduced as "SONG."
Lines [240–43], in which the brothers say they cannot
sing and must speak the words, may have been added
because the particular actors who played Arviragus and
Guiderius were not good singers.
4. Referring to traditional symbols of weakness and
strength, respectively.
5. Submit to the same terms as you.
6. May spirits who have not been laid to rest leave you
alone.

These herblets shall,° which we upon you strow.       *shall wither*
Come on, away; apart upon our knees[7]
290 [                               ]
The ground that gave them° first has them again.       *gave them life*
Their pleasures here are past, so is their pain.

*Exeunt* [BELARIUS, ARVIRAGUS, *and* GUIDERIUS]

INNOGEN *awakes*   Yes, sir, to Milford Haven. Which is the way?
I thank you. By yon bush? Pray, how far thither?
295 'Od's pitykins,° can it be six mile yet?       *By God's pity (mild oath)*
I have gone° all night. 'Faith, I'll lie down and sleep.       *walked*

[*She sees* CLOTEN]

But soft,° no bedfellow! O gods and goddesses!       *wait*
These flowers are like the pleasures of the world,
This bloody man the care on't.[8] I hope I dream,
300 For so° I thought I was a cavekeeper,       *For then*
And cook to honest creatures. But 'tis not so.
'Twas but a bolt° of nothing, shot of° nothing,       *an arrow / from*
Which the brain makes of fumes.[9] Our very eyes
Are sometimes like our judgements, blind. Good faith,
305 I tremble still with fear; but if there be
Yet left in heaven as small a drop of pity
As a wren's eye, feared gods, a part of it!
The dream's here still. Even when I wake it is
Without me as within me; not imagined, felt.
310 A headless man? The garments of Posthumus?
I know the shape of 's leg; this is his hand,
His foot Mercurial, his Martial[1] thigh,
The brawns° of Hercules; but his Jovial[2] face—       *muscles*
Murder in heaven! How? 'Tis gone. Pisanio,
315 All curses madded Hecuba[3] gave the Greeks,
And mine to boot, be darted on thee! Thou,
Conspired° with that irregulous° devil Cloten,       *Conspiring / lawless*
Hath here cut off my lord. To write and read
Be henceforth treacherous! Damned Pisanio
320 Hath with his forgèd letters—damned Pisanio—
From this most bravest° vessel of the world       *splendid*
Struck the main-top!° O Posthumus, alas,       *top of the mast; his head*
Where is thy head? Where's that? Ay me, where's that?
Pisanio might have killed thee at the heart
325 And left thy head on. How should this be? Pisanio?
'Tis he and Cloten. Malice and lucre° in them       *greed*
Have laid this woe here. O, 'tis pregnant,° pregnant!       *clear*
The drug he gave me, which he said was precious
And cordial° to me, have I not found it       *restorative*
330 Murd'rous to th' senses? That confirms it home.°       *completely*
This is Pisanio's deed, and Cloten—O,
Give colour to my pale cheek with thy blood,
That we the horrider° may seem to those       *more terrifying*
Which chance to find us!

---

7. Some other place ("apart"), let us pray (be "upon our knees"). Because the previous two lines rhyme, as do the next two lines, it is probable that a line is missing here. The sense of "apart upon our knees" also seems obscure, probably because the thought is truncated.
8. This bloody man is like the sorrow of the world.
9. "Fumes" (vapors) were thought to rise from the stom-

ach and cause dreams and distortions of the imagination.
1. Fashioned for battle, like that of Mars, the god of war. *Mercurial:* Like that of Mercury, the fleet-footed messenger of the gods.
2. Majestic like the face of Jove, king of the gods.
3. The Queen of Troy, Priam's wife, whose desire for revenge against the Greeks made her insane ("madded").

[*She smears her face with blood*]
     O my lord, my lord!
  [*She faints.*]
  *Enter* LUCIUS, [*Roman*] *Captains, and a* SOOTHSAYER
 A ROMAN CAPTAIN [*to* LUCIUS] To them° the legions garrisoned   *In addition to them*
335  in Gallia
  After your will⁴ have crossed the sea, attending°     *waiting for*
  You here at Milford Haven with your ships.
  They are hence in readiness.
 LUCIUS       But what from Rome?
 A ROMAN CAPTAIN The senate hath stirred up the confiners°   *inhabitants*
340 And gentlemen of Italy, most willing spirits
  That promise noble service, and they come
  Under the conduct of bold Giacomo,
  Siena's° brother.             *The Duke of Siena's*
 LUCIUS     When expect you them?
 A ROMAN CAPTAIN With the next benefit o'th' wind.
 LUCIUS         This forwardness°   *readiness*
345 Makes our hopes fair. Command our present numbers
  Be mustered; bid the captains look to't.  [*Exit one or more*]
  [*To* SOOTHSAYER]     Now, sir,
  What have you dreamed of late of this war's purpose?°  *outcome*
 SOOTHSAYER Last night the very gods showed me a vision—
  I fast,° and prayed for their intelligence°—thus:  *fasted / information*
350 I saw Jove's bird, the Roman eagle, winged
  From the spongy° south to this part of the west,   *damp*
  There vanished in the sunbeams; which portends,
  Unless my sins abuse° my divination,      *falsify*
  Success to th' Roman host.
 LUCIUS     Dream often so,
  And never false.°            *dream falsely*
  [*He sees Cloten's body*]
355     Soft, ho, what trunk is here
  Without his top? The ruin speaks that sometime°   *once*
  It was a worthy building. How, a page?
  Or° dead or sleeping on him? But dead rather,   *Either*
  For nature doth abhor to make his bed
360 With the defunct, or sleep upon the dead.
  Let's see the boy's face.
 A ROMAN CAPTAIN    He's alive, my lord.
 LUCIUS He'll then instruct us of this body. Young one,
  Inform us of thy fortunes, for it seems
  They crave to be demanded. Who is this
365 Thou mak'st thy bloody pillow? Or who was he
  That, otherwise than noble nature did,⁵
  Hath altered that good picture? What's thy interest
  In this sad wreck?° How came't? Who is't?    *ruin*
  What art thou?
 INNOGEN    I am nothing; or if not,
370 Nothing to be were better.⁶ This was my master,
  A very valiant Briton, and a good,
  That here by mountaineers lies slain. Alas,

---

4. According to your command.     6. It were better to be nothing.
5. Who, in a manner different from nature's workings.

There is no more such masters. I may wander
From east to occident, cry out for service,
375　Try many, all good; serve truly, never
Find such another master.
LUCIUS　　　　　　　　　　'Lack,° good youth,　　　　　　　*Alack*
Thou mov'st no less with thy complaining than
Thy master in bleeding. Say his name, good friend.
INNOGEN　Richard du Champ.[7] [*Aside*] If I do lie and do
380　No harm by it, though the gods hear I hope
They'll pardon it. [*Aloud*] Say you, sir?
LUCIUS　　　　　　　　　　　Thy name?
INNOGEN　　　　　　　　　　　　　　Fidele, sir.
LUCIUS　Thou dost approve° thyself the very same.　　　*show*
Thy name well fits thy faith,° thy faith thy name.　　*fidelity*
Wilt take thy chance with me? I will not say
385　Thou shalt be so well mastered, but be sure,
No less beloved. The Roman Emperor's letters
Sent by a consul to me should not sooner
Than thine own worth prefer° thee. Go with me.　　*recommend*
INNOGEN　I'll follow, sir. But first, an't° please the gods,　*if it*
390　I'll hide my master from the flies as deep
As these poor pickaxes° can dig; and when　　　　　*(her hands)*
With wild-wood leaves and weeds I ha' strewed his grave
And on it said a century of° prayers,　　　　　　　*a hundred*
Such as I can, twice o'er I'll weep and sigh,
395　And leaving so his service, follow you,
So please you entertain° me.　　　　　　　　　　*employ*
LUCIUS　　　　　　　　　Ay, good youth,
And rather father thee than master thee. My friends,
The boy hath taught us manly duties. Let us
Find out the prettiest daisied plot we can,
400　And make him with our pikes and partisans[8]
A grave. Come, arm° him. Boy, he is preferred°　*lift / recommended*
By thee to us, and he shall be interred
As soldiers can. Be cheerful. Wipe thine eyes.
Some falls are means the happier to arise.°

　　　　　　　　　　　*Exeunt* [*with Cloten's body*]

## 4.3

*Enter* CYMBELINE, LORDS, *and* PISANIO
CYMBELINE　Again, and bring me word how 'tis with her.
　　　　　　　　　　　　*Exit one or more*
A fever with° the absence of her son,　　　　　　*on account of*
A madness of which her life's in danger—heavens,
How deeply you at once do touch° me! Innogen,　　*afflict*
5　The great part of my comfort, gone; my queen
Upon a desperate bed,° and in a time　　　　*Extremely ill in bed*
When fearful wars point at me; her son gone,
So needful for this present!° It strikes me past　　*So needed now*
The hope of comfort. [*To* PISANIO] But for thee, fellow,

---

7. This French name translates as "Richard of the
Field," perhaps an allusion to a well-known London
printer named Richard Field, who was born in
Stratford-upon-Avon and printed Shakespeare's *Rape of
Lucrece* and *Venus and Adonis* in the 1590s.

8. With our spears and our halberds (long-handled
weapons with axlike blades).
9. Some falls are means by which good fortune arises.
4.3 Location: Cymbeline's court, Britain.

10  Who needs must know of her departure and
    Dost seem so ignorant, we'll enforce it from thee
    By a sharp torture.
    PISANIO                    Sir, my life is yours.
    I humbly set it at your will. But for my mistress,
    I nothing know° where she remains, why gone,                    *know nothing about*
15  Nor when she purposes° return. Beseech° your highness,          *intends to / I beseech*
    Hold me° your loyal servant.                                    *Regard me as*
    A LORD                    Good my liege,
    The day that she was missing he was here.
    I dare be bound he's true, and shall perform
    All parts of his subjection° loyally. For Cloten,               *duty as a subject*
20  There wants° no diligence in seeking him,                       *is lacking*
    And will° no doubt be found.                                    *he will*
    CYMBELINE                    The time is troublesome.°          *dire*
    [*To* PISANIO] We'll slip you° for a season, but our jealousy   *let you go*
    Does yet depend.[1]
    A LORD              So please your majesty,
    The Roman legions, all from Gallia drawn,
25  Are landed on your coast with a supply
    Of Roman gentlemen by the senate sent.
    CYMBELINE    Now for° the counsel of my son and queen!         *If only I now had*
    I am amazed° with matter.°                                     *overwhelmed / business*
    A LORD                    Good my liege,
    Your preparation can affront no less
30  Than what you hear of.[2] Come more, for more you're ready.
    The want° is but to put those powers in motion                 *The only thing needed*
    That long to move.
    CYMBELINE              I thank you. Let's withdraw,
    And meet the time as it seeks us. We fear not
    What can from Italy annoy° us, but                              *harm*
35  We grieve at chances° here. Away.                               *events*
                    *Exeunt* [CYMBELINE *and* LORDS]
    PISANIO    I heard no letter from my master since
    I wrote him Innogen was slain. 'Tis strange.
    Nor hear I from my mistress, who did promise
    To yield me often tidings. Neither know I
40  What is betid° to Cloten, but remain                            *has happened*
    Perplexed in all. The heavens still must work.
    Wherein I am false I am honest; not true, to be true.
    These present wars shall find I love my country
    Even to the note° o'th' King, or I'll fall in them.            *notice*
45  All other doubts, by time let them be cleared:
    Fortune brings in some boats that are not steered.    *Exit*

### 4.4

*Enter* BELARIUS, GUIDERIUS, *and* ARVIRAGUS
    GUIDERIUS    The noise is round about us.
    BELARIUS                    Let us from it.
    ARVIRAGUS    What pleasure, sir, find we in life to lock it°    *shut it off*
    From action and adventure?
    GUIDERIUS                    Nay, what hope

---

1. *but . . . depend:* but our suspicions still hold.       have heard of.
2. *Your . . . of:* Your forces can confront all those you    4.4 Location: Before the cave of Belarius, Wales.

|  | Have we in hiding us? This way° the Romans | *By this course of action* |
| 5 | Must or° for Britains slay us, or receive us | *either* |
|  | For barbarous and unnatural revolts° | *rebels* |
|  | During their use,[1] and slay us after. | |

BELARIUS                                             Sons,
We'll higher to the mountains; there secure us.
To the King's party there's no going. Newness

| 10 | Of Cloten's death—we being not known, not mustered | |
|  | Among the bands°—may drive us to a render° | *troops / an account* |
|  | Where we have lived, and so extort from 's that | |
|  | Which we have done, whose answer would be death | |
|  | Drawn on° with torture. | *Prolonged* |

GUIDERIUS                               This is, sir, a doubt
In such a time nothing becoming you
Nor satisfying us.

ARVIRAGUS                               It is not likely
That when they hear the Roman horses neigh,

|  | Behold their quartered files,° have both their eyes | *orderly troops* |
|  | And ears so cloyed importantly[2] as now, | |
| 20 | That they will waste their time upon our note,° | *in observing us* |
|  | To know from whence we are. | |

BELARIUS                                   O, I am known

| | Of° many in the army. Many years, | *By* |
| | Though Cloten then° but young, you see, not wore° him | *was then / did not wear* |

From my remembrance. And besides, the King
25  Hath not deserved my service nor your loves,
Who find in my exile the want of breeding,
The certainty of this hard life;[3] aye hopeless
To have the courtesy your cradle promised,[4]

|  | But to be still° hot summer's tanlings,[5] and | *always* |

The shrinking slaves of winter.
30  GUIDERIUS                               Than be so,
Better to cease to be. Pray, sir, to th'army.
I and my brother are not known; yourself

|  | So out of thought, and thereto° so o'ergrown,[6] | *in addition* |

Cannot be questioned.
ARVIRAGUS                               By this sun that shines,
35  I'll thither. What thing is't[7] that I never
Did see man die, scarce ever looked on blood

|  | But that of coward hares, hot° goats, and venison, | *lecherous* |

Never bestrid a horse save one that had
A rider like myself, who ne'er wore rowel[8]
40  Nor iron on his heel! I am ashamed
To look upon the holy sun, to have
The benefit of his blest beams, remaining
So long a poor unknown.
GUIDERIUS                               By heavens, I'll go.
If you will bless me, sir, and give me leave,

| 45 | I'll take the better care;° but if you will not, | *be the more careful* |

---

1. While they have need of us.
2. So completely taken up with important matters.
3. *Who . . . life:* (You) who experience as a result of my exile a lack of proper education, the enduring fact of this hard life.
4. *aye . . . promised:* yes, without hope to have the cultivated existence your noble birth promised.
5. People exposed to the sun. In England at this time, tanned skin denoted low social status.
6. So overgrown with hair or beard; so grown in years; so grown out of memory.
7. What a bad state of affairs it is.
8. Small rotating disk at the end of a spur. Wearing spurs was the privilege of gentlemen.

The hazard therefore due[9] fall on me by
The hands of Romans.

ARVIRAGUS                    So say I, amen.

BELARIUS    No reason I, since of your lives you set
So slight a valuation, should reserve

50  My cracked° one to more care. Have with you,° boys!          weakened / Come then
If in your country° wars you chance to die,                          country's
That is my bed, too, lads, and there I'll lie.
Lead, lead. [Aside] The time seems long. Their blood thinks scorn°    disdains itself
Till it fly out and show them princes born.          Exeunt

## 5.1

Enter POSTHUMUS [dressed as an Italian
gentleman, carrying a bloody cloth]

POSTHUMUS    Yea, bloody cloth, I'll keep thee, for I once wished
Thou shouldst be coloured thus. You married ones,
If each of you should take this course, how many
Must murder wives much better than themselves

5   For wrying° but a little! O Pisanio,                                 erring
Every good servant does not all commands,
No bond but° to do just ones. Gods, if you               No obligation except
Should have ta'en vengeance on my faults, I never
Had lived to put on this;° so had you saved          to undertake this deed

10  The noble Innogen to repent, and struck
Me, wretch, more worth your vengeance. But alack,
You snatch some hence for little faults; that's love,
To have them fall no more.[1] You some permit
To second° ills with ills, each elder° worse,                reinforce / later fault

15  And make them dread ill, to the doer's thrift.[2]
But Innogen is your own. Do your blest wills,
And make me blest to obey. I am brought hither
Among th'Italian gentry, and to fight
Against my lady's kingdom. 'Tis enough

20  That, Britain, I have killed thy mistress-piece;[3]
I'll give no wound to thee. Therefore, good heavens,
Hear patiently my purpose. I'll disrobe me
Of these Italian weeds, and suit° myself                              dress
As does a Briton peasant.
        [He disrobes himself]
                    So I'll fight

25  Against the part° I come with; so I'll die                           side
For thee, O Innogen, even for whom my life
Is every breath a death; and, thus unknown,
Pitied° nor hated, to the face of peril                         Neither pitied
Myself I'll dedicate. Let me make men know

30  More valour in me than my habits° show.                          garments
Gods, put the strength o'th' Leonati in me.
To shame the guise° o'th' world, I will begin            customs; dress
The fashion—less without and more within.          Exit

9. May the danger due to me (as a result of my disobedience).
5.1 Location: The Roman camp, Britain.
1. that's . . . more: that is a sign of love, to have them no longer sin.
2. And make them fear punishment, to their own benefit.
3. Punning on "masterpiece." Most editions, following

F, read: "'Tis enough / That, Britain, I have killed thy mistress; peace." "Mistress-piece," which can be found in other texts from the period, suggests the extraordinary excellence of Innogen. "Piece" could be spelled "peace" in the early modern period, and the unfamiliar compound might have been misread by the person setting type for the play.

## 5.2

[*A march.*] *Enter* LUCIUS, GIACOMO, *and the Roman
army at one door, and the Briton army at another, Leonatus* POSTHUMUS *following like a poor soldier. They
march over and go out.* [*Alarums.*] *Then enter again in
skirmish* GIACOMO *and* POSTHUMUS: *he vanquisheth and
disarmeth* GIACOMO, *and then leaves him*

GIACOMO    The heaviness and guilt within my bosom
  Takes off° my manhood. I have belied° a lady,            *Destroys / slandered*
  The princess of this country, and the air on't°              *of it*
  Revengingly enfeebles me; or° could this carl,°       *otherwise / peasant*
5  A very drudge° of nature's, have subdued me                *slave*
  In my profession? Knighthoods and honours borne
  As I wear mine are titles but° of scorn.                   *merely*
  If that thy gentry, Britain, go before°                 *surpass*
  This lout as he exceeds our lords, the odds
10 Is that we scarce are men and you are gods.        *Exit*

## 5.3[1]

*The battle continues.* [*Alarums. Excursions. The trumpets sound a retreat.*] *The Britons fly,* CYMBELINE *is
taken. Then enter to his rescue* BELARIUS, GUIDERIUS,
*and* ARVIRAGUS

BELARIUS    Stand, stand, we have th'advantage of the ground.
  The lane is guarded. Nothing routs us but
  The villainy of our fears.
GUIDERIUS *and* ARVIRAGUS    Stand, stand, and fight.
  *Enter* POSTHUMUS [*like a poor soldier*], *and seconds the
  Britons. They rescue* CYMBELINE *and exeunt*

## 5.4

[*The trumpets sound a retreat,*] *then enter* LUCIUS, GIA-
COMO, *and* INNOGEN
LUCIUS [*to* INNOGEN]    Away, boy, from the troops, and save thyself;
  For friends kill friends, and the disorder's such
  As war were hoodwinked.[1]
GIACOMO                     'Tis their fresh supplies.
LUCIUS    It is a day turned strangely. Or betimes
5 Let's reinforce, or fly.[2]                       *Exeunt*

## 5.5

*Enter* POSTHUMUS [*like a poor soldier*], *and a Briton*
    LORD
LORD    Cam'st thou from where they made the stand?
POSTHUMUS                        I did,
  Though you, it seems, come from the fliers.
LORD                           Ay.
POSTHUMUS    No blame be to you, sir, for all was lost,
  But° that the heavens fought. The King himself      *Had it not been*

---

5.2 Location: A field between the British and Roman
camps, Britain.
5.3 Location: Scene continues.
1. In F and most modern editions, there is no new
scene marked here or at 5.4, since 5.2, 5.3, and 5.4
form one continuous battle sequence. However, the
stage is temporarily cleared where the Oxford editors

have marked 5.3 and 5.4, and a cleared stage is the
usual signal of a new scene on the Renaissance stage.
5.4 Location: Scene continues.
1. As if war were blindfolded.
2. *Or betimes . . . fly:* Let us either promptly reinforce
our troops or flee.
5.5 Location: Scene continues.

| | | |
|---|---|---|
| 5 | Of his wings destitute,[1] the army broken, | |
| | And but° the backs of Britons seen, all flying | *only* |
| | Through a strait° lane; the enemy full-hearted,° | *narrow / bold* |
| | Lolling the tongue with slaught'ring,[2] having work | |
| | More plentiful than tools to do't, struck down | |
| 10 | Some mortally, some slightly touched,° some falling | *wounded* |
| | Merely through fear, that the strait pass was dammed° | *clogged* |
| | With dead men hurt behind,[3] and cowards living | |
| | To die with lengthened shame.[4] | |

LORD                                              Where was this lane?

POSTHUMUS    Close by the battle, ditched, and walled with turf;

| | | |
|---|---|---|
| 15 | Which gave advantage to an ancient soldier, | |
| | An honest one, I warrant, who deserved | |
| | So long a breeding as his white beard came to,[5] | |
| | In doing this for 's country. Athwart° the lane | *Across* |
| | He with two striplings—lads more like° to run | *likely* |
| 20 | The country base[6] than to commit such slaughter; | |
| | With faces fit for masks,[7] or rather fairer | |
| | Than those for preservation cased, or shame[8]— | |
| | Made good° the passage, cried to those that fled | *Secured* |
| | 'Our Britain's harts die flying, not her men. | |
| 25 | To darkness fleet° souls that fly backwards. Stand, | *rush* |
| | Or we are Romans,[9] and will give you that° | *(death)* |
| | Like beasts which you shun beastly,° and may save | *in cowardly fashion* |
| | But to look back in frown.[1] Stand, stand.' These three, | |
| | Three thousand confident,[2] in act as many— | |
| 30 | For three performers are the file° when all | *entire force* |
| | The rest do nothing—with this word 'Stand, stand', | |
| | Accommodated° by the place, more charming[3] | *Assisted* |
| | With their own nobleness, which could have turned | |
| | A distaff to a lance,[4] gilded° pale looks; | *brought color to* |
| 35 | Part shame, part spirit renewed,[5] that some, turned coward | |
| | But by example[6]—O, a sin in war, | |
| | Damned in the first beginners![7]—gan° to look | *began* |
| | The way that they° did and to grin[8] like lions | *(the three)* |
| | Upon the pikes o'th' hunters. Then began | |
| 40 | A stop° i'th' chaser, a retire. Anon° | *halt / Soon* |
| | A rout, confusion thick; forthwith they fly | |
| | Chickens the way which they stooped eagles;[9] slaves, | |
| | The strides they victors made;[1] and now our cowards, | |
| | Like fragments° in hard voyages, became | *scraps of food* |

---

1. Deprived of his wings (that is, the troops to either side of the main division of the army).
2. With their tongues hanging out either from the labor of slaughter or from eagerness to commit the slaughter.
3. Hurt on their backs (as they were fleeing).
4. To die later after a life of prolonged shame.
5. *who . . . to:* who deserved to live so long again as his white beard indicated he had already lived.
6. *to run . . . base:* to play a children's game (prisoner's house) that involves running between two bases.
7. Gentlewomen wore masks to protect their complexions from the elements.
8. *fairer . . . shame:* more delicate than those covered with masks for protection ("preservation") or out of modesty.
9. Or we will behave like Romans.
1. *and may . . . frown:* and may prevent only by turning

back upon the enemy with threatening face.
2. As confident as if they were three thousand.
3. *more charming:* casting a spell on others.
4. *could . . . lance:* that is, could have made women fight. The distaff, an instrument used in spinning wool, was a proverbial symbol of womanhood.
5. Shame inspired some, courage others.
6. Because of the example set by others.
7. In those who first set the example (of cowardly behavior).
8. To bare their teeth.
9. *forthwith . . . eagles:* straightway they (the Romans) fled like chickens along the passage down which they had just swooped like eagles.
1. *slaves . . . made:* like slaves, they retrace the steps they had made as victors.

45     The life o'th' need.[2] Having found the back door open
    Of the unguarded hearts,[3] heavens, how they wound!
    Some slain before,[4] some dying, some their friends
    O'erborne° i'th' former wave, ten chased by one,           *Overwhelmed*
    Are now each one the slaughterman of twenty.
50     Those that would die or ere° resist are grown      *before they would*
    The mortal bugs° o'th' field.                               *deadly terrors*
   LORD                    This was strange chance:
    A narrow lane, an old man, and two boys.
   POSTHUMUS    Nay, do not wonder at it. Yet you are made
    Rather to wonder at the things you hear
55     Than to work° any. Will you rhyme upon't,            *perform*
    And vent it[5] for a mock'ry? Here is one:
    'Two boys, an old man twice a boy,° a lane,     *in his second childhood*
    Preserved the Britons, was the Romans' bane.'
   LORD    Nay, be not angry, sir.
   POSTHUMUS              'Lack,° to what end?          *Alas*
60     Who dares not stand° his foe, I'll be his friend,      *confront*
    For if he'll do as he is made° to do,           *inclined*
    I know he'll quickly fly my friendship too.
    You have put° me into rhyme.                    *forced*
   LORD              Farewell; you're angry.   *Exit*
   POSTHUMUS    Still going?° This a lord? O noble misery,[6]   *Still running away*
65     To be i'th' field and ask 'What news?' of me!
    Today how many would have given their honours
    To have saved their carcasses—took heel to do't,
    And yet died too!° I, in mine own woe charmed,[7]     *anyway*
    Could not find death where I did hear him groan,
70     Nor feel him where he struck. Being an ugly monster,
    'Tis strange he hides him in fresh cups, soft beds,
    Sweet words, or hath more ministers° than we     *other agents*
    That draw his knives i'th' war. Well, I will find him;
    For being now a favourer to the Briton,[8]
75     No more° a Briton, I have resumed again       *I am no more*
    The part° I came in. Fight I will no more,          *role*
    But yield me to the veriest hind° that shall        *peasant*
    Once touch my shoulder.° Great the slaughter is   *try to arrest me*
    Here made by th' Roman; great the answer be°   *great the retaliation*
80     Britons must take. For me, my ransom's death,
    On either side I come to spend my breath,°      *give up my life*
    Which neither here I'll keep nor bear° again,     *carry away*
    But end it by some means for Innogen.
        *Enter two [Briton]* CAPTAINS, *and soldiers*
   FIRST CAPTAIN    Great Jupiter be praised, Lucius is taken.
85     'Tis thought the old man and his sons were angels.
   SECOND CAPTAIN    There was a fourth man, in a seely habit,°   *rustic garments*
    That gave th'affront with them.
   FIRST CAPTAIN            So 'tis reported,
    But none of 'em can be found. Stand, who's there?
   POSTHUMUS    A Roman,

---

2. Vital in the time of crisis.
3. *Having . . . hearts:* Having found unprotected the weak spot of these undefended souls (that is, the Romans).
4. Some that earlier were as good as dead.
5. And circulate ("vent") your rhymes.
6. What noble wretchedness.
7. In my despair preserved, as if by a charm.
8. Since death is now looking kindly upon Britons.

90      Who had not now been drooping here if seconds°         *supporters*
     Had answered him.°                                 *followed him*
     SECOND CAPTAIN [*to soldiers*]   Lay hands on him, a dog!
     A leg of Rome shall not return to tell
     What crows have pecked them here. He brags his service
     As if he were of note.° Bring him to th' King.          *high rank*
     [*Flourish.*] *Enter* CYMBELINE [*and his train*], BELARIUS,
        GUIDERIUS, ARVIRAGUS, PISANIO, *and Roman captives.*
     *The* CAPTAINS *present* POSTHUMUS *to* CYMBELINE, *who*
     *delivers him over to a* JAILER. [*Exeunt all but* POSTHU-
     MUS *and two* JAILERS *who lock gyves*° *on his legs*][9]     *fetters*
95      FIRST JAILER   You shall not now be stol'n. You have locks upon you,
     So graze as you find pasture.
     SECOND JAILER           Ay, or a stomach.   [*Exeunt* JAILERS]
     POSTHUMUS   Most welcome, bondage, for thou art a way,
     I think, to liberty. Yet am I better
     Than one that's sick o'th' gout, since he had rather
100     Groan so in perpetuity than be cured
     By th' sure physician, death, who is the key
     T'unbar these locks. My conscience, thou art fettered
     More than my shanks° and wrists. You good gods give me     *legs*
     The penitent instrument to pick that bolt,
105     Then free for ever.[1] Is't enough I am sorry?
     So children temporal fathers do appease;
     Gods are more full of mercy. Must I repent,
     I cannot do it better than in gyves
     Desired more than constrained.° To satisfy,°     *forced (upon me) / atone*
110     If of my freedom 'tis the main part,[2] take
     No stricter render° of me than my all.              *repayment*
     I know you are more clement° than vile men         *merciful*
     Who of their broken° debtors take a third,          *bankrupt*
     A sixth, a tenth, letting them thrive again
115     On their abatement.° That's not my desire.       *reduced amount*
     For Innogen's dear life take mine, and though
     'Tis not so dear,° yet 'tis a life; you coined it.      *valuable*
     'Tween man and man they weigh not every stamp;
     Though light, take pieces for the figure's sake;[3]
120     You rather mine, being yours.[4] And so, great powers,
     If you will make this audit,° take this life,      *settle this account*
     And cancel these cold bonds.[5] O Innogen,
     I'll speak to thee in silence!

---

9. F and most modern editions mark a new scene here. Confusion arises because in F, no exit is marked for any character after Posthumus is handed over to a Jailer. Either everyone exits and Posthumus then reenters with two Jailers, indicating a new scene, or, as here, Posthumus and Jailers stay onstage continuously. The latter option means that Posthumus is fettered in the open fields, giving new point to the First Jailer's injunction to "graze as you find pasture" (5.5.96). Usually, Posthumus is assumed to be fettered inside a British prison.
1. *The . . . ever:* Give me penitence, the instrument to pick that lock (the lock on his conscience, which is fettered by guilt). Then (I am) free forever; then free me

(by death).
2. If it is the most important element in freeing me from guilt.
3. *'Tween . . . sake:* In business dealings between men, they do not weigh every coin ("stamp"). Even though some coins are deficient in weight ("light"), they accept them because of the image (of the King) stamped on them.
4. You should be more inclined to accept my coin (me), since your image is stamped on me. This line refers to the Christian belief that humans are made in the image of God.
5. These old legal agreements; these cruel links with life; these harsh fetters.

[*He sleeps.*] *Solemn music. Enter, as in an apparition,*
SICILIUS *Leonatus (father to Posthumus, an old man),*
*attired like a warrior, leading in his hand an ancient*
*matron, his wife, and* MOTHER *to Posthumus, with music*
*before them. Then, after other music, follows the two*
*young Leonati,* BROTHERS *to Posthumus, with wounds as*
*they died in the wars. They circle* POSTHUMUS *round as*
*he lies sleeping*

SICILIUS  No more, thou thunder-master,[6] show
125 Thy spite on mortal flies.°                                *frail creatures*
With Mars° fall out, with Juno° chide,        *god of war / Jove's wife*
That° thy adulteries                                          *Who*
Rates° and revenges.                                       *Berates*
Hath my poor boy done aught but well,
130 Whose face I never saw?
I died whilst in the womb he stayed,
Attending nature's law,[7]
Whose father then—as men report
Thou orphans' father art—
135 Thou shouldst have been, and shielded him
From this earth-vexing smart.[8]
MOTHER  Lucina° lent not me her aid,                 *goddess of childbirth*
But took me in my throes,
That from me was Posthumus ripped,
140 Came crying 'mongst his foes,
A thing of pity.
SICILIUS  Great nature like his ancestry
Moulded the stuff° so fair                                *substance*
That he deserved the praise o'th' world
145 As great Sicilius' heir.
FIRST BROTHER  When once he was mature for man,°    *had matured into manhood*
In Britain where was he
That could stand up his parallel,
Or fruitful° object be                                      *life-giving*
150 In eye of Innogen, that best
Could deem° his dignity?°                            *Judge / worth*
MOTHER  With marriage wherefore° was he mocked,          *why*
To be exiled, and thrown
From Leonati seat and cast
155 From her his dearest one,
Sweet Innogen?
SICILIUS  Why did you suffer Giacomo,
Slight° thing of Italy,                                    *Worthless*
To taint his nobler heart and brain
160 With needless jealousy,
And to become the geck° and scorn                        *dupe*
O'th' other's villainy?
SECOND BROTHER  For this from stiller seats[9] we come,
Our parents and us twain,
165 That striking in our country's cause
Fell bravely and were slain,

---

6. Jupiter, or Jove, the king of the gods, often made himself known to humans through thunder and lightning.
7. Awaiting the decree of nature (for his birth).
8. From this suffering that afflicts all humans.
9. From calmer regions (alluding to the Elysian Fields—in classical mythology the abode of the blessed after death).

Our fealty and Tenantius'° right                    (*Cymbeline's father*)
    With honour to maintain.
FIRST BROTHER    Like hardiment° Posthumus hath    *Similar bold deeds*
170    To Cymbeline performed.
    Then, Jupiter, thou king of gods,
    Why hast thou thus adjourned°                    *deferred*
    The graces for his merits due,
    Being all to dolours° turned?                    *sorrows*
175 SICILIUS    Thy crystal window ope;° look out;    *open*
    No longer exercise
    Upon a valiant race thy harsh
    And potent injuries.
MOTHER    Since, Jupiter, our son is good,
180    Take off his miseries.
SICILIUS    Peep through thy marble mansion. Help,
    Or we poor ghosts will cry
    To th' shining synod° of the rest°    *assembly / rest of the gods*
    Against thy deity.°                    *godhead*
185 BROTHERS    Help, Jupiter, or we appeal,
    And from thy justice fly.

       JUPITER *descends in thunder and lightning, sitting upon*
       *an eagle. He throws a thunderbolt. The ghosts fall on*
       *their knees*

JUPITER    No more, you petty spirits of region low,
    Offend our hearing. Hush! How dare you ghosts
    Accuse the thunderer, whose bolt, you know,
190    Sky-planted,° batters all rebelling coasts?    *Rooted in the heavens*
    Poor shadows of Elysium, hence, and rest
    Upon your never-withering banks of flowers.
    Be not with mortal accidents° oppressed;         *events*
    No care of yours it is; you know 'tis ours.
195    Whom best I love, I cross,° to make my gift,    *thwart*
    The more delayed, delighted.° Be content.    *the more pleasing*
    Your low-laid son our godhead will uplift.
    His comforts thrive, his trials well are spent.°    *ended*
    Our Jovial star° reigned at his birth, and in    *The planet Jupiter*
200    Our temple was he married. Rise, and fade.
    He shall be lord of Lady Innogen,
    And happier much by his affliction made.
    This tablet lay upon his breast, wherein
    Our pleasure his full fortune doth confine.[1]
       [*He gives the ghosts a tablet which they lay upon Posthu-*
       *mus' breast*]
205 And so away. No farther with your din
    Express impatience, lest you stir up mine.
    Mount, eagle, to my palace crystalline.    [*He*] *ascends* [*into the heavens*]
SICILIUS    He came in thunder. His celestial breath
    Was sulphurous to smell.[2] The holy eagle
210    Stooped, as to foot us.[3] His ascension is
    More sweet than our blest fields. His royal bird

---

1. *wherein . . . confine:* wherein it is our pleasure his
great fortune precisely to set forth.
2. Sulfur was popularly associated with thunder and
lightning. As a constituent of gunpowder, its smell may
have been detectable in the theater when gunpowder
was used.
3. Swooped as if to seize us in its talons.

Preens the immortal wing and claws his beak
As when his god is pleased.
ALL THE GHOSTS                    Thanks, Jupiter.
SICILIUS   The marble pavement⁴ closes, he is entered
215     His radiant roof. Away, and, to be blest,
Let us with care perform his great behest.   [*The ghosts*] *vanish*
            [POSTHUMUS *awakes*]
POSTHUMUS   Sleep, thou hast been a grandsire, and begot
A father to me; and thou hast created
A mother and two brothers. But, O scorn,°                    *bitter mockery*
220     Gone! They went hence so soon as they were born,
And so I am awake. Poor wretches that depend
On greatness' favour dream as I have done,
Wake and find nothing. But, alas, I swerve.°                    *go astray*
Many dream not to find, neither deserve,
225     And yet are steeped in favours; so am I,
That have this golden chance and know not why.
What fairies haunt this ground? A book? O rare one,
Be not, as is our fangled world,⁵ a garment
Nobler than that it covers. Let thy effects
230     So follow to° be most unlike our courtiers,                    *that they*
As good as promise.
            [*He*] *reads*
'Whenas° a lion's whelp shall, to himself unknown, without                    *When*
seeking find, and be embraced by a piece of tender air; and
when from a stately cedar shall be lopped branches which,
235     being dead many years, shall after revive, be jointed to the old
stock, and freshly grow; then shall Posthumus end his miseries,
Britain be fortunate and flourish in peace and plenty.'
'Tis still a dream, or else such stuff as madmen
Tongue,° and brain° not; either both, or nothing,                    *Speak / understand*
240     Or senseless speaking,° or a speaking such                    *Either meaningless speech*
As sense° cannot untie. Be what it is,                    *reason*
The action of my life is like it, which I'll keep,
If but for sympathy.⁶
            *Enter* JAILER
JAILER   Come, sir, are you ready for death?
245     POSTHUMUS   Over-roasted rather; ready long ago.
JAILER   Hanging⁷ is the word, sir. If you be ready for that, you
are well cooked.
POSTHUMUS   So, if I prove a good repast to the spectators, the
dish pays the shot.⁸
250     JAILER   A heavy reckoning for you, sir. But the comfort is, you
shall be called to no more payments, fear no more tavern bills,
which are as often the sadness of parting as the procuring of
mirth. You come in faint for want of meat, depart reeling with
too much drink, sorry that you have paid too much and sorry
255     that you are paid too much;⁹ purse and brain both empty: the
brain the heavier for being too light,° the purse too light, being                    *foolish*

---

4. Referring to the closing of the trapdoor in the ceil-ing above the stage, which represents the floor ("pave-ment") of the heavens.
5. Our world so obsessed with fashions.
6. If only because of the similarity.

7. Death by hanging, with a pun on "hanging" as referring to the practice of hanging up raw meat before cooking.
8. The food pays the reckoning; I am worth what it costs to hang me.
9. Subdued by too much drink.

drawn of heaviness.[1] Of this contradiction you shall now be
quit. O, the charity of a penny cord! It sums up thousands in a
trice.° You have no true debitor and creditor[2] but it: of what's
260 past, is, and to come the discharge.° Your neck, sir, is pen,
book, and counters;[3] so the acquittance° follows.

POSTHUMUS   I am merrier to die than thou art to live.

JAILER   Indeed, sir, he that sleeps feels not the toothache; but a
man that were to° sleep your sleep, and a hangman to help him
265 to bed, I think he would change places with his officer;° for
look you, sir, you know not which way you shall go.

POSTHUMUS   Yes, indeed do I, fellow.

JAILER   Your death has eyes in 's head, then. I have not seen him
so pictured.[4] You must either be directed by some that take
270 upon them° to know, or take upon yourself that which I am
sure you do not know, or jump° the after-enquiry on your own
peril; and how you shall speed° in your journey's end I think
you'll never return to tell on.°

POSTHUMUS   I tell thee, fellow, there are none want° eyes to
275 direct them the way I am going but such as wink° and will not
use them.

JAILER   What an infinite mock is this, that a man should have
the best use of eyes to see the way of blindness!° I am sure
hanging's the way of winking.

*Enter a* MESSENGER

280 MESSENGER   Knock off his manacles, bring your prisoner to the
King.

POSTHUMUS   Thou bring'st good news, I am called to be made
free.[5]

JAILER   I'll be hanged then.

285 POSTHUMUS   Thou shalt be then freer than a jailer; no bolts for
the dead.[6]

JAILER [*aside*]   Unless a man would marry a gallows and beget
young gibbets, I never saw one so prone.° Yet, on my conscience, there are verier knaves desire to live, for all° he be a
290 Roman; and there be some of them, too, that die against their
wills; so should I if I were one. I would we were all of one
mind, and one mind good. O, there were desolation° of jailers
and gallowses! I speak against my present profit, but my wish
hath a preferment[7] in't.                                          *Exeunt*

| | |
|---|---|
| *an instant* | |
| *release from debt* | |
| *deliverance* | |
| | |
| | |
| *were about to* | |
| *(the hangman)* | |
| | |
| | |
| *some who profess* | |
| *risk* | |
| *succeed* | |
| *of* | |
| *lacking* | |
| *shut their eyes* | |
| | |
| *the way to death* | |
| | |
| | |
| | |
| | |
| | |
| | |
| *eager* | |
| *even though* | |
| | |
| *the ruin* | |

## 5.6

[*Flourish.*] *Enter* CYMBELINE, BELARIUS, GUIDERIUS,
ARVIRAGUS, PISANIO, *and lords*

CYMBELINE [*to* BELARIUS, GUIDERIUS, *and* ARVIRAGUS]   Stand by
my side, you whom the gods have made
Preservers of my throne. Woe is my heart

---

1. Being emptied of the money that makes it heavy.
2. Account book.
3. Metal tokens used for making calculations.
4. So depicted (referring to visual representations of
death as a skeleton or skull with no eyes).
5. Posthumus means "set free by death." The Jailer
thinks he means "set free from prison."
6. Most editions, following F2, have everyone leave the
stage here except the Jailer. However, the Jailer himself

has been ordered to bring the prisoner to the King,
which would mean that he must not be separated from
Posthumus. Rather than being a monologue, the ensuing speech may be largely spoken in asides to the audience as the Jailer unlocks Posthumus's fetters and
prepares to take him to Cymbeline.
7. Had a promotion in it (implying that a world without
the need for jailers could offer him better employment).
5.6 Location: The camp of Cymbeline, Britain.

That the poor soldier that so richly fought,
Whose rags shamed gilded arms, whose naked breast

5      Stepped before targs of proof,¹ cannot be found.
He shall be happy that can find him, if
Our grace can make him so.

BELARIUS                          I never saw
Such noble fury in so poor a thing,
Such precious deeds in one that promised naught
But beggary and poor looks.

10   CYMBELINE                          No tidings of him?
PISANIO   He hath been searched° among the dead and living,       sought
But no trace of him.

CYMBELINE                          To my grief I am
The heir of his reward, which I will add
[*To* BELARIUS, GUIDERIUS, *and* ARVIRAGUS] To you, the liver,
heart, and brain of Britain,

15   By whom I grant she lives. 'Tis now the time
To ask of whence you are. Report it.

BELARIUS                               Sir,
In Cambria° are we born, and gentlemen.                              Wales
Further to boast were neither true nor modest,
Unless I add we are honest.

CYMBELINE                          Bow your knees.
         [*They kneel. He knights them*]

20   Arise, my knights o'th' battle.² I create you
Companions to our person, and will fit° you                          supply
With dignities becoming your estates.°                               (new) rank
         [BELARIUS, GUIDERIUS, *and* ARVIRAGUS *rise.*]
         *Enter* CORNELIUS *and* LADIES
There's business in these faces. Why so sadly
Greet you our victory? You look like Romans,
And not o'th' court of Britain.

25   CORNELIUS                          Hail, great King!
To sour your happiness I must report
The Queen is dead.

CYMBELINE                          Who worse than a physician
Would this report become? But I consider
By medicine life may be prolonged, yet death

30   Will seize the doctor too. How ended she?
CORNELIUS   With horror, madly dying, like her life,
Which being cruel to the world, concluded
Most cruel to herself. What she confessed
I will report, so please you. These her women

35   Can trip me° if I err, who with wet cheeks                      point out my mistakes
Were present when she finished.

CYMBELINE                          Prithee, say.
CORNELIUS   First, she confessed she never loved you, only
Affected° greatness got by you, not you;                             Desired
Married your royalty, was wife to your place,°                       position
Abhorred your person.

40   CYMBELINE                          She alone knew this,
And but° she spoke it dying, I would not                             except that

---

1. *targs of proof*: shields whose strength had been tested.
2. A special group of knights who won their titles for extraordinary bravery on the battlefield.

Believe her lips in opening it. Proceed.
CORNELIUS   Your daughter, whom she bore in hand° to love          *she pretended*
　　With such integrity, she did confess
45　Was as a scorpion to her sight, whose life,
　　But that her flight prevented it, she had
　　Ta'en off° by poison.                                                                *Ended*
CYMBELINE                         O most delicate° fiend!                      *subtle*
　　Who is't can read a woman? Is there more?
CORNELIUS   More, sir, and worse. She did confess she had
50　For you a mortal mineral° which, being took,                    *a deadly poison*
　　Should by the minute feed on life, and, ling'ring,
　　By inches waste you. In which time she purposed
　　By watching,° weeping, tendance,³ kissing, to                 *staying awake*
　　O'ercome you with her show;° and in fine,°         *performance / finally*
55　When she had fit you with° her craft, to work              *shaped you by*
　　Her son into th'adoption of the crown;⁴
　　But failing of her end by his strange absence,
　　Grew shameless-desperate, opened° in despite                 *revealed*
　　Of heaven and men her purposes, repented
60　The evils she hatched were not effected; so
　　Despairing died.
CYMBELINE              Heard you all this, her women?
LADIES   We did, so please your highness.
CYMBELINE                                      Mine eyes
　　Were not in fault, for she was beautiful;
　　Mine ears that heard her flattery, nor my heart
65　That thought her like her seeming.° It had been vicious°   *appearance / wrong*
　　To have mistrusted her. Yet, O my daughter,
　　That it was folly in me thou mayst say,
　　And prove it in thy feeling.⁵ Heaven mend all!
　　　　*Enter* LUCIUS, GIACOMO, SOOTHSAYER, *and other Roman*
　　　　*prisoners,* POSTHUMUS *behind, and* INNOGEN [*dressed as*
　　　　*a man, all guarded by Briton soldiers*]
　　Thou com'st not, Caius, now for tribute. That
70　The Britons have razed out,° though with the loss            *erased*
　　Of many a bold one; whose kinsmen have made suit
　　That their good souls° may be appeased with slaughter   *(of the dead Britons)*
　　Of you, their captives, which ourself have granted.
　　So think of your estate.°                                                       *condition*
75　LUCIUS   Consider, sir, the chance of war. The day
　　Was yours by accident. Had it gone with us,
　　We should not, when the blood was cool, have threatened
　　Our prisoners with the sword. But since the gods
　　Will have it thus, that nothing but our lives
80　May be called ransom, let it come. Sufficeth
　　A Roman with a Roman's heart can suffer.
　　Augustus lives to think on't;⁶ and so much
　　For my peculiar care.° This one thing only                   *concern for myself*
　　I will entreat:
　　　　[*He presents* INNOGEN *to* CYMBELINE]
　　　　　　my boy, a Briton born,

---

3. Showing attention to you.
4. *to work . . . crown:* to work her son into the position
of heir to the crown.
5. And find it true by your experience.
6. Augustus lives and can consider what to do.

85 Let him be ransomed. Never master had
A page so kind, so duteous, diligent,
So tender over his occasions,° true,                    *thoughtful of his needs*
So feat,° so nurse-like; let his virtue join              *graceful*
With my request, which I'll make bold your highness
90 Cannot deny. He hath done no Briton harm,
Though he have served a Roman. Save him, sir,
And spare no blood beside.°                             *no one else*
CYMBELINE                        I have surely seen him.
His favour° is familiar to me. Boy,                      *face*
Thou hast looked thyself into my grace,[7]
95 And art mine own. I know not why, wherefore,
To say 'Live, boy'. Ne'er thank thy master. Live,
And ask of Cymbeline what boon° thou wilt               *reward*
Fitting my bounty and thy state,° I'll give it,          *rank*
Yea, though thou do demand a prisoner
The noblest ta'en.
100 INNOGEN                      I humbly thank your highness.
LUCIUS  I do not bid thee beg my life, good lad,
And yet I know thou wilt.
INNOGEN                       No, no. Alack,
There's other work in hand. I see a thing[8]
Bitter to me as death. Your life, good master,
Must shuffle° for itself.                                *shift*
105 LUCIUS                        The boy disdains me.
He leaves me, scorns me. Briefly die their joys
That place them on the truth of girls and boys.[9]
Why stands he so perplexed?
CYMBELINE [*to* INNOGEN]          What wouldst thou, boy?
I love thee more and more; think more and more
110 What's best to ask. Know'st him thou look'st on? Speak,
Wilt have him live? Is he thy kin, thy friend?
INNOGEN  He is a Roman, no more kin to me
Than I to your highness, who, being born your vassal,
Am something nearer.
CYMBELINE            Wherefore ey'st him so?
115 INNOGEN  I'll tell you, sir, in private, if you please
To give me hearing.
CYMBELINE           Ay, with all my heart,
And lend my best attention. What's thy name?
INNOGEN  Fidele, sir.
CYMBELINE            Thou'rt my good youth, my page.
I'll be thy master. Walk with me, speak freely.
          [CYMBELINE *and* INNOGEN *speak apart*]
BELARIUS [*aside to* GUIDERIUS *and* ARVIRAGUS]  Is not this boy
      revived from death?
120 ARVIRAGUS               One sand° another                *One grain of sand*
Not more resembles that° sweet rosy lad                   *than he resembles that*
Who died, and was Fidele. What think you?
GUIDERIUS  The same dead thing alive.
BELARIUS  Peace, peace, see further. He eyes us not. Forbear.

---

7. You have by your appearance gained my favor.
8. Referring to the ring that she gave to Posthumus and
that is now on Giacomo's finger.

9. *Briefly . . . boys:* Quickly dies the happiness of those
who depend on the fidelity of girls and boys.

125     Creatures may be alike. Were't he, I am sure
      He would have spoke to us.
      GUIDERIUS               But we see° him dead.          *saw*
      BELARIUS    Be silent; let's see further.
      PISANIO [*aside*]              It is my mistress.
      Since she is living, let the time run on
      To good or bad.
      CYMBELINE [*to* INNOGEN]    Come, stand thou by our side,
130     Make thy demand aloud. [*To* GIACOMO]   Sir, step you forth.
      Give answer to this boy, and do it freely,
      Or, by our greatness and the grace of it,
      Which is our honour, bitter torture shall
      Winnow° the truth from falsehood.        *Separate*
      [*To* INNOGEN]             On, speak to him.
135     INNOGEN    My boon is that this gentleman may render°     *declare*
      Of whom he had this ring.
      POSTHUMUS [*aside*]        What's that to him?
      CYMBELINE [*to* GIACOMO]    That diamond upon your finger, say,
      How came it yours?
      GIACOMO    Thou'lt torture me to leave° unspoken that     *for leaving*
      Which to be spoke would torture thee.
140     CYMBELINE               How, me?
      GIACOMO    I am glad to be constrained to utter that°       *what*
      Torments me to conceal. By villainy
      I got this ring; 'twas Leonatus' jewel,
      Whom thou didst banish; and, which more may grieve thee,
145     As it doth me, a nobler sir ne'er lived
      'Twixt sky and ground. Wilt thou hear more, my lord?
      CYMBELINE    All that belongs to this.
      GIACOMO              That paragon thy daughter,
      For whom my heart drops blood, and my false spirits
      Quail to remember—give me leave, I faint.
150     CYMBELINE    My daughter? What of her? Renew thy strength.
      I had rather thou shouldst live while nature will°     *as long as nature allows*
      Than die ere I hear more. Strive, man, and speak.
      GIACOMO    Upon a time—unhappy was the clock
      That struck the hour—it was in Rome—accursed
155     The mansion where—'twas at a feast—O, would
      Our viands had been poisoned, or at least
      Those which I heaved to head!°—the good Posthumus—     *raised to my mouth*
      What should I say?—he was too good to be
      Where ill men were, and was the best of all
160     Amongst the rar'st of good ones—sitting sadly,
      Hearing us praise our loves of Italy
      For beauty that made barren the swelled boast[1]
      Of him that best could speak; for feature laming
      The shrine of Venus or straight-pitched Minerva,[2]
165     Postures beyond brief nature;[3] for condition,°         *character*
      A shop of all the qualities that man
      Loves woman for; besides that hook of wiving,°     *bait for marriage*
      Fairness which strikes the eye—

1. For beauty so great that it rendered hollow even the exaggerated boasts.
2. *for . . . Minerva:* for looks rendering deficient even the body (shrine) of the goddess of love (Venus) or the magisterial goddess of the arts (Minerva). *straight-pitched:* with erect posture.
3. Forms surpassing those of mere mortals.

CYMBELINE                      I stand on fire.
Come to the matter.
GIACOMO               All too soon I shall,
170   Unless thou wouldst grieve quickly. This Posthumus,
Most like a noble lord in love and one
That had a royal lover, took his hint,
And not dispraising whom we praised—therein
He was as calm as virtue—he began
175   His mistress' picture, which by his tongue being made,
And then a mind put in't, either our brags
Were cracked° of kitchen-trulls, or his description         *uttered in defense*
Proved us unspeaking sots.°                          *fools incapable of speech*
CYMBELINE                Nay, nay, to th' purpose.
GIACOMO   Your daughter's chastity—there it begins.
180   He spake of her as° Dian had hot° dreams                 *as if / lustful*
And she alone were cold,° whereat I, wretch,               *chaste*
Made scruple of° his praise, and wagered with him       *Disputed*
Pieces of gold 'gainst this which then he wore
Upon his honoured finger, to attain
185   In suit° the place of 's bed and win this ring            *By urging my suit*
By hers and mine adultery. He, true knight,
No lesser of her honour confident
Than I did truly find her, stakes this ring—
And would so had it been a carbuncle
190   Of Phoebus' wheel,[4] and might so safely had it
Been all the worth of 's car.° Away to Britain        *worth the entire chariot*
Post° I in this design. Well may you, sir,               *Hasten*
Remember me at court, where I was taught
Of° your chaste daughter the wide difference             *By*
195   'Twixt amorous and villainous. Being thus quenched
Of hope, not longing,° mine Italian brain           *though not of desire*
Gan° in your duller Britain[5] operate                  *Began*
Most vilely; for my vantage,° excellent.               *profit*
And, to be brief, my practice° so prevailed             *deceit*
200   That I returned with simular° proof enough        *pretended; specious*
To make the noble Leonatus mad
By wounding his belief in her renown°                 *reputation*
With tokens thus and thus; averring° notes             *confirming*
Of chamber-hanging, pictures, this her bracelet—
205   O cunning, how I got it!—nay, some marks
Of secret on her person, that he could not
But think her bond of chastity quite cracked,
I having ta'en the forfeit.[6] Whereupon—
Methinks I see him now—
POSTHUMUS [*coming forward*]   Ay, so thou dost,
210   Italian fiend! Ay me, most credulous fool,
Egregious murderer, thief, anything
That's due[7] to all the villains past, in being,
To come! O, give me cord, or knife, or poison,
Some upright justicer!° Thou, King, send out           *judge*
215   For torturers ingenious. It is I

---

4. *had . . . wheel:* even if it had been a precious stone from the wheel of the sun god's chariot.
5. Alluding to the belief that England's northern climate made its inhabitants sluggish and slow of wit.
6. Believing I had taken what she gave up (her chastity).
7. *anything / That's due:* any name that's owed.

That all th'abhorrèd things o'th' earth amend[8]
By being worse than they. I am Posthumus,
That killed thy daughter—villain-like, I lie:
That caused a lesser villain than myself,
220　A sacrilegious thief, to do't. The temple
Of virtue was she; yea, and she herself.°　　　　　she was virtue herself
Spit and throw stones, cast mire upon me, set
The dogs o'th' street to bay me. Every villain
Be called Posthumus Leonatus, and
225　Be 'villain' less than 'twas![9] O Innogen!
My queen, my life, my wife, O Innogen,
Innogen, Innogen!
INNOGEN [approaching him]　Peace, my lord. Hear, hear.
POSTHUMUS　Shall 's have a play of this? Thou scornful page,
There lie thy part.°　　　　　　　　　　　Your role is to lie there
　　　[He strikes her down]
PISANIO [coming forward]　O gentlemen, help!
230　Mine and your mistress! O my lord Posthumus,
You ne'er killed Innogen till now. Help, help!
[To INNOGEN] Mine honoured lady.
CYMBELINE　　　　　　　　　Does the world go round?
POSTHUMUS　How comes these staggers[1] on me?
PISANIO [to INNOGEN]　　　　　　　　Wake, my mistress.
CYMBELINE　If this be so, the gods do mean to strike me
235　To death with mortal° joy.　　　　　　　death-causing
PISANIO [to INNOGEN]　How fares my mistress?
INNOGEN　O, get thee from my sight!
Thou gav'st me poison. Dangerous fellow, hence.
Breathe not where princes are.
CYMBELINE　　　　　　　　　The tune of Innogen.
240　PISANIO　Lady, the gods throw stones of sulphur° on me if　　thunderbolts
That box I gave you was not thought by me
A precious thing. I had it from the Queen.
CYMBELINE　New matter still.
INNOGEN　　　　　　　　　　It poisoned me.
CORNELIUS　　　　　　　　　　　　O gods!
I left out one thing which the Queen confessed
245　[To PISANIO] Which must approve° thee honest. 'If Pisanio　　prove
Have', said she, 'given his mistress that confection°　　　compound
Which I gave him for cordial, she is served
As I would serve a rat.'
CYMBELINE　　　　　　　　What's this, Cornelius?
CORNELIUS　The Queen, sir, very oft importuned me
250　To temper° poisons for her, still° pretending　　　　mix / always
The satisfaction of her knowledge only
In killing creatures vile, as cats and dogs
Of no esteem.° I, dreading that her purpose　　　　　value
Was of more danger, did compound for her
255　A certain stuff which, being ta'en, would cease
The present power of life, but in short time

---

8. Who makes all loathsome things seem better.
9. Every . . . 'twas: May the word "villain" be less abhorrent
than it was, since "Posthumus Leonatus" has replaced

it.
1. A disease, usually of horses, that causes an unsteady
walk; dizziness.

All offices of nature° should again         *All natural faculties*
Do their due functions. [*To* INNOGEN] Have you ta'en of it?
INNOGEN   Most like° I did, for I was dead.                *likely*
BELARIUS [*aside to* GUIDERIUS *and* ARVIRAGUS]   My boys,
    There was our error.
260   GUIDERIUS            This is sure Fidele.
INNOGEN [*to* POSTHUMUS]   Why did you throw your wedded
       lady from you?
Think that you are upon a lock,² and now
Throw me again.
    [*She throws her arms about his neck*]
POSTHUMUS         Hang there like fruit, my soul,
  Till the tree die.
CYMBELINE [*to* INNOGEN]   How now, my flesh, my child?
265   What, mak'st thou me a dullard° in this act?      *sluggish performer*
  Wilt thou not speak to me?
INNOGEN [*kneeling*]        Your blessing, sir.
BELARIUS [*aside to* GUIDERIUS *and* ARVIRAGUS]   Though you did
       love this youth, I blame ye not.
You had a motive° for't.                      *reason*
CYMBELINE           My tears that fall
Prove holy water on thee!
    [*He raises her*]
                Innogen,
Thy mother's dead.
270   INNOGEN           I am sorry for't, my lord.
CYMBELINE   O, she was naught,° and 'long° of her it was   *worthless / because*
That we meet here so strangely.° But her son      *like strangers*
Is gone, we know not how nor where.
PISANIO               My lord,
Now fear is from me I'll speak truth. Lord Cloten,
275   Upon my lady's missing,° came to me           *absence*
With his sword drawn, foamed at the mouth, and swore
If I discovered° not which way she was gone       *revealed*
It was my instant death. By accident°          *chance*
I had a feignèd letter of my master's³
280   Then in my pocket, which directed him
  To seek her on the mountains near to Milford,
Where in a frenzy, in my master's garments,
Which he enforced from me, away he posts°        *hastens*
With unchaste purpose, and with oath to violate
285   My lady's honour. What became of him
I further know not.
GUIDERIUS          Let me end the story.
  I slew him there.
CYMBELINE        Marry, the gods forfend!
I would not thy good deeds° should from my lips   *(on the battlefield)*
Pluck a hard sentence. Prithee, valiant youth,
290   Deny't again.°                        *Take it back*
GUIDERIUS   I have spoke it, and I did it.
CYMBELINE   He was a prince.
GUIDERIUS   A most incivil° one. The wrongs he did me    *barbarous*

---

2. You are in a wrestling hold. This is a disputed passage; F here reads "rock."

3. Referring to the letter written by Posthumus to mislead Innogen.

Were nothing prince-like, for he did provoke me
295 With language that would make me spurn the sea
If it could so roar to me. I cut off 's head,
And am right glad he is not standing here
To tell this tale of mine.[4]

CYMBELINE                    I am sorrow for thee.
By thine own tongue thou art condemned, and must
Endure our law. Thou'rt dead.

300 INNOGEN                              That headless man
I thought had been my lord.

CYMBELINE [to soldiers]         Bind the offender,
And take him from our presence.

BELARIUS                         Stay, sir King.
This boy is better than the man he slew,
As well descended as thyself, and hath
305 More of thee merited than a band of Clotens
Had ever scar for.[5] Let his arms alone;
They were not born for bondage.

CYMBELINE                         Why, old soldier,
Wilt thou undo the worth thou art unpaid for[6]
By tasting of our wrath? How of descent
As good as we?

310 ARVIRAGUS          In that he spake too far.

CYMBELINE [to BELARIUS][7]   And thou shalt die for't.

BELARIUS                                        We will die all three
But I will prove° that two on 's° are as good          *Unless I prove / of us*
As I have given out him. My sons, I must
For mine own part unfold a dangerous speech,
Though haply° well for you.                              *perhaps*

315 ARVIRAGUS                  Your danger's ours.

GUIDERIUS   And our good his.

BELARIUS                      Have at it then. By leave,[8]
Thou hadst, great King, a subject who
Was called Belarius.

CYMBELINE              What of him? He is
A banished traitor.

BELARIUS              He it is that hath
320 Assumed° this age. Indeed, a banished man;          *Reached*
I know not how a traitor.

CYMBELINE [to soldiers]      Take him hence.
The whole world shall not save him.

BELARIUS                             Not too hot.°          *fast*
First pay me for the nursing of thy sons,
And let it° be confiscate all so soon                    *(the payment)*
As I have received it.

325 CYMBELINE          Nursing of my sons?

BELARIUS   I am too blunt and saucy. [Kneeling] Here's my knee.
Ere I arise I will prefer° my sons,                      *advance*
Then spare not the old father. Mighty sir,

---

4. To tell a tale of cutting off my head.
5. *than . . . for*: than an army of Clotens ever earned by
their battle scars.
6. The merit you are not yet rewarded for.
7. It is unclear to whom—Arviragus or Belarius—
Cymbeline speaks the next line. Arviragus has just

addressed Cymbeline, and one might expect the King's
reply to be directed to him. Belarius, however, made the
offending remark about Guiderius being of as good
birth as Cloten, and the threat of death probably applies
to him.
8. Let's begin, then. With your permission.

These two young gentlemen that call me father
330 And think they are my sons are none of mine.
They are the issue° of your loins, my liege,                    *offspring*
And blood of your begetting.
CYMBELINE                          How, my issue?
BELARIUS  So sure as you your father's. I, old Morgan,⁹
Am that Belarius whom you sometime° banished.                         *once*
335 Your pleasure was my mere offence,¹ my punishment
Itself, and all my treason. That I suffered
Was all the harm I did. These gentle princes—
For such and so they are—these twenty years
Have I trained up. Those arts° they have as I              *accomplishments*
340 Could put into them. My breeding was, sir,
As your highness knows. Their nurse Euriphile,
Whom for the theft I wedded, stole these children
Upon my banishment. I moved° her to't,                           *persuaded*
Having received the punishment before
345 For that which I did then. Beaten° for loyalty          *Having been beaten*
Excited me to treason. Their dear loss,
The more of you 'twas felt, the more it shaped°                    *suited*
Unto° my end° of stealing them. But, gracious sir,          *With / purpose*
Here are your sons again, and I must lose
350 Two of the sweet'st companions in the world.
The benediction of these covering heavens
Fall on their heads like dew, for they are worthy
To inlay heaven with stars.°              *To become constellations*
CYMBELINE                          Thou weep'st, and speak'st.
The service that you three have done is more
355 Unlike° than this thou tell'st. I lost my children.              *Improbable*
If these be they, I know not how to wish
A pair of worthier sons.
BELARIUS [*rising*]            Be pleased a while.
This gentleman, whom I call Polydore,
Most worthy prince, as yours, is true Guiderius.
[GUIDERIUS *kneels*]
360 This gentleman, my Cadwal, Arviragus,
Your younger princely son.
[ARVIRAGUS *kneels*]
He, sir, was lapped°                                              *wrapped*
In a most curious° mantle wrought by th' hand        *delicately fashioned*
Of his queen mother, which for more probation°                      *proof*
I can with ease produce.
CYMBELINE                          Guiderius had
365 Upon his neck a mole, a sanguine° star.                        *blood-red*
It was a mark of wonder.
BELARIUS                          This is he,
Who hath upon him still that natural stamp.
It was wise nature's end in the donation°          *purpose in giving it*
To be his evidence now.
CYMBELINE                          O, what am I?
370 A mother to the birth of three? Ne'er mother

9. Morgan was the Welsh name Belarius assumed dur-     1. What you pleased (to accuse me of) was my entire
ing the years he spent in Wales.                      offense.

Rejoiced deliverance more.[2] Blest pray you be,
That, after this strange starting from your orbs,[3]
You may reign in them now!

    [GUIDERIUS *and* ARVIRAGUS *rise*]

                  O Innogen,
Thou hast lost by this a kingdom.

INNOGEN                      No, my lord,

375   I have got two worlds by't. O my gentle brothers,
Have we thus met? O, never say hereafter
But I am truest speaker. You called me brother
When I was but your sister; I you brothers
When ye were so indeed.

CYMBELINE              Did you e'er meet?

ARVIRAGUS   Ay, my good lord.

380 GUIDERIUS              And at first meeting loved,
Continued so until we thought he died.

CORNELIUS   By the Queen's dram she swallowed.

CYMBELINE                      O rare instinct!
When shall I hear all through? This fierce° abridgement      *drastic*
Hath to it circumstantial branches which

385 Distinction should be rich in.[4] Where? How lived you?
And when came you to serve our Roman captive?
How parted with your brothers? How first met them?
Why fled you from the court? And whither? These,
And your three motives° to the battle, with      *the motives of you three*

390 I know not how much more, should be demanded,
And all the other by-dependences,°      *circumstances*
From chance° to chance. But nor° the time nor place      *occurrence / neither*
Will serve our long inter'gatories.° See,      *lengthy questioning*
Posthumus anchors upon Innogen,

395 And she, like harmless lightning, throws her eye
On him, her brothers, me, her master, hitting
Each object with a joy. The counterchange
Is severally in all.[5] Let's quit this ground,
And smoke° the temple with our sacrifices.      *fill with smoke*

400 [*To* BELARIUS] Thou art my brother; so we'll hold thee ever.

INNOGEN [*to* BELARIUS]   You are my father too, and did relieve° me      *save*
To see this gracious season.

CYMBELINE               All o'erjoyed,
Save these in bonds. Let them be joyful too,
For they shall taste our comfort.

INNOGEN [*to* LUCIUS]            My good master,
I will yet do you service.

405 LUCIUS              Happy be you!

CYMBELINE   The forlorn° soldier that so nobly fought,      *wretched*
He would have well becomed this place, and graced
The thankings of a king.

POSTHUMUS            I am, sir,
The soldier that did company these three

---

2. Never did giving birth cause a mother to rejoice more.
3. After this unnatural displacement from your rightful positions. Referring to astrological theories that each heavenly body moved in its proper orb, or circle, around the earth. For a planet to move outside its orb caused disturbances in the heavens.
4. *circumstantial . . . in:* many ramifications that will provide particulars in rich abundance.
5. *The . . . all:* The exchange (of glances) passes from each to each.

410 In poor beseeming.° 'Twas a fitment⁶ for       *appearance*
    The purpose I then followed. That I was he,
    Speak, Giacomo; I had you down, and might
    Have made you finish.°                             *die*
    GIACOMO [*kneeling*]       I am down again,
    But now my heavy conscience sinks my knee
415  As then your force did. Take that life, beseech you,
    Which I so often owe;° but your ring first,    *owe so many times over*
    And here the bracelet of the truest princess
    That ever swore her faith.
    POSTHUMUS [*raising him*]     Kneel not to me.
    The power that I have on you is to spare you,
420  The malice towards you to forgive you. Live,
    And deal with others better.
    CYMBELINE              Nobly doomed!°       *sentenced*
    We'll learn our freeness of a son-in-law.
    Pardon's the word to all.
    ARVIRAGUS [*to* POSTHUMUS]   You holp° us, sir,     *helped*
    As° you did mean indeed to be our brother.      *As if*
425  Joyed are we that you are.
    POSTHUMUS   Your servant, princes. [*To* LUCIUS] Good my lord of Rome,
    Call forth your soothsayer. As I slept, methought
    Great Jupiter, upon his eagle backed,°     *riding on his eagle*
    Appeared to me with other spritely° shows     *ghostly*
430  Of mine own kindred. When I waked I found
    This label° on my bosom, whose containing°    *tablet / contents*
    Is so from sense in hardness that I can
    Make no collection of it.⁷ Let him show
    His skill in the construction.°           *interpretation*
    LUCIUS                Philharmonus.
    SOOTHSAYER   Here, my good lord.
435  LUCIUS               Read, and declare the meaning.
    SOOTHSAYER *reads* [*the tablet*]  'Whenas a lion's whelp shall, to
    himself unknown, without seeking find, and be embraced by a
    piece of tender air; and when from a stately cedar shall be
    lopped branches which, being dead many years, shall after
440  revive, be jointed to the old stock, and freshly grow: then shall
    Posthumus end his miseries, Britain be fortunate and flourish
    in peace and plenty.'
    Thou, Leonatus, art the lion's whelp.
    The fit and apt construction of thy name,
445  Being *leo-natus*,° doth import so much.       *lion-born*
    [*To* CYMBELINE] The piece of tender air thy virtuous daughter,
    Which we call '*mollis aer*';⁸ and '*mollis aer*'
    We term it '*mulier*', [*to* POSTHUMUS] which '*mulier*' I divine
    Is this most constant wife, who even now,
450  Answering the letter of the oracle,⁹
    Unknown to you, unsought, were clipped about°     *embraced*
    With this most tender air.
    CYMBELINE           This hath some seeming.
    SOOTHSAYER   The lofty cedar, royal Cymbeline,

---

6. A suitable disguise.
7. *Is . . . it:* Is so difficult to make sense of that I can draw no conclusion from it.

8. Latin for "gentle air." An ancient (and erroneous) etymology for *mulier*, Latin for "woman" or "wife."
9. Fulfilling the exact terms of the oracle.

Personates° thee, and thy lopped branches point       *Stands for*
455    Thy two sons forth, who, by Belarius stol'n,
For many years thought dead, are now revived,
To the majestic cedar joined, whose issue
Promises Britain peace and plenty.

CYMBELINE                        Well,
My peace we will begin; and, Caius Lucius,
460    Although the victor, we submit to Caesar
And to the Roman empire, promising
To pay our wonted tribute, from the which
We were dissuaded by our wicked queen,
Whom° heavens in justice both on her and hers      *On whom*
465    Have laid most heavy hand.

SOOTHSAYER    The fingers of the powers above do tune
The harmony of this peace. The vision,
Which I made known to Lucius ere the stroke
Of this yet scarce-cold battle,[1] at this instant
470    Is full° accomplished. For the Roman eagle,           *entirely*
From south to west on wing soaring aloft,
Lessened herself,[2] and in the beams o'th' sun
So vanished; which foreshowed our princely eagle
Th'imperial Caesar should again unite
475    His favour with the radiant Cymbeline,
Which shines here in the west.

CYMBELINE                 Laud we the gods,
And let our crookèd° smokes climb to their nostrils    *curling*
From our blest altars. Publish° we this peace        *Proclaim*
To all our subjects. Set we forward,° let       *Let us go forth*
480    A Roman and a British ensign° wave           *banner*
Friendly together. So through Lud's town march,
And in the temple of great Jupiter
Our peace we'll ratify, seal it with feasts.
Set on there.° Never was a war did cease,       *March forth*
485    Ere bloody hands were washed, with such a peace.

[*Flourish.*] *Exeunt* [*in triumph*]

---

1. *ere . . . battle:* before the action of this battle, which   2. Made herself small (by flying into the distance).
has only just ceased.

# The Tempest

Near the close of *King Lear*, the ruined old king, stripped of the last vestiges of his power, dreams of being locked away happily in prison with his beloved Cordelia. Father and daughter have a more tragic fate in store for them, but Shakespeare returns to the dream in *The Tempest*. The play opens on a remote island of exile where Prospero, deposed from power and thrust out of Milan by his wicked brother, has found shelter with his only daughter, Miranda. Unlike many of Shakespeare's plays, *The Tempest* does not appear to have a single dominant source for its plot, but it is a kind of echo chamber of Shakespearean motifs. Its story of loss and recovery and its air of wonder link it closely to the group of late plays that modern editors generally call "romances" (*Pericles, The Winter's Tale, Cymbeline*), but it resonates as well with issues that haunted Shakespeare's imagination throughout his career: the painful necessity for a father to let his daughter go (*Othello, King Lear*); the treacherous betrayal of a legitimate ruler (*Richard II, Julius Caesar, Hamlet, Macbeth*); the murderous hatred of one brother for another (*Richard III, As You Like It, Hamlet, King Lear*); the passage from court society to the wilderness and the promise of a return (*A Midsummer Night's Dream, As You Like It*); the young heiress, torn from her place in the social hierarchy (*Twelfth Night, Pericles, The Winter's Tale*); the dream of manipulating others by means of art, especially by staging miniature plays within plays (*1 Henry IV, Much Ado About Nothing, Hamlet*); the threat of a radical loss of identity (*The Comedy of Errors, Richard II, King Lear*); the relationship between nature and nurture (*Pericles, The Winter's Tale*); the harnessing of magical powers (*The First Part of the Contention [2 Henry VI], A Midsummer Night's Dream, Macbeth*).

Though it is the first play printed in the First Folio (1623), *The Tempest* is probably one of the last that Shakespeare wrote. It can be dated fairly precisely: it uses material that was not available until late 1610, and there is a record of a performance before the king on Hallowmas Night, 1611. Since Shakespeare retired soon after to Stratford, *The Tempest* has seemed to many to be his valedictory to the theater. In this view, Prospero's strangely anxious and moving epilogue—"Now my charms are all o'erthrown, / And what strength I have's mine own"—is the expression of Shakespeare's own professional leave-taking. There are reasons to be skeptical: after finishing *The Tempest*, he collaborated on at least two other plays, *All Is True (Henry VIII)* and *The Two Noble Kinsmen*, and it is perilous to identify Shakespeare too closely with any of his characters, let alone an exiled, embittered, manipulative princely wizard. Yet the echo-chamber effect is striking, and when Prospero and others speak of his powerful "art," it is difficult not to associate the skill of the great magician with the skill of the great playwright. Near the end of the play, the association is made explicit when Prospero uses his magic powers to produce what he terms "some vanity of mine art" (4.1.41), a betrothal masque performed by spirits whom he calls forth "to enact / My present fancies" (4.1.121–22). The masque, typically a lavish courtly performance with music and dancing, may have seemed particularly appropriate on the occasion of another early performance: *The Tempest* was one of fourteen plays provided as part of the elaborate festivities in honor of the betrothal and marriage of King James's daughter Elizabeth to Frederick, the elector palatine. As Prospero's gift of the beautiful spectacle displays his magnificence and authority, so *The Tempest* and the other plays commanded by the king for his daughter's wedding would have enhanced his own prestige.

*The Tempest* opens with a spectacular storm that recalls *King Lear* not only in its violence but in its indifference to the ruler's authority: "What cares these roarers for

Magical storm. From Olaus Magnus, *Historia de Gentibus Septentrionalibus* (1555 ed.).

the name of king?" (1.1.15–16), shouts the exasperated Boatswain at the aristocrats who are standing in his way. The Boatswain's outburst seems unanswerable: like the implacable thunder in *King Lear,* the tempest marks the point at which exalted titles are revealed to be absurd pretensions, substanceless in the face of the elemental forces of nature and the desperate struggle for survival. But we soon learn that this tempest is not in fact natural and that it emphatically does hear and respond to human power, a power that is terrifying but, at least by its own account, benign: "The direful specta- cle of the wreck," Prospero tells his daughter, "I have with such provision in mine art / So safely ordered" (1.2.26, 28–29) that no one on board has been harmed.

Shakespeare's contemporaries were fascinated by the figure of the magus, the great magician who by dint of deep learning, ascetic discipline, and patient skill could com- mand the secret forces of the natural and supernatural world. Distinct from the village witch and "cunning man," figures engaged in local acts of healing and malice, and dis- tinct, too, from alchemical experimenters bent on turning base metal into gold, the magus, cloaked in a robe covered with mysterious symbols, pronounced his occult charms, called forth spirits, and ranged in his imagination through the heavens and the earth, conjoining contemplative wisdom with virtuous action in order to confer great benefits upon his age. But there was a shiver of fear mingled with the popular admira- tion: when the person in Shakespeare's time most widely identified as a magus, the wizard John Dee, was away from his house, his library, one of the greatest private collections of books in England, was set on fire and burned to the ground.

Book, costume, powerful language, the ability to enact the fancies of the brain: these are key elements of both magic and theater. "I have bedimmed / The noontide sun," Prospero declares (5.1.41–42), beginning an enumeration of extraordinary accomplishments that culminates with the revelation that

> graves at my command
> Have waked their sleepers, oped, and let 'em forth
> By my so potent art.
>
> (5.1.48–50)

For the playwright who conjured up the ghosts of Caesar and old Hamlet, the claim does not seem extravagant, but for a magician it amounts to an extremely dangerous confession. Necromancy—communing with the spirits of the dead—was the very essence of black magic, the hated practice from which Prospero is careful to distinguish himself throughout the play. Before his exile, the island had been the realm of the "damned witch Sycorax," who was banished there "for mischiefs manifold and sorceries terrible" (1.2.265–66). The legitimacy of Prospero's power, including power over his slave Caliban, Sycorax's son, depends on his claims to moral authority, but for one disturbing moment it is difficult to see the difference between "foul witch" and princely magician. Small wonder that as soon as he has disclosed that he has trafficked with the dead, Prospero declares that he abjures his "rough magic" (5.1.50).

Prospero does not give an explicit reason for this abjuration, but it appears to be a key stage in the complex process that has led, before the time of the play, to his overthrow and will lead, after the play's events are over, to his return to power. This process in its entirety requires years to unfold, but the play depicts only a small, though crucially important, fragment of it. Together with his early *Comedy of Errors*, *The Tempest* is unusual among Shakespeare's plays in observing what literary critics of the age called the unities of time and place; unlike *Antony and Cleopatra*, for example, which ranges over a huge territory, or *The Winter's Tale*, which covers a huge span of time, the actions of *The Tempest* all take place in a single locale, the island, during the course of a single day. In a long scene of exposition just after the spectacular opening storm, Prospero tells Miranda that he is at a critical moment; everything depends on his seizing the opportunity that fortune has granted him. The whole play, then, is the spectacle of his timing, timing that might be cynically termed political opportunism or theatrical cunning but that Prospero himself associates with the working out of "providence divine" (1.2.160). The opportunity he seizes has its tangled roots in what he calls "the dark backward and abyss of time" (1.2.50). Many years before, when he was Duke of Milan, Prospero's preoccupation with "secret studies" gave his ambitious and unscrupulous brother Antonio the opportunity to topple him from power. Now those same studies, perfected during his long exile, have enabled Prospero to cause

The conjurer. Engraving by Theodore de Bry after a drawing by John White. From Thomas Hariot, *A Briefe and True Report of the New Found Land of Virginia* (1590).

Antonio and his shipmates, sailing back to Italy from Tunis, to be shipwrecked on his island, where they have fallen unwittingly under his control. His magic makes it possible not only to wrest back his dukedom but to avenge himself for the terrible wrong that his brother and his brother's principal ally, Alonso, the King of Naples, have done him: "They now are in my power" (3.3.90). Audiences in Shakespeare's time would have had an all too clear image of how horrendous the vengeance of enraged princes usually was. That Prospero restrains himself from the full exercise of his power to harm his enemies, that he breaks his magic staff and drowns his book, is his highest moral achievement, a triumphant display of self-mastery: "The rarer action is / In virtue than in vengeance" (5.1.27–28).

All of those who are shipwrecked on the island undergo the same shock of terror and unexpected survival, but their experiences, as they cross the yellow sands and make their way toward the interior of the island, differ markedly. The least affected are the mariners, including the feisty Boatswain; after their exhausting labors in the storm, they have sunk into a strange, uneasy sleep, only to be awakened in time to sail the miraculously restored ship back to Italy. The others are put through more complex trials; exposed to varying degrees of anxiety, temptation, grief, fear, and penitence, they are in effect subjects in a psychological experiment carefully conducted by Prospero, who attempts to instill in them moral self-control and work-discipline. The most generously treated is Ferdinand, the only son of the King of Naples, whom Prospero, in what is essentially a carefully planned dynastic alliance, has secretly chosen to be his son-in-law. As Ferdinand bewails what he assumes is his father's death by drowning, he hears strange, haunting music, including the remarkable song of death and metamorphosis, "Full fathom five thy father lies" (1.2.400). Ferdinand is the only one of the shipwrecked company, until the play's final scene, to encounter Prospero directly; the magician makes the experience menacing, humiliating, and frustrating, but this is the modest, salutary price the young man must pay to win the hand of the beautiful Miranda, who seems to him a goddess and who, for her part, has fallen in love with him at first sight.

Prospero directs the experience of the rest as well, but not in person; instead they principally encounter his diligent servant, Ariel. Ariel is not human, although at a crucial moment he is able to imagine what he would feel "were I human" (5.1.20). He is, as the cast of characters describes him, an "airy spirit," capable of moving at immense speed, altering the weather, and producing vivid illusions. We learn that Ariel possesses an inherent moral "delicacy," a delicacy that in the past (that is, before the time depicted in the play) has brought him pain. For, as Prospero reminds him, he had been Sycorax's servant and was, for refusing "to act her earthy and abhorred commands" (1.2.275), imprisoned by the witch for many years in a cloven pine. Prospero freed him from confinement and now demands in return a fixed term of service, which Ariel provides with a mixture of brilliant alacrity and grumbling. Prospero responds in turn with mingled affection and anger, alternating warm praises and dire threats. Although Prospero's "art," through which he commands Ariel and the lesser spirits, seems to foresee and control everything, this control is purchased by constant discipline.

And, for all his godlike powers, there are limits to what Prospero can do. He can make the loathed Antonio and the others know something of the bitterness of loss and isolation; he can produce in them irresistible drowsiness and startled awakenings; he can command Ariel to lay before them a splendid banquet and then make it suddenly vanish; he can drive them to desperation and madness. But in the case of his own brother and Alonso's similarly wicked brother Sebastian, Prospero cannot reshape their inner lives and effect a moral transformation. The most he can do with these men without conscience is to limit through continual vigilance any further harm they might do and to take back what is rightfully his. When, with an obvious effort, Prospero declares that he forgives his brother's "rankest fault" (5.1.134), Antonio is conspicuously silent.

But the higher moral purpose of Prospero's art is not all a failure. With Alonso, the project of provoking repentance by generating intense grief and fear succeeds admirably: Alonso not only gives up his power over the dukedom of Milan but begs Prospero's pardon for the wrong he committed in conspiring to overthrow him. (Both rulers, Alonso and Prospero, can look forward to a unification of their states in the next generation, through the marriage of Ferdinand and Miranda.) Moreover, Prospero's carefully contrived scenarios succeed in confirming the decency, loyalty, and goodness of Alonso's counselor, Gonzalo, who had years before provided the exiled Duke and his daughter with the means necessary for their survival.

It is Gonzalo's goodness that at the end of the play enables him to grasp the dynastic providence in the bewildering tangle of events—"Was Milan thrust from Milan, that his issue / Should become kings of Naples?" (5.1.208–09)—and that earlier inspires him to sense the miraculous nature of their survival. Indifferent to the contemptuous mockery of the cynical Antonio and Sebastian, Gonzalo responds to shipwreck on the strange island by speculating on how he would govern it were he responsible for its "plantation":

> I'th' commonwealth I would by contraries
> Execute all things. For no kind of traffic
> Would I admit, no name of magistrate;
> Letters should not be known; riches, poverty,
> And use of service, none; contract, succession,
> Bourn, bound of land, tilth, vineyard, none;
> No use of metal, corn, or wine, or oil;
> No occupation, all men idle, all.
>
> (2.1.147–54)

Shakespeare adapted Gonzalo's utopian speculations from a passage in "Of Cannibals" (1580), a remarkably free-spirited essay by the French humanist Michel de Montaigne. The Brazilian Indians, Montaigne admiringly writes (in John Florio's 1603 translation), have "no kind of traffic, no knowledge of letters, no intelligence of numbers, no name

America. Engraving by Theodor Galle after a drawing by Jan van der Straet (c. 1580).

of magistrate nor of politic superiority, no use of service, of riches or of poverty, no contracts, no successions . . . no occupation but idle, no respect of kindred but common,
no apparel but natural, no manuring of lands, no use of wine, corn, or metal." For Montaigne, the European adventurers and colonists, confident in their cultural superiority,
are the real barbarians, while the American natives, with their cannibalism and free
love, live in accordance with nature.

The issues raised by Montaigne, and more generally by New World voyages, may
have been particularly interesting to *The Tempest's* early audiences as news reached
London of the extraordinary adventures of the Virginia Company's colony at Jamestown.
Shakespeare seems to have read a detailed account of these adventures in a letter written by the colony's secretary, William Strachey; although the letter was not printed until
1625, it was evidently circulating in manuscript in 1610. In 1609, a fleet carrying more
than four hundred persons sent out to reinforce the colony was struck by a hurricane
near the Virginia coast. Two of the vessels reached their destination, but the third, the
ship carrying the governor, Sir Thomas Gates, ran aground on an uninhabited island
in the Bermudas. Remarkably enough, all of the passengers and crew survived; but their
tribulations were not over. By forcing everyone to labor side by side in order to survive,
the violence of the storm had weakened the governor's authority, and both the natural
abundance and the isolation of the island where they were shipwrecked weakened it
further. Gates ordered the company to build new ships in order to sail to Jamestown,
but his command met with ominous grumblings and threats of mutiny. According to
Strachey's letter, the main troublemaker directly challenged Gates's authority: "therefore let the Governour (said he) kiss, etc." In response, Gates had the troublemaker
shot to death. New ships were built, and in an impressive feat of navigation, the entire
company reached Jamestown. The group found the settlement deeply demoralized: illness was rampant, food was scarce, and relations with the neighboring Indians, once
amicable, had completely broken down. Only harsh military discipline kept the English
colony from falling apart.

With the possible exception of some phrases from Strachey's description of the
storm and a few scattered details, *The Tempest* does not directly use any of this vivid
narrative. Prospero's island is evidently in the Mediterranean, and the New World is
only mentioned as a far-off place, "the still-vexed Bermudas" (1.2.230), where the swift
Ariel flies to fetch dew. Yet Shakespeare's play seems constantly to echo precisely the
issues raised by the Bermuda shipwreck and its aftermath. What does it take to survive?
How do men of different classes and moral character react during a state of emergency?
What is the proper relation between theoretical understanding and practical experience
or between knowledge and power? Is obedience to authority willing or forced? How can
those in power protect themselves from the conspiracies of malcontents? Is it possible
to detect a providential design in what looks at first like a succession of accidents? If
there are natives to contend with, how should colonists establish friendly and profitable
relations with them? What is to be done if relations turn sour? How can those who rule
prevent an alliance between hostile natives and the poorer colonists, often disgruntled
and themselves exploited? And—Montaigne's more radical questions—what is the justification of one person's rule over another? Who is the civilized man, and who is the
barbarian?

The unregenerate nastiness of Antonio and Sebastian, conjoined with the goodness
of Gonzalo, might seem indirectly to endorse Montaigne's critique of the Europeans
and his praise of the cannibals, were it not for the disturbing presence in *The Tempest*
of the character whose name is almost an anagram for "cannibal," Caliban. Caliban,
whose god Setebos is mentioned in accounts of Magellan's voyages as a Patagonian
deity, is anything but a noble savage. Shakespeare does not shrink from the darkest
European fantasies about the Wild Man. Indeed, he exaggerates them: Caliban is
deformed, lecherous, evil-smelling, treacherous, naive, drunken, lazy, rebellious, violent, and devil-worshipping. According to Prospero, he is not even human: "A devil, a

born devil, on whose nature / Nurture can never stick" (4.1.188–89). When he first came to the island, Prospero recalls, he treated Caliban "with human care" (1.2.349), lodging him in his own cell until the savage tried to rape Miranda. The arrival of the other Europeans brings out still worse qualities. Encountering the basest of the company, Alonso's jester, Trinculo, and drunken butler, Stefano, Caliban falls at their feet in brutish worship and then devises a conspiracy to murder Prospero in his sleep. Were the conspiracy to succeed, Caliban would get neither the girl for whom he lusts nor the freedom for which he shouts—he would become "King" Stefano's "foot-licker" (4.1.218)—but he would satisfy the enormous hatred he feels for Prospero.

Prospero's power, Caliban reasons, derives from his superior knowledge. "Remember / First to possess his books," he urges the louts, "for without them / He's but a sot as I am. . . . Burn but his books" (3.2.86–90). The strategy is a canny one, in recognizing an underlying link between literacy and authority, but the problem is not only that Stefano and Trinculo are hopeless fools but also that Prospero, like all Renaissance princes, has a diligent spy network: the invisible Ariel overhears the conspirators and warns his master of the approaching danger. Prospero's sudden recollection of the warning leads him to break off the betrothal masque with one of the most famous speeches in all of Shakespeare, "Our revels now are ended" (4.1.148ff.). This brooding meditation on the theatrical insubstantiality of the entire world and the dreamlike nature of human existence has seemed to many the pinnacle of the play's visionary wisdom. But it does not subsume in its rich cadences the other voices in *The Tempest*; specifically, it does not silence the surprising power of Caliban's voice.

That voice has been amplified in the centuries that followed the first performances of *The Tempest*, as European colonialism saw its grand political, moral, and economic claims disputed and, after violent struggles, dismantled. During these struggles, many anticolonial writers and critics rewrote Shakespeare's play, casting Prospero as a smugly racist, sexist oppressor, Ariel as a native coopted and corrupted by his colonial master, and Caliban as a victimized hero. "Prospero invaded the islands," declared the Cuban writer Roberto Fernández Retamar, "killed our ancestors, enslaved Caliban, and taught him his language to make himself understood. What else can Caliban do but use that same language—today he has no other—to curse him, to wish that the 'red plague' would fall on him?"

Shakespeare, who wrote when the colonialist project was still in its early stages, could not have anticipated this afterlife, and some scholars have argued that the relevance to *The Tempest* of the New World voyages has been greatly exaggerated. But, as the Barbadian writer George Lamming puts it, "Caliban keeps answering back." Caliban enters the play cursing, grumbling, and, above all, disputing Prospero's authority: "This island's mine, by Sycorax my mother, / Which thou tak'st from me" (1.2.334–35). By the close, his attempt to kill Prospero foiled and his body racked with cramps and bruises, Caliban declares that he will "be wise hereafter, / And seek for grace" (5.1.298–99). Yet it is not his mumbled reformation but his vehement protests that leave an indelible mark on *The Tempest*. The play may depict Caliban, in Prospero's ugly term, as "filth," but it gives him a remarkable, unforgettable eloquence. To Miranda's taunting reminder that she taught him to speak, Caliban retorts, "You taught me language, and my profit on't / Is I know how to curse" (1.2.366–67). It is not only in cursing, however, that Caliban is gifted: in richly sensuous poetry, he speaks of the island's natural resources and of his dreams. Caliban can be beaten into submission, but the master cannot eradicate his slave's desires, his pleasures, and his inconsolable pain. And across the vast gulf that divides the triumphant prince and the defeated savage, there is a momentary, enigmatic glimpse of a hidden bond: "This thing of darkness," Prospero says of Caliban, "I / Acknowledge mine" (5.1.278–79). The words need only be a claim of ownership, but they seem to hint at a deeper, more disturbing link between father and monster, legitimate ruler and savage, judge and criminal. Perhaps the link is only an illusion, a trick of the imagination on a strange island, but as Prospero leaves the island, it is he who begs for pardon.

STEPHEN GREENBLATT

## TEXTUAL NOTE

The only authoritative printed text of *The Tempest* is in the First Folio of 1623 (F), where it appears as the first play, at the head of the comedies. The text seems to have been prepared with care. It includes a list of characters (*"Names of the Actors"*) printed at the end of the play and supplies act and scene divisions that this edition follows. There are also unusually full stage directions, although scholars have argued about whether these were written entirely by Shakespeare or were supplied or elaborated by the person who transcribed the author's manuscript for the compositors. Certain features of this transcription have led scholars to the conclusion that it was done by Ralph Crane, an experienced scribe who was responsible for the preparation of at least four other Shakespeare plays.

Most of the songs in *The Tempest* are preserved in early to mid-seventeenth-century manuscripts. These manuscripts indicate repeats and refrains, which have accordingly been accepted in the text of this edition.

## SELECTED BIBLIOGRAPHY

Albanese, Denise. "Admiring Miranda and Enslaving Nature." *New Science, New World*. Durham, N.C.: Duke University Press, 1996. 59–91. Miranda as the feminine locus of the play's exploration of nature and culture.

Barker, Francis, and Peter Hulme. "Nymphs and Reapers Heavily Vanish: The Discursive Con-texts of *The Tempest*." *Alternative Shakespeares*. Vol. I. Ed. John Drakakis. London: Methuen, 1985. 191–205. English colonialism as a discursive context for the play's interest in the usurpation of power.

Brotton, Jerry. " 'This Tunis, sir, was Carthage': Contesting Colonialism in *The Tempest*." *Post-Colonial Shakespeares*. Ed. Ania Loomba and Martin Orkin. London: Routledge, 1998. 23–42. The play's Mediterranean geography exposes a bifurcated interest in both the Old and the New Worlds.

Brown, Paul. " 'This Thing of Darkness I Acknowledge Mine': *The Tempest* and the Discourse of Colonialism." *Political Shakespeare: New Essays in Cultural Materialism*. Ed. Jonathan Dollimore and Alan Sinfield. Ithaca, N.Y.: Cornell University Press, 1985. 48–71. Shakespeare's ambivalent depictions of political, social, and sexual authority read in relation to contemporary colonial practice.

Callaghan, Dympna. "Irish Memories in *The Tempest*." *Shakespeare Without Women: Representing Gender and Race on the Renaissance Stage*. London: Routledge, 2000. 97–138. Using the play's Irish echoes, considers how selective colonial recollection suppresses the cultural memory of the colonized.

Cartelli, Thomas. "Prospero in Africa: *The Tempest* as Colonialist Text and Pretext." *Repositioning Shakespeare: National Formations, Postcolonial Appropriations*. London: Routledge, 1999. 87–104. *The Tempest* can be made to operate both for and against the interests of modern Western ideology.

Greenblatt, Stephen. "Martial Law in the Land of Cockaigne." *Shakespearean Negotiations: The Circulation of Social Energy in Renaissance England*. Berkeley: University of California Press, 1988. 129–63. The play apparently celebrates the restoration of patriarchal order yet also ironically scrutinizes the political manipulation of anxiety.

Hulme, Peter, and William H. Sherman, eds. *"The Tempest" and Its Travels.* Philadelphia: University of Pennsylvania Press, 2000. A range of critical and creative materials, situating the play amid the local and global contexts of its time and beyond.

Orgel, Stephen. *The Illusion of Power: Political Theater in the English Renaissance.* Berkeley: University of California Press, 1975. Compares public and court theater practice, highlighting the masque's role in the allegorized expression of sovereign power.

Vaughan, Virginia Mason, and Alden T. Vaughan. *Critical Essays on Shakespeare's "The Tempest."* New York: Hall, 1998. Eleven essays illustrating the breadth and diversity of critical and cultural engagement with the play.

## FILMS

*Forbidden Planet.* 1956. Dir. Fred M. Wilcox. USA. 98 min. A science-fiction cult classic in which Ariel is a robot and Caliban a monster of the id.

*The Tempest.* 1960. Dir. George Schaefer. USA. 76 min. A made-for-TV, one-camera film of a solid, though short stage rendition, with Richard Burton standing out as Caliban.

*The Tempest.* 1979. Dir. Derek Jarman. UK. 95 min. Part Gothic, part punk. Renders Juno's masque as a Broadway musical number.

*Tempest.* 1982. Dir. Paul Mazursky. USA. 140 min. Disenchanted New York architect escapes to a Greek island to reexamine his life.

*Prospero's Books.* 1991. Dir. Peter Greenaway. UK. 129 min. Surreal and baroque, focusing on the imagined contents of Prospero's library. John Gielgud stars.

# The Tempest

## The Persons of the Play

PROSPERO, the rightful Duke of Milan
MIRANDA, his daughter
ANTONIO, his brother, the usurping Duke of Milan
ALONSO, King of Naples
SEBASTIAN, his brother
FERDINAND, Alonso's son
GONZALO, an honest old counsellor of Naples
ADRIAN
FRANCISCO } lords
ARIEL, an airy spirit attendant upon Prospero
CALIBAN, a savage and deformed native of the island, Prospero's slave
TRINCULO, Alonso's jester
STEFANO, Alonso's drunken butler
The MASTER of a ship
BOATSWAIN
MARINERS
SPIRITS
    *The Masque*
Spirits appearing as:
IRIS
CERES
JUNO
Nymphs, reapers

## 1.1

*A tempestuous noise of thunder and lightning heard.*
*Enter a* SHIPMASTER *and a* BOATSWAIN[1] [*at separate*
*doors*]

MASTER   Boatswain!

BOATSWAIN   Here, Master. What cheer?

MASTER   Good,[2] speak to th' mariners. Fall to't yarely,° or we run          *promptly*
   ourselves aground. Bestir, bestir!          *Exit*
      *Enter* MARINERS

5   BOATSWAIN   Heigh, my hearts!° Cheerly, cheerly, my hearts!       *hearties*
   Yare, yare! Take in the topsail![3] Tend° to th' Master's whistle!—   *Attend*
   Blow till thou burst thy wind, if room enough.[4]
        *Enter* ALONSO, SEBASTIAN, ANTONIO, FERDINAND, GON-
        ZALO, *and others*

ALONSO   Good Boatswain, have care. Where's the Master?
   [*To the* MARINERS] Play the men!°          *Act like men*

10  BOATSWAIN   I pray now, keep below.

ANTONIO   Where is the Master, Boatswain?

---

1.1 Location: A ship at sea.
1. The Boatswain probably enters after the shipmaster calls him; the latter is perhaps on the upper stage.
2. Acknowledging the Boatswain's presence; or perhaps short for "good man."

3. To reduce the surface area of the sail, and thereby lessen the force of the wind pushing the ship toward the island.
4. The wind may blow until it splits itself, provided there is enough sea room to maneuver in.

BOATSWAIN  Do you not hear him? You mar our labour. Keep
your cabins; you do assist the storm.

GONZALO  Nay, good,° be patient.                                      *good man*

15 BOATSWAIN  When the sea is. Hence! What cares these roarers
for the name of king?[5] To cabin! Silence; trouble us not.

GONZALO  Good, yet remember whom thou hast aboard.

BOATSWAIN  None that I more love than myself. You are a councillor;[6] if you can command these elements to silence and work
20 peace of the present,[7] we will not hand° a rope more. Use your      *handle*
authority. If you cannot, give thanks you have lived so long and
make yourself ready in your cabin for the mischance of the
hour, if it so hap.° [*To the* MARINERS] Cheerly, good hearts! [*To*    *happen*
GONZALO] Out of our way, I say!                          *Exit*

25 GONZALO  I have great comfort from this fellow. Methinks he
hath no drowning mark[8] upon him; his complexion is perfect
gallows.[9] Stand fast, good Fate, to his hanging. Make the rope
of his destiny our cable,[1] for our own doth little advantage.° If     *use*
he be not born to be hanged, our case is miserable.
                                            *Exit* [*Courtiers*]

*Enter* BOATSWAIN

30 BOATSWAIN  Down with the topmast![2] Yare! Lower, lower! Bring
her to try wi'th' main-course![3]
              *A cry within*
A plague upon this howling! They are louder than the weather,
or our office.[4]
              *Enter* SEBASTIAN, ANTONIO, *and* GONZALO
Yet again? What do you here? Shall we give o'er° and drown?       *up*
35 Have you a mind to sink?

SEBASTIAN  A pox o'your throat, you bawling, blasphemous,
incharitable dog!

BOATSWAIN  Work you, then.

ANTONIO  Hang, cur, hang, you whoreson insolent noisemaker.
40 We are less afraid to be drowned than thou art.
                                            [*Exeunt* MARINERS]

GONZALO  I'll warrant him for drowning,[5] though° the ship were    *even if*
no stronger than a nutshell and as leaky as an unstanched°         *a freely menstruating*
wench.

BOATSWAIN  Lay her a-hold, a-hold! Set her two courses![6] Off to
45 sea again! Lay her off!
              *Enter* MARINERS, *wet*
MARINERS  All lost! To prayers, to prayers! All lost!
                                            [*Exeunt* MARINERS]

BOATSWAIN  What, must our mouths be cold?[7]

GONZALO  The King and Prince at prayers! Let's assist them,
For our case is as theirs.

---

5. "Roarers," referring here to the waves, was also a term for riotous people.
6. Member of the King's council; also an adviser or persuader.
7. Of the present circumstances.
8. Birthmark whose position was held to portend death by drowning. "He that was born to be hanged will never be drowned" was proverbial.
9. His physiognomy, appearance, shows that he will certainly be hanged.
1. Anchor cable (an anchor is actually useless in a storm).

2. To reduce the top weight of the ship and make it more stable.
3. Bring the ship close to the wind sailing only with the mainsail.
4. Duties (in shouting orders).
5. I'll guarantee him against drowning.
6. Set the foresail in addition to the mainsail.
7. To be cold in the mouth—to be dead—was proverbial; may also suggest that the mariners warm their mouths with liquor (line 50).

SEBASTIAN                      I'm out of patience.
50   ANTONIO   We are merely° cheated of our lives by drunkards.          *utterly*
      This wide-chopped° rascal—would thou mightst lie drowning          *large-mouthed*
      The washing of ten tides.[8]
GONZALO                      He'll be hanged yet,
      Though every drop of water swear against it
      And gape at wid'st to glut° him.                                    *its widest to swallow*
           *A confused noise within*
MARINERS [*within*]                      Mercy on us!
55   We split, we split! Farewell, my wife and children!
      Farewell, brother! We split, we split, we split!
                                    [*Exit* BOATSWAIN]
ANTONIO   Let's all sink wi'th' King.
SEBASTIAN                      Let's take leave of him.
                           *Exit* [ANTONIO *and* SEBASTIAN]
GONZALO   Now would I give a thousand furlongs of sea for an
      acre of barren ground: long heath, broom, furze,[9] anything.
60   The wills above be done, but I would fain die a dry death.
                                                               *Exit*

## 1.2

      *Enter* PROSPERO [*in his magic cloak, with a staff*], *and*
           MIRANDA
MIRANDA[1]   If by your art,[2] my dearest father, you have
      Put the wild waters in this roar, allay them.
      The sky, it seems, would pour down stinking pitch,
      But that the sea, mounting to th' welkin's° cheek,               *sky's*
5    Dashes the fire out. O, I have sufferèd
      With those that I saw suffer! A brave° vessel,                    *splendid*
      Who had, no doubt, some noble creature in her,
      Dashed all to pieces! O, the cry did knock
      Against my very heart! Poor souls, they perished.
10   Had I been any god of power, I would
      Have sunk the sea within the earth, or ere°                       *before*
      It should the good ship so have swallowed and
      The fraughting souls[3] within her.
PROSPERO[4]                      Be collected.
      No more amazement.° Tell your piteous° heart            *consternation / pitying*
      There's no harm done.
MIRANDA                      O woe the day!
15   PROSPERO                      No harm.
      I have done nothing but in care of thee,
      Of thee, my dear one, thee, my daughter, who
      Art ignorant of what thou art, naught knowing
      Of whence I am, nor that I am more better°                        *higher in rank*

---

8. Pirates were hanged on the shore at low-water mark
and left there for the ebbing and flowing of three tides.
9. Heather, yellow shrubs, and gorse—all shrubs that
grow in poor soil.
1.2 Location: The rest of the play is set in various parts
of Prospero's island.
1. *Miranda* in Latin means "admirable" or "wonder-

ing." Miranda uses the formal "you," contrasting with
Prospero's more familiar "thou."
2. Skill; magic; learning; science.
3. Souls constituting the freight; perhaps also suggesting "burdened."
4. *Prospero* in Italian and Spanish means "fortunate" or
"prosperous."

20 Than Prospero, master of a full poor cell[5]
And thy no greater father.

MIRANDA                                    More to know
Did never meddle with° my thoughts.                    *intrude upon*

PROSPERO                                    'Tis time
I should inform thee farther. Lend thy hand,
And pluck my magic garment from me.
        [MIRANDA *removes Prospero's cloak, and he lays it on the
        ground*]
                                        So.

25 Lie there, my art.—Wipe thou thine eyes; have comfort.
The direful spectacle of the wreck, which touched
The very virtue of compassion in thee,
I have with such provision° in mine art                    *foresight*
So safely ordered that there is no soul—

30 No, not so much perdition° as an hair                    *loss*
Betid° to any creature in the vessel,                    *Happened*
Which° thou heard'st cry, which thou saw'st sink. Sit down,    *Whom*
For thou must now know farther.
        [MIRANDA *sits*]

MIRANDA                                    You have often
Begun to tell me what I am, but stopped

35 And left me to a bootless inquisition,°                    *profitless inquiry*
Concluding 'Stay; not yet'.

PROSPERO                            The hour's now come.
The very minute bids thee ope° thine ear,                    *open*
Obey, and be attentive. Canst thou remember
A time before we came unto this cell?

40 I do not think thou canst, for then thou wast not
Out° three years old.                                        *Fully*

MIRANDA                            Certainly, sir, I can.

PROSPERO    By° what? By any other house or person?        *About*
Of anything the image tell me that
Hath kept with thy remembrance.

MIRANDA                                    'Tis far off,

45 And rather like a dream than an assurance°                *a certainty*
That my remembrance warrants.° Had I not                    *guarantees is true*
Four or five women once that tended me?

PROSPERO    Thou hadst, and more, Miranda. But how is it
That this lives in thy mind? What seest thou else

50 In the dark backward° and abyss of time?                    *past*
If thou rememb'rest aught° ere thou cam'st here,            *anything*
How thou cam'st here thou mayst.

MIRANDA                                    But that I do not.

PROSPERO    Twelve year since, Miranda, twelve year since,
Thy father was the Duke of Milan,[6] and
A prince of power—

55 MIRANDA                            Sir, are not you my father?

PROSPERO    Thy mother was a piece° of virtue,° and        *perfect example / chastity*
She said thou wast my daughter; and thy father
Was Duke of Milan, and his only heir
And princess no worse issued.°                            *no less nobly born*

5. Suggesting a hermit's or a poor man's dwelling. *full:* very.    6. Pronounced with stress on the first syllable.

MIRANDA                     O the heavens!
60    What foul play had we that we came from thence?
       Or blessèd° was't we did?                            *providential*
      PROSPERO              Both, both, my girl.
       By foul play, as thou sayst, were we heaved thence,
       But blessedly holp° hither.                        *helped*
      MIRANDA                O, my heart bleeds
       To think o'th' teen° that I have turned you to,        *sorrow; trouble*
65    Which is from° my remembrance. Please you, farther.   *out of*
      PROSPERO   My brother and thy uncle called Antonio—
       I pray thee mark me, that a brother should
       Be so perfidious—he whom next° thyself             *after*
       Of all the world I loved, and to him put
70    The manage° of my state—as at that time           *control*
       Through all the signories° it was the first,         *lordships*
       And Prospero the prime° duke—being so reputed    *foremost*
       In dignity, and for the liberal arts[7]
       Without a parallel—those being all my study,
75    The government I cast upon my brother,
       And to my state grew stranger, being transported[8]
       And rapt in secret studies. Thy false uncle—
       Dost thou attend me?
      MIRANDA             Sir, most heedfully.
      PROSPERO   Being once perfected how to grant suits,[9]
80    How to deny them, who t'advance and who
       To trash for over-topping,[1] new created
       The creatures° that were mine, I say—or changed 'em   *dependents*
       Or else new formed 'em;[2] having both the key°     *control*
       Of officer and office, set all hearts i'th' state
85    To what tune pleased his ear, that° now he was     *so that*
       The ivy which had hid my princely trunk
       And sucked my verdure° out on't. Thou attend'st not!  *vitality; power*
      MIRANDA   O good sir, I do.
      PROSPERO             I pray thee mark me.
       I, thus neglecting worldly ends, all dedicated
90    To closeness° and the bettering of my mind        *seclusion*
       With that which but° by being so retired           *merely*
       O'er-priced all popular rate,[3] in my false brother
       Awaked an evil nature; and my trust,
       Like a good parent,[4] did beget of him
95    A falsehood, in its contrary° as great          *inverse qualities*
       As my trust was, which had indeed no limit,
       A confidence sans° bound. He being thus lorded     *without*
       Not only with what my revenue yielded
       But what my power might else exact, like one
100   Who having into° truth, by telling oft,             *unto*
       Made such a sinner of his memory
       To credit his own lie,[5] he did believe

7. As opposed to the "mechanical arts," the "liberal arts"
encompassed the trivium (grammar, logic, and rhetoric)
and the quadrivium (arithmetic, geometry, music, and
astronomy).
8. Enraptured, with suggestions of "conveyed to another
place." *grew stranger*: grew alienated from; became a foreigner to.
9. Having mastered handling formal requests.
1. For rising too high. *trash*: restrain, hold back (as by a

leash).
2. *changed . . . 'em*: changed the duties and allegiance of
existing officials, or created new ones.
3. Became too precious for the people to value, or understand.
4. From the colloquial "Good parents breed bad children."
5. *like one . . . lie*: like someone who comes to believe his
own repeatedly stated lie. *To*: So as to.

He was indeed the Duke. Out o'th'° substitution, *As a consequence of the*
And executing° th'outward face° of royalty *portraying / image*
105 With all prerogative, hence his ambition growing—
Dost thou hear?
MIRANDA               Your tale, sir, would cure deafness.
PROSPERO   To have no screen between this part he played
And him he played it for, he needs will be
Absolute Milan.[6] Me,° poor man—my library *As for me*
110 Was dukedom large enough—of temporal royalties° *rule*
He thinks me now incapable; confederates,° *(he) plots*
So dry° he was for sway,° wi'th' King of Naples *thirsty / power*
To give him annual tribute, do him homage,
Subject his coronet to his crown,[7] and bend
115 The dukedom, yet unbowed—alas, poor Milan—
To most ignoble stooping.[8]
MIRANDA                    O the heavens!
PROSPERO   Mark his condition° and th'event,° then tell me *treaty / outcome*
If this might be a brother.
MIRANDA               I should sin
To think but° nobly of my grandmother. *anything but*
Good wombs have borne bad sons.[9]
120 PROSPERO                         Now the condition.
This King of Naples, being an enemy
To me inveterate, hearkens my brother's suit;
Which was that he, in lieu o'th' premises[1]
Of homage and I know not how much tribute,
125 Should presently extirpate me and mine
Out of the dukedom, and confer fair Milan,
With all the honours, on my brother. Whereon,
A treacherous army levied, one midnight
Fated to th' purpose did Antonio open
130 The gates of Milan; and, i'th' dead of darkness,
The ministers° for th' purpose hurried thence *agents*
Me and thy crying self.
MIRANDA               Alack, for pity!
I, not rememb'ring how I cried out then,
Will cry it o'er again; it is a hint° *an occasion*
That wrings mine eyes to't.
135 PROSPERO [*sitting*]       Hear a little further,
And then I'll bring thee to the present business
Which now's upon's, without the which this story
Were most impertinent.° *irrelevant*
MIRANDA               Wherefore did they not
That hour destroy us?
PROSPERO               Well demanded, wench;[2]
140 My tale provokes that question. Dear, they durst not,
So dear the love my people bore me; nor set
A mark so bloody on the business, but
With colours fairer painted their foul ends.
In few,° they hurried us aboard a barque,° *short / ship*

---

6. *To have . . . Milan:* He wanted to be the Duke of
Milan in actual fact, rather than merely exercising power
as the Duke's proxy. *screen:* partition, barrier.
7. Subject Antonio's coronet to Alonso's crown. *coronet:*
a lesser crown indicating the wearer's inferiority to the
sovereign.
8. *and bend . . . stooping:* by making Milan, previously

free, a tributary subject of Naples.
9. Antonio's character need not imply that his mother
was a bad parent (see line 94).
1. In return for the conditions agreed upon.
2. A young woman; also term of endearment to wife,
daughter, or sweetheart.

145 Bore us some leagues to sea, where they prepared
A rotten carcass of a butt,[3] not rigged,
Nor tackle, sail, nor mast—the very rats
Instinctively have quit it. There they hoist us,
To cry to th' sea that roared to us, to sigh
150 To th'winds, whose pity, sighing back again,
Did us but loving wrong.[4]

MIRANDA                              Alack, what trouble
Was I then to you!

PROSPERO                      O, a cherubin
Thou wast that did preserve me. Thou didst smile,
Infusèd with a fortitude from heaven,
155 When I have decked° the sea with drops° full salt,                    *covered; adorned / tears*
Under my burden groaned;[5] which° raised in me                    *(Miranda's smile)*
An undergoing stomach,° to bear up                    *A courage to endure*
Against what should ensue.

MIRANDA    How came we ashore?

160 PROSPERO    By providence divine.
Some food we had, and some fresh water, that
A noble Neapolitan, Gonzalo,
Out of his charity—who being then appointed
Master of this design—did give us; with
165 Rich garments, linens, stuffs, and necessaries
Which since have steaded° much. So, of his gentleness,[6]                    *been useful*
Knowing I loved my books, he furnished me
From mine own library with volumes that
I prize above my dukedom.

MIRANDA                              Would I might
But ever see that man!

170 PROSPERO                      Now I arise.[7]
[*He stands and puts on his cloak*][8]
Sit still,° and hear the last of our sea-sorrow.                    *Continue to sit*
Here in this island we arrived, and here
Have I thy schoolmaster made thee more profit°                    *profit more*
Than other princes[9] can, that have more time
175 For vainer hours and tutors not so careful.°                    *caring*

MIRANDA    Heavens thank you for't. And now I pray you, sir—
For still 'tis beating in my mind—your reason
For raising this sea-storm.

PROSPERO                      Know thus far forth.
By accident most strange, bountiful Fortune,
180 Now my dear lady,[1] hath mine enemies
Brought to this shore; and by my prescience
I find my zenith[2] doth depend upon
A most auspicious star,[3] whose influence
If now I court not, but omit,° my fortunes                    *disregard*

---

3. Cask or tub: here, deprecatory for "boat."
4. The winds, responding sympathetically to our sighs, only blew us farther out to sea.
5. The secondary sense provides an image of giving birth.
6. Nobility; kindness.
7. Referring to the action of standing; or to Prospero's rising fortunes (as in lines 179–85). The former might visually reinforce the latter, especially if Prospero also resumes his magical powers by putting on his cloak.

8. This direction, necessary before Prospero can charm Miranda to sleep, follows naturally from the reference to Prospero's books, his other source of power.
9. *princes*: a generic plural for "princes and princesses."
1. Traditional characterization of Fortune as a woman changeable in her affections.
2. Highest point, as of a star in the sky.
3. Referring to the belief that celestial bodies had astrological influence on people and events.

185 Will ever after droop. Here cease more questions.
Thou art inclined to sleep; 'tis a good dullness,°          *drowsiness*
And give it way. I know thou canst not choose.
    [MIRANDA *sleeps*]
Come away,° servant, come! I am ready now.          *Come here*
Approach, my Ariel,[4] come!
    *Enter* ARIEL
190 ARIEL    All hail, great master, grave sir, hail. I come
To answer thy best pleasure. Be't to fly,
To swim, to dive into the fire, to ride
On the curled clouds, to thy strong bidding task
Ariel and all his quality.°          *cohorts; faculties*
PROSPERO          Hast thou, spirit,
195 Performed to point° the tempest that I bade thee?          *in detail*
ARIEL    To every article.
I boarded the King's ship. Now on the beak,°          *prow*
Now in the waste,° the deck,° in every cabin,          *midship / poop*
I flamed amazement.[5] Sometime I'd divide,
200 And burn in many places;[6] on the top-mast,
The yards, and bowsprit, would I flame distinctly;
Then meet and join. Jove's lightning, the precursors
O'th' dreadful thunderclaps, more momentary
And sight-outrunning° were not. The fire and cracks          *quicker than the eye*
205 Of sulphurous[7] roaring the most mighty Neptune
Seem to besiege, and make his bold waves tremble,
Yea, his dread trident shake.
PROSPERO          My brave spirit!
Who was so firm, so constant, that this coil°          *turmoil*
Would not infect his reason?
ARIEL          Not a soul
210 But felt a fever of the mad,° and played          *such as madmen feel*
Some tricks of desperation. All but mariners
Plunged in the foaming brine and quit the vessel,
Then all afire with me. The King's son Ferdinand,
With hair upstaring°—then like reeds, not hair—          *standing on end*
215 Was the first man that leaped; cried 'Hell is empty,
And all the devils are here'.
PROSPERO          Why, that's my spirit!
But was not this nigh shore?
ARIEL          Close by, my master.
PROSPERO    But are they, Ariel, safe?
ARIEL          Not a hair perished.
On their sustaining[8] garments not a blemish,
220 But fresher than before. And, as thou bad'st° me,          *commanded*
In troops° I have dispersed them 'bout the isle.          *groups*
The King's son have I landed by himself,
Whom I left cooling of ° the air with sighs          *cooling*
In an odd angle° of the isle, and sitting,          *corner*
His arms in this sad knot.[9]

4. Ariel's name, along with sounding like "airy," also means in Hebrew "lion of God." The name appears as a magical spirit in various occult texts.
5. I appeared as flames, causing terror.
6. The phosphorescent effect of St. Elmo's fire, caused in a thunderstorm by the charge of static electricity that builds up particularly around metal projections.
7. Sulphur was popularly associated with thunder and lightning.
8. Buoying up, and thus suggesting "life-giving."
9. Folded sadly, like this (folded arms implied sorrow).

225 PROSPERO                    Of the King's ship,
    The mariners, say how thou hast disposed,
    And all the rest o'th' fleet.
    ARIEL                         Safely in harbour
    Is the King's ship, in the deep nook where once
    Thou called'st me up at midnight to fetch dew
230 From the still-vexed° Bermudas, there she's hid;                    *ever-stormy*
    The mariners all under hatches stowed,
    Who, with° a charm joined to° their suffered labour,        *by virtue of / with*
    I have left asleep. And for the rest o'th' fleet,
    Which I dispersed, they all have met again,
235 And are upon the Mediterranean float°                                 *billow; sea*
    Bound sadly home for Naples,
    Supposing that they saw the King's ship wrecked,
    And his great person perish.
    PROSPERO                    Ariel, thy charge
    Exactly is performed; but there's more work.
    What is the time o'th' day?
240 ARIEL                        Past the mid season.°                          *noon*
    PROSPERO    At least two glasses.° The time 'twixt six and now        *hourglasses*
    Must by us both be spent most preciously.
    ARIEL    Is there more toil? Since thou dost give me pains,°              *tasks*
    Let me remember° thee what thou hast promised                          *remind*
    Which is not yet performed me.
245 PROSPERO                         How now? Moody?
    What is't thou canst demand?
    ARIEL                         My liberty.
    PROSPERO    Before the time be out? No more!
    ARIEL                                 I prithee,
    Remember I have done thee worthy service,
    Told thee no lies, made thee no mistakings, served
250 Without or° grudge or grumblings. Thou did promise                   *either*
    To bate° me a full year.                                       *remit; excuse*
    PROSPERO               Dost thou forget
    From what a torment I did free thee?
    ARIEL                         No.
    PROSPERO    Thou dost, and think'st it much to tread the ooze
    Of the salt deep,
255 To run upon the sharp wind of the north,
    To do me business in the veins¹ o'th' earth
    When it is baked° with frost.                              *dried and hardened*
    ARIEL                         I do not, sir.
    PROSPERO    Thou liest, malignant thing. Hast thou forgot
    The foul witch Sycorax, who with age and envy
260 Was grown into a hoop?° Hast thou forgot her?            *bent over with age*
    ARIEL    No, sir.
    PROSPERO    Thou hast. Where was she born? Speak, tell me!
    ARIEL    Sir, in Algiers.
    PROSPERO               O, was she so! I must
    Once in a month recount what thou hast been,
265 Which thou forget'st. This damned witch Sycorax,
    For mischiefs manifold and sorceries terrible
    To enter human hearing, from Algiers

1. Mineral veins or subterranean rivers.

Thou know'st was banished. For one thing she did
They would not take her life.[2] Is not this true?
270 ARIEL Ay, sir.
PROSPERO This blue-eyed[3] hag was hither brought with child,
And here was left by th' sailors. Thou, my slave,
As thou report'st thyself, was then her servant;
And for° thou wast a spirit too delicate                                          *because*
275 To act her earthy[4] and abhorred commands,
Refusing her grand hests,° she did confine thee                                  *commands*
By help of her more potent ministers,°                                          *agents; slaves*
And in her most unmitigable rage,
Into a cloven pine; within which rift
280 Imprisoned thou didst painfully remain
A dozen years, within which space she died
And left thee there, where thou didst vent thy groans
As fast as mill-wheels strike.° Then was this island—                           *hit the water*
Save for the son that she did litter° here,                                       *give birth to*
285 A freckled whelp, hag-born—not honoured with
A human shape.
ARIEL                    Yes, Caliban her son.
PROSPERO Dull thing, I say so:[5] he, that Caliban
Whom now I keep in service. Thou best know'st
What torment I did find thee in. Thy groans
290 Did make wolves howl, and penetrate° the breasts                            *arouse sympathy in*
Of ever-angry bears; it was a torment
To lay upon the damned, which Sycorax
Could not again undo. It was mine art,
When I arrived and heard thee, that made gape
The pine and let thee out.
295 ARIEL                         I thank thee, master.
PROSPERO If thou more murmur'st, I will rend an oak,
And peg thee in his° knotty entrails till                                        *its*
Thou hast howled away twelve winters.
ARIEL                                    Pardon, master.
I will be correspondent° to command,                                           *compliant*
300 And do my spriting gently.°                                                 *graciously*
PROSPERO Do so, and after two days
I will discharge thee.[6]
ARIEL                    That's my noble master!
What shall I do? Say what, what shall I do?
PROSPERO Go make thyself like to a nymph o'th' sea. Be subject
305 To no sight but thine and mine, invisible
To every eyeball else.[7] Go take this shape,°                                  *appearance; disguise*
And hither come in't. Go; hence with diligence!    *Exit* [ARIEL]
Awake, dear heart, awake! Thou hast slept well;
Awake.
MIRANDA [*awaking*] The strangeness of your story put
Heaviness° in me.                                                              *Sleepiness*
310 PROSPERO                 Shake it off. Come on;

---

2. *For . . . life:* Only because she got pregnant. Capital
sentences were commuted for pregnant women; ordinarily, condemned witches were either hanged or burned
at the stake.
3. Blue eyelids were thought to be a sign of pregnancy.
4. Difficult for Ariel, whose element is air; also, grossly

material, coarse.
5. You dullard, that's just what I said.
6. Prospero reduces this to within two days at line 425
and actually releases Ariel in about four hours' time.
7. *Be . . . else:* Ariel may wear a conventional costume,
indicating his invisibility to other characters onstage.

We'll visit Caliban my slave, who never
Yields us kind answer.

MIRANDA                         'Tis a villain, sir,
I do not love to look on.

PROSPERO                         But as 'tis,
We cannot miss° him. He does make our fire,                    *avoid; do without*
315   Fetch in our wood, and serves in offices°                         *capacities; duties*
That profit us.—What ho! Slave, Caliban!
Thou earth, thou, speak!

CALIBAN (*within*)              There's wood enough within.

PROSPERO   Come forth, I say! There's other business for thee.
Come, thou tortoise! When?

*Enter* ARIEL, *like a water-nymph*
320   Fine apparition! My quaint[8] Ariel,
Hark in thine ear.
[*He whispers*]

ARIEL                         My lord, it shall be done.              *Exit*

PROSPERO   Thou poisonous slave, got° by the devil[9] himself              *begot*
Upon thy wicked dam,° come forth!              *harmful, foul mother*

*Enter* CALIBAN

CALIBAN   As wicked dew as e'er my mother brushed[1]
325   With raven's feather from unwholesome fen°                         *bog*
Drop on you both! A southwest[2] blow on ye,
And blister you all o'er!

PROSPERO   For this be sure tonight thou shalt have cramps,
Side-stitches that shall pen thy breath up. Urchins[3]
330   Shall forth at vast of° night, that they may work              *during the boundless*
All exercise on thee.[4] Thou shalt be pinched
As thick as honeycomb,[5] each pinch more stinging
Than bees that made 'em.°                         *(honeycomb cells)*

CALIBAN                         I must eat my dinner.
This island's mine, by Sycorax my mother,
335   Which thou tak'st from me. When thou cam'st first,
Thou strok'st me and made much of me, wouldst give me
Water with berries in't, and teach me how
To name the bigger light, and how the less,[6]
That burn by day and night; and then I loved thee,
340   And showed thee all the qualities o'th' isle,
The fresh springs, brine-pits, barren place and fertile—
Cursed be I that did so! All the charms°                         *spells*
Of Sycorax, toads, beetles, bats, light on you;
For I am all the subjects that you have,
345   Which first was mine own king, and here you sty me°              *pen me up*
In this hard rock, whiles you do keep from me
The rest o'th' island.

PROSPERO                         Thou most lying slave,
Whom stripes° may move, not kindness! I have used° thee,              *lashes / treated*

8. The term could simultaneously mean "ingenious," "curious in appearance," and "elegant."
9. Not merely an insult, but also an allusion to Caliban's birth from the devil (incubus) and witch.
1. Brushed up, collected. Dew was a common ingredient of magical potions.
2. A southerly wind was considered plague-bearing.
3. Hedgehogs; but here indicates spirits disguised as hedgehogs.

4. *that . . . thee*: in order that they may perform their habitual activity.
5. *Thou . . . honeycomb*: The pinch marks will be as closely packed as, and of similar texture to, the cells of a honeycomb.
6. Recalls Genesis 1:16: "God then made two great lights: the greater light to rule the day, and the less light to rule the night."

Filth as thou art, with human care, and lodged thee
350 In mine own cell, till thou didst seek to violate
The honour of my child.

CALIBAN    O ho, O ho! Would't had been done!
Thou didst prevent me; I had peopled else
This isle with Calibans.

MIRANDA[7]                        Abhorrèd slave,
355 Which any print° of goodness wilt not take,                    *impression*
Being capable of° all ill! I pitied thee,                          *susceptible to*
Took pains to make thee speak, taught thee each hour
One thing or other. When thou didst not, savage,
Know thine own meaning, but wouldst gabble like
360 A thing most brutish, I endowed thy purposes
With words that made them known. But thy vile race,°              *hereditary nature*
Though thou didst learn, had that in't which good natures
Could not abide to be with; therefore wast thou
Deservedly confined into this rock,
365 Who hadst deserved more than a prison.

CALIBAN    You taught me language, and my profit on't
Is I know how to curse. The red plague rid you[8]
For learning me your language!

PROSPERO                        Hag-seed,° hence!                  *Offspring of a hag*
Fetch us in fuel. And be quick, thou'rt best,
370 To answer other business.°—Shrug'st thou, malice?             *perform other tasks*
If thou neglect'st or dost unwillingly
What I command, I'll rack thee with old[9] cramps,
Fill all thy bones with aches,[1] make thee roar,
That beasts shall tremble at thy din.

CALIBAN                              No, pray thee.
375 [*Aside*] I must obey. His art is of such power
It would control my dam's god Setebos,[2]
And make a vassal of him.

PROSPERO                        So, slave, hence!    *Exit* CALIBAN

*Enter* FERDINAND *and* ARIEL, *invisible, playing and*
*singing.*[3] [PROSPERO *and* MIRANDA *stand aside*]

                              *Song*

ARIEL        Come unto these yellow sands,
                And then take hands;
380            Curtsied when you have and kissed—
                The wild waves whist[4]—
                Foot it featly° here and there,                   *Dance nimbly*
                And, sweet sprites, bear°                         *sing*
                The burden.° Hark, hark.                          *refrain*
385 SPIRITS (*dispersedly* [*within*]) Bow-wow!
ARIEL        The watch-dogs bark.
SPIRITS [*within*]  Bow-wow!

7. Many editors assign this speech to Prospero, believing
it to be out of character for Miranda.
8. The plague that gives red sores destroy, kill you.
9. As of aged people; long-accustomed.
1. As a noun, this was probably pronounced "aitches."
2. A name found in travel narratives as a god of the Pata-
gonians.

3. This probably does not imply that Ferdinand enters
first, even though such a staging is possible if Ferdinand
is bewildered as to where this music is coming from. Ariel
is invisible to all but Prospero and the audience. He is
probably still dressed as a water nymph.
4. Become hushed and attentive.

ARIEL            Hark, hark, I hear
                  The strain of strutting Chanticleer
390                 Cry 'cock-a-diddle-dow'.

FERDINAND    Where should this music be? I'th' air or th'earth?
It sounds no more; and sure it waits° upon              *attends*
Some god o'th' island. Sitting on a bank,
Weeping again the King my father's wreck,
395   This music crept by me upon the waters,
Allaying both their fury and my passion°           *grief*
With its sweet air.° Thence I have followed it—     *melody*
Or it hath drawn me rather. But 'tis gone.
No, it begins again.

### Song

400 ARIEL          Full fathom five thy father lies.
                  Of his bones are coral made;
             Those are pearls that were his eyes;
                  Nothing of him that doth fade
                  But doth suffer a sea-change
405                Into something rich and strange.
              Sea-nymphs hourly ring his knell:
SPIRITS [*within*]   Ding dong.
ARIEL          Hark, now I hear them.
SPIRITS [*within*]                   Ding-dong bell. [*etc.*]
FERDINAND   The ditty does remember⁵ my drowned father.
410   This is no mortal° business, nor no sound      *human; of death*
That the earth owes.°                       *owns*
       [*Music*]
            I hear it now above me.
PROSPERO [*to* MIRANDA]   The fringèd curtains of thine eye advance,°   *raise*
And say what thou seest yon.
MIRANDA               What is't? A spirit?
Lord, how it looks about! Believe me, sir,
415   It carries a brave° form. But 'tis a spirit.      *splendid; gallant*
PROSPERO   No, wench, it eats and sleeps, and hath such senses
As we have, such. This gallant° which thou seest     *fine gentleman*
Was in the wreck, and but° he's something° stained   *except that / somewhat*
With grief, that's beauty's canker,⁶ thou mightst call him
420   A goodly person. He hath lost his fellows,
And strays about to find 'em.
MIRANDA             I might call him
A thing divine, for nothing natural
I ever saw so noble.
PROSPERO [*aside*]⁷     It° goes on, I see,          *(My plan)*
As my soul prompts it. [*To* ARIEL] Spirit, fine spirit, I'll free thee
Within two days for this.
425 FERDINAND [*aside*]         Most sure the goddess
On whom these airs attend.⁸ [*To* MIRANDA] Vouchsafe° my prayer   *Grant*
May know if you remain° upon this island,         *dwell*

5. Commemorate. *ditty:* the words of the song.
6. Cankerworm; caterpillar ("beauty" being seen as a flower); spreading sore.
7. Prospero's asides here and at lines 442, 454, and 497 may be either private utterances or addressed to Ariel. If the former, Ariel may nevertheless hear them; Prospero speaks to Ariel after all these instances. Their import may well be purposefully enigmatic.
8. *Most . . . attend:* Probably spoken aside, but possibly an invocation. *Most sure the goddess:* Echoes Aeneas's reaction to seeing Venus after his shipwreck, "o dea certe" (*Aeneid* I.328). *airs:* Ariel's melodies.

And that you will some good instruction give
How I may bear me° here. My prime request,    *conduct myself*
430 Which I do last pronounce, is—O you wonder⁹—
If you be maid¹ or no?

MIRANDA                No wonder, sir,
But certainly a maid.

FERDINAND                My language! Heavens!
I am the best² of them that speak this speech,
Were I but where 'tis spoken.

PROSPERO                How, the best?
435 What wert thou if the King of Naples heard thee?

FERDINAND    A single³ thing, as I am now that wonders
To hear thee speak of Naples. He does hear me,⁴
And that he does I weep. Myself am Naples,°    *King of Naples*
Who with mine eyes, never since at ebb,° beheld    *ceasing to flow*
The King my father wrecked.

440 MIRANDA                Alack, for mercy!

FERDINAND    Yes, faith, and all his lords, the Duke of Milan
And his brave son⁵ being twain.

PROSPERO [*aside*]                The Duke of Milan
And his more braver daughter could control⁶ thee,
If now 'twere fit to do't. At the first sight
445 They have changed eyes.⁷—Delicate° Ariel,    *Graceful; artful*
I'll set thee free for this. [*To* FERDINAND] A word, good sir.
I fear you have done yourself some wrong.⁸ A word.

MIRANDA [*aside*]    Why speaks my father so ungently?° This    *discourteously*
Is the third man that e'er I saw, the first
450 That e'er I sighed for. Pity move my father
To be inclined my way.

FERDINAND                O, if a virgin,
And your affection not gone forth,⁹ I'll make you
The Queen of Naples.

PROSPERO                Soft, sir! One word more.
[*Aside*] They are both in either's powers. But this swift business
455 I must uneasy° make, lest too light¹ winning    *difficult*
Make the prize light. [*To* FERDINAND] One word more. I charge thee
That thou attend me. Thou dost here usurp
The name thou ow'st° not; and hast put thyself    *own*
Upon this island as a spy, to win it
From me the lord on't.°    *of it*

460 FERDINAND                No, as I am a man.

MIRANDA    There's nothing ill can dwell in such a temple.²
If the ill spirit have so fair a house,
Good things will strive to dwell with't.

PROSPERO [*to* FERDINAND]                Follow me.
[*To* MIRANDA] Speak not you for him; he's a traitor. [*To* FERDINAND] Come!

---

9. Miracle, punning on the meaning of Miranda's name.
1. Unmarried virgin; made (human).
2. Highest in rank, assuming he has succeeded his father.
3. Weak and helpless; solitary; one and the same.
4. "He" and "me" both refer to Ferdinand. Presuming his father to be dead, Ferdinand takes himself to be the new King of Naples (and as such, he hears himself speaking). Alternatively, Ferdinand thinks his father's spirit hears him.
5. The only instance in which Antonio is mentioned as

having a son.
6. Challenge; take to task; exercise power over.
7. Exchanged loving glances; fallen in love at first sight.
8. Euphemistic for "told a lie about yourself."
9. Given over to someone else.
1. Easy; playing on the meanings of "little valued" and also "promiscuous" in line 456.
2. A common metaphor for the body; also a conventional Renaissance notion that moral qualities were physically manifest.

465 I'll manacle thy neck and feet together.
Sea-water shalt thou drink; thy food shall be
The fresh-brook mussels,³ withered roots, and husks
Wherein the acorn cradled. Follow!

FERDINAND                                No.
I will resist such entertainment° till                          *treatment*
Mine enemy has more power.
            *He draws, and is charmed from moving*
470 MIRANDA                                O dear father,
Make not too rash a trial of him, for
He's gentle, and not fearful.⁴

PROSPERO                                What, I say,
My foot° my tutor? Put thy sword up, traitor,                   *inferior*
Who mak'st a show but dar'st not strike, thy conscience
475 Is so possessed with guilt. Come from thy ward,°             *defensive stance*
For I can here disarm thee with this stick°                     *magician's wand*
And make thy weapon drop.

MIRANDA                                Beseech you, father!

PROSPERO   Hence! Hang not on my garments.

MIRANDA                                Sir, have pity.
I'll be his surety.

PROSPERO                Silence! One word more
480 Shall make me chide thee, if not hate thee. What,
An advocate for an impostor? Hush!
Thou think'st there is no more such shapes° as he,             *forms; men*
Having seen but him and Caliban. Foolish wench!
To° th' most of men this is a Caliban,                         *Compared to*
And they to him are angels.

485 MIRANDA                                My affections
Are then most humble. I have no ambition
To see a goodlier man.

PROSPERO [*to* FERDINAND]   Come on; obey.
Thy nerves° are in their infancy again,                        *sinews*
And have no vigour in them.

FERDINAND                                So they are.
490 My spirits,° as in a dream, are all bound up.                *mental powers*
My father's loss, the weakness which I feel,
The wreck of all my friends, nor this man's threats
To whom I am subdued, are but light to me,
Might I but through my prison once a day
495 Behold this maid. All corners else o'th' earth
Let liberty make use of; space enough
Have I in such a prison.

PROSPERO [*aside*]                It works. [*To* ARIEL] Come on.—
Thou hast done well, fine Ariel. [*To* FERDINAND] Follow me.
[*To* ARIEL] Hark what thou else shalt do me.

MIRANDA [*to* FERDINAND]                Be of comfort.
500 My father's of a better nature, sir,
Than he appears by speech. This is unwonted°                   *unusual*
Which now came from him.

PROSPERO [*to* ARIEL]                Thou shalt be as free
As mountain winds; but then° exactly do                        *until then*
All points of my command.

---

3. Freshwater mussels are inedible.          4. He's noble and, therefore, not cowardly. Alternatively,
                                                not fearsome.

505 ARIEL   To th' syllable.

PROSPERO [*to* FERDINAND]   Come, follow. [*To* MIRANDA] Speak
not for him.                                                         *Exeunt*

## 2.1

*Enter* ALONSO, SEBASTIAN, ANTONIO, GONZALO, ADRIAN,
*and* FRANCISCO

GONZALO [*to* ALONSO]   Beseech you, sir, be merry. You have cause,
So have we all, of joy; for our escape
Is much beyond our loss. Our hint° of woe                            *occasion*
Is common; every day some sailor's wife,
5   The masters of some merchant, and the merchant,[1]
Have just° our theme of woe. But for the miracle,                   *exactly*
I mean our preservation, few in millions
Can speak like us. Then wisely, good sir, weigh
Our sorrow with° our comfort.                                       *against*

ALONSO                              Prithee, peace.[2]

10   SEBASTIAN [*to* ANTONIO]   He receives comfort like cold porridge.°   *broth*
ANTONIO   The visitor[3] will not give him o'er so.°               *leave him alone*
SEBASTIAN   Look, he's winding up the watch of his wit. By and
by it will strike.

GONZALO [*to* ALONSO]   Sir—
15   SEBASTIAN [*to* ANTONIO]   One: tell.°                          *keep count*
GONZALO [*to* ALONSO]   When every grief is entertained° that's    *harbored*
offered,
Comes to th'entertainer[4]—

SEBASTIAN   A dollar.[5]

GONZALO   Dolour° comes to him indeed. You have spoken truer        *Sorrow*
20   than you purposed.

SEBASTIAN   You have taken it wiselier than I meant you should.

GONZALO [*to* ALONSO]   Therefore my lord—

ANTONIO [*to* SEBASTIAN]   Fie, what a spendthrift is he of his
tongue!

25   ALONSO [*to* GONZALO]   I prithee, spare.°                      *spare your words*

GONZALO   Well, I have done. But yet—

SEBASTIAN [*to* ANTONIO]   He will be talking.

ANTONIO   Which of he or Adrian, for a good wager, first begins
to crow?[6]

30   SEBASTIAN   The old cock.

ANTONIO   The cockerel.[7]

SEBASTIAN   Done. The wager?

ANTONIO   A laughter.[8]

SEBASTIAN   A match!

35   ADRIAN [*to* GONZALO]   Though this island seem to be desert°—   *uninhabited*

ANTONIO [*to* SEBASTIAN]   Ha, ha, ha!

SEBASTIAN   So, you're paid.[9]

ADRIAN   Uninhabitable, and almost inaccessible—

SEBASTIAN [*to* ANTONIO]   Yet—

40   ADRIAN   Yet—

---

2.1
1. The chief officers of some merchant ship and its
owner.
2. Sebastian takes this as "pease," as in "pease porridge."
3. Antonio compares Gonzalo with one who visits and
comforts the sick and distressed.
4. There comes to the person who accepts that grief.

5. *dollar:* English name for the German thaler.
6. Which of the two will first begin to speak ("crow")?
7. "The young cock crows as the old hears" was proverbial. "Old cock" refers to Gonzalo and "cockerel" to
Adrian.
8. From the proverb "He laughs that wins."
9. Antonio's laugh is his prize.

ANTONIO [*to* SEBASTIAN]   He could not miss't.
ADRIAN   It must needs be of subtle, tender, and delicate[1]
    temperance.°                                                                                                                                *climate*
ANTONIO [*to* SEBASTIAN]   Temperance was a delicate wench.[2]
45   SEBASTIAN   Ay, and a subtle, as he most learnedly delivered.[3]
ADRIAN [*to* GONZALO]   The air breathes upon us here most
    sweetly.
SEBASTIAN [*to* ANTONIO]   As if it had lungs, and rotten ones.
ANTONIO   Or as 'twere perfumed by a fen.°                                                                                *bog*
50   GONZALO [*to* ADRIAN]   Here is everything advantageous to life.
ANTONIO [*to* SEBASTIAN]   True, save° means to live.                                                                *except*
SEBASTIAN   Of that there's none, or little.
GONZALO [*to* ADRIAN]   How lush and lusty° the grass looks!                           *tender and luxuriant*
    How green!
55   ANTONIO   The ground indeed is tawny.
SEBASTIAN   With an eye[4] of green in't.
ANTONIO   He misses not much.
SEBASTIAN   No, he doth but mistake the truth totally.
GONZALO [*to* ADRIAN]   But the rarity[5] of it is, which is indeed
60       almost beyond credit—
SEBASTIAN [*to* ANTONIO]   As many vouched° rarities are.                                        *alleged, accepted*
GONZALO [to ADRIAN]   That our garments being, as they were,
    drenched in the sea, hold notwithstanding their freshness and
    glosses, being rather new-dyed than stained with salt water.
65   ANTONIO [*to* SEBASTIAN]   If but one of his pockets[6] could speak,
    would it not say he lies?
SEBASTIAN   Ay, or very falsely pocket up his report.[7]
GONZALO [*to* ADRIAN]   Methinks our garments are now as fresh
    as when we put them on first in Afric, at the marriage of the
70       King's fair daughter Claribel to the King of Tunis.
SEBASTIAN   'Twas a sweet marriage, and we prosper well in our
    return.
ADRIAN   Tunis was never graced before with such a paragon to°                             *for*
    their queen.
75   GONZALO   Not since widow Dido's[8] time.
ANTONIO [*to* SEBASTIAN]   Widow?[9] A pox o'that! How came that
    'widow' in? Widow Dido!
SEBASTIAN   What if he had said 'widower Aeneas' too? Good
    Lord, how you take° it!                                                                                                                *fuss about*
80   ADRIAN [*to* GONZALO]   'Widow Dido' said you? You make me
    study of ° that: she was of Carthage, not of Tunis.                                                   *examine*
GONZALO   This Tunis, sir, was Carthage.[1]
ADRIAN   Carthage?
GONZALO   I assure you, Carthage.

---

1. Exquisite, but in Antonio's usage (line 44), "given to pleasure." *subtle:* fine, but in Sebastian's usage (line 45), "sexually expert" or "crafty."
2. Antonio takes "Temperance" to be the name of a girl. *delicate:* voluptuous, given to pleasure.
3. "Learnedly delivered" was a popular phrase among Puritans who wanted to appear pious.
4. A tinge. In Antonio's reply, an "eye of green" refers to Gonzalo's optimistic capacity to see green.
5. Exceptional quality; but in Sebastian's usage (line 61), "uncommon thing."
6. Seen as the garments' "mouth"; also implying that

Gonzalo's pockets are stained.
7. The evidence of stained pockets would confute Gonzalo's words and reputation for honesty. *pocket up:* suppress, or keep silent; also, receive unprotestingly.
8. Queen of ancient Carthage, whose tragic love affair with Aeneas is related in Virgil's *Aeneid*.
9. Antonio picks on this designation for a woman abandoned by her lover as being either irrelevant or conspicuously prudish. Dido, however, was in fact a widow when she met Aeneas.
1. The city of Tunis was actually built 10 miles from the site of Carthage.

85 ANTONIO [*to* SEBASTIAN]   His word is more than the miraculous harp.[2]

SEBASTIAN   He hath raised the wall, and houses too.

ANTONIO   What impossible matter will he make easy next?

SEBASTIAN   I think he will carry this island home in his pocket,

90 and give it his son for an apple.

ANTONIO   And sowing the kernels° of it in the sea, bring forth          seeds
more islands.

GONZALO [*to* ADRIAN]   Ay.[3]

ANTONIO [*to* SEBASTIAN]   Why, in good time.

95 GONZALO [*to* ALONSO]   Sir, we were talking that our garments
seem now as fresh as when we were at Tunis, at the marriage
of your daughter, who is now queen.

ANTONIO   And the rarest that e'er came there.

SEBASTIAN   Bate,[4] I beseech you, widow Dido.

100 ANTONIO   O, widow Dido? Ay, widow Dido.

GONZALO [*to* ALONSO]   Is not, sir, my doublet as fresh as the first
day I wore it? I mean in a sort.[5]

ANTONIO [*to* SEBASTIAN]   That 'sort' was well fished for.

GONZALO [*to* ALONSO]   When I wore it at your daughter's

105 marriage.

ALONSO   You cram these words into mine ears against
The stomach of my sense.[6] Would I had never
Married my daughter there! For, coming thence,
My son is lost; and, in my rate,° she too,          consideration

110 Who is so far from Italy removed
I ne'er again shall see her. O thou mine heir
Of Naples and of Milan, what strange fish
Hath made his meal on thee?

FRANCISCO                              Sir, he may live.
I saw him beat the surges under him

115 And ride upon their backs. He trod the water,
Whose enmity he flung aside, and breasted
The surge, most swoll'n, that met him. His bold head
'Bove the contentious waves he kept, and oared
Himself with his good arms in lusty° stroke          vigorous

120 To th' shore, that o'er his wave-worn basis bowed,[7]
As° stooping to relieve him. I not° doubt          As if / do not
He came alive to land.

ALONSO                              No, no; he's gone.

SEBASTIAN [*to* ALONSO]   Sir, you may thank yourself for this great loss,
That would not bless our Europe with your daughter,

125 But rather loose° her to an African,          lose; release
Where she, at least, is banished from your eye,
Who° hath cause to wet the grief° on't.          (Claribel) / weep

ALONSO                              Prithee, peace.

SEBASTIAN   You were kneeled to and importuned otherwise[8]
By all of us, and the fair soul herself

130 Weighed between loathness and obedience at

---

2. Referring to Amphion's harp, to the music of which the walls (but not the houses) of Thebes arose.
3. Affirming his belief that Tunis was Carthage; Antonio mocks the length of time this took.
4. Except (as a verb); don't mention.
5. Comparatively speaking; Antonio plays on "drawing

lots."
6. *You . . . sense:* The image is of one being force-fed words against the appetite ("stomach") for hearing them.
7. *that . . . bowed:* that extended out and drooped over the foot of the cliff, which had been eroded by waves.
8. *otherwise:* to act differently.

Which end o'th' beam should bow.[9] We have lost your son,
I fear, for ever. Milan and Naples have
More widows in them of this business' making
Than we bring men to comfort them. The fault's your own.
ALONSO   So is the dear'st o'th' loss.[1]

135   GONZALO                                     My lord Sebastian,
The truth you speak doth lack some gentleness
And time to speak it in. You rub the sore[2]
When you should bring the plaster.
SEBASTIAN [*to* ANTONIO]   Very well.

140   ANTONIO   And most chirurgeonly.°                        surgeonlike
GONZALO [*to* ALONSO]   It is foul weather in us all, good sir,
When you are cloudy.
SEBASTIAN [*to* ANTONIO]   Fowl weather?[3]
ANTONIO                                     Very foul.
GONZALO [*to* ALONSO]   Had I plantation[4] of this isle, my lord—
ANTONIO [*to* SEBASTIAN]   He'd sow't with nettle-seed.
SEBASTIAN                                     Or docks,
   or mallows.[5]

145   GONZALO   And were the king on't, what would I do?
SEBASTIAN [*to* ANTONIO]   Scape being drunk, for want of wine.
GONZALO   I'th' commonwealth I would by contraries
Execute all things.[6] For no kind of traffic°                 commerce
Would I admit, no name of magistrate;

150   Letters° should not be known; riches, poverty,           Writing; erudition
And use of service,° none; contract, succession,[7]            servants
Bourn,° bound of land, tilth,° vineyard, none;          Boundary / tillage
No use of metal, corn,° or wine, or oil;                        grain
No occupation, all men idle, all;

155   And women too—but innocent and pure;[8]
No sovereignty—
SEBASTIAN [*to* ANTONIO]   Yet he would be king on't.
ANTONIO   The latter end of his commonwealth forgets the
   beginning.
GONZALO [*to* ALONSO]   All things in common° nature should   for communal use
   produce

160   Without sweat or endeavour. Treason, felony,
Sword, pike, knife, gun, or need of any engine,°               weapon
Would I not have; but nature should bring forth
Of it° own kind all foison,° all abundance,                    its / plenty
To feed my innocent people.

165   SEBASTIAN [*to* ANTONIO]   No marrying[9] 'mong his subjects?
ANTONIO   None, man, all idle: whores and knaves.
GONZALO [*to* ALONSO]   I would with such perfection govern, sir,
   T'excel the Golden Age.[1]

---

9. *Weighed . . . bow:* Weighed loathness to marry against
obedience to her father to find out which end of the
scales' beam would sink.
1. That is, the most grievous, or costliest, part of the loss
is also my own.
2. "To rub the sore" was proverbial. *plaster* (line 138): a
soothing remedy.
3. Perhaps recalling lines 28–31.
4. Had I responsibility for colonization of the island, but
also interpreted as "planting" by Antonio and Sebastian.
5. Cited as wild plants prone to grow on uncultivated
land; but dock is a traditional soother of nettle stings, and

mallow roots were used to make soothing ointment.
6. *I would . . . things:* I would advance the opposite to
what would be usual. This speech is based on a passage
in John Florio's translation of Montaigne's essay "Of the
Cannibals."
7. Inheritance of property.
8. Idleness proverbially begets lust.
9. Seen as irrelevant to sexually innocent people; also a
form of contract (line 151).
1. In classical mythology, the earliest of the ages—a time
without strife, labor, or injustice, when abundant food
grew without cultivation.

SEBASTIAN Save° his majesty! *God save*

ANTONIO Long live Gonzalo!

GONZALO [*to* ALONSO] And—do you mark me, sir?

170 ALONSO Prithee, no more. Thou dost talk nothing to me.

GONZALO I do well believe your highness, and did it to minister
occasion² to these gentlemen, who are of such sensible° and *sensitive*
nimble lungs that they always use° to laugh at nothing. *are accustomed*

ANTONIO 'Twas you we laughed at.

175 GONZALO Who, in this kind of merry fooling, am nothing to
you. So you may continue, and laugh at nothing still.

ANTONIO What a blow was there given!

SEBASTIAN An it had not fallen flat-long.³

GONZALO You are gentlemen of brave mettle.⁴ You would lift

180 the moon out of her sphere, if she would continue in it five
weeks without changing.⁵

*Enter* ARIEL, [*invisible,*] *playing solemn music*

SEBASTIAN We would so, and then go a-bat-fowling.⁶

ANTONIO [*to* GONZALO] Nay, good my lord, be not angry.

GONZALO No, I warrant you, I will not adventure my discretion

185 so weakly.⁷ Will you laugh me asleep? For I am very heavy.° *tired; serious*

ANTONIO Go sleep, and hear us.

[GONZALO, ADRIAN, *and* FRANCISCO *sleep*]

ALONSO What, all so soon asleep? I wish mine eyes
Would, with themselves, shut up my thoughts.—I find
They are inclined to do so.

SEBASTIAN Please you, sir,

190 Do not omit° the heavy offer° of it. *neglect / opportunity*
It seldom visits sorrow; when it doth,
It is a comforter.

ANTONIO We two, my lord,
Will guard your person while you take your rest,
And watch your safety.

ALONSO Thank you. Wondrous heavy.

[*He sleeps. Exit* ARIEL]

195 SEBASTIAN What a strange drowsiness possesses them!

ANTONIO It is the quality o'th' climate.

SEBASTIAN Why
Doth it not then our eyelids sink? I find
Not myself disposed to sleep.

ANTONIO Nor I; my spirits are nimble.
They fell together all, as by consent;° *consensus*

200 They dropped as by a thunderstroke. What might,
Worthy Sebastian, O, what might—? No more!—
And yet methinks I see it in thy face.
What thou shouldst be th'occasion speaks° thee, and *opportunity reveals to*
My strong imagination sees a crown
Dropping upon thy head.

205 SEBASTIAN What, art thou waking?° *awake*

ANTONIO Do you not hear me speak?

---

2. *minister occasion:* afford opportunity.

3. If it had not fallen on the flat, harmless side of the
sword.

4. Courage; punning on "metal," as of a sword blade.

5. *You would . . . changing:* If the moon were to remain
in her orbit ("sphere") one week longer than usual (five
weeks), you would steal her from her place.

6. Trapping birds by using light to attract them and bats
to strike them down; may also mean swindling and vic-
timizing the simple.

7. I will not put my sound judgment at risk so foolishly.

SEBASTIAN                                    I do, and surely
It is a sleepy language, and thou speak'st
Out of thy sleep. What is it thou didst say?
This is a strange repose, to be asleep
210    With eyes wide open; standing, speaking, moving,
And yet so fast asleep.
ANTONIO                          Noble Sebastian,
Thou letst thy fortune sleep, die rather; wink'st°                    shut your eyes
Whiles thou art waking.
SEBASTIAN                          Thou dost snore distinctly;°            meaningfully
There's meaning in thy snores.
215    ANTONIO    I am more serious than my custom. You
Must be so too if heed° me, which to do                        if you heed
Trebles thee o'er.
SEBASTIAN                Well, I am standing water.[8]
ANTONIO    I'll teach you how to flow.
SEBASTIAN                                    Do so; to ebb
Hereditary sloth[9] instructs me.
ANTONIO                          O,
220    If you but knew how you the purpose cherish
Whiles thus you mock it;[1] how in stripping it
You more invest° it! Ebbing° men, indeed,               clothe / Declining
Most often do so near the bottom run
By their own fear or sloth.
SEBASTIAN                          Prithee, say on.
225    The setting° of thine eye and cheek proclaim                     fixed look
A matter° from thee, and a birth, indeed,            Something important
Which throes[2] thee much to yield.
ANTONIO                                    Thus, sir.
Although this lord° of weak remembrance,° this,          (Gonzalo) / memory
Who shall be of as little memory°                              remembered
230    When he is earthed,° hath here almost persuaded—              buried
For he's a spirit of persuasion, only
Professes[3] to persuade—the King his son's alive,
'Tis as impossible that he's undrowned
As he that sleeps here swims.
SEBASTIAN                          I have no hope
That he's undrowned.
235    ANTONIO                          O, out of that 'no hope'
What great hope have you! No hope that way° is          (that he's not drowned)
Another way so high a hope that even
Ambition cannot pierce a wink° beyond,                    catch a glimpse
But doubt discovery there.[4] Will you grant with me
That Ferdinand is drowned?
SEBASTIAN                          He's gone.
240    ANTONIO                                    Then tell me,
Who's the next heir of Naples?
SEBASTIAN                          Claribel.

8. Between tides, and thus open to suggestion; also associated with being slothful. *Trebles thee o'er:* Makes you
three times as great.
9. Inherited laziness, or the slowness to attain prosperity
arising from being born a younger brother.
1. *If . . . it:* If you only understood that your mockery
reveals how great your aspirations really are; also, the

hereditary position you mock is actually to your advantage. *cherish:* hold dear; cultivate.
2. Which puts in agony, as in childbirth.
3. *only / Professes:* his sole vocation is.
4. Doubt that there is anything to achieve beyond the
high hope of the crown.

ANTONIO    She that is Queen of Tunis; she that dwells
 Ten leagues beyond man's life;° she that from Naples    *lifetime journey*
 Can have no note°—unless the sun were post°—   *information / messenger*
245 The man i'th' moon's too slow—till new-born chins
 Be rough and razorable; she that from° whom     *returning from*
 We all were sea-swallowed, though some cast again[5]—
 And by that destiny, to perform an act
 Whereof what's past is prologue, what to come
 In yours and my discharge.°            *performance*
250 SEBASTIAN       What stuff is this? How say you?
 'Tis true my brother's daughter's Queen of Tunis;
 So is she heir of Naples; 'twixt which regions
 There is some space.
 ANTONIO      A space whose every cubit°   *about 18 to 22 inches*
 Seems to cry out 'How shall that Claribel
255 Measure us° back to Naples? Keep° in Tunis,   *(the cubits) / Stay*
 And let Sebastian wake.'° Say this were death   *(to his opportunity)*
 That now hath seized them; why, they were no worse
 Than now they are. There be that° can rule Naples   *those that*
 As well as he that sleeps, lords that can prate
260 As amply and unnecessarily
 As this Gonzalo; I myself could make
 A chough of as deep chat.[6] O, that you bore
 The mind that I do, what a sleep were this
 For your advancement! Do you understand me?
 SEBASTIAN    Methinks I do.
265 ANTONIO       And how does your content
 Tender° your own good fortune?       *Regard; care for*
 SEBASTIAN         I remember
 You did supplant your brother Prospero.
 ANTONIO           True;
 And look how well my garments sit upon me,
 Much feater° than before. My brother's servants   *more trimly*
270 Were then my fellows; now they are my men.
 SEBASTIAN    But for your conscience.
 ANTONIO    Ay, sir, where lies that? If 'twere a kibe[7]
 'Twould put me to° my slipper; but I feel not   *make me wear*
 This deity in my bosom. Twenty consciences
275 That stand 'twixt me and Milan, candied[8] be they,
 And melt ere they molest. Here lies your brother,
 No better than the earth he lies upon
 If he were that which now he's like—that's dead;
 Whom I with this obedient steel,° three inches of it,   *sword*
280 Can lay to bed for ever; whiles you, doing thus,
 To the perpetual wink for aye° might put    *sleep forever*
 This ancient morsel, this Sir Prudence, who
 Should not upbraid our course. For all the rest,
 They'll take suggestion° as a cat laps milk;   *prompting to evil*
285 They'll tell the clock° to any business that    *chime; agree*
 We say befits the hour.
 SEBASTIAN      Thy case, dear friend,

---

5. Regurgitated, cast ashore; also, possibly, theatrical
role-playing.
6. I . . . chat: I could train a jackdaw (known for imitat-

ing speech) to speak as profoundly.
7. Chilblain; sore on the heel.
8. Turned to sugar; crystallized in sugar.

Shall be my precedent. As thou got'st Milan,
I'll come by Naples. Draw thy sword. One stroke
Shall free thee from the tribute which thou payest,
And I the King shall love thee.

290 ANTONIO                    Draw together,
And when I rear my hand, do you the like
To fall it on Gonzalo.
          [*They draw*]
SEBASTIAN                    O, but one word.
          *Enter* ARIEL, [*invisible,*] *with music and song*
ARIEL [*to* GONZALO]    My master through his art foresees the danger
That you his friend are in—and sends me forth,
295 For else° his project dies, to keep them⁹ living.                    *otherwise*
          [*He*] *sings in Gonzalo's ear*
                    While you here do snoring lie,
                    Open-eyed conspiracy
                        His time° doth take.                    *opportunity*
                    If of life you keep a care,
                    Shake off slumber, and beware.
300                         Awake, awake!
ANTONIO [*to* SEBASTIAN]    Then let us both be sudden.
GONZALO [*awaking*]                    Now good angels
Preserve the King!
ALONSO [*awaking*]    Why, how now? Ho, awake!
          [*The others awake*]
          [*To* ANTONIO *and* SEBASTIAN]                    Why are you° drawn?    *your weapons*
          [*To* GONZALO] Wherefore this ghastly° looking?                    *fearful*
305 GONZALO                    What's the matter?
SEBASTIAN    Whiles we stood here securing° your repose,                    *guarding*
Even now we heard a hollow burst of bellowing,
Like bulls, or rather lions. Did't not wake you?
It struck mine ear most terribly.
ALONSO                    I heard nothing.
310 ANTONIO    O, 'twas a din to fright a monster's ear,
To make an earthquake! Sure it was the roar
Of a whole herd of lions.
ALONSO                    Heard you this, Gonzalo?
GONZALO    Upon mine honour, sir, I heard a humming,
And that a strange one too, which did awake me.
315 I shaked you, sir, and cried.° As mine eyes opened                    *called out*
I saw their weapons drawn. There was a noise,
That's verily.° 'Tis best we stand upon our guard,                    *the truth*
Or that we quit this place. Let's draw our weapons.
ALONSO    Lead off this ground, and let's make further search
For my poor son.
320 GONZALO                    Heavens keep him from these beasts!
For he is sure i'th' island.
ALONSO                    Lead away.    [*Exeunt all but* ARIEL]¹
ARIEL    Prospero my lord shall know what I have done.
So, King, go safely on to seek thy son.                    *Exit*

---

9. Gonzalo and Alonso.
1. Ariel's following lines are spoken as the other characters depart; he probably exits in another direction.

## 2.2

*Enter* CALIBAN, [*wearing a gaberdine,*[1] *and*] *with a bur-*
*den of wood*

CALIBAN [*throwing down his burden*]   All the infections that the
    sun sucks up
From bogs, fens, flats,° on Prosper fall, and make him         *marshes*
By inch-meal° a disease!         *inch by inch*
    [*A noise of thunder heard*][2]
            His spirits hear me,
And yet I needs must curse. But they'll nor pinch,
5  Fright me with urchin-shows,[3] pitch me i'th' mire,
Nor lead me like a fire-brand in the dark
Out of my way, unless he bid 'em. But
For every trifle are they set upon me;
Sometime like apes, that mow° and chatter at me       *grimace*
10  And after bite me; then like hedgehogs, which
Lie tumbling in my barefoot way and mount
Their pricks at my footfall; sometime am I
All wound with° adders, who with cloven tongues     *entwined by*
Do hiss me into madness.
    *Enter* TRINCULO[4]
          Lo now, lo!
15  Here comes a spirit of his, and to torment me
For bringing wood in slowly. I'll fall flat.
Perchance he will not mind° me.         *notice*
    [*He lies down*]
TRINCULO   Here's neither bush nor shrub to bear off° any     *ward off*
    weather at all, and another storm brewing. I hear it sing i'th'
20    wind. Yon same black cloud, yon huge one, looks like a foul
    bombard[5] that would shed his liquor. If it should thunder as it
    did before, I know not where to hide my head. Yon same cloud
    cannot choose but fall by pailfuls. [*Seeing* CALIBAN] What have
    we here, a man or a fish? Dead or alive?—A fish, he smells
25    like a fish; a very ancient and fish-like smell; a kind of not-of-
    the-newest poor-john.[6] A strange fish! Were I in England now,
    as once I was, and had but this fish painted,[7] not a holiday-fool
    there but would give a piece of silver. There would this mon-
    ster make a man.[8] Any strange beast there makes a man. When
30    they will not give a doit° to relieve a lame beggar, they will lay     *small coin*
    out ten to see a dead Indian.[9] Legged like a man, and his fins
    like arms! Warm, o'my troth! I do now let loose my opinion,
    hold it no longer. This is no fish, but an islander that hath
    lately suffered by a thunderbolt.
    [*Thunder*]
35    Alas, the storm is come again. My best way is to creep under
    his gaberdine; there is no other shelter hereabout. Misery
    acquaints a man with strange bedfellows. I will here shroud°     *take cover*
    till the dregs[1] of the storm be past.

---

2.2
1. A loose smock made of coarse material.
2. Caliban takes this as a response to his curse; in F, the direction comes before Caliban speaks.
3. With the sight of hedgehoglike spirits.
4. Trinculo is probably dressed in traditional fool's mot-ley (many-colored garment).
5. Large leather drinking vessel; stone-throwing military engine.
6. Dried hake, a poor person's staple.
7. On a sign to attract spectators.
8. Make a fortune for a man; become a man.
9. An allusion to exhibitions of American Indians in London.
1. Drinks, as from a "bombard" of wine.

[*He hides under Caliban's gaberdine.*]
*Enter* STEFANO, *singing* [*with a wooden bottle in his hand*]

STEFANO          I shall no more to sea, to sea,
40                          Here shall I die ashore—
This is a very scurvy tune to sing at a man's funeral.
Well, here's my comfort.
          [*He*] *drinks,* [*then*] *sings*
          The master, the swabber, the boatswain, and I,
                    The gunner and his mate,
45          Loved Mall, Meg, and Marian, and Margery,
                    But none of us cared for Kate.
                    For she had a tongue with a tang,°                    sting
                    Would cry to a sailor 'Go hang!'
          She loved not the savour of tar nor of pitch,
50          Yet a tailor might scratch her where'er she did itch.²
                    Then to sea, boys, and let her go hang!
                    Then to sea [*etc.*].
This is a scurvy tune, too. But here's my comfort.
          [*He*] *drinks*

CALIBAN [*to* TRINCULO]   Do not torment me! O!
55   STEFANO   What's the matter?° Have we devils here? Do you put          What's going on?
          tricks upon's with savages and men of Ind,° ha? I have not          India
          scaped drowning to be afeard now of your four legs. For it hath
          been said: 'As proper a man as ever went on four legs³ cannot
          make him give ground.' And it shall be said so again, while
60          Stefano breathes at'° nostrils.                                        at the
CALIBAN   The spirit torments me. O!
STEFANO   This is some monster of the isle with four legs, who
          hath got, as I take it, an ague.° Where the devil should he learn          a fit of fever
          our language? I will give him some relief, if it be but for that.
65          If I can recover° him and keep him tame and get to Naples          cure
          with him, he's a present for any emperor that ever trod on neat's
          leather.°                                                              cowhide; shoes
CALIBAN [*to* TRINCULO]   Do not torment me, prithee! I'll bring
          my wood home faster.
70   STEFANO   He's in his fit now, and does not talk after° the wisest.          in the manner of
          He shall taste of my bottle. If he have never drunk wine afore,
          it will go near to° remove his fit. If I can recover him and keep          almost
          him tame, I will not take too much for him.⁴ He shall pay for
          him that hath° him, and that soundly.                                  gets
75   CALIBAN [*to* TRINCULO]   Thou dost me yet but little hurt. Thou
          wilt anon, I know it by thy trembling. Now Prosper works upon
          thee.
STEFANO   Come on your ways.° Open your mouth. Here is that          Come on
          which will give language to you, cat.⁵ Open your mouth. This
80          will shake° your shaking, I can tell you, and that soundly. You          dislodge
          cannot tell who's your friend. Open your chaps again.
          [CALIBAN *drinks*]

2. Implying sexual desire and gratification. Tailors were
often mocked for supposed lack of virility.
3. Comically varying "on two legs" (upright); also suggesting "on crutches."
4. No sum can be too high for him.
5. "Ale will make a cat speak" was proverbial.

TRINCULO  I should know that voice. It should be—but he is
drowned, and these are devils. O, defend me!

STEFANO  Four legs and two voices—a most delicate° monster!  *exquisitely made*
His forward voice now is to speak well of his friend; his backward voice is to utter foul speeches and to detract. If all the
wine in my bottle will recover him,⁶ I will help his ague.
Come.

[CALIBAN *drinks*]

Amen.° I will pour some in thy other mouth.  *Enough*

TRINCULO  Stefano!

STEFANO  Doth thy other mouth call me? Mercy, mercy! This is
a devil, and no monster. I will leave him. I have no long
spoon.⁷

TRINCULO  Stefano! If thou beest Stefano, touch me and speak
to me, for I am Trinculo. Be not afeard. Thy good friend Trinculo.

STEFANO  If thou beest Trinculo, come forth. I'll pull thee by
the lesser legs. If any be Trinculo's legs, these are they.

[*He pulls out* TRINCULO *by the legs*]

Thou art very° Trinculo indeed! How cam'st thou to be the  *actual*
siege° of this moon-calf ?⁸ Can he vent° Trinculos?  *excrement / defecate*

TRINCULO [*rising*]  I took him to be killed with a thunderstroke.
But art thou not drowned, Stefano? I hope now thou art not
drowned. Is the storm overblown? I hid me under the dead
moon-calf 's gaberdine for fear of the storm. And art thou living,
Stefano? O Stefano, two Neapolitans scaped!

[*He dances* STEFANO *round*]

STEFANO  Prithee, do not turn me about. My stomach is not
constant.

CALIBAN  These be fine things, an if ° they be not spirits.  *an if = if*
That's a brave° god, and bears celestial liquor.  *an excellent; a fine*
I will kneel to him.

[*He kneels*]

STEFANO [*to* TRINCULO]  How didst thou scape? How cam'st thou
hither? Swear by this bottle how thou cam'st hither. I escaped
upon a butt of sack⁹ which the sailors heaved o'erboard, by this
bottle—which I made of the bark of a tree with mine own
hands since I was cast ashore.

CALIBAN  I'll swear upon that bottle to be thy true subject, for
the liquor is not earthly.

STEFANO [*offering* TRINCULO *the bottle*]  Here. Swear then how
thou escapedst.

TRINCULO  Swum ashore, man, like a duck. I can swim like a
duck, I'll be sworn.

STEFANO  Here, kiss the book.¹

[TRINCULO *drinks*]

Though thou canst swim like a duck, thou art made like a
goose.²

---

6. If it takes all the wine in my bottle to cure him.
7. From the proverbial "He should have a long spoon
that sups with the devil."
8. Deformed creature; miscarriage, owing to the supposed detrimental influence of the moon.
9. Cask of Spanish or Canary wine.

1. Confirming an oath by kissing the Bible; or the proverbial "Kiss the cup" ("Drink").
2. Probably alluding to Trinculo's outstretched neck with
the bottle as a beak; also a byword for giddiness and
unsteadiness on the feet.

125 TRINCULO O Stefano, hast any more of this?
STEFANO The whole butt, man. My cellar is in a rock by th' sea-
side, where my wine is hid.
      [CALIBAN *rises*]
How now, moon-calf ? How does thine ague?
CALIBAN Hast thou not dropped from heaven?
130 STEFANO Out o'th' moon, I do assure thee. I was the man i'th'
moon when time was.°                                       *once upon a time*
CALIBAN I have seen thee in her, and I do adore thee.
My mistress° showed me thee, and thy dog and thy bush.[3]     *(Miranda)*
STEFANO Come, swear to that. Kiss the book. I will furnish it
135 anon with new contents. Swear.
      [CALIBAN *drinks*]
TRINCULO By this good light,° this is a very shallow monster! I    *sun*
afeard of him? A very weak monster! The man i'th' moon? A
most poor, credulous monster! Well drawn,° monster, in good   *drunk*
sooth!
140 CALIBAN [*to* STEFANO] I'll show thee every fertile inch o'th' island,
And I will kiss thy foot. I prithee, be my god.
TRINCULO By this light, a most perfidious and drunken monster!
When's god's asleep, he'll rob his bottle.
CALIBAN [*to* STEFANO] I'll kiss thy foot. I'll swear myself thy subject.
145 STEFANO Come on then; down, and swear.
      [CALIBAN *kneels*]
TRINCULO I shall laugh myself to death at this puppy-headed
monster. A most scurvy monster! I could find in my heart to
beat him—
STEFANO [*to* CALIBAN] Come, kiss.
      [CALIBAN *kisses his foot*]
150 TRINCULO But that the poor monster's in drink.° An abominable   *drunk*
monster!
CALIBAN I'll show thee the best springs; I'll pluck thee berries;
I'll fish for thee, and get thee wood enough.
A plague upon the tyrant that I serve!
155 I'll bear him no more sticks, but follow thee,
Thou wondrous man.
TRINCULO A most ridiculous monster, to make a wonder of a
poor drunkard!
CALIBAN [*to* STEFANO] I prithee, let me bring thee where crabs°   *crab apples*
grow,
160 And I with my long nails will dig thee pig-nuts,°      *edible tubers*
Show thee a jay's nest, and instruct thee how
To snare the nimble marmoset. I'll bring thee
To clust'ring filberts, and sometimes I'll get thee
Young seamews° from the rock. Wilt thou go with me?    *seagulls*
165 STEFANO I prithee now, lead the way without any more talking.—Trinculo, the King and all our company else being
drowned, we will inherit here.—Here, bear my bottle.[4]—Fellow Trinculo, we'll fill him° by and by again.                       *it*
CALIBAN (*sings drunkenly*)[5] Farewell, master, farewell, farewell!
170 TRINCULO A howling monster, a drunken monster!

---

3. A dog and a thornbush were traditional attributes of
the man in the moon; cf. *A Midsummer Night's Dream*
5.1.248–49.

4. Probably spoken to Caliban.
5. This stage direction may be misplaced and may actually refer to the following song, "No more dams."

CALIBAN [*sings*]   No more dams I'll make for° fish,                                    *to trap*
                    Nor fetch in firing°                                                  *firewood*
                    At requiring,
                    Nor scrape trenchering,⁶ nor wash dish.
175                 'Ban, 'ban, Cacaliban
                    Has a new master.—Get a new man!⁷
          Freedom, high-day!° High-day, freedom! Freedom, high-day,         *holiday*
          freedom!
STEFANO   O brave° monster! Lead the way.          *Exeunt*          *excellent; fine*

## 3.1

*Enter* FERDINAND, *bearing a log*

FERDINAND   There be some sports are painful, and their labour
     Delight in them sets off.¹ Some kinds of baseness
     Are nobly undergone, and most poor matters
     Point to rich ends. This my mean° task                                *lowly*
5    Would be as heavy to me as odious, but°                                *except that*
     The mistress which I serve quickens° what's dead,                      *enlivens*
     And makes my labours pleasures. O, she is
     Ten times more gentle than her father's crabbed,
     And he's composed of harshness. I must remove
10   Some thousands of these logs and pile them up,
     Upon a sore° injunction. My sweet mistress                            *harsh*
     Weeps when she sees me work, and says such baseness
     Had never like executor. I forget,
     But these sweet thoughts do even refresh my labours,
     Most busil'est² when I do it.°                                        *(labor)*

*Enter* MIRANDA, *and* PROSPERO [*following at a distance*]

15   MIRANDA                          Alas now, pray you
     Work not so hard. I would the lightning had
     Burnt up those logs that you are enjoined to pile.
     Pray set it down, and rest you. When this burns
     'Twill weep³ for having wearied you. My father
20   Is hard at study. Pray now, rest yourself.
     He's safe° for these three hours.                    *We are safe from him*
FERDINAND                          O most dear mistress,
     The sun will set before I shall discharge
     What I must strive to do.
MIRANDA                          If you'll sit down
     I'll bear your logs the while. Pray give me that;
     I'll carry it to the pile.
25   FERDINAND                          No, precious creature.
     I had rather crack my sinews, break my back,
     Than you should such dishonour undergo
     While I sit lazy by.
MIRANDA                          It would become me
     As well as it does you; and I should do it
30   With much more ease, for my good will is to it,
     And yours it is against.

---

6. Trenchers, or wooden plates.
7. Addressed to the old master, Prospero.
**3.1**
1. *their . . . off*: the greater effort invested amounts to

more pleasure; the labor of painful activities ("sports") is
offset by whatever delight we take in them.
2. Most busily (giving a double superlative).
3. By exuding drops of resin.

PROSPERO [*aside*]         Poor worm, thou art infected.[4]
    This visitation[5] shows it.
MIRANDA [*to* FERDINAND]   You look wearily.
FERDINAND   No, noble mistress, 'tis fresh morning with me
    When you are by at night. I do beseech you,
35    Chiefly that I might set it in my prayers,
    What is your name?
MIRANDA             Miranda. O my father,
    I have broke your hest° to say so!           *disobeyed your command*
FERDINAND            Admired[6] Miranda!
    Indeed the top of admiration, worth
    What's dearest to the world. Full many a lady
40    I have eyed with best regard, and many a time
    Th'harmony of their tongues hath into bondage
    Brought my too diligent° ear. For several virtues     *attentive*
    Have I liked several° women; never any            *various*
    With so full soul but some defect in her
45    Did quarrel with the noblest grace she owed°     *owned*
    And put it to the foil.[7] But you, O you,
    So perfect and so peerless, are created
    Of every creature's best.
MIRANDA           I do not know
    One of my sex, no woman's face remember
50    Save from my glass° mine own; nor have I seen     *mirror*
    More that I may call men than you, good friend,
    And my dear father. How features are abroad[8]
    I am skilless° of ; but, by my modesty,°     *ignorant / virginity*
    The jewel in my dower,° I would not wish       *dowry*
55    Any companion in the world but you;
    Nor can imagination form a shape
    Besides° yourself to like of. But I prattle     *Other than*
    Something° too wildly, and my father's precepts     *Somewhat*
    I therein do forget.
FERDINAND        I am in my condition°           *rank*
60    A prince, Miranda, I do think a king—
    I would° not so—and would no more endure     *wish it were*
    This wooden slavery[9] than to suffer
    The flesh-fly[1] blow my mouth. Hear my soul speak.
    The very instant that I saw you did
65    My heart fly to your service; there resides
    To make me slave to it. And for your sake
    Am I this patient log-man.
MIRANDA           Do you love me?
FERDINAND   O heaven, O earth, bear witness to this sound,
    And crown what I profess with kind event°     *favorable outcome*
70    If I speak true! If hollowly,° invert           *falsely*
    What best is boded° me to mischief !° I,     *foretold to / misfortune*
    Beyond all limit of what° else i'th' world,     *whatsoever*
    Do love, prize, honour you.

---

4. Inflicted with lovesickness. *worm*: an expression of tenderness; but a worm was often thought to carry disease.
5. Suggesting a pastoral or charitable visit to the sick; or may indicate a visit by the plague, here lovesickness.
6. Playing on the meaning of Miranda's name.

7. Foiled it, or made it ineffectual; challenged it, as in a fencing match (compare "quarrel" in line 45).
8. What people look like elsewhere.
9. The log as a symbol of Prospero's oppression.
1. Species of fly that deposits its eggs ("blows") in dead flesh.

MIRANDA [*weeping*]      I am a fool
  To weep at what I am glad of.
PROSPERO [*aside*]        Fair encounter
75  Of two most rare affections! Heavens rain grace
  On that which breeds between 'em.
FERDINAND [*to* MIRANDA]       Wherefore weep you?
MIRANDA  At mine unworthiness, that dare not offer
  What I desire to give, and much less take
  What I shall die to want.[2] But this is trifling,
80  And all the more it seeks to hide itself
  The bigger bulk it shows.[3] Hence, bashful cunning,°      *artful shyness*
  And prompt me, plain and holy innocence.
  I am your wife, if you will marry me.
  If not, I'll die your maid.° To be your fellow°      *virgin; servant / equal*
85  You may deny me, but I'll be your servant
  Whether you will or no.
FERDINAND [*kneeling*]     My mistress,° dearest;      *sweetheart*
  And I thus humble ever.
MIRANDA  My husband then?
FERDINAND  Ay, with a heart as willing°      *desirous*
90  As bondage e'er of freedom. Here's my hand.[4]
MIRANDA  And mine, with my heart in't. And now farewell
  Till half an hour hence.
FERDINAND       A thousand thousand.°      *(farewells)*
      *Exeunt* [*severally*° MIRANDA *and* FERDINAND]      *separately*
PROSPERO  So glad of this as they I cannot be,
  Who are surprised with all;° but my rejoicing      *overwhelmed by all*
95  At nothing can be more. I'll to my book,°      *book of magic*
  For yet ere supper-time must I perform
  Much business appertaining.      *Exit*

### 3.2

*Enter* CALIBAN, STEFANO, *and* TRINCULO

STEFANO [*to* CALIBAN]    Tell not me. When the butt is out we will
  drink water, not a drop before. Therefore bear up and board
  'em.[1] Servant monster, drink to me.
TRINCULO  Servant monster? The folly° of this island! They say      *absurdity*
5  there's but five upon this isle. We are three of them; if th'other
  two be brained° like us, the state totters.      *have brains*
STEFANO  Drink, servant monster, when I bid thee. Thy eyes are
  almost set° in thy head.      *fixed by drunkenness*
TRINCULO  Where should they be set° else? He were a brave      *placed*
10  monster indeed if they were set in his tail.
STEFANO  My man-monster hath drowned his tongue in sack.
  For my part, the sea cannot drown me. I swam, ere I could
  recover the shore, five and thirty leagues,° off and on.[2] By this      *about 100 miles*

---

2. *At . . . want:* Miranda is not at liberty to bestow her virginity nor to obtain the consummation that she desires and lacs.
3. *all . . . shows:* an image of secret pregnancy.
4. *I am your wife . . . hand:* Such an exchange could actually have constituted a marriage ceremony. In Shakespeare's time, weddings did not need to be wit-

nessed and performed in a church to be valid (compare 4.1.14–19).
**3.2**
1. Force a way aboard, continuing the naval-warfare terminology; take onboard (drink). *bear up:* sail to the attack.
2. Tacking away from and toward the shore.

light, thou shalt be my lieutenant, monster, or my standard.³

15 TRINCULO    Your lieutenant if you list;° he's no standard.                                    *wish*

STEFANO    We'll not run, Monsieur Monster. .

TRINCULO    Nor go° neither; but you'll lie⁴ like dogs, and yet say                         *walk*
nothing neither.

STEFANO    Moon-calf, speak once in thy life, if thou beest a good
20    moon-calf.

CALIBAN    How does thy honour? Let me lick thy shoe.
I'll not serve him; he is not valiant.

TRINCULO    Thou liest, most ignorant monster! I am in case° to                      *prepared*
jostle a constable. Why, thou debauched fish, thou, was there
25    ever man a coward that hath drunk so much sack as I today?
Wilt thou tell a monstrous lie, being but half a fish and half a
monster?

CALIBAN [*to* STEFANO]    Lo, how he mocks me! Wilt thou let him,
my lord?

30 TRINCULO    'Lord' quoth he? That a monster should be such a
natural!⁵

CALIBAN [*to* STEFANO]    Lo, lo, again! Bite him to death, I prithee.

STEFANO    Trinculo, keep a good tongue in your head. If you
prove a mutineer, the next tree.° The poor monster's my sub-              *(for a gallows)*
35    ject, and he shall not suffer indignity.

CALIBAN    I thank my noble lord. Wilt thou be pleased
To hearken once again to the suit I made to thee?

STEFANO    Marry, will I. Kneel and repeat it. I will stand, and so
shall Trinculo.
                [CALIBAN *kneels*.]
                *Enter* ARIEL, *invisible*

40 CALIBAN    As I told thee before, I am subject to a tyrant, a sor-
cerer, that by his cunning hath cheated me of the island.

ARIEL    Thou liest.

CALIBAN [*to* TRINCULO]    Thou liest, thou jesting monkey, thou.
I would my valiant master would destroy thee.
45    I do not lie.

STEFANO    Trinculo, if you trouble him any more in's tale, by this
hand, I will supplant° some of your teeth.                                             *uproot*

TRINCULO    Why, I said nothing.

STEFANO    Mum, then, and no more. [*To* CALIBAN] Proceed.

50 CALIBAN    I say by sorcery he got this isle;
From me he got it. If thy greatness will
Revenge it on him—for I know thou dar'st,
But this thing⁶ dare not—

STEFANO    That's most certain.

55 CALIBAN    Thou shalt be lord of it, and I'll serve thee.

STEFANO    How now shall this be compassed?° Canst thou bring                *accomplished*
me to the party?°                                                                           *person concerned*

CALIBAN    Yea, yea, my lord. I'll yield him thee asleep
Where thou mayst knock a nail into his head.⁷

60 ARIEL    Thou liest, thou canst not.

---

3. Standard-bearer, but in Trinculo's reply "one who can
stand up."
4. Lie (down); tell lies; excrete.
5. An idiot, punning on the idea that monsters were

unnatural.
6. Trinculo; or perhaps Caliban himself.
7. As Jael murdered sleeping Sisera in Judges 4:21 and
5:26.

CALIBAN  What a pied ninny's° this! [*To* TRINCULO] Thou scurvy    *fool in motley*
    patch!°    *jester; idiot*
[*To* STEFANO] I do beseech thy greatness give him blows,
And take his bottle from him. When that's gone
He shall drink naught but brine, for I'll not show him
65  Where the quick freshes° are.    *fast-flowing springs*
STEFANO  Trinculo, run into no further danger. Interrupt the
    monster one word further, and, by this hand, I'll turn my mercy
    out o'doors and make a stockfish of thee.[8]
TRINCULO  Why, what did I? I did nothing. I'll go farther off.
70  STEFANO  Didst thou not say he lied?
ARIEL  Thou liest.
STEFANO  Do I so? [*Striking* TRINCULO] Take thou that. As you
    like this, give me the lie° another time.    *call me a liar*
TRINCULO  I did not give the lie. Out o'your wits and hearing
75  too? A pox o'your bottle! This can sack and drinking do. A
    murrain° on your monster, and the devil take your fingers.    *plague*
CALIBAN  Ha, ha, ha!
STEFANO  Now forward with your tale. [*To* TRINCULO] Prithee,
    stand further off.
80  CALIBAN  Beat him enough; after a little time
    I'll beat him too.
STEFANO [*to* TRINCULO]
                Stand farther. [*To* CALIBAN] Come, proceed.
CALIBAN  Why, as I told thee, 'tis a custom with him
    I'th' afternoon to sleep. There° thou mayst brain him,    *Then*
    Having first seized his books; or with a log
85  Batter his skull, or paunch° him with a stake,    *disembowel*
    Or cut his weasand° with thy knife. Remember    *windpipe*
    First to possess his books, for without them
    He's but a sot° as I am, nor hath not    *stupid fool*
    One spirit to command—they all do hate him
90  As rootedly as I. Burn but his books.
    He has brave utensils,[9] for so he calls them,
    Which when he has a house he'll deck withal.
    And that most deeply to consider is
    The beauty of his daughter. He himself
95  Calls her a nonpareil.° I never saw a woman    *one without equal*
    But only Sycorax my dam and she,
    But she as far surpasseth Sycorax
    As great'st does least.
STEFANO                Is it so brave° a lass?    *excellent; fine*
CALIBAN  Ay, lord. She will become thy bed, I warrant,
100  And bring thee forth brave brood.
STEFANO  Monster, I will kill this man. His daughter and I will
    be king and queen—save° our graces!—and Trinculo and thy-    *God save*
    self shall be viceroys. Dost thou like the plot, Trinculo?
TRINCULO  Excellent.
105  STEFANO  Give me thy hand. I am sorry I beat thee. But while
    thou liv'st, keep a good tongue in thy head.

8. Proverbial allusion to the beating of dried fish before    9. Perhaps confusing implements for magic and house-
cooking it.    hold goods.

CALIBAN    Within this half hour will he be asleep.
    Wilt thou destroy him then?
STEFANO    Ay, on mine honour.
110    ARIEL [aside]    This will I tell my master.
CALIBAN    Thou mak'st me merry; I am full of pleasure.
    Let us be jocund. Will you troll° the catch°        *sing / round; song*
    You taught me but while-ere?°        *a short time ago*
STEFANO    At thy request, monster, I will do reason, any rea-
115    son.°—Come on, Trinculo, let us sing.        *anything reasonable*
    (*Sings*)        Flout 'em and cout[1] 'em,
            And scout° 'em and flout 'em.        *mock*
            Thought is free.
CALIBAN    That's not the tune.
    ARIEL *plays the tune on a tabor and pipe*[2]
120    STEFANO    What is this same?
TRINCULO    This is the tune of our catch, played by the picture
    of Nobody.[3]
STEFANO [*calls towards* ARIEL]    If thou beest a man, show thyself
    in thy likeness. If thou beest a devil, take't as thou list.°        *wish*
125    TRINCULO    O, forgive me my sins!
STEFANO    He that dies pays all debts.[4] [*Calls*] I defy thee.—
    Mercy upon us![5]
CALIBAN    Art thou afeard?
STEFANO    No, monster, not I.
130    CALIBAN    Be not afeard. The isle is full of noises,
    Sounds, and sweet airs,° that give delight and hurt not.        *tunes*
    Sometimes a thousand twangling instruments
    Will hum about mine ears, and sometime voices
    That if I then had waked after long sleep
135    Will make me sleep again; and then in dreaming
    The clouds methought would open and show riches
    Ready to drop upon me, that when I waked
    I cried to dream again.
STEFANO    This will prove a brave kingdom to me, where I shall
140    have my music for nothing.[6]
CALIBAN    When Prospero is destroyed.
STEFANO    That shall be by and by.° I remember the story.        *very soon*
            [*Exit* ARIEL, *playing music*]
TRINCULO    The sound is going away. Let's follow it, and after do
    our work.
145    STEFANO    Lead, monster; we'll follow.—I would I could see this
    taborer. He lays it on.[7]
TRINCULO [*to* CALIBAN]    Wilt come? I'll follow Stefano.    *Exeunt*

---

1. Probably a dialectal form of "colt" (cheat). The stage direction ("Sings") suggests that the others cannot manage the catch and remain in bewildered silence. But Trinculo, and perhaps Caliban, may attempt to join in.
2. The tabor was a small drum slung on the left-hand side of the body; the tabor pipe was a long narrow pipe played with the left hand. The combination was associated with rustic dances and merrymaking.
3. "Nobody" was a character in a comedy who was depicted on the title page of the printed text. Large breeches up to his neck made him appear to have no trunk.
4. Varying the proverbial "Death pays all debts."
5. Stefano's defiance comically collapses.
6. James I spent large sums on court music, but not typically of the popular kind Ariel now plays.
7. He sets himself to his music vigorously. Stefano deserts Caliban in order to follow the music. Trinculo and Caliban in turn follow Stefano (line 147).

### 3.3

*Enter* ALONSO, SEBASTIAN, ANTONIO, GONZALO, ADRIAN,
*and* FRANCISCO

GONZALO [*to* ALONSO]    By'r la'kin,[1] I can go no further, sir.
My old bones ache. Here's a maze trod indeed
Through forthrights and meanders.° By your patience,                    *direct and winding paths*
I needs must rest me.

ALONSO        Old lord, I cannot blame thee,
5   Who am myself attached° with weariness                                    *seized*
To th' dulling of my spirits. Sit down and rest.
Even° here I will put off my hope, and keep it                             *Exactly*
No longer for° my flatterer. He is drowned                                 *as*
Whom thus we stray to find, and the sea mocks
10  Our frustrate° search on land. Well, let him go.                        *vain*
[*They sit*]

ANTONIO [*aside to* SEBASTIAN]    I am right glad that he's so out of hope.
Do not for° one repulse forgo the purpose                                  *on account of*
That you resolved t'effect.

SEBASTIAN [*aside to* ANTONIO] The next advantage
Will we take throughly.°                                                   *thoroughly*

ANTONIO [*aside to* SEBASTIAN] Let it be tonight,
15  For now they are oppressed with travel.° They                          *journey; travail*
Will not nor cannot use such vigilance
As when they are fresh.

SEBASTIAN [*aside to* ANTONIO] I say tonight. No more.
                    *Solemn and strange music.* [*Enter*] PROSPERO *on the*
                    *top,*[2] *invisible*

ALONSO   What harmony is this? My good friends, hark.

GONZALO   Marvellous sweet music.
                    *Enter* [*spirits, in*] *several strange shapes, bringing in* [*a*
                    *table and*] *a banquet, and dance about it with gentle*
                    *actions of salutations, and, inviting the King and* [*his*
                    *companions*] *to eat, they depart*

20  ALONSO   Give us kind keepers,° heavens! What were these?            *guardian angels*

SEBASTIAN   A living drollery.[3] Now I will believe
That there are unicorns; that in Arabia
There is one tree, the phoenix' throne, one phoenix[4]
At this hour reigning there.

ANTONIO                              I'll believe both;
25  And what does else want credit° come to me,                          *lack belief*
And I'll be sworn 'tis true. Travellers ne'er did lie,[5]
Though fools at home condemn 'em.

GONZALO                              If in Naples
I should report this now, would they believe me—
If I should say I saw such islanders?
30  For certes° these are people of the island,                          *certainly*
Who though they are of monstrous shape, yet note
Their manners are more gentle-kind than of
Our human generation you shall find
Many, nay, almost any.

---

**3.3**
1. Ladykin: a colloquial form of reference to the Virgin
Mary.
2. A small acting area above the upper stage.
3. A puppet show with live actors.

4. The unicorn and phoenix, a bird, were two mythological creatures that sometimes figured in travelers' tales.
Only one phoenix was said to exist in the world at any one
time.
5. Proverbially, "A traveler may lie with authority."

PROSPERO [aside]                    Honest lord,
35    Thou hast said well, for some of you there present
      Are worse than devils.
ALONSO                        I cannot too much muse.°                         *marvel*
      Such shapes, such gesture, and such sound, expressing—
      Although they want the use of tongue°—a kind                           *language*
      Of excellent dumb discourse.
PROSPERO [aside]                    Praise in departing.[6]
FRANCISCO    They vanished strangely.
40    SEBASTIAN                          No matter, since
      They have left their viands° behind, for we have stomachs.°    *food / good appetites*
      Will't please you taste of what is here?
ALONSO                          Not I.
GONZALO    Faith, sir, you need not fear. When we were boys,
      Who would believe that there were mountaineers°              *mountain dwellers*
45    Dewlapped like bulls, whose throats had hanging at 'em
      Wallets° of flesh? Or that there were such men                         *Pouches*
      Whose heads stood in their breasts? Which now we find
      Each putter-out of five for one[7] will bring us
      Good warrant of.
ALONSO [rising]    I will stand to and feed,°                             *begin eating*
50    Although my last—no matter, since I feel
      The best is past. Brother, my lord the Duke,
      Stand to, and do as we.
             [ALONSO, SEBASTIAN, *and* ANTONIO *approach the table.*]
             *Thunder and lightning. Enter* ARIEL [*descending*] *like a*
             *harpy,*[8] *claps his wings upon the table, and, with a*
             *quaint device,*° *the banquet vanishes*[9]          *an ingenious mechanism*
ARIEL    You are three men of sin, whom destiny—
      That hath to° instrument this lower world                                  *as its*
55    And what is in't—the never-surfeited sea
      Hath caused to belch up you, and on this island
      Where man doth not inhabit, you 'mongst men
      Being most unfit to live. I have made you mad,
      And even with suchlike valour[1] men hang and drown
      Their proper selves.°                                                       *Themselves*
             [ALONSO, SEBASTIAN, *and* ANTONIO *draw*][2]
60                        You fools! I and my fellows
      Are ministers of fate. The elements
      Of whom your swords are tempered[3] may as well
      Wound the loud winds, or with bemocked-at stabs
      Kill the still-closing[4] waters, as diminish
65    One dowl° that's in my plume.° My fellow ministers     *featherlet / plumage*
      Are like° invulnerable. If you could hurt,                              *similarly*

6. Reserve your praise until the end of the event.
7. A traveler could profit from a voyage by laying down a sum with a broker before departing and undertaking to bring back evidence of having reached his destination; if successful, he was repaid fivefold.
8. A mythological monster with a vulture's wings and claws and a woman's face. Aeneas and his companions encountered these harpies, who stole their meals and threatened to punish them with slow starvation. *Thunder and lightning*: Both spectacular and functional for disguising the mechanics of the "quaint device."
9. The simplest effective staging is by means of a rotating tabletop with the vessels of the banquet fixed to its surface. Leg-to-leg planks supporting the tabletop or a hang-ing cloth would conceal the vanished banquet. The harpy's wings would hide the mechanics from the audience, and clapping them would provide a visual distraction.
1. *suchlike valour*: fearlessness that comes from madness.
2. Ariel perhaps ascends beyond their reach here. Aeneas's companions, like Alonso here, similarly attempted to kill the harpies with swords.
3. Compounded and hardened. Metal was sometimes thought of as being compounded of earth and fire, here contrasted with winds and waters.
4. Self-healing, since they close immediately once parted.

Your swords are now too massy° for your strengths      *heavy*
And will not be uplifted.
       [ALONSO, SEBASTIAN, *and* ANTONIO *stand amazed*°]      *crazed; bewildered*
                But remember,
For that's my business to you, that you three
70 From Milan did supplant good Prospero;
Exposed unto the sea, which hath requit it,
Him and his innocent child; for which foul deed,
The powers, delaying not forgetting,[5] have
Incensed the seas and shores, yea, all the creatures,[6]
75 Against your peace. Thee of thy son, Alonso,
They have bereft, and do pronounce by me
Ling'ring perdition[7]—worse than any death
Can be at once—shall step by step attend
You and your ways; whose[8] wraths to guard you from—
80 Which here in this most desolate[9] isle else falls
Upon your heads—is nothing° but heart's sorrow      *there is no alternative*
And a clear life° ensuing.      *a life innocent of sin*
         *He [ascends and] vanishes[1] in thunder. Then, to soft*
         *music, enter the [spirits] again, and dance with mocks*
         *and mows,° and [they depart,] carrying out the table*      *grimaces*
PROSPERO    Bravely the figure of this harpy hast thou
Performed, my Ariel; a grace it had devouring.[2]
85 Of my instruction hast thou nothing bated°      *omitted*
In what thou hadst to say. So with good life[3]
And observation strange[4] my meaner ministers°      *lesser spirits*
Their several kinds° have done.° My high charms work,      *various roles / performed*
And these mine enemies are all knit up
90 In their distractions. They now are in my power;
And in these fits I leave them, while I visit
Young Ferdinand, whom they suppose is drowned,
And his and mine loved darling.          [*Exit*]
       [GONZALO, ADRIAN, *and* FRANCISCO *go towards the*
       *others*]
GONZALO    I'th' name of something holy, sir, why stand you
In this strange stare?
95 ALONSO               O, it is monstrous, monstrous!
Methought the billows spoke and told me of it,
The winds did sing it to me, and the thunder,
That deep and dreadful organ-pipe, pronounced
The name of Prosper. It did bass my trespass.[5]
100 Therefor° my son i'th' ooze is bedded, and      *For that*
I'll seek him deeper than e'er plummet sounded,
And with him there lie mudded.         *Exit*
SEBASTIAN             But one fiend at a time,
I'll fight their legions o'er.°      *from beginning to end*

---

5. Related to the proverb "God stays long but strikes at last."
6. Compare Genesis 1:21: "Then God created . . . everything living and moving."
7. Slow starvation; hell on earth of spiritual suffering. The phrase is first the object of "pronounce" and then the subject of "shall . . . attend."
8. Refers to "the powers" in line 73.
9. Joyless, wretched; barren, deserted.

1. Ariel is raised out of sight into the canopy.
2. In clapping his wings, Ariel has created the illusion of having devoured the banquet.
3. Convincingly; with vitality. *So:* In the same way.
4. Remarkable attention to the requirements of their parts, or instructions.
5. The thunder proclaimed my sin ("trespass") in a bass voice, or with a bass background; perhaps wordplay on the "utter baseness" of trespass.

ANTONIO                                    I'll be thy second.
                        *Exeunt* [SEBASTIAN *and* ANTONIO]
   GONZALO   All three of them are desperate.° Their great guilt,                    *in despair; reckless*
105   Like poison given to work° a great time after,                                              *take effect*
   Now 'gins to bite the spirits. I do beseech you
   That are of suppler joints, follow them swiftly,
   And hinder them from what this ecstasy°                                                   *madness*
   May now provoke them to.
   ADRIAN                                    Follow, I pray you.          *Exeunt*

## 4.1

*Enter* PROSPERO, FERDINAND, *and* MIRANDA

   PROSPERO [*to* FERDINAND]   If I have too austerely punished you,
   Your compensation makes amends, for I
   Have given you here a third[1] of mine own life—
   Or that for which I live—who° once again                                                  *whom*
5   I tender° to thy hand. All thy vexations                                                       *offer*
   Were but my trials of thy love, and thou
   Hast strangely° stood the test. Here, afore heaven,                                     *wonderfully*
   I ratify this my rich gift. O Ferdinand,
   Do not smile at me that I boast of her,
10   For thou shalt find she will outstrip all praise,
   And make it halt° behind her.                                                             *limp*
   FERDINAND                                    I do believe it
   Against an oracle.[2]
   PROSPERO   Then, as my gift and thine own acquisition
   Worthily purchased,° take my daughter. But                                              *Gained by effort*
15   If thou dost break her virgin-knot° before                                                  *virginity*
   All sanctimonious° ceremonies may                                                         *holy*
   With full and holy rite be ministered,
   No sweet aspersion° shall the heavens let fall                                           *shower of grace*
   To make this contract grow; but barren hate,
20   Sour-eyed disdain, and discord, shall bestrew
   The union of your bed with weeds[3] so loathly
   That you shall hate it both. Therefore take heed,
   As Hymen's[4] lamps shall light you.
   FERDINAND                                    As I hope
   For quiet days, fair issue,° and long life                                               *children*
25   With such love as 'tis now, the murkiest den,°                                              *cave*
   The most opportune place, the strong'st suggestion°                                     *temptation*
   Our worser genius can,[5] shall never melt
   Mine honour into lust to take away
   The edge° of that day's celebration;                                                     *unblunted desire*
30   When I shall think or° Phoebus' steeds are foundered[6]                                    *either*
   Or night kept chained below.
   PROSPERO                                    Fairly spoke.

---

**4.1**
1. *Miranda.* The usual poetic conceit was a half; commentators variously conjecture the other third to be his
dukedom, his books, or his late wife.
2. *I . . . oracle:* I would believe it even if an oracle said
otherwise.
3. Weeds in place of the flowers traditionally strewn on
the marriage bed; wordplay on both "marriage bed" and

"seed-bed."
4. Classical god of marriage.
5. Is capable of. *worser genius:* evil spirit corresponding
to a guardian angel.
6. Collapsed and made lame. *Phoebus' steeds:* the mythological horses that drew the chariot of the sun. Ferdinand
anticipates that on his wedding day he will in his impatience think that the night will never come.

Sit, then, and talk with her. She is thine own.
[FERDINAND *and* MIRANDA *sit and talk together*]
What,° Ariel, my industrious servant Ariel!                            *Now, then*
        *Enter* ARIEL
ARIEL   What would my potent master? Here I am.
35  PROSPERO   Thou and thy meaner° fellows your last service          *lesser*
    Did worthily perform, and I must use you
    In such another trick. Go bring the rabble,[7]
    O'er whom I give thee power, here to this place.
    Incite them to quick motion, for I must
40  Bestow upon the eyes of this young couple
    Some vanity[8] of mine art. It is my promise,
    And they expect it from me.
ARIEL                          Presently?°                             *At once*
PROSPERO   Ay, with a twink.[9]
ARIEL             Before you can say 'Come' and 'Go',
45            And breathe twice, and cry 'So, so',
              Each one tripping on his toe
              Will be here with mop and mow.[1]
              Do you love me, master? No?
PROSPERO   Dearly, my delicate Ariel. Do not approach
    Till thou dost hear me call.
50  ARIEL                    Well; I conceive.°      *Exit*            *understand*
PROSPERO [*to* FERDINAND]   Look thou be true.[2] Do not give dalliance
    Too much the rein.[3] The strongest oaths are straw
    To th' fire i'th' blood. Be more abstemious,
    Or else, good night your vow.
FERDINAND                        I warrant you, sir,
55  The white cold virgin snow upon my heart
    Abates the ardour of my liver.[4]
PROSPERO                          Well.—
    Now come, my Ariel! Bring a corollary°                            *surplus*
    Rather than want° a spirit. Appear, and pertly.°                 *lack / briskly*
        *Soft music*
    [*To* FERDINAND *and* MIRANDA] No tongue, all eyes! Be silent.
        *Enter* IRIS[5]
60  IRIS   Ceres, most bounteous lady, thy rich leas[6]
    Of wheat, rye, barley, vetches,[7] oats, and peas;
    Thy turfy mountains where live nibbling sheep,
    And flat meads° thatched with stover,[8] them to keep;           *meadows*
    Thy banks with peonied and twillèd[9] brims
65  Which spongy° April at thy hest betrims[1]                       *wet*
    To make cold nymphs chaste crowns; and thy broom-groves,[2]
    Whose shadow the dismissèd bachelor° loves,                      *rejected suitor*

---

7. Troupe of lesser spirits: *trick:* theatrical device, or clever artifice.
8. Trifle; conceit; illusion; display.
9. In the twinkling of an eye.
1. With derisive and grimacing gestures.
2. Take care that you remain faithful to your promise. Prospero may have caught the lovers just indulging in dalliance.
3. To "give the rein" is to make a horse gallop.
4. *The . . . liver:* Virgin snow lies on his heart because he has remained chaste, never having given in to his ardent liver. The liver was held to be the seat of passion.

5. Goddess of the rainbow and messenger of Juno; her apparel is in the colors of the rainbow, and she wears "saffron wings" (line 78).
6. Arable land. Ceres was the Roman goddess of agriculture and generative nature.
7. Pealike plants grown for fodder.
8. Hay for winter fodder.
9. Reinforced with entwined branches to prevent riverbank erosion. *peonied:* covered with peonies.
1. Adorns with flowers; recalls the colloquial "April showers bring forth May flowers."
2. Thickets of gorse, yellow-flowered shrubs. *cold:* chaste.

Being lass-lorn; thy pole-clipped vineyard,³
And thy sea-marge,° sterile and rocky-hard,          *seashore*
70  Where thou thyself dost air:° the Queen o'th' Sky,°      *take fresh air / Juno*
Whose wat'ry arch° and messenger am I,              *rainbow*
Bids thee leave these, and with her sovereign grace
          JUNO [*appears in the air*]⁴
Here on this grass-plot,⁵ in this very place,
To come and sport.—Her peacocks fly amain.⁶
75  Approach, rich Ceres, her to entertain.
          *Enter* [ARIEL *as*] CERES⁷
CERES  Hail, many-coloured messenger, that ne'er
Dost disobey the wife of Jupiter;°                  *Juno*
Who with thy saffron wings upon my flowers
Diffusest honey-drops, refreshing showers,
80  And with each end of thy blue bow dost crown
My bosky⁸ acres and my unshrubbed down,
Rich scarf⁹ to my proud earth. Why hath thy queen
Summoned me hither to this short-grassed green?
IRIS  A contract of true love to celebrate,
85  And some donation freely to estate°               *bestow*
On the blest lovers.
CERES              Tell me, heavenly bow,°            *rainbow*
If Venus or her son,¹ as° thou dost know,           *as far as*
Do now attend the Queen. Since they did plot
The means that dusky Dis² my daughter got,
90  Her and her blind boy's scandalled° company       *scandalous; notorious*
I have forsworn.
IRIS                Of her society
Be not afraid. I met her deity
Cutting the clouds towards Paphos,³ and her son
Dove-drawn⁴ with her. Here thought they to have done
95  Some wanton charm upon⁵ this man and maid,
Whose vows are that no bed-right⁶ shall be paid
Till Hymen's torch be lighted⁷—but in vain.
Mars's hot minion° is returned again.               *lover; Venus*
Her waspish-headed⁸ son has broke his arrows,
100  Swears he will shoot no more, but play with sparrows,⁹
And be a boy right out.°                            *an ordinary boy*
          [*Music.* JUNO *descends to the stage*]¹
CERES              Highest queen of state,
Great Juno, comes; I know her by her gait.°         *majestic bearing*

---

3. Vineyard with vines embracing, twined around, their supporting poles; pruned vineyard. "Vineyard" was pronounced as three syllables. *lass-lorn:* abandoned by the girl he wooed.
4. Juno was queen of the heavens and goddess of women, held to protect marriages and preside over childbirth. Her chair is ornamented with a peacock motif. She descends by a "flight" mechanism to a position suspended in the air above the stage. Music may be played. Juno remains in view aloft until line 101. If, however, F's direction here is misplaced, she may not appear until line 101.
5. Compare "this short-grassed green" (line 83) and "this green land" (line 130): a green carpet on the acting area is indicated.
6. In haste. Peacocks, sacred to Juno, drew her chariot.
7. Her part is probably played by Ariel (see line 167).
8. Covered with bushes and thickets.
9. Ornamental and hung across the body rather than

around the neck.
1. Cupid, proverbially blind.
2. King of the underworld in classical mythology. Venus and her son Cupid made him fall in love with Ceres' daughter Proserpine, whom he abducted (Ovid, *Metamorphoses* 5.395ff.).
3. City in Cyprus: associated with Venus.
4. Doves were sacred to Venus and drew her chariot.
5. *done . . . upon:* cast a lustful spell upon.
6. Right to consummate the marriage; also suggesting a rite, as in line 17.
7. Until the wedding ceremony is performed.
8. Peevish, irritable, and with arrows like the wasp's sting.
9. Sparrows were associated with Venus because they were proverbially lustful.
1. This completes Juno's flight to the stage; again, music may be played.

JUNO   How does my bounteous sister? Go with me
　　　To bless this twain, that they may prosperous be,
105　　And honoured in their issue.
　　　　　　　[CERES *joins* JUNO, *and*] *they sing*[2]
　JUNO　　　　Honour, riches, marriage-blessing,
　　　　　　　Long continuance and increasing,
　　　　　　　Hourly joys be still° upon you!　　　　　　　　　*always*
　　　　　　　Juno sings her blessings on you.
110　CERES　　Earth's increase, and foison° plenty,　　　　　　*abundance*
　　　　　　　Barns and garners° never empty,　　　　　　　　*granaries*
　　　　　　　Vines with clust'ring bunches growing,
　　　　　　　Plants with goodly burden bowing;
　　　　　　　Spring come to you at the farthest,
115　　　　　　In the very end of harvest.[3]
　　　　　　　Scarcity and want shall shun you,
　　　　　　　Ceres' blessing so is on you.
　FERDINAND　This is a most majestic vision, and
　　　Harmonious charmingly.[4] May I be bold°　　　　　　　*Would I be right*
　　　To think these spirits?
120　PROSPERO　　　　　　　Spirits, which by mine art
　　　I have from their confines[5] called to enact
　　　My present fancies.
　FERDINAND　　　　　　　Let me live here ever!
　　　So rare a wondered° father and a wise　　　　　　*endowed with wonders*
　　　Makes this place paradise.
　　　　　　JUNO *and* CERES *whisper, and send* IRIS *on employment*
　　　PROSPERO　　　　　　　　Sweet° now, silence.　　　　　　*Softly*
125　Juno and Ceres whisper seriously.
　　　There's something else to do. Hush, and be mute,
　　　Or else our spell is marred.
　IRIS　　You nymphs called naiads of the wind'ring[6] brooks,
　　　With your sedged crowns° and ever-harmless looks,　　*garlands of reeds*
130　Leave your crisp channels, and on this green land
　　　Answer your summons; Juno does command.
　　　Come, temperate nymphs, and help to celebrate
　　　A contract of true love. Be not too late.
　　　　　　*Enter certain nymphs*
　　　You sunburned sicklemen,° of August weary,　　　　　*harvesters*
135　Come hither from the furrow and be merry;
　　　Make holiday, your rye-straw hats put on,
　　　And these fresh nymphs encounter every one
　　　In country footing.
　　　　　　*Enter certain reapers, properly habited.*[7] *They join with*
　　　　　　*the nymphs in a graceful dance; towards the end whereof*
　　　　　　PROSPERO *starts suddenly, and speaks*
　PROSPERO [*aside*]　I had forgot that foul conspiracy
140　Of the beast Caliban and his confederates
　　　Against my life. The minute of their plot

2. Ceres and Juno might be raised together in the flight apparatus and sing suspended above the stage. They would then vanish (line 142 stage direction) by being raised into the heavens.
3. Let spring return immediately after harvest, without any intervening winter. (In Greek mythology, winter was originally caused by Ceres abandoning the earth in search of Proserpine.)
4. Delightfully; magically; harmoniously.
5. Regions of dwelling. Word is accented on the second syllable.
6. Perhaps a conflation of "wandering" and "winding." The naiads were mythical river nymphs.
7. Either properly or finely dressed.

Is almost come. [*To the spirits*] Well done! Avoid;° no more!                *Begone*
   *To a strange, hollow, and confused noise, the [spirits in*
   *the pageant] heavily vanish.*[8]
   [FERDINAND *and* MIRANDA *rise*]
FERDINAND [*to* MIRANDA]    This is strange. Your father's in some passion
   That works° him strongly.                                               *agitates*
MIRANDA                  Never till this day
145   Saw I him touched with anger so distempered.°                *troubled; distracted*
PROSPERO    You do look, my son, in a moved sort,°                  *disturbed manner*
   As if you were dismayed. Be cheerful, sir.
   Our revels[9] now are ended. These our actors,
   As I foretold you,° were all spirits, and                            *told you before*
150   Are melted into air, into thin air;
   And like the baseless fabric[1] of this vision,
   The cloud-capped towers, the gorgeous palaces,
   The solemn temples, the great globe[2] itself,
   Yea, all which it inherit,[3] shall dissolve;
155   And, like this insubstantial pageant faded,
   Leave not a rack° behind. We are such stuff                       *wisp of cloud*
   As dreams are made on,° and our little life                             *of*
   Is rounded[4] with a sleep. Sir, I am vexed.
   Bear with my weakness. My old brain is troubled.
160   Be not disturbed with my infirmity.
   If you be pleased, retire into my cell,
   And there repose. A turn or two I'll walk
   To still my beating mind.
FERDINAND *and* MIRANDA    We wish your peace.
                *Exeunt* [FERDINAND *and* MIRANDA]
PROSPERO    Come with a thought![5] I thank thee, Ariel. Come!
   *Enter* ARIEL
ARIEL    Thy thoughts I cleave to. What's thy pleasure?
165 PROSPERO                 Spirit,
   We must prepare to meet with Caliban.
ARIEL    Ay, my commander. When I presented[6] Ceres
   I thought to have told thee of it, but I feared
   Lest I might anger thee.
170 PROSPERO    Say again: where didst thou leave these varlets?°          *ruffians*
ARIEL    I told you, sir, they were red-hot with drinking;
   So full of valour that they smote the air
   For breathing in their faces, beat the ground
   For kissing of their feet; yet always bending°                        *aiming*
175   Towards their project. Then I beat my tabor,°                     *side drum*
   At which like unbacked° colts they pricked their ears,           *never-ridden*
   Advanced° their eyelids, lifted up their noses                        *Opened*
   As° they smelt music. So I charmed their ears                        *As if*
   That calf-like they my lowing° followed, through                    *mooing*
180   Toothed briars, sharp furzes, pricking gorse,° and thorns,    *prickly shrubs*
   Which entered their frail shins. At last I left them
   I'th' filthy-mantled[7] pool beyond your cell,

---

8. Sorrowfully depart (probably not implying a trick of staging).
9. Entertainment, in both festive and theatrical senses.
1. An edifice or substance without foundations; insubstantial, alluding to buildings in masque scenery.
2. World; also with a passing allusion to the Globe Theatre.

3. All who come into possession of it.
4. Rounded off; surrounded; or, possibly, crowned.
5. Come as fast as thought, a colloquial simile.
6. Acted; produced the masque of; introduced while playing Iris.
7. Covered with filthy scum.

There dancing up to th' chins, that° the foul lake          *so that*
O'er-stunk[8] their feet.
PROSPERO                    This was well done, my bird.°          *chick; dear*
185 Thy shape invisible retain thou still.
The trumpery° in my house, go bring it hither          *cheap goods*
For stale° to catch these thieves.          *decoy; bait*
ARIEL                          I go, I go.          *Exit*
PROSPERO    A devil, a born devil, on whose nature
Nurture can never stick; on whom my pains,
190 Humanely taken, all, all lost, quite lost,
And, as with age his body uglier grows,
So his mind cankers.° I will plague them all,          *festers*
Even to roaring.
          *Enter* ARIEL, *laden with glistening apparel, etc.*
          Come, hang them on this lime.[9]
          [ARIEL *hangs up the apparel. Exeunt* PROSPERO *and*
                                                        ARIEL]
          *Enter* CALIBAN, STEFANO, *and* TRINCULO, *all wet*
CALIBAN    Pray you, tread softly, that the blind mole may
195 Not hear a foot fall. We now are near his cell.
STEFANO    Monster, your fairy, which you say is a harmless fairy,
has done little better than played the Jack° with us.          *knave; will o' the-wisp*
TRINCULO    Monster, I do smell° all horse-piss, at which my          *smell of*
nose is in great indignation.
200 STEFANO    So is mine. Do you hear, monster? If I should take a
displeasure against you, look you—
TRINCULO    Thou wert but a lost monster.
CALIBAN    Good my lord, give me thy favour still.
Be patient, for the prize I'll bring thee to
205 Shall hoodwink[1] this mischance. Therefore speak softly.
All's hushed as midnight yet.
TRINCULO    Ay, but to lose our bottles in the pool!
STEFANO    There is not only disgrace and dishonour in that,
monster, but an infinite loss.
210 TRINCULO    That's more to me than my wetting. Yet this is your
harmless fairy, monster.
STEFANO    I will fetch off[2] my bottle, though I be o'er ears° for          *drowned*
my labour.
CALIBAN    Prithee, my king, be quiet. Seest thou here;
215 This is the mouth o'th' cell. No noise, and enter.
Do that good mischief which may make this island
Thine own for ever, and I thy Caliban
For aye° thy foot-licker.          *ever*
STEFANO                          Give me thy hand.
I do begin to have bloody thoughts.
220 TRINCULO [*seeing the apparel*]    O King Stefano, O peer! O wor-
thy Stefano, look what a wardrobe here is for thee![3]
CALIBAN    Let it alone, thou fool, it is but trash.
TRINCULO [*putting on a gown*]    O ho, monster, we know what
belongs to a frippery!° O King Stefano!          *old-clothes shop*

---

8. Made smelly; smelled worse than.
9. Lime tree, indicating a stage property.
1. Blind with a hood, as was done to pacify a hawk—
hence, make harmless; also, put out of sight.

2. Recover; rescue; drink off.
3. Recalling "King Stephen was and a worthy peer, / His
breeches cost him but a crown," a popular ballad about
King Stephen, sung in part in *Othello* 2.3.77ff.

| | | |
|---|---|---|
| 225 | STEFANO Put off that gown, Trinculo. By this hand, I'll have that gown. | |
| | TRINCULO Thy grace shall have it. | |
| | CALIBAN The dropsy⁴ drown this fool! What do you mean | |
| | To dote thus on such luggage?° Let't alone, | *encumbrances* |
| 230 | And do the murder first. If he awake, | |
| | From toe to crown he'll fill our skins with pinches, | |
| | Make us° strange stuff. | *Turn us into* |
| | STEFANO Be you quiet, monster.—Mistress lime, is not this my | |
| | jerkin?° Now is the jerkin under the line.⁵ Now, jerkin, you are | *leather jacket* |
| 235 | like to lose your hair and prove a bald jerkin.⁶ | |

[STEFANO *and* TRINCULO *take garments*]

TRINCULO  Do, do! We steal by line and level,⁷ an't like° your       *if it please*
grace.

STEFANO  I thank thee for that jest. Here's a garment for't. Wit
shall not go unrewarded while I am king of this country. 'Steal
240    by line and level' is an excellent pass of pate.⁸ There's another
garment for't.

TRINCULO  Monster, come, put some lime upon your fingers,⁹
and away with the rest.

CALIBAN  I will have none on't. We shall lose our time,
245    And all be turned to barnacles,¹ or to apes
With foreheads villainous° low.       *wretchedly*

STEFANO  Monster, lay to° your fingers. Help to bear this away       *apply*
where my hogshead of wine is, or I'll turn you out of my kingdom. Go to, carry this.

250  TRINCULO  And this.

STEFANO  Ay, and this.

[*They load* CALIBAN *with apparel.*]
*A noise of hunters heard. Enter divers° spirits in shape of*       *various*
*dogs and hounds, hunting them about;* PROSPERO *and*
ARIEL *setting them on*

PROSPERO  Hey, Mountain, hey!

ARIEL                              Silver! There it goes, Silver!

PROSPERO  Fury, Fury! There, Tyrant, there! Hark, hark!
[*Exeunt* STEFANO, TRINCULO, *and* CALIBAN, *pursued by spirits*]
[*To* ARIEL]  Go, charge my goblins that they grind their joints
255    With dry convulsions,² shorten up their sinews
With agèd cramps, and more pinch-spotted³ make them
Than pard or cat o'mountain.⁴
                    [*Cries within*]

ARIEL                              Hark, they roar!

PROSPERO  Let them be hunted soundly.° At this hour       *thoroughly*
Lies at my mercy all mine enemies.

---

4. A disease characterized by the accumulation of fluid
in connective tissue.
5. Below the lime tree; south of the equator; below the
waist. Also a possible allusion to the proverb "Thou hast
stricken the ball under the line," meaning "You have
cheated." Stefano has taken the jerkin from the lime tree.
6. Baldness caused either through tropical disease or by
sailors who customarily shaved the heads of passengers
when they crossed the line of the equator for the first
time. "Under the [waist]line" (line 234) could also be an
allusion to baldness from syphilis.
7. An idiomatic expression for "properly, by the rules"—
literally, "by plumb line and carpenter's level"; also pun-

ning on "lime." *Do, do*: an expression of approval.
8. Thrust of wit (fencing term).
9. Be "lime-fingered," sticky-fingered (alluding to bird-
lime, a gluey substance used to catch birds).
1. Barnacle geese, also known as "tree geese" and supposed to begin life as barnacle shells.
2. Afflicting "sapless," or old, people.
3. Spotted with bruises from pinches. *agèd cramps*: the
convulsions of old age.
4. Both terms are synonymous with "leopard"; the second
is from Jeremiah 13:23: "May a man of Ind change his
skin, and the cat of the mountain her spots?" (Bishops'
Bible).

260 Shortly shall all my labours end, and thou
Shalt have the air at freedom. For a little,
Follow, and do me service.                          *Exeunt*

### 5.1

*Enter* PROSPERO, *in his magic robes, and* ARIEL

PROSPERO   Now does my project gather to a head.[1]
My charms crack not, my spirits obey, and time
Goes upright with his carriage.[2] How's the day?
ARIEL   On the sixth hour; at which time, my lord,
You said our work should cease.
5 PROSPERO                           I did say so
When first I raised the tempest. Say, my spirit,
How fares the King and's° followers?                          *and his*
ARIEL                                 Confined together
In the same fashion as you gave in charge,
Just as you left them; all prisoners, sir,
10 In the lime-grove which weather-fends[3] your cell.
They cannot budge till your release.° The King,          *you release them*
His brother, and yours, abide all three distracted,°          *out of their wits*
And the remainder mourning over them,
Brimful of sorrow and dismay; but chiefly
15 Him that you termed, sir, the good old lord Gonzalo:
His tears run down his beard like winter's drops
From eaves of reeds.° Your charm so strongly works 'em          *thatched roofs*
That if you now beheld them your affections°                    *feelings*
Would become tender.
PROSPERO                  Dost thou think so, spirit?
ARIEL   Mine would, sir, were I human.
20 PROSPERO                                   And mine shall.
Hast thou, which art but air, a touch,° a feeling                    *sense*
Of their afflictions, and shall not myself,
One of their kind, that relish all as sharply
Passion as they,[4] be kindlier[5] moved than thou art?
25 Though with their high° wrongs I am struck to th' quick,          *great*
Yet with my nobler reason 'gainst my fury
Do I take part.° The rarer action is                                    *side*
In virtue than in vengeance. They being penitent,
The sole drift of my purpose doth extend
30 Not a frown further. Go release them, Ariel.
My charms I'll break, their senses I'll restore,
And they shall be themselves.
ARIEL                              I'll fetch them, sir.          *Exit*
[PROSPERO *draws a circle with his staff*][6]
PROSPERO[7]   Ye elves of hills, brooks, standing lakes and groves,
And ye that on the sands with printless foot
35 Do chase the ebbing Neptune, and do fly him
When he comes back; you demi-puppets[8] that

---

5.1
1. Draw to its fulfillment. "Project" suggests an alchemical projection or "experiment."
2. Because his carriage, or burden, is now light.
3. Which protects from the weather.
4. *that . . . they:* who feel as much strong emotion as they do.
5. More tenderly; more naturally.
6. The original text does not indicate when the circle is drawn. Other possibilities are at the beginning of the scene or before the entry at line 57.
7. Prospero's speech closely follows Ovid's *Metamorphoses* 7.265–77, in Arthur Golding's translation (1567); the speaker in Ovid is the sorceress Medea, who uses her witchcraft to vengeful ends.
8. Puppets; elves; quasi puppets.

By moonshine do the green sour ringlets[9] make
Whereof the ewe not bites; and you whose pastime
Is to make midnight° mushrooms, that rejoice                    *springing up overnight*
40   To hear the solemn curfew;[1] by whose aid,
Weak masters[2] though ye be, I have bedimmed
The noontide sun, called forth the mutinous winds,
And 'twixt the green sea and the azured vault°                  *the sky*
Set roaring war—to the dread rattling thunder
45   Have I given fire, and rifted° Jove's stout oak              *split*
With his own bolt;° the strong-based promontory                *lightning bolt*
Have I made shake, and by the spurs° plucked up                *roots*
The pine and cedar; graves at my command
Have waked their sleepers, oped, and let 'em forth
50   By my so potent art. But this rough[3] magic
I here abjure. And when I have required°                        *summoned*
Some heavenly music—which even now I do—
To work mine end upon their senses that°                        *the senses of whom*
This airy[4] charm is for, I'll break my staff,
55   Bury it certain° fathoms in the earth,                       *several*
And deeper than did ever plummet sound
I'll drown my book.
            *Solemn music. Here enters [first]* ARIEL *[invisible]; then*
            ALONSO, *with a frantic gesture, attended by* GONZALO;
            SEBASTIAN *and* ANTONIO, *in like manner, attended by*
            ADRIAN *and* FRANCISCO. *They all enter the circle which*
            PROSPERO *had made, and there stand charmed; which*
            PROSPERO *observing, speaks*
*[To* ALONSO*]*[5] A solemn air,° and° the best comforter        *song / which is*
To an unsettled fancy,° cure thy brains,                         *imagination*
Now useless, boiled within thy skull.
60   *[To* SEBASTIAN *and* ANTONIO*]*[6]          There stand,
For you are spell-stopped.—
Holy Gonzalo, honourable man,
Mine eyes, ev'n sociable° to the show° of thine,                *sympathetic / appearance*
Fall fellowly drops. *[Aside]* The charm dissolves apace,
65   And as the morning steals upon the night,
Melting the darkness, so their rising senses
Begin to chase the ignorant fumes[7] that mantle°               *envelop*
Their clearer° reason.—O good Gonzalo,                          *growing clearer*
My true preserver, and a loyal sir°                             *gentleman*
70   To him thou follow'st, I will pay° thy graces               *requite*
Home° both in word and deed.—Most cruelly                       *Fully*
Didst thou, Alonso, use me and my daughter.
Thy brother was a furtherer° in the act.—                       *an accomplice*
Thou art pinched° for't now, Sebastian.                         *tortured; afflicted*
*[To* ANTONIO*]*                          Flesh and blood,
75   You, brother mine, that entertained ambition,
Expelled remorse and nature,[8] whom,° with Sebastian—          *who*

---

9. Fairy rings: distinctive circles of grass supposed to be
caused by dancing fairies but actually caused by mushrooms.
1. The bell rung at nightfall, indicating the time when
spirits are abroad.
2. Ineffectual when acting independently; without supernatural power; subordinate spirits.
3. Violent; discordant; crudely approximate.

4. Wrought by spirits of the air.
5. Prospero remains invisible and inaudible to Alonso
and his party until he greets Alonso at line 108.
6. Or perhaps to all the shipwrecked lords.
7. Fogs of ignorance; the image is of the sun ("rising
senses") dissipating morning mist.
8. Pity and brotherly affection.

Whose inward pinches therefore are most strong,—
Would here have killed your king, I do forgive thee,
Unnatural though thou art. [*Aside*] Their understanding
80  Begins to swell,° and the approaching tide                    *(as does a tide)*
Will shortly fill the reasonable shores
That now lie foul and muddy. Not° one of them                   *There is not*
That yet looks on me, or would know me.—Ariel,
Fetch me the hat and rapier[9] in my cell.
85  I will discase° me, and myself present                        *undress*
As I was sometime Milan.[1] Quickly, spirit!
Thou shalt ere long be free.
      ARIEL *sings and helps to attire him* [*as Duke of Milan*]
   ARIEL  Where the bee sucks, there suck I:
     In a cowslip's bell I lie;
90       There I couch when owls do cry.
     On the bat's back I do fly
     After summer merrily.
     Merrily, merrily shall I live now
     Under the blossom that hangs on the bough.
95       Merrily, merrily shall I live now
     Under the blossom that hangs on the bough.
   PROSPERO  Why, that's my dainty Ariel! I shall miss thee,
But yet thou shalt have freedom.—So, so, so.[2]—
To the King's ship, invisible as thou art!
100  There shalt thou find the mariners asleep
Under the hatches. The Master and the Boatswain
Being awake, enforce them to this place,
And presently,° I prithee.                                      *immediately*
   ARIEL  I drink the air before me, and return
105  Or ere° your pulse twice beat.      *Exit*   *Before*
   GONZALO  All torment, trouble, wonder, and amazement°    *bewilderment*
Inhabits here. Some heavenly power guide us
Out of this fearful° country!                                   *fearsome*
   PROSPERO       Behold, sir King,
The wrongèd Duke of Milan, Prospero.
110  For more assurance that a living prince
Does now speak to thee, I embrace thy body;
And to thee and thy company I bid
A hearty welcome.
     [*He embraces* ALONSO]
   ALONSO      Whe'er° thou beest he or no,    *Whether*
Or some enchanted trifle[3] to abuse° me,                       *delude; maltreat*
115  As late I have been, I not know. Thy pulse
Beats as of flesh and blood; and since I saw thee
Th'affliction of my mind amends, with which
I fear a madness held me. This must crave°—                    *requires, as explanation*
An if this be at all[4]—a most strange story.
120  Thy dukedom[5] I resign, and do entreat

---

9. Elements of normal aristocratic dress.
1. Formerly, when Duke of Milan.
2. Prospero arranges his attire approvingly.
3. With a suggestion of the old sense of "trifle" as "decep-

tion."
4. If this is really happening.
5. Alonso's rights of homage and tribute from it.

Thou pardon me my wrongs. But how should Prospero
Be living and be here?

PROSPERO [to GONZALO]     First, noble friend,
Let me embrace thine age,° whose honour cannot                    *old body*
Be measured or confined.
     [*He embraces* GONZALO]

GONZALO                              Whether this be
Or be not, I'll not swear.

125  PROSPERO                         You do yet taste
Some subtleties⁶ o'th' isle that will not let you
Believe things certain.—Welcome, my friends all.
     [*Aside to* SEBASTIAN *and* ANTONIO]
But you, my brace° of lords, were I so minded,                     *pair*
I here could pluck his highness' frown upon you

130  And justify° you traitors. At this time                           *prove*
I will tell no tales.

SEBASTIAN [*to* ANTONIO] The devil speaks in him.

PROSPERO                                        No.
     [*To* ANTONIO]     For you, most wicked sir, whom° to call brother    *who*
Would even infect my mouth, I do forgive
Thy rankest fault, all of them, and require

135  My dukedom of thee, which perforce° I know                        *necessarily*
Thou must restore.

ALONSO                       If thou beest Prospero,
Give us particulars of thy preservation,
How thou hast met us here, whom three hours since
Were wrecked upon this shore, where I have lost—

140  How sharp the point of this remembrance is!—
My dear son Ferdinand.

PROSPERO                         I am woe° for't, sir.                 *I grieve*

ALONSO     Irreparable is the loss, and patience
Says it is past her cure.

PROSPERO                       I rather think
You have not sought her help, of° whose soft grace°               *by / mercy*

145  For the like loss I have her sovereign aid,
And rest myself content.

ALONSO                         You the like loss?

PROSPERO     As great to me as late;° and supportable              *recent*
To make the dear loss⁷ have I means much weaker
Than you may call to comfort you, for I
Have lost my daughter.⁸

150  ALONSO                         A daughter?
O heavens, that they were living both in Naples,
The king and queen there! That they were, I wish
Myself were mudded in that oozy bed
Where my son lies. When did you lose your daughter?

155  PROSPERO     In this last tempest. I perceive these lords
At this encounter do so much admire°                              *wonder*
That they devour their reason,⁹ and scarce think
Their eyes do offices of truth,° these words                      *function accurately*

---

6. *You . . . subtleties:* You still experience some of the illusions. "Subtleties" were also sweet confections shaped like castles, temples, beasts, allegorical figures, etc., and arranged like a pageant.
7. *supportable . . . loss:* in order to make the heartfelt loss bearable.
8. Prospero apparently means that Alonso still has a child, his daughter Claribel, to comfort him.
9. "Reason" has the additional sense of "discourse"; hence the phrase is an extension of "swallow their words."

Are natural breath. But howsoe'er you have
160 Been jostled from your senses, know for certain
That I am Prospero, and that very Duke
Which was thrust forth of Milan, who most strangely,
Upon this shore where you were wrecked, was landed
To be the lord on't. No more yet of this,
165 For 'tis a chronicle of day by day,
Not a relation for a breakfast, nor
Befitting this first meeting. Welcome, sir.
This cell's my court. Here have I few attendants,
And subjects none abroad.¹ Pray you, look in.
170 My dukedom since you have given me again,
I will requite you with as good a thing;
At least bring forth a wonder to content ye
As much as me my dukedom.

> *Here* PROSPERO *discovers*² FERDINAND *and* MIRANDA,
> *playing at chess*

MIRANDA     Sweet lord, you play me false.°                                    *trick me*
175 FERDINAND     No, my dearest love,
I would not for the world.
MIRANDA     Yes, for a score of kingdoms you should wrangle,
An I would call it fair play.³
ALONSO                                    If this prove
A vision of the island, one dear son
Shall I twice lose.
180 SEBASTIAN                    A most high miracle.
FERDINAND [*coming forward*]     Though the seas threaten, they are merciful.
I have cursed them without cause.

> [*He kneels*]

ALONSO                                    Now all the blessings
Of a glad father compass thee about.°                                    *surround you*
Arise and say how thou cam'st here.

> [FERDINAND *rises*]

MIRANDA [*coming forward*]                    O wonder!
185 How many goodly creatures are there here!
How beauteous mankind is! O brave new world
That has such people in't!
PROSPERO                                    'Tis new to thee.
ALONSO [*to* FERDINAND]     What is this maid with whom thou
          wast at play?
Your eld'st° acquaintance cannot be three hours.                                    *longest*
190 Is she the goddess that hath severed us,
And brought us thus together?
FERDINAND                                    Sir, she is mortal;
But by immortal providence she's mine.
I chose her when I could not ask my father
For his advice, nor thought I had one. She
195 Is daughter to this famous Duke of Milan,
Of whom so often I have heard renown,
But never saw before; of whom I have

---

1. Elsewhere about the island; beyond the cell.
2. Reveals by drawing back a curtain hanging in front of the discovery space.
3. *for . . . play*: if I would not accuse you of cheating, you would quarrel for twenty kingdoms. Other editions read "And" for "An" (i.e., you could quarrel for twenty kingdoms, and I would still call it fair play.)

Received a second life; and second father
This lady makes him to me.

ALONSO                    I am hers.[4]

200 But O, how oddly will it sound, that I
Must ask my child° forgiveness!                          *(Miranda)*

PROSPERO                    There, sir, stop.
Let us not burden our remembrance with
A heaviness° that's gone.                                *sorrow*

GONZALO                    I have inly wept,
Or should have spoke ere this. Look down, you gods,
205 And on this couple drop a blessèd crown,
For it is you that have chalked forth° the way          *marked out*
Which brought us hither.

ALONSO                    I say amen, Gonzalo.

GONZALO    Was Milan° thrust from Milan, that his issue   *the Duke of Milan*
Should become kings of Naples? O rejoice
210 Beyond a common joy! And set it down
With gold on lasting pillars:[5] in one voyage
Did Claribel her husband find at Tunis,
And Ferdinand her brother found a wife
Where he himself was lost; Prospero his dukedom
215 In a poor isle; and all of us ourselves,
When no man was his own.[6]

ALONSO *[to* FERDINAND *and* MIRANDA*]* Give me your hands.
Let grief and sorrow still° embrace his heart           *always*
That° doth not wish you joy.                             *Who*

GONZALO                    Be it so! Amen!

*Enter* ARIEL, *with the* MASTER *and* BOATSWAIN *amazedly*
*following*

O look, sir, look, sir, here is more of us!
220 I prophesied if a gallows were on land
This fellow could not drown. *[To the* BOATSWAIN*]* Now,
blasphemy,°                                              *blasphemer*
That swear'st grace o'erboard: not an oath on shore?
Hast thou no mouth by land? What is the news?

BOATSWAIN    The best news is that we have safely found
225 Our King and company. The next, our ship,
Which but three glasses° since we gave out° split,      *hourglasses / declared*
Is tight and yare[7] and bravely rigged, as when
We first put out to sea.

ARIEL *[aside to* PROSPERO*]* Sir, all this service
Have I done since I went.

PROSPERO *[aside to* ARIEL*]*    My tricksy° spirit!       *capricious; neat*
230 ALONSO    These are not natural events; they strengthen°  *increase*
From strange to stranger. Say, how came you hither?

BOATSWAIN    If I did think, sir, I were well awake
I'd strive to tell you. We were dead of ° sleep,        *with*
And—how we know not—all clapped° under hatches,         *shut up*
235 Where but even now, with strange and several° noises   *various*
Of roaring, shrieking, howling, jingling chains,
And more diversity of sounds, all horrible,

4. I will be her second father, Alonso's assent to the betrothal.
5. Suggesting, perhaps, the triumphal arches commissioned to celebrate notable occasions.
6. When we all had lost our senses.
7. Is sound and ready to sail.

We were awaked; straightway at liberty;
Where we in all her trim freshly beheld
240 Our royal, good, and gallant ship, our Master
Cap'ring to eye° her. On° a trice, so please you,          *Dancing to see / In*
Even in a dream, were we divided from them,
And were brought moping° hither.          *dazed*
ARIEL [*aside to* PROSPERO]          Was't well done?
PROSPERO [*aside to* ARIEL]          Bravely, my diligence. Thou shalt be free.
245 ALONSO   This is as strange a maze as e'er men trod,
And there is in this business more than nature
Was ever conduct° of. Some oracle          *conductor*
Must rectify our knowledge.
PROSPERO                              Sir, my liege,
Do not infest° your mind with beating on[8]          *trouble*
250 The strangeness of this business. At picked leisure,
Which shall be shortly, single° I'll resolve you,          *in private*
Which to you shall seem probable,° of every          *plausible*
These happened accidents;° till when be cheerful,          *occurrences*
And think of each thing well. [*Aside to* ARIEL] Come hither, spirit.
255 Set Caliban and his companions free.
Untie the spell.          [*Exit* ARIEL]
[*To* ALONSO]   How fares my gracious sir?
There are yet missing of your company
Some few odd lads that you remember not.
          *Enter* ARIEL, *driving in* CALIBAN, STEFANO, *and* TRIN-
          CULO, *in their stolen apparel*
STEFANO   Every man shift for all the rest, and let no man take
260 care for himself,[9] for all is but fortune. Coragio, bully-monster,[1]
coragio!
TRINCULO   If these° be true spies which I wear in my head, here's          *these eyes*
a goodly sight.
CALIBAN   O Setebos, these be brave spirits indeed!
265 How fine° my master is! I am afraid          *splendidly dressed*
He will chastise me.
SEBASTIAN   Ha, ha! What things are these, my lord Antonio?
Will money buy 'em?
ANTONIO                              Very like;° one of them          *likely*
Is a plain° fish, and no doubt marketable.          *mere*
270 PROSPERO   Mark but the badges[2] of these men, my lords,
Then say if they° be true. This misshapen knave,          *(the men); (the badges)*
His mother was a witch, and one so strong
That could control the moon, make flows and ebbs,
And deal in her command without her power.[3]
275 These three have robbed me, and this demi-devil,[4]
For he's a bastard one, had plotted with them
To take my life. Two of these fellows you
Must know and own.[5] This thing of darkness I
Acknowledge mine.
CALIBAN                              I shall be pinched to death.
280 ALONSO   Is not this Stefano, my drunken butler?

8. With repeatedly worrying about.
9. Stefano drunkenly confuses the saying "Every man for himself."
1. Gallant monster. *Coragio:* Take courage (Italian).
2. Livery. Servants often wore their master's emblem,
but Prospero probably refers to the stolen apparel.
3. And wield her (the moon's) power without her authority, or beyond the reach of her might.
4. Being the offspring of Sycorax and the devil.
5. And acknowledge to be yours.

SEBASTIAN   He is drunk now. Where had he wine?

ALONSO   And Trinculo is reeling ripe.° Where should they                    *drunk*
   Find this grand liquor that hath gilded⁶ 'em?
   [*To* TRINCULO] How cam'st thou in this pickle?⁷

285   TRINCULO   I have been in such a pickle since I saw you last that,
   I fear me, will never out of my bones. I shall not fear flyblowing.⁸

SEBASTIAN   Why, how now, Stefano?

STEFANO   O, touch me not! I am not Stefano, but a cramp.

290   PROSPERO   You'd be king o'the isle, sirrah?

STEFANO   I should have been a sore° one, then.                    *an inept; severe; pained*

ALONSO [*pointing to* CALIBAN]   This is a strange thing as e'er I
   looked on.

PROSPERO   He is as disproportioned in his manners⁹

295   As in his shape. [*To* CALIBAN] Go, sirrah, to my cell.
   Take with you your companions. As you look
   To have my pardon, trim° it handsomely.                    *tidy; decorate*

CALIBAN   Ay, that I will; and I'll be wise hereafter,
   And seek for grace. What a thrice-double ass

300   Was I to take this drunkard for a god,
   And worship this dull fool!

PROSPERO                    Go to, away!          [*Exit* CALIBAN]¹

ALONSO [*to* STEFANO *and* TRINCULO]
   Hence, and bestow your luggage where you found it.

SEBASTIAN   Or stole it, rather.     [*Exeunt* STEFANO *and* TRINCULO]

PROSPERO [*to* ALONSO]   Sir, I invite your highness and your train

305   To my poor cell, where you shall take your rest
   For this one night; which part of it° I'll waste°                    *part of which / spend*
   With such discourse as I not doubt shall make it
   Go quick away: the story of my life,
   And the particular accidents° gone by                    *events*

310   Since I came to this isle. And in the morn
   I'll bring you to your ship, and so to Naples,
   Where I have hope to see the nuptial
   Of these our dear-belovèd solemnized;
   And thence retire me to my Milan, where
   Every third thought shall be my grave.

315   ALONSO                    I long
   To hear the story of your life, which must
   Take° the ear strangely.                    *Captivate*

PROSPERO                    I'll deliver° all,                    *relate*
   And promise you calm seas, auspicious gales,
   And sail so expeditious that shall° catch                    *it will*

320   Your royal fleet far off. [*Aside to* ARIEL] My Ariel, chick,
   That is thy charge. Then to the elements
   Be free, and fare thou well.                    [*Exit* ARIEL]
                    Please you, draw near.°                    *go in*
                    *Exeunt* [*all but* PROSPERO]²

---

6. Probably alluding to the alchemical elixir ("liquor") known as *aurum potabile* (drinkable gold); hence "gilded" (flushed).
7. Sorry plight; Trinculo takes up the literal sense of "preserving liquid," recalling both his drunkenness and his drenching in the lake.
8. Not fear being infested with flies, since he has been

"pickled" (preserved).
9. Behavior; moral character.
1. The Folio does not explicitly say that Caliban leaves the stage in response to Prospero's command.
2. The general exeunt is through Prospero's cell; Ariel departs in another direction.

## Epilogue

PROSPERO   Now my charms are all o'erthrown,
And what strength I have's mine own,
Which is most faint. Now 'tis true
I must be here confined by you
5   Or sent to Naples. Let me not,
Since I have my dukedom got,
And pardoned the deceiver, dwell
In this bare island° by your spell;                          *(the stage)*
But release me from my bands°                               *fetters*
10   With the help of your good hands.°                       *(applause)*
Gentle breath° of yours my sails                   *Favorable comment*
Must fill, or else my project fails,
Which was to please. Now I want°                               *lack*
Spirits to enforce, art to enchant;
15   And my ending[1] is despair
Unless I be relieved by prayer,
Which pierces so, that it assaults
Mercy itself, and frees all faults.
As you from crimes would pardoned be,
20   Let your indulgence[2] set me free.
              *[He awaits applause, then] exit*

---

**Epilogue**
1. Punning on the sense "death."            2. Approval; appeasement; remission for sin.

# Cardenio

Many plays acted in Shakespeare's time have failed to survive; they may easily include some that he wrote. The mystery of *Love's Labour's Won* is discussed above. Certain manuscript records of the seventeenth century suggest that at least one other play in which he had a hand may have disappeared. On 9 September 1653 the London publisher Humphrey Moseley entered in the Stationers' Register a batch of plays including 'The History of Cardenio, by Mr Fletcher and Shakespeare'. Cardenio is a character in Part One of Cervantes' *Don Quixote*, published in English translation in 1612. Two earlier allusions suggest that the King's Men owned a play on this subject at the time that Shakespeare was collaborating with John Fletcher (1579–1625). On 20 May 1613 the Privy Council authorized payment of £20 to John Heminges, as leader of the King's Men, for the presentation at court of six plays, one listed as 'Cardenno'. On 9 July of the same year Heminges received £6 13s. 4d. for his company's performance of a play 'called Cardenna' before the ambassador of the Duke of Savoy.

No more information about this play survives from the seventeenth century, but in 1728 Lewis Theobald published a play based on the story of Cardenio called *Double Falsehood, or The Distrest Lovers*, which he claimed to have 'revised and adapted' from one 'written originally by W. Shakespeare'. It had been successfully produced at Drury Lane on 13 December 1727, and was given thirteen times up to 1 May 1728. Other performances are recorded in 1740, 1741, 1767 (when it was reprinted), 1770, and 1847. In 1770 a newspaper stated that 'the original manuscript' was 'treasured up in the Museum of Covent Garden Playhouse'; fire destroyed the theatre, including its library, in 1808.

Theobald claimed to own several manuscripts of an original play by Shakespeare, and remarked that some of his contemporaries thought the style was Fletcher's, not Shakespeare's. When he himself came to edit Shakespeare's plays he did not include either *Double Falsehood* or the play on which he claimed to have based it; he simply edited the plays of the First Folio, not adding either *Pericles* or *The Two Noble Kinsmen*, though he believed they were partly by Shakespeare. It is quite possible that *Double Falsehood* is based (however distantly) on a play of Shakespeare's time; if so, the play is likely to have been the one performed by the King's Men and ascribed by Moseley in 1653 to Fletcher and Shakespeare.

*Double Falsehood* is a tragicomedy; the characters' names differ from those in *Don Quixote*; and the story is varied. Henriquez rapes Violante, then falls in love with Leonora, loved by his friend Julio. Her parents agree to the marriage, but Julio interrupts the ceremony. Leonora (who had intended to kill herself) swoons and later takes sanctuary in a nunnery. Julio goes mad with desire for vengeance on his false friend; and the wronged Violante, disguised as a boy, joins a group of shepherds, and is almost raped by one of them. Henriquez's virtuous brother, Roderick, ignorant of his villainy, helps him to abduct Leonora. Leonora and Violante both denounce Henriquez to Roderick. Finally Henriquez repents and marries Violante, while Julio (now sane) marries Leonora.

Some of the motifs of *Double Falsehood*, such as the disguised heroine wronged by her lover, the hero's descent into madness, and the ultimate restoration of sundered relationships, recall Shakespeare's late plays. But most of the dialogue seems un-Shakespearean. Theobald's play stands as a tantalizing reminder of what has been lost.

THE OXFORD EDITORS
*Revised by Stephen Greenblatt*

# The Two Noble Kinsmen

When Prospero proclaims near the end of *The Tempest* (1611), "But this rough magic / I here abjure" (5.1.50–51), audiences often think they are hearing Shakespeare's farewell to the theater. But the final passage Shakespeare wrote for the stage is more likely to be found at the conclusion of *The Two Noble Kinsmen* (1613–14). Theseus, Duke of Athens, the play's highest-ranking character, attempts to grasp the ironic, paradoxical twists of fate he has witnessed:

>                               Never fortune
> Did play a subtler game—the conquered triumphs,
> The victor has the loss. Yet in the passage
> The gods have been most equal.
> . . . . . . . . . . . . . . . . . . . . . . . . . . . . . . . . . . . . . . . . . . .
>                             Let us be thankful
> For that which is, and with you [the gods] leave dispute
> That are above our question. Let's go off
> And bear us like the time.
>                                 (5.6.112–37)

It is thus tempting to interpret Theseus's resigned disillusionment as Shakespeare's last word—perhaps on life, certainly on *The Two Noble Kinsmen*. The message of the play is not that easy to determine, however. Theseus's emphasis on the gods, his confidence in their justice (they "have been most equal"), and his counsel of an ambivalent mixture of joy and sorrow ("bear us like the time") underestimate the grim cynicism that accompanies the undeniable pathos of the play. Chivalric military and sexual norms give a touching nobility to the action; but, arguably, they also generate the misery and destruction to which the bewildered Theseus attempts to respond.

    The problem of determining the work's tone is related to the question of authorship. Shakespeare probably wrote *The Two Noble Kinsmen* with John Fletcher, a younger contemporary who succeeded him as the leading dramatist of Shakespeare's acting company, the King's Men. Several of Shakespeare's very early and very late plays may have involved collaboration. In his final years, he worked with Fletcher—on the lost *Cardenio* (1612–13; probably based on an episode of Part One of Cervantes's *Don Quixote*, 1605; translated 1612), on *All Is True* (*Henry VIII*; 1613), and on *The Two Noble Kinsmen*. For this last play, Shakespeare seems to have written most of the first and last acts plus a few other scenes, while his colleague composed the rest and, hence, slightly more than half of the work as a whole. (There may also be a third hand involved; see the Textual Note). The two main dramatists differ in style, presentation, and outlook. The rhetorically knotty, ritualistic, near-tragic grandeur in Shakespeare's share contrasts with the syntactically simpler, dramatically more dynamic, near-absurd deflation in Fletcher's. The play as a whole is, therefore, neither simply Shakespearean nor simply Fletcherian. It is the product of their collaboration and is accordingly marked by dissonance as well as unity.

    Broadly speaking, *The Two Noble Kinsmen* represents a moment of transition from the more popular theater of Shakespeare's time to the more elite drama of Fletcher's. In many respects, it is typical of the very last phase of Shakespeare's career, and it offers a particularly illuminating comparison to other tragicomic romances written separately by Shakespeare and Fletcher in the preceding six or seven years. Among Shakespeare's leading works in this genre—*Pericles, The Winter's Tale, Cymbeline,* and *The Tempest*—one finds parallels to *The Two Noble Kinsmen*'s medieval source, pseudo-historical ancient Greek setting, emphasis on spectacle and ceremony, defense of innocence in the midst of corruption, striving for self-mastery, and transcendence of self-interest. There are further similarities in the insistence on death as a necessary price of the survivors' happiness, successful supplication to the gods for aid, and consequent sense of a controlling metaphysical presence that orders events in a way that is beyond human control. Although *The Two Noble Kinsmen* occurs exclusively on dry land, the work replicates even the trademark maritime imagery of Shakespearean romance, with its focus on peril and destruction: the dying Arcite "such a vessel 'tis that floats but for / The surge that next approaches" (5.6.83–84).

Yet *The Two Noble Kinsmen* has a very different feel from other romances of the time. As the Prologue explains, "Chaucer, of all admired, the story gives" (line 13). The main plot is taken—with greater freedom by Shakespeare than by Fletcher—from *The Knight's Tale,* which immediately follows *The General Prologue* in *The Canterbury Tales* (late fourteenth century). Its subject is the mortal rivalry between Palamon and Arcite, the two cousins referred to in the title, for the hand of Emilia. But the play's atypicality stems only partly from its resulting stylized chivalric ethos and accompanying acts of courtesy, acts that go beyond even what is found in Chaucer. What sets *The Two Noble Kinsmen* apart is its unusually somber resolution to the impossible dilemmas of the plot. Despite Theseus's assertions, the behavior of the gods does not restore confidence in a benevolent Providence. Indeed, Mars, whose intercession Arcite requests, and Venus, to whom Palamon prays, emblematize the chaos reigning in human affairs. The play is also structurally distinctive. Shakespearean romance reveals the passage from suffering to serenity, the redemption of the older generation by the younger (and particularly by the virtuous daughter). But Shakespeare and Fletcher's play has no interest in the restorative workings of time. All relationships occur within a single generation, and the young woman (Emilia) incites violence rather than reconciliation.

For these reasons, *The Two Noble Kinsmen* is sometimes viewed as an antiromance. As such, it bears comparison both to Shakespeare's other collaborations with Fletcher, noted earlier, and to a number of Shakespeare's earlier plays, which are pervasively echoed particularly in Fletcher's scenes. Palamon and Arcite's initial resignation in prison recalls *Richard II;* their conflict over Emilia, *The Two Gentlemen of Verona;* Emilia's comparison of pictures, *Hamlet.* When Arcite asks for a sign before his decisive battle with Palamon, he correctly takes Mars's answering thunder as a promise of victory. But this reassurance is no less duplicitous than the guarantee that "none of woman born / Shall harm Macbeth" (*Macbeth,* 4.1.96–97), with the important difference that Macbeth is a usurping mass murderer whereas Arcite is guilty only of desiring a woman his cousin saw first. The divine poetic justice often thought to be operating, however deviously, in *Macbeth* seems like little more than a dirty trick in *The Two Noble Kinsmen.*

A similar indebtedness to previous Shakespearean plays marks the subplot, which has no known source and which dramatizes the unrequited love of the Jailer's Daughter for Palamon. It is mainly the work of Fletcher, who borrowed the morris dance before Theseus and Hippolyta in 3.5 not from Shakespeare but from a masque (an aristocratic theatrical event emphasizing song, dance, and spectacle) that Francis Beaumont had composed for court performance in February 1613. (The morris dance itself is a rural folk form often performed on May Day by dancers in outlandish costumes who employ stock characters to partly mime traditional stories.) Otherwise, the Shakespearean legacy is pronounced. The Daughter's fall into madness when ignored by Palamon is modeled on Ophelia's in *Hamlet,* complete with an attempted suicide. Her willow song (4.1.79–80) was earlier sung by Desdemona in *Othello*. The Doctor who prescribes her cure previously ministered to King Lear and rather more unsuccessfully to Lady Macbeth. When the Daughter joins the people whom "ruder tongues distinguish 'villager'" (3.5.106) in the morris dance, the allusion is to another play indebted to *The Knight's Tale*: in *A Midsummer Night's Dream*, "rude mechanicals" (artisans, 3.2.9) also perform before Theseus and Hippolyta on the occasion of their wedding, and unrequited lovers wander through the forest.

But *The Two Noble Kinsmen* is *A Midsummer Night's Dream* with a difference. One of Shakespeare's previous romances, *The Winter's Tale*, might be understood as the tragic jealousy of *Othello* lightened and redeemed by the pastoral experience of a romantic comedy, *As You Like It*. By contrast, in *The Two Noble Kinsmen*, the comic tone of *A Midsummer Night's Dream* is darkened by the intervening experience of *Measure for Measure*, *All's Well That Ends Well*, and especially *Troilus and Cressida*, a work also drawing on Chaucerian narrative to depict a combination of chivalry and sensuality that leads to self-destructive violence and an indifference to the desires of the idealized woman. Indeed, Theseus's final words, quoted earlier, have been likened to Gloucester's metaphysical despair in *King Lear*:

> As flies to wanton boys are we to th' gods;
> They kill us for their sport.
>
> (Folio, 4.1.37–38)

A geographical and legendary legacy lies behind this outlook. Although the opening scene and the vast majority of the remainder of the play are set in and around Athens, the darker influence of Thebes is immediately felt. In an episode greatly expanded from the source, three widowed queens beg Theseus to come to their aid against Thebes, thus introducing the military dimension of chivalric conduct. Theseus reluctantly yields to Hippolyta's and Emilia's entreaties to defer his own pleasure (marriage to Hippolyta) to help dowagers in distress. His intervention pits him against Palamon and Arcite, who conclude that they must fight for their home city despite their hatred of its ruler, Creon. This initial sequence implicitly invokes Thebes' history of intrafamilial violence. According to ancient Greek narratives, Cadmus sows the soil with serpent's teeth, from which armed men grow; these men slaughter each other and, together with Cadmus, the few survivors found Thebes. Later, Oedipus unwittingly murders his father, and as the play opens, his two sons have killed each other in a battle for the throne that has also widowed the three queens.

The two cousins, imprisoned following Theseus's victory over Thebes, are compelled to repeat this history. When Theseus catches them fighting each other over Emilia, he orders their death, only to reverse his decision at Hippolyta's and Emilia's request. He ultimately proposes a chivalric combat in which each cousin is to be aided by three knights and all members of the losing side are to be executed. This plan increases the expected death toll beyond what is necessary and, indeed, beyond what is found in Chaucer. It is thwarted by the accidental death of Arcite, a death that is hard to see as providential but that undeniably makes Theseus's strategy look bad by comparison. Earlier, Palamon laments "Mars's so-scorned altar" and yearns for war "to get the soldier work, that peace might purge / For her repletion" (1.2.20, 23–24). This image of war as the virtuous means of purging the excesses of peace is echoed in Arcite's prayer to Mars, who

> heal'st with blood
> The earth when it is sick, and cur'st the world
> O'th' plurisy of people.
>
> (5.1.63–65)

Yet *The Two Noble Kinsmen* sees in war and chivalric combat less a cure for society than a loss of life.

A compulsive sexuality bears much of the blame for the havoc that is wreaked. As Theseus says, "Being sensually subdued / We lose our human title" (1.1.231–32). Arcite and especially Palamon are willing to kill and die for a woman about whom they know nothing except her appearance, and even that only at a distance. Arcite seems partly motivated by competitive emulation, by a desire to spite Palamon. He tells his cousin that when he sees Emilia, he will "pitch between her arms to anger thee" (2.2.221). The kinsmen claim rights to Emilia while serving life sentences in prison and without her being aware of their existence, much less expressing any interest in them. Her feelings don't matter to them. From this perspective, chivalric combat seems an appropriate mechanism for determining which cousin deserves her. In the event, this stance is validated by their society through the intervention of Theseus. Emilia really doesn't have the choice of rejecting them both. When, bowing to the inevitable, she temporarily is attracted to them, she is unable to decide between "two such young handsome men" (4.2.3). She, too, looks only to looks.

Palamon's prayer to Venus unwittingly reveals a simultaneous approval and denigration of sexuality:

> I knew a man
> Of eighty winters, this I told them, who
> A lass of fourteen brided—'twas thy power
> To put life into dust. The agèd cramp
> Had screwed his square foot round,
> The gout had knit his fingers into knots,
> Torturing convulsions from his globy eyes
> Had almost drawn their spheres, that what was life
> In him seemed torture. This anatomy
> Had by his young fair fere a boy, and I
> Believed it was his, for she swore it was,
> And who would not believe her?
>
> (5.2.39–50)

The power of love is thus exalted through deliberately repellent description. The reference to the "boy" anticipates imagery of sexuality and reproduction at the conclusion—"consummation," "miscarry," "conceives," "deliver" (5.5.94, 101, 137, 138)—that is unremittingly associated with loss. And the account ends with an apparently rhetorical but actually open question that undermines both Venus's sovereignty and female chastity. The very celebration of love has the effect of raising anxieties about women's fidelity and childbirth.

Heterosexual desire is rendered even more unappealing in *The Two Noble Kinsmen* by the extended representation of what it destroys. This positive alternative is same-sex attachment, whether understood as the Renaissance ideal of male friendship, as girlish intimacy, or as homoerotic attraction. In a romantic comedy such as *Much Ado About Nothing*, the rejection of heterosexual bonding is seen as an immature

The beginning of *The Knight's Tale*, from *The Workes of Our Ancient and Learned English Poet, Geffrey Chaucer* (1602 ed.).

The imprisoned Palamon and Arcite gazing at Emilia in the garden below. From a French translation of about 1455 of Giovanni Boccaccio's *Teseida* (the source of Chaucer's *Knight's Tale*), by René of Anjou.

foible to be overcome. Here, however, the movement from same-sex innocence to heterosexual experience is figured primarily as loss—comically in the Prologue, with its comparison of "new plays and maidenheads" (line 1), more grimly thereafter. Although in no other respect an Amazon, Emilia emphatically does prefer virginity and the company of females to the prospect of marriage. She tells Theseus that if he does not grant her petition, she will not "be so hardy / Ever to take a husband" (1.1.203–4). In her sexual joking with her Woman, she says that "men are mad things" (2.2.126) and praises the rose above all other flowers because "it is the very emblem of a maid" (2.2.137). Even after coming to admire the cousins, she still prays to Diana either that the more loving and deserving win her or that she be allowed to continue a virgin "in thy band" (5.3.26). When Theseus tells her, "If you can love, end this difference" by choosing one of the kinsmen, she evasively replies, "I cannot, sir. They are both too excellent" (3.6.277, 285).

This stance is explained by Emilia's earlier touching recollection of her intimacy with Flavina, who died when each was eleven. Her account of two girls who "loved for [simply because] we did" (1.3.61) culminates in this exchange:

> EMILIA    . . . the true love 'tween maid and maid may be
> More than in sex dividual.
> HIPPOLYTA                                You're out of breath,
> And this high-speeded pace is but to say
> That you shall never, like the maid Flavina,
> Love any that's called man.
> EMILIA    I am sure I shall not.
>
>                                    (1.3.81–86)

Female friendship thus stands against the absolute monarch's commitment to enforced marriage. Neither she nor the play repudiates this position.

Palamon and Arcite do so, however, choosing to kill and die—and hence to ruin the most precious thing in their lives, their love for each other—out of desire for Emilia. This resolution of the standard Renaissance debate over the respective claims of love and friendship has a paradoxical effect. The very depreciation of the cousins' attachment, which is not emphasized in Chaucer, only highlights its value. When they are first imprisoned, though they regret that life imprisonment precludes marriage and family, their thoughts quickly turn to each other. Arcite recommends "the enjoying of our griefs together" (2.2.60) and misogynistically notes the danger of freedom, which "might, like women / Woo us to wander from" "the ways of honour" (lines 75–76, 73). "Were we at liberty / A wife might part us lawfully," but in prison "we are one another's wife, ever begetting / New births of love" (lines 88–89, 80–81).

As they boast of their loving friendship, Palamon's first sight of Emilia undermines their resolution. She is talking to her Woman about the narcissus flower. This leads her to reflect upon the myth of Narcissus, who fell in love with his own beautiful reflection in a pool and died pining for it: "That was a fair boy, certain, but a fool / To love himself. Were there not maids enough?" (2.2.120–21). This implicit connection between Palamon and Narcissus is made explicit when Emilia remarks that Palamon shows

> not a smile.
> Yet these that we count errors may become him:
> Narcissus was a sad boy, but a heavenly.
> (4.2.30–32)

Palamon's suggested autoeroticism and preference for males over females is anticipated in Emilia's immediately preceding, unequivocally homosexual description of Arcite:

> Just such another wanton Ganymede
> Set Jove afire once, and enforced the god
> Snatch up the goodly boy and set him by him.
> (4.2.15–17)

Similarly, as the cousins prepare to arm and then battle each other, Arcite admiringly remarks, "Defy me in these fair terms, and you show / More than a mistress to me" (3.6.25–26). And most strikingly of all, when Arcite is released from prison, Palamon imagines what would happen if the roles were reversed:

> Were I at liberty I would do things
> Of such a virtuous greatness that this lady,
> This blushing virgin, should take manhood to her
> And seek to ravish me.
> (2.2.260–63)

Even the thought of the woman he loves becomes a fantasy of homosexual rape.

If the play anywhere offers an ideal balance between same-sex and other-sex bonding, it is in Theseus, whose friendship with Pirithous coexists comfortably with his impending marriage to Hippolyta. As suggested earlier, however, Theseus's conduct is open to question. Moreover, it is at least suggested that marriage to Hippolyta will never measure up to friendship with Pirithous. Most important, the catastrophic experience of Emilia and the kinsmen carries far more weight than Theseus's greater success in negotiating potentially antagonistic emotional and sexual attachments. Nonetheless, the figure of Theseus may be crucial to an extended allusion to the Jacobean court in *The Two Noble Kinsmen*. Theseus is perhaps an idealized image of King James, who combined marriage with homosexual behavior. In this interpretation, Arcite's death corresponds to the death of James's oldest son, Prince Henry, in the fall of 1612. The concluding, bittersweet union of Emilia with Palamon similarly parallels the marriage a few months later of James's daughter Elizabeth with the Elector Palatine. The probable revivals of 1619–20 and 1625–26, as well as the publication of the First Quarto in 1634, may also have resonated with court life. On the other hand, the evidence is not overwhelming for a direct connection of the play to the Jacobean court, whose members in any case might not have been flattered by the comparison. Such questions could not much matter to subsequent audiences, however, and with the exception of an adaptation in the late 1660s, *The Two Noble Kinsmen* seems to have remained unstaged until 1928. Since then, performances have tended to be effective when they have eschewed realism for ritual. But an interesting alternative is provided by a 1979 production, where the decision to employ an all-male cast emphasized the work's homoerotic motifs.

A joust celebrating the marriage of Henry IV of England to Joan of Navarre. From the Beauchamp Pageant (1485–90).

In general, however, beginning with the late seventeenth-century adaptation, the most consistently successful feature of the staging has been the Jailer's Daughter, who, though isolated and powerless, often emerges as the drama's central figure. Her four successive soliloquies in the middle of the play (2.4, 2.6, 3.2, 3.4), three of them probably—and the fourth perhaps—by Fletcher, are marked by exclamations, questions, and a consequent intimacy with the audience denied the other characters. The Daughter's special stage position thus helps win sympathy for her. In Shakespeare's plays, this position is characteristically reserved for a lower-class male character, especially the clown or fool, with whom the groundlings might identify. Here, however, we see a meshing of Shakespeare's interest in the folk with Fletcher's in strong women.

The Daughter stands at the center of a subplot that interacts with and critically reflects on the main action. Immediately following some frank sexual talk by the morris dancers in 2.3, she delivers her first soliloquy and then frees Palamon from prison in the hope that he will satisfy her sexual desire for him. Even though the genders are reversed, the situation is the same as in the main plot: the person in love knows little of the beloved, who, in turn, is almost completely oblivious of the lover. When the Daughter later joins the morris dance, she is appropriately cast as the "She-fool" (3.5.138 stage direction). In a dramaturgical sense, she *is* the female equivalent of the fool, for by this time Palamon's indifference has driven her mad. Her illness is cured pragmatically and amorally. On the advice of the Doctor and over the principled objections of her father (the Jailer), the Wooer pretends to be Palamon and makes love with her. Tricked into losing a virginity she was not trying to preserve, "she's well restored / And to be married shortly" (5.6.27–28) to the man who is socially and emotionally right for her. (Earlier, he foils her attempted suicide.) This outcome makes perfect sense in light of Renaissance medicine, which believed hysteria was caused by a wandering womb that could be returned to its proper place by intercourse. More cynically, however, one might conclude that the only thing women really need is sex and that any man will do.

The Daughter thinks she is marrying one man only to end up with another. Similarly, as Emilia settles into her fate, fate forces her to resettle her affections. Neither woman is given a choice—which is just as well, since neither is capable of making distinctions. The generic names in the subplot—Daughter, Jailer, Wooer, Doctor, Brother, Friends—highlight lack of individuality while pointing toward a similar absence in the main plot. The critical effort to discriminate between Palamon and Arcite inadvertently reaffirms what it seeks to deny: that it takes an effort to tell the cousins apart.

Even the Daughter's madness is arguably no more deviant and certainly much less destructive than the suicidal and homicidal behavior of Palamon and Arcite. Yet the two noble kinsmen are taken seriously in a way that she is not. Either because she is a woman or because she is from the lower class or both, she has no right to expect her feelings to be reciprocated, even though she has done more for Palamon than either of the cousins has for Emilia. It is unclear, however, whether the play aims to call attention to this obvious double standard. Ironically, her service to Palamon leads to Arcite's death after earlier bringing Palamon within a hair's breadth of the executioner's ax. Palamon meets the Jailer on his way to the block, graciously acknowledges his gratitude to "your gentle daughter" (5.6.24), and "gives his purse" (5.6.32 stage direction) as part of the dowry for her impending marriage. His generosity infects the other knights slated to die with him:

> FIRST KNIGHT  Nay, let's be offerers all.
> SECOND KNIGHT  Is it a maid?
> PALAMON                                    Verily, I think so—
> (5.6.32–33)

Thus, with the play's characteristic irony, "they give their purses" (5.6.35 stage direction) on a doubly false assumption—that they are doomed and that they are contributing to a virgin's dowry. But in another sense, the Daughter is bought off. Palamon

speaks with greater accuracy than he knows in saying she is "more to me deserving /
Than I can quit [requite] or speak of" (5.6.34–35).

Long before this, the Daughter's sequence of soliloquies has come to an end. In the
second half of the play, having moved from one form of folly to another, she appears
only in dialogue scenes and hence partly loses her unique contact with the audience.
Yet even here, her vigorous language and stage presence produce an immediacy that
effectively combines with the pathos of her predicament. It is, finally, a pathos she
shares with the characters in the main plot, who watch in bewildered incomprehension
as their most cherished ideals fail them when it matters most.

WALTER COHEN

## TEXTUAL NOTE

*The Two Noble Kinsmen* dates from between February 20, 1613, and October 31,
1614. The mention of "our losses" in the Prologue (line 32) has sometimes been taken
as a reference to the burning of the Globe Theatre on June 29, 1613. If so, this is
Shakespeare's final play, perhaps performed at Blackfriars, the King's Men's indoor
theater, in the fall of 1613 or winter of 1614, or at the opening of the rebuilt Globe,
their outdoor theater, a year after the fire. Both the only substantive text, the Quarto
of 1634 (Q), and an entry from earlier the same year in the Stationers' Register (a listing of books approved for publication), which calls the play a "TragiComedy," attribute it to John Fletcher and Shakespeare. The exclusion of *The Two Noble Kinsmen*
from the First Folio of 1623 (F) has sometimes led to doubts about Shakespeare's
authorship, but most scholars accept the attribution, which is supported by other
internal and external evidence.

Although the exact division of labor between the two playwrights cannot be determined with certainty, Shakespeare probably wrote a little less than half the play:
1.1–2.1 (although some scholars give Fletcher 1.4–1.5), perhaps 2.3, 3.1, perhaps 3.2,
perhaps 4.3, 5.1.34–5.3 (although 5.2 is sometimes attributed to Fletcher), and
5.5–5.6. These attributions are necessarily tentative, given the likelihood that the plan
of the play changed a bit in the course of composition and that Fletcher undertook
some revision to bring the play to its final form—perhaps of Shakespeare's text, perhaps
of his own in light of Shakespeare's sections. A further complication is the possible
presence of a third, less central, author—either Francis Beaumont, a major collaborator with Fletcher, or, more likely, Nathan Field, who also collaborated with Fletcher at
this time and might have been one of the leading actors in the performance of the play.

Q is based either on the authors' manuscript or on a scribal transcript. The latter is
the more likely alternative. The manuscript apparently underwent some revision, possibly by an author, perhaps in the Prologue, more probably in 4.2, and especially in 4.3.
Whether authorial or scribal, it was annotated with stage directions and other indications (for instance, about props) in preparation for performance, perhaps more than
once—for the original production and again for a revival in 1625–26 by Edward Knight,
who worked for the King's Men at the time.

Two compositors probably set the type for Q, alternating work quite frequently. The
printed text is a good one, but it contains two scenes headed 2.4 (followed by 2.6); editors routinely convert the second 2.4 to 2.5. Q also follows 3.4 with 3.6 and 3.7, perhaps a sign of an original 3.5 that was cut without the subsequent scenes being
renumbered, as they are here (as 3.5 and 3.6). In addition, it missets verse as prose and,
more often (2.1, 4.3), prose as verse. Some editors have ignored Q's scene break
between 2.1 and 2.2 on the grounds that the scene is continuous. As the notes explain,
the present edition proposes a staging for the two scenes that justifies the scene division. On the other hand, though again for reasons of staging, this edition expands Q's

5.1 into three scenes: the final three scenes in the play are, therefore, converted from 5.2–4 to 5.4–6.

## SELECTED BIBLIOGRAPHY

Berggren, Paula S. "'For what we lack / We laugh': Incompletion and *The Two Noble Kinsmen*." *Modern Language Studies* 14.4 (1984): 3–17. Sees the play as an antiromance marked by frustrated attempts at action, intensified through the imagery, and by lack of either divine justice or redemptive reconciliation.

Briggs, Julia. "Tears at the Wedding: Shakespeare's Last Phase." *Shakespeare's Late Plays: New Readings*. Ed. Jennifer Richards and James Knowles. Edinburgh: Edinburgh University Press, 1999. 210–27. *The Two Noble Kinsmen* as typical of Shakespeare's late collaborations with Fletcher in its grim posing of irreconcilable choices in the absence of metaphysical consolation.

Bruster, Douglas. "The Jailer's Daughter and the Politics of Madwomen's Language." *Shakespeare Quarterly* 46 (1995): 277–300. Sees the Daughter as powerless and isolated but nonetheless central to the play, her unique language marked by class and gender, her madness constituting a form of resistance; more generally, her depiction understood as the intersection of Shakespeare's interest in the folk and Fletcher's in strong women characters, and also as indicative of a transition to a less popular drama.

Finkelpearl, Philip J. "Two Distincts, Division None: Shakespeare's and Fletcher's *The Two Noble Kinsmen* of 1613." *Elizabethan Theater: Essays in Honor of S. Schoenbaum*. Ed. R. B. Parker and S. P. Zitner. Newark: University of Delaware Press, 1996. 184–99. Shakespearean cosmological concerns versus Fletcher's more worldly and irreverent approach, united by a critical independence from views of honor and chivalry associated with the royal family.

Frey, Charles, ed. *Shakespeare, Fletcher, and "The Two Noble Kinsmen."* Columbia: University of Missouri Press, 1989. A collection of modern criticism together with a review of scholarship on the play.

Herman, Peter C. "'Is This Winning?': Prince Henry's Death and the Problem of Chivalry in *The Two Noble Kinsmen*." *South Atlantic Review* 62 (1997): 1–31. The death of King James's son and heir as a blow to chivalry, generating in the play a skepticism about its martial and erotic implications.

Potter, Lois, ed. *The Two Noble Kinsmen*. 3rd ed. Walton-on-Thames, Surrey: Thomas Nelson, 1997. Outstanding scholarly edition with a lengthy critical introduction.

Shannon, Laurie J. "Emilia's Argument: Friendship and 'Human Title' in *The Two Noble Kinsmen*." *English Literary Renaissance* 64 (1997): 657–682. Emilia as Amazonian rational advocate of female friendship (understood as chastity, homoeroticism, and conscience) against irrational absolute power (understood as imposing the obligation to marry).

Spencer, Theodore. "*The Two Noble Kinsmen*." *Modern Philology* 36 (1939): 255–76. Contrasts the ritualistic action and convoluted rhetoric of Shakespeare's scenes with the greater emotional intensity but slighter thematic depth of Fletcher's.

Stewart, Alan. "'Near Akin': The Trials of Friendship in *The Two Noble Kinsmen*." *Shakespeare's Late Plays: New Readings*. Ed. Jennifer Richards and James Knowles. Edinburgh: Edinburgh University Press, 1999. 57–71. The main plot as the failure of idealized male friendship and especially kinship, showing the incompatibility of classical and chivalric ideals with Jacobean social reality.

# The Two Noble Kinsmen

### THE PERSONS OF THE PLAY

PROLOGUE
THESEUS, Duke of Athens
HIPPOLYTA, Queen of the Amazons, later wife of Theseus
EMILIA, her sister
PIRITHOUS, friend of Theseus
PALAMON ⎫ the two noble kinsmen, cousins, nephews of
ARCITE ⎭ Creon, the King of Thebes
Hymen, god of marriage
A BOY, who sings
ARTESIUS, an Athenian soldier
Three QUEENS, widows of kings killed in the siege of Thebes
VALERIUS, a Theban
A HERALD
WOMAN, attending Emilia
An Athenian GENTLEMAN
MESSENGERS
Six KNIGHTS, three attending Arcite and three Palamon
A SERVANT
A JAILER in charge of Theseus' prison
The JAILER'S DAUGHTER
The JAILER'S BROTHER
The WOOER of the Jailer's daughter
Two FRIENDS of the Jailer
A DOCTOR
Six COUNTRYMEN, one dressed as a babion, or baboon
Gerald, a SCHOOLMASTER
NELL, a country wench
Four other country wenches: Friz, Madeline, Luce, and
    Barbara
Timothy, a TABORER
EPILOGUE
Nymphs, attendants, maids, executioner, guard

## Prologue

*Flourish.*° [*Enter* PROLOGUE]                    *Trumpet call*
PROLOGUE    New plays and maidenheads are near akin:
    Much followed both, for both much money giv'n
    If they stand sound and well.[1] And a good play,
    Whose modest scenes blush on his marriage day
    And shake to lose his honour,[2] is like her
    That after holy tie° and first night's stir              *marriage*
    Yet still is modesty, and still retains

---

Prologue
1. *stand sound and well:* sexual wordplay about virility and lack of venereal disease.
2. *Whose . . . honour:* Whose previously unwatched

scenes are "modest" and shy (they "blush") on opening night and "shake" with fear at the thought of being viewed (losing their virginity).

More of the maid to sight than husband's pains.³
We pray our play may be so,° for I am sure                    (*modest*)
10    It has a noble breeder° and a pure,                          *begetter*
A learnèd, and a poet never went
More famous yet 'twixt Po and silver Trent.⁴
Chaucer, of° all admired, the story gives:                    *by*
There° constant to eternity it lives.                         *In his words*
15    If we let fall° the nobleness of this°        *demean* / (*the poem*)
And the first sound this child° hear be a hiss,              *play*
How will it shake the bones of that good man,°             (*Chaucer*)
And make him cry from under ground, 'O fan
From me the witless chaff of such a writer,
20    That blasts my bays and my famed works makes lighter
Than Robin Hood'?⁵ This is the fear we bring,
For to say truth, it were an endless° thing    *never-ending; pointless*
And too ambitious to aspire to him,°                         (*Chaucer*)
Weak as we are, and almost breathless swim
25    In this deep water. Do but you hold out
Your helping hands and we shall tack about
And something do to save us.⁶ You shall hear
Scenes, though below his art, may yet appear
Worth two hours' travail.⁷ To his bones, sweet sleep;
30    Content to you. If this play do not keep
A little dull time from us,⁸ we perceive
Our losses fall so thick we must needs leave.⁹    *Flourish.* [*Exit*]

### 1.1

*Music. Enter Hymen*° *with a torch burning, a* BOY *in a*     *god of marriage*
*white robe before, singing and strewing flowers. After*
*Hymen, a nymph encompassed in her tresses, bearing a*
*wheaten garland.*¹ *Then* THESEUS *between two other*
*nymphs with wheaten chaplets*° *on their heads. Then*        *wreaths*
HIPPOLYTA,² *the bride, led by* [PIRITHOUS] *and another*
*holding a garland over her head, her tresses likewise*
*hanging. After her,* EMILIA *holding up her train.* [*Then*
ARTESIUS *and other attendants*]
BOY [*sings during procession*]
          Roses, their sharp spines being gone,
          Not royal in their smells alone,
               But in their hue;

---

3. *still . . . pains:* still looks more like a virgin ("maid") than like a married woman who has experienced her husband's sexual exertions.
4. *a poet . . . Trent:* there has never been a more famous poet from Italy to England. The Po is a river in Italy, the Trent an English waterway.
5. *That . . . Hood:* Who disgraces my fame as a poet (garlands of bay or laurel were awarded to great poets, hence the name "poet laureate") and makes my renowned creations seem more trivial than a popular tale or ballad (such as Robin Hood).
6. *Do but . . . us:* Help us by applauding, and we will turn like a sailboat in the breeze produced by your clapping hands, thereby saving our reputation.
7. *two hours' travail:* the actors' labor ("travail") for two hours in performing the play (standard length was two to three hours); also, since Q reads "travel," the audience will take part in a two-hour imaginative journey

while watching the play. "Travail" continues the metaphor of childbirth and rearing begun in line 10, which itself develops from the image of the loss of virginity on the marriage night.
8. *keep . . . us:* keep us amused.
9. Our losses will be so great that we will need to quit the theater. The "losses" refer to the decline in reputation from a poorly received play and perhaps also to the burning of the Globe Theatre on June 29, 1613, during a performance of *All Is True* (*Henry VIII*).
1.1 Location: Athens, near the temple where Hippolyta and Theseus are to be married.
1. The young woman's hair hangs loose, indicating virginity; her garland signifies fertility.
2. According to legend, Hipployta was Queen of the Amazons before Theseus conquered her race of women warriors and brought her to Thebes as his captive and bride.

Maiden pinks, of odour faint,
Daisies smell-less, yet most quaint,°      *fine*
   And sweet thyme true;

Primrose, first-born child of Ver,°      *spring*
Merry springtime's harbinger,
   With harebells dim;°      *dark hyacinths*
Oxlips,° in their cradles growing,      *Flowering herbs*
Marigolds, on deathbeds blowing,°      *flowering on graves*
   Lark's-heels trim;°      *Fine larkspur*
All dear nature's children sweet,
Lie fore bride and bridegroom's feet,
   *[IIe] strew[s] flowers*
   Blessing their sense.
Not an angel of the air,°      *bird*
Bird melodious, or bird fair,
   Is absent hence.

The crow, the sland'rous[3] cuckoo, nor
The boding° raven, nor chough hoar,[4]      *ominous*
   Nor chatt'ring pie,°      *magpie*
May on our bridehouse° perch or sing,      *wedding venue*
Or with them any discord bring,
   But from it fly.

*Enter three* QUEENS *in black, with veils stained,° with*      *dyed black*
*imperial crowns. The* FIRST QUEEN *falls down at the*
*foot of* THESEUS; *the* SECOND *falls down at the foot of*
HIPPOLYTA; *the* THIRD, *before* EMILIA
FIRST QUEEN [*to* THESEUS]    For pity's sake and true gentility's,
Hear and respect° me.      *attend to*
SECOND QUEEN [*to* HIPPOLYTA]    For your mother's sake,
And as you wish your womb may thrive with fair ones,
Hear and respect me.
THIRD QUEEN [*to* EMILIA]    Now for the love of him whom Jove
    hath marked°      *singled out for*
The honour of your bed, and for the sake
Of clear° virginity, be advocate      *unspotted*
For us and our distresses. This good deed
Shall raze you out o'th' Book of Trespasses
All you are set down there.[5]
THESEUS [*to* FIRST QUEEN]    Sad lady, rise.
HIPPOLYTA [*to* SECOND QUEEN]       Stand up.
EMILIA [*to* THIRD QUEEN]         No knees to me.
What woman I may stead° that is distressed      *assist*
Does bind me to her.
THESEUS [*to* FIRST QUEEN]    What's your request? Deliver° you      *Speak*
    for all.
FIRST QUEEN [*kneeling still*]    We are three queens whose sovereigns
    fell before
The wrath of cruel Creon;[6] who° endured      *(the sovereigns)*

---

3. Because it yelled out "cuckold" (husband of an adulterous wife), impugning faithful wives.
4. A jackdaw—a small, rare, gray-headed ("hoar"), red-beaked, cliff-dwelling member of the crow family.
5. *Shall . . . there:* Will expunge your sins from the divine ledger.
6. Brother to Jocasta and, hence, both brother-in-law

and uncle to Oedipus, Creon succeeded Oedipus's son Eteocles as King of Thebes following the siege known as the "Seven Against Thebes," in which both Eteocles and all the attackers, led by Eteocles' brother Polynices, were killed. Creon refused to bury any of the seven, including the husbands of the Three Queens.

The beaks of ravens, talons of the kites,
And pecks of crows in the foul fields° of Thebes.          *battlefields*
He will not suffer us to burn their bones,
To urn their ashes, nor to take th'offence
45  Of mortal loathsomeness from the blest eye
Of holy Phoebus,° but infects the winds               *the sun*
With stench of our slain lords. O pity, Duke!
Thou purger of the earth,[7] draw thy feared sword
That does good turns to th' world; give us the bones
50  Of our dead kings that we may chapel° them;          *entomb*
And of° thy boundless goodness take some note          *in*
That for our crownèd heads we have no roof,
Save this,° which is the lion's and the bear's,         *(the sky)*
And vault° to everything.                               *ceiling*
THESEUS                    Pray you, kneel not:
55  I was transported with° your speech, and suffered      *moved by*
Your knees to wrong themselves.° I have heard the fortunes   *(by kneeling)*
Of your dead lords, which gives me such lamenting
As wakes my vengeance and revenge for 'em.
King Capaneus was your lord: the day
60  That he should° marry you—at such a season             *was about to*
As now it is with me—I met your groom
By Mars's altar. You were that time fair,
Not Juno's mantle fairer than your tresses,
Nor in more bounty spread her.[8] Your wheaten wreath
65  Was then nor° threshed nor blasted;° fortune at you     *neither / withered*
Dimpled her cheek with smiles; Hercules our kinsman—
Then weaker than° your eyes—laid by his club.          *overwhelmed by*
He tumbled down upon his Nemean hide
And swore his sinews thawed.[9] O grief and time,
70  Fearful° consumers, you will all devour.                *Terrifying*
FIRST QUEEN [*kneeling still*]  O, I hope some god,
Some god hath put his mercy in your manhood,
Whereto he'll infuse power and press you forth
Our undertaker.°                                        *champion*
THESEUS              O no knees, none, widow:
[*The* FIRST QUEEN *rises*]
75  Unto the helmeted Bellona° use them                   *Roman goddess of war*
And pray for me, your soldier. Troubled I am.
[*He*] *turns away*
SECOND QUEEN [*kneeling still*]  Honoured Hippolyta,
Most dreaded Amazonian, that hast slain
The scythe-tusked boar,[1] that with thy arm, as strong
80  As it is white, wast near to° make the male            *almost managed to*
To thy sex captive, but that this, thy lord—
Born to uphold creation in that honour
First nature styled it in[2]—shrunk thee into

7. Like his cousin Hercules (see 1.1.66, 3.6.175), Theseus was known for ridding the world of monsters and
evildoers.
8. Nor is Juno (goddess of marriage) more luxuriantly
wrapped in her mantle than you were in your hanging
tresses.
9. *He . . . thawed:* He (Hercules) flopped down on the
hide of the Nemean lion (which he wore after killing it
as one of his twelve labors) and swore his muscles were
turned to water by your beauty. Most powerful of Greek

mythological heroes, performer of "twelve strong
labours" set for him by his cousin (3.6.175), Hercules
was typically portrayed armed with a club.
1. *Honored . . . boar:* Hippolyta is here confused with
Atalanta, another Amazon, who participated with
Meleager in the hunt for the Calydonian boar. See note
to 3.5.18.
2. *Born . . . in:* Born to sustain the natural order of
creation—the order of man over woman.

The bound thou wast o'erflowing,[3] at once subduing
85  Thy force and thy affection; soldieress,
That equally canst poise° sternness with pity,                    *balance*
Whom now I know hast much more power on° him                      *over*
Than ever he had on thee, who ow'st° his strength,               *owns*
And his love too, who is a servant for
90  The tenor of thy speech;[4] dear glass of° ladies,             *mirror for*
Bid him that we, whom flaming war doth scorch,
Under the shadow of his sword may cool us.
Require him he° advance it o'er our heads.                        *Ask him to*
Speak't in a woman's key, like such a woman
95  As any of us three. Weep ere you fail.
Lend us a knee:[5]
But touch the ground for us no longer time
Than a dove's motion when the head's plucked off.
Tell him, if he i'th' blood-sized° field lay swoll'n,            *blood-soaked*
100  Showing the sun his teeth, grinning at the moon,
What you would do.

HIPPOLYTA          Poor lady, say no more.
I had as lief trace[6] this good action with you
As that° whereto I am going, and never yet                       *(marriage)*
Went I so willing way. My lord is taken°                         *affected*
105  Heart-deep with your distress. Let him consider.
I'll speak anon.°                                                 *soon*
     [*The* SECOND QUEEN *rises*]

THIRD QUEEN (*kneel[ing still] to* EMILIA)   O, my petition was
Set down in ice,[7] which by hot grief uncandied°               *thawed*
Melts into drops; so sorrow, wanting form,
Is pressed with deeper matter.[8]

EMILIA                         Pray stand up:
Your grief is written in your cheek.
110  THIRD QUEEN                        O woe,
You cannot read it there; there,° through my tears,            *in my eye*
Like wrinkled pebbles in a glassy stream,
You may behold 'em.°                                             *(my sorrows)*
     [*The* THIRD QUEEN *rises*]
                    Lady, lady, alack—
He that will all the treasure know o'th' earth
115  Must know° the centre too; he that will fish               *dig deep throughout*
For my least minnow, let him lead° his line                     *weight with lead*
To catch one at my heart. O, pardon me:
Extremity, that sharpens sundry wits,
Makes me a fool.[9]

EMILIA                 Pray you, say nothing, pray you.
120  Who cannot feel nor see the rain, being in't,
Knows neither wet nor dry. If that you were
The ground-piece of some painter,[1] I would buy you
T'instruct me 'gainst a capital° grief, indeed                  *deadly*

---

3. *shrunk . . . o'erflowing:* returned you to the limits of your sex, which you had previously exceeded.
4. *who is . . . speech:* who, like a good lover, obeys your every spoken desire.
5. *Speak't . . . knee:* Don't speak like an Amazon. Use tears to avoid defeat. Join us in kneeling.
6. I would as willingly follow through.
7. *my . . . ice:* my former speech was cold and formal.

8. *so . . . matter:* so sorrow, lacking a way to express itself, is made yet more oppressive by its inarticulateness; or, perhaps, receives the stamp of "deeper" impulses.
9. *Extremity . . . fool:* Extreme suffering, which makes some minds more clear, has made me speak inappropriately.
1. *If . . . painter:* If you were merely the subject (model; preliminary sketch?) of a painting.

| | |
|---|---|
| 125 | Such heart-pierced° demonstration; but, alas, |
| | Being a natural sister of our sex,[2] |
| | Your sorrow beats so ardently° upon me |
| | That it shall make a counter-reflect 'gainst[3] |
| | My brother's° heart, and warm it to some pity, |
| | Though it were made of stone. Pray have good comfort. |

Marginal glosses (right column):
- *heartrending* (line 124)
- *burningly* (line 126)
- *brother-in-law's* (line 128)

THESEUS   Forward to th' temple.° Leave not out a jot      *(for the wedding)*
130  O'th' sacred ceremony.

FIRST QUEEN                O, this celebration
Will longer last and be more costly than
Your suppliants' war. Remember that your fame
Knolls° in the ear o'th' world: what you do quickly      *Tolls like a bell*
135  Is not done rashly; your first thought is more
Than others' laboured meditance;° your premeditating      *careful meditation*
More than their actions. But, O Jove, your actions,
Soon as they move, as ospreys do the fish,[4]
Subdue before they touch. Think, dear Duke, think
What beds our slain kings have.

140  SECOND QUEEN                What griefs our beds,
That our dear lords have none.

THIRD QUEEN                None fit for th' dead.
Those that with cords, knives, drams,° precipitance,°      *poisons / leaps*
Weary of this world's light, have to themselves
Been death's most horrid agents, human grace°      *mercy*
Affords them dust and shadow.

145  FIRST QUEEN                But our lords
Lie blist'ring fore the visitating° sun,      *inspecting*
And were good kings, when living.

THESEUS                It is true,
And I will give you comfort to give° your dead lords graves,      *by giving*
The which to do must make some work with Creon.

150  FIRST QUEEN   And that work presents itself to th' doing.[5]
Now 'twill take form, the heats are gone tomorrow.[6]
Then, bootless° toil must recompense itself      *fruitless*
With its own sweat; now he's secure,°      *unaware of danger*
Not dreams we stand before your puissance°      *power*
155  Rinsing our holy begging in our eyes
To make petition clear.°      *pure; manifest*

SECOND QUEEN                Now you may take him,
Drunk with his victory.

THIRD QUEEN                And his army full
Of bread and sloth.

THESEUS                Artesius, that best knowest
How to draw out,° fit to this enterprise      *select*
160  The prim'st° for this proceeding and the number      *best soldiers*
To carry° such a business: forth and levy      *conduct; win*
Our worthiest instruments, whilst we dispatch
This grand act of our life, this daring deed
Of fate[7] in wedlock.

---

2. Since you are actually a live woman (rather than a representation of a grieving wife).
3. That, like a mirror, I'll reflect your (sunlike) sorrow back toward.
4. According to popular legend, ospreys had the power to compel fish to rise to the surface and turn over, making themselves available for capture.

5. And that work needs to be done as soon as possible.
6. While the plan, like molten metal, is still hot, it can be transformed into something—once it grows cold, it can no longer be shaped.
7. *this daring deed / Of fate:* this act (marriage) that challenges fate.

FIRST QUEEN [*to the other two* QUEENS]    Dowagers,° take hands;    *Widows*
165    Let us be widows to our woes; delay
Commends us to a famishing hope.[8]
ALL THREE QUEENS                            Farewell.
SECOND QUEEN    We come unseasonably,° but when could grief    *at a bad time*
Cull forth,° as unpanged° judgement can, fitt'st time    *Choose / untormented*
For best solicitation?
THESEUS                    Why, good ladies,
170    This is a service whereto I am going
Greater than any war—it more imports me°    *means more to me*
Than all the actions that I have foregone,°    *done to date*
Or futurely can cope.°    *achieve*
FIRST QUEEN                The more proclaiming°    *Clearly showing that*
Our suit shall be neglected when her arms,
175    Able to lock Jove from a synod,[9] shall
By warranting° moonlight corslet thee![1] O when    *authorizing*
Her twinning cherries° shall their sweetness fall°    *lips / let fall*
Upon thy tasteful° lips, what wilt thou think    *tasting*
Of rotten kings or blubbered° queens? What care    *tear-soaked*
180    For what thou feel'st not, what thou feel'st being able
To make Mars spurn his drum?° O, if thou couch    *(battle signal)*
But one night with her, every hour in't will
Take hostage of thee° for a hundred,° and    *Commit you / (more)*
Thou shalt remember nothing more than what
That banquet bids° thee to.    *appetizer invites*
185    HIPPOLYTA [*to* THESEUS]        Though much unlike
You should be so transported, as much sorry
I should be such a suitor[2]—yet I think
Did I not by th'abstaining of my joy,
Which breeds a deeper longing, cure their surfeit°    *excess of grief*
190    That craves a present medicine,° I should pluck    *an immediate relief*
All ladies' scandal° on me. [*Kneels*] Therefore, sir,    *reproach*
As I shall here make trial of my prayers,
Either presuming them to have some force,
Or sentencing for aye their vigour dumb,[3]
195    Prorogue° this business we are going about, and hang    *Delay*
Your shield afore your heart—about that neck
Which is my fee,° and which I freely lend    *property*
To do these poor queens service.
ALL THREE QUEENS [*to* EMILIA]        O, help now,
Our cause cries for your knee.
EMILIA [*kneels to* THESEUS]        If you grant not
200    My sister her petition in that force°    *with that energy*
With that celerity and nature° which    *spontaneous speed*
She makes it in, from henceforth I'll not dare
To ask you anything, nor be so hardy°    *bold*
Ever to take a husband.
THESEUS                    Pray stand up.

---

8. *Let . . . hope:* Let us mourn our misfortunes as we
mourned our husbands (or, let us, widowlike, part from
our woes), since by delaying the battle until his marriage is completed, Theseus consigns us to failure.
9. Able to keep Jupiter from a meeting of the gods.
1. Encircle you like a "corslet," close-fitting defensive
armor. Theseus has traded arms (armor) for arms
(embraces).

2. *Though . . . suitor:* Although it's highly unlikely
you'd be so carried away, and just as unlikely I'd now
request you to postpone the wedding.
3. Or forever "sentencing" my prayers to silence, than
which they are no more effectual.

[*They rise*]

205 I am entreating of myself to do
That which you kneel to have me.°—Pirithous,  have me do
Lead on the bride: get you° and pray the gods  go
For success and return; omit not anything
In the pretended° celebration.—Queens,  intended
210 Follow your soldier.° [*To* ARTESIUS] As before, hence you,  Theseus
And at the banks of Aulis⁴ meet us with
The forces you can raise, where we shall find
The moiety of a number for a business
More bigger looked.⁵  [*Exit* ARTESIUS]
[*To* HIPPOLYTA]  Since that our theme is haste,
215 I stamp this kiss upon thy current lip—
Sweet, keep it as my token.⁶ [*To the wedding party*] Set you
  forward,
For I will see you gone.
[*To* EMILIA] Farewell, my beauteous sister.—Pirithous,
Keep the feast full:° bate° not an hour on't.°  fully / abate / of it
PIRITHOUS  Sir,
220 I'll follow you at heels. The feast's solemnity°  ceremonial splendor
Shall want° till your return.  be lacking
THESEUS  Cousin,° I charge you  Friend
Budge not from Athens. We shall be returning
Ere you can end this feast, of which, I pray you,
Make no abatement.°—Once more, farewell all.  reduction
  *Exeunt* [HIPPOLYTA, EMILIA, PIRITHOUS, *and train*]
  *towards the temple*
FIRST QUEEN  Thus dost thou still make good the tongue o'th'
225  world.⁷
SECOND QUEEN  And earn'st a deity equal with Mars—
THIRD QUEEN  If not above him, for
Thou being but mortal mak'st affections° bend  sexual urges
To godlike honours;⁸ they themselves, some say,
Groan under such a mast'ry.⁹
230 THESEUS  As we are men,
Thus should we do; being sensually subdued°  overcome by appetites
We lose our human title.° Good cheer, ladies.  claim to humanity
Now turn we towards your comforts.  *Flourish. Exeunt*

## 1.2
*Enter* PALAMON *and* ARCITE
ARCITE  Dear Palamon, dearer in love than blood,
And our prime cousin,° yet unhardened in  nearest kin
The crimes of nature,¹ let us leave the city,

4. Port where the Greek troops assembled before sailing for Troy.
5. *where . . . looked:* where we shall find part of an army
already assembled for a larger campaign than this one.
6. *I . . . token:* puns on coining and engraving. *stamp:*
press (a kiss); make a coin by impressing an image on
metal. *current:* flowing away (like a stream); red (cur-
rant); genuine, not counterfeit. *token:* memento (often
of love); metal stamped and used as a coin.
7. In this way, you (Theseus) prove true everything the
world says of you.
8. *mak'st . . . honours:* subordinate your human passions to godlike deeds.

9. *they . . . mast'ry:* the gods themselves complain of
such self-restraint; suffer because their passions master them.
1.2 Location: Thebes.
1. *unhardened . . . nature:* inexperienced in the natural
vices of man. In this scene, a number of the most
important themes of the play are introduced: that
maturity and experience necessitate a loss of innocence; that friendship constitutes a stronger tie than
either marriage / love relations or blood; and that duty
to the knightly virtue of honor is stronger than duty to
human laws and sovereigns (except in times of war).

*temptations*

Thebes, and the temptings° in't, before we further

5 Sully our gloss of° youth.              *Tarnish our pristine*

And here to keep in abstinence we shame

As in incontinence;[2] for not to swim

I'th' aid o'th' current° were almost to sink—     *With the flow*

At least to frustrate striving;[3] and to follow

10 The common stream 'twould bring us to an eddy

Where we should turn° or drown; if labour through,    *spin endlessly*

Our gain but life and weakness.[4]

PALAMON                  Your advice

Is cried up with example.[5] What strange ruins°     *ruined men*

Since first we went to school may we perceive

15 Walking in Thebes? Scars and bare weeds°      *tattered clothes*

The gain o'th' martialist° who did propound        *soldier*

To his bold ends[6] honour and golden ingots,

Which though he won, he had not;[7] and now flirted°    *(is) mocked*

By peace for whom he fought. Who then shall offer

20 To Mars's so-scorned altar? I do bleed

When such I meet, and wish great Juno[8] would

Resume her ancient° fit of jealousy            *former*

To get the soldier work, that peace might purge

For her repletion[9] and retain° anew           *take into service*

25 Her° charitable heart, now hard and harsher    *(Juno's); (peace's)*

Than strife or war could be.

ARCITE               Are you not out?°      *off the point*

Meet you no ruin but the soldier in

The cranks and turns° of Thebes? You did begin    *winding streets*

As if you met decays of many kinds.

30 Perceive you none that do arouse your pity

But th'unconsidered° soldier?             *neglected*

PALAMON                Yes, I pity

Decays where'er I find them, but such most

That, sweating in an honourable toil,

Are paid with ice° to cool 'em.            *treated coldly*

ARCITE                  'Tis not this

35 I did begin to speak of. This is virtue,

Of no respect in Thebes. I spake of Thebes,

How dangerous, if we will keep our honours,

It is for our residing where every evil

Hath a good colour,° where every seeming good's    *appearance*

40 A certain evil, where not to be ev'n jump

As they are here were to be strangers, and

Such things to be, mere monsters.[1]

PALAMON              'Tis in our power,

Unless we fear that apes can tutor's,° to     *that we're mere mimics*

Be masters of our manners. What need I

45 Affect another's gait, which is not catching°    *infectious; attractive*

---

2. *here . . . incontinence:* we incur as much shame here (in a corrupt city) by remaining innocent as we would elsewhere by debauching ourselves.

3. And at least renders our exertions (on behalf of goodness) pointless.

4. *if . . . weakness:* if we were to pass through such a whirlpool ("eddy"), we would gain only our lives in a weakened state.

5. Is borne out by numerous examples.

6. *propound . . . ends:* propose as recompense for his

courage.

7. Which, though victorious in battle, he didn't receive.

8. Juno's jealousy led to the Trojan War and other conflicts.

9. *purge / For her repletion:* take medicine to alleviate her (peace's) overeating (the indulgent life of peacetime).

1. *where . . . monsters:* where failure to conform exactly ("jump") makes you a foreigner and perfect conformity makes you a monster.

Where there is faith?[2] Or to be fond° upon        *to dote*
Another's way of speech, when by mine own
I may be reasonably conceived°—saved, too—       *understood*
Speaking it° truly? Why am I bound       *If I speak*
50 By any generous° bond to follow him       *noble*
Follows° his tailor, haply° so long until    *Who heeds / at least*
The followed make pursuit?° Or let me know    *(for unpaid bills)*
Why mine own barber is unblest—with him
My poor chin, too—for 'tis not scissored just
55 To such a favourite's glass?° What canon° is there    *image / law*
That does command my rapier from my hip
To dangle't in my hand? Or to go tiptoe
Before the street be foul?[3] Either I am
The fore-horse in the team or I am none
60 That draw i'th' sequent trace.[4] These poor slight sores
Need not a plantain.[5] That which rips my bosom
Almost to th' heart's—
ARCITE             Our uncle Creon.
PALAMON                   He,
A most unbounded° tyrant, whose successes    *unrestrained*
Makes heaven unfeared and villainy assured°    *assured that*
65 Beyond its power there's nothing; almost puts
Faith in a fever,[6] and deifies alone
Voluble chance;° who only attributes       *Variable fortune*
The faculties of other instruments
To his own nerves and act;[7] commands men's service,
70 And what they win in't, boot° and glory; one    *booty; gain*
That fears not to do harm, good dares not.° Let    *dares not do good*
The blood of mine that's sib° to him be sucked    *related*
From me with leeches. Let them break° and fall    *burst*
Off me with that° corruption.       *(Creon's)*
ARCITE            Clear-spirited° cousin,    *Noble-spirited*
75 Let's leave his court that we may nothing share
Of his loud° infamy: for our milk       *well-known*
Will relish of the pasture,[8] and we must
Be vile or disobedient; not his kinsmen
In blood unless in quality.[9]
PALAMON           Nothing truer.
80 I think the echoes of his shames have deafed
The ears of heav'nly justice. Widows' cries
Descend again into their throats and have not
    *Enter* VALERIUS
Due audience of° the gods—Valerius.    *Proper notice from*
VALERIUS   The King calls for you; yet be leaden-footed°    *go slowly*
85 Till his great rage be off him. Phoebus, when
He broke his whipstock and exclaimed against
The horses of the sun,[1] but whispered to°    *compared to*

2. Self-reliance. Palamon's speech echoes familiar criticisms of the contrived, "effeminate" manners of
courtiers and men of fashion, here contrasted with
implicit religious norms ("faith"; "saved," line 48;
"canon," line 55).
3. *go . . . foul:* tiptoe on a clean street.
4. *Either . . . trace:* I will not pull behind the lead
("fore-") horse (follow fashion).
5. Herb used for treating wounds.
6. *puts . . . fever:* undermines religion.

7. *attributes . . . act:* takes credit for others' successes.
8. Like cows whose milk absorbs the taste of whatever
they eat.
9. *not . . . quality:* we ought not to act like his kinsmen
unless we're willing to act like him; we're not his kinsmen unless we act like him.
1. After his son Phaeton died driving the horses of the
sun, Phoebus (the sun) vented his grief at the horses—
hence the broken whip handle ("whipstock").

The loudness of his fury.
PALAMON            Small winds shake him.
  But what's the matter?
90  VALERIUS    Theseus, who where he threats, appals, hath sent
  Deadly defiance to him° and pronounces              *(Creon)*
  Ruin to Thebes, who° is at hand to seal             *(Theseus)*
  The promise of his wrath.[2]
ARCITE             Let him approach.
  But that we fear the gods in him,° he brings not   *justness of his cause*
95  A jot of terror to us. Yet what man
  Thirds his own worth—the case is each of ours—
  When that his action's dregged with mind assured
  'Tis bad he goes about.[3]
PALAMON            Leave that unreasoned.°        *Forget that*
  Our services stand now for Thebes, not Creon,
100  Yet to be neutral to him were dishonour,
  Rebellious° to oppose. Therefore we must        *Treasonable*
  With him stand to the mercy of° our fate,        *submit to*
  Who hath bounded our last minute.[4]
ARCITE             So we must.
  Is't said this war's afoot? Or it shall be
  On fail of° some condition?           *If Thebes rejects*
105  VALERIUS           'Tis in motion,
  The intelligence of state° came in the instant   *official announcement*
  With the defier.°                    *herald of Theseus*
PALAMON        Let's to the King, who, were he
  A quarter carrier of that honour which
  His enemy come in, the blood we venture
110  Should be as for our health,[5] which were not spent,°   *wasted*
  Rather laid out for purchase.° But, alas,    *invested for profit*
  Our hands advanced before° our hearts, what will   *beyond*
  The fall o'th' stroke do damage?[6]
ARCITE             Let th'event°—        *outcome*
  That never-erring arbitrator—tell us
115  When we know all ourselves,[7] and let us follow
  The becking° of our chance.       *Exeunt*     *calling*

## 1.3

*Enter* PIRITHOUS, HIPPOLYTA, *and* EMILIA
PIRITHOUS    No further.
HIPPOLYTA          Sir, farewell. Repeat my wishes
  To our great lord, of whose success I dare not
  Make any timorous question; yet I wish him
  Excess and overflow of power, an't might be,°     *if possible*
5  To dure° ill-dealing fortune. Speed to him;     *endure*
  Store[1] never hurts good governors.
PIRITHOUS             Though I know
  His ocean needs not my poor drops, yet they
  Must yield their tribute there. [*To* EMILIA] My precious maid,

---

2. *seal . . . wrath:* turn anger to action.
3. *Yet . . . about:* Yet any man reduces his worth by two-thirds—as we do—when he knows the action he undertakes is unworthy.
4. *Who . . . minute:* Which has determined when we die.
5. *the blood . . . health:* our loss of blood in combat

would be equivalent to a therapeutic bloodletting.
6. *what . . . damage:* what harm will "the fall o'th' stroke" do?
7. *tell . . . ourselves:* speak for itself.
1.3 Location: The outskirts of Athens.
1. Abundant resources (here, good men like Pirithous).

| | | |
|---|---|---|
| | Those best affections° that the heavens infuse | *inclinations* |
| 10 | In their best-tempered pieces° keep enthroned | *greatest creations* |
| | In your dear heart. | |

EMILIA                    Thanks, sir. Remember me

| | | |
|---|---|---|
| | To our all-royal brother, for whose speed° | *success* |
| | The great Bellona I'll solicit; and | |
| | Since in our terrene state° petitions are not | *earthly condition* |
| 15 | Without gifts understood, I'll offer to her | |
| | What I shall be advised she likes. Our hearts | |
| | Are in his army, in his tent. | |

HIPPOLYTA                    In's bosom.

| | | |
|---|---|---|
| | We have been soldiers,° and we cannot weep | *(as Amazons)* |
| | When our friends don their helms,° or put to sea, | *helmets* |
| 20 | Or tell of babes broached° on the lance, or women | *speared* |
| | That have sod° their infants in—and after eat them— | *boiled* |
| | The brine they wept at killing 'em:[2] then if | |
| | You stay to see of us such spinsters, we | |
| | Should hold you here forever.[3] | |

PIRITHOUS                    Peace be to you

| | | |
|---|---|---|
| 25 | As I pursue this war, which° shall be then | *(peace)* |
| | Beyond further requiring.°        *Exit* PIRITHOUS | *In no need of prayer* |

EMILIA                    How his longing

| | | |
|---|---|---|
| | Follows his friend! Since his depart,° his sports, | *Theseus's departure* |
| | Though craving° seriousness and skill, passed slightly | *requiring* |
| | His careless execution,[4] where nor° gain | *neither* |
| 30 | Made him regard or loss consider, but | |
| | Playing one business in his hand, another | |
| | Directing in his head, his mind nurse equal | |
| | To these so diff'ring twins.[5] Have you observed him | |
| | Since our great lord departed? | |

HIPPOLYTA                    With much labour;°

| | | |
|---|---|---|
| | | *diligence* |
| 35 | And I did love him for't. They two have cabined° | *shared quarters* |
| | In many as dangerous as poor a corner, | |
| | Peril and want contending;[6] they have skiffed° | *sailed across* |
| | Torrents whose roaring tyranny and power | |
| | I'th' least of these° was dreadful, and they have | *At the weakest point* |
| 40 | Fought out together where death's self was lodged;[7] | |
| | Yet fate hath brought them off. Their knot of love, | |
| | Tied, weaved, entangled with so true, so long, | |
| | And with a finger of so deep a cunning,° | *skill* |
| | May be outworn,° never undone. I think | *worn out (in death)* |
| 45 | Theseus cannot be umpire to himself, | |
| | Cleaving his conscience into twain and doing | |
| | Each side like° justice, which[8] he loves best. | *equal* |

EMILIA                    Doubtless

| | |
|---|---|
| | There is a best, and reason has no manners |
| | To say it is not you. I was acquainted |
| 50 | Once with a time when I enjoyed a playfellow; |
| | You were at wars when she the grave enriched, |

2. Miriam killed, cooked, and ate her son during the Roman siege of Jerusalem, adding her own tears for sauce.
3. *then if . . . forever:* if you wait long enough for us to turn into spinners (housewives), you'll wait forever.
4. *passed . . . execution:* were pursued carelessly.

5. *his . . . twins:* his attention divided equally between sports and Theseus.
6. Contending for which was the greater hardship.
7. *where . . . lodged:* the underworld, to rescue Proserpina.
8. Pirithous or Hippolyta.

Who made too proud the bed;° took leave o'th' moon[9]— *grave*
Which then looked pale at parting—when our count° *age*
Was each eleven.

HIPPOLYTA             'Twas Flavina.

EMILIA                         Yes.

55  You talk of Pirithous' and Theseus' love:
Theirs has more ground,° is more maturely seasoned, *a stronger base*
More buckled° with strong judgement, and their needs *joined together*
The one of th'other may be said to water
Their intertangled roots of love; but I
60  And she I sigh and spoke of were things innocent,
Loved for° we did, and like the elements,[1] *simply because*
That know not what, nor why, yet do effect° *create*
Rare issues° by their operance, our souls *Amazing results*
Did so to one another. What she liked
65  Was then of° me approved; what not, condemned— *by*
No more arraignment.° The flower that I would pluck *inquiry*
And put between my breasts—O then but beginning
To swell about the blossom—she would long° *desire*
Till she had such another, and commit it
70  To the like innocent cradle, where, phoenix-like,
They died in perfume.[2] On my head no toy° *trifle*
But was her pattern.° Her affections— pretty, *model*
Though happily her careless wear—I followed
For my most serious decking.[3] Had mine ear
75  Stol'n some new air,° or at adventure° hummed one, *tune / by chance*
From musical coinage,° why, it was a note *improvisation*
Whereon her spirits would sojourn—rather dwell on—
And sing it in her slumbers. This rehearsal—
Which, seely innocence wots well, comes in
80  Like old emportment's bastard[4]—has this end:
That the true love 'tween maid and maid may be
More than in sex dividual.[5]

HIPPOLYTA                     You're out of breath,
And this high-speeded pace is but to say
That you shall never, like the maid Flavina,
85  Love any that's called man.

EMILIA   I am sure I shall not.

HIPPOLYTA   Now alack, weak sister,
I must no more believe thee in this point—
Though in't I know thou dost believe thyself—
90  Than I will trust a sickly appetite
That loathes even as it longs. But sure, my sister,
If I were ripe for your persuasion,° you *open to your views*
Have said enough to shake me from the arm

---

9. Diana (the moon goddess), who watched over virgins and Amazons; hence Emilia's (equivocal) patron.
1. Air, fire, earth, and water—constituents of all matter.
2. The phoenix died by being burned on aromatic wood, only to be reborn from its own ashes.
3. *Her affections . . . decking:* Whatever she wore— even though she wasn't aware of how appealing it was—I'd imitate with utmost seriousness. For "happily" Q has "happely," which could also mean "haply" (by chance).

4. *This . . . bastard:* This narrative, which, as any happy innocent well knows, is an illegitimate descendant (poor likeness) of my former passion (or, the former significance of the relationship). For "seely innocence" Q has "fury-innocent" (innocent passionate love), which may be correct.
5. *in sex dividual:* between two sexes. Q has "individuall," which in the seventeenth century could mean the indivisible unity of male and female, and hence may be correct.

Of the all-noble Theseus, for whose fortunes
95 I will now in and kneel, with great assurance
That we more than his Pirithous possess
The high throne in his heart.

EMILIA                                    I am not
Against your faith, yet I continue mine.          *Exeunt*

### 1.4

*Cornetts. A battle struck within. Then a retreat.*
*Flourish.[1] Then enter* THESEUS, *victor. The three* QUEENS
*meet him and fall on their faces before him. [Also enter*
*a* HERALD, *and attendants bearing]* PALAMON *and*
ARCITE [*on*] *two hearses°*                                        biers

FIRST QUEEN [*to* THESEUS]   To thee no star be dark.°          unfavorable
SECOND QUEEN [*to* THESEUS]                   Both heaven and earth
Friend thee for ever.
THIRD QUEEN [*to* THESEUS]   All the good that may
Be wished upon thy head, I cry 'Amen' to't.
THESEUS   Th'impartial gods, who from the mounted° heavens          high
5 View us their mortal herd, behold who err
And in their time chastise. Go and find out
The bones of your dead lords and honour them
With treble ceremony: rather than a gap
Should be in their dear° rites we would supply't.                    valued
10 But those we will depute which shall invest°                       clothe
You in your dignities, and even° each thing                          rectify
Our haste does leave imperfect. So adieu,
And heaven's good eyes look on you.          *Exeunt* [*the*] QUEENS
                                        What are those?
HERALD   Men of great quality,° as may be judged                     rank
15 By their appointment.° Some of Thebes have told's        armor and weapons
They are sisters' children, nephews to the King.
THESEUS   By th' helm° of Mars I saw them in the war,               helmet
Like to a pair of lions smeared with prey,
Make lanes in troops aghast. I fixed my note°                      attention
20 Constantly on them, for they were a mark°                   striking sight
Worth a god's view. What prisoner was't that told me
When I enquired their names?
HERALD                                    Wi' leave, they're called
Arcite and Palamon.
THESEUS                         'Tis right: those, those.
They are not dead?
25 HERALD   Nor in a state of life. Had they been taken
When their last hurts were given, 'twas possible
They might have been recovered.° Yet they breathe,                  healed
And have the name of men.
THESEUS                         Then like men use 'em.
The very lees of such, millions of rates
30 Exceed the wine of others.[2] All our surgeons
Convent° in their behoof;° our richest balms,        Assemble / behalf
Rather than niggard,° waste. Their lives concern us           use stingily

---

1.4 Location: On the outskirts of Thebes.
1. Small horns sound offstage, signaling the start of
battle, a retreat, and then a triumphal entrance.

2. *The very . . . others:* The dregs of such men far
exceed the best that others can offer.

Much more than Thebes is worth. Rather than have 'em
Freed of this plight and in their morning° state—      *former (healthy)*
35  Sound and at liberty—I would 'em dead;
But forty-thousandfold we had rather have 'em
Prisoners to us, than death. Bear 'em speedily
From our kind air, to them unkind,³ and minister
What man to man may do—for our sake, more,
40  Since I have known frights, fury, friends' behests,
Love's provocations, zeal, a mistress' task,
Desire of liberty, a fever, madness,
Hath set a mark which nature could not reach to
Without some imposition, sickness in will
45  O'er-wrestling strength in reason.⁴ For our love
And great Apollo's° mercy, all our best      *god of healing*
Their best skill tender.—Lead into the city
Where, having bound things scattered,° we will post°      *reimposed order / hurry*
To Athens fore our army.      *Flourish. Exeunt*

1.5

*Music. Enter the [three]* QUEENS *with the hearses of
their [lords] in a funeral solemnity [with attendants]*
Song

Urns and odours, bring away,
Vapours, sighs, darken the day;
  Our dole° more deadly looks than dying.      *mourning*
Balms and gums¹ and heavy cheers,°      *sad countenances*
5  Sacred vials filled with tears,
  And clamours through the wild air flying:

Come all sad and solemn shows,
That are quick-eyed pleasure's foes.
We convent naught else but woes,
10    We convent naught else but woes.
THIRD QUEEN    This funeral path brings° to your household's      *leads*
    grave—
Joy seize on you again, peace sleep with him.
SECOND QUEEN    And this to yours.
FIRST QUEEN                                  Yours this way. Heavens lend
A thousand differing ways to one sure end.°      *death*
15  THIRD QUEEN    This world's a city full of straying streets,
And death's the market-place where each one meets.
*Exeunt severally°*      *separately*

2.1

*Enter [the]* JAILER *and [the]* WOOER
JAILER    I may depart with° little, while I live; something I may      *may spare*
cast° to you, not much. Alas, the prison I keep, though it be for      *give (as a dowry)*
great ones, yet they seldom come; before one salmon you shall
take a number of minnows. I am given out to be better lined°      *said to be richer*
5  than it can appear to me report° is a true speaker. I would I      *rumor*

---

3. Fresh air was thought dangerous to wounds.
4. *Since . . . reason:* Since compelling incentives can impel men to perform beyond their normal abilities, whereas otherwise weak will triumphs over strong reason. *mark:* target. *imposition:* command.
1.5 Scene continues.

1. Aromatic substances used in mourning rituals.
2.1 Location: The palace garden in Athens, perhaps with the second, or higher, gallery above representing the window of the cell where Palamon and Arcite are being held.

were really that° I am delivered° to be. Marry¹, what I have—    *what / reported*
be it what it will—I will assure upon° my daughter at the day    *bequeath to*
of my death.

WOOER   Sir, I demand no more than your own offer, and I will
10   estate° your daughter in what I have promised.    *settle*

JAILER   Well, we will talk more of this when the solemnity² is
past. But have you a full promise of° her?    *from*
     *Enter [the* JAILER'S] DAUGHTER [*with rushes*]°    *(as floor coverings)*
When that shall be seen, I tender my consent.

WOOER   I have, sir. Here she comes.

15 JAILER [*to* DAUGHTER]   Your friend and I have chanced to name
you here, upon the old business—but no more of that now. So
soon as the court hurry is over we will have an end of it. I'th'
mean time, look tenderly° to the two prisoners. I can tell you    *carefully*
they are princes.

20 JAILER'S DAUGHTER   These strewings° are for their chamber. 'Tis    *rushes*
pity they are in prison, and 'twere pity they should be out. I do
think they have patience to make any adversity ashamed; the
prison itself is proud of 'em, and they have all the world in
their chamber.³

25 JAILER   They are famed° to be a pair of absolute° men.    *reputed / perfect*

JAILER'S DAUGHTER   By my troth, I think fame but stammers°    *underrates*
'em—they stand a grece° above the reach of report.    *step*

JAILER   I heard them reported in the battle to be the only doers.°    *supreme achievers*

JAILER'S DAUGHTER   Nay, most likely, for they are noble sufferers.⁴
30   I marvel how they would have looked had they been victors, that
with such a constant nobility enforce a freedom out of bondage,
making misery their mirth, and affliction a toy° to jest at.    *trifle*

JAILER   Do they so?

JAILER'S DAUGHTER   It seems to me they have no more sense of
35   their captivity than I of ruling Athens. They eat well, look merrily, discourse of many things, but° nothing of their own    *but say*
restraint° and disasters. Yet sometime a divided° sigh—martyred    *captivity / half-audible*
as 'twere i'th' deliverance—will break from one of them, when
the other presently° gives it so sweet a rebuke that I could wish    *immediately*
40   myself a sigh to be so chid, or at least a sigher to be comforted.

WOOER   I never saw 'em.

JAILER   The Duke himself came privately in the night,
     PALAMON *and* ARCITE [*appear at a window*] *above*
and so did they.⁵ What the reason of it is I know not. Look,
yonder they are. That's Arcite looks out.

45 JAILER'S DAUGHTER   No, sir, no—that's Palamon. Arcite is the
lower° of the twain—[*pointing at* ARCITE] you may perceive a    *shorter*
part of him.

JAILER   Go to,° leave your pointing. They would not make us    *Come now*
their object.⁶ Out of their sight.

50 JAILER'S DAUGHTER   It is a holiday to look on them. Lord, the difference of ° men!                     *Exeunt*    *between*

---

1. To be sure (originally, by the Virgin Mary).
2. Theseus and Hippolyta's wedding.
3. They have everything they need in their prison cell, because they have each other. See 2.2.60.
4. For they endure nobly what others do to them. To do

and to suffer are antithetical.
5. Theseus brought them secretly at night.
6. They would not be so rude as to point at us; they don't want to look at us.

## 2.2

*Enter* PALAMON *and* ARCITE *in prison* [*in shackles,
above*]

PALAMON How do you, noble cousin?

ARCITE How do you, sir?

PALAMON Why, strong enough to laugh at misery

And bear the chance° of war. Yet we are prisoners,     *uncertainties*

I fear, for ever, cousin.

ARCITE I believe it,

And to that destiny have patiently

5 Laid up my hour to come.°     *Consigned my future*

PALAMON O, cousin Arcite,

Where is Thebes now?[1] Where is our noble country?

Where are our friends and kindreds? Never more

Must we behold those comforts, never see

The hardy youths strive for° the games of honour,     *in*

10 Hung with the painted favours° of their ladies,     *love tokens*

Like tall ships under sail; then start amongst 'em

And, as an east wind, leave 'em all behind us,

Like lazy clouds, whilst Palamon and Arcite,

Even in the wagging of a wanton leg,[2]

15 Outstripped the people's praises, won the garlands

Ere they have time to wish 'em ours. O never

Shall we two exercise, like twins of honour,

Our arms again and feel our fiery horses

Like proud seas under us. Our good swords, now—

20 Better° the red-eyed god of war ne'er wore—     *Better swords*

Ravished° our sides, like age must run to rust     *Torn from*

And deck the temples of those gods that hate us.

These hands shall never draw 'em out like lightning

To blast° whole armies more.     *annihilate*

ARCITE No, Palamon,

25 Those hopes are prisoners with us. Here we are,

And here the graces of our youths must wither,

Like a too-timely° spring. Here age must find us     *buds in a premature*

And, which is heaviest,° Palamon, unmarried—     *what is saddest*

The sweet embraces of a loving wife

30 Loaden with kisses, armed with thousand Cupids,

Shall never clasp our necks; no issue° know us;     *offspring*

No figures° of ourselves shall we e'er see     *images*

To glad our age, and, like young eagles, teach 'em

Boldly to gaze against bright arms[3] and say,

35 'Remember what your fathers were, and conquer.'

The fair-eyed maids shall weep our banishments,

And in their songs curse ever-blinded fortune,

Till she for shame see what a wrong she has done

To youth and nature. This is all our world.

40 We shall know nothing here but one another,

---

2.2 Location: The prison in Athens, perhaps represented by the principal upper stage, located on the first, or lower, gallery; as in 2.1, the garden is located on the main stage. The shift of Palamon and Arcite from the higher to the lower gallery is implied by the stage directions and start of a new scene here in Q.

1. The kinsmen's view of Thebes in 1.2 is very different, perhaps because Shakespeare probably wrote the earlier scene and Fletcher this one.
2. *Even . . . leg*: Effortlessly.
3. Eagles supposedly could gaze at the sun without being blinded.

Hear nothing but the clock that tells° our woes.                                     *counts*
The vine shall grow, but we shall never see it;
Summer shall come, and with her all delights,
45    But dead-cold winter must inhabit here still.
PALAMON   'Tis too true, Arcite. To our Theban hounds
That shook the agèd forest with their echoes,
No more now must we holler; no more shake
Our pointed javelins whilst the angry swine°                              *the wild boar*
50    Flies like a Parthian quiver⁴ from our rages,
Struck with our well-steeled darts. All valiant uses°—                      *activities*
The food and nourishment of noble minds—
In us two here shall perish; we shall die—
Which is the curse of honour—lastly,°                                          *at last*
Children of grief and ignorance.°                                   *Sad and unknown*
55  ARCITE                   Yet, cousin,
Even from the bottom of these miseries,
From all that fortune can inflict upon us,
I see two comforts rising—two mere° blessings,                                 *pure*
If the gods please, to hold here a brave patience
60    And the enjoying of our griefs together.
Whilst Palamon is with me, let me perish
If I think this our prison.
PALAMON              Certainly
'Tis a main° goodness, cousin, that our fortunes                          *the greatest*
Were twined together. 'Tis most true, two souls
65    Put in two noble bodies, let 'em suffer
The gall of hazard,° so° they grow together,                   *bitterest luck / if*
Will never sink;° they must not, say° they could.              *succumb / even if*
A willing man dies sleeping⁵ and all's done.
ARCITE   Shall we make worthy uses of this place
That all men hate so much?
70  PALAMON               How, gentle cousin?
ARCITE   Let's think this prison holy sanctuary,
To keep us from corruption of worse men.
We are young, and yet desire the ways of honour
That liberty and common conversation,°                         *worldly acquaintances*
75    The poison of pure spirits, might, like women,
Woo us to wander from. What worthy blessing
Can be, but our imaginations
May make it ours? And here being thus together,
We are an endless mine° to one another:                                     *resource*
80    We are one another's wife, ever begetting
New births of love; we are father, friends, acquaintance;
We are in one another, families—
I am your heir, and you are mine; this place
Is our inheritance: no hard oppressor
85    Dare take this from us. Here, with a little patience,
We shall live long and loving. No surfeits° seek us—             *diseases from excess*
The hand of war hurts none here, nor the seas
Swallow their youth. Were we at liberty

---

4. During the era of ancient Rome's supremacy, the Parthians were renowned archers, famous for shooting behind them at their enemies as they pretended to flee.

5. A man resigned to his fate dies in peace, as if merely falling asleep.

A wife might part us lawfully, or business;
90 Quarrels consume us; envy of ill men
Crave our acquaintance.⁶ I might sicken, cousin,
Where you should never know it, and so perish
Without your noble hand to close mine eyes,
Or prayers to the gods. A thousand chances,
Were we from hence, would sever us.

95 PALAMON                                        You have made me—
I thank you, cousin Arcite—almost wanton°                    *frolicsome*
With my captivity. What a misery
It is to live abroad,° and everywhere!                    *out of captivity*
'Tis like a beast, methinks. I find the court here;
100 I am sure, a more content;° and all those pleasures    *greater happiness*
That woo the wills of men to vanity
I see through now, and am sufficient
To tell the world 'tis but a gaudy shadow,
That old Time, as he passes by, takes with him.
105 What had we been, old° in the court of Creon,                *grown old*
Where sin is justice, lust and ignorance
The virtues of the great ones? Cousin Arcite,
Had not the loving gods found this place for us,
We had died as they do, ill° old men, unwept,                *wicked*
110 And had° their epitaphs, the people's curses.               *had for*
Shall I say more?

ARCITE                        I would hear you still.°           *forever*

PALAMON                                        Ye shall.
Is there record of any two that loved
Better than we do, Arcite?

ARCITE                                Sure there cannot.

PALAMON    I do not think it possible our friendship
Should ever leave us.

115 ARCITE                        Till our deaths it cannot,

*Enter* EMILIA *and her* WOMAN [*below.*° PALAMON *sees*      (in the garden)
EMILIA *and is silent*]

And after death our spirits shall be led
To those that love eternally.° Speak on, sir.                (in Elysium)

EMILIA [*to her* WOMAN]    This garden has a world of pleasure in't.
What flower is this?

WOMAN                        'Tis called narcissus, madam.

120 EMILIA    That was a fair boy, certain, but a fool
To love himself.⁷ Were there not maids enough?

ARCITE [*to* PALAMON]    Pray forward.°                       *go on speaking*

PALAMON                                        Yes.

EMILIA [*to her* WOMAN]                        Or were they all hard-hearted?

WOMAN    They could not be to one so fair.

EMILIA                                        Thou wouldst not.

WOMAN    I think I should not, madam.

EMILIA                                        That's a good wench—
But take heed to your kindness, though.

125 WOMAN                                        Why, madam?

EMILIA    Men are mad things.

---

6. *envy . . . acquaintance:* the malice (or, our envy) of
evil men might infect us.
7. Narcissus fell in love with his own reflection in a

pool and drowned trying to embrace it. After his death,
he was turned into a flower.

ARCITE [*to* PALAMON]                    Will ye go forward, cousin?
EMILIA [*to her* WOMAN]   Canst not thou work° such flowers in                    *embroider*
    silk, wench?
WOMAN                    Yes.
EMILIA   I'll have a gown full of 'em, and of these.
    This is a pretty colour—will't not do
    Rarely° upon a skirt, wench?                    *Beautifully*
130  WOMAN                    Dainty,° madam.                    *Very nicely*
ARCITE [*to* PALAMON]    Cousin, cousin, how do you, sir? Why,
    Palamon!
PALAMON   Never till now was I in prison, Arcite.
ARCITE   Why, what's the matter, man?
PALAMON                    Behold and wonder!
       [ARCITE *sees* EMILIA]
    By heaven, she is a goddess!
ARCITE                    Ha!
PALAMON                    Do reverence.
    She is a goddess, Arcite.
135  EMILIA [*to her* WOMAN]    Of all flowers
    Methinks a rose is best.
WOMAN                    Why, gentle madam?
EMILIA   It is the very emblem of a maid—
    For when the west wind courts her gently,
    How modestly she blows,° and paints the sun[8]                    *blooms*
140      With her chaste blushes! When the north° comes near her,                    *north wind*
    Rude and impatient, then, like chastity,
    She locks her beauties in her bud again,
    And leaves him to base briers.°                    *thorns*
WOMAN                    Yet, good madam,
    Sometimes her modesty will blow° so far                    *open*
145      She falls for't°—a maid,                    *because of it*
    If she have any honour, would be loath
    To take example by her.
EMILIA                    Thou art wanton.
ARCITE [*to* PALAMON]    She is wondrous fair.
PALAMON                    She is all the beauty extant.
EMILIA [*to her* WOMAN]    The sun grows high—let's walk in.
    Keep these flowers.
150  We'll see how close art can come near their colours.
    I am wondrous merry-hearted—I could laugh now.
WOMAN   I could lie down, I am sure.[9]
EMILIA                    And take one° with you?                    *(a rose); (a lover)*
WOMAN   That's as we bargain, madam.
EMILIA                    Well, agree° then.                    *let's bargain*
      *Exeunt* EMILIA *and* [*her*] WOMAN
PALAMON   What think you of this beauty?
ARCITE                    'Tis a rare one.
PALAMON   Is't but a rare one?
155  ARCITE                    Yes, a matchless beauty.
PALAMON   Might not a man well lose himself and love her?
ARCITE   I cannot tell what you have done; I have,
    Beshrew mine eyes° for't. Now I feel my shackles.                    *Curse me (an oath)*

---

8. Tints the sunlight pink; the inside of a rose looks like
an image of the sun.

9. "Laugh and lie down" was an Elizabethan card
game; sexual allusion.

PALAMON    You love her then?

160  ARCITE    Who would not?

PALAMON    And desire her?

ARCITE    Before my liberty.

PALAMON    I saw her first.

ARCITE                                That's nothing.

PALAMON                                             But it shall be.

ARCITE    I saw her too.

PALAMON                         Yes, but you must not love her.

165  ARCITE    I will not, as you do, to worship her
         As she is heavenly and a blessèd goddess!
         I love her as a woman, to enjoy her—
         So both may love.

PALAMON                         You shall not love at all.

ARCITE    Not love at all—who shall deny me?

170  PALAMON    I that first saw her, I that took possession
         First with mine eye of all those beauties
         In her revealed to mankind. If thou[1] lov'st her,
         Or entertain'st a hope to blast my wishes,
         Thou art a traitor, Arcite, and a fellow°                    *(contemptuous)*

175      False as thy title to° her. Friendship, blood,                    *claim to possess*
         And all the ties between us I disclaim,
         If thou once think upon her.

ARCITE                                   Yes, I love her—
         And if the lives of all my name lay° on it,                    *my family depended*
         I must do so. I love her with my soul—

180      If that will lose ye, farewell, Palamon!
         I say again,
         I love her, and in loving her maintain
         I am as worthy and as free° a lover,                           *noble*
         And have as just a title to her beauty,

185      As any Palamon, or any living
         That is a man's son.

PALAMON                         Have I called thee friend?

ARCITE    Yes, and have found me so. Why are you moved° thus?          *incensed*
         Let me deal coldly° with you. Am not I                         *dispassionately*
         Part of your blood, part of your soul? You have told me
         That I was Palamon and you were Arcite.

190  PALAMON                                             Yes.

ARCITE    Am not I liable to those affections,°                        *passions*
         Those joys, griefs, angers, fears, my friend shall suffer?

PALAMON    Ye may be.

ARCITE                      Why then would you deal so cunningly,
         So strangely, so unlike a noble kinsman,

195      To love alone? Speak truly. Do you think me
         Unworthy of her sight?

PALAMON                             No, but unjust
         If thou pursue that sight.

ARCITE                               Because another
         First sees the enemy, shall I stand still,
         And let mine honour down, and never charge?

PALAMON    Yes, if he be but one.°                                     *be alone*

---

1. The contemptuous "thou" replaces the more polite "you." Arcite follows suit at line 218.

| | | |
|---|---|---|
| 200 | **ARCITE** But say that one | |
| | Had rather combat me? | |
| | **PALAMON** Let that one say so, | |
| | And use thy freedom; else, if thou pursuest her, | |
| | Be as that cursèd man that hates his country, | |
| | A branded villain. | |
| | **ARCITE** You are mad. | |
| | **PALAMON** I must be. | |
| 205 | Till thou art worthy, Arcite, it concerns me; | |
| | And in this madness if I hazard° thee | *endanger* |
| | And take thy life, I deal but truly.° | *fairly* |
| | **ARCITE** Fie, sir. | |
| | You play the child extremely. I will love her, | |
| | I must, I ought to do so, and I dare— | |
| | And all this justly. | |
| 210 | **PALAMON** O, that now, that now | |
| | Thy false self and thy friend had but this fortune— | |
| | To be one hour at liberty and grasp | |
| | Our good swords in our hands! I would quickly teach thee | |
| | What 'twere to filch affection from another. | |
| 215 | Thou art baser in it than a cutpurse.° | *thief* |
| | Put but thy head out of this window more | |
| | And, as I have a soul, I'll nail thy life to't.° | *to the window frame* |
| | **ARCITE** Thou dar'st not, fool; thou canst not; thou art feeble. | |
| | Put my head out? I'll throw my body out | |
| 220 | And leap° the garden when I see her next, | *jump down to* |
| | *Enter [the* JAILER *above]* | |
| | And pitch° between her arms to anger thee. | *hurl myself* |
| | **PALAMON** No more—the keeper's coming. I shall live | |
| | To knock thy brains out with my shackles. | |
| | **ARCITE** Do. | |
| | **JAILER** By your leave, gentlemen. | |
| | **PALAMON** Now, honest keeper? | |
| 225 | **JAILER** Lord Arcite, you must presently to th' Duke. | |
| | The cause I know not yet. | |
| | **ARCITE** I am ready, keeper. | |
| | **JAILER** Prince Palamon, I must a while bereave you | |
| | Of your fair cousin's company. | |
| | *Exeunt* ARCITE *and [the* JAILER*]* | |
| | **PALAMON** And me, too, | |
| | Even when you please, of life. Why is he sent for? | |
| 230 | It may be he shall marry her—he's goodly,° | *handsome* |
| | And like enough the Duke hath taken notice | |
| | Both of his blood° and body. But his falsehood! | *noble family* |
| | Why should a friend be treacherous? If that | |
| | Get him a wife so noble and so fair, | |
| 235 | Let honest men ne'er love again. Once more | |
| | I would but see this fair one. Blessèd garden, | |
| | And fruit and flowers more blessèd, that still° blossom | *perpetually* |
| | As her bright eyes shine on ye! Would I were, | |
| | For all the fortune of my life hereafter, | |
| 240 | Yon little tree, yon blooming apricot— | |
| | How I would spread and fling my wanton arms | |
| | In at her window! I would bring her fruit | |
| | Fit for the gods to feed on; youth and pleasure | |

Still as° she tasted should be doubled on her;                    *Whenever*
245    And if she be not heavenly, I would make her
       So near the gods in nature they should fear her—
              *Enter* [the JAILER *above*]
       And then I am sure she would love me. How now, keeper,
       Where's Arcite?
JAILER                    Banished—Prince Pirithous
       Obtained his liberty;[2] but never more,
250    Upon his oath and life, must he set foot
       Upon this kingdom.
PALAMON [*aside*]          He's a blessèd man.
       He shall see Thebes again, and call to arms
       The bold young men that, when he bids 'em charge,
       Fall on like fire. Arcite shall have a fortune,°                *chance*
255    If he dare make himself a worthy lover,
       Yet in the field to strike a battle for her;
       And if he lose her then, he's a cold coward.
       How bravely may he bear himself to win her
       If he be noble Arcite; thousand ways!
260    Were I at liberty I would do things
       Of such a virtuous greatness that this lady,
       This blushing virgin, should take manhood to her
       And seek to ravish me.
JAILER                         My lord, for you
       I have this charge° to—                                        *order*
PALAMON                        To discharge my life.
265 JAILER    No, but from this place to remove your lordship—
       The windows are too open.
PALAMON                        Devils take 'em
       That are so envious° to me—prithee kill me.                    *spiteful*
JAILER    And hang for't afterward?
PALAMON                        By this good light,
       Had I a sword I would kill thee.
JAILER                         Why, my lord?
270 PALAMON    Thou bring'st such pelting° scurvy news continually,    *paltry*
       Thou art not worthy life. I will not go.
JAILER    Indeed you must, my lord.
PALAMON                        May I° see the garden?               *Will I be able to*
JAILER    No.
PALAMON    Then I am resolved—I will not go.
JAILER    I must constrain you, then; and for° you are dangerous,     *because*
       I'll clap more irons on you.
275 PALAMON                        Do, good keeper.
       I'll shake 'em so ye shall not sleep:
       I'll make ye a new morris.[3] Must I go?
JAILER    There is no remedy.
PALAMON                        Farewell, kind window.
       May rude wind never hurt thee. O, my lady,
280    If ever thou hast felt what sorrow was,
       Dream how I suffer. Come, now bury me.[4]
              *Exeunt* PALAMON *and* [*the* JAILER]

2. The motives behind Pirithous's intercession are not          4. Palamon's new cell will be like a grave because he
explained.                                                      will be banished from Emilia.
3. Morris dancers wore bells on their clothes.

## 2.3

*Exeunt* ARCITE

ARCITE Banished the kingdom? 'Tis a benefit,
A mercy I must thank 'em for; but banished
The free enjoying of that face I die for—
O, 'twas a studied° punishment, a death                                    *deliberate*
5    Beyond imagination; such a vengeance
That, were I old and wicked, all my sins
Could never pluck upon me. Palamon,
Thou hast the start° now—thou shalt stay and see                      *advantage*
Her bright eyes break° each morning 'gainst thy window,              *(like dawn)*
10   And let in life into thee. Thou shalt feed
Upon the sweetness of a noble beauty
That nature ne'er exceeded, nor ne'er shall.
Good gods! What happiness has Palamon!
Twenty to one he'll come to speak to her,
15   And if she be as gentle as she's fair,
I know she's his—he has a tongue will tame
Tempests and make the wild rocks wanton.°                              *full of joy*
Come what can come,
The worst is death. I will not leave the kingdom.
20   I know mine own° is but a heap of ruins,                              *(Thebes)*
And no redress there. If I go he has her.
I am resolved another shape° shall make me,                            *a disguise*
Or end my fortunes. Either way I am happy—
I'll see her and be near her, or no more.°                              *or die*

*Enter four* COUNTRY [MEN], *one [of whom carries] a
garland before them.* [ARCITE *stands apart*]

25   FIRST COUNTRYMAN   My masters, I'll be there—that's certain.
SECOND COUNTRYMAN   And I'll be there.
THIRD COUNTRYMAN   And I.
FOURTH COUNTRYMAN   Why then, have with ye,° boys! 'Tis but           *I'll come too*
a chiding[1]—
Let the plough play° today, I'll tickle't out                          *be idle*
Of the jades' tails tomorrow.[2]
30   FIRST COUNTRYMAN                  I am sure
To have my wife as jealous as a turkey[3]—
But that's all one. I'll go through, let her mumble.°                  *grumble*
SECOND COUNTRYMAN   Clap her aboard tomorrow night and
stow her,[4]
And all's made up again.
THIRD COUNTRYMAN          Ay, do but put
35   A fescue° in her fist and you shall see her                          *teacher's pointer*
Take a new lesson out° and be a good wench.                            *Learn a new lesson*
Do we all hold against the maying?[5]
FOURTH COUNTRYMAN   Hold? What should ail us?°                          *prevent us*
THIRD COUNTRYMAN                              Arcas will be there.
SECOND COUNTRYMAN   And Sennois, and Rycas, and three bet-
40   ter lads ne'er danced under green tree; and ye know what
wenches, ha? But will the dainty dominie,° the schoolmaster,          *fussy teacher*

---

2.3 Location: The countryside outside Athens.
1. The worst punishment I'll get (for not working) is a scolding.
2. *I'll . . . tomorrow:* I'll whip extra work out of the horses ("jades") tomorrow.

3. Thought to be jealously territorial.
4. Sexual metaphor: board her (like a ship) and fill up her cargo hold.
5. Are we still going to participate in the May Day celebrations (of fertility and the coming of spring)?

keep touch,° do you think? For he does all,[6] ye know.                    *keep this promise*

THIRD COUNTRYMAN    He'll eat a hornbook[7] ere he fail. Go to, the
matter's too far driven° between him and the tanner's daughter     *affair's gone too far*
to let slip now, and she must see the Duke, and she must dance too.

FOURTH COUNTRYMAN    Shall we be lusty?°                              *lively*

SECOND COUNTRYMAN    All the boys in Athens blow wind i'th'
breech on's![8] And here I'll be and there I'll be, for our town,
and here again and there again—ha, boys, hey for the weavers![9]

FIRST COUNTRYMAN    This must be done i'th' woods.

FOURTH COUNTRYMAN    O, pardon me.

SECOND COUNTRYMAN    By any° means, our thing of learning°      *all / our teacher*
said so; where he himself will edify the Duke most parlously°         *cleverly*
in our behalfs— he's excellent i'th' woods, bring him to th'
plains, his learning makes no cry.°                                   *falls silent*

THIRD COUNTRYMAN    We'll see the sports, then every man to's
tackle°—and, sweet companions, let's rehearse, by any means,      *morris-dancing gear*
before the ladies see us, and do sweetly, and God knows what
may come on't.

FOURTH COUNTRYMAN    Content—the sports once ended, we'll
perform. Away boys, and hold.°                                       *keep your word*

ARCITE [*coming forward*]    By your leaves, honest friends, pray
            you whither go you?

FOURTH COUNTRYMAN    Whither? Why, what a° question's that?          *what sort of a*

ARCITE    Yet 'tis a question
To me that know not.

THIRD COUNTRYMAN    To the games, my friend.

SECOND COUNTRYMAN    Where were you bred, you know it not?

ARCITE                                                    Not far, sir—
Are there such games today?

FIRST COUNTRYMAN                    Yes, marry, are there,
And such as you never saw. The Duke himself
Will be in person there.

ARCITE                          What pastimes are they?

SECOND COUNTRYMAN    Wrestling and running. [*To the others*]
        'Tis a pretty fellow.

THIRD COUNTRYMAN [*to* ARCITE]
    Thou wilt not go along?

ARCITE                      Not yet, sir.

FOURTH COUNTRYMAN                    Well, sir,
Take your own time. [*To the others*] Come, boys.

FIRST COUNTRYMAN                            My mind misgives me—
This fellow has a vengeance trick o'th' hip:[1]
Mark how his body's made for't.

SECOND COUNTRYMAN                I'll be hanged though
If he dare venture; hang him, plum porridge![2]
He wrestle? He roast eggs![3] Come, let's be gone, lads.
                        *Exeunt* [*the*] *four* [COUNTRYMEN]

ARCITE    This is an offered° opportunity                            *unsought*
I durst not° wish for. Well I could have wrestled[4]—       *would not have dared*

---

6. For he arranges everything.
7. A primer or tablet, protected by a translucent plate
of horn, inscribed with the alphabet.
8. Will try—and fail—to keep up with us.
9. Hooray for the weavers (the profession to which the
speaker apparently belongs).
1. *My . . . hip*: I fear that this man may be a skillful
wrestler.
2. Contemptuous, suggesting that Arcite is out of
shape. Plum porridge was a heavy dessert of stewed
dried fruits eaten at Christmas.
3. He'd be a better cook than wrestler (?); he probably
can't cook an egg (?).
4. I knew how to wrestle.

The best men called it excellent—and run
80  Swifter than wind upon a field of corn,°                                    *wheat*
Curling the wealthy° ears, never° flew. I'll venture,                *abundant / ever*
And in some poor disguise be there. Who knows
Whether my brows may not be girt with garlands,
And happiness prefer° me to a place                                   *good fortune promote*
85  Where I may ever dwell in sight of her?                     *Exit*

### 2.4

*Enter [the]* JAILER'S DAUGHTER
JAILER'S DAUGHTER   Why should I love this gentleman? 'Tis
odds°                                                                            *Chances are*
He never will affect° me. I am base,                                              *love*
My father the mean° keeper of his prison,                                        *lowly*
And he a prince. To marry him is hopeless,
5   To be his whore¹ is witless. Out upon't,°                    *(Expressing abhorrence)*
What pushes° are we wenches driven to                                        *extremities*
When fifteen° once has found us? First, I saw him;                         *(the age)*
I, seeing, thought he was a goodly man;
He has as much to please a woman in him—
10  If he please to bestow it so—as ever
These eyes yet looked on. Next, I pitied him,
And so would any young wench, o'my conscience,
That ever dreamed or vowed her maidenhead
To a young handsome man. Then, I loved him,
15  Extremely loved him, infinitely loved him—
And yet he had a cousin fair as he, too.
But in my heart was Palamon, and there,
Lord, what a coil he keeps!° To hear him                              *turmoil he makes*
Sing in an evening, what a heaven it is!
20  And yet his songs are sad ones. Fairer spoken
Was never gentleman. When I come in
To bring him water in a morning, first
He bows his noble body, then salutes° me, thus:                                 *greets*
'Fair, gentle maid, good morrow. May thy goodness
25  Get thee a happy husband.' Once he kissed me—
I loved my lips the better ten days after.
Would he would do so every day! He grieves much,
And me as much to see his misery.
What should I do to make him know I love him?
30  For I would fain° enjoy him. Say I ventured                                *eagerly*
To set him free? What says the law then? Thus much
For law or kindred! I will do it,
And this night; ere tomorrow he shall love me.          *Exit*

### 2.5

*Short flourish of cornetts and shouts within. Enter* THE-
SEUS, HIPPOLYTA, PIRITHOUS, EMILIA, ARCITE *[disguised]*
*with a garland [and attendants]*
THESEUS   You have done worthily. I have not seen
Since Hercules a man of tougher sinews.°                                        *muscles*
Whate'er you are, you run the best and wrestle°                         *wrestle the best*
That these times can allow.°                                                      *show*

---

2.4 Location: The prison in Athens.          2.5 Location: Athens, near the site of the athletic
1. Premarital sex, not prostitution.          games.

| ARCITE | I am proud to please you. | |
| THESEUS | What country bred you? | |
| 5 ARCITE | This—but far off, prince. | |
| THESEUS | Are you a gentleman? | |
| ARCITE | My father said so, | |

And to those gentle uses gave me life.[1]

THESEUS  Are you his heir?

| ARCITE | His youngest, sir. | |
| THESEUS | Your father | |

Sure is a happy sire, then. What proves you?°                          (*a gentleman*)

10 ARCITE   A little of all noble qualities.°                          *accomplishments*
I could have kept° a hawk and well have hollered                          *I knew how to keep*
To a deep° cry of dogs; I dare not praise                          *loud*
My feat in horsemanship, yet they that knew me
Would say it was my best piece;° last and greatest,                          *attribute*
I would° be thought a soldier.                          *used to*

| 15 THESEUS | You are perfect. | |
| PIRITHOUS | Upon my soul, a proper° man. | *handsome* |
| EMILIA | He is so. | |

PIRITHOUS [*to* HIPPOLYTA]   How do you like him, lady?

| HIPPOLYTA | I admire° him. | *am amazed at* |

I have not seen so young a man so noble—
If he say true—of his sort.°                          *rank*

| EMILIA | Believe° | *Be sure* |

20 His mother was a wondrous handsome woman—
His face methinks goes that way.˘                          *demonstrates that*

| HIPPOLYTA | But his body | |

And fiery mind illustrate° a brave father.                          *indicate; copy*

PIRITHOUS   Mark how his virtue,° like a hidden sun,                          *excellence*
Breaks through his baser garments.

| HIPPOLYTA | He's well got,° sure. | *wellborn* |

THESEUS [*to* ARCITE]   What made you seek this place, sir?

| 25 ARCITE | Noble Theseus, | |

To purchase name° and do my ablest service                          *get a reputation*
To such a well-found° wonder as thy worth,                          *well-deserved*
For only in thy court of all the world
Dwells fair-eyed honour.

| PIRITHOUS | All his words are worthy. | |

30 THESEUS [*to* ARCITE]   Sir, we are much indebted to your travel,°                          *journey; effort*
Nor shall you lose your wish.—Pirithous,
Dispose of° this fair gentleman.                          *Place*

| PIRITHOUS | Thanks, Theseus. | |

[*To* ARCITE] Whate'er you are, you're mine, and I shall give you
To a most noble service, to this lady,
35 This bright young virgin; pray observe° her goodness.                          *respect*
You have honoured her fair birthday with your virtues,
And as your due you're hers. Kiss her fair hand, sir.

ARCITE   Sir, you're a noble giver. [*To* EMILIA] Dearest beauty,
Thus let me seal my vowed faith.
[*He kisses her hand*]

|  | When your servant, | |

Your most unworthy creature, but offends you,
Command him die, he shall.

40

1. And raised me for those genteel pursuits.

EMILIA                              That were too cruel.
If you deserve well, sir, I shall soon see't.
You're mine, and somewhat better than your rank° I'll use you.          *position*
PIRITHOUS [*to* ARCITE]   I'll see you furnished,° and, because you          *equipped*
   say
45    You are a horseman, I must needs entreat you
This afternoon to ride—but 'tis a rough one.°          *(horse)*
ARCITE   I like him better, prince—I shall not then
Freeze in my saddle.
THESEUS [*to* HIPPOLYTA]   Sweet, you must be ready—
And you, Emilia, [*to* PIRITHOUS] and you, friend—and all,
50    Tomorrow by the sun,° to do observance          *by sunrise*
To flow'ry May in Dian's wood. [*To* ARCITE] Wait well, sir,
Upon your mistress.—Emily, I hope
He shall not go afoot.
EMILIA                        That were a shame, sir,
While I have horses. [*To* ARCITE] Take your choice, and what
55    You want,° at any time, let me but know it.          *lack*
If you serve faithfully, I dare assure you,
You'll find a loving mistress.
ARCITE                              If I do not,
Let me find that° my father ever hated—          *that which*
Disgrace and blows.
THESEUS                  Go, lead the way—you have won it.[2]
60    It shall be so: you shall receive all dues
Fit for the honour you have won. 'Twere wrong else.
[*To* EMILIA] Sister, beshrew my heart, you have a servant
That, if I were a woman, would be master.
But you are wise.
EMILIA                  I hope too wise for that, sir. *Flourish. Exeunt*

## 2.6

*Enter [the]* JAILER'S DAUGHTER

JAILER'S DAUGHTER   Let all the dukes and all the devils roar—
He is at liberty! I have ventured° for him,          *taken a risk*
And out I have brought him. To a little wood
A mile hence I have sent him, where a cedar
Higher than all the rest spreads like a plane,°          *plane tree*
Fast° by a brook—and there he shall keep close°          *Close / shall hide*
5    Till I provide him files and food, for yet
His iron bracelets° are not off. O Love,°          *shackles / Cupid*
What a stout-hearted child thou art! My father
Durst better have endured cold iron than done it.[1]
I love him beyond love and beyond reason
10    Or wit° or safety. I have made him know it—          *sense*
I care not, I am desperate. If the law
Find me and then condemn me for't, some wenches,
Some honest-hearted maids, will sing my dirge
And tell to memory my death was noble,
15    Dying almost a martyr. That way he takes,
I purpose, is my way too. Sure, he cannot

---

2. Won the honor of leading the procession.
2.6 Location: Near the prison in Athens.

1. *My . . . it:* My father would sooner have been run
through than have freed a prisoner.

Be so unmanly as to leave me here.
20   If he do, maids will not so easily
Trust men again. And yet, he has not thanked me
For what I have done—no, not so much as kissed me—
And that, methinks, is not so well. Nor scarcely
Could I persuade him to become a free man,
25   He made such scruples of the wrong he did
To me and to my father. Yet, I hope
When he considers more, this love of mine
Will take more root within him. Let him do
What he will with me—so he use me kindly.²
30   For use me,° so he shall, or I'll proclaim him,      *(sexually)*
And to his face, no man.° I'll presently      *(sexually)*
Provide him necessaries and pack my clothes up,
And where there is a patch of ground I'll venture,
So he be with me. By him, like a shadow,
35   I'll ever dwell. Within this hour the hubbub
Will be all o'er the prison—I am then
Kissing the man they look for. Farewell, father:
Get° many more such prisoners and such daughters,      *Catch; beget*
And shortly you may keep yourself.³ Now to him.      [*Exit*]

### 3.1

[*A bush in place.*] *Cornetts in sundry*° *places. Noise and*      *various (offstage)*
*hollering as [of ] people a-Maying.*¹
    *Enter* ARCITE

ARCITE   The Duke has lost Hippolyta—each took°      *went to*
A several laund.° This is a solemn rite      *A different clearing*
They owe bloomed May, and the Athenians pay° it      *observe*
To th' heart of° ceremony. O, Queen Emilia,      *With the utmost*
5   Fresher than May, sweeter
Than her gold buttons° on the boughs, or all      *buds*
Th'enamelled knacks° o'th' mead° or garden—yea,      *flowers / meadow*
We challenge too the bank of any nymph
That makes the stream seem flowers;² thou, O jewel
10   O'th' wood, o'th' world, hast likewise blessed a pace°      *path through the woods*
With thy sole presence in thy [
           ]³ rumination
That I, poor man, might eftsoons come between
And chop on some cold thought.⁴ Thrice blessèd chance
15   To drop on° such a mistress, expectation      *run into*
Most guiltless on't!° Tell me, O Lady Fortune,      *unexpectedly*
Next after Emily my sovereign, how far
I may be proud. She takes strong note of me,
Hath made me near her, and this beauteous morn,

2. Provided that he treat me gently; naturally; nobly, in a manner befitting a man of his kind.
3. You yourself may use the jail, since everyone else will either have escaped or been freed.
3.1 Location: All of Act 3 takes place in a forest near Athens.
1. May Day celebrations included feasts, hunting, music, entertainments (such as the morris dance of 3.5.139), and dancing around the maypole. See note to 2.3.37.

2. *We . . . flowers*: Emilia surpasses in beauty even a nymph's flowered riverbank, whose reflection makes the river itself seem covered with flowers.
3. Q has a comma after "presence" and lacks this gap. Editors often strengthen the punctuation by starting a new sentence with "In thy rumination." It is unclear how Arcite could "come between" (line 13) a "rumination," however—hence the hypothesis of a missing line.
4. *might . . . thought*: might suddenly come upon you and seize some chaste thought.

20　The prim'st° of all the year, presents me with　　　　　　　　　*best*
　　A brace° of horses—two such steeds might well　　　　　　　　*pair*
　　Be by a pair of kings backed,° in a field　　　　　　　　　　*ridden*
　　That their crowns' titles tried.⁵ Alas, alas,
　　Poor cousin Palamon, poor prisoner—thou
25　So little dream'st upon my fortune that
　　Thou think'st thyself the happier thing to be
　　So near Emilia. Me thou deem'st at Thebes,
　　And therein wretched, although free. But if
　　Thou knew'st my mistress breathed on me, and that
30　I eared her language,° lived in her eye—O, coz,　　　　*listened to her*
　　What passion would enclose° thee!　　　　　　　　　*rage would possess*
　　　　　　*Enter* PALAMON *as out of a bush with his shackles.* [*He*]
　　　　　　*bends° his fist at* ARCITE　　　　　　　　　　　　*shakes*
PALAMON　　　　　　　　　　　Traitor kinsman,
　　Thou shouldst perceive my passion if these signs
　　Of prisonment⁶ were off me, and this hand
　　But owner of a sword. By all oaths in one,
35　I and the justice of my love would make thee
　　A confessed traitor. O thou most perfidious
　　That ever gently looked,° the void'st of honour　　　*seemed gentlemanly*
　　That e'er bore gentle token,° falsest cousin　　　　*wore noble emblems*
　　That ever blood made kin—call'st thou her thine?
40　I'll prove it in my shackles, with these hands,
　　Void of appointment,° that thou liest and art　　　*Devoid of weapons*
　　A very thief in love, a chaffy° lord　　　　　　　　　*worthless*
　　Not worth the name of villain. Had I a sword
　　And these house-clogs° away—　　　　　　　　　　*fetters*
ARCITE　　　　　　　　　　　　Dear cousin Palamon—
45　PALAMON　　Cozener° Arcite, give me language such　　*Cheater (punning)*
　　As thou hast showed me feat.⁷
ARCITE　　　　　　　　　　　Not finding in
　　The circuit of my breast any gross stuff
　　To form me like your blazon holds me to
　　This gentleness of answer⁸—'tis your passion
50　That thus mistakes, the which, to you being enemy,
　　Cannot to me be kind.⁹ Honour and honesty
　　I cherish and depend on, howsoe'er
　　You skip° them in me, and with them, fair coz,　　　*ignore*
　　I'll maintain my proceedings. Pray be pleased
55　To show in generous° terms your griefs,° since that　*genteel / grievances*
　　Your question's° with your equal, who professes　　*dispute is*
　　To clear his own way¹ with the mind and sword
　　Of a true gentleman.
PALAMON　　　　　　　　That thou durst,° Arcite!　　*You wouldn't dare*
ARCITE　　My coz, my coz, you have been well advertised°　*informed*
60　How much I dare; you've seen me use my sword
　　Against th'advice° of fear. Sure, of° another　　　*warning / by*

5. *in . . . tried:* on a battlefield where they were fighting
for each other's kingdoms.
6. *signs / Of prisonment:* shackles.
7. *give . . . feat:* use words that accord better with your
(perfidious) actions.
8. *Not . . . answer:* Since I find nothing in me that fits
your description of me, I answer gently. *blazon:* (descrip-

tion of a) coat of arms.
9. *'tis . . . kind:* your anger ("passion") is your enemy
(distorts your judgment) and thus to me cannot be kind
(because you are my kinsman—"kind" also means
"kin"—and friend, and hence we share all enemies).
1. To justify; to make his own way.

You would not hear me doubted, but your silence
Should break out, though i'th' sanctuary.[2]

PALAMON                                    Sir,
    I have seen you move in such a place° which well        *battle; tournament*
65    Might justify your manhood; you were called
    A good knight and a bold. But the whole week's not fair
    If any day it rain: their valiant temper°              *attitude*
    Men lose when they incline to treachery,
    And then they fight like compelled bears[3]—would fly
    Were they not tied.

70  ARCITE             Kinsman, you might as well
    Speak this and act it in your glass° as to            *mirror*
    His ear which now disdains you.

PALAMON              Come up to me,
    Quit° me of these cold gyves,° give me a sword,    *Free / chains*
    Though it be rusty, and the charity
75    Of one meal lend me. Come before me then,
    A good sword in thy hand, and do but say
    That Emily is thine—I will forgive
    The trespass° thou hast done me, yea, my life,      *wrong*
    If then thou carry't;° and brave souls in shades°   *beat me / Hades*
80    That have died manly, which will seek of me
    Some news from earth, they shall get none but this—
    That thou art brave and noble.

ARCITE             Be content,
    Again betake you to° your hawthorn house.      *go back into*
    With counsel of the night[4] I will be here
85    With wholesome viands.° These impediments°   *food / shackles*
    Will I file off. You shall have garments and
    Perfumes to kill the smell o'th' prison. After,
    When you shall stretch yourself and say but 'Arcite,
    I am in plight',° there shall be at your choice     *I am ready*
    Both sword and armour.

90  PALAMON          O, you heavens, dares any
    So noble bear a guilty business!° None       *act shamefully*
    But only Arcite, therefore none but Arcite
    In this kind is so bold.

ARCITE           Sweet Palamon.

PALAMON  I do embrace you and your offer—for
95    Your offer do't I only, sir; your person,
    Without hypocrisy, I may not wish
        *Wind° horns [within]*                *Sound*
    More than my sword's edge on't.

ARCITE           You hear the horns—
    Enter your muset° lest this match between's     *gap in a thicket*
    Be crossed ere met.° Give me your hand, farewell. *prevented before begun*
100    I'll bring you every needful thing—I pray you,
    Take comfort and be strong.

PALAMON          Pray hold your promise,
    And do the deed with a bent brow.° Most certain   *stern countenance*
    You love me not—be rough with me and pour

---

2. *your . . . sanctuary*: you would speak to defend me
even if you were hiding in a safe place (or in a church).
3. In bearbaiting competitions (a popular pastime with

connections to the theater), bears were tied to a stake.
4. With darkness to assist (and hide) me.

This oil° out of your language. By this air,                    *smoothness; flattery*
105   I could for each word give a cuff, my stomach°             *anger*
Not reconciled by reason.
ARCITE                             Plainly spoken,
Yet—pardon me—hard language: when I spur
*Wind horns [within]*
My horse I chide him not. Content and anger
In me have but one face.° Hark, sir, they call            *the same expression*
110   The scattered to the banquet. You must guess
I have an office° there.                                   *assigned duty*
PALAMON                        Sir, your attendance
Cannot please heaven, and I know your office
Unjustly is achieved.°                                    *Was earned unfairly*
ARCITE                          'Tis a good title.°        *It was won justly*
I am persuaded this question, sick between's,
115   By bleeding must be cured.⁵ I am a suitor°             *I beg*
That to your sword you will bequeath this plea°           *lawsuit*
And talk of it no more.
PALAMON                        But this one word:
You are going now to gaze upon my mistress—
For note you, mine she is—
ARCITE                          Nay then—
PALAMON                                        Nay, pray you—
120   You talk of feeding me to breed me strength—
You are going now to look upon a sun
That strengthens what it looks on. There you have
A vantage° o'er me, but enjoy it till                      *advantage*
I may enforce my remedy. Farewell.
*Exeunt [severally, PALAMON as into the bush]*

### 3.2

*Enter [the] JAILER'S DAUGHTER [with a file]*
JAILER'S DAUGHTER   He has mistook the brake° I meant, is gone    *thicket*
After¹ his fancy. 'Tis now wellnigh morning.
No matter—would it were perpetual night,
And darkness lord o'th' world. Hark, 'tis a wolf!
5    In me hath grief slain fear, and, but for one thing,
I care for nothing—and that's Palamon.
I reck° not if the wolves would jaw° me, so°            *care / gnaw / if*
He had this file. What if I hollered for him?
I cannot holler. If I whooped, what then?
10   If he not answered, I should call a wolf
And do him but that service.² I have heard
Strange howls this livelong night—why may't not be
They have made prey of him? He has no weapons;
He cannot run; the jangling of his gyves°              *fetters*
15   Might call fell° things to listen, who have in them   *wild*
A sense to know a man unarmed, and can
Smell where resistance is. I'll set it down°           *take it as fact*
He's torn to pieces: they howled many together

---

5. *I am . . . cured:* I am convinced that the dispute       **3.2**
between us (here, imagined as a sick person) can only       1. *is gone / After:* is led by (only).
be settled (cured) by a bloodletting.                        2. I would at least serve him by calling a wolf to attack
him (ironic).

And then they fed on him. So much for that.
20   Be bold to ring the bell.° How stand I then?                    *ring his death knell*
All's chared° when he is gone. No, no, I lie:                        *My work is all done*
My father's to be hanged for his escape,
Myself to beg, if I prized life so much
As to deny my act—but that I would not,
25   Should I try death by dozens.³ I am moped°—                      *dazed*
Food took I none these two days,
Sipped some water. I have not closed mine eyes
Save when my lids scoured off their brine.⁴ Alas,
Dissolve, my life; let not my sense unsettle,°                      *reason come unhinged*
30   Lest I should drown or stab or hang myself.
O state of nature,° fail together° in me,                           *life / entirely*
Since thy best props° are warped. So which way now?                *supports*
The best way is the next° way to a grave,                          *nearest*
Each errant step beside⁵ is torment. Lo,
35   The moon is down, the crickets chirp, the screech-owl
Calls in the dawn. All offices are done
Save what I fail in:⁶ but the point is this,
An end,° and that is all.                             *Exit*       *A death*

### 3.3

*Enter* ARCITE *with [a bundle containing] meat, wine,*
*and files*

ARCITE   I should be near the place. Ho, cousin Palamon!
*Enter* PALAMON [*as from the bush*]
PALAMON   Arcite.
ARCITE                    The same. I have brought you food and files.
Come forth and fear not, here's no Theseus.
PALAMON   Nor none so honest, Arcite.
ARCITE                                That's no matter—
5   We'll argue that hereafter. Come, take courage—
You shall not die thus beastly.° Here, sir, drink;                  *like an animal*
I know you are faint. Then I'll talk further with you.
PALAMON   Arcite, thou mightst now poison me.
ARCITE                          I might—
But I must⁸ fear you first. Sit down and, good now,                 *should need to*
10   No more of these vain parleys.° Let us not,                     *pointless comments*
Having our ancient¹ reputation with us,
Make talk for² fools and cowards. To your health, sir.
PALAMON   Do.°                                                       *You drink first*
[ARCITE *drinks*]
ARCITE                    Pray sit down, then, and let me entreat you,
By all the honesty and honour in you,
15   No mention of this woman—'twill disturb us.
We shall have time enough.
PALAMON                          Well, sir, I'll pledge you.°         *drink your health*
[PALAMON *drinks*]
ARCITE   Drink a good hearty draught; it breeds good blood,° man.   *makes you strong*

---

3. Even if I had to die dozens of times (ways).
4. Except when I blinked to clear my eyes of tears.
5. Each step that wanders from the direct path to the grave.
6. *All . . . in:* All tasks are done, except the one I've failed to complete (either giving the file to Palamon or

killing herself).
**3.3**
1. Of long standing; former (now reestablished through escape).
2. Talk as though we were; make ourselves the talk of.

Do not you feel it thaw you?

PALAMON                          Stay, I'll tell you
After a draught or two more.
            [PALAMON *drinks*]

ARCITE                          Spare it not—
The Duke has more, coz. Eat now.

PALAMON                          Yes.
            [PALAMON *eats*]

20  ARCITE                          I am glad
You have so good a stomach.°                                    *an appetite; an anger*

PALAMON                          I am gladder
I have so good meat° to't.                                      *(to feed my anger)*

ARCITE                          Is't not mad,° lodging                *strange; maddening*
Here in the wild woods,³ cousin?

PALAMON                          Yes, for them
That have wild° consciences.                                    *uncivilized*

ARCITE                          How tastes your victuals?
Your hunger needs no sauce, I see.

25  PALAMON                          Not much.
But if it did, yours is too tart,⁴ sweet cousin.
What is this?

ARCITE          Venison.

PALAMON                          'Tis a lusty° meat—              *hearty*
Give me more wine. Here, Arcite, to the wenches
We have known in our days. [*Drinking*] The lord steward's
      daughter.
Do you remember her?

30  ARCITE                          After you,⁵ coz.

PALAMON          She loved a black-haired man.

ARCITE                          She did so; well, sir.

PALAMON          And I have heard some call him Arcite, and—

ARCITE          Out with't, faith.

PALAMON                          She met him in an arbour—
What did she there, coz? Play o'th' virginals?⁶

ARCITE          Something° she did, sir—                        *To some extent*

35  PALAMON                          Made her groan a month for't—
Or two, or three, or ten.°                                     *(in pregnancy)*

ARCITE                          The marshal's sister
Had her share too, as I remember, cousin,
Else there be tales° abroad. You'll pledge her?                *false rumors*

PALAMON                          Yes.
            [*They drink*]

ARCITE          A pretty brown° wench 'tis. There was a time    *brunette*
40  When young men went a-hunting, and a wood,
And a broad beech, and thereby hangs a tale—
Heigh-ho!°                                                     *(a sigh)*

PALAMON          For Emily, upon my life! Fool,
Away with this strained mirth. I say again,
That sigh was breathed for Emily. Base cousin,
Dar'st thou break⁷ first?

ARCITE                          You are wide.°                  *wide of the mark*

---

3. *woods:* Pun on "wode" (mad).
4. Your insolence ("sauce," line 25) is too bitter ("tart").
5. Finish your toast first, before I propose mine.
6. Small keyboard instrument; (sexual).
7. Break our agreement (not to refer to Emilia).

45 PALAMON                                    By heaven and earth,
    There's nothing in thee honest.
    ARCITE                              Then I'll leave you—
      You are a beast° now.                                    *behaving savagely*
    PALAMON                        As thou mak'st me, traitor.
    ARCITE [*pointing to the bundle*]    There's all things needful: files
        and shirts and perfumes—
      I'll come again some two hours hence and bring
      That that shall quiet° all.                                    *silence*
50 PALAMON                        A sword and armour.
    ARCITE    Fear° me not. You are now too foul.° Farewell.    *Doubt / beastly*
      Get off your trinkets:° you shall want naught.                *shackles*
    PALAMON                                    Sirrah°—              *(an insult)*
    ARCITE    I'll hear no more.                          *Exit*
    PALAMON              If he keep touch°, he dies for't.    *keeps his promise*
                                    *Exit* [*as into the bush*]

## 3.4

    *Enter* [*the*] JAILER'S DAUGHTER
    JAILER'S DAUGHTER    I am very cold, and all the stars are out too,
      The little stars and all, that look like aglets°—            *shiny ornaments*
      The sun has seen my folly. Palamon!
      Alas, no, he's in heaven. Where am I now?
5     Yonder's the sea and there's a ship—how't tumbles!
      And there's a rock lies watching under water—
      Now, now, it° beats upon it—now, now, now,                   *(the ship)*
      There's a leak sprung, a sound° one—how they cry!            *large*
      Open her¹ before the wind—you'll lose all else.
10    Up with a course° or two and tack° about, boys.          *lower sail / turn*
      Good night, good night, you're gone. I am very hungry.
      Would I could find a fine frog—he would tell me
      News from all parts o'th' world, then would I make
      A carrack° of a cockle-shell, and sail                        *cargo ship*
15    By east and north-east to the King of Pygmies,
      For he tells fortunes rarely.° Now my father,                *wonderfully*
      Twenty to one, is trussed up in a trice°               *to be hanged quickly*
      Tomorrow morning. I'll say never a word.
      [*She*] *sing*[*s*]
      For I'll cut my green coat, a foot above my knee,
20    And I'll clip my yellow locks, an inch below mine eye,
          Hey nonny, nonny, nonny,
      He s'buy° me a white cut,² forth for to ride,                 *He shall buy*
      And I'll go seek him, through the world that is so wide,
          Hey nonny, nonny, nonny.
25    O for a prick now, like a nightingale,
      To put my breast against.³ I shall sleep like a top° else.  *Exit*    *soundly*

---

**3.4**
1. Open her sails (so she can run).
2. Horse (called a "cut" because it was a gelding or had
a cropped tail).

3. O . . . *against*: nightingales supposedly pricked themselves to stay awake at night. "Prick" also carries a sexual meaning; compare the sexual punning here with
that in Ophelia's "mad" speeches in *Hamlet*.

## 3.5

*Enter [Gerald] a* SCHOOLMASTER, *[five]* COUNTRYMEN,
*[one of whom is dressed as a]* BABION, *[five]* Wenches,
*[and Timothy,] a* TABORER. *[All are attired as morris
dancers]*[1]

SCHOOLMASTER Fie, fie,
  What tediosity and disinsanity[2]
  Is here among ye! Have my rudiments°                                        lessons; rehearsals
  Been laboured so long with ye, milked unto ye,
5  And, by a figure,° even the very plum-broth                                figure of speech
  And marrow[3] of my understanding laid upon ye?
  And do you still cry 'where?' and 'how?' and 'wherefore?'
  You most coarse frieze capacities, ye jean judgements,[4]
  Have I said, 'thus let be', and 'there let be',
10  And 'then let be', and no man understand me?
  *Proh deum, medius fidius*[5]—ye are all dunces.
  Forwhy, here stand I. Here the Duke comes. There are you,
  Close° in the thicket. The Duke appears. I meet him,                        Hidden
  And unto him I utter learnèd things
15  And many figures. He hears, and nods, and hums,°                          murmurs approval
  And then cries, 'Rare!', and I go forward.° At length                       continue
  I fling my cap up—mark there—then do you,
  As once did Meleager and the boar,[6]
  Break comely out° before him, like true lovers,[7]                         Appear decorously
20  Cast yourselves in a body decently,[8]
  And sweetly, by a figure, trace° and turn, boys.                           follow the steps
FIRST COUNTRYMAN And sweetly we will do it, master Gerald.
SECOND COUNTRYMAN Draw up the company. Where's the
    taborer?
THIRD COUNTRYMAN Why, Timothy!
TABORER                         Here, my mad boys, have at ye!°             go ahead; I'm ready
SCHOOLMASTER But I say, where's these women?
25 FOURTH COUNTRYMAN                      Here's Friz and Madeline.
SECOND COUNTRYMAN And little Luce with the white legs, and
    bouncing° Barbara.                                                       robust
FIRST COUNTRYMAN And freckled Nell, that never failed her
    master.°                                                                (with sexual overtone)
SCHOOLMASTER Where be your ribbons,[9] maids? Swim° with        Dance gracefully
    your bodies
  And carry it° sweetly and deliverly,°                                      move / nimbly
30  And now and then a favour° and a frisk.°                                 kiss; bow / leap
NELL Let us alone,° sir.                                                     Leave it to us
SCHOOLMASTER             Where's the rest o'th' music?°                      musicians
THIRD COUNTRYMAN Dispersed° as you commanded.                              Placed here and there
SCHOOLMASTER                                    Couple,° then,              Pair up
  And see what's wanting.° Where's the babion?                               who's missing

---

3.5
1. The morris dance was a rural folk dance of north
English origin, performed in costume. *babion:* one morris dancer, who took the part of the fool, always wore
the costume of an ape or a baboon. *taborer:* drummer.
2. What tedium and folly (pedantic).
3. "Plum-broth" (hearty stew of dried fruits and suet)
and "marrow" both suggest essence or fortifying sustenance.
4. *You . . . judgements:* You people of rudimentary
intellects. "Frieze" and "jean" were coarse fabrics worn

by laborers.
5. O God, heaven help me (Latin).
6. Meleager was a Greek warrior who killed the great
Calydonian boar and brought its head to the Amazon
warrior Atalanta.
7. Like loving subjects of Theseus; in couples, as lovers
do.
8. Position yourselves appropriately for the dance.
9. Morris dancers carried ribbons or streamers as
props.

[*To the* BABION] My friend, carry your tail without offence°                    *sexual offense*
35  Or scandal to the ladies; and be sure
    You tumble with audacity and manhood,°                                       *bravery*
    And when you bark,[1] do it with judgement.
BABION                                    Yes, sir.
SCHOOLMASTER   *Quousque tandem?*[2] Here is a woman wanting!
FOURTH COUNTRYMAN   We may go whistle—all the fat's i'th'
    fire.[3]
40  SCHOOLMASTER   We have,
    As learnèd authors utter, washed a tile;°                                    *worked in vain*
    We have been *fatuus,*° and laboured vainly.                                 *foolish*
SECOND COUNTRYMAN   This is that scornful piece, that scurvy
    hilding°                                                                     *worthless woman*
    That gave her promise faithfully she would be here—
45  Cicely, the seamstress' daughter.
    The next gloves that I give her shall be dogskin.°                           *cheap leather*
    Nay, an° she fail me once—you can tell, Arcas,                               *if*
    She swore by wine and bread she would not break.°                           *(her solemn oath)*
SCHOOLMASTER   An eel and woman,
50  A learnèd poet says, unless by th' tail
    And with thy teeth thou hold, will either° fail—                            *both*
    In manners this was false position.[4]
FIRST COUNTRYMAN   A fire-ill take her!° Does she flinch now?                    *A pox infect her*
THIRD COUNTRYMAN                                           What
    Shall we determine,° sir?                                                    *decide to do*
SCHOOLMASTER                     Nothing;
55  Our business is become a nullity,
    Yea, and a woeful and a piteous nullity.
FOURTH COUNTRYMAN   Now, when the credit of our town lay on it,
    Now to be frampold, now to piss o'th' nettle![5]
    Go thy ways—I'll remember thee, I'll fit thee!°                             *get even with you*
    *Enter [the]* JAILER'S DAUGHTER
JAILER'S DAUGHTER [*sings*]
60      The *George Alow*[6] came from the south,
            From the coast of Barbary-a;
        And there he met with brave gallants of war,°                           *warships*
            By one, by two, by three-a.
        'Well hailed, well hailed, you jolly gallants,
65          And whither now are you bound-a?
        O let me have your company
            Till I come to the sound-a.'

    There was three fools fell out about an owlet—

        The one he said it was an owl,
70          The other he said nay,
        The third he said it was a hawk,
            And her bells were cut away.[7]

---

1. Baboons were considered half man, half dog.
2. How much longer (must I wait)? (Latin, as throughout the scene.) Expression of impatience that opens the ancient Roman writer Cicero's first oration against Catiline but here indicates the Schoolmaster's pomposity.
3. We may as well give up, since all our work has produced nothing. Both phrases were proverbial, although the second has a different meaning today.

4. A false (pro)position is a logical fallacy. The Schoolmaster compares Cicely's flawed manners to faulty logic.
5. Now to be temperamental, to lose her temper.
6. Probably taken from "The George Aloe and the Sweepstake," a ballad published in 1611. The *George Aloe* was a ship.
7. Hawks used for falconry wore bells in order to make them easier to catch.

THIRD COUNTRYMAN   There's a dainty° madwoman, master,                    *fine*
Comes i'th' nick,° as mad as a March hare.                    *nick (of time)*
75   If we can get her dance, we are made again.°                    *all will be well*
I warrant her, she'll do the rarest gambols.°                    *finest capers*
FIRST COUNTRYMAN   A madwoman? We are made, boys.
SCHOOLMASTER [*to the* JAILER'S DAUGHTER]   And are you mad,
    good woman?
JAILER'S DAUGHTER   I would be sorry else.
    Give me your hand.
SCHOOLMASTER          Why?
JAILER'S DAUGHTER                    I can tell your fortune.
    [*She examines his hand*]
80   You are a fool. Tell ten—I have posed him.[8] Buzz!°                    *Silence*
Friend, you must eat no white bread—if you do,
Your teeth will bleed extremely. Shall we dance, ho?
I know you—you're a tinker.° Sirrah tinker,                    *mender of kettles*
Stop no more holes but what you should.°                    *(sexual)*
SCHOOLMASTER                    *Dii boni*°—                    *Good gods*
A tinker, damsel?
85   JAILER'S DAUGHTER   Or a conjurer°—                    *magician*
Raise me a devil now and let him play
*Qui passa* o'th' bells and bones.[9]
SCHOOLMASTER                    Go, take her,
And fluently persuade her to a peace.°                    *to do what we want*
*Et opus exegi, quod nec Iovis ira, nec ignis*[1]—
Strike up, and lead her in.
90   SECOND COUNTRYMAN          Come, lass, let's trip it.°                    *let's dance*
JAILER'S DAUGHTER   I'll lead.
THIRD COUNTRYMAN   Do, do.
SCHOOLMASTER   Persuasively and cunningly°—                    *skillfully*
    *Wind horns* [*within*]          away, boys,
I hear the horns. Give me some meditation,°                    *time to think*
And mark° your cue.                    *don't forget*
          *Exeunt all but* [*Gerald the*] SCHOOLMASTER
95          Pallas° inspire me.                    *goddess of wisdom*
    *Enter* THESEUS, PIRITHOUS, HIPPOLYTA, EMILIA, ARCITE,
    *and train*
THESEUS   This way the stag took.
SCHOOLMASTER   Stay and edify.°                    *be edified*
THESEUS   What have we here?
PIRITHOUS   Some country sport, upon my life, sir.
THESEUS [*to the* SCHOOLMASTER]   Well, sir, go forward—we will
100          edify.
Ladies, sit down—we'll stay it.°                    *stay to watch*
    [*They sit:* THESEUS *in a chair, the others on stools*]
SCHOOLMASTER   Thou doughty Duke, all hail! All hail, sweet
    ladies.
THESEUS   This is a cold° beginning.                    *(punning on "hail")*

---

8. *Tell . . . him:* Count to ten (a common test for insanity or idiocy)—I have stumped ("posed") him. The Jailer's Daughter tests the Schoolmaster for idiocy and fails him.
9. *Chi passa* (Italian: who passes) were the first words of a common dance tune. Bones were used as percus-
sion instruments, along with bells.
1. "And I have created a work which neither Jove's anger nor fire [can destroy]." Slightly misquoted from Ovid's *Metamorphoses* 15.871.

SCHOOLMASTER  If you but favour,[2] our country pastime made is.
105  We are a few of those collected here,
That ruder tongues distinguish° 'villager';  *call*
And to say verity, and not to fable,
We are a merry rout, or else a rabble,
Or company, or, by a figure,° chorus,  *figure of speech*
110  That fore thy dignity will dance a morris.
And I, that am the rectifier° of all,  *director; connector*
By title *pedagogus*,° that let fall  *teacher*
The birch upon the breeches of the small ones,
And humble with a ferula° the tall ones,  *cane*
115  Do here present this machine, or this frame;[3]
And dainty Duke, whose doughty dismal° fame  *awe-inspiring*
From Dis to Daedalus,[4] from post to pillar,
Is blown abroad, help me, thy poor well-willer,°  *well-wisher*
And with thy twinkling eyes, look right and straight
120  Upon this mighty 'Moor'—of mickle° weight—  *much*
'Ice' now comes in,[5] which, being glued together,
Makes 'morris', and the cause that we came hither.
The body of our sport, of no small study,[6]
I first appear, though rude, and raw, and muddy,
125  To speak, before thy noble grace, this tenor[7]
At whose great feet I offer up my penner.°  *pen case*
The next,° the Lord of May and Lady bright;  *next to appear*
The Chambermaid and Servingman, by night
That seek out silent hanging;[8] then mine Host
130  And his fat Spouse, that welcomes, to their cost,
The gallèd° traveller, and with a beck'ning  *tired*
Informs the tapster° to inflame the reck'ning;°  *bartender / overcharge*
Then the beest-eating Clown;[9] and next, the Fool;
The babion with long tail and eke long tool,°  *penis*
135  *Cum multis aliis*° that make a dance—  *With many others*
Say 'ay', and all shall presently° advance.  *at once*
THESEUS  Ay, ay, by any means, dear dominie.°  *teacher*
PIRITHOUS                                                      Produce.°  *Put on (your show)*
SCHOOLMASTER  (*knock[s] for the dance*)
*Intrate filii*,[1] come forth and foot it.
[*He flings up his cap.*] *Music.*
[*The* SCHOOLMASTER *ushers in*
*May Lord,          May Lady.*
*Servingman,        Chambermaid.*
*A Country Clown,*
*or Shepherd,       Country Wench.*

---

2. Approve. Compare Quince's speech to Theseus in *A Midsummer Night's Dream* 5.1.126–50.
3. Both "machine" and "frame" mean "structure" or "production."
4. Dis was god of the underworld; Daedalus was creator of the Cretan labyrinth and inventor of wings for human flight. Theseus triumphed over both the underworld and the labyrinth. Daedalus is invoked for the sake of alliteration and, because of his association with flight and hence the heavens, for contrast to Dis.
5. The Schoolmaster displays the word "morris" from two placards, possibly held by the dancers. In Q, the word is split into two syllables, "Morr" and "Is" (here emended to "Moor" and "Ice"). They may have been

spelled out, or perhaps pictograms were used, with the first placard depicting a Moor and the second the allegorical figure Winter.
6. The main part in our entertainment, carefully prepared.
7. Argument; tenner (ten-syllable line).
8. Curtain behind which they can make love.
9. Clown or country shepherd (see stage direction at line 138) who likes "beest," the thick milk produced by a cow for the first few days after calving.
1. Come in, my sons (children). The masculine *filii* is especially appropriate, since the women's parts were played by boy actors.

An Host,              Hostess.
A He-babion,          She-babion.
A He-fool,            The JAILER'S DAUGHTER as
                          She-fool.
*All these persons apparelled to the life,° the men issuing*      in lifelike costume
*out of one door and the wenches from the other. They*
*dance a morris*]
    Ladies, if we have been merry,
140     And have pleased ye with a derry,
    And a derry, and a down,°                               (song refrain words)
    Say the schoolmaster's no clown.
    Duke, if we have pleased thee too,
    And have done as good boys should do,
145     Give us but a tree or twain
    For a maypole, and again,
    Ere another year run out,
    We'll make thee laugh, and all this rout.°               company
THESEUS   Take twenty, dominie. [*To* HIPPOLYTA] How does my
    sweetheart?
HIPPOLYTA   Never so pleased, sir.
150 EMILIA                 'Twas an excellent dance,
    And for a preface,° I never heard a better.                as for the prologue
THESEUS   Schoolmaster, I thank you. One see 'em all rewarded.
PIRITHOUS   And here's something to paint your pole withal.
    [*He gives them money*]
THESEUS   Now to our sports again.
SCHOOLMASTER
155     May the stag thou hunt'st stand long,°                  give a good chase
    And thy dogs be swift and strong;
    May they kill him without lets,°                         obstacles
    And the ladies eat his dowsets.°                         testicles (a delicacy)
    [*Exeunt* THESEUS *and train.*] *Wind horns* [*within*]
    Come, we are all made. *Dii deaeque omnes,*°              Gods and goddesses all
160     Ye have danced rarely, wenches.                          *Exeunt*

## 3.6

*Enter* PALAMON *from the bush*

PALAMON   About this hour my cousin gave his faith°            word
    To visit me again, and with him bring
    Two swords and two good armours;° if he fail,           suits of armor
    He's neither man nor soldier. When he left me,
5     I did not think a week could have restored
    My lost strength to me, I was grown so low
    And crest-fall'n with my wants. I thank thee, Arcite,
    Thou art yet a fair foe, and I feel myself,
    With this refreshing, able once again
10     To out-dure° danger. To delay it longer                 endure; outlast
    Would make the world think, when it comes to hearing,°   when word gets out
    That I lay fatting, like a swine, to fight,
    And not a soldier.¹ Therefore this blest morning

---

**3.6**
1. *fatting . . . soldier:* being fattened like a swine for the slaughter, rather than preparing myself like a warrior for
the fight.

Shall be the last; and that sword he refuses,°                    *(in choosing first)*
15  If it but hold,° I kill him with; 'tis justice.                      *Unless it breaks*
So, love and fortune for me!
    *Enter* ARCITE *with [two] armours and [two] swords*
         O, good morrow.
ARCITE Good morrow, noble kinsman.
PALAMON        I have put you
To too much pains, sir.
ARCITE      That too much, fair cousin,
Is but a debt to honour, and my duty.
20  PALAMON Would you were so in all, sir—I could wish ye
As kind a kinsman, as you force me find
A beneficial foe, that my embraces
Might thank ye, not my blows.
ARCITE       I shall think either,
Well done, a noble recompense.
PALAMON      Then I shall quit° you.                 *repay*
25  ARCITE Defy me in these fair terms, and you show°        *show youself to be*
More than a mistress to me—no more anger,
As you love anything that's honourable.
We were not bred to talk, man. When we are armed
And both upon our guards, then let our fury,
30  Like meeting of two tides, fly strongly from us;
And then to whom the birthright° of this beauty              *rightful possession*
Truly pertains°—without upbraidings, scorns,                      *belongs*
Despisings of our persons, and such poutings
Fitter for girls and schoolboys—will be seen,
35  And quickly, yours or mine. Will't please you arm, sir?
Or, if you feel yourself not fitting° yet,                            *ready*
And furnished with your old strength, I'll stay,° cousin,           *wait*
And every day discourse you into health,
As I am spared.° Your person I am friends with,             *In my spare time*
40  And I could wish I had not said I loved her,
Though I had died;[2] but loving such a lady,
And justifying° my love, I must not fly from't.                   *affirming*
PALAMON Arcite, thou art so brave an enemy
That no man but thy cousin's fit to kill thee.
I am well and lusty°—choose your arms                     *eager to do battle*
45  ARCITE       Choose you, sir.
PALAMON Wilt thou exceed in all,[3] or dost thou do it
To make me spare thee?
ARCITE      If you think so, cousin,
You are deceived, for as I am a soldier,
I will not spare you.
PALAMON     That's well said.
ARCITE       You'll find it.°                    *find it so*
50  PALAMON Then as I am an honest man, and love
With all the justice of affection,[4]
I'll pay thee soundly.°                                       *punish you properly*
    *[He chooses one armour]*
      This I'll take.

---

2. Although it would have killed me to keep silent.
3. Will you always outdo me in courtesy (as here, by
letting me choose my arms first)?

4. Palamon's love of Emilia is just; Palamon will deal
justly (honorably) with Arcite because he loves him.

ARCITE [*indicating the remaining armour*]  That's mine, then.
  I'll arm you first.
PALAMON      Do.
        [ARCITE *arms* PALAMON]
                    Pray thee tell me, cousin,
  Where gott'st thou this good armour?
ARCITE                'Tis the Duke's,
  And to say true, I stole it. Do I pinch you?
55  PALAMON                  No.
ARCITE   Is't not too heavy?
PALAMON           I have worn a lighter—
  But I shall make it serve.
ARCITE           I'll buckle't close.°             *tightly*
PALAMON   By any means.
ARCITE           You care not for a grand guard?[5]
PALAMON   No, no, we'll use no horses. I perceive
  You would fain be at that fight.°       *rather fight mounted*
60  ARCITE           I am indifferent.
PALAMON   Faith, so am I. Good cousin, thrust the buckle
  Through far enough.
ARCITE         I warrant you.°          *Trust me*
PALAMON           My casque° now.       *helmet*
ARCITE   Will you fight bare-armed?
PALAMON           We shall be the nimbler.
ARCITE   But use your gauntlets, though—those are o'th' least.°   *too small*
  Prithee take mine, good cousin.
65  PALAMON          Thank you, Arcite.
  How do I look? Am I fall'n much away?°     *much thinner*
ARCITE   Faith, very little—love has used you kindly.
PALAMON   I'll warrant thee, I'll strike home.
ARCITE              Do, and spare not—
  I'll give you cause, sweet cousin.
PALAMON          Now to you, sir.
        [PALAMON *arms* ARCITE]
70  Methinks this armour's very like that, Arcite,
  Thou wor'st that day the three kings fell, but lighter.
ARCITE   That was a very good one, and that day,
  I well remember, you outdid me, cousin.
  I never saw such valour. When you charged
75  Upon the left wing of the enemy,
  I spurred hard to come up,° and under me     *keep up with you*
  I had a right good horse.
PALAMON         You had indeed—
  A bright bay, I remember.
ARCITE         Yes. But all
  Was vainly laboured in me—you outwent me,
80  Nor could my wishes reach you.[6] Yet a little
  I did by imitation.
PALAMON        More by virtue°—     *valor*
  You are modest, cousin.
ARCITE         When I saw you charge first,
  Methought I heard a dreadful clap of thunder
  Break from the troop.

---

5. Chest plate for fighting on horseback.      6. My wishes to keep up with you were not answered.

| | | |
|---|---|---|
| PALAMON | But still before that flew | |
| 85 | The lightning of your valour. Stay a little, | |
| | Is not this piece too strait?° | *tight* |
| ARCITE | No, no, 'tis well. | |
| PALAMON | I would have nothing hurt thee but my sword— | |
| | A bruise would be dishonour. | |
| ARCITE | Now I am perfect°. | *ready* |
| PALAMON | Stand off,° then. | *Step back* |
| ARCITE | Take my sword; I hold° it better. | *consider* |
| 90 | PALAMON I thank ye. No, keep it—your life lies° on it. | *depends* |
| | Here's one—if it but hold,° I ask no more | *holds together* |
| | For all my hopes. My cause and honour guard me. | |
| ARCITE | And me, my love. | |

*They bow several ways,*[7] *then advance and stand*

Is there aught else to say?

PALAMON   This only, and no more. Thou art mine aunt's son,
95   And that blood we desire to shed is mutual:
In me, thine, and in thee, mine. My sword
Is in my hand, and if thou kill'st me,
The gods and I forgive thee. If there be
A place prepared for those that sleep in honour,
100   I wish his weary soul that falls may win it.
Fight bravely, cousin. Give me thy noble hand.
ARCITE   Here, Palamon. This hand shall never more
Come near thee with such friendship.

| | | |
|---|---|---|
| PALAMON | I commend thee.° | *(to God)* |

ARCITE   If I fall, curse me, and say I was a coward—
105   For none but such dare die in these just trials.
Once more farewell, my cousin.
PALAMON                    Farewell, Arcite.

*Fight. Horns within; they stand*

ARCITE   Lo, cousin, lo, our folly has undone us.
PALAMON                              Why?
ARCITE   This is the Duke a-hunting, as I told you.
If we be found, we are wretched. O, retire,
110   For honour's sake, and safely, presently,
Into your bush again. Sir, we shall find

| | | |
|---|---|---|
| Too many° hours to die. In, gentle cousin— | | *More than enough* |

If you be seen, you perish instantly
For breaking prison, and I, if you reveal me,
115   For my contempt.[8] Then all the world will scorn us,
And say we had a noble difference,

| | | |
|---|---|---|
| But base disposers of it.° | | *settled it ignobly* |

PALAMON                    No, no, cousin,
I will no more be hidden, nor put off

| | | |
|---|---|---|
| This great adventure° to a second trial. | | *undertaking* |
| 120   I know your cunning and I know your cause°— | | *motive (for delay)* |
| He that faints° now, shame take him! Put thyself | | *is fainthearted* |
| Upon thy present guard°— | | *At once on guard* |

ARCITE                    You are not mad?

| | | |
|---|---|---|
| PALAMON   Or° I will make th'advantage of this hour | | *Either I'm mad or* |

---

7. They make ceremonial bows in various directions, as if they were jousting in a tournament.

8. For my disobedience to Theseus's order that I be banished.

Mine own, and what to come shall threaten me
125 I fear less than my fortune.° Know, weak cousin,                    (in this fight)
I love Emilia, and in that I'll bury
Thee and all crosses else.°                                          all other obstacles
ARCITE                     Then come what can come,
Thou shalt know, Palamon, I dare as well
Die as discourse or sleep. Only this fears° me,                     frightens
130 The law will have the honour of our ends.⁹
Have at thy life!
PALAMON          Look to thine own well, Arcite!
        [*They*] *fight again.*
        *Horns. Enter* THESEUS, HIPPOLYTA, EMILIA, PIRITHOUS,
        *and train.* [THESEUS *separates* PALAMON *and* ARCITE]
THESEUS   What ignorant and mad malicious° traitors                 evil-minded
Are you, that 'gainst the tenor° of my laws                         purport
Are making battle, thus like knights appointed,°                    armed
135 Without my leave and officers of arms?¹
By Castor,² both shall die.
PALAMON                     Hold° thy word, Theseus.                 Keep
We are certainly both traitors, both despisers°                     disobedient
Of thee and of thy goodness. I am Palamon,
That cannot love thee, he that broke thy prison—
140 Think well what that deserves. And this is Arcite;
A bolder traitor never trod thy ground,
A falser ne'er seemed friend. This is the man
Was begged° and banished; this is he contemns thee,                 petitioned for
And what thou dar'st do; and in this disguise,
145 Against thine own edict, follows thy sister,°                    sister-in-law
That fortunate bright° star, the fair Emilia,                       luck-bringing
Whose servant°—if there be a right in seeing                        courtly lover
And first bequeathing of the soul to—justly
I am; and, which is more, dares think her his.
150 This treachery, like a most trusty lover,
I called him now to answer. If thou be'st
As thou art spoken,° great and virtuous,                           reported to be
The true decider of all injuries,
Say, 'Fight again', and thou shalt see me, Theseus,
155 Do such a justice thou thyself wilt envy.
Then take my life—I'll woo thee to't.
PIRITHOUS                              O heaven,
What more than man is this!
THESEUS                     I have sworn.
ARCITE                                We seek not
Thy breath of mercy, Theseus. 'Tis to me
A thing as soon to die as thee to say it,
160 And no more moved. Where this man calls me traitor
Let me say thus much—if in love be treason,
In service of so excellent a beauty,
As I love most, and in that faith will perish,
As I have brought my life here to confirm it,
165 As I have served her truest, worthiest,
As I dare kill this cousin that denies it,

9. We will die by execution rather than combat.          2. Common Roman oath. Castor and Pollux, twins,
1. Overseers of chivalric combat.                        were sons of Jupiter.

So let me be most traitor and ye please me.
For° scorning thy edict, Duke, ask that lady          *As for*
Why she is fair, and why her eyes command me
170 Stay here to love her, and if she say, 'Traitor',
I am a villain fit to lie unburied.
PALAMON    Thou shalt have pity of° us both, O Theseus,          *on*
If unto neither thou show mercy. Stop,
As thou art just, thy noble ear against us;
175 As thou art valiant, for thy cousin's° soul,          *(Hercules')*
Whose twelve strong labours crown his memory,
Let's die together, at one instant, Duke.
Only a little let him fall before me,
That I may tell my soul he shall not have her.
180 THESEUS   I grant your wish; for to say true, your cousin
Has ten times more offended, for I gave him
More mercy than you found, sir, your offences
Being no more than his. None here speak for 'em,
For ere the sun set both shall sleep for ever.
185 HIPPOLYTA [*to* EMILIA]    Alas, the pity! Now or never, sister,
Speak, not to be denied. That face of yours
Will bear the curses else of after ages
For these lost cousins.
EMILIA                              In my face, dear sister,
I find no anger to 'em, nor no ruin.
190 The misadventure of their own eyes kill° 'em.          *kills*
Yet that° I will be woman and have pity,          *to show that*
  [*She kneels*]
My knees shall grow to th' ground, but° I'll get mercy.          *unless*
Help me, dear sister—in a deed so virtuous
The powers of all women will be with us.
  [HIPPOLYTA *kneels*]
Most royal brother—
HIPPOLYTA                    Sir, by our tie of marriage—
EMILIA   By your own spotless honour—
195 HIPPOLYTA                              By that faith,
That fair hand, and that honest heart you gave me—
EMILIA   By that you would have pity in another,[3]
By your own virtues infinite—
HIPPOLYTA                    By valour,
By all the chaste° nights I have ever pleased you—          *faithful only to you*
THESEUS   These are strange conjurings.°          *incantations*
200 PIRITHOUS                              Nay, then, I'll in too.
  [*He kneels*]
By all our friendship, sir, by all our dangers,
By all you love most: wars, and this sweet lady—
EMILIA   By that° you would have trembled to deny          *(chivalric aid)*
A blushing maid—
HIPPOLYTA                    By your own eyes, by strength—
In which you swore I went beyond° all women,          *I excelled*
205 Almost all men—and yet I yielded, Theseus—
PIRITHOUS   To crown all this, by your most noble soul,
Which cannot want° due mercy, I beg first—          *lack*

---

3. By whatever you would expect someone else to pity.

HIPPOLYTA    Next hear my prayers—

210  EMILIA                                Last let me entreat, sir—

PIRITHOUS    For mercy.

HIPPOLYTA                    Mercy.

EMILIA                                Mercy on these princes.

THESEUS    Ye make my faith reel.[4] Say I felt
    Compassion to 'em both, how would you place° it?        *have me bestow*
    [*They rise*]

EMILIA    Upon their lives—but with their banishments.

215  THESEUS    You are a right° woman, sister: you have pity,       *typical*
    But want the understanding where to use it.
    If you desire their lives, invent a way
    Safer than banishment. Can these two live,
    And have the agony of love about 'em,
220      And not kill one another? Every day
    They'd fight about you, hourly bring your honour
    In public question with their swords.[5] Be wise, then,
    And here forget 'em. It concerns your credit°       *reputation*
    And my oath equally. I have said—they die.
225      Better they fall by th' law than one another.
    Bow not my honour.[6]

EMILIA                                O my noble brother,
    That oath was rashly° made, and in your anger.     *impulsively*
    Your reason will not hold° it. If such vows        *sustain*
    Stand for express will,° all the world must perish.   *steadfast resolve*
230      Beside, I have another oath 'gainst yours,
    Of more authority, I am sure more love—
    Not made in passion, neither, but good heed.°     *thoughtfulness*

THESEUS    What is it, sister?

PIRITHOUS [*to* EMILIA]        Urge it home, brave lady.

EMILIA    That you would ne'er deny me anything
235      Fit for my modest suit and your free granting.
    I tie you to your word now; if ye fail in't,
    Think how you maim your honour—
    For now I am set a-begging, sir. I am deaf
    To all but your compassion—how their lives
240      Might breed the ruin of my name, opinion.°     *my reputation*
    Shall anything that loves me perish for° me?     *because of*
    That were a cruel wisdom: do men prune
    The straight young boughs that blush with thousand blossoms
    Because they may be° rotten? O, Duke Theseus,    *become*
245      The goodly mothers that have groaned for these,°  *(in childbirth)*
    And all the longing maids that ever loved,
    If your vow stand,° shall curse me and my beauty,    *holds*
    And in their funeral songs for these two cousins
    Despise my cruelty and cry woe worth° me,      *befall*
250      Till I am nothing but the scorn of women.
    For heaven's sake, save their lives and banish 'em.

THESEUS    On what conditions?

EMILIA                                Swear 'em° never more    *Have them swear*
    To make me their contention, or to know me,°    *think of me*

---

4. You make my constancy to my own oath (to kill the kinsmen) waver.
5. *They'd . . . swords:* They'd fight publicly over you, thus compromising your honor.
6. Don't force me to lower (bend) my standards of honor.

To tread upon thy dukedom; and to be,
255 Wherever they shall travel, ever strangers
To one another.
PALAMON            I'll be cut a-pieces
Before I take this oath—forget I love her?
O all ye gods, despise me, then. Thy banishment
I not mislike, so we may fairly carry
260 Our swords and cause along—else, never trifle,
But take our lives, Duke. I must love, and will;
And for that love must and dare kill this cousin
On any piece° the earth has.                    *spot of ground*
THESEUS                  Will you, Arcite,
Take these conditions?
PALAMON            He's a villain then.
PIRITHOUS                      These are men!
265 ARCITE   No, never, Duke. 'Tis worse to me than begging,
To take° my life so basely. Though I think         *value*
I never shall enjoy her, yet I'll preserve
The honour of affection and die for her,
Make death a devil.°                          *Even horribly*
270 THESEUS   What may be done? For now I feel compassion.
PIRITHOUS   Let it not fall° again, sir.            *diminish*
THESEUS                  Say, Emilia,
If one of them were dead—as one must—are you
Content to take the other to your husband?
They cannot both enjoy you. They are princes
275 As goodly as your own eyes, and as noble
As ever fame yet spoke of. Look upon 'em,
And if you can love, end this difference.
I give consent. [*To* PALAMON *and* ARCITE] Are you content too,
      princes?
PALAMON *and* ARCITE   With all our souls.
THESEUS                  He that she refuses
Must die, then.
280 PALAMON *and* ARCITE   Any death thou canst invent, Duke.
PALAMON   If I fall from that mouth,° I fall with favour,   *(because of her decision)*
And lovers yet unborn shall bless my ashes.
ARCITE   If she refuse me, yet my grave will wed me,
And soldiers sing my epitaph.
THESEUS [*to* EMILIA]         Make choice, then.
285 EMILIA   I cannot, sir. They are both too excellent.
For° me, a hair shall never fall of these men.       *On account of*
HIPPOLYTA [*to* THESEUS]   What will become of 'em?
THESEUS                  Thus I ordain it,
And by mine honour once again it stands,
Or both shall die. [*To* PALAMON *and* ARCITE] You shall both to your country,
290 And each within this month, accompanied
With three fair knights, appear again in this place,
In which I'll plant° a pyramid; and whether,°      *fix / whichever*
Before us that are here, can force his cousin,
By fair and knightly strength, to touch the pillar,
295 He shall enjoy her; the other lose his head,
And all his friends; nor shall he grudge to fall,[7]

7. And all his friends will die with him; nor should he consider his execution unjust.

Nor think he dies with interest in° this lady.  *a rightful claim to*
Will this content ye?
PALAMON                    Yes. Here, cousin Arcite,
I am friends again till that hour.
ARCITE                           I embrace ye.
THESEUS [*to* EMILIA]   Are you content, sister?
300  EMILIA                                        Yes, I must, sir,
Else both miscarry.°  *perish*
THESEUS [*to* PALAMON *and* ARCITE]
                    Come, shake hands again, then,
And take heed, as you are gentlemen, this quarrel
Sleep till the hour prefixed, and hold your course.°  *keep your resolve*
PALAMON   We dare not fail thee, Theseus.
THESEUS                                Come, I'll give ye
305  Now usage like to princes and to friends.
When ye return, who wins I'll settle here,°  *set up in Athens*
Who loses, yet I'll weep upon his bier.
                    *Exeunt. [In the act-time the bush is removed]*


## 4.1

                *Enter [the]* JAILER *and his* FRIEND
JAILER   Hear you no more? Was nothing said of me
Concerning the escape of Palamon?
Good sir, remember.
FRIEND                      Nothing that I heard,
For I came home before the business
5   Was fully ended. Yet I might perceive,
Ere I departed, a great likelihood
Of both their pardons: for Hippolyta
And fair-eyed Emily upon their knees
Begged with such handsome pity that the Duke,
10  Methought, stood staggering° whether he should follow  *wavering as to*
His rash oath or the sweet compassion
Of those two ladies; and to second them
That truly noble prince, Pirithous—
Half his own heart[1]—set in too, that° I hope  *so that*
15  All shall be well. Neither heard I one question
Of your name or his scape.
                *Enter [the]* SECOND FRIEND
JAILER                      Pray heaven it hold° so.  *continue*
SECOND FRIEND   Be of good comfort, man. I bring you news,
Good news.
JAILER            They are welcome.
SECOND FRIEND                        Palamon has cleared you,
And got your pardon, and discovered° how  *exposed*
20  And by whose means he scaped—which was your daughter's,
Whose pardon is procured too; and the prisoner,
Not to be held ungrateful to her goodness,
Has given a sum of money to her marriage—
A large one, I'll assure you.
JAILER                      Ye are a good man,
And ever bring good news.
25  FIRST FRIEND                 How was it ended?

---

**4.1** Location: The prison          1. Hippolyta is (has) the other half.

SECOND FRIEND   Why, as it should be: they that ne'er begged,
But° they prevailed, had their suits fairly granted—                              *Still*
The prisoners have their lives.
FIRST FRIEND                    I knew 'twould be so.
SECOND FRIEND   But there be new conditions which you'll hear of
At better time.
JAILER             I hope they are good.
30  SECOND FRIEND                    They are honourable—
How good they'll prove I know not.
            *Enter [the]* WOOER
FIRST FRIEND                    'Twill be known.
WOOER   Alas, sir, where's your daughter?
JAILER                    Why do you ask?
WOOER   O, sir, when did you see her?
SECOND FRIEND                    How he looks!
JAILER   This morning.
WOOER             Was she well? Was she in health?
Sir, when did she sleep?
35  FIRST FRIEND             These are strange questions.
JAILER   I do not think she was very well: for now
You make me mind° her, but this very day                              *remind me of*
I asked her questions and she answered me
So far from what she was,° so childishly,                              *her usual manner*
40  So sillily, as if she were a fool,
An innocent—and I was very angry.
But what of her, sir?
WOOER             Nothing, but my pity²—
But you must know it, and as good by me
As by another that less loves her—
JAILER   Well, sir?
FIRST FRIEND             Not right?°                              *in her right mind*
WOOER             No, sir, not well.
45  SECOND FRIEND                              Not well?
WOOER   'Tis too true—she is mad.
FIRST FRIEND                    It cannot be.
WOOER   Believe, you'll find it so.
JAILER                    I half suspected
What you told me—the gods comfort her!
Either this was her love to Palamon,
50  Or fear of my miscarrying on³ his scape,
Or both.
WOOER   'Tis likely.
JAILER                    But why all this haste, sir?
WOOER   I'll tell you quickly. As I late was angling°                              *fishing*
In the great lake that lies behind the palace,
From the far shore, thick set with reeds and sedges,
55  As patiently I was attending sport,°                              *awaiting a fish*
I heard a voice—a shrill one—and attentive
I gave my ear, when I might well perceive
'Twas one that sung, and by the smallness° of it                              *high pitch*
A boy or woman. I then left my angle°                              *fishing rod*
60  To his own skill,° came near, but yet perceived not                              *To fish by itself*
Who made the sound, the rushes and the reeds

2. My pity for you and her makes me speak.          3. My being punished because of.

Had so encompassed it.° I laid me down                    *overgrown the place*
And listened to the words she sung, for then,
Through a small glade cut by the fishermen,
I saw it was your daughter.
65  JAILER                              Pray go on, sir.
WOOER   She sung much, but no sense; only I heard her
Repeat this often—'Palamon is gone,
Is gone to th' wood to gather mulberries;
I'll find him out tomorrow.'
FIRST FRIEND                    Pretty soul!
70  WOOER   'His shackles will betray him—he'll be taken,
And what shall I do then? I'll bring a bevy,°           *company*
A hundred black-eyed maids that love as I do,
With chaplets° on their heads of daffodillies,          *wreaths*
With cherry lips and cheeks of damask roses,
75  And all we'll dance an antic° fore the Duke           *a grotesque dance*
And beg his pardon.'⁴ Then she talked of you, sir—
That you must lose your head tomorrow morning,
And she must gather flowers to bury you,
And see the house made handsome.° Then she sung        *neat*
80  Nothing but 'willow, willow, willow',⁵ and between
Ever was 'Palamon, fair Palamon',
And 'Palamon was a tall° young man'. The place          *valiant*
Was knee-deep° where she sat; her careless tresses      *(in rushes)*
A wreath of bull-rush rounded;° about her stuck         *encircled*
85  Thousand freshwater flowers of several° colours—     *various*
That° she appeared, methought, like the fair nymph      *Such that*
That feeds the lake with waters, or as Iris⁶
Newly dropped down from heaven. Rings she made
Of rushes that grew by,⁷ and to 'em spoke
90  The prettiest posies⁸—'Thus our true love's tied',
'This you may lose, not me', and many a one.
And then she wept, and sung again, and sighed—
And with the same breath smiled and kissed her hand.
SECOND FRIEND   Alas, what pity it is!
WOOER                                  I made in to° her:   *approached*
95  She saw me and straight sought the flood°—I saved her, *at once jumped in*
And set her safe to land, when presently
She slipped away and to the city made,
With such a cry and swiftness that, believe me,
She left me far behind her. Three or four
100  I saw from far off cross° her—one of 'em              *intercept*
I knew to be your brother, where she stayed°            *stopped*
And fell, scarce to be got away. I left them with her,
> *Enter [the* JAILER'S] BROTHER, [*the* JAILER'S] DAUGHTER,
> *and others*
And hither came to tell you—here they are.
JAILER'S DAUGHTER [*sings*]   'May you never more enjoy the
           light . . .'°—                                *(unknown song)*
Is not this a fine song?
105  JAILER'S BROTHER          O, a very fine one.

---

4. Beg Duke Theseus to pardon Palamon.
5. Refrain of a popular song, also sung by Desdemona in *Othello* 4.3.
6. Goddess of the rainbow and Juno's messenger.

7. *Rings . . . by*: sometimes used as wedding rings in rural (or mock) wedding ceremonies.
8. Mottoes and aphorisms, sometimes engraved on the inside of rings.

JAILER'S DAUGHTER    I can sing twenty more.
JAILER'S BROTHER                              I think you can.
JAILER'S DAUGHTER    Yes, truly can I—I can sing 'The Broom'
   And 'Bonny Robin'⁹—are not you a tailor?
JAILER'S BROTHER    Yes.
JAILER'S DAUGHTER       Where's my wedding gown?
JAILER'S BROTHER                              I'll bring it tomorrow.
110 JAILER'S DAUGHTER    Do, very rarely°—I must be abroad else,°    *early / or I'll be out*
   To call the maids and pay the minstrels,
   For I must lose my maidenhead by cocklight,°    *before dawn*
   'Twill never thrive else.¹ (*Sings*)    'O fair, O sweet . . .'²
JAILER'S BROTHER [*to the* JAILER]    You must e'en take it
      patiently.
JAILER                'Tis true.
JAILER'S DAUGHTER    Good ev'n, good men. Pray, did you ever
115    hear
   Of one young Palamon?
JAILER                              Yes, wench, we know him.
JAILER'S DAUGHTER    Is't not a fine young gentleman?
JAILER                                            'Tis, love.
JAILER'S BROTHER    By no mean cross her, she is then distempered
   Far worse than now she shows.³
FIRST FRIEND [*to the* JAILER'S DAUGHTER]    Yes, he's a fine man.
JAILER'S DAUGHTER    O, is he so? You have a sister.
120 FIRST FRIEND                              Yes.
JAILER'S DAUGHTER    But she shall never have him, tell her so,
   For° a trick that I know. You'd best look to her,    *Because of*
   For if she see him once, she's gone—she's done
   And undone in an hour. All the young maids
125    Of our town are in love with him, but I laugh at 'em
   And let 'em all alone. Is't not a wise course?
FIRST FRIEND                              Yes.
JAILER'S DAUGHTER    There is at least two hundred now with
      child by him,
   There must be four;° yet I keep close⁴ for all this,    *four hundred*
   Close as a cockle;° and all these° must be boys—    *clam / (the offspring)*
130    He has the trick on't°—and at ten years old    *of producing boys*
   They must be all gelt for musicians⁵
   And sing the wars of Theseus.
SECOND FRIEND                    This is strange.
JAILER'S BROTHER    As ever you heard, but say nothing.
FIRST FRIEND                              No.
JAILER'S DAUGHTER    They come from all parts of the dukedom
      to him.
135    I'll warrant ye, he had not so few last night
   As twenty to dispatch. He'll tickle't up°    *do the (sexual) job*
   In two hours, if his hand be in.°    *if he's in good shape*
JAILER                              She's lost
   Past all cure.

---

9. "The Broom" and "Bonny Robin" were popular songs (Ophelia sings a line of the latter in *Hamlet* 4.5). "Robin" could mean "penis."
1. Otherwise things (or possibly the marriage) won't prosper for me.
2. A song adapted from the seventh of Sir Philip Sid-ney's *Certain Sonnets* (1598).
3. *By . . . shows:* Don't contradict her in any way, or she'll become far worse deranged than she is now.
4. Keep my mouth (and thighs) closed.
5. They must all be castrated so that their voices do not break and they can become singers.

JAILER'S BROTHER   Heaven forbid, man!

JAILER'S DAUGHTER   [*to the* JAILER]   Come hither—you are a
    wise man.

FIRST FRIEND   Does she know him?°            *recognize her father*

SECOND FRIEND   No—would she did.

140    JAILER'S DAUGHTER               You are master of a ship?

JAILER   Yes.

JAILER'S DAUGHTER   Where's your compass?

JAILER                       Here.

JAILER'S DAUGHTER             Set it to th' north.

And now direct your course to th' wood where Palamon

Lies longing for me. For the tackling,°        *rigging*

Let me alone.° Come, weigh,° my hearts, cheerly all.   *I'll do it / (anchor)*

145    Uff, uff, uff !⁶ 'Tis up.° The wind's fair. Top° the bowline.  *(the anchor) / Tighten*

Out with the mainsail. Where's your whistle, master?

JAILER'S BROTHER   Let's get her in.°        *inside (an aside)*

JAILER   Up to the top,° boy!          *top of the mast*

JAILER'S BROTHER        Where's the pilot?

FIRST FRIEND                 Here.

JAILER'S DAUGHTER   What kenn'st thou?°     *What do you see*

SECOND FRIEND            A fair wood.

JAILER'S DAUGHTER          Bear for° it, master.  *Steer toward*

150    Tack about!

(*Sings*) 'When Cynthia° with her borrowed light . . .'⁷   *the moon*

                              *Exeunt*

## 4.2

      *Enter* EMILIA, *with two pictures*°    *(Palamon and Arcite)*

EMILIA Yet I may bind those wounds up that must open

And bleed to death for my sake else—I'll choose,

And end their strife. Two such young handsome men

Shall never fall for° me; their weeping mothers    *die because of*

5    Following the dead cold ashes of their sons,

Shall never curse my cruelty. Good heaven,

What a sweet face has Arcite! If wise nature,

With all her best endowments, all those beauties

She sows into the births of noble bodies,

10    Were here a mortal woman and had in her

The coy° denials of young maids, yet doubtless    *modest*

She would run mad for this man. What an eye,

Of what a fiery sparkle and quick° sweetness    *lively*

Has this young prince! Here° love himself sits smiling!  *In his eye*

15    Just such another wanton Ganymede

Set Jove afire once, and enforced the god

Snatch up the goodly boy and set him by him,

A shining constellation.¹ What a brow,

Of what a spacious majesty, he carries!

20    Arched like the great-eyed Juno's, but far sweeter,

Smoother than Pelops' shoulder!° Fame and honour,   *(made of ivory)*

---

6. Grunts of exertion; possibly the sound of the wind in
the sails.
7. Line from an unknown song.

**4.2** Location: Theseus's palace in Athens.
1. Ganymede was a beautiful youth whom Jupiter
became enamored of and carried off to be his cupbearer
on Mt. Olympus. In the end, Ganymede was transformed into the constellation Aquarius.

|  | | |
|---|---|---|
| | Methinks, from hence,° as from a promontory | *his brow* |
| | Pointed° in heaven, should clap their wings and sing | *Reaching its peak* |
| | To all the under world° the loves and fights | *the earth* |
| 25 | Of gods, and such men near 'em.° Palamon | *men most like gods* |
| | Is but his foil;² to him a mere dull shadow; | |
| | He's swart and meagre,° of an eye as heavy° | *dark and thin / sad* |
| | As if he had lost his mother; a still temper,° | *lethargic disposition* |
| | No stirring in him, no alacrity, | |
| 30 | Of all this° sprightly sharpness, not a smile.° | *(Arcite's) / trace* |
| | Yet these° that we count errors may become him: | *these qualities* |
| | Narcissus was a sad° boy, but a heavenly.° | *serious / beautiful* |
| | O, who can find the bent of woman's fancy?³ | |
| | I am a fool, my reason is lost in me, | |
| 35 | I have no choice,⁴ and I have lied so lewdly° | *wickedly* |
| | That women ought to beat me. On my knees | |
| | I ask thy pardon, Palamon, thou art alone° | *uniquely* |
| | And only beautiful, and these the eyes, | |
| | These the bright lamps of beauty, that command | |
| 40 | And threaten love—and what young maid dare cross° 'em? | *oppose* |
| | What a bold gravity, and yet inviting, | |
| | Has this brown manly face? O, love, this only | |
| | From this hour is complexion.⁵ Lie there, Arcite, | |
| | Thou art a changeling to him, a mere gypsy,⁶ | |
| 45 | And this the noble body. I am sotted,° | *made stupid* |
| | Utterly lost—my virgin's faith⁷ has fled me. | |
| | For if my brother, but even now, had asked me | |
| | Whether I loved, I had run mad for Arcite; | |
| | Now if my sister, more for Palamon. | |
| 50 | Stand both together.° Now come ask me, brother— | *(comparing portraits)* |
| | Alas, I know not; ask me now, sweet sister— | |
| | I may go look.° What a mere child is fancy, | *seek further* |
| | That having two fair gauds° of equal sweetness, | *toys* |
| | Cannot distinguish,° but must cry for both! | *choose* |

*Enter [a]* GENTLEMAN

How now, sir?

55 GENTLEMAN     From the noble Duke your brother,
Madam, I bring you news. The knights are come.

EMILIA  To end the quarrel?

GENTLEMAN          Yes.

EMILIA                 Would I might end first!

|  | | |
|---|---|---|
| | What sins have I committed, chaste Diana,⁸ | |
| | That my unspotted youth must now be soiled° | *defiled* |
| 60 | With blood of princes, and my chastity | |
| | Be made the altar where the lives of lovers— | |
| | Two greater and two better never yet | |
| | Made mothers joy—must be the sacrifice | |
| | To my unhappy beauty? | |

2. Piece of thin, reflective metal in which a jewel was set, enhancing the jewel's brilliance (setting it off by contrast).
3. Who can discern which way a woman's affections will tend?
4. I am incapable of choosing.
5. *this only . . . complexion*: the only "complexion" I'll appreciate from now on is a dark one.
6. A changeling was an ugly or deformed child left by fairies in exchange for one they stole. Gypsies were also thought to steal children; otherwise the meaning is unclear, since the word generally referred to a swarthy person and Palamon has the dark complexion. Perhaps if a dark complexion is "fair," Arcite's fair skin will be considered the "gypsy" one.
7. My prior oath (1.3.86ff.) to remain a virgin.
8. Virgin goddess of the moon and of the Amazons. See 1.3.52 and note.

*Enter* THESEUS, HIPPOLYTA, PIRITHOUS, *and attendants*

THESEUS                          Bring 'em in

65   Quickly, by any means, I long to see 'em.   [*Exit one or more*]
[*To* EMILIA] Your two contending lovers are returned,
And with them their fair knights. Now, my fair sister,
You must love one of them.

EMILIA                          I had rather both,
So° neither for my sake should fall untimely.°                    So that / prematurely
*Enter* [*a*] MESSENGER

THESEUS   Who saw 'em?

PIRITHOUS                          I a while.

70   GENTLEMAN                          And I.

THESEUS [*to the* MESSENGER]
From whence come you, sir?

MESSENGER                          From the knights.

THESEUS                          Pray speak,
You that have seen them, what they are.

MESSENGER                          I will, sir,
And truly what I think. Six braver spirits
Than these they have brought, if we judge by the outside,

75   I never saw nor read of.⁹ He that stands
In the first place with Arcite, by his seeming,°                   appearance
Should be a stout° man; by his face, a prince.                     brave
His very looks so say° him: his complexion,                        declare
Nearer a brown than black, stern and yet noble,

80   Which shows him hardy, fearless, proud° of dangers.             scornful
The circles of his eyes show fire within him,
And, as a heated° lion, so he looks.                               an angry
His hair hangs long behind him, black and shining,
Like ravens' wings. His shoulders, broad and strong;

85   Armed long and round;¹ and on his thigh a sword
Hung by a curious baldric, when he frowns
To seal his will with.² Better,° o' my conscience,                A better sword
Was never soldier's friend.

THESEUS   Thou hast well described him.

90   PIRITHOUS   Yet a great deal short,
Methinks, of him that's first with Palamon.

THESEUS   Pray speak° him, friend.                                 describe

PIRITHOUS                          I guess he is a prince too,
And, if it may be, greater—for his show°                          appearance
Has all the ornament of honour in't.

95   He's somewhat bigger than the knight he° spoke of,             (the messenger)
But of a face far sweeter. His complexion
Is as a ripe grape, ruddy. He has felt,
Without doubt, what he fights for,° and so apter                  (love)
To make this cause his own. In's face appears

100  All the fair hopes of ° what he undertakes,                    confidence about
And when he's angry, then a settled° valour,                      steady
Not tainted with extremes, runs through his body
And guides his arm to brave things. Fear he cannot—

---

9. *nor read of:* possibly a joke on the playwright's part;
the following descriptions closely follow Chaucer's
*Knight's Tale* 2129–78.
1. With long, well-muscled arms.

2. *Hung . . . with:* Hung from an artfully crafted ("curious") sword belt ("baldric"), which he uses to carry out
his will when he is angry.

He shows no such soft temper. His head's yellow,
105 Hard-haired[3] and curled, thick twined: like ivy tods,°    *bushes*
Not to undo with° thunder. In his face    *Not destroyed by*
The livery of the warlike maid[4] appears,
Pure red and white—for yet no beard has blessed him—
And in his rolling° eyes sits victory,    *passionate*
110 As if she ever° meant to court his valour.    *(victory) always*
His nose stands high, a character° of honour;    *distinguishing mark*
His red lips, after fights, are fit for ladies.

EMILIA    Must these men die too?

PIRITHOUS                When he speaks, his tongue
Sounds like a trumpet. All his lineaments°    *body parts*
115 Are as a man would wish 'em—strong and clean.°    *perfectly shaped*
He wears a well-steeled° axe, the staff ° of gold.    *well-honed / handle*
His age, some five-and-twenty.

MESSENGER            There's another—
A little man, but of a tough soul, seeming
As great° as any. Fairer promises    *noble*
120 In such a body yet I never looked on.

PIRITHOUS    O, he that's freckle-faced?

MESSENGER              The same, my lord.
Are they° not sweet ones?    *(the freckles)*

PIRITHOUS        Yes, they are well.

MESSENGER                 Methinks,
Being so few and well disposed,° they show    *arranged*
Great and fine art in nature. He's white-haired°—    *blond*
125 Not wanton white,° but such a manly colour    *effeminately fair*
Next to an auburn, tough and nimble set,°    *and lithe*
Which shows an active soul. His arms are brawny,
Lined with strong sinews—to the shoulder piece
Gently they swell, like women new-conceived,°    *starting pregnancy*
130 Which speaks him prone to labour, never fainting
Under the weight of arms; stout-hearted, still,°    *when motionless*
But when he stirs, a tiger. He's grey-eyed,[5]
Which yields compassion where he conquers; sharp
To spy advantages, and where he finds 'em,
135 He's swift to make 'em his. He does no wrongs,
Nor takes none.° He's round-faced, and when he smiles    *tolerates any*
He shows° a lover; when he frowns, a soldier.    *looks like*
About his head he wears the winner's oak,[6]
And in it stuck the favour of his lady.
140 His age, some six-and-thirty. In his hand
He bears a charging staff ° embossed with silver.    *lance*

THESEUS    Are they all thus?

PIRITHOUS           They are all the sons of honour.

THESEUS    Now as I have a soul, I long to see 'em.
[*To* HIPPOLYTA] Lady, you shall see men fight now.

HIPPOLYTA                 I wish it,
145 But not the cause, my lord. They would show

---

3. Perhaps influenced by Thomas Speght's 1602 edition of Chaucer's *Knight's Tale,* where King Emetrius's hair "was of yron" (was made of iron) instead of "yronne" (curled).
4. *The . . . maid:* His allegiance to Bellona, goddess of war (or possibly to Athena, also associated with warlike powers).
5. With eyes of blue or blue-gray. Eyes of this color supposedly implied compassion.
6. Valiant soldiers received a wreath of oak leaves, particularly if they saved their friends in battle.

Bravely about the titles of two kingdoms[7]—
'Tis pity love should be so tyrannous.
[*To* EMILIA] O my soft-hearted sister, what think you?
Weep not till they weep blood. Wench, it must be.
THESEUS [*to* EMILIA]
    You have steeled 'em° with your beauty.       *made them determined*
150   [*To* PIRITHOUS]                Honoured friend,
To you I give the field:° pray order it        *charge of the combat*
Fitting the persons that must use it.
PIRITHOUS              Yes, sir.
THESEUS   Come, I'll go visit 'em—I cannot stay,°       *wait*
Their fame° has fired me so. Till they appear,     *This account of them*
Good friend, be royal.°                  *treat them royally*
155 PIRITHOUS         There shall want no bravery.°     *splendor*
EMILIA [*aside*]   Poor wench, go weep—for whosoever wins
Loses a noble cousin for thy sins.           *Exeunt*

## 4.3

*Enter* [*the*] JAILER, [*the*] WOOER, [*and the*] DOCTOR
DOCTOR   Her distraction is more at some time of the moon than
    at other some,° is it not?                     *at others*
JAILER   She is continually in a harmless distemper:° sleeps little;   *state of confusion*
    altogether without appetite, save often drinking; dreaming of
5   another world, and a better; and what broken piece of matter
    soe'er she's about, the name 'Palamon' lards it,[1] that she
    farces° every business                         *stuffs*
    *Enter* [*the* JAILER'S] DAUGHTER
    withal,° fits it to every question. Look where she comes—you   *with it*
    shall perceive her behaviour.
    [*They stand apart*]
10 JAILER'S DAUGHTER   I have forgot it quite—the burden on't° was   *refrain of the song*
    'Down-a, down-a', and penned by no worse man than Giraldo,
    Emilia's schoolmaster. He's as fantastical,° too, as ever he may   *fanciful*
    go upon's legs°— for in the next world will Dido see Palamon,   *as any man*
    and then will she be out of love with Aeneas.[2]
15 DOCTOR   What stuff 's here? Poor soul.
JAILER   E'en thus all day long.
JAILER'S DAUGHTER   Now for this charm that I told you of—you
    must bring a piece of silver on the tip of your tongue, or no
    ferry:[3] then, if it be your chance to come where the blessed
20   spirits are—there's a sight now! We maids that have our livers
    perished,[4] cracked to pieces with love, we shall come there and
    do nothing all day long but pick flowers with Proserpine.[5] Then
    will I make Palamon a nosegay, then let him mark me,° then—   *notice me*
DOCTOR   How prettily she's amiss! Note her a little further.
25 JAILER'S DAUGHTER   Faith, I'll tell you: sometime we go to barley-

---

7. *They . . . kingdoms*: It would be more appropriate if
they were fighting for each other's kingdoms.
**4.3** Location: The prison.
1. Whatever disjointed piece of business she tries to
do (or discuss), Palamon's name is inserted into it (like
a piece of fat into lean meat in order to make it cook
better).
2. Presumably the Schoolmaster has written a song
about Dido and her lover, Aeneas, who abandons her in
Virgil's *Aeneid*. The Jailer's Daughter imagines a new
ending in which Dido falls in love with Palamon rather

than Aeneas in the afterlife.
3. Charon demanded payment for ferrying dead souls
across the river Styx to the underworld. Hence the custom of placing a coin on the tongues of the dead.
4. Shrivel up from unrequited love. The liver was supposed to be the seat of the passions.
5. One day while she was picking flowers, Proserpine
was spotted by Pluto, who carried her off to the underworld to be his queen. Her mother, Demeter, got Zeus
to allow her to spend six months on earth each year.

break,[6] we of the blessed. Alas, 'tis a sore life they have i'th'
other place—such burning, frying, boiling, hissing, howling,
chattering, cursing—O they have shrewd measure°—take                    *harsh retribution*
heed! If one be mad or hang or drown themselves, thither they
30   go, Jupiter bless us, and there shall we be put in a cauldron of
lead and usurers' grease,[7] amongst a whole million of cutpurses, and there boil like a gammon° of bacon that will never          *side*
be enough.°                                                             *cooked enough*

DOCTOR   How her brain coins!°                                          *invents*

35   JAILER'S DAUGHTER   Lords and courtiers that have got maids with
child—they are in this place. They shall stand in fire up to the
navel and in ice up to th' heart, and there th'offending part
burns, and the deceiving part freezes—in truth a very grievous
punishment as one would think for such a trifle. Believe me,
40   one would marry a leprous witch to be rid on't, I'll assure you.

DOCTOR   How she continues this fancy! 'Tis not an engrafted
madness, but a most thick and profound melancholy.[8]

JAILER'S DAUGHTER   To hear there a proud° lady and a proud city         *an aristocratic*
wife° howl together! I were a beast an° I'd call it good sport.          *merchant's wife / if*
45   One cries, 'O this smoke!', th'other, 'This fire!'; one cries, 'O
that ever I did it behind the arras!',° and then howls—th'other          *wall hanging*
curses a suing fellow and her garden-house.[9]
(*Sings*) 'I will be true, my stars, my fate . . .'°   *Exit* DAUGHTER    *(unknown song)*

JAILER [*to the* DOCTOR]   What think you of her, sir?

50   DOCTOR   I think she has a perturbed mind, which I cannot
minister to.

JAILER   Alas, what then?

DOCTOR   Understand you she ever affected° any man ere she             *loved*
beheld Palamon?

55   JAILER   I was once, sir, in great hope she had fixed her liking on
this gentleman, my friend.

WOOER   I did think so too, and would account I had a great pen-
n'orth° on't to give half my state° that both she and I, at this        *bargain / property*
present, stood unfeignedly on the same terms.

60   DOCTOR   That intemperate surfeit of her eye hath distempered
the other senses.[1] They may return and settle again to execute
their preordained faculties, but they are now in a most extrav-
agant vagary.° This you must do: confine her to a place where          *errant wandering*
the light may rather seem to steal in than be permitted; take
65   upon you, young sir her friend, the name of Palamon; say you
come to eat with her and to commune of love. This will catch
her attention, for this her mind beats upon°—other objects that        *is obsessed with*
are inserted 'tween her mind and eye become the pranks and
friskins° of her madness. Sing to her such green songs[2] of love       *tricks and frolics*
70   as she says Palamon hath sung in prison; come to her stuck in°       *decorated with*
as sweet flowers as the season is mistress of, and thereto make
an addition of some other compounded odours° which are                 *blended perfumes*

---

6. A game played with male-female couples: one
couple assigned to a place in the field called "hell"
attempted to entrap the other couples.
7. The traditional punishment for avarice was boiling
in oil (here, imagined as the sweat, "grease," given off
by usurers).
8. It is not a rooted ("an engrafted"), true madness,
but a deep depression (what today might be called love

sickness).
9. *a suing . . . garden-house:* the persuasive Wooer who
lured her into a garden house, a site notorious for
amorous trysts.
1. Her excessive gazing at Palamon has thrown her
other senses off.
2. Songs typical of youth.

grateful° to the sense. All this shall become° Palamon, for     *pleasant / befit*
Palamon can sing, and Palamon is sweet and every good thing.
75 Desire to eat with her, carve° her, drink to her, and still among³     *carve for*
intermingle your petition of grace and acceptance into her
favour. Learn what maids have been her companions and play
feres,° and let them repair to her, with Palamon in their mouths,     *playmates*
and appear with tokens as if they suggested° for him. It is a     *interceded*
80 falsehood° she is in, which is with falsehoods to be combated.     *delusion*
This may bring° her to eat, to sleep, and reduce what's now out     *induce*
of square° in her into their former law and regiment.° I have     *disordered / rule*
seen it approved,⁴ how many times I know not, but to make the
number more I have great hope in this. I will between the
85 passages° of this project come in with my appliance.⁵ Let us     *stages*
put it in execution, and hasten the success,° which doubt not     *outcome*
will bring forth comfort.                                   *Exeunt*

## 5.1

[*An altar prepared.*] *Flourish. Enter* THESEUS, PIRI-
THOUS, HIPPOLYTA, *attendants*

THESEUS   Now let 'em enter and before the gods
Tender their holy prayers. Let the temples
Burn bright with sacred fires, and the altars
In hallowed clouds commend° their swelling incense     *deliver*
5 To those above us. Let no due° be wanting.     *proper ritual*
    *Flourish of cornetts*
They have a noble work in hand, will° honour     *which will*
The very powers that love 'em.
    *Enter* PALAMON [*with his three*] *Knights* [*at one door*],
    *and* ARCITE [*with his three Knights at the other door*]

PIRITHOUS                         Sir, they enter.

THESEUS   You valiant and strong-hearted enemies,
You royal german° foes that this day come     *closely related*
10 To blow that nearness° out that flames between ye,     *close kinship*
Lay by your anger for an hour and, dove-like,
Before the holy altars of your helpers,
The all-feared gods, bow down your stubborn bodies.
Your ire° is more than mortal—so° your help be;     *anger / so may*
15 And as the gods regard° ye, fight with justice.     *are watching*
I'll leave you to your prayers, and betwixt ye
I part my wishes.°                          *divide my hopes*

PIRITHOUS           Honour crown the worthiest.
    *Exit* THESEUS *and his train*

PALAMON [*to* ARCITE]   The glass° is running now that cannot     *hourglass*
    finish
Till one of us expire. Think you but thus,
20 That were there aught in me which strove to show°     *to expose itself as*
Mine enemy in this business, were't one eye
Against another, arm oppressed by arm,
I would destroy th'offender—coz, I would,

---

3. Among these pastimes.
4. I have seen this type of treatment successfully carried out.
5. My final mode of treatment (see 5.4).
**5.1** Location: The forest. A single altar is probably visible upstage, perhaps on the inner stage, for this scene

(at least from line 34) and the next two. Here, it is dedicated to Mars. Q treats these first three scenes as a
single one. This makes sense if there are three altars
onstage, rather than, as assumed here, only one, which
successively represents three different altars, presumably in different locations.

Though parcel° of myself. Then from this gather     *it were a piece*
How I should tender° you.     *treat*

25 ARCITE                    I am in labour
To push your name, your ancient love, our kindred,°     *kinship*
Out of my memory, and i'th' selfsame place
To seat something I would confound.° So hoist we     *destroy*
The sails that must these vessels port even where°     *carry wherever*
The heavenly limiter° pleases.     *(of life)*

30 PALAMON                 You speak well.
Before I turn,° let me embrace thee, cousin—     *turn away*
This I shall never do again.

ARCITE                 One farewell.

PALAMON   Why, let it be so—farewell, coz.

ARCITE                    Farewell, sir.

*Exeunt* PALAMON *and his [three] Knights*

Knights, kinsmen, lovers—yea, my sacrifices,[1]
35 True worshippers of Mars, whose spirit in you
Expels the seeds of fear and th'apprehension
Which still is father of it,[2] go with me
Before the god of our profession.° There     *god we worship*
Require° of him the hearts of lions and     *Request*
40 The breath° of tigers, yea, the fierceness too,     *endurance*
Yea, the speed also—to go on,° I mean,     *go forward*
Else° wish we to be snails. You know my prize     *Otherwise (in retreat)*
Must be dragged out of blood—force and great feat
Must put my garland on me, where she sticks,
45 The queen of flowers.[3] Our intercession, then,
Must be to him° that makes the camp a cistern     *(Mars)*
Brimmed with the blood of men—give me your aid,
And bend your spirits towards him.

*They kneel [before the altar, fall on their faces, then on
their knees again]*

[*Praying to Mars*]           Thou mighty one,
That with thy power hast turned green Neptune° into purple;[4]     *god of the sea*
50 Whose havoc in vast field comets prewarn,°     *forecast*
Unearthèd° skulls proclaim; whose breath blows down     *As yet unburied*
The teeming Ceres' foison;[5] who dost pluck°     *pull down*
With hand armipotent° from forth blue clouds     *powerful in arms*
The masoned° turrets, that both mak'st and break'st     *stone*
55 The stony girths° of cities; me thy pupil,     *walls*
Youngest follower of thy drum, instruct this day
With military skill, that to thy laud°     *praise*
I may advance my streamer,° and by thee     *banner*
Be styled° the lord o'th' day. Give me, great Mars,     *named*
60 Some token of thy pleasure.

*Here they fall on their faces, as formerly, and there is
heard clanging of armour, with a short thunder, as the
burst of a battle, whereupon they all rise and bow to
the altar*

---

1. The three knights may literally become human sacrifices from Arcite to Mars if Arcite loses the battle.
2. *th'apprehension . . . it*: the anticipation of a daunting situation, which always breeds fear.
3. *Must put . . . flowers*: Will win for my head (where Emilia already resides) the victor's laurels, of which

she, as the most beautiful of flowers, is part.
4. Red with blood.
5. *whose breath . . . foison*: whose breath (wind) destroys the plenty of the fields produced by Ceres, goddess of agriculture.

O great corrector of enormous° times,                             disordered
Shaker of o'er-rank° states, thou grand decider                   overripe
Of dusty and old titles, that heal'st with blood°        through bloodletting
The earth when it is sick, and cur'st the world
65   O'th' plurisy° of people, I do take                                excess
Thy signs auspiciously, and in thy name,
To my design, march boldly. [*To his Knights*] Let us go.

*Exeunt*

## 5.2

*Enter* PALAMON *and his Knights with the former*
*observance*

PALAMON [*to his Knights*]   Our stars must glister° with new fire,   fortunes must glisten
or be
Today extinct.° Our argument is love,                            extinguished
Which if the goddess of it grant, she gives
Victory too. Then blend your spirits with mine,
5   You whose free nobleness° do make my cause             generous nobility
Your personal hazard. To the goddess Venus
Commend° we our proceeding, and implore                         Commit
Her power unto our party.
        *Here they kneel* [*before the altar, fall on their faces then*
        *on their knees again*]
[*Praying to Venus*] Hail, sovereign queen of secrets,[1] who hast
        power
10   To call the fiercest tyrant from his rage
And weep unto a girl;[2] that hast the might,
Even with an eye-glance, to choke° Mars's drum                   silence
And turn th'alarum° to whispers; that canst make           call to arms
A cripple flourish with° his crutch, and cure him            brandish
15   Before Apollo;[3] that mayst force the king
To be his subject's vassal, and induce
Stale gravity° to dance; the polled° bachelor         old men / bald
Whose youth, like wanton boys through bonfires,
Have skipped° thy flame, at seventy thou canst catch       Has escaped
20   And make him to the scorn° of his hoarse throat      (by listeners)
Abuse young lays of love.[4] What godlike power
Hast thou not power upon? To Phoebus° thou                       the sun
Add'st flames hotter than his—the heavenly fires
Did scorch his mortal son,[5] thine him. The huntress,
25   All moist and cold, some say, began to throw
Her bow away and sigh.[6] Take to thy grace
Me, thy vowed soldier, who do bear thy yoke
As 'twere a wreath of roses, yet is° heavier         though the yoke is
Than lead itself, stings more than nettles.
30   I have never been foul-mouthed against thy law;
Ne'er revealed secret, for I knew none; would not,
Had I kenned° all that were. I never practised                   known
Upon[7] man's wife, nor would the libels° read          (against love)

---

5.2 Location: The altar, here dedicated to Venus.
1. As the rest of the speech (lines 31ff.) indicates,
secrecy and discretion were essential components of
the chivalric love code.
2. Make him weep for a girl (or, weep so much that he
becomes like a girl).
3. Even more quickly than Apollo, the god of medicine.

4. Botch young lovers' love songs.
5. See note to 1.2.85–87.
6. *The huntress . . . sigh:* Diana, notwithstanding her
vow of chastity, fell in love with the shepherd
Endymion. *cold:* chaste.
7. *practised / Upon:* wooed.

Of liberal° wits. I never at great feasts           *licentious*
35 Sought to betray° a beauty, but have blushed    *expose the affairs of*
At simp'ring sirs that did. I have been harsh
To large confessors,[8] and have hotly asked them
If they had mothers—I had one, a woman,
And women 'twere they wronged. I knew a man
40 Of eighty winters, this I told them, who
A lass of fourteen brided°—'twas thy° power     *wedded / Venus's*
To put life into dust. The agèd cramp°         *cramp of old age*
Had screwed° his square foot round,             *twisted*
The gout had knit his fingers into knots,
45 Torturing convulsions from his globy eyes°     *swollen sockets*
Had almost drawn their spheres,° that° what was life  *eyeballs / so that*
In him seemed torture. This anatomy°           *skeleton*
Had by his young fair fere° a boy, and I           *mate*
Believed it was his, for she swore it was,
50 And who would not believe her? Brief °—I am     *In short*
To those that prate and have done,[9] no companion;
To those that boast and have not,° a defier;    *have done nothing*
To those that would and cannot, a rejoicer.
Yea, him I do not love that tells close offices°    *secret matters*
55 The foulest way, nor names concealments[1] in
The boldest language. Such a one I am,
And vow that lover never yet made sigh
Truer than I. O, then, most soft sweet goddess,
Give me the victory of this question,° which     *conflict*
60 Is true love's merit,° and bless me with a sign    *just deserts*
Of thy great pleasure.
     *Here music is heard, doves° are seen to flutter. They fall*   *(sacred to Venus)*
     *again upon their faces, then on their knees*
O thou that from eleven to ninety reign'st
In mortal bosoms, whose chase° is this world     *hunting ground*
And we in herds thy game, I give thee thanks
65 For this fair token, which, being laid unto°     *added to*
Mine innocent true heart, arms in assurance
My body to this business. [*To his Knights*] Let us rise
And bow before the goddess.
     *They [rise and] bow*
               Time comes on.           *Exeunt*

### 5.3

     *Still° music of record[er]s. Enter* EMILIA *in white, her*    *Soft*
     *hair about her shoulders, [with] a wheaten wreath; one*
     *in white holding up her train, her hair stuck with flow-*
     *ers; one before her carrying a silver hind° in which is*   *(sacred to Diana)*
     *conveyed incense and sweet odours, which being set*
     *upon the altar, her maids standing [apart], she sets fire*
     *to it. Then they curtsy and kneel*
EMILIA [*praying to Diana*]   O sacred, shadowy, cold,[1] and con-
     stant queen,
    Abandoner of revels, mute contemplative,

---

8. To those who boast of their love conquests.
9. To those who talk of deeds they have actually done.
1. Nor exposes what should remain hidden.
**5.3** Location: The altar, here dedicated to Diana.

1. *shadowy*: a goddess of the moon, Diana was associated with the night. *cold*: chaste. See 1.3.52, 4.2.58, and notes to these lines.

Sweet, solitary, white as chaste, and pure
As wind-fanned° snow, who to thy female knights                                           *windblown*
5      Allow'st no more blood° than will make a blush,                                             *sexual desire*
Which is their order's robe: I here, thy priest,
Am humbled fore thine altar. O, vouchsafe
With that thy rare green eye, which never yet
Beheld thing maculate,° look on thy virgin;                                                     *tainted*
10    And, sacred silver mistress, lend thine ear—
Which ne'er heard scurril° term, into whose port°                                    *scurrilous / opening*
Ne'er entered wanton° sound—to my petition,                                                       *lewd*
Seasoned with holy fear.° This is my last                                                      *pious awe*
Of vestal office.² I am bride-habited,°                                                   *dressed as a bride*
15    But maiden-hearted. A husband I have 'pointed,°                                        *have been assigned*
But do not know him. Out of two, I should
Choose one and pray for his success, but I
Am guiltless of election.³ Of mine eyes
Were I to lose one, they are equal precious—
20    I could doom neither: that which perished should
Go to't unsentenced. Therefore, most modest queen,
He of the two pretenders° that best loves me                                                     *suitors*
And has the truest title in't,° let him                                                        *claim to me*
Take off my wheaten garland,° or else grant                                               *Take my virginity*
25    The file and quality I hold I may
Continue in thy band.⁴

> *Here the hind vanishes under the altar and in the place*
> *ascends a rose tree having one rose° upon it*                                       *(symbol of virginity)*

[*To her women*] See what our general of ebbs and flows⁵
Out from the bowels of her holy altar,
With sacred act, advances—but one rose!
30    If well inspired,⁶ this battle shall confound°                                           *destroy*
Both these brave knights, and I a virgin flower
Must grow alone, unplucked.

> *Here is heard a sudden twang of instruments and the*
> *rose falls from the tree*

The flower is fall'n, the tree descends. [*To Diana*] O mistress,
Thou here dischargest me—I shall be gathered.⁷
35    I think so, but I know not thine own will.
Unclasp thy mystery.° [*To her women*] I hope she's pleased;                         *Reveal your meaning*
Her signs were gracious.                       *They curtsy and exeunt*

## 5.4

> *Enter [the]* DOCTOR, [*the*] JAILER, *and [the]* WOOER *in*
> [*the*] *habit of°* Palamon                                                                  *dressed as*

DOCTOR    Has this advice I told you done any good upon her?
WOOER    O, very much. The maids that kept her company have
half persuaded her that I am Palamon. Within this half-hour
she came smiling to me, and asked me what I would eat, and
5      when I would kiss her. I told her presently,° and kissed her                            *at once*
twice.

---

2. *my . . . office*: my last duty as your virginal devotee.            5. Our ruler of the moon and, hence, of tides.
3. Am not guilty of having made a choice (and hence            6. If this is a true omen.
of having betrayed my vows).                                          7. I shall be married; I shall lose my virginity.
4. *grant . . . band*: grant that I may continue to hold the        5.4 Location: The prison.
rank and condition (of virginity) as one of your devotees.

DOCTOR 'Twas well done—twenty times had been far better,
    For there° the cure lies mainly.              *(in kissing)*
WOOER                   Then she told me
    She would watch° with me tonight, for well she knew     *stay up*
    What hour my fit° would take me.        *urgent inclination*
10 DOCTOR                     Let her do so,
    And when your fit comes, fit her home,[1]
    And presently.
WOOER           She would have me sing.
DOCTOR    You did so?
WOOER          No.
DOCTOR              'Twas very ill done, then.
    You should observe° her every way.       *accommodate*
WOOER                    Alas,
15     I have no voice, sir, to confirm° her that way.     *assure*
DOCTOR    That's all one,° if ye make a noise.    *That doesn't matter*
    If she entreat° again, do anything—          *beg*
    Lie with her if she ask you.
JAILER             Ho there, Doctor.
DOCTOR    Yes, in the way of cure.
JAILER               But first, by your leave,
    I'th' way of honesty.°              *(after marriage)*
20 DOCTOR            That's but a niceness°—   *an excessive scruple*
    Ne'er cast your child away for honesty.[2]
    Cure her first this way, then if she will° be honest,   *wants to*
    She has the path° before her.         *(of marriage)*
JAILER              Thank ye, Doctor.
DOCTOR    Pray bring her in and let's see how she is.
25 JAILER    I will, and tell her her Palamon stays° for her.   *waits*
    But, Doctor, methinks you are i'th' wrong still.   *Exit* JAILER
DOCTOR    Go, go. You fathers are fine fools—her honesty?
    An we should give her physic till we find that[3]—
WOOER    Why, do you think she is not honest, sir?
DOCTOR    How old is she?
WOOER             She's eighteen.
30 DOCTOR                 She may be—
    But that's all one. 'Tis nothing to our purpose.°   *It makes no difference*
    Whate'er her father says, if you perceive
    Her mood inclining that way that I spoke of,
    Videlicet,° the way of flesh—you have me?     *Namely*
WOOER    Yes, very well, sir.
35 DOCTOR              Please her appetite,
    And do it home°—it cures her, *ipso facto*,[4]    *completely*
    The melancholy humour° that infects her.    *mood (medical)*
WOOER    I am of your mind, Doctor.
             *Enter [the]* JAILER *and [his]* DAUGHTER *[mad]*
DOCTOR    You'll find it so—she comes: pray humour her.
          *[The* DOCTOR *and the* WOOER *stand apart]*
JAILER *[to his* DAUGHTER]    Come, your love Palamon stays for
40     you, child,

---

1. Fully serve her needs (have sex with her).
2. A paradox: don't lose your daughter (to her madness) in order to keep her (honest).
3. If we were to treat her until we could be sure of her virginity (the obvious continuation of the unfinished thought being, we'd be treating her forever).
4. By the very act (*ipso facto*) of having sex, she'll be cured. The Doctor assumes, correctly in the event, that the Daughter suffers from hysteria, thought to be caused by a wandering womb and cured by intercourse.

And has done this long hour, to visit you.
JAILER'S DAUGHTER  I thank him for his gentle patience.
He's a kind gentleman, and I am much bound° to him.    *obliged*
Did you ne'er see the horse he gave me?
JAILER                                            Yes.
JAILER'S DAUGHTER  How do you like him?
45 JAILER                                        He's a very fair° one.    *beautiful*
JAILER'S DAUGHTER  You never saw him dance?
JAILER                                            No.
JAILER'S DAUGHTER                              I have, often.
He dances very finely, very comely,
And, for a jig, come cut and long-tail to him,[5]
He turns ye like a top.
JAILER                        That's fine, indeed.
50 JAILER'S DAUGHTER  He'll dance the morris twenty mile an hour,
And that will founder the best hobbyhorse,[6]
If I have any skill,° in all the parish—            *judgment*
And gallops to the tune of 'Light o' love'.[7]
What think you of this horse?
JAILER                              Having these virtues
55 I think he might be brought° to play at tennis.    *taught*
JAILER'S DAUGHTER  Alas, that's nothing.
JAILER                                  Can he write and read too?
JAILER'S DAUGHTER  A very fair hand, and casts himself th'accounts[8]
Of all his hay and provender. That ostler
Must rise betime that cozens° him. You know    *get up early to cheat*
The chestnut mare the Duke has?
60 JAILER                              Very well.
JAILER'S DAUGHTER  She is horribly in love with him, poor beast,
But he is like his master—coy° and scornful.      *aloof*
JAILER  What dowry has she?
JAILER'S DAUGHTER              Some two hundred bottles°    *bales of hay*
And twenty strike° of oats, but he'll ne'er have her.    *bushels*
65 He lisps in's neighing, able to entice
A miller's mare.[9] He'll be the death of her.
DOCTOR  What stuff she utters!
JAILER  Make curtsy—here your love comes.
WOOER [*coming forward*]  Pretty soul,
How do ye?
            [*She curtsies*]
70              That's a fine maid, there's a curtsy.
JAILER'S DAUGHTER  Yours to command, i'th' way of honesty—
How far is't now to th' end o'th' world, my masters?
DOCTOR  Why, a day's journey, wench.
JAILER'S DAUGHTER [*to* WOOER]      Will you go with me?
WOOER  What shall we do there, wench?

5. *He . . . him:* He dances finely no matter what horse he is compared with. *cut:* a horse with a docked tail (see note to 3.4.22). There is sexual wordplay throughout this scene.
6. That will lame ("founder") the best morris dancer. *hobbyhorse:* one extremely agile morris dancer was dressed as a horse and imitated its movements.
7. Popular ballad, also referred to in *Much Ado About*

*Nothing* 3.4.39 and *The Two Gentlemen of Verona* 1.2.83. The title means "inconstant in love."
8. He has beautiful penmanship and reckons his own expenses.
9. *He . . . mare:* He's such a smooth talker he could seduce even a miller's mare—a workhorse renowned for its steadfast, circular plodding and, hence, least likely to be distracted.

JAILER'S DAUGHTER            Why, play at stool-ball[1]—
   What is there else to do?

75   WOOER               I am content
   If we shall keep our wedding° there.          *As long as we marry*

JAILER'S DAUGHTER           'Tis true—
   For there, I will assure you, we shall find
   Some blind priest for the purpose that will venture
   To marry us, for here they are nice,° and foolish.      *too scrupulous*

80    Besides, my father must be hanged tomorrow,
   And that would be a blot i'th' business.
   Are not you Palamon?

WOOER            Do not you know me?

JAILER'S DAUGHTER    Yes, but you care not for me. I have nothing
   But this poor petticoat and two coarse smocks.°      *undergarments*

WOOER    That's all one—I will have you.

85   JAILER'S DAUGHTER           Will you surely?

WOOER    Yes, by this fair hand, will I.

JAILER'S DAUGHTER          We'll to bed then.

WOOER    E'en when you will.°                 *Whenever you like*
    [*He kisses her*]

JAILER'S DAUGHTER [*rubbing off the kiss*]
               O, sir, you would fain be nibbling.

WOOER    Why do you rub my kiss off?

JAILER'S DAUGHTER          'Tis a sweet one,
   And will perfume me finely against° the wedding.      *in preparation for*
   [*Indicating the* DOCTOR] Is not this your cousin Arcite?

90   DOCTOR                     Yes, sweetheart,
   And I am glad my cousin Palamon
   Has made so fair a choice.

JAILER'S DAUGHTER         Do you think he'll have me?

DOCTOR    Yes, without doubt.

JAILER'S DAUGHTER [*to the* JAILER]    Do you think so too?

JAILER                          Yes.

JAILER'S DAUGHTER    We shall have many children. [*To the* DOCTOR]
   Lord, how you're grown!

95    My Palamon, I hope, will grow too,[2] finely,
   Now he's at liberty. Alas, poor chicken,
   He was kept down with hard meat° and ill lodging,      *coarse food*
   But I'll kiss him up again.
    *Enter a* MESSENGER

MESSENGER    What do you here? You'll lose the noblest sight
   That e'er was seen.

JAILER           Are they i'th' field?

100  MESSENGER              They are—
   You bear a charge° there too.                *have a duty*

JAILER            I'll away straight.
   [*To the others*] I must e'en leave you here.

DOCTOR           Nay, we'll go with you—
   I will not lose the sight.

JAILER         How did you like her?

DOCTOR    I'll warrant you, within these three or four days

---

1. A game, somewhat like cricket, played with ball and bat by women or by men and women together.      2. Get fat; have an erection.

I'll make her right again.

[*Exit the* JAILER *with the* MESSENGER]

105    [*To the* WOOER]         You must not from her,
But still preserve° her in this way.            *keep treating*

WOOER                 I will.

DOCTOR   Let's get her in.

WOOER   [*to the* JAILER'S DAUGHTER]
                 Come, sweet, we'll go to dinner,
And then we'll play at cards.

JAILER'S DAUGHTER        And shall we kiss too?

WOOER   A hundred times.

JAILER'S DAUGHTER      . And twenty.

WOOER                     Ay, and twenty.

JAILER'S DAUGHTER   And then we'll sleep together.

110 DOCTOR [*to the* WOOER]             Take her offer.

WOOER [*to the* JAILER'S DAUGHTER]
    Yes, marry, will we.

JAILER'S DAUGHTER   But you shall not hurt me.

WOOER   I will not, sweet.

JAILER'S DAUGHTER       If you do, love, I'll cry.       *Exeunt*

## 5.5

*Flourish. Enter* THESEUS, HIPPOLYTA, EMILIA,
PIRITHOUS, *and some attendants*

EMILIA   I'll no step further.

PIRITHOUS            Will you lose this sight?

EMILIA   I had rather see a wren hawk at° a fly      *attack in midair*
Than this decision. Every blow that falls
Threats a brave life; each stroke laments
5   The place whereon it falls, and sounds more like
A bell° than blade. I will stay here.          *death knell*
It is enough my hearing shall be punished
With what shall happen, 'gainst the which there is
No deafing, but to hear;[1] not taint mine eye
With dread sights it may shun.

10 PIRITHOUS [*to* THESEUS]       Sir, my good lord,
Your sister will no further.

THESEUS            O, she must.
She shall see deeds of honour in their kind,°    *true nature*
Which sometime show well pencilled.° Nature now   *even when just drawn*
Shall make and act° the story, the belief      *invent and perform*
Both sealed with eye and ear.[2] [*To* EMILIA] You must be
15     present—
You are the victor's meed,° the price and garland    *reward*
To crown the question's title.[3]

EMILIA             Pardon me,
If I were there I'd wink.°           *keep my eyes closed*

THESEUS          You must be there—
This trial is, as 'twere, i'th' night, and you
The only star to shine.

20 EMILIA          I am extinct.°          *extinguished*

---

5.5 Location: The forest, near the tournament field.    by all that is seen and heard.
1. *there . . . hear:* there is no way to block out the noise    3. To crown the rightful victor in the dispute.
in order not to hear.
2. *the belief . . . ear:* the story will be rendered credible

There is but envy° in that light which shows         *malice*
The one the other. Darkness, which ever was
The dam° of horror, who does stand accursed        *mother*
Of many mortal millions, may even now,
25   By casting her black mantle over both,
That° neither could find other, get herself        *So that*
Some part of a good name, and many a murder
Set off whereto° she's guilty.          *Atone for of which*
**HIPPOLYTA**               You must go.
**EMILIA**   In faith, I will not.
**THESEUS**            Why, the knights must kindle
30   Their valour at your eye. Know, of this war
You are the treasure, and must needs be by°      *nearby*
To give the service pay.°          *reward the winner*
**EMILIA**              Sir, pardon me—
The title of a kingdom may be tried
Out of itself.°              *Outside the kingdom*
**THESEUS**      Well, well—then at your pleasure.
35   Those that remain with you could wish their office
To any of their enemies.
**HIPPOLYTA**          Farewell, sister.
I am like to know your husband fore yourself,
By some small start of time. He whom the gods
Do of the two know° best, I pray them he     *know to be*
40   Be made your lot.         *Exeunt [all but* EMILIA]
     [EMILIA *takes out two pictures, one from her right side,*
     *and one from her left*]
**EMILIA**  Arcite is gently visaged,° yet his eye    *has a gentle expression*
Is like an engine bent[4] or a sharp weapon
In a soft sheath. Mercy and manly courage
Are bedfellows in his visage. Palamon
45   Has a most menacing aspect. His brow
Is graved° and seems to bury what it frowns on,    *frowned*
Yet sometime 'tis not so, but alters to°     *according to*
The quality° of his thoughts. Long time his eye    *nature*
Will dwell upon his object. Melancholy
50   Becomes° him nobly—so does Arcite's mirth.    *Suits*
But Palamon's sadness is a kind of mirth,
So mingled as if mirth did make him sad
And sadness merry. Those darker humours° that    *moods*
Stick misbecomingly° on others, on them    *Seem misplaced*
55   Live in fair dwelling.[5]
      *Cornetts. Trumpets sound as to a charge*
Hark, how yon spurs to spirit° do incite     *bravery*
The princes to their proof.° Arcite may win me,   *to prove themselves*
And yet may Palamon wound Arcite to
The spoiling of his figure.° O, what pity   *(so as to disfigure him)*
60   Enough for such a chance![6] If I were by°    *near*
I might do hurt, for they would glance their eyes
Toward my seat, and in that motion might
Omit a ward or forfeit an offence

---

4. Is like a weapon, such as a bow, ready to be released.   6. Would be sufficient for such a (sad) turn of events.
5. *on them . . . dwelling:* suit them well.

Which craved that very time.[7] It is much better
    *Cornetts. A great cry and noise within, crying,*
    *'A Palamon'*
65     I am not there. O better never born,
Than minister to such harm.
    *Enter* SERVANT
               What is the chance?°        *Who won*
SERVANT   The cry's 'A Palamon'.
EMILIA   Then he has won. 'Twas ever likely—
He looked all grace and success, and he is
70     Doubtless the prim'st° of men. I prithee run    *most perfect*
And tell me how it goes.
    *Shout and cornetts, crying, 'A Palamon'*
SERVANT             Still 'Palamon'.
EMILIA   Run and enquire.          [*Exit* SERVANT]
    [*She speaks to the picture in her right hand*]
               Poor servant,° thou hast lost.    *lover (Arcite)*
Upon my right side still I° wore thy picture,    *I always*
Palamon's on the left. Why so, I know not.
75     I had no end° in't, else chance would have it so.    *purpose*
    *Another cry and shout within and cornetts*
On the sinister side the heart lies—Palamon
Had the best-boding chance.[8] This burst of clamour
Is sure the end o'th' combat.
    *Enter* SERVANT
SERVANT   They said that Palamon had Arcite's body
80     Within an inch o'th' pyramid—that the cry
Was general 'A Palamon'. But anon
Th'assistants° made a brave redemption,° and    *knights / rescue*
The two bold titlers° at this instant are    *fighters for the title*
Hand to hand at it.
EMILIA           Were they° metamorphosed    *I wish they were*
85     Both into one! O why? There were no woman
Worth so composed a man:[9] their single share,
Their nobleness peculiar to them, gives
The prejudice of disparity, value's shortness,
To any lady breathing[1]—
    *Cornetts. Cry within, 'Arcite, Arcite'*
               More exulting?
'Palamon' still?
90   SERVANT          Nay, now the sound is 'Arcite'.
EMILIA   I prithee, lay attention to the cry.
    *Cornetts. A great shout and cry, 'Arcite, victory!'*
Set both thine ears to th' business.
SERVANT             The cry is
'Arcite' and 'Victory'—hark, 'Arcite, victory!'
The combat's consummation° is proclaimed    *conclusion*
By the wind instruments.
95   EMILIA          Half sights saw°    *Mere glimpses showed*
That Arcite was no babe. God's lid,° his richness    *By God's eyelid*

---

7. *might . . . time:* might miss the perfect moment for
a defensive parry or an offensive move.
8. *On . . . chance:* The location of Palamon's picture—
on Emilia's left ("sinister") side, where her heart is—
portended victory, since the contest is about love.

9. *There . . . man:* No woman could be worthy of this
composite man made up of both Palamon and Arcite.
1. *their single . . . breathing:* no woman could have as
much nobility as either one of them. *their single share:*
each one's value.

And costliness of spirit looked through him—it could
No more be hid in him than fire in flax,°            *straw*
Than humble banks can go to law with° waters      *can battle*
100    That drift° winds force to raging. I did think          *driving*
Good Palamon would miscarry, yet I knew not
Why I did think so. Our reasons are not prophets
When oft our fancies are. They are coming off°—     *leaving the field*
Alas, poor Palamon.
        [*She puts away the pictures.*]
        *Cornetts. Enter* THESEUS, HIPPOLYTA, PIRITHOUS, ARCITE
        *as victor, and attendants*
105   THESEUS    Lo, where our sister is in expectation,
Yet quaking and unsettled. Fairest Emily,
The gods by their divine arbitrament
Have given you this knight. He is a good one
As ever struck at head. [*To* ARCITE *and* EMILIA] Give me your
        hands.
[*To* ARCITE] Receive you her, [*to* EMILIA] you him: [*to both*]
110       be plighted with
A love that grows as you decay.
ARCITE                 Emilia,
To buy you I have lost what's dearest to me
Save what is bought,° and yet I purchase cheaply     *(Emilia)*
As I do rate your value.
THESEUS [*to* EMILIA]        O lovèd sister,
115   He speaks now of as brave a knight as e'er
Did spur a noble steed. Surely the gods
Would have him die a bachelor lest his race
Should show i'th' world too godlike. His behaviour
So charmed me that, methought, Alcides° was       *Hercules*
120   To him a sow[2] of lead. If I could praise
Each part of him to th'all I have spoke,[3] your Arcite
Did° not lose by't; for he that was thus good,       *Would*
Encountered yet his better. I have heard
Two emulous Philomels[4] beat the ear o'th' night
125   With their contentious throats, now one the higher,
Anon the other, then again the first,
And by and by out-breasted, that the sense[5]
Could not be judge between 'em—so it fared
Good space° between these kinsmen, till heavens did   *For a good while*
130   Make hardly° one the winner. [*To* ARCITE] Wear the garland   *Barely make*
With joy that you have won.—For the subdued,°      *losers*
Give them our present° justice, since I know       *immediate*
Their lives but pinch° 'em. Let it here be done.       *torment*
The scene's not for our seeing; go we hence
135   Right joyful, with some sorrow. [*To* ARCITE] Arm° your prize;   *Give your arm to*
I know you will not lose her. Hippolyta,
I see one eye of yours conceives a tear,
The which it will deliver.
        *Flourish*

---

2. Smelted metal taken from a furnace.
3. *to . . . spoke:* in the same way I have praised Palamon as a whole.
4. Two rival nightingales. In Greek mythology,
Philomela was raped by her sister's husband, who cut

out her tongue so she couldn't accuse him. By weaving
the story into cloth, she nonetheless informed her sister, who fed her husband their son. The gods turned the
sister into a nightingale and Philomela into a swallow.
5. And by and by outsung, so that the sense of hearing.

EMILIA                              Is this winning?
O all you heavenly powers, where is your mercy?
140  But that your wills have said it must be so,
And charge me live to comfort this unfriended,°          deprived of his friend
This miserable prince, that cuts away
A life more worthy from him than all women,
I should and would die too.

HIPPOLYTA                            Infinite pity
145  That four such eyes should be so fixed on one°          one woman
That two must needs be blind for't.⁶

THESEUS                                         So it is.          Exeunt

## 5.6

*Enter [guarded] PALAMON and his [three] KNIGHTS pin-*
*ioned; [enter with them the] JAILER [and an] execu-*
*tioner [with block and axe]*

PALAMON    There's many a man alive that hath outlived
The love o'th' people; yea, i'th' selfsame state
Stands many a father with his child: some comfort
We have by so considering. We expire,
5    And not without men's pity; to live still,
Have their good wishes.¹ We prevent°                        avoid
The loathsome misery of age, beguile°                       cheat
The gout and rheum° that in lag° hours attend              coughing / final
For grey approachers;° we come towards the gods            (to death)
10   Young and unwappered,° not halting° under crimes        untired / limping morally
Many and stale°—that sure shall please the gods            long gone
Sooner than such,° to give us nectar with 'em,             (sinful old men)
For we are more clear° spirits. My dear kinsmen,           innocent
Whose lives for this poor comfort are laid down,
You have sold 'em° too too cheap.                          (your lives)

15   FIRST KNIGHT                          What ending could be
Of more content? O'er us the victors have
Fortune, whose title° is as momentary                      claim
As to us death is certain—a grain of honour
They not o'erweigh us.²

SECOND KNIGHT                      Let us bid farewell,
20   And with our patience anger tott'ring° fortune,          unstable
Who at her certain'st reels.³

THIRD KNIGHT                       Come, who begins?

PALAMON    E'en he that led you to this banquet shall
Taste to you all.⁴ [*To the* JAILER] Aha, my friend, my friend,
Your gentle daughter gave me freedom once;
25   You'll see't done° now for ever. Pray, how does she?      see me set free
I heard she was not well; her kind of ill°                 illness
Gave me some sorrow.

JAILER                          Sir, she's well restored
And to be married shortly.

PALAMON                          By my short life,

---

6. That two eyes must be blinded (in death); that two
men could be so blind as to fight to the death for one
woman.
5.6 Location: Scene continues.
1. *We expire . . . wishes:* Even though we are to die, we
have men's good wishes that we might go on living.

2. *a grain . . . us:* they have no more honor than we do.
3. Who, when she seems most certain, suddenly
changes direction.
4. Taste (death) first, like the servant at a state banquet
who was required to taste the food before the king and
guests to make sure it wasn't poisoned.

I am most glad on't. 'Tis the latest° thing     *last*
30   I shall be glad of. Prithee, tell her so;
Commend me to her, and to piece her portion°     *increase her dowry*
Tender her this.
      [*He gives his purse*]
FIRST KNIGHT     Nay, let's be offerers all.
SECOND KNIGHT     Is it a maid?°     *virgin*
PALAMON              Verily, I think so—
A right good creature more to me° deserving     *from me*
Than I can quit° or speak of.     *requite*
35 ALL THREE KNIGHTS         Commend us to her.
      *They give their purses*
JAILER     The gods requite you all, and make her thankful.
PALAMON     Adieu, and let my life be now as short
As my leave-taking.
      [*He*] *lies on the block*
FIRST KNIGHT         Lead, courageous cousin.
SECOND AND THIRD KNIGHTS     We'll follow cheerfully.
      *A great noise within: crying, 'Run! Save! Hold!'*
      *Enter in haste a* MESSENGER
40 MESSENGER     Hold! Hold! O, hold! Hold! Hold!
      *Enter* PIRITHOUS *in haste*
PIRITHOUS     Hold, ho! It is a cursèd haste you made
If you have done° so quickly! Noble Palamon,     *finished*
The gods will show their glory in a life
That thou art yet to lead.
PALAMON             Can that be,
45   When Venus, I have said, is false? How do things fare?
PIRITHOUS     Arise, great sir, and give the tidings ear
That are most rarely sweet and bitter.
PALAMON                What
Hath waked us from our dream?
PIRITHOUS          List,° then: your cousin,     *Listen*
Mounted upon a steed that Emily
50   Did first bestow on him, a black one owing°     *owning*
Not a hair-worth of white which some will say
Weakens his price⁵ and many will not buy
His goodness with this note;° which superstition     *distinctive mark*
Here finds allowance°—on this horse is Arcite     *gains support*
55   Trotting the stones of Athens, which the calkins
Did rather tell than trample;⁶ for the horse
Would make his length° a mile, if 't pleased his rider     *length of stride*
To put pride in him. As he thus went counting
The flinty pavement, dancing, as 'twere, to th' music
60   His own hooves made—for, as they say, from iron
Came music's origin⁷—what envious flint,°     *cobblestone*
Cold as old Saturn⁸ and like him possessed
With fire malevolent, darted a spark,

---

5. Makes him less valuable, because dark horses were considered vicious or ill omened.
6. *which . . . trample:* the horse's gait was so long and light that its feet seemed more to count ("tell") the cobbles one by one than to trample them. *calkins:* turned-down edges of a horseshoe.
7. Pythagoras is supposed to have discovered music

when walking through a blacksmith's forge.
8. According to Chaucer's *Knight's Tale,* Saturn, father of Jupiter, was responsible for the reversal of fortune described here, because he had promised Venus that Palamon would win Emilia. Shakespeare and Fletcher limit Saturn's responsibility to a simile.

Or what fierce sulphur else, to this end made,⁹

65 I comment not—the hot horse, hot as fire,
Took toy° at this and fell to what disorder                    *a capricious dislike*
His power could give his will; bounds; comes on end;
Forgets school-doing,° being therein trained                  *school training*
And of kind manège;° pig-like he whines                       *well disciplined*
70 At the sharp rowel,° which he frets at rather                *spur*
Than any jot obeys; seeks all foul means
Of boist'rous and rough jad'ry° to disseat                    *behavior like a nag*
His lord, that kept it° bravely. When naught served,          *who kept his seat*
When neither curb would crack, girth break, nor diff'ring°    *various*
      plunges
75 Disroot his rider whence he grew,° but that                 *was fixed*
He kept him 'tween his legs, on his hind hooves—
On end he stands—
That Arcite's legs, being higher than his head,
Seemed with strange art to hang. His victor's wreath
80 Even then fell off his head; and presently
Backward the jade comes o'er and his full poise°             *weight*
Becomes the rider's load. Yet is he living;
But such a vessel 'tis that floats but for
The surge that next approaches.¹ He much desires
85 To have some speech with you—lo, he appears.
      *Enter* THESEUS, HIPPOLYTA, EMILIA, [*and*] ARCITE *in a*
      *chair* [*borne by attendants*]
PALAMON    O miserable end of our alliance!
The gods are mighty. Arcite, if thy heart,
Thy worthy manly heart, be yet unbroken,
Give me thy last words. I am Palamon,
One that yet loves thee dying.
90 ARCITE                                Take Emilia,
And with her all the world's joy. Reach° thy hand—            *Give me*
Farewell—I have told° my last hour. I was false,             *counted*
Yet never treacherous.² Forgive me, cousin—
One kiss from fair Emilia—[*they kiss*] 'tis done.
Take her; I die.                                [*He dies*]
95 PALAMON              Thy brave soul seek Elysium.
EMILIA [*to Arcite's body*]    I'll close thine eyes, Prince. Blessèd
      souls be with thee.
Thou art a right good man, and, while I live,
This day I give to tears.
PALAMON                  And I to honour.
THESEUS    In this place first you fought, e'en very here
100 I sundered you.° Acknowledge to the gods                   *separated your fight*
Our thanks that you are living.
His part is played, and, though it were too short,
He did it well. Your day is lengthened and
The blissful dew of heaven does arrouse° you.                 *sprinkle*
105 The powerful Venus well hath graced her altar,
And given you your love; our master, Mars,

---

9. Or some spark of hellfire made for this purpose.
1. *But such . . . approaches:* But he can live only until
the next onslaught (like a boat that can stay afloat only
until the next wave hits).

2. *I was . . . treacherous:* I was "false" to our friendship
(because Palamon did see Emilia first) but "never
treacherous" in vying for Emilia's love.

Hath vouched° his oracle, and to Arcite gave                                    *made good on*
The grace of the contention.° So the deities                                    *victory in the battle*
Have showed due justice.—Bear this hence.

[*Exeunt attendants with Arcite's body*]

PALAMON                                                O cousin,

110    That we should things desire which do cost us
The loss of our desire! That naught could buy
Dear love, but loss of dear love!

THESEUS                                        Never fortune
Did play a subtler game—the conquered triumphs,
The victor has the loss. Yet in the passage°                                    *proceedings*

115    The gods have been most equal.° Palamon,                                 *impartial*
Your kinsman hath confessed the right o'th' lady°                               *the right to Emilia*
Did lie in you,° for you first saw her and                                      *Was yours*
Even then proclaimed your fancy. He restored her
As your stol'n jewel, and desired your spirit

120    To send him hence forgiven. The gods my justice
Take from my hand, and they themselves become
The executioners.° Lead your lady off,                                          *executors of justice*
And call your lovers from the stage of death,°                                  *friends from the scaffold*
Whom I adopt my friends. A day or two

125    Let us look sadly and give grace unto
The funeral of Arcite, in whose end°                                            *after which*
The visages of bridegrooms we'll put on
And smile with Palamon, for whom an hour,
But one hour since, I was as dearly sorry

130    As glad of Arcite, and am now as glad
As for him sorry. O you heavenly charmers,°                                     *gods who enchant us*
What things you make of us! For what we lack
We laugh, for what we have, are sorry; still
Are children in some kind. Let us be thankful

135    For that which is, and with you leave dispute
That are above our question.³ Let's go off
And bear us like° the time.           *Flourish. Exeunt*                        *act in accordance with*

## Epilogue

[*Enter* EPILOGUE]

EPILOGUE    I would now ask ye how ye like the play,
But, as it is with schoolboys, cannot say.°                                     *speak*
I am cruel fearful.° Pray yet stay awhile,¹                                     *horribly afraid*
And let me look upon ye. No man smile?

5    Then it goes hard, I see. He that has
Loved a young handsome wench, then, show his face—
'Tis strange if none be here—and, if he will,
Against his conscience let him hiss and kill
Our market.° 'Tis in vain, I see, to stay ye.                                   *Our chance of success*

10    Have at the worst can come,° then! Now, what say ye?                       *Do your worst*
And yet mistake me not—I am not bold—
We have no such cause.° If the tale we have told—                              *purpose*
For 'tis no other—any way content° ye,                                         *please*
For to that honest purpose it was meant ye,°                                    *intended for you*

---

3. *with . . . question:* cease to dispute with you, who
are beyond our questioning.    **Epilogue**
1. Don't hiss or applaud yet.

15    We have our end;° and ye shall have ere long,     *achieved our aim*
    I dare say, many a better to prolong
    Your old loves to us. We and all our might°     *all we can do*
    Rest at your service. Gentlemen, good night.    *Flourish.* [*Exit*]

# POEMS

POEMS

# Venus and Adonis

When Shakespeare wrote the narrative poem *Venus and Adonis,* he was already an up-and-coming playwright; but he called his poem "the first heir of my invention" because, in 1593, it was his earliest work to see print. While plays were considered the property of the theater company and found their way to the printing house erratically if at all, an author could publish nondramatic works like *Venus and Adonis* and *The Rape of Lucrece* without impediment. It was customary to dedicate such published poems to aristocrats who might provide financial support or other form of patronage. Shakespeare dedicated *Venus and Adonis* to Henry Wriothesley, Earl of Southampton, a handsome nineteen-year-old aristocrat with sophisticated literary tastes, who was soon to come into a substantial fortune. But despite the conventionally flattering language of the dedication, Shakespeare intended to appeal to a larger audience than merely the patron to whom the poem was nominally addressed. Indeed, *Venus and Adonis* was exceedingly popular in Shakespeare's lifetime: it went through nine editions, and his contemporaries quote passages from it more often than they quote from any other Shakespearean play or poem.

Part of the attraction of the poem for Shakespeare's contemporaries was its extended and apparently effortless deployment of an elaborate poetic form. The poem's *ababcc* stanza, a quatrain followed by a couplet, was popular among many Elizabethan poets—George Gascoigne, Thomas Lodge, Edmund Spenser, and Philip Sidney, among others—but Shakespeare's virtuosity was so widely recognized that it has henceforth been known in English not by its Italian name, *sesta rima,* but as the "Venus and Adonis stanza." A sort of abbreviated sonnet, this stanza, in Shakespeare's hands, tends often to proffer a snatch of narrative in the quatrain, followed by a summarizing or reflective couplet, thus alternating between advancing the plot and commenting, pithily and wittily, upon the action.

Shakespeare found the story of Venus and Adonis in Ovid's *Metamorphoses,* a poem in fifteen books that retells, in beautiful Latin, more than two hundred pagan myths of transformation. Since Elizabethan schoolboys were required to memorize long passages from the *Metamorphoses,* many of Shakespeare's readers knew Ovid in the original; others read him in a popular 1567 English translation by Arthur Golding. Shakespeare would have been aware that the cult of Adonis was widespread in antiquity, a cult that involved rites of fertility and seasonal renewal and was associated with the adoration of a mother goddess variously identified as Venus, Aphrodite, Astoreth, Isis, or Cybele. In the Old Testament, the Israelites are periodically chastised for abandoning their male divinity for the worship of this heathen goddess; her cult thus seems, at least for the Jews of antiquity, to have constituted an alluring alternative to patriarchal monotheism. For Christian interpreters, the myth of the mutilated, transformed Adonis resembles the story of Christ closely enough to be read, on the one hand, as a pagan analogue to Christ's death and resurrection and, on the other hand, as a demonstration of the superior power of the Judeo-Christian God, who, unlike Venus, can confer true immortality.

Shakespeare was not the only Elizabethan writer to adapt Ovid's stories to an English idiom. *Venus and Adonis* is an erotic narrative poem of a type that had become popular in the 1580s and grew even more so in the 1590s, partly because of the success of Shakespeare's poem and of Christopher Marlowe's roughly contemporaneous *Hero and Leander.* The writers of such poems acquired their plots from classical sources, but they got their idea of how to treat those plots from a medieval and Renaissance tradition of erotic

Two horses mating. From Antonio Tempesta, *Horses of Different Lands*.

poetry, deriving from the Italian poet Petrarch and developed in English by such poets as Thomas Wyatt, Philip Sidney, and Edmund Spenser. In *Venus and Adonis,* Shakespeare reconceives his mythological protagonists so that his poem might in some respects more closely approximate a Petrarchan norm. When Ovid's Venus is dazzled by Adonis, she resolves to appeal to him by feigning an interest in his favorite sport. By donning hunting gear and resolutely chasing rabbits, she successfully captures the gorgeous huntsman, her true quarry. Shakespeare's Venus declares herself in a much more forthright fashion, but his Adonis, unlike Ovid's, remains unresponsive to her charms. Thus *Venus and Adonis* reproduces a dynamic that Petrarch and his followers had made familiar by the late sixteenth century, in which a yearning lover pleads endlessly with a chilly love object.

The enduring fascination of this scenario for Renaissance poets lay in their recognition that the absence of sexual gratification can enhance erotic desire: "An oven that is stopped, or river stayed, / Burneth more hotly, swelleth with more rage" (lines 331–32). In Petrarchan poetry, little of consequence seems to happen, but the apparent lack of momentum is actually a prime stimulus to creativity. Frustration hones techniques of erotic persuasion; it energizes lament; it interestingly complicates the poet-lover's state of mind. The sophisticated pleasure of intense self-awareness replaces the straightforward, even mindless pleasure of the sex act itself. In *Venus and Adonis,* Shakespeare's concentration on psychological detail produces an extraordinary slowing-down and drawing-out of the action. Ovid spends about eighty-five lines on Adonis, beginning with a brisk description of his birth and ending with an equally succinct account of his metamorphosis into an anemone flower. Shakespeare manages to devote almost twelve hundred lines to the last twenty-four hours of Adonis's life.

In some important respects, however, Shakespeare departs from his Petrarchan precedents. The Ovidian retelling of the story of Venus and Adonis appears in *Metamor-*

*phoses* 10, a book that, as Ovid's translator Arthur Golding writes, "chiefly doth contain one kind of argument / Reproving most prodigious lusts." Taken together, the stories of Book 10 treat necrophilia, homosexuality, bestiality, fetishism, and incest; in this context, the story of Venus and Adonis seems relatively tame. But the "prodigiousness" of the Venus and Adonis story becomes clear when it is compared with similar Ovidian tales, which usually involve gods—Jove, Neptune, Apollo, or Pluto—who rape or attempt to rape beautiful young women. The story of Venus and Adonis reverses the "normal" gender of eager divinity and reluctant mortal.

Shakespeare's revisions of the story exaggerate the effects of this transposition. He attributes some conventionally "masculine" traits to his heroine and some conventionally "feminine" ones to his hero. His Venus is experienced, immensely strong, and apparently quite a bit larger than the Adonis whom she effortlessly tucks under one arm. Shakespeare's Adonis is dimpled, tender, coy, and virginal. At the same time, a female, even one as formidable as Venus, is imagined to be incapable of rape, so Venus cannot simply overpower her beloved as Apollo or Jove might do. Anatomical constraints force her to play a quite different but also conventionally masculine part: the pleading, unsatisfied role conventionally assigned to the male lover in Petrarchan poetry.

Since in Renaissance erotic poetry the positions of actively desiring, rhetorically fluent male and passive, unwilling female are ordinarily strictly demarcated, the sexual transpositions in the Venus and Adonis story have immediate consequences for Shakespeare's use of poetic conventions. Obviously they give those conventions a fresh twist. In Shakespeare's hands, such novelty is often comic: the aggressive, rhetorically hyperbolic Venus and the fastidious Adonis are funny, because now as then they violate conventional notions of appropriate gender-specific behavior. Some of these reversals are obvious to a modern reader, since our courtship rituals retain vestiges of the assumption that males are naturally dominant and inclined to take the sexual initiative. Other reversals are more specific to the poetic tradition in which Shakespeare wrote. In traditional love poetry, for instance, the enamored man "blazons," or elaborately describes, the features of the woman he desires, dwelling on the incomparable beauty of her eyes, hair, lips, hands, voice, gestures, and so forth. But in *Venus and Adonis*, Venus is compelled to blazon her own charms, because Adonis will not do it for her.

> Mine eyes are grey, and bright, and quick in turning.
> My beauty as the spring doth yearly grow.
> My flesh is soft and plump, my marrow burning.
> . . . . . . . . . . . . . . . . . . . . . . .
> Bid me discourse, I will enchant thine ear,
> Or like a fairy, trip upon the green;
> Or like a nymph, with long, dishevelled hair,
> Dance on the sands, and yet no footing seen.
> (lines 140–48)

While in the conventional love situation the blazon is a man's cry of yearning for an exquisite object, here it becomes a woman's calculated, but unsuccessful, advertising campaign.

Shakespeare also dwells on the comic quality of Venus's divine attributes, such as the miraculous weightlessness of her robust body. At one point, Venus describes herself as a kind of giant balloon: "Witness this primrose bank whereon I lie: / These forceless flowers like sturdy trees support me" (lines 151–52). Her physical strength contrasts vividly with her quintessentially feminine body: when Venus "locks her lily fingers one in one" (line 228), she turns out to have a grip of steel. Shakespeare's interest in such apparent incongruities foreshadowed his much more elaborate exploration of the effects of transvestism and sexual reversal in such plays as *As You Like It, Twelfth Night, All's Well That Ends Well, Macbeth,* and *Antony and Cleopatra*. The humor of *Venus and Adonis* is two-edged, however, for it implicitly mocks not merely the aberrant protagonists but the standards from which they deviate. In what sense are particular

Cupid taking aim. From George Wither, *A Collection of Emblemes* (1635). The motto reads: "Be wary, whosoe're thou be, / For from Love's arrows, none are free."

traits or behaviors "naturally" masculine or feminine if actual males and females do not possess them?

The upending of gender stereotypes in *Venus and Adonis* is only one of the strategies of reversal that structure the imagery of the poem. Again and again, its metaphors and similes insist on the similarity of what seems different, the difference in what seems the same. Hunting is and is not like sexual pursuit; killing is and is not like loving; female sexual desire is and is not like maternal nurture; the boar, savagely rooting in Adonis's groin, is and is not like Venus; Adonis is and is not like the sun god or the flower into which he eventually transforms. Many of these comparisons or implied comparisons are traditional ones; Shakespeare's virtuosity is evident not as much in the originality of his individual conceits as in their extraordinary profusion and in the surprising way in which apparently incompatible images are tellingly juxtaposed.

The handling of imagery corresponds with the poem's abrupt reversals of mood and with the unpredictable, accidental quality of the story. The frank comedy of the beginning swerves into tragedy, or at least pathos, at the close, as the immortal goddess confronts the death of her reluctant beloved. Over the course of the poem, our estimation of both characters undergoes dizzying shifts. Venus—goddess, whore, cradle robber, and queen—is funny, scary, eloquent, and pitiable by turns. Adonis's sexual diffidence at first seems as ridiculous to the readers as it does to Venus; but he suddenly seems less absurd when he replies, gravely even if rather too sanctimoniously, to Venus's importunities.

Venus's frank joy in the pleasures of sex suggests an uninhibited pagan universe, in which gods, animals, and human beings all are ruled by the same laws of generation and sensual enjoyment. Shakespeare's lavish attention to the forest setting in which the poem takes place suggests his keen appreciation of the sensuous possibilities of a purely natural world. The bodies of animals—Adonis's splendid courser, inflamed by lust; the ferocious boar, bursting through the thorniest thickets; the zigzagging hunted hare—all are accorded blazons of their own, as if they, not merely the human lovers, were full participants in the story of love and death. At such moments, the poem seems enthusiastically to endorse the original religious significance of the Venus and Adonis story, which linked human lives with the rhythms of a natural environment.

But Shakespeare's poem hardly evokes a sexual utopia. Even though the pagan setting of the poem presumably frees the characters from the sexually abstemious culture of Christianity, the heroine and hero still disagree vehemently about the value of sexual indulgence. Chastity has its attractions even apart from whatever supernatural reinforcement Christian faith might lend to it—especially, as Adonis notes, for those who are not yet fully adult. The

The boar attacking Adonis. From Henry Peacham, *Minerva Britanna* (1612).

immortal Venus thinks of experience as an endless series of pleasurable present-tense moments; the mortal Adonis wants to conceive of his life in terms of narrative development, building slowly and coherently to a future maturity. His untimely death suggests the risks of thinking of one's life in this fashion; he seems unwisely to have forgone present satisfaction in the hope of a reward that will never materialize.

On the other hand, why should Adonis, the victim of a sexual attack, enjoy caresses he has neither invited nor encouraged? Just as Shakespeare's reversal of gender stereotypes calls into question the adequacy of those stereotypes, so Adonis's recoil from Venus calls into question the naturalness of reproductive sexuality. Venus, the goddess of love, is supposed to be the apex of heterosexual desirability, both source and goal of every man's desire. Adonis, however, does not desire her even when she presses herself upon him. The congress of male and female thus seems simultaneously natural—what Adonis's palfrey and a passing mare know without tutelage—and optional, a possibility that some males, at any rate, may be willing to do without.

Shakespeare writes almost entirely from Venus's perspective: the boy, not the woman, is the sex object of *Venus and Adonis.* In an age lacking our comparatively rigid conception of sexual orientation, lovely androgynous boys were assumed to be attractive to adult men and women alike. Shakespeare returned to the subject of the adolescent boy's ambiguous, half-conscious sexiness in his transvestite comedies, and to the adult man's reluctance to commit himself to exclusively heterosexual alliances in those plays as well as in *The Merchant of Venice. Venus and Adonis* can thus be read both as a narrative of frustrated heterosexual desire and, perhaps, as a parable of desire for a beautiful, aloof boy by a male poet—a scenario also sketched in many of Shakespeare's sonnets.

What is the meaning of sexuality? *Venus and Adonis* suggests a wide variety of possibilities: it is both a joke and a cosmic principle, a function of stern reproductive necessity and of sheer animal exuberance, a link with the animal world and an escape from it, a necessity and an option, a reminder of mortality and an intimation of immortality, a celebration of personal uniqueness and a threat to the formation of an individual identity. The shifting perspectives of the poem exploit the ambivalence with which Shakespeare's culture, as well as our own, treats sexual matters as simultaneously comical and deeply serious. The language of *Venus and Adonis* is especially good at capturing the confusing, contradictory array of sensations produced by another person's unfamiliar body close to one's own, a sensation at once grand, comic, oppressive, arousing, and repellant. The sweating, reeking, melting, and liquefying that at first seem specific to Venus's courtship of Adonis appear, by the end of the poem, to represent a principle of mortal existence and moral evaluation, as one thing merges unsteadily, unexpectedly, into another.

Biographical critics have found in *Venus and Adonis* ample grounds for speculation. Does the sexual dynamic of this poem reflect Shakespeare's experience with the older

Anne Hathaway, hauling him into some bosky nook outside Stratford, or alternatively an infatuation with Henry Wriothesley, the gorgeous youth to whom, some speculate, the early sonnets are devoted in both senses of the word? Given the scanty biographical data that have come down to us, it is impossible to know. What is clear is that *Venus and Adonis* inaugurates many of the distinctive features of Shakespeare's later work: a fascination, and capacity to sympathize, with sexually assertive women and self-contained, immature young men; an erotic energy that is both exuberant and hard to pin down; a complex moral sensibility capable of apprehending contradictory ethical imperatives at the same time; and an uncanny ability to combine comic, tragic, pathetic, and sensuous effects in a single work, even in a single poetic moment.

KATHARINE EISAMAN MAUS

## TEXTUAL NOTE

The textual history of *Venus and Adonis* is much less tangled than that of most of the plays. Critics have theorized that Shakespeare wrote the narrative poems in 1592 and 1593, when an epidemic of bubonic plague forced the London theaters to close. At the time, it was unclear whether the playhouses would be allowed to reopen, so Shakespeare may have had not merely plenty of time on his hands but an urgent practical motive for establishing his credentials as a nondramatic writer. *Venus and Adonis* was first published in quarto in 1593 by the printer Richard Field, who was, like Shakespeare, a native of Stratford-upon-Avon. Only one copy of this edition survives. It contains very few obvious misprints and was presumably prepared from Shakespeare's manuscript, perhaps under his direct supervision. *Venus and Adonis* was frequently reprinted during Shakespeare's lifetime, but there is little substantive variation from one printing to another.

## SELECTED BIBLIOGRAPHY

Bate, Jonathan. "Sexual Poetry." *Shakespeare and Ovid*. Oxford: Clarendon, 1993. 48–65. Shakespeare's adaptation of Ovid's story of transgressive desire.

Hughes, Ted. "Conception and Gestation of the Equation's Tragic Myth." *Shakespeare and the Goddess of Complete Being*. London: Faber and Faber, 1992. 49–92. *Venus and Adonis* as Shakespeare's version of an ancient myth, filtered through Roman Catholicism, of goddess and sacrificed consort.

Hulse, Clark. *Metamorphic Verse: The Elizabethan Minor Epic*. Princeton: Princeton University Press, 1981. 141–75. *Venus and Adonis* in relation to its sources and immediate predecessors.

Kahn, Coppélia. "Self as Eros in *Venus and Adonis*." *Man's Estate: Masculine Identity in Shakespeare*. Berkeley: University of California Press, 1981. 21–46. Adonis as narcissist.

Keach, William. "Venus and Adonis." *Elizabethan Erotic Narratives: Irony and Pathos in the Ovidian Poetry of Shakespeare, Marlowe, and Their Contemporaries*. New Brunswick, N.J.: Rutgers University Press, 1977. 52–84. The poem considered among others of its genre.

Kolin, Philip C. *Venus and Adonis: Critical Essays*. New York: Garland, 1997. A collection of articles.

Rambuss, Richard. "What It Feels Like for a Boy: Shakespeare's *Venus and Adonis*." *A Companion to Shakespeare's Works*, vol. IV: *Poems, Problem Comedies, Late Plays*. Ed. Richard Dutton and Jean Howard. Malden, Mass.: Blackwell, 2003. *Venus and Adonis* as a "proto-gay" poem.

# Venus and Adonis

*Vilia miretur vulgus; mihi flavus Apollo*
*Pocula Castalia plena ministret aqua.*[1]

TO THE RIGHT HONOURABLE
HENRY WRIOTHESLEY,
EARL OF SOUTHAMPTON, AND
BARON OF TITCHFIELD[2]

Right Honourable, I know not how I shall offend in dedicating my unpolished lines to your lordship, nor how the world will censure° me for choosing so strong a prop to support so weak a burden. Only, if your honour seem but pleased, I account myself highly praised, and vow to take advantage of all idle hours till I have honoured you with some graver labour. But if the first heir[3] of my invention prove deformed, I shall be sorry it had so noble a godfather, and never after ear° so barren a land for fear it yield me still° so bad a harvest. I leave it to your honourable survey, and your honour to your heart's content, which I wish may always answer your own wish and the world's hopeful expectation.

        YOUR HONOUR'S IN ALL DUTY,
        WILLIAM SHAKESPEARE

*judge*

*cultivate*
*always*

---

Even as the sun with purple-coloured face
Had ta'en his last leave of the weeping morn,[1]
Rose-cheeked Adonis hied him° to the chase.
Hunting he loved, but love he laughed to scorn.
   Sick-thoughted° Venus makes amain° unto him,
   And like a bold-faced suitor 'gins to woo him.

*hurried*

*Lovesick / speedily*

'Thrice fairer than myself,' thus she began,
'The fields' chief flower, sweet above compare,
Stain to all nymphs,° more lovely than a man,
More white and red than doves or roses are—
   Nature that made thee with herself at strife
   Saith that the world hath ending with thy life.[2]

*Eclipsing all women*

'Vouchsafe, thou wonder, to alight thy steed
And rein his proud head to the saddle-bow;

5

10

**Dedication**
1. "Let vile people admire vile things; may fair-haired Apollo serve me goblets filled with Castalian water" (Ovid, *Amores* 1.15.35–36). Apollo is the god of poetry; the Castalian spring is sacred to the Muses.
2. Prominent courtier, nineteen years old at the time of *Venus and Adonis*'s publication. Shakespeare also dedicated *The Rape of Lucrece* to him.

3. *Venus and Adonis* was Shakespeare's first published work.
**Poem**
1. Aurora, goddess of the dawn, weeps tears of dew when forsaken each morning by her lover, the sun.
2. *Nature . . . life*: Nature, who strove to surpass herself in making you, says that if you die, the world will end.

15    If thou wilt deign this favour, for thy meed°          *reward*
      A thousand honey secrets shalt thou know.
          Here come and sit where never serpent hisses;
          And, being sat, I'll smother thee with kisses,

      'And yet not cloy thy lips with loathed satiety,
20    But rather famish them amid their plenty,
      Making them red, and pale, with fresh variety;
      Ten kisses short as one, one long as twenty.
          A summer's day will seem an hour but short,
          Being wasted° in such time-beguiling sport.'          *spent*

25    With this, she seizeth on his sweating palm,
      The precedent of pith and livelihood,³
      And, trembling in her passion, calls it balm—
      Earth's sovereign° salve to do a goddess good.          *potent*
          Being so enraged, desire doth lend her force
30        Courageously to pluck him from his horse.

      Over one arm, the lusty courser's rein;
      Under her other was the tender boy,
      Who blushed and pouted in a dull disdain
      With leaden appetite, unapt to toy.⁴
35        She red and hot as coals of glowing fire;
          He red for shame, but frosty in desire.

      The studded bridle on a ragged bough
      Nimbly she fastens—O, how quick is love!
      The steed is stallèd° up, and even now          *fastened*
40    To tie the rider she begins to prove.°          *try*
          Backward she pushed him, as she would be thrust,
          And governed him in strength, though not in lust.

      So soon was she along° as he was down,          *alongside him*
      Each leaning on their elbows and their hips.
45    Now doth she stroke his cheek, now doth he frown
      And 'gins to chide, but soon she stops his lips,
          And, kissing, speaks, with lustful language broken:°          *interrupted*
          'If thou wilt chide, thy lips shall never open.'

      He burns with bashful shame; she with her tears
50    Doth quench the maiden burning of his cheeks.
      Then, with her windy sighs and golden hairs,
      To fan and blow them dry again she seeks.
          He saith she is immodest, blames her miss;°          *misbehavior*
          What follows more she murders with a kiss.

55    Even as an empty eagle, sharp by fast,°          *hungry from fasting*
      Tires° with her beak on feathers, flesh, and bone,          *Tears*
      Shaking her wings, devouring all in haste
      Till either gorge° be stuffed or prey be gone,          *stomach*
          Even so she kissed his brow, his cheek, his chin,
60        And where she ends she doth anew begin.

---

3. The evidence of strength and liveliness.          4. Uninterested in sex play.

Forced to content,° but never to obey,°                                    *acquiesce / respond*
Panting he lies and breatheth in her face.
She feedeth on the steam as on a prey
And calls it heavenly moisture, air of grace,
65      Wishing her cheeks were gardens full of flowers,
      So they were dewed with such distilling° showers.        *gently dropping*

Look how a bird lies tangled in a net,
So fastened in her arms Adonis lies.
Pure shame and awed° resistance made him fret,                    *overpowered*
70   Which bred more beauty in his angry eyes.
      Rain added to a river that is rank°                                         *full*
      Perforce will force it overflow the bank.

Still she entreats, and prettily entreats,
For to a pretty ear she tunes her tale.
75   Still is he sullen, still he lours° and frets                              *frowns*
'Twixt crimson shame and anger ashy-pale.
      Being red, she loves him best; and being white,
      Her best is bettered with a more delight.

Look how he can, she cannot choose but love;
80   And by her fair immortal hand she swears
From his soft bosom never to remove
Till he take truce° with her contending tears,                       *come to terms*
      Which long have rained, making her cheeks all wet;
      And one sweet kiss shall pay this countless debt.

85   Upon this promise did he raise his chin,
Like a divedapper[5] peering through a wave
Who, being looked on, ducks as quickly in—
So offers he to give what she did crave.
      But when her lips were ready for his pay,
90     He winks,° and turns his lips another way.                          *shuts his eyes*

Never did passenger° in summer's heat                                    *traveler*
More thirst for drink than she for this good turn.
Her help she sees, but help she cannot get.
She bathes in water, yet her fire must burn.
95     'O pity,' gan she cry, 'flint-hearted boy!
      'Tis but a kiss I beg—why art thou coy?

'I have been wooed as I entreat thee now
Even by the stern and direful god of war,°                               *Mars*
Whose sinewy neck in battle ne'er did bow,
100  Who conquers where he comes in every jar.°                        *conflict*
      Yet hath he been my captive and my slave,
      And begged for that which thou unasked shalt have.

'Over my altars hath he hung his lance,
His battered shield, his uncontrollèd° crest,                           *unvanquished*
105  And for my sake hath learned to sport and dance,

---

5. Grebe (small English waterbird).

To toy, to wanton, dally, smile, and jest,
　　Scorning his churlish drum and ensign red,
　　Making my arms° his field, his tent my bed.　　　　　　　　　　*(a pun)*

'Thus he that over-ruled I overswayed,
110　Leading him prisoner in a red-rose chain.
Strong-tempered steel his stronger strength obeyed,
Yet was he servile to my coy disdain.
　　O, be not proud, nor brag not of thy might,
　　For mast'ring her that foiled° the god of fight.　　　　　　　　*conquered*

115　'Touch but my lips with those fair lips of thine—
Though mine be not so fair, yet are they red—
The kiss shall be thine own as well as mine.
What seest thou in the ground? Hold up thy head.
　　Look in mine eyeballs: there thy beauty lies.°　　　　　　　*lies reflected*
120　　Then why not lips on lips, since eyes in eyes?

'Art thou ashamed to kiss? Then wink again,
And I will wink. So shall the day seem night.
Love keeps his revels where there are but twain.
Be bold to play—our sport is not in sight.°　　　　　　　　*unobserved*
125　These blue-veined violets whereon we lean
　　Never can blab, nor know not⁶ what we mean.

'The tender spring° upon thy tempting lip　　　　　*growth of new beard*
Shows thee unripe; yet mayst thou well be tasted.
Make use of time; let not advantage slip.
130　Beauty within itself should not be wasted.
　　Fair flowers that are not gathered in their prime
　　Rot, and consume themselves in little time.

'Were I hard-favoured,° foul, or wrinkled-old,　　　　　　　　*ugly*
Ill-nurtured, crooked, churlish, harsh in voice,
135　O'er-worn,° despisèd, rheumatic, and cold,　　　　　　　　*Worn out*
Thick-sighted,° barren, lean, and lacking juice,　　　　　　*Partly blind*
　　Then mightst thou pause, for then I were not for thee.
　　But having no defects, why dost abhor me?

'Thou canst not see one wrinkle in my brow.
140　Mine eyes are grey,⁷ and bright, and quick in turning.
My beauty as the spring doth yearly grow.°　　　　　　　　*rejuvenate*
My flesh is soft and plump, my marrow° burning.　　　　　*vital spirits*
　　My smooth moist hand, were it with thy hand felt,
　　Would in thy palm dissolve, or seem to melt.

145　'Bid me discourse, I will enchant thine ear;
Or like a fairy, trip upon the green;
Or like a nymph, with long, dishevelled hair,
Dance on the sands, and yet no footing° seen.　　　　　　　*footprint*
　　Love is a spirit all compact° of fire,　　　　　　　　　　*made up*
150　　Not gross° to sink, but light, and will aspire.°　　　　*heavy / rise*

---

6. The double negative ("nor . . . not") was acceptable in Elizabethan English.

7. Considered the best eye color by medieval and Renaissance love poets.

'Witness this primrose bank whereon I lie:
These forceless flowers like sturdy trees support me.
Two strengthless doves[8] will draw me through the sky
From morn till night, even where I list° to sport me.          *wherever I wish*
155     Is love so light, sweet boy, and may it be
      That thou should think it heavy unto thee?

'Is thine own heart to thine own face affected?°          *attracted*
Can thy right hand seize love upon thy left?°          *by clasping the left*
Then woo thyself, be of thyself rejected;
160 Steal thine own freedom,° and complain on theft.          *Capture your affections*
    Narcissus[9] so himself himself forsook,
    And died to kiss his shadow in the brook.

'Torches are made to light, jewels to wear,
Dainties to taste, fresh beauty for the use,
165 Herbs for their smell, and sappy plants to bear.
Things growing to themselves° are growth's abuse.          *only for themselves*
    Seeds spring from seeds, and beauty breedeth beauty:
    Thou wast begot; to get° it is thy duty.          *beget*

'Upon the earth's increase why shouldst thou feed
170 Unless the earth with thy increase be fed?
By law of nature thou art bound to breed,
That thine° may live when thou thyself art dead;          *(your children)*
    And so in spite of death thou dost survive,
    In that thy likeness still is left alive.'

175 By this,° the lovesick queen began to sweat,          *By this time*
For where they lay the shadow had forsook them,
And Titan,° tired in the midday heat,          *the sun god*
With burning eye did hotly overlook them,
    Wishing Adonis had his team° to guide          *(of sun horses)*
180     So he° were like him,° and by Venus' side.          *(Titan) / (Adonis)*

And now Adonis, with a lazy sprite°          *dull spirit*
And with a heavy, dark, disliking eye,
His louring brows o'erwhelming° his fair sight,          *overhanging*
Like misty vapours when they blot the sky,
185     Souring his cheeks,° cries, 'Fie, no more of love!          *Frowning*
    The sun doth burn my face; I must remove.'°          *leave*

'Ay me,' quoth Venus, 'young, and so unkind?°          *unnatural*
What bare° excuses mak'st thou to be gone?          *poor*
I'll sigh celestial breath, whose gentle wind
190 Shall cool the heat of this descending sun.
    I'll make a shadow for thee of my hairs;
    If they burn too, I'll quench them with my tears.

'The sun that shines from heaven shines but warm,°          *merely warms me*
And lo, I lie between that sun and thee.

---

8. Traditionally, Venus's chariot was drawn by swans or doves; see lines 1190–92.
9. In classical mythology, a young man who fell in love with his own image reflected in the water; after he pined to death, he was turned into a flower.

195 The heat I have from thence doth little harm;
Thine eye darts forth the fire that burneth me,
And were I not immortal, life were done°                       *destroyed*
Between this heavenly and earthly sun.

'Art thou obdurate, flinty, hard as steel?
200 Nay, more than flint, for stone at rain relenteth.°            *wears away*
Art thou a woman's son, and canst not feel
What 'tis to love, how want of love° tormenteth?               *being denied love*
O, had thy mother borne so hard a mind,
She had not brought forth thee, but died unkind.

205 'What am I, that thou shouldst contemn° me this?             *deny; scorn*
Or what great danger dwells upon my suit?
What were thy lips the worse for one poor kiss?
Speak, fair; but speak fair words, or else be mute.
Give me one kiss, I'll give it thee again,
210 And one for int'rest, if thou wilt have twain.

'Fie, lifeless picture, cold and senseless° stone,             *insensible*
Well painted idol, image dull and dead,
Statue contenting but the eye alone,
Thing like a man, but of no woman bred:
215 Thou art no man, though of a man's complexion,°             *appearance*
For men will kiss even by their own direction.'°              *inclination*

This said, impatience chokes her pleading tongue,
And swelling passion doth provoke a pause.
Red cheeks and fiery eyes blaze forth° her wrong.             *display; flame out*
220 Being judge in love, she cannot right her cause;[1]
And now she weeps, and now she fain° would speak,            *gladly*
And now her sobs do her intendments° break.                   *intended words*

Sometime she shakes her head, and then his hand;
Now gazeth she on him, now on the ground.
225 Sometime her arms enfold him like a band;°                  *fetter*
She would, he will not in her arms be bound.
And when from thence he struggles to be gone,
She locks her lily fingers one in one.

'Fondling,'° she saith, 'since I have hemmed thee here         *Foolish one; beloved*
230 Within the circuit of this ivory pale,°                      *fence*
I'll be a park, and thou shalt be my deer.
Feed where thou wilt, on mountain or in dale;
Graze on my lips, and if those hills be dry,
Stray lower, where the pleasant fountains lie.

235 'Within this limit is relief[2] enough,
Sweet bottom-grass,[3] and high delightful plain,
Round rising hillocks, brakes obscure and rough,°             *dark, shaggy thickets*
To shelter thee from tempest and from rain.

1. Although (or because) she is love's arbiter, she cannot win her own case.
2. Pasture; variety of landscape; sexual gratification.
3. Valley grass (pubic hair); Venus's body-landscape is
intentionally suggestive throughout.

Then be my deer, since I am such a park;
240 No dog shall rouse thee,° though a thousand bark.'  *drive you from cover*

At this Adonis smiles as in disdain,
That in each cheek appears a pretty dimple.
Love made those hollows, if° himself were slain,  *so that if*
He might be buried in a tomb so simple,
245    Foreknowing well, if there he came to lie,
   Why, there love lived, and there he could not die.

These lovely caves, these round enchanting pits,
Opened their mouths to swallow Venus' liking.°  *to engulf her desire*
Being mad before, how doth she now for wits?[4]
250 Struck dead at first, what needs a second striking?
   Poor queen of love, in thine own law forlorn,°  *condemned to suffer*
   To love a cheek that smiles at thee in scorn!

Now which way shall she turn? What shall she say?
Her words are done, her woes the more increasing.
255 The time is spent; her object will away,
And from her twining arms doth urge releasing.
   'Pity,' she cries; 'some favour, some remorse!'°  *compassion*
   Away he springs, and hasteth to his horse.

But lo, from forth a copse° that neighbours by  *thicket*
260 A breeding jennet,° lusty, young, and proud,  *mare in heat*
Adonis' trampling courser doth espy,
And forth she rushes, snorts, and neighs aloud.
   The strong-necked steed, being tied unto a tree,
   Breaketh his rein, and to her straight goes he.

265 Imperiously he leaps, he neighs, he bounds,
And now his woven girths he breaks asunder.
The bearing[5] earth with his hard hoof he wounds,
Whose hollow womb resounds like heaven's thunder.
   The iron bit he crusheth 'tween his teeth,
270    Controlling what he was controllèd with.

His ears up-pricked, his braided hanging mane
Upon his compassed crest° now stand on end;  *arched neck*
His nostrils drink the air, and forth again,
As from a furnace, vapours doth he send.
275    His eye, which scornfully glisters like fire,
   Shows his hot courage° and his high desire.  *lust*

Sometime he trots, as if he told° the steps,  *counted*
With gentle majesty and modest pride.
Anon he rears upright, curvets,[6] and leaps,
280 As who° should say, 'Lo, thus my strength is tried,°  *one who / tested*
   And this I do to captivate the eye
   Of the fair breeder that is standing by.'

4. How does she keep her sanity now?       6. Bounds on his hind legs with raised forelegs.
5. Supporting; suffering; generative.

What recketh he° his rider's angry stir,°                                    *cares he about / noise*
His flattering° 'Holla', or his 'Stand, I say!'?                             *cajoling*
285  What cares he now for curb° or pricking spur,                           *bit*
For rich caparisons or trappings gay?
　　He sees his love, and nothing else he sees,
　　For nothing else with his proud sight agrees.

Look when° a painter would surpass the life                                  *Just as*
290  In limning out° a well proportioned steed,                             *depicting*
His art with nature's workmanship at strife,
As if the dead the living should exceed:
　　So did this horse excel a common one
　　In shape, in courage, colour, pace, and bone.°                           *frame*

295  Round-hoofed, short-jointed, fetlocks shag and long,[7]
Broad breast, full eye, small head, and nostril wide,
High crest, short ears, straight legs, and passing° strong;                  *extremely*
Thin mane, thick tail, broad buttock, tender hide—
　　Look what° a horse should have he did not lack,                          *Whatever*
300  　Save a proud rider on so proud a back.

Sometime he scuds far off, and there he stares;
Anon he starts at stirring of a feather.
To bid the wind a base[8] he now prepares,
And whe'er° he run or fly they know not whether;°                            *whether / which*
305  For through his mane and tail the high wind sings,
　　Fanning the hairs, who wave like feathered wings.

He looks upon his love, and neighs unto her;
She answers him as if she knew his mind.
Being proud, as females are, to see him woo her,
310  She puts on outward strangeness,° seems unkind,                         *reserve*
　　Spurns at° his love, and scorns the heat he feels,                       *Repels; kicks*
　　Beating his kind° embracements with her heels.                           *amorous; natural*

Then, like a melancholy malcontent,
He vails° his tail that, like a falling plume,                               *lowers*
315  Cool shadow to his melting buttock lent.
He stamps, and bites the poor flies in his fume.°                            *anger*
　　His love, perceiving how he was enraged,
　　Grew kinder, and his fury was assuaged.

His testy° master goeth about° to take him,                                  *angry / tries*
320  When lo, the unbacked breeder,[9] full of fear,
Jealous of catching,° swiftly doth forsake him,                             *Fearful of being caught*
With her the horse, and left Adonis there.
　　As they were mad unto the wood they hie them,
　　Outstripping crows that strive to overfly them.

325  All swoll'n with chafing,° down Adonis sits,                           *anger*
Banning° his boist'rous and unruly beast;                                    *Cursing*

---

7. *short-jointed . . . long:* with short pasterns (the bone just above the horse's hoof) and shaggy joints above the hooves.

8. To dare the wind to run (from a children's game, prisoner's base).
9. Mare without mount (rider or stallion).

And now the happy season once more fits°          *is suited*
That lovesick love by pleading may be blessed;
   For lovers say the heart hath treble wrong
330    When it is barred the aidance of the tongue.

An oven that is stopped, or river stayed,°        *dammed*
Burneth more hotly, swelleth with more rage.
So of concealèd sorrow may be said
Free vent of words love's fire doth assuage.
335    But when the heart's attorney° once is mute,      *pleader (the tongue)*
   The client breaks,[1] as desperate in his suit.

He sees her coming, and begins to glow,
Even as a dying coal revives with wind,
And with his bonnet° hides his angry brow,          *hat*
340 Looks on the dull earth with disturbèd mind,
   Taking no notice that she is so nigh,
   For all askance he holds her in his eye.

O, what a sight it was wistly° to view          *intently*
How she came stealing to the wayward boy,
345 To note the fighting conflict of her hue,
How white and red each other did destroy!
   But now her cheek was pale; and by and by
   It flashed forth fire, as lightning from the sky.

Now was she just before him as he sat,
350 And like a lowly lover down she kneels;
With one fair hand she heaveth up his hat;
Her other tender hand his fair cheek feels.
   His tend'rer cheek receives her soft hand's print
   As apt as new-fall'n snow takes any dint.°         *dent*

355 O, what a war of looks was then between them,
Her eyes petitioners to his eyes suing!
His eyes saw her eyes as they had not seen them,
Her eyes wooed still; his eyes disdained the wooing;
   And all this dumb play had his° acts made plain       *its*
360    With tears which, chorus-like, her eyes did rain.[2]

Full gently now she takes him by the hand,
A lily prisoned in a jail of snow,
Or ivory in an alabaster band;
So white a friend engirds so white a foe.
365    This beauteous combat, wilful and unwilling,
   Showed° like two silver doves that sit a-billing.      *Looked*

Once more the engine of her thoughts began:
'O fairest mover on this mortal round,°          *earth*
Would thou wert as I am, and I a man,
370 My heart all whole as thine, thy heart my wound;°     *suffering my wound*

---

1. Breaks apart; goes bankrupt.
2. Venus's tears interpret her mute gestures as the chorus in a play explains a dumb show.

For one sweet look thy help I would assure thee,
Though nothing but my body's bane° would cure thee.'     *destruction*

'Give me my hand,' saith he. 'Why dost thou feel it?'
'Give me my heart,' saith she, 'and thou shalt have it.
375  O, give it me, lest thy hard heart do steel it,³
And, being steeled, soft sighs can never grave° it;     *engrave*
   Then love's deep groans I never shall regard,
   Because Adonis' heart hath made mine hard.'

'For shame,' he cries, 'let go, and let me go!
380  My day's delight is past; my horse is gone,
And 'tis your fault I am bereft him so.
I pray you hence, and leave me here alone;
   For all my mind, my thought, my busy care
   Is how to get my palfrey° from the mare.'     *riding horse*

385  Thus she replies: 'Thy palfrey, as he should,
Welcomes the warm approach of sweet desire.
Affection° is a coal that must be cooled,     *Passion*
Else, suffered,° it will set the heart on fire.     *allowed to persist*
   The sea hath bounds, but deep desire hath none;
390     Therefore no marvel though thy horse be gone.

'How like a jade° he stood tied to the tree,     *nag*
Servilely mastered with a leathern rein!
But when he saw his love, his youth's fair fee,°     *reward*
He held such petty bondage in disdain,
395     Throwing the base thong from his bending crest,
   Enfranchising his mouth, his back, his breast.

'Who sees his true-love in her naked bed,
Teaching the sheets a whiter hue than white,
But when his glutton eye so full hath fed
400  His other agents° aim at like delight?     *faculties*
   Who is so faint that dares not be so bold
   To touch the fire, the weather being cold?

'Let me excuse thy courser, gentle boy;
And learn of him, I heartily beseech thee,
405  To take advantage on° presented joy.     *of*
Though I were dumb, yet his proceedings teach thee.
   O, learn to love! The lesson is but plain,
   And, once made perfect,° never lost again.'     *learned by heart*

'I know not love,' quoth he, 'nor will not know it,
410  Unless it be a boar, and then I chase it.
'Tis much to borrow, and I will not owe it.
My love to love is love but to disgrace it;⁴
   For I have heard it is a life in death,
   That laughs and weeps, and all but with a breath.

3. Turn my heart to steel; steal my heart.    4. My only interest in love is in discrediting it.

415 'Who wears a garment shapeless and unfinished?
Who plucks the bud before one leaf put forth?
If springing° things be any jot diminished,                    *immature*
They wither in their prime, prove nothing worth.
    The colt that's backed° and burdened being young,          *ridden*
420    Loseth his pride, and never waxeth strong.

'You hurt my hand with wringing. Let us part,
And leave this idle° theme, this bootless° chat.              *useless / pointless*
Remove your siege from my unyielding heart;
To love's alarms° it will not ope the gate.                    *assaults*
425    Dismiss your vows, your feignèd tears, your flatt'ry;
    For where a heart is hard they make no batt'ry.'°           *breach*

'What, canst thou talk?' quoth she. 'Hast thou a tongue?
O, would thou hadst not, or I had no hearing!
Thy mermaid's voice⁵ hath done me double wrong.
430 I had my load before, now pressed° with bearing:            *oppressed*
    Melodious discord, heavenly tune harsh sounding,
    Ears' deep-sweet music, and heart's deep-sore wounding.

'Had I no eyes but ears, my ears would love
That inward beauty and invisible;
435 Or were I deaf, thy outward parts would move
Each part in me that were but sensible.°                       *perceiving*
    Though neither eyes nor ears to hear nor see,
    Yet should I be in love by touching thee.

'Say that the sense of feeling were bereft me,
440 And that I could not see, nor hear, nor touch,
And nothing but the very smell were left me,
Yet would my love to thee be still as much;
    For from the stillitory⁶ of thy face excelling°            *incomparable*
    Comes breath perfumed, that breedeth love by smelling.

445 'But O, what banquet wert thou to the taste,
Being nurse and feeder of the other four!
Would they not wish the feast might ever last
And bid suspicion° double-lock the door                       *wariness*
    Lest jealousy, that sour unwelcome guest,
450    Should by his stealing-in disturb the feast?'

Once more the ruby-coloured portal° opened                    *threshold (mouth)*
Which to his speech did honey passage yield,
Like a red morn that ever yet betokened
Wrack° to the seaman, tempest to the field,                   *Shipwreck*
455    Sorrow to shepherds, woe unto the birds,
    Gusts and foul flaws° to herdmen and to herds.             *winds*

This ill presage advisedly she marketh.⁷
Even as the wind is hushed before it raineth,
Or as the wolf doth grin° before he barketh,                  *show his teeth*

5. Which, irresistible in song, was supposed to lure      6. Apparatus used to distill perfume.
sailors onto rocks.                                        7. She notices this bad omen carefully.

460 Or as the berry breaks before it staineth,
   Or like the deadly bullet of a gun,
   His meaning struck her ere his words begun,

And at his look she flatly falleth down,
For looks kill love, and love by looks reviveth;
465 A smile recures° the wounding of a frown,          *cures*
But blessèd bankrupt that by loss so thriveth!
   The silly° boy, believing she is dead,          *naive*
   Claps her pale cheek till clapping makes it red,

And, all amazed,° brake° off his late intent,      *perplexed / broke*
470 For sharply he did think to reprehend her,
Which cunning love did wittily prevent.
   Fair fall[8] the wit that can so well defend her!
   For on the grass she lies as she were slain,
   Till his breath breatheth life in her again.

475 He wrings her nose, he strikes her on the cheeks,
He bends her fingers, holds her pulses hard;°      *takes her pulse*
He chafes her lips; a thousand ways he seeks
To mend the hurt that his unkindness marred.°    *caused to injure her*
   He kisses her; and she, by her good will,°        *consent*
480   Will never rise, so he will kiss her still.°      *keep kissing her*

The night of sorrow now is turned to day.
Her two blue windows° faintly she upheaveth,      *(her eyes)*
Like the fair sun when, in his fresh array,
He cheers the morn, and all the earth relieveth;
485   And as the bright sun glorifies the sky,
   So is her face illumined with her eye,

Whose beams upon his hairless face are fixed,
As if from thence they borrowed all their shine.
Were never four such lamps together mixed,
490 Had not his clouded with his brow's repine.°      *discontent*
   But hers, which through the crystal tears gave light,
   Shone like the moon in water seen by night.

'O, where am I?' quoth she; 'in earth or heaven,
Or in the ocean drenched,° or in the fire?        *submerged*
495 What hour is this: or° morn or weary even?°    *either / evening*
Do I delight to die, or life desire?
   But now I lived, and life was death's annoy;°      *deathly pain*
   But now I died, and death was lively° joy.        *living*

'O, thou didst kill me; kill me once again!
500 Thy eyes' shrewd° tutor, that hard heart of thine,    *stern*
Hath taught them scornful tricks, and such disdain
That they have murdered this poor heart of mine,
   And these mine eyes, true leaders° to their queen,    *guides*
   But for thy piteous° lips no more had seen.      *pitying*

8. Good luck befall (with wordplay on "fall down").

505 'Long may they kiss each other, for this cure!
O, never let their crimson liveries wear,°         *wear out*
And as they last, their verdure⁹ still endure
To drive infection from the dangerous year,
    That the star-gazers, having writ on death,°      *predicted plague*
510     May say the plague is banished by thy breath!

'Pure lips, sweet seals in my soft lips imprinted,
What bargains may I make still to be sealing?°     *kissing; making deals*
To sell myself I can be well contented,
So° thou wilt buy, and pay, and use good dealing;           *If*
515     Which purchase if thou make, for fear of slips°       *fraud*
    Set thy seal manual° on my wax-red lips.     *identifying stamp*

'A thousand kisses buys my heart from me;
And pay them at thy leisure, one by one.
What is ten hundred touches° unto thee?         *(of the lips)*
520 Are they not quickly told,° and quickly gone?       *counted*
    Say for non-payment that the debt should double,
    Is twenty hundred kisses such a trouble?' –

'Fair queen,' quoth he, 'if any love you owe me,
Measure my strangeness° with my unripe years.     *Explain my coldness*
525 Before I know myself, seek not to know me.
No fisher but the ungrown fry forbears.¹
    The mellow plum doth fall, the green sticks fast,
    Or, being early plucked, is sour to taste.

'Look, the world's comforter° with weary gait       *(the sun)*
530 His day's hot task hath ended in the west.
The owl, night's herald, shrieks 'tis very late;
The sheep are gone to fold, birds to their nest,
    And coal-black clouds, that shadow heaven's light,
    Do summon us to part and bid good night.

535 'Now let me say good night, and so say you.
If you will say so, you shall have a kiss.'
'Good night,' quoth she; and ere he says adieu
The honey° fee of parting tendered° is.        *sweet / given*
    Her arms do lend his neck a sweet embrace.
540     Incorporate° then they seem; face grows to face,    *United in one body*

Till breathless he disjoined, and backward drew
The heavenly moisture, that sweet coral mouth,
Whose precious taste her thirsty lips well knew,
Whereon they surfeit, yet complain on drought.
545     He with her plenty pressed, she faint with dearth,
    Their lips together glued, fall to the earth.

Now quick desire hath caught the yielding prey,
And glutton-like she feeds, yet never filleth.
Her lips are conquerors, his lips obey,

---

9. Literally, greenness; here, freshness. The lips ward    1. Every fisherman spares the young fish.
off disease as fresh parsley was believed to do.

550 Paying what ransom the insulter° willeth,                    *conqueror*
        Whose vulture° thought doth pitch the price so high       *ravenous*
        That she will draw his lips' rich treasure dry,

        And, having felt the sweetness of the spoil,
        With blindfold fury she begins to forage.
555 Her face doth reek° and smoke, her blood doth boil,           *steam*
        And careless° lust stirs up a desperate courage,          *reckless*
            Planting° oblivion, beating reason back,              *Implanting*
            Forgetting shame's pure blush and honour's wrack.°    *ruin*

        Hot, faint, and weary with her hard embracing,
560 Like a wild bird being tamed with too much handling,
        Or as the fleet-foot roe that's tired with chasing,
        Or like the froward° infant stilled with dandling,       *fretful*
            He now obeys, and now no more resisteth,
            While she takes all she can, not all she listeth.°    *desires*

565 What wax so frozen but dissolves with temp'ring°             *fingering*
        And yields at last to every light impression?
        Things out of° hope are compassed° oft with vent'ring,   *beyond / accomplished*
        Chiefly in love, whose leave° exceeds commission.°        *liberty / warrant*
            Affection faints° not, like a pale-faced coward,      *Passion relents*
570     But then woos best when most his choice is froward.

        When he did frown, O, had she then gave over,
        Such nectar from his lips she had not sucked.
        Foul° words and frowns must not repel a lover.            *Harsh*
        What though the rose have prickles, yet 'tis plucked!
575     Were beauty under twenty locks kept fast,
            Yet love breaks through, and picks them all at last.

        For pity now she can no more detain him.
        The poor fool° prays her that he may depart.             *(term of affection)*
        She is resolved no longer to restrain him,
580 Bids him farewell, and look well to° her heart,             *take good care of*
            The which, by Cupid's bow she doth protest,
            He carries thence encagèd in his breast.

        'Sweet boy,' she says, 'this night I'll waste in sorrow,
        For my sick heart commands mine eyes to watch.
585 Tell me, love's master, shall we meet tomorrow?
        Say, shall we, shall we? Wilt thou make the match?'
            He tells her no, tomorrow he intends
            To hunt the boar with certain of his friends.

        'The boar!' quoth she; whereat a sudden pale,
590 Like lawn° being spread upon the blushing rose,             *fine linen*
        Usurps her cheek. She trembles at his tale,
        And on his neck her yoking arms she throws.
            She sinketh down, still hanging by his neck.
            He on her belly falls, she on her back.

595 Now is she in the very lists² of love,
Her champion mounted for the hot encounter.
All is imaginary she doth prove.³
He will not manage her,° although he mount her,    *ride her (like a horse)*
    That worse than Tantalus' is her annoy,⁴
600     To clip Elysium,⁵ and to lack her joy.

Even so poor birds, deceived with painted grapes,
Do surfeit by the eye, and pine the maw;⁶
Even so she languisheth in her mishaps
As° those poor birds that helpless° berries saw.    *Like / unusable*
605     The warm effects° which she in him finds missing    *outward signs*
    She seeks to kindle with continual kissing.

But all in vain, good queen! It will not be.
She hath assayed° as much as may be proved;°    *attempted / tried*
Her pleading hath deserved a greater fee:⁷
610 She's Love; she loves; and yet she is not loved.
    'Fie, fie,' he says, 'you crush me. Let me go.
    You have no reason to withhold me so.'

'Thou hadst been gone,' quoth she, 'sweet boy, ere this,
But that thou told'st me thou wouldst hunt the boar.
615 O, be advised; thou know'st not what it is
With javelin's point a churlish swine to gore,
    Whose tushes,° never sheathed, he whetteth still,°    *tusks / continually*
    Like to a mortal° butcher, bent° to kill.    *deadly / intending*

'On his bow-back° he hath a battle⁸ set    *arched back*
620 Of bristly pikes that ever threat his foes.
His eyes like glow-worms shine; when he doth fret
His snout digs sepulchres where'er he goes.
    Being moved,° he strikes, whate'er is in his way,    *angered*
    And whom he strikes his crooked tushes slay.

625 'His brawny sides with hairy bristles armed
Are better proof° than thy spear's point can enter.    *armor*
His short thick neck cannot be easily harmed.
Being ireful,° on the lion he will venture.    *angry*
    The thorny brambles and embracing bushes,
630     As° fearful of him, part; through whom° he rushes.    *As if / which*

'Alas, he naught esteems that face of thine,
To which love's eyes pays tributary gazes,
Nor thy soft hands, sweet lips, and crystal eyne,°    *eyes (archaic)*
Whose full perfection all the world amazes;
635     But having thee at vantage°—wondrous dread!—    *his mercy*
    Would root° these beauties as he roots the mead.°    *root up / meadow*

---

2. Enclosed tournament arena.
3. The hot encounter is only imaginary, she finds.
4. Torment. In classical mythology, Tantalus was punished by eternal hunger and thirst; food and water were always visible but receded at his approach.
5. In classical mythology, the abode of the blessed

dead. *clip*: embrace.
6. Starve the stomach. The ancient Greek artist Zeuxis painted grapes so realistic that birds pecked at them.
7. A legal metaphor: Venus, acting as an attorney, deserves a better payment.
8. Row of armed soldiers.

'O, let him keep° his loathsome cabin° still.                         *stay in / lair*
Beauty hath naught to do with such foul fiends.
Come not within his danger by thy will.
640   They that thrive well take counsel of their friends.
      When thou didst name the boar, not to dissemble,⁹
      I feared thy fortune, and my joints did tremble.

'Didst thou not mark my face? Was it not white?
Saw'st thou not signs of fear lurk in mine eye?
645   Grew I not faint, and fell I not downright?
Within my bosom, whereon thou dost lie,
      My boding heart pants, beats, and takes no rest,
      But like an earthquake shakes thee on my breast.

'For where love reigns, disturbing jealousy°                         *apprehension*
650   Doth call himself affection's sentinel,
Gives false alarms, suggesteth mutiny,°                               *incites rebellion*
And in a peaceful hour doth cry, "Kill, kill!",°                      *(a battle cry)*
      Distemp'ring° gentle love in his desire,                       *Quenching*
      As air and water do abate the fire.

655   'This sour informer, this bate-breeding° spy,                   *conflict-breeding*
This canker° that eats up love's tender spring,°                     *cankerworm / sprout*
This carry-tale, dissentious jealousy,
That sometime true news, sometime false doth bring,
      Knocks at my heart, and whispers in mine ear
660   That if I love thee, I thy death should fear;

'And, more than so, presenteth to mine eye
The picture of an angry chafing boar,
Under whose sharp fangs on his back doth lie
An image like thyself, all stained with gore,
665   Whose blood upon the fresh flowers being shed
      Doth make them droop with grief, and hang the head.

'What should I do, seeing thee so indeed,
That tremble at th'imagination?
The thought of it doth make my faint heart bleed,
670   And fear doth teach it divination.
      I prophesy thy death, my living sorrow,
      If thou encounter with the boar tomorrow.

'But if thou needs wilt hunt, be ruled by me:
Uncouple° at the timorous flying° hare,                              *Unleash the dogs / fleeing*
675   Or at the fox which lives by subtlety,
Or at the roe which no encounter dare.
      Pursue these fearful° creatures o'er the downs,                *timid*
      And on thy well-breathed horse keep with thy hounds.

'And when thou hast on foot the purblind° hare,                      *dim-sighted*
680   Mark the poor wretch, to overshoot° his troubles,               *run past*
How he outruns the wind, and with what care
He cranks and crosses° with a thousand doubles.                      *twists and turns*

---

9. *not to dissemble*: to tell the truth.

The many musits° through the which he goes         *hedge gaps*
Are like a labyrinth to amaze° his foes.         *confuse*

685 'Sometime he runs among a flock of sheep
To make the cunning hounds mistake their smell,
And sometime where earth-delving conies° keep,         *rabbits*
To stop the loud pursuers in their yell;
    And sometime sorteth° with a herd of deer.         *consorts*
690     Danger deviseth shifts;° wit waits on fear.         *tricks*

'For there his smell with others being mingled,
The hot scent-snuffing hounds are driven to doubt,
Ceasing their clamorous cry till they have singled,
With much ado, the cold fault° cleanly out.         *lost scent*
695     Then do they spend their mouths.° Echo replies,         *give tongue*
    As if another chase were in the skies.

'By this, poor Wat,° far off upon a hill,         *(name for a hare)*
Stands on his hinder legs with list'ning ear,
To hearken if his foes pursue him still.
700 Anon their loud alarums he doth hear,
    And now his grief may be comparèd well
    To one sore sick that hears the passing-bell.[1]

'Then shalt thou see the dew-bedabbled wretch
Turn, and return, indenting° with the way.         *zigzagging*
705 Each envious° brier his weary legs do scratch;         *malicious*
Each shadow makes him stop, each murmur stay;
    For misery is trodden on by many,
    And, being low, never relieved by any.

'Lie quietly, and hear a little more;
710 Nay, do not struggle, for thou shalt not rise.
To make thee hate the hunting of the boar
Unlike myself thou hear'st me moralize,[2]
    Applying° this to that, and so to so,         *Showing the pertinence of*
    For love can comment upon every woe.

715 'Where did I leave?'° 'No matter where,' quoth he;         *leave off*
'Leave me, and then the story aptly ends.
The night is spent.' 'Why what of that?' quoth she.
'I am,' quoth he, 'expected of° my friends,         *by*
    And now 'tis dark, and going I shall fall.'
720     'In night,' quoth she, 'desire sees best of all.

'But if thou fall, O, then imagine this:
The earth, in love with thee, thy footing trips,
And all is but to rob thee of a kiss.
Rich preys° make true° men thieves; so do thy lips         *spoils / honest*
725     Make modest Dian[3] cloudy and forlorn
    Lest she should steal a kiss, and die forsworn.[4]

---

1. Bell tolled for one who has just died.
2. Although I (the goddess of love) do not usually make moral points, I do so now.
3. Goddess of the moon, hunting, and virginity, also called "Cynthia" (line 728); "cloudy" because covered with clouds and because made sorrowful by her love of Adonis.
4. Die having violated her oath of chastity.

'Now of this dark night I perceive the reason.
Cynthia, for shame, obscures her silver shine
Till forging° nature be condemned of treason                    *counterfeiting*
730  For stealing moulds from heaven, that were divine,
        Wherein she framed thee, in high heaven's despite,°           *defiance*
        To shame the sun by day and her by night.

'And therefore hath she bribed the destinies
To cross the curious° workmanship of nature,                    *elaborate*
735  To mingle beauty with infirmities,
        And pure perfection with impure defeature,°                  *disfigurement*
        Making it subject to the tyranny
        Of mad mischances and much misery;

'As burning fevers, agues pale and faint,
740  Life-poisoning pestilence, and frenzies wood,°              *insane fits*
        The marrow-eating sickness⁵ whose attaint°                  *infection*
        Disorder breeds by heating of the blood;
        Surfeits, impostumes,° grief, and damned despair          *abscesses*
        Swear nature's death for framing° thee so fair.          *making*

745  'And not the least of all these maladies
        But in one minute's fight brings beauty under.
        Both favour, savour,° hue, and qualities,                  *beauty; smell*
        Whereat th'impartial gazer late did wonder,
        Are on the sudden wasted,° thawed, and done,              *wasted away*
750  As mountain snow melts with the midday sun.

'Therefore, despite of fruitless° chastity,                    *defying barren*
Love-lacking vestals and self-loving nuns,
That on the earth would breed a scarcity
And barren dearth of daughters and of sons,
755  Be prodigal. The lamp that burns by night
        Dries up his oil to lend the world his light.

'What is thy body but a swallowing grave,
Seeming to bury that posterity
Which, by the rights of time, thou needs must have
760  If thou destroy them not in dark obscurity?
        If so, the world will hold thee in disdain,
        Sith° in thy pride so fair a hope is slain.                *Since*

'So in thyself thyself art made away,°                        *destroyed*
A mischief° worse than civil, home-bred strife,                *An evil*
765  Or theirs whose desperate hands themselves do slay,
        Or butcher sire that reaves° his son of life.              *robs*
        Foul cank'ring rust the hidden treasure frets,°          *eats away*
        But gold that's put to use more gold begets.'

'Nay, then,' quoth Adon, 'You will fall again
770  Into your idle,° over-handled theme.                          *unprofitable*
The kiss I gave you is bestowed in vain,
And all in vain you strive against the stream;

_____
5. Syphilis, which attacks the bones.

For, by this black-faced night, desire's foul nurse,
Your treatise° makes me like you worse and worse.                    *discussion; plea*

775 'If love have lent you twenty thousand tongues,
And every tongue more moving than your own,
Bewitching like the wanton mermaid's songs,
Yet from mine ear the tempting tune is blown;
    For know, my heart stands armèd in mine ear,
780     And will not let a false sound enter there,

'Lest the deceiving harmony should run
Into the quiet closure° of my breast,                                *enclosure*
And then my little heart were quite undone,
In his bedchamber to be barred of rest.
785     No, lady, no. My heart longs not to groan,
    But soundly sleeps, while now it sleeps alone.

'What have you urged that I cannot reprove?
The path is smooth that leadeth on to danger.
I hate not love, but your device° in love,                           *tactics*
790 That lends embracements unto every stranger.
    You do it for increase—O strange excuse,
    When reason is the bawd to lust's abuse!

'Call it not love, for love to heaven is fled
Since sweating lust on earth usurped his name,
795 Under whose simple° semblance he hath fed                          *innocent*
Upon fresh beauty, blotting it with blame;
    Which the hot tyrant stains, and soon bereaves,
    As caterpillars do the tender leaves.

'Love comforteth, like sunshine after rain,
800 But lust's effect is tempest after sun.
Love's gentle spring doth always fresh remain;
Lust's winter comes ere summer half be done.
    Love surfeits not; lust like a glutton dies.
    Love is all truth, lust full of forgèd lies.

805 'More I could tell, but more I dare not say;
The text is old, the orator too green.
Therefore in sadness° now I will away;                               *truly*
My face is full of shame, my heart of teen.°                         *grief*
    Mine ears that to your wanton talk attended
810     Do burn themselves for having so offended.'

With this he breaketh from the sweet embrace
Of those fair arms which bound him to her breast,
And homeward through the dark laund° runs apace,                     *glade*
Leaves love upon her back, deeply distressed.
815     Look how a bright star shooteth from the sky,
    So glides he in the night from Venus' eye,

Which after him she darts, as one on shore
Gazing upon a late-embarkèd friend
Till the wild waves will have him seen no more,

820 Whose ridges with the meeting clouds contend.
    So did the merciless and pitchy night
    Fold in the object that did feed her sight.

    Whereat amazed,° as one that unaware                   *shocked*
    Hath dropped a precious jewel in the flood,
825 Or stonished,° as night wand'rers often are,          *confused*
    Their light blown out in some mistrustful° wood:   *anxiety-producing*
      Even so, confounded in the dark she lay,
      Having lost the fair discovery of her way.[6]

    And now she beats her heart, whereat it groans,
830 That all the neighbour caves, as seeming troubled,
    Make verbal repetition of her moans;
    Passion° on passion deeply is redoubled.          *Lamentation*
      'Ay me,' she cries, and twenty times 'Woe, woe!'
      And twenty echoes twenty times cry so.

835 She, marking them, begins a wailing note,
    And sings extemporally a woeful ditty,
    How love makes young men thrall,° and old men dote,   *enslaved*
    How love is wise in folly, foolish-witty.
      Her heavy° anthem still concludes in woe,      *sorrowful*
840     And still the choir of echoes answer so.

    Her song was tedious, and outwore the night;
    For lovers' hours are long, though seeming short.
    If pleased themselves, others, they think, delight
    In such-like circumstance, with such-like sport.
845     Their copious stories oftentimes begun
    End without audience, and are never done.

    For who hath she to spend the night withal°        *with*
    But idle sounds resembling parasites,°     *flattering hangers-on*
    Like shrill-tongued tapsters° answering every call,   *tavern keepers*
850 Soothing the humour of fantastic wits?[7]
      She says ''Tis so'; they answer all ''Tis so',
      And would say after her, if she said 'No'.

    Lo, here the gentle lark, weary of rest,
    From his moist cabinet° mounts up on high       *nest*
855 And wakes the morning,° from whose silver breast   *(Aurora)*
    The sun ariseth in his majesty,
      Who doth the world so gloriously behold
      That cedar tops and hills seem burnished gold.

    Venus salutes him with this fair good-morrow:
860 'O thou clear° god, and patron of all light,       *bright*
    From whom each lamp and shining star doth borrow
    The beauteous influence[8] that makes him bright:

---

6. *the fair . . . way:* a clear view of her path; a beautiful
guide.
7. Catering to the moods of erratic people.

8. The ethereal stream that in Renaissance astrology
was supposed to flow from stars and planets.

> There lives a son° that sucked an earthly mother            *(Adonis)*
> May° lend thee light, as thou dost lend to other.'           *Who may*

865   This said, she hasteth to a myrtle grove,
Musing° the morning is so much o'erworn°                        *Wondering / spent*
And yet she hears no tidings of her love.
She hearkens for his hounds, and for his horn.
> Anon she hears them chant it lustily,°                        *sing out heartily*
870   And all in haste she coasteth° to the cry.                 *rushes*

And as she runs, the bushes in the way
Some catch her by the neck, some kiss her face,
Some twine about her thigh to make her stay.
She wildly breaketh from their strict° embrace,                 *restricting*
875   Like a milch° doe whose swelling dugs° do ache,            *milk / udders*
> Hasting to feed her fawn hid in some brake.°                  *thicket*

By this° she hears the hounds are at a bay,⁹                    *By now*
Whereat she starts, like one that spies an adder
Wreathed up in fatal folds just in his way,
880   The fear whereof doth make him shake and shudder;
> Even so the timorous yelping of the hounds
> Appals her senses, and her spirit confounds.

For now she knows it is no gentle chase,
But the blunt° boar, rough bear, or lion proud,                *rude*
885   Because the cry remaineth in one place,
Where fearfully the dogs exclaim aloud.
> Finding their enemy to be so curst,°                          *vicious*
> They all strain court'sy¹ who shall cope° him first.         *contend with*

This dismal cry rings sadly in her ear,
890   Through which it enters to surprise° her heart,            *assault*
Who, overcome by doubt and bloodless fear,
With cold-pale weakness numbs each feeling part;°              *sense organ*
> Like soldiers when their captain once doth yield,
> They basely fly, and dare not stay° the field.              *remain in*

895   Thus stands she in a trembling ecstasy,°                   *stupor*
Till, cheering up her senses all dismayed,
She tells them 'tis a causeless fantasy
And childish error that they are afraid;
> Bids them leave quaking, bids them fear no more;
900   And with that word she spied the hunted boar,

Whose frothy mouth, bepainted all with red,
Like milk and blood being mingled both together,
A second fear through all her sinews spread,
Which madly hurries her, she knows not whither.
905   This way she runs, and now she will no further,
> But back retires to rate° the boar for murder.                *berate*

9. Stopped by the quarry, which is making a stand.      1. Politely defer to one another.

A thousand spleens° bear her a thousand ways.                    *impulses*
She treads the path that she untreads again.
Her more than haste is mated° with delays,                      *counteracted*
910   Like the proceedings of a drunken brain,
        Full of respects,° yet naught at all respecting;         *considerations*
        In hand with all things, naught at all effecting.[2]

Here kennelled in a brake she finds a hound,
And asks the weary caitiff° for his master;                     *wretch*
915   And there another licking of his wound,
        'Gainst venomed sores the only sovereign plaster.°       *effective remedy*
        And here she meets another, sadly scowling,
        To whom she speaks; and he replies with howling.

When he hath ceased his ill-resounding noise,
920   Another flap-mouthed mourner, black and grim,
Against the welkin° volleys out his voice.                      *sky*
Another, and another, answer him,
        Clapping their proud tails to the ground below,
        Shaking their scratched ears, bleeding as they go.

925   Look how the world's poor people are amazed
At apparitions, signs, and prodigies,°                          *strange occurrences*
Whereon with fearful eyes they long have gazed,
Infusing them with° dreadful prophecies:                        *Reading into them*
        So she at these sad signs draws up her breath,
930   And, sighing it again, exclaims on° death.                 *berates*

'Hard-favoured tyrant, ugly, meagre, lean,
Hateful divorce of love'—thus chides she death;
'Grim-grinning° ghost, earth's worm: what dost thou mean       *(like a skull)*
To stifle beauty, and to steal his breath
935   Who, when he lived, his breath and beauty set
        Gloss on the rose, smell to the violet?

'If he be dead—O no, it cannot be,
Seeing his beauty, thou shouldst strike at it.
O yes, it may; thou hast no eyes to see,[3]
940   But hatefully, at random dost thou hit.
        Thy mark° is feeble age; but thy false dart             *target*
        Mistakes that aim, and cleaves an infant's heart.

'Hadst thou but bid beware, then he° had spoke,                 *(Adonis)*
And, hearing him, thy power had lost his° power.                *its*
945   The destinies will curse thee for this stroke.
They bid thee crop a weed; thou pluck'st a flower.
        Love's golden arrow at him should have fled,°           *flown*
        And not death's ebon dart to strike him dead.

'Dost thou drink tears, that thou provok'st such weeping?
950   What may a heavy groan advantage° thee?                   *benefit*
Why hast thou cast into eternal sleeping
Those eyes that taught all other eyes to see?

2. Full of notions, yet actually attending to nothing.    3. Death's eye sockets are empty, like a skull's.

Now nature cares not for thy mortal vigour,[4]
Since her best work is ruined with thy rigour.'

955 Here overcome, as one full of despair,
She vailed° her eyelids, who like sluices stopped     *lowered*
The crystal tide that from her two cheeks fair
In the sweet channel of her bosom dropped.
    But through the flood-gates breaks the silver rain,
960     And with his strong course opens them again.

O, how her eyes and tears did lend and borrow!°     *(by reflection)*
Her eye seen in the tears, tears in her eye,
Both crystals, where they viewed each other's sorrow:
Sorrow, that friendly° sighs sought still to dry,     *consoling; like-minded*
965     But, like a stormy day, now wind, now rain,
    Sighs dry her cheeks, tears make them wet again.

Variable passions throng her constant woe,
As striving who should best become° her grief.     *fit*
All entertained,° each passion labours so     *permitted to enter*
970 That every present sorrow seemeth chief,
    But none is best. Then join they all together,
    Like many clouds consulting° for foul weather.     *gathering*

By this, far off she hears some huntsman hollo;°     *(hunting call)*
A nurse's song ne'er pleased her babe so well.
975 The dire imagination° she did follow     *train of thought*
This sound of hope doth labour to expel;
    For now reviving joy bids her rejoice
    And flatters her it is Adonis' voice.

Whereat her tears began to turn their tide,°     *to ebb*
980 Being prisoned in her eye like pearls in glass;
Yet sometimes falls an orient° drop beside,     *a glistening*
Which her cheek melts, as° scorning it should pass     *as if*
    To wash the foul° face of the sluttish ground,     *dirty*
    Who is but drunken when she seemeth drowned.

985 O hard-believing love—how strange it seems
Not to believe, and yet too credulous!
Thy weal° and woe are both of them extremes.     *prosperity*
Despair, and hope, makes thee ridiculous.
    The one doth flatter thee in thoughts unlikely;
990     In likely thoughts the other kills thee quickly.

Now she unweaves the web that she hath wrought.
Adonis lives, and death is not to blame.
It was not she that called him all to naught.[5]
Now she adds honours to his hateful name.
995     She clepes° him king of graves, and grave for kings,     *calls (archaic)*
    Imperious supreme° of all mortal things.     *Imperial ruler*

---

4. Nature does not heed your lethal power.     5. She who called Death everything bad.

'No, no,' quoth she, 'sweet death, I did but jest.
Yet pardon me, I felt a kind of fear
Whenas I met the boar, that bloody beast,
1000  Which knows no pity, but is still severe.
　　　Then, gentle shadow—truth I must confess—
　　　I railed on thee, fearing my love's decease.

'' 'Tis not my fault; the boar provoked my tongue.
Be wreakèd° on him, invisible commander.　　　　　　　　　　　　　　*revenged*
1005  'Tis he, foul creature, that hath done thee wrong.
I did but act;° he's author of thy slander.　　　　　　　　　　　*(as an agent)*
　　　Grief hath two tongues,° and never woman yet　　　　　*is doubly loud*
　　　Could rule them both, without ten women's wit.'

Thus, hoping that Adonis is alive,
1010  Her rash suspect° she doth extenuate,　　　　　　　　　　　　*suspicion*
And, that his beauty may the better thrive,
With death she humbly doth insinuate;°　　　　　　　　　　　*curry favor*
　　　Tells him of trophies, statues, tombs; and stories
　　　His victories, his triumphs, and his glories.

1015  'O Jove,' quoth she, 'how much a fool was I
To be of such a weak and silly mind
To wail his death who lives, and must not die
Till mutual° overthrow of mortal kind!　　　　　　　　　　　*universal*
　　　For he being dead, with him is beauty slain,
1020  　　And beauty dead, black chaos comes again.

'Fie, fie, fond° love, thou art as full of fear　　　　　*foolish; affectionate*
As one with treasure laden, hemmed with thieves.
Trifles unwitnessèd with eye or ear
Thy coward heart with false bethinking° grieves.'　　　　*imagination*
1025  　　Even at this word she hears a merry horn,
　　　Whereat she leaps,° that was but late° forlorn.　　　*(for joy) / lately*

As falcons to the lure, away she flies.
The grass stoops not, she treads on it so light;
And in her haste unfortunately spies
1030  The foul boar's conquest on her fair delight;
　　　Which seen, her eyes, as murdered with the view,
　　　Like stars ashamed of° day, themselves withdrew.°　　*put to shame by / shut*

Or as the snail, whose tender horns being hit
Shrinks backward in his shelly cave with pain,
1035  And there, all smothered up, in shade doth sit,
Long after fearing to creep forth again;
　　　So at his bloody view her eyes are fled
　　　Into the deep dark cabins of her head,

Where they resign their office and their light
1040  To the disposing of her troubled brain,
Who bids them still consort with° ugly night,　　　　　　*always accompany*
And never wound the heart with looks again,
　　　Who,° like a king perplexèd° in his throne,　　　*(the heart) / troubled*
　　　By their suggestion° gives a deadly groan,　　　*(the eyes') incitement*

1045    Whereat each tributary subject[6] quakes,
       As when the wind, imprisoned in the ground,
       Struggling for passage, earth's foundation shakes,[7]
       Which with cold terror doth men's minds confound.
          This mutiny each part doth so surprise°          *assail*
1050       That from their dark beds once more leap her eyes,

       And, being opened, threw unwilling light
       Upon the wide wound that the boar had trenched
       In his soft flank, whose wonted° lily-white         *usual*
       With purple tears that his wound wept was drenched.
1055         No flower was nigh, no grass, herb, leaf, or weed,
          But stole his blood, and seemed with him to bleed.

       This solemn sympathy poor Venus noteth.
       Over one shoulder doth she hang her head.
       Dumbly° she passions,° franticly she doteth.     *Mutely / suffers*
1060       She thinks he could not die, he is not dead.
         Her voice is stopped, her joints forget to bow,°    *cannot bend*
         Her eyes are mad that they have wept till° now.     *before*

       Upon his hurt she looks so steadfastly
       That her sight, dazzling,° makes the wound seem three;   *blurring*
1065       And then she reprehends her mangling eye,
       That makes more gashes where no breach should be.
         His face seems twain; each several limb is doubled;
         For oft the eye mistakes, the brain being troubled.

       'My tongue cannot express my grief for one,
1070       And yet,' quoth she, 'behold two Adons dead!
       My sighs are blown away, my salt tears gone,
       Mine eyes are turned to fire, my heart to lead.
         Heavy heart's lead, melt at mine eyes' red fire!
         So shall I die by drops of hot desire.

1075      'Alas, poor world, what treasure hast thou lost,
       What face remains alive that's worth the viewing?
       Whose tongue is music now? What canst thou boast
       Of things long since, or anything ensuing?
         The flowers are sweet, their colours fresh and trim;
1080         But true sweet beauty lived and died with him.

       'Bonnet nor veil henceforth no creature wear:°   *(to preserve complexion)*
       Nor sun nor wind will ever strive to kiss you.
       Having no fair° to lose, you need not fear.       *beauty*
       The sun doth scorn you, and the wind doth hiss you.
1085         But when Adonis lived, sun and sharp air
         Lurked like two thieves to rob him of his fair;

       'And therefore would he put his bonnet on,
       Under whose brim the gaudy sun would peep.
       The wind would blow it off, and, being gone,

---

6. Each inferior organ of Venus's body.        7. Sixteenth-century explanation of earthquakes.

1090 Play with his locks; then would Adonis weep,
    And straight,° in pity of his tender years,          *immediately*
    They both would strive who first should dry his tears.

'To see his face the lion walked along
Behind some hedge, because he would not fear° him.     *frighten*
1095 To recreate° himself° when he hath sung,     *entertain / (Adonis)*
The tiger would be tame, and gently hear him.
    If he had spoke, the wolf would leave his prey,
    And never fright the silly° lamb that day.     *innocent*

'When he beheld his shadow in the brook,
1100 The fishes spread on it their golden gills.
When he was by, the birds such pleasure took
That some would sing, some other in their bills
    Would bring him mulberries and ripe-red cherries.
    He fed them with his sight, they him with berries.

1105 'But this foul, grim, and urchin-snouted° boar,     *hedgehog-snouted*
Whose downward eye still looketh for a grave,
Ne'er saw the beauteous livery[8] that he wore:
    Witness the entertainment° that he gave.     *reception*
    If he did see his face, why then, I know
1110 He thought to kiss him, and hath killed him so.

' 'Tis true, 'tis true; thus was Adonis slain;
He ran upon the boar with his sharp spear,
Who did not whet his teeth at him again,°     *in return*
But by a kiss thought to persuade him° there,     *win him over*
1115     And, nuzzling in his flank, the loving swine
    Sheathed unaware the tusk in his soft groin.

'Had I been toothed like him, I must confess
With kissing him I should have killed him first;
But he is dead, and never did he bless
1120 My youth with his, the more am I accursed.'
    With this she falleth in the place she stood,
    And stains her face with his congealèd blood.

She looks upon his lips, and they are pale.
She takes him by the hand, and that is cold.
1125 She whispers in his ears a heavy tale,
As if they heard the woeful words she told.
    She lifts the coffer-lids° that close his eyes,     *treasure-chest lids*
    Where lo, two lamps burnt out in darkness lies;

Two glasses, where herself herself beheld
1130 A thousand times, and now no more reflect,
Their virtue° lost, wherein they late excelled,     *power*
And every beauty robbed of his° effect.     *its*
    'Wonder of time,' quoth she, 'this is my spite,°     *torment*
    That, thou being dead, the day should yet be light.

8. His appearance (literally, garment).

1135 'Since thou art dead, lo, here I prophesy
     Sorrow on love hereafter shall attend.
     It° shall be waited on with jealousy,                                    *(Love)*
     Find sweet beginning, but unsavoury end;
        Ne'er settled equally, but high or low,⁹
1140    That all love's pleasure shall not match his woe.

     'It shall be fickle, false, and full of fraud,
     Bud, and be blasted,° in a breathing-while:°           *blighted / moment*
     The bottom poison, and the top o'erstrawed°                   *strewn over*
     With sweets that shall the truest sight beguile.
1145 The strongest body shall it make most weak,
        Strike the wise dumb,° and teach the fool to speak.               *mute*

     'It shall be sparing,° and too full of riot,°           *miserly / excess*
     Teaching decrepit age to tread the measures.¹
     The staring° ruffian shall it keep in quiet,                      *glaring*
1150 Pluck down the rich, enrich the poor with treasures;
        It shall be raging-mad, and silly-mild;
        Make the young old, the old become a child.

     'It shall suspect where is no cause of fear;
     It shall not fear where it should most mistrust.
1155 It shall be merciful, and too severe,
     And most deceiving when it seems most just.°                      *honest*
        Perverse it shall be where it shows most toward,²
        Put fear to valour, courage to the coward.

     'It shall be cause of war and dire events,
1160 And set dissension 'twixt the son and sire;
     Subject and servile to all discontents,³
     As dry combustious matter is to fire.
        Sith° in his prime death doth my love destroy,                   *Since*
        They that love best their loves shall not enjoy.'

1165 By this, the boy that by her side lay killed
     Was melted like a vapour from her sight,
     And in his blood that on the ground lay spilled
     A purple flower sprung up, chequered with white,°         *(the anemone)*
        Resembling well his pale cheeks, and the blood
1170    Which in round drops upon their whiteness stood.

     She bows her head the new-sprung flower to smell,
     Comparing it to her Adonis' breath,
     And says within her bosom it shall dwell,
     Since he himself is reft° from her by death.                        *torn*
1175    She crops the stalk, and in the breach appears
        Green-dropping sap, which she compares to tears.

     'Poor flower,' quoth she, 'this was thy father's guise°—            *habit*
     Sweet issue° of a more sweet-smelling sire—            *offspring; emission*

---

9. *Ne'er . . . low:* Love shall involve extremes of happiness and grief rather than equanimity; lovers shall come from different social stations.

1. To dance (inappropriately).
2. It shall be stubborn where it seems most compliant.
3. Cause and slave of all discontentedness.

For every little grief to wet his eyes.
1180 To grow unto himself° was his desire,                    *mature independently*
   And so 'tis thine; but know it is as good
   To wither in my breast as in his blood.

'Here was thy father's bed, here in my breast.
Thou art the next of blood,° and 'tis thy right.                    *heir (with wordplay)*
1185 Lo, in this hollow cradle take thy rest;
   My throbbing heart shall rock thee day and night.
   There shall not be one minute in an hour
   Wherein I will not kiss my sweet love's flower.'

Thus, weary of the world, away she hies,
1190 And yokes her silver doves, by whose swift aid
   Their mistress, mounted, through the empty skies
   In her light chariot quickly is conveyed,
     Holding their course to Paphos,⁴ where their queen
     Means to immure° herself, and not be seen.                    *confine*

4. Venus's abode in Cyprus.

# The Rape of Lucrece

In the dedication to *Venus and Adonis* in 1593, Shakespeare promised his patron the Earl of Southampton a "graver labor"; a year later, *The Rape of Lucrece* delivered on his pledge. Like most nondramatic poems of the period, in other words, this one was dedicated to a wealthy individual whom Shakespeare hoped would reward his efforts, and presumably reflected Shakespeare's awareness of that individual's literary preferences. Perhaps not surprisingly, then, the two poems have much in common: their classical inspiration; their lush, highly rhetorical narrative verse; their interest in the dynamic of a one-sided sexual passion. Yet both poems were intended for a wider audience, and both were popular successes: *The Rape of Lucrece* was reprinted at least six times during Shakespeare's lifetime. Moreover, as Shakespeare suggests in his dedication, whereas *Venus and Adonis,* despite its sad end, remains playful even in its pathos, *The Rape of Lucrece* treats a tragic subject of political as well as sexual consequence. It is written in rime royal, a seven-line iambic-pentameter stanza with the rhyme scheme *ababbcc,* a verse form reserved since the time of Chaucer for elevated, tragic subjects. Shakespeare's contemporary Gabriel Harvey captures the difference in the two poems when he comments that *Venus and Adonis* pleases "the younger sort," while *The Rape of Lucrece,* like *Hamlet,* pleases "the wiser sort."

Today *The Rape of Lucrece* is commonly regarded far less highly than the play with which Harvey classifies it. The change in estimation suggests that Shakespeare's original readers came to the poem with generic expectations, literary tastes, and interpretive equipment different from our own. One important difference is the greater familiarity many Renaissance readers would have had with Shakespeare's sources, a familiarity that left them free to concentrate on the ways in which the poet was varying or amplifying on well-known prototypes. Slightly different versions of the tale of Tarquin and Lucretia were available in Livy's history of Rome and in Ovid's *Fasti,* both commonly read in Elizabethan grammar schools. In 509 B.C.E., Rome's King was Tarquin the Proud, a good military leader but an oppressive ruler over his own subjects. Sextus Tarquinius, the King's son, raped Lucretia, the wife of Collatinus, one of his aristocratic retainers. Lucretia committed suicide after revealing the crime to her male relatives and exhorting them to revenge her. After her corpse was exhibited in the Roman Forum, a wholesale revolt against the Tarquins erupted, led by the King's nephew Lucius Junius Brutus. The royal family was exiled, and Rome became a republic, ruled by a senate and administered by one or more elected "consuls," of which Lucius Junius Brutus was the first.

For the Renaissance as well as for its original Roman audience, the story of Tarquin and Lucrece displayed vividly the inextricability of domestic and civic order, of public and private realms, of sexual and political violence. As a political fable, it suggested circumstances in which subjects were permitted, even obliged, to challenge the authority of their sovereign. When Tarquin rapes Lucrece, he does not merely perpetrate an act of brutal violence against her, but he defies Collatinus's exclusive claim on his wife's body, imagined as the husband's property. The story thus exemplifies a ruler's reckless disregard for the rights of his *male* subjects. In the late sixteenth century, when monarchies in western Europe were strengthening their power at the expense of parliaments and the higher aristocracy, the story could be cited as a precedent for resisting tyranny.

Purely as a sexual melodrama too, the story had wide appeal. Again and again, Renaissance painters portrayed Tarquin stealing into Lucretia's bed, Lucretia stabbing herself, and Lucius Junius Brutus exhorting over her body in the marketplace, often incorporating all three scenes into the same picture. Lucretia became a focus of especially fierce

*Lucretia.* Raphael.

debate. On the one hand, she seemed a model of wifely duty, a woman to whom marital fidelity was not merely a matter of social respectability but a fundamental life principle. On the other hand, suicide by the sword—the traditional last, defiant gesture of heroic Roman men—could seem improperly self-assertive in a woman. Moreover, some Christian writers considered Lucretia's suicide not merely indecorous but sinful. In *The City of God,* Augustine argued that since virtues are properties of the will and not the body, Lucretia was innocent of unchastity. But ironically, her sexual blamelessness rendered her suicide completely inexcusable; Augustine considered her a murderess who had taken her own life out of unchristian pride. By Shakespeare's time, therefore, Lucretia could be held up, variously, as a model of female propriety and as an example of pagan willfulness, as a woman who both upholds and breaks from the usual constraints upon her sex.

Adapting the story to his own purposes, Shakespeare makes interesting changes of detail and emphasis. As Ovid and Livy recount it, the story of violation, suicide, and revolution is full of turbulent physical action and unexpected revelations: and in Livy especially, the political consequences of the rape receive much more attention than the sexual assault itself. Shakespeare's version downplays—though it does not eliminate—the political aspects of the story, and it contains most of the feverish momentum of the original story in the prefatory "Argument": "The same night he treacherously stealeth into her chamber, violently ravished her, and early in the morning speedeth away. Lucrece, in this lamentable plight, hastily dispatcheth messengers." The poem itself, by contrast, concentrates not upon moments of violence or haste but upon what precedes and follows those moments: what Tarquin thinks on his way to Lucrece's bedchamber, how Lucrece occupies herself between the time she sends off her messenger and Collatine's return.

Like *Venus and Adonis, The Rape of Lucrece* eschews eventfulness for elaborate psychological analysis, attempting to capture in verse the uneven surge and flow of troubled, self-divided consciousnesses. In Shakespeare's hands, the story of Tarquin and Lucrece becomes a story about how people make choices that lead to violence. Everything in the poem is the consequence of a decision, not an accident of fate, and nothing seems inevitable. The poem teases the reader with alternative possibilities. What if Collatine had kept his marital happiness to himself? What if Tarquin's conscience had overcome his lust? What if Lucrece's beauty had blinded Tarquin permanently instead of temporarily? What if Collatine had arrived to save Lucrece at the last moment? What if Lucrece had resolved to kill Tarquin rather than herself?

In large part, these alternatives receive so much attention because both Tarquin and Lucrece make decisions that fail to reflect their best interests. The poem is constantly suggesting that they would be better off doing something else; and, interestingly, the characters themselves at times seem lucidly aware of that fact. Tarquin tells himself that his assault will desecrate the very virtue he admires in Lucrece, destroy his own self-respect, and bring dishonor upon his family. Then he rapes Lucrece. Lucrece argues to herself what her husband and father will tell her later: that she cannot incur guilt by a sexual act to which she has not consented, and that therefore she need not take her own life. Then she commits suicide.

In both cases, the characters' stubborn refusal to acknowledge the obvious seems to follow from their tendency to conceive of themselves in terms of a few crucial metaphors. In Tarquin's case, the metaphors are military: "Affection is my captain, and he leadeth, / . . . My heart shall never countermand mine eye" (lines 271, 276). Such images attract Tarquin because they portray a rash, grossly disorderly act in terms of strict discipline. Even as he overturns the proper subordination of passion to reason, he elaborates a clear, if perverse, hierarchy of priorities. Moreover, by casting himself as a warrior and Lucrece as an enemy territory, Tarquin minimizes the blame that attaches to rape, an act conventionally associated with (and often excused in) soldiers pillaging an enemy town.

Of course, as Lucrece reminds him, she is not his foe, and Tarquin's actions violate not only her bodily integrity but her husband's trust in a friend and superior. Her pleas show how tendentious are Tarquin's interpretations of the metaphors he attaches to himself. When Tarquin describes himself as an "uncontrollèd tide," and therefore intractable to entreaties, Lucrece attempts to modify the sense of the metaphor:

> 'Thou art,' quoth she, 'a sea, a sovereign king,
> And lo, there falls into thy boundless flood
> Black lust, dishonour, shame, misgoverning,
> Who seek to stain the ocean of thy blood.'
> (lines 652–55)

Likewise, her account of his psychological state replaces the military metaphor of battle against an enemy with one of civil order temporarily disrupted:

> I sue for exiled majesty's repeal;
> Let him return, and flatt'ring thoughts retire.
> His true respect will prison false desire.
> (lines 640–42)

Eventually, the rape that Tarquin tries to think of as an orderly military maneuver leads not only to his psychological fragmentation and self-torment but to literal exile, an exile Lucrece describes as already having occurred metaphorically.

After the rape and Tarquin's departure, the narrative focus shifts to Lucrece. Although she knows that she is not intentionally guilty of breaking her marital vows, she nonetheless construes herself as culpable. Like her violator, Lucrece thinks of herself and her body in symbolic terms, although in her case the governing metaphors are fortress, house, mansion, temple, tree. By emphasizing the protective function of the body, these metaphors make it easy for Lucrece to think of herself as irreparably damaged once her body has been assaulted by Tarquin's lust:

> Ay me, the bark peeled from the lofty pine
> His leaves will wither and his sap decay;
> So must my soul, her bark being peeled away.
> (lines 1167–69)

Once Tarquin sacks and batters Lucrece's fortress, she suffers regardless of her innocence, like the inhabitant of a plundered town. Of course, like Tarquin, Lucrece interprets such metaphors tendentiously: she could just as well think of the "bark" or the "house" that shelters her soul as a morally insignificant excrescence. Instead, when the condition of her body seems to conflict with the condition of her soul, she desperately attempts to resolve the inconsistency by declaring herself irredeemably contaminated. In doing so, she endorses—indeed, almost celebrates—a literally fatal ambivalence in the definition of female chastity. For despite Augustine's objections, female chastity ordinarily refers to a physical condition as well as to a mental attitude in cultures that value female bodily intactness; this ambivalence still haunts rape survivors today, who often blame themselves for their own victimization.

Comprehensible though Lucrece's suicide may be in these terms, however, it is ironically fraught with the very contradictions she seeks to avoid. She "revenges" herself

*Tarquino e Lucrezia.* Titian (c. 1570).

upon Tarquin by completing the assault he began, plunging the phallic blade into what Shakespeare calls the "sheath" of her breast (the Latin word for "sheath" is *vagina*). She insists that she is acting in Collatine's interests even while she ignores his wishes; she proves her innocence by demanding of herself that she pay the penalty for guilt; she validates her version of the rape story by silencing herself more effectively than Tarquin had with the bedclothes.

Although the metaphors Tarquin and Lucrece use to think about their respective situations are, therefore, highly problematic, they are definitely not arbitrary. Both protagonists derive their figures of speech from the same medieval and Renaissance poetic tradition Shakespeare had already drawn upon in *Venus and Adonis.* The configuration of characters—the warrior-lover desperately pursuing his passion, the beautiful woman whose chastity makes her irresistibly desirable—is likewise conventional. Shakespeare suggests the importance of this poetic mentality for *The Rape of Lucrece* by anachronistically importing the language of chivalry into a poem about ancient Rome: Tarquin agonizes about the consequences of his transgression for his family's coat of arms, and Lucrece accuses him of breaking "knighthood, gentry, and sweet friendship's oath" (line 569). This is closer to the world of Thomas Malory's Arthurian romances, Thomas Wyatt's sonnets, Philip Sidney's *Arcadia,* or Edmund Spenser's *Faerie Queene* than it is to the world of Livy or Ovid.

In fact, it is possible to see *The Rape of Lucrece,* like *Venus and Adonis,* as attempting to renovate a rhetoric of sexual passion that had begun to seem trite by Shakespeare's time. But the two poems employ almost exactly opposite strategies of renewal. *Venus and Adonis* surprises the reader by turning conventional expectations of gendered behavior upside down, assigning the aggressive, desiring role to the woman and casting the male as an uncorrupted fortress of virtue. *The Rape of Lucrece,* on the other hand, pushes the conventional language of love poetry in a relentlessly literal direction, making it interesting by unleashing the latent ferocity and misogyny of a courtly love aesthetic. Lovers in the poetry of Spenser and Sidney, Petrarch and Wyatt, think of themselves as soldiers of desire, but they are so awed by their mistresses that aggressive thoughts are quenched by a mere glance from their imperious beloveds. Shakespeare's Tarquin, in contrast, more consistent and less exquisitely sensitive, uses the implicitly coercive rhetoric of love poetry as a pretext for rape.

Given the poem's intense concern with the use and misuse of language, it is not surprising that *The Rape of Lucrece* is also attentive to the relationship of rhetoric to other forms of representation. Again and again, the poem pauses to consider the relative power and conviction of linguistic and visual experience, of the ear and the eye. At some points in the poem, vision seems the privileged sense, giving immediate access to the unquestionably real. "Beauty itself doth of itself persuade / The eyes of men without an orator," the narrator declares; "To see sad sights moves more than hear them told" (lines 29–30, 1324). Yet Shakespeare alters his sources to have Tarquin provoked to lust not by the sight of Lucrece but by Collatine's report of her; and he dwells too on Lucrece's inability to divine Tarquin's motives from his appearance.

The rape and death of Lucretia. From Jost Amman, *Icones Livianae* (1572).

This persistent concern with the relative adequacy of different representational modes culminates in a long passage in which Lucrece contemplates a tapestry of Troy. In multiple ways, the tapestry is relevant to her own case, for the Trojan War was the consequence of a rape, and after the city's destruction, Trojan exiles were supposed to have founded Rome. After Lucrece's suicide, the account of her rape will provide the pretext for another founding, that of the Roman Republic. Eventually, her story will be displayed by artists in the same way that the legend of Troy is illustrated here—a series of chronologically distinct episodes represented simultaneously on the same panel. As Lucrece gazes at the painter's vast panorama of violation, the poet emphasizes both the vivid realism of the depiction and the artificial means by which that realism is produced: "Here one man's hand leaned on another's head, / His nose being shadowed by his neighbour's ear" (lines 1415–16). Portraying people according to the laws of perspective makes them look "natural," but it also reduces them to a collection of grotesquely amputated shapes. Like *Venus and Adonis*, *The Rape of Lucrece* invokes nature as a category of value and then subverts it; but whereas the earlier poem undermines "nature" by suggesting that its supposed precepts are inadequate, the later poem undermines "nature" by suggesting that its effect is only achieved by extraordinary artifice. Shakespeare will consider the issue again in such plays as *A Midsummer Night's Dream*, *The Winter's Tale*, *The Tempest*, and, of course, *Hamlet*.

KATHARINE EISAMAN MAUS

## TEXTUAL NOTE

Richard Field was the printer for *The Rape of Lucrece*, published in 1594, as he had been for *Venus and Adonis* the previous year. Like *Venus and Adonis*, *Lucrece* in its printed state probably derives directly from Shakespeare's manuscript, and it presents relatively few textual difficulties. Some editors question whether Shakespeare wrote the prefatory "Argument." A few variations among surviving copies of the First Quarto represent proof corrections; in Elizabethan times, proofreading was done while the work was in the process of being printed, so corrections could appear in some copies but not in others.

## SELECTED BIBLIOGRAPHY

Belsey, Catherine. "Tarquin Dispossessed: Expropriation and Consent in *The Rape of Lucrece*." *Shakespeare Quarterly* 52 (2001): 45–70. Lucrece as property and as person.

Donaldson, Ian. *The Rapes of Lucretia: A Myth and Its Transformations*. Oxford: Clarendon, 1982. Discusses Shakespeare's poem alongside other literary and artistic treatments of the story.

Fineman, Joel. "Shakespeare's Will: The Temporality of Rape." *Representations* 20 (Fall 1987): 25–76. Features an ingenious discussion of the "let" as both hindering Tarquin and spurring him to action.

Hadfield, Andrew. "Tarquin's Everlasting Banishment: Republicanism and Constitutionalism in *The Rape of Lucrece* and *Titus Andronicus*." *Parergon: Journal of the Australian and New Zealand Association for Medieval and Renaissance Studies* 19 (2002): 77–104. A discussion of the political issues in the poem.

Kahn, Coppélia. "The Rape in Shakespeare's *Lucrece*." *Shakespeare Studies* 9 (1976): 45–72. Feminist account of rape and patriarchy in the poem.

Maus, Katharine Eisaman. "Taking Tropes Seriously: Language and Violence in Shakespeare's *Rape of Lucrece*." *Shakespeare Quarterly* 37 (1986): 66–82. *The Rape of Lucrece* as a literalization of Petrarchan metaphors.

Vickers, Nancy. "The Blazon of Sweet Beauty's Best: Shakespeare's *Lucrece*." *Shakespeare and the Question of Theory*. Ed. Patricia Parker and Geoffrey Hartman. New York: Methuen, 1985. 95–115. The sexual politics of the blazon or detailed description of Lucrece's body.

# The Rape of Lucrece

TO THE RIGHT HONOURABLE
HENRY WRIOTHESLEY,
EARL OF SOUTHAMPTON AND
BARON OF TITCHFIELD[1]

The love I dedicate to your lordship is without end, whereof this
pamphlet° without beginning[2] is but a superfluous moiety.° The
warrant° I have of your honourable disposition, not the worth of
my untutored lines, makes it assured of acceptance. What I have
done is yours; what I have to do is yours, being part in all I have,
devoted yours. Were my worth greater my duty would show
greater, meantime, as it is, it is bound to your lordship, to whom
I wish long life still° lengthened with all happiness.

*short work / part*
*assurance*

*continually*

YOUR LORDSHIP'S IN ALL DUTY,
WILLIAM SHAKESPEARE

## THE ARGUMENT°

*plot*

Lucius Tarquinius (surnamed Superbus for his excessive
pride),° after he had caused his own father-in-law Servius Tullius
to be cruelly murdered, and, contrary to the Roman laws and
customs, not requiring[3] or staying for the people's suffrages° had
possessed himself of the kingdom, went accompanied with his
sons and other noblemen of Rome to besiege Ardea,[4] during
which siege the principal men of the army meeting one evening
at the tent of Sextus Tarquinius, the King's son, in their discourses after supper everyone commended the virtues of his
own wife, among whom Collatinus extolled the incomparable
chastity of his wife, Lucretia. In that pleasant humour° they all
posted° to Rome, and, intending by their secret and sudden
arrival to make trial of that which everyone had before
avouched, only Collatinus finds his wife (though it were late in
the night) spinning amongst her maids. The other ladies were all
found dancing, and revelling, or in several disports.° Whereupon
the noblemen yielded Collatinus the victory and his wife the
fame. At that time Sextus Tarquinius, being enflamed with
Lucrece' beauty, yet smothering his passions for the present,
departed with the rest back to the camp, from whence he shortly
after privily° withdrew himself and was, according to his estate,°
royally entertained and lodged by Lucrece at Collatium.[5] The
same night he treacherously stealeth into her chamber, violently

*"the Proud"*

*approval*

*merry mood*
*hurried*

*diversions*

*secretly / rank*

**Dedication** and **Argument**
1. See *Venus and Adonis*, note 2 to Dedication.
2. *The Rape of Lucrece* begins *in medias res* (in the
middle of the story), as the Latin poet Horace recommends in *The Art of Poetry*.

3. Not asking for.
4. City 25 miles south of Rome.
5. Town 10 miles east of Rome; the ancestral home of
Collatinus's family.

ravished her, and early in the morning speedeth away. Lucrece, in this lamentable plight, hastily dispatcheth messengers—one to Rome for her father, another to the camp for Collatine. They came, the one accompanied with Junius Brutus, the other with Publius Valerius, and, finding Lucrece attired in mourning habit, demanded the cause of her sorrow. She, first taking an oath of them for her revenge, revealed the actor° and whole manner of his dealing, and withal° suddenly stabbed herself. Which done, with one consent they all vowed to root out the whole hated family of the Tarquins, and, bearing the dead body to Rome, Brutus acquainted the people with the doer and manner of the vile deed, with a bitter invective against the tyranny of the King; wherewith the people were so moved that with one consent and a general acclamation the Tarquins were all exiled and the state government changed from kings to consuls.[6]

*doer*
*moreover*

---

From the besieged Ardea all in post,°
Borne by the trustless wings of false desire,
Lust-breathèd° Tarquin leaves the Roman host
And to Collatium bears the lightless° fire
5   Which, in pale embers hid, lurks to aspire°
    And girdle with embracing flames the waist
    Of Collatine's fair love, Lucrece the chaste.

*haste*

*Lust-inspired*
*smoldering*
*rise up*

Haply° that name of chaste unhapp'ly° set
This bateless° edge on his keen appetite,
10  When Collatine unwisely did not let°
To praise the clear unmatchèd red and white
Which triumphed in that sky of his delight,°
    Where mortal stars° as bright as heaven's beauties
    With pure aspects[1] did him peculiar° duties.

*Perhaps / unfortunately*
*unbluntable*
*forbear*

*(Lucrece's face)*
*(her eyes)*
*exclusive*

15  For he the night before in Tarquin's tent
Unlocked the treasure of his happy state,
What priceless wealth the heavens had him lent
In the possession of his beauteous mate,
Reck'ning his fortune at such high-proud rate
20    That kings might be espousèd to more fame,
    But° king nor peer to such a peerless dame.

*But neither*

O happiness enjoyed but of° a few,
And, if possessed, as soon decayed and done
As is the morning's silver melting dew
25  Against the golden splendour of the sun,
An expired date° cancelled ere well begun!
    Honour and beauty in the owner's arms
    Are weakly fortressed from a world of harms.

*only by*

*time limit*

Beauty itself doth of° itself persuade
30  The eyes of men without an orator.
What needeth then apology be made

*by*

6. Chief magistrates, elected for one-year terms.    **Poem**
                                       1. Looks; astral influences.

To set forth that which is so singular?°             *unique*
Or why is Collatine the publisher°             *publicizer*
    Of that rich jewel he should keep unknown
35     From thievish ears, because it is his own?

Perchance his boast of Lucrece' sov'reignty°        *superiority*
Suggested° this proud issue° of a king,        *Tempted / offspring*
For by our ears our hearts oft tainted be.
Perchance that envy of so rich a thing,
40   Braving compare,° disdainfully did sting        *Defying comparison*
    His high-pitched thoughts, that meaner° men should vaunt°    *inferior / boast*
    That golden hap° which their superiors want.°        *luck / lack*

But some untimely thought did instigate
His all-too-timeless° speed, if none of those.        *untimely; rapid*
45   His honour, his affairs, his friends, his state°        *rank*
Neglected all, with swift intent he goes
To quench the coal which in his liver° glows.        *(seat of lust)*
    O rash false heat, wrapped in repentant cold,
    Thy hasty spring still blasts° and ne'er grows old!        *is always frostbitten*

50   When at Collatium this false lord arrived,
Well was he welcomed by the Roman dame,
Within whose face beauty and virtue strived
Which of them both should underprop her fame.
When virtue bragged, beauty would blush for shame;
55     When beauty boasted blushes, in despite°        *defiance*
    Virtue would stain° that or° with silver white.        *dye / gold*

But beauty, in that white entitulèd°        *claiming title*
From Venus' doves, doth challenge that fair field.[2]
Then virtue claims from beauty beauty's red,
60   Which virtue gave the golden age to gild[3]
Their silver cheeks, and called it then their shield,
    Teaching them thus to use it in the fight:
    When shame assailed, the red should fence° the white.        *defend*

This heraldry in Lucrece' face was seen,
65   Argued° by beauty's red and virtue's white.        *Demonstrated; disputed*
Of either's colour was the other queen,
Proving from world's minority° their right.        *earliest age*
Yet their ambition makes them still to fight,
    The sovereignty of either being so great
70     That oft they interchange each other's seat.

This silent war of lilies and of roses
Which Tarquin viewed in her fair face's field
In their pure ranks his traitor eye encloses,
Where, lest between them both it should be killed,
75   The coward captive vanquishèd doth yield
    To those two armies that would let him go
    Rather than triumph in° so false a foe.        *over*

2. Territory; battlefield; surface on which a coat of arms is displayed. *Venus' doves:* white turtledoves draw the chariot of Venus, the love goddess.

3. Coat with gold; cover with red (as in a blush). *the golden age:* a mythical, ideal era of innocence and plenty.

Now thinks he that her husband's shallow tongue,
The niggard prodigal that praised her so,
80  In that high task hath done her beauty wrong,
Which far exceeds his barren skill to show.°                    *describe*
Therefore that praise which Collatine doth owe°               *fail to render*
   Enchanted Tarquin answers° with surmise              *compensates for*
   In silent wonder of still-gazing eyes.

85  This earthly saint adorèd by this devil
Little suspecteth the false worshipper,
For unstained thoughts do seldom dream on evil.
Birds never limed° no secret bushes fear,                       *trapped*
So guiltless she securely° gives good cheer⁴                   *unsuspectingly*
90     And reverent welcome to her princely guest,
   Whose inward ill no outward harm expressed,

For that he coloured° with his high estate,                    *disguised*
Hiding base sin in pleats° of majesty,                          *folds*
That° nothing in him seemed inordinate                         *So that*
95  Save sometime too much wonder of his eye,
Which, having all, all could not satisfy,
   But poorly rich so wanteth in his store°              *plenty*
   That, cloyed with much, he pineth still for more.

But she that never coped with stranger° eyes                   *strangers'*
100  Could pick no meaning from their parling° looks,           *persuasive*
Nor read the subtle shining secrecies
Writ in the glassy margins⁵ of such books.
She touched no unknown baits nor feared no hooks,
   Nor could she moralize° his wanton sight°         *interpret / looking*
105     More than his eyes were opened to the light.⁶

He stories to her ears her husband's fame
Won in the fields of fruitful Italy,
And decks with praises Collatine's high name
Made glorious by his manly chivalry
110  With bruisèd arms° and wreaths of victory.                 *dented weapons*
   Her joy with heaved-up hand she doth express,
   And wordless so greets heaven for his success.

Far from the purpose of his coming thither
He makes excuses for his being there.
115  No cloudy show of stormy blust'ring weather
Doth yet in his fair welkin° once appear                        *sky (face)*
Till sable° night, mother of dread and fear,                   *black*
   Upon the world dim darkness doth display
   And in her vaulty prison stows the day.

120  For then is Tarquin brought unto his bed,
Intending° weariness with heavy sprite;°               *Pretending / spirit*
For after supper long he questionèd°                            *conversed*
With modest Lucrece, and wore out the night.

---

4. Hospitable entertainment.
5. Where summaries and interpretive remarks were

often placed.
6. Were made obvious.

Now leaden slumber with life's strength doth fight,
125 And everyone to rest himself betakes
  Save thieves, and cares, and troubled minds that wakes.

As one of which doth Tarquin lie revolving°       *considering*
The sundry dangers of his will's obtaining,°     *gratifying his desire*
Yet ever to obtain his will resolving,
130 Though weak-built hopes[7] persuade him to abstaining.
  Despair to gain doth traffic oft for gaining,[8]
   And when great treasure is the meed° proposed,    *prize*
   Though death be adjunct,[9] there's no death supposed.°  *thought of*

Those that much covet are with gain so fond°      *infatuated*
135 That what° they have not, that which they possess,   *That for what*
They scatter and unloose it from their bond,°     *ownership*
And so by hoping more they have but less,
Or, gaining more, the profit° of excess        *advantage*
  Is but to surfeit and such griefs[1] sustain
140 That they° prove bankrupt in this poor-rich gain.  *(the covetous)*

The aim of all is but to nurse the life
With honour, wealth, and ease in waning age,
And in this aim there is such thwarting strife
That one for all, or all for one, we gage,°       *risk*
145 As° life for honour in fell° battle's rage,   *For instance / cruel*
  Honour for wealth; and oft that wealth doth cost
  The death of all, and all together lost.

So that, in vent'ring ill,[2] we leave to be
The things we are for that which we expect,
150 And this ambitious foul infirmity
In having° much, torments us with defect     *While we have*
Of that we have; so then we do neglect
  The thing we have, and all for want of wit°   *lack of sense*
  Make something nothing by augmenting it.

155 Such hazard now must doting Tarquin make,
Pawning his honour to obtain his lust,
And for himself himself he must forsake.
Then where is truth if there be no self-trust?°   *truth to oneself*
When shall he think to find a stranger just
160 When he himself himself confounds, betrays
  To sland'rous tongues and wretched hateful days?

Now stole upon the time the dead of night
When heavy sleep had closed up mortal eyes.
No comfortable star did lend his° light,       *its*
165 No noise but owls' and wolves' death-boding cries
  Now serves the season, that they may surprise
   The silly° lambs. Pure thoughts are dead and still,  *innocent*
   While lust and murder wakes to stain° and kill.   *defile*

---

7. The fact that his hopes are flimsy.
8. Despair of gaining her (rightfully) often encourages him to gain her (by any means possible).
9. Be joined with it.
1. That is, the ills that accompany excess.
2. In taking serious risks; in undertaking evil deeds.

And now this lustful lord leapt from his bed,
170 Throwing his mantle rudely o'er his arm,
Is madly tossed between desire and dread.
Th'one sweetly flatters, th'other feareth harm,
But honest fear, bewitched with lust's foul charm,
    Doth too-too oft betake him to retire,°                                    *retreat*
175 Beaten away by brainsick rude desire.

His falchion° on a flint he softly smiteth,                                 *curved sword*
That from the cold stone sparks of fire do fly,
Whereat a waxen torch forthwith he lighteth,
Which must be lodestar° to his lustful eye,                                 *guiding light*
180 And to the flame thus speaks advisedly:°                                    *deliberately*
    'As from this cold flint I enforced this fire,
    So Lucrece must I force to my desire.'

Here pale with fear he doth premeditate
The dangers of his loathsome enterprise,
185 And in his inward mind he doth debate
What following sorrow may on this arise.
Then, looking scornfully, he doth despise
    His naked armour of still-slaughtered lust,[3]
    And justly thus controls° his thoughts unjust:                          *rebukes; restrains*

190 'Fair torch, burn out thy light, and lend it not
To darken her whose light excelleth thine;
And die, unhallowed thoughts, before you blot
With your uncleanness that which is divine.
Offer pure incense to so pure a shrine.
195     Let fair humanity abhor the deed
    That spots and stains love's modest snow-white weed.°                   *attire (chastity)*

'O shame to knighthood and to shining arms!
O foul dishonour to my household's grave!°                                  *ancestral tomb*
O impious act including° all foul harms!                                    *encompassing*
200 A martial man to be soft fancy's° slave!                                 *love's*
True valour still a true respect[4] should have;
    Then my digression° is so vile, so base,                                *error*
    That it will live engraven in my face.

'Yea, though I die the scandal will survive
205 And be an eyesore in my golden coat.°                                    *(of arms)*
Some loathsome dash[5] the herald will contrive
To cipher me how fondly° I did dote,                                        *To show how foolishly*
That my posterity, shamed with the note,°                                   *stigma*
    Shall curse my bones and hold it for no sin
210     To wish that I their father had not been.

'What win I if I gain the thing I seek?
A dream, a breath, a froth of fleeting joy.
Who buys a minute's mirth to wail a week,

---

3. His ineffective defense against his lust, always
quenched in the moment of fulfillment; his not-yet-erect
penis.

4. A suitable awareness of virtue.
5. Bar in a coat of arms, indicating a dishonorable
action by an ancestor.

Or sells eternity to get a toy?°                                              *trifle*
215  For one sweet grape who will the vine destroy?
　　Or what fond beggar, but to touch the crown,
　　Would with the sceptre straight be strucken down?

'If Collatinus dream of my intent
Will he not wake, and in a desp'rate rage
220  Post hither this vile purpose to prevent?—
This siege that hath engirt° his marriage,                                    *surrounded*
This blur° to youth, this sorrow to the sage,                                 *blot*
　　This dying virtue, this surviving shame,
　　Whose crime will bear an ever-during° blame.                            *everlasting*

225  'O what excuse can my invention° make                                   *ingenuity*
When thou shalt charge me with so black a deed?
Will not my tongue be mute, my frail joints shake,
Mine eyes forgo their light,° my false heart bleed?                          *power of vision*
The guilt being great, the fear doth still exceed,
230  　And extreme fear can neither fight nor fly,
　　But coward-like with trembling terror die.

'Had Collatinus killed my son or sire,
Or lain in ambush to betray my life,
Or were he not my dear friend, this desire
235  Might have excuse to work upon his wife
As in revenge or quittal° of such strife.                                     *requital*
　　But as he is my kinsman, my dear friend,
　　The shame and fault finds no excuse nor end.

'Shameful it is—ay, if the fact° be known.                                    *deed*
240  Hateful it is—there is no hate in loving.
I'll beg her love—but she is not her own.
The worst is but denial and reproving;
My will is strong past reason's weak removing.
　　Who fears a sentence° or an old man's saw°                            *maxim / proverb*
245  　Shall by a painted cloth be kept in awe.'⁶

Thus graceless holds he disputation
'Tween frozen conscience and hot-burning will,
And with good thoughts makes dispensation,°                                  *dispenses*
Urging the worser sense for vantage still;
250  Which in a moment doth confound and kill
　　All pure effects,° and doth so far proceed                              *tendencies*
　　That what is vile shows like a virtuous deed.

Quoth he, 'She took me kindly by the hand,
And gazed for tidings in my eager eyes,
255  Fearing some hard news from the warlike band
Where her belovèd Collatinus lies.
O how her fear did make her colour rise!
　　First red as roses that on lawn° we lay,                                *fine linen*
　　Then white as lawn, the roses took away.

6. Will be awed by a tapestry (often depicting morally significant narratives, as in lines 1366ff.).

260 'And how her hand, in my hand being locked,
Forced it to tremble with her loyal fear,
Which struck her sad, and then it faster rocked
Until her husband's welfare she did hear,
Whereat she smilèd with so sweet a cheer°          *an expression*
265     That had Narcissus[7] seen her as she stood
Self-love had never drowned him in the flood.

'Why hunt I then for colour° or excuses?          *pretext*
All orators are dumb when beauty pleadeth.
Poor wretches have remorse in poor abuses;°          *regret minor lapses*
270 Love thrives not in the heart that shadows° dreadeth;          *illusory scruples*
Affection° is my captain, and he leadeth,          *Passion*
    And when his gaudy banner is displayed,
    The coward fights, and will not be dismayed.

'Then childish fear avaunt,° debating die,          *begone*
275 Respect° and reason wait on° wrinkled age!          *Circumspection / attend*
My heart shall never countermand mine eye,
Sad° pause and deep regard beseems the sage.          *Serious*
My part is youth, and beats these from the stage.[8]
    Desire my pilot is, beauty my prize.°          *pirate's booty*
280     Then who fears sinking where such treasure lies?'

As corn° o'ergrown by weeds, so heedful fear          *grain*
Is almost choked by unresisted lust.
Away he steals, with open list'ning ear,
Full of foul hope and full of fond° mistrust,          *foolish; passionate*
285 Both which as servitors to the unjust
    So cross him with their opposite persuasion
    That now he vows a league, and now invasion.

Within his thought her heavenly image sits,
And in the selfsame seat sits Collatine.
290 That eye which looks on her confounds his wits,
That eye which him beholds, as° more divine,          *because it is*
Unto a view so false will not incline,
    But with a pure appeal seeks° to the heart,          *applies*
    Which once corrupted, takes the worser part,

295 And therein heartens up his servile powers[9]
Who, flattered by their leader's jocund show,
Stuff up his lust as minutes fill up hours,
And as their captain, so their pride doth grow,
Paying more slavish tribute than they owe.[1]
300     By reprobate desire thus madly led
    The Roman lord marcheth to Lucrece' bed.

The locks between her chamber and his will,
Each one by him enforced, retires his ward;°          *withdraws its bolt*
But as they open they all rate° his ill,          *berate (by squeaking)*

---

7. In classical mythology, a youth who fell in love with his reflection in a pool; in some versions of the tale, he drowned attempting to kiss the image.
8. Like the Vice character in the medieval morality play.

9. Appetites or passions, imagined as servants of the heart, the seat of conscience.
1. That is, debasing themselves by collaborating and encouraging the corrupted heart.

305    Which drives the creeping thief to some regard.°         *caution*
       The threshold grates the door to have him heard,
          Night-wand'ring weasels² shriek to see him there.
          They fright him, yet he still pursues his fear.°       *what makes him fear*

       As each unwilling portal yields him way,
310    Through little vents and crannies of the place
       The wind wars with his torch to make him stay,
       And blows the smoke of it into his face,
       Extinguishing his conduct° in this case.          *guide; behavior*
          But his hot heart, which fond desire doth scorch,
315       Puffs forth another wind that fires the torch,

       And being lighted, by the light he spies
       Lucretia's glove wherein her needle sticks.
       He takes it from the rushes where it lies,
       And gripping it, the needle his finger pricks,
320    As who should say 'This glove to wanton tricks
          Is not inured. Return again in haste.
          Thou seest our mistress' ornaments are chaste.'

       But all these poor forbiddings could not stay him;
       He in the worst sense consters° their denial.        *construes*
325    The doors, the wind, the glove that did delay him
       He takes for accidental things of trial,°        *tests of resolve*
       Or as those bars which stop the hourly dial,³
          Who with a ling'ring stay his course doth let°       *hinder; permit*
          Till every minute pays the hour his debt.

330    'So, so,' quoth he, 'these lets attend the time,
       Like little frosts that sometime threat the spring
       To add a more rejoicing to the prime,°           *spring*
       And give the sneapèd° birds more cause to sing.     *pinched with cold*
       Pain pays the income° of each precious thing.       *is the price of*
335       Huge rocks, high winds, strong pirates, shelves,° and sands    *reefs*
          The merchant fears, ere rich at home he lands.'

       Now is he come unto the chamber door
       That shuts him from the heaven of his thought,
       Which with a yielding latch, and with no more,
340    Hath barred him from the blessèd thing he sought.
       So from° himself impiety hath wrought°         *unlike / made him*
          That for his prey to pray he doth begin,
          As if the heavens should countenance his sin.

       But in the midst of his unfruitful prayer
345    Having solicited th'eternal power
       That his foul thoughts might compass° his fair fair,⁴     *obtain; embrace*
       And they would stand auspicious to the hour,
       Even there he starts.° Quoth he, 'I must deflower.     *is startled*
          The powers to whom I pray abhor this fact;°       *deed*
350       How can they then assist me in the act?

2. Weasels were kept to catch vermin.        before jerking forward.
3. The marks on a clock face, where the hands pause     4. His virtuous and beautiful one.

'Then love and fortune be my gods, my guide!
My will is backed with resolution.
Thoughts are but dreams till their effects be tried;
The blackest sin is cleared with absolution.
355   Against love's fire fear's frost hath dissolution.
    The eye of heaven is out,° and misty night         *extinguished*
    Covers the shame that follows sweet delight.'

This said, his guilty hand plucked up the latch,
And with his knee the door he opens wide.
360   The dove sleeps fast that this night-owl will catch.
Thus treason works ere traitors be espied.
Who sees the lurking serpent steps aside,
    But she, sound sleeping, fearing no such thing,
    Lies at the mercy of his mortal° sting.         *lethal*

365   Into the chamber wickedly he stalks,°         *steals*
And gazeth on her yet-unstainèd bed.
The curtains being close,° about he walks,         *shut*
Rolling his greedy eye-balls in his head.
By their high treason is his heart misled,
370    Which gives the watchword to his hand full soon
    To draw the cloud° that hides the silver moon.         *(the bed curtain)*

Look as° the fair and fiery-pointed sun         *See how*
Rushing from forth a cloud bereaves our sight,
Even so, the curtain drawn, his eyes begun
375   To wink,° being blinded with a greater light.         *close*
Whether it is that she reflects so bright
    That dazzleth them, or else some shame supposed,
    But blind they are, and keep themselves enclosed.

O had they in that darksome prison died,
380   Then had they seen the period° of their ill.         *end*
Then Collatine again by Lucrece' side
In his clear° bed might have reposèd still.         *undefiled*
But they must ope, this blessèd league° to kill,         *marriage*
    And holy-thoughted Lucrece to their sight
385    Must sell her joy, her life, her world's delight.

Her lily hand her rosy cheek lies under,
Coz'ning° the pillow of a lawful kiss,         *Cheating*
Who therefore angry seems to part in sunder,°         *in two*
Swelling on either side to want his bliss;[5]
390   Between whose hills her head entombèd is,
    Where like a virtuous monument she lies
    To be admired of lewd unhallowed eyes.

Without the bed her other fair hand was,
On the green coverlet, whose perfect white
395   Showed like an April daisy on the grass,
With pearly sweat resembling dew of night.

5. Because it is denied its pleasure (of her lips touching its surface).

Her eyes like marigolds[6] had sheathed their light,
   And canopied in darkness sweetly lay
   Till they might open to adorn the day.

400 Her hair like golden threads played with her breath—
   O modest wantons, wanton modesty!—
   Showing life's triumph in the map° of death,            *image*
   And death's dim look in life's mortality.
   Each° in her sleep themselves so beautify        *(life and death)*
405    As if between them twain there were no strife,
    But that life lived in death, and death in life.

Her breasts like ivory globes circled with blue,
   A pair of maiden[7] worlds unconquerèd,
   Save of their lord no bearing yoke they knew,
410 And him by oath they truly honourèd.
   These worlds in Tarquin new ambition bred,
    Who like a foul usurper went about
    From this fair throne to heave the owner out.

What could he see but mightily he noted?
415 What did he note but strongly he desired?
   What he beheld, on that he firmly doted,
   And in his will° his wilful eye he tired.[8]           *lust*
   With more than admiration he admired
    Her azure veins, her alabaster skin,
420    Her coral lips, her snow-white dimpled chin.

As the grim lion fawneth° o'er his prey,         *shows delight*
   Sharp hunger by the conquest satisfied,
   So o'er this sleeping soul doth Tarquin stay,
   His rage of lust by gazing qualified,°          *mollified*
425 Slaked not suppressed for standing by her side.
   His eye which late this mutiny restrains
   Unto a greater uproar tempts his veins,

And they like straggling slaves° for pillage fighting,   *lowborn soldiers*
   Obdurate vassals fell° exploits effecting,        *fierce*
430 In bloody death and ravishment delighting,
   Nor children's tears nor mothers' groans respecting,
   Swell in their pride, the onset still° expecting.    *at any moment*
    Anon his beating heart, alarum° striking,     *signal to attack*
    Gives the hot charge, and bids them do their liking.

435 His drumming heart cheers up his burning eye,
   His eye commends° the leading to his hand.      *entrusts*
   His hand, as proud of such a dignity,
   Smoking with pride marched on to make his stand
   On her bare breast, the heart of all her land,
440    Whose ranks of blue veins as his hand did scale°    *climb*
   Left their round turrets destitute and pale.

6. The pot marigold folds up its flowers at day's end.    8. Wearied; fed greedily (as a hawk tears flesh with its
7. Used of an unconquered citadel.                 beak).

They, must'ring° to the quiet cabinet°                    *gathering / room (heart)*
Where their dear governess° and lady lies,                            *ruler*
Do tell her she is dreadfully beset,
445    And fright her with confusion of their cries.
She much amazed breaks ope her locked-up eyes,
    Who, peeping forth this tumult to behold,
    Are by his flaming torch dimmed and controlled.°            *overwhelmed*

Imagine her as one in dead of night
450    From forth dull sleep by dreadful fancy waking,
That thinks she hath beheld some ghastly sprite
Whose grim aspect sets every joint a-shaking.
What terror 'tis! But she in worser taking,°                        *plight*
    From sleep disturbèd, heedfully doth view
455    The sight which makes supposèd terror true.

Wrapped and confounded in a thousand fears,
Like to a new-killed bird she trembling lies.
She dares not look, yet, winking,° there appears        *shutting her eyes*
Quick-shifting antics,° ugly in her eyes.                  *grotesque shapes*
460    Such shadows are the weak brain's forgeries,
    Who, angry that the eyes fly from their lights,
    In darkness daunts them with more dreadful sights.

His hand that yet remains upon her breast—
Rude ram,° to batter such an ivory wall—                  *battering ram*
465    May feel her heart, poor citizen, distressed,
Wounding itself to death, rise up and fall,
Beating her bulk,° that his hand shakes withal.°        *chest / as well*
    This moves in him more rage and lesser pity
    To make the breach and enter this sweet city.

470    First like a trumpet doth his tongue begin
To sound a parley⁹ to his heartless° foe,                       *terrified*
Who o'er the white sheet peers her whiter chin,
The reason of this rash alarm to know,
Which he by dumb demeanour° seeks to show.                    *mute gesture*
475    But she with vehement prayers urgeth still
    Under what colour° he commits this ill.                      *pretext*

Thus he replies: 'The colour in thy face,
That even for anger makes the lily pale
And the red rose blush at her own disgrace,
480    Shall plead for me and tell my loving tale.
Under that colour° am I come to scale                    *pretext; hue; flag*
    Thy never-conquered fort. The fault is thine,
    For those thine eyes betray thee unto mine.

'Thus I forestall thee, if thou mean to chide:
485    Thy beauty hath ensnared thee to this night,
Where thou with patience must my will abide,
My will that marks thee for my earth's° delight,            *earthly; bodily*
Which I to conquer sought with all my might.

9. A call to a negotiation.

But as reproof and reason beat it° dead,        *(my lust)*
490   By thy bright beauty was it newly bred.

'I see what crosses° my attempt will bring,       *misfortunes*
I know what thorns the growing rose defends;
I think° the honey guarded with a sting;       *know*
All this beforehand counsel° comprehends.       *wisdom*
495   But will is deaf, and hears no heedful friends.
     Only he hath an eye to gaze on beauty,
     And dotes on what he looks, 'gainst law or duty.

'I have debated even in my soul
What wrong, what shame, what sorrow I shall breed;
500   But nothing can affection's° course control,       *passion's*
Or stop the headlong fury of his speed.
I know repentant tears ensue° the deed,       *follow*
     Reproach, disdain, and deadly enmity,
     Yet strive I to embrace mine infamy.'

505   This said, he shakes aloft his Roman blade,
Which like a falcon tow'ring in the skies
Coucheth the fowl° below with his wings' shade       *Makes the prey crouch*
Whose crooked beak threats, if he° mount he dies.       *(the fowl)*
So under his insulting° falchion lies       *triumphantly exulting*
510      Harmless Lucretia, marking what he tells
     With trembling fear, as fowl hear falcons' bells.[1]

'Lucrece,' quoth he, 'this night I must enjoy thee.
If thou deny, then force must work my way,
For in thy bed I purpose to destroy thee.
515   That done, some worthless slave of thine I'll slay
To kill thine honour with thy life's decay;[2]
     And in thy dead arms do I mean to place him,
     Swearing I slew him seeing thee embrace him.

'So thy surviving husband shall remain
520   The scornful mark of every open eye,°       *observer*
Thy kinsmen hang their heads at this disdain,
Thy issue blurred with nameless bastardy,[3]
And thou, the author of their obloquy,
     Shalt have thy trespass cited up in rhymes°       *described in ballads*
525      And sung by children in succeeding times.

'But if thou yield, I rest thy secret friend.
The fault unknown is as a thought unacted.
A little harm done to a great good end
For lawful policy remains enacted.[4]
530   The poisonous simple° sometime is compacted°       *ingredient / mixed*
     In a pure° compound; being so applied,       *benign*
     His venom in effect is purified.

---

1. Hunting falcons had bells attached to their legs.   father's name is unknown.
2. To destroy your reputation along with your life.   4. *For . . . enacted:* Is allowed as proper statesmanship.
3. Your children suspected of being bastards whose

'Then for thy husband and thy children's sake
Tender my suit;° bequeath not to their lot                    *Regard my plea*
535  The shame that from them no device[5] can take,
The blemish that will never be forgot,
Worse than a slavish wipe or birth-hour's blot;[6]
    For marks descried in men's nativity
    Are nature's faults, not their own infamy.'

540  Here with a cockatrice'[7] dead-killing eye
He rouseth up himself, and makes a pause,
While she, the picture of pure piety,
Like a white hind° under the gripe's° sharp claws,            *doe / griffin*
Pleads in a wilderness where are no laws
545    To the rough beast that knows no gentle right,°          *law of gentility*
    Nor aught obeys but his foul appetite.

But when a black-faced cloud the world doth threat,
In his dim mist th'aspiring mountains hiding,
From earth's dark womb some gentle gust doth get
550  Which blows these pitchy vapours from their biding,°       *place*
Hind'ring their present° fall by this dividing;              *immediate*
    So his unhallowed haste her words delays,
    And moody Pluto winks while Orpheus plays.[8]

Yet, foul night-waking cat, he doth but dally
555  While in his holdfast foot the weak mouse panteth.
Her sad behaviour feeds his vulture folly,°                   *ravenous insanity*
A swallowing gulf° that even in plenty wanteth.             *whirlpool; belly*
His ear her prayers admits, but his heart granteth
    No penetrable entrance to her plaining.°               *lament*
560    Tears harden lust, though marble wear with raining.

Her pity-pleading eyes are sadly fixed
In the remorseless wrinkles of his face.
Her modest eloquence with sighs is mixed,
Which to her oratory adds more grace.
565  She puts the period often from his° place,                   *its*
    And midst the sentence so her accent breaks
    That twice she doth begin ere once she speaks.

She conjures him by high almighty Jove,
By knighthood, gentry,° and sweet friendship's oath,        *noble birth*
570  By her untimely tears, her husband's love,
By holy human law and common troth,[9]
By heaven and earth and all the power of both,
    That to his borrowed° bed he make retire,              *(guest)*
    And stoop[1] to honour, not to foul desire.

---

5. Ingenuity; heraldic emblem.
6. A slave's brand or birthmark.
7. Legendary monster whose glance was deadly.
8. When Orpheus, a legendary musician and poet, attempted to regain his dead wife from the underworld, he charmed Pluto, god of the underworld, by playing on the lyre.
9. *common troth:* the good faith that binds communities together.
1. Swoop down to a lure (in falconry); lie down; subject himself.

575 Quoth she, 'Reward not hospitality
With such black payment as thou hast pretended.° *offered*
Mud not the fountain that gave drink to thee;
Mar not the thing that cannot be amended;
End thy ill aim before thy shoot be ended.
580     He is no woodman° that doth bend his bow *sportsman*
    To strike a poor unseasonable° doe. *out-of-season*

'My husband is thy friend; for his sake spare me.
Thyself art mighty; for thine own sake leave me;
Myself a weakling; do not then ensnare me.
585 Thou look'st not like deceit; do not deceive me.
My sighs like whirlwinds labour hence to heave thee.
    If ever man were moved with woman's moans,
    Be movèd with my tears, my sighs, my groans.

'All which together, like a troubled ocean,
590 Beat at thy rocky and wreck-threat'ning heart
To soften it with their continual motion,
For stones dissolved to water do convert.
    O, if no harder than a stone thou art,
    Melt at my tears, and be compassionate.
595     Soft pity enters at an iron gate.

'In Tarquin's likeness I did entertain thee.
Hast thou put on his shape to do him shame?
To all the host of heaven I complain me.
Thou wrong'st his honour, wound'st his princely name.
600 Thou art not what thou seem'st, and if the same,
    Thou seem'st not what thou art, a god, a king,
    For kings like gods should govern everything.

'How will thy shame be seeded° in thine age *ripened*
When thus thy vices bud before thy spring?
605 If in thy hope° thou dar'st do such outrage, *If not yet in power*
What dar'st thou not when once thou art a king?
O be remembered, no outrageous thing
    From vassal actors° can be wiped away; *lowborn criminals*
    Then kings' misdeeds cannot be hid in clay.° *(even after death)*

610 'This deed will make thee only loved for° fear, *obeyed out of*
But happy monarchs still° are feared for love. *always*
With foul offenders thou perforce must bear
When they in thee the like offences prove.
If but for fear of this, thy will remove;
615     For princes are the glass,° the school, the book *mirror*
    Where subjects' eyes do learn, do read, do look.

'And wilt thou be the school where lust shall learn?
Must he in thee read lectures of such shame?
Wilt thou be glass wherein it shall discern
620 Authority for sin, warrant for blame,
    To privilege° dishonour in thy name? *justify*
    Thou back'st° reproach against long-living laud,° *support / praise*
    And mak'st fair reputation but a bawd.

'Hast thou command?° By him° that gave it thee,         *authority / (God)*
625  From a pure heart command thy rebel will.
Draw not thy sword to guard iniquity,
For it was lent thee all that brood° to kill.         *kind of thing*
Thy princely office how canst thou fulfil
When, patterned° by thy fault, foul sin may say     *given a precedent*
630  He learned to sin, and thou didst teach the way?

'Think but how vile a spectacle it were
To view thy present trespass in another.
Men's faults do seldom to themselves appear;
Their own transgressions partially they smother.°     *hide (from themselves)*
635  This guilt would seem death-worthy in thy brother.
   O, how are they wrapped in with infamies
   That from their own misdeeds askance° their eyes!     *turn away*

'To thee, to thee my heaved-up hands appeal,
Not to seducing lust, thy rash relier.[2]
640  I sue for exiled majesty's repeal;°         *recall from exile*
Let him return, and flatt'ring thoughts retire.
His true respect° will prison false desire,         *judgment*
   And wipe the dim mist from thy doting eyne,°     *eyes (archaic)*
   That thou shalt see thy state, and pity mine.'

645  'Have done,' quoth he; 'my uncontrollèd tide
Turns not, but swells the higher by this let.°         *restraint*
Small lights are soon blown out; huge fires abide,
And with the wind in greater fury fret.
The petty streams, that pay a daily debt
650    To their salt sovereign,° with their fresh falls' haste     *(the sea)*
   Add to his flow, but alter not his taste.'

'Thou art,' quoth she, 'a sea, a sovereign king,
And lo, there falls into thy boundless flood
Black lust, dishonour, shame, misgoverning,
655  Who seek to stain the ocean of thy blood.°     *disposition; birthright*
If all these petty ills shall change thy good,
   Thy sea within a puddle's womb is hearsed,°     *enclosed*
   And not the puddle in thy sea dispersed.

'So shall these slaves° be king, and thou their slave;     *(lust, dishonor, etc.)*
660  Thou nobly base, they basely dignified;
Thou their fair life, and they thy fouler grave;
Thou loathèd in their shame, they in thy pride.
The lesser thing should not the greater hide.
   The cedar stoops not to the base shrub's foot,
665    But low shrubs wither at the cedar's root.

'So let thy thoughts, low vassals to thy state'—
'No more,' quoth he, 'by heaven, I will not hear thee.
Yield to my love. If not, enforcèd hate
Instead of love's coy° touch shall rudely tear thee.     *gentle*
670  That done, despitefully° I mean to bear thee     *maliciously*

2. *thy rash relier*: on which you rashly rely.

Unto the base bed of some rascal groom°                    *servant*
To be thy partner in this shameful doom.'

This said, he sets his foot upon the light;
For light and lust are deadly enemies.
675   Shame folded up in blind concealing night
When most unseen, then most doth tyrannize.
The wolf hath seized his prey, the poor lamb cries,
    Till with her own white fleece° her voice controlled°    *(bedclothes) / overpowered*
    Entombs her outcry in her lips' sweet fold.°            *crevice; sheep pen*

680   For with the nightly linen that she wears
He pens her piteous clamours in her head,
Cooling his hot face in the chastest tears
That ever modest eyes with sorrow shed.
O that prone° lust should stain so pure a bed,            *headlong; eager*
685     The spots whereof could weeping purify,
    Her tears should drop on them perpetually!

But she hath lost a dearer thing than life,
And he hath won what he would lose again.
This forcèd league doth force a further strife,
690   This momentary joy breeds months of pain;
This hot desire converts to cold disdain.
    Pure chastity is rifled of her store,
    And lust, the thief, far poorer than before.

Look° as the full-fed hound or gorgèd hawk,               *Just*
695   Unapt for tender° smell or speedy flight,              *delicate*
Make slow pursuit, or altogether balk°                    *turn from*
The prey wherein by nature they delight,
So surfeit-taking Tarquin fares° this night.             *behaves; feeds*
    His taste delicious, in digestion souring,
700     Devours his will that lived by foul devouring.

O deeper sin than bottomless conceit°                     *unlimited fantasy*
Can comprehend in still imagination!
Drunken desire must vomit his receipt°                    *what he swallowed*
Ere he can see his own abomination.
705   While lust is in his pride, no exclamation
    Can curb his heat or rein his rash desire,
    Till like a jade° self-will himself doth tire.         *recalcitrant horse*

And then with lank and lean discoloured cheek,
With heavy eye, knit brow, and strengthless pace,
710   Feeble desire, all recreant,[3] poor, and meek,
Like to a bankrupt beggar wails his case.
The flesh being proud, desire doth fight with grace,
    For there it revels, and when that decays,°            *subsides*
    The guilty rebel for remission° prays.                *pardon*

715   So fares it with this faultful lord of Rome
Who this accomplishment so hotly chased;

---

3. Cowardly; faithless; exhausted.

For now against himself he sounds° this doom,°    *pronounces / sentence*
That through the length of times he stands disgraced.
Besides, his soul's fair temple is defaced,
720  To whose weak ruins muster troops of cares·
  To ask the spotted princess° how she fares.    *(the defiled soul)*

She says her subjects with foul insurrection
Have battered down her consecrated wall,
And by their mortal° fault brought in subjection    *deadly*
725 Her immortality, and made her thrall
To living death and pain perpetual,
  Which° in her prescience she controllèd still,    *(the soul's subjects)*
  But her foresight could not forestall their will.

Ev'n in this thought through the dark night he stealeth,
730 A captive victor that hath lost in gain,
Bearing away the wound that nothing healeth,
The scar that will, despite of cure, remain;
Leaving his spoil° perplexed in greater pain.    *prey*
  She bears the load of lust he left behind,
735  And he the burden of a guilty mind.

He like a thievish dog creeps sadly thence;
She like a wearied lamb lies panting there.
He scowls, and hates himself for his offence;
She, desperate, with her nails her flesh doth tear.
740 He faintly flies, sweating with guilty fear;
  She stays, exclaiming on° the direful night.    *denouncing*
  He runs, and chides his vanished loathed delight.

He thence departs, a heavy convertite;°    *sad penitent*
She there remains, a hopeless castaway.
745 He in his speed looks for the morning light;
She prays she never may behold the day.
'For day,' quoth she, 'night's scapes° doth open lay,    *sins*
  And my true eyes have never practised how
  To cloak offences with a cunning brow.

750 'They think not but that every eye can see
The same disgrace which they themselves behold,
And therefore would they still in darkness be,
To have their unseen sin remain untold.
For they their guilt with weeping will unfold,
755  And grave,° like water that doth eat in steel,⁴    *engrave*
  Upon my cheeks what helpless shame I feel.'

Here she exclaims against repose and rest,
And bids her eyes hereafter still be blind.
She wakes her heart by beating on her breast,
760 And bids it leap from thence where it may find
Some purer chest to close° so pure a mind.    *enclose*
  Frantic with grief, thus breathes she forth her spite°    *reproach*
  Against the unseen secrecy of night:

4. Aqua fortis (literally, "strong water"), nitric acid.

'O comfort-killing night, image of hell,
765  Dim register° and notary of shame,                                    *recorder*
Black stage for tragedies and murders fell,
Vast sin-concealing chaos, nurse of blame!
Blind muffled bawd, dark harbour for defame,°                         *infamy*
     Grim cave of death, whisp'ring conspirator
770       With close-tongued treason and the ravisher!

'O hateful, vaporous, and foggy night,
Since thou art guilty of my cureless crime,
Muster thy mists to meet the eastern light,
Make war against proportioned° course of time.                        *orderly*
775  Or if thou wilt permit the sun to climb
     His wonted height, yet ere he go to bed
     Knit poisonous clouds about his golden head.

'With rotten damps° ravish the morning air,                            *vapors*
Let their exhaled unwholesome breaths make sick
780  The life of purity, the supreme fair,°                            *(the sun)*
Ere he arrive his weary noon-tide prick;°                     *mark on a clock*
And let thy musty vapours march so thick
     That in their smoky ranks his smothered light
     May set at noon, and make perpetual night.

785  'Were Tarquin night, as he is but night's child,
The silver-shining queen⁵ he would distain;°                           *stain*
Her twinkling handmaids° too, by him defiled,                     *(the stars)*
Through night's black bosom should not peep again.
So should I have co-partners in my pain,
790       And fellowship in woe doth woe assuage,
     As palmers'° chat makes short their pilgrimage.                  *pilgrims'*

'Where now I have no one to blush with me,
To cross their arms⁶ and hang their heads with mine,
To mask their brows and hide their infamy,
795  But I alone, alone must sit and pine,
Seasoning the earth with showers of silver brine,
     Mingling my talk with tears, my grief with groans,
     Poor wasting monuments° of lasting moans.                *short-lived tokens*

'O night, thou furnace of foul reeking smoke,
800  Let not the jealous° day behold that face                       *suspicious*
Which underneath thy black all-hiding cloak
Immodestly lies martyred with disgrace!
Keep still possession of thy gloomy place,
     That all the faults which in thy reign are made
805       May likewise be sepulchred in thy shade.

'Make me not object° to the tell-tale day:                           *manifest*
The light will show charactered° in my brow                           *written*
The story of sweet chastity's decay,
The impious breach of holy wedlock vow.
810  Yea, the illiterate that know not how

---

5. The moon, symbol of chastity.          6. This is a conventional gesture of melancholy.

To cipher° what is writ in learnèd books                    *decipher*
Will quote° my loathsome trespass in my looks.              *note*

'The nurse to still her child will tell my story,
And fright her crying babe with Tarquin's name.
815   The orator to deck his oratory
Will couple my reproach to Tarquin's shame.
Feast-finding minstrels⁷ tuning my defame
    Will tie the hearers to attend° each line,              *listen to*
    How Tarquin wrongèd me, I Collatine.

820   'Let my good name, that senseless° reputation,         *intangible*
For Collatine's dear love be kept unspotted;
If that be made a theme for disputation,
The branches of another root are rotted,⁸
And undeserved reproach to him allotted
825   That is as clear from this attaint° of mine            *stain*
    As I ere this was pure to Collatine.

'O unseen shame, invisible disgrace!
O unfelt sore, crest-wounding⁹ private scar!
Reproach° is stamped in Collatinus' face,                   *Reproof; dishonor*
830   And Tarquin's eye may read the mot° afar,             *motto*
How he in peace is wounded, not in war.
    Alas, how many bear such shameful blows,
    Which not themselves but he that gives them knows!

'If, Collatine, thine honour lay in me,
835   From me by strong assault it is bereft;
My honey lost, and I, a drone-like bee,
Have no perfection of my summer left,¹
But robbed and ransacked by injurious theft.
    In thy weak hive a wandering wasp hath crept,
840   And sucked the honey which thy chaste bee kept.

'Yet am I guilty of thy honour's wrack;°                    *ruin*
Yet for thy honour did I entertain him.
Coming from thee, I could not put him back,
For it had been dishonour to disdain him.
845   Besides, of weariness he did complain him,
    And talked of virtue—O unlooked-for evil,
    When virtue is profaned in such a devil!

'Why should the worm intrude the maiden bud,
Or hateful cuckoos hatch in sparrows' nests,
850   Or toads infect fair founts with venom° mud,         *venomous*
Or tyrant folly° lurk in gentle breasts,                    *cruel lewdness*
Or kings be breakers of their own behests?°                 *commands*
    But no perfection is so absolute
    That some impurity doth not pollute.

---

7. Minstrels were paid to perform at banquets.                lines 204–10).
8. That is, Collatine's reputation is also destroyed.          1. Have nothing left of what I made in the summer;
9. Damaging the coat of arms, hence family honor (cf.          have none of the purity of my prime remaining.

855 'The agèd man that coffers up his gold
Is plagued with cramps, and gouts, and painful fits,
And scarce hath eyes his treasure to behold,
But like still-pining Tantalus² he sits,
And useless barns° the harvest of his wits,                    *hoards*
860     Having no other pleasure of his gain
        But torment that it cannot cure his pain.

'So then he hath it when he cannot use it,
And leaves it to be mastered° by his young,°        *possessed / children*
Who in their pride do presently° abuse it.                  *immediately*
865 Their father was too weak and they too strong
To hold their cursèd-blessèd fortune long.
        The sweets we wish for turn to loathèd sours
        Even in the moment that we call them ours.

'Unruly blasts wait on the tender spring,
870 Unwholesome weeds take root with precious flowers,
The adder hisses where the sweet birds sing,
What virtue breeds, iniquity devours.
We have no good that we can say is ours
        But ill-annexèd opportunity³
875     Or° kills his life or else his quality.                   *Either*

'O opportunity, thy guilt is great!
'Tis thou that execut'st the traitor's treason;
Thou sets the wolf where he the lamb may get;
Whoever plots the sin, thou point'st° the season.          *appoint*
880 'Tis thou that spurn'st at right, at law, at reason;
        And in thy shady cell where none may spy him
        Sits sin, to seize the souls that wander by him.

'Thou mak'st the vestal⁴ violate her oath,
Thou blow'st the fire when temperance is thawed,
885 Thou smother'st honesty, thou murd'rest troth,
Thou foul abettor, thou notorious bawd;°                  *procurer*
Thou plantest scandal and displacest laud.
        Thou ravisher, thou traitor, thou false thief,
        Thy honey turns to gall, thy joy to grief.

890 'Thy secret pleasure turns to open shame,
Thy private feasting to a public fast,
Thy smoothing° titles to a ragged name,                  *flattering*
Thy sugared tongue to bitter wormwood taste.
Thy violent vanities can never last.
895     How comes it then, vile opportunity,
        Being so bad, such numbers seek for thee?

'When wilt thou be the humble suppliant's friend,
And bring him where his suit may be obtained?
When wilt thou sort° an hour great strifes to end,          *select*

2. A mythological figure who was punished in Hades by
eternal hunger and thirst; food and water were always
visible but receded at his approach.
3. Bad circumstances joined to or following from the
good.
4. The priestess of Vesta, Roman goddess of the hearth
and household; vestals were sworn to lifelong virginity.

900 Or free that soul which wretchedness hath chained,
 Give physic° to the sick, ease to the pained?       *medicine*
  The poor, lame, blind, halt,° creep, cry out for thee,     *limp*
  But they ne'er meet with opportunity.

'The patient dies while the physician sleeps,
905 The orphan pines while the oppressor feeds,
 Justice is feasting while the widow weeps,
 Advice° is sporting while infection breeds.       *(medical advice)*
 Thou grant'st no time for charitable deeds.
  Wrath, envy, treason, rape, and murder's rages,
910   Thy heinous hours wait on them as their pages.

'When truth and virtue have to do with thee
 A thousand crosses° keep them from thy aid.      *impediments*
 They buy° thy help, but sin ne'er gives a fee;     *(must pay for)*
 He gratis comes, and thou art well appaid°      *satisfied*
915 As well to hear as grant what he hath said.
  My Collatine would else have come to me
  When Tarquin did, but he was stayed by thee.

'Guilty thou art of murder and of theft,
 Guilty of perjury and subornation,[5]
920 Guilty of treason, forgery, and shift,°         *fraud*
 Guilty of incest, that abomination:
 An accessory by thine inclination°        *nature*
  To all sins past and all that are to come
  From the creation to the general doom.

925 'Misshapen time, copesmate° of ugly night,      *comrade*
 Swift subtle post,° carrier of grisly care,      *messenger*
 Eater of youth, false slave to false delight,
 Base watch° of woes, sin's pack-horse, virtue's snare,  *town crier; announcer*
 Thou nursest all, and murd'rest all that are.
930   O hear me then, injurious shifting° time;    *changing; traitorous*
  Be guilty of my death, since° of my crime.     *as thou art*

'Why hath thy servant opportunity
 Betrayed the hours thou gav'st me to repose,
 Cancelled my fortunes, and enchainèd me
935 To endless date° of never-ending woes?      *duration*
 Time's office is to fine° the hate of foes,     *end; punish*
  To eat up errors by opinion° bred,       *rumor*
  Not spend the dowry of a lawful bed.

'Time's glory is to calm contending kings,
940 To unmask falsehood and bring truth to light,
 To stamp the seal of time in agèd things,
 To wake the morn and sentinel° the night,      *guard*
 To wrong the wronger till he render right,
  To ruinate proud buildings with thy hours
945   And smear with dust their glitt'ring golden towers;

5. Bribing others to give false testimony.

'To fill with worm-holes stately monuments,
To feed oblivion with decay of things,
To blot old books and alter their contents,
To pluck the quills from ancient ravens' wings,
950   To dry the old oak's sap and blemish° springs,      *contaminate*
     To spoil antiquities of hammered steel,
     And turn the giddy round of fortune's wheel;

'To show the beldame° daughters of her daughter,    *old woman*
To make the child a man, the man a child,
955   To slay the tiger that doth live by slaughter,
To tame the unicorn and lion wild,
To mock the subtle in themselves beguiled,[6]
     To cheer the ploughman with increaseful crops,
     And waste huge stones with little water drops.

960   'Why work'st thou mischief in thy pilgrimage,
Unless thou couldst return to make amends?
One poor retiring[7] minute in an age
Would purchase thee a thousand thousand friends,
Lending him wit that to bad debtors lends.
965     O this dread night, wouldst thou one hour come back,
     I could prevent this storm and shun thy wrack!

'Thou ceaseless lackey° to eternity,    *eternal servant*
With some mischance cross Tarquin in his flight.
Devise extremes beyond extremity
970   To make him curse this cursèd crimeful night.
Let ghastly shadows his lewd eyes affright,
     And the dire thought of his committed evil
     Shape every bush a hideous shapeless devil.

'Disturb his hours of rest with restless trances;°    *dreams; seizures*
975   Afflict him in his bed with bedrid groans;
Let there bechance him pitiful mischances
To make him moan, but pity not his moans.
Stone him with hardened hearts harder than stones,
     And let mild women to him lose their mildness,
980     Wilder to him than tigers in their wildness.

'Let him have time to tear his curlèd hair,
Let him have time against himself to rave,
Let him have time of time's help to despair,
Let him have time to live a loathèd slave,
985   Let him have time a beggar's orts° to crave,    *scraps*
     And time to see one that by alms doth live
     Disdain to him disdainèd scraps to give.

'Let him have time to see his friends his foes,
And merry fools to mock at him resort.°    *gather*
990   Let him have time to mark how slow time goes
In time of sorrow, and how swift and short

---

6. The cunning, taken in by their own schemes.
7. Returning (thus permitting people to do things differently).

His time of folly and his time of sport;
　　And ever let his unrecalling crime[8]
　　Have time to wail th'abusing of his time.

995 'O time, thou tutor both to good and bad,
Teach me to curse him that thou taught'st this ill;
At his own shadow let the thief run mad,
Himself himself seek every hour to kill;
Such wretched hands such wretched blood should spill,
1000 　　For who so base would such an office have
　　As sland'rous deathsman° to so base a slave?　　　　　　　*detested executioner*

'The baser is he, coming from a king,
To shame his hope with deeds degenerate.
The mightier man, the mightier is the thing
1005 That makes him honoured or begets him hate,
For greatest scandal waits on greatest state.[9]
　　The moon being clouded presently° is missed,　　　　　　　*immediately*
　　But little stars may hide them when they list.°　　　　　　　*wish*

'The crow may bathe his coal-black wings in mire
1010 And unperceived fly with the filth away,
But if the like the snow-white swan desire,
The stain upon his silver down will stay.
Poor grooms° are sightless° night, kings glorious day.　　　　*servants / dark*
　　Gnats are unnoted wheresoe'er they fly,
1015 　　But eagles gazed upon with every eye.

'Out, idle words, servants to shallow fools,
Unprofitable sounds, weak arbitrators!
Busy yourselves in skill-contending schools,°　　　　　　　　*(of rhetoric)*
Debate where leisure serves with dull debaters,
1020 To trembling clients be you mediators;
　　For me, I force° not argument a straw,　　　　　　　　　　　*value*
　　Since that my case is past the help of law.

'In vain I rail at opportunity,
At time, at Tarquin, and uncheerful night.
1025 In vain I cavil with° mine infamy,　　　　　　　　　　　　　*object to*
In vain I spurn at my confirmed despite.°　　　　　　　　*irreparable injury*
This helpless° smoke of words doth me no right;　　　　　*unhelpful; weak*
　　The remedy indeed to do me good
　　Is to let forth my foul defilèd blood.

1030 'Poor hand, why quiver'st thou at this decree?
Honour thyself to rid me of this shame,
For if I die, my honour lives in thee,
But if I live, thou liv'st in my defame.°　　　　　　　　　　　*infamy*
Since thou couldst not defend thy loyal dame,
1035 　　And wast afeard to scratch her wicked foe,
　　Kill both thyself and her for yielding so.'

8. Crime that cannot be undone.　　　　　　　9. Attends those of highest rank.

This said, from her betumbled couch she starteth,
To find some desp'rate instrument of death.
But this, no slaughterhouse, no tool imparteth°                    *furnishes*
1040 To make more vent° for passage of her breath,                    *a bigger hole*
Which thronging through her lips so vanisheth
   As smoke from Etna that in air consumes,
   Or that which from dischargèd cannon fumes.

'In vain,' quoth she, 'I live, and seek in vain
1045 Some happy mean to end a hapless life.
I feared by Tarquin's falchion to be slain,
Yet for the selfsame purpose seek a knife.
But when I feared I was a loyal wife;
   So am I now—O no, that cannot be,
1050    Of that true type° hath Tarquin rifled me.                    *pattern of virtue*

'O, that is gone for which I sought to live,
And therefore now I need not fear to die.
To clear this spot by death, at least I give
A badge of fame to slander's livery,°                    *servant's uniform*
1055 A dying life to living infamy.
   Poor helpless help, the treasure stol'n away,
   To burn the guiltless casket where it lay!

'Well, well, dear Collatine, thou shalt not know
The stainèd taste of violated troth.
1060 I will not wrong thy true affection so
To flatter thee with an infringèd oath.
This bastard graft[1] shall never come to growth.
   He shall not boast, who did thy stock pollute,
   That thou art doting father of his fruit,

1065 'Nor shall he smile at thee in secret thought,
Nor laugh with his companions at thy state.
But thou shalt know thy int'rest° was not bought                    *property*
Basely with gold, but stol'n from forth thy gate.
For me, I am the mistress of my fate,
1070    And with my trespass never will dispense°                    *dispense with = excuse*
   Till life to death acquit° my forced offence.                    *atone for*

'I will not poison thee with my attaint,°                    *contamination*
Nor fold° my fault in cleanly coined excuses.                    *envelop*
My sable ground[2] of sin I will not paint
1075 To hide the truth of this false night's abuses.
My tongue shall utter all; mine eyes, like sluices,
   As from a mountain spring that feeds a dale
   Shall gush pure streams to purge my impure tale.'

1080 By this, lamenting Philomel[3] had ended
The well-tuned warble of her nightly sorrow,

---

1. Lucrece assumes that Tarquin has made her pregnant. Her image is from the grafting of plants, in which
two different kinds of plants are artificially forced to
grow as one; a "bastard slip" is an unwanted shoot.
2. Black background (a heraldic term).

3. The nightingale. In classical mythology, Philomela
was raped by King Tereus, her sister's husband, and
with her sister took vengeance on him. All three were
changed into birds (see Ovid, *Metamorphoses* 6).

And solemn night with slow sad gait descended
To ugly hell, when lo, the blushing morrow
Lends light to all fair eyes that light will borrow.
But cloudy° Lucrece shames° herself to see,　　　　　　　　　　*melancholy / is ashamed*
1085　And therefore still in night would cloistered be.

Revealing day through every cranny spies,
And seems to point her out where she sits weeping;
To whom she sobbing speaks, 'O eye of eyes,
Why pry'st thou through my window? Leave thy peeping,
1090　Mock with thy tickling beams eyes that are sleeping,
　　　Brand not my forehead with thy piercing light,
　　　For day hath naught to do what's done by night.'

Thus cavils she with everything she sees:
True grief is fond° and testy as a child　　　　　　　　　　　*foolish*
1095　Who, wayward once,° his mood with naught agrees;　　　*once out of sorts*
Old woes, not infant sorrows, bear them mild.°　　　　　*bear themselves mildly*
Continuance tames the one; the other wild,
　　　Like an unpractised swimmer plunging still,°　　　　　*constantly*
　　　With too much labour drowns for want of skill.

1100　So she, deep drenchèd in a sea of care,
Holds disputation with each thing she views,
And to herself all sorrow doth compare;
No object but her passion's strength renews,
And as one shifts,° another straight° ensues.　　　　　　*moves / immediately*
1105　　Sometime her grief is dumb° and hath no words,　　　*mute*
　　　Sometime 'tis mad and too much talk affords.

The little birds that tune their morning's joy
Make her moans mad with their sweet melody,
For mirth doth search° the bottom of annoy;°　　　　　　*probe / vexation*
1110　Sad souls are slain° in merry company;　　　　　　　*overcome with distress*
Grief best is pleased with grief's society.
　　　True sorrow then is feelingly sufficed°　　　　　　　*properly contented*
　　　When with like semblance it is sympathized.°　　　　*matched*

'Tis double death to drown in ken° of shore;　　　　　　　*sight*
1115　He ten times pines° that pines beholding food;　　　　　*starves*
To see the salve doth make the wound ache more;
Great grief grieves most at that would do it good;
Deep woes roll forward like a gentle flood
　　　Who, being stopped, the bounding° banks o'erflows.　　*confining*
1120　　Grief dallied° with nor° law nor limit knows.　　　　*trifled / neither*

'You mocking birds,' quoth she, 'your tunes entomb
Within your hollow-swelling feathered breasts,
And in my hearing be you mute and dumb;
My restless discord loves no stops nor rests;
1125　A woeful hostess brooks° not merry guests.　　　　　　*tolerates*
　　　Relish° your nimble notes to pleasing ears;　　　*Warble; make pleasing*
　　　Distress likes dumps° when time is kept with tears.　　*sad songs*

'Come, Philomel, that sing'st of ravishment,
Make thy sad grove in my dishevelled hair.
1130 As the dank earth weeps at thy languishment,°    *lamentation*
So I at each sad strain will strain a tear,
And with deep groans the diapason° bear;    *bass accompaniment*
 For burden-wise[4] I'll hum on Tarquin still,
 While thou on Tereus descants better skill.[5]

1135 'And whiles against a thorn[6] thou bear'st thy part
To keep thy sharp woes waking, wretched I,
To imitate thee well, against my heart
Will fix a sharp knife to affright mine eye,
Who° if it wink° shall thereon fall and die.   *(I) / (my eye) close*
1140  These means, as frets° upon an instrument,  *(punning on "vexation")*
 Shall tune our heart-strings to true languishment.

'And for, poor bird, thou sing'st not in the day,
As shaming any eye should thee behold,
Some dark deep desert seated from the way,[7]
1145 That knows not parching heat nor freezing cold,
Will we find out, and there we will unfold
 To creatures stern sad tunes to change their kinds.°  *natures*
 Since men prove beasts, let beasts bear gentle minds.'

As the poor frighted deer that stands at gaze,
1150 Wildly determining which way to fly,
Or one encompassed with a winding maze,
That cannot tread the way out readily,
So with herself is she in mutiny,
 To live or die which of the twain were better
1155  When life is shamed and death reproach's debtor.°  *will incur reproach*

'To kill myself,' quoth she, 'alack, what were it
But with my body my poor soul's pollution?[8]
They that lose half with greater patience bear it
Than they whose whole is swallowed in confusion.°  *ruin*
1160 That mother tries a merciless conclusion°  *experiment*
 Who, having two sweet babes, when death takes one
 Will slay the other and be nurse to none.

'My body or my soul, which was the dearer,
When the one pure the other made divine?
1165 Whose love of either to myself was nearer,
When both were kept for heaven and Collatine?
Ay me, the bark peeled from the lofty pine
 His leaves will wither and his sap decay;
 So must my soul, her bark being peeled away.

1170 'Her house is sacked, her quiet interrupted,
Her mansion battered by the enemy,
Her sacred temple spotted, spoiled, corrupted,

4. Like a bass line; playing on "burden" as sorrow,
weight.
5. Sings the treble part more skillfully.
6. The nightingale was imagined to press against a

thorn to keep itself awake during the night.
7. Some uninhabited place located far from the road.
8. To pollute my poor soul, as my body has already
been polluted.

Grossly engirt with daring° infamy.                              *unrestrained*
Then let it not be called impiety
1175   If in this blemished fort° I make some hole                   *(my body)*
       Through which I may convey° this troubled soul.             *steal away*

'Yet die I will not till my Collatine
Have heard the cause of my untimely death,
That he may vow in that sad hour of mine
1180   Revenge on him that made me stop my breath.
My stainèd blood to Tarquin I'll bequeath,
    Which by him tainted shall for him be spent,
    And as his due writ° in my testament.°                        *written / last will*

'My honour I'll bequeath unto the knife
1185   That wounds my body so dishonourèd.
'Tis honour to deprive° dishonoured life;                         *take away*
The one° will live, the other° being dead.                        *(honor) / (life)*
So of shame's ashes shall my fame be bred,[9]
    For in my death I murder shameful scorn;
1190   My shame so dead, mine honour is new born.

'Dear lord of that dear jewel° I have lost,                       *(chastity)*
What legacy shall I bequeath to thee?
My resolution, love, shall be thy boast,
By whose example thou revenged mayst be.
1195   How Tarquin must be used, read it in me.
    Myself, thy friend, will kill myself, thy foe;
    And for my sake serve° thou false Tarquin so.                 *treat*

'This brief abridgement of my will I make:
My soul and body to the skies and ground;
1200   My resolution, husband, do thou take;
Mine honour be the knife's that makes my wound;
My shame be his that did my fame confound;
    And all my fame that lives disbursèd be°                      *that remains be paid out*
    To those that live and think no shame of me.

1205   'Thou, Collatine, shalt oversee° this will.                 *execute*
How was I overseen° that thou shalt see it!                       *deluded*
My blood shall wash the slander of mine ill;
My life's foul deed my life's fair end shall free it.
Faint not, faint heart, but stoutly say "So be it".
1210   Yield to my hand, my hand shall conquer thee;
    Thou dead, both die, and both shall victors be.'

This plot of death when sadly she had laid,
And wiped the brinish° pearl from her bright eyes,               *salty*
With untuned° tongue she hoarsely calls her maid,               *inharmonious*
1215   Whose swift obedience to her mistress hies;°                *hastens*
For fleet-winged duty with thought's feathers flies.
    Poor Lucrece' cheeks unto her maid seem so
    As winter meads when sun doth melt their snow.

9. My honor will be like the mythological phoenix, consumed in fire only to be reborn from the ashes.

Her mistress she doth give demure good-morrow
1220  With soft slow tongue, true mark of modesty,
And sorts° a sad look to her lady's sorrow,         *suits*
For why° her face wore sorrow's livery;°        *Because / attire*
But durst not ask of her audaciously
    Why her two suns were cloud-eclipsèd so,
1225     Nor why her fair cheeks over-washed with woe.

But as the earth doth weep, the sun being set,
Each flower moistened like a melting eye,
Even so the maid with swelling drops gan wet
Her circled° eyne, enforced° by sympathy     *rounded / compelled*
1230  Of those fair suns set in her mistress' sky,
    Who in a salt-waved ocean quench their light;
    Which makes the maid weep like the dewy night.

A pretty while° these pretty creatures stand,     *fair amount of time*
Like ivory conduits coral cisterns filling.
1235  One justly weeps, the other takes in hand°     *acknowledges*
No cause but company of her drops' spilling.
Their gentle sex to weep are often willing,
    Grieving themselves to guess at° others' smarts,°     *conjecture / pains*
    And then they drown their eyes or break their hearts.

1240  For men have marble, women waxen minds,
And therefore are they formed as marble will.
The weak oppressed, th'impression of strange kinds°     *alien natures*
Is formed in them by force, by fraud, or skill.
Then call them not the authors of their ill,
1245     No more than wax shall be accounted evil
    Wherein is stamped the semblance of a devil.

Their smoothness like a goodly champaign plain°     *open field*
Lays open° all the little worms that creep;     *Reveals*
In men as in a rough-grown grove remain
1250  Cave-keeping° evils that obscurely° sleep.     *Concealed / unseen*
Through crystal walls each little mote° will peep;     *speck*
    Though men can cover crimes with bold stern looks,
    Poor women's faces are their own faults' books.

No man° inveigh against the withered flower,     *Let no man*
1255  But chide rough winter that the flower hath killed.
Not that devoured, but that which doth devour
Is worthy blame. O, let it not be held
Poor women's faults that they are so full-filled
    With men's abuses. Those proud lords, to blame,
1260     Make weak-made women tenants to their shame.

The precedent° whereof in Lucrece view,     *proof*
Assailed by night with circumstances strong
Of present° death, and shame that might ensue     *immediate*
By that her death, to do her husband wrong.
1265  Such danger to resistance did belong
    That dying fear through all her body spread;
    And who cannot abuse a body dead?

By this,° mild patience bid fair Lucrece speak
To the poor counterfeit of her complaining.°

*this time*
*(the weeping maid)*

1270 'My girl,' quoth she, 'on what occasion break
Those tears from thee that down thy cheeks are raining?
If thou dost weep for grief of my sustaining,°
    Know, gentle wench, it small avails° my mood.
    If tears could help, mine own would do me good.

*borne by me*
*little helps*

1275 'But tell me, girl, when went'—and there she stayed,
Till after a deep groan—'Tarquin from hence?'
'Madam, ere I was up,' replied the maid,
'The more to blame my sluggard negligence.
Yet with the fault I thus far can dispense:°

*excuse*

1280     Myself was stirring ere the break of day,
    And ere I rose was Tarquin gone away.

'But lady, if your maid may be so bold,
She would request to know your heaviness.'°
'O, peace,' quoth Lucrece, 'if it should be told,

*sorrow*

1285 The repetition cannot make it less;
For more it is than I can well express,
    And that deep torture may be called a hell
    When more is felt than one hath power to tell.

'Go, get me hither paper, ink, and pen;
1290 Yet save that labour, for I have them here.
What should I say? One of my husband's men
Bid thou be ready by and by to bear
A letter to my lord, my love, my dear.
    Bid him with speed prepare to carry it;
1295     The cause craves° haste, and it will soon be writ.'

*requires*

Her maid is gone, and she prepares to write,
First hovering o'er the paper with her quill.
Conceit° and grief an eager combat fight;
What wit° sets down is blotted straight with will;°

*Imagination*
*thought / passion*

1300 This is too curious-good,° this blunt and ill.
    Much like a press° of people at a door
    Throng her inventions, which shall go before.°

*elaborate*
*crowd*
*first*

At last she thus begins: 'Thou worthy lord
Of that unworthy wife that greeteth thee,
1305 Health to thy person! Next, vouchsafe t'afford—
If ever, love, thy Lucrece thou wilt see—
Some present° speed to come and visit me.
    So I commend me,° from our house in grief;
    My woes are tedious, though my words are brief.'

*immediate*
*ask to be remembered*

1310 Here folds she up the tenor° of her woe,
Her certain sorrow writ uncertainly.
By this short schedule° Collatine may know
Her grief, but not her grief's true quality.
She dares not thereof make discovery,°

*gist*
*summary*
*revelation*

1315     Lest he should hold it her own gross abuse,°
    Ere she with blood had stained her stain's excuse.

*trespass*

Besides, the life and feeling of her passion
She hoards, to spend when he is by to hear her,
When sighs and groans and tears may grace the fashion°          appearance; fashioning
1320   Of her disgrace, the better so to clear her
From that suspicion which the world might bear her.
   To shun this blot she would not blot the letter
   With words, till action might become° them better.          suit

To see sad sights moves more than hear them told,
1325   For then the eye interprets to the ear
The heavy motion° that it doth behold,          sad action
When every part a part of woe doth bear.
'Tis but a part of sorrow that we hear;
   Deep sounds make lesser noise than shallow fords,
1330   And sorrow ebbs, being blown with wind of words.

Her letter now is sealed, and on it writ
'At Ardea to my lord with more than haste'.
The post attends,° and she delivers it,          messenger waits
Charging the sour-faced groom to hie as fast
1335   As lagging fowls before the northern blast.
   Speed more than speed° but dull and slow she deems;          Even unusual speed
   Extremity still urgeth such extremes.

The homely villain° curtsies to her low,          unpolished menial
And blushing on her with a steadfast eye
1340   Receives the scroll without or° yea or no,          either
And forth with bashful innocence doth hie.
But they whose guilt within their bosoms lie
   Imagine every eye beholds their blame,
   For Lucrece thought he blushed to see her shame,

1345   When, silly groom,° God wot,° it was defect          simple servant / knows
Of spirit, life, and bold audacity.
Such harmless creatures have a true respect
To talk in deeds,[1] while others saucily
Promise more speed, but do it leisurely.
1350   Even so this pattern of the worn out age°          old-fashioned model
   Pawned° honest looks, but laid no words to gage.°          Offered / as a pledge

His kindled duty[2] kindled her mistrust,
That two red fires in both their faces blazed.
She thought he blushed as knowing Tarquin's lust,
1355   And blushing with him, wistly° on him gazed.          attentively
Her earnest eye did make him more amazed.°          bewildered
   The more she saw the blood his cheeks replenish,
   The more she thought he spied in her some blemish.

But long she thinks° till he return again,          she thinks it long
1360   And yet the duteous vassal scarce is gone.
The weary time she cannot entertain,°          while away
For now 'tis stale to sigh, to weep, and groan.

1. have . . . deeds: rightly express their deference by     2. His blushing bow; his ardent loyalty.
their actions (rather than merely by their words).

So woe hath wearied woe, moan tired moan,
   That she her plaints a little while doth stay,
1365    Pausing for means to mourn some newer way.

At last she calls to mind where hangs a piece
Of skilful painting made for° Priam's Troy,              *representing*
Before the which is drawn the power° of Greece,       *army*
For Helen's rape the city to destroy,
1370  Threat'ning cloud-kissing Ilion° with annoy;°   *high-built Troy / injury*
   Which the conceited° painter drew so proud      *ingenious*
   As heaven, it seemed, to kiss the turrets bowed.

A thousand lamentable objects there,
In scorn of° nature, art gave lifeless life.           *Defying*
1375  Many a dry drop seemed a weeping tear
Shed for the slaughtered husband by the wife.
The red blood reeked° to show the painter's strife,[3]    *smoked*
   And dying eyes gleamed forth their ashy lights
   Like dying coals burnt out in tedious nights.

1380  There might you see the labouring pioneer°     *trench digger*
Begrimed with sweat and smearèd all with dust,
And from the towers of Troy there would appear
The very eyes of men through loop-holes thrust,
Gazing upon the Greeks with little lust.°         *pleasure*
1385   Such sweet observance° in this work was had   *verisimilitude*
   That one might see those far-off eyes look sad.

In great commanders grace and majesty
You might behold, triumphing in their faces;
In youth, quick° bearing and dexterity;           *lively*
1390  And here and there the painter interlaces
Pale cowards marching on with trembling paces,
   Which heartless° peasants did so well resemble   *dejected*
   That one would swear he saw them quake and tremble.

In Ajax and Ulysses, O what art
1395  Of physiognomy might one behold!
The face of either ciphered° either's heart;      *represented*
Their face their manners most expressly told.
In Ajax' eyes blunt° rage and rigour rolled,        *rude*
   But the mild glance that sly Ulysses lent
1400   Showed deep regard° and smiling government.°  *judgment / self-control*

There pleading° might you see grave Nestor stand,  *persuading*
As 'twere encouraging the Greeks to fight,
Making such sober action with his hand
That it beguiled attention, charmed the sight.
1405  In speech it seemed his beard all silver-white
   Wagged up and down, and from his lips did fly
   Thin winding breath which purled° up to the sky.   *curled*

---

3. Conflict between Trojans and Greeks; conflict between nature and art.

About him were a press of gaping faces
Which seemed to swallow up his sound advice,
1410 All jointly list'ning, but with several graces,°                    *various attitudes*
As if some mermaid did their ears entice;
Some high, some low, the painter was so nice.°                      *skillful; subtle*
    The scalps of many, almost hid behind,
    To jump up higher seemed, to mock the mind.°              *(by artistic illusion)*

1415 Here one man's hand leaned on another's head,
His nose being shadowed by his neighbour's ear;
Here one being thronged bears° back, all boll'n° and red;          *crowded pushes / swollen*
Another, smothered, seems to pelt° and swear,                      *scold*
And in their rage such signs of rage they bear
1420 As but for loss of° Nestor's golden words                      *That except they might miss*
    It seemed they would debate with angry swords.

For much imaginary° work was there;                                *creative*
Conceit deceitful, so compact,° so kind,°                          *efficient / natural*
That for Achilles' image stood his spear
1425 Gripped in an armèd hand; himself behind
Was left unseen save to the eye of mind;
    A hand, a foot, a face, a leg, a head,
    Stood for the whole to be imaginèd.

And from the walls of strong-besiegèd Troy
1430 When their brave hope, bold Hector, marched to field,
Stood many Trojan mothers sharing joy
To see their youthful sons bright weapons wield;
And to their hope they such odd action° yield                      *contrary gestures*
    That through their light joy seemèd to appear,
1435    Like bright things stained, a kind of heavy fear.

And from the strand° of Dardan where they fought                   *shore*
To Simois'° reedy banks the red blood ran,                         *Trojan river*
Whose waves to imitate the battle sought
With swelling ridges, and their ranks began
1440 To break upon the gallèd° shore, and then                      *eroded; injured*
    Retire again, till meeting greater ranks
    They join, and shoot their foam at Simois' banks.

To this well painted piece is Lucrece come,
To find a face where all distress is stelled.°                     *engraved*
1445 Many she sees where cares have carvèd some,
But none where all distress and dolour dwelled
Till she despairing Hecuba° beheld                                 *Queen of Troy*
    Staring on Priam's° wounds with her old eyes,            *King of Troy*
    Which bleeding under Pyrrhus' proud foot lies.

1450 In her the painter had anatomized°                            *laid open*
Time's ruin, beauty's wreck, and grim care's reign.
Her cheeks with chaps° and wrinkles were disguised;°              *cracks / disfigured*
Of what she was no semblance did remain.
Her blue blood changed to black in every vein,
1455    Wanting° the spring that those shrunk pipes had fed,  *Lacking*
    Showed life imprisoned in a body dead.

On this sad shadow Lucrece spends her eyes,
And shapes her sorrow to the beldame's° woes, *old woman's*
Who nothing wants to answer her[4] but cries
1460 And bitter words to ban° her cruel foes. *curse*
The painter was no god to lend her those,
   And therefore Lucrece swears he did her wrong
   To give her so much grief, and not a tongue.

'Poor instrument,' quoth she, 'without a sound,
1465 I'll tune° thy woes with my lamenting tongue, *sing*
And drop sweet balm in Priam's painted wound,
And rail on Pyrrhus that hath done him wrong,
And with my tears quench Troy that burns so long,
   And with my knife scratch out the angry eyes
1470    Of all the Greeks that are thine enemies.

'Show me the strumpet° that began this stir,° *(Helen) / dispute*
That with my nails her beauty I may tear.
Thy heat of lust, fond Paris, did incur
This load of wrath that burning Troy doth bear;
1475 Thine eye kindled the fire that burneth here,
   And here in Troy, for trespass of thine eye,
   The sire, the son, the dame and daughter die.

'Why should the private pleasure of someone
Become the public plague of many moe?° *more*
1480 Let sin alone° committed light alone *by one person*
Upon his head that hath transgressèd so;
Let guiltless souls be freed from guilty woe.
   For one's offence why should so many fall,
   To plague a private sin in general?° *collectively*

1485 'Lo, here weeps Hecuba, here Priam dies,
Here manly Hector faints, here Troilus swoons,
Here friend by friend in bloody channel° lies, *gutter*
And friend to friend gives unadvisèd° wounds, *unintended*
And one man's lust these many lives confounds.
1490    Had doting Priam checked his son's desire,
   Troy had been bright with fame, and not with fire.'

Here feelingly she weeps Troy's painted woes;
For sorrow, like a heavy hanging bell
Once set on ringing, with his° own weight goes; *its*
1495 Then little strength rings out the doleful knell.
So Lucrece, set a-work, sad tales doth tell
   To pencilled pensiveness and coloured sorrow.
   She lends them words, and she their looks doth borrow.

She throws her eyes about the painting round,
1500 And who she finds forlorn she doth lament.
At last she sees a wretched image bound,
That piteous looks to Phrygian shepherds lent.[5]

---

4. Who lacks nothing to resemble her.
5. That made Phrygian shepherds look on in pity (Phrygia was the area around Troy).

His face, though full of cares, yet showed content.
　　Onward to Troy with the blunt swains° he goes,　　　　　　*rough rustics*
1505　So mild that patience° seemed to scorn his woes.　　　　　*his patience*

In him the painter laboured with his skill
To hide deceit and give the harmless show°　　　　　　　　*appearance*
An humble gait, calm looks, eyes wailing still,°　　　　*weeping continually*
A brow unbent that seemed to welcome woe;
1510　Cheeks neither red nor pale, but mingled so
　　That blushing red no guilty instance° gave,　　　　　　　　*sign*
　　Nor ashy pale the fear that false hearts have.

But like a constant and confirmèd devil
He entertained° a show so seeming just,　　　　　　　　　　*maintained*
1515　And therein so ensconced° his secret evil　　　　　　　　*concealed*
That jealousy° itself could not mistrust°　　　　　*suspicion / suspect*
False creeping craft and perjury should thrust
　　Into so bright a day such blackfaced storms,
　　Or blot with hell-born sin such saint-like forms.

1520　The well skilled workman this mild image drew
For perjured Sinon,[6] whose enchanting° story　　　　　　　*deluding*
The credulous old Priam after slew;
Whose words like wildfire[7] burnt the shining glory
Of rich-built Ilion, that the skies were sorry,
1525　And little stars shot from their fixèd places
　　When their glass° fell wherein they viewed their faces.　　*mirror (Troy)*

This picture she advisedly° perused,　　　　　　　　　　　*carefully*
And chid° the painter for his wondrous skill,　　　　　　　*scolded*
Saying some shape° in Sinon's was abused,　　　*(other person's shape)*
1530　So fair a form lodged not a mind so ill;
And still on him she gazed, and gazing still,
　　Such signs of truth in his plain° face she spied　　　　　　*open*
　　That she concludes the picture was belied.°　　　　*shown to be false*

'It cannot be,' quoth she, 'that so much guile'—
1535　She would have said 'can lurk in such a look',
But Tarquin's shape came in her mind the while,
And from her tongue 'can lurk' from 'cannot' took.
'It cannot be' she in that sense forsook,
　　And turned it thus: 'It cannot be, I find,
1540　But such a face should bear a wicked mind.

'For even as subtle Sinon here is painted,
So sober-sad, so weary, and so mild,
As if with grief or travail he had fainted,
To me came Tarquin armèd, too beguiled°　　　　　　　　*disguised*
1545　With outward honesty, but yet defiled
　　With inward vice. As Priam him did cherish,
　　So did I Tarquin, so my Troy did perish.

6. Sinon was a Greek who pretended to have fled from　　their city.
his own people; once "rescued" and brought to Troy, he　　7. A mixture of sulfur, tar, and other combustible sub-
persuaded the Trojans to receive the wooden horse into　　stances, used to set fires during battle.

'Look, look, how list'ning Priam wets his eyes
To see those borrowed° tears that Sinon sheds.    *inauthentic*
1550 Priam, why art thou old and yet not wise?
For every tear he falls° a Trojan bleeds.    *(Sinon) lets fall*
His eye drops fire, no water thence proceeds.
    Those round clear pearls of his that move thy pity
    Are balls of quenchless fire to burn thy city.

1555 'Such devils steal effects° from lightless hell,    *illusions*
For Sinon in his fire doth quake with cold,
And in that cold hot-burning fire doth dwell.
These contraries such unity do hold
Only to flatter° fools and make them bold;    *encourage*
1560     So Priam's trust false Sinon's tears doth flatter
    That he finds means to burn his Troy with water.'

Here, all enraged, such passion her assails
That patience is quite beaten from her breast.
She tears the senseless° Sinon with her nails,    *unfeeling*
1565 Comparing him to that unhappy° guest    *misfortune-bringing*
Whose deed hath made herself herself detest.
    At last she smilingly with this gives o'er:
    'Fool, fool,' quoth she, 'his wounds will not be sore.'

Thus ebbs and flows the current of her sorrow,
1570 And time doth weary time with her complaining.
She looks for night, and then she longs for morrow,
And both she thinks too long with her remaining.
Short time seems long in sorrow's sharp sustaining.°    *painful enduring*
    Though woe be heavy, yet it seldom sleeps,
1575     And they that watch° see time how slow it creeps.    *remain awake*

Which all this time hath overslipped her thought
That she with painted images hath spent,
Being from the feeling of her own grief brought
By deep surmise° of others' detriment,°    *contemplation / suffering*
1580 Losing her woes in shows of discontent.°    *pictures of sorrow*
    It easeth some, though none it ever cured,
    To think their dolour others have endured.

But now the mindful° messenger come back    *dutiful*
Brings home his lord and other company,
1585 Who finds his Lucrece clad in mourning black,
And round about her tear-distainèd° eye    *tear-stained*
Blue circles streamed, like rainbows in the sky.
    These water-galls° in her dim element°    *rainbow fragments / sky*
    Foretell new storms to° those already spent.    *in addition to*

1590 Which when her sad beholding husband saw,
Amazedly in her sad face he stares.
Her eyes, though sod° in tears, looked red and raw,    *sodden*
Her lively colour killed with deadly cares.
He hath no power to ask her how she fares.
1595     Both stood like old acquaintance in a trance,
    Met far from home, wond'ring each other's chance.°    *fortune*

At last he takes her by the bloodless hand,
And thus begins: 'What uncouth° ill event                              *strange*
Hath thee befall'n, that thou dost trembling stand?
1600  Sweet love, what spite° hath thy fair colour spent?                 *harm*
Why art thou thus attired in discontent?[8]
    Unmask,° dear dear, this moody heaviness,                *Disclose*
    And tell thy grief, that we may give redress.'

Three times with sighs she gives her sorrow fire[9]
1605  Ere once she can discharge one word of woe.
At length addressed° to answer his desire,                    *ready*
She modestly prepares to let them know
Her honour is ta'en prisoner by the foe,
    While Collatine and his consorted° lords            *accompanying*
1610    With sad attention long to hear her words.

And now this pale swan in her wat'ry nest
Begins the sad dirge of her certain ending.[1]
'Few words,' quoth she, 'shall fit the trespass best,
Where no excuse can give the fault amending.
1615  In me more woes than words are now depending,°     *weighing; belonging*
    And my laments would be drawn out too long
    To tell them all with one poor tired tongue.

'Then be this all the task it hath to say:
Dear husband, in the interest° of thy bed        *claiming possession*
1620  A stranger came, and on that pillow lay
Where thou wast wont to rest thy weary head;
And what wrong else may be imaginèd
    By foul enforcement might be done to me,
    From that, alas, thy Lucrece is not free.

1625  'For in the dreadful dead of dark midnight
With shining falchion in my chamber came
A creeping creature with a flaming light,
And softly cried, "Awake, thou Roman dame,
And entertain° my love; else lasting shame            *receive*
1630    On thee and thine this night I will inflict,
    If thou my love's desire do contradict.

"'For some hard-favoured° groom of thine," quoth he,   *ugly*
"Unless thou yoke thy liking to my will,
I'll murder straight,° and then I'll slaughter thee,     *immediately*
1635  And swear I found you where you did fulfil
The loathsome act of lust, and so did kill
    The lechers in their deed. This act will be
    My fame, and thy perpetual infamy."

'With this I did begin to start and cry,
1640  And then against my heart he set his sword,
Swearing unless I took all patiently

---

8. Black; see line 1585.
9. As sixteenth-century gunners lighted firearms with matches.

1. Swans were supposed to sing only when they were on the point of death.

I should not live to speak another word.
So should my shame still rest upon record,
   And never be forgot in mighty Rome
1645   Th'adulterate° death of Lucrece and her groom.       *adulterous*

'Mine enemy was strong, my poor self weak,
And far the weaker with so strong a fear.
My bloody judge forbade my tongue to speak;
No rightful plea might plead for justice there.
1650   His scarlet lust came° evidence to swear       *gave*
   That my poor beauty had purloined his eyes;
   And when the judge is robbed, the prisoner dies.

'O teach me how to make mine own excuse,
Or at the least this refuge let me find:
1655   Though my gross blood be stained with this abuse,
Immaculate and spotless is my mind.
That was not forced, that never was inclined
   To accessory yieldings,² but still pure
   Doth in her poisoned closet yet endure.'

1660   Lo, here the hopeless merchant° of this loss,       *owner (Collatine)*
With head declined° and voice dammed up with woe,       *bent*
With sad set eyes and wreathèd arms across,³
From lips new waxen° pale begins to blow       *newly grown*
The grief away that stops his answer so;
1665     But wretched as he is, he strives in vain.
   What he breathes out, his breath drinks up again.

As through an arch° the violent roaring tide       *(under a bridge)*
Outruns the eye that doth behold his haste,
Yet in the eddy boundeth in his pride
1670   Back to the strait that forced him on so fast,
In rage sent out, recalled in rage being past;
   Even so his sighs, his sorrows, make a saw,⁴
   To push grief on, and back the same grief draw.

Which speechless woe of his poor she attendeth,°       *poor Lucrece notes*
1675   And his untimely frenzy° thus awaketh:       *delirium*
'Dear lord, thy sorrow to my sorrow lendeth
Another power;° no flood by raining slaketh.       *Greater strength*
My woe too sensible° thy passion maketh,       *acutely felt*
   More feeling-painful. Let it then suffice
1680     To drown on woe one pair of weeping eyes.

'And for my sake, when I might charm thee so,⁵
For she that was thy Lucrece, now attend me.
Be suddenly revengèd on my foe—
Thine, mine, his own. Suppose thou dost defend me
1685   From what is past. The help that thou shalt lend me

---

2. To yielding that would make me an accessory to the crime.
3. See line 793 and note.
4. Go back and forth (inhaling and exhaling), like a saw cutting wood.
5. As I used to be when I charmed you (before the rape).

Comes all too late, yet let the traitor die,
For sparing° justice feeds° iniquity. *lenient / encourages*

'But ere I name him, you fair lords,' quoth she,
Speaking to those that came with Collatine,
1690 'Shall plight° your honourable faiths to me *pledge*
With swift pursuit to venge this wrong of mine;
For 'tis a meritorious fair design° *intention*
    To chase injustice with revengeful arms.
    Knights, by their oaths, should right poor ladies' harms.'

1695 At this request with noble disposition° *purpose*
Each present lord began to promise aid,
As bound in knighthood to her imposition,° *imposed task*
Longing to hear the hateful foe bewrayed.° *revealed*
But she that yet her sad task hath not said° *completed*
1700     The protestation stops. 'O speak,' quoth she;
    'How may this forcèd stain be wiped from me?

'What is the quality of my offence,
Being constrained with dreadful circumstance?
May my pure mind with the foul act dispense,
1705 My low-declinèd honour to advance?° *raise*
May any terms acquit me from this chance?° *mishap*
    The poisoned fountain clears itself again,
    And why not I from this compellèd stain?'

With this they all at once began to say
1710 Her body's stain her mind untainted clears,
While with a joyless smile she turns away
The face, that map which deep impression bears
Of hard misfortune, carved in it with tears.
    'No, no,' quoth she, 'no dame hereafter living
1715     By my excuse shall claim excuse's giving.'

Here with a sigh as if her heart would break
She throws forth Tarquin's name. 'He, he,' she says—
But more than he her poor tongue could not speak,
Till after many accents° and delays, *sighs*
1720 Untimely breathings, sick and short essays,° *attempts*
    She utters this: 'He, he, fair lords, 'tis he
    That guides this hand to give this wound to me.'

Even here she sheathèd in her harmless° breast *innocent*
A harmful knife, that thence her soul unsheathed.
1725 That blow did bail° it from the deep unrest *liberate*
Of that polluted prison where it breathed.
Her contrite sighs unto the clouds bequeathed
    Her wingèd sprite,° and through her wounds doth fly *spirit*
    Life's lasting date[6] from cancelled destiny.

---

6. Eternal duration. The line is difficult, and could mean that Lucrece's immortal soul separates from her earthly life and body (canceled destiny), or that Lucrece, by taking her fate into her own hands (canceling her destiny), makes her fame eternal.

1730  Stone-still, astonished° with this deadly deed                            *stunned*
       Stood Collatine and all his lordly crew,
       Till Lucrece' father that beholds her bleed
       Himself on her self-slaughtered body threw;
       And from the purple fountain Brutus[7] drew
1735      The murd'rous knife; and as it left the place
          Her blood in poor revenge held it in chase,

       And bubbling from her breast it doth divide
       In two slow rivers, that the crimson blood
       Circles her body in on every side,
1740  Who like a late-sacked° island vastly° stood,            *just-looted / devastated*
       Bare and unpeopled in this fearful° flood.                               *fearsome*
          Some of her blood still pure and red remained,
          And some looked black, and that false Tarquin-stained.

       About the mourning and congealèd face
1745  Of that black blood a wat'ry rigol° goes,                                   *circle*
       Which seems to weep upon the tainted place;
       And ever since, as pitying Lucrece' woes,
       Corrupted blood some watery token shows;
          And blood untainted still doth red abide,
1750      Blushing at that which is so putrefied.

       'Daughter, dear daughter,' old Lucretius cries,
       'That life was mine which thou hast here deprived.
       If in the child the father's image lies,
       Where shall I live now Lucrece is unlived?°                                 *slain*
1755  Thou wast not to this end from me derived.
          If children predecease progenitors,
          We are their offspring, and they none of ours.

       'Poor broken glass,° I often did behold                                   *mirror*
       In thy sweet semblance my old age new born;
1760  But now that fair fresh mirror, dim and old,
       Shows me a bare-boned death° by time outworn.                              *skull*
       O, from thy cheeks my image thou hast torn,
          And shivered all the beauty of my glass,
          That I no more can see what once I was.

1765  'O time, cease thou thy course and last no longer,
       If they surcease° to be that should survive!                               *cease*
       Shall rotten death make conquest of the stronger,
       And leave the falt'ring feeble souls alive?
       The old bees die, the young possess their hive.
1770      Then live, sweet Lucrece, live again and see
          Thy father die, and not thy father thee.'

       By this starts Collatine as from a dream,
       And bids Lucretius give his sorrow place;
       And then in key-cold° Lucrece' bleeding stream                       *cold as metal*
1775  He falls, and bathes the pale fear in his face,

---

7. Lucius Junius Brutus. Tarquin the Proud, the        pretending to be mentally retarded. After Lucrece's
rapist's father, had killed Brutus's brother, but Brutus,   rape, he led the coup that overthrew the Tarquins and
whose name means "stupid," escaped royal suspicion by    established republican government in Rome.

And counterfeits to die with her a space,
   Till manly shame bids him possess his breath,
   And live to be revengèd on her death.

The deep vexation of his inward soul
1780  Hath served a dumb arrest° upon his tongue,         *silent injunction*
   Who, mad that sorrow should his use control,°        *prevent*
   Or keep him from heart-easing words so long,
   Begins to talk; but through his lips do throng
      Weak words, so thick come in his poor heart's aid
1785     That no man could distinguish what he said.

Yet sometime 'Tarquin' was pronouncèd plain,
   But through his teeth, as if the name he tore.
   This windy tempest, till it blow up rain,
   Held back his sorrow's tide to make it more.
1790  At last it rains, and busy winds give o'er.
      Then son and father weep with equal strife
      Who should weep most, for daughter or for wife.

The one doth call her his, the other his,
   Yet neither may possess the claim they lay.
1795  The father says 'She's mine'; 'O, mine she is,'
   Replies her husband, 'do not take away
   My sorrow's interest;° let no mourner say        *title of possession*
      He weeps for her, for she was only mine,
      And only must be wailed by Collatine.'

1800  'O,' quoth Lucretius, 'I did give that life
   Which she too early and too late hath spilled.'
   'Woe, woe,' quoth Collatine, 'she was my wife.
   I owed° her, and 'tis mine that she hath killed.'       *owned*
   'My daughter' and 'my wife' with clamours filled
1805     The dispersed air, who, holding Lucrece' life,[8]
      Answered° their cries, 'my daughter' and 'my wife'.    *Echoed*

Brutus, who plucked the knife from Lucrece' side,
   Seeing such emulation° in their woe           *competition*
   Began to clothe his wit in state° and pride,       *dignity*
1810  Burying in Lucrece' wound his folly's show.°   *pretended stupidity*
   He with the Romans was esteemèd so
      As silly jeering idiots° are with kings,       *court jesters*
      For sportive words and utt'ring foolish things.

But now he throws that shallow habit° by     *foolish appearance*
1815  Wherein deep policy° did him disguise,       *shrewdness*
   And armed his long-hid wits advisedly°       *prudently*
   To check the tears in Collatinus' eyes.
   'Thou wrongèd lord of Rome,' quoth he, 'arise.
      Let my unsounded° self, supposed a fool,    *of unknown depth*
1820     Now set thy long-experienced wit to school.

'Why, Collatine, is woe the cure for woe?
   Do wounds help wounds, or grief help grievous deeds?

8. See lines 1727ff.

Is it revenge to give thyself a blow
For his foul act by whom thy fair wife bleeds?
1825 Such childish humour° from weak minds proceeds;   *silly behavior*
    Thy wretched wife mistook the matter so
    To slay herself, that should have slain her foe.

'Courageous Roman, do not steep thy heart
In such relenting dew of lamentations,
1830 But kneel with me, and help to bear thy part
To rouse our Roman gods with invocations
That they will suffer° these abominations—   *allow*
    Since Rome herself in them doth stand disgraced—
    By our strong arms from forth her fair streets chased.°   *to be chased*

1835 'Now by the Capitol that we adore,
And by this chaste blood so unjustly stained,
By heaven's fair sun that breeds the fat° earth's store,°   *fertile / plenty*
By all our country° rights in Rome maintained,   *civic*
And by chaste Lucrece' soul that late complained
1840     Her wrongs to us, and by this bloody knife,
    We will revenge the death of this true wife.'

This said, he struck his hand upon his breast,
And kissed the fatal knife to end his vow,
And to his protestation urged the rest,
1845 Who, wond'ring at him, did his words allow.°   *approve*
    Then jointly to the ground their knees they bow,
    And that deep vow which Brutus made before
    He doth again repeat, and that they swore.

When they had sworn to this advisèd doom°   *considered judgment*
1850 They did conclude to bear dead Lucrece thence,
To show her bleeding body thorough° Rome,   *throughout*
And so to publish° Tarquin's foul offence;   *publicize*
Which being done with speedy diligence,
    The Romans plausibly° did give consent   *with applause*
1855     To Tarquin's everlasting banishment.

# The Sonnets and
# "A Lover's Complaint"

Shakespeare's plays often seem indifferent to high-cultural rules of construction. His sonnets (composed from about 1591 to 1604, possibly revised thereafter, and published in 1609) are the opposite: they faithfully adhere to the norms of an international tradition inspired by the fourteenth-century Italian poet Petrarch. Paradoxically, the very strictness of sonnet structure is the condition of possibility for Shakespeare's originality. The rigor of the form encourages a logical, rationalist approach to the standard topic of the Renaissance sonnet—love and its attendant emotions (desire, jealousy, and the like). The conflict between passionate feelings and a mobile intellect often skeptical of those feelings accordingly becomes a central theme of the poems. And that mobility is conveyed through a linguistic virtuosity marked by metaphors and puns that can work either with or against the larger structure of the sonnet.

Thematically, the sonnets are equally distinctive. The typical object of love—the unapproachable, exalted lady—is displaced so as to make room for a daring representation of homoerotic and adulterous passions. Almost the entire sequence can be divided along these lines. Sonnets 1–126 recount the speaker's idealized, sometimes painful love for a femininely beautiful, well-born male youth; 127–52 his unidealized, ultimately bitter affair with a darkly attractive, unaristocratic "mistress"—where this term invokes, however ironically, the vocabulary of courtly love rather than the derogatory modern meaning. The two love relationships are complicated by a lovers' triangle (40–42, 133–34, 144) and a poetic rival for the youth's affections (78–80, 82–86). These topics provide the occasion for a complex meditation upon a range of issues— time, nature, human mortality, economics, perhaps class and race, and, not least, an artistic immortality. And this self-referential reflection upon the sonnets' very composition is heightened by the reader's intense proximity to a speaker who is and is not Shakespeare.

The poems are best approached by locating their formal specificity against the background of two artistic practices through which Shakespeare came to the poems: his work in the theater, and the prior tradition of the sonnet. The standard verse line of Shakespearean drama and Shakespearean sonnet alike is iambic pentameter. But there the similarity ends. Roughly two-thirds of all lines in the plays are composed in unrhymed iambic pentameter, or blank verse; less than 10 percent employ rhyme. By contrast, Shakespeare's sonnets almost always consist of fourteen rhyming iambic-pentameter lines. Blank verse easily accommodates enjambment, the runover of sense from one line to the next. Rhyme encourages congruence between syntax and verse line: a unit of meaning ends when the line does. Blank verse supports the narrative logic of Shakespearean drama, rhyme the lyric impulse of the Shakespearean sonnet. You watch a play to see what happens next; you read a sonnet to discover the original expression of feelings and thoughts. Language is thus more obtrusively part of meaning in poetry than in drama.

It is easy to find exceptions to these claims. The crucial consideration, however, is the significance for Shakespeare of inherited conventions. The sonnet originated in Italy a century before Petrarch. Petrarch's decisive poetic sequence chronicles the author's passionately complex emotions in relation to his beloved Laura. The Petrarchan sonnet is divided into two frequently contrasting units, an octave (eight lines) and a sestet (six lines), by its rhyme scheme—*abbaabba cdecde,* where each letter represents a line and a repeated letter indicates a rhyme. The Petrarchan mode reached England by the early sixteenth century in the works of Wyatt and Surrey, whose modified rhyme scheme (*abab cdcd efef gg*), later taken over by Shakespeare, divides the sonnet into three quatrains (four-line groupings) and a couplet. This organization offers greater conceptual range than does the Petrarchan model. The quatrains can operate in parallel, represent steps in a logical argument, or contradict each other. They may be grouped into larger units of eight-and-four lines or eight-and-six lines (if the couplet is included) that are set against each other, with the result in the latter case that the Petrarchan octave-sestet structure is approximated. In turn, the epigrammatic concluding couplet, whose analytical tendencies contrast with the more experiential approach of at least the first two quatrains, can summarize the preceding lines, generalize from them, draw appropriate inferences, contribute a new thought, or even reverse the preceding argument.

Sonnet structure often guides Shakespeare's pervasive use of imagery and metaphor. In Sonnet 73, each quatrain pursues a different metaphor as part of a single argument:

> That time of year thou mayst in me behold
> When yellow leaves, or none, or few, do hang
> Upon those boughs which shake against the cold,
> Bare ruined choirs where late the sweet birds sang.
> In me thou seest the twilight of such day
> As after sunset fadeth in the west,
> Which by and by black night doth take away,
> Death's second self, that seals up all in rest.
> In me thou seest the glowing of such fire
> That on the ashes of his youth doth lie
> As the death-bed whereon it must expire,
> Consumed with that which it was nourished by.
> This thou perceiv'st, which makes thy love more strong,
> To love that well which thou must leave ere long.

The evocation of fall in the opening quatrain nostalgically communicates the sadness of aging. Enjambment supports the imagistic pattern: it causes meaning to "hang" in the balance at the end of the line, just as "yellow leaves . . . do hang / Upon those boughs." The "yellow leaves" are also leaves of a book, "bare ruined choirs," or quires (manuscript gatherings). Similarly, the birds' former song, together with the primary meaning of "choirs" (the part of a church where the choir sings), may refer to the speaker's own voice and hence to a lost poetic creativity. In short, the experience of aging is compared to the annual movement toward colder seasons and to the decline of artistic inspiration. In the second quatrain, the unit of time constricts: "That time of year" is replaced by "the twilight of such day." Although, like autumn, sunset is a natural process, it is not an organic one. Emphasis accordingly shifts away from bodily degeneration. These lines also look forward in a way the first quatrain does not. Twilight is taken away by "black night . . . , / Death's second self, that seals up all in rest." The rest that night brings is a source of comfort, but night is compared with death, and the syntax, at odds with the literal meaning, suggests that it is death rather than night "that seals up all in [eternal] rest."

The third quatrain opens like the second, with "In me thou seest," a phrase also partly anticipated in the first line of the poem. This repetition reinforces the parallelism among the quatrains and suggests that the poem proceeds less by narrative progression than by thematic variation. Yet this quatrain, while highlighting the transition from aging to mortality, narrows time further, to the "glowing" fire, in effect abandoning the temporal model of the first two quatrains for a spatial metaphor. Only the ashes remain from the fire's and, by implication, the speaker's "youth" (line 10); they are also the fire's and the speaker's "death-bed" (line 11). The earlier idealization of youth, now reduced to "ashes," has disappeared; conversely, although the fire of old age no longer rages, it is still "glowing"—it still gives off heat. The present is thus a continuation of the past. Furthermore, the metaphorical relationship is reversed. The dying fire is a metaphor for human aging, but that aging becomes a metaphor for the dying fire.

Paradoxically, the fire is "Consumed with that which it was nourished by"; it is "consumed" (or choked) by—and along with—the very ashes that, as fuel, previously "nourished" it. Normally, the fire consumes the fuel, not the other way around. Both "consumed" and "nourished" metaphorically explain the already metaphorical fire, which they connect back to humanity through their allusions to eating. The speaker's fiery passion for the youth he addresses nourished him when he was young but consumes him now. Indeed, the line structurally enacts the tacit thematic rejection of a temporal model of decline. It is an example of chiasmus, in which the elements of the first half ("Consumed . . . that") are repeated in reverse order in the second half ("which . . . nourished"), thus producing an *abba* semantic pattern. Accordingly, this quatrain has no equivalent to the earlier "cold" or "night," which are metaphorically responsible for the approach of death. Life and death have the same source.

All three quatrains employ cyclical metaphors of life, death, and rebirth. But the cycle remains incomplete. Autumn does not lead to spring or night to day. The "long-lived phoenix" (19.4), the legendary self-resurrecting bird that dies in flames and is reborn from the ashes, doesn't quite appear. Perhaps these suppressed allusions to cyclical patterns raise and then frustrate expectations, denying the consolation of the future. The concluding couplet, which moves away from metaphor and toward a new idea, suggests this interpretation. Recognizing the speaker's literally consuming passion makes the youth's "love more strong" (line 13). The youth, therefore, loves well what he "must leave ere long" (line 14)—explicitly, the speaker; implicitly, his own life, partly because that leaving recalls the "yellow leaves" with which the poem opened. There is no answer to the destructive power of time, but that power is partly counteracted by love.

Sonnet 73 suggests how conformity to sonnet convention can enable a thoughtful interplay among time, love, death, and art. Sonnet 81, on the other hand, offers a radical disjunction of syntax and rhyme scheme: almost any two consecutive lines can produce a complete sentence, depending on how you punctuate:

> And toungs to be, your beeing shall rehearse,
> When all the breathers of this world are dead,
> You still shall liue (such vertue hath my Pen).
> (81.11–13)

This three-line sequence, presented as it appears in the first edition of 1609, runs over the end of a quatrain but nonetheless produces two possible sentences that are grammatically correct and semantically effective (lines 11 and 12 or 12 and 13). Conceptually, the unorthodox move here is the implicit equation of the speaker with his social superior, the youth. The poet's literary prowess promises enduring renown for both the writer and his subject. Or does it? If you take lines 11 and 12 together, as modern editions do, the emphasis falls on "dead." But if you instead take lines 12 and 13 as a unit, the center of interest becomes "liue" and "my Pen." The poem thus promises both death and immortality, just as the wordplay on "rehearse" (line 11) predicts a future in which the youth is both still spoken about and literally re-hearsed.

The relationship between formal and thematic innovation can also be approached by considering the sonnets as a sequence. English enthusiasm for such sequences was triggered by the posthumous printing of Sir Philip Sidney's collection *Astrophel and Stella* (1591). Sonnets also circulated in manuscript form, since print culture was often considered beneath the dignity of (would-be) gentlemen or courtier-poets. The vogue for sonnet sequences responded to poets' ambitions as well as to the gender politics of the late Elizabethan court. Middle-class writers, for instance, sought financial assistance for their work by praising their aristocratic patrons. Expressions of love in this hierarchical relationship may be less indications of deep feeling than competitive strategies of advancement. Shakespeare's rival poet sonnets seem to convert this competition into literary theme. In general, then, it is often hard to determine where authentic sentiment ends and professional calculation begins.

The sonnet sequence itself is not the only larger formal category, however. When Shakespeare's sonnets first appeared in print, they were immediately followed in the same collection by "A Lover's Complaint." This work belongs to the genre of complaint poetry in which a woman laments her (usually) sexual ruin amid doleful reflections on life. Between 1593 and 1596, six poets published works consisting of a sonnet sequence, a brief intermediate piece usually based on ancient Greek form or subject matter (Cupid, for example), and a concluding complaint. The sonnets section of one such work, from which Shakespeare probably borrowed, is addressed to an attractive male youth. Another poet anticipates Shakespeare's sequence in dividing his sonnets into two main groups. It would be wrong to overstate the homogeneity of this mini-tradition. Nonetheless, the 1609 Quarto—a sonnet sequence divided into two parts, the first concerning a beautiful male youth and the second a woman; two concluding sonnets on Cupid; and a poetic complaint—is less miscellaneous collection than multi-generic form. Recent critics have had no trouble in demonstrating such connections between Shakespeare's sonnets and "A Lover's Complaint"—voyeurism, seduction, abandonment, and a similar cast of characters, among others. Nonetheless, the differences are obvious—for instance, the longer poem's ornamental, archaic diction and lack of emotional intensity. More important, the most detailed scholarship on the subject argues powerfully that not Shakespeare but John Davies of Hereford wrote "A Lover's Complaint." If so, as seems likely, Shakespeare could not have authorized the publication of the 1609 Quarto.

This line of reasoning raises questions about the internal organization of the sonnets as well (although not about their authorship). It has been suggested that the division of the sequence into two main groups is unwarranted. Most of the poems are not explicitly about either the youth or the mistress and do not even designate the sex of the person discussed. Only their relative position in the collection has produced the standard simplification adopted here. Furthermore, the sequence as a whole is relatively uninterested in plot. The poems to the mistress in particular show little sign of organization or process, combining occasional affection with chaos, bitterness, self-abasement, shame, unwilling sexual desire, and self-loathing. Perhaps, in 1609, they had not yet been placed in a particular order; perhaps they were intended for a separate collection. But the first 126 sonnets, too, evince only intermittent interest in linear movement, emphasizing longing, jealousy, and a fear of separation, while anticipating both the desire and the anguish of the subsequent poems.

Nonetheless, many of the sonnets are carefully ordered in pairs or longer groups. More important, the two main sections of the sequence are of compelling thematic interest. For the two centuries ending about a generation ago, the homoerotic attachment to the youth, now a routine part of critical discussion, provoked revulsion or denial. Sonnet 20 was—and still is—at the center of the debate:

> A woman's face with nature's own hand painted
> Hast thou, the master-mistress of my passion;
> A woman's gentle heart, but not acquainted
> With shifting change as is false women's fashion;
> An eye more bright than theirs, less false in rolling,
> Gilding the object whereupon it gazeth;
> A man in hue, all hues in his controlling,
> Which steals men's eyes and women's souls amazeth.

And for a woman wert thou first created,
Till nature as she wrought thee fell a-doting,
And by addition me of thee defeated
By adding one thing to my purpose nothing. [one thing = a penis]
    But since she pricked thee out for women's pleasure,
    Mine be thy love and thy love's use their treasure.

Nature originally intended the youth to be a woman (the octave). But she fell in love with her creation and hence turned him into a male, a change that benefited her but forced the speaker to limit his relationship to the youth to love without sexual consummation (the sestet). Thus, the poem wittily plays with gender boundaries—"master-mistress," "A woman's face," "one thing," "A man in hue" (with a further sexual reference if "hue" was pronounced like "you"; lines 2, 1, 12, 7). "Acquainted" and "controlling" pun on "cunt"; "nothing" and "treasure" refer to the female sexual organ as well (lines 3, 7, 12, 14). As someone "pricked . . . out for women's pleasure" (line 13), the youth is equipped to give women pleasure but also to be "pricked" and hence experience women's pleasure.

"Thy beauty's form in table of my heart" (24.2). Here a man is holding a "table" (tablet) in front of his heart while another man engraves the first man's portrait on it. From Geffrey Whitney, *A Choice of Emblemes* (1586).

Even the form gets into the act: this is the only sonnet where all the rhymes have "feminine" endings—the term since the Renaissance for a two-syllable rhyme with the second syllable unstressed. Finally, the misogyny of the poem's complaint about "false" women (lines 4, 5) is consistent with its homoeroticism. Women are to be resented because the speaker prefers males, or at least the youth, and also because they get to enjoy "love's use," while he must content himself merely with "love" (line 14)—where the contrast suggests that "love" carries both its Renaissance meaning of "friendship" and its modern sense of romantic and sexual desire.

Sonnet 20 looks forward to poems that express passionate, erotic love for the youth, apparently without sexual fulfillment. But they also look back to the opening seventeen sonnets, in which the speaker urges the youth to marry and produce an heir. Hence, the speaker solicits the youth's love for someone else, since the point is procreation and, therefore, an immortality comparable to the artistic immortality promised later in the sequence. The exhortation cuts against both the conventional aspiration of the love sonnet and the speaker's unconventional aim of winning the youth. But this is because the multiple possible meanings of "love" in Sonnet 20 characterize the poems to the youth more generally.

How the case for marriage is argued is instructive. Shakespeare's reversal of the metaphorical relationship in sonnet 73, it will be recalled, removes any fixed point of reference. A comparable reversal also marks economic imagery of the first seventeen sonnets. As in Sonnet 20 (line 14), that imagery frequently turns on usury. Long subject to denunciation, usury in Renaissance England was just beginning its conversion into the respectable financial category of interest. Shakespeare shared the prevailing repugnance at the idea of making money out of money. Thus, the speaker condemns his mistress for her affair with the young man, represented as collecting a debt:

    The statute of thy beauty thou wilt take,
    Thou usurer that putt'st forth all to use.
                    (134.9–10)

She will "take" the full amount owed to her financially (sexually) because, like a "usurer," she employs "all" her wealth (her body) for profit ("use" means both "engage in usury" and "engage in sexual activity"). Elsewhere, more ambivalently, the youth is criticized for being, paradoxically, both "unthrifty" and a "niggard" (4.1, 5):

> Profitless usurer, why dost thou use
> So great a sum of sums yet canst not live?
> (4.7–8)

Here, "use" antithetically means both "use up" and "lend at interest." Literally, how can the youth lend vast "sums" for profit and be unable to support himself? Metaphorically, he acts in a "profitless" manner in wasting his endowments. Hence, he cannot "live" on in his children. By implication, a usurer is always without value.

But the lines also imagine the opposite. If there is a profitless usurer, there might be a profitable one. This good usurer predominates in the sonnets:

> That use is not forbidden usury
> Which happies those that pay the willing loan.
> (6.5–6)

Is "forbidden" an attribute of all, or just unallowable, usury? Keeping one's "treasure" to oneself merits only "thriftless praise"; "beauty's use" deserves "much more praise" if a child results (2.6–9). At least "an unthrift" allows the world to enjoy his wealth; "beauty's waste" is indefensible—"kept unused, the user so destroys it" (9.9–12). And sonnet 20 ends, as we've seen, with the speaker declaring, as if to console himself: "Mine be thy love and thy love's use their treasure" (line 14). The speaker gets the youth's love, whereas the "treasure" women get is merely the "use" (metaphorically, children) of that love. He obtains the principal, they the interest. These passages activate metaphorical meanings of "use" to promote marriage and family. But in so doing, they connect the proper use of beauty with usury, which comes to be understood as the economic equivalent of human reproduction, the early sonnet's highest ideal. The neofeudal celebration of tradition as lineage smuggles in a defense of economic behavior destructive of tradition. Usury is transformed into a potentially noble activity. Through metaphor, then, Shakespeare entertains ideas that might have been less accessible as bald statements.

The poems to the speaker's mistress are also scandalously unconventional—in their focus on a sordid, adulterous affair with an unfaithful woman that is marked by passionate desire and equally passionate recrimination. Even the relatively serene sonnets in this section self-consciously undermine convention:

> My mistress' eyes are nothing like the sun;
> . . . . . . . . . . . . . . . . . . . . . . . . . . . . . . .
> And yet, by heaven, I think my love as rare
> As any she belied with false compare.
> (130.1, 13–14)

Here the target is the standard Petrarchan mode of praise. More generally, the aim is to dismantle falsely idealizing rhetoric:

> When my love swears that she is made of truth
> I do believe her though I know she lies,
> . . . . . . . . . . . . . . . . . . . . . . . . . . . . . .
> Therefore I lie with her, and she with me,
> And in our faults by lies we flattered be.
> (138.1–2, 13–14)

In Sonnet 130, true love requires the speaker to reject "false compare." In Sonnet 138, love paradoxically requires the speaker to "credit . . . false-speaking," to suppress "simple truth" (lines 7–8), and to embrace "lies." The sequence ends, however, with the bitter deployment of the same rhetoric against speaker and woman alike:

> For I have sworn thee fair—more perjured eye
> To swear against the truth so foul a lie.
> (152.13–14)

This concluding couplet recalls the opening of the sequence on the mistress:

> In the old age black was not counted fair,
> . . . . . . . .
> But now is black beauty's successive heir.
> (127.1, 3)

Black is the color of the woman's eyes, eyebrows, breasts, hair (127.9–10, 132.3, 130.3–4), and skin:

> Then I will swear beauty herself is black,
> And all they foul that thy complexion lack.
> (132.13–14)

As in other poetry of the time, this paradoxical, anticonventional praise of blackness echoes the biblical Song of Songs as well as sixteenth-century Continental and English poetry, including Sidney's. The praise is often inseparable from a misogynistic denunciation of the use of cosmetics to produce artificial beauty (127.4–12). Black hair and eyes gained prestige in the 1590s through a shift in fashion from blond hair to dark. Thus the speaker's personal views accord with broader social change.

The mistress's color may or may not be racialized, however, since even dark skin might merely distinguish her from falsely idealized women or aristocratic ladies able to avoid the sun. Nonetheless, *Titus Andronicus, Othello, Antony and Cleopatra*, and *The Tempest* feature actual or threatened interracial coupling. The mistress's combination of blackness and promiscuity may provoke both desire and fear of powerfully exotic female sexuality. The valence of blackness accordingly moves from the paradoxical to the conventional: "In nothing art thou black save in thy deeds" (131.13); "For I have sworn thee fair, and thought thee bright, / Who art as black as hell, and dark as night" (147.13–14). Like usury, then, blackness oscillates between conventional norms and radical innovation. Such is the case with the sonnets more generally.

Finally, the intense emotion here and elsewhere, the psychological complexity with which it is scrutinized, the unconventional subject matter, the sense that one is overhearing snatches of conversation, the first-person speaker, that speaker's self-conscious identification with Shakespeare (135–136)—all encourage a biographical interpretation of the sonnets. For two centuries, such interpretation has proven risky either to undertake or to avoid. There has been a major but unsuccessful scholarly effort to discover the real people whom Shakespeare discusses but does not name. The youth has most often been identified with Henry Wriothesley, Earl of Southampton, or William Herbert, Earl of Pembroke. The sonnets' dedication is to "Mr. W. H.," Pembroke's initials and the reverse of Southampton's. But neither is likely to have been addressed as "Mr." Proposals about the identity of the mistress are much shakier. Christopher Marlowe and George Chapman are among those suggested as the rival poet—on the basis of no real evidence. This inconclusiveness led mid-twentieth-century critics to focus on formal concerns. But the resulting advances often entailed evading the disconcerting biographical material that the poems do seem to provide. Shakespeare's sonnets, like his plays, combine verbal artistry and conceptual unorthodoxy with psychological exploration. Their special fascination, however, is that the soul they examine is apparently Shakespeare's own.

WALTER COHEN

## TEXTUAL NOTE

The sonnets and "A Lover's Complaint" were printed for the first time in "SHAKESPEARES SONNETS," a Quarto that appeared in 1609. The type for the volume was set by two compositors, who probably worked from a scribal transcript of an authorial manuscript. It is likely that the arrangement of the sonnets is primarily, or perhaps entirely, Shakespearean. But since the compositors punctuated in different ways, the Quarto's punctuation cannot be regarded as authorial. Indeed, it is unlikely that Shakespeare had anything to do with the printing of the Quarto; it is also unlikely that this was an authorized edition—although the second point is more controversial than the first. Finally, it now appears that "A Lover's Complaint" was written not by Shakespeare but by John Davies. (See Vickers in the Selected Bibliography.)

The Quarto was reprinted in *Poems: Written by W. Shakespeare, Gent.* (1640), in which the sonnets (with eight omitted) and "A Lover's Complaint" were joined by additional poetry of Shakespeare and other writers, individual sonnets were run together to produce longer works, the sonnets were titled, their order was rearranged, and a few pronouns were changed or (in the titles) invented. This collection has no independent textual value. *The Passionate Pilgrim* (first edition, 1599 or earlier; second edition, 1599–1600), an unauthorized volume attributed to Shakespeare by its publisher, is a different matter. The second edition includes twenty poems—three from *Love's Labour's Lost* (the 1598 Quarto of which presumably had already appeared in print), four others more reliably attributed to other writers, eleven pieces by unknown authors, and versions of sonnets 138 and 144 that seem to be both erroneous and unrevised.

Another dozen sonnets survive in various manuscripts, all from 1620 or later. Although many derive from the Quarto, a few may preserve—amid mistakes in transcription—authentically Shakespearean phrasing from versions earlier than those in the 1609 edition. It is possible that one or more of these transcripts derive directly from an authorial manuscript and in that sense are closer to what Shakespeare wrote than is the Quarto. The Alternative Versions, printed after "A Lover's Complaint" in this edition, include manuscript renditions of sonnets 2 (the most popular, judging by the number of extant copies) and 106, as well as sonnets 138 and 144 as they appeared in *The Passionate Pilgrim*. Sonnets 8 and 128, for which additional versions are not included here, could also possibly derive from authorial manuscripts. From the four included in the Alternative Versions, one may perhaps learn something of Shakespeare's process of revision.

The poems were probably composed over more than a decade. *The Passionate Pilgrim* and, more inferentially, some of the manuscripts show that Shakespeare wrote a number of the sonnets in the 1590s at the latest. So, too, does Francis Meres's reference in 1598 to Shakespeare's "sugred Sonnets among his priuate friends." The circulation of manuscripts was a common form of "publication" at the time. It should be noted, however, that a "sonnet" could be any short lyric poem. The best candidate for early composition is probably 145, on the basis of its vocabulary, its use of tetrameters rather than pentameters, and the words "hate away" (line 13)—a possible pun on the name of the poet's wife, Anne Hathaway. Further chronological hints are provided by the boom in love-sonnet sequences during the 1590s as well as by Shakespeare's own plays from 1594 to 1596—*Love's Labour's Lost, A Midsummer Night's Dream, Romeo and Juliet*, and *Richard II*—plays that, despite belonging to a variety of genres, are all linked to the sonnets in vocabulary, lyrical feel, and (by the standards of Shakespearean drama) high incidence of rhyme.

Recent scholarship, however, has suggested a later composition or revision for a considerable number of the sonnets. Although no consensus currently exists, a plausible recent estimate is as follows:

|        |                              |
|--------|------------------------------|
| 1–60:  | c. 1595–1596 (later revised?)|
| 61–103:| c. 1594–1595                 |
| 104–26:| c. 1598–1604                 |
| 127–54:| c. 1591–1595                 |

Even if this dating is only roughly accurate, it indicates that the sequence of the sonnets as published in 1609 sharply deviates from the chronology of composition. Beyond revealing that Shakespeare—and perhaps not Shakespeare alone—rearranged the sonnets according to other criteria, this conclusion also implies a disconnect between autobiographical impulse and chronological narrative (unless the sonnets that were composed later uniformly refer back to an earlier time). If the poems are in fact autobiographical, they cannot provide a linear account of events. This nonnarrative hypothesis is supported by internal evidence, specifically the references to the love triangle involving the speaker, the youth, and the mistress both early and late in the sequence (40–42, 133–34, 144). Alternatively, if the sequence does provide a linear narrative, it cannot be autobiographical. And, of course, the sequence may offer neither chronological narrative nor actual autobiography.

## SELECTED BIBLIOGRAPHY

Bloom, Harold, ed. *Shakespeare's Sonnets*. New York: Chelsea House, 1987. Five leading critical essays from 1960 to 1985.

Booth, Stephen. *An Essay on Shakespeare's Sonnets*. New Haven: Yale University Press, 1969. Detailed evidence for multiple overlapping structures within individual sonnets, structures that expand possible meaning without cohering into a unified whole.

————, ed. *Shakespeare's Sonnets*. New Haven: Yale University Press, 1977. Same argument as above, but in the form of a detailed poem-by-poem commentary, together with both the 1609 Quarto of the sonnets and a modernized version.

Fineman, Joel. *Shakespeare's Perjured Eye: The Invention of Poetic Subjectivity in the Sonnets*. Berkeley: University of California Press, 1986. Psychoanalytical study that distinguishes the narcissistic, homosexual visual identification of sonnets 1–126 from the misogynistic heterosexual desire and conflict of 127–52, the latter being the founding moment of modern subjectivity.

Halpern, Richard. *Shakespeare's Perfume: Sodomy and Sublimity in the Sonnets, Wilde, Freud, and Lacan*. Philadelphia: University of Pennsylvania Press, 2002. 11–31. Links sodomy, aesthetics, sublimation, and the sublime.

Hernstein, Barbara, ed. *Discussions of Shakespeare's Sonnets*. Boston: Heath, 1964. Brief pre-twentieth-century accounts plus thirteen important essays from 1930 to 1960.

Schoenfeldt, Michael, ed. *A Companion to Shakespeare's Sonnets*. Malden, Mass.: Blackwell, 2007. The sonnets and "A Lover's Complaint" together with twenty-three essays from the current century plus contributions from Booth (1969) and Vendler (1997).

Vendler, Helen. *The Art of Shakespeare's Sonnets*. Cambridge, Mass.: Belknap Press, 1997. Detailed sonnet-by-sonnet interpretation, focusing on formal considerations, together with the 1609 Quarto and a modernized version of the text, as well as a CD-ROM of Vendler reading the poems.

Vickers, Brian. *Shakespeare, "A Lover's Complaint," and John Davies of Hereford*. New York: Cambridge University Press, 2007. Argues that Davies, not Shakespeare, wrote "A Lover's Complaint."

Willen, Gerald, and Victor B. Reed, eds. *A Casebook on Shakespeare's Sonnets*. New York: Crowell, 1964. Annotated modern edition of the sonnets together with six major critical essays from the 1930s to the early 1950s and very brief explications of a few individual sonnets.

# Sonnets

TO.THE.ONLY.BEGETTER.OF.
THESE.ENSUING.SONNETS.
M^R. W. H.[1] ALL.HAPPINESS.
AND.THAT.ETERNITY.
PROMISED.
BY.
OUR.EVER-LIVING.POET.[2]
WISHETH.
THE.WELL-WISHING.
ADVENTURER.IN.
SETTING.
FORTH.
T. T.[3]

### 1

| | |
|---|---|
| From fairest creatures we desire increase,° | *offspring* |
| That thereby beauty's rose[1] might never die, | |
| But as the riper should by time decease, | |
| His tender[2] heir might bear his memory; | |
| 5 But thou, contracted° to thine own bright eyes, | *engaged; reduced* |
| Feed'st thy light's flame with self-substantial fuel,[3] | |
| Making a famine where abundance lies, | |
| Thyself thy foe, to thy sweet self too cruel. | |
| Thou that art now the world's fresh ornament | |
| 10 And only herald to the gaudy° spring | *brilliant* |
| Within thine own bud buriest thy content,° | *substance; happiness* |
| And, tender churl,° mak'st waste in niggarding. | *young old miser* |
| Pity the world, or else this glutton be: | |
| To eat the world's due, by the grave and thee.[4] | |

**Dedication**

1. The identity of W. H. has generated much speculation. As "the only begetter of these ensuing sonnets," "W. H." is probably a misprint for "W. S." or "W. SH." (William Shakespeare). Other candidates include the person who obtained the manuscript for the publisher and the youth who apparently inspired most of the poems. For biographical speculation about the sonnets, see the Introduction.

2. God, literally "ever-living," who promises eternity to Shakespeare (if, as suggested in the previous note, "W.H." refers to Shakespeare); or, less probably, Shakespeare, who promises "eternity" to the young man.

3. Thomas Thorpe, the printer, is the "well-wishing adventurer."

**Sonnet 1**

1. In Q, "rose," unlike most other nouns, is always capitalized (35.2; 54.3, 6, 11; 67.8; 95.2; 98.10; 99.8; 109.14; and 130.5, 6). Here, it is also italicized. These printing conventions, combined with the placement of the word near the beginning of the first sonnet and its frequent repetition thereafter, suggest that "rose" is the poet's name for the object of his desire, on the model of, for instance, Stella in Sir Philip Sidney's influential sonnet sequence *Astrophel and Stella* (published 1591). The rose had long been associated with female genitalia, most notably in the thirteenth-century French narrative poem *The Romance of the Rose*, by Guillaume de Lorris and Jean de Meun. In Shakespeare's case, however, the object of desire is male. He is most frequently referred to as "youth," almost never as "boy" or "man." Shakespeare's "mistress" in the later sonnets is contrasted with "roses" (130.5, 6).

2. The rose's (the youth's) young.

3. Are consuming yourself like a candle.

4. *this . . . thee:* be a glutton by causing what is due to the world (your posterity) to be consumed both by the grave and within yourself.

## 2[1]

When forty winters shall besiege thy brow
And dig deep trenches in thy beauty's field,
Thy youth's proud livery,° so gazed on now,          *uniform; appearance*
Will be a tattered weed,° of small worth held.          *clothing; plant*
5   Then being asked where all thy beauty lies,
Where all the treasure of thy lusty days,
To say within thine own deep-sunken eyes
Were an all-eating shame and thriftless praise.[2]
How much more praise deserved thy beauty's use[3]
10  If thou couldst answer 'This fair child of mine
Shall sum my count, and make my old excuse',[4]
Proving his beauty by succession thine.°          *inherited from you*
   This were° to be new made when thou art old,          *would be*
   And see thy blood warm when thou feel'st it cold.

## 3

Look in thy glass,° and tell the face thou viewest          *mirror*
Now is the time that face should form another,
Whose fresh repair° if now thou not renewest          *state*
Thou dost beguile° the world, unbless° some mother.          *swindle / leave childless*
5   For where is she so fair whose uneared° womb          *unplowed*
Disdains the tillage of thy husbandry?[1]
Or who is he so fond will be the tomb
Of his self-love to stop posterity?[2]
Thou art thy mother's glass, and she in thee
10  Calls back the lovely April of her prime;
So thou through windows of thine age[3] shalt see,
Despite of wrinkles, this thy golden time.
   But if thou live remembered not to be,[4]
   Die single, and thine image dies with thee.

## 4

Unthrifty loveliness, why dost thou spend
Upon thyself thy beauty's legacy?
Nature's bequest gives nothing, but doth lend,
And being frank, she lends to those are free.[1]
5   Then, beauteous niggard, why dost thou abuse
The bounteous largess given thee to give?
Profitless usurer, why dost thou use°          *lend for profit; spend*
So great a sum of sums yet canst not live?[2]
For having traffic° with thyself alone,          *(commercial); (sexual)*
10  Thou of thyself thy sweet self dost deceive.°          *defraud*
Then how when nature calls thee to be gone:
What acceptable audit canst thou leave?
   Thy unused[3] beauty must be tombed with thee,
   Which usèd, lives th'executor to be.

**Sonnet 2**
1. See *Spes Altera* in the Alternative Versions.
2. Would be a shameful admission of gluttony and boast of excessive expenditure.
3. How much more would the use (employment; investment or usurious lending) of your beauty merit.
4. Shall make my accounts balance and defend (absolve) me in my age.
**Sonnet 3**
1. Cultivation; acting as a husband.

2. *who . . . posterity:* who is so foolish that he will selfishly deny posterity a child?
3. Eyes weakened by old age; your children.
4. But if you live to be forgotten.
**Sonnet 4**
1. And being generous, she lends to those who (also) are generous.
2. Make a living; live on in your children.
3. Not put to use; not interest-bearing.

**5**

Those hours that with gentle work did frame°                    *form*
The lovely gaze° where every eye doth dwell                     *face*
Will play the tyrants to the very same,
And that unfair which fairly doth excel;[1]
5   For never-resting time leads summer on
To hideous winter, and confounds° him there,                   *destroys*
Sap checked with frost, and lusty leaves quite gone,
Beauty o'er-snowed, and bareness everywhere.
Then were not summer's distillation left
10   A liquid prisoner pent in walls of glass,
Beauty's effect with beauty were bereft,[2]
Nor° it nor no remembrance what it was.                        *Neither*
       But flowers distilled, though they with winter meet,
       Lose[3] but their show; their substance still lives sweet.

**6**[1]

Then let not winter's ragged° hand deface                       *rough*
In thee thy summer ere thou be distilled.
Make sweet some vial,° treasure° thou some place          *womb / enrich*
With beauty's treasure ere it be self-killed.
5   That use° is not forbidden usury                           *lending for profit*
Which happies those that pay the willing loan:[2]
That's for thyself° to breed another thee,                     *So you would do*
Or ten times happier, be it ten for one;°                      *1,000% interest*
Ten times thyself were happier than thou art,
10   If ten of thine ten times refigured° thee.                *copied*
Then what could death do if thou shouldst depart,
Leaving thee living in posterity?
       Be not self-willed,[3] for thou art much too fair
       To be death's conquest and make worms thine heir.

**7**

Lo, in the orient° when the gracious light°                    *east / sun*
Lifts up his burning head, each under° eye                     *earthly*
Doth homage to his new-appearing sight,
Serving with looks his sacred majesty,
5   And having climbed the steep-up heavenly hill,
Resembling strong youth in his middle age,°                    *noon*
Yet mortal looks adore his beauty still,
Attending on his golden pilgrimage.
But when from highmost pitch, with weary car,°                 *sun god's chariot*
10   Like feeble age he reeleth from the day,
The eyes, 'fore duteous, now converted° are                    *turned*
From his low tract,° and look another way.                     *path*
       So thou, thyself outgoing in thy noon,
       Unlooked on diest unless thou get° a son.°              *beget / (sun)*

**Sonnet 5**
1. Will make unattractive that which now excels in
beauty.
2. *Then . . . bereft:* Then if there were no perfume distilled from flowers bottled in glass vials, both beauty and
its effect would be lost.
3. Q has "Leese," understood in this edition as a cognate
of "lose." This is Shakespeare's only use of "Leese," which

allows a pun on "lease." See 13.5.
**Sonnet 6**
1. This sonnet links with 5.
2. Which makes happy those who willingly lend, or who
willingly repay the loan with interest (in the form of
children).
3. Stubborn; leaving everything in a will to yourself
alone.

### 8

Music to hear,[1] why hear'st thou music sadly?
Sweets° with sweets war not, joy delights in joy.      *Sweet things*
Why lov'st thou that which thou receiv'st not gladly,
Or else receiv'st with pleasure thine annoy?
5  If the true concord of well-tunèd sounds
By unions° married do offend thine ear,      *harmony*
They do but sweetly chide thee, who confounds°      *destroys*
In singleness the parts[2] that thou shouldst bear.
Mark how one string, sweet husband to another,
10  Strikes each in each° by mutual ordering,      *Resonates*
Resembling sire and child and happy mother,
Who all in one one pleasing note do sing;
    Whose speechless° song, being many, seeming one,      *The strings' wordless*
    Sings this to thee: 'Thou single wilt prove none.'[3]

### 9

Is it for fear to wet a widow's eye
That thou consum'st thyself in single life?
Ah, if thou issueless° shalt hap to die,      *childless*
The world will wail thee like a makeless° wife.      *widowed*
5  The world will be thy widow, and still° weep      *continually*
That thou no form of thee hast left behind,
When every private° widow well may keep      *individual*
By children's eyes her husband's shape in mind.
Look what° an unthrift in the world doth spend      *Whatever*
10  Shifts but his° place, for still the world enjoys it;      *its*
But beauty's waste hath in the world an end,
And kept unused, the user° so destroys it.      *spender; lender*
    No love toward others in that bosom sits
    That on himself such murd'rous shame commits.

### 10

For shame deny that thou bear'st love to any,
Who for thyself art so unprovident.
Grant, if thou wilt, thou art beloved of many,
But that thou none lov'st is most evident;
5  For thou art so possessed with murd'rous hate
That 'gainst thyself thou stick'st not to conspire,°      *don't balk at conspiring*
Seeking that beauteous roof to ruinate
Which to repair should be thy chief desire.
O, change thy thought, that I may change my mind!°      *judgment*
10  Shall hate be fairer lodged than gentle love?
Be as thy presence° is, gracious and kind,      *appearance*
Or to thyself at least kind-hearted prove.
    Make thee another self for love of me,
    That beauty still may live in thine or thee.

---

**Sonnet 8**
1. You whose voice is music.
2. Musical parts; roles as husband and father.

3. Without an heir, death will render you nothing (alluding to the proverb "One is no number").

## 11

As fast as thou shalt wane, so fast thou grow'st
In one of thine from that which thou departest,[1]
And that fresh blood which youngly thou bestow'st
Thou mayst call thine when thou from youth convertest.°     *turn away*
5   Herein lives wisdom, beauty, and increase;
Without this, folly, age, and cold decay.
If all were minded so, the times should cease,
And threescore year would make the world away.
Let those whom nature hath not made for store,°     *breeding*
10   Harsh,° featureless,° and rude,° barrenly perish.     *ugly (all three words)*
Look whom she best endowed she gave the more,[2]
Which bounteous gift thou shouldst in bounty° cherish.     *by using bountifully*
    She carved thee for her seal,[3] and meant thereby
    Thou shouldst print more, not let that copy die.

## 12

When I do count the clock° that tells the time,     *hours as they strike*
And see the brave° day sunk in hideous night;     *fine*
When I behold the violet past prime,
And sable° curls ensilvered o'er with white;     *black*
5   When lofty trees I see barren of leaves,
Which erst° from heat did canopy the herd,     *once*
And summer's green all girded up in sheaves
Borne on the bier with white and bristly beard:[1]
Then of thy beauty do I question make
10   That thou among the wastes of time must go,
Since sweets° and beauties do themselves forsake,     *sweet things*
And die as fast as they see others grow;
    And nothing 'gainst time's scythe can make defence
    Save breed to brave him° when he takes thee hence.     *children to defy time*

## 13

O that you were yourself![1] But, love, you are
No longer yours than you yourself here live.
Against° this coming end you should prepare,     *For*
And your sweet semblance to some other give.
5   So should that beauty which you hold in lease
Find no determination;° then you were°     *never end / would be*
Yourself again after your self's decease,
When your sweet issue your sweet form should bear.
Who lets so fair a house fall to decay,
10   Which husbandry[2] in honour might uphold
Against the stormy gusts of winter's day,
And barren rage of death's eternal cold?
    O, none but unthrifts,° dear my love, you know.     *spendthrifts*
    You had a father; let your son say so.

**Sonnet 11**
1. In a child begotten in youth (with suggestions of sexual intercourse and of death).
2. To whomever nature gave most (made best-looking) she gave even more (extra reproductive abilities). The near circularity of "best endowed" and "more" alludes to Matthew 25:29, the paradoxical parable of the talents: "For unto every man that hath, it shall be given."

3. Literally, a stamp of authority.
**Sonnet 12**
1. An . . . beard: And sheaves of mature ("bearded") grain carried away on the harvest cart; old man borne on a funeral bier.
**Sonnet 13**
1. If only you could remain your (eternal) self.
2. Stewardship; being a husband.

## 14

Not from the stars do I my judgement pluck,
And yet methinks I have astronomy;°       *astrological knowledge*
But not to tell of good or evil luck,
Of plagues, of dearths, or seasons' quality.
5  Nor can I fortune to brief minutes° tell,       *precisely*
'Pointing to each his thunder, rain, and wind,
Or say with princes if it shall go well
By oft predict° that I in heaven find;       *numerous signs*
But from thine eyes my knowledge I derive,
10  And, constant stars, in them I read such art
As[1] truth and beauty shall together thrive
If from thyself to store thou wouldst convert.[2]
    Or else of thee this I prognosticate:
    Thy end is truth's and beauty's doom and date.°       *final judgment and end*

## 15

When I consider every thing that grows
Holds° in perfection but a little moment,       *Remains*
That this huge stage presenteth naught but shows
Whereon the stars in secret influence° comment;       *(astrologically)*
5  When I perceive that men as plants increase,
Cheerèd and checked even by the selfsame sky;
Vaunt° in their youthful sap,° at height decrease,       *Gloat / strength*
And wear their brave state out of memory:[1]
Then the conceit° of this inconstant stay°       *imagination / (on earth)*
10  Sets you most rich in youth before my sight,
Where wasteful time debateth° with decay       *competes*
To change your day of youth to sullied night;
    And all in war with time for love of you,
    As he takes from you, I engraft you new.[2]

## 16[1]

But wherefore do not you a mightier way
Make war upon this bloody tyrant, time,
And fortify yourself in your decay
With means more blessèd than my barren rhyme?
5  Now stand you on the top of happy hours,°       *in your prime*
And many maiden gardens yet unset°       *unplanted*
With virtuous wish would bear your living flowers,
Much liker than your painted counterfeit.°       *image in art or poetry*
So should the lines of life[2] that life repair°       *restore*
10  Which this time's pencil or my pupil pen[3]
Neither in inward worth nor outward fair
Can make you live yourself° in eyes of men.       *as yourself*
    To give away yourself keeps yourself still,°       *(as children)*
    And you must live drawn by your own sweet skill.

---

**Sonnet 14**
1. *such art / As:* such predictions as that.
2. If you would provide for the future.
**Sonnet 15**
1. Wear their splendid clothing until they are forgotten
(with a sense of "wearing out").
2. *And . . . new:* And I, in competition with time because

I love you, restore you with my verse.
**Sonnet 16**
1. This sonnet links with 15.
2. Lineage; living lines (unlike those of poet or painter).
3. Neither today's painters ("pencil" means "paintbrush")
nor I, who imitate painting in my verse.

## 17

Who will believe my verse in time to come
If it were filled with your most high deserts?—
Though yet, heaven knows, it is but as a tomb
Which hides your life, and shows not half your parts.°      *attributes*
5   If I could write the beauty of your eyes
And in fresh numbers° number all your graces,      *lively verses*
The age to come would say 'This poet lies;
Such heavenly touches ne'er touched earthly faces.'
So should my papers, yellowed with their age,
10   Be scorned, like old men of less truth than tongue,
And your true rights° be termed a poet's rage°      *praises / hyperbole*
And stretchèd metre° of an antique song.      *overwrought poetry*
    But were some child of yours alive that time,
    You should live twice: in it, and in my rhyme.

## 18

Shall I compare thee to a summer's day?
Thou art more lovely and more temperate.
Rough winds do shake the darling buds of May,
And summer's lease° hath all too short a date.      *fixed span of time*
5   Sometime too hot the eye of heaven shines,
And often is his gold complexion dimmed,
And every fair from fair[1] sometime declines,
By chance or nature's changing course untrimmed;°      *rendered ordinary*
But thy eternal summer shall not fade
10   Nor lose possession of that fair thou ow'st,°      *own*
Nor shall death brag thou wander'st in his shade
When in eternal lines to time thou grow'st.[2]
    So long as men can breathe or eyes can see,
    So long lives this, and this gives life to thee.

## 19

Devouring time, blunt thou the lion's paws,
And make the earth devour her own sweet brood;
Pluck the keen teeth from the fierce tiger's jaws,
And burn the long-lived phoenix[1] in her blood.°      *alive*
5   Make glad and sorry seasons as thou fleet'st,
And do whate'er thou wilt, swift-footed time,
To the wide world and all her fading sweets.°      *sweet things*
But I forbid thee one most heinous crime:
O, carve not with thy hours my love's fair brow,
10   Nor draw no lines there with thine antique° pen.      *old; capricious*
Him in thy course untainted do allow
For beauty's pattern to succeeding men.
    Yet do thy worst, old time; despite thy wrong
    My love shall in my verse ever live young.

---

**Sonnet 18**
1. Lovely thing from loveliness.
2. When in immortal poetry you become engrafted to time.

**Sonnet 19**
1. Legendary, self-resurrecting bird believed to live in cycles of several centuries, dying in flames and reborn from the ashes. See also 73.9–12.

### 20

A woman's face with nature's own hand° painted                                                                   (*without cosmetics*)
Hast thou, the master-mistress[1] of my passion;[2]
A woman's gentle heart, but not acquainted°                                                     (*pun on "quaint," "cunt"*)
With shifting change as is false women's fashion;
5    An eye more bright than theirs, less false in rolling,°                                              *wandering (sexually)*
Gilding the object whereupon it gazeth;
A man in hue, all hues in his controlling,[3]
Which steals men's eyes and women's souls amazeth.°                                                            *overwhelms*
And for° a woman wert thou first created,                                                            *to be; to be with*
10   Till nature as she wrought thee fell a-doting,°                                               *behaved foolishly*
And by addition me of thee defeated°                                                                *cheated me of you*
By adding one thing to my purpose nothing.[4]
    But since she pricked° thee out for women's pleasure,[5]                                             *chose; (sexual)*
    Mine be thy love and thy love's use their treasure.[6]

### 21

So is it not with me as with that muse°                                                                              *poet*
Stirred by a painted° beauty to his verse,                                                               (*with cosmetics*)
Who heaven itself for ornament° doth use,                                                                 *poetic imagery*
And every fair with his fair doth rehearse,[1]
5    Making a couplement of proud compare[2]
With sun and moon, with earth, and sea's rich gems,
With April's first-born flowers, and all things rare
That heaven's air in this huge rondure hems.°                                                            *globe surrounds*
O let me, true in love, but truly write,
10   And then believe me my love is as fair
As any mother's child, though not so bright
As those gold candles° fixed in heaven's air.                                                                 (*the stars*)
    Let them say more that like of hearsay° well;                                                              *clichés*
    I will not praise that purpose not° to sell.                                                        *since I don't intend*

### 22

My glass° shall not persuade me I am old                                                                          *mirror*
So long as youth and thou are of one date;°                                                         *While you're young*
But when in thee time's furrows I behold,
Then look I° death my days should expiate.°                                                          *I expect / conclude*
5    For all that beauty that doth cover thee
Is but the seemly° raiment of my heart,                                                                        *fitting*
Which in thy breast doth live, as thine in me;
How can I then be elder than thou art?
O therefore, love, be of thyself so wary
10   As I, not for myself, but for thee will,
Bearing thy heart, which I will keep so chary°                                                              *cautiously*
As tender nurse her babe from faring ill.

---

**Sonnet 20**
1. Both patron and sexual mistress (hence, homoerotic); referring to the youth's feminine looks.
2. Object of my love; controller of my feelings; controller of my passionate poetry.
3. A man whose looks enable him to attract and dominate all others; a man whose looks encompass all other appearances (both male and female). "Hue" may pun on "you" with possible sexual connotations. "Hues" may pun on "use"; see line 14 and note. "Controlling" puns on "cunt."
4. *one . . . nothing*: something (a penis) of no use to me;

"thing" meant sexual organ; "nothing" meant female sexual organ.
5. To give women pleasure; to have the pleasure women have.
6. I'll have the main part of your love (the capital or principal), while women get just the "use" (interest; pleasure; children) of it (or, while you use women sexually).
**Sonnet 21**
1. And compares every beautiful thing with his beloved.
2. Making a link in proud comparison.

Presume not on[1] thy heart when mine is slain:
Thou gav'st me thine not to give back again.

### 23

As an unperfect actor on the stage
Who with his fear is put besides° his part,                                    *forgets*
Or some fierce thing replete with too much rage
Whose strength's abundance weakens his own heart,
5   So I, for fear of trust,° forget to say                              *lack of confidence*
The perfect ceremony of love's rite,[1]
And in mine own love's strength seem to decay,
O'er-charged with burden of mine own love's might.
O let my books be then the eloquence
10  And dumb presagers° of my speaking breast,                           *mute presenters*
Who plead for love, and look for recompense
More than that tongue that more hath more expressed.[2]
    O learn to read what silent love hath writ;
    To hear with eyes belongs to love's fine wit.

### 24

Mine eye hath played the painter,[1] and hath steeled[2]
Thy beauty's form in table° of my heart.                                    *the painted tablet*
My body is the frame wherein 'tis held,
And perspective[3] it is best painter's art;
5   For through the painter must you see his skill
To find where your true image pictured lies,
Which in my bosom's shop° is hanging still,                                  *heart's workshop*
That hath his windows glazèd with thine eyes.[4]
Now see what good turns eyes for eyes have done:
10  Mine eyes have drawn thy shape, and thine for me
Are windows to my breast, wherethrough the sun
Delights to peep, to gaze therein on thee.
    Yet eyes this cunning want° to grace their art:                        *lack this talent*
    They draw but what they see, know not the heart.

### 25

Let those who are in favour with their stars
Of public honour and proud titles boast,
Whilst I, whom fortune of such triumph bars,
Unlooked-for joy in that I honour most.[1]
5   Great princes' favourites their fair leaves spread°                    *bloom*
But as the marigold at the sun's eye,[2]
And in themselves their pride lies° burièd,                                 *will lie*
For at a frown they in their glory die.
The painful warrior famousèd for might,

**Sonnet 22**
1. Do not expect to get back.
**Sonnet 23**
1. Q reads "right," suggesting love's due as well as ritual.
2. More than that (rival) speaker who has more often said more.
**Sonnet 24**
1. The running conceit is of the speaker and addressee looking into one another's eyes, seeing both the other and himself reflected.
2. Engraved. Editors often emend Q's "steeld" to "stell'd" (fixed, placed) for a better fit with "painter."
3. Seen from the proper angle, through the painter's eyes. A "perspective" was a distorted painting that looked right only if viewed from the correct angle.
4. The addressee looks into the speaker's eyes ("windows"), which seem fitted with glass ("glazèd") by the reflection there of the addressee's own eyes. The eyes are the heart's ("his" [its], referring to "bosom's," line 7) windows, through which the addressee can therefore see his own image in the speaker's heart.
**Sonnet 25**
1. Unexpectedly (privately) take pleasure in what I most esteem (the youth).
2. Only at the prince's pleasure or whim.

10 After a thousand victories once foiled
Is from the book of honour razèd° quite,                    *deleted*
And all the rest forgot for which he toiled.
    Then happy I, that love and am beloved
    Where I may not remove nor be removed.

### 26

Lord of my love, to whom in vassalage°                     *feudal allegiance*
Thy merit hath my duty strongly knit,
To thee I send this written embassage°                     *missive*
To witness duty, not to show my wit;
5 Duty so great which wit so poor as mine
May make seem bare in wanting° words to show it,           *lacking*
But that I hope some good conceit° of thine                *opinion*
In thy soul's thought, all naked,¹ will bestow° it,        *provide a place for*
Till whatsoever star that guides my moving°                *actions*
10 Points on me graciously with fair aspect,°              *astrological influence*
And puts apparel on my tattered loving
To show me worthy of thy sweet respect.
    Then may I dare to boast how I do love thee;
    Till then, not show my head where thou mayst prove° me.    *test*

### 27

Weary with toil I haste me to my bed,
The dear repose for limbs with travel° tired;              *work; journeying*
But then begins a journey in my head
To work my mind when body's work's expired;
5 For then my thoughts, from far where I abide,
Intend a zealous pilgrimage to thee,
And keep my drooping eyelids open wide,
Looking on darkness which the blind do see:
Save that my soul's imaginary sight
10 Presents thy shadow° to my sightless view,              *picture*
Which like a jewel hung in ghastly night
Makes black night beauteous and her old face new.
    Lo, thus by day my limbs, by night my mind,
    For° thee, and for myself, no quiet find.            *Because of*

### 28¹

How can I then return in happy plight,°                    *condition*
That am debarred the benefit of rest,
When day's oppression is not eased by night,
But day by night and night by day oppressed,
5 And each, though enemies to either's° reign,             *each other's*
Do in consent shake hands to torture me,
The one by toil, the other to complain²
How far I toil, still farther off from thee?
I tell the day to please him thou art bright,
10 And do'st him grace when clouds do blot the heaven;³
So flatter I the swart°-complexioned night                *dark*
When sparkling stars twire not thou gild'st the even.⁴

---

**Sonnet 26**
1. Refers to his "bare"-seeming "duty."
**Sonnet 28**
1. This sonnet links with 27.

2. *one:* day. *other:* night, making me "complain."
3. And confer beauty on him as a substitute for the sun.
4. By saying that when stars aren't twinkling, you brighten the evening.

But day doth daily draw my sorrows longer,
And night doth nightly make grief's strength seem stronger.

### 29

When, in disgrace with fortune and men's eyes,
I all alone beweep my outcast state,
And trouble deaf heaven with my bootless° cries,          *unavailing*
And look upon myself and curse my fate,
5  Wishing me like to one more rich in hope,
Featured like him, like him with friends possessed,[1]
Desiring this man's art° and that man's scope,°          *skill / range*
With what I most enjoy° contented least:          *like; own*
Yet in these thoughts myself almost despising,
10  Haply[2] I think on thee, and then my state,°          *mood; fortunes*
Like to the lark at break of day arising
From sullen earth, sings hymns at heaven's gate;
    For thy sweet love remembered such wealth brings
    That then I scorn to change my state with kings'.

### 30

When to the sessions° of sweet silent thought          *court sittings*
I summon up remembrance of things past,
I sigh° the lack of many a thing I sought,          *mourn*
And with old woes new wail my dear time's waste.[1]
5  Then can I drown an eye unused to flow
For precious friends hid in death's dateless° night,          *endless*
And weep afresh love's long-since-cancelled° woe,          *repaid (with sorrow)*
And moan th'expense° of many a vanished sight.          *passing*
Then can I grieve at grievances foregone,°          *bygone*
10  And heavily° from woe to woe tell° o'er          *sadly / say; count*
The sad account° of fore-bemoanèd moan,          *story; finances*
Which I new pay as if not paid before.
    But if the while I think on thee, dear friend,
    All losses are restored, and sorrows end.

### 31

Thy bosom is endearèd with° all hearts          *loved by; enriched by*
Which I by lacking have supposèd dead,
And there reigns love, and all love's loving parts,
And all those friends which I thought burièd.
5  How many a holy and obsequious° tear          *dutifullly mourning*
Hath dear religious° love stol'n from mine eye          *devoted*
As interest of° the dead, which° now appear          *due payment to / who*
But things removed° that hidden in thee lie!          *absent*
Thou art the grave where buried love doth live,
10  Hung with the trophies° of my lovers gone,          *memorials*
Who all their parts° of me to thee did give:          *shares*
    That due of many[1] now is thine alone.

---

**Sonnet 29**
1. *Wishing . . . possessed:* Three people he wants to be like—"like to one" with better prospects, better looking "like him," and having friends "like him."
2. By chance; also, pun on "happily."

**Sonnet 30**
1. *my . . . waste:* the frittering or wasting away of my precious time.
**Sonnet 31**
1. What was owed to many (myself).

Their images I loved I view in thee,
And thou, all they,[2] hast all the all of me.

### 32

If thou survive my well-contented day[1]
When that churl death my bones with dust shall cover,
And shalt by fortune° once more resurvey                           *chance*
These poor rude° lines of thy deceasèd lover,                      *rough*
5  Compare them with the bett'ring° of the time,              *progress; better art*
And though they be outstripped by every pen,
Reserve them for my love, not for their rhyme
Exceeded by the height of happier men.[2]
O then vouchsafe me but this loving thought:
10  'Had my friend's muse grown with this growing age,
A dearer birth° than this his love had brought                     *worthier poem*
To march in ranks of better equipage;°                             *poems*
    But since he died, and poets better prove,°          *have improved*
    Theirs for their style I'll read, his for his love.'

### 33

Full many a glorious morning have I seen
Flatter the mountain tops with sovereign eye,°                     *sunlight*
Kissing with golden face the meadows green,
Gilding pale streams with heavenly alchemy;
5  Anon° permit the basest° clouds to ride                  *(But) soon / darkest*
With ugly rack° on his celestial face,                             *cloudy mask*
And from the forlorn world his visage hide,
Stealing unseen to west with this disgrace.
Even so my sun one early morn did shine
10  With all triumphant splendour on my brow;
But out, alack,° he was but one hour mine;                         *alas*
The region° cloud hath masked him from me now.                     *high*
    Yet him for this my love no whit disdaineth:
    Suns of the world may stain° when heaven's sun staineth.  *darken*

### 34[1]

Why didst thou promise such a beauteous day
And make me travel forth without my cloak,
To let base clouds o'ertake me in my way,
Hiding thy brav'ry° in their rotten smoke?°                        *finery / noxious mists*
5  'Tis not enough that through the cloud thou break
To dry the rain on my storm-beaten face,
For no man well of such a salve can speak
That heals the wound and cures not the disgrace.[2]
Nor can thy shame° give physic to° my grief;                      *remorse / cure*
10  Though thou repent, yet I have still the loss.
Th'offender's sorrow lends but weak relief
To him that bears the strong offence's cross.°                     *consequences*

---

2. And you, who are made up of all of them.
**Sonnet 32**
1. Day of my death, which I shall willingly accept.
2. *Reserve . . . men:* Keep them because you love me, not
for their value as poetry, which is surpassed by poets more
fortunate in their talent than I.
**Sonnet 34**
1. This sonnet links with 33.
2. Disfigurement; dishonor done the poet by the youth's
neglect.

Ah, but those tears are pearl which thy love sheds,
And they are rich, and ransom° all ill deeds.                    *atone for*

### 35

No more be grieved at that which thou hast done:
Roses have thorns, and silver fountains mud.
Clouds and eclipses stain° both moon and sun,                    *darken*
And loathsome canker° lives in sweetest bud.                     *(worm)*
5    All men make faults, and even I in this,
Authorizing thy trespass with compare,[1]
Myself corrupting salving thy amiss,[2]
Excusing thy sins more than thy sins are;[3]
For to thy sensual fault I bring in sense[4]—
10   Thy adverse party is thy advocate—
And 'gainst myself a lawful plea commence.
Such civil war is in my love and hate
    That I an accessory needs must be
    To that sweet thief which sourly robs from me.

### 36

Let me confess that we two must be twain[1]
Although our undivided loves are one;
So shall those blots° that do with me remain       *flaws; sources of shame*
Without thy help by me be borne alone.
5    In our two loves there is but one respect,°         *focus of attention*
Though in our lives a separable spite[2]
Which, though it alter not love's sole° effect,         *single-minded*
Yet doth it steal sweet hours from love's delight.
I may not evermore acknowledge thee
10   Lest my bewailèd guilt should do thee shame,
Nor thou with public kindness honour me
Unless thou take° that honour from thy name.                     *lose*
    But do not so. I love thee in such sort°           *such a way*
    As, thou being mine, mine is thy good report.[3]

### 37

As a decrepit father takes delight
To see his active child do deeds of youth,
So I, made lame by fortune's dearest° spite,                    *direst*
Take all my comfort of° thy worth and truth;                    *in*
5    For whether beauty, birth, or wealth, or wit,
Or any of these all, or all, or more,
Entitled in thy parts[1] do crownèd sit,
I make my love engrafted to this store.[2]
So then I am not lame, poor, nor despised,
10   Whilst that this shadow° doth such substance give          *idea*
That I in thy abundance am sufficed

Sonnet 35
1. Justifying your offense with comparisons.
2. Corrupting myself in minimizing your transgression.
3. Excusing you (overindulgently) from worse sins than
the ones you've committed.
4. I use reason to defend your sensual offense.
Sonnet 36
1. Separated; but also, paradoxically, two of a kind or
bound together.

2. Separation that causes vexation; vexation that causes
separation.
3. Reputation. This couplet also ends 96.
Sonnet 37
1. Enrolled among your good qualities.
2. I engraft my love onto this abundance (of good qualities).

And by a part of all thy glory live.
Look what° is best, that best I wish in thee;                    *whatever*
This° wish I have, then ten times happy me.                     *When this*

### 38

How can my muse want subject to invent°                         *lack subject matter*
While thou dost breathe, that pour'st into my verse
Thine own sweet argument,° too excellent                        *theme*
For every vulgar paper to rehearse?[1]
5   O, give thyself the thanks if aught in me
Worthy perusal stand against thy sight;[2]
For who's so dumb that cannot write to thee,
When thou thyself dost give invention light?
Be thou the tenth muse, ten times more in worth
10  Than those old nine which rhymers invocate,
And he that calls on thee, let him bring forth
Eternal numbers° to outlive long° date.                         *verses / a distant*
    If my slight muse do please these curious° days,            *finicky*
    The pain° be mine, but thine shall be the praise.           *pains; effort*

### 39

O, how thy worth with manners° may I sing                       *modesty*
When thou art all the better part of me?
What can mine own praise to mine own self bring,
And what is't but mine own when I praise thee?
5   Even for° this let us divided live,                         *Because of*
And our dear love lose name of single one,°                     *the reputation of unity*
That by this separation I may give
That due to thee which thou deserv'st alone.
O absence, what a torment wouldst thou prove
10  Were it not thy sour leisure gave sweet leave
To entertain° the time with thoughts of love,                  *enliven*
Which time and thoughts so sweetly doth deceive,
    And that thou teachest how to make one twain
    By praising him here° who doth hence remain!               *in this poem*

### 40[1]

Take all my loves, my love, yea, take them all:
What hast thou then more than thou hadst before?
No love, my love, that thou mayst true love call—
All mine was thine before thou hadst this more.
5   Then if for my love thou my love receivest,[2]
I cannot blame thee for my love thou usest;[3]
But yet be blamed if thou this self[4] deceivest
By wilful taste of what thyself° refusest.                      *your better nature*
I do forgive thy robb'ry, gentle thief,
10  Although thou steal thee all my poverty;°                   *what little I own*
And yet love knows it is a greater grief

---

**Sonnet 38**
1. Every ordinary, commonplace piece of writing to set forth.
2. *if . . . sight:* if you see anything in my writing worth reading.
**Sonnet 40**
1. Sonnets 40–42 concern a situation that may be identi-

cal to the love triangle described in 133–34 and 144.
2. Then if for love of me you take my beloved.
3. *for . . . usest:* because you use my beloved (sexually).
4. The poet (often emended, perhaps rightly, to "thyself").

To bear love's wrong than hate's known injury.
   Lascivious grace,° in whom all ill well shows,         *Charming wanton*
   Kill me with spites,° yet we must not be foes.          *offenses*

### 41

Those pretty° wrongs that liberty° commits         *minor / licentiousness*
When I am sometime absent from thy heart
Thy beauty and thy years full well befits,
For still° temptation follows where thou art.             *continually*
5  Gentle° thou art, and therefore to be won;       *Tender; upper-class*
Beauteous thou art, therefore to be assailed;
And when a woman woos, what woman's son
Will sourly leave her till he have prevailed?[1]
Ay me, but yet thou mightst my seat[2] forbear,
10  And chide thy beauty and thy straying youth
Who lead thee in their riot° even there         *depraved conduct*
Where thou art forced to break a two-fold troth:
   Hers, by thy beauty tempting her to thee,
   Thine, by thy beauty being false to me.

### 42

That thou hast her, it is not all my grief,
And yet it may be said I loved her dearly;
That she hath thee is of my wailing chief,°         *chief reason*
A loss in love that touches me more nearly.
5  Loving offenders, thus I will excuse ye:
Thou dost love her because thou know'st I love her,
And for my sake even so doth she abuse° me,        *mistreat*
Suff'ring my friend for my sake to approve her.[1]
If I lose thee, my loss is my love's gain,
10  And losing° her, my friend hath found that loss:     *I losing*
Both find each other, and I lose both twain,
And both for my sake lay on me this cross.°       *affliction*
   But here's the joy: my friend and I are one.
   Sweet flattery!° Then she loves but me alone.    *Pleasing delusion*

### 43

When most I wink,° then do mine eyes best see,     *shut my eyes*
For all the day they view things unrespected;°   *unheeded; unworthy*
But when I sleep, in dreams they look on thee,
And, darkly bright, are bright in dark directed.[1]
5  Then thou, whose shadow shadows doth make bright,[2]
How would thy shadow's form° form happy show°   *substance / sight*
To the clear day with thy much clearer light,
When to unseeing eyes[3] thy shade shines so!
How would, I say, mine eyes be blessèd made
10  By looking on thee in the living day,
When in dead night thy fair imperfect° shade       *incorporeal*

---

**Sonnet 41**
1. Until he has had his way. But Q's "he" could easily be a misprint for "she."
2. Rightful place (my mistress).
**Sonnet 42**
1. To put her to the test (sexually).

**Sonnet 43**
1. (My eyes) seeing in the dark turn toward your bright eyes in the dark.
2. Whose image lightens darkness.
3. Because closed in sleep.

Through heavy sleep on sightless eyes doth stay!
    All days are nights to see till I see thee,
    And nights bright days when dreams do show thee me.°          *to me*

### 44

If the dull° substance of my flesh were thought,                *heavy*
Injurious distance should not stop my way;
For then, despite of space, I would be brought
From limits° far remote where° thou dost stay.         *places / to where*
5   No matter then although my foot did stand
Upon the farthest earth removed from thee;
For nimble thought can jump both sea and land
As soon as think the place where he° would be.          *(thought)*
But ah, thought kills me that I am not thought,
10  To leap large lengths of miles when thou art gone,
But that, so much of earth and water wrought,[1]
I must attend time's leisure[2] with my moan,
    Receiving naught by elements so slow
    But heavy tears, badges of either's woe.[3]

### 45[1]

The other two,[2] slight° air and purging fire,             *light*
Are both with thee wherever I abide;
The first my thought, the other my desire,
These present-absent[3] with swift motion slide;
5   For when these quicker° elements are gone          *livelier*
In tender embassy of love to thee,
My life, being made of four, with two alone
Sinks down to death, oppressed with melancholy,
Until life's composition be recured°             *renewed*
10  By those swift messengers returned from thee,
Who even but now come back again assured
Of thy fair health, recounting it to me.
    This told, I joy; but then no longer glad,
    I send them back again and straight° grow sad.    *suddenly*

### 46

Mine eye and heart are at a mortal° war              *lethal*
How to divide the conquest of thy sight.[1]
Mine eye my heart thy picture's sight would bar,
My heart, mine eye the freedom° of that right.     *free enjoyment*
5   My heart doth plead that thou in him dost lie,
A closet° never pierced with crystal eyes;           *room*
But the defendant doth that plea deny,
And says in him thy fair appearance lies.
To 'cide° this title is empanellèd°        *decide / enrolled*
10  A quest° of thoughts, all tenants to the heart,

---

**Sonnet 44**
1. Being compounded of so much earth and water (the heavy elements).
2. I must wait humbly (as if on a great man) for time to reunite us.
3. Emblems of the grief of each of the poet's elements (of earth because heavy [sad], of water because wet).
**Sonnet 45**
1. This sonnet links with 44.

2. Of the poet's four elements. See 44.11.
3. Now present, now absent; constantly coming and going.
**Sonnet 46**
1. The spoils of the sight of you (possibly in a painting; see 47.5–14).

And by their verdict is determinèd
The clear eye's moiety° and the dear heart's part,     *jury*
   As thus: mine eye's due is thy outward part,     *share*
   And my heart's right thy inward love of heart.

### 47[1]

Betwixt mine eye and heart a league is took,°     *truce is made*
And each doth good turns now unto the other.
When that mine eye is famished for a look,
Or heart in love with sighs himself doth smother,[2]
5  With my love's picture then my eye doth feast,
And to the painted banquet bids my heart.
Another time mine eye is my heart's guest
And in his thoughts of love doth share a part.
So either by thy picture or my love,
10 Thyself away art present still with me;
For thou no farther than my thoughts canst move,
And I am still° with them, and they with thee;     *constantly*
   Or if they sleep, thy picture in my sight
   Awakes my heart to heart's and eye's delight.

### 48

How careful was I when I took my way°     *set off*
Each trifle under truest° bars to thrust,     *most reliable*
That to my use° it might unusèd stay     *benefit*
From hands of falsehood, in sure wards° of trust.     *safe places*
5  But thou, to° whom my jewels trifles are,     *compared to*
Most worthy comfort, now my greatest grief,[1]
Thou best of dearest and mine only care
Art left the prey of every vulgar thief.
Thee have I not locked up in any chest
10 Save where thou art not, though I feel thou art—
Within the gentle closure of my breast,
From whence at pleasure thou mayst come and part;°     *go*
   And even thence thou wilt be stol'n, I fear,
   For truth° proves thievish for a prize so dear.     *even honesty*

### 49

Against° that time—if ever that time come—     *In preparation for*
When I shall see thee frown on my defects,
Whenas thy love hath cast his utmost sum,[1]
Called to that audit by advised respects;°     *judicious reasons*
5  Against that time when thou shalt strangely° pass     *as a stranger*
And scarcely greet me with that sun, thine eye,
When love converted from the thing it was
Shall reasons find of settled gravity:[2]
Against that time do I ensconce me° here     *secure myself*
10 Within the knowledge of mine own desert,[3]
And this my hand against myself uprear°     *testify against myself*

---

**Sonnet 47**
1. This sonnet links with 46.
2. Or when my loving heart smothers itself with sighs.
**Sonnet 48**
1. Because absent and in danger of being stolen.

**Sonnet 49**
1. When your love has calculated the bottom line.
2. Shall find reasons for a dignified reserve; shall find reasons of well-established seriousness (for leaving me).
3. My (lack of?) worthiness to be loved.

To guard the lawful reasons on thy part.°                    *defend your case*
   To leave poor me thou hast the strength of laws,
   Since why to love° I can allege no cause.                 *why you should love*

### 50

How heavy° do I journey on the way,                          *wearily*
When what I seek—my weary travel's end—
Doth teach that ease and that repose to say[1]
'Thus far the miles are measured from thy friend.'
5  The beast that bears me, tired with my woe,
Plods dully on to bear° that weight in me,                   *while bearing*
As if by some instinct the wretch did know
His rider loved not speed, being made[2] from thee.
The bloody spur cannot provoke him on
10 That sometimes anger thrusts into his hide,
Which heavily he answers with a groan
More sharp to me than spurring to his side;
   For that same groan doth put this in my mind:
   My grief lies onward and my joy behind.

### 51[1]

Thus can my love excuse the slow offence°                    *offense of slowness*
Of my dull bearer when from thee I speed:
From where thou art why should I haste me thence?
Till I return, of posting° is no need.                       *riding quickly*
5  O what excuse will my poor beast then find
When swift extremity° can seem but slow?                     *extreme (return) speed*
Then should I spur, though mounted on the wind;
In wingèd speed no motion shall I know.[2]
Then can no horse with my desire keep pace;
10 Therefore desire, of perfect'st love being made,
Shall rein° no dull flesh in his fiery race;                 *curb*
But love, for love,° thus shall excuse my jade:             *on love's behalf*
   Since from thee going he went wilful-slow,
   Towards thee I'll run and give him leave to go.°        *walk*

### 52

So am I as the rich° whose blessèd key                       *rich man*
Can bring him to his sweet up-lockèd treasure,
The which he will not ev'ry hour survey,
For° blunting the fine point of seldom° pleasure.            *To avoid / occasional*
5  Therefore are feasts° so solemn° and so rare            *feast days / dignified*
Since, seldom coming, in the long year set
Like stones of worth they thinly placèd are,
Or captain° jewels in the carcanet.°                         *chief / jeweled collar*
So is the time that keeps you as° my chest,°                 *like / jewel case*
10 Or as the wardrobe which the robe doth hide,
To make some special instant special blest

---

**Sonnet 50**
1. Teach the comforts at the end of the road to remind me that.
2. *speed, being made*: hastening away; haste, when and because it is.
**Sonnet 51**
1. This sonnet links with 50.

2. I will feel no motion when desire carries me back through the air. See line 11 and sonnets 44–45 for the association of fire and air with desire and thought, and of earth and water with dull, slow flesh.

By new unfolding his imprisoned pride.
　　Blessèd are you whose worthiness gives scope,
　　Being had, to triumph; being lacked, to hope.[1]


### 53

What is your substance, whereof are you made,
That millions of strange shadows on you tend?°　　　　　*attend*
Since every one hath, every one, one shade,[1]
And you, but one, can every shadow lend.[2]
5　Describe° Adonis, and the counterfeit°　　　*Draw / likeness*
Is poorly imitated after you.
On Helen's cheek all art of beauty set,
And you in Grecian tires are painted new.[3]
Speak of the spring and foison° of the year:　　　　*harvest time*
10　The one doth shadow of your beauty show,
The other as your bounty doth appear;
And you in every blessèd shape we know.°　　　　　*recognize*
　　In all external grace you have some part,
　　But you like none, none you, for constant heart.


### 54

O how much more doth beauty beauteous seem
By° that sweet ornament which truth doth give!　　　*Because of*
The rose looks fair, but fairer we it deem
For that sweet odour which doth in it live.
5　The canker blooms[1] have full as deep a dye
As the perfumèd tincture° of the roses,　　　　　　*color*
Hang on such thorns, and play as wantonly°　　*flatter as playfully*
When summer's breath their maskèd buds discloses;
But for° their virtue only is° their show　　　*since / lies wholly in*
10　They live unwooed and unrespected° fade,　　　*unappreciated*
Die to themselves.° Sweet roses do not so;　*alone; without influence*
Of their sweet deaths are sweetest odours made:
　　And so of you, beauteous and lovely youth,
　　When that° shall fade, by verse distils your truth.[2]　　　*beauty*


### 55

Not marble nor the gilded monuments
Of princes shall outlive this powerful rhyme,
But you shall shine more bright in these contents
Than unswept stone besmeared with sluttish° time.　　*slovenly*
5　When wasteful war shall statues overturn,
And broils° root out the work of masonry,　　　　　*battles*
Nor Mars his° sword nor war's quick fire shall burn　*Neither Mars's*
The living record of your memory.
'Gainst death and all oblivious enmity
10　Shall you pace forth; your praise shall still find room

---

**Sonnet 52**
1. *gives . . . hope:* allows me to exult when with you and
to hope when not with you.
**Sonnet 53**
1. Since each person has an individual shadow.
2. Can cast all shadows (are visible in every image).
3. *On . . . new:* If one were to use every art to reproduce
the beauty of Helen of Troy (or use artful cosmetics

on Helen's cheek) it would look like you in Grecian
headgear.
**Sonnet 54**
1. Dog roses (having little scent).
2. See sonnet 5. Q's "vade" is a variant of "fade," the reading adopted here, but it probably has the secondary meaning of "depart," from the Latin *vadere*.

Even in the eyes of all posterity
That wear this world out to the ending doom.[1]
 So, till the judgement that yourself arise,
 You live in this, and dwell in lovers' eyes.

### 56

Sweet love,[1] renew thy force. Be it not said
Thy edge should blunter be than appetite,
Which but° today by feeding is allayed,     *merely for*
Tomorrow sharpened in his former might.
5 So, love, be thou; although today thou fill
Thy hungry eyes even till they wink° with fullness,   *close (to sleep)*
Tomorrow see again, and do not kill
The spirit of love with a perpetual dullness.
Let this sad int'rim like the ocean be
10 Which parts the shore where two contracted new
Come daily to the banks, that when they see
Return of love, more blessed may be the view;[2]
 Or call it winter, which, being full of care,
 Makes summer's welcome, thrice more wished, more rare.°   *valuable*

### 57

Being your slave, what should I do but tend°     *wait*
Upon the hours and times of your desire?
I have no precious time at all to spend,
Nor services to do, till you require;
5 Nor dare I chide the world-without-end° hour   *endless*
Whilst I, my sovereign, watch the clock for you,
Nor think the bitterness of absence sour
When you have bid your servant once adieu.
Nor dare I question with my jealous thought
10 Where you may be, or your affairs suppose,°   *speculate on*
But like a sad slave stay and think of naught
Save, where you are, how happy you make those.
 So true a fool is love that in your will,[1]
 Though you do anything, he thinks no ill.

### 58[1]

That god forbid, that made me first your slave,
I should in thought control your times of pleasure,
Or at your hand th'account of hours to crave,[2]
Being your vassal° bound to stay° your leisure.   *slave / wait upon*
5 O let me suffer, being at your beck,
Th'imprisoned absence of your liberty,[3]
And patience, tame to sufferance, bide each check,[4]
Without accusing you of injury.

---

**Sonnet 55**
1. Doomsday: in Christianity, the Day of Judgment, when dead bodies are supposed to "arise" (line 13) from the grave and be united with their souls.
**Sonnet 56**
1. The feeling (not the beloved).
2. *Let . . . view*: The "sad" interval between periods of feeling love is like an ocean dividing shores where two lovers come daily hoping for the (emotionally renewing) sight of a boat bringing the other. *contracted new*: newly betrothed.

**Sonnet 57**
1. Desire (including sexual desire); capitalized in Q, perhaps punning on Shakespeare's name. See 135–36.
**Sonnet 58**
1. This sonnet links with 57.
2. Or should seek an account of how you pass your time.
3. The imprisoned feeling caused by your licentiousness when you're away.
4. And (let me) patient, acquiescent in suffering, endure each setback.

Be where you list,° your charter° is so strong          *wish / freedom*
10   That you yourself may privilege° your time          *allocate*
To what you will; to you it doth belong
Yourself to pardon of self-doing° crime.          *committed by you*
   I am to wait, though waiting so be hell,
   Not blame your pleasure, be it ill or well.

### 59

If there be nothing new, but that which is
Hath been before, how are our brains beguiled,°          *cheated*
Which, labouring° for invention, bear amiss          *working; giving birth*
The second burden of a former child![1]
5   O that record° could with a backward look          *recollection*
Even of five hundred courses of the sun
Show me your image in some antique book
Since mind at first in character was done,[2]
That I might see what the old world could say
10   To this composèd wonder of your frame;[3]
Whether we are mended° or whe'er better they,          *improved*
Or whether revolution be the same.[4]
   O, sure I am the wits° of former days          *clever writers*
   To subjects worse have given admiring praise.

### 60

Like as the waves make towards the pebbled shore,
So do our minutes hasten to their end,
Each changing place with that which goes before;
In sequent toil all forwards do contend.[1]
5   Nativity,° once in the main of light,°          *A newborn / in the world*
Crawls to maturity, wherewith being crowned
Crookèd° eclipses 'gainst his glory fight,          *Pernicious*
And time that gave doth now his gift confound.°          *ruin*
Time doth transfix the flourish[2] set on youth,
10   And delves the parallels° in beauty's brow;          *carves the wrinkles*
Feeds on the rarities of nature's truth,[3]
And nothing stands but for his scythe to mow.
   And yet to times in hope° my verse shall stand,          *future days*
   Praising thy worth despite his cruel hand.

### 61

Is it thy will thy image should keep open
My heavy eyelids to the weary night?
Dost thou desire my slumbers should be broken
While shadows° like to thee do mock my sight?          *visions*
5   Is it thy spirit that thou send'st from thee
So far from home into my deeds to pry,
To find out shames and idle hours in me,
The scope and tenor of thy jealousy?[1]
   O no; thy love, though much, is not so great.

Sonnet 59
1. *bear . . . child:* mistakenly ("amiss") give birth for a second time to a child that has already been born.
2. Since writing was invented.
3. To the wonderful composition of your form (perhaps referring to the sonnet itself as well).
4. Whether the revolving of the ages makes no difference.

Sonnet 60
1. Toiling one after the other, all seek to move forward.
2. Time pierces and destroys the ornament (beauty).
3. On the most precious products of nature's perfection.

Sonnet 61
1. The object and intent of your distrust (that is, "shames and idle hours," line 7).

10  It is my love that keeps mine eye awake,
    Mine own true love that doth my rest defeat,
    To play the watchman ever for thy sake.
        For thee watch I° whilst thou dost wake elsewhere,    *I remain awake*
        From me far off, with others all too near.

### 62

    Sin of self-love possesseth all mine eye,
    And all my soul, and all my every part;
    And for this sin there is no remedy,
    It is so grounded inward in my heart.
5   Methinks no face so gracious is as mine,
    No shape so true,° no truth of such account,    *perfect*
    And for myself mine own worth do define
    As° I all other° in all worths surmount.    *As if / others*
    But when my glass° shows me myself indeed,    *mirror*
10  Beated and chapped with tanned antiquity,
    Mine own self-love quite contrary I read;
    Self so self-loving were iniquity.
        'Tis thee, my self,° that for° myself I praise,    *you, my other self / as*
        Painting my age with beauty of thy days.

### 63

    Against° my love shall be as I am now,    *Preparing for when*
    With time's injurious hand crushed and o'erworn;
    When hours have drained his blood and filled his brow
    With lines and wrinkles; when his youthful morn
5   Hath travelled° on to age's steepy¹ night,    *progressed; toiled*
    And all those beauties whereof now he's king
    Are vanishing, or vanished out of sight,
    Stealing away the treasure of his spring:
    For such a time do I now fortify
10  Against confounding° age's cruel knife,    *devastating*
    That he shall never cut from memory
    My sweet love's beauty, though° my lover's life.    *though he will sever*
        His beauty shall in these black lines be seen,
        And they shall live, and he in them still green.°    *perpetually youthful*

### 64

    When I have seen by time's fell° hand defaced    *fierce*
    The rich proud cost° of outworn buried age;    *expense*
    When sometime°-lofty towers I see down razed,    *once*
    And brass eternal slave to mortal rage;¹
5   When I have seen the hungry ocean gain
    Advantage on the kingdom of the shore,
    And the firm soil win of° the wat'ry main,    *win ground from*
    Increasing store with loss and loss with store;²
    When I have seen such interchange of state,
10  Or state³ itself confounded to decay,°    *reduced to ruins*
    Ruin hath taught me thus to ruminate:

**Sonnet 63**
1. Precipitous (like the path of the setting sun).
**Sonnet 64**
1. And eternal brass forever succumbs to death's violence.

2. Adding to the stock of one by loss of the other, and vice versa.
3. *state* (line 9): condition; sovereign territory. *state* (line 10): pomp.

That time will come and take my love away.
  This thought is as a death, which° cannot choose          *since thought*
  But weep to have° that which it fears to lose.              *at having*

65

Since° brass, nor stone, nor earth, nor boundless sea,     *Since there is neither*
But sad mortality o'ersways their power,
How with this rage shall beauty hold a plea,[1]
Whose action is no stronger than a flower?
5  O how shall summer's honey breath hold out
Against the wrackful° siege of battering days            *damaging*
When rocks impregnable are not so stout,
Nor gates of steel so strong, but time decays?°        *decays them*
O fearful meditation! Where, alack,
10  Shall time's best jewel° from time's chest[2] lie hid,     *(the beloved)*
Or what strong hand can hold his swift foot back,
Or who his spoil° of beauty can forbid?           *destruction*
  O none, unless this miracle have might:
  That in black ink my love may still shine bright.

66

Tired with all these°, for restful death I cry:      *(the ensuing wrongs)*
As,° to behold desert° a beggar born,        *For example / merit*
And needy nothing trimmed in jollity,[1]
And purest faith unhappily forsworn,°         *betrayed; perjured*
5  And gilded honour shamefully misplaced,
And maiden virtue rudely strumpeted,
And right perfection wrongfully disgraced,
And strength by limping sway° disablèd,          *feeble leaders*
And art made tongue-tied° by authority,        *learning silenced*
10  And folly, doctor-like, controlling skill,[2]
And simple truth miscalled simplicity,°          *naïveté*
And captive good attending° captain ill.         *serving*
  Tired with all these, from these would I be gone,
  Save that to die I leave my love alone.

67

Ah, wherefore with infection[1] should he live
And with his presence grace impiety,
That° sin by him advantage should achieve         *So that*
And lace° itself with his society?            *decorate*
5  Why should false painting imitate his cheek,
And steal dead seeming of[2] his living hue?
Why should poor° beauty indirectly seek         *lesser*
Roses of shadow,° since his rose is true?     *Cosmetic beauty*
Why should he live now nature bankrupt is,
10  Beggared of blood to blush through lively veins,
For she hath no exchequer° now but his,         *treasury*

---

**Sonnet 65**
1. How can beauty make a (legal) case against such a power to destroy?
2. Treasure chest; coffin.
**Sonnet 66**
1. And ungifted (or impoverished) worthlessness adorned with finery.

2. And folly, feigning erudition, dominating true wisdom or ability. Before modern medicine, doctors were often portrayed as fools or con artists.
**Sonnet 67**
1. The world's ills (as in 66).
2. *dead seeming of*: an inanimate outward resemblance from.

And proud of many, lives upon his gains?[3]
    O, him she stores° to show what wealth she had                     *keeps*
    In days long since, before these last so bad.

### 68[1]

Thus is his cheek the map° of days outworn,                          *image*
When beauty lived and died as flowers do now,
5    Before these bastard signs of fair° were borne°     *cosmetics / worn; born*
Or durst inhabit on a living brow;
Before the golden tresses of the dead,
The right of sepulchres,[2] were shorn away
To live a second life on second head;
Ere beauty's dead fleece made another gay.
In him those holy antique hours° are seen               *good old days*
10   Without all ornament, itself and true,
Making no summer of another's green,
Robbing no old to dress his beauty new;
    And him as for a map doth nature store,°                *keep*
    To show false art what beauty was of yore.

### 69

Those parts of thee that the world's eye doth view
Want° nothing that the thought of hearts can mend.°    *Lack / imagine better*
All tongues, the voice of souls, give thee that due,
Utt'ring bare truth even so as foes commend.[1]
5    Thy outward thus with outward praise is crowned,
But those same tongues that give thee so thine own°         *your due*
In other accents° do this praise confound°         *words / undermine*
By seeing farther than the eye hath shown.
They look into the beauty of thy mind,
10   And that in guess they measure by thy deeds.
Then, churls, their thoughts—although their eyes were kind
To thy fair flower add the rank smell of weeds.
    But why thy odour matcheth not thy show,°            *appearance*
    The soil is this: that thou dost common grow.[2]

### 70[1]

That thou are blamed shall not be thy defect,
For slander's mark° was ever yet the fair.                   *target*
The ornament of beauty is suspect,°                    *suspicion*
A crow that flies in heaven's sweetest air.
5    So° thou be good, slander doth but approve             *So long as*
Thy worth the greater, being wooed of time;[2]
For canker vice[3] the sweetest buds doth love,
And thou present'st a pure unstainèd prime.°              *youth*
Thou hast passed by the ambush of young days
10   Either not assailed, or victor being charged;

---

3. Though (falsely) taking pride in her abundance (of offspring?), lives off the interest he earns (from his endowment of beauty).
**Sonnet 68**
1. This sonnet links with 67.
2. Properly belonging to tombs (wigs were made from the
hair of corpses).
**Sonnet 69**
1. Uttering minimal truth, in the way that enemies

praise.
2. The ground (reason; also, stain) is this: you are becoming low (promiscuous).
**Sonnet 70**
1. This sonnet links with 69.
2. *slander . . . time:* the gossip merely proves that you're
so popular ("wooed of time") that you're worth even
more.
3. Slander, like a cankerworm.

Yet this thy praise cannot be so° thy praise           *enough*
To tie up envy, evermore enlarged.°           *forever at large*
  If some suspect of ill masked not thy show,°       *appearance*
  Then thou alone kingdoms of hearts shouldst owe.°       *own*

### 71

No longer mourn for me when I am dead
Than you shall hear the surly sullen bell
Give warning to the world that I am fled
From this vile world with vilest[1] worms to dwell.
5  Nay, if you read this line, remember not
The hand that writ it; for I love you so
That I in your sweet thoughts would be forgot
If thinking on me then should make you woe.
O, if, I say, you look upon this verse
10  When I perhaps compounded am° with clay,        *am mixed*
Do not so much as my poor name rehearse,°      *repeat; rebury*
But let your love even with my life decay,
  Lest the wise world should look into your moan
  And mock you with me° after I am gone.       *for loving me*

### 72

O, lest the world should task you to recite
What merit lived in me that you should love,
After my death, dear love, forget me quite;
For you in me can nothing worthy prove—
5  Unless you would devise some virtuous lie
To do more for me than mine own desert,
And hang more praise upon deceasèd I
Than niggard truth would willingly impart.
O, lest your true love may seem false in this,
10  That you for love speak well of me untrue,°       *untruthfully*
My° name be buried where my body is,          *Let my*
And live no more to shame nor me nor you;
  For I am shamed by that which I bring forth,[1]
  And so should you,° to love things nothing worth.    *you be*

### 73

That time of year thou mayst in me behold
When yellow leaves, or none, or few, do hang
Upon those boughs which shake against the cold,
Bare ruined choirs where late the sweet birds sang.[1]
5  In me thou seest the twilight of such day
As after sunset fadeth in the west,
Which by and by black night doth take away,
Death's second self, that seals up all in rest.
In me thou seest the glowing of such fire
10  That° on the ashes of his youth[2] doth lie        *As*

---

**Sonnet 71**
1. Q's "vildest" is an archaic form of "vilest" that may also carry the connotation of "most reviled."
**Sonnet 72**
1. Presumably alluding to the writer's poems or to his profession as actor and playwright.
**Sonnet 73**
1. *choirs:* the area in a church where the choir ("sweet

birds") sings; gatherings of manuscript "leaves" (line 2), or quires ("quiers" in Q).
2. Perhaps referring to the phoenix, a legendary self-resurrecting bird believed to live in cycles of several centuries, dying in flames and being reborn from the ashes. See also 19.4.

As the death-bed whereon it must expire,
Consumed with that which it was nourished by.[3]
   This thou perceiv'st, which makes thy love more strong,
   To love that° well which thou must leave ere long.     *(the speaker); (life)*

### 74[1]

But be contented when that fell arrest°     *fearful death*
Without all bail shall carry me away.
My life hath in this line° some interest,°     *verse / legal claim*
Which for memorial still with thee shall stay.
5  When thou reviewest° this, thou dost review     *reread*
The very part° was consecrate to thee.     *part of me that*
The earth can have but earth, which is his due;
My spirit is thine, the better part of me.
So then thou hast but lost the dregs of life,
10  The prey of worms, my body being dead,
The coward conquest of a wretch's knife,[2]
Too base of° thee to be rememberèd.     *by*
   The worth of that° is that which it contains,     *(the body)*
   And that is this,° and this with thee remains.     *this spirit (his poetry)*

### 75

So are you to my thoughts as food to life,
Or as sweet-seasoned° showers are to the ground;     *spring*
And for the peace of you° I hold such strife     *you provide*
As 'twixt a miser and his wealth is found:
5  Now proud as an enjoyer, and anon
Doubting the filching age[1] will steal his treasure;
Now counting° best to be with you alone,     *estimating*
Then bettered° that the world may see my pleasure;     *better contented*
Sometime all full with feasting on your sight,
10  And by and by clean° starvèd for a look;     *wholly*
Possessing or pursuing no delight
Save what is had or must from you be took.
   Thus do I pine and surfeit day by day,
   Or° gluttoning on all, or all away.°     *Either / having nothing*

### 76

Why is my verse so barren of new pride,°     *adornments*
So far from variation or quick° change?     *lively*
Why, with the time,° do I not glance aside     *following the fashion*
To new-found methods and to compounds[1] strange?
5  Why write I still all one, ever the same,
And keep invention in a noted weed,[2]
That every word doth almost tell my name,
Showing their birth and where° they did proceed?     *whence*
O know, sweet love, I always write of you,

---

3. Ironically, the fire is choked ("consumed") by (along with) the ashes, which are the residue of the fuel that the fire previously fed upon ("was nourished by").
**Sonnet 74**
1. This sonnet links with 73.
2. The cowardly conquest of a wretch such as Death (who was thought to carry a scythe).

**Sonnet 75**
1. Fearing that these dishonest times.
**Sonnet 76**
1. *compounds*: stylistic or formal mixtures; compound words; elaborate medicines (with "methods," which also refers to both literary and medical treatments).
2. And keep literary creativity in such familiar clothing.

10 And you and love are still my argument;° *always my topic*
So all my best is dressing old words new,
Spending again what is already spent;
   For as the sun is daily new and old,
   So is my love, still telling what is told.

## 77[1]

Thy glass° will show thee how thy beauties wear,[2] *mirror*
Thy dial° how thy precious minutes waste, *sundial*
The vacant leaves thy mind's imprint° will bear, *written ideas*
And of this book this learning mayst thou taste:
5 The wrinkles which thy glass will truly show
Of mouthèd° graves will give thee memory;° *gaping / remind you*
Thou by thy dial's shady stealth° mayst know *stealing shadow*
Time's thievish progress to eternity;
Look what° thy memory cannot contain *Whatever*
10 Commit to these waste blanks,° and thou shalt find *empty pages*
Those children nursed,° delivered from thy brain, *preserved*
To take a new acquaintance of thy mind.° *strike you afresh*
   These offices° so oft as thou wilt look *functions*
   Shall profit thee and much enrich thy book.

## 78[1]

So oft have I invoked thee for my muse
And found such fair assistance in my verse
As every alien pen hath got my use,[2]
And under thee° their poesy disperse. *with you as patron*
5 Thine eyes, that taught the dumb on high° to sing *aloud*
And heavy ignorance aloft to fly,
Have added feathers to the learned's wing[3]
And given grace° a double majesty. *excellence*
Yet be most proud of that which I compile,° *write*
10 Whose influence° is thine and born of thee. *power to move*
In others' works thou dost but mend° the style, *improve*
And arts° with thy sweet graces gracèd be; *(their) artistry*
   But thou art all my art, and dost advance
   As high as learning my rude ignorance.

## 79

Whilst I alone did call upon thy aid
My verse alone had all thy gentle grace;
But now my gracious numbers are decayed,
And my sick muse doth give another place.° *way to another poet*
5 I grant, sweet love, thy lovely argument[1] *labor*
Deserves the travail° of a worthier pen,
Yet what of thee thy poet doth invent
He robs thee of, and pays it thee again.
He lends thee virtue, and he stole that word
10 From thy behaviour; beauty doth he give,
And found it in thy cheek: he can afford° *extend*

<hr>

**Sonnet 77**
1. This sonnet appears to have accompanied the gift of a notebook.
2. Last; wear away; "were" (Q's spelling).
**Sonnet 78**
1. This sonnet begins the rival poet sequence (78–80,

82–86).
2. That every other poet imitates me.
3. Have improved the poetic "flights" of even accomplished poets.
**Sonnet 79**
1. The subject of your loveliness.

No praise to thee but what in thee doth live.
    Then thank him not for that which he doth say,
    Since what he owes thee thou thyself dost pay.

### 80

O, how I faint° when I of you do write,                      *get discouraged*
Knowing a better spirit° doth use your name,             *(the rival poet)*
And in the praise thereof spends all his might,
To make me tongue-tied, speaking of your fame!
5  But since your worth, wide as the ocean is,
The humble as° the proudest sail doth bear,               *as well as*
My saucy barque,° inferior far to his,               *impudent boat*
On your broad main° doth wilfully appear.                 *waters*
Your shallowest help will hold me up afloat
10  Whilst he upon your soundless° deep doth ride;        *bottomless*
Or, being wrecked, I am a worthless boat,
He of tall building[1] and of goodly pride.°            *magnificence*
    Then if he thrive and I be cast away,
    The worst was this: my love was my decay.

### 81[1]

Or° I shall live your epitaph to make,                      *Either*
Or you survive when I in earth am rotten.
From hence° your memory death cannot take,      *the world; my poetry*
Although in me each part° will be forgotten.      *each of my attributes*
5  Your name from hence° immortal life shall have,    *henceforth; my poetry*
Though I, once gone, to all the world must die.
The earth can yield me but a common grave
When you entombèd in men's eyes shall lie.
Your monument shall be my gentle verse,
10  Which eyes not yet created shall o'er-read,
And tongues to be° your being shall rehearse°     *future tongues / recite*
When all the breathers of this world are dead.
    You still shall live—such virtue° hath my pen—       *power*
    Where breath most breathes, even in° the mouths of men.   *right in*

### 82

I grant thou wert not married to my muse,
And therefore mayst without attaint o'erlook°        *dishonor read*
The dedicated[1] words which writers° use           *other writers*
Of their fair subject, blessing every book.
5  Thou art as fair in knowledge as in hue,°         *appearance*
Finding thy worth a limit° past my praise,            *region*
And therefore art enforced to seek anew
Some fresher stamp of these time-bettering days.[2]
And do so, love; yet when they have devised
10  What strainèd touches rhetoric can lend,
Thou, truly fair, wert truly sympathized[3]
In true plain words by thy true-telling friend;

---

**Sonnet 80**
1. Tall, strong build.
**Sonnet 81**
1. Except for lines 2–3 and 10–11, any two consecutive
lines in this sonnet form a complete sentence.

**Sonnet 82**
1. Devoted; referring to a prefatory dedication.
2. Some more recent imprint (commendation) of these
culturally progressive times.
3. Would be accurately represented.

And their gross painting° might be better used        *cosmetics; flattery*
Where cheeks need blood: in thee it is abused.°        *used wrongly*

### 83

I never saw that you did painting° need,        *cosmetics*
And therefore to your fair° no painting set.        *beauty*
I found—or thought I found—you did exceed
The barren tender° of a poet's debt;        *payment*
5 And therefore have I slept in your report:[1]
That° you yourself, being extant, well might show        *So that*
How far a modern° quill doth come too short,        *trite; fashionable*
Speaking of worth, what worth[2] in you doth grow.
This silence for° my sin you did impute,        *to be*
10 Which shall be most my glory, being dumb;
For I impair not beauty, being mute,
When others would give life, and bring a tomb.[3]
    There lives more life in one of your fair eyes
    Than both your poets can in praise devise.

### 84

Who is it that says most which[1] can say more
Than this rich praise: that you alone are you,[2]
In whose confine immurèd is the store
Which should example where your equal grew?[3]
5 Lean penury within that pen doth dwell
That to his subject lends not some small glory;
But he that writes of you, if he can tell
That you are you, so dignifies his story.
Let him but copy what in you is writ,
10 Not making worse what nature made so clear,°        *purely excellent*
And such a counterpart shall fame° his wit,        *copy will make famous*
Making his style admirèd everywhere.
    You to your beauteous blessings add a curse,[4]
    Being fond on praise, which makes your praises worse.[5]

### 85

My tongue-tied muse in manners holds her still°        *tactfully says nothing*
While comments of° your praise, richly compiled,        *commentaries in*
Reserve thy character° with golden quill        *Hoard up your features*
And precious phrase by all the muses filed.°        *polished*
5 I think good thoughts whilst other° write good words,        *others*
And like unlettered clerk still cry 'Amen'
To every hymn[1] that able spirit affords°        *offers*
In polished form of well-refinèd pen.
Hearing you praised I say ' 'Tis so, 'tis true,'

**Sonnet 83**
1. Neglected to sing your praises.
2. In speaking of value of the worth that.
3. When others who try to make you live in their writings only end up burying you.
**Sonnet 84**
1. *Who . . . which:* What hyperbolical enthusiast.
2. The line is a poetical in-joke, echoing a passage in Gervase Markham's *Devoreux* (published 1597) that addresses and praises Penelope Rich, a famous beauty of the Elizabethan court. Like *Devoreux*, Q has *"Rich"* rather than "rich." See also 85.2.

3. *In . . . grew:* Within whom is contained the stock that would be needed to produce your equal?
4. Personality flaw; vexation (for those who would praise you).
5. Being (too) fond of praise, which makes the praise seem like flattery; being (too) fond of the sort of praise that detracts from you.
**Sonnet 85**
1. *like . . . hymn:* like an illiterate parish clerk reflexively approve ("cry 'Amen'" after) every poem ("hymn") of praise.

10   And to the most° of praise add something more;      *highest*
But that is in my thought,° whose love to you,      *unspoken*
Though words come hindmost, holds his rank before.°    *before all others*
   Then others for the breath of words respect,°      *regard*
   Me for my dumb thoughts, speaking in effect.°      *in reality*

## 86

Was it the proud full sail of his° great verse      *(a rival poet's)*
Bound for the prize° of all-too-precious you      *pirate's spoils*
That did my ripe thoughts in my brain inhearse,°      *bury*
Making their tomb the womb wherein they grew?
5   Was it his spirit, by spirits taught to write
Above a mortal pitch,° that struck me dead?      *height*
No, neither he nor his compeers[1] by night
Giving him aid my verse astonishèd.°      *made silent*
He nor that affable familiar ghost°      *spirit*
10   Which nightly gulls° him with intelligence,°      *fools / ideas*
As victors, of my silence cannot boast;
I was not sick of any fear from thence.
   But when your countenance filled up[2] his line,
   Then lacked I matter; that enfeebled mine.

## 87

Farewell—thou art too dear° for my possessing,      *costly*
And like° enough thou know'st thy estimate.°      *it is likely / value*
The charter of thy worth gives thee releasing;[1]
My bonds in thee are all determinate.°      *terminated*
5   For how do I hold thee but by thy granting,
And for that riches where is my deserving?
The cause of this fair gift in me is wanting,
And so my patent back again is swerving.[2]
Thyself thou gav'st, thy own worth then not knowing,
10   Or me to whom thou gav'st it else mistaking;°      *overestimating*
So thy great gift, upon misprision growing,°      *based on error*
Comes home again, on better judgement making.[3]
   Thus have I had thee as a dream doth flatter:°      *creates an illusion*
   In sleep a king, but waking no such matter.

## 88

When thou shalt be disposed to set me light°      *value me little*
And place my merit in the eye of scorn,
Upon thy side against myself I'll fight,
And prove thee virtuous though thou art forsworn.
5   With mine own weakness being best acquainted,
Upon thy part I can set down a story
Of faults concealed wherein I am attainted,
That thou in losing me shall win much glory;
And I by this will be a gainer too;
10   For bending all my loving thoughts on thee,
   The injuries that to myself I do,
   Doing thee vantage, double vantage me.

**Sonnet 86**
1. Colleagues (the "spirits" in line 5).
2. Your features gave subject matter to; your approval made up for any lack in.

**Sonnet 87**
1. The privilege you derive from your worth releases you from love's bonds.
2. My rights of possession revert to you.
3. on . . . *making*: when you realize your error.

Such is my love, to thee I so belong,
That for thy right myself will bear all wrong.

## 89

Say that thou didst forsake me for some fault,
And I will comment° upon that offence;                    elaborate
Speak of my lameness, and I straight will halt,[1]
Against thy reasons making no defence.
5   Thou canst not, love, disgrace me half so ill,
To set a form upon desirèd change,[2]
As I'll myself disgrace, knowing thy will.
I will acquaintance strangle and look strange,[3]
Be absent from thy walks,° and in my tongue            familiar places
10  Thy sweet belovèd name no more shall dwell,
Lest I, too much profane, should do it wrong,
And haply° of our old acquaintance tell.                  by chance
    For thee, against myself I'll vow debate;°            combat
    For I must ne'er love him whom thou dost hate.

## 90[1]

Then hate me when thou wilt, if ever, now,
Now while the world is bent my deeds to cross,°          foil
Join with the spite of fortune, make me bow,
And do not drop in for an after-loss.[2]
5   Ah do not, when my heart hath scaped this sorrow,
Come in the rearward of a conquered woe;[3]
Give not a windy night a rainy morrow
To linger out a purposed overthrow.[4]
If thou wilt leave me, do not leave me last,
10  When other petty griefs have done their spite,
But in the onset come; so shall I taste
At first the very worst of fortune's might,
    And other strains° of woe, which now seem woe,        types; burdens
    Compared with loss of thee will not seem so.

## 91

Some glory in their birth, some in their skill,
Some in their wealth, some in their body's force,
Some in their garments (though new-fangled ill),°        fashionably ugly
Some in their hawks and hounds, some in their horse,°    horses
5   And every humour hath his° adjunct pleasure           temperament has its
Wherein it finds a joy above the rest.
But these particulars are not my measure;°               (of joy)
All these I better° in one general best.                 exceed
Thy love is better than high birth to me,
10  Richer than wealth, prouder than garments' cost,
Of more delight than hawks or horses be,
And having thee of all men's pride[1] I boast,

---

**Sonnet 89**
1. Talk of my disability (perhaps alluding to the lame meter of line 2), and I at once will limp (stop objecting).
2. To lend justification to the change you seek.
3. I will end our familiarity and act like a stranger.
**Sonnet 90**
1. This sonnet links with 89.

2. Do not fall upon me to inflict a later disaster.
3. Assault me again after I have overcome my present grief.
4. *To . . . overthrow:* By protracting or delaying your intended assault.
**Sonnet 91**
1. Of everything in which others take pride.

Wretched in this alone: that thou mayst take
All this away, and me most wretched make.

### 92[1]

But do thy worst to steal thyself away,
For term of° life thou art assurèd mine,　　　　　　　　　*the duration of my*
And life no longer than thy love will stay,
For it depends upon that love of thine.
5　Then need I not to fear the worst of wrongs
When in the least of them[2] my life hath end.
I see a better state to me belongs
Than that which on thy humour doth depend.
Thou canst not vex me with inconstant mind,
10　Since that my life on thy revolt doth lie.[3]
O, what a happy title[4] do I find—
Happy to have thy love, happy to die!
　　But what's so blessèd fair that fears no blot?
　　Thou mayst be false, and yet I know it not.

### 93[1]

So shall I live supposing thou art true
Like a deceivèd husband; so love's face°　　　　　　　　*appearance*
May still seem love to me, though altered new—
Thy looks with me, thy heart in other place.
5　For there can live no hatred in thine eye,
Therefore in that I cannot know thy change.
In many's looks the false heart's history
Is writ in moods and frowns and wrinkles strange,[2]
But heaven in thy creation did decree
10　That in thy face sweet love should ever dwell;
Whate'er thy thoughts or thy heart's workings be,
Thy looks should nothing thence but sweetness tell.
　　How like Eve's apple doth thy beauty grow
　　If thy sweet virtue answer not thy show![3]

### 94

They that have power to hurt and will do none,
That do not do the thing they most do show,[1]
Who moving others are themselves as stone,
Unmovèd, cold,° and to temptation slow—　　　　　　　*composed*
5　They rightly° do inherit heaven's graces,　　　　　　　*truly*
And husband nature's riches from expense;[2]
They are the lords and owners of their faces,
Others but stewards° of their excellence.　　　　　　　*hired managers*
The summer's flower is to the summer sweet
10　Though to itself it only live and die,[3]
But if that flower with base infection meet

---

Sonnet 92
1. This sonnet links with 91.
2. In the slightest sign of your displeasure.
3. Since change in your affections would kill me.
4. What a claim to be considered happy.
Sonnet 93
1. This sonnet links with 92.
2. In signs of anger and frowns and displeased

expressions.
3. Does not correspond to your looks.
Sonnet 94
1. *they most do show:* that their appearance implies.
2. And protect nature's rich endowment from waste.
3. *is . . . die:* emits its sweetness to others even though it lives and dies in apparent isolation (unpollinated: compare 54.5–11).

The basest weed outbraves his dignity;[4]
    For sweetest things turn sourest by their deeds:
    Lilies that fester smell far worse than weeds.[5]

### 95

How sweet and lovely dost thou make the shame
Which, like a canker° in the fragrant rose,              *cankerworm*
Doth spot the beauty of thy budding name!°            *fame*
O, in what sweets dost thou thy sins enclose!
5    That tongue that tells the story of thy days,
Making lascivious comments on thy sport,°     *amorous adventures*
Cannot dispraise, but in a kind of praise,
Naming thy name, blesses° an ill report.         *makes positive*
O, what a mansion have those vices got
10   Which for their habitation chose out thee,
Where beauty's veil doth cover every blot
And all things turns to fair that eyes can see!
    Take heed, dear heart, of this large privilege:
    The hardest knife ill used doth lose his° edge.     *its*

### 96

Some say thy fault is youth, some wantonness;°     *promiscuity; frivolity*
Some say thy grace is youth and gentle sport.[1]
Both grace and faults are loved of more and less;°     *by people of all ranks*
Thou mak'st faults graces that to thee resort.
5    As on the finger of a thronèd queen
The basest jewel will be well esteemed,
So are those errors that in thee are seen
To truths translated° and for true things deemed.     *converted*
How many lambs might the stern° wolf betray     *vicious*
10   If like° a lamb he could his looks translate!     *into*
How many gazers mightst thou lead away
If thou wouldst use the strength of all thy state!°     *power*
    But do not so: I love thee in such sort°     *such a way*
    As, thou being mine, mine is thy good report.[2]

### 97

How like a winter hath my absence been
From thee, the pleasure of the fleeting year!
What freezings have I felt, what dark days seen,
What old December's bareness everywhere!
5    And yet this time removed° was summer's time,     *away*
The teeming autumn big° with rich increase,     *pregnant*
Bearing the wanton burden of the prime°     *harvest of wanton spring*
Like widowed wombs after their lords' decease.
Yet this abundant issue seemed[1] to me
10   But hope of orphans and unfathered fruit,
For summer and his pleasures wait° on thee,     *attend*
And thou away, the very birds are mute;

---

4. Exceeds the flower in magnificence.
5. This line also occurs in *The Reign of King Edward III,* a play printed anonymously in 1596 and sometimes attributed, in whole or in part, to Shakespeare.

**Sonnet 96**
1. A gentleman's sexual prerogative.
2. Reputation. The same couplet ends 36.
**Sonnet 97**
1. Offspring seemed in prospect, before the beloved's absence.

Or if they sing, 'tis with so dull a cheer°        *such a dismal mood*
That leaves look pale, dreading the winter's near.

### 98

From you have I been absent in the spring
When proud-pied° April, dressed in all his trim,°     *multicolored / finery*
Hath put a spirit of youth in everything,
That heavy Saturn[1] laughed and leapt with him.
5  Yet nor the lays° of birds nor the sweet smell     *not the songs*
Of different flowers° in odour and in hue     *flowers differing*
Could make me any summer's story tell,°     *speak (write) happily*
Or from their proud lap° pluck them where they grew;     *(the ground)*
Nor did I wonder at the lily's white,
10  Nor praise the deep vermilion in the rose.
They were but sweet, but figures° of delight     *merely emblems*
Drawn after you, you pattern of all those;
    Yet seemed it winter still, and, you away,
    As with your shadow I with these did play.[2]

### 99[1]

The forward° violet thus did I chide:     *early*
Sweet thief, whence didst thou steal thy sweet° that smells,     *perfume*
If not from my love's breath? The purple pride°     *beauty*
Which on thy soft cheek for complexion dwells
5  In my love's veins thou hast too grossly° dyed.     *obviously*
The lily I condemnèd for thy hand,[2]
And buds of marjoram[3] had stol'n thy hair;
The roses fearfully on thorns did stand,
One blushing shame, another white despair;
10  A third, nor red nor white, had stol'n of both,°     *(making it pink)*
And to° his robb'ry had annexed thy breath;     *in addition to*
But for his theft in pride of all his growth
A vengeful canker° ate him up to death.     *cankerworm*
    More flowers I noted, yet I none could see
    But sweet° or colour it had stol'n from thee.     *perfume*

### 100

Where are thou, muse, that thou forget'st so long
To speak of that which gives thee all thy might?
Spend'st thou thy fury[1] on some worthless song,
Dark'ning° thy power to lend base subjects light?     *Debasing*
5  Return, forgetful muse, and straight° redeem     *immediately*
In gentle numbers° time so idly spent;     *noble poetry*
Sing to the ear that doth thy lays esteem
And gives thy pen both skill and argument.°     *substance*
Rise, resty° muse, my love's sweet face survey     *lazy*
10  If° time have any wrinkle graven there.     *To see if*
If any, be a satire to° decay     *satirist of*
And make time's spoils despisèd everywhere.

---

**Sonnet 98**
1. The planet Saturn was regarded as cold and slow, exerting a melancholy influence.
2. As if with your image I played with these flowers.
**Sonnet 99**
1. This sonnet has an extra opening line.

2. For stealing whiteness from your (the beloved's) hand.
3. The herb, sweet of scent and auburn in color.
**Sonnet 100**
1. Inspiration (the "poet's rage" of 17.11).

Give my love fame faster than time wastes life;
So, thou prevene'st° his scythe and crookèd knife.                    *impede*

### 101[1]

O truant muse, what shall be thy amends
For thy neglect of truth in beauty dyed?
Both truth and beauty on my love depends;
So dost thou too, and therein° dignified.                    *therein are you*
5    Make answer, muse. Wilt thou not haply° say                    *perhaps*
'Truth needs no colour with his colour fixed,[2]
Beauty no pencil beauty's truth to lay,[3]
But best is best if never intermixed'?°                    *(with cosmetics)*
Because he needs no praise wilt thou be dumb?
10    Excuse not silence so, for't lies in thee
To make him much outlive a gilded tomb,
And to be praised of° ages yet to be.                    *by*
    Then do thy office,° muse; I teach thee how                    *duty*
    To make him seem long° hence as he shows° now.        *a long time / appears*

### 102

My love is strengthened, though more weak in seeming.°                    *appearance*
I love not less, though less the show appear.
That love is merchandized[1] whose rich esteeming°                    *appraisal*
The owner's tongue doth publish everywhere.
5    Our love was new and then but in the spring°                    *just beginning*
When I was wont to greet it with my lays,
As Philomel[2] in summer's front° doth sing,                    *beginning*
And stops her pipe in growth of riper days—
Not that the summer is less pleasant now
10    Than when her mournful hymns did hush the night,
But that wild music burdens[3] every bough,
And sweets grown common lose their dear delight.
    Therefore like her I sometime hold my tongue,
    Because I would not dull° you with my song.                    *overfeed*

### 103

Alack, what poverty my muse brings forth
That, having such a scope to show her pride,[1]
The argument all bare° is of more worth                    *subject by itself*
Than when it hath my added praise beside!
5    O blame me not if I no more can write!
Look in your glass° and there appears a face                    *mirror*
That overgoes my blunt invention[2] quite,
Dulling° my lines and doing me disgrace.                    *(by contrast)*
Were it not sinful then, striving to mend,°                    *improve*
10    To mar the subject that before was well?—
For to no other pass° my verses tend                    *end*

---

**Sonnet 101**
1. This sonnet links with 100.
2. Truth needs no artificial color to be added to his natural coloring.
3. True beauty need apply no (cosmetic) brush.
**Sonnet 102**
1. (Debased by being) turned into merchandise for sale.
2. Nightingale; with ambiguous hints of the myth of Philomel, whose brother-in-law raped her and ripped out her

tongue to ensure her silence. See Book 6 of Ovid's *Metamorphoses*.
3. Loads; provides a musical refrain (probably from many other poets) on.
**Sonnet 103**
1. Considering that she has such opportunity (in you) to display her skill (her pride in you).
2. That surpasses my dull powers of invention.

Than of your graces and your gifts to tell;
And more, much more, than in my verse can sit
Your own glass shows you when you look in it.

### 104

To me, fair friend, you never can be old;
For as you were when first your eye I eyed,
Such seems your beauty still. Three winters cold
Have from the forests shook three summers' pride;°      *splendor*
5  Three beauteous springs to yellow autumn turned
In process° of the seasons have I seen,      *the progress*
Three April perfumes in three hot Junes burned
Since first I saw you fresh, which yet° are green.      *who still*
Ah yet doth beauty, like a dial hand,
10  Steal from his figure and no pace perceived;[1]
So your sweet hue,° which methinks still doth stand,      *appearance*
Hath motion, and mine eye may be deceived.
    For fear of which, hear this, thou age unbred:°      *future age*
    Ere you were born was beauty's summer dead.

### 105

Let not my love be called idolatry,
Nor my belovèd as an idol show,
Since all alike my songs and praises be
To one, of one, still° such, and ever so.      *continually*
5  Kind is my love today, tomorrow kind,
Still constant in a wondrous excellence.
Therefore my verse, to constancy confined,
One thing expressing, leaves out difference.°      *diversity (of theme)*
'Fair, kind, and true' is all my argument,
10  'Fair, kind, and true' varying to other words,
And in this change is my invention spent,[1]
Three themes in one, which wonderous scope affords.
    Fair, kind, and true have often lived alone,°      *separately*
    Which three till now never kept seat° in one.      *dwelt permanently*

### 106[1]

When in the chronicle of wasted° time      *past*
I see descriptions of the fairest wights,°      *people*
And beauty making beautiful old rhyme
In praise of ladies dead and lovely knights;
5  Then in the blazon[2] of sweet beauty's best,
Of hand, of foot, of lip, of eye, of brow,
I see their antique pen would have expressed
Even such a beauty as you master° now.      *possess*
So all their praises are but prophecies
10  Of this our time, all you prefiguring,
And for° they looked but with divining° eyes      *as / prophetic*
They had not skill enough your worth to sing;      *want to*

---

**Sonnet 104**
1. *doth . . . perceived*: beauty imperceptibly "steals" (departs stealthily from; robs from) the youthful appearance ("figure") of the beloved as the hand of the watch ("dial") stealthily progresses ("steals") away from the number ("figure") on the watch face.

**Sonnet 105**
1. And in varying the words alone my inventiveness is expended.
**Sonnet 106**
1. See "On his Mistress' Beauty" in the Alternative Versions.
2. Poetic catalog of virtues.

For we° which now behold these present days      *even we*
Have eyes to wonder, but lack tongues to praise.

## 107

Not mine own fears nor the prophetic soul
Of the wide world dreaming on things to come
Can yet the lease° of my true love control,      *allotted term*
Supposed as forfeit to a confined doom.[1]
5   The mortal moon hath her eclipse endured,[2]
And the sad augurs mock their own presage;[3]
Incertainties now crown themselves assured,[4]
And peace proclaims olives of endless age.[5]
Now with the drops[6] of this most balmy time
10   My love looks fresh, and death to me subscribes,°      *submits*
Since spite of him I'll live in this poor rhyme
While he insults° o'er dull and speechless tribes,[7]      *prevails*
   And thou in this shalt find thy monument
   When tyrants' crests and tombs of brass are spent.°      *ruined*

## 108

What's in the brain that ink may character°      *express*
Which hath not figured° to thee my true spirit?      *shown*
What's new to speak, what now to register,°      *record*
That may express my love or thy dear merit?
5   Nothing, sweet boy; but yet like prayers divine
I must each day say o'er the very same,
Counting no old thing old, thou mine, I thine,
Even as when first I hallowed thy fair name.
So that eternal love in love's fresh case°      *covering*
10   Weighs not° the dust and injury of age,      *Overlooks*
Nor gives to necessary° wrinkles place,°      *inevitable / priority*
But makes antiquity for aye his page,[1]
   Finding the first conceit of love there bred[2]
   Where time and outward form would° show it dead.      *want to*

## 109

O never say that I was false of heart,
Though absence seemed my flame to qualify°—      *reduce*
As easy might I from myself depart
As from my soul, which in thy breast doth lie.
5   That is my home of love. If I have ranged,
Like him that travels I return again,
Just to the time,° not with the time exchanged,°      *Punctually / changed*
So that myself bring water for my stain.[1]

---

**Sonnet 107**
1. Imagined as limited to a finite term.
2. Survived. The line is variously taken to refer to an eclipse of the moon, to an event in the life (or, more likely, to the death in 1603) of Queen Elizabeth (often known as Diana, the moon goddess), or, less probably, to the defeat of the Spanish Armada (1588).
3. And prophets of doom now ridicule their own prophecies.
4. Desired but doubtful possibilities now celebrate their realization; uncertainty is now unavoidable.
5. And peace declares the olive branches that symbolize it to be everlasting. Perhaps a reference to the peace treaty

with Spain signed by King James, who succeeded Elizabeth.
6. Soothing drops of dew, rain, or balm. Balm was used in the coronation ceremony.
7. Over those legions of dead who have no poetic legacy.
**Sonnet 108**
1. But makes (old) age forever the (youthful) servant to love; perhaps referring to the pages of poetry written when the "sweet boy" (line 5) was still young.
2. The first feeling (poetic expression) of love generated in that place (the beloved; the poem).
**Sonnet 109**
1. *for my stain:* to cleanse the stain of my absence.

Never believe, though in my nature reigned
10　All frailties that besiege all kinds of blood,°　　　　　　　　*disposition*
That it could so preposterously be stained
To leave for° nothing all thy sum of good;　　　　　　　　　*exchange for*
　　For nothing this wide universe I call
　　Save thou my rose; in it thou art my all.

### 110

Alas, 'tis true, I have gone here and there
And made myself a motley to the view,°　　　　　　　　*clown to the world*
Gored° mine own thoughts, sold cheap what is most dear,　　　　*Injured*
Made old offences of affections new.[1]
5　Most true it is that I have looked on truth°　　　　　　　*fidelity*
Askance and strangely.° But, by all above,　　　　　　　　*coldly*
These blenches° gave my heart another youth,　　　　　　　*alterations*
And worse essays° proved thee my best of love　　　　　　　*experiments*
Now all is done, have what shall have no end;[2]
10　Mine appetite I never more will grind
On newer proof to try[3] an older friend,
A god in love, to whom I am confined.
　　Then give me welcome, next my heaven the best,°　　　*next best to heaven*
　　Even to thy pure and most most loving breast.

### 111

O, for my sake do you with[1] fortune chide,
The guilty goddess of my harmful deeds,
That did not better for my life provide
Than public means which public manners breeds.[2]
5　Thence comes it that my name receives a brand,°　　　　　*stigma*
And almost thence my nature is subdued
To what it works in, like the dyer's hand.
Pity me then, and wish I were renewed,°　　　　　　　　*cured*
Whilst like a willing patient I will drink
10　Potions of eisel° 'gainst my strong infection;　　　*medicinal vinegar*
No° bitterness that I will bitter think,　　　　　　　　*There is no*
Nor double penance to correct correction.°　　　　*correct me twice over*
　　Pity me then, dear friend, and I assure ye
　　Even that your pity is enough to cure me.

### 112[1]

Your love and pity doth th'impression fill°　　　　*eliminates the scar*
Which vulgar° scandal stamped upon my brow;　　　　　　*public*
For what care I who calls me well or ill,
So you o'er-green my bad, my good allow?[2]
5　You are my all the world, and I must strive
To know my shames and praises from your tongue—
None else to me, nor I to none alive,

---

Sonnet 110
1. Repeated traditional misbehavior (infidelity)—or offended old friends—in (my treatment of) new attachments.
2. *have . . . end:* take that (my love) which will not expire.
3. *grind . . . try:* sharpen with new experience to test.
Sonnet 111
1. Q has "wish," which gives a more problematic array of

alternative meanings.
2. Probably: Than employment as an actor, which requires one to curry favor with the public.
Sonnet 112
1. This sonnet links with 111.
2. So long as you allow new growth to cover what is bad in me, and give credit for what is good.

That my steeled sense or changes, right or wrong.[3]
In so profound abyss I throw all care
10   Of others' voices that my adder's sense°                                    *deaf ears*
To critic and to flatterer stoppèd are.
Mark how with my neglect I do dispense:[4]
        You are so strongly in my purpose bred[5]
        That all the world besides, methinks, they're dead.


### 113

Since I left you mine eye is in my mind,[1]
And that which governs me to go about°                              *And my real sight*
Doth part his° function and is partly blind,                           *Divides its*
Seems seeing, but effectually is out;°                                        *blind*
5   For it no form delivers to the heart
Of bird, of flower, or shape which it doth latch.°              *catch sight of*
Of his quick objects° hath the mind no part,                 *fleeting impressions*
Nor his own vision holds[2] what it doth catch;
For if it see the rud'st or gentlest° sight,                      *coarsest or noblest*
10   The most sweet favour[3] or deformèd'st creature,
The mountain or the sea, the day or night,
The crow or dove, it shapes them to your feature.[4]
        Incapable of more, replete with you,
        My most true mind thus makes mine eye untrue.


### 114[1]

Or whether doth my mind, being crowned with you,[2]
Drink up the monarch's plague, this flattery,
Or whether shall I say mine eye saith true,
And that your love taught it this alchemy,[3]
5   To make of monsters and things indigest°                              *chaotic*
Such cherubins° as your sweet self resemble,                            *angels*
Creating every° bad a perfect best                                       *from every*
As fast as objects to his beams assemble?[4]
O, 'tis the first, 'tis flatt'ry in my seeing,
10   And my great° mind most kingly drinks it up.                         *pompous*
Mine eye well knows what with his gust is 'greeing,[5]
And to his palate doth prepare the cup.
        If it be poisoned, 'tis the lesser sin
        That mine eye loves it and doth first begin.[6]


### 115

Those lines that I before have writ do lie,
Even those that said I could not love you dearer;
Yet then my judgement knew no reason why

---

3. *None . . . wrong*: perhaps, There being no one else to influence me, and no one else's influence being capable of positively or negatively affecting my hardened disposition.
4. How I excuse my neglect (of "other's voices," line 10).
5. Nurtured in all my plans.
**Sonnet 113**
1. I see with my mind's eye.
2. Nor does the eye's vision hold on to.
3. Face; perhaps Q's "sweet-favor" means "sweet-favored," or "good-looking."
4. It makes them look like you.

**Sonnet 114**
1. This sonnet links with 113.
2. Being made a King by having you. "Or whether" introduces alternatives.
3. And that love of you taught my eye how thus to transform things.
4. As fast as objects come before its gaze. (The eye was thought to emit beams of light).
5. What pleases the mind's appetite.
6. And drinks first (like a King's taster).

My most full flame should afterwards burn clearer.
5 But reckoning time,[1] whose millioned accidents
Creep in 'twixt vows° and change decrees of kings,                    *(and their performance)*
Tan° sacred beauty, blunt the sharp'st intents,                    *Darken*
Divert strong minds to th' course of alt'ring things—
Alas, why, fearing of time's tyranny,
10 Might I not then say[2] 'Now I love you best',
When I was certain o'er° incertainty,                    *beyond*
Crowning° the present, doubting of the rest?                    *Exalting*
   Love is a babe; then might I not say so,[3]
   To give° full growth to that which still doth grow.                    *Thereby giving*

## 116

Let me not to the marriage of true minds
Admit impediments.° Love is not love                    *legal barriers to marriage*
Which alters when it alteration finds,
Or bends with the remover to remove.[1]
5 O no, it is an ever fixèd mark[2]
That looks on tempests and is never shaken;
It is the star to every wand'ring barque,
Whose worth's unknown although his height be taken.[3]
Love's not time's fool,° though rosy lips and cheeks                    *plaything*
10 Within his bending sickle's compass[4] come;
Love alters not with his brief hours and weeks,
But bears it out even to the edge of doom.[5]
   If this be error and upon° me proved,                    *against*
   I never writ, nor no man ever loved.

## 117

Accuse me thus: that I have scanted° all                    *neglected*
Wherein I should your great deserts repay,
Forgot upon your dearest love to call
Whereto all bonds do tie me day by day;
5 That I have frequent° been with unknown minds,°                    *friendly / strangers*
And given to time your own dear-purchased right;[1]
That I have hoisted sail to all the winds
Which should° transport me farthest from your sight.                    *were likely to*
Book both my wilfulness and errors down,
10 And on just proof surmise accumulate;[2]
Bring me within the level° of your frown,                    *aim*
But shoot not at me in your wakened hate,
   Since my appeal says I did strive to prove[3]
   The constancy and virtue of your love.

---

**Sonnet 115**
1. But taking time into account; but time, which settles accounts.
2. Was I not then right to have said.
3. Thus I shouldn't say, "Now I love you best" (line 10).
**Sonnet 116**
1. Or abandons the relationship when the loved one is unfaithful or has departed or died, or when time ("the remover") alters things for the worse.
2. An unmoving sea mark, such as a lighthouse or a beacon, which provides a constant reference point for sailors.
3. *Whose . . . taken:* The star's (great) intrinsic value can-
not be assessed, although navigators at sea can measure height above the horizon.
4. Within range of time's curved (and hostile) scythe. "Compass" also recalls the imagery of the second quatrain.
5. But endures until the eve of doomsday.
**Sonnet 117**
1. And wasted idly what should have been your right (rite) because acquired by your great worth and affection (because acquired at your great cost).
2. And pile suspicion on top of your proof.
3. Since my defense is that I was trying to test.

### 118

Like° as, to make our appetites more keen,                          *Just*
With eager° compounds we our palate urge;°          *sharp / stimulate*
As to prevent° our maladies unseen                            *forestall*
We sicken to shun sickness when we purge:[1]
5  Even so, being full of your ne'er cloying sweetness,
To bitter sauces did I frame° my feeding,                      *adjust*
And, sick of welfare,[2] found a kind of meetness°         *suitability*
To be diseased ere that there was true needing.
Thus policy° in love, t'anticipate                            *strategy*
10  The ills that were not, grew to faults assured,
And brought to[3] medicine a healthful state
Which, rank of goodness, would by ill be cured.[4]
    But thence I learn, and find the lesson true:
    Drugs poison him that so° fell sick of you.         *thus; so badly*

### 119

What potions have I drunk of siren[1] tears
Distilled from limbecks° foul as hell within,                    *stills*
Applying° fears to hopes and hopes to fears,          *(as a medicine)*
Still° losing when I saw myself° to win!          *Always / expected*
5  What wretched errors hath my heart committed
Whilst it hath thought itself so blessèd never!
How have mine eyes out of their spheres been fitted[2]
In the distraction° of this madding° fever!       *delirium / fit-inducing*
O benefit of ill! Now I find true
10  That better is by evil still made better,
And ruined love when it is built anew
Grows fairer than at first, more strong, far greater.
    So I return rebuked to my content,
    And gain by ills thrice more than I have spent.

### 120

That you were once unkind befriends me now,
And for° that sorrow which I then did feel               *because of*
Needs must I under my transgression bow,
Unless my nerves° were brass or hammered steel.              *sinews*
5  For if you were by my unkindness shaken
As I by yours, you've past a hell of time,
And I, a tyrant, have no leisure taken
To weigh° how once I suffered in° your crime.    *contemplate / from*
O that our night of woe[1] might have remembered°        *reminded*
10  My deepest sense how hard true sorrow hits,
And soon to you as you to me then tendered°             *offered*
The humble salve which wounded bosoms fits![2]

---

**Sonnet 118**
1. We make ourselves sick with medicine that causes vomiting or bowel movements so as to prevent greater illness.
2. Made ill by good food.
3. Treated with; brought to the need of.
4. Overfull with goodness (health, the beloved), sought to be cured by disease (evil).
**Sonnet 119**
1. Deceitfully and dangerously alluring. Sirens were

mythological creatures, part bird, part woman, said to lure sailors to their death with their irresistible songs.
2. Been driven convulsively out of their sockets.
**Sonnet 120**
1. Our earlier time of suffering (caused by the youth's unfaithfulness).
2. The salve of apology that is just the thing for an injured heart.

But that your trespass° now becomes a fee;° — *offense / compensation*
Mine ransoms° yours, and yours must ransom me. — *absolves*

### 121

'Tis better to be vile than vile esteemed° — *reputed vile*
When not to be receives reproach of being,° — *being so (vile)*
And the just pleasure lost, which is so deemed
Not by our feeling but by others' seeing.[1]
5  For why should others' false adulterate° eyes — *corrupted*
Give salutation to my sportive blood?[2]
Or on my frailties why are frailer spies,
Which in their wills[3] count bad what I think good?
No, I am that I am, and they that level° — *aim*
10 At my abuses reckon up their own.
I may be straight, though they themselves be bevel;° — *crooked*
By their rank° thoughts my deeds must not be shown,° — *foul / measured*
   Unless this general evil they maintain:
   All men are bad and in their badness reign.° — *thrive*

### 122

Thy gift, thy tables,° are within my brain — *notebook*
Full charactered° with lasting memory, — *written*
Which shall above that idle rank[1] remain
Beyond all date, even to eternity;
5  Or at the least so long as brain and heart
Have faculty° by nature to subsist, — *power*
Till each to razed° oblivion yield his part — *destroying*
Of thee, thy record never can be missed.° — *lost*
That poor retention[2] could not so much hold,
10 Nor need I tallies thy dear love to score;[3]
Therefore to give them° from me was I bold, — *(the "tables")*
To trust those tables° that receive thee more. — *memory*
   To keep an adjunct° to remember thee — *aid*
   Were to import° forgetfulness in me. — *imply*

### 123

No, time, thou shalt not boast that I do change!
Thy pyramids built up with newer might[1]
To me are nothing° novel, nothing strange, — *in no way*
They are but dressings of a former sight.[2]
5  Our dates° are brief, and therefore we admire — *lives*
What thou dost foist upon us that is old,
And rather make them born to our desire[3]

---

**Sonnet 121**
1. *And . . . seeing:* And we are denied the appropriate, innocent pleasure (or, we don't even get to enjoy the sin we've supposedly committed), which is considered sinful not by us but by others.
2. Wink knowingly at my lustful behavior.
3. *Or . . . wills:* Why should my failings be pried into by even more culpable people, who wilfully (who licentiously; who in Will Shakespeare).
**Sonnet 122**
1. Trivial status (of the "tables" as opposed to "memory").
2. That inadequate container (the "tables"); that faulty

memory.
3. Nor do I need the notched sticks used in calculating sums (to which the "tables" are contemptuously compared) to reckon up your precious love.
**Sonnet 123**
1. Grand buildings constructed by more modern means. Possibly referring to structures erected in Rome in 1586 or in London in 1603 (for James's coronation), but retaining a sense of almost timeless Egyptian antiquity.
2. Replicas of what's been seen before.
3. And consider them made just for us.

Than think that we before have heard them told.°       *described*
Thy registers° and thee I both defy,       *records*
10 Not wond'ring at the present nor the past;
For thy records and what we see doth lie,
Made more or less by thy continual haste.[4]
    This I do vow, and this shall ever be:
    I will be true despite thy scythe and thee.

### 124

If my dear love° were but the child of state[1]       *(for you)*
It might for fortune's bastard be unfathered,[2]
As subject to time's love or to time's hate,
Weeds among weeds or flowers with flowers gathered.[3]
5 No, it was builded far from accident;°       *chance*
It suffers° not in smiling pomp, nor falls       *changes*
Under the blow of thrallèd° discontent       *captive*
Whereto th'inviting time our fashion calls.[4]
It fears not policy,° that heretic       *expediency*
10 Which works on leases of short-numbered hours,°       *short-term contracts*
But all alone stands hugely politic,°       *prudent*
That it nor° grows with heat° nor drowns with showers.       *neither / prosperity*
    To this I witness call the fools of time,
    Which die for goodness, who have lived for crime.[5]

### 125

Were't aught to me I bore the canopy,[1]
With my extern° the outward honouring,       *exterior action*
Or laid great bases for eternity[2]
Which proves more short than waste° or ruining?       *decay*
5 Have I not seen dwellers on form and favour[3]
Lose all and more by paying too much rent,°       *overdoing homage*
For compound sweet forgoing simple savour,[4]
Pitiful thrivers in their gazing spent?[5]
No, let me be obsequious° in thy heart,       *dutiful*
10 And take thou my oblation,° poor but free,°       *offering / freely given*
Which is not mixed with seconds,[6] knows no art°       *artifice*
But mutual render,° only me for thee.       *exchange*
    Hence, thou suborned informer![7] A true soul
    When most impeached° stands least in thy control.       *accused*

---

4. Raised and destroyed by time's swift passage; made to seem more or less majestic by virtue of newness or antiquity and the tastes of the times.
**Sonnet 124**
1. Were simply the result of circumstances; of your high position.
2. It might be disinherited as a passing fancy, a product of fortune (chance, wealth).
3. *As . . . gathered*: Regarded as useless or valuable as time and fortune decide.
4. To which ("pomp" and "discontent") we are driven by the latest trend ("fashion").
5. *To . . . crime*: I call as witness those playthings of time

who, having lived wicked lives, reform or repent at death.
**Sonnet 125**
1. Would I care if I enhanced my status by carrying a ceremonial canopy for a royal person?
2. Laid foundations for eternal monuments.
3. Seen those who depend (linger) on ceremony and appearance.
4. For obsequious praise giving up plain candor.
5. Pitiful in their empty achievements, ruined by love of show.
6. The second-rate.
7. Paid spy: jealousy or the detractor whose charges the poem answers.

### 126[1]

O thou my lovely boy, who in thy power
Dost hold time's fickle glass,[2] his sickle-hour;[3]
Who hast by waning grown,[4] and therein show'st
Thy lovers withering as thy sweet self grow'st—
5   If nature, sovereign mistress over wrack,°                              *decay*
As thou goest onwards still° will pluck thee back,              *constantly*
She keeps thee to this purpose: that her skill
May time disgrace, and wretched minutes kill.
Yet fear her, O thou minion° of her pleasure!                     *darling*
10  She may detain but not still keep her treasure.
     Her audit,° though delayed, answered° must be,   *debt (to time) / paid*
     And her quietus° is to render° thee.            *settlement / relinquish*

### 127[1]

In the old age° black was not counted fair,[2]                    *old days*
Or if it were, it bore not beauty's name;
But now is black beauty's successive heir,°            *heir by succession*
And beauty slandered with a bastard shame:[3]
5   For since each hand hath put on° nature's power,            *usurped*
Fairing° the foul with art's false borrowed face,       *Beautifying*
Sweet beauty hath no name, no holy bower,
But is profaned, if not lives in disgrace.
Therefore my mistress' eyes are raven-black,
10  Her brow so suited,[4] and they mourners seem
At such who, not born fair, no beauty lack,
Sland'ring creation with a false esteem.[5]
     Yet so° they mourn, becoming of° their woe,   *in such a way / adorning*
     That every tongue says beauty should look so.

### 128

How oft, when thou, my music, music play'st
Upon that blessèd wood whose motion° sounds          *mechanism*
With thy sweet fingers when thou gently sway'st°         *govern*
The wiry concord that mine ear confounds,°        *amazes (with delight)*
5   Do I envy those jacks[1] that nimble leap
To kiss the tender inward of thy hand
Whilst my poor lips, which should that harvest reap,
At the wood's boldness by thee blushing stand!
To be so tickled they would change their state
10  And situation with those dancing chips

**Sonnet 126**
1. This "sonnet" or envoi, of six couplets, concludes the part of the sequence apparently addressed to the youth and formally signals a change in tone and subject matter in the remaining sonnets.
2. Capricious, treacherous hourglass (?); mirror showing changing images (?).
3. Reaping time. "Sickle-hour" emends Q's "sickle, hower," which may be an error for "sickle o'er." A familiar emblem for time placed the hourglass below and the sickle above.
4. Become more beautiful with age. As the sand in the top half of an hourglass wanes, the sand in the bottom part grows.
**Sonnet 127**
1. Sonnets 127–52 have been traditionally known as the "dark lady" group, although their subject matter is not uniform and their object is only once called "dark" (147.14)

and never a "lady." She is referred to as the poet's "mistress" (127.9; 130.1, 8, 12), however, and often described as "black" (127.1, 3, 9; 130.4; 131.12, 13; 132.3, 13; 147.14). The celebration of black beauty goes back to the biblical Song of Songs, 1:4: "I am blacke . . . but comelie." See the Introduction.
2. Beautiful; light-colored.
3. And (fair) beauty accused of illegitimacy (by use of cosmetics).
4. Her brow dressed (matched) in an eyebrow black like her eyes (and for the same reason).
5. *At . . . esteem:* Because of those who, not being fair, make up for it with cosmetics, so that even natural beauty is presumed artificial.
**Sonnet 128**
1. Keys of the virginal, a harpsichordlike instrument; fellows.

O'er whom thy fingers walk with gentle gait,
Making dead wood more blessed than living lips.
    Since saucy° jacks so happy are in this,      *impudent*
    Give them thy fingers, me thy lips to kiss.

### 129

Th'expense of spirit in a waste of shame
Is lust in action;[1] and till action, lust
Is perjured, murd'rous, bloody, full of blame,
Savage, extreme, rude,° cruel, not to trust,°     *harsh / be trusted*
5 Enjoyed no sooner but despisèd straight,°     *immediately*
Past reason° hunted, and no sooner had     *Madly*
Past reason hated as a swallowed bait
On purpose laid to make the taker mad;
Mad in pursuit and in possession so,°     *(mad)*
10 Had, having, and in quest to have, extreme;
A bliss in proof and proved,[2] a very woe;
Before, a joy proposed; behind, a dream.
    All this the world well knows, yet none knows well
    To shun the heaven that leads men to this hell.

### 130

My mistress' eyes are nothing like the sun;
Coral is far more red than her lips' red.
If snow be white, why then her breasts are dun;°     *grayish brown*
If hairs be wires,[1] black wires grow on her head.
5 I have seen roses damasked,° red and white,     *dappled*
But no such roses see I in her cheeks;
And in some perfumes is there more delight
Than in the breath that from my mistress reeks.°     *issues; smells*
I love to hear her speak, yet well I know
10 That music hath a far more pleasing sound.
I grant I never saw a goddess go:°     *walk*
My mistress when she walks treads on the ground.
    And yet, by heaven, I think my love as rare
    As any she belied with false compare.[2]

### 131

Thou art as tyrannous so as thou art[1]
As those whose beauties proudly make them cruel,
For well thou know'st to my dear° doting heart     *fond(ly)*
Thou art the fairest and most precious jewel.
5 Yet, in good faith, some say that thee behold
Thy face hath not the power to make love groan.
To say they err I dare not be so bold,
Although I swear it to myself alone;
And, to be sure° that is not false I swear,     *for proof; surely*
10 A thousand groans but thinking on° thy face     *just thinking about*
One on another's neck° do witness bear     *In quick succession*

**Sonnet 129**
1. *Th'expense . . . action*: The expenditure of vital energy (semen) in a shameful waste (waist) is consummated lust.
2. *in proof*: while being experienced. *proved*: having been experienced.
**Sonnet 130**
1. Elizabethan poets often compared women's hair to golden wires.
2. As any woman misrepresented by false comparison.
**Sonnet 131**
1. As cruel as you are dark (hence not conventionally beautiful).

    Thy black° is fairest in my judgment's place.[2]       *dark appearance*
       In nothing art thou black° save in thy deeds,          *ugly*
       And thence this slander,[3] as I think, proceeds.

### 132

    Thine eyes I love, and they, as° pitying me—        *as if*
       Knowing thy heart torment° me with disdain—    *to torment*
       Have put on black, and loving mourners be,
       Looking with pretty ruth° upon my pain;         *pity*
5   And truly, not the morning sun of heaven
       Better becomes° the gray cheeks° of the east,   *beautifies / clouds*
       Nor that full star that ushers in the even°   *(Venus, the evening star)*
       Doth° half that glory to the sober west,        *Imparts*
       As those two mourning° eyes become thy face.   *(pun on "morning")*
10  O, let it then as well beseem° thy heart        *become*
       To mourn for me, since mourning doth thee grace,
       And suit thy pity like in every part.[1]
        Then will I swear beauty herself is black,
       And all they foul° that thy complexion lack.      *ugly*

### 133

    Beshrew° that heart that makes my heart to groan   *Curse (a mild term)*
       For that deep wound it gives my friend and me!
       Is't not enough to torture me alone,
       But slave to slavery° my sweet'st friend must be?  *utterly enslaved*
5   Me from myself thy cruel eye hath taken,
       And my next self thou harder hast engrossed.[1]
       Of him, myself, and thee I am forsaken—
       A torment thrice threefold thus to be crossed.°    *afflicted*
       Prison° my heart in thy steel bosom's ward,°   *Imprison / cell*
10  But then my friend's heart let my poor heart bail;
       Whoe'er keeps° me, let my heart be his guard;[2]   *guards*
       Thou canst not then use rigour° in my jail.      *severity*
       And yet thou wilt; for I, being pent° in thee,    *locked up*
       Perforce am thine, and° all that is in me.       *as is*

### 134[1]

    So, now° I have confessed that he is thine,      *now that*
       And I myself am mortgaged to thy will,°   *intent; sexual desire*
       Myself I'll forfeit, so that other mine[2]
       Thou wilt restore to be my comfort still.
5   But thou wilt not, nor he will not° be free,     *doesn't want to*
       For thou art covetous, and he is kind.
       He learned but surety-like° to write° for me   *as guarantor / sign*
       Under that bond° that him as fast[3] doth bind.    *(of infatuation)*
       The statute[4] of thy beauty thou wilt take,
10  Thou usurer that putt'st forth all to use,°   *at interest; for sex*
       And sue a friend came° debtor for my sake;    *who became*

---

2. In my opinion.
3. See line 6 for "this slander."
**Sonnet 132**
1. And dress your pity similarly, in heart as well as eyes.
**Sonnet 133**
1. And my second self, or closest friend, you have even more cruelly monopolized.

2. My friend's prison.
**Sonnet 134**
1. This sonnet links with 133.
2. So long as my other self.
3. As firmly as myself.
4. The total guaranteed by the bond.

So him I lose through my unkind abuse.[5]
    Him have I lost; thou hast both him and me;
    He pays the whole,° and yet am I not free.          *(pun on "hole")*

### 135[1]

Whoever hath her wish, thou hast thy Will,
And Will to boot,° and Will in overplus.          *in addition*
More than enough am I that vex thee still,°      *always (by wooing)*
To thy sweet will making addition thus.
5  Wilt thou, whose will is large and spacious,
Not once vouchsafe to hide my will in thine?
Shall will in others° seem right gracious,        *others' wills*
And in my will no fair acceptance shine?[2]
The sea, all water, yet receives rain still,
10  And in abundance addeth to his° store;          *its*
So thou, being rich in Will, add to thy Will
One will of mine to make thy large Will more.
    Let no unkind no fair beseechers kill;[3]
    Think all but one,° and me in that one Will.      *one suitor*

### 136[1]

If thy soul check° thee that I come so near,[2]        *chide*
Swear to thy blind soul that I was thy Will,[3]
And will, thy soul knows, is admitted there;
Thus far for love my love-suit, sweet, fulfil.°        *grant*
5  Will will fulfill the treasure° of thy love,    *fill up the treasury*
Ay, fill it full with wills, and my will one.°      *one of them*
In things of great receipt° with ease we prove      *volume*
Among a number one is reckoned none.[4]
Then in the number let me pass untold,°       *uncounted*
10  Though in thy store's account° I one must be;   *tally (of lovers)*
For nothing hold me, so it please thee hold
That nothing me a something, sweet, to thee.[5]
    Make but my name thy love,[6] and love that still,°    *always*
    And then thou lov'st me for my name is Will.

### 137

Thou blind fool love, what dost thou to mine eyes
That they behold and see not what they see?
They know what beauty is, see where it lies,
Yet what the best is take the worst to be.[1]
5  If eyes corrupt° by over-partial° looks    *corrupted / overly doting*

---

5. Through your ill treatment of me; through my ill-treatment of the youth.
**Sonnet 135**
1. This sonnet, as well as 136, 143, and "A Lover's Complaint," lines 126–33, puns elaborately on different senses of "will": wishes, sexual desire, futurity, testament, the name "Will" (applied to one or more persons, including Shakespeare, and capitalized and sometimes italicized in Q), and the male and female sexual organs. See also 57.13 and note.
2. And my will not be greeted with a kind reception.
3. Let no unkindness of yours kill any of your worthy suitors.

**Sonnet 136**
1. This sonnet links with 135.
2. I am so forthright; I am so physically close.
3. See sonnet 135, note 1.
4. Proverbially, one is no number.
5. For . . . thee: Think me worthless so long as, my darling, you treasure worthless me. Q's punctuation, "something sweet to thee," emphasizes the sexual implications.
6. Love only my name, "Will"; that is, act on your desire.
**Sonnet 137**
1. Yet take the worst to be the best.

Be anchored in the bay where all men ride,[2]
Why of eyes' falsehood hast thou forgèd hooks
Whereto the judgement of my heart is tied?
Why should my heart think that a several plot°                    *private land*
10   Which my heart knows the wide world's common place?[3]—
Or° mine eyes, seeing this, say this is not,                        *Or why should*
To put fair truth upon so foul a face?
    In things right true my heart and eyes have erred,
    And to this false plague[4] are they now transferred.

### 138[1]

When my love swears that she is made of truth
I do believe her though I know she lies,
That° she might think me some untutored youth               *So that*
Unlearnèd in the world's false subtleties.
5    Thus vainly° thinking that she thinks me young,           *in vain; with vanity*
Although she knows my days are past the best,
Simply I credit[2] her false-speaking tongue;
On both sides thus is simple truth suppressed.
But wherefore says she not she is unjust,°                       *unfaithful*
10   And wherefore say not I that I am old?
O, love's best habit is in seeming trust,[3]
And age in love loves not to have years told.°                  *counted*
    Therefore I lie° with her, and she with me,                 *tell lies; lie down*
    And in our faults by lies we flattered be.

### 139

O, call° not me to justify° the wrong                            *ask / approve*
That thy unkindness° lays upon my heart.                        *infidelity*
Wound me not with thine eye[1] but with thy tongue;
Use power with power,[2] and slay me not by art.°              *by deceit*
5    Tell me thou lov'st elsewhere, but in my sight,
Dear heart, forbear to glance thine eye aside.
What° need'st thou wound with cunning when thy might          *Why*
Is more than my o'erpressed defence can bide?°                 *endure*
Let me excuse thee: 'Ah, my love well knows
10   Her pretty looks have been mine enemies,
And therefore from my face she turns my foes
That they elsewhere might dart their injuries.'
    Yet do not so; but since I am near slain,
    Kill me outright with looks, and rid° my pain.             *put an end to*

### 140

Be wise as thou art cruel; do not press
My tongue-tied patience with too much disdain,
Lest sorrow lend me words, and words express

---

2. Harbor for general use (suggesting a promiscuous woman).
3. *the wide . . . place:* common land, open to all (suggesting promiscuity); a commonplace known by all.
4. This plague of false perception; this deceitful woman.
**Sonnet 138**
1. Another version of this sonnet appears in *The Passionate Pilgrim.* See the Textual Note and the Alternative Versions.
2. Naively (foolishly; giving the appearance of folly) I (pretend to) believe.
3. Love is best dressed in apparent fidelity (apparent trust).
**Sonnet 139**
1. By looking elsewhere, at other men (see line 6).
2. Use power frankly; fairly.

The manner of my pity-wanting[1] pain.
5  If I might teach thee wit,° better it were,         *wisdom*
Though not to love, yet, love, to tell me so—
As testy sick men when their deaths be near
No news but health from their physicians know.°      *learn*
For if I should despair I should grow mad,
10  And in my madness might speak ill of thee.
Now this ill-wresting world[2] is grown so bad
Mad slanderers by mad ears believèd be.
   That I may not be so, nor thou belied,°        *maligned*
   Bear thine eyes straight,[3] though thy proud heart go wide.°   *astray*

## 141

In faith, I do not love thee with mine eyes,
For they in thee a thousand errors note;
But 'tis my heart that loves what they despise,
Who in despite of view° is pleased to dote.      *despite what it sees*
5  Nor are mine ears with thy tongue's tune delighted,
Nor tender feeling to base touches prone;[1]
Nor taste nor smell desire to be invited
To any sensual feast with thee alone;
But my five wits[2] nor my five senses can
10  Dissuade one foolish heart from serving thee,
Who leaves unswayed the likeness of a man.[3]
Thy proud heart's slave and vassal-wretch to be.
   Only my plague thus far° I count my gain:      *to this extent*
   That she that makes me sin awards me pain.[4]

## 142[1]

Love is my sin, and thy dear virtue hate,
Hate of my sin grounded on sinful loving.[2]
O, but with mine compare thou thine own state,
And thou shalt find it° merits not reproving;     *(my state)*
5  Or if it do, not from those lips of thine
That have profaned their scarlet ornaments[3]
And sealed[4] false bonds of love as oft as mine,
Robbed others' beds' revenues of their rents.[5]
Be it lawful° I love thee as thou lov'st those     *let it be lawful that*
10  Whom thine eyes woo as mine importune thee.
Root pity in thy heart, that when it grows
Thy pity may deserve to pitied be.°      *make you pitiable*
   If thou dost seek to have what thou dost hide,°    *(pity)*
   By self example mayst thou be denied!

**Sonnet 140**
1. Unpitied; desiring pity; pitiable.
2. Now this world, that tends to interpret in the worst light.
3. Keep looking only at me (see 139).
**Sonnet 141**
1. Nor is my keen sense of touch susceptible to "base" sexual contact.
2. Mental faculties (common sense, imagination, fancy, judgment, memory).
3. Which (the heart, serving you) leaves without a commander the mere semblance of a man.
4. By making me sin, she causes me to suffer punitive penance, which will reduce my sufferings after death.

**Sonnet 142**
1. This sonnet links with 141.
2. *Love . . . loving:* My only sin is love, and your most valuable virtue is hatred, hatred of my sin in loving you (but also, your most valuable virtue is the haughty rejection of my wooing) based on (your) immoral sexual affairs.
3. Lips, which are scarlet, like a cardinal's robe.
4. "Sealed" with a kiss: comparing the mistress's lips to the red wax used to seal official documents.
5. Stolen the sexual and emotional intimacy ("rents" paid by a tenant) from others' marriages by committing adultery, thus reducing the possibility that these marriages will result in children ("revenues," estates that yield income).

### 143

Lo, as a care-full° housewife runs to catch         *busy*
One of her feathered creatures broke away,
Sets down her babe and makes all swift dispatch°     *hurries*
In pursuit of the thing she would have stay,
5  Whilst her neglected child holds her in chase,
Cries to catch her whose busy care is bent
To follow that which flies before her face,
Not prizing° her poor infant's discontent:       *regarding*
So runn'st thou after that which flies from thee,
10  Whilst I, thy babe, chase thee afar behind;
But if thou catch thy hope, turn back to me
And play the mother's part: kiss me, be kind.
    So will I pray that thou mayst have thy Will[1]
    If thou turn back and my loud crying still.

### 144[1]

Two loves I have, of comfort and despair,
Which like two spirits do suggest° me still.      *entice*
The better angel is a man right fair,
The worser spirit a woman coloured ill.°        *darkly*
5  To win me soon to hell my female evil
Tempteth my better angel from my side,
And would corrupt my saint to be a devil,
Wooing his purity with her foul pride;
And whether that my angel be turned fiend
10  Suspect I may, yet not directly tell;
But being both from me, both to each friend,[2]
I guess one angel in another's hell.[3]
    Yet this shall I ne'er know, but live in doubt
    Till my bad angel fire my good one out.[4]

### 145[1]

Those lips that love's own hand did make
Breathed forth the sound that said 'I hate'
To me that languished for her sake;
But when she saw my woeful state,
5  Straight in her heart did mercy come,
Chiding that tongue that ever sweet
Was used in giving gentle doom,°         *judgment*
And taught it thus anew to greet:
'I hate' she altered with an end
10  That followed it as gentle day
Doth follow night who, like a fiend,
From heaven to hell is flown away.
    'I hate' from hate away she threw,[2]
    And saved my life, saying 'not you.'

---

**Sonnet 143**
1. A pun; see sonnet 135, note 1.
**Sonnet 144**
1. Another version of this sonnet appears in *The Passionate Pilgrim*. See Textual Note and Alternative Versions.
2. Both away from me and lovers to one another.
3. Each torments the other; they are in the "hell," or middle den, of a (sexual) game called barley-break; the man occupies the sex organ ("hell") of the woman.
4. Until my bad angel expels my good one, who has

become an animal to be smoked out of a burrow; until my bad angel infects my good one with venereal disease; until bad money ("angel" = gold coin) drives out good.
**Sonnet 145**
1. Unlike the other sonnets, which are in iambic pentameter, 145 is composed of eight-syllable (iambic tetrameter) lines.
2. She converted the normal meaning of the phrase "I hate" away from "hate." A pun on "hate away" and "(Anne) Hathaway," Shakespeare's wife, is possible.

### 146

Poor soul, the centre of my sinful earth,
[          ] these rebel powers that thee array;[1]
Why dost thou pine within and suffer dearth,
Painting thy outward walls so costly gay?
5  Why so large cost, having so short a lease,
Dost thou upon thy fading mansion° spend?          *(the body)*
Shall worms, inheritors of this excess,
Eat up thy charge?° Is this thy body's end?          *expense*
Then, soul, live thou upon thy servant's° loss,      *(the body's)*
10  And let that pine to aggravate thy store.[2]
Buy terms divine° in selling hours of dross;°    *eternal life / waste*
Within be fed, without be rich no more.
   So shalt thou feed on death, that feeds on men,
   And death once dead, there's no more dying then.

### 147

My love is as a fever, longing still°           *continually*
For that which longer nurseth° the disease,       *nourishes*
Feeding on that which doth preserve° the ill,       *prolong*
Th'uncertain° sickly appetite to please.        *capricious*
5  My reason, the physician to my love,
Angry that his prescriptions are not kept,
Hath left me, and I desperate now approve
Desire is death, which physic did except.[1]
Past cure I am, now reason is past care,[2]
10  And frantic mad with evermore° unrest.         *constant*
My thoughts and my discourse as madmen's are,
At random from° the truth vainly° expressed;  *unconnected to / idly*
   For I have sworn thee fair, and thought thee bright,
   Who art as black as hell, as dark as night.

### 148

O me, what eyes hath love put in my head,
Which have no correspondence with true sight!
Or if they have, where is my judgement fled,
That censures falsely[1] what they see aright?
5  If that be fair whereon my false eyes dote,
What means the world to say it is not so?
If it be not, then love doth well denote[2]
Love's eye is not so true as all men's. No,[3]
How can it, O, how can love's eye be true,
10  That is so vexed with watching° and with tears?    *staying awake*

---

**Sonnet 146**
1. This rebellious body in which you are clothed. At the beginning of the line, Q repeats "My sinful earth" from the previous line. There is no way of discovering what Shakespeare wrote; among the guesses are "Starved by," "Foiled by," "Spoiled by," and "Feeding."
2. And let the body dwindle to add to your wealth.
**Sonnet 147**
1. *now . . . except:* now discover that desire, which rejected medicine, is fatal.
2. Medical care: inverting the proverb "Past cure, past

care" (don't worry about what you can't control). In the proverb, you don't care because you can't cure; here, because you don't care, you can't cure.
**Sonnet 148**
1. That judges inaccurately (dishonestly). "False" (line 5) has similar meanings.
2. Then my self-delusion in love proves that.
3. Not so true as all other men's eye. On the contrary, Q's "all men's, no" is often emended to "all men's 'No,'" suggesting a pun on "eye/aye" (yes).

No marvel then though I° mistake my view:       *that I (eye)*
The sun itself sees not till heaven clears.
    O cunning love, with tears thou keep'st me blind
    Lest eyes, well seeing, thy foul faults should find!

## 149

Canst thou, O cruel, say I love thee not
When I against myself with thee partake?°       *take sides*
Do I not think on thee when I forgot
Am of myself, all-tyrant,[1] for thy sake?
5  Who hateth thee that I do call my friend?
On whom frown'st thou that I do fawn upon?
Nay, if thou lour'st° on me, do I not spend°     *scowl / wreak*
Revenge upon myself with present moan?°     *instant anguish*
What merit do I in myself respect°     *value; note*
10 That is so proud thy service to despise,[2]
When all my best° doth worship thy defect,°     *best qualities / flaws*
Commanded by the motion of thine eyes?
    But, love, hate on; for now I know thy mind.
    Those that can see thou lov'st, and I am blind.[3]

## 150

O, from what power hast thou this powerful might
With insufficiency° my heart to sway,     *By your flaws*
To make me give the lie to my true sight
And swear that brightness doth not grace the day?[1]
5 Whence hast thou this becoming of things ill,[2]
That in the very refuse of thy deeds°     *your basest behavior*
There is such strength and warrantise° of skill     *guarantee*
That in my mind thy worst all best exceeds?
Who taught thee how to make me love thee more
10 The more I hear and see just cause of hate?
O, though I love what others do abhor,
With others thou shouldst not abhor my state.
    If thy unworthiness raised love in me,
    More worthy I to be beloved of thee.

## 151

Love is too young° to know what conscience is,     *(Cupid being a boy)*
Yet who knows not conscience[1] is born of love?
Then, gentle cheater, urge° not my amiss,°     *stress / fault*
Lest guilty of my faults thy sweet self prove.
5 For, thou betraying me, I do betray
My nobler part° to my gross body's treason.     *soul*
My soul doth tell my body that he may
Triumph in love; flesh stays no farther reason,[2]

**Sonnet 149**
1. *when . . . all-tyrant:* when I tyrannically neglect myself.
2. So proud as to scorn to serve you.
3. You love those who see you accurately and thus admire you, but I am blinded (by love and thus, from your point of view, unworthy of being loved). The first clause may have the opposite sense, however: you love those who see your defects well enough not to love you.
**Sonnet 150**
1. *To . . . day:* the speaker is so blindly in love that he finds beauty only in the blackness he associates with his mistress.
2. This capacity to render the ugly attractive.
**Sonnet 151**
1. Moral sense; carnal knowledge.
2. Flesh, specifically the sexual organ, needs no further encouragement.

10    But rising at thy name doth point out thee
    As his triumphant prize. Proud of this pride,[3]
    He is contented thy poor drudge to be,
    To stand° in thy affairs, fall by thy side.          *assist; be erect*
      No want of conscience hold it that I call
      Her 'love' for whose dear love I rise and fall.

### 152

    In loving thee thou know'st I am forsworn,[1]
    But thou art twice forsworn to me love swearing°    *in swearing love to me*
    In act thy bed-vow° broke, and new faith torn    *to husband (or lover)*
5   In vowing new hate after new love bearing.[2]
    But why of two oaths' breach do I accuse thee
    When I break twenty? I am perjured most,
    For all my vows are oaths but to misuse° thee,    *deceive*
    And all my honest faith in thee is lost.
10    For I have sworn deep oaths of thy deep kindness,
    Oaths of thy love, thy truth, thy constancy,
    And to enlighten thee gave eyes to blindness,[3]
    Or made them swear against the thing they see.
      For I have sworn thee fair—more perjured eye°    *(punning on "I")*
      To swear against the truth so foul a lie.

### 153[1]

    Cupid laid by his brand° and fell asleep.    *torch*
    A maid of Dian's[2] this advantage found,°    *seized*
    And his love-kindling fire did quickly steep
5   In a cold valley-fountain of that ground,
    Which borrowed from this holy fire of love
    A dateless° lively heat, still° to endure,    *An endless / always*
    And grew a seething bath which yet men prove
    Against strange maladies a sovereign cure.[3]
10    But at my mistress' eye love's brand new fired,°    *being newly lit*
    The boy for trial° needs would touch my breast.    *to test it*
    I, sick withal,° the help of bath desired,    *from it*
    And thither hied, a sad distempered° guest,    *seriously ill*
      But found no cure; the bath for my help lies
      Where Cupid got new fire: my mistress' eyes.

3. Swelling with pride (and lust).
**Sonnet 152**
1. Forsworn presumably in breaking loving vows—perhaps to his wife, to the youth to whom he promised unswerving devotion in earlier sonnets, or to both.
2. *new faith . . . bearing:* the "new faith" followed by "new hate" may be addressed either to the speaker's young friend or to the speaker himself.
3. And to make you fair (give you insight), I looked blindly on your failings (pretended to see what I couldn't).

**Sonnet 153**
1. This and the following sonnet derive indirectly from classical fifth-century Greek epigrams.
2. Diana, goddess of chastity.
3. *And grew . . . cure:* And became a boiling-hot medicinal bath (used, among other purposes, for the treatment of venereal disease), which men still find to be an outstanding remedy for foreign illnesses (venereal diseases were associated with foreigners). There may be an allusion here and in 154 to the town of Bath, which became a famous health spa in the eighteenth century.

## 154[1]

5   The little love-god lying once asleep
     Laid by his side his heart-inflaming brand,°           *torch*
     Whilst many nymphs that vowed chaste life to keep
     Came tripping by; but in her maiden hand
     The fairest votary took up that fire
10   Which many legions of true hearts had warmed,
     And so the general° of hot desire         *commander (Cupid)*
     Was sleeping by a virgin hand disarmed.
     This brand she quenchèd in a cool well by,°      *close by*
     Which from love's fire took heat perpetual,
     Growing a bath and healthful remedy
     For men diseased; but I, my mistress' thrall,°       *slave*
       Came there for cure; and this° by that I prove:    *the following*
       Love's fire heats water, water cools not love.

**Sonnet 154**
1. This sonnet varies the topic of 153.

# A Lover's Complaint

From off a hill whose concave womb re-worded°         *hollow side echoed*
A plaintful story from a sist'ring° vale,         *nearby*
My spirits t'attend° this double voice accorded,°     *hear / agreed*
And down I laid to list° the sad-tuned tale;      *listen to*
5  Ere long espied a fickle° maid full pale,       *a disturbed*
Tearing of papers, breaking rings a-twain,°       *in two*
Storming her world with sorrow's wind and rain.

Upon her head a plaited hive° of straw          *hat*
Which fortified° her visage from the sun,        *protected*
10  Whereon the thought° might think sometime it saw  *imagination*
The carcass of a beauty spent and done.
Time had not scythèd all that youth begun,
Nor youth all quit; but spite° of heaven's fell° rage,   *in spite / fierce*
Some beauty peeped through lattice of seared° age.   *withered*

15  Oft did she heave her napkin to her eyne,[1]
Which on it had conceited characters,°      *imaginative designs*
Laund'ring the silken figures in the brine
That seasoned° woe had pelleted in tears,     *experienced; salted*
And often reading what contents it bears;
20  As often shrieking undistinguished° woe      *inarticulate*
In clamours of all size, both high and low.

Sometimes her levelled eyes their carriage ride[2]
As° they did batt'ry to the spheres° intend;     *As if / planets*
Sometime diverted their poor balls° are tied  *eyeballs; cannonballs*
25  To th'orbèd° earth; sometimes they do extend    *spherical*
Their view right on;° anon their gazes lend       *straight*
To every place at once, and nowhere fixed,
The mind and sight distractedly commixed.°      *confused*

Her hair, nor° loose nor tied in formal plait,      *neither*
30  Proclaimed in her a careless hand of pride;[3]
For some, untucked, descended her sheaved° hat,  *fell from her straw*
Hanging her pale and pinèd cheek beside.
Some in her threaden fillet° still did bide,       *headband*
And, true to bondage, would not break from thence,
35  Though slackly braided in loose negligence.

A thousand favours° from a maund° she drew   *love tokens / basket*
Of amber, crystal, and of beaded jet,°     *beads of black stone*
Which one by one she in a river threw
Upon whose weeping margin she was set;°      *seated*
40  Like usury applying wet to wet,[4]

---

1. Often did she raise her handkerchief to her eyes.
2. Sometimes her eyes, aimed (like a cannon), glare (are mounted on a swivel).
3. A hand careless of pride; a hand proud in its care-lessness (knowing that she could attract with no effort).
4. Like usury making wealth wealthier (by adding tears to the stream).

Or monarch's hands that lets not bounty fall
Where want cries some, but where excess begs all.[5]

Of folded schedules° had she many a one         *letters*
Which she perused, sighed, tore, and gave the flood;
45  Cracked many a ring of posied gold and bone,[6]
Bidding them find their sepulchres in mud;
Found yet more letters sadly penned in blood,
With sleided silk feat and affectedly
Enswathed[7] and sealed to curious° secrecy.      *careful*

50  These often bathed she in her fluxive° eyes,     *flowing*
And often kissed, and often 'gan to tear;
Cried 'O false blood, thou register° of lies,     *record*
What unapprovèd° witness dost thou bear!    *unreliable*
Ink would have seemed more black and damnèd here!'
55  This said, in top of rage the lines she rents,°     *rips*
Big° discontent so breaking their contents.    *Powerful*

A reverend man that grazed his cattle nigh
Sometime a blusterer that the ruffle knew[8]
Of court, of city, and had let go by
60  The swiftest hours observèd as they flew,[9]
Towards this afflicted fancy fastly[1] drew,
And, privileged by age, desires to know
In brief the grounds and motives of her woe.

So slides he down upon his grainèd bat,[2]
65  And comely° distant sits he by her side,      *politely*
When he again desires her, being sat,
Her grievance with his hearing to divide.°     *share*
If that from him there may be aught applied
Which may her suffering ecstasy° assuage,    *grief*
70  'Tis promised in the charity of age.

'Father,' she says, 'though in me you behold
The injury of many a blasting° hour,     *disfiguring*
Let it not tell your judgement I am old;
Not age, but sorrow over me hath power.
75  I might as yet have been a spreading° flower,   *blooming*
Fresh to myself, if I had self-applied
Love to myself, and to no love beside.

'But, woe is me, too early I attended
A youthful suit—it was° to gain my grace°—   *was designed / favor*
80  O, one by nature's outwards° so commended   *external appearance*
That maidens' eyes stuck over all° his face.   *were glued to*
Love lacked a dwelling and made him her place,

---

5. *Or . . . all*: Or like the monarch who, rather than give a little to the truly needy, gives a great deal to those who already have plenty.
6. A ring of gold and ivory inscribed with messages (of love).
7. *With . . . / Enswathed*: Delicately and affectionately wrapped in strands of separated ("sleided") silk.

8. Once a man of the world who was accustomed to the busier life.
9. *had . . . flew*: was past the prime of life, but had learned from experience.
1. Toward this person afflicted by love rapidly (close by).
2. So he comes down the bank with the help of his forked herdsman's staff.

And when in his fair parts she did abide
She was new-lodged and newly deified.

85 'His browny locks did hang in crookèd curls,
And every light occasion° of the wind                      *chance stirring*
Upon his lips their silken parcels° hurls.                  *(of hair)*
What's sweet to do, to do will aptly find.[3]
Each eye that saw him did enchant the mind,
90 For on his visage was in little° drawn                     *miniature*
What largeness thinks in paradise was sawn.[4]

'Small show of man was yet upon his chin;
His phoenix° down began but to appear,                     *singularly lovely*
Like unshorn velvet, on that termless skin[5]
95 Whose bare outbragged the web[6] it seemed to wear;
Yet showed his visage by that cost more dear,[7]
And nice affections° wavering stood in doubt             *discriminating tastes*
If best were as it was, or best without.°                 *(shaven)*

'His qualities were beauteous as his form,
100 For maiden-tongued° he was, and thereof free.°          *modest / well spoken*
Yet if men moved° him, was he such a storm               *angered*
As oft twixt May and April is to see
When winds breathe sweet, unruly though they be.
His rudeness so with his authorized youth
105 Did livery falseness in a pride of truth.[8]

'Well could he ride, and often men would say
"That horse his mettle from his rider takes;
Proud of subjection, noble by the sway,°                  *control*
What rounds, what bounds, what course,° what stop he makes!"  *gallop*
110 And controversy hence a question takes,
Whether the horse by him became his deed,
Or he his manège by th' well-doing steed.[9]

'But quickly on this side the verdict went:
His real habitude° gave life and grace                    *disposition*
115 To appertainings° and to ornament,                      *external attributes*
Accomplished in himself, not in his case.°               *mere appearance*
All aids, themselves made fairer by their place,
Came for additions;[1] yet their purposed trim
Pieced not[2] his grace, but were all graced by him.

120 'So on the tip of his subduing tongue
All kind of arguments and question deep,
All replication prompt,° and reason strong,              *quick reply*

3. Ways are easily found to do pleasant things (look, love).
4. What one would imagine seeing on a larger scale in paradise.
5. Like velvet with its nap unclipped, on that indescribable (invulnerable to time) skin.
6. Whose naked surface showed more beautiful than the down covering.
7. Yet his face looked more precious (attractive) because

of its rich clothing.
8. *His . . . truth:* His roughness, sanctioned by his "youth," employed falseness in truth's uniform.
9. *Whether . . . steed:* Whether he performed so well because of his horsemanship or because his grace in horsemanship (French: *manège*) was a result of the horse's skill.
1. Attempted to increase his worth.
2. *their . . . not:* their anticipated decorative effect did not increase.

For his advantage still did wake and sleep.[3]
To make the weeper laugh, the laugher weep,
125   He had the dialect and different skill,[4]
Catching all passions in his craft of will,[5]

'That° he did in the general bosom reign                                    *So that*
Of young, of old, and sexes both enchanted,
To dwell with him in thoughts, or to remain
130   In personal duty, following where he haunted.°                      *often went*
Consents[6] bewitched, ere he desire,° have granted,          *before he asks*
And dialogued for him what he would say,
Asked their own wills, and made their wills obey.

'Many there were that did his picture get
135   To serve their eyes, and in it put their mind,
Like fools that in th'imagination set
The goodly objects° which abroad° they find              *sights / traveling*
Of lands and mansions, theirs in thought assigned,
And labour in more pleasures to bestow them[7]
140   Than the true gouty landlord which doth owe° them.              *own*

'So many have, that never touched his hand,
Sweetly supposed them mistress of his heart.
My woeful self, that did in freedom stand,
And was my own fee-simple,[8] not in part,
145   What with his art in youth, and youth in art,
Threw my affections in his charmèd° power,                    *magical*
Reserved the stalk and gave him all my flower.

'Yet did I not, as some my equals° did,                      *young girls of my rank*
Demand of him, nor being desired yielded.°                   *yielded sexual favors*
150   Finding myself in honour so forbid,
With safest distance I mine honour° shielded.                *chastity*
Experience° for me many bulwarks builded                     *(of "my equals")*
Of proofs new bleeding, which remained the foil[9]
Of this false jewel and his amorous spoil.

155   'But ah, who ever shunned by precedent
The destined ill she must herself assay,°                    *try out*
Or forced examples 'gainst her own content
To put the by-past perils in her way?[1]
Counsel may stop a while what will not stay,°               *stop for good*
160   For when we rage,° advice is often seen,                  *(with lust)*
By blunting° us, to make our wills more keen.               *repressing*

---

3. *For . . . sleep:* (Like servants) adjusted their waking
and sleeping hours for the benefit of their master.
4. The manner of speech and versatile skill.
5. His faculty of persuasion. Here and in the next stanza,
there are suggestions of other senses of "will." See sonnets
135–36.
6. Powers of (sexual) consent; consenting people.
7. *theirs . . . them:* imagining the "lands and mansions"
their own, they try harder to use them pleasurably.
8. And had absolute control of myself (as of land in free-
hold).

9. *Of . . . foil:* Fresh examples of seduction, which
remained the defense (or sword—picking up the military,
specifically fencing, imagery of "distance," "shielded,"
"bulwarks," "bleeding," lines 151–53). But "foil" as the
dark material in which gems are set to make them look
more brilliant also works with "false jewel" in the following line, to suggest that the young man's sexual escapades
made him more attractive.
1. *Or . . . way:* Or reminded herself, to counter her present inclinations, of bygone dangers. *forced:* urged.

'Nor gives it satisfaction to our blood°          *sexuality*
That we must curb it upon others' proof,°          *experience*
To be forbod° the sweets that seems so good          *forbidden*
165  For fear of harms that preach in our behoof.°          *for our benefit*
O appetite, from judgement stand aloof!
The one a palate hath that needs will taste,
Though reason weep, and cry it is thy last.

'For further I could say this man's untrue,[2]
170  And knew the patterns° of his foul beguiling;          *instances*
Heard where his plants in others' orchards° grew,          *(wombs)*
Saw how deceits were gilded in his smiling,
Knew vows were ever brokers° to defiling,          *go-betweens*
Thought characters and words merely but art,[3]
175  And bastards of his foul adulterate heart.

'And long upon these terms I held my city°          *chastity*
Till thus he gan° besiege me: "Gentle maid,          *began to*
Have of my suffering youth some feeling pity,
And be not of my holy vows afraid.
180  That's° to ye sworn to none was ever said;          *What is*
For feasts of love I have been called unto,
Till now did ne'er invite nor never woo.

'"All my offences that abroad° you see°          *in the world / learn of*
Are errors of the blood,° none of the mind.          *sexual passion*
185  Love made them not; with acture they may be,[4]
Where neither party is nor true nor kind.°          *faithful or loving*
They sought their shame that so their shame did find,
And so much less of shame in me remains
By how much of me their reproach contains.[5]

190  '"Among the many that mine eyes have seen,
Not° one whose flame my heart so much as warmèd          *There is not*
Or my affection put to th' smallest teen,°          *pain*
Or any of my leisures° ever charmèd.          *hours of leisure*
Harm have I done to them, but ne'er was harmèd;
195  Kept hearts in liveries,° but mine own was free,          *in uniform (service)*
And reigned commanding in his monarchy.

'"Look here what tributes wounded fancies° sent me          *lovers*
Of pallid pearls and rubies red as blood,
Figuring° that they their passions likewise lent me          *Showing*
200  Of grief and blushes, aptly understood
In bloodless white and the encrimsoned mood°—          *form (of rubies)*
Effects of terror and dear modesty,
Encamped in hearts, but fighting outwardly.[6]

---

2. I am able to say more about this man's perfidy.
3. Written and spoken words were merely instruments of skill (in seduction).
4. *with . . . be:* by a mere physical act they may be performed.

5. *By . . . contains:* The more they name me in their reproaches (thus revealing that they are unchaste and, hence, by this logic, to blame).
6. *Effects . . . outwardly:* White ("terror") and red (blushing "modesty") fighting on their faces.

'"And lo, behold, these talents° of their hair,                                                      *riches*
205  With twisted mettle amorously impleached,[7]
I have received from many a several fair,°                                                 *a different beauty*
Their kind acceptance weepingly beseeched,
With th'annexations° of fair gems enriched,                                                       *additions*
And deep-brained sonnets that did amplify°                                                  *expound; increase*
210  Each stone's dear nature, worth, and quality.

'"The diamond?—why, 'twas beautiful and hard,
Whereto his invised[8] properties did tend;
The deep-green em'rald, in whose fresh regard
Weak sights their sickly radiance do amend;[9]
215  The heaven-hued sapphire and the opal blend[1]
With objects manifold; each several° stone,                                                       *distinct*
With wit well blazoned,° smiled or made some moan.                                            *described*

'"Lo, all these trophies of affections° hot,                                                      *passions*
Of pensived° and subdued desires the tender,°                                            *saddened / gifts*
220  Nature hath charged me that I hoard them not,
But yield them up where I myself must render—
That is to you, my origin and ender;°                                                  *alpha and omega; all*
For these of force must your oblations[2] be,
Since I their altar, you enpatron me.[3]

225  '"O then advance of yours that phraseless° hand                                    *beyond description*
Whose white weighs down the airy scale of praise.[4]
Take all these similes[5] to your own command,
Hallowed with sighs that burning° lungs did raise.                                           *(with love)*
What me, your minister for you, obeys,
230  Works under you,[6] and to your audit° comes                                                *account*
Their distract parcels° in combinèd sums.                                              *component parts*

'"Lo, this device was sent me from a nun,
A sister sanctified of holiest note,°                                                            *reputation*
Which late her noble suit° in court did shun,                                          *attendance; suitors*
235  Whose rarest havings° made the blossoms° dote;                                  *qualities / young nobles*
For she was sought by spirits of richest coat,°                                             *coat of arms*
But kept cold distance, and did thence remove
To spend her living° in eternal love.°                                                       *life / (of God)*

'"But O, my sweet, what labour is't to leave
240  The thing we have not, mast'ring what not strives,°                                   *does not resist*
Planing° the place which did no form[7] receive,                                              *Smoothing*
Playing patient sports in unconstrainèd gyves![8]
She that her fame so to herself contrives[9]

---

7. With misdirected courage (confused spirit?) lovingly
intertwined. Many editors emend "mettle" to "metal."
8. Its unseen—referring to the diamond but also, perhaps, to the equally "beautiful and hard" young man.
9. *in . . . amend:* which, when looked at, can heal weak
vision.
1. Blended: many-colored; accompanying other "objects" (line 216).
2. For these necessarily must be offerings at your altar.
3. Since I am the altar (on which they were offered), you
must necessarily be the patron saint of the altar (me).

4. Whose white exceeds any measure of praise.
5. These emblematic gifts and the sonnets that explain
them.
6. *What . . . under you:* Whatever pays homage to me,
your agent, serves you.
7. No impression (of love, on the heart).
8. Patiently enduring shackles ("gyves") that have not
been forced upon one and that can be removed (or that
do not constrain). (The entire sentence is ironic.)
9. She who thus contrives for herself the reputation of
disinterest in love.

The scars of battle scapeth by the flight,
245 And makes her absence valiant, not her might.[1]

'"O, pardon me, in that my boast is true!
The accident which brought me to her eye
Upon the moment° did her force° subdue,          *Immediately / resolve*
And now she would the cagèd cloister fly.
250 Religious° love put out religion's eye.          *Devoted (sexual)*
Not to be tempted would she be immured,°          *walled up*
And now, to tempt, all liberty procured.

'"How mighty then you are, O hear me tell!
The broken bosoms° that to me belong          *hearts*
255 Have emptied all their fountains in my well,
And mine I pour° your ocean all among.          *pour into*
I strong o'er them, and you o'er me being strong,
Must for your victory us all congest,°          *gather*
As compound° love to physic° your cold breast.          *medicinal / treat*

260 '"My parts° had power to charm a sacred nun,          *attributes*
Who disciplined, ay dieted in° grace,          *sustained by*
Believed her eyes when they t' assail begun,[2]
All vows and consecrations giving place.°          *yielding*
O most potential love: vow, bond, nor space
265 In thee hath neither sting, knot, nor confine,[3]
For thou art all, and all things else are thine.

'"When thou impressest,[4] what are precepts worth
Of stale example? When thou wilt inflame,
How coldly those impediments stand forth
270 Of wealth, of filial fear, law, kindred, fame.
Love's arms are° peace, 'gainst rule, 'gainst sense, 'gainst shame;          *Love's power compels*
And° sweetens in the suff'ring pangs it bears          *And love*
The aloes° of all forces, shocks, and fears.          *bitterness*

'"Now all these hearts that do on mine depend,
275 Feeling it break, with bleeding groans they pine,[5]
And supplicant° their sighs to you extend          *as supplicants*
To leave° the batt'ry that you make 'gainst mine,          *cease*
Lending soft audience to my sweet design,[6]
And credent° soul to that strong-bonded oath          *trustful*
280 That shall prefer and undertake° my troth."          *advance and guarantee*

'This said, his wat'ry eyes he did dismount,°          *lower (military)*
Whose sights till then were levelled° on my face.          *aimed*
Each cheek a river running from a fount
With brinish current downward flowed apace.
285 O, how the channel° to the stream° gave grace,          *cheeks / tears*

---

1. And achieves a reputation for valor by avoiding the temptation of love, not by strongly resisting it.
2. When my attributes ("parts") began to assail her heart.
3. *potential . . . confine:* powerful love: a "vow" has no force ("sting"), a "bond" does not tie ("knot"), and "space" does not restrain ("confine").

4. When you draft someone into your (military) service; make an impression on the heart.
5. Because each sigh supposedly robbed the heart of a drop of blood.
6. Looking favorably on my intentions.

Who glazed with crystal gate the glowing roses
That flame through water which their hue encloses.[7]

'O father, what a hell of witchcraft lies
In the small orb of one particular° tear!       *single*
290    But with the inundation of the eyes
What rocky heart to water will not wear?°       *wear away*
What breast so cold that is not warmèd here?
O cleft° effect! Cold modesty, hot wrath,°    *divided / passion*
Both fire from hence and chill extincture hath.[8]

295    'For lo, his passion,° but an art of craft,    *passionate speech*
Even there resolved° my reason into tears.      *dissolved*
There my white stole of chastity I daffed,°    *took off*
Shook off my sober guards and civil° fears;    *seemly*
Appear to him as he to me appears,
300    All melting, though our drops this diff'rence bore:
His poisoned me, and mine did him restore.

'In him a plenitude of subtle matter,°    *raw material; cunning*
Applied to cautels,° all strange forms receives,[9]    *tricky devices*
Of burning blushes or of weeping water,
305    Or swooning paleness; and he takes and leaves,°    *uses this and shuns that*
In either's aptness,° as it best deceives,    *As each is appropriate*
To blush at speeches rank,° to weep at woes,    *offensive*
Or to turn white and swoon at tragic shows,

'That not a heart which in his level° came    *range (of fire)*
310    Could scape the hail of his all-hurting aim,
Showing fair nature is[1] both kind and tame,
And, veiled in them,° did win whom he would maim.    *(kindness and tameness)*
Against the thing he sought he would exclaim;
When he most burned in heart-wished luxury,°    *lust*
315    He preached pure maid° and praised cold chastity.    *virginal purity*

'Thus merely with the garment of a grace°    *with external appeal*
The naked and concealèd fiend he covered,
That th'unexperient° gave the tempter place,°    *inexperienced / entry*
Which like a cherubin above them hovered.°    *(as if protectively)*
320    Who, young and simple, would not be so lovered?[2]
Ay me, I fell, and yet do question make°    *wonder*
What I should do again for such a sake.°    *person; pleasure*

'O that infected° moisture of his eye,    *tainted*
O that false fire which in his cheek so glowed,
325    O that forced thunder from° his heart did fly,    *that from*
O that sad breath his spongy lungs bestowed,°    *emitted*
O all that borrowed motion seeming owed[3]
Would yet again betray the fore-betrayed,
And new pervert a reconcilèd° maid.'    *penitent*

---

7. *Who . . . encloses:* The river is seen as a kind of glass covering ("crystal gate") over the cheeks ("roses"), whose color shines through the "water," like a jewel enclosed in glass. *Who:* (the stream).
8. *Both . . . hath:* Tears heat up cold modesty and extin-guish hot passion (as the following stanza elaborates).
9. *all . . . receives:* is shaped into novel forms.
1. Pretending his nature is.
2. Would not desire such a lover.
3. That emotion apparently his own.

## Alternative Versions

Each of the four sonnets below exists in an alternative version. The text on top is the version as it appeared in the 1609 Quarto. *"Spes Altera"* and "On his Mistress' Beauty" derive from seventeenth-century manuscripts. The alternative versions of sonnets 138 and 144 are from *The Passionate Pilgrim* (1599).

### 2

When forty winters shall besiege thy brow
And dig deep trenches in thy beauty's field,
Thy youth's proud livery, so gazed on now,
Will be a tattered weed, of small worth held.
5  Then being asked where all thy beauty lies,
Where all the treasure of thy lusty days,
To say within thine own deep-sunken eyes
Were an all-eating shame and thriftless praise.
How much more praise deserved thy beauty's use
10  If thou couldst answer 'This fair child of mine
Shall sum my count, and make my old excuse',
Proving his beauty by succession thine.
    This were to be new made when thou art old,
    And see thy blood warm when thou feel'st it cold.

*Spes Altera°*             *Another Hope*

When forty winters shall besiege thy brow
And trench deep furrows in that lovely field,
Thy youth's fair liv'ry, so accounted° now,      *esteemed*
Shall be like rotten weeds of no worth held.
5  Then being asked where all thy beauty lies,
Where all the lustre of thy youthful days,
To say 'Within these hollow sunken eyes'
Were an all-eaten truth[1] and worthless praise.
O how much better were thy beauty's use
10  If thou couldst say 'This pretty child of mine
Saves my account[2] and makes my old excuse',
Making his beauty by succession thine.
    This were to be new born when thou art old,
    And see thy blood warm when thou feel'st it cold.

### 106

When in the chronicle of wasted time
I see description of the fairest wights,
And beauty making beautiful old rhyme
In praise of ladies dead and lovely knights;
5  Then in the blazon of sweet beauty's best,
Of hand, of foot, of lip, of eye, of brow,
I see their antique pen would have expressed
Even such a beauty as you master now.
So all their praises are but prophecies
10  Of this our time, all you prefiguring,
And for they looked but with divining eyes
They had not skill enough your worth to sing;

---

*Spes Altera*
1. An accurate statement that you had been gluttonous.    2. Preserves (increases) my wealth (my moral record).

For we which now behold these present days
Have eyes to wonder, but lack tongues to praise.

## On his Mistress' Beauty

When in the annals of all-wasting time
I see descriptions of the fairest wights,
And beauty making beautiful old rhyme
In praise of ladies dead and lovely knights;
5   Then in the blazon of sweet beauty's best,
Of face, of hand, of lip, of eye, or brow,
I see their antique pen would have expressed
E'en such a beauty as you master now.
So all their praises were but prophecies
10   Of these our days, all you prefiguring,
And for they saw but with divining eyes
They had not skill enough your worth to sing;
    For we which now behold these present days
    Have eyes to wonder, but no tongues to praise.

---

## 138

When my love swears that she is made of truth
I do believe her though I know she lies,
That she might think me some untutored youth
Unlearnèd in the world's false subtleties.
5   Thus vainly thinking that she thinks me young,
Although she knows my days are past the best,
Simply I credit her false-speaking tongue;
On both sides thus is simple truth suppressed.
But wherefore says she not she is unjust,
10   And wherefore say not I that I am old?
O, love's best habit is in seeming trust,
And age in love loves not to have years told.
    Therefore I lie with her, and she with me,
    And in our faults by lies we flattered be.

---

## 138

When my love swears that she is made of truth
I do believe her though I know she lies,
That she might think me some untutored youth
Unskilful in the world's false forgeries.
5   Thus vainly thinking that she thinks me young,
Although I know my years be past the best,
I, smiling, credit her false-speaking tongue,
Outfacing° faults in love with love's ill rest.[1]                    *Defying*
But wherefore says my love that she is young,
10   And wherefore say not I that I am old?
O, love's best habit's in a soothing tongue,
And age in love loves not to have years told.
    Therefore I'll lie with love,° and love with me,          *my lover; lovingly*
    Since that our faults in love thus smothered be.

---

**Sonnet 138**
1. With the "rest" of what's bad in love; restlessness.

### 144

Two loves I have, of comfort and despair,
Which like two spirits do suggest me still.
The better angel is a man right fair,
The worser spirit a woman coloured ill.
5  To win me soon to hell my female evil
Tempteth my better angel from my side,
And would corrupt my saint to be a devil,
Wooing his purity with her foul pride;
And whether that my angel be turned fiend
10  Suspect I may, yet not directly tell;
But being both from me, both to each friend,
I guess one angel in another's hell.
    Yet this shall I ne'er know, but live in doubt
    Till my bad angel fire my good one out.

### 144

Two loves I have, of comfort and despair,
That like two spirits do suggest me still.
My better angel is a man right fair,
My worser spirit a woman coloured ill.
5  To win me soon to hell my female evil
Tempteth my better angel from my side,
And would corrupt my saint to be a devil,
Wooing his purity with her fair pride;
And whether that my angel be turned fiend,
10  Suspect I may, yet not directly tell;
For being both to me, both to each friend,
I guess one angel in another's hell.
    The truth I shall not know, but live in doubt
    Till my bad angel fire my good one out.

# Various Poems

The short poems included here are occasional pieces. That is, they were written not as part of a longer work by a single author but for specific occasions. They are arranged in the order in which Shakespeare might have written them from the early 1590s until shortly before his death, if in fact he wrote them all—an extremely unlikely supposition. (See the Textual Note.) Unlike the sonnets, which collectively possess considerable coherence, these poems employ a number of meters, line lengths, rhyme schemes, and stanzaic forms. Until very recently, scholarly discussion generally focused on the relationship of the poems to Shakespeare's biography and on the question of whether Shakespeare actually wrote them.

"A Song," one of the two longer poems printed here, is noteworthy mainly as a virtuoso display of rhyming: there are usually eight pairs of rhyme words in each ten-line stanza, with the rhymes occurring as often as every three syllables and on occasion every two syllables ("Being set, lips met," line 39). *The Passionate Pilgrim* appeared under Shakespeare's name in 1599, apparently without his approval. Of its twenty poems, five are lifted from Shakespeare's other works and hence appear elsewhere in this volume, four are clearly by other writers, and eleven remain unattributed and are accordingly printed here. Numbers 4, 6, and 9—all sonnets—are noteworthy for their focus on the theme of *Venus and Adonis*, to which they may be a response. By 1599, Shakespeare's name had considerable cachet. *The Passionate Pilgrim* very possibly seeks to exploit that cachet, interweaving a few pieces by Shakespeare with other poems so as to produce a thematically resonant sequence that obscures the homoeroticism of some of the sonnets and in effect becomes a testament to poetic artifice.

Several of the other poems are elegies—compositions in memory of the dead, though sometimes written while the subject was still alive. The first of the two epitaphs on the usurer John Combe reveals a conventional hostility to usury. The second, however, deploys the complex, sometimes positive, metaphorical relationship between usury and breeding characteristic of the early sonnets. Combe

> did gather [wealth from usury]
> To make the poor his issue [heirs]; he, their father,
> . . . [made] record of his tilth and seed.
> (lines 3–5)

Urging marriage and a family, sonnet 3 speaks of "the tillage of thy husbandry" (line 6). And sonnet 6 argues:

> That use is not forbidden usury
> Which happies those that pay the willing loan:
> That's for thyself to breed another thee,
> Or ten times happier, be it ten for one.
> (lines 5–8)

Thus, in the sonnets, the language of usury helps clarify paternity, whereas in the second epitaph, the language of paternity helps clarify usury. In both, however, the two terms are mutually illuminating. The last line quoted from sonnet 6 is also reminiscent of the opening of the first epitaph: "Ten in the hundred here lies engraved; / A hundred to ten his soul is not saved." Both refer to the highest legal interest rate—ten in a hundred, or 10 percent—although only the sonnet converts the allusion into a positive image.

Similarly, "Verses upon the Stanley Tomb at Tong" closely parallels the language of some of Shakespeare's sonnets concerned with the destructive power of time. The "register" of the first of the two poems (1.3) and the "sky-aspiring pyramids" of the second (2.2) also appear in sonnet 123 ("pyramids built up," "registers," lines 2, 9). Closer still is the connection to sonnet 55: "Not marble nor the gilded monuments / Of princes shall outlive this powerful rhyme" (lines 1–2). Stanley's "fame is more perpetual than these stones" (1.4); "Not monumental stone preserves our fame" (2.1). Stanley's "memory," however, "shall outlive marble and defacers' hands" as well as "time's consumption" (2.3, 4, 5), just as "memory" need not worry that "war shall statues overturn" and is not dependent on "unswept stone besmeared with sluttish time" in sonnet 55 (lines 8, 5, 4). Although the guarantee of immortality seems to be Stanley's life rather than the "powerful rhyme" of the sonnet (line 2), the end is the same: Stanley "is not dead; he doth but sleep" (1.2), while in the sonnet, " 'gainst death and all oblivious enmity / Shall you pace forth" (lines 9–10). Ultimately, poetic fame in the sonnet lasts only "till the judgement that yourself arise" (on Judgment Day; line 13); analogously, "Stanley for whom this stands shall stand in heaven" (2.6). The pun on the name in this concluding line ("Stanley/stands/stand") is similar to the sign of the author's hand left in "Upon a pair of gloves that master sent to his mistress," where "the will is all" recalls Shakespeare's emphatic references to his first name in sonnets 135 and 136.

"Upon a pair of gloves" seems to reveal the poet intruding himself into a composition ostensibly from Alexander Aspinall to his (future?) wife; the "Epitaph on Himself" is strikingly impersonal. The lack of specificity may in this case be a poetic signature, however. By 1616, perhaps only Shakespeare could have written about Shakespeare without reference to his theatrical or literary career. This modesty coincides with an open threat: "cursed be he that moves my bones" (line 4). The apparently conventional warning was designed to forestall the very real danger of his body being dug up to make room for fresh corpses; in this case, it proved successful.

The second relatively long occasional poem, "The Phoenix and Turtle," is another matter. The one work in this section whose literary quality has been widely admired, it was one of several poems—others were by George Chapman, Ben Jonson, and John Marston—appended to Robert Chester's *Loves Martyr* (1601). An abstruse philosophical composition, "The Phoenix and Turtle" may represent Shakespeare's effort to refashion himself as a different kind of poet from the one who appeared two years earlier in unauthorized form in *The Passionate Pilgrim*. Literary innovation here may also have an element of poetic competition with his three fellow contributors to Chester's volume, all of whom were also dramatists. With two of them, Johnson and Marston, Shakespeare was then probably engaged in the satirical Poets' War, a battle of rival playwrights.

"The Phoenix and Turtle" is divided into three sections and composed in trochaic tetrameter, an atypical meter for Shakespeare. In the first five quatrains, which may be indebted to Chaucer's *Parliament of Fowls*, a language of elaborate circumlocution merely calls the birds together to mourn the deaths of two remarkably constant lovers—the proverbially faithful turtledove (here, male) and the legendary phoenix (here, female). Supposedly, only one phoenix was alive at any given moment, and the bird died only to be reborn from its own ashes. Neither of the two birds is named yet, however. The anthem, which constitutes the next eight stanzas, is presumably intoned by the birds. In a reversal of the procedure of the opening twenty lines, this epithalamion, or marriage hymn, turns to a deceptively simple vocabulary that conceals dense argumentation. Behind the emphasis on the paradoxical unity of two separate beings lies the mystery of the Christian Trinity as understood in Scholastic theology—medieval Europe's assimilation of the recently translated writings of Aristotle, which began in the twelfth century. The ideal love of the two birds ultimately defies the efforts at comprehension by Reason, which cannot understand how

> . . . love in twain
> Had the essence but in one,
> Two distincts, division none,

or how

> . . . the self was not the same.
> Single nature's double name
> Neither two nor one was called.
> (lines 25–27, 38–40)

In other words, the rationalist vocabulary of this section ultimately undermines its own legitimacy. Perhaps the lines vindicate the more mystical understanding of ideal love that Renaissance thought derived from Plato, whose doctrines Aristotle had sought to answer. In any case, the heterosexual love praised in this self-contradictory fashion parallels the celebration of homoerotic love in the sonnets to the young man: "Let me confess that we two must be twain / Although our undivided loves are one" (36.1–2). Following the anthem, Reason delivers the concluding section of the poem, the *threnos,* or mourning song, in which Shakespeare returns to the central genre of his occasional poetry—the elegy. Retaining the straightforwardly abstract diction of the anthem and the trochaic-tetrameter meter of both of the first two parts but abandoning quatrains (rhyming *abba*) for tercets (rhyming *aaa*), the last five stanzas emphasize the finality of the death of the couple, which apparently excludes both rebirth (even on the part of the immortal phoenix) and "posterity"—the latter as a result of a "married chastity" (lines 59, 61) that has the same (lack of) consequences as the love for the young man in the sonnets. The result is the diminution of life: the only authentic or perhaps ideal "truth and beauty buried be" (line 64).

"The Phoenix and Turtle" raises all sorts of interpretive problems. Since the *threnos* is spoken by Reason, who has been defeated by the phoenix and turtle, should the concluding stanzas be seen not as authorial statement but as the position of a fallible character who lets fly a crow of triumph at the couple's death? Moreover, the concluding summons of all "that are either true or fair" (line 66) sits oddly with the immediately preceding insistence that genuine truth and beauty no longer exist: perhaps now they exist only separately. And why does Shakespeare, through Reason, insist on the lack of offspring and, apparently rejecting a central feature of the legend, on the mortality of the phoenix? This last question is only emphasized by the occasion of publication. All of the poems with which "The Phoenix and Turtle" were printed are on the subject of the phoenix and turtle, and all but Shakespeare's deny the finality of the phoenix's death. "The Phoenix and Turtle" alone forgoes the possibility of exploiting the standard treatment of the phoenix as the intersection of the temporal and the timeless.

The title page of the volume advertises Chester's long poem as "allegorically shadowing the truth of Love, in the constant Fate of the Phoenix and Turtle." This claim, the abstract language of "The Phoenix and Turtle," and the avowed purpose of the volume—to honor Sir John Salusbury of Lleweni, knighted by the Queen in June 1601—have all encouraged a search in Shakespeare's poem for allegorical meaning (beyond the praise of ideal human union through a tale of two birds). The marriage of phoenix and turtle has been seen as the joining of the literal and the metaphorical in poetry, so that the poem self-referentially becomes a metaphor for metaphor itself. Historical readings have found candidates for the parts of the turtle and the phoenix in Salusbury and his wife, as well as in the Earl of Essex, Salusbury, or the English people in relation to Queen Elizabeth. Although none of these theories is convincing, in part because of a failure to explain what real "tragic scene" is being allegorically represented by the couple's deaths (line 52), all testify to the poem's ability to hint at hidden meanings. Perhaps it is safer to explain the poem's suggestiveness simply by saying that "The Phoenix and Turtle" labors to construct an ideal image of love while simultaneously circumscribing the real utility of that ideal. Marriage and funeral, celebration and dirge, ideal affirmation and pragmatic denial, the poem is a characteristically Shakespearean venture in having it both ways.

WALTER COHEN

## TEXTUAL NOTE

"A Song" survives in two related manuscript collections of poetry by different authors, dating from 1637 and 1639. It is untitled in both manuscripts, unattributed in the later collection, and ascribed to Shakespeare in the earlier one. The text printed here is based on the earlier version, although the choice between the two is not very important. Both manuscripts of "A Song" derive from a scribal transcript of the writer's original version, but it is impossible to determine how many intermediate copies there may have been. The poem was first assigned in print to Shakespeare in 1985, a claim that has aroused considerable skepticism. The name in the 1637 manuscript and the independent analysis of the poem's language carried out by statisticians make attribution to Shakespeare possible (c. 1592–95) though unlikely. It probably dates from 1613–30.

"Upon a pair of gloves" is found in a manuscript compiled around 1629 by Sir Francis Fane of Bulbeck (1611–80). The poem supposedly accompanied gloves presented by Alexander Aspinall, a Stratford schoolmaster, to his second wife, whom he married in 1594. The poem's second line, "The will is all," could refer to Shakespeare or to William Shaw, a glover who was the son of Aspinall's second wife. Hence, the attribution to Shakespeare is conjectural.

The eleven poems from *The Passionate Pilgrim* (1599) printed here are of uncertain authorship, although probably not by Shakespeare. This collection of twenty lyrics published under Shakespeare's name includes five pieces that are clearly his. Three come from *Love's Labour's Lost;* the other two are sonnets 138 and 144, and are included in this edition as Alternative Versions at the end of the section on the sonnets and "A Lover's Complaint." Four poems are apparently by other writers—Richard Barnfield, Bartholomew Griffin, and Christopher Marlowe. "The Phoenix and Turtle" was printed in 1601, untitled and ascribed to Shakespeare, among the "Poeticall Essaies" that follow Robert Chester's *Loves Martyr: or Rosalins Complaint.* The ascription is widely accepted.

The remaining poems are about specific people, and in each instance, as in "Upon a pair of gloves," there is a plausible London or Stratford connection between Shakespeare and the person(s) in question. The "Verses upon the Stanley Tomb at Tong," perhaps by Shakespeare (c. 1600–03) even though there are possible chronological difficulties, are first attributed to him in a manuscript from around 1630. It is not clear whether the lines constitute one poem or two, whether they are addressed to one member of the Stanley family or two, and which member or members are referred to. If they are intended as a single poem, it is not certain which group of six lines should come first. "On Ben Jonson" is first attributed to Shakespeare, improbably, in a manuscript from roughly 1650. "An Epitaph on Elias James," published in the 1633 edition of John Stow's *Survey of London,* is more likely to be Shakespeare's. James died in 1610. "An extemporary epitaph on John Combe," who died in 1614, employs a joke about usurers that became popular starting in 1608. The earliest manuscripts do not assign the poem to Shakespeare. There is an ambiguous attribution to Shakespeare in 1634 and an unambiguous ascription of the last one and a half lines in a manuscript from around 1650. On balance, Shakespeare probably did not write the poem. "Another Epitaph on John Combe" is first attributed to Shakespeare in the same manuscript (c. 1650); the case for Shakespearean authorship of this poem is stronger, however. "Upon the King" was printed, unattributed, beneath an engraving of King James that was the frontispiece to the 1616 edition of the King's *Works.* The earliest ascription is found in a manuscript of about 1633–34, where the poem is entitled "Shakespeare on the King." Again, late attribution following earlier lack of attribution casts doubt on Shakespearean authorship. "Epitaph on Himself" appears on Shakespeare's gravestone in Stratford. The earliest other attribution occurs in a manuscript compiled by Sir Francis Fane, about 1655–56. The lines may be Shakespearean.

## SELECTED BIBLIOGRAPHY

Adams, Joseph Quincy. "Shakespeare as a Writer of Epitaphs." *The Manly Anniversary Studies in Language and Literature*. 1923; repr.: Freeport, N.Y.: Books for Libraries Press, 1968. 78–89. Defends Shakespeare's authorship.

Bednarz, James P. "*The Passionate Pilgrim* and 'The Phoenix and Turtle.'" *The Cambridge Companion to Shakespeare's Poetry*. Ed. Patrick Cheney. New York: Cambridge University Press, 2007. 108–24. Locates these works in the context of late Elizabethan poetic publication and literary and theatrical competition.

Cunningham, V. J. "'Essence' and 'The Phoenix and Turtle.'" *English Literary History* 19 (1952): 265–76. Discusses the theological language of the poem.

Hobday, C. H. "Shakespeare's Venus and Adonis Sonnets." *Shakespeare Survey* 26 (1973): 103–09. Discussion of the poems on this topic in *The Passionate Pilgrim*.

Honigmann, E. A. J. *Shakespeare: The Lost Years*. Totowa, N.J.: Barnes & Noble, 1985. 77–83, 90–113. "The Phoenix and Turtle" as a celebration of Salusbury's marriage in 1586; briefer comments on Shakespeare's elegies.

Hyland, Peter. *An Introduction to Shakespeare's Poems*. Houndmills, Basingstoke: Palgrave Macmillan, 2002. 194–213. Survey of Shakespeare's occasional poetry, with special attention paid to "The Phoenix and Turtle."

Hume, Anthea. "*Love's Martyr*, 'The Phoenix and Turtle,' and the Aftermath of the Essex Rebellion." *Review of English Studies* n.s., 40 (1989): 48–71. Reads the poem as an allegory of Essex's relationship to Elizabeth.

Kay, Dennis. *William Shakespeare: Sonnets and Poems*. New York: Twayne, 1998. 77–95. Surveys the occasional poems.

Roberts, Sasha. *Reading Shakespeare's Poems in Early Modern England*. Houndmills, Basingstoke: Palgrave Macmillan, 2003. 154–58, 177–90. *The Passionate Pilgrim*, both in print form and in manuscript transcription of individual poems, seen as suppressing the homoeroticism of Shakespeare's sonnets, contributing to misogynistic literature, and celebrating erotic poetic art. Emphasis on the various interpretive contexts generated by different collections.

Underwood, Richard Allan. *Shakespeare's "The Phoenix and Turtle": A Survey of Scholarship*. Salzburg Studies in English Literature 15. Salzburg: Institut für Englische Sprache und Literatur, Universität Salzburg, 1974. Overview of previous criticism of the poem.

# Various Poems

## A Song[1]

### 1

Shall I die? Shall I fly
Lovers' baits and deceits,
   sorrow breeding?
Shall I tend?° Shall I send?                   *wait passively*
5    Shall I sue, and not rue
   my proceeding?[2]
In all duty her beauty
Binds me her servant for ever.
   If she scorn, I mourn,
10   I retire to despair, joining° never.      *(sexually; militarily)*

### 2

Yet I must vent my lust
And explain inward pain
   by my love conceiving.[3]
If she smiles, she exiles
15    All my moan; if she frown,
   all my hopes deceiving—
Suspicious doubt,° O keep out,           *fear (of rejection)*
For thou art my tormentor.
   Fie away, pack away;
20   I will love, for hope bids me venture.

### 3

'Twere abuse to accuse
My fair love, ere I prove°                      *test*
   her affection.
Therefore try! Her reply
25    Gives thee joy—or annoy,
   or affliction.[4]
Yet howe'er, I will bear
Her pleasure with patience, for beauty
   Sure will not seem to blot
30   Her deserts, wronging him doth her duty.[5]

### 4

In a dream it did seem—
But alas, dreams do pass
   as do shadows—
I did walk, I did talk
35    With my love, with my dove,

---

1. This poem may or may not have been set to music.
2. Both "sue" (line 5) and "proceeding" refer to lawsuits.
3. Yet I must give expression to my lust by explaining (in poetry) the pain caused by my love. "Conceiving" may also refer to conceiving a child (line 13).
4. "Affliction" may also suggest a sexually transmitted disease.
5. *for beauty . . . duty:* for true beauty will not allow her reputation to appear tarnished by wronging him who serves her faithfully.

through fair meadows.
Still° we passed till at last                                    *Continually*
We sat to repose us for pleasure.
Being set, lips met,
40    Arms twined, and did bind my heart's treasure.

**5**

Gentle wind sport did find
Wantonly° to make fly                                            *Capriciously*
    her gold tresses.
As they shook I did look,
45    But her fair° did impair                                   *beauty*
    all my senses.
As amazed, I gazed
On more than a mortal complexion.
You that love can prove[6]
50    Such force in beauty's inflection.°                        *bending*

**6**

Next° her hair, forehead fair,                                   *Next to*
Smooth and high; neat doth lie
    without wrinkle,
Her fair brows;° under those,                                    *forehead*
55    Star-like eyes win love's prize
    when they twinkle.
In her cheeks who° seeks                                         *whoever*
Shall find there displayed beauty's banner;°                     *(a blush)*
O admiring desiring
60    Breeds, as I look still upon her.

**7**

Thin lips red, fancy's[7] fed
With all sweets when he meets,
    and is granted
There to trade,[8] and is made
65    Happy, sure, to endure
    still undaunted.
Pretty chin doth win
Of all their culled commendations;[9]
Fairest neck, no speck;
70    All her parts merit high admirations.

**8**

Pretty bare, past compare,
Parts those plots which besots
    still asunder.[1]
It is meet naught but sweet
75    Should come near that so rare
    'tis a wonder.[2]
No mis-shape, no scape°                                          *transgression*

---

6. You who are in love are able to test.
7. Affection is; imagination is.
8. *granted / There to trade:* allowed to kiss there.
9. Wins from all people their specially chosen praises.
1. *Pretty . . . asunder:* Incomparably pretty "bare" skin

and breasts (exposed above a low neckline) separate the
nipples ("plots") that, always separated, (always) cause
infatuation.
2. It is proper that nothing but good should come near
that which is so wonderfully valuable.

Inferior to nature's perfection;
No blot, no spot:
80    She's beauty's queen in election.

### 9

Whilst I dreamt, I exempt
From all care, seemed to share
   pleasure's plenty;
But awake, care take—
85    For I find to my mind
   pleasures scanty.
Therefore I will try
To compass° my heart's chief contenting.          *accomplish*
To delay, some say,
90    In such a case causeth repenting.

## 'Upon a pair of gloves that master sent to his mistress'

The gift is small,
The will is all:[3]
Alexander Aspinall[4]

## Poems from *The Passionate Pilgrim*

### 4

Sweet Cytherea,[5] sitting by a brook
With young Adonis, lovely, fresh, and green,°    *young; inexperienced*
Did court the lad with many a lovely° look,    *amorous*
Such looks as none could look but beauty's queen.
5   She told him stories to delight his ear,
She showed him favours to allure his eye;
To win his heart she touched him here and there—
Touches so soft still° conquer chastity.    *always*
But whether unripe years did want conceit,°    *lack understanding*
10  Or he refused to take her figured° proffer,    *implied*
The tender nibbler would not touch the bait,
But smile and jest at every gentle offer.
   Then fell she on her back, fair queen and toward:°    *ready*
   He rose and ran away—ah, fool too froward!°    *obstinate*

### 6

Scarce had the sun dried up the dewy morn,
And scarce the herd gone to the hedge for shade,
When Cytherea, all in love forlorn,
A longing tarriance° for Adonis made    *waiting*
5   Under an osier° growing by a brook,    *a willow*
A brook where Adon used to cool his spleen.°    *hot temper*
Hot was the day, she hotter, that did look
For his approach that often there had been.
Anon he comes and throws his mantle by,

---

3. With a characteristic pun on the poet's name: the goodwill behind the gift is all-encompassing; it's the thought that counts.
4. Stratford schoolmaster from 1582 to 1624.

5. Sonnets 4, 6, and 9 all treat the unsuccessful wooing of the beautiful but unresponsive young man Adonis by Venus ("Cytherea"), the goddess of love.

10 And stood stark naked on the brook's green brim.
The sun looked on the world with glorious eye,
Yet not so wistly° as this queen on him.                    *eagerly; longingly*
    He, spying her, bounced in whereas he stood.[6]
    'O Jove,' quoth she, 'why was not I a flood?'°         *body of water*

### 7

Fair is my love, but not so fair as fickle,
Mild as a dove, but neither true nor trusty,°              *trustworthy*
Brighter than glass, and yet, as glass is, brittle;
Softer than wax, and yet as iron rusty;°                  *corrupt (morally)*
5   A lily pale, with damask° dye to grace her,          *red*
    None fairer, nor none falser to deface her.[7]

Her lips to mine how often hath she joined,
Between each kiss her oaths of true love swearing.
How many tales to please me hath she coined,°            *invented*
10 Dreading my love, the loss whereof still fearing.[8]
    Yet in the midst of all her pure protestings
    Her faith, her oaths, her tears, and all were jestings.

She burnt with love as straw with fire flameth,
She burnt out love as soon as straw out burneth,
15 She framed° the love, and yet she foiled° the framing,   *built / ruined*
She bade love last, and yet she fell a-turning.°          *(to another lover)*
    Was this a lover or a lecher whether,°               *which of the two*
    Bad in the best, though excellent in neither?[9]

### 9

Fair was the morn when the fair queen of love,°           *Venus*
[                      ]¹
Paler for sorrow than her milk-white dove,
For Adon's sake, a youngster proud and wild,
5 Her stand she takes upon a steep-up hill.
Anon° Adonis comes with horn and hounds.                  *Soon*
She, seely° queen, with more than love's good will        *foolish*
Forbade the boy he should not pass those grounds.°        *cross those valleys*
'Once,' quoth she, 'did I see a fair sweet youth
10 Here in these brakes° deep-wounded with° a boar,        *thickets / by*
Deep in the thigh, a spectacle of ruth.°                  *pity*
See in my thigh,' quoth she, 'here was the sore.'
    She showèd hers; he saw more wounds than one,°       *(sexual)*
    And blushing fled, and left her all alone.

### 10

Sweet rose, fair flower, untimely plucked, soon faded—
Plucked in the bud and faded in the spring;
Bright orient pearl, alack, too timely shaded;[2]
Fair creature, killed too soon by death's sharp sting,

---

6. Jumped in from where he stood.
7. Nor is anyone more false, to her discredit; with a possible reference to cosmetics in "falser" and "deface."
8. Continually being anxious about losing my love.
9. Bad in romance, but not outstanding merely as a sex-

ual partner either.
1. A line is missing here in the original edition.
2. Darkened too soon. "Orient" pearls were valued as more lustrous than their European counterparts.

5  Like a green plum that hangs upon a tree
   And falls through wind before the fall should be.

   I weep for thee, and yet no cause I have,
   For why:° thou left'st me nothing in thy will,                          *Because*
   And yet thou left'st me more than I did crave,
10 For why: I cravèd nothing of thee still.[3]
        O yes, dear friend, I pardon crave of thee:[4]
        Thy discontent° thou didst bequeath to me.                        *unhappiness*

## 12

   Crabbèd° age and youth cannot live together:                          *Ill-tempered*
   Youth is full of pleasance, age is full of care;
   Youth like summer morn, age like winter weather;
   Youth like summer brave,° age like winter bare.                        *well dressed*
5  Youth is full of sport, age's breath is short.
   Youth is nimble, age is lame,
   Youth is hot and bold, age is weak and cold.
   Youth is wild and age is tame.
        Age, I do abhor thee; youth, I do adore thee.
10      O my love, my love is young.
        Age, I do defy thee. O sweet shepherd, hie thee,°                 *hurry up*
        For methinks thou stay'st° too long.                             *delay*

## 13

   Beauty is but a vain and doubtful good,
   A shining gloss that fadeth suddenly,
   A flower that dies when first it 'gins to bud,
   A brittle glass that's broken presently.°                             *immediately*
5      A doubtful good, a gloss, a glass, a flower,
        Lost, faded, broken, dead within an hour.
   And as goods lost are seld° or never found,                           *seldom*
   As faded gloss no rubbing will refresh,
   As flowers dead lie withered on the ground,
10 As broken glass no cement can redress,°                               *repair*
        So beauty blemished once, for ever lost,
        In spite of physic,° painting, pain,° and cost.                  *medicine / labor*

## 14

   Good night, good rest—ah, neither be my share.
   She bade good night that kept my rest away,
   And daffed° me to a cabin hanged° with care                           *dismissed / adorned*
   To descant on the doubts° of my decay.                                *expand upon the fears*
5  'Farewell,' quoth she, 'and come again tomorrow.'
   Fare well I could not, for I supped with sorrow.

   Yet at my parting sweetly did she smile,
   In scorn or friendship nill I conster whether.[5]
   'Tmay be she joyed to jest at my exile

3. "Nothing" (lines 8, 10) evokes the tangibility of
absence caused by death. But "nothing" also may denote
female sexual organs. In line 8, it would go with "will"
(testament; lust) to suggest that the dead woman's desire
(formerly) made her sexually available to the speaker. In
line 10, the speaker would be saying that he always

("still") desired her.
4. This line seems to contradict the previous one by
claiming that the speaker did, after all, "crave" something—"pardon."
5. I will not guess which of the two.

10 'Tmay be, again to make me wander thither.
    'Wander'—a word for shadows like myself,
    As take the pain but cannot pluck the pelf.°             *reward*

Lord, how mine eyes throw gazes to the east!
My heart doth charge the watch, the morning rise[6]
15 Doth cite° each moving° sense from idle rest,         *summon / living*
Not daring trust the office of mine eyes.
    While Philomela° sings I sit and mark,°    *the nightingale / listen*
    And wish her lays were tunèd like the lark.[7]

For she doth welcome daylight with her dite,°         *song*
20 And daylight drives away dark dreaming night.
The night so packed,° I post° unto my pretty;    *sent off / hasten*
Heart hath his hope, and eyes their wishèd sight,
    Sorrow changed to solace, and solace mixed with sorrow,
    Forwhy° she sighed and bade me come tomorrow.    *Because*

25 Were I with her, the night would post too soon,
But now are minutes added to the hours.
To spite me now each minute seems a moon,
Yet not for me, shine sun[8] to succour flowers!
    Pack night, peep day, good day, of night now borrow;
30     Short night tonight, and length thyself tomorrow.[9]

## Sonnets
## to Sundry Notes of Music

### 15

It was a lording's° daughter, the fairest one of three,    *lord's*
That likèd of her master° as well as well might be,    *tutor*
Till looking on an Englishman, the fairest that eye could see,
    Her fancy fell a-turning.°    *(to another lover)*

5 Long was the combat doubtful° that love with love did fight:    *uncertain*
To leave the master loveless, or kill the gallant knight.
To put in practice either, alas, it was a spite°    *would be a vexation*
    Unto the seely° damsel.    *helpless*
But one must be refusèd, more mickle° was the pain    *great*
10 That nothing could be usèd° to turn them both to gain.    *done*
For of the two the trusty knight was wounded with disdain—
    Alas, she could not help it.

Thus art° with arms contending was victor of the day,    *learning*
Which by a gift of learning did bear the maid away.
15 Then lullaby, the learned man hath got the lady gay;
    For now my song is ended.

---

6. My heart blames those on watch, the break of day. Or, perhaps: My heart orders the "eyes" (line 13) to watch for morning; my heart urges the night watch to hurry or proclaim morning.
7. And wish her (nighttime) songs were the songs of the (morning) lark.
8. Let the sun shine, not for my sake, but.
9. The speaker is asking night to shorten now and to lengthen tomorrow, when he's with his mistress.

## 17

My flocks feed not, my ewes breed not,
   My rams speed° not, all is amiss.             *thrive*
Love is dying, faith's defying,[1]
   Heart's denying causer of this.
5    All my merry jigs are quite forgot,
All my lady's love is lost, God wot.°          *knows*
Where her faith was firmly fixed in love,
There a nay is placed without remove.°      *immovably*
   One seely cross° wrought all my loss—    *foolish mishap*
10    O frowning fortune, cursèd fickle dame!
   For now I see inconstancy
   More in women than in men remain.

   In black mourn I, all fears scorn I,
   Love hath forlorn me, living in thrall.°   *enslaved (to love)*
15   Heart is bleeding, all help needing—
   O cruel speeding,° freighted with gall.     *fortune*
My shepherd's pipe can sound no deal,°    *not at all*
My wether's[2] bell rings doleful knell,
My curtal dog[3] that wont to° have played   *formerly liked to*
20   Plays not at all, but seems afraid,
   With sighs so deep procures to weep
   In howling wise° to see my doleful plight.     *fashion*
   How sighs resound through heartless ground,
   Like a thousand vanquished men in bloody fight!

25   Clear wells spring not, sweet birds sing not,
   Green plants bring not forth their dye.
Herd stands weeping, flocks all sleeping,
   Nymphs back peeping fearfully.
All our pleasure known to us poor swains,
30   All our merry meetings on the plains,
All our evening sport from us is fled,
All our love is lost, for love is dead.
   Farewell, sweet lass, thy like ne'er was
   For as sweet content, the cause of all my moan.
35   Poor Corydon[4] must live alone,
   Other help for him I see that there is none.

## 18

Whenas° thine eye hath chose the dame      *When*
And stalled° the deer that thou shouldst strike,  *entrapped*
Let reason rule things worthy blame
As well as fancy, partial might.[5]
5    Take counsel of some wiser head,
   Neither too young nor yet unwed,
And when thou com'st thy tale to tell,
Smooth not thy tongue with filèd° talk   *rehearsed; scheming*

---

1. Faith's rejection; "de-fying" means de-faithing.
2. A male sheep castrated while still immature. The "bell-wether" is the lead sheep of the flock.
3. Dog with a cut tail.
4. Conventional name for a shepherd (from one of

Virgil's *Eclogues,* which were pastoral poems).
5. Let reason as well as desire (fancy), which is biased and by itself inadequate, govern your potentially blameworthy love affairs.

Lest she some subtle practice° smell:            *deception*
10   A cripple soon can find a halt.[6]
     But plainly say thou lov'st her well,
     And set her person forth to sale,[7]

And to her will° frame all thy ways.°       *desire / habits*
   Spare not to spend, and chiefly there
15   Where thy desert may merit praise
   By ringing in thy lady's ear.[8]
     The strongest castle, tower, and town,
     The golden bullet° beats it down.      *words; money*

Serve always with assurèd trust,°        *reliability*
20   And in thy suit be humble-true;
   Unless thy lady prove unjust,°         *unfaithful*
   Press never thou to choose anew.[9]
     When time° shall serve, be thou not slack    *occasion*
     To proffer, though she put thee back.[1]

25   What though° her frowning brows be bent,    *Although*
   Her cloudy looks will calm ere night,
   And then too late she will repent
   That thus dissembled her delight,[2]
     And twice desire,° ere it be day,    *(sexual gratification)*
30     That which with scorn she put away.°    *rejected*

What though she strive to try her strength,
   And ban,° and brawl,° and say thee nay,    *curse / shout*
   Her feeble force will yield at length
   When craft° hath taught her thus to say:    *craftiness*
35     'Had women been so strong as men,
     In faith you had not had it then.'

The wiles and guiles that women work,°      *employ*
   Dissembled with an outward show,
   The tricks and toys° that in them lurk      *whims*
40   The cock that treads them[3] shall not know.
     Have you not heard it said full oft
     A woman's nay doth stand for nought?[4]

Think women still to strive with men,
   To sin and never for to saint.[5]
45   There is no heaven; be holy then
   When time with age shall them attaint.[6]
     Were kisses all the joys in bed,
     One woman would another wed.

---

6. Those practiced in deceit can easily sense deception. *find a halt*: detect a limp.

7. Like a salesman, start praising her qualities. One of the manuscript versions of this poem has "& set thy body forth to sell."

8. Don't be stingy about spending your money in ways that will draw your lady's attention to your merit.

9. Don't make attempts to choose someone else (?)

1. Even if she resists you. The "proffer," at first an offer, becomes outright rape here and in the following stanzas.

2. She who in this way concealed her desire.

3. The man who copulates with them.

4. Nothing; (sexual) naughtiness; a vulva.

5. Expect women always to engage (compete) with men in sin but not in saintliness, or chastity.

6. There is no thought of heaven (purity) in women seeking sexual pleasure. Let them be holy when they're old and unattractive.

But soft, enough—too much, I fear,
50  Lest that my mistress hear my song
She will not stick to round me on th'ear[7]
To teach my tongue to be so long.
    Yet will she blush (here be it said)
    To hear her secrets so bewrayed.°                    revealed

## The Phoenix and Turtle[8]

Let the bird of loudest lay[9]
On the sole Arabian tree[1]
Herald sad and trumpet be,
To whose sound chaste wings° obey.                       virtuous birds

5   But thou shrieking harbinger,°                        the screech owl
Foul precurrer of the fiend,[2]
Augur of the fever's end°—                              Prophet of death or cure
To this troupe[3] come thou not near.

From this session° interdict°                            (of a court) / forbid
10  Every fowl of tyrant wing°                            bird of prey
Save the eagle, feathered king.
Keep the obsequy° so strict.                            funeral rite

Let the priest in surplice white[4]
That defunctive music can,[5]
15  Be the death-divining swan,
Lest the requiem lack his right.°                       its due; its rite

And thou treble-dated° crow,                            long-lived
That thy sable gender mak'st
With the breath thou giv'st and tak'st,[6]
20  'Mongst our mourners shalt thou go.

Here the anthem doth commence:
Love and constancy is dead,
Phoenix and the turtle fled
In a mutual flame from hence.

25  So they loved as° love in twain                      that
Had the essence but in one,
Two distincts, division none.
Number there in love was slain.[7]

7. She won't refrain from scolding me (boxing me) on the ear.
8. *Phoenix*: a legendary, self-resurrecting bird believed to live in cycles of several centuries, dying in flames and reborn from its own ashes—here, regarded as female. *Turtle*: turtledove, symbol of constancy—here, regarded as male.
9. Song. It is unclear which bird this refers to—possibly the phoenix, unless one reads "Death is now the phoenix' nest" (line 56) not as part of a cycle but as a final resting place. Alternately, it is some other bird (the rooster?) known for its loud voice.
1. Supposedly, a unique tree on which sits the phoenix, which is similarly unique: only one exists at any given time.
2. Precursor of the devil: screech owls were thought to foretell death.
3. The troupe of mourning birds called forth by "the bird of loudest lay" (line 1).
4. The swan. A "surplice" is a loose clerical outer garment.
5. That is skilled in funereal music. Swans were thought to sing beautifully just before (their own) death (hence the phrase "swan song").
6. *That . . . tak'st*: crows were believed to conceive by billing (kissing)—hence, "With the breath." *sable gender*: black offspring.
7. The stanza toys with the commonplace paradox of lovers' simultaneous unity and separateness, ending with the hyperbolic claim that being neither one nor two, the love of the phoenix and the turtle killed the very notion of "number" (line 28).

Hearts remote° yet not asunder,      *separate*
30  Distance and no space was seen
'Twixt this turtle and his queen.
But in them it were a wonder.[8]

So° between them love did shine      *So much*
That the turtle saw his right°      *due; possession; nature*
35  Flaming in the Phoenix' sight.°      *eyesight; appearance*
Either was the other's mine.°      *self; wealth*

Property was thus appalled
That the self was not the same.[9]
Single nature's double name[1]
40  Neither two nor one was called.

Reason, in itself confounded,°      *thoroughly destroyed*
Saw division° grow together      *things divided*
To themselves, yet either neither,[2]
Simple were so well compounded[3]

45  That it cried 'How true° a twain      *faithful; truly*
Seemeth this concordant one!
Love hath reason, reason none,
If what parts can so remain.'[4]

Whereupon it made this threne[5]
50  To the phoenix and the dove,
Co-supremes° and stars of love,      *Joint rulers*
As chorus to their tragic scene.

*Threnos*

Beauty, truth,° and rarity,      *fidelity*
Grace in all simplicity,
55  Here enclosed in cinders lie.

Death is now the phoenix' nest,[6]
And the turtle's loyal breast
To eternity doth rest.[7]

Leaving no posterity
60  'Twas not their infirmity,°      *sterility*
It was married chastity.

Truth may seem but cannot be,
Beauty brag, but 'tis not she.[8]
Truth and beauty buried be.

8. It would have seemed extraordinary in any creatures but them.
9. The notion of an essential self was thus weakened by the fact that the self was not identical to itself.
1. An indivisible essence with two separate names.
2. Saw separate entities paradoxically become one, but each one was neither single nor united.
3. Single elements were so perfectly combined (appearing to remain "simple" rather than "compounded").
4. Love represents a higher reason than reason itself because of this embodiment of the paradox of unity of separate elements.
5. Reason made this threnody (a mourning song or epitaph).
6. The phoenix's nest, ordinarily a site of regeneration, is finally a place of death; alternatively, the regenerative qualities of the phoenix's nest will overcome death.
7. Rests eternally; endures forever.
8. Any appearances of fidelity or beauty will only be illusions.

65　To this urn let those repair°　　　　　　　　　　　　　　　*go*
　　That are either true or fair.
　　For these dead birds sigh a prayer.

## Verses upon the Stanley Tomb[9] at Tong

### Written upon the east end of the tomb

　　Ask who lies here, but do not weep.
　　He is not dead; he doth but sleep.
　　This stony register° is for his bones;　　　　　　　　　　*record*
　　His fame is more perpetual than these stones,
5　And his own goodness, with himself being gone,
　　Shall live when earthly monument is none.

### Written upon the west end thereof

　　Not monumental stone preserves our fame,
　　Nor sky-aspiring pyramids[1] our name.
　　The memory of him for whom this stands
　　Shall outlive marble and defacers' hands.
5　When all to time's consumption shall be given,
　　Stanley for whom this stands shall stand in heaven.

## On Ben Jonson[2]

Master Ben Jonson and master William Shakespeare being merry
at a tavern, Master Jonson having begun this for his epitaph:

　　Here lies Ben Jonson
　　That was once one,°　　　　　　　　　　　　　　　　　*alive*

he gives it to Master Shakespeare to make up who presently
writes:

　　Who while he lived was a slow thing,[3]
　　And now, being dead, is nothing.

## An Epitaph on Elias James[4]

　　When God was pleased, the world unwilling yet,[5]
　　Elias James to nature paid his debt,
　　And here reposeth. As he lived, he died,
　　The saying strongly in him verified:
5　'Such life, such death'.° Then, a known truth to tell,　　*One dies as one lives*
　　He lived a godly life, and died as well.

---

9. Shakespeare had various connections to the Stanley family. It is unclear whether these verses, still visible on the tombstone, memorialize Sir Edward Stanley, Sir Thomas Stanley, or both (with one verse devoted to each).
1. Grand buildings constructed by more modern means. Possibly referring to structures erected in Rome in 1586 or in London in 1603 (for James's coronation), but retaining from their association with Egypt a sense of almost timeless antiquity.
2. One of the best-known of Shakespeare's fellow playwrights (1572–1637).
3. Jonson was a notoriously slow writer.
4. A London brewer of Shakespeare's acquaintance who gave 10 pounds to the parish poor when he died. His tomb was destroyed in the Great Fire of London (1666).
5. Though the world was still unwilling.

### An extemporary epitaph on John Combe,[6] a noted usurer

Ten in the hundred[7] here lies engraved;
A hundred to ten° his soul is not saved.                    (*odds*)
If anyone ask who lies in this tomb,
'O ho!' quoth the devil, ''tis my John-a-Combe.'

### Another Epitaph on John Combe

He being dead, and making the poor his heirs,[8] William
Shakespeare after writes this for his epitaph:

Howe'er he livèd judge not,
John Combe shall never be forgot
While poor hath memory, for he did gather[9]
To make the poor his issue;° he, their father,          *offspring; heirs*
As record of his tilth and seed[1]
Did crown him° in his latter deed.                            *himself*

### Upon the King
At the foot of the effigy of King James I, before his *Works*
(1616)[2]

Crowns have their compass;° length of days, their date;°   *boundaries / limit*
Triumphs, their tombs; felicity, her fate.
Of more than earth can earth make none partaker,[3]
But knowledge makes the king most like his maker.

### Epitaph on Himself[4]

Good friend, for Jesus' sake forbear
To dig the dust enclosèd here.
Blessed be the man that spares these stones,
And cursed be he that moves my bones.

---

6. Combe, a wealthy Stratford bachelor, left Shakespeare
5 pounds—a fairly generous sum—in his will.
7. A slang term for "usurer," suggesting one who lends
money at 10-percent interest.
8. Combe left generous bequests to the poor of Stratford
in his will, including a provision that 100 pounds continue to be lent out, with the interest given as alms.

9. Accumulate wealth (through usury).
1. Tillage and planting (offspring).
2. These lines appear below a picture of James that was
the frontispiece to the 1616 edition of his works.
3. No earthly power (not even a King) has power over the
afterlife.
4. Carved above Shakespeare's grave in Stratford.

# APPENDICES

APPENDICES

# Early Modern Map Culture

In the early modern period, maps were often considered rare and precious objects, and seeing a map could be an important and life-changing event. This was so for Richard Hakluyt, whose book *The Principal Navigations, Voiages, Traffiques and Discoveries of the English Nation* (1598–1600) was the first major collection of narratives describing England's overseas trading ventures. Hakluyt tells how, as a boy still at school in London, he visited his uncle's law chambers and saw a book of cosmography lying open there. Perceiving his nephew's interest in the maps it contained, the uncle turned to a modern map and "pointed with his wand to all the knowen Seas, Gulfs, Bayes, Straights, Capes, Rivers, Empires, Kingdomes, Dukedomes, and Territories of ech part, with declaration also of their speciall commodities and particular wants, which by the benefit of traffike, and entercourse of merchants, are plentifully supplied. From the Mappe he brought me to the Bible, and turning to the 107 Psalme, directed mee to the 23 and 24 verses, where I read, that they which go downe to the sea in ships, and occupy [work] by the great waters, they see the works of the Lord, and his woonders in the deepe." This event, Hakluyt records, made so deep an impression upon him, that he vowed he would devote his life to the study of this kind of knowledge. *The Principal Navigations* was the result, a book that mixes a concern with the profit to be made from trade and from geographical knowledge with praise for the Christian god who made the "great waters" and, in Hakluyt's view, looked with special favor on the English merchants and sailors who voyaged over them.

In the early modern period, access to maps was far less easy than it is today. Before the advent of printing in the late fifteenth century, maps were drawn and decorated by hand. Because they were rare and expensive, these medieval maps were for the most part owned by the wealthy and the powerful. Sometimes adorned with pictures of fabulous sea monsters and exotic creatures, maps often revealed the Christian worldview of those who composed them. Jerusalem appeared squarely in the middle of many maps (called T and O maps), with Asia, Africa, and Europe, representing the rest of the known world, arranged symmetrically around the Holy City. Because they had not yet been discovered by Europeans, North and South America were not depicted.

Mapping practices changed markedly during the late fifteenth and sixteenth centuries both because of the advent of print and also because European nations such as Portugal and Spain began sending ships on long sea voyages to open new trade routes to the East and, eventually, to the Americas. During this period, monarchs competed to have the best cartographers supply them with accurate maps of their realms and especially of lands in Africa, Asia, or the Americas, where they hoped to trade or plant settlements. Such knowledge was precious and jealously guarded. The value of such maps and the secrecy that surrounded them are indicated by a story published in Hakluyt's *The Principal Navigations*. An English ship had captured a Portuguese vessel in the Azores, and a map was discovered among the ship's valuable cargo, which included spices, silks, carpets, porcelain, and other exotic commercial objects. The map was "inclosed in a case of sweete Cedar wood, and lapped up almost an hundred fold in fine calicut-cloth, as though it had been some incomparable jewell." The value of the map and what explains the careful way in which it was packed lay in the particular information it afforded the English about Portuguese trading routes. More than beautiful objects, maps like this one were crucial to the international race to find safe sea routes to the most profitable trading centers in the East.

In the sixteenth century, books of maps began to be printed, making them more affordable for ordinary people, though some of these books, published as big folio volumes, remained too dear for any but wealthy patrons to buy. Yet maps were increasingly a part of daily life, and printing made many of them more accessible. Playgoers in Shakespeare's audiences must have understood in general the value and uses of maps, for they appear as props in a number of his plays. Most famously, at the beginning of *King Lear,* the old king has a map brought onstage showing the extent of his kingdom. He then points on the map to the three separate parts into which he is dividing his realm to share among his daughters. The map, often unfurled with a flourish on a table or held up for view by members of Lear's retinue, signals the crucial relationship of the land to the monarch. He is his domains, and the map signifies his possession of them. To divide the kingdom, in essence to tear apart the map, would have been judged foolish and destructive by early modern political theorists. Similarly, in *1 Henry IV,* when rebels against the sitting monarch, Henry IV, plot to overthrow him, they bring a map onstage in order to decide what part of the kingdom will be given to each rebel leader. Their proposed dismemberment of the realm signifies the danger they pose. Treasonously, they would rend in pieces the body of the commonwealth.

Maps, of course, had other uses besides signifying royal domains. In some instances, they were used pragmatically to help people find their way from one place to another. A very common kind of map, a portolan chart, depicted in minute detail the coastline of a particular body of water. Used by sailors, these maps frequently were made by people native to the region they described. Many world or regional maps, because they were beautifully decorated and embellished with vivid colors, were used for decorative purposes. John Dee, a learned adviser to Queen Elizabeth and a great book collector, wrote that some people used maps "to beautifie their Halls, Parlers, Chambers, Galeries, Studies, or Libraries." He also spoke of more scholarly uses for these objects. They could, for example, be useful aids in the study of history or geography, enabling people to locate "thinges past, as battels fought, earthquakes, heavenly fyringes, and such occurents in histories mentioned." Today we make similar use of maps, like those included in this volume, when, in reading Shakespeare's plays, we resort to a map to find out where the Battle of Agincourt took place or where Othello sailed when he left Venice for Cyprus.

This edition of the *Norton Shakespeare* includes six maps. Three of them are modern maps drawn specifically to show the location of places important to Shakespeare's plays. They depict London, the British Isles and France, and the eastern Mediterranean. This edition also includes three early modern maps that indicate some of the different kinds of printed maps that people might have seen in Shakespeare's lifetime. The earliest is a map of London that appeared in a 1574 edition of a famous German atlas, *Civitates Orbis Terrarum (Cities of the World)*, compiled by George Braun with engravings by Franz Hogenberg. This remarkable atlas includes maps and information on cities throughout Europe, Asia, and North Africa; the first of its six volumes appeared in 1572, the last in 1617. Being included in the volume indicated a city's status as a recognized metropolitan center. In a charming touch, Braun added to his city maps pictures of figures in local dress. At the bottom of the map of London, for example, there are four figures who appear to represent the city's prosperous citizens. In the center, a man in a long robe holds the hand of soberly dressed matron. On either side of them are younger and more ornately dressed figures. The young man sports a long sword and a short cloak, the woman a dress with elaborate skirts. In the atlas, the map is colored, and the clothes of the two young people echo one another in shades of green and red.

At the time the map was made, London was a rapidly expanding metropolis. In 1550, it contained about 55,000 people; by 1600, it would contain nearly 200,000. The map shows the densely populated old walled city north of the Thames River, in the middle of which was Eastcheap, the commercial district where, in Shakespeare's plays about the reign of Henry IV, Falstaff holds court in a tavern. The map also shows that by 1570 London was spreading westward beyond the wall toward Westminster Palace. This medieval structure, which appears on the extreme left side of the map, was where English monarchs resided when in London and where, at the end of *2 Henry IV,* the king dies in the fabled Jerusalem Chamber of the Westminster complex. On the far right of the map, one can see the Tower of London, where Edward IV's young sons were imprisoned by Richard III, an event depicted in Shakespeare's *The Tragedy of King Richard the Third*. The map also indicates the centrality of the Thames to London's commercial life. It shows the river full of boats, some of those on the east side of London Bridge large oceangoing vessels with several masts. South of the river, where many of the most famous London theaters, including Shakespeare's Globe, were to be constructed in the 1590s, there are relatively few buildings. By 1600, this would change, as Southwark, as it was known, came to be an increasingly busy entertainment, residential, and commercial district.

The map of the Christian Holy Lands at the eastern tip of the Mediterranean Sea had extremely wide distribution because it was included in the many editions of the Geneva Bible, an English translation of the Scriptures put together by a group of Puritan scholars working in Geneva in the 1550s. Moderately sized and priced, the Geneva Bible became the most popular Bible in English until the King James version was produced in 1611. Even after that date, many ordinary Protestant readers continued to use the popular Geneva Bible, which underwent refinements, changes, and additions throughout the second half of the sixteenth century, including in 1576 a new translation of the New Testament heavily indebted to the scholarship of the French theologian Théodore de Bèze.

The map included here is from a 1592 edition of this Bible, printed in London by Christopher Barker. The map was placed before Matthew, the first book of the New Testament, and it shows places mentioned in the first four Gospels (Matthew, Mark, Luke, and John), which collectively tell of the life and deeds of Jesus. It indicates, for example, the location of Bethlehem, where he was born; Nazareth, where he spent his youth; and Cana of Galilee, where he turned water into wine at a marriage. It suggests that, to the English reader, this particular territory was overwritten by and completely intertwined with Christian history. Yet in the Mediterranean Sea, on the left of the map, several large ships are visible, and they are reminders of another fact about this region: it was a vigorous trading arena where European Christian merchants did business with local merchants—Christian, Jew, and Muslim—and with traders bringing luxury goods by overland routes from the East. A number of Shakespeare's plays are set in this complex eastern Mediterranean region where several religious traditions laid claim to its territories and many commercial powers competed for preeminence. *Pericles*, for example, has a hero who is the ruler of Tyre, a city on the upper right side of the map. In the course of his wanderings, Pericles visits many cities along the eastern coasts of the Mediterranean. The conclusion of the play, in which the hero is reunited both with his long-lost daughter and the wife he believes dead, has seemed to many critics to share in a sense of Christian miracle, despite the fact of its ostensibly pagan setting. *The Comedy of Errors* and parts of *Othello* and of *Antony and Cleopatra* are also set in the eastern Mediterranean. One of Shakespeare's earliest plays, *The Comedy of Errors*, is an urban comedy in which the protagonists are merchants deeply involved in commercial transactions. It is also the first play in which Shakespeare mentions the Americas in an extended joke in which he compares parts of a serving woman's body to the countries on a map including Ireland, France, and the Americas. In *Othello*, the eastern Mediterranean island of Cyprus is represented as a tense Christian outpost defending Venetian interests against the Muslim Turks. In *Antony and Cleopatra*, Egypt figures as the site of Eastern luxury and also of imperial conquest, an extension of the Roman Empire. Clearly, this region was to Shakespeare and his audiences one of the most complex and most highly charged areas of the world: a site of religious, commercial, and imperial significance.

The map of Great Britain and Ireland comes from a 1612 edition of John Speed's *The Theatre of the Empire of Great Britaine*, an innovative atlas containing individual maps of counties and towns in England and Wales, as well as larger maps that include Scotland and Ireland. Speed was by trade a tailor who increasingly devoted his time to the study of history and cartography. Befriended by the antiquarian scholar William Camden, he eventually won patronage from Sir Fulke Greville, who gave him a pension that allowed him to devote full time to his scholarly endeavors. *The Theatre* was one product of this newfound freedom. The map included here is one of his most ambitious. It shows the entire British Isles, nominated by Speed as "The Kingdome of Great Britaine and Ireland," though at this time Ireland was far from under the control of the English crown and Scotland was still an independent kingdom, despite the fact that James I, a Scot by birth, had tried hard to forge a formal union between England and Scotland. This problem of the relationship of the parts of the British Isles to one another, and England's assertion of power over the others, is treated in *Henry V,* in which officers from Wales, Ireland, and Scotland are sharply delineated yet all depicted as loyal subjects of the English king.

One striking aspect of Speed's map is the balance it strikes between the two capital cities, London on the left, prominently featuring the Thames and London Bridge, and Edinburgh on the right. This would have pleased James, whose interest in his native country Shakespeare played to in his writing of *Macbeth*, based on material from Scottish history. Speed's map acknowledges the claims of the monarch to the territory it depicts. In the upper left corner, the British lion and the Scottish unicorn support a roundel topped with a crown. When James became king of England in 1603, he created this merged symbol of Scottish-English unity. The motto of the Royal Order of the Garter, "Honi soit qui mal y pense" (Shamed be he who thinks ill of it), is inscribed around the circumference. In the bottom left corner of the map, another locus of authority is established. Two cherubs, one holding a compass, the other a globe, sit beneath a banner on which is inscribed the words: "Performed by John Speede." If the territory is the monarch's, the craft that depicts it belongs to the tailor turned cartographer.

Today, maps are readily available from any gasoline station or on the Internet, but in early modern England they were still rare and valuable objects that could generate great excitement in those who owned or beheld them. Along with other precious items, maps were sometimes put on display in libraries and sitting rooms, but they had functions beyond the ornamental. They helped to explain and order the world, indicating who claimed certain domains, showing where the familiar stories of the Bible or of English history occurred, helping merchants find their way to distant markets. As John Dee, the early modern map enthusiast concluded, "Some, for one purpose: and some, for an other, liketh, loveth, getteth, and useth, Mappes, Chartes, and Geographicall Globes."

JEAN E. HOWARD

Ireland, Scotland, Wales, England, and Western France: Places Important to Shakespeare's Plays.

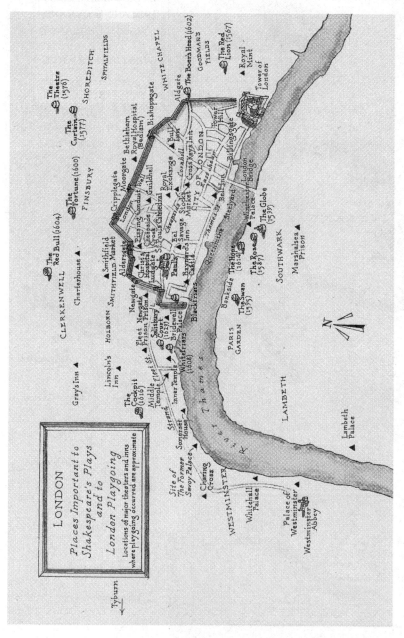

London: Places Important to Shakespeare's Plays and London Playgoing.

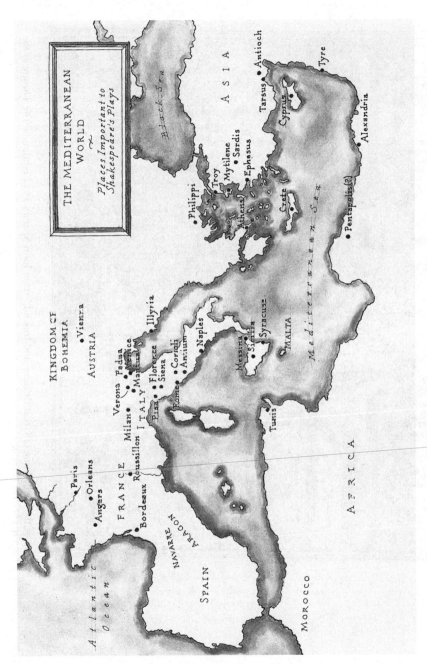

The Mediterranean World: Places Important to Shakespeare's Plays.

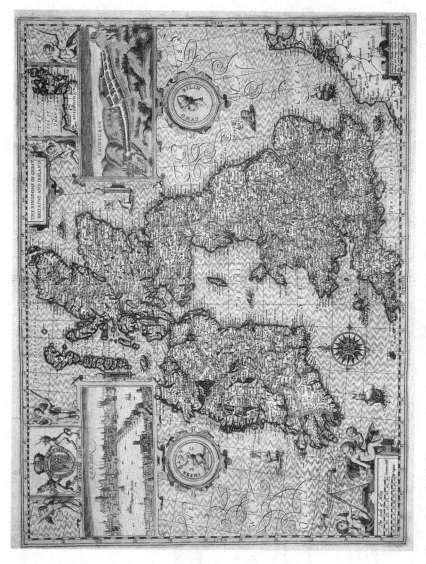

Map of the "Kingdome of Great Britaine and Ireland," from John Speed's 1612 edition of *The Theatre of the Empire of Great Britaine.*

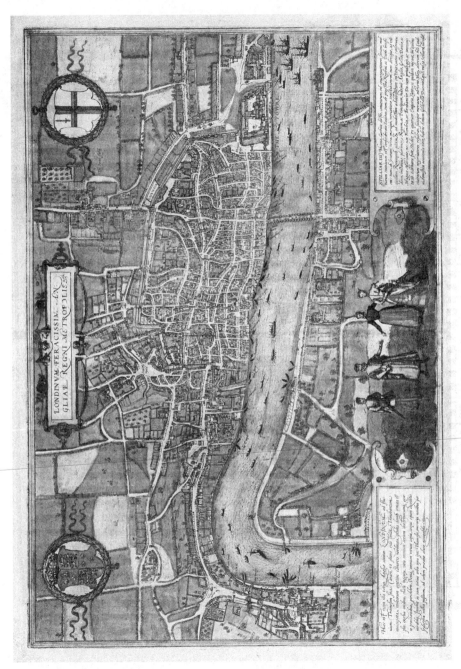

Printed map of London, 1574, taken from a German atlas of European cities by George Braun and Franz Hogenberg.

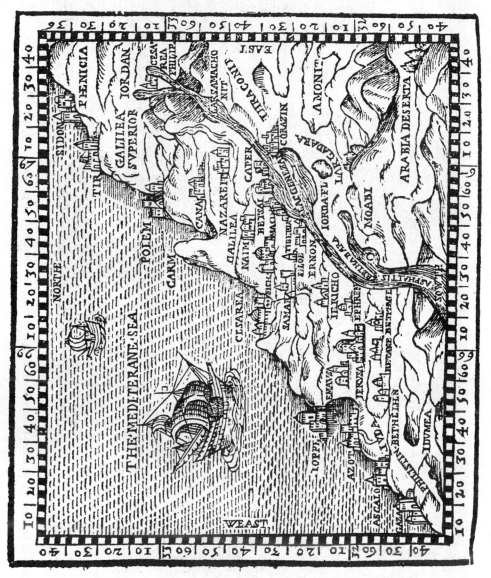

Map of the Holy Land, from the Théodore de Bèze Bible, printed in London, 1592.

# Documents

This selection of documents provides a range of contemporary testimony about Shakespeare's character, his work, and the social and institutional conditions under which it was produced. In the absence of newspapers and reviewers, few references to the theater survive. The availability of such hints and fragments as are presented here serves as a mark of Shakespeare's distinction, for the theater was perceived by much of the literate population as ephemeral popular entertainment. The reports of spectators whose accounts we have are more like reviews than any other texts the period has to offer; hence the importance even of brief notes such as Nashe's or Platter's, and the particular value of extended accounts such as those of Simon Forman. The government documents included here offer a vivid glimpse of the institutional procedures by which the theater was regulated. The legal documents—a contract for the construction of a theater modeled on the Globe, and Shakespeare's will—provide the most detailed account available of the material conditions of his life and work. The extracts from criticism and other literary texts show the diversity of contemporary response to his art.

The source for each text is given at the end of the introductory headnote. Additional documents can be found at wwnorton.com/shakespeare.

WS: E. K. Chambers, *William Shakespeare: A Study of Facts and Problems*, 2 vols. (Oxford: Clarendon Press, 1930).
ES: E. K. Chambers, *The Elizabethan Stage*, 4 vols. (Oxford: Clarendon Press, 1923).

## Robert Greene on Shakespeare (1592)

[Robert Greene (1560–1592), a prolific author of plays, romances, and pamphlets, attacked Shakespeare in his *Greenes, Groats-worth of Witte, bought with a million of Repentance*. Greene had studied at Cambridge, and his "M.A." was prominently displayed on his title pages. Shakespeare's lack of a university education is clearly one motive for the professional resentment of the following excerpt. Another is probably that Greene was poor and very ill and felt forsaken while writing the *Groats-worth of Witte*; the preface refers to it as his "Swanne-like song," and the narrative is framed as the repentance of a dying man. (Some scholars have held that the posthumously published work contains fabrications by a publisher attempting to capitalize on Greene's name.) The three colleagues Greene addresses are likely to be Christopher Marlowe, Thomas Nashe, and George Peele. The text is that of 1596, as printed in Alexander B. Grosart's *Life and Complete Works in Prose and Verse of Robert Greene*, vol. 12 (New York: Russell and Russell).]

> *To those Gentlemen his Quondam acquaintance,*
> *that spend their wits in making Plaies, R. G.*
> *wisheth a better exercise, and wisdome*
> *to prevent his extremities. . . .*

Base minded men al three of you, if by my miserie ye be not warned: for unto none of you (like me) fought those burres to cleave: those Puppits (I meane) that speake from our mouths, those Anticks garnisht in our colours. Is it not strange that I, to whom they al have beene beholding: is it not like that you, to whome they all have beene beholding, shall (were ye in that case that I am now) be both at once of them forsaken? Yes trust them not: for there is an upstart Crow, beautified with our feathers, that with his *Tygers heart wrapt in a Players hide,*[1] *supposes he is as well able to bumbast out a blanke verse as the best of you: and being an absolute Johannes fac totum,*[2] is in his owne conceit the onely Shake-scene in a countrie. O that I might intreate your rare wits to be imployed in more profitable courses: & let those Apes imitate your past excellence, and never more acquaint them with your admired inventions. I know the best husband[3] of you all will never prove an Usurer, and the kindest of them / all will never proove a kinde nurse: yet whilst you may, seeke you better Maisters; for it is pittie men of such rare wits, should be subject to the pleasures of such rude groomes.

## Thomas Nashe on *1 Henry VI* (1592)

[Thomas Nashe (1567–1601), Greene's fellow playwright and pamphleteer, protests the attribution to himself of the *Groats-worth of Witte* in the preface to the 1592 edition of a pamphlet of his own, *Pierce Penilisse; His Supplication to the Devil.* The satire of *Pierce Penilisse* is more general and political than that of the *Groats-worth,* attacking the manners of the middle class. The allusion to the Talbot scenes of *1 Henry VI* (4.2–7) comes in a section subtitled "The defence of Playes." Talbot is supposed to have been played by Richard Burbage, later the leading actor of the Lord Chamberlain's and King's Men. The text is from Ronald B. McKerrow's 1904 edition of Nashe's *Works,* vol. 1 (London: Bullen).]

How would it have joyed brave *Talbot* (the terror of the French) to thinke that after he had lyne two hundred yeares in his Tombe, hee should triumphe againe on the Stage, and have his bones newe embalmed with the teares of ten thousand spectators at least (at severall times), who, in the Tragedian that represents his person, imagine they behold him fresh bleeding.

## Francis Meres on Shakespeare (1598)

[Francis Meres (1565–1647) was educated at Cambridge and was active in London literary circles in 1597–98, after which he became a rector and schoolmaster in the country. The descriptions of Shakespeare are taken from a section on poetry in *Palladis Tamia, Wits Treasury,* a work largely consisting of translated classical quotations and exempla. Unlike the main body of the work, the subsections on poetry, painting, and music include comparisons of English artists to figures of antiquity. Meres goes on after the extract below to list Shakespeare among the best English writers for lyric, tragedy, comedy, elegy, and love poetry. The text is from Don Cameron Allen's 1933 edition of the section "Poetrie" (Urbana: University of Illinois).]

### From XI

As the Greeke tongue is made famous and eloquent by *Homer, Hesiod, Euripedes, Aeschilus, Sophocles, Pindarus, Phocylides* and *Aristophanes;* and the Latine tongue by *Virgill, Ovid, Horace, Silius Italicus, Lucanus, Lucretius, Ausonius* and *Claudianus:* so the English tongue is mightily enriched, and gorgeouslie invested

---

1. A parody of *Richard Duke of York* (*3 Henry VI*) 1.4.138: "O tiger's heart wrapped in a woman's hide!" This obvious allusion and the following pun on Shakespeare's name make it certain that Shakespeare is the

"crow" described here.
2. Jack-of-all-trades. *conceit:* imagination.
3. Steward.

in rare ornaments and resplendent abiliments by Sir *Philip Sidney, Spencer, Daniel, Drayton, Warner, Shakespeare, Marlow* and *Chapman*.

## From XIV

As the soule of *Euphorbus* was thought to live in *Pythagoras*: so the sweete wittie soule of Ovid lives in mellifluous & honytongued *Shakespeare*, witnes his *Venus* and *Adonis*, his *Lucrece*, his sugred Sonnets.

## From XV

As *Plautus* and *Seneca* are accounted the best for Comedy and Tragedy among the Latines: so *Shakespeare* among $y^e$ English is the most excellent in both kinds for the stage; for Comedy, witnes his *Gētlemē of Verona*, his *Errors*, his *Love labors lost*, his *Love labours wonne*,[1] his *Midsummers night dreame*, & his *Merchant of Venice*: for Tragedy his *Richard the 2. Richard the 3. Henry the 4. King John, Titus Andronicus* and his *Romeo* and *Juliet*.

As *Epius Stolo* said, that the Muses would speake with *Plautus* tongue, if they would speak Latin: so I say that the Muses would speak with *Shakespeares* fine filed phrase, if they would speake English.

## Thomas Platter on *Julius Caesar* (September 21, 1599)

[Thomas Platter (b. 1574), a Swiss traveler, recorded his experience at the Globe playhouse in an account of his travels. The German text is printed in WS 2:322.]

Den 21 Septembris nach dem Imbissessen, etwan umb zwey vhren, bin ich mitt meiner geselschaft vber daz wasser gefahren, haben in dem streüwinen Dachhaus die Tragedy vom ersten Keyser Julio Caesare mitt ohngefahr 15 personen schen gar artlich agieren; zu endt der Comedien dantzeten sie ihrem gebraucht nach gar vberausz zierlich, ye zwen in mannes vndt 2 in weiber kleideren angethan, wunderbahrlich mitt einanderen.

On the 21st of September after lunch, about two o'clock, I crossed the water [the Thames] with my party, and we saw the tragedy of the first emperor Julius Caesar acted very prettily in the house with the thatched roof, with about fifteen characters; at the end of the comedy, according to their custom, they danced with exceeding elegance, two each in men's and two in women's clothes, wonderfully together.

[Translated by Noah Heringman]

## Gabriel Harvey on *Hamlet, Venus and Adonis,* and *The Rape of Lucrece* (1598–1603)

[Gabriel Harvey (c. 1550–1631), a scholar perhaps best remembered as the particular friend of Spenser, gave the following account of Shakespeare and other contemporaries in a long manuscript note in his copy of Speght's 1598 edition of Chaucer. The date of the note is uncertain, but internal evidence makes it highly unlikely to be later than 1603. The references to Shakespeare are brief but suggestive, and the note is useful both in providing a context for the appreciation of Shakespeare and for its characteris-

---

1. The play—or at least the title—has not survived; a bookseller's record of the title does survive, however.

tically keen assessment of the state of modern literature. The text is from G. C. Moore Smith's edition of *Gabriel Harvey's Marginalia* (Stratford-upon-Avon: Shakespeare Head Press, 1913).]

And now translated Petrarch, Ariosto, Tasso, & Bartas himself deserve curious comparison with Chaucer, Lidgate, & owre best Inglish, auncient & moderne. Amongst which, the Countesse of Pembrokes Arcadia, & the Faerie Queene ar now freshest in request: & Astrophil, & Amyntas ar none of the idlest pastimes of sum fine humanists. The Earle of Essex much commendes Albions England:[1] and not unworthily for diverse notable pageants, before, & in the Chronicle. Sum Inglish, & other Histories nowhere more sensibly described, or more inwardly discovered. The Lord Mountjoy makes the like account of Daniels peece of the Chronicle,[2] touching the Usurpation of Henrie of Bullingbrooke, which in deede is a fine, sententious, & politique peece of Poetrie: as proffitable, as pleasurable. The younger sort takes much delight in Shakespeares Venus, & Adonis: but his Lucrece, & his tragedie of Hamlet, Prince of Denmarke, have it in them, to please the wiser sort. Or such poets: or better: or none.

> Vilia miretur vulgus: mihi flavus Apollo
> Pocula Castaliæ plena ministret aquæ:[3]

quoth Sir Edward Dier, betwene jest, & earnest. Whose written devises farr excell most of the sonets, and cantos in print. His Amaryllis, & Sir Walter Raleighs Cynthia, how fine & sweet inventions? Excellent matter of emulation for Spencer, Constable, France, Watson, Daniel, Warner, Chapman, Silvester, Shakespeare, & the rest of owr florishing metricians. I looke for much, aswell in verse, as in prose, from mie two Oxford frends, Doctor Gager, & M. Hackluit: both rarely furnished for the purpose: & I have a phansie to Owens new Epigrams, as pithie as elegant, as plesant as sharp, & sumtime as weightie as breife: & amongst so manie gentle, noble, & royall spirits meethinkes I see sum heroical thing in the clowdes: mie soveraine hope. Axiophilus[4] shall forgett himself, or will remember to leave sum memorials behinde him: & to make an use of so manie rhapsodies, cantos, hymnes, odes, epigrams, sonets, & discourses, as at idle howers, or at flowing fitts he hath compiled. God knowes what is good for the world, & fitting for this age.

## Contract for the Building of the Fortune Theatre (1600)

[This contract was drawn up between Philip Henslowe and Edward Alleyn, partners in the venture, and Peter Street, the carpenter (or general contractor) in charge of the construction. In fact, Alleyn seems to have put up all the money, £440 for the work specified in the contract in addition to £80 for decoration and considerable sums to acquire the lot and surrounding properties. Alleyn faced opposition from residents of the neighborhood, but he had secured the favor of key supporters, so that he was able to proceed with the construction. As the new home of the Lord Admiral's Men, the Fortune did in fact become a center of disturbances, with complaints coming to the Middlesex Bench of assaults, petty thefts, and riotous behavior. Alleyn had been the leading actor of the Lord Admiral's Men, chief competitors of the Lord Chamberlain's Men, and the Fortune was conceived to compete with the Globe, meanwhile replacing the decaying and poorly situated Rose Theatre. The contract's

1. By William Warner (1586).
2. *The Ciuile Wars Between the Two Houses of Lancaster and Yorke* (1595).
3. "Let what is cheap excite the marvel of the crowd; for me may golden Apollo minister full cups from the

Castalian fount" (Ovid, *Amores* 1.15.35–36, Loeb translation). These lines also appear on the title page of Shakespeare's *Venus and Adonis* (1592–93).
4. Probably Harvey himself.

descriptions and frequent references to the Globe, given this background, can be seen as providing some of our best evidence on the nature of the Globe itself. The text is reprinted in *ES*, vol. 2.]

'This Indenture made the Eighte daie of Januarye 1599,[1] and in the Twoe and Fortyth yeare of the Reigne of our sovereigne Ladie Elizabeth, by the grace of god Queene of Englande, Fraunce and Irelande, defender of the Faythe, &c. betwene Phillipp Henslowe and Edwarde Allen of the parishe of S^te Saviours in Southwark in the Countie of Surrey, gentlemen, on thone parte, and Peeter Streete, Cittizen and Carpenter of London, on thother parte witnesseth That whereas the saide Phillipp Henslowe & Edward Allen, the daie of the date hereof, have bargayned, compounded & agreed with the saide Peter Streete ffor the erectinge, buildinge & settinge upp of a new howse and Stadge for a Plaiehouse in and uppon a certeine plott or parcell of grounde appoynted oute for that purpose, scytuate and beinge nere Goldinge lane in the parishe of S^te Giles withoute Cripplegate of London,[2] to be by him the saide Peeter Streete or somme other sufficyent woorkmen of his provideinge and appoyntemente and att his propper costes & chardges, for the consideracion hereafter in theis presentes expressed, made, erected, builded and sett upp in manner & forme followinge (that is to saie); The frame of the saide howse to be sett square[3] and to conteine ffowerscore foote of lawfull assize everye waie square withoutt and fiftie five foote of like assize square everye waie within, with a good suer and stronge foundacion of pyles, brick, lyme and sand bothe without & within, to be wroughte one foote of assize att the leiste above the grounde; And the saide fframe to conteine three Stories in heighth, the first or lower Storie to conteine Twelve foote of lawfull assize in heighth, the second Storie Eleaven foote of lawfull assize in heigth, and the third or upper Storie to conteine Nyne foote of lawfull assize in heigth; All which Stories shall conteine Twelve foote and a halfe of lawfull assize in breadth througheoute, besides a juttey forwardes in either of the saide twoe upper Stories of Tenne ynches of lawfull assize, with ffower convenient divisions for gentlemens roomes,[4] and other sufficient and convenient divisions for Twoe pennie roomes, with necessarie seates to be placed and sett, aswell in those roomes as througheoute all the rest of the galleries of the saide howse, and with suchelike steares, conveyances & divisions withoute & within, as are made & contryved in and to the late erected Plaiehowse on the Banck in the saide parishe of S^te Saviours called the Globe; With a Stadge and Tyreinge howse[5] to be made, erected & settupp within the saide fframe, with a shadowe or cover[6] over the saide Stadge, which Stadge shalbe placed & sett, as alsoe the stearecases of the saide fframe, in suche sorte as is prefigured in a plott[7] thereof drawen, and which Studge shall conteine in length Fortie and Three foote of lawfull assize and in breadth to extende to the middle of the yarde[8] of the saide howse; The same Stadge to be paled in belowe with good, stronge and sufficyent newe oken bourdes, and likewise the lower Storie of the saide fframe withinside, and the same lower storie to be alsoe laide over and fenced with stronge yron pykes; And the saide Stadge to be in all other proporcions contryved and fashioned like unto the Stadge of the saide Plaie howse called the Globe; With convenient windowes and lightes glazed to the saide Tyreinge howse; And the saide fframe, Stadge and Stearecases to be covered with Tyle, and to have a sufficient gutter of lead to carrie & convey the water frome the coveringe of the saide Stadge to fall backwardes; And also all the saide fframe and the Stairecases thereof

---

1. 1600 (New Style).
2. *nere . . . London*: an area then in the northwest suburbs, literally outside Cripplegate and, like the Globe across the water, outside the jurisdiction of a City Council often inimical to the theater.
3. This square shape was unusual; the outlines of comparable theaters of the period were round or polygonal (with more than four sides).
4. Something like the VIP boxes of the present day.

5. "Attiring house," a dressing room and backstage area extending onto the rear of the stage.
6. A roof (known as "the heavens") partially covering the stage, supported by the pillars that also served as versatile pieces of scenery.
7. Plan.
8. *in breadth . . . yarde*: the stage would then extend about 27 feet into the yard, specified earlier as 55 feet square.

to be sufficyently enclosed withoute with lathe, lyme & haire, and the gentlemens roomes and Twoe pennie roomes to be seeled[9] with lathe, lyme & haire, and all the fflowers of the saide Galleries, Stories and Stadge to be bourded with good & sufficyent newe deale bourdes of the whole thicknes, wheare need shalbe; And the saide howse and other thinges beforemencioned to be made & doen to be in all other contrivitions, conveyances, fashions, thinge and thinges effected, finished and doen accordinge to the manner and fashion of the saide howse called the Globe, saveinge only that all the princypall and maine postes of the saide fframe and Stadge forwarde shalbe square and wroughte palasterwise,[1] with carved proporcions called Satiers[2] to be placed & sett on the topp of every of the same postes, and saveinge alsoe that the said Peeter Streete shall not be chardged with anie manner of pay[ntin]ge in or aboute the saide fframe howse or Stadge or anie parte thereof, nor rendringe[3] the walls within, nor seeling anie more or other roomes then the gentlemens roomes, Twoe pennie roomes and Stadge before remembred. Nowe theiruppon the saide Peeter Streete dothe covenant, promise and graunte ffor himself, his executours and administratours, to and with the saide Phillipp Henslowe and Edward Allen and either of them, and thexecutours and administratours of them and either of them, by theis presentes in manner & forme followeinge (that is to saie); That he the saide Peeter Streete, his executours or assignes, shall & will att his or their owne propper costes & chardges well, woorkmanlike & substancyallie make, erect, sett upp and fully finishe in and by all thinges, accordinge to the true meaninge of theis presentes, with good, stronge and substancyall newe tymber and other necessarie stuff, all the saide fframe and other woorkes whatsoever in and uppon the saide plott or parcell of grounde (beinge not by anie aucthoretie restrayned, and haveinge ingres, egres & regres to doe the same) before the ffyve & twentith daie of Julie next commeinge after the date hereof; And shall alsoe at his or theire like costes and chardges provide and finde all manner of woorkmen, tymber, joystes, rafters, boordes, dores, boltes, hinges, brick, tyle, lathe, lyme, haire, sande, nailes, lade, iron, glasse, woorkmanshipp and other thinges whatsoever, which shalbe needefull, convenyent & necessarie for the saide fframe & woorkes & everie parte thereof; And shall alsoe make all the saide fframe in every poynte for Scantlinges[4] lardger and bigger in assize then the Scantlinges of the timber of the saide newe erected howse called the Globe; And alsoe that he the saide Peeter Streete shall furthwith, aswell by himself as by suche other and soemanie woorkmen as shalbe convenient & necessarie, enter into and uppon the saide buildinges and woorkes, and shall in reasonable manner proceede therein withoute anie wilfull detraccion untill the same shalbe fully effected and finished. In consideracion of all which buildinges and of all stuff & woorkemanshipp thereto belonginge, the saide Phillipp Henslowe & Edward Allen and either of them, ffor themselves, theire, and either of theire executours & administratours, doe joynctlie & severallie covenante & graunte to & with the saide Peeter Streete, his executours & administratours by theis presentes, that they the saide Phillipp Henslowe & Edward Allen or one of them, or the executours administratours or assignes of them or one of them, shall & will well & truelie paie or cawse to be paide unto the saide Peeter Streete, his executours or assignes, att the place aforesaid appoynted for the erectinge of the saide fframe, the full somme of Fower hundred & Fortie Poundes of lawfull money of Englande in manner & forme followeinge (that is to saie), att suche tyme and when as the Tymberwoork of the saide fframe shalbe rayzed & sett upp by the saide Peeter Streete his executours or assignes, or within seaven daies then next followeinge, Twoe hundred & Twentie poundes, and att suche time and when as the saide fframe & woorkes shalbe fullie effected & ffynished as is aforesaide, or within seaven daies then next followeinge, thother Twoe hundred and Twentie poundes,

9. Coated both on the "ceiling" (a related word) and the walls.
1. Finished in the form of pilasters, ornamental columns in the classical style.

2. Satyrs. *proporcions*: figures.
3. Plastering.
4. Prescribed dimensions of the beams.

withoute fraude or coven.[5] Provided allwaies, and it is agreed betwene the saide parties, that whatsoever somme or sommes of money the saide Phillipp Henslowe & Edward Allen or either of them, or thexecutours or assignes of them or either of them, shall lend or deliver unto the saide Peter Streete his executours or assignes, or anie other by his appoyntemente or consent, ffor or concerninge the saide woorkes or anie parte thereof or anie stuff thereto belonginge, before the raizeinge & setteinge upp of the saide fframe, shalbe reputed, accepted, taken & accoumpted in parte of the firste paymente aforesaid of the saide some of Fower hundred & Fortie poundes, and all suche somme & sommes of money, as they or anie of them shall as aforesaid lend or deliver betwene the razeinge of the saide fframe & finishinge thereof and of all the rest of the saide woorkes, shalbe reputed, accepted, taken & accoumpted in parte of the laste pamente aforesaid of the same somme of Fower hundred & Fortie poundes, anie thinge abovesaid to the contrary notwithstandinge. In witnes whereof the parties abovesaid to theis presente Indentures Interchaungeably have sett theire handes and seales. Geoven[6] the daie and yeare ffirste abovewritten.

P S

Sealed and delivered by the saide Peter Streete in the presence of me William Harris Pub[lic] Scr[ivener] And me Frauncis Smyth appr[entice] to the said Scr[ivener]
[*Endorsed:*] Peater Streat ffor The Building of the Fortune.

## Augustine Phillips, Francis Bacon, et al. on *Richard II* (1601)

[These extracts from testimony submitted at the Earl of Essex's trial for treason, and related documents, show that some of Essex's supporters had contracted with the Lord Chamberlain's Men to revive *Richard II*, apparently in order to provide a model for the justified deposition of a monarch and thus propitiate the coup in which Essex planned to depose Elizabeth. The play was performed on February 7, and "it was on the same day," according to E. K. Chambers, "that Essex received a summons to appear before the Privy Council. This interrupted his plans for securing possession of the Queen's person and arresting her ministers, and precipitated his futile outbreak of February 8." Augustine Phillips was one of Shakespeare's colleagues in the Lord Chamberlain's Men. Sir Edward Coke was, for a time, chief justice under King James. The last excerpt is a contemporary record of a conversation between the queen and her archivist several months after Essex was executed. The texts are from *WS*, vol. 2.]

### From the Abstract of Evidence

The Erle of Essex is charged with high Treason, namely, That he plotted and practised with the Pope and king of Spaine for the disposing and settling to himself Aswell the Crowne of England, as of the kingdom of Ireland.

### From the Examination of Augustine Phillips, February 18, 1601

The Examination of Augustyne Phillypps servant unto the L Chamberlyne and one of hys players taken the xviij[th] of Februarij 1600 upon hys oth
He sayeth that on Fryday last was sennyght or Thursday S[r] Charles Percy S[r] Josclyne Percy and the L. Montegle with some thre more spak to some of the play-

ers in the presans of thys examinate to have the play of the deposyng and kyllyng of
Kyng Rychard the second to be played the Saterday next promysyng to gete them xls.
more then their ordynary to play yt. Wher thys Examinate and hys fellowes were
determyned to have played some other play, holdyng that play of Kyng Richard to be
so old & so long out of use as that they shold have small or no Company at yt. But
at their request this Examinate and his fellowes were Content to play yt the Saterday and had their xls. more then their ordynary for yt and so played yt accordyngly

Augustine Phillipps

### From the speech of Sir Edward Coke at Essex's trial, February 19

I protest upon my soul and conscience I doe beleeve she should not have long
lived after she had been in your power. Note but the precedents of former ages,
how long lived Richard the Second after he was surprised in the same manner? The
pretence was alike for the removing of certain counsellors, but yet shortly after it
cost him his life.

### From [Francis Bacon's] "A Declaration of the . . . Treasons . . . by Robert late Earle of Essex"

The afternoone before the rebellion, Merricke,[1] with a great company of others, that afterwards were all in the action, had procured to bee played before them,
the play of deposing King Richard the second. Neither was it casuall, but a play
bespoken by Merrick. And not so onely, but when it was told him by one of the
players, that the play was olde, and they should have losse in playing it, because
fewe would come to it: there was fourty shillings extraordinarie given to play it, and
so thereupon playd it was. So earnest hee was to satisfie his eyes with the sight of
that tragedie which hee thought soone after his lord should bring from the stage
to the state, but that God turned it upon their owne heads.

### From a Memorandum in the Lambard family manuscript, August 4

. . . so her Majestie fell upon[2] the reign of King Richard II. saying, 'I am Richard II. know ye not that?'
W.L. 'Such a wicked imagination was determined and attempted by a most
unkind Gent. the most adorned creature that ever your Majestie made.'
Her Majestie. 'He that will forget God, will also forget his benefactors; this tragedy was played 40[tie] times in open streets and houses.'

# John Manningham on Twelfth Night and Richard III (1602)

[John Manningham (d. 1622) kept a diary during his time as a law student at the
Middle Temple, recording the witticisms of his colleagues and a rich variety of anecdotes. The vibrant and boisterous life of the Inns of Court is also illustrated by the Gesta
Grayorum (see above). The February entry describes the festivities organized for Can-
dlemas Day at the Middle Temple, while the second recounts an anecdote related to
Manningham by one Mr. Touse (this name is difficult to read in the manuscript). As
with all the documents in this section, any date before March 25 is assigned to the following year according to our calendar, so that 1601 here becomes 1602 (New Style).

1. Sir Gilly Merrick, one of Essex's supporters, was
later tried separately for treason.
2. Came across (in reading). The memorandum

describes a scene in which the queen is reading over
the archives that have been in the keeping of her
interlocutor, William Lambard.

The text is from the 1976 edition of Robert Sorlien (Hanover, N.H.: University Press of New England).]

## Febr. 1601

2. At our feast wee had a play called "Twelve night, or what you will"; much like the commedy of errores, or Menechmi[1] in Plautus, but most like and neere to that in Italian called Inganni.[2] A good practise in it to make the steward beleeve his Lady widdowe[3] was in Love with him, by counterfayting a letter, as from his Lady, in generall termes, telling him what shee liked best in him, and prescribing his gesture in smiling, his apparraile, &c., and then when he came to practise, making him beleeve they tooke him to be mad.

## Marche. 1601

13. . . . Upon a tyme when Burbidge played Rich[ard] 3. there was a Citizen grewe soe farr in liking with him, that before shee went from the play shee appointed him to come that night unto hir by the name of Ri[chard] the 3. Shakespeare, overhearing their conclusion, went before, was intertained, and at his game ere Burbidge came. Then message being brought that Richard the 3[d]. was at the dore, Shakespeare caused returne to be made that William the Conquerour was before Rich[ard] the 3. Shakespeare's name William. (Mr. Touse.)

## Letters Patent Formalizing the Adoption of the Lord Chamberlain's Men as the King's Men (May 19, 1603)

[James I issued the warrant ordering this patent shortly after his coronation, enhancing the status of Shakespeare's company. As retainers of the royal household with the title of Grooms of the Chamber, they performed at the court with increasing frequency (177 times between 1603 and 1616) and assisted occasionally with other court functions; but, more important, they acted throughout the kingdom under the authority of the royal patent, whose scope the forceful wording below makes clear. The patent, bearing the Great Seal, was issued May 19 as ordered in the warrant of May 17. There is some evidence to suggest that James was particularly taken with Shakespeare's poetry, and the playwright's valorization of James's ancestry (as originating with Banquo) in Macbeth certainly suggests that Shakespeare cultivated his esteem. The text is from ES, vol. 2.]

Commissio specialis pro Laurencio Fletcher & Willelmo Shackespeare et aliis[2]

James by the grace of god &c. To all Justices, Maiors, Sheriffes, Constables, hedborowes,[1] and other our Officers and lovinge Subjectes greetinge. Knowe yee that Wee of our speciall grace, certeine knowledge, & mere motion[3] have licenced and aucthorized and by theise presentes[4] doe licence and aucthorize theise our Servauntes Lawrence Fletcher, William Shakespeare, Richard Burbage, Augustyne Phillippes, John Heninges, Henrie Condell, William Sly, Robert Armyn, Richard Cowly, and the rest of theire Assosiates freely to use and exercise the Arte and faculty of playinge

---

1. Source for The Comedy of Errors.
2. The two plays with this exact title (1562 and 1592) seem less likely to be "most like" Twelfth Night than another Italian play, Ingannati (1537), which has characters named Fabio and Malevolti and makes reference to Twelfth Night (Epiphany).
3. Olivia is not a widow in the version of Shakespeare's play that has come down to us, though she is

so described in one of Shakespeare's principal sources for the play.
1. A parish officer similar to a petty constable.
2. Commissio . . . aliis: By special commission on behalf of . . . and others.
3. Inclination, desire.
4. The present document.

Comedies, Tragedies, histories, Enterludes, moralls,[5] pastoralls, Stageplaies, and Suche others like as theie have alreadie studied or hereafter shall use or studie, aswell for the recreation of our lovinge Subjectes, as for our Solace and pleasure when wee shall thincke good to see them, duringe our pleasure. And the said Commedies, tragedies, histories, Enterludes, Morralles, Pastoralls, Stage-playes, and suche like to shewe and exercise publiquely to theire best Com-moditie,[6] when the infection of the plague shall decrease, aswell within theire nowe usual howse called the Globe within our County of Surrey, as alsoe within anie towne halls or Moute halls[7] or other conveniente places within the liberties and freedome of anie other Cittie, universitie, towne, or Boroughe whatsoever within our said Realmes and domynions. Willinge and Commaundinge you and everie of you, as you tender our pleasure, not onelie to permitt and suffer them herein without anie your lettes hindrances or molestacions during our said pleasure, but alsoe to be aidinge and assistinge to them, yf anie wronge be to them offered, And to allowe them such former Curtesies as hath bene given to men of theire place and quallitie,[8] and alsoe what further favour you shall shewe to theise our Servauntes for our sake wee shall take kindlie at your handes. In wytnesse whereof &c. witnesse our selfe at Westminster the nyntenth day of May

per breve de privato sigillo[9] &c.

## Master of the Wardrobe's Account (March 1604)

[This entry offers us a rare glimpse of the players in the entourage of King James, sport-ing festive regalia in their capacity as Grooms of the Chamber. The royal procession took place March 15, 1604. The text is from WS, vol. 2.]

Red Clothe bought of sondrie persons and given by his Majestie to diverse persons against[1] his Majesties sayd royall proceeding through the Citie of London, viz.:— . . .

| The Chamber . . . | |
|---|---|
| Fawkeners[2] &c. &c. | Red cloth |
| William Shakespeare | iiii yardes di. |
| Augustine Phillipps | " |
| Lawrence Fletcher | " |
| John Hemminges | " |
| Richard Burbidge | " |
| William Slye | " |
| Robert Armyn | " |
| Henry Cundell | " |
| Richard Cowley | " |

## Simon Forman on *Macbeth, Cymbeline,* and *The Winter's Tale* (1611)

[Simon Forman (1552–1611) was a largely self-educated physician and astrologer who rose from humble beginnings to establish a successful London practice. A large parcel of his manuscripts, including scientific and autobiographical material as well as the diary from which this account of the plays is taken, has survived, making his life one of the best-documented Elizabethan lives. These manuscripts provide

5. Morality plays.
6. Advantage.
7. Council chambers.
8. Profession.
9. In sum, from the privy seal.

1. For.
2. Obsolete form of "falconers," very likely the men who trained the falcons used for James's fowl-hunting expeditions. The falconers might owe their place in the retinue to James's well-known passion for hunting.

detailed information about Forman's many sidelines, such as the manufacture of talismans, alchemy, and necromancy, as well about his sex life. The text is from *WS*, vol. 2.]

### The Bocke of Plaies and Notes therof per formane for Common Pollicie[1]

In Mackbeth at the Glob, 1610 ⟨1611⟩, the 20 of Aprill ♄ (Saturday), ther was to be observed, firste, howe Mackbeth and Bancko, 2 noble men of Scotland, Ridinge thorowe a wod, the ⟨r⟩ stode before them 3 women feiries or Nimphes, And saluted Mackbeth, sayinge, 3 tyms unto him, haille Mackbeth, king of Codon;[2] for thou shalt be a kinge, but shalt beget No kinges, &c. Then said Bancko, What all to Mackbeth And nothing to me. Yes, said the nimphes, haille to thee Bancko, thou shalt beget kinges, yet be no kinge. And so they departed & cam to the Courte of Scotland to Dunkin king of Scotes, and yt was in the dais of Edward the Confessor. And Dunkin bad them both kindly wellcome, And made Mackbeth forth with Prince of Northumberland,[3] and sent him hom to his own castell, and appointed Mackbeth to provid for him, for he would sup with him the next dai at night, & did soe. And Mackebeth contrived to kill Dunkin, & thorowe the persuasion of his wife did that night Murder the kinge in his own Castell, beinge his guest. And ther were many prodigies seen that night & the dai before. And when Mack Beth had murdred the kinge, the blod on his handes could not be washed of by Any meanes, nor from his wives handes, which handled the bloddi daggers in hiding them, By which means they became both moch amazed & Affronted. The murder being knowen, Dunkins 2 sonns fled, the on to England, the ⟨other to⟩ Walles, to save them selves, they being fled, they were supposed guilty of the murder of their father, which was nothinge so. Then was Mackbeth crowned kinge, and then he for feare of Banko, his old companion, that he should beget kinges but be no kinge him selfe, he contrived the death of Banko, and caused him to be Murdred on the way as he Rode. The next night, beinge at supper with his noble men whom he had bid to a feaste to the which also Banco should have com, he began to speake of Noble Banco, and to wish that he wer ther. And as he thus did, standing up to drincke a Carouse to him, the ghoste of Banco came and sate down in his cheier behind him. And he turninge About to sit down Again sawe the goste of Banco, which fronted him so, that he fell into a great passion of fear and fury, Utterynge many wordes about his murder, by which, when they hard that Banco was Murdred they Suspected Mackbet.

Then MackDove fled to England to the kinges sonn, And soe they Raised an Army, And cam into Scotland, and at Dunston Anyse overthruc Mackbet. In the meantyme whille Mardovec was in England, Mackbet slewe Mackdoves wife & children, and after in the battelle Mackdove slewe Mackbet.

Observe Also howe Mackbetes quen did Rise in the night in her slepe, & walke and talked and confessed all, & the docter noted her wordes.

### Of Cimbalin king of England.

Remember also the storri of Cymbalin king of England, in Lucius tyme, howe Lucius Cam from Octavus Cesar for Tribut, and being denied, after sent Lucius with a greate Arme of Souldiars who landed at Milford haven, and Affter wer vanquished by Cimbalin, and Lucius taken prisoner, and all by means of 3 outlawes, of the which 2 of them were the sonns of Cimbalim, stolen from him when they were but 2 yers old by an old man whom Cymbalin banished, and he kept them as his own sonns 20 yers with him in A cave. And howe ⟨one⟩ of them slewe Clotan, that was the quens sonn, goinge to Milford haven to sek the love of Innogen the

---

1. *Common Pollicie:* practical use. Forman's title for his notes on plays is not printed in Chambers, but interpolated here from G. Blakemore Evans's transcription in the *Riverside Shakespeare.*

2. Cawdor.
3. Probably Forman's error; Duncan gives Macbeth the title Thane of Cawdor. Duncan's son Malcolm is the Prince of Northumberland.

kinges daughter, whom he had banished also for lovinge his daughter,[4] and howe the Italian that cam from her love conveied him selfe into A Cheste, and said yt was a chest of plate sent from her love & others, to be presented to the kinge. And in the depest of the night, she being aslepe, he opened the cheste, & cam forth of yt, And vewed her in her bed, and the markes of her body, & toke awai her braslet, & after Accused her of adultery to her love, &c. And in thend howe he came with the Romains into England & was taken prisoner, and after Reveled to Innogen, Who had turned her self into mans apparrell & fled to mete her love at Milford haven, & chanchsed to fall on the Cave in the wodes wher her 2 brothers were, & howe by eating a sleping Dram they thought she had bin deed, & laid her in the wodes, & the body of Cloten by her, in her loves apparrell that he left behind him, & howe she was found by Lucius, &c.

In the Winters Talle at the glob 1611 the 15 of maye ☿ ⟨Wednesday⟩.

Observe ther howe Lyontes the kinge of Cicillia was overcom with Jelosy of his wife with the kinge of Bohemia his frind that came to see him, and howe he contrived his death and wold have had his cup berer to have poisoned, who gave the king of Bohemia warning therof & fled with him to Bohemia.

Remember also howe he sent to the Orakell of Appollo & the Annswer of Apollo, that she was giltles and that the king was jelouse &c. and howe Except the child was found Again that was loste the kinge should die without yssue, for the child was caried into Bohemia & ther laid in a forrest & brought up by a sheppard And the kinge of Bohemia his sonn maried that wentch & howe they fled into Cicillia to Leontes, and the sheppard having showed the letter of the nobleman by whom Leontes sent a was ⟨away?⟩ that child and the jewells found about her, she was knowen to be Leontes daughter and was then 16 yers old.

Remember also the Rog[5] that cam in all tottered like coll pixci[6] and howe he feyned him sicke & to have bin Robbed of all that he had and howe he cosened the por man of all his money, and after cam to the shep sher[7] with a pedlers packe & ther cosened them Again of all their money And howe he changed apparrell with the kinge of Bomia his sonn, and then howe he turned Courtier &c. Beware of trustinge feined beggars or fawninge fellouss.

## Sir Henry Wotton on *All Is True* (*Henry VIII*) and the Burning of the Globe (1613)

[Sir Henry Wotton (1568–1639), a highly educated poet and essayist, distinguished diplomat, and finally provost of Eton College, wrote to his nephew Sir Edmund Bacon shortly after the burning of the Globe. Chambers includes several other accounts of this incident in *The Elizabethan Stage,* vol. 2, pp. 419ff. The event is also recorded in John Stow's chronicles and was lamented by poets, including (several years later) Ben Jonson, and held up by Puritan divines like Prynne as an intimation of God's wrath. The excerpt below is from the earliest extant text, *Letters of Sir Henry Wotton to Sir Edmund Bacon* (London, 1661), p. 29.]

Now, to let matters of State sleep, I will entertain you at the present with what hath happened this week at the banks side. The Kings Players had a new Play, called *All is true,* representing some principall pieces of the raign of *Henry* 8, which was set forth with many extraordinary circumstances of Pomp and Majesty, even to the matting of the stage; the Knights of the Order, with their Georges and Garter, the Guards with their embroidered Coats, and the like: sufficient in truth within a while to make

---

4. Morgan/Belarius is not banished in the version of the play that comes down to us.
5. Rogue (Autolycus).

6. Probably "colt-pixie," a mischievous sprite or fairy.
7. Sheep shearing.

greatness very familiar, if not ridiculous. Now, King *Henry* making a Masque at the Cardinal, *Wolsey's* house, and certain Chambers[1] being shot off at his entry, some of the paper, or other stuff wherewith one of them was stopped, did light on the thatch, where being thought at first but an idle smoak, and their eyes more attentive to the show, it kindled inwardly, and ran round like a train, consuming within less then an hour the whole house to the very grounds.

This was the fatal period of that vertuous fabrique, wherein yet nothing did perish, but wood and straw, and a few forsaken cloaks; only one man had his breeches set on fire, that would perhaps have broyled him, if he had not by the benefit of a provident wit put it out with bottle Ale. The rest when we meet.

## Ben Jonson on *The Tempest* (and *Titus Andronicus*) (1614)

[This extract from *Bartholomew Fair* contains one of several allusions to Shakespeare in the plays of his associate and sometime rival. The first paragraph alludes to the fashion for revenge plays such as Shakespeare's *Titus Andronicus* and Kyd's *Spanish Tragedy*, at its height roughly twenty-five years before *Bartholomew Fair* was written. The second paragraph refers disapprovingly to *The Tempest* (1613), first produced shortly before *Bartholomew Fair*. The text is that reprinted in *WS*, vol. 2, from the 1631 edition of Jonson's play (from the play's Induction).]

Hee that will sweare, *Jeronimo*, or *Andronicus* are the best playes, yet, shall passe uncxcepted at,[1] heere, as a man whose Judgement shewes it is constant, and hath stood still, these five and twentie, or thirtie yeeres. . . .

If there bee never a *Servant-monster* i' the Fayre; who can helpe it? he[2] sayes; nor a nest of Antiques?[3] Hee is loth to make Nature afraid[4] in his *Playes*, like those that beget *Tales, Tempests*, and such like *Drolleries*, to mix his head with other mens heeles; let the concupisence of *Jigges* and *Dances*, raigne as strong as it will amongst you.[5]

## Shakespeare's Will (March 25, 1616)

[Shakespeare probably dictated this will sometime around January 1616. The first draft seems to have been dated in January, and 1616 is the most likely inference for the year (see note 1). The final revision was certainly made on the date given, but no clean copy was prepared, so the manuscript contains a substantial number of insertions and deletions. The text here has been silently emended to assist in ease of reading. Deleted passages have been eliminated; the most significant of these is reproduced in the notes, where significant interlineations are also identified. Most of the altered passages, as Chambers writes, simply "correct slips, make the legal terminology more precise, or incorporate afterthoughts." The revision of the will was occasioned chiefly by the February marriage of Shakespeare's daughter Judith. Our text is adapted from E. A. J. Honigmann and Susan Brock, eds., *Playhouse Wills, 1558–1642* (Manchester: Manchester University Press, 1993). For a facsimile and thorough discussion of the will, see *WS* 2:169–80.]

1. Small pieces of artillery, used for firing salutes.
1. Uncriticized.
2. The author.
3. Variant spelling of "antics," grotesque or ludicrous representations, or the actors (such as the clowns in *The Tempest*) playing such parts.
4. Make nature afraid by inexact imitation or too much

fantasy.
5. *concupisence . . . you:* a reference to the dance generally incorporated into theatrical performance (see, for example, Platter's account above). Jonson suggests he is refusing to cater to the vulgar taste for more dancing in plays.

Testamentum willelmij Shackspeare
Vicesimo Quinto die martij Anno Regni Domini nostri Jacobi nunc Regis Anglie &c
decimo quarto & Scotie xlixo Annoque domini 1616[1]
In the name of god Amen I William Shackspeare of Stratford upon Avon in the countie of warrwick gentleman in perfect health & memorie god be praysed doe make &
Ordayne this my last will & testament in manner & forme followeing That ys to saye
ffirst I Comend my Soule into the handes of god my Creator hoping & assuredlie
beleeving through thonelie merittes of Jesus Christe my Saviour to be made partaker
of lyfe everlastinge And my bodye to the Earth whereof yt ys made Item I Gyve &
bequeath unto my Daughter Judyth One Hundred & ffyftie poundes of lawfull English money to be paied unto her in manner & forme followeing That ys to saye One
Hundred Poundes in discharge of her marriage porcion[2] within one yeare after my
Deceas with consideracion[3] after the Rate of twoe shillinges in the pound for soe
long tyme as the same shalbe unpaied unto her after my deceas & the ffyftie poundes
Residewe thereof upon her Surrendring of or gyving of such sufficient securitie as
the overseers of this my Will shall like of to Surrender or graunnte All her[4] estate &
Right that shall discend or come unto her after my deceas or that shee nowe hath of
in or to one Copiehold tenemente with thappurtenaunces lyeing & being in Stratford upon Avon aforesaied in the saied countie of warrwick being parcell or holden
of the mannour of Rowington unto my Daughter Susanna Hall & her heires for ever
Item I Gyve & bequeath unto my saied Daughter Judith One Hundred & ffyftie
Poundes more if shee or Anie issue of her bodie be Lyvinge att thend of three Yeares
next ensueing the daie of the Date of this my Will during which tyme my executours
to paie her consideracion from my deceas according to the Rate afore saied And if
she dye within the saied terme without issue of her bodye then my will ys & I doe
gyve & bequeath One Hundred Poundes thereof to my Neece Elizabeth Hall & the
ffiftie Poundes to be sett fourth by my executours during the lief of my Sister Johane
Harte & the use & proffitt thereof Cominge shalbe payed to my saied Sister Jone &
after her deceas the saied l li[5] shall Remaine Amongst the children of my saied Sister Equallie to be Devided Amongst them But if my saied Daughter Judith be lyving
att thend of the saied three Yeares or anie yssue of her bodye then my Will ys & soe
I devise & bequeath the saied Hundred & ffyftie poundes to be sett out by my executours & overseers for the best benefitt of her & her issue & the stock[6] not to be paied
unto her soe long as she shalbe marryed & Covert Baron[7] but my will ys that she shall
have the consideracon yearelie paied unto her during her lief & after her deceas the
saied stock and consideracion to bee paied to her children if she have Anie & if not
to her executours or assignes she lyving the saied terme after my deceas Provided that
if such husbond as she shall att thend of the saied three Yeares be marryed unto
or attaine after doe sufficientle Assure unto her & thissue of her bodie landes
Awnswereable to the porcion by this my will gyven unto her & to be adjudged soe by
my executours & overseers then my will ys that the saied Cl li[8] shalbe paied to such
husbond as shall make such assurance to his owne use Item I gyve & bequeath unto
my saied sister Jone xx li & all my wearing Apparrell to be paied & Delivered within
one yeare after my deceas And I doe Will & devise unto her the house with thappurtenaunces in Stratford wherein she dwelleth for her naturall lief under the yearelie Rent of xii d. Itm I gyve & bequeath unto her three sonns William Harte[9]

---

1. *Testamentum . . . 1616:* The Will of William
Shakespeare (marginal heading). On the twenty-fifth
day of March, in the fourteenth year of the reign of
our lord James now King of England, etc., and of Scotland the forty-ninth, in the year of our Lord 1616.
(The abbreviation for "January" is crossed out in the
manuscript, "March" having been substituted at the
time the will was revised.)
2. The phrase "in discharge of her marriage porcion"
was inserted during the course of revision.

3. Compensation, or interest.
4. Susanna Hall's. (The preceding "All" marks the
beginning of a new sentence.)
5. *l li:* £50.
6. Principal.
7. *Covert Baron:* under the protection of a husband.
8. *Cl li:* £150.
9. A blank in the manuscript. Shakespeare appears to
have forgotten the name of one of his nephews,
Thomas.

hart & Michaell Harte ffyve poundes A peece to be payed within one Yeare after my deceas[1] Item I gyve & bequeath unto her the saied Elizabeth Hall All my Plate (except my brod silver & gilt bole)[2] that I nowe have att the Date of this my Will Itm I gyve & bequeath unto the Poore of Stratford aforesaied tenn poundes to mr Thomas Combe my Sword to Thomas Russell Esquier ffyve poundes & to ffrauncis Collins of the Borough of Warrwick in the countie of Warrwick gentleman thirteene poundes Sixe shillinges & Eight pence to be paied within one Yeare after my Deceas Itm I gyve & bequeath to Hamlett Sadler xxvi s viii d[3] to buy him A Ringe to William Raynoldes gentleman xxvi s viii d to buy him A Ringe to my godson William Walker xx s in gold to Anthonye Nashe gentleman xxvi s viii d & to mr John Nashe xx vi s viii d & to my fellows John Hemynnges Richard Burbage & Henry Cundell xxvi s viii d A peece to buy them Ringes[4] Item I Gyve Will bequeath & Devise unto my Daughter Susanna Hall for better enabling of her to performe this my will & towardes the performans thereof All that Capitall messuage or tenemente[5] with thappurtenaunces in Stratford aforesaied Called the newe place Wherein I nowe Dwell & twoe messuages or tenementes with thappurtenaunces scituat lyeing & being in Henley streete within the borough of Stratford aforesaied And all my barnes stables Orchardes gardens landes tenementes & hereditamentes[6] Whatsoever scituat lyeing & being or to be had Receyved perceyved or taken within the townes Hamlettes villages ffieldes & groundes of Stratford upon Avon Oldstratford Bushopton & Welcombe or in anie of them in the saied countie of warrwick And alsoe All that Messuage or tememente with thappurtenaunces wherein one John Robinson dwelleth scituat lyeing & being in the blackfriers in London nere the Wardrobe & all other my landes tenementes & hereditamentes Whatsoever To Have & to hold All & singuler the saied premisses with their Appurtenaunces unto the saied Susanna Hall for & During the terme of her naturall lief & after her Deceas to the first sonne of her bodie lawfullic Issueing & to the heires males of the bodie of the saied first Sonne lawfullie Issueinge & for defalt of such issue to the second Sonne of her bodie lawfullie issueinge & to the heires males of the bodie of the saied Second Sonne lawfullie issueinge & for defalt of such heires to the third Sonne of the bodie of the saied Susanna Lawfullie issueing & of the heries males of the bodie of the saied third sonne lawfullic issueing And for defalt of such issue the same soe to be & Remaine to the ffourth ffyfth sixte & Seaventh sonnes of her bodic lawfullie issueing one after Another & to the heires[7] Males of the bodies of the saied ffourth fifth Sixte & Seaventh sonnes lawfullie issueing in such manner as yt ys before Lymitted to be & Remaine to the first second & third Sonns of her bodie & to their heires males And for defalt of such Issue the saied premisses to be & Remaine to my sayed Neece Hall[8] & the heires Males of her bodie Lawfullie yssueing for Defalt of such issue to my Daughter Judith & the heires Males of her bodie lawfullie issueinge And for Defalt of such issue to the Right heires of me the saied William

1. *unto . . . deceas*: this passage was inserted at the top of the second page, probably when the will was revised. The following lines, with which the page originally began, are crossed out in the original: "to be sett out for her within one Yeare after my Deceas by my executours with thadvise & direccions of my overseers for her best proffitt untill her Marriage & then the same with the increase thereof to be paied unto her." These lines evidently referred to Judith Shakespeare as unmarried.
2. This parenthetical clause is an insertion, and has sparked some debate about Shakespeare's opinion of Judith's marriage.
3. The "s" stands for "shillings," the "d" for "pence."
4. *to my fellows . . . Ringes*: Shakespeare's "fellows," or colleagues, Heminges, Burbage, and Condell, had worked with him in the Lord Chamberlain's Men and

King's Men for many years. Many other wills and documents of the period provide evidence of the practice of wearing mourning rings alluded to here.
5. Residence. *messuage*: dwelling house with its outbuildings or adjoining lands.
6. Heritable property.
7. In addition to the signature near the end, Shakespeare signed the will here, in the bottom right-hand corner of the second page.
8. Susanna Hall's daughter Elizabeth, actually Shakespeare's granddaughter (the sense of "niece" is less restricted in early modern usage). Elizabeth proved to be Susanna's only surviving child, and since Susanna was already thirty-three in 1616, the hypothetical series of seven sons preceding this mention of Elizabeth is doubly remarkable.

Shackspere for ever Itm I gyve unto my wief my second best bed[9] with the furniture Item I gyve & bequeath to my saied Daughter Judith my broad silver gilt bole
All the Rest of my goodes Chattelles Leases plate Jewels & household stuffe
Whatsoever after my dettes and Legasies paied & my funerall expences discharged
I gyve Devise & bequeath to my Sonne in Lawe John Hall gentleman & my Daughter Susanna his wief Whom I ordaine & make executours of this my Last Will &
testament And I doe intreat & Appoint the saied Thomas Russell Esquier &
ffrauncis Collins gentleman to be overseers hereof And doe Revoke All former
wills & publishe this to be my last Will & testament In Witnes Whereof I have here
unto put my hand the Daie & Yeare first above Written. /                    By me
William Shakespeare witnes to the publishing hereof Fra: Collyns Julyus Shawe
John Robinson Hamnet Sadler Robert Whattcott[1]

## Front Matter from the First Folio of Shakespeare's Plays (1623)

[John Heminges and Henry Condell, friends and colleagues of Shakespeare, organized
this first publication of his collected (thirty-six) plays. Eighteen of the plays had not
appeared in print before, and for these the First Folio is the sole surviving source. Only
*Pericles, The Two Noble Kinsmen,* and *Sir Thomas More* are not included in the volume.
Four of the first twelve (printed) pages of the Folio are reproduced below in reduced facsimile. They include Jonson's brief address "To the Reader," Droeshout's portrait of
Shakespeare, a table of contents, and a list of actors.]

9. This bequest to Shakespeare's wife, Anne, was
inserted in the course of his revision of the will. She
is not mentioned elsewhere in the will at least partly
because, as Shakespeare's widow, she would be guaranteed a certain portion of the estate by law. The
appearance of this inserted bequest is nevertheless
strange enough to have evoked much speculation.
1. After Shakespeare's death, the will was endorsed
here at the bottom of the third page with a Latin
inscription indicating that the will had gone to pro-
bate before a magistrate on June 22, 1616.

# To the Reader.

This Figure, that thou here feeſt put,
    It vvas for gentle Shakeſpeare cut;
Wherein the Grauer had a ſtrife
    with Nature, to out-doo the life :
O, could he but haue dravvne his vvit
    As well in braſſe, as he hath hit
His face, the Print vvould then ſurpaſſe
    All, that vvas euer vvrit in braſſe.
But, ſince he cannot, Reader, looke
    Not on his Picture, but his Booke.

B. I.

Mr. William
SHAKESPEARES
COMEDIES,
HISTORIES, &
TRAGEDIES.

Published according to the True Originall Copies.

Martin Droeshout sculpsit London.

*LONDON*
Printed by Isaac Iaggard, and Ed. Blount. 1623.

# A CATALOGVE

of the ſeuerall Comedies, Hiſtories, and Tragedies contained in this Volume.

# The Workes of William Shakespeare,

## containing all his Comedies, Histories, and
### Tragedies: Truely set forth, according to their first
#### ORIGINALL.

## The Names of the Principall Actors
### in all these Playes.

*William Shakespeare.*

*Richard Burbadge.*

*John Hemmings.*

*Augustine Phillips.*

*William Kempt.*

*Thomas Poope.*

*George Bryan.*

*Henry Condell.*

*William Slye.*

*Richard Cowly.*

*John Lowine.*

*Samuell Crosse.*

*Alexander Cooke.*

*Samuel Gilburne.*

*Robert Armin.*

*William Ostler.*

*Nathan Field.*

*John Underwood.*

*Nicholas Tooley.*

*William Ecclestone.*

*Joseph Taylor.*

*Robert Benfield.*

*Robert Goughe.*

*Richard Robinson.*

*Iohn Shancke.*

*Iohn Rice.*

# John Milton on Shakespeare (1630)

[John Milton (1608–1674) was born in London and as a boy might conceivably have seen Shakespeare's company act. This poem first appeared prefixed to the Second Folio of Shakespeare's works in 1632 and again in the 1640 *Poems* of Shakespeare. The text is from the 1645 edition of Milton's *Poems*, as reprinted in *WS*, vol. 2, but the title given is from the Second Folio version.]

## An Epitaph on the admirable Dramaticke Poet, W. Shakespeare

What needs my *Shakespear* for his honour'd Bones,
The labour of an age in piled Stones,
Or that his hallow'd reliques should be hid
Under a star-ypointing[1] *Pyramid?*
Dear son of memory, great heir of Fame,
What need'st thou such weak witnes of thy name?
Thou in our wonder and astonishment
Hast built thy self a live-long Monument.
For whilst toth' shame of slow-endeavouring art,
They easie numbers flow, and that each heart
Hath from the leaves of thy unvalu'd[2] Book,
Those Delphick[3] lines with deep impression took,
Then thou our fancy of itself bereaving,[4]
Dost make us Marble with too much conceaving;
And so Sepulcher'd in such pomp dost lie,
That Kings for such a Tomb would wish to die.

# Ben Jonson on Shakespeare (1623–37)

[In addition to numerous allusions to Shakespeare in his plays, Ben Jonson (1573–1637) writes explicitly about his friend, colleague, and rival in a number of places, most significantly in the two commendatory poems prefixed to the First Folio (see above) and in the published extracts from his notebooks entitled *Timber: or, Discoveries; Made upon Men and Matter*, first published in his *Works* of 1640. It is impossible to date the original entries precisely; Chambers's conjecture is that the following entry on Shakespeare was made after 1630. The text is from the authoritative edition by C. H. Herford and Percy Simpson, vol. 8 (Oxford: Clarendon Press, 1952).]

*Indeed,* the multitude commend Writers, as they doe Fencers, or Wrastlers; who if they come in robustiously, and put for it, with a deale of violence, are received for the *braver-fellowes:* when many times their owne rudenesse is a cause of their disgrace; and a slight touch of their Adversary, gives all that boisterous force the foyle. But in these things, the unskilfull are naturally deceiv'd, and judging wholly by the bulke, thinke rude things greater then polish'd; and scatter'd more numerous, then compos'd: Nor thinke this only to be true in the sordid multitude, but the neater sort of our *Gallants:* for all are the multitude; only they differ in cloaths, not in judgement or understanding.

*I remember,* the Players have often mentioned it as an honour to *Shakespeare,*

---

1. Pointing to the stars.
2. Invaluable.
3. Reference to Apollo, god of poetry, whose most famous shrine was at Delphi.

4. *our . . . bereaving:* "our imaginations are rapt 'out of ourselves,' leaving behind our soulless bodies like statues"—Isabel MacCaffrey.

that in his writing, (whatsoever he penn'd) hee never blotted out line.[1] My answer hath beene, Would he had blotted a thousand. Which they thought a malevolent speech. [I had not told posterity this,] but for their ignorance, who choose that circumstance to commend their friend by, wherein he most faulted. And to justifie mine owne candor, (for I lov'd the man, and doe honour his memory (on this side Idolatry) as much as any.) Hee was (indeed) honest, and of an open, and free nature: had an excellent *Phantsie*[2]; brave notions, and gentle expressions: wherein hee flow'd with that facility, that sometime it was necessary he should be stop'd: *Sufflaminandus erat;*[3] as *Augustus* said of *Haterius.*[4] His wit was in his owne power; would the rule of it had beene so too. Many times hee fell into those things, could not escape laughter: As when hee said in the person of *Cæsar*, one speaking to him; *Cæsar, thou dost me wrong.* Hee replyed: *Cæsar did never wrong, but with just cause*[5]: and such like; which were ridiculous. But hee redeemed his vices, with his vertues. There was ever more in him to be praysed, then to be pardoned.

# John Aubrey on Shakespeare (1681)

[What Chambers calls "the Shakespeare-mythos" was already well under way by the time John Aubrey (1626–1697) collected these anecdotes for the biographies in his *Brief Lives*, first anthologized in 1692. Aubrey's chief sources were prominent figures of the Restoration stage, which had seen increasingly popular revivals and adaptations of *Hamlet, The Tempest*, and many other plays of Shakespeare. Numerous actors and critics in the latter part of the seventeenth century helped to "rehabilitate" Shakespeare; if at the time of the Restoration his plays had seemed terribly musty and old-fashioned, by the 1680s his reputation as an author of lasting value was well established, thanks to the enthusiasm of Restoration playgoers. Aubrey's first source, Christopher Beeston, was the son of a one-time member of Shakespeare's company. William Davenant was a formidable entrepreneur as well as a dramatist, and Thomas Shadwell a prolific playwright perhaps best remembered as Dryden's King of Dullness. The text is from Chambers's transcription (*WS*, vol. 2), with a few silent emendations for ease of reading. Some of the material is from the published version of *Brief Lives*, and some of it from manuscript notes apparently used in writing the *Lives*.]

> the more to be admired q[uia][1] he was not a company keeper[2]
> lived in Shoreditch, wouldnt be debauched, & if invited to
> writ; he was in paine.[3]
>
> W. Shakespeare.

M[r]. William Shakespear. [*bay-wreath in margin*] was borne at Stratford upon Avon, in the County of Warwick; his father was a Butcher, & I have been told heretofore by some of the neighbours, that when he was a boy he exercised his father's Trade, but when he kill'd a Calfe, he would doe it in a *high style*, & make a Speech. There was at that time another Butcher's son in this Towne, that was held not at all inferior to him for a naturall witt, his acquaintance & coetanean,[4] but dyed young. This Wm. being inclined naturally to Poetry and acting, came to London I guesse about 18. and was an Actor at one of the Play-houses and did act

1. Compare Heminges and Condell's address to the reader in the First Folio: "And what he thought, he uttered with that easinesse, that wee have scarse received from him a blot in his papers."
2. Imagination.
3. "He needed the drag-chain" (adapted from Marcus Seneca's *Controversiae* 4, Preface).
4. Quintus Haterius, Roman rhetorician (d. 26 c.e.).
5. See *Julius Caesar* 3.1.47.

1. Because.
2. "Company keeper" can mean "libertine" or "reveler"; the general sense of the passage is that Shakespeare is "the more to be admired" for his temperance and modesty.
3. The embarrassment ("paine") at being asked to write is presumably due to the same alleged modesty.
4. Contemporary.

exceedingly well: now B. Johnson was never a good Actor, but an excellent Instructor. He began early to make essayes at Dramatique Poetry, which at that time was very lowe; and his Playes tooke well: He was a handsome well shap't man: very good company, and of a very readie and pleasant smooth Witt. The Humour[5] of . . . the Constable in a Midsomersnight's Dreame, he happened to take at Grendon [*In margin*, 'I thinke it was Midsomer night that he happened to lye there'.] in Bucks[6] which is the roade from London to Stratford, and there was living that Constable about 1642 when I first came to Oxon.[7] M[r]. Jos. Howe is of that parish and knew him. Ben Johnson and he did gather Humours of men dayly where ever they came. One time as he was at the Tavern at Stratford super[8] Avon, one Combes an old rich Usurer was to be buryed, he makes there this extemporary[9] Epitaph

> Ten in the Hundred[1] the Devill allowes
> But *Combes* will have twelve, he sweares & vowes:
> If any one askes who lies in this Tombe:
> Hoh! quoth the Devill, 'Tis my John o' Combe.

He was wont to goe to his native Country once a yeare. I thinke I have been told that he left 2 or 300[li] per annum[2] there and therabout: to a sister. [*In margin*, 'V.[3] his Epitaph in Dugdales Warwickshire'.] I have heard S[r] Wm. Davenant and M[r]. Thomas Shadwell (who is counted the best Comœdian we have now) say, that he had a most prodigious Witt, and did admire his naturall parts beyond all other Dramaticall writers. He was wont to say, That he never blotted out a line in his life: sayd Ben: Johnson, I wish he had blotted out a thousand. [*In margin*, 'B. Johnsons Underwoods'.] His Comœdies will remaine witt, as long as the English tongue is understood; for that he handles mores hominum;[4] now our present writers reflect so much upon particular persons, and coxcombeities, that 20 yeares hence, they will not be understood. Though as Ben: Johnson sayes of him, that he had but little Latine and lesse Greek, He understood Latine pretty well: for he had been in his younger yeares a Schoolmaster in the Countrey. [*In margin*, 'from M[r] —— Beeston'.]

S[r] William Davenant Knight Poet Laureate was borne in _____ street in the City of Oxford, at the Crowne Tavern. His father was John Davenant a Vintner there, a very grave and discreet Citizen: his mother was a very beautifull woman, & of a very good witt and of conversation extremely agreable. . . . M[r] William Shakespeare was wont to goe into Warwickshire once a yeare, and did commonly in his journey lye at this house in Oxon: where he was exceedingly respected. I have heard parson Robert D[avenant] say that here M[r] W. Shakespeare here gave him a hundred ..lsses. Now S[r] Wm. would sometimes when he was pleasant over a glasse of wine with his most intimate friends e.g. Sam: Butler (author of Hudibras) &c. say, that it seemed to him that he writt with the very spirit that Shakespeare,[5] and seemed contented enough to be thought his Son: he would tell them the story as above. in which way his mother had a very light report, whereby she was called a whore.

---

5. Character, personality.
6. Buckinghamshire.
7. Oxford.
8. Upon.
9. Extemporaneous.
1. 10-percent interest. (Combe is damned because he charges 12 percent on his loans, 2 percent above the maximum allowed for usury not to be a mortal sin.)
2. £300 a year.
3. See.
4. *for that . . . hominum*: because he treats of (general) human manners or customs.
5. A word such as "had" seems to be missing.

# TIMELINE

| TEXT | CONTEXT |
|---|---|
| | **1558**   Queen Mary I, a Roman Catholic, dies; her sister Elizabeth, raised Protestant, is proclaimed queen. |
| | **1559**   Church of England is reestablished under the authority of the sovereign with the passage of the Act of Uniformity and the Act of Supremacy. |
| **1562**   *The Tragedy of Gorboduc*, by Thomas Norton and Thomas Sackville, is performed; it is the first English play in blank verse. | **1563**   The Church of England adopts the Thirty-nine Articles of Religion, detailing its points of doctrine and clarifying its differences both from Roman Catholicism and from more extreme forms of Protestantism. |
| | **1564**   William Shakespeare is born in Stratford to John and Mary Arden Shakespeare; he is christened a few days later, on April 23. |
| | **1565**   John Shakespeare is made an alderman of Stratford. |
| | **1567**   Mary Queen of Scots is imprisoned on suspicion of the murder of her husband, Lord Darnley. Their infant son, Charles James, is crowned James VI of Scotland. |
| | **1568**   John Shakespeare is elected Bailiff of Stratford, the town's highest office. Performances in Stratford by the Queen's Players and the Earl of Worcester's men. |
| | **1572**   An act is passed that severely punishes vagrants and wanderers, including actors not affiliated with a patron. Performances in Stratford by the Earl of Leicester's men. |
| | **1574**   The Earl of Warwick's and Earl of Worcester's men perform in Stratford. |
| | **1576**   James Burbage, father of Richard, later the leading actor in Shakespeare's company, builds the Theatre in Shoreditch, a suburb of London. |
| | **1577**   The Curtain Theatre opens in Shoreditch. |

| TEXT | CONTEXT |
|---|---|
| | **1577–1580** Sir Francis Drake circumnavigates the globe. |
| | **1578** Mary Shakespeare pawns her lands, suggesting that the family is in financial distress. Lord Strange's Men and Lord Essex's Men perform at Stratford. |
| | **1580** A Jesuit mission is established in England with the aim of reconverting the nation to Roman Catholicism. |
| | **1582** Shakespeare marries Anne Hathaway. |
| | **1583** The birth of Shakespeare's older daughter, Susanna. |
| | **1584** Sir Walter Ralegh establishes the first English colony in the New World at Roanoke Island in modern North Carolina; the colony fails. |
| | **1585** The birth of Shakespeare's twin son and daughter, Hamnet and Judith. John Shakespeare is fined for not going to church |
| | **1586** Sir Philip Sidney dies from battle wounds. |
| **1587** Thomas Kyd's *The Spanish Tragedy* (pub. c. 1592) and Christopher Marlowe's *Tamburlaine* (pub. 1590) are performed. | **1587** Mary Queen of Scots is executed for treason against Elizabeth I. Francis Drake defeats the Spanish fleet at Cádiz. John Shakespeare loses his position as an alderman. Philip Henslowe builds the Rose theater at Bankside, on the Thames. |
| | **1588** The Spanish Armada attempts an invasion of England but is defeated. |
| **1589** Robert Greene, *Friar Bacon and Friar Bungay.* Thomas Kyd, *Hamlet* (not extant; perhaps a source for Shakespeare's *Hamlet*). Christopher Marlowe, *The Jew of Malta.* | **1589** Shakespeare is probably affiliated with the amalgamated Lord Strange's and Lord Admiral's Men from about this time until 1594. |
| **1590** Anonymous, *The True Chronicle History of King Leir, and his Three Daughters.* | **1590** James VI of Scotland marries Anne of Denmark, but believes himself to be bewitched on his honeymoon when he cannot consummate the marriage. Witch trials in Scotland. |
| **1591** Shakespeare's *1, 2,* and *3 Henry VI* performed. | **1592** The theatrical manager of the Admiral's Men, Philip Henslowe, begins his diary, continued until 1604, recording his business |

| TEXT | CONTEXT |
|---|---|
| | transactions, an important source for theater historians. |
| **1592–1593** *Richard III.*<br>*Venus and Adonis.*<br>*The Comedy of Errors.*<br>*Titus Andronicus.*<br>*The Taming of the Shrew.* | From June 1592 to June 1594, London theaters are shut down because of the plague; acting companies tour the provinces. |
| **1594** Shakespeare dedicates *The Rape of Lucrece* to Henry Wriothesley, Earl of Southampton. | **1594** Roderigo Lopez, Portuguese physician and a Jewish convert to Christianity, is executed on slight evidence for having plotted to poison Elizabeth I. |
| **1594–1596** *A Midsummer Night's Dream.*<br>*Richard II.*<br>*Romeo and Juliet.* | The birth of James VI's first son, Henry.<br><br>**1595** Shakespeare lives in St. Helen's Parish, Bishopsgate, London.<br>Shakespeare apparently becomes a sharer in (provides capital for) the newly re-formed Lord Chamberlain's Men.<br>The Swan Theatre is built in Bankside.<br>Hugh O'Neill, Earl of Tyrone, rebels against English rule in Ireland.<br>Walter Ralegh explores Guiana, on the north coast of South America. |
| **1596** *King John.*<br>*The Merchant of Venice.*<br>*1 Henry IV.* | **1596** John Shakespeare is granted a coat of arms; hence the title of "gentleman."<br>William Shakespeare's son Hamnet dies. |
| **1597** *The Merry Wives of Windsor.* | **1597** James Burbage builds the second Blackfriars Theatre. But the Lord Chamberlain's Men are not permitted to play in it, so they rent it to boys' companies for a number of years.<br>The landlord refuses to renew the lease on the land under the Theatre in Shoreditch. |
| **1598** *2 Henry IV.*<br>*Much Ado About Nothing.*<br>Ben Jonson, *Every Man in His Humor,* which lists Shakespeare as one of the actors. | **1598** The Edict of Nantes ends the French civil wars, granting toleration to Protestants.<br>Materials from the demolished Theatre in Shoreditch are transported across the Thames to be used in building the Globe Theatre. |
| **1599** *Henry V.*<br>*Julius Caesar.*<br>*As You Like it.* | **1599** The queen's favorite, Robert Devereux, Earl of Essex, leads an expedition to Ireland in March but returns home without permission in October and is imprisoned.<br>Satires and other offensive books are prohibited by ecclesiastical order. Extant copies are gathered and burned. Two notorious satirists, Thomas Nashe and Gabriel Harvey, are forbidden to publish. |

| TEXT | CONTEXT |
|---|---|
| **1600** *Hamlet.* Michael Drayton and several collaborators, who object to Shakespeare's depiction of Oldcastle-Falstaff in the *Henry IV* plays, write *The First Part of the True and Honorable History of the Life of Sir John Oldcastle, the Good Lord Cobham.* | **1600** The Earl of Essex is suspended from some of his offices and confined to house arrest. The birth of James VI's second son, Charles. The founding of the East India Company. Edward Alleyn and Philip Henslowe build the Fortune Theatre for the Lord Admiral's Men, competing with the Lord Chamberlain's Men at the Globe. |
| **1601** "The Phoenix and the Turtle" published in Robert Chester's *Love's Martyr.* *Twelfth Night.* In the "War of the Theaters," Ben Jonson, John Marston, and Thomas Dekker write a series of satiric plays mocking one another. | **1601** The Earl of Essex leads some gentlemen against Elizabeth I, but the rising is quickly quelled. A few of the rebels, including Shakespeare's patron, the Earl of Southampton, arrange a staging of *Richard II* at the Globe, apparently to incite rebellion. Essex is convicted of treason and beheaded. Shakespeare's father dies. |
| **1602** *Troilus and Cressida.* | **1602** Shakespeare makes substantial real-estate purchases in Stratford. The opening of the Bodleian Library in Oxford. |
| | **1603** Queen Elizabeth dies; she is succeeded by her cousin, James VI of Scotland (now James I of England). Shakespeare's name appears for the last time in Ben Jonson's lists of actors, as a "principal tragedian" in *Sejanus.* Plague closes the London theaters from mid-1603 to April 1604. Hugh O'Neill surrenders in Ireland. |
| **1604** *Measure for Measure.* *Othello.* | **1604** The conclusion of a peace with Spain makes travel across the Atlantic safer, encouraging plans for English colonies in the Americas. |
| **1605** *All's Well That Ends Well.* *King Lear.* | **1605** The discovery of the Gunpowder Plot by some radical Catholics to blow up the Houses of Parliament during its opening ceremonies, when the royal family, Lords, and Commons are assembled in one place. The Red Bull Theatre built. |
| **1606** *Macbeth.* *Antony and Cleopatra.* Ben Jonson, *Volpone.* Anonymous, *The Revenger's Tragedy.* | **1606** The London and Plymouth Companies receive charters to colonize Virginia. Parliament passes "An Act to Restrain Abuses of Players," prohibiting oaths or blasphemy onstage. |
| **1607** *Timon of Athens.* *Pericles.* | **1607** An English colony is established in Jamestown, Virginia. Shakespeare's daughter Susanna marries John Hall. Shakespeare's brother Edmund (described as a player) dies. |

| TEXT | CONTEXT |
|---|---|
| 1608  *Coriolanus.* | 1608  The King's Men obtain permission to play at the second Blackfriars Theatre, a smaller indoor venue. |
| 1609  *Cymbeline.*<br>Unauthorized publication of the sonnets. | |
| 1610  *The Winter's Tale.*<br>Ben Jonson, *The Alchemist.* | 1610  Henry is made Prince of Wales.<br>Shakespeare probably returns to Stratford and settles there. |
| 1611  *The Tempest.*<br>Francis Beaumont and John Fletcher,<br>  *A King and No King.*<br>Publication of the Authorized (King James)<br>  Bible. | 1611  Plantation of Ulster in Ireland, a colony of English and Scottish Protestants settled on land confiscated from Irish rebels. |
| 1612  *All Is True (Henry VIII)*, with<br>  John Fletcher.<br>John Webster, *The White Devil.* | 1612  Prince Henry dies. |
| 1613  *The Two Noble Kinsmen,*<br>  with John Fletcher. | 1613  Princess Elizabeth marries Frederick V, Elector Palatine.<br>The Globe Theatre burns down during a performance of *All Is True.* |
| 1614  Ben Jonson, *Bartholomew Fair.*<br>John Webster, *The Duchess of Malfi.* | 1614  Philip Henslowe and Jacob Meade build the Hope Theatre, used both for play performances and as a bearbaiting arena.<br>The Globe Theatre reopens. |
| 1616  Ben Jonson publishes *The Works of Benjamin Jonson,* the first collection of plays by an English author. | 1616  William Harvey describes the circulation of the blood.<br>Shakespeare's daughter Judith marries.<br>Shakespeare dies on April 23. |
| 1623  Members of the King's Men publish the First Folio of Shakespeare's plays. | |

# Textual Variants

CONTROL TEXT: Q1

Q1: The Quarto of 1609
Q2: The Quarto of 1609
Q3: The Quarto of 1611
Q4: The Quarto of 1619
Q5: The Quarto of 1630
Q6: The Quarto of 1635
Qa, Qb: Successive states of Q1 incorporating various print-shop corrections and changes
PA: George Wilkins, THE Painfull Aduentures of *Pericles* Prince of Tyre. *Being* The true History of the Play of *Pericles*, as it was lately presented by the worthy and ancient Poet *Iohn Gower*

Title: Pericles, Prynce of Tyre [Stationers' Register entry] THE LATE, / And much admired Play, / Called / Pericles, Prince of Tyre. / With the true Relation of the whole Historie, / aduentures, and fortunes of the said Prince: / As also, / The no lesse strange, and worthy accidents, / in the Birth and Life, of his Daughter / *MARIANA*. [Q1 title page] The Play of Pericles / Prince of Tyre. &c. [Q1 head title] *The Play of Pericles Prince of Tyre* [Q1 running titles]
Scene 1 [not in Q1; see note to Scene 1] 6 holy-ales Holydayes 11 these [Q2] those 17 This' This 21 fere Peere 29 By But 30 account' account'd 39 a wight of wight 42 s.d. *lords and peers in their richest ornaments* [PA] *fellowers* 50 Fit for th' For 54 In her their best perfections to knit To knit in her, their best perfections 60 razed racte 67 boundless bondlesse 73 heav'n-like face face like Heauen 79 semblants semblance bloodless pale 83 From For 99 s.p. ANTIOCHUS [not in Q1] s.d. *He . . . riddle* [not in Q1] which the tyrant receiuing with an angry brow, threw downe the Riddle [PA] 102 'sayed sayd 107 s.d. *He . . . riddle* [not in Q1] which the Prince taking vp, read aloude [PA] 113 this [PA] they 139 like is like 152 He's he ha's 154 our your 156 cancel counsell 163 your worth and our degree our honour and your worth 170 you're you 171 uncomely vntimely 179 'schew shew 186 the which which 194–95 And . . . your And our minde pertakes her priuat actions, / To your secrecie; and for your 202 s.d. *hastily* [PA; not in Q1]

204 Your majesty My Lord 205 after; like after, and like 208 it be to say thou say 209 Your majesty [not in Q1] 210–11 If . . . highness My Lord, if I can get him within my Pistols length, Ile make him sure enough, so farewell to your highnesse. [prose] 212 s.p. ANTIOCHUS [Q4; not in Q1]
Scene 2 [not in Q1] s.d. *distempered* [not in Q1] Princes distemperature [PA] 3 Be my By me 7 feared, 's fearde is 10 care's author's the others 20 honour him honour 25 th'ostent the stint 30 am once 33 s.d. *among them old* HELICANUS [not in Q1] olde [PA, describing Helicanus] 37–42 You . . . contradict it [not in Q1] he did not wel so to abuse himselfe, to waste his body there with pyning sorrow, vpon whose safety depended the liues and proserity of a whole kingdome, that it was ill in him to doe it, and no lesse in his counsell to suffer him, without contradicting it [PA; Helicanus to Pericles] 46 wind sparke 49 a [not in Q1] 55 Helicane *Hellicans* 59 brows face 63 you but [Q4] but you 64 s.d. *lifting him up* [PA; not in Q1] 65 for it [Q4] fort the heav'ns heauē 68 mak'st makes 70 you you your selfe 75 Where, as [Q2] Whereas 78 As children are heav'n's blessings: to parents, objects [not in Q1] 86 of of a 88 me [not in Q1] 89 fears feare 91 doubt—as doubt no doubt doo't, as no doubt 105 grieve griue for 113 Or or til the 117 in my absence wrong thy liberties wrong my liberties in my absence 120 Tarsus *Thursus* 126 sure crack cracke 127 we'll will
Scene 3 [not in Q1] 2–3 and am caught . . . but if I do it [not in Q1] 10–40 You . . . Tyre [prose in Q1] 11 question question mee 21 lest that he lest hee 27 King's ears it Kings seas 28 on the seas at the Sea 30 Lord Thaliart am I, of Antioch [not in Q1] 31 s.p. HELICANUS [Q4; not in Q1] of Antioch from *Antiochus* 32 King Antiochus him 35 lord's Lord has betoke [Q2] betake 36 Now my now 37 enquire desire
Scene 4 [not in Q1] 8 they're they are midges' mischiefs 13 our sorrows and sorrowes 15 lungs toungs 17 helps helpers 20 As you think best Ile doe my best 22 o'er on 23 the [Q3] her 34 Those These 36 they [Q2] thy 39 two summers [PA] too sauers 47 Here weeping stands a lord, there lies a lady dying Heere stands a Lord,

and there a Ladie weeping; heere standes one weeping, and there lies another dying [PA] **54 heed** heare **55 s.d.** *fainting . . . slowly* a fainting messenger came slowely into them [PA] **57 thou** [Q4] thee **58 t'expect** to expect **64 neighbour** [PA] neighbouring **66 Hath** That these the **68 men** mee **72 not** not as **73 him's** himnes **77 grave's** grounds **79 whence he comes.** whence he comes, and what he craues? **82 s.d.** the LORD *again conducting* [not in Q1] he demaunded of the fellow where the Gouernour was, and foorthwith to be conducted to him [PA] **87–88 Since entering your unshut gates have witnessed / The widowed desolation** And seene the desolation; Pericles . . . no sooner entred into their unshut gates, but his princely eies were partaking witnesses of their widowed desolation [PA] **89 hearts** teares **92 fraught** stuft; fraughted [PA] **93 importing** expecting **96 s.p. ALL OF TARSUS** *Omnes.* **s.d.** *falling . . . weeping* [not in Q1] the feeble soules . . . fell on their knees, and wept [PA] **99 me, my selfe,** our **104 ne'er** neare

Scene 5 [not in Q1] **4 Prove** That Will prove **11 Tarsus** *Tharstill* **12 speken** spoken **14 His statue build** Build his Statue **17 Helicane** [Q3] *Helicon* **19 for that** for though **22 Sent word** Sau'd one **24 hid intent to murden** hid in Tent to murdred [Qa] had intent to murder [Qb] **25 Tarsus** *Tharsis* **27 deeming** doing **36 aught** ought **51 s.d.** *two poor* three; pore Fishermen [PA; in this edition, the Third Fisherman enters after the first two.] **52 s.p. MASTER I.**; the maister Fisherman [PA; changed throughout, except at line 80, where "I." is changed to "THIRD FISHERMAN"] **What ho, Pilch** What, to pelch **54 s.d. He . . . repair** [not in Q1] certayne *Fishermen . . .* were come out from their homely cottages to dry and repaire their nettes [PA] **56–72, 74–75, 77–81, 83–84, 90–92, 93–94, 99–101, 123, 136–37, 139–40, 144–47, 152–54, 195–97** [verse in Q1] **70 devours** deuowre **77 s.p. THIRD FISHERMAN** [Q4] 3. FISHER-MAN I. **110 crave** aske **112 pray** [Q4] pray you **113 quotha** ke-tha an and **114 s.d. To . . . ground** the chiefe of these fishermen . . . lifting him vp from the ground [PA] **116 holidays** all day **117 moreo'er** more; or **123 an** and **124 all your** you **128–30 beadle. MASTER** Thine office, knave— SECOND FISHERMAN Is to draw up the other nets. I'll go Beadle: But Maister, Ile goe draw vp the Net; goe dragge vp some other nettes [PA; the Master commanding his servants—hence, this edition introduces an interjection by the Master into the Second Fisherman's speech.] **133 s.d.** *seating . . . Pericles* [not in Q1] the maister . . . seated

himselfe by him [PA] **136 is** [Q2] I **141–42 from his subjects / He gains** he gaines from / His subjects **144 some half** [PA] halfe **148 Were but** [PA] Were answerable [PA] equall **151 get himself** get for with for **153 s.d. Before . . . prize** [not in Q1] before helpe came, vp came the Fish expected, but prooued indeede to be a rusty armour. [PA] **155 pray** [Qb] pary [Qa] **156 thy** [not in Q1] all her crosses [PA] **157 losses** selfe **164 forfend, the same may** protect thee, Fame may **169 in 's** [Q4] in his **176 with't** with it **180 learned** [PA] borne **185 this** them **187 I'm** I am **188 rapture** rupture **191 delightsome** delight **193 friends** friend **198 equal** a Goale

Scene 6 [not in Q1] **s.d.** *and sit on two thrones* [not in Q1] They thus seated [PA] **4 daughter** daughter heere **8 my** my royall **13 renown** Renownes **14 office** honour **16 s.d.** *richly . . . THAISA* [not in Q1] richly armed, their Pages before them bearing their Deuices on their shields being by the knights Page deliuered to the Lady [PA; repeated for each knight in this edition] **21 s.d. She . . . KING** [not in Q1] from her presented to the King her father [PA; repeated for each knight in this edition] **22 s.d.** [See note to 6.16.] **26 An armèd** Is an Armed **27 thus** thus in Spanish **Piùe per dolcezza che per forza** *Pue Per doleera kee per forsa* **s.d.** [See note to 6.21.] **28 You . . . force** [not in Q1] more by lenitie than by force [PA] **s.d.** [See note to 6.16.] **29 what's** [Q4] with **31 pompae** *Pompey; pompa* [PA] **s.d.** [See note to 6.21.] **32–33 Desire . . . enterprise** [not in Q1] desire of renowne drew him to this enterprise [PA] **33 s.d.** [See note to 6.16.] **34 A knight of Athens bearing** [not in Q1] The fift of *Athens,* and his Deuice was [PA] **36 s.d.** [See note to 6.21.] **37 this** his **38 s.d.** [See note to 6.16.] **39 And who the fifth?** [not in Q1] **39–40 a prince of Corinth / Presents** [not in Q1] a prince of *Corinth* [PA] **43 So . . . into** [PA; not in Q1] **s.d. PERICLES . . . THAISA** [not in Q1] The sixt and last was *Pericles,* Prince of *Tyre,* who hauing neither Page to deliuer his shield, nor shield to deliuer . . . Himselfe with a most gracefull curtesie presented it vnto her . . . being himselfe in a rusty Armour [PA] **45 delivereth** deliuered **49 From** A pretty morrall frō **54 T'have** To haue **56 Unto** To **60 for** by

Scene 7 [not in Q1] **s.d.** *A stately banquet is brought in* [not in Q1] a most stately banquet [PA] *a* MARSHAL *conducting* [not in Q1] by the Kings Marshall conducted [PA] **1 to the KNIGHTS** To say Knights, to say **2 To I** 7 **You're** You are **11 yours** [Q4] your **13 artists** an Artist **15 You are** And you are **24**

**Envied** Enuies **25 s.d. PERICLES . . . THAISA** placed directly ouer-against where the king and his daughter sate [*PA* (said of Pericles)] **27 distaste** resist but not **29 I am amazed** [not in Q1] **34 broke** broken **36 Yon** [Q2] You **37 me** [Q4; not in Q1] **what that 42 son's** sonne a like a **48 s.p. THE OTHER KNIGHTS** *Knights* **49 stored** stur'd **50 you do** [Q4] do you **full** fill **51 s.p. THE OTHER KNIGHTS** *Knight.* **59 so doing** doing so **like** like to **61 entertain** entraunce **62 bear** say wee drinke **69 Furthermore** And furthermore **know** know of him **71–72 THAISA The King . . . Wishing** *Tha.* The king my father (sir) has drunke to you / *Peri.* I thanke him / *Tha.* Wishing **79 unconstant** [not in Q1] and vnconstant [*PA*] **79–80 bereft / Unfortunately** both reft [Q1] most vnfortunately bereft both [*PA*] **83–84 seeking adventures / Was** [not in Q1] **83 84 A gentleman . . . seas** A Gentleman of *Tyre*: who onely by misfortune of the seas **84 solely** onely **86 mishaps** misfortune **87 s.d.–95 SIMONIDES . . . accept** [not in Q1] Which mishaps of his the king vnderstanding of, hee was strucke with present pitty to him, and rising from his state, he came foorthwith and imbraced him, bade him be cheered, and tolde him, that whatsoeuer misfortune had impayred him of, fortune, by his helpe, could repayre to him, for both himselfe and Countrey should be his friendes, and presently calling for a goodly milke white Steede, and a payre of golden spurres, them first hee bestowed vppon him, telling him, they were the prises due to his merite, and ordained for that dayes enterprise: which kingly curtesie Pericles as thankefully accepting. Much time beeing spent in daancing and other reuells [*PA*] **99 Your limbs will** Will **104 Come** Come sir **105 sir, that the** you **112 Lights, pages, to** Pages and lights to **114 should** [not in Q1] **116 s.p. KING SIMONIDES** [Q3; not in Q1, where the speech continues as Pericles']

**Scene 8** [not in Q1] **4 hold** with-hold **9 both apparelled all in jewels** [*PA*; not in Q1] **11 Their** those **13 hands** hand **29 step** breath **33 death indeed's** death in deed, **34 this— kingdoms** this Kingdome is **36 utter** [not in Q1] **38 unto** as vnto our **40 By** Try **44 But . . . love** [follows line 48 in Q1] **45 longer then let me** longer, let me **46 Further to bear** To forbeare **49 seek your noble prince** search like nobles, **55 us** [not in Q1] **56–57 If . . . out / If . . . there** [after line 29 in Q1]

**Scene 8a** [not in Q1] Prince *Pericles* hauing had (as before is mentioned) his lodging directed next adioyning to the kings bedchamber, whereas all the other Princes

vppon their comming to their lodgings betooke themselues to their pillowes, and to the nourishment of a quiet sleepe, he of the Gentlemen that attended him, (for it is to be noted, that vpon the grace that the king had bestowed on him, there was of his Officers toward him no attendance wanting) hee desired that hee might be left priuate, onely that for his instant solace they would pleasure him with some delightfull Instrument, with which, and his former practise hee intended to passe away the tediousnesse of the night insteade of more fitting slumbers. His wil was presently obeyed in all things since their master had commaunded he should be disobeyed in nothing: the Instrument is brought him, and as hee had formerly wished, the Chamber is disfurnished of any other company but himselfe [*PA*, from which this scene is reconstructed] **8 s.d. a stringed instrument** [implied by *PA*, which refers to the "fingering" of the instrument and describes Pericles singing as he plays] **9–10 Now . . . sleep** all the other Princes . . . betooke themselues to their pillowes [*PA*] **10 s.d. PERICLES plays and sings** [*PA* elaborately describes the performance.] **11–13 Day . . . on.** But day that hath still that soueraigntie to drawe backe the empire of the night, though a while shee in darkenesse vsurpe, brought the morning on [*PA*] **14–15 I . . . me** euen in the instant came in *Pericles*, to giue his Grace that salutation which the morning required of him [*PA*]

**Scene 9** [not in Q1] **5 none can** by no meanes can I **6 have get 7–8 It . . . chamber** she hath so strictly / Tyed her to her Chamber, that t'is impossible **15 light** light / T'is well Mistris, your choyce agrees with mine **18 Mistress, 'tis well** Well, your her **20–21 that / In show, I have determined on in heart** it; the king intending to dissemble that in shew, which hee had determined on in heart [*PA*] **24–25 night. My ears, / I do protest** night: / I do protest, my eares **30 think you of my daughter** do you thinke of my Daughter, sir **31 And** And she is **33 My daughter, sir** Sir, my Daughter **34 So well indeed** I so well **39 s.d. He . . . feet** [not in Q1] foorthwith prostrating himselfe at the kings feete [*PA*] **43 her** her. / *king.* Thou has bewicht my daughter, / And thou art a villaine. / *Peri.* By the Gods I haue not **47 Thou liest like a traitor** Traytor, thou lyest **48–50 That . . . child** [not in Q1] I, traytour, quoth the king, that thus disguised, art stolne into my Court, with the witchcraft of thy actions to bewitch, the yeelding spirit of my tender Childe [*PA*] **51–52 Who calls me traitor, unless it be the King, / Ev'n in his**

bosom I will write the lie Even in his throat, vnless it be the King, / That cals me Traytor, I returne the lye [Q1] were it any in his Court, except himselfe, durst call him traytor, even in his bosome he would write the lie [PA] **54 blood** thoughts **56 in search of honour** [PA] for Honours cause **57 your state** her state [Q1] his State [PA] **60–62 I . . . witness** No? heere comes my Daughter, she can witnesse it [Q1] answered, he should prooue it otherwise, since by his daughters hand, it there was euident, both his practise and her consent therein [PA] **64–65 By what . . . fulfilled** [not in Q1] demaunded of her by the hope she had of heauen, or the desire she had to haue her best wished fulfilled heere in the worlde [PA] **68 made** that made **71 How, minion** [PA] Yea Mistris **72–96 I am glad on't . . . only child** I am glad on't with all my heart [Q1] How minion, quoth her Father (taking her off at the very word, who dare be displeased withalle) Is this a fit match for you? a stragling *Theseus* borne we knowe not where, one that hath neither bloud nor merite for thee to hope for, or himselfe to challenge euen the least allowaunce of thy perfections, when she humbling her princely knees before her Father, besought him to consider, that suppose his birth were base (when his life shewed him not to be so) yet hee had vertue, which is the very ground of all nobilitie, enough to make him noble: she intreated him to remember that she was in loue, the power of which loue was not to be confined by the power of his will. And my most royall Father, quoth shee, what with my penne I haue in secret written vnto you, with my tongue now I openly confirme, which is, that I have no life but his loue, neither any being but in the enioying of his worth. But daughter (quoth *Symonides*) equalles to equalls, good to good is ioyned, this not being so, the bauine of your minde in rashnesse kindled, must againe be quenched, or purchase our displeasure, And for you sir (speaking to prince *Pericles*) first learne to know, I banish you my Court, and yet scorning that our kingly inragement should stoope so lowe, for that your ambition sir, Ile haue your life. Be constant quoth *Thaysa,* for euerie droppe of blood hee sheades of yours, he shall draw an other from his onely childe [PA] **97 yea** [not in Q1] **102 s.d.** He . . . hand [not in Q1] catching them both rashly by the handes [PA] **103 s.d.** He . . . hand [not in Q1; see note to line 102 s.d.] **105 I shall** Ile **s.d.** He . . . together [not in Q1] heclapt them hand in hand [PA] **106 s.d.** PERICLES and THAISA kiss [not in Q1] while they as louingly ioyned lip to lip [PA] **108 your fur-**

ther further you you both **112 s.p.** PERICLES and THAISA *Ambo.* **113 Then** And then

**Scene 10** [not in Q1] **2 the house about** about the house **6 fore** from **7 crickets** Cricket **8 As** Are **10 Where** by [Q2] Whereby **13 eche** each **14 s.d.** *comes hastily in to meetes;* came hastily in to them [PA] **17 coigns** Crignes **21 stead** steed **29 mutiny there he** mutanie, hee there **t'appease** t'oppresse **46 fortune's mood** fortune mou'd **60 sea-tossed** seas tost **speke** speake

**Scene 11** [not in Q1] **7 Thou stormest** then storme **8 spit** speat **11 patroness** [Q4] patrioness **midwife** my wife **27 s.d.** *She . . . infant* [not in Q1] vp comes *Lycorida* the Nurse . . . and into his armies deliuers his Sea-borne Babe [PA] **s.d.** PERICLES . . . *weeps* [not in Q1] *Pericles* looking mournfully vpon it, shooke his head, and wept [PA] **34 Poor inch of nature** [PA; not in Q1] **36 partage** portage **37 s.d.** *the* MASTER *and a* SAILOR *two Saylers* **38, 43, 47, 51 s.p.** MASTER *1. Sayl.* **40 its worst** the worst **43–53** [verse in Q1] **43 Slack** Slacke [Qb] Slake [Qa] **bow-lines** bolins **45 s.p.** SAILOR 2. *Sayl.* **an** and **50 but** [not in Q1] **52 custom** easterne **52–54** yield 'er . . . queen! yeeld'er, / *Per.* As you thinke meet; for she must ouer board straight: / Most wretched Queene. **59 ooze** oare **61 And** The **aye-remaining** ayre remayning **64 paper** [Q2] Taper **66 coffer** coffin **69 s.p.** SAILOR 2. **72, 74 s.p.** MASTER 2. **73 from** for **74 Make** O make

**Scene 12** [not in Q1] **s.d.** *poor man and a* some that came to him both for helpe for themselues, and reliefe for others [PA] **2 those** these **4 seen** been in **5 ne'er** neare **7 in** to **8 to th'** to the **19–20 lordship** should, / Having . . . you, at Lordship, / Hauing . . . you, should at **20 this hour** these early howers **22 to** should **23 held** hold **26 dispend** [PA] expend **34 so** [not in Q1] **36 and cause** in course **39 glad** please **42 alone** [not in Q1] **46 48, 53 s.p.** PHILEMON *Seru⟨ant⟩* [variously abbreviated] **49 The sea tossed up** did the sea tosse vp **52–53 Did . . . sir** [Question and answer occur after "bitumed" at line 58 in Q1.] **54 Or a more eager** as tost it vpon shore **s.p.** CERIMON [not in Q1; see last note to line 58] **56 by** [not in Q1] **queasy** [not in Q1] **58 bitumed** bottomed **soft** *Cer.* Wrench it open soft. **62 and crowned** [not in Q1] crowned [PA] **65 i'th'** in the **75 even** [Q4] euer **77 rash** rough **82 have heard** heard **83 nine hours dead** that had 9. howers lien dead **84 appliances** applyaunce **84 s.d.** PHILEMON *one* **86 still** rough **87 vial** Violl **90–91**

warmth / Breathes warmth breath **94 set**
sets **104 gentle** my gentle
**Scene 13** [not in Q1] **5 strokes** shakes **6**
**hurt** hant **7 woundingly** wondringly **8**
**you'd** you had **9 T'have** to haue **10 Should**
Could **14 and leave** leauing **25 th'** the **29**
**Unscissored** vncisserd [*PA*] vnsisterd **29**
**hair** heyre **32 s.p. DIONYZA I** [Q1] *Cler.* I
[Q1 catchword] **35 s.p. CLEON** *Cler.* **36 th'**
**masted** the mask'd
**Scene 14** [not in Q1] **s.d. THAISA** *Tharsa* **2**
**are all** are **5 eaning** learning **6 th'** the **11**
**s.p. CERIMON** *Cler.* **13 till your date expire**
you may abide you may abide till your date
expire **16 s.p. THAISA** [Q4] *Thin.*
**Scene 15** [not in Q1] **8 music** Musicks **10**
**her** hie **the heart** the art **14 Seeks** Seeke
**15 has** hath **16 lass** wench **17 ripe** [Q2]
**right rite** sight **26 bird** bed **32 WIth dove of**
**Paphos might the** The Doue of *Paphos* might
with the **38 murder** murderer **42 s.d.** *A*
*tomb is revealed* a monument in remembrance [*PA*] **47 carry** carried **55 i'th'** in the
**57–58 or fanning love thy bosom /**
**Unflame** in flaming, thy loue bosome,
enflame **63 weeping** weeping for **nurse's**
Mistresse **66 grave** greene **68 tomb** graue
**71 but** [not in Q1] **ceaseless** lasting **76–77**
**favour / Is changed** fauours / Changd **78**
**Give me your flowers. Come** Come giue me
your flowers **o'er** ere **margin** marre it **79 is**
**piercing** is quicke **80 And quick; it sharps**
And it perces and sharpens **81 th'** the
**81–151 No . . . slain** [prose in Q1; many of
the following emendations help create metrical verse lines] **90 resume** reserue **94 truly**
yet **95 Nay Come,** come **99 Pray you** pray
**104 mariners** Saylers **105 with** [not in Q1]
**111 Once** and **114 stem** stern **120 The**
for the **121 would** will **128 once on a**
**worm** vpon a worme **129 for it** [Q4] fort
**131 danger** any danger **139 s.d.** *drawing*
*out his sword* [*PA*] **140 s.d.** *running* [*PA*]
**144 s.d. PIRATES** *carrying* **MARINA** the
pyrates who had thus rescued *Marina,* carried her to their shippes [*PA*] **LEONINE** *steals*
*back* Enter Leonine; he secretly stole back
[*PA*] **146 An** and **147 she'll** shee will
**Scene 16** [not in Q1] **4 lose** lost **too much**
[Q2] too much much **4 wenchless** too
wenchlesse **17 They're too** ther's two **33**
**mystery** trade **37 s.p. A PIRATE** *Sayler.* **45**
**hundred sesterces** [*PA*] thousand peeces
**58 had but** had not **59 To** for to **66 like**
[Q4; not in Q1] **80 must stir** [Q4] stir **88**
**watered as** watred, and **92 Veroles** *Verollus*
**98 of** in **100 all** [not in Q1] **103 to despise**
despise **111 s.p. BAWD** *Mari⟨na⟩* **123–24**
**reapest the harvest out of thine own set-**
**ting forth** hast the haruest out of thine owne
report **133 with me** with vs

**Scene 17** [not in Q1] **s.d.** *in mourning gar-*
*ments* mourning garments [*PA*] **1 are** ere
**5–47 Were . . . done** [prose in Q1] **6 A lady**
O Ladie **12 fact** face **13 demands** shall
demaund **15 is not** it, not **17 pious** [*PA*]
impious **25 cowed** coward **27 prime** prince
**28 sources** courses **31 distain** disdaine **33**
**Marina's** [Q2] *Marianas* **34 malkin** Mawkin
**48 angel** Angells **49 in thine eagle talons**
with thine Eagles talents
**Scene 18** [not in Q1] **1 make we** make **3**
**take** take our **7 scene** sceanes **8 i'th'** with
**10 the** [Q2] thy **14 govern, if** gouerne it,
**16 Tyre** time **18 his** this **19 go on** grone
**24 true-owed** true olde **29 puts out 34**
**sweetest, best** *sweetest, and best* **36–37**
**In . . . good** [*PA*; not in Q1. For the eight
lines from Q1 omitted here, see Additional
Passage.] **42 scene** Steare
**Scene 19** [not in Q1] **2 s.p. SECOND GENTLE-**
**MAN** [Qa, Qb, Qb catchword] *Gower.* [Qa
catchword] **13 the whole of** a whole **24**
**loon** Lowne **25 custom** customers **27 to-**
**bless** to blesse **34 deed** deedes **41 dignifies**
dignities **42 noble** number **52 honourably**
know worthie note **63 hers** her **64 139**
**Fair . . . Away** [prose in Q1; many of the following emendations help create metrical
verse lines] **64 Fair** Now prittie **66 I Why** I
**name it but** name but **71 or** or at **73 Pro-**
**claimeth you** proclaimes you to be **74 And**
[not in Q1] **75 into it** intoo't **76 blood** parts
**77 whole province** place **78 What** Why
**informed** made knowne vnto **80 seeds of**
**shame, roots of** seeds and rootes of shame
and **s.d. MARINA** *weeps* [not in Q1] teares
[*PA*] **81 you've** you haue **82 off aloof for a**
aloft for **84–89 can . . . ling'ring shall not**
see thee, or else looke friendly vpon thee; vrg-
ing her, that he was the Gouernour, whose
authoritie coulde wincke at those blemishes,
her selfe, and that sinnefull house could cast
vppon her, or his displeasure punish at his
owne pleasure, which displeasure of mine, thy
beauty shall not priuiledge thee from, nor my
affection, which hath drawen me vnto this
place abate, if thou with further lingering
withstand me [*PA*] **85 or can on faults look**
**friendly** or else looke friendly vpon thee [not
in *PA*] **91–93 Let . . . yourself** [not in Q1] If
as you say (my Lorde) you are the Gouernour,
let not your authoritie, which should teach
you to rule others, be the meanes to make
you misgouerne your selfe [*PA*] **96–106**
**What . . . impoverish me** [not in Q1] What
reason is there in your Justice, who hath
power ouer all, to vndoe any? If you take from
mee mine honour, you are like him, that
makes a gappe into forbidden ground, after
whome too many enter, and you are guiltie of
all their euilles: my life is yet vnspotted, my

chastitie vnstained in thought. Then if your violence deface this building, the workemanship of heauen, made vp for good, and not to be the exercise of sinnes intemperaunce, you do kill your owne honour, abuse your owne iustice, and impouerish me. . . . Is there a necessitie (my yet good Lord) if there be fire before me, that I must strait then thither flie and burne my selfe? Or if suppose this house, (which too too many feele such houses are) should be the Doctors patrimony, and Surgeons feeding; folowes it therefore, that I must needs infect my self to giue them maintenaunce? [*PA*] **114 s.d.** *kneeling* [not in Q1] which wordes (being spoken vpon her knees) [*PA*] **115 franked** plac't **119 s.d.** *moved* [*PA*; not in Q1] **120 s.d.** *He . . . hands* [not in Q1] hee lift her vp with his hands [*PA*] **121 Though** Had **122 hath** had **s.d.** *He . . . eyes* [not in Q1] in steede of willing her to drie her eyes, he wiped the wet himselfe off [*PA*] **and my foul thoughts** [not in Q1] I hither came with thoughte intemperate, foule and deformed [*PA*] **123 Thy . . . white** [not in Q1] the which your paines so well hath laued, that they are now white [*PA*] **124–26 I . . . honesty** holde, heeres golde for thee [Q1] and for my parte, who hither came but to haue payd the price, a peece of golde for your virginitie, now giue you twenty to releeue your honesty [*PA*] **127 Persever still** perseuer **128 The** For me be you thoughten, that I came with no ill intent, for to me the **131 The . . . made** [*PA*; not in Q1] **132 not** not but noble noble, hold, heeres more golde for thee **134 honour. Hold, here's more gold. / If** goodnes, if [A shorter version of the words omitted at line 132 is reintroduced here.] **135 s.d.** *Enter . . . out* [not in Q1] the bawde standing ready at the doore, as hee should go out, making his obeysaunce vnto him as hee should returne [*PA*] **146 executioner shall do** hãg-man shal execute **We'll** come your way, weele **152 She** He **158 s.p. PANDER** *Bawd.* **159 ice** glass **167 s.d.** *catching . . . hand* [*PA*; not in Q1] **176–84 Neither . . . lungs** [prose in Q1; many of the following emendations help create metrical verse lines] **176 can be** are **178 place** place **for which 179 change with thee** change **180 Thou** Thou art the **182 To th'** To the **ev'ry** euery **190 sew'rs** shores **190 public** common **191 these** these wayes **193 dear** deere, that the gods wold safely deliuer me from this place **Here's** here, heers **194 make gain** gaine **197 I will** will **206 women** [Q4] woman
Scene 20 [not in Q1] **8 twin** Twine **13 We** Where wee **Waves there him tossed** wee there him left **14 Whence** Where **tofore**

before **20 fervour** [Qb] former [Qa] **22 the** his
Scene 21 [not in Q1] **1 s.p. SAILOR OF TYRE** 1 *Say.* **1–53 Where . . . prevented** [prose in Q1] **1 Lord Helicanus can resolve you, sir** Where is Lord *Helicanus?* hee can resolue you, O here he is Sir **3 In it** and in it is **6 s.p. SAILOR OF TYRE** 2 *Say.* **6 Ho Ho Gentlemen What is your lordship's pleasure** Doeth your Lordship call **7 some** there is some **8 you** [not in Q1] **9 s.p. SAILOR OF MYTILENE** *Hell.* [Qa] 1 *Say* [Qb] **This** Sir, this **aught** ought you would **11 sir** [not in Q1] **12–16 You wish me well. / I . . . Mytilene; / Being . . . are** *Li⟨simachus⟩* You wish mee well, beeing . . . are. *Hell⟨icanus⟩* First what is your place? *Ly⟨simachus⟩* I . . . this place you lie before [Helicanus's question in Q1 is omitted, and an emended version of Lysimachus's reply ("I . . . before") is moved to an earlier position, after "You wish me well."] **17 Our** Syr our **our king** the King **21 grew** is **22 tell it ouer** repeat **23 precious** [not in Q1] **25 See him, sir, you may** You may **26 sight. He** [Qb] sight see [Qa] **27 any.** LYSIMACHUS **Let me yet** any, yet let me [speech continued by Helicanus in Q1, with different word order] **28 s.p. HELICANUS** [Q4] *Lys⟨imachus⟩* **s.d.** *lying . . . sack-cloth* [not in Q1] so attired from the ordinary habite of other men, as with a long ouer-growne beard, diffused hayre, vndecent nayles on his fingers, and himselfe lying vppon his cowch groueling on his face [*PA*; when Pericles first learns of Marina's death, *PA* reports that "hee apparrelles himselfe in sacke-cloth."] **28–29 person, / Till** [Q4] person. / *Hell⟨icanus⟩* Till [In this edition, Helicanus is already speaking.] **29 of** that **night** wight **30 all hail** all haile, the Gods preserue you **s.d.** PERICLES . . . pillow hee shruncke himselfe downe vppon his pillow [*PA*] **35 choice** chosen **alarum** allure **36 deafened ports** defend parts **37 in all** is all **38 among** and **39 Dwells now i'th'** now vpon the **40 Go fetch her hither** [not in Q1] **47 gods** God **51 it** it to you **54 presence** present **57 of** of a or and **I'd** [Q4] I do **58 to** and **wed** [Q4] to wed **59 one on bounty** beautie **60 feat** fate **64–140 Sir . . . end here** [prose in Q1; many of the following emendations help to create metrical verse lines] **65 recure** recouerie **67 Let** Come, let **68 prosper her** make her prosperous **Marked** [Q4] Marke **69 s.p. MAID** *Mar⟨ina⟩* **84 Stay** go not **88 My lord** [after "said," line 87, in Q1] **90–91 what . . . shores?** what Countrey women heare of these shewes? **93 seem** appeare **95 such** sucha one **99 cased** caste **109 palace** *Pallas* **111 make my senses** [Q4] makes senses **112 Thou show'st** for thou lookest **114 say** stay **121**

circumstance thoughts 123 thousandth thousand 128 lost thou them? Thy name lost thou thy name 130 sir, [not in Q1] 142 Motion as well? Motion well 146 when the minute 147 recounted deliuered 153 You will scarce believe me You scorne, beleeue me 159 wooed hauing wood 160 the deed it 162 To Mytilene they brought me Brought me to *Metaline* 163 What will you of me whither wil you haue me? 164 impostor imposture 167 s.p. PERICLES *Hell⟨icanus⟩* 174 would never neuer would 192 rest rest you sayd 193 So prove but true in that, thou art my daughter [not in Q1] 194 life like 196 name? name was *Thaisa* 199 Thou art [Q4] th'art s.d. *He kisses her* he falls on hir necke, and kisses her [PA] 201 Not shee is not 207 sir [not in Q1] 211 doubt doat 217–18 LYSIMACHUS Music, my lord? / PERICLES I hear most *Lys.* Musicke my Lord? I heare. / *Per.* Most 219 raps nips 220 eyelids eyes s.d. *He sleeps* he fell into a slumber [PA] 221 A . . . head. Companion A Pillow for his head, so leaue him all. / Well my companion 223 So leave him all [after "head" (line 222) in Q1] 227–28 At large . . . voice [not in Q1] 231 life like 232 Perform or performe 233 rest [not in Q1] 238 Th' The
Scene 22 [not in Q1] 9 well [not in Q1] 23 espouse [PA] wed 24 The fair Thaisa . . . at Pentapolis at *Pentapolis,* the faire *Thaisa* s.d. THAISA *starts* At the naming of whome, she her selfe being by, could not choose but starte [PA] 26 who whom 28 whom who 30 Bore brought 31 our barque vs 35 nun mum 39 same verie 42 one in 48 upon him [not in Q1] 70 s.d. *embracing* MARINA [not in Q1] giuing his daughter to her armes to embrace her as a child [PA] 72 s.p. PERICLES [Q4] *Hell⟨icanus⟩* 82 is the [not in Q1] 90 And told how in this temple she came placed How shee came plac'ste heere in the Temple [Q1] for in this Temple was she placed [PA] 91 Diana *Dian* 92 I [not in Q1] 93 Nightly Night Beloved [not in Q1] 95 At Pentapolis shall marry her shall marrie her at *Pentapolis* 101 from Pentapolis [not in Q1] 102 Heav'n Heauens [Q1] Heauen [Q1 catchword] 112 preserved preferd 113 Led [Q2] Led 119 their [Q4] his deed to th' deede, the 123 that [not in Q1]

## THE WINTER'S TALE

### CONTROL TEXT: F

F: The Folio of 1623
**s.p.** OLD SHEPHERD [F's use of *"Shep⟨heard⟩."* has been changed throughout.]

**s.p.** FIRST LADY [F's use of *"Lady"* has been changed at 2.1.2, 5, 14, 16.]
**s.p.** A LORD [F's use of *"Lord"* has been changed throughout 2.1; at 2.3.26, 147, and 197; and at 3.2.114, 172, 200, and 214.]

**1.2.106** And A **160** ornament Ornaments **209** they [not in F] **278** hobby-horse Holy-Horse
**2.2.56** let't le't **69** twixt betwixt
**2.3.39** What Who
**3.2.10** Silence. [italicized and set as stage direction in F] **31** Who Whom **166** certain [not in F]
**3.3.67** bairn Barne **73** hallooed hallow'd **110** made mad
**4.2.3** sixteen fifteene
**4.3.10** With heigh, with heigh, *With heigh,*
**4.4.12** it [not in F] **13** swoon sworne **98** your you **148** so [not in F] **160** out on't **237** kiln-hole kill-hole **239** Clammer clamor **298** gentlemen Gent. **347** who whom **407** acknowledged acknowledge **411** who whom **416** see neuer see **427** hoop hope **455** your my **577** so [not in F] **597** could would **685** know not know **713** to at
**5.1.21** spoke spoken **58–59** stage, / Where . . . mourn, appear Stage / ⟨Where . . . now appeare⟩ **61** just iust such **78** your you a
**5.3.5** young contracted your contracted **18** Lonely Louely **67** fixture fixure **96** Or those On: those **150** This' This

## CYMBELINE, KING OF BRITAIN

### CONTROL TEXT: F

F: The Folio of 1623
Fa, Fb: Successive states of F incorporating various print-shop corrections and changes

Title: *Cymbeline King of Britaine* [F table of contents] *The Tragedie of Cymbeline* [F head title]

**s.p.** INNOGEN [F's use of *Imogen* is changed throughout.]
**s.p.** GIACOMO [F's use of *Iachimo* is modernized throughout.]
**s.p.** HELEN [In 2.2, F's use of *La.* is changed throughout.]
**s.p.** FILARIO [F's use of *Philario* is modernized throughout.]
**s.p.** A ROMAN CAPTAIN [F's *Captain* is changed at 4.2.335, 339, 344, and 361.]
**s.p.** A LORD [F's use of *Lord* is changed at 4.3.16, 23, 28.]

s.p. FIRST JAILER [F's use of *Gao* is changed at 5.5.95.]

1.1.3 King Kings 15 of at 30 Cassibelan *Cassibulan* 98 Filario's *Filorio's*
1.2.9 steel if he Steele if it
1.3.9 this his
1.4.40 not to to 62 Britain Britanie 63 not but not 72 purchase purchases 90 five [Fb] fine [Fa] 111 thousand thousands
1.5.28 factor for for 85 words, Pisanio words
1.6.7 desire desires 25 truest *trust.* 29 takes take 37 th'unnumbered the number'd 81 count account 126 lend to lend 163 me [Fb] ma [Fa] 169 men's men 170 descended defended 187 Best The best
2.1.21 an and 24 your you 31 tonight night 58 husband, than husband then.
2.2.2 hour houre [Fb] houe [Fa] 43 riveted riueted [Fb] riuete [Fa] 49 bare beare
2.3.6 s.p. CLOTEN [not in text] 17 s.p. MUSICIAN [not in F] heaven *Heauens* 24 s.p. CLOTEN [not in F] 25 vice voyce 27 amend amed 39 out on't 43 solicits solicity 96 cure are 116 foil foyle 132 garment Garments 149 you your
2.4.6 seared hopes fear'd hope 14 Ere Or 18 legions Legion 24 courage courages 34 through thorough 37 s.p. FILARIO *Post.* 41 had haue 47 not note 57 you yon 60 leaves leaue 76 Such since 116 her woman her women 135 the her 151 follow follow him
2.5.2 bastards all all Bastards 16 German one Iarmen on 27 man can name name
3.1.5 Cassibelan *Cassibulan* 11 There will There 20 banks Oakes 30, 39–40 Cassibelan *Cassibulan*
3.2.2 accuser accuse 10 to hers to her 14 to do good [Fb] to go do od [Fa] 22 here [Fb] her [Fa] 64 Till And 67 score store ride rid 78 Nor here, nor nor heere, not
3.3.2 Stoop Sleepe 15–16 war; / That Warre. / This 23 bauble Babe 25 'em him 28 know knowes 33 travelling abed trauailing a bed 34 prison for Prison, or 83 wherein they bow whereon the Bowe 86 Polydore *Poladour* 106 Morgan *Mergan*
3.4.78 afore't a-foot 88 make makes 100 out [not in F] 132 churlish, noble noble
3.5.32 looks looke 40 strokes, stroke; 44 loud'st lowd of 86 tongue heart
3.6.68 Ay I I'd I do 74 price prize
3.7.9 commends commands
4.2.2 from after 47 hath he hath 51 s.p. BELARIUS *Arui⟨ragus⟩.* 59 him them 60 patience patient 123 thanks, ye thanks the 133 humour Honor 171 how thou 187 ingenious ingenuous 203 not not the 206

crare care 207 Might Might'st 225 ruddock Raddocke 230 winter-gown winter-ground 238 once once to 258 begin. begin. / SONG. 286 th'earth's face their Faces 288 strow strew 292 is are 325 thy this 338 are hence are heere 392 wild-wood leaves wild wood-leaues 401 he is hee's
4.3.40 betid betide
4.4.2 find we we finde 17 the their 18 files Fires 27 hard heard
5.1.1 once wished am wisht 15 dread ill dread it 16 blest best 20 mistress-piece Mistris: Peace
5.5.2 Ay I did 24 harts hearts her our 42 stooped stopt 43 they the 53 Yet you you 64 This This is 121 make take 161 geck geeke 163 come came 175 look looke / looke 212 Preens Prunes claws cloyes 252 are as are 257 Of Oh, of 260 sir Sis 270 or take or to take 273 on one
5.6.54 and in fine and in time 55 fit fitted 62 s.p. LADIES *La.* 64 heard heare 134 On One 142 Torments Which torments 205 got it got 225 villain villany 261 from fro 262 lock Rocke 303 boy man 335 mere neere 352 like liks 379 you we 387 brothers Brother 393 inter'gatories Interrogatories 406 so no 469 this yet yet this

## THE TEMPEST

### CONTROL TEXT: F

F: The Folio of 1623
Fa, Fb: Successive states of F incorporating various print-shop corrections and changes

1.1.18–19 councillor Councellor 19–20 work peace worke the peace 31 wi'th' with 54 s.p. MARINERS [not in F] 57 wi'th' with' 59 broom Browne furze firrs
1.2.100 oft of it. 112 wi'th' with 153 wast was't 174 princes Princesse 201 bowsprit Bore-spritt 230 Bermudas *Bermoothes* 262 Algiers *Argier* 284 she he 304 to [not in F] 330 forth at for that 349 human humane 383 sprites *Sprights* 385–88 s.p. SPIRITS . . . ARIEL . . . SPIRITS [Only the last refrain, "Hark, hark, I hear," is assigned to Ar⟨iel⟩. in F.] 390 cock-a-diddle-dow *cockadidle-dowe* 407 s.p. SPIRITS . . . *dong* Burthen ding dong 408 s.p. SPIRITS [*within*] [not in F] 470 power pow'r
2.1.37 s.p. ANTONIO . . . Sebastian *Seb⟨ast-ian⟩.* . . . . *Ant⟨onio⟩.* 133 More Mo 140 chirurgeonly Chirurgeonly 253 every eu'ry
2.2.52 Then to sea [*etc.*] [not in F] 108 spirits sprights 120 Swum Swom 164 seamews Scamels
3.1.2 sets set 15 busil'est busie lest 47 peerless peetlesse

**3.2.24 debauched** debosh'd **30 s.p. TRIN-CULO** [F (text)] *Cal⟨iban⟩*. [F (catchword)]
**3.3.2 ache** akes **15 travel** trauaile **29 islanders** Islands **33 human** humaine **65 plume** plumbe **99 bass** base
**4.1.9 of her** her of **13 gift** guest **17 rite** right **52 rein** raigne **53 abstemious** abstenious **61 vetches** Fetches **peas** Pease **64 peonied** pioned **74 Her** here **81 bosky** boskie **83 short-grassed** short gras'd **110 s.p. CERES** [not in F] **and** [not in F] **123 wise** wife **136 holiday** holly day **180 gorse** gosse **193 them on** on them **lime** line **229 Let't alone** let's alone
**5.1.10 lime-grove** *Line-groue* **16 run** runs **60 boiled** boile **72 Didst** [F (catchword)] **Did** [F (text)] **75 entertained** entertaine **81 shores** shore **93–96 Merrily . . . bough** [In F, these lines are not repeated.] **113 Whe'er** Where **126 not** nor **158 these** Their **178 An** And **202 remembrance** remembrances **230 events** [Fb] euens [Fa] **237 more** mo **239 her** our **288 Why** [Fb] Who [Fa]

THE TWO NOBLE KINSMEN

CONTROL TEXT: Q

Q: The Quarto of 1634
Qa, Qb: The uncorrected (Qa) and corrected (Qb) states of Q

Title: *The Two Noble Kinsmen* [Q] a Tragi-Comedy called the two noble kinsmen [Stationers' Register]

**s.p. PROLOGUE , EPILOGUE** [Q simply titles each section "PROLOGVE" and "EPILOGVE," which could be interpreted either as speech prefixes or as section headings.]
**s.p. JAILER** [Q alternates between *Jailer* and *Keeper*. Standardized throughout.]
**s.p. JAILER'S DAUGHTER** [Q's consistent use of *Daughter* is expanded throughout.]
**s.p. JAILER'S BROTHER** [Q's consistent use of *Brother* is expanded throughout.]
**s.p. COUNTRYMEN** [Q uses only numbers to refer to the Countrymen, except in 3.5, when one of the Countrymen, who is dressed as a baboon, is referred to as *Baum* or *Bavian* ("babion," old form of "baboon") in Q and "babion" in this edition.]
**Prologue s.d.** *Enter* PROLOGUE / **s.p. PROLOGUE** PROLOGVE. **26 tack** take

**1.1. s.d. PIRITHOUS** Theseus **1 s.p. BOY** The Song. [In Q, the song is not assigned to a particular character. It is clear from the preceding stage direction, however, that it is the boy who sings.] **7 born** borne **9 harebells** *her bels*

**13–14 children sweet,** / **Lie** *children: sweete-* / *Ly* **20 chough** hoar *Clough hee* **68 Nemean** Nenuan **90 thy** the **112 glassy** glasse **132 longer** long **138 move** mooves **155 Rinsing** Wrinching **158 Artesius** *Artesuis* **166 s.p. ALL THREE QUEENS** *All.* **171 war** was **177 twinning** twyning. ["Twined" remains a possible alternative modernization. Compare 2.2.64.] **211 Aulis** Anly
**1.2.55 canon** Cannon **69 men's service** men service **70 glory; one** glory on
**1.3.31 one** ore **54 eleven** a eleven **54 Flavina** Flauia **73 happily** happely **73 wear** were **75 one** on **79 seely innocence** fury-innocent **82 dividual** individuall **82 out** ont
**1.4.18 smeared** [Qb] succard [Qa] **22 Wi'leave** We leave **45 O'erwrestling** Or wrastling **49 fore** for
**1.5. s.d.** *Song* [not in Q] **9–10 woes,** / **We . . .** woes. woes. *We convent, &c.*
**2.2.21 wore** were **22 Ravished** Bravishd **64 twined** twyn'd **118–19 s.p. EMILIA This . . . in't.** / **What** This . . . in't. / *Emil.* What [In Q, Arcite continues speaking until the end of line 118.] **132 was I** I was **150 close** neere **182 love her** love **189 your blood** you blood **264 to** too **272 you** yon
**2.3.6 sins** [Qb] fins [Qa] **24 s.d.** *garland* garlond [Qb] *Garlon* [Qa] **40 ye** yet **53 said** sees **64 Yet** Yes
**2.4.33 night; ere tomorrow** night, or to-morrow
**2.5 Scaena 4 28 For** Fo
**2.6.33 patch** path
**3.1.2 laund** land **11 12 With . . . rumination** [Q prints as one line with no lacuna marked.] **37 looked, the void'st** lookd the voydes **43 Not** Nor **96 s.d. within** *of Cornets*. [In Q's "Winde hornes of Cornets," "Cornets" may be a playhouse addition; "of" could mean "off," or "offstage," here rendered as "within."] **98 muset** Musicke **108 not** nor **113 'Tis** If **123 enjoy it** enjoy't
**3.2.1 mistook the brake** mistooke; the Beake **7 reck** wreake **19 fed** feed **28 brine** bine
**3.3.12 sir &c. 23 them** then **52 Sirrah—** Sir ha:
**3.4.9 Open** Vpon **10 tack** take **19 a foot** *afoote*
**3.5 Scaena 6 s.d. BABION** Baum **8 jean** jave **25 these** their **33, 134 babion** *Bavian* **67 I** [not in Q] **68 There . . . owlet—** *There . . . howlet* [Q's italics appear to derive from the compositor mistakenly interpreting this line as part of the song.] **69 he** [not in Q] **100 s.p. THESEUS** *Per.* [Pirithous] **120 'Moor'** Morr **121 'Ice' Is 125 tenor** tenner **133 beest-eating** beast eating **138 s.p. SCHOOLMASTER** [not in Q] **139–48 Ladies . . . rout** [italics in Q. The compositor possibly misinterpreted this speech as a song.] **140 ye** thee **143 thee** three **152 you** yon

3.6 Scaena 7 **145 thine** this **236 fail** fall **272
must** muff **273 the other** th'other **279, 280
s.p.** PALAMON *and* ARCITE *Both.*
4.1.**11 oath** o'th **20 he scaped** he escapt **45
WOOER** No, Sir, not well. SECOND FRIEND
**Not well?** 2 *Fr.* Not well?—*Wooer,* No Sir
not well. **63 sung** song **84 wreath** wreake
**86 she appeared, methought,** me thought
she appeard **104 light . . .'** *light, &c.* [Here
and at 4.1.113 and 151 and 4.3.48, Q's
"&c." suggests that more than the single
line of the song printed in the text was
sung.] **113 sweet . . .'** *sweete, &c.* **119 Far
For 133 s.p.** JAILER'S BROTHER *Daugh.*
[Jailer's Daughter] **140 s.p.** SECOND
FRIEND *I. Fr.* [First Friend] **144–45
Cheerly all. / Uff** cheerely. / *All.* Owgh [In
Q, the *"All"* pretend to join in.] **150 Tack**
Take **151 light . . .'** *light, &c.*
4.2.**16 Jove afire once** Loue a fire with **54–55
both! / s.d.** *Enter* [a] GENTLEMAN HOW
both. / s.d. *Enter Emil⟨ia⟩ and Gent⟨leman⟩:*
s.p. *Emil⟨ia⟩.* How [Q's superfluous references to Emilia in the s.d. and s.p. are omitted.] **76 first** fitst **81 fire** faire **105 tods** tops
**110 court** corect
4.3.**20 spirits are** spirits, as **27 i'th' other** i'th
/ Thother **41 engrafted** engraffed **45
th'other** another **46 behind** [Qb] behold
[Qa] **48 fate . . .'** *fate, &c.* **75 carve** crave
5.1.**37 father of** farther off **44 me** [not in Q]
**49–50 purple; / Whose havoc in vast field
comets prewarn,** purple. / Comets pre-
warne, whose havocke in vaste Feild **53
armipotent** armenypotent
**5.2, 5.3** [Q continues as part of 5.1]
**5.4** Scaena 2 **34 Yes,** Yet **38 s.d.** *mad Maide* **39
humour** honour **53 tune** turne **103 lose the
sight** loose the Fight
**5.5** Scaena 3 **78 the end** th'end **111 Emilia**
*Emily* **139 your** you
**5.6** Scaena 4 **1 s.p.** PALAMON [not in Q] **39
s.p.** SECOND *and* THIRD KNIGHTS *I.2.
K⟨nights⟩.* **47 rarely** early **79 victor's** [Qb]
victoros [Qa] **107 Hath** Hast
**Epilogue s.d.** *Enter* EPILOGUE / **s.p.** EPI-
LOGUE EPILOGVE.

## Venus and Adonis

### Control text: Q1

Q1: The Quarto of 1593
Q2, Q3, Q7: Successive printings of Q1 that
incorporate various corrections.

**466 loss** loue
**680 overshoot** ouer-shut [The Oxford editors
point out that "shut" is a spelling variant of
"shoot" in the early modern period.]
**748 th'impartial** [Q2] the th'impartiall

**1031 as** [Q3] are
**1054 was** [Q7] had

## The Rape of Lucrece

### Control text: Q1

Q1: The Quarto of 1594

The poem is called "LUCRECE" on the title page
but *"The Rape of Lucrece"* in the head title
and running titles.

**550 blows** blow
**950 blemish** cherish
**1316 stain's** stain'd
**1475 Thine** Thy
**1544 armèd, too** armed to
**1662 wreathèd** wretched
**1713 in it** it in

## The Sonnets and "A Lover's Complaint"

### Control text: Q

Q: The Quarto of 1609
Qa, Qb: Qa is the uncorrected version, Qb the
corrected version
Other texts cited:
B1—British Library Add. MS 10309, fol. 143
(c. 1630; Margaret Bellasys)
B2—British Library Add. MS 21433, fol. 114ᵛ
(c. 1630; Inns of Court)
B3—British Library Add. MS 25303, fol. 119ᵛ
(c. 1620s–30s; Inns of Court)
M—Pierpont Morgan MA 1057, p. 96 (c.
1630s)
MS—St. John's, Cambridge, MS S. 23 (James
416), fols. 38ʳ–38ᵛ (c. 1630s–40s)
*Passionate Pilgrim,* c. 1599
R—Rosenbach MS 1083 / 16, p. 256 (c. 1630)
W—Westminster Abbey, MS 41, fol. 49
(1619–30s; George Morley)

**Sonnets**
1 [number not in Q]
2 [For another version of this sonnet, present
in eleven manuscripts, see the Alternative
Versions.] **4 tattered** [MS] totter'd
5.14 **Lose** Leese
12.4 **ensilvered o'er** or siluer'd ore
13.7 **Yourself** You selfe
20.7 **hues** *Hews*
23.14 **with . . . wit** wit . . . wiht
25.9 **might** worth
26.12 **thy** their
27.10 **thy** their
28.12 **gild'st the even** guil'st th'eauen **14
strength** length

31.8 **thee** there
34.12 **cross** losse
35.8 **thy . . . thy** their . . . their
37.7 **thy** their
39.12 **doth** dost
41.12 **troth** truth
43.11 **thy** their
44.13 **naught** naughts
45.12 **thy** their
46.3, 8, 13, 14 **thy** their 9 **'cide** side
47.10 **art** are 11 **no** nor
50.6 **dully** duly
51.10 **perfect'st** perfects 11 **rein** naigh
54.14 **fade** vade
55.1 **monuments** monument
56.13 **Or** As
61.8 **tenor** tenure
62.10 **chapped** chopt
63.5 **travelled** trauaild
65.12 **of** or
67.6 **seeming** seeing
69.3 **due** end 5 **Thy** Their 14 **soil** solye
70.6 **Thy** their
71.4 **vilest** vildest
73.4 **ruined choirs** rn'wd quiers
76.7 **tell** fel
77.10 **blanks** blacks
82.8 **these** the
85.3 **thy** their
86.13 **filled** fild
89.11 **profane** prophane [Qb]; proface [Qa]
90.11 **shall** stall
91.9 **better** bitter
99.9 **One** Our 13 **ate** eate
100.14 **prevene'st** preuenst
102.8 **her** his
106 [For another version of this sonnet, present in two manuscripts, see the Alternative Versions.] 12 **skill** [MSS] still
111.1 **with** wish
112.14 **they're dead** y'are dead
113.6 **latch** lack 14 **makes mine eye** maketh mine
116 119 [all but one extant copy of Q]
126.2 **sickle-hour** sickle, hower 8 **minutes** mynuit 12 [After this line, Q prints parentheses for each line of an imagined couplet.]
127.10 **brow** eyes
128.11, 14 **thy** their
129.9 **Mad** Made 11 **proved** proud **a** and
132.6 **the east** th'East 9 **mourning** morning
135.1, 2, 11, 12, 14 **Will** *Will*
136.2, 5, 14 **Will** *Will* 6 **Ay** I
138 [For another version of this sonnet, see the Alternative Versions.] 12 **to have** [*Passionate Pilgrim*] t'haue
140.13 **belied** be lyde
143.13 **Will** *Will*
144 [For another version of this sonnet, see the Alternative Versions.] 6 **side** [*Passionate Pilgrim*] sight 9 **fiend** finde

146.2 [            ] **My sinfull earth**
153.8 **strange** strang 14 **eyes** eye

**"A Lover's Complaint"**
7 **sorrow's** sorrowes,
37 **beaded** bedded
51 **'gan** gaue
112 **manège** mannad'g
118 **Came** Can
131 **Consents** Consent's
139 **labour** labouring
161 **wills** wits
182 **woo** vovv
198 **pallid** palyd [sometimes interpreted as "palèd," which properly means "having grown pale"]
204 **hair** heir
208 **th'annexations** th'annexions
228 **Hallowed** Hollowed
233 **A** Or
241 **Planing** Playing
251 **immured** enur'd
252 **procured** procure
260 **nun** Sunne
261 **ay** I
270 **kindred,** kindred
293 **O** Or

**Alternative Versions**

*Spes Altera*
Control text: W
*Spes Altera* [B1, B2, B3] To one yᵗ would dye a Mayd
3 **liv'ry** [B1] liuery
5 **lies** lye [cropped control-text ms.]
8 **praise** prays [cropped control-text ms.]

**On his Mistress' Beauty**
Control text: M
2 **descriptions** [R] discription
3 **rhyme** [R] mine [but with "rime" written in the margin as a correction]
6 **hand** [R] hands
8 **E'en** Ev'n [M] Euen [R]
10 **these** [R] those
12 **your** thy

VARIOUS POEMS

TITLE VARIANTS ARE NOT INCLUDED IN THE LISTS BELOW.

**A Song**
Control text: B
B: Bodleian MS Rawlinson poet. 160, fols. 108ʳ–109ᵛ
Y: Yale Osborn b. 197
5 **sue** shewe 10 **joining** [Y] ioying 13 **conceiving** breeding 19 **Fie** [Y] Fly 29 **will** [Y] wit 30 **stanza number 4** [Y] [no number in

B] **38 pleasure** [Y] our pleasure **49 You** [Y] Then **52 neat** next **68 their culled** thats cald **commendations** [B may instead read "commendatious."] **71 Pretty** [Y] A pretty **77 mis-shape** mishap **82 From** For **83 plenty** [Y] in plenty

## Upon a pair of gloves
Control text: Shakespeare Birthplace Trust Record Office (MS ER.93)

## Poems from *The Passionate Pilgrim*
Control text, poems 4, 17, 18: O1; remaining poems: O2
O1: The First Octavo of 1599
O2: The Second Octavo of 1599
Fo2: Folger Library MS V.a.339, fol. 203
*Madrigals*: Thomas Weelkes, *Madrigals* (1597)
*Helicon*: *England's Helicon* (1600)
**4.5 ear** [Fo2] eares **10 her** [O2] his
**10.1, 2 faded** vaded **8, 9 left'st** leftts
**12.12 stay'st** staies
**13.2, 6, 8 fadeth ... faded ... faded** vadeth ... vaded ... vaded
**14.17 Philomela sings** Philomela sits and sings **19 dite** ditte **20 daylight** [not in O2] **24 sighed** sight **27 a moon** an houre
**17.3 faith's** Faithes **4 Heart's** harts **16 freighted** fraughted **27 Herd** Heards **28 back** [*Madrigals*] blacke **33 lass** [*Madrigals*] loue **34 moan** [*Helicon*] woe
**18.45 be** [Fo2] by

## The Phoenix and Turtle
Control text: Robert Chester, *Loves Martyr: or Rosalins Complaint. Allegorically shadowing the truth of Loue, in the constant Fate of the Phoenix and Turtle* (1601), sigs. Z3ᵛ–Z4ᵛ

## Verses upon the Stanley Tomb at Tong
Control text: Inscription on the Stanley tomb at Tong

## On Ben Jonson
Control text: Bodleian MS Ashmole 38, p. 181 (c. 1650), a transcript, probably in the hand of Nicholas Burgh

## An Epitaph on Elias James
Control text: John Stow, *Survey of London* (1633), p. 825
B: Bodleian MS Rawlinson poet. 160, fol. 41
**3 reposeth** [B] reposes

## An extemporary epitaph on John Combe, a noted usurer
Control text: Fo1
Fo1: Folger MS V.a. 147, fol. 72ʳ (1673), a transcript, probably in the hand of Robert Dobyns
Fo2: Folger MS V.a. 345, p. 232
**1 here lies** here lyeth **2 not** now **3 lies** [Fo2] lyeth

## Another Epitaph on John Combe
Control text: Bodleian MS Ashmole 38, p. 180 (c. 1650), a transcript, probably in the hand of Nicholas Burgh
**William Shakespeare** hee [The epitaph is attributed at the end to "W. Shak."]

## Upon the King
Control text: King James I, *Works* (1616), beneath the engraving of the King on the frontispiece

## Epitaph on Himself
Control text: Shakespeare's grave at Stratford

# General Bibliography*

There is a huge and ever-expanding scholarly literature about Shakespeare and his culture. This general list and the lists that accompany the individual plays and the poems in this volume are only a small sampling of the available resources. Journals devoted to Shakespeare studies include *Shakespeare Bulletin, Shakespeare Jahrbuch* (Germany), *Shakespeare Quarterly, Shakespeare Studies,* and *Shakespeare Survey* (England); other journals, such as *English Literary History, English Literary Renaissance, Renaissance Quarterly, Representations,* or *Studies in English Literature,* also frequently publish essays on Shakespeare's works. The categories below are only approximate; many of the texts could properly belong in more than one category.

## Guides and Companions to Shakespeare Studies

Callaghan, Dympna, ed. *A Feminist Companion to Shakespeare.* Malden, Mass.: Blackwell, 2000.

De Grazia, Margreta, and Stanley Wells, eds. *The Cambridge Companion to Shakespeare.* Cambridge, Eng.: Cambridge University Press, 2001.

Drakakis, John, ed. *Alternative Shakespeares.* 2nd ed. London: Routledge, 1985.

Dutton, Richard, and Jean E. Howard, eds. *A Companion to Shakespeare's Works,* I: *The Tragedies.* Malden, Mass.: Blackwell, 2003.

———, eds. *A Companion to Shakespeare's Works,* II: *The Histories.* Malden, Mass.: Blackwell, 2003.

———, eds. *A Companion to Shakespeare's Works,* III: *The Comedies.* Malden, Mass.: Blackwell, 2003.

———, eds. *A Companion to Shakespeare's Works,* IV: *Poems, Problem Comedies, Late Plays.* Malden, Mass.: Blackwell, 2003.

Hattaway, Michael, ed. *The Cambridge Companion to Shakespeare's History Plays.* Cambridge, Eng.: Cambridge University Press, 2002.

Hawkes, Terence, ed. *Alternative Shakespeares, Volume 2.* London: Routledge, 1996.

Hodgdon, Barbara, and W. B. Worthen, eds. *A Companion to Shakespeare and Performance.* Malden, Mass.: Blackwell, 2005.

Jackson, Russell, ed. *The Cambridge Companion to Shakespeare on Film.* 2nd ed. Cambridge, Eng.: Cambridge University Press, 2007.

Kasten, David Scott, ed. *A Companion to Shakespeare.* Malden, Mass.: Blackwell, 1999.

Kinney, Arthur F. *Shakespeare by Stages: An Historical Introduction.* Malden, Mass.: Blackwell, 2003.

Leggatt, Alexander, ed. *The Cambridge Companion to Shakespearean Comedy.* Cambridge, Eng.: Cambridge University Press, 2002.

McDonald, Russ, ed. *The Bedford Companion to Shakespeare: An Introduction with Documents.* 2nd ed. Houndmills, Basingstoke: Palgrave Macmillan, 2001.

———, ed. *Shakespeare: An Anthology of Criticism and Theory, 1945–2000.* Malden, Mass.: Blackwell, 2004.

McEachern, Claire, ed. *The Cambridge Companion to Shakespearean Tragedy.* Cambridge, Eng.: Cambridge University Press, 2002.

*Edited by Holger Schott Syme, Department of English, University of Toronto.

Schoenfeldt, Michael. *A Companion to Shakespeare's Sonnets*. Malden, Mass.: Blackwell, 2006.

Smith, Emma, ed. *Shakespeare's Comedies: A Guide to Criticism*. Malden, Mass.: Blackwell, 2003.

———, ed. *Shakespeare's Histories: A Guide to Criticism*. Malden, Mass.: Blackwell, 2003.

———, ed. *Shakespeare's Tragedies: A Guide to Criticism*. Malden, Mass.: Blackwell, 2003.

Wells, Stanley, and Lena Cowen Orlin, eds. *Shakespeare: An Oxford Guide*. Oxford: Oxford University Press, 2003.

Wells, Stanley, and Sarah Stanton, eds. *The Cambridge Companion to Shakespeare on Stage*. New York: Cambridge University Press, 2002.

# Shakespeare's World

## Social, Political, and Economic History

Amussen, Susan Dwyer. *An Ordered Society: Gender and Class in Early Modern England*. New York: Columbia University Press, 1993.

Archer, Ian W. *The Pursuit of Stability: Social Relations in Elizabethan London*. New York: Cambridge University Press, 1991.

Ariès, Philippe, and Georges Duby, general eds. *A History of Private Life,* Volume III: *Passions of the Renaissance*. Ed. Roger Chartier. Trans. Arthur Goldhammer. Cambridge, Mass.: Belknap Press, 1989.

Armitage, David, and Michael J. Braddick, eds. *The British Atlantic World, 1500–1800*. New York: Palgrave Macmillan, 2002.

Barry, Jonathan, ed. *The Tudor and Stuart Town: A Reader in English Urban History, 1530–1688*. London: Longman, 1990.

Barry, Jonathan, and Christopher Brooks. *The Middling Sort of People: Culture, Society and Politics in England, 1550–1800*. Houndmills, Basingstoke: Palgrave Macmillan, 1994.

Barthelmey, Anthony Gerard. *Black Face, Maligned Race: The Representation of Blacks in English Drama from Shakespeare to Southerne*. Baton Rouge: Louisiana State University Press, 1987.

Beier, A. L. *Masterless Men: The Vagrancy Problem in England, 1560–1640*. New York: Methuen, 1985.

Beier, A. L., and Roger Finlay, eds. *London 1500–1700: The Making of the Metropolis*. New York: Longman, 1986.

Ben-Amos, Ilana Krausman. *Adolescence and Youth in Early Modern England*. New Haven: Yale University Press, 1994.

Bridenbaugh, Carl. *Vexed and Troubled Englishmen, 1590–1642*. New York: Oxford University Press, 1976.

Brigden, Susan. *New Worlds, Lost Worlds: The Rule of the Tudors, 1485–1603*. New York: Viking, 2001.

Burgess, Glenn. *The Politics of the Ancient Constitution: An Introduction to English Political Thought, 1603–1642*. University Park: Pennsylvania State University Press, 1993.

Capp, Bernard S. *When Gossips Meet: Women, Family, and Neighbourhood in Early Modern England*. Oxford: Oxford University Press, 2003.

Clark, Alice. *Working Life of Women in the Seventeenth Century.* Introduction by Amy Louise Erickson. 1968. New York: Routledge, 1992.

Clay, C. G. A. *Economic Expansion and Social Change: England 1500–1700*. 2 vols. New York: Cambridge University Press, 1984.

Cressy, David. *Birth, Marriage, and Death: Ritual, Religion, and the Life-Cycle in Tudor and Stuart England*. Oxford: Oxford University Press, 1997.

Cruickshank, Charles Greig. *Elizabeth's Army.* 2nd ed. Oxford: Clarendon, 1966.

Elliot, John Huxtable. *The Old World and the New, 1492–1650.* New York: Cambridge University Press, 1970.

Ellis, Steven G. *Tudor Ireland: Crown, Community, and the Conflict of Cultures, 1470–1603.* London: Longman, 1985.

Elton, G. R. *England Under the Tudors.* 3rd ed. New York: Routledge, 1991.

———. *The Tudor Revolution in Government: Administrative Changes in the Reign of Henry VIII.* Cambridge, Eng.: Cambridge University Press, 1959.

Emmison, F. G. *Elizabethan Life.* Chelmsford: Essex County Council, 1970.

Erickson, Amy Louise. *Women and Property in Early Modern England.* New York: Routledge, 1993.

Finlay, Roger. *Population and Metropolis: The Demography of London, 1580–1650.* Cambridge, Eng.: Cambridge University Press, 1981.

Fletcher, Anthony. *Gender, Sex, and Subordination in England, 1500–1800.* New Haven: Yale University Press, 1995.

Fletcher, Anthony, and John Stevenson, eds. *Order and Disorder in Early Modern England.* New York: Cambridge University Press, 1985.

Gaskill, Malcolm. *Crime and Mentalities in Early Modern England.* New York: Cambridge University Press, 2000.

Gittings, Clare. *Death, Burial and the Individual in Early Modern England.* London: Croom Helm, 1984.

Gowing, Laura. *Common Bodies: Women, Touch and Power in Seventeenth-Century England.* New Haven: Yale University Press, 2003.

Griffiths, Paul. *Youth and Authority: Formative Experiences in England, 1560–1640.* Oxford: Clarendon, 1996.

Griffiths, Paul, Adam Fox, and Steve Hindle, eds. *The Experience of Authority in Early Modern England.* New York: St. Martin's, 1996.

Guy, John A. *Queen of Scots: The True Life of Mary Stuart.* Boston: Houghton Mifflin, 2004.

———, ed. *The Reign of Elizabeth I: Court and Culture in the Last Decade.* Cambridge, Eng.: Cambridge University Press, 1995.

———. *Tudor England.* New York: Oxford University Press, 1988.

Heal, Felicity, and Clive Holmes. *The Gentry in England and Wales, 1500–1700.* Basingstoke: Macmillan, 1994.

Herrup, Cynthia B. *The Common Peace: Participation and the Criminal Law in Seventeenth-Century England.* New York: Cambridge University Press, 1987.

Hindle, Steve. *The State and Social Change in Early Modern England, c.1550–1640.* New York: St. Martin's, 2000.

Hirst, Derek. *Authority and Conflict: England, 1603–1658.* Cambridge, Mass.: Harvard University Press, 1986.

Ingram, Martin. *Church Courts, Sex, and Marriage in England, 1570–1640.* New York: Cambridge University Press, 1987.

James, Mervyn. *Society, Politics and Culture: Studies in Early Modern England.* New York: Cambridge University Press, 1986.

King, John N. *Tudor Royal Iconography: Literature and Art in an Age of Religious Crisis.* Princeton: Princeton University Press, 1989.

Kishlansky, Mark A. *A Monarchy Transformed: Britain 1603–1714.* New York: Penguin Books, 1996.

Klein, Joan Larsen. *Daughters, Wives, and Widows: Writings by Men about Women and Marriage in England, 1500–1640.* Urbana: University of Illinois Press, 1992.

Lake, Peter, with Michael Questier. *The Anti-Christ's Lewd Hat: Protestants, Papists and Players in Post-Reformation England.* New Haven: Yale University Press, 2002.

Laslett, Peter. *The World We Have Lost: Further Explored.* 3rd ed. New York: Scribner, 1984.

Levin, Carole. *The Heart and Stomach of a King: Elizabeth I and the Politics of Sex and Power.* Philadelphia: University of Pennsylvania Press, 1994.

Lockyer, Roger. *The Early Stuarts: A Political History of England, 1603–1642.* 2nd ed. London: Longman, 1999.

MacCaffrey, Wallace T. *Elizabeth I: War and Politics, 1588–1603.* Princeton: Princeton University Press, 1992.

Manning, Roger B. *Village Revolts: Social Protest and Popular Disturbances in England, 1509–1640.* Oxford: Clarendon, 1988.

Matar, Nabil I. *Islam in Britain, 1558–1685.* New York: Cambridge University Press, 1998.

———. *Turks, Moors, and Englishmen in the Age of Discovery.* New York: Columbia University Press, 1999.

Mendelson, Sara Heller, and Patricia Crawford. *Women in Early Modern England, 1550–1720.* Oxford: Clarendon, 1998.

Moody, T. W., F. X. Martin, and F. J. Byrne, eds. *A New History of Ireland,* Volume 3: *Early Modern Ireland, 1534–1691.* Oxford: Oxford University Press, 2001.

Mukerji, Chandra. *From Graven Images: Patterns of Modern Materialism.* New York: Columbia University Press, 1983.

Neale, J. E. *Elizabeth I and Her Parliaments, 1559–1581.* London: Cape, 1971.

———. *Queen Elizabeth I.* London: Pimlico, 1998.

Nichols, John, ed. *The Progresses and Public Processions of Queen Elizabeth.* 3 vols. London: J. Nichols, 1823.

Palliser, D. M. *The Age of Elizabeth: England under the Later Tudors, 1547–1603.* 2nd ed. New York: Longman, 1992.

Parry, J. H. *The Age of Reconnaissance: Discovery, Exploration, and Settlement, 1450 to 1650.* New York: Praeger, 1969.

Pearson, Lu Emily Hess. *Elizabethans at Home.* Stanford: Stanford University Press, 1967.

Peck, Linda Levy. *Court Patronage and Corruption in Early Stuart England.* Boston: Unwin Hyman, 1990.

Peters, Christine. *Women in Early Modern Britain, 1450–1640.* New York: Palgrave Macmillan, 2004.

Pocock, J. G. A. *The Ancient Constitution and the Feudal Law: Study of English Historical Thought in the Seventeenth Century—A Reissue with a Retrospect.* Rev. ed. New York: Cambridge University Press, 1987.

Rappaport, Steve. *Worlds within Worlds: Structures of Life in Sixteenth-Century London.* New York: Cambridge University Press, 1989.

Sharpe, J. A. *Crime in Early Modern England, 1550–1750.* 2nd ed. New York: Longman, 1999.

———. *Early Modern England: A Social History, 1550–1760.* 2nd ed. London: Arnold, 1997.

Slack, Paul. *The Impact of Plague in Tudor and Stuart England.* Boston: Routledge and Kegan Paul, 1985.

———. *Poverty and Policy in Tudor and Stuart England.* New York: Longman, 1988.

———, ed. *Rebellion, Popular Protest, and the Social Order in Early Modern England.* New York: Cambridge University Press, 1984.

Stone, Lawrence. *The Causes of the English Revolution, 1529–1642.* New York: Routledge, 2002.

———. *The Crisis of the Aristocracy, 1558–1641.* Oxford: Clarendon, 1965.

———. *The Family, Sex and Marriage in England, 1500–1800.* New York: Harper & Row, 1979.

Thirsk, Joan. *Economic Policy and Projects: The Development of a Consumer Society in Early Modern England.* Oxford: Clarendon, 1978.

Thomas, Keith. *Religion and the Decline of Magic: Studies in Popular Beliefs in Sixteenth and Seventeenth Century England.* New York: Scribner, 1971.

Underdown, David. *Fire from Heaven: Life in an English Town in the Seventeenth Century.* London: HarperCollins, 1992.

———. *Revel, Riot, and Rebellion: Popular Politics and Culture in England, 1603–1660.* Oxford: Clarendon, 1985.

Williams, Penry. *The Later Tudors: England, 1547–1603*. New York: Oxford University Press, 1995.

Wrightson, Keith. *Earthly Necessities: Economic Lives in Early Modern Britain*. New Haven: Yale University Press, 2000.

———. *English Society, 1580–1680*. London: Hutchinson, 1982.

Yates, Frances Amelia. *Astraea: The Imperial Theme in the Sixteenth Century*. London: Routledge and Kegan Paul, 1975.

Zagorin, Perez. *Rebels and Rulers, 1500–1660*. 2 vols. New York: Cambridge University Press, 1982.

## Intellectual and Religious History

Armitage, David. *The Ideological Origins of the British Empire*. New York: Cambridge University Press, 2000.

Baker, Herschel Clay. *The Race of Time: Three Lectures on Renaissance Historiography*. Toronto: University of Toronto Press, 1967.

Barkan, Leonard. *Nature's Work of Art: The Human Body as Image of the World*. New Haven: Yale University Press, 1975.

Bossy, John. *Christianity in the West, 1400–1700*. New York: Oxford University Press, 1985.

Bouwsma, William James. *John Calvin: A Sixteenth-Century Portrait*. New York: Oxford University Press, 1988.

Cassirer, Ernst. *The Individual and the Cosmos in Renaissance Philosophy*. Trans. Mario Domandi. Philadelphia: University of Pennsylvania Press, 1972.

Clark, Stuart. *Thinking with Demons: The Idea of Witchcraft in Early Modern Europe*. New York: Oxford University Press, 1997.

Collinson, Patrick. *The Birthpangs of Protestant England: Religion and Cultural Change in the Sixteenth and Seventeenth Centuries*. New York: St. Martin's, 1988.

———. *The Elizabethan Puritan Movement*. New York: Oxford University Press, 1990.

———. *The Religion of Protestants: The Church in English Society, 1559–1625*. Oxford: Clarendon, 1982.

Doran, Susan, and Christopher Durston. *Princes, Pastors, and People: The Church and Religion in England, 1500–1700*. Rev. ed. New York: Routledge, 2003.

Duffy, Eamon. *The Stripping of the Altars: Traditional Religion in England, c. 1400–c. 1580*. 2nd ed. New Haven: Yale University Press, 1992.

Gadd, Ian, and Alexandra Gillespie, eds. *John Stow (1525–1605) and the Making of the English Past*. London: British Library, 2004.

Haigh, Christopher. *English Reformations: Religion, Politics, and Society under the Tudors*. New York: Oxford University Press, 1993.

Hill, Christopher. *Society and Puritanism in Pre-Revolutionary England*. New York: Schocken Books, 1964.

Houlbrooke, Ralph A. *Death, Religion, and the Family in England, 1480–1700*. New York: Oxford University Press, 1998.

Kelly, Henry Ansgar. *Divine Providence in the England of Shakespeare's Histories*. Cambridge, Mass.: Harvard University Press, 1970.

Kilroy, Gerard. *Edmund Campion. Memory and Transcription*. Aldershot, Eng.: Ashgate, 2005.

Klaits, Joseph. *Servants of Satan: The Age of the Witch Hunts*. Bloomington: Indiana University Press, 1985.

Kristeller, Paul Oskar. *Renaissance Thought: The Classic, Scholastic, and Humanistic Strains*. New York: Harper & Row, 1961.

Levao, Ronald. *Renaissance Minds and Their Fictions: Cusanus, Sidney, Shakespeare*. Berkeley: University of California Press, 1985.

Levin, Harry. *The Myth of the Golden Age in the Renaissance*. Bloomington: University of Indiana Press, 1969.

Levy, Fred Jacob. *Tudor Historical Thought*. San Marino, Calif.: Huntington Library Press, 1967.

MacCulloch, Diarmaid. *The Later Reformation in England, 1547–1603*. 2nd ed. New York: Palgrave, 2001.

———. *The Reformation*. New York: Viking, 2004.

Mack, Peter, ed. *Renaissance Rhetoric*. New York: St. Martin's, 1994.

Marotti, Arthur F. *Religious Ideology and Cultural Fantasy: Catholic and Anti-Catholic Discourses in Early Modern England*. Notre Dame, Ind.: University of Notre Dame Press, 2005.

Marshall, Peter. *Beliefs and the Dead in Reformation England*. London: Oxford University Press, 2002.

Oldridge, Darren, ed. *The Witchcraft Reader*. London: Routledge, 2001.

Patterson, Annabel M. *Reading Holinshed's Chronicles*. Chicago: University of Chicago Press, 1994.

Popkin, Richard H. *The History of Skepticism from Erasmus to Spinoza*. Berkeley: University of California Press, 1979.

Sharpe, James. *Instruments of Darkness: Witchcraft in England 1550–1750*. New York: Penguin Books, 1996.

Shuger, Debora Kuller. *Habits of Thought in the English Renaissance: Religion, Politics, and the Dominant Culture*. Berkeley: University of California Press, 1990.

Sonnino, Lee A. *A Handbook to Sixteenth-Century Rhetoric*. London: Routledge and Kegan Paul, 1968.

Strong, Roy. *The Cult of Elizabeth: Elizabethan Portraiture and Pageantry*. London: Thames and Hudson, 1977.

———. *The English Icon: Elizabethan & Jacobean Portraiture*. New York: Pantheon Books, 1969.

Walsham, Alexandra. *Providence in Early Modern England*. New York: Oxford University Press, 1999.

Watt, Tessa. *Cheap Print and Popular Piety, 1560–1649*. New York: Cambridge University Press, 1991.

Wind, Edgar. *Pagan Mysteries in the Renaissance*. Rev. and enl. ed. London: Oxford University Press, 1980.

Woolf, D. R. *Reading History in Early Modern England*. New York: Cambridge University Press, 2000.

———. *The Social Circulation of the Past: English Historical Culture, 1500–1730*. New York: Oxford University Press, 2003.

## Cultural History and Early Modern Cultural Studies

Aers, David, Bob Hodge, and Gunther Kress. *Literature, Language, and Society in England, 1589–1680*. Totowa, N.J.: Barnes & Noble Books, 1981.

Agnew, Jean-Christophe. *Worlds Apart: The Market and the Theater in Anglo-American Thought, 1550–1750*. New York: Cambridge University Press, 1986.

Andersen, Jennifer, and Elizabeth Sauer, eds. *Books and Readers in Early Modern England: Material Studies*. Philadelphia: University of Pennsylvania Press, 2001.

Bakhtin, Mikhail. *Rabelais and His World*. Trans. Hélène Iswolsky. Rev. ed. Bloomington: Indiana University Press, 1984.

Baldwin, Thomas Whitfield. *William Shakespere's Small Latine & Lesse Greeke*. Urbana: University of Illinois Press, 1944.

Barkan, Leonard. *The Gods Made Flesh: Metamorphosis & the Pursuit of Paganism*. New Haven: Yale University Press, 1986.

Barker, Francis. *The Tremulous Private Body: Essays on Subjection*. New York: Methuen, 1984.

Baron, Sabrina Alcorn, ed. *The Reader Revealed*. Washington, D.C.: Folger Shakespeare Library, 2001.

Bartels, Emily Carroll. *Spectacles of Strangeness: Imperialism, Alienation, and Marlowe.* Philadelphia: University of Pennsylvania Press, 1993.

Beilin, Elaine V. *Redeeming Eve: Women Writers of the English Renaissance.* Princeton: Princeton University Press, 1987.

Blank, Paula. *Broken English: Dialects and the Politics of Language in Renaissance Literature.* New York: Routledge, 1996.

Bloom, Gina. *Voice in Motion: Staging Gender, Shaping Sound in Early Modern England.* Philadelphia: Pennsylvania University Press, 2007.

Bray, Alan. *Homosexuality in Renaissance England.* Rev. ed. New York: Columbia University Press, 1995.

Brayman Hackel, Heidi. *Reading Material in Early Modern England: Print, Gender, and Literacy.* New York: Cambridge University Press, 2005.

Briggs, Julia. *This Stage-Play World: Texts and Contexts, 1580–1625.* 2nd ed. New York: Oxford University Press, 1997.

Bristol, Michael D. *Carnival and Theater: Plebeian Culture and the Structure of Authority in Renaissance England.* New York: Methuen, 1985.

Brotton, Jerry. *Trading Territories: Mapping the Early Modern World.* London: Reaktion Books, 1997.

Brown, Pamela Allen. *Better a Shrew than a Sheep: Women, Drama, and the Culture of Jest in Early Modern England.* Ithaca, N.Y.: Cornell University Press, 2003.

Burke, Peter. *Popular Culture in Early Modern Europe.* New York: New York University Press, 1978.

Burt, Richard, and John Michael Archer, eds. *Enclosure Acts: Sexuality, Property, and Culture in Early Modern England.* Ithaca, N.Y.: Cornell University Press, 1994.

Bushnell, Rebecca W. *A Culture of Teaching: Early Modern Humanism in Theory and Practice.* Ithaca, N.Y.: Cornell University Press, 1996.

Buxton, John. *Elizabethan Taste.* London: Macmillan, 1963.

Caldwell, John. *The Oxford History of English Music.* New York: Oxford University Press, 1991.

Carroll, William C. *Fat King, Lean Beggar: Representations of Poverty in the Age of Shakespeare.* Ithaca, N.Y.: Cornell University Press, 1996.

Clegg, Cyndia Susan. *Press Censorship in Elizabethan England.* New York: Cambridge University Press, 1997.

———. *Press Censorship in Jacobean England.* New York: Cambridge University Press, 2001.

Cox, John D. *The Devil and the Sacred in English Drama, 1350–1642.* New York: Cambridge University Press, 2000.

Crane, Mary Thomas. *Framing Authority: Sayings, Self, and Society in Sixteenth-Century England.* Princeton: Princeton University Press, 1993.

Crawford, Julie. *Marvelous Protestantism: Monstrous Births in Post-Reformation England.* Baltimore: Johns Hopkins University Press, 2005.

Cressy, David. *Literacy and the Social Order: Reading and Writing in Tudor and Stuart England.* New York: Cambridge University Press, 1980.

De Grazia, Margreta, Maureen Quilligan, and Peter Stallybrass, eds. *Subject and Object in Renaissance Culture.* New York: Cambridge University Press, 1996.

Diehl, Huston. *Staging Reform, Reforming the Stage: Protestantism and Popular Theater in Early Modern England.* Ithaca, N.Y.: Cornell University Press, 1997.

Dolan, Frances E. *Dangerous Familiars: Representations of Domestic Crime in England, 1550–1700.* Ithaca, N.Y.: Cornell University Press, 1994.

———. *Whores of Babylon: Catholicism, Gender, and Seventeenth-Century Print Culture.* Ithaca, N.Y.: Cornell University Press, 1999.

Eisenstein, Elizabeth L. *The Printing Press as an Agent of Change: Communications and Cultural Transformations in Early-Modern Europe.* 2 vols. New York: Cambridge University Press, 1979.

Ferguson, Margaret W. *Dido's Daughters: Literacy, Gender, and Empire in Early Modern England and France*. Chicago: University of Chicago Press, 2003.

Ferguson, Margaret W., Maureen Quilligan, and Nancy J. Vickers, eds. *Rewriting the Renaissance: The Discourses of Sexual Difference in Early Modern Europe*. Chicago: University of Chicago Press, 1986.

Fisher, Will. *Materializing Gender in Early Modern English Literature and Culture*. New York: Cambridge University Press, 2006.

Fleming, Juliet. *Graffiti and the Writing Arts of Early Modern England*. Philadelphia: University of Pennsylvania Press, 2001.

Frye, Susan. *Elizabeth I: The Competition for Representation*. New York: Oxford University Press, 1993.

Fumerton, Patricia. *Cultural Aesthetics: Renaissance Literature and the Practice of Social Ornament*. Chicago: University of Chicago Press, 1991.

———. *Unsettled: The Culture of Mobility and the Working Poor in Early Modern England*. Chicago: University of Chicago Press, 2006.

Gillies, John. *Shakespeare and the Geography of Difference*. New York: Cambridge University Press, 1994.

Goldberg, Jonathan. *James I and the Politics of Literature: Jonson, Shakespeare, Donne, and Their Contemporaries*. Baltimore: Johns Hopkins University Press, 1983.

———. *Writing Matter: From the Hands of the English Renaissance*. Stanford: Stanford University Press, 1990.

———, ed. *Queering the Renaissance*. Durham, N.C.: Duke University Press, 1994.

Greenblatt, Stephen. *Learning to Curse: Essays in Early Modern Culture*. New York: Routledge, 1990.

———. *Renaissance Self-Fashioning: From More to Shakespeare*. Chicago: University of Chicago Press, 1980.

———, ed. *New World Encounters*. Berkeley: University of California Press, 1993.

———, ed. *Representing the English Renaissance*. Berkeley: University of California Press, 1988.

Grout, Donald Jay, and Hermine Weigel Williams. *A Short History of Opera*. 4th ed. New York: Columbia University Press, 2003.

Hall, Kim F. *Things of Darkness: Economies of Race and Gender in Early Modern England*. Ithaca, N.Y.: Cornell University Press, 1995.

Harris, Jonathan Gil. *Foreign Bodies and the Body Politic: Discourses of Social Pathology in Early Modern England*. New York: Cambridge University Press, 1998.

Harvey, Elizabeth D., ed. *Sensible Flesh: On Touch in Early Modern Culture*. Philadelphia: University of Pennsylvania Press, 2003.

Haselkorn, Anne M., and Betty S. Travitsky, eds. *The Renaissance Englishwoman in Print: Counterbalancing the Canon*. Amherst: University of Massachusetts Press, 1990.

Helgerson, Richard. *Forms of Nationhood: The Elizabethan Writing of England*. Chicago: University of Chicago Press, 1992.

Henderson, Katherine Usher, and Barbara F. McManus. *Half Humankind: Contexts and Texts of the Controversy About Women in England, 1540–1640*. Urbana: University of Illinois Press, 1985.

Hendricks, Margo, and Patricia Parker, eds. *Women, "Race," and Writing in the Early Modern Period*. New York: Routledge, 1994.

Hillman, David, and Carla Mazzio, eds. *The Body in Parts: Fantasies of Corporeality in Early Modern Europe*. New York: Routledge, 1997.

Hoeniger, F. David. *Medicine and Shakespeare in the English Renaissance*. Newark: University of Delaware Press, 1992.

Huizinga, Johan. *The Autumn of the Middle Ages*. Trans. Rodney J. Payton and Ulrich Mammitzsch. Chicago: University of Chicago Press, 1996.

Hull, Suzanne W. *Chaste, Silent & Obedient: English Books for Women, 1475–1640*. San Marino, Calif.: Huntington Library, 1982.

Hutson, Lorna. *The Usurer's Daughter: Male Friendship and Fictions of Women in Sixteenth-Century England.* New York: Routledge, 1994.

Javitch, Daniel. *Poetry and Courtliness in Renaissance England.* Princeton: Princeton University Press, 1978.

Jones, Ann Rosalind, and Peter Stallybrass. *Renaissance Clothing and the Materials of Memory.* New York: Cambridge University Press, 2000.

Jordan, Constance. *Renaissance Feminism: Literary Texts and Political Models.* Ithaca, N.Y.: Cornell University Press, 1990.

Knapp, Jeffrey. *Shakespeare's Tribe: Church, Nation, and Theater in Renaissance England.* Chicago: University of Chicago Press, 2002.

Laqueur, Thomas Walter. *Making Sex: Body and Gender from the Greeks to Freud.* Cambridge, Mass.: Harvard University Press, 1990.

MacDonald, Joyce Green. *Women and Race in Early Modern Texts.* New York: Cambridge University Press, 2002.

Magnusson, Lynne. *Shakespeare and Social Dialogue: Dramatic Language and Elizabethan Letters.* New York: Cambridge University Press, 1999.

Manley, Lawrence. *Literature and Culture in Early Modern London.* New York: Cambridge University Press, 1995.

Marcus, Leah S. *The Politics of Mirth: Jonson, Herrick, Milton, Marvell, and the Defense of Old Holiday Pastimes.* Chicago: University of Chicago Press, 1986.

McJannet, Linda. *The Sultan Speaks: Dialogue in English Plays and Histories about the Ottoman Turks.* New York: Palgrave Macmillan, 2006.

Meron, Theodor. *Bloody Constraint: War and Chivalry in Shakespeare.* New York: Oxford University Press, 1998.

Miller, David Lee, Sharon O'Dair, and Harold Weber, eds. *The Production of English Renaissance Culture.* Ithaca, N.Y.: Cornell University Press, 1994.

Montrose, Louis. *The Subject of Elizabeth: Authority, Gender, and Representation.* Chicago: University of Chicago Press, 2006.

Neill, Michael. *Issues of Death: Mortality and Identity in English Renaissance Tragedy.* Oxford: Clarendon, 1997.

Netzloff, Mark. *England's Internal Colonies: Class, Capital, and the Literature of Early Modern English Colonialism.* New York: Palgrave Macmillan, 2003.

Orlin, Lena Cowen. *Private Matters and Public Culture in Post-Reformation England.* Ithaca, N.Y.: Cornell University Press, 1994.

———, ed. *Material London, ca. 1600.* Philadelphia: University of Pennsylvania Press, 2000.

Parry, Graham. *The Golden Age Restor'd: The Culture of the Stuart Court, 1603–42.* New York: St. Martin's, 1981.

Paster, Gail Kern. *The Body Embarrassed: Drama and the Disciplines of Shame in Early Modern England.* Ithaca, N.Y.: Cornell University Press, 1993.

———. *Humoring the Body: Emotions and the Shakespearean Stage.* Chicago: University of Chicago Press, 2004.

Paster, Gail Kern, Katherine Rowe, and Mary Floyd-Wilson, eds. *Reading the Early Modern Passions: Essays in the Cultural History of Emotion.* Philadelphia: University of Pennsylvania Press, 2004.

Patterson, Annabel M. *Censorship and Interpretation: The Conditions of Writing and Reading in Early Modern England.* Madison: University of Wisconsin Press, 1984.

Peck, Linda Levy. *Consuming Splendor: Society and Culture in Seventeenth-Century England.* New York: Cambridge University Press, 2005.

Platt, Peter G. *Reason Diminished: Shakespeare and the Marvelous.* Lincoln: University of Nebraska Press, 1997.

Pollard, Tanya. *Drugs and Theater in Early Modern England.* New York: Oxford University Press, 2005.

Sanders, Eve Rachele. *Gender and Literacy on Stage in Early Modern England.* New York: Cambridge University Press, 1998.

Sawday, Jonathan. *The Body Emblazoned: Dissection and the Human Body in Renaissance Culture*. New York: Routledge, 1995.

Schoenfeldt, Michael C. *Bodies and Selves in Early Modern England: Physiology and Inwardness in Spenser, Shakespeare, Herbert, and Milton*. New York: Cambridge University Press, 1999.

Schwyzer, Philip. *Literature, Nationalism, and Memory in Early Modern England and Wales*. New York: Cambridge University Press, 2004.

Shapiro, James. *Shakespeare and the Jews*. New York: Columbia University Press, 1996.

Sharpe, Kevin, and Peter Lake, eds. *Culture and Politics in Early Stuart England*. Stanford: Stanford University Press, 1993.

Sherman, William H. *John Dee: The Politics of Reading and Writing in the English Renaissance*. Amherst: University of Massachusetts Press, 1995.

Shuger, Debora. *Censorship and Cultural Sensibility: The Regulation of Language in Tudor-Stuart England*. Philadelphia: University of Pennsylvania Press, 2006.

Simon, Joan. *Education and Society in Tudor England*. Cambridge, Eng.: Cambridge University Press, 1966.

Singh, Jyotsna G. *Colonial Narratives/Cultural Dialogues: 'Discoveries' of India in the Language of Colonialism*. New York: Routledge, 1996.

Smith, Bruce R. *The Acoustic World of Early Modern England: Attending to the O-Factor*. Chicago: University of Chicago Press, 1999.

———. *Homosexual Desire in Shakespeare's England: A Cultural Poetics*. Chicago: University of Chicago Press, 1994.

Smuts, R. Malcolm. *Court Culture and the Origins of a Royalist Tradition in Early Stuart England*. Philadelphia: University of Pennsylvania Press, 1987.

Stallybrass, Peter, and Allon White. *The Politics and Poetics of Transgression*. Ithaca, N.Y.: Cornell University Press, 1986.

Traub, Valerie, M. Lindsay Kaplan, and Dympna Callaghan, eds. *Feminist Readings of Early Modern Culture: Emerging Subjects*. New York: Cambridge University Press, 1996.

Turner, Henry S. *The English Renaissance Stage: Geometry, Poetics, and the Practical Spatial Arts 1580–1630*. New York: Oxford University Press, 2006.

Turner, James Grantham, ed. *Sexuality and Gender in Early Modern Europe: Institutions, Texts, Images*. New York: Cambridge University Press, 1993.

Wall, Wendy. *Staging Domesticity: Household Work and English Identity in Early Modern Drama*. New York: Cambridge University Press, 2002.

Watson, Robert N. *The Rest Is Silence: Death as Annihilation in the English Renaissance*. Berkeley: University of California Press, 1994.

Whigham, Frank. *Ambition and Privilege: The Social Tropes of Elizabethan Courtesy Theory*. Berkeley: University of California Press, 1984.

Woodbridge, Linda. *Vagrancy, Homelessness, and English Renaissance Literature*. Urbana: University of Illinois Press, 2001.

———. *Women and the English Renaissance: Literature and the Nature of Womankind, 1540 to 1620*. Urbana: University of Illinois Press, 1984.

## Shakespeare's Generic, Literary, and Theatrical Contexts

Alpers, Paul. *What Is Pastoral?* Chicago: University of Chicago Press, 1996.

Altman, Joel. *The Tudor Play of Mind: Rhetorical Inquiry and the Development of Elizabethan Drama*. Berkeley: University of California Press, 1978.

Barish, Jonas. *The Antitheatrical Prejudice*. Berkeley: University of California Press, 1981.

Bate, Jonathan. *Shakespeare and Ovid*. Oxford: Clarendon, 1993.

Bates, Catherine. *The Rhetoric of Courtship in Elizabethan Language and Literature*. New York: Cambridge University Press, 1992.

Beckwith, Sarah. *Signifying God: Social Relation and Symbolic Act in the York Corpus Christi Plays.* Chicago: University of Chicago Press, 2001.

Belsey, Catherine. *The Subject of Tragedy: Identity and Difference in Renaissance Drama.* New York: Methuen, 1985.

Bevington, David M. *From "Mankind" to Marlowe: Growth of Structure in the Popular Drama of Tudor England.* Cambridge, Mass.: Harvard University Press, 1962.

———. *Tudor Drama and Politics: A Critical Approach to Topical Meaning.* Cambridge, Mass.: Harvard University Press, 1968.

Bly, Mary. *Queer Virgins and Virgin Queans on the Early Modern Stage.* New York: Oxford University Press, 2000.

Bowers, Fredson Thayer. *Elizabethan Revenge Tragedy, 1587–1642.* Princeton: Princeton University Press, 1940.

Braden, Gordon. *Renaissance Tragedy and the Senecan Tradition: Anger's Privilege.* New Haven: Yale University Press, 1985.

Bruster, Douglas. *Drama and the Market in the Age of Shakespeare.* New York: Cambridge University Press, 1992.

Bullough, Geoffrey, ed. *Narrative and Dramatic Sources of Shakespeare.* 8 vols. New York: Columbia University Press, 1957–75.

Butler, Martin. *Theatre and Crisis, 1632–1642.* New York: Cambridge University Press, 1984.

Carroll, William C. *The Metamorphoses of Shakespearean Comedy.* Princeton: Princeton University Press, 1985.

Cartwright, Kent. *Theatre and Humanism: English Drama in the Sixteenth Century.* New York: Cambridge University Press, 1999.

Clubb, Louise George. *Italian Drama in Shakespeare's Time.* New Haven: Yale University Press, 1989.

Cohen, Walter. *Drama of a Nation: Public Theater in Renaissance England and Spain.* Ithaca, N.Y.: Cornell University Press, 1985.

Crewe, Jonathan. *Trials of Authorship: Anterior Forms and Poetic Reconstruction from Wyatt to Shakespeare.* Berkeley: University of California Press, 1990.

Danson, Lawrence. *Shakespeare's Dramatic Genres.* New York: Oxford University Press, 2000.

Dawson, Anthony B., and Paul Yachnin. *The Culture of Playgoing in Shakespeare's England: A Collaborative Debate.* New York: Cambridge University Press, 2001.

Dillon, Janette. *Language and Stage in Medieval and Renaissance England.* New York: Cambridge University Press, 1998.

Felperin, Howard. *Shakespearean Romance.* Princeton: Princeton University Press, 1972.

Finkelpearl, Philip J. *John Marston of the Middle Temple: An Elizabethan Dramatist in His Social Setting.* Cambridge, Mass.: Harvard University Press, 1969.

Gardiner, Harold C. *Mysteries' End: An Investigation of the Last Days of the Medieval Religious Stage.* New Haven: Yale University Press, 1946.

Halasz, Alexandra. *The Marketplace of Print: Pamphlets and the Public Sphere in Early Modern England.* New York: Cambridge University Press, 1997.

Harbage, Alfred. *Shakespeare and the Rival Traditions.* New York: Macmillan, 1952.

Hardison, O. B. *Christian Rite and Christian Drama in the Middle Ages: Essays in the Origin and Early History of Modern Drama.* Baltimore: Johns Hopkins University Press, 1965.

Heinemann, Margot. *Puritanism and Theatre: Thomas Middleton and Opposition Drama under the Early Stuarts.* New York: Cambridge University Press, 1980.

Honan, Park. *Christopher Marlowe: Poet & Spy.* New York: Oxford University Press, 2005.

Honigmann, E. A. J., ed. *Shakespeare and His Contemporaries: Essays in Comparison.* Manchester: Manchester University Press, 1986.

———, ed. *Shakespeare's Impact on His Contemporaries.* London: Macmillan, 1982.

Howard, Jean E. *Theater of a City: The Places of London Comedy, 1598–1642*. Philadelphia: University of Pennsylvania Press, 2007.

Hunter, G. K. *John Lyly: The Humanist as Courtier*. Cambridge, Mass.: Harvard University Press, 1962.

Jones, Emrys. *The Origins of Shakespeare*. Oxford: Clarendon, 1977.

———. *Scenic Form in Shakespeare*. Oxford: Clarendon, 1971.

Kastan, David Scott, and Peter Stallybrass, eds. *Staging the Renaissance: Reinterpretations of Elizabethan and Jacobean Drama*. New York: Routledge, 1991.

Kermode, Lloyd Edward, Jason Scott-Warren, and Martine van Elk, eds. *Tudor Drama Before Shakespeare, 1485–1590: New Directions for Research, Criticism, and Pedagogy*. New York: Palgrave Macmillan, 2004.

Kolve, V. A. *The Play Called Corpus Christi*. Stanford: Stanford University Press, 1966.

Leggatt, Alexander. *Citizen Comedy in the Age of Shakespeare*. Toronto: University of Toronto Press, 1973.

———. *Introduction to English Renaissance Comedy*. Manchester: Manchester University Press, 1999.

Levin, Harry. *Shakespeare and the Revolution of the Times: Perspectives and Commentaries*. New York: Oxford University Press, 1976.

Levith, Murray J. *Shakespeare's Italian Settings and Plays*. Basingstoke: Macmillan, 1989.

Lomax, Marion. *Stage Images and Traditions: Shakespeare to Ford*. New York: Cambridge University Press, 1987.

Martindale, Charles, and A. B. Taylor, eds. *Shakespeare and the Classics*. New York: Cambridge University Press, 2004.

Masten, Jeffrey. *Textual Intercourse: Collaboration, Authorship, and Sexualities in Renaissance Drama*. New York: Cambridge University Press, 1997.

McLuskie, Kathleen. *Renaissance Dramatists*. New York: Harvester Wheatsheaf, 1989.

McMillin, Scott. *The Elizabethan Theatre and the Book of Sir Thomas More*. Ithaca, N.Y.: Cornell University Press, 1987.

McMillin, Scott, and Sally-Beth MacLean. *The Queen's Men and Their Plays*. New York: Cambridge University Press, 1998.

McMullan, Gordon, and Jonathan Hope, eds. *The Politics of Tragicomedy: Shakespeare and After*. New York: Routledge, 1991.

Miola, Robert S. *Shakespeare's Reading*. New York: Oxford University Press, 2000.

———. *Shakespeare's Rome*. New York: Cambridge University Press, 1983.

Newcomb, Lori Humphrey. *Reading Popular Romance in Early Modern England*. New York: Columbia University Press, 2002.

Norbrook, David. *Poetry and Politics in the English Renaissance*. London: Routledge and Kegan Paul, 1984.

Orgel, Stephen. *The Illusion of Power: Political Theater in the English Renaissance*. Berkeley: University of California Press, 1975.

Peters, Julie Stone. *Theatre of the Book, 1480–1880: Print, Text, and Performance in Europe*. New York: Oxford University Press, 2000.

Riggs, David. *Ben Jonson: A Life*. Cambridge, Mass.: Harvard University Press, 1989.

———. *The World of Christopher Marlowe*. London: Faber and Faber, 2004.

Rose, Mark. *Shakespearean Design*. Cambridge, Mass.: Belknap Press, 1972.

Rose, Mary Beth. *The Expense of Spirit: Love and Sexuality in English Renaissance Drama*. Ithaca, N.Y.: Cornell University Press, 1988.

Salingar, Leo. *Dramatic Form in Shakespeare and the Jacobeans: Essays*. New York: Cambridge University Press, 1986.

———. *Shakespeare and the Traditions of Comedy*. New York: Cambridge University Press, 1974.

Schwyzer, Philip. *Archaeologies of English Renaissance Literature*. New York: Oxford University Press, 2007.

Shapiro, James. *Rival Playwrights: Marlowe, Jonson, Shakespeare*. New York: Columbia University Press, 1991.

Snyder, Susan. *The Comic Matrix of Shakespeare's Tragedies: Romeo and Juliet, Hamlet, Othello, and* King Lear. Princeton: Princeton University Press, 1979.

Spivack, Bernard. *Shakespeare and the Allegory of Evil: The History of a Metaphor in Relation to His Major Villains.* New York: Columbia University Press, 1958.

Thomas, Vivian. *The Moral Universe of Shakespeare's Problem Plays.* New York: Routledge, 1991.

Vickers, Brian, ed. *English Renaissance Literary Criticism.* New York: Oxford University Press, 1999.

Vitkus, Daniel. *Turning Turk: English Theater and the Multicultural Mediterranean, 1570–1630.* New York: Palgrave Macmillan, 2003.

Weimann, Robert. *Shakespeare and the Popular Tradition in the Theater: Studies in the Social Dimension of Dramatic Form and Function.* Ed. Robert Schwartz. Baltimore: Johns Hopkins University Press, 1978.

Whitney, Charles. *Early Responses to Renaissance Drama.* New York: Cambridge University Press, 2006.

Woolf, Rosemary. *The English Mystery Plays.* Berkeley: University of California Press, 1972.

## The Playing Field: Theaters, Actors, Patrons, and the State

Astington, John H. *English Court Theatre, 1558–1642.* Cambridge, Eng.: Cambridge University Press, 1999.

———, ed. *The Development of Shakespeare's Theater.* New York: AMS Press, 1992.

Barroll, J. Leeds. *Politics, Plague, and Shakespeare's Theater: The Stuart Years.* Ithaca, N.Y.: Cornell University Press, 1991.

Beckerman, Bernard. *Shakespeare at the Globe, 1599–1609.* New York: Macmillan, 1962.

Bentley, Gerald Eades. *The Jacobean and Caroline Stage.* 7 vols. Oxford: Clarendon, 1941–68.

———. *The Profession of Dramatist in Shakespeare's Time, 1590–1642.* Princeton: Princeton University Press, 1971.

———. *The Profession of Player in Shakespeare's Time, 1590–1642.* Princeton: Princeton University Press, 1984.

Berry, Herbert. *Shakespeare's Playhouses.* Illustrated by C. Walter Hodges. New York: AMS Press, 1987.

Bradbrook, M. C. *The Rise of the Common Player: A Study of Actor and Society in Shakespeare's England.* Cambridge, Mass.: Harvard University Press, 1962.

Chambers, E. K. *The Elizabethan Stage.* 4 vols. Oxford: Clarendon, 1923.

———. *The Mediaeval Stage.* 2 vols. Oxford: Clarendon, 1903.

Clare, Janet. *Art Made Tongue-Tied by Authority: Elizabethan and Jacobean Dramatic Censorship.* 2nd ed. Manchester: Manchester University Press, 1999.

Cook, Ann Jennalie. *The Privileged Playgoers of Shakespeare's London: 1576–1642.* Princeton: Princeton University Press, 1981.

Cox, John D., and David Scott Kastan, eds. *A New History of Early English Drama.* New York: Columbia University Press, 1997.

Dessen, Alan C. *Elizabethan Stage Conventions and Modern Interpreters.* Cambridge, Eng.: Cambridge University Press, 1984.

———. *Recovering Shakespeare's Theatrical Vocabulary.* New York: Cambridge University Press, 1995.

Dessen, Alan C., and Leslie Thomson. *A Dictionary of Stage Directions in English Drama, 1580–1642.* New York: Cambridge University Press, 1999.

Dillon, Janette. *The Cambridge Introduction to Early English Theatre.* New York: Cambridge University Press, 2006.

Dutton, Richard. *Licensing, Censorship and Authorship in Early Modern England: Buggeswords.* Houndmills, Basingstoke: Palgrave Macmillan, 2000.

———. *Mastering the Revels: The Regulation and Censorship of English Renaissance Drama*. London: Macmillan, 1991.

Dutton, Richard, Alison Findlay, and Richard Wilson, eds. *Region, Religion, and Patronage: Lancastrian Shakespeare*. Manchester: Manchester University Press, 2003.

Erne, Lukas. *Shakespeare as Literary Dramatist*. New York: Cambridge University Press, 2003.

Foakes, R. A. *Illustrations of the English Stage, 1580–1642*. Stanford: Stanford University Press, 1985.

Gair, W. Reavley. *The Children of Paul's: The Story of a Theatre Company, 1553–1608*. New York: Cambridge University Press, 1982.

Greg, W. W., ed. *Dramatic Documents from the Elizabethan Playhouses: Stage Plots: Actor's Parts: Prompt Books*. 2 vols. Oxford: Clarendon, 1931.

Gurr, Andrew. *Playgoing in Shakespeare's London*. 3rd ed. New York: Cambridge University Press, 2004.

———. *The Shakespeare Company, 1594–1642*. New York: Cambridge University Press, 2004.

———. *The Shakespearian Playing Companies*. Oxford: Clarendon, 1996.

———. *The Shakespearean Stage, 1574–1642*. 3rd ed. New York: Cambridge University Press, 1992.

Gurr, Andrew, and John Orrell. *Rebuilding Shakespeare's Globe*. London: Weidenfeld & Nicolson, 1989.

Harris, Jonathan Gil, and Natasha Korda, eds. *Staged Properties in Early Modern Drama*. New York: Cambridge University Press, 2002.

Hattaway, Michael. *Elizabethan Popular Theatre: Plays in Performance*. London: Routledge and Kegan Paul, 1982.

Henslowe, Philip. *Henslowe's Diary*. Ed. R. A. Foakes. 2nd ed. New York: Cambridge University Press, 2002.

Hodges, C. Walter. *The Globe Restored: A Study of the Elizabethan Theatre*. New York: Norton, 1973.

Holland, Peter, and Stephen Orgel, eds. *From Performance to Print in Shakespeare's England*. New York: Palgrave Macmillan, 2006.

———, eds. *From Script to Stage in Early Modern England*. Houndmills, Basingstoke: Palgrave Macmillan, 2004.

Ingram, William. *The Business of Playing: The Beginnings of Adult Professional Theater in Elizabethan London*. Ithaca, N.Y.: Cornell University Press, 1992.

Kernan, Alvin. *Shakespeare, the King's Playwright: Theater in the Stuart Court, 1603–1613*. New Haven: Yale University Press, 1995.

King, T. J. *Shakespearean Staging, 1599–1642*. Cambridge, Mass.: Harvard University Press, 1971.

Knutson, Roslyn Lander. *Playing Companies and Commerce in Shakespeare's Time*. Cambridge, Eng.: Cambridge University Press, 2001.

———. *The Repertory of Shakespeare's Company, 1594–1613*. Fayetteville: University of Arkansas Press, 1991.

Laroque, François. *Shakespeare's Festive World: Elizabethan Seasonal Entertainment and the Professional Stage*. New York: Cambridge University Press, 1991.

Lopez, Jeremy. *Theatrical Convention and Audience Response in Early Modern Drama*. New York: Cambridge University Press, 2002.

MacIntyre, Jean. *Costumes and Scripts in the Elizabethan Theatres*. Edmonton: University of Alberta Press, 1992.

Milling, Jane, and Peter Thomson, eds. *The Cambridge History of British Theatre*, Vol. 1: *Origins to 1660*. New York: Cambridge University Press, 2004.

Mulryne, J. R., and Margaret Shewring, eds. *Shakespeare's Globe Rebuilt*. New York: Cambridge University Press, 1997.

Munro, Lucy. *Children of the Queen's Revels: A Jacobean Theatre Repertory*. New York: Cambridge University Press, 2005.

Palfrey, Simon, and Tiffany Stern. *Shakespeare in Parts*. Oxford: Oxford University Press, 2007.

Shapiro, Michael. *Children of the Revels: The Boy Companies of Shakespeare's Time and Their Plays*. New York: Columbia University Press, 1977.

Smith, Irwin. *Shakespeare's Blackfriars Playhouse: Its History and Its Design*. New York: New York University Press, 1964.

Stern, Tiffany. *Making Shakespeare: From Stage to Page*. New York: Routledge, 2004.

———. *Rehearsal from Shakespeare to Sheridan*. Oxford: Clarendon, 2000.

White, Paul Whitfield, and Suzanne Westfall, eds. *Shakespeare and Theatrical Patronage in Early Modern England*. New York: Cambridge University Press, 2002.

Wickham, Glynne. *Early English Stages, 1300 to 1660*. 4 vols. New York: Routledge, 2002.

Wickham, Glynne, Herbert Berry, and William Ingram, eds. *English Professional Theatre, 1530–1660*. New York: Cambridge University Press, 2000.

# Shakespeare's Life

Alexander, Peter. *Shakespeare's Life and Art*. New ed. New York: New York University Press, 1961.

Bate, Jonathan. *The Genius of Shakespeare*. London: Picador, 1997.

Bradbrook, M. C. *Shakespeare: The Poet in His World*. New York: Columbia University Press, 1978.

Chambers, E. K. *William Shakespeare: A Study of Facts and Problems*. 2 vols. Oxford: Clarendon, 1930.

Duncan-Jones, Katherine. *Ungentle Shakespeare: Scenes from His Life*. London: Arden Shakespeare, 2001.

Eccles, Mark. *Shakespeare in Warwickshire*. Madison: University of Wisconsin Press, 1961.

Edwards, Philip. *Shakespeare: A Writer's Progress*. New York: Oxford University Press, 1986.

Fraser, Russell A. *Shakespeare, The Later Years*. New York: Columbia University Press, 1992.

———. *Young Shakespeare*. New York: Columbia University Press, 1988.

Greenblatt, Stephen. *Will in the World: How Shakespeare Became Shakespeare*. New York: Norton, 2004.

Greer, Germaine. *Shakespeare*. New York: Oxford University Press, 1986.

Honan, Park. *Shakespeare: A Life*. New York: Oxford University Press, 1998.

Honigmann, E. A. J. *Shakespeare: The Lost Years*. 2nd ed. Manchester: Manchester University Press, 1998.

Hotson, Leslie. *Shakespeare Versus Shallow*. Boston: Little, Brown, and Company, 1931.

Levi, Peter. *The Life and Times of William Shakespeare*. New York: Macmillan, 1988.

Matus, Irvin Leigh. *Shakespeare, The Living Record*. Houndmills, Basingstoke: Macmillan, 1991.

Reese, M. M. *Shakespeare: His World and His Work*. Rev. ed. London: Edward Arnold, 1980.

Sams, Eric. *The Real Shakespeare: Retrieving the Early Years, 1564–1594*. New Haven: Yale University Press, 1995.

Schmidgall, Gary. *Shakespeare and the Poet's Life*. Lexington: University Press of Kentucky, 1990.

Schoenbaum, Samuel. *Shakespeare's Lives*. New ed. New York: Oxford University Press, 1991.

———. *William Shakespeare: A Compact Documentary Life*. Rev. ed. New York: Oxford University Press, 1987.

Shapiro, James. *A Year in the Life of William Shakespeare: 1599*. New York: Harper-Collins, 2005.

Taylor, Gary. *Reinventing Shakespeare: A Cultural History, from the Restoration to the Present*. New York: Weidenfeld & Nicolson, 1989.

Thomson, Peter. *Shakespeare's Professional Career*. New York: Cambridge University Press, 1992.

Wells, Stanley. *Shakespeare: A Life in Drama*. New York: Norton, 1995.

———. *Shakespeare: For All Time*. London: Macmillan, 2002.

Wood, Michael. *In Search of Shakespeare*. London: BBC, 2003.

# Critical Approaches

## Classics of Shakespeare Criticism

Barber, C. L. *Shakespeare's Festive Comedy: A Study of Dramatic Form and Its Relation to Social Custom*. Princeton: Princeton University Press, 1959.

Bradley, A. C. *Shakespearean Tragedy: Lectures on Hamlet, Othello, King Lear, Macbeth*. 3rd ed. New York: St. Martin's Press, 1992.

Coleridge, Samuel Taylor. *Coleridge on Shakespeare: The Text of the Lectures of 1811–12*. Ed. R. A. Foakes. Charlottesville: University Press of Virginia, 1971.

———. *Shakespearean Criticism*. 2 vols. Ed. T. M. Raysor. 2nd ed. New York: Dutton, 1969.

Eliot, T. S. "Shakespeare and the Stoicism of Seneca." *Selected Essays, 1917–1932*. New ed. New York: Harcourt, Brace, 1950.

Empson, William. *The Structure of Complex Words*. 3rd ed. London: Chatto & Windus, 1977.

Frye, Northrop. *Fools of Time: Studies in Shakespearean Tragedy*. Toronto: University of Toronto Press, 1967.

———. *A Natural Perspective: The Development of Shakespearean Comedy and Romance*. New York: Columbia University Press, 1965.

Hazlitt, William. *Characters of Shakespear's Plays*. London, 1817.

Johnson, Samuel. *Samuel Johnson on Shakespeare*. Ed. H. R. Woudhuysen. New York: Penguin, 1989.

Jones, Ernest. *Hamlet and Oedipus*. New York: Norton, 1949.

Kermode, Frank, ed. *Four Centuries of Shakespearian Criticism*. 1965. New York: Avon, 1965.

Knight, G. Wilson. *The Wheel of Fire: Interpretations of Shakespearean Tragedy, with Three New Essays*. 4th ed. New York: Harper & Row, 1977.

Kott, Jan. *Shakespeare Our Contemporary*. Trans. Boleslaw Taborski. Garden City, N.Y.: Anchor Books, 1966.

Morgann, Maurice. *Shakespearean Criticism*. Ed. Daniel A. Fineman. Oxford: Clarendon, 1972.

Spurgeon, Caroline F. E. *Shakespeare's Imagery, and What It Tells Us*. New York: Macmillan, 1935.

Tillyard, E. M. W. *Shakespeare's History Plays*. London: Chatto and Windus, 1944.

Vickers, Brian, ed. *Shakespeare: The Critical Heritage*. 6 vols. London: Routledge and Kegan Paul, 1974–1981.

## General Studies

Barton, Anne. *Essays, Mainly Shakespearean*. New York: Cambridge University Press, 1994.

Bloom, Harold. *Shakespeare: The Invention of the Human*. New York: Riverhead Books, 1998.

Burckhardt, Sigurd. *Shakespearean Meanings*. Princeton: Princeton University Press, 1968.

Garber, Marjorie. *Shakespeare After All*. New York: Pantheon, 2004.

Hibbard, G. R. *The Making of Shakespeare's Dramatic Poetry*. Toronto: University of Toronto Press, 1981.

Honigmann, E. A. J. *Myriad-Minded Shakespeare: Essays on the Tragedies, Problem Comedies, and Shakespeare the Man*. 2nd ed. New York: St. Martin's Press, 1998.

Jones, John. *Shakespeare at Work*. New York: Oxford University Press, 1995.

Nuttall, A. D. *Shakespeare the Thinker*. New Haven: Yale University Press, 2007.

Ryan, Kiernan. *Shakespeare*. 3rd ed. New York: Palgrave Macmillan, 2001.

## Language and Style

Baxter, John. *Shakespeare's Poetic Styles: Verse into Drama*. London: Routledge and Kegan Paul, 1980.

Blake, N. F. *Shakespeare's Language: An Introduction*. New York: St. Martin's Press, 1983.

Cercignani, Fausto. *Shakespeare's Works and Elizabethan Pronunciation*. New York: Oxford University Press, 1981.

Clemen, Wolfgang. *Shakespeare's Soliloquies*. Trans. Charity Scott Stokes. New York: Methuen, 1987.

———. *The Development of Shakespeare's Imagery*. New York: Hill and Wang, 1962.

Danson, Lawrence. *Tragic Alphabet: Shakespeare's Drama of Language*. New Haven: Yale University Press, 1974.

Donawerth, Jane. *Shakespeare and the Sixteenth-Century Study of Language*. Urbana: University of Illinois Press, 1984.

Edwards, Philip, Inga-Stina Ewbank, and G. K. Hunter, eds. *Shakespeare's Styles: Essays in Honour of Kenneth Muir*. New York: Cambridge University Press, 1980.

Gross, Kenneth. *Shakespeare's Noise*. Chicago: University of Chicago Press, 2001.

Hope, Jonathan. *Shakespeare's Grammar*. London: Arden Shakespeare, 2003.

Houston, John Porter. *Shakespearean Sentences: A Study in Style and Syntax*. Baton Rouge: Louisiana State University Press, 1988.

Hussey, S. S. *The Literary Language of Shakespeare*. 2nd ed. New York: Longman, 1992.

Kökeritz, Helge. *Shakespeare's Pronunciation*. New Haven: Yale University Press, 1953.

Mahood, M. M. *Shakespeare's Wordplay*. London: Methuen, 1957.

McDonald, Russ. *Shakespeare and the Arts of Language*. New York: Oxford University Press, 2001.

———. *Shakespeare's Late Style*. New York: Cambridge University Press, 2006.

Miriam Joseph, Sister. *Shakespeare's Use of the Arts of Language*. New York: Columbia University Press, 1947.

Palfrey, Simon. *Late Shakespeare: A New World of Words*. Oxford: Clarendon, 1997.

Parker, Patricia. *Literary Fat Ladies: Rhetoric, Gender, Property*. New York: Methuen, 1987.

———. *Shakespeare from the Margins: Language, Culture, Context*. Chicago: University of Chicago Press, 1996.

Partridge, Eric. *Shakespeare's Bawdy: A Literary & Psychological Essay and a Comprehensive Glossary*. 3rd ed. New York: Routledge, 1991.

Trousdale, Marion. *Shakespeare and the Rhetoricians*. Chapel Hill: University of North Carolina Press, 1982.

Vickers, Brian. *The Artistry of Shakespeare's Prose*. London: Methuen, 1968.

———. "Shakespeare's Use of Rhetoric." *A New Companion to Shakespeare Studies*. Ed. Kenneth Muir and S. Schoenbaum. Cambridge, Eng.: Cambridge University Press, 1971. 83–98.

Wright, George T. *Shakespeare's Metrical Art*. Berkeley: University of California Press, 1988.

Young, David. *The Action to the Word: Structure and Style in Shakespearean Tragedy.* New Haven: Yale University Press, 1990.

## Psychoanalytic Criticism

Adelman, Janet. *Suffocating Mothers: Fantasies of Maternal Origin in Shakespeare's Plays,* Hamlet *to* The Tempest. New York: Routledge, 1992.

Armstrong, Philip. *Shakespeare in Psychoanalysis.* New York: Routledge, 2001.

Berger, Harry Jr. *Making Trifles of Terrors: Redistributing Complicities in Shakespeare.* Stanford: Stanford University Press, 1997.

Charnes, Linda. *Notorious Identity: Materializing the Subject in Shakespeare.* Cambridge, Mass.: Harvard University Press, 1993.

Enterline, Lynn. *The Rhetoric of the Body from Ovid to Shakespeare.* Cambridge, Eng.: Cambridge University Press, 2000.

Fineman, Joel. *Shakespeare's Perjured Eye: The Invention of Poetic Subjectivity in the Sonnets.* Berkeley: University of California Press, 1986.

Freedman, Barbara. *Staging the Gaze: Postmodernism, Psychoanalysis, and Shakespearean Comedy.* Ithaca, N.Y.: Cornell University Press, 1991.

Garber, Marjorie. *Coming of Age in Shakespeare.* New York: Methuen, 1981.

———. *Shakespeare's Ghost Writers: Literature as Uncanny Causality.* New York: Methuen, 1987.

Girard, René. *A Theater of Envy: William Shakespeare.* New York: Oxford University Press, 1991.

Holland, Norman N. *Psychoanalysis and Shakespeare.* New York: Octagon, 1966.

Lupton, Julia Reinhard, and Kenneth Reinhard. *After Oedipus: Shakespeare in Psychoanalysis.* Ithaca, N.Y.: Cornell University Press, 1993.

Marshall, Cynthia. *The Shattering of the Self: Violence, Subjectivity, and Early Modern Texts.* Baltimore: Johns Hopkins University Press, 2002.

Mazzio, Carla, and Douglas Trevor, eds. *Historicism, Psychoanalysis, and Early Modern Culture.* New York: Routledge, 2000.

Pye, Christopher. *The Regal Phantasm: Shakespeare and the Politics of Spectacle.* New York: Routledge, 1990.

———. *The Vanishing: Shakespeare, the Subject, and Early Modern Culture.* Durham, N.C.: Duke University Press, 2000.

Schwartz, Murray M., and Coppélia Kahn, eds. *Representing Shakespeare: New Psychoanalytic Essays.* Baltimore: Johns Hopkins University Press, 1982.

Skura, Meredith Anne. *The Literary Use of the Psychoanalytic Process.* New Haven: Yale University Press, 1981.

———. *Shakespeare the Actor and the Purposes of Playing.* Chicago: University of Chicago Press, 1993.

Wheeler, Richard P. *Shakespeare's Development and the Problem Comedies: Turn and Counter-Turn.* Berkeley: University of California Press, 1981.

Zimmerman, Susan, ed. *Erotic Politics: Desire on the Renaissance Stage.* New York: Routledge, 1992.

## Feminism, Gender Studies, and Queer Studies

Bamber, Linda. *Comic Women, Tragic Men: A Study of Gender and Genre in Shakespeare.* Stanford: Stanford University Press, 1982.

Barker, Deborah, and Ivo Kamps, eds. *Shakespeare and Gender: A History.* New York: Verso, 1995.

Boose, Lynda E. "The Father and the Bride in Shakespeare." *PMLA* 97 (1982): 325–47.

Callaghan, Dympna. *Shakespeare Without Women: Representing Gender and Race on the Renaissance Stage.* New York: Routledge, 2000.

————. *Women and Gender in Renaissance Tragedy: A Study of* King Lear, Othello, The Duchess of Malfi, *and* The White Devil. Atlantic Highlands, N.J.: Humanities Press International, 1989.

Chedgzoy, Kate, ed. *Shakespeare, Feminism and Gender*. Houndmills, Basingstoke: Palgrave Macmillan, 2001.

Dash, Irene G. *Wooing, Wedding, and Power: Women in Shakespeare's Plays*. New York: Columbia University Press, 1981.

DiGangi, Mario. *The Homoerotics of Early Modern Drama*. New York: Cambridge University Press, 1997.

Dusinberre, Juliet. *Shakespeare and the Nature of Women*. 3rd ed. New York: Palgrave Macmillan, 2003.

Erickson, Peter. *Patriarchal Structures in Shakespeare's Drama*. Berkeley: University of California Press, 1985.

French, Marilyn. *Shakespeare's Division of Experience*. New York: Summit Books, 1981.

Garner, Shirley Nelson, and Madelon Sprengnether, eds. *Shakespearean Tragedy and Gender*. Bloomington: Indiana University Press, 1996.

Goldberg, Jonathan. *Sodometries: Renaissance Texts, Modern Sexualities*. Stanford: Stanford University Press, 1992.

Howard, Jean E., and Phyllis Rackin. *Engendering a Nation: A Feminist Account of Shakespeare's English Histories*. New York: Routledge, 1997.

Jardine, Lisa. *Still Harping on Daughters: Women and Drama in the Age of Shakespeare*. 2nd ed. New York: Columbia University Press, 1989.

Kahn, Coppélia. *Man's Estate: Masculine Identity in Shakespeare*. Berkeley: University of California Press, 1981.

————. *Roman Shakespeare: Warriors, Wounds, and Women*. New York: Routledge, 1997.

Korda, Natasha. *Shakespeare's Domestic Economies: Gender and Property in Early Modern England*. Philadelphia: University of Pennsylvania Press, 2002.

Lenz, Carolyn, Ruth Swift, Gayle Greene, and Carol Thomas Neely, eds. *The Woman's Part: Feminist Criticism of Shakespeare*. Urbana: University of Illinois Press, 1980.

Neely, Carol Thomas. *Broken Nuptials in Shakespeare's Plays*. New Haven: Yale University Press, 1985.

————. *Distracted Subjects: Madness and Gender in Shakespeare and Early Modern Culture*. Ithaca, N.Y.: Cornell University Press, 2004.

Newman, Karen. *Fashioning Femininity and English Renaissance Drama*. Chicago: University of Chicago Press, 1991.

Novy, Marianne. *Love's Argument: Gender Relations in Shakespeare*. Chapel Hill: University of North Carolina Press, 1984.

————, ed. *Women's Re-Visions of Shakespeare: On the Responses of Dickinson, Woolf, Rich, H.D., George Eliot, and Others*. Urbana: University of Illinois Press, 1990.

Orgel, Stephen. *Impersonations: The Performance of Gender in Shakespeare's England*. New York: Cambridge University Press, 1996.

Shapiro, Michael. *Gender in Play on the Shakespearean Stage: Boy Heroines and Female Pages*. Ann Arbor: University of Michigan Press, 1994.

Shepherd, Simon. *Amazons and Warrior Women: Varieties of Feminism in Seventeenth Century Drama*. New York: St. Martin's, 1981.

Traub, Valerie. *Desire and Anxiety: Circulations of Sexuality in Shakespearean Drama*. New York: Routledge, 1992.

————. *The Renaissance of Lesbianism in Eary Modern England*. New York: Cambridge University Press, 2002.

Wayne, Valerie, ed. *The Matter of Difference: Materialist Feminist Criticism of Shakespeare*. Ithaca, N.Y.: Cornell University Press, 1991.

### Historical Approaches: Materialism, New Historicism, and Cultural Materialism

Archer, John Michael. *Citizen Shakespeare: Freemen and Aliens in the Language of the Plays*. New York: Palgrave Macmillan, 2005.

Arnold, Oliver. *The Third Citizen: Shakespeare's Theater and the Early Modern House of Commons*. Baltimore: Johns Hopkins University Press, 2007.

Belsey, Catherine. *Shakespeare and the Loss of Eden: The Construction of Family Values in Early Modern Culture*. New Brunswick, N.J.: Rutgers University Press, 1999.

Berry, Ralph. *Shakespeare and Social Class*. Atlantic Highlands, N.J.: Humanities Press International, 1988.

Bristol, Michael D. *Shakespeare's America, America's Shakespeare*. New York: Routledge, 1990.

Bruster, Douglas. *Shakespeare and the Question of Culture: Early Modern Literature and the Cultural Turn*. New York: Palgrave Macmillan, 2003.

Cox, John D. *Shakespeare and the Dramaturgy of Power*. Princeton: Princeton University Press, 1989.

Dollimore, Jonathan. *Radical Tragedy: Religion, Ideology, and Power in the Drama of Shakespeare and His Contemporaries*. 3rd ed. New York: Palgrave Macmillan, 2004.

Dollimore, Jonathan, and Alan Sinfield, eds. *Political Shakespeare: Essays in Cultural Materialism*. 2nd ed. Ithaca, N.Y.: Cornell University Press, 1994.

Dubrow, Heather, and Richard Strier, eds. *The Historical Renaissance: New Essays on Tudor and Stuart Literature and Culture*. Chicago: University of Chicago Press, 1988.

Eagleton, Terry. *William Shakespeare*. Malden, Mass.: Blackwell, 1986.

Greenblatt, Stephen. *Hamlet in Purgatory*. Princeton: Princeton University Press, 2001.

———. *Shakespearean Negotiations: The Circulation of Social Energy in Renaissance England*. Berkeley: University of California Press, 1988.

Hadfield, Andrew. *Shakespeare and Republicanism*. New York: Cambridge University Press, 2005.

Hawkes, Terence. *Meaning by Shakespeare*. New York: Routledge, 1992.

———. *That Shakespeherian Rag: Essays on a Critical Process*. New York: Methuen, 1986.

Holderness, Graham, ed. *The Shakespeare Myth*. Manchester: Manchester University Press, 1988.

———, ed. *Shakespeare's History Plays: Richard II to Henry V*. Houndmills, Basingstoke: Palgrave Macmillan, 1992.

Howard, Jean E. *The Stage and Social Struggle in Early Modern England*. New York: Routledge, 1994.

Howard, Jean E., and Scott Cutler Shershow, eds. *Marxist Shakespeares*. New York: Routledge, 2001.

Howard, Jean E., and Marion F. O'Connor, eds. *Shakespeare Reproduced: The Text in History and Ideology*. New York: Methuen, 1987.

Jardine, Lisa. *Reading Shakespeare Historically*. New York: Routledge, 1996.

Jordan, Constance. *Shakespeare's Monarchies: Ruler and Subject in the Romances*. Ithaca, N.Y.: Cornell University Press, 1997.

Kamps, Ivo, ed. *Materialist Shakespeare: A History*. New York: Verso, 1995.

Kastan, David Scott. *Shakespeare After Theory*. London: Routledge, 1999.

———. *Shakespeare and the Shapes of Time*. Hanover, N.H.: University Press of New England, 1982.

Mallin, Eric S. *Inscribing the Time: Shakespeare and the End of Elizabethan England*. Berkeley: University of California Press, 1995.

Marcus, Leah S. *Puzzling Shakespeare: Local Reading and Its Discontents*. Berkeley: University of California Press, 1988.

Maus, Katharine Eisaman. *Inwardness and Theater in the English Renaissance*. Chicago: University of Chicago Press, 1995.

Montrose, Louis. *The Purpose of Playing: Shakespeare and the Cultural Politics of the Elizabethan Theatre.* Chicago: University of Chicago Press, 1996.

Mullaney, Steven. *The Place of the Stage: License, Play, and Power in Renaissance England.* Chicago: University of Chicago Press, 1988.

Orgel, Stephen. *The Authentic Shakespear: and Other Problems of the Early Modern Stage.* New York: Routledge, 2002.

Patterson, Annabel. *Shakespeare and the Popular Voice.* Malden, Mass.: Blackwell, 1989.

Rackin, Phyllis. *Stages of History: Shakespeare's English Chronicles.* Ithaca, N.Y.: Cornell University Press, 1990.

Siemon, James R. *Word Against Word: Shakespearean Utterance.* Amherst: University of Massachusetts Press, 2002.

Sinfield, Alan. *Shakespeare, Authority, Sexuality: Unfinished Business in Cultural Materialism.* New York: Routledge, 2006.

Tennenhouse, Leonard. *Power on Display: The Politics of Shakespeare's Genres.* New York: Methuen, 1986.

Weimann, Robert. *Author's Pen and Actor's Voice: Playing and Writing in Shakespeare's Theatre.* Ed. Helen Higbee and William West. New York: Cambridge University Press, 2000.

Wells, Robin Headlam. *Shakespeare, Politics, and the State.* Houndmills, Basingstoke: Palgrave Macmillan, 1986.

Wilson, Richard. *Secret Shakespeare: Studies in Theatre, Religion and Resistance.* Manchester: Manchester University Press, 2004.

———. *Will Power: Essays on Shakespearean Authority.* Detroit: Wayne State University Press, 1993.

## Postcolonial Criticism, Race, and Ethnicity

Alexander, Catherine M. S., and Stanley Wells, eds. *Shakespeare and Race.* New York: Cambridge University Press, 2000.

Cartelli, Thomas. *Repositioning Shakespeare: National Formations, Postcolonial Appropriations.* New York: Routledge, 1999.

de Sousa, Geraldo U. *Shakespeare's Cross-Cultural Encounters.* Houndmills, Basingstoke: Palgrave Macmillan, 2002.

Floyd-Wilson, Mary. *English Ethnicity and Race in Early Modern Drama.* New York: Cambridge University Press, 2003.

Hendricks, Margo. " 'Obscured by dreams:' Race, Empire, and Shakespeare's *A Midsummer Night's Dream.*" *Shakespeare Quarterly* 47 (1996): 37–60.

Hulme, Peter. *Colonial Encounters: Europe and the Native Caribbean, 1492–1797.* New York: Methuen, 1986.

Knapp, Jeffrey. *An Empire Nowhere: England, America, and Literature from Utopia to The Tempest.* Berkeley: University of California Press, 1992.

Loomba, Ania. *Gender, Race, Renaissance Drama.* Manchester: Manchester University Press, 1989.

Loomba, Ania, and Martin Orkin, eds. *Post-colonial Shakespeares.* New York: Routledge, 1998.

Maley, Willy. *Nation, State, and Empire in English Renaissance Literature: Shakespeare to Milton.* New York: Palgrave Macmillan, 2003.

Vaughan, Virginia Mason. *Performing Blackness on English Stages, 1500–1800.* New York: Cambridge University Press, 2005.

## Other Philosophical and Theoretical Approaches

Booth, Stephen. *King Lear, Macbeth, Indefinition, and Tragedy.* New Haven: Yale University Press, 1983.

Cavell, Stanley. *Disowning Knowledge in Seven Plays of Shakespeare.* Updated ed. New York: Cambridge University Press, 2003.

Engle, Lars. *Shakespearean Pragmatism: Market of His Time.* Chicago: University of Chicago Press, 1993.

Evans, Malcolm. *Signifying Nothing: Truth's True Contents in Shakespeare's Text.* Athens: University of Georgia Press, 1986.

Felperin, Howard. *The Uses of the Canon: Elizabethan Literature and Contemporary Theory.* New York: Oxford University Press, 1990.

Goldberg, Jonathan. *Shakespeare's Hand.* Minneapolis: University of Minnesota Press, 2003.

Grady, Hugh. *The Modernist Shakespeare: Critical Texts in a Material World.* Oxford: Clarendon, 1991.

———. *Shakespeare, Machiavelli, and Montaigne: Power and Subjectivity from Richard II to Hamlet.* Oxford: Oxford University Press, 2002.

Grady, Hugh, and Terence Hawkes, eds. *Presentist Shakespeares.* New York: Routledge, 2006.

Hawkes, Terence. *Shakespeare in the Present.* New York: Routledge, 2002.

Knapp, Robert S. *Shakespeare—The Theater and the Book.* Princeton: Princeton University Press, 1989.

Lukacher, Ned. *Daemonic Figures: Shakespeare and the Question of Conscience.* Ithaca, N.Y.: Cornell University Press, 1994.

Lupton, Julia Reinhard. *Citizen-Saints: Shakespeare and Political Theology.* Chicago: University of Chicago Press, 2005.

Parker, Patricia, and Geoffrey Hartman, eds. *Shakespeare and the Question of Theory.* New York: Methuen, 1985.

Pechter, Edward. *What Was Shakespeare?: Renaissance Plays and Changing Critical Practice.* Ithaca, N.Y.: Cornell University Press, 1995.

Rabkin, Norman. *Shakespeare and the Problem of Meaning.* Chicago: University of Chicago Press, 1981.

Schalkwyk, David. *Speech and Performance in Shakespeare's Sonnets and Plays.* Cambridge, Eng.: Cambridge University Press, 2002.

## Textual Criticism and Bibliography

Allen, Michael J. B., and Kenneth Muir, eds. *Shakespeare's Plays in Quarto: A Facsimile Edition of Copies Primarily from the Henry E. Huntington Library.* Berkeley: University of California Press, 1981.

Blayney, Peter W. M. *The First Folio of Shakespeare.* Washington, D.C.: Folger Library Publications, 1991.

———. *The Texts of* King Lear *and Their Origins. Vol. 1: Nicholas Okes and the First Quarto.* New York: Cambridge University Press, 1982.

Bowers, Fredson. *On Editing Shakespeare.* Charlottesville: University Press of Virginia, 1966.

Brooks, Douglas A. *From Playhouse to Printing House: Drama and Authorship in Early Modern England.* New York: Cambridge University Press, 2000.

De Grazia, Margreta. "Homonyms Before and After Lexical Standardization." *Deutsche Shakespeare-Gesellschaft West* (Jahrbuch 1990): 143–56.

———. *Shakespeare Verbatim: The Reproduction of Authenticity and the 1790 Apparatus.* New York: Oxford University Press, 1991.

De Grazia, Margreta, and Peter Stallybrass. "The Materiality of the Shakespearean Text." *Shakespeare Quarterly* 44 (1993): 255–83.

Erne, Lukas, and Margaret Jane Kidnie, eds. *Textual Performances: The Modern Reproduction of Shakespeare's Drama.* New York: Cambridge University Press, 2004.

Franklin, Colin. *Shakespeare Domesticated: The Eighteenth-Century Editions*. Brookfield, Vt.: Gower Publishing Company, 1991.

Hinman, Charlton, ed. *The First Folio of Shakespeare*. 2nd ed. New York: Norton, 1996.

———. *The Printing and Proof-Reading of the First Folio of Shakespeare*. 2 vols. Oxford: Clarendon, 1963.

Honigmann, E. A. J. *The Stability of Shakespeare's Text*. London: E. Arnold, 1965.

Ioppolo, Grace. *Dramatists and Their Manuscripts in the Age of Shakespeare, Jonson, Middleton and Heywood: Authorship, Authority and the Playhouse*. New York: Routledge, 2006.

———. *Revising Shakespeare*. Cambridge, Mass.: Harvard University Press, 1991.

Irace, Kathleen O. *Reforming the "Bad" Quartos: Performance and Provenance of Six Shakespearean First Editions*. Newark: University of Delaware Press, 1994.

Jackson, MacDonald P. *Defining Shakespeare: Pericles as Test Case*. New York: Oxford University Press, 2003.

Kastan, David Scott. *Shakespeare and the Book*. New York: Cambridge University Press, 2001.

Lesser, Zachary. *Renaissance Drama and the Politics of Publication: Readings in the English Book Trade*. New York: Cambridge University Press, 2004.

Maguire, Laurie E. *Shakespearean Suspect Texts: The "Bad" Quartos and Their Contexts*. New York: Cambridge University Press, 1996.

Maguire, Laurie E., and Thomas L. Berger, eds. *Textual Formations and Reformations*. Newark: University of Delaware Press, 1998.

Marcus, Leah S. *Unediting the Renaissance: Shakespeare, Marlowe, Milton*. New York: Routledge, 1996.

McKerrow, Ronald B. *Prolegomena for the Oxford Shakespeare: A Study in Editorial Method*. Oxford: Clarendon, 1939.

McLeod, Randall, ed. *Crisis in Editing: Texts of the English Renaissance*. New York: AMS Press, 1994.

———. "UN *Editing* Shak-speare." *SubStance* 33/34 (1982): 26–55.

———[as Random Cloud]. "The Psychopathology of Everyday Art." *The Elizabethan Theatre IX*. Ed. G. R. Hibbard. Port Credit, Ontario: P. D. Meany, 1986. 100–68.

Murphy, Andrew. *Shakespeare in Print: A History and Chronology of Shakespeare Publishing*. New York: Cambridge University Press, 2003.

———, ed. *The Renaissance Text: Theory, Editing, Textuality*. Manchester: Manchester University Press, 2000.

Pollard, Alfred W. *Shakespeare's Folios and Quartos: A Study in the Bibliography of Shakespeare's Plays, 1594–1685*. London: Methuen, 1909.

Seary, Peter. *Lewis Theobald and the Editing of Shakespeare*. Oxford: Clarendon, 1990.

Taylor, Gary, and Michael Warren, eds. *The Division of the Kingdoms: Shakespeare's Two Versions of King Lear*. Oxford: Clarendon, 1986.

Urkowitz, Steven. *Shakespeare's Revision of King Lear*. Princeton: Princeton University Press, 1980.

Vickers, Brian. *Shakespeare, Co-Author: A Historical Study of Five Collaborative Plays*. New York: Oxford University Press, 2002.

Walker, Alice. *Textual Problems of the First Folio: Richard III, King Lear, Troilus & Cressida, 2 Henry IV, Hamlet, Othello*. Cambridge, Eng.: Cambridge University Press, 1953.

Wells, Stanley. *Re-Editing Shakespeare for the Modern Reader*. New York: Oxford University Press, 1984.

Wells, Stanley, and Gary Taylor. *Modernizing Shakespeare's Spelling*. Oxford: Clarendon, 1979.

———. *William Shakespeare: A Textual Companion*. Oxford: Clarendon, 1987.

Werstine, Paul. "A Century of 'Bad' Shakespeare Quartos." *Shakespeare Quarterly* 50 (1999): 310–33.

———. "Narratives about Printed Shakespeare Texts: 'Foul Papers' and 'Bad' Quartos." *Shakespeare Quarterly* 41 (1990): 65–86.

Williams, George Walton. *The Craft of Printing and the Publication of Shakespeare's Works*. Washington, D.C.: Folger Shakespeare Library, 1985.

Wilson, J. Dover. *The Manuscript of Shakespeare's "Hamlet" and the Problems of Its Transmission: An Essay in Critical Bibliography*. 2 vols. New York: Macmillan, 1934.

## Shakespeare and Performance

Aebischer, Pascale. *Shakespeare's Violated Bodies: Stage and Screen Performance*. New York: Cambridge University Press, 2003.

Aebischer, Pascale, Edward J. Esche, and Nigel Wheale, eds. *Remaking Shakespeare: Performance Across Media, Genres, and Cultures*. New York: Palgrave Macmillan, 2003.

Bartholomeusz, Dennis. *"Macbeth" and the Players*. Cambridge, Eng.: Cambridge University Press, 1969.

Barton, John. *Playing Shakespeare*. London: Methuen, 1984.

Bate, Jonathan, and Russell Jackson, eds. *Shakespeare: An Illustrated Stage History*. New York: Oxford University Press, 1996.

Berger, Harry Jr. *Imaginary Audition: Shakespeare on Stage and Page*. Berkeley: University of California Press, 1989.

Berry, Francis. *The Shakespeare Inset: Word and Picture*. London: Routledge and Kegan Paul, 1965.

Berry, Ralph. *Changing Styles in Shakespeare*. Boston: Allen & Unwin, 1981.

Bevington, David M. *Action Is Eloquence: Shakespeare's Language of Gesture*. Cambridge, Mass.: Harvard University Press, 1984.

———. *This Wide and Universal Theater: Shakespeare in Performance, Then and Now*. Chicago: University of Chicago Press, 2007.

Branam, George Curtis. *Eighteenth-Century Adaptations of Shakespearean Tragedy*. Berkeley: University of California Press, 1956.

Bratton, Jacky, and Julie Hankey, gen. eds. The Shakespeare in Production Series. Cambridge, Eng.: Cambridge University Press, 1996–.

Brennan, Anthony. *Onstage and Offstage Worlds in Shakespeare's Plays*. New York: Routledge, 1989.

———. *Shakespeare's Dramatic Structures*. Boston: Routledge and Kegan Paul, 1986.

Brown, Ivor. *Shakespeare and the Actors*. London: Bodley Head, 1970.

Brown, John Russell. *Shakespeare and the Theatrical Event*. Houndmills, Basingstoke: Palgrave Macmillan, 2002.

———. *Shakespeare's Dramatic Style: Romeo and Juliet, As You Like It, Julius Caesar, Twelfth Night, Macbeth*. London: Heinemann, 1970.

Bulman, James C., ed. *Shakespeare, Theory, and Performance*. New York: Routledge, 1996.

Calderwood, James. *Shakespearean Metadrama: The Argument of the Play in Titus Andronicus, Love's Labour's Lost, Romeo and Juliet, A Midsummer Night's Dream, and Richard II*. Minneapolis: University of Minnesota Press, 1971.

Carlisle, Carol Jones. *Shakespeare from the Greenroom: Actors' Criticisms of Four Major Tragedies*. Chapel Hill: University of North Carolina Press, 1969.

Cohn, Ruby. *Modern Shakespeare Offshoots*. Princeton: Princeton University Press, 1976.

Dean, Winton. "Shakespeare in the Opera House." *Shakespeare Survey* 18 (1965): 75–93.

Dobson, Michael. *The Making of the National Poet: Shakespeare, Adaptation and Authorship, 1660–1769*. Oxford: Clarendon, 1992.

————, ed. *Performing Shakespeare's Tragedies Today: The Actor's Perspective.* New York: Cambridge University Press, 2006.

Downer, Alan S. *The Eminent Tragedian William Charles Macready.* Cambridge, Mass.: Harvard University Press, 1966.

Duffin, Ross W. *Shakespeare's Songbook.* New York: Norton, 2004.

Foulkes, Richard, ed. *Shakespeare and the Victorian Stage.* New York: Cambridge University Press, 1986.

Goldman, Michael. *Acting and Action in Shakespearean Tragedy.* Princeton: Princeton University Press, 1985.

Hirsch, James E. *The Structure of Shakespearean Scenes.* New Haven: Yale University Press, 1981.

Hogan, Charles Beecher, ed. *Shakespeare in the Theatre, 1701–1800.* 2 vols. Oxford: Clarendon, 1952–57.

Holland, Peter. *English Shakespeares: Shakespeare on the English Stage in the 1990's.* New York: Cambridge University Press, 1997.

Homan, Sidney, ed. *Shakespeare's "More Than Words Can Witness": Essays on Visual and Nonverbal Enactment in the Plays.* Lewisburg, Pa.: Bucknell University Press, 1980.

————, ed. *When the Theater Turns to Itself: The Aesthetic Metaphor in Shakespeare.* Lewiston, Pa.: Bucknell University Press, 1981.

Hoenselaars, Ton, ed. *Shakespeare's History Plays: Performance, Translation and Adaptation in Britain and Abroad.* Cambridge, Eng.: Cambridge University Press, 2004.

Howard, Jean E. *Shakespeare's Art of Orchestration: Stage Technique and Audience Response.* Urbana: University of Illinois Press, 1984.

Jones, Emrys. *Scenic Form in Shakespeare.* Oxford: Clarendon, 1971.

Kennedy, Dennis. *Looking at Shakespeare: A Visual History of Twentieth-Century Performance.* 2nd ed. New York: Cambridge University Press, 2001.

————, ed. *Foreign Shakespeare: Contemporary Performance.* New York: Cambridge University Press, 1993.

Marshall, Gail, and Adrian Poole, eds. *Victorian Shakespeare.* New York: Palgrave Macmillan, 2003.

McGuire, Philip C. *Speechless Dialect: Shakespeare's Open Silences.* Berkeley: University of California Press, 1985.

McGuire, Philip C., and David A. Samuelson. *Shakespeare: The Theatrical Dimension.* New York: AMS Press, 1979.

Mooney, Michael E. *Shakespeare's Dramatic Transactions.* Durham, N.C.: Duke University Press, 1990.

Mowat, Barbara A. *The Dramaturgy of Shakespeare's Romances.* Athens: University of Georgia Press, 1976.

Odell, George Clinton Densmore. *Shakespeare from Betterton to Irving.* 2 vols. New York: Scribner, 1920.

Parsons, Keith, and Pamela Mason, eds. *Shakespeare in Performance.* London: Salamander, 1995.

Poel, William. *Shakespeare in the Theater.* London: Sidgwick and Jackson, 1913.

Rosenberg, Marvin. *The Masks of King Lear.* Berkeley: University of California Press, 1972.

Rosenberg, Marvin, et al. *Clamorous Voices: Shakespeare's Women Today.* London: Women's Press, 1988.

Rutter, Carol, gen. ed. The Shakespeare in Performance Series. Manchester: Manchester University Press, 1982–.

Shattuck, Charles H. *Shakespeare on the American Stage,* vol. 1: *From the Hallams to Edwin Booth.* Washington, D.C.: Folger Shakespeare Library, 1976.

————. *Shakespeare on the American Stage,* vol. 2: *From Booth and Barrett to Sothern and Marlowe.* Washington, D.C.: Folger Shakespeare Library, 1987.

————. *The Shakespeare Promptbooks: A Descriptive Catalogue.* Urbana: University of Illinois Press, 1965.

Slater, Ann. *Shakespeare, the Director.* Totowa, N.J.: Barnes & Noble Books, 1982.

Smallwood, Robert, ed. *Players of Shakespeare.* 6 vols. New York: Cambridge University Press, 1985–2004.

————, gen. ed. The Shakespeare at Stratford series. London: Arden Shakespeare, 2002– .

Speaight, Robert. *Shakespeare on the Stage: An Illustrated History of Shakespearian Performance.* London: Collins, 1973.

————. *William Poel and the Elizabethan Revival.* Cambridge, Mass.: Harvard University Press, 1954.

Spencer, Hazelton. *Shakespeare Improved: The Restoration Versions in Quarto and On the Stage.* Cambridge, Mass.: Harvard University Press, 1927.

Styan, J. L. *The Shakespeare Revolution: Criticism and Performance in the Twentieth Century.* New York: Cambridge University Press, 1977.

————. *Shakespeare's Stagecraft.* Cambridge, Eng.: Cambridge University Press, 1967.

————. "Sight and Space: The Perception of Shakespeare on Stage and Screen." *Shakespeare, Pattern of Excelling Nature: Shakespeare Criticism in Honor of America's Bicentennial.* Ed. David Bevington and Jay L. Halio. Newark: University of Delaware Press, 1978.

Thompson, Marvin and Ruth, eds. *Shakespeare and the Sense of Performance.* Newark: University of Delaware Press, 1989.

Trewin, J. C. *Shakespeare on the English Stage, 1900–1964.* London: Barrie and Rockliff, 1964.

Wells, Stanley. *Royal Shakespeare: Four Major Productions at Stratford-upon-Avon.* Manchester: Manchester University Press, 1977.

————, ed. *Shakespeare in the Theatre: An Anthology of Criticism.* New York: Oxford University Press, 1997.

Worthen, William B. *Shakespeare and the Authority of Performance.* New York: Cambridge University Press, 1997.

————. *Shakespeare and the Force of Modern Performance.* New York: Cambridge University Press, 2003.

## Shakespeare on Film

Ball, Robert Hamilton. *Shakespeare on Silent Film: A Strange Eventful History.* London: Allen & Unwin, 1968.

Burt, Richard, and Lynda E. Boose, eds. *Shakespeare the Movie: Popularizing the Plays on Film, TV, and Video.* New York: Routledge, 1997.

————. *Shakespeare the Movie II: Popularizing the Plays on Film, TV, Video, and DVD.* New York: Routledge, 2003.

Bristol, Michael D. *Big-Time Shakespeare.* New York: Routledge, 1996.

Buchanan, Judith. *Shakespeare on Film.* New York: Pearson Longman, 2005.

Buchman, Lorne Michael. *Still in Movement: Shakespeare on Screen.* New York: Oxford University Press, 1991.

Bulman, J. C., and H. R. Coursen, eds. *Shakespeare on Television: An Anthology of Essays and Reviews.* Hanover, N.H.: University Press of New England, 1988.

Burnett, Mark Thornton, and Ramona Wray, eds. *Shakespeare, Film, Fin de Siècle.* New York: St. Martin's, 2000.

Burt, Richard. *Shakespeare After Mass Media.* New York: Palgrave Macmillan, 2002.

Cartelli, Thomas, and Katherine Rowe, eds. *New Wave Shakespeare on Screen.* Malden, Mass.: Polity Press, 2007.

Crowl, Samuel. *Shakespeare at the Cineplex: The Kenneth Branagh Era.* Athens: Ohio University Press, 2003.

————. *Shakespeare and Film*. New York: Norton, 2008.

Davies, Anthony, and Stanley Wells, eds. *Shakespeare and the Moving Image: The Plays on Film and Television*. New York: Cambridge University Press, 1994.

Donaldson, Peter S. *Shakespearean Films/Shakespearean Directors*. Boston: Unwin Hyman, 1990.

Henderson, Diana E. *Collaborations with the Past: Reshaping Shakespeare Across Time and Media*. Ithaca, N.Y.: Cornell University Press, 2006.

————. *A Concise Companion to Shakespeare on Screen*. Malden, Mass.: Blackwell, 2007.

Hindle, Maurice. *Studying Shakespeare on Film*. New York: Palgrave Macmillan, 2007.

Kliman, Bernice W. *Hamlet: Film, Television, and Audio Performance*. Madison, N.J.: Fairleigh Dickinson University Press, 1988.

Lehmann, Courtney. *Shakespeare Remains: Theater to Film, Early Modern to Postmodern*. Ithaca, N.Y.: Cornell, 2002.

Lehmann, Courtney, and Lisa S. Starks, eds. *Spectacular Shakespeare: Critical Theory and Popular Cinema*. Madison, N.J.: Fairleigh Dickinson University Press, 2002.

Rothwell, Kenneth S. *A History of Shakespeare on Screen: A Century of Film and Television*. 2nd ed. Cambridge, Eng.: Cambridge University Press, 2004.

# Glossary

## STAGE TERMS

**"Above"** The gallery on the upper level of the *frons scenae*. In open-air theaters, such as the Globe, this space contained the lords' rooms. The central section of the gallery was sometimes used by the players for short scenes. Indoor theaters such as Blackfriars featured a curtained alcove for musicians above the stage.

**"Aloft"** See *"Above."*

**Amphitheater** An open-air theater, such as the Globe.

**Arras** See *Curtain.*

**Cellerage** See *Trap.*

**Chorus** In the works of Shakespeare and other Elizabethan playwrights, a single individual (not, as in Greek tragedy, a group) who speaks before the play (and often before each act), describing events not shown on stage as well as commenting on the action witnessed by the audience.

**Curtain** Curtains, or arras (hanging tapestries), covered a part of the *frons scenae,* thus concealing the discovery space, and may also have been draped around the edge of the stage to conceal the open area underneath.

**Discovery space** A central opening or alcove concealed behind a curtain in the center of the *frons scenae.* The curtain could be drawn aside to "discover" tableaux such as Portia's caskets, the body of Polonius, or the statue of Hermione. Shakespeare appears to have used this stage device only sparingly.

**Doubling** The common practice of having one actor play multiple roles, so that a play with a large cast of characters might be performed by a relatively small company.

**Dumb shows** Mimed scenes performed before a play (or before each act), summarizing or foreshadowing the plot. Dumb shows were popular in early Elizabethan drama; although they already seemed old-fashioned in Shakespeare's time, they were employed by writers up to the 1640s.

**Epilogue** A brief speech or poem addressed to the audience by an actor after the play. In some cases, as in *2 Henry IV,* the epilogue could be combined with, or could merge into, the jig.

**Forestage** The front of the stage, closest to the audience.

**Frons scenae** The wall at the back of the stage, behind which lay the players' tiring-house. The *frons scenae* of the Globe featured two doors flanking the central discovery space, with a gallery "above."

**Gallery** Covered seating areas surrounding the open yard of the public amphitheaters. There were three levels of galleries at the Globe; admission to these seats cost an extra penny (in addition to the basic admission fee of one penny to the yard), and seating in the higher galleries another penny yet. In indoor theaters such as Blackfriars, where there was no standing room, gallery seating was less expensive than seating in the pit; indeed, seats nearest the stage were the most expensive.

**Gatherers** Persons employed by the playing company to take money at the entrances to the theater.

**Groundlings** Audience members who paid the minimum price of admission (one penny) to stand in the yard of the open-air theaters; also referred to as "understanders."

**Heavens** The canopied roof over the stage in the open-air theaters, protecting the players and their costumes from rain. The "heavens" would be brightly decorated with sun, moon, and stars, and perhaps the signs of the zodiac.

**Hut** A structure on the top of the cover over the stage, where stagehands produced the effects of thunder and lightning and operated the machinery by which gods, such as Jupiter in *Cymbeline,* descended through the trapdoor in the "heavens."

**Jig** A song-and-dance performance by the clown and other members of the company at the conclusion of a play. These performances were frequently bawdy and were officially banned in 1612.

**Lords' rooms** Partitioned sections of the gallery "above," where the most prestigious and expensive seats in the public playhouses were located. These rooms were designed not to provide the best view of the action on the stage below, but to make their privileged occupants conspicuous to the rest of the audience.

**Open-air theaters** Unroofed public playhouses in the suburbs of London, such as The Theatre, the Rose, and the Globe.

**Part** The character played by an actor. In Shakespeare's theater, actors were given a roll of paper called a "part" containing all of the speeches and all of the cues belonging to their character. The term "role," synonymous with "part," is derived from such rolls of paper.

**Patrons** Important nobles and members of the royal family under whose protection the theatrical companies of London operated; players not in the service of patrons were punishable as vagabonds. The companies were referred to as their patrons' "Men" or "Servants." Thus the name of the company to which Shakespeare belonged for most of his career was first the Lord Chamberlain's Men, then was changed to the King's Men in 1603, when James I became their patron.

**Pillars** The "heavens" were supported by two tall painted pillars or posts near the front of the stage. These occasionally played a role in stage action, allowing a character to "hide" while remaining in full view of the audience.

**Pit** The area in front of the stage in indoor theaters such as Blackfriars, where the most expensive and prestigious bench seating was to be had.

**Posts** See *Pillars.*

**Proscenium** The space of the transparent "fourth wall," which divides the actors from the orchestra and audience in the standard modern theater. The stages on which Shakespeare's plays were first performed had no proscenium.

**Rearstage** The back of the stage, farthest from the audience.

**Repertory** The stock of plays a company had ready for performance at a given time. Companies generally performed a different play each day, often more than a dozen plays in a month and more than thirty in the course of the season.

**Role**  See *Part*.

**Sharers**  Senior actors holding shares in a joint-stock theatrical company; they paid for costumes, hired hands, and new plays, and they shared profits and losses equally. Shakespeare was not only a longtime "sharer" of the Lord Chamberlain's Men but, from 1599, a "housekeeper," the holder of a one-eighth share in the Globe playhouse.

**Tiring-house**  The players' dressing (attiring) room, a structure located at the back of the stage and connected to the stage by two or more doors in the *frons scenae*.

**Trap**  A trapdoor near the front of the stage that allowed access to the "cellarage" beneath and was frequently associated with hell's mouth. Another trapdoor in the "heavens" opened for the descent of gods to the stage below.

**"Within"**  The tiring-house, from which offstage sound effects such as shouts, drums, and trumpets were produced.

**Yard**  The central space in open-air theaters such as the Globe, into which the stage projected and in which audience members stood. Admission to the yard in the public theaters cost a penny, the cheapest admission available.

## TEXTUAL TERMS

**Aside**  See *Stage direction*.

**Autograph**  Text written in the author's own hand. With the possible exception of a few pages of the collaborative play *Sir Thomas More*, no dramatic works or poems written in Shakespeare's hand are known to survive.

**Canonical**  Of an author, the writings generally accepted as authentic. In the case of Shakespeare's dramatic works, only two plays that are not among the thirty-six plays contained in the First Folio, *Pericles* and *The Two Noble Kinsmen*, have won widespread acceptance into the Shakespearean canon. (This sense of "canonical" should not be confused with the use of "the canon" to denote the entire body of literary works, including but not limited to Shakespeare's, that have traditionally been regarded as fit objects of admiration and study.)

**Catchword**  A word printed below the text at the bottom of a page, matching the first word on the following page. The catchword enabled the printer to keep the pages in their proper sequence. Where the catchword fails to match the word at the top of the next page, there is reason to suspect that something has been lost or misplaced.

**Compositor**  A person employed in a print shop to set type. To speed the printing process, most of Shakespeare's plays were set by more than one compositor. Compositors frequently followed their own standards in spelling and punctuation. They inevitably introduced some errors into the text, often by selecting the wrong piece from the type case or by setting the correct letter upside down.

**Conflation**  A version of a play created by combining readings from more than one substantive edition. Since the early eighteenth century, for example, most versions of *King Lear* and of several other plays by Shakespeare have been conflations of quarto and First Folio texts.

**Control text**   The text upon which a modern edition is based.

**Dramatis personae**   A list of the characters appearing in the play. In the First Folio such lists were printed at the end of some but not all of the plays. The editor Nicholas Rowe (1709) first provided lists of dramatis personae for all of Shakespeare's dramatic works.

**Exeunt / Exit**   See *Stage direction*.

**Fair copy**   A transcript of the "foul papers" made either by a scribe or by the playwright.

**Folio**   A bookmaking format in which each large sheet of paper is folded once, making two leaves (four pages front and back). This format produced large volumes, generally handsome and expensive. The First Folio of Shakespeare's plays was printed in 1623.

**Foul papers**   An author's first completed draft of a play, typically full of blotted-out passages and revisions. None of Shakespeare's foul papers is known to survive.

**Licensing**   By an order of 1581, new plays could not be performed until they had received a license from the Master of the Revels. A separate license, granted by the Court of High Commission, was required for publication, though in practice plays were often printed without license. From 1610, the Master of the Revels had the authority to license plays for publication as well as for performance.

**Manent / Manet**   See *Stage direction*.

**Memorial reconstruction**   The conjectured practice of reconstructing the text of a play from memory. Companies touring in the provinces without access to promptbooks may have resorted to memorial reconstruction. This practice also provides a plausible explanation for the existence of the so-called bad Quartos.

**Octavo**   A bookmaking format in which each large sheet of paper is folded three times, making eight leaves (sixteen pages front and back). Only one of Shakespeare's plays, *Richard Duke of York* (3 *Henry VI*, 1595), was published in octavo format.

**Playbook**   See *Promptbook*.

**Press variants**   Minor textual variations among books of the same edition, resulting from corrections made in the course of printing or from damaged or slipped type.

**Promptbook**   A manuscript of a play (either foul papers or fair copy) annotated and adapted for performance by the theatrical company. The promptbook incorporated stage directions, notes on properties and special effects, and revisions, sometimes including those required by the Master of the Revels. Promptbooks are usually identifiable by the replacement of characters' names with actors' names.

**Quarto**   A bookmaking format in which each large sheet of paper is folded twice, making four leaves (eight pages front and back). Quarto volumes were smaller and less expensive than books printed in the folio format.

**Scribal copy**   A transcript of a play produced by a professional scribe (or "scrivener"). Scribes tended to employ their own preferred spellings and abbreviations and could be responsible for introducing a variety of errors.

**Speech prefix (s.p.)**   The indication of the identity of the speaker of the following line or lines. Early editions of Shakespeare's plays often use different prefixes at different points to designate the same person. On occasion, the name of the actor who was to play the role appears in place of the name of the character.

**Stage direction (s.d.)** The part of the text that is not spoken by any character but that indicates actions to be performed onstage. Stage directions in the earliest editions of Shakespeare's plays are sparse and are sometimes grouped together at the beginning of a scene rather than next to the spoken lines they should precede, accompany, or follow. By convention, the most basic stage directions were written in Latin. "Exit" indicates the departure of a single actor from the stage, "exeunt" the departure of more than one. "Manet" indicates that a single actor remains onstage, "manent" that more than one remains. Lines accompanied by the stage direction "aside" are spoken so as not to be heard by the others onstage. This stage direction appeared in some early editions of Shakespeare plays, but other means were also used to indicate such speech (such as placing the words within parentheses), and sometimes no indication was provided.

**Stationers' Register** The account books of the Company of Stationers (of which all printers were legally required to be members), recording the fees paid for permission to print new works as well as the fines exacted for printing without permission. The Stationers' Register thus provides a valuable if incomplete record of publication in England.

**Substantive text** The text of an edition based upon access to a manuscript, as opposed to a derivative text based only on an earlier edition.

**Variorum editions** Comprehensive editions of a work or works in which the various views of previous editors and commentators are compiled.

# ILLUSTRATION ACKNOWLEDGMENTS

**General Introduction**   Plague death bill: By permission of the Folger Shakespeare Library • Webbe: By permission of the British Library • Amman: Spencer Collection, The New York Public Library, Astor, Lenox and Tilden Foundation • *Swetnam* title page: By permission of The Huntington Library, San Marino, California • Pope as Antichrist: By permission of the Folger Shakespeare Library • de Heere: The National Museum of Wales • Armada portrait: By kind permission of Marquess of Tavistock and Trustees of the Bedford Estate • Boaistuau: By permission of The Huntington Library, San Marino, California • Mandeville: By permission of the Houghton Library, Harvard University • Funeral procession: Additional Ms. 35324, folio 37v. By permission of the British Library • Gheeraerts: By permission of the Trustees of Dulwich Picture Gallery • van den Broek: Fitzwilliam Museum, University of Cambridge • Swimming: Bodleian Library, University of Oxford, 4° G.17.Art • Panorama of London: By permission of the British Library • Tarleton: Harley 3885, folio 19. By permission of the British Library • Hanging: Pepys Library, Magdalene College, Cambridge • Syphilis victim: By permission of The Huntington Library, San Marino, California • *Spanish Tragedy* title page: By permission of the Folger Shakespeare Library • Stratford-upon-Avon: By permission of City of York Libraries • Cholmondeley sisters: Tate Gallery, London • Alleyn: By permission of the Trustees of Dulwich Picture Library • *If You Know Not Me* title page: By permission of The Huntington Library, San Marino, California • van der Straet: By permission of the Folger Shakespeare Library
**The Shakespearean Stage**   Braun and Hogenburg: 8.Tab.c.4. Bk.1.pl.1. By permission of the British Library • Hollar: Guildhall Library, Corporation of London • Interior of the "new" Globe: Courtesy of The International Shakespeare Globe Center Ltd. Photo: John Tramper • Exterior of the "new" Globe: Courtesy of The International Shakespeare Globe Center Ltd. Photo: Richard Kalina • *Frons scenae* of the "new" Globe: Courtesy of The International Shakespeare Globe Center Ltd. Photo: Richard Kalina • Oliver: The Burghley House Collection. Photograph: Courtauld Institute of Art • Peacham: Reproduced by permission of the Marquess of Bath, Longleat House, Warminster, Wiltshire, Great Britain. Photograph: Courtauld Institute of Art • de Witt: University Library, Utrecht, MS 842, f.132r • Middle Temple Hall: The Benchers of the Honorable Society of the Middle Temple, London • Hollar: Guildhall Library, Corporation of London

**Shakespearean Romance**
*Le Naufrage*: By permission of the Fine Arts Museums of San Francisco • Venus and Jupiter (astride an eagle): By permission of the Abaris Books • Portolan atlas: By permission of the Library of Congress, Geography and Map Division, Washington, D.C.
**Venus and Adonis**   Tempesta: © British Museum • Wither: By permission of the Houghton Library, Harvard University • Peacham: By permission of the Folger Shakespeare Library
**The Rape of Lucrece**   Raphael: Private collection • Titian: Fitzwilliam Museum, University of Cambridge • Amman: Rare Books and Manuscripts Division, The New York Public Library, Astor, Lenox and Tilden Foundations
**Sonnets**   Whitney: By permission of the Folger Shakespeare Library
**Pericles**   Gower title page: C.34.L.8. By permission of the British Library • Inigo Jones: Devonshire Collection, Chatsworth. Reproduced by permission of the Duke of Devonshire and the Chatsworth Settlement Trustees. Photo credit: The Courtauld Institute of Art
**The Winter's Tale**   *Bloudy Mother* title page: By permission of the Houghton Library, Harvard University • Rüff: By permission of the Folger Shakespeare Library • Pedlar: Pepys Library, Magdalene College, Cambridge
**Cymbeline**   van de Passe: © British Museum • Enea Vico: By permission of Abaris Books
**The Tempest**   Magnus: Reproduced by permission of the Huntington Library • Galle: The Burndy Library, Norwalk, Connecticut
**The Two Noble Kinsmen**   "The Knight's Tale" extract: Division of Rare Books and Manuscript Collections, Cornell University Library • René of Anjou: Österreichische Nationalbibliothek, Vienna • Beauchamp Pageant: Cotton Julius E IV art 6, folio 3. By permission of the British Library.
**Early Modern Map Culture**   Speed: © British Library/HIP/Art Resource, NY • Braun and Hogenberg: HIP/Art Resource, NY. Museum of London, London, Great Britain
**Contemporary Documents**
First Folio front matter: *The Norton Facsimile of the First Folio of Shakespeare*, 2nd ed. (1996)

# Index of Poems: Titles and First Lines

# THE HOUSE OF LANCASTER

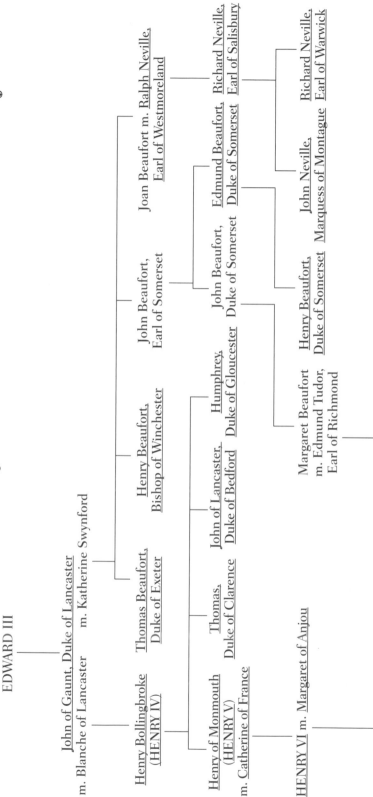

EDWARD III

John of Gaunt, Duke of Lancaster    m. Katherine Swynford
m. Blanche of Lancaster

Henry Beaufort,
Bishop of Winchester

Joan Beaufort m. Ralph Neville,
Earl of Westmoreland

John Beaufort,
Earl of Somerset

Edmund Beaufort,    Richard Neville,
Duke of Somerset    Earl of Salisbury

John Beaufort,
Duke of Somerset

Thomas Beaufort,
Duke of Exeter

Henry Bollingbroke
(HENRY IV)

John of Lancaster,    Humphrey,
Duke of Bedford    Duke of Gloucester

Thomas,
Duke of Clarence

John Neville,
Marquess of Montague

Richard Neville,
Earl of Warwick

Henry Beaufort,
Duke of Somerset

Margaret Beaufort
m. Edmund Tudor,
Earl of Richmond

Henry of Monmouth
(HENRY V)
m. Catherine of France

HENRY VI m. Margaret of Anjou

Henry Tudor, Earl of Richmond (HENRY VII) m. Elizabeth of York

Edward, Prince of Wales m. Anne Neville

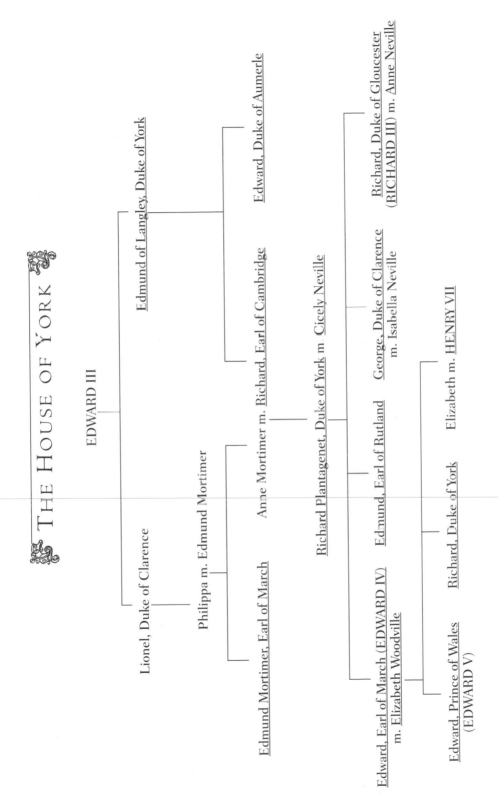

# THE HOUSE OF YORK

**EDWARD III**

- Lionel, Duke of Clarence
  - Philippa m. Edmund Mortimer
    - Edmund Mortimer, Earl of March
    - Anne Mortimer m. Richard, Earl of Cambridge
      - Richard Plantagenet, Duke of York m. Cicely Neville
        - Edward, Earl of March (EDWARD IV) m. Elizabeth Woodville
          - Edward, Prince of Wales (EDWARD V)
          - Richard, Duke of York
          - Elizabeth m. HENRY VII
        - Edmund, Earl of Rutland
        - George, Duke of Clarence m. Isabella Neville
        - Richard, Duke of Gloucester (RICHARD III) m. Anne Neville
- Edmund of Langley, Duke of York
  - Edward, Duke of Aumerle

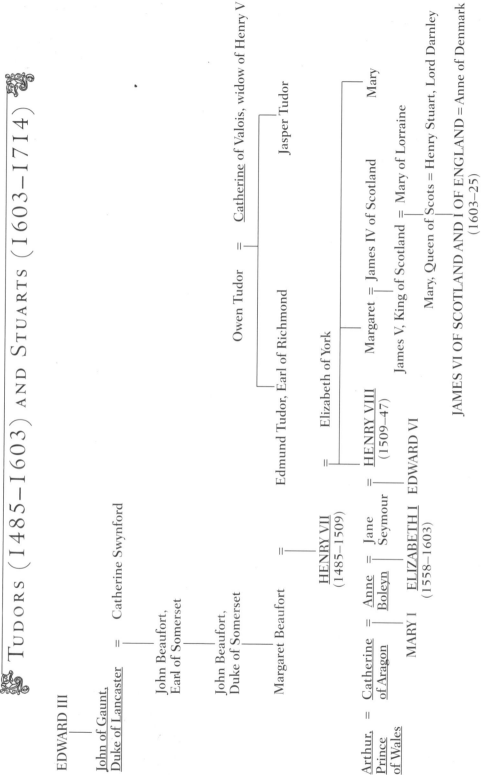

# Tudors (1485–1603) and Stuarts (1603–1714)

EDWARD III

John of Gaunt, Duke of Lancaster = Catherine Swynford

John Beaufort, Earl of Somerset

John Beaufort, Duke of Somerset

Margaret Beaufort = Edmund Tudor, Earl of Richmond

Owen Tudor = Catherine of Valois, widow of Henry V

Jasper Tudor

HENRY VII (1485–1509) = Elizabeth of York

Arthur, Prince of Wales = Catherine of Aragon = HENRY VIII (1509–47) = Anne Boleyn, Jane Seymour

MARY I, ELIZABETH I (1558–1603), EDWARD VI

Margaret = James IV of Scotland

Mary

James V, King of Scotland = Mary of Lorraine

Mary, Queen of Scots = Henry Stuart, Lord Darnley

JAMES VI OF SCOTLAND AND I OF ENGLAND = Anne of Denmark (1603–25)

An equal sign (=) stands for marriage. Underlined names indicate characters in the plays. Capitals note reigning Kings and Queens.